GOVERNMENT IN AMERICA

GOVERNMENT IN AMERICA

PEOPLE, POLITICS, AND POLICY

Eighth Edition

George C. Edwards III
Texas A & M University

Martin P. Wattenberg
University of California, Irvine

Robert L. Lineberry
University of Houston

An imprint of Addison Wesley Longman, Inc.

New York • Reading, Massachusetts • Menlo Park, California • Harlow, England
Don Mills, Ontario • Sydney • Mexico City • Madrid • Amsterdam

Executive Editor: *Pam Gordon*
Acquisitions Editor: *Peter Glovin*
Developmental Editor: *Barbara A. Conover*
Supplements Editors: *Jessica Bayne, Jen McCaffery*
Senior Marketing Manager: *Suzanne Daghlian*
Project Coordination, Text Design, and Electronic Page Makeup: *Thompson Steele Production Services*
Cover Designer: *Kay Petronio*
Cover Photograph: *Pienee Lynn/Tony Stone*
Photo Researcher: *Mira Schachne*
Full-Service Production Manager: *Eric Jorgensen*
Manufacturing Manager: *Hilda Kaparanian*
Printer and Binder: *RR Donnelley & Sons Company*
Cover Printer: *The Lehigh Press, Inc.*

Library of Congress Cataloging-in-Publication Data

Edwards, George C.
Government in America : people, politics, and policy / George C. Edwards III, Martin P. Wattenberg, Robert L. Lineberry. -- 8th ed.
p. cm.
Includes bibliographical references and index.
ISBN 0-321-01287-9
1. United States--Politics and government. I. Wattenberg, Martin P., 1956- . II. Lineberry, Robert L. III. Government in America.
JK271.E25 1997b
320.473--dc21 97-23749
CIP

ISBN 0-321-01287-9 (College Edition)
ISBN 0-321-04495-9 (School Edition)

3 4 5 6 7 8 9 10 11 - DOW - 03 02 01 00 99 98

BRIEF CONTENTS

PART THREE The Policymakers

PART FOUR Policies

CONTENTS

5 CIVIL RIGHTS AND PUBLIC POLICY 111

PART TWO

People and Politics

6 PUBLIC OPINION AND POLITICAL ACTION 140

7 THE MASS MEDIA AND THE POLITICAL AGENDA 166

8 POLITICAL PARTIES 187

9 NOMINATIONS AND CAMPAIGNS 216

10 ELECTIONS AND VOTING BEHAVIOR 238

11 INTEREST GROUPS 257

PART THREE

The Policymakers

12 CONGRESS 284

13 THE PRESIDENCY 317

14 THE CONGRESS, THE PRESIDENT, AND THE BUDGET: THE POLITICS OF TAXING AND SPENDING 353

15 THE FEDERAL BUREAUCRACY 378

16 THE FEDERAL COURTS 408

PART FOUR

Policies

17 ECONOMIC POLICYMAKING 440

20 FOREIGN AND DEFENSE POLICYMAKING 498

21 THE NEW IMPORTANCE OF STATE AND LOCAL GOVERNMENT 526

LIST OF SELECTED FEATURES

YOU ARE THE POLICYMAKER

YOU ARE THE JUDGE

THE COURT DECIDES

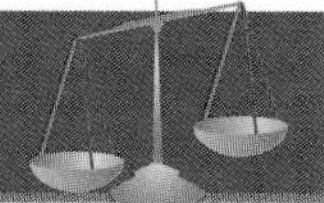

AMERICA IN PERSPECTIVE

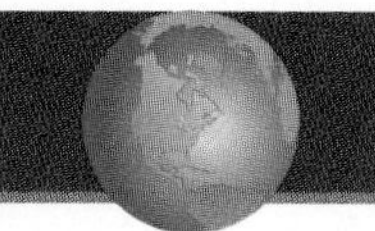

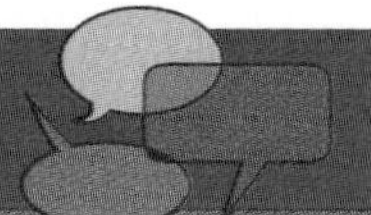

THE PEOPLE SPEAK

SINCE KENNEDY

IN THE TWENTY-FIRST CENTURY

PREFACE

Americans elected a conservative majority to both the House and the Senate in 1994, the first Republican Congress in 40 years. Two years later they reelected Bill Clinton, the first Democrat to win reelection since Franklin Roosevelt, 60 years earlier. Decisionmakers of both political parties face important challenges as they determine the scope of our government as we enter the twenty-first century. Students need a framework in which to understand these new challenges.

FOCUS

We write *Government in America* to provide our readers with a better understanding of our fascinating political system. We focus on four core subject areas: constitutional foundations, patterns of political behavior, political institutions, and public policy outputs. This eighth edition of *Government in America* continues to frame its content with a public policy approach to government in the United States. We do not discuss policy at the expense of politics, however. Instead we ask, "What difference does politics make to the policies governments produce?" Because the principal reason for studying politics is to understand these policies, this focus engages students' interest and stimulates consideration of the most important aspects of governing.

We uniquely devote Chapter 14 to the federal budget. The federal budget codifies who gets what, a central issue in public policy. We discuss the size of federal spending, taxation, and deficits, as well as the political interactions among the president, the executive branch, and Congress. The annual budget debates on the Hill are some of the most colorful. The book also treats economic policy specifically, making it a separate chapter, because this topic deserves coverage of its own. We place the budget chapter after those on the presidency and Congress so that the reader may apply knowledge of these institutions to a core policymaking process. Discussion of policy occurs throughout the chapters, as well as in every chapter's conclusion, where the two major themes of democracy and the scope of government are discussed to offer readers a consistent framework oriented toward policy outputs.

TWO THEMES

To render the policy focus in concrete terms, we have expanded two important themes throughout the book: the nature of democracy and the scope of government. Each chapter begins with an anecdote and introductory text, tinted to highlight the relevance of these themes to the chapter's subject. Each chapter ends with specific sections on the two themes under the heading "Understanding . . . " that show how the themes help illuminate the chapter's subject matter.

The first theme, democracy, deals with the first great question central to governing: *How should we govern*? We evaluate how well the American system lives up to citizens' expectations of democratic government. In Chapter 1, we define democracy as a means of selecting policymakers and of organizing government so that policy represents and responds to citizens' preferences. As with previous editions, we continue to incorporate theoretical issues in our discussions of different models of American democracy. We also raise questions about democracy in the context of our discussion of the various components of American government. For example, Is a strong presidency good for democracy? Do our mass media make us more democratic? Are powerful courts compatible with democracy? We try to encourage students to think analytically about the theories and to develop independent assessments of the American government's politics and policies.

The question of whether America's diversity and open political process frequently produce gridlock emerges as a subtheme to our discussion of democracy. The diversity of the American people is reflected in the diversity of political interests represented in the political system. This system is so open that many different interests find access to policymakers. In our system of checks and balances, the opposition by one set of policymakers can sometimes frustrate the will of the majority. We leave it to the reader to determine whether the difficulty of achieving policy change, be it the Clinton health care reform plan or the Republicans' Contract with America, is a positive feature of our system. Our goal is to promote understanding of the consequences of the American democratic system and provoke discussion about these consequences.

Our second theme, the scope of government, focuses on another great question of governing: *What should government do*? Here we discuss alternative views concerning the proper role and size for American government and the influence that the workings of government and politics have on the scope of government. The government's scope is the core question around which politics revolves in contemporary America, pervading many crucial issues: To what degree should Washington impose national standards on state policies? How high should taxes be? Do elections encourage politicians to promise more governmental services?

A subtheme of the scope of government is the role of individualism in American political life. The people who immigrated to America may have been diverse, but many adopted a common dream of America as a place where people could make it on their own without interference from government. Today, individualism remains a powerful influence in the United States. Americans' strong preference for free markets and limited government has important consequences for public policy. Thus, we often employ the concept of individualism in our analysis of the scope of government.

We hope that readers employ these perennial questions embodied in the nature of our democracy and the scope of our government when they examine political events long after reading the book.

CURRENCY

This eighth edition is completely up-to-date and incorporates the best recent scholarship on U.S. government. We have expanded our coverage of several topics to reflect their importance in contemporary American politics. Our emphasis in each chapter on the scope of government is also very timely.

There is expanded coverage of theories of democracy in Chapter 1. In Chapter 3, we have included substantial material on fiscal federalism, an area at the core of much of the current debate over public policy. We have added material on the Constitution and religion in Chapter 4, addressing both the free exercise and the establishment of religion—another issue animating American politics today. Similarly, in Chapter 5, we have devoted substantial attention to both women's rights and affirmative action, as well as to racial gerrymandering and voting rights. The latest Supreme Court decisions, including *Reno v. ACLU, Vecco v. Quill and Washington v. Glucksberg, Agostini v. Felton, Boerne v. Flores, Printz v. U.S.,* and *Raines v. Byrd,* are, of course, included wherever they are relevant.

A section on individualism and the media about the increased focus on presidential politics and candidate-centered politics appears in Chapter 7. Chapter 8 on political parties devotes more attention to divided government, to reflect the first Republican-controlled Congresses to face a Democratic president since 1948. Chapter 11 has a discussion of how interest groups campaigned successfully against President Clinton's health care reform proposal.

We have included in Chapters 10, 11, and 12 comprehensive coverage of the historic 1994 congressional elections and the 1996 presidential and congressional elections, both the campaigns and the results. We have also provided up-to-date coverage of the recent changes in congressional leadership, organization, and procedures in Chapter 12. Naturally, we have devoted considerable attention, in Chapter 13, to the Clinton administration (including its relations with Congress, the public and the press, the organization of the White House, and the president's actions as commander in chief) and, in Chapter 14, to the efforts of both the president and Congress to deal with the budget, which has become central to American politics and policy. President Clinton's judicial appointments are discussed in Chapter 16. Chapter 18 on social welfare policymaking includes discussion of the historic welfare reform of 1996. Chapter 21 on state and local politics has been revised to reflect the resurgence of the states in American politics.

FIVE FEATURES

Five special features appear throughout Government in America: (1) **You Are the Policymaker/Judge;** (2) **Since Kennedy;** (3) **The People Speak;** (4) **America in Perspective;** and (5) **In the Twenty-first Century.** These features may outline a case study, present some specific research on a question, provide a historical or comparative perspective, or offer figures and tables that illustrate important points—valuable learning aids for students. Each of the five features plays a particular role in the text to support our approach to American Government.

We believe it is important for students to recognize and think critically about difficult policy choices they must face as citizens. **"You Are the Policymaker"** asks students to read arguments on both sides of a specific current issue, such as whether the minimum wage should be raised, and then to make a policy decision.

In chapters dealing with legal questions, this feature is titled **"You Are the Judge,"** and it presents the student with an actual court case and concludes with **"The Court Decides,"** showing how the case was actually resolved.

In order to maintain strong historical coverage, we again include a feature titled **"Since Kennedy"** for the eighth edition. Each chapter contains a box analyzing some aspect of how politics or public policy has changed since the 1960s, such as the public's declining trust in government or the rise of the negative press. In some instances, we specifically compare the early 1960s to the early 1990s. In other instances, we trace the continuous changes from President Kennedy to President Clinton.

Complementing our theme of democracy are boxes called **"The People Speak,"** which provide recent opinion poll data regarding a matter discussed in the text. Some examples include whether the government in Washington is becoming too powerful, whether abortion should be outlawed, and whether big interests have too much influence on government.

Instructors who wish to incorporate a comparative element into their courses will appreciate our **"America in Perspective"** boxes. This feature examines how the United States compares to other countries in areas such as tax rates, voter turnout, or the delivery of public services.

In addition to our regular examination of the past, we also look toward the future at several points in our new feature titled "**In the 21st Century.**" We do not have any crystal balls to tell us how the future will unfold, but we do believe that these plausible scenarios are worth pondering as American democracy heads into the next millennium.

Each chapter ends with a contemporary bibliography, a listing of key terms, and, new to the eighth edition, a list of Internet resources relevent to the chapter. Additional study aids appear at the back of the book: a glossary of terms, the Declaration of Independence, *Federalist Papers* No. 10 and No. 51, the Constitution, and tables on presidents and presidential elections, party control of the presidency and Congress in the twentieth century, and Supreme Court justices serving in this century.

SUPPLEMENTS

A comprehensive selection of teaching and learning resources has been developed to supplement the eighth edition of *Government in America.*

FOR QUALIFIED ADOPTERS

Instructor's Manual A complete resource manual by Jan Leighley of Texas A&M University is available for the instructor. Each chapter of the instructor's manual includes learning objectives, a synopsis, glossary terms, lecture outlines, sources for other lecture material, and suggested projects and activities.

Test Banks The test bank by Jan Leighley of Texas A&M University consists of about 4000 multiple-choice, true/false, and completion test questions. Each question is coded with the correct response and referenced to the page in *Government in America* on which the correct answer is indicated.

Test Gen EQ Computerized Testing System This flexible, easy-to-master computer test bank includes all the test items in the printed test bank. The software allows you to edit existing questions and add your own items. Tests can be printed in several different formats and can include figures such as graphs and tables. The test bank is available for Windows and Macintosh Computers.

Politics in Action *Laser Disc* Eleven "Lecture Launchers," covering broad subjects such as social movements, conducting a campaign, and the passage of a bill, are examined through narrated videos, interviews, edited documentaries, original footage, and political ads. *Politics in Action* is available as an easy-to-use laser disc or videotape, and is accompanied by an extensive *User's Manual,* which provides background on the segments, links to topics in textbooks, discussion questions, and bar codes (for easy access when using the laser disc version).

Transparencies Transparency acetates of figures in the text are available free to instructors who want to help students interpret visual data. These transparencies facilitate the integration of student reading with classroom lectures. Electronic transparencies on 3.5" disks are available from Longman upon adoption.

FOR STUDENTS

Study Guide This comprehensive study guide by Charles Matzke helps students not only to remember the essential text material but also to examine and discover further perspectives on American government. Each chapter of the study guide contains learning objectives, a chapter synopsis/overview, review questions, key terms, and discussion questions.

Super Shell *Student Tutorial Software* The *SuperShell* by John Soares, is a computerized student tutorial guide. The program was developed to help students retain the key concepts and ideas they have read. This versatile drill and-practice software contains multiple-choice, true/false, and short answer questions for each chapter in the text. Diagnostic graphics provide the student with immediate reinforcement and indicate areas in which further study might prove beneficial. Students can print out narrative chapter outlines or consult an easy-to-use tutorial guide. In addition, a flash card program is included to drill students on the terms in the text's glossary. Available for Windows and Macintosh Computers.

Anthologies There are two different American government anthologies available from Longman to complement this textbook. Woll, *American Government: Readings and Cases,* Twelfth Edition, is a best-selling, comprehensive anthology of major Supreme Court cases, essential political documents, and seminal essays in the history of American political thought. Grover/Peschek, *Voices of Dissent,* Second Edition, is an anthology of 40 critical essays, including coverage of media bias, Clinton's presidency, Republican Congress, voter discontent, health care, NAFTA, and free trade.

The HarperCollins Political Pamphleteer To help instructors and students incorporate the expertise of others into lectures and reading, HarperCollins asked specialists in various areas of political science to write essays appropriate for 50-minute classes. Each pamphlet in the series complements or elaborates on the themes raised in *Government in America*. Pamphlet titles include "Women and Politics"; "The Environment and Politics"; "Urban Politics"; "Latinos and Politics"; "National Health Care"; "Bill of Rights"; "Blacks and Politics"; "Landmark Supreme Court Decisions"; and "Affirmitive Action and the Supreme Court."

ACKNOWLEDGMENTS

Many, many colleagues have kindly given us counsel on the drafts of this edition. They include the following:

Christine Arnold-Laurie, Charles County Community College
Michael Caldwell, University of Illinois, Urbana
Willie Curtis, United States Military Academy
Joel Franke, Blinn College
Barbara Hedrick, Moorehead State University
Brinck Kerr, University of Arkansas
Michael Postiglione, Quincey University
Joseph Rudolph, Towsend State University
Robert Toburen, Louisiana Technical University
Joseph Trachtenberg, Clayton State College

A number of editors have provided valuable assistance in the production of this edition of *Government in America.* Barbara Conover was a superb developmental editor, coordinating every aspect of the book. Elinor Stapleton was a dedicated project editor, tirelessly attending to details. Political science editor Peter Glovin provided valuable guidance, helping keep the project on course and on schedule. Suzanne Daghlian was invaluable in developing a marketing plan for the book. We are grateful to all of them. Finally, we owe a special debt of gratitude to Professor John Pelissero of Loyola University Chicago, who did an excellent job drafting Chapter 21.

—George C. Edwards III
—Martin P. Wattenberg
—Robert L. Lineberry

ABOUT THE AUTHORS

GEORGE C. EDWARDS III is Distinguished Professor of Political Science at Texas A&M University and Director of The Center for Presidential Studies. He also holds the Jordan Professorship in Liberal Arts and has held visiting appointments at the U.S. Military Academy at West Point, Peking University in Beijing, Hebrew University of Jerusalem, and the University of Wisconsin in Madison. One of the country's leading scholars of the presidency, he has written or edited 15 books on American politics and public policymaking, including *At the Margins: Presidential Leadership of Congress, Presidential Leadership, Presidential Approval,* and *National Security and the U.S. Constitution.*

Professor Edwards has served as President of the Presidency Research Section of the American Political Science Association and on many editorial boards. He has also received the Decoration for Distinguished Civilian Service from the U.S. Army. A frequent speaker at universities around the country, he often lectures abroad as well.

Professor Edwards also applies his scholarship to practical issues of government. In 1988, he went to Brasilia to advise those writing the new constitution for Brazil. He was an issue leader for the National Academy of Public Administration's Project on the 1988 Presidential Transition, providing advice to the new president. In 1993, he spent 6 weeks in China lecturing on democracy. In 1994, he was a consultant to Russian democratic leaders on building a political party system in that country.

When not writing, speaking, or advising, he prefers to spend his time with his wife Carmella sailing, skiing, scuba diving, playing tennis, traveling, or attending art auctions.

MARTIN P. WATTENBERG is Professor of Political Science at the University of California, Irvine. His first regular paying job was with the Washington Redskins in 1977, from which he moved on to receive a Ph.D. at the University of Michigan in 1982.

While at Michigan, Professor Wattenberg authored *The Decline of American Political Parties* (Harvard University Press), currently in its fifth edition. Most recently, he has written *The Rise of Candidate-Centered Politics: Presidential Elections of the 1980s,* also published by Harvard. In addition, he has contributed many professional articles to such journals as the *American Political Science Review, American Journal of Political Science, American Politics Quarterly, Public Opinion Quarterly,* and *Public Opinion.*

Professor Wattenberg has also lectured in Australia, Europe, Asia, and Africa about American politics. Presently, he is working with a colleague in Canberra on a project comparing American and Australian electoral behavior.

When not writing, lecturing, or surfing the web, he can most often be found on the beach at Newport or at the local tennis courts.

ROBERT L. LINEBERRY is Professor of Political Science at the University of Houston and has been its Senior Vice President. He served from 1981 to 1988 as Dean of the College of Liberal Arts and Sciences at the University of Kansas in Lawrence.

A native of Oklahoma City, he received a B.A. degree from the University of Oklahoma in 1964 and a Ph.D. in political science from the University of North Carolina in 1968. He taught for 7 years at Northwestern University.

Dr. Lineberry has been President of the Policy Studies Section of the American Political Science Association and is currently the editor of *Social Science Quarterly.* He is the author or coauthor of numerous books and articles in political science. In addition, for the past 30 years he has taught regularly the introductory course in American government.

He has been married to Nita Lineberry for 30 years. They have two children, Nikki, who works in Glenwood Springs, Colorado, and Keith, who works in Houston, Texas. They have three grandchildren—Lee, Callie, and Hunter.

GOVERNMENT IN AMERICA

Introducing Government in America

The twenty-first century is fast approaching, bringing with it unimagined challenges. We want to be able to respond to these challenges individually, as citizens, and collectively, as a nation. Indeed, during the 1996 presidential campaign, President Clinton chose for his theme the phrase "building a bridge to the twenty-first century." Clinton spoke of bringing the lofty ideals of America's past into this new century while at the same time being prepared for the challenges of the new age. Many believe that the coming years will be known as the "information age." Information is now power, so it is said, both in business and in government. It is our hope that *Government in America* will help you become a well-informed citizen, a citizen better able to lead our country into the next century.

TWO CENTRAL QUESTIONS

We begin Chapter 1 by introducing three important concepts: government, politics, and public policy. We also raise two fundamental questions about governing that will serve as themes throughout the book:

1. *How should we be governed*? Americans take great pride in calling their government democratic. Today there is a rush to establish democracy in many countries, but not everyone agrees on what democracy means. This chapter will examine the workings of democratic government. The chapters that follow will evaluate the way American government actually works compared to the standards of an "ideal" democracy. We will continually ask, "Who holds power and who influences the policies adopted by government?"

2. *What should government do*? This text will explore the relationship between how American government works and what the government does. In other words, "Does our government do what we want it to do?" This second theme is closely linked to the first—the process of government is tied to the substance of public policy.

What government should do can be examined in terms of "the scope of government." Debates about the scope of government, including its functions and budget, are among the most important in American political life. These debates are at the core of disputes between the major political parties and between liberals and conservatives.

The purpose of Chapter 1 is to lay a foundation for understanding government in America. This foundation begins with the notion of government.

GOVERNMENT, POLITICS, AND PUBLIC POLICY

Government, politics, and public policy are interrelated. Government is important because of what it does for us—and to us. It can protect us, feed us, educate us, send us to war, tax us, and affect just about every aspect of our lives. All of these actions involve setting public policies. This chapter will first examine government itself to see how it works and how these procedures affect the policies it produces.

GOVERNMENT

Whether you have been interested in government or not, your life has been, and will be, greatly shaped by it. Few things have more to do with your standard of living, your freedoms, and your opportunities than government. Clearly, it is a topic that bears close examination.

***What Is Government*?** The institutions that make public policy for a society are collectively known as **government.** In our national government, these institutions are Congress, the president, courts, and federal administrative agencies (often called "the bureaucracy"). We also have thousands of state and local governments in the United States that make policies that affect us.

Occasionally a society's form of government undergoes radical change. This occurred in America with the rebellion against British colonial rule in 1776 and with the transfer of power from the government under the Articles of Confederation to that under the Constitution. Since then, we have regularly had the chance to change officeholders in our government at election time. There are roughly 500,000 elected officials in the United States; that means that somewhere, on almost every day of the year, someone is running for office.

Every government has a means of changing its leaders. Some changes, like those in American government, are orderly and peaceful. Just before noon on January 20, 1993, a crowd of Clinton staffers stood patiently right outside the main gate to the White House. As President Clinton prepared to take his oath of office, they anxiously awaited the chance to take their posts in the new administration. When the clock struck twelve, the gates swung open and

In the United States, the transfer of power is achieved through peaceful means. In 1995, the Republicans gained control of the House of Representatives for the first time in 40 years. Here, Democratic leader Richard Gephardt symbolically passes the gavel to the new Republican Speaker of the House, Newt Gingrich.

the new White House aides went in to move into their offices.

Not all governments change in such a peaceful and orderly fashion. The twentieth century has been a time of revolutionary upheaval. The Russians in 1917 and the Chinese in 1949 changed their governments through violent revolution in order to adopt communist governments. Sometimes a change in government is less orderly than in America, but less bloody than a revolution. In 1989, massive protest marches in East Germany led to a toppling of the communist government, free elections, and soon thereafter reunification with West Germany. Regardless of how they assumed power, however, all governments have certain functions in common.

What Governments Do Big or small, democratic or not, governments in the modern world are similar to one another in the following ways:

1. *Governments maintain national defense.* A government seeks to protect its national sovereignty, usually by maintaining armed forces. In the nuclear age, some governments possess awesome power to make war, maintaining large armies and deploying highly sophisticated weapons. The United States spends nearly $300 billion a year on national defense. Some politicians think the United States spends too much on defense; others think this amount provides only minimal defensive capabilities. On both sides, there are those who think that military expenditures are not made efficiently.

2. *Governments provide public goods.* **Public goods** are things that everyone can share. Contrast a loaf of bread, a private good, with clean air, a public good. You can buy a loaf of bread and easily consume it by yourself. Clean air, however, is available to everyone. A public good, unlike a loaf of bread, is indivisible and nonexclusive. Everyone can use a public good; no one can be denied its use.

A central principle of modern political science and economics is that individuals have little incentive to provide public goods because no one can make a profit from them. For instance, many businesses seem unconcerned with cleaning the air, because they do not make a profit from providing clean air. Thus, governments are usually left to provide things like highways, public parks, and pollution control.

3. *Governments have police powers to provide order.* Every government has some means of maintaining order. When people protest *en masse,* governments may resort to extreme measures to restore order. Chinese security forces occupied streets around Tiananmen Square in 1989 to crush the student protest. Even in the United States, governments consider the responsibility to maintain order one of their most important jobs. When riots broke out in Los Angeles after the 1992 Rodney King verdict, the National Guard was called in to stop the looting and arson.

4. *Governments provide public services.* Hospitals and many other public services are maintained by governments. Governments in this country spend billions of dollars on schools, libraries, weather forecasting, halfway houses, and dozens of other public services.

5. *Governments socialize the young into the political culture.* Most modern governments pay for education and use it to develop support for national principles among the young. School curricula typically offer a course on the philosophy and practice of the country's government. Rituals like the daily Pledge of Allegiance foster patriotism and love of country.

6. *Governments collect taxes to pay for the services they provide.* In 1997, one of every three dollars earned by an American citizen was used to pay national, state, and local taxes. Although Americans often complain about the high cost of government, our tax burden is actually much lower than that of citizens in most other democratic nations.

All these tasks of government add up to tremendous responsibilities for our political leaders. Many important and difficult decisions must be made

Many American public schools begin each day with the Pledge of Allegiance. Like most governments around the world, the U.S. government uses the public schools to socialize its children. Required civics courses and governmental approval of curricula and textbooks help ensure that the young understand and support the American system of government.

regarding what government should do. For example, how much should we spend on national defense? How high should taxes for Social Security be? The way we answer such questions is through politics.

POLITICS

When Ronald Reagan competed in Republican primaries, he espoused what became known as his eleventh commandment: "Thou shall not speak ill of a fellow party member." During the 1996 primaries, the Republican candidates regularly violated Reagan's commandment—especially when the subject turned to Bob Dole. Pat Buchanan regularly called him "Beltway Bob," attempting to paint Dole as an out-of-touch Washington insider. Steve Forbes launched negative ads claiming that Dole had often voted for wasteful government spending programs and higher taxes. Lamar Alexander said that this was not Dole's time to be president, implying that he was too old for the job. But when the Republican Convention rolled around, all three men endorsed Dole without reservation. When they were asked about their previous remarks, the standard answer from Dole's defeated rivals was "That's just politics." Indeed, we are now used to one candidate's attacking another—sometimes in ugly language—in order to gain votes. However, politics is a lot more than merely what candidates do to win elections.

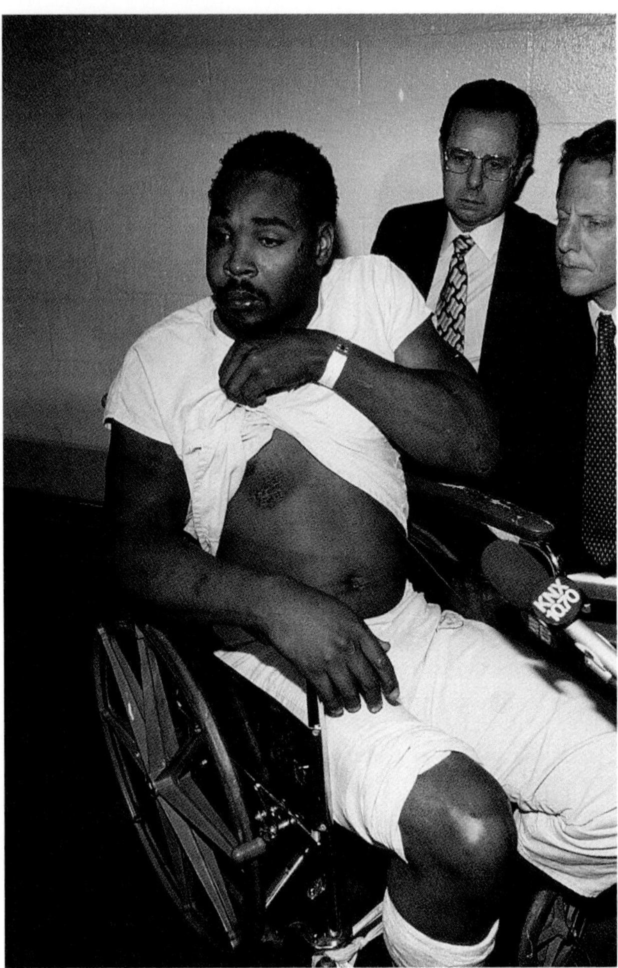

The videotaped beating of Rodney King outraged many individuals. Here, King displays his wounds for the press. When a jury acquitted the police officers charged with assaulting King, one of the worst riots in U.S. history broke out in Los Angeles. A second trial, in which the officers were charged with violating King's civil rights, took place almost a year after the riots.

WHAT POLITICS IS

Politics determines whom we select as our governmental leaders and what policies they pursue. Political scientists often cite a famous definition of **politics** by Harold D. Lasswell: "Who gets what, when, and how."[1] It is one of the briefest and most useful definitions of politics ever penned. Admittedly, this broad definition covers a lot of ground (office politics, sorority politics, and so on) in which political scientists are not interested. They are interested primarily in politics related to governmental decision making.

The media usually focus on the *who* of politics. At a minimum, this includes voters, candidates, groups, and parties. *How* people participate in politics is important, too. They get what they want through bargaining, supporting, compromising, lobbying, and so forth. *What* refers to the substance of politics and government—

the public policies that come from government. Governments distribute benefits, such as new roads, and burdens, such as new taxes. In this sense, government and politics involve winners and losers.

POLITICAL INVOLVEMENT

People get involved in politics for many reasons. Some of these reasons, no doubt, are noble, and others are not. The ways in which people get involved in politics—whether as candidates for office or simply by voting for the local school board—make up their **political participation.** Many people judge the health of a government, especially a democratic government, by how widespread political participation is. When judged by voter turnout, America does quite poorly, with one of the lowest turnout rates in the world. Low voter turnout has an effect on who holds political power. As Wolfinger and Rosenstone have shown in their study of voter turnout, "voters are not a microcosm of the entire body of citizens, but a distorted sample that exaggerates the size of some groups and minimizes that of others."[2] Voting is only one way of participating. For a few Americans—a very few—politics is a vocation rather than an avocation. They run for office, and some even earn their livelihood from holding political office.

There are thousands of Americans who treat politics not as a casual civic duty, but as something critical to them and their interests. Many of these people are members of interest groups or single-issue groups, which have recently come to prominence in American politics. One of the most important factors in modern politics is the **single-issue groups:** interest groups so concerned with one matter that their members will cast their votes on the basis of that issue only, ignoring a politician's stand on everything else.[3] Groups of activists dedicated either to outlawing abortion or to preserving abortion rights are good examples of single-issue groups.

When the Supreme Court handed down its decision in a case called *Webster v. Reproductive Health Services* in 1989, it narrowed a woman's right to an abortion by allowing states to decide whether to provide funds to women who want abortions but cannot afford them. People on the pro-choice and the pro-life sides—and note the loaded term each uses for itself—have turned to state politics to achieve their goals. Pro-lifers attempted to convince their legislators to restrict abortion funding by picketing abortion clinics and lobbying legislatures in many states. Pro-choicers have worked on legislators to keep the right to abortion as broad as possible. Neither group considers a middle course. For this reason, many politicians feel that single-issue groups such as these get in the way of policymaking. Single-issue groups have little taste for compromise, an approach that most politicians take as the heart and soul of their job. The influence of single-issue groups on voters and elected officials complicates efforts to seek the middle ground on various issues. Individual citizens and organized groups get involved in politics because they understand that the public policy choices made by governments affect them in significant ways. Will they have access to medical care? Will they be taken care of in their old age? Is the water they drink pure? These and other questions tie politics to public policy.

PUBLIC POLICY

More and more, Americans expect government to do something about their problems. The president and members of Congress are expected to keep the economy humming along; voters will penalize them at the

polls if they do not. When people confront government officials with problems that they expect them to solve, they are trying to influence the government's **policy agenda.** John Kingdon defined a policy agenda as "the list of subjects or problems to which government officials, and people outside of government closely associated with those officials, are paying serious attention at any given time."[4] Like individuals, governments have priorities. Some issues will be considered, and others will not. One of the key elements of democratic government is that public officials, if they want to get elected, must pay attention to the problems that concern the voters. When you vote, you are partly looking at whether a candidate shares your agenda. If you are worried about rising health care costs and unemployment, and a certain candidate talks only about America's moral decay and ending legalized abortions, you will probably support another candidate.

Pro-life and pro-choice groups are single-minded and usually uncompromising. With the reelection of President Clinton, abortion will probably remain legal for some time.

A government's policy agenda changes regularly. When jobs are scarce and business productivity is falling, economic problems occupy a high position on the government's agenda. If the economy is doing well and trouble spots around the world occupy the headlines, foreign policy questions are bound to dominate the agenda. Nothing works better than a crisis to elevate an issue on a policy agenda. An oil spill, an airline crash, or a brutal murder will increase the probability that ecology, air safety, or gun control will rise to near the top of a government's agenda.

Public policy is a choice that government makes in response to some issue on its agenda (see Table 1.1). It is also worth noting that policymakers can establish a policy by doing nothing, as well as by doing something. Doing nothing—or doing nothing different—is a choice. Often a debate about public policy centers on whether government should do something rather than nothing. Reporter Randy Shilts' book about the American government's response to the AIDS crisis tells a sad tale of inaction, even when the AIDS epidemic reached crisis levels.[5] Shilts traces the staggering growth in the number of people with AIDS and reveals how governments in Washington and elsewhere did little or debated quietly about what to do. Shilts claims that, because politicians viewed AIDS as a gay person's disease, they were reluctant to support measures to deal with it, fearful of losing the votes of anti-gay constituents. The issue thus remained a low priority on the government's policy agenda until infections started to spread to the general population, including celebrities like basketball star Magic Johnson.

Government in America will constantly ask you to sharpen your ability to make policy choices. The "You Are the Policymaker" sections throughout the text present actual policy questions that have confronted Congress, the president, the Supreme Court, or a governmental bureaucracy. These sections challenge you to exercise your best judgment as a citizen, to analyze each issue and make a policy choice.

THE POLITICAL SYSTEM

A **political system** is a set of institutions and activities that link together government, politics, and public policy.[6] Most systems, political or not, can be diagrammed. We can create simple renderings of how a nuclear power plant or an automobile works. Figure 1.1 (see page 8) is a model of how a political system works. The rest of this book will flesh out this skeletal version of our political system, but for now the model will help you to identify several key elements.

TABLE 1.1 TYPES OF PUBLIC POLICIES

There are many types of public policies. Every decision that government makes—a law it passes, a budget it establishes, and even a decision not to act on an issue—is public policy. Here are the most important types of public policies:

TYPE	DEFINITION	EXAMPLE
Congressional statute	Law passed by Congress	Social Security Act
Presidential action	Decision by president	American troops sent to Haiti
Court decision	Opinion by Supreme Court or other court	Supreme Court ruling that school segregation is unconstitutional
Budgetary choices	Legislative enactment of taxes and expenditures	The federal budget
Regulation	Agency adoption of regulation	Food and Drug Administration approval of a new drug

POLITICAL ISSUES AND LINKAGE INSTITUTIONS

Politics begins, of course, with people, and people do not always agree on the best course of action. A **political issue** arises when people disagree about a problem or about a public policy choice made to combat a problem. There is never a shortage of political issues in this country; government, however, will not act upon an issue until it is high on the agenda.

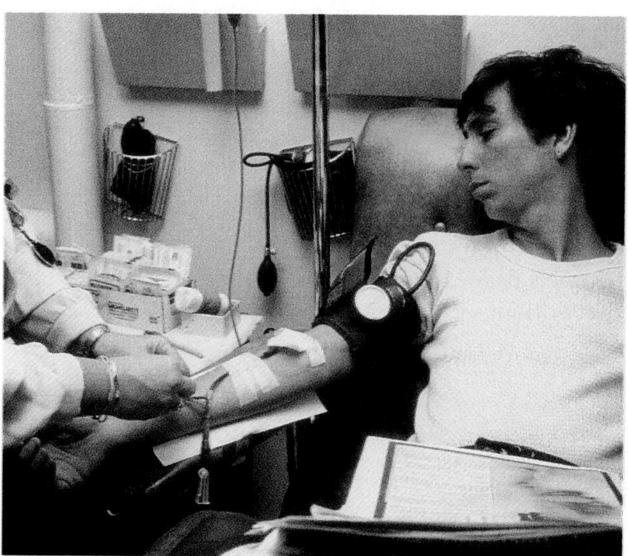

AIDS was relatively low on the political agenda until well-known celebrities started to die from the disease. AIDS activists have found, however, that getting the problem on the agenda is only half the political battle. Getting the government to take aggressive action to find and approve new treatments has proved to be at least as difficult.

In a democratic society, political parties, elections, interest groups, and the media are key **linkage institutions** between the preferences of citizens and the government's policy agenda. Parties and interest groups exert much effort to get the issues they believe are important to the top of the government's agenda. Elections and the media are two major forums through which potential agenda items receive public attention.

MAKING PUBLIC POLICY: THE POLICYMAKING INSTITUTIONS

Policymakers stand at the core of the political system. Working within the government's institutions, policymakers scan the issues on the policy agenda, select some for attention, and make policies concerning them. The U.S. Constitution establishes three policymaking institutions: Congress, the presidency, and the courts. Today the power of the bureaucracy is so great that most political scientists consider it a fourth policymaking institution.

Very few policies are made by a single policymaking institution. Part Three discusses these institutions separately, but they do not operate independently. Environmental policy is a good example. Some presidents have used their influence with Congress to urge clean-air and clean-water policies. When Congress responds by passing legislation to clean up the environment, bureaucracies have to implement the new policies. Rules and regulations issued by the bureaucratic agencies fill fat volumes. In addition, every law passed and every rule made can be challenged in the courts. Courts make decisions about what the policies mean and whether they conflict with the Constitution. In policymaking, every political institution gets involved.

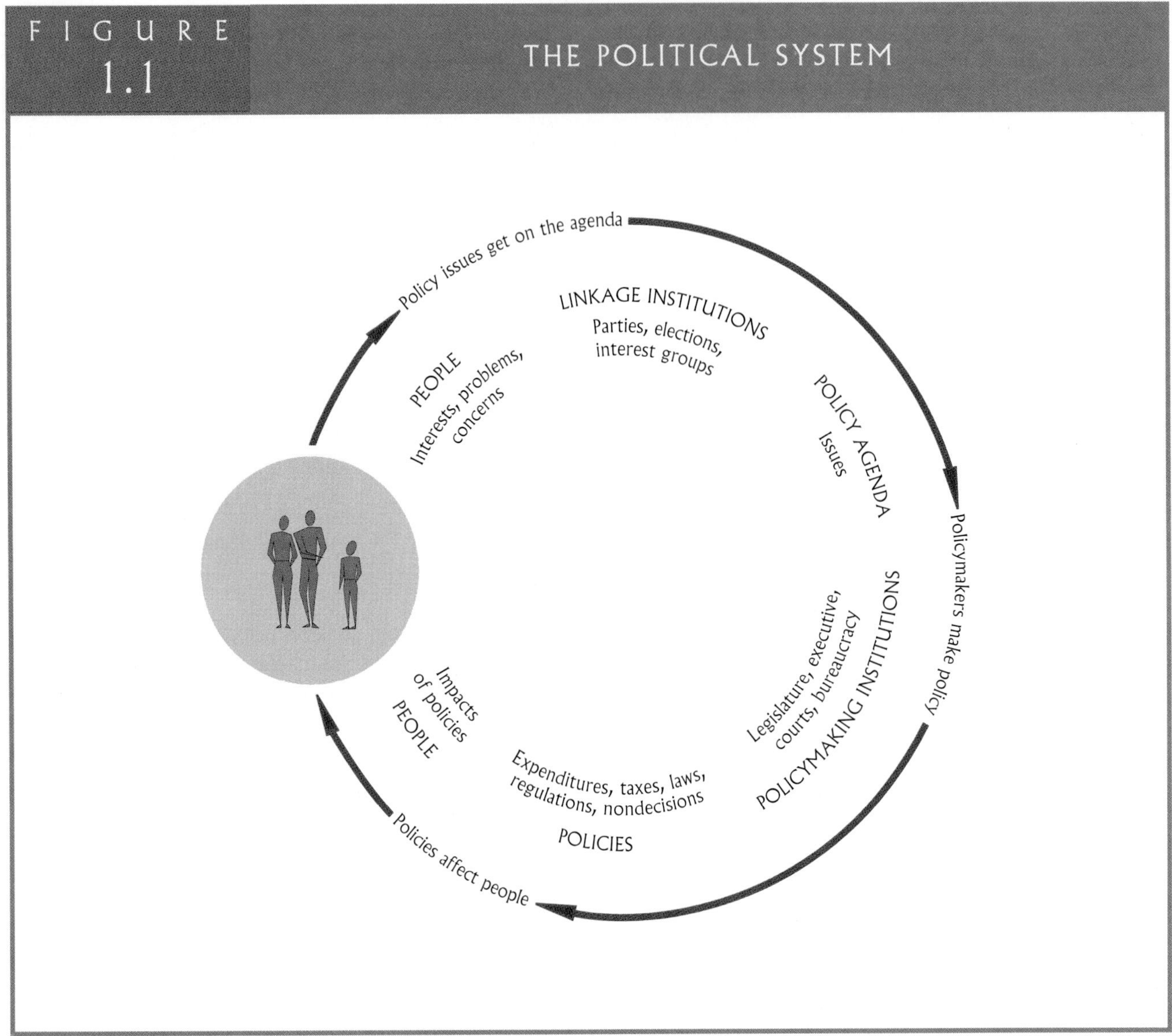

FIGURE 1.1 THE POLITICAL SYSTEM

POLICIES HAVE IMPACTS

Policy impacts are the effects that policy has on people and on society's problems. People who raise a policy issue usually want more than just a new law, a fancy proclamation, a bureaucratic rule, or a court judgment. They want a policy that works. Environmentalists want an industrial emissions policy that not only claims to prevent air pollution but also does so. Consumers want an economic policy that actually reduces inflation. Minority groups want a civil rights policy that not only promises them equal treatment but also ensures it.

Having a policy implies a goal. Whether we want to reduce poverty, cut crime, clean the water, or hold down inflation, we have a goal in mind. Analysts of policy impacts ask how well the policy achieves its goal—and at what cost. The analysis of policy impacts carries the political system back to its point of origin: people's interests, problems, and concerns. Translating people's desires into suitable public policy is crucial to the workings of democracy.

DEMOCRATIC GOVERNMENT

In 1848, the intellectual founders of modern communism, Karl Marx and Friedrich Engels, published *The Communist Manifesto,* one of the most famous political documents ever written. It began with these words: "A specter is haunting Europe. It is the specter of communism." Today one could write, "A specter is haunting Europe (and everywhere else). It is the specter of democracy."

From the Russian Revolution in 1917 through the recent end of the Cold War, American foreign policy was concerned with preventing the spread of communism. This was especially true immediately after World War II, when the Soviet Union expanded its sphere of influence throughout Eastern Europe. As Winston Churchill warned, an "Iron Curtain" had descended across Europe. From then on, a cold war existed between the United States and the Soviet Union—a struggle between democracy and communism for control of governments around the world. In one famous televised encounter (known as "The Kitchen Debate" because it occurred in a model kitchen of the future), Soviet Premier Nikita Khrushchev predicted to then Vice President Nixon that Nixon's grandchildren would be communists. Nixon naturally responded that Khrushchev's grandchildren would live in a democracy. Nixon later recalled that at the time, he was sure that Khrushchev would be wrong about America but that he was unsure whether his prediction about the Soviet Union would ever be realized. Over three decades later, it was. All the countries that once were part of the Soviet Empire now practice democracy, holding regular elections and permitting freedom of speech.

The resounding demands for democracy were not heard only in Eastern Europe, however. In Argentina, Brazil, Nicaragua, and other Latin American countries, one-party or military regimes gave way to competitive party systems and civilian governments. In South Africa, over three centuries of white rule came to an end in 1994 as a result of the first election open to all races. Yet despite this global move toward democracy, not everyone defines democracy the way Americans do—or think they do.

A statue of Vladimir Lenin, leader of Russia's Communist revolution, is hauled away in Bucharest, Romania, after the Communist government there was toppled. Like Romania's Communist regime, Lenin did not go down without a fight—it took two days to remove the statue.

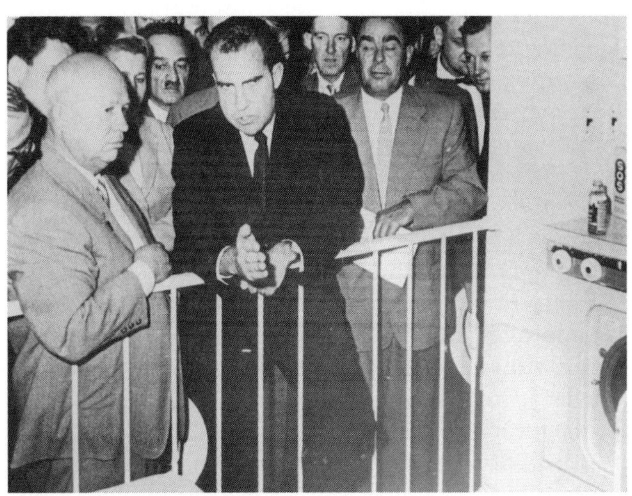

In 1959, then Vice President Nixon journeyed to Moscow to meet with Soviet Premier Khrushchev. Outside an exhibit of a model kitchen of the future, Nixon and Khrushchev had an impromptu debate in front of reporters as to which system—capitalism or communism—was the best course for a prosperous future.

DEFINING DEMOCRACY

The word *democracy* is overused. It takes its place among terms like *freedom, justice,* and *peace* as a word that has, seemingly, only positive connotations. Democracy is now the sort of loaded word Humpty Dumpty spoke of in *Through the Looking Glass:* "When I make a word do a lot of work like that, I pay it extra." However, democracy was not always so popular. The writers of the U.S. Constitution had no fondness for democracy. Elbridge Gerry of Massachusetts, a delegate to the Constitutional

Convention, said that "the evils we experience flow from the excesses of democracy." Another delegate, Roger Sherman, said that the people "should have as little to do as may be with the government." Only much later did Americans come to cherish democracy.

Today, most Americans would probably say that democracy is "government by the people." This phrase, of course, is part of Abraham Lincoln's famous definition of democracy from his Gettysburg Address: "government of the people, by the people, and for the people." The best that can be said of this definition is that it is brief; it is not, however, very informative. The late E. E. Schattschneider claimed that "we ought to get rid of confusing language such as 'government by the people.' To say that 270 million Americans 'govern' does not shed much light on the role of people in the American political system."[7] Schattschneider further remarked that an all-American town meeting would be the largest, longest, and most boring and frustrating meeting imaginable.

If democracy means government by the people, Giovanni Sartori asks "Which people?" There are six ways, he says, to interpret *people:*

1. Literally everybody
2. An undetermined large part, a great many
3. The lower class as opposed to some elite
4. An indivisible entity as an organic whole
5. An absolute majority (the majority has absolute power)
6. A limited majority (the majority has limited power).[8]

These are very different interpretations of *people.* No democracy permits government by literally everybody; for instance, children, felons, and noncitizens residing in the country have no voice in American government. What, then, do we mean when we say that democracy is government by the people? Here is a basic definition used throughout this book: **Democracy** is a means of selecting policymakers and of organizing government so that policy represents and responds to citizens' preferences.

TRADITIONAL DEMOCRATIC THEORY

What we call **traditional democratic theory** rests upon several principles.[9] These principles specify how a democratic government makes its decisions. One contemporary democratic theorist, Robert Dahl, suggests that "an ideal democratic process would satisfy five criteria."[10] Here are his five cornerstones of an ideal democracy:

1. *Equality in voting.* The principle of "one person, one vote" is basic to democracy. When citizens have different preferences about policies or leaders, they all need an equal chance to express their views.

2. *Effective participation.* Citizens must act on their opinions by participating in political institutions. Political participation need not be universal, but it must be representative. If high-income people vote at higher rates, the result is the same as if the wealthy had literally been given extra votes.

3. *Enlightened understanding.* A democratic society must be a marketplace of ideas. A free press and free speech are essential to civic understanding. When one group monopolizes or distorts information, citizens cannot truly understand issues.

4. *Citizen control of the agenda.* Citizens should have the collective right to control the government's policy agenda. If wealthy or powerful individuals or groups distort the agenda, citizens cannot make government address the issues they feel are most important.

5. *Inclusion.* The government must include, and extend rights to, all those subject to its laws. Citizenship must be open to all within a nation if the nation is to call itself democratic.

Only by following these principles can a political system be called "democratic." In addition, democracies must practice **majority rule** and preserve **minority rights.** In a democracy, choosing among alternatives (whether policies or officeholders) means weighing the desires of the majority.

Nothing is more fundamental to democratic theory than majority rule. Alexis de Tocqueville, the great French intellectual who traveled through America in the 1830s, wrote that "the very essence of democratic government consists in the absolute sovereignty of the majority. The power of the majority in America is not only preponderant, but irresistible."[11]

Interestingly, de Tocqueville was only describing, not approving. In fact, his observations about majority rule in America concluded with this harsh judgment: "This state of things is harmful in itself, and dangerous for the future." Today most Americans would disagree.

In addition, although Americans believe in majority rule, most also feel it is vital to protect minority rights such as freedom of speech and assembly. In a society too large to make its decisions in open meetings, a few will have to look after the concerns of the many. The relationship between the few leaders and the many followers is one of **representation.** The closer the correspondence between representatives and their electoral majority, the closer the approximation to democracy. Three contemporary theories presenting different views on how the representation process works are discussed in the following section.

THREE CONTEMPORARY THEORIES OF AMERICAN DEMOCRACY

All bodies of knowledge use theories to simplify and explain a mass of detail. In physics, there are Newtonian theories, atomic theories, and theories of relativity. One way that the history of science can be written is in terms of the conflict of different theories over the centuries.

Theories of American politics are also plentiful. There are elite theories, rational-choice theories, cultural theories, and psychological theories, among others. Each focuses on a key element of politics, and each reaches a somewhat different conclusion. Theories of American democracy are essentially theories about who has power and influence. All, in one way or another, ask the question "Who really governs in our nation?"

Pluralism One important theory of American democracy, **pluralist theory,** contends that many centers of influence vie for power and control. Groups compete with one another for control over public policy, and no one group or set of groups dominates. Pluralists' views of American government are thus generally positive. There are, they say, multiple access points to our government. Given that power is dispersed among the various branches and levels of government, groups that lose in one arena can take their case to another. According to pluralists, bargaining and compromise are essential ingredients in our democracy. The result is a rough approximation of the public interest in public policy.

Pluralists doubt that electoral majorities can or do really rule. Robert Dahl had this to say about majority rule: "On matters of specific policy the majority rarely rules."[12] Rather, he said, "A central, guiding thread of American constitutional development has been the evolution of a political system in which all active and legitimate groups in the population can make themselves heard at some crucial stage in the process."[13]

Group politics is certainly as American as apple pie. Alexis de Tocqueville called us a "nation of joiners." And we continue to be, especially given the recent explosion of interest group activity. Groups are without a doubt on the rise in American political life, as will be discussed at length in Chapter 11. Groups and their lobbyists—the groups' representatives in Washington—have become masters of the technology of politics. Computers, mass mailing lists, sophisticated media advertising, and hard-sell techniques are their stock-in-trade. As a result, some observers believe that Dahl's pluralist vision that all groups are heard via the American political process is more true now than ever before.

Elite and Class Theory Critics of pluralism believe that this view paints too rosy a picture of American political life. By arguing that almost every group can get a piece of the pie, they say, pluralists miss the larger question of how the pie is distributed. The poor may get their food stamps, but the rich still get their tax deductions. Governmental programs may help minorities, but the income gap between African Americans and whites remains wide.

Elite and class theory contends that our society, like all societies, is divided along class lines and that an upper-class elite rules regardless of the formal niceties of governmental organization. Wealth—the holding of assets such as property, stocks, and bonds—is the basis of this power. Over a third of the nation's wealth is currently held by just 1 percent of the population. Elite and class theorists believe that this 1 percent of Americans controls most policy decisions because they can afford to finance election campaigns and control key institutions, such as large corporations. According to elite and class theory, a few powerful Americans do not merely influence policymakers—they *are* the policymakers.

At the center of all theories of elite dominance is, of course, big business. Around the turn of the century, Woodrow Wilson charged that "the masters of the Government of the United States are the combined capitalists and manufacturers of the United States." One of his successors as president, Calvin Coolidge, expressed his favorable attitude toward business when he stated that "The business of America is business." No recent president has tried harder to help big business than

Ronald Reagan, and many elite theorists believe that he succeeded beyond all expectations. As Kevin Phillips wrote in his best seller *The Politics of Rich and Poor,* "The 1980s were the triumph of upper America—an ostentatious celebration of wealth, the political ascendancy of the richest third of the population and a glorification of capitalism, free markets and finance."[14]

It is doubtful that anything quite like this will be written about the Clinton Administration. However, big business is still very influential. Journalist Bob Woodward's account of Clinton's first year in office argues that many promises made in Clinton's "Putting People First" program were sacrificed to satisfy the demands of Wall Street.[15] Reflecting on the source of *real* power, Clinton's 1992 campaign manager, James Carville, is reported to have said, "I used to think if there was reincarnation, I wanted to come back as the president or the pope or a .400 baseball hitter. But now I want to come back as the bond market. You can intimidate everybody."[16] Elite theorists maintain that who holds office in Washington is of marginal consequence; it is the corporate giants that always have the power.

Hyperpluralism A third theory, **hyperpluralism,** offers a different critique of pluralism. Hyperpluralism is pluralism gone sour. In this view, groups are so strong that government is weakened, as the influence of many groups cripples government's ability to make policy. Hyperpluralism states that many groups—not just the elite ones—are so strong that government is unable to act.

Whereas pluralism maintains that input from groups is a good thing for the political decision-making process, hyperpluralism asserts that there are *too* many ways for groups to control policy. Our fragmented federal political system containing governments with overlapping jurisdictions is one major factor that contributes to hyperpluralism. Too many governments can make it hard to coordinate policy implementation. Any policy requiring the cooperation of several levels of government can be hampered by the reluctance of any one of them. Too many cooks may spoil the broth; so can too many governments.

According to hyperpluralists, groups have become sovereign and government is merely their servant. Groups that lose policymaking battles in Congress these days do not give up the battle; they carry it to the courts. Recently, the number of cases brought to state and federal courts has soared. Environmentalists use legal procedures to delay the construction of nuclear power plants; businesses take federal regulatory agencies to court to fight the implementation of regulations; religious groups drag local school districts into court to secure injunctions against sex education. The courts have become one more battleground in which policies can be effectively opposed as each group tries to bend policy to suit its own purposes.

These powerful groups divide the government and its authority. Hyperpluralist theory holds that government gives in to every conceivable interest and single-issue group. When politicians try to placate every group, the result is confusing, contradictory, and muddled policy—if politicians manage to make policy at all. Like elite and class theorists, hyperpluralist theorists suggest that the public interest is rarely translated into public policy.

CHALLENGES TO DEMOCRACY

Regardless of which theory is most convincing, there are a number of continuing challenges to democracy. Many of these challenges apply to American democracy as well as to the fledgling democracies around the world.

How Can the People Confront Complex Issues? Traditional democratic theory holds that ordinary citizens have the good sense to reach political judgments and that government has the capacity to act on those judgments. Today, however, we live in a society of experts, whose technical knowledge overshadows the knowledge of most people. What, after all, does the average citizen—however conscientious—know about chemical dumps, oil spills, Japanese competition, eligibility criteria for welfare, and the hundreds of other issues that confront government each year? Alexander Hamilton, the architect of the American economic system and George Washington's secretary of the treasury, once said that every society is divided into the few and the many. He argued that the few will rule; the many will be ruled. Years ago, the power of the few—the elite—might have been based on property holdings. Today, the elite are likely to be those who command knowledge, the experts. Even the most rigorous democratic theory does not demand that citizens be experts on everything; but as human knowledge has expanded, it has become increasingly difficult for individual citizens to make well-informed decisions.

Are Citizens Doing Their Job? When citizens do not seem to take their citizenship seriously, democracy's defenders worry. There is plenty of evidence that Americans know little about who their leaders are, much less about their policy decisions, as we will discuss at length in Chapter 6. Furthermore, Americans do not take full advantage of their opportunities to shape government or select its leaders.

Only 49 percent of eligible voters participated in the 1996 presidential election. These facts worry many democratic thinkers.

Is American Democracy Too Dependent on Money? Many political observers worry about the close connection between money and politics, especially in congressional elections. Winning a congressional seat these days usually requires a campaign war chest of *at least* half a million dollars. Candidates have become increasingly dependent on Political Action Committees (PACs) to fund their campaigns because of the escalation of campaign costs. These PACs often represent specific economic interests, and they care little about how members of Congress vote on most issues—just the issues that particularly affect them. Critics charge that when it comes to the issues the PACs care about, the members of Congress listen, lest they be denied the money they need for their reelection. When democracy confronts the might of money, the gap between democratic theory and reality widens further. Free elections are a cornerstone of democracy. When elections are bought, manipulated, sold, or sullied, democracy suffers.

Can the Political System Adapt to Today's Rapidly Changing World? Politics is always in a constant state of change, but over the last three decades the *rate* of change has been dizzying. Some commentators question whether, with the world's oldest constitutional framework—one that was designed to resist change—the American political system can be responsive to changing demands. James Sundquist writes that "A government too inefficient to embark on adventurous efforts to change society is also liable to be, by necessity, too inefficient to meet its inescapable, imperative responsibilities."[17]

In 1963, Bill Clinton was inspired to pursue a political career by shaking hands with President Kennedy during a White House ceremony for high school students. The concepts of American politics and government that Clinton learned while he was in college were shaped by the Kennedy years, just as the current political situation shapes much of the material in this book. However, a comparison of this textbook to the one that Bill Clinton used three decades ago would reveal tremendous differences. To cite just a few examples, the Kennedy era was one when voters trusted those in public office, political parties were strong, and the budget deficit was rarely a political issue; today, cynicism about politics is pervasive, parties are weak, and the deficit is a continuing major problem.

Anthony King writes that "Political scientists, more than many of them realize, are takers of snapshots rather than moving pictures."[18] In particular, he notes that those who study political institutions explain how and why they function as they do without addressing how they have functioned differently in the past. Although this book is mostly a snapshot of government in America at the present time, we believe it is important to present a regular focus on change over the last four decades as well. In subsequent chapters, you will find a feature entitled "Since Kennedy" that will help you understand how the American political system has adapted to change between these two eras.

In addition to examining how American politics has adapted to a changing society and world, we also look

In 1963, 16-year-old Bill Clinton made his first trip to Washington as one of Arkansas' representatives to Boys Nation. At a White House ceremony, Clinton shook hands with President John F. Kennedy. Clinton has often said that it was at this moment that he decided to pursue a career in politics.

Cartoonists & Writers Syndicate

toward the future in an attempt to illuminate possible developments that may impact politics and government in the coming decades. Because any discussion of the future is necessarily speculative, we include this "In the Twenty-First Century" feature only where issues that are likely to be of consequence during a student's lifetime can be readily identified.

Does America's Diversity Produce Governmental Gridlock? The diversity of the American people is reflected in the diversity of political interests represented in the political system. As we will see, this system is so open that interests find it easy to gain effective access to policymakers. Moreover, the distribution of power within the government is so decentralized that access to a few policymakers may be enough to determine the outcome of battles over public policy.

When interests disagree, which they often do, no coalition may be strong enough to form a majority and establish policy. But each interest may use its influence to thwart those whose policy proposals they oppose. In effect, they have a veto over policy, creating what is often referred to as **policy gridlock.** This problem is magnified when voters choose a president of one party and congressional majorities of the other party, as has often been the case in recent years.

The result is that nothing may get done, even if action is widely desired by a clear majority of voters. For example, in the past few years, most people in the United States felt that the country faced a crisis in health care. Yet President Clinton was unable to overcome the opposition of various interests and fashion a comprehensive proposal that could pass Congress—even with a Democratic majority in both Houses in 1993–1994.

Business owners gathered at an entrance to Yellowstone National Park to protest the federal shutdown that occured in 1996 when President Clinton vetoed the budget plans of the Republican Congress.

Democracy is not necessarily an end in itself. For many, evaluations of democracy depend on what democratic government produces. Thus, a major challenge to democracy in America is to overcome the diversity of interests and fragmentation of power in order to deliver policies that are responsive to citizens' needs.

SOME KEY QUESTIONS ABOUT DEMOCRACY

Throughout *Government in America* you will be asked to evaluate American democracy. The chapters that follow will acquaint you with the development of democracy in the United States. For example, the next chapter will show that the U.S. Constitution was not originally designed to promote democracy but has slowly evolved to its current form. Much of America's move toward greater democracy has centered on the extension of civil liberties and civil rights (which Chapters 4 and 5 will review). Probably the most important civil right is the right to vote. Upcoming chapters will examine voting behavior and elections and ask the following questions about how people form their opinions and to what extent they express these opinions via elections.

- Are people knowledgeable about matters of public policy?
- Do they apply what knowledge they have to their voting choices?
- Are American elections designed to facilitate public participation?

These are the sorts of questions you will need to ask about the people's input into government.

Linkage institutions, such as interest groups, political parties, and the media, help translate input from the public into output from the policymakers. When you explore these institutions, you will consider the extent to which they either help or hinder democracy.

- Does the interest group system allow for all points of view to be heard, or do significant biases give advantages to particular groups?
- Do political parties provide voters with clear choices, or do they obscure their stands on issues in order to get as many votes as possible?
- If there are choices, do the media help citizens understand them?

It is up to public officials actually to make the policy choices, because American government is a representative democracy rather than a pure democracy. For democracy to work well, elected officials must be responsive to public opinion.

- Is the Congress representative of American society, and is it capable of reacting to changing times?
- Does the president look after the general welfare of the public, or has the office become too focused on the interests of the elite?

These are some of the crucial questions you will address in discussing the executive and legislative branches of government. In addition, the way our nonelected institutions—the bureaucracy and the courts—function is crucial to evaluating how well American democracy works. These institutions are designed to implement and interpret the law, but bureaucrats and judges often cannot avoid making public policy as well. When they do so, are they violating democratic principles for policy decisions, given that neither institution can be held accountable at the ballot box?

All of these questions concerning democracy in America have more than one answer. A goal of *Government in America* is to familiarize you with the different ways to approach, and answer, these questions. One way to approach all of the preceding questions is to address one of the most important questions facing modern American democracy: Is the scope of government responsibilities too vast, just about right, or not comprehensive enough?

THE SCOPE OF GOVERNMENT IN AMERICA

In his first presidential address to Congress in 1993, Bill Clinton stated, "I want to talk to you about what government can do because I believe government must do more." Toward this end, President Clinton later proposed a comprehensive government program to require businesses to provide a basic level of health insurance for their employees. Congressional Republicans lined up solidly against Clinton's plan for national health insurance, arguing that government intervention in the affairs of individual citizens and businesses does more harm than good.

Those who are inclined to support government involvement in matters such as health care argue that intervention is the only means of achieving important goals in American society. How else, they ask, can we ensure that everyone has enough to eat, clean air and water, and affordable housing? How else can we ensure that the disadvantaged are given opportunities for education and jobs and are not discriminated against? Opponents of widening the scope of government agree that these are worthwhile goals but challenge whether involving the federal government is an effective way to pursue them. Dick Armey, a key Republican leader in the House, expresses this view well when he writes, "There is more wisdom in millions of individuals making decisions in their own self-interest than there is in even the most enlightened bureaucrat (or congressman!) making decisions on their behalf."[19]

To understand the dimensions of this debate, it is important first to get some sense of the current scope of the federal government's activities.

HOW ACTIVE IS AMERICAN GOVERNMENT?

In terms of dollars spent, government in America is vast. Altogether, our governments—national, state, and local—spend about one out of every three dollars of our **gross domestic product**, the total value of all goods and services produced annually by the United States. In 1997, expenditures for all American governments amounted to about $2.4 trillion. Government not only spends large sums of money but also employs large numbers of people. About 18 million Americans work for one of our governments, mostly at the state and local level: teachers teach America's children, police officers deal with crime, university professors teach college students, and so on.

Consider some facts about the size of our national government:

- It spends more than $1.5 trillion annually (printed as a number, that's $1,500,000,000,000 a year).
- It employs nearly 5 million people.
- It owns one-third of the land in the United States.
- It occupies 2.6 billion square feet of office space, more than four times the office space located in the nation's ten largest cities.
- It owns and operates 437,000 nonmilitary vehicles.[20]

How does the American national government spend almost $1.5 trillion a year? National defense takes about one-sixth of the federal budget, a much smaller percentage than it did three decades ago. Social Security consumes more than one-fifth of the budget. Medicare is another big-ticket item, requiring nearly $160 billion a year, a little over one-tenth of the budget. State and local governments also get important parts of the federal government's budget. The federal government helps fund highway construction, airport construction, police departments, school districts, and other state and local functions. Americans often complain about the high cost of government, but most Americans approve of what government does with its money. There is little support to cut spending on most specific government programs.

When expenditures grow, tax revenues must grow to pay the additional costs. When taxes do not grow as fast as spending, a budget deficit results. Budget deficits have occurred for decades in the United States. The national government has recently fallen short of paying its bills by as much as $290 billion a year. Each year's deficit is piled onto the previous deficits, and the entire sum equals the national debt, all the money owed by the national government. Today the national debt is nearing $5 trillion.

Whatever the national problem—pollution, AIDS, earthquake relief, homelessness, hunger, sexism—many people expect Congress to solve the problem with legislation. Thus, American government certainly is large in terms of dollars spent, persons employed, and laws passed. Our concern, however, is less about the absolute size of government and more about whether government activity is what we want it to be.

LIBERAL AND CONSERVATIVE VIEWS OF THE SCOPE OF GOVERNMENT

Of all the issues that divide liberals and conservatives, probably the most important is their differing views on the appropriate scope of government. In the United States, **liberals** support a more active role for government in most spheres, together with higher spending and more regulation. In general, liberals favor

- More governmental regulation of the economy to promote such goals as health care, consumer protection, and a pollution-free environment.
- More policies to help disadvantaged groups, including policies to ensure and expand opportunities for poor people, minorities, and women.
- More policies to redistribute income, through taxation, from those with more to those with less.

Conservatives, on the other hand, favor

- Fewer governmental regulations and a greater reliance on the market to provide such things as jobs, health care, and pollution control.
- Fewer governmental policies in the name of disadvantaged groups, who conservatives believe will benefit most from a strong economy free from governmental intervention.
- Fewer tax laws that discourage business growth by establishing high rates for capital investment.

However, liberals do not always favor governmental action, and conservatives do not always oppose it. Liberals, for example, typically oppose using the power of government to restrict or prohibit abortions and to organize prayers in public schools, whereas conservatives generally favor such policies. Liberals are more likely to support restrictions on individual freedom in the economic sphere, whereas conservatives often support governmental involvement with individual freedom in noneconomic matters.

A COMPARATIVE PERSPECTIVE ON THE SCOPE OF GOVERNMENT

A useful way to think about political issues, such as the scope of government, is to compare the United States with other countries, especially other democracies with developed economies. Throughout *Government in America,* a feature entitled "America in Perspective" provides an opportunity to understand our country's government better by comparing the United States with other nations. For example, it is possible to compare the size of the gross domestic product spent by all levels of government in the United States with similar expenditures in other prosperous nations. Compared to most other economically developed nations, the United States devotes a smaller percentage of its resources to government. As we will see in Chapter 14, the tax burden on Americans is small compared to other democratic nations.

Further, most advanced industrial democracies have a system of national insurance that provides most health care; the United States does not, though President Clinton unsuccessfully tried to establish such a system. In other countries, national governments have taken it upon themselves to start up airline, telephone, and communications companies. Governments have built much of the housing in most Western nations, compared to only a small fraction of the housing in America. Thus, in terms of its impact on citizens' everyday lives, government in the United States actually does less than the governments of similar countries.

AMERICAN INDIVIDUALISM

One of the primary reasons for the comparatively small scope of American government is the prominence of **individualism** in American political thought and practice. Alexis de Tocqueville observed that

> Individualism is a mature and calm feeling, which disposes each member of the community to sever himself from the mass of his fellows and to draw apart with his family and his friends, so that after

Former President Ronald Reagan and former British Prime Minister Margaret Thatcher were close both personally and politically. Both leaders were great supporters of free-market policies and were opposed to government interventionism, and both effected major changes in their countries to this end.

> he has thus formed a little circle of his own, he willingly leaves society to itself.[21]

The immigrants who founded American society may have been diverse, but many shared a common dream of America as a place where one could make it on one's own without interference from government. Louis Hartz's *The Liberal Tradition in America* is a classic analysis of the dominant political beliefs during America's formative years.[22] Hartz argues that the major force behind limited government in America is that it was settled by people who fled from the feudal and clerical oppressions of the Old World. Once in the New World, such people wanted little from government other than for it to leave them alone.

Another reason for American individualism is the existence of a bountiful frontier—at least up until the turn of the twentieth century. Thus, not only did many people come to America to escape from governmental interference, but the frontier allowed them to get away from government almost entirely once they arrived. Frederick Jackson Turner's famous work on the significance of the frontier in American history argues that "the frontier is productive of individualism."[23] According to Turner, being in the wilderness and having to survive on one's own left settlers with an aversion to any control from the outside world—particularly from the government.

The results of these historical influences are evident in American politics today. Individualism remains highly valued in the United States, and the public policy consequences are a strong preference for free markets and limited government. The analysis of the scope of government in this book will return to the importance of individualism in American politics at various relevant points.

SOME KEY QUESTIONS ABOUT THE SCOPE OF GOVERNMENT

Debate over the scope of government is central to contemporary American politics, and it is a theme this text will examine in each chapter. Our goal is not to determine for you the proper role of the national government. Instead, you will explore the implications of the way politics, institutions, and policy in America affect the scope of government. By raising questions such as those listed in the next few paragraphs, you may draw your own conclusions about the appropriate role of government in America. Part One of *Government in America* examines the constitutional foundations of American government. A concern with the proper scope of government leads to a series of questions regarding the constitutional structure of American politics, including

- What role did the Constitution's authors foresee for the federal government?
- Does the Constitution favor a government with a broad scope, or is it neutral on this issue?
- Why did the functions of government increase, and why did they increase most at the national rather than the state level?
- Has bigger, more active government constrained freedom—as some feared?
- Or does the increased scope of government serve to protect civil liberties and civil rights?

Part Two focuses on those who make demands on government, including the public, political parties, interest groups, and the media. Here you will seek answers to questions such as

- Does the public favor a large, active government?

- Do competing political parties predispose the government to provide more public services?
- Do elections help control the scope of government, or do they legitimize an increasing role for the public sector?
- Are pressures from interest groups necessarily translated into more governmental regulations, bigger budgets, and the like?
- Has media coverage of government enhanced government's status and growth, or have the media been an instrument for controlling government?

Governmental institutions themselves obviously deserve close examination. Part Three discusses these institutions and asks

- Has the presidency been a driving force behind increasing the scope and power of government (and thus of the president)?
- Can the president control a government with so many programs and responsibilities?
- Is Congress, because it is subject to constant elections, predisposed toward big government?
- Is Congress too responsive to the demands of the public and organized interests?

The nonelected branches of government, which are also discussed in these chapters, are especially interesting when we consider the issue of the scope of government. For instance,

- Are the federal courts too active in policymaking, intruding on the authority and responsibility of other branches and levels of government?
- Is the bureaucracy too acquisitive, constantly seeking to expand its budgets and authority, or is it simply a reflection of the desires of elected officials?
- Is the bureaucracy too large, and thus a wasteful menace to efficient and fair implementation of public policies?

The next 20 chapters will search for answers to these and many other questions regarding the scope of government. And you will undoubtedly add a few questions of your own as you seek to resolve the issue of the proper scope of government involvement.

SUMMARY

This first chapter serves several important purposes. First, it introduces you to the meaning of government. Government consists of those institutions that make authoritative public policies for society as a whole. In the United States, four key institutions make policy at the national level: Congress, the presidency, the courts, and the bureaucracy. Politics is, very simply, who gets what, when, and how. People engage in politics for a variety of reasons, and all their activities in politics are collectively called political participation. The result of government and politics is public policy. Public policy includes all of the decisions and nondecisions by government.

The first question central to governing is "How should we be governed?" Americans are fond of calling their government democratic. Democratic government includes, above all else, a commitment to majority rule and minority rights. This text will help you compare the way American government works with the standards of democracy and will continually address questions about who holds power and who influences the policies adopted by government.

The second fundamental question regarding governing is "What should government do?" One of the most important issues about government in America has to do with the scope of government. Conservatives often talk about the evils of intrusive government; liberals see the national government as rather modest in comparison both to what it could do and to the functions governments perform in other democratic nations. *Government in America* will explore how the workings of American government affect what government actually does.

KEY TERMS

government
public goods
politics
political participation
single-issue groups
policy agenda
public policy
political system
political issue
linkage institutions
policy impacts
democracy
traditional democratic theory
majority rule
minority rights
representation
pluralist theory
elite and class theory
hyperpluralism
policy gridlock
gross domestic product
liberals
conservatives
individualism

FOR FURTHER READING

Bok, Derek. *The State of the Nation: Government and the Quest for a Better Society.* Cambridge, MA: Harvard University Press, 1996. An excellent analysis of how America is doing, compared to other major democracies, on a wide variety of policy aspects.

Dahl, Robert A. *Democracy and Its Critics.* New Haven, CT: Yale University Press, 1989. Dahl is one of the world's most articulate thinkers about democracy.

de Tocqueville, Alexis. *Democracy in America.* New York: Mentor Books, 1956. This classic by a nineteenth-century French aristocrat remains one of the most insightful works on the nature of American society and government.

Hartz, Louis. *The Liberal Tradition in America.* New York: Harcourt, Brace, 1955. A classic piece of analysis concerning why the scope of government has been more limited in America than in other democracies.

Kettl, Donald F. *Sharing Power: Public Governance and Private Markets.* Washington, DC: Brookings Institution, 1993. Explores the problems with contracting out government services to the private sector.

King, Anthony, ed. *The New American Political System,* 2nd version. Washington, DC: American Enterprise Institute, 1990. Reviews the profound changes in American politics and government since Kennedy was president.

Kingdon, John W. *Agendas, Alternatives, and Public Policies,* 2nd ed. New York: HarperCollins, 1995. One of the first efforts by a political scientist to examine the political agenda.

Savas, E. S. *Privatization: The Key to Better Government.* Chatham, NJ: Chatham House, 1987. His subtitle calls privatization the key to better government; liberals might not agree.

Smith, Hedrick. *The Power Game: How Washington Works.* New York: Ballantine, 1988. A good introduction to the political life of our nation's capital.

Stanley, Harold W., and Richard G. Niemi. *Vital Statistics on American Politics,* 5th ed. Washington, DC: Congressional Quarterly, 1995. Useful data on government, politics, and policy in the United States.

INTERNET RESOURCES

www.policy.com

Contains discussion of major policy issues of the day and links to resources about them.

www.vote-smart.org/reference/histdocs/fedlist/index.htm

The complete collection of *The Federalist Papers.*

www.c-span.org/alexis

Information and discussion about Tocqueville's classic work, *Democracy in America.*

www.yahoo.com/Government

The place to go to search for information about government and politics.

NOTES

1. Harold D. Lasswell, *Politics: Who Gets What, When, and How* (New York: McGraw-Hill, 1938).
2. Raymond E. Wolfinger and Steven J. Rosenstone, *Who Votes* (New Haven, CT: Yale University Press, 1980), 198.
3. On the growth of interest groups, see Jack L. Walker, "The Origins and Maintenance of Interest Groups in America," *American Political Science Review* 77 (June 1983): 390–406.
4. John Kingdon, *Agendas, Alternatives, and Public Policies* (Boston: Little, Brown, 1984), 3.
5. Randy Shilts, *And the Band Played On: Politics, People, and the AIDS Epidemic* (New York: Penguin Books, 1987).
6. All models of political systems are indebted to David Easton, "An Approach to the Analysis of Political Systems," *World Politics* 9 (April 1957): 379–389.
7. E. E. Schattschneider, *Two Hundred Million Americans in Search of a Government* (New York: Holt, Rinehart & Winston, 1969), 63.
8. Giovanni Sartori, *Theory of Democracy Revisited,* vol. 1 (Chatham, NJ: Chatham House, 1987), 22.
9. This conception of traditional democratic theory is derived from Robert A. Dahl, *Preface to Democratic Theory* (Chicago: University of Chicago Press, 1956), chaps. 2, 3; Joseph A. Schumpeter, *Capitalism, Socialism, and Democracy* (New York: Harper & Row, 1942), chap. 21; Anthony Downs, *An Economic Theory of Democracy* (New York: Harper & Row, 1957), 22-24; and Carl Cohen, *Democracy* (Athens, GA: University of Georgia Press, 1971).
10. Robert A. Dahl, *Dilemmas of Pluralist Democracy* (New Haven, CT: Yale University Press, 1983), 6.
11. Alexis de Tocqueville, *Democracy in America* (New York: Mentor Books, 1956), 112–113.
12. Dahl, *Preface,* 124.
13. Dahl, *Preface,* 137.
14. Kevin Phillips, *The Politics of Rich and Poor: Wealth and the American Electorate in the Reagan Aftermath* (New York: Random House, 1990), 1.
15. Bob Woodward, *The Agenda: Inside the Clinton White House* (New York: Simon & Schuster, 1994).
16. Woodward, *The Agenda,* 145.

17. James L. Sundquist, *Constitutional Reform and Effective Government,* revised ed. (Washington, D.C.: Brookings Institution, 1992), 5.
18. Anthony King, "Introduction," in King, ed., *The New American Political System* (Washington, DC: American Enterprise Institute, 1978), 1.
19. Dick Armey, *The Freedom Revolution* (Washington, D.C.: Regnery, 1995), 316.
20. E. S. Savas, *Privatization: The Key to Better Government* (Chatham, NJ: Chatham House, 1987), 13.
21. de Tocqueville, *Democracy in America,* vol. 2, 104.
22. See Louis Hartz, *The Liberal Tradition in America* (New York: Harcourt, Brace, 1955).
23. Frederick Jackson Turner, *The Significance of the Frontier in American History* (New York: Readex Microprint, 1966), 221.

PART ONE

Constitutional Foundations

No one pretends that democracy is perfect or all-wise. Indeed, it has been said that democracy is the worst form of Government except all those other forms that have been tried from time to time.

— *WINSTON CHURCHILL, 1947*

2 The Constitution

During the 1984 Republican National Convention in Dallas, Gregory Lee Johnson burned an American flag in front of city hall to protest nuclear weapons buildup. He was convicted of "desecration of a venerated object," sentenced to 1 year in prison, and fined $2,000. Johnson appealed his conviction, and in 1989 the U.S. Supreme Court, in the case of *Texas v. Gregory Lee Johnson,* found that the law under which he was prosecuted—and similar laws across the country—was unconstitutional because it violated freedom of speech. Burning the flag, the Court said, constituted speech and not just dramatic action.

Although Johnson was pleased, he was nearly alone. The public howled its opposition to the decision, and President Bush called for a constitutional amendment authorizing punishment of flag desecraters. Many public officials vowed to support the amendment; organized opposition to the amendment was scarce. However, an amendment to prohibit burning the American flag did *not* obtain the two-thirds vote in each house of Congress necessary to send a constitutional amendment to the states for ratification.

Congress did, however, pass a regular law—the Flag Protection Act of 1989—that outlawed the desecration of the American flag. The next year, in *United States v. Eichman,* the Supreme Court found the act an impermissible infringement on free speech.

In the end, after years of political posturing, legislation, and litigation, little had changed. Burning the flag remains a legally protected form of political expression despite the objections of the overwhelming majority of the American public.

Understanding how unpopular protestors could win against the combined forces of the public and its elected officials is central to understanding the American system of government. The Constitution supersedes ordinary law, even when the law represents the wishes of a majority of citizens. The Constitution not only guarantees individual rights but also decentralizes power. Even the president, "the leader of the free world," cannot force Congress to act, as Bush could not force Congress to start the process of amending the Constitution. Power is not concentrated efficiently in one person's hands, such as the president's. Instead, there are numerous checks on the exercise of power and many obstacles to change. Some complain that this system produces stalemate, while others praise the way it protects minority views. Both positions are correct.

Gregory Johnson's case, then, raises some important questions about government in America. What does democracy mean if the majority does not get its way? Is this how we should be governed? And is it appropriate that the many limits, both direct and indirect, on the scope of government action prevent action desired by most people?

A **constitution** is a nation's basic law. It creates political institutions, allocates power within government, and often provides guarantees to citizens. A constitution is also an unwritten accumulation of traditions and precedents that have established acceptable styles of behavior and policy outcomes.

A constitution sets the broad rules of the game of politics, allowing certain types of competition among certain players. *These rules are never neutral,* however. Instead, they give some participants and some policy options advantages over others in the policymaking process. This is why understanding these rules is so important to understanding government and to

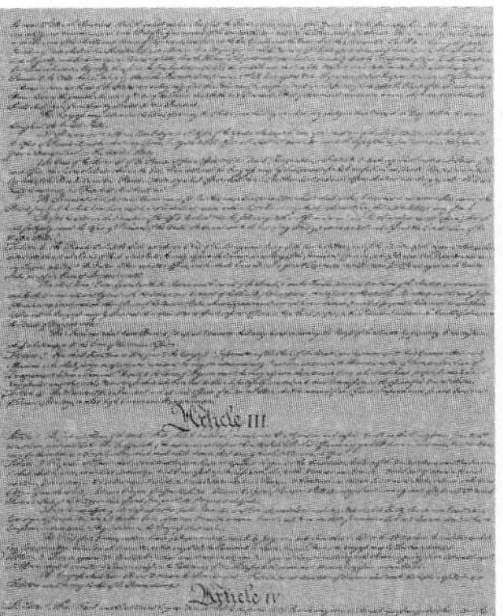
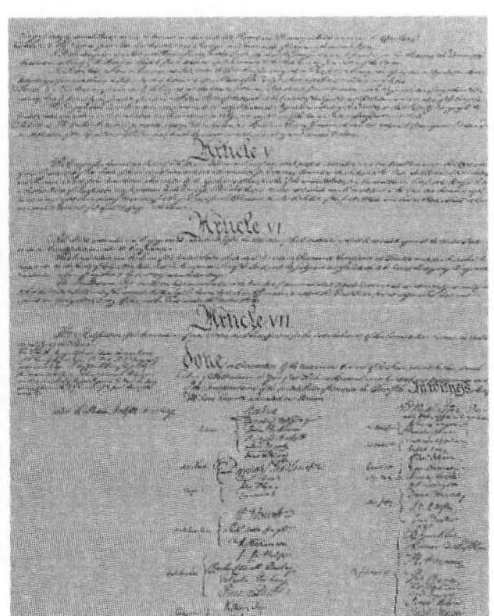

The original of the United States Constitution

answering questions about how we are governed and what government does.

THE ORIGINS OF THE CONSTITUTION

In the summer of 1776, a small group of men met in Philadelphia and passed a resolution that began an armed rebellion against the government of the most powerful nation on earth. The resolution was, of course, the Declaration of Independence; the armed rebellion was the American Revolution.

The attempt to overthrow a government forcibly is a serious and unusual act. It is considered treasonous everywhere, including in the United States. Typically, it is punishable by death. A set of compelling ideas drove our forefathers to take such drastic and risky action. It is important to understand these ideas in order to understand the Constitution.

THE ROAD TO REVOLUTION

By eighteenth-century standards, life was not bad for most people in America at the time of the Revolution (slaves and indentured servants being major exceptions). In fact, white colonists "were freer, more equal, more prosperous, and less burdened with cumbersome feudal and monarchical restraints than any other part of mankind."[1] Although the colonies were part of the British empire, the king and Parliament generally confined themselves to governing America's foreign policy and trade. Almost everything else was left to the discretion of individual colonial governments. Although commercial regulations irritated colonial shippers, planters, land speculators, and merchants, these rules had little influence on the vast bulk of the population who were self-employed farmers or artisans.

As you can see in Figure 2.1, Britain obtained an enormous new territory in North America after the French and Indian War ended in 1763. The cost of defending this territory against foreign adversaries was large, and Parliament reasoned that it was only fair that those who were the primary beneficiaries—the colonists—should contribute to their own defense. Thus, in order to raise revenue for colonial administration and defense, the British legislature passed a series of taxes on official documents, newspapers, paper, glass, paint, and, of course, tea. Britain also began tightening enforcement of its trade regulations, which were designed to benefit the mother country, not the colonists.

Colonists resented these taxes, especially because they were imposed without the colonists' enjoying any direct representation in Parliament. They protested, boycotted the taxed goods, and as a symbolic act of disobedience even threw 342 chests of tea into Boston Harbor. Britain reacted by applying economic pressure through a naval blockade of the harbor, further fueling the colonists' anger. The colonists responded by forming the First Continental Congress in September 1774, sending delegates from each colony to Philadelphia to discuss the future of relations with Britain.

DECLARING INDEPENDENCE

As colonial discontent with the English festered, the Continental Congress was in almost continuous session during 1775 and 1776. Talk of independence was common among the delegates. Virginia, as it often did in those days, played a leading role at the Philadelphia meeting of the Congress. It sent seven delegates to join the serious discussion of repudiating the rule of King George III. These delegates were joined later by a last-minute substitute for Peyton Randolph, who was needed back in Williamsburg to preside over Virginia's House of Burgesses.

The substitute, Thomas Jefferson, was a young, well-educated Virginia lawmaker who had just written a resolution in the Virginia legislature objecting to new British policies. He traveled to Philadelphia attended by his slaves Richard and Jesse and, being in no great hurry to get there, stopped along the way to purchase some books and a new stallion.[2] Jefferson brought to the Continental Congress his talent as an author and the knowledge of a careful student of political philosophy. Jefferson was not a rabble-rousing pamphleteer like Thomas Paine, whose fiery tract *Common Sense* had appeared in January 1776 and fanned the already hot flames of revolution. Jefferson was steeped in the philosophical writings of European moral philosophers, and his rhetoric matched his reading.

In May and June of 1776, the Continental Congress began debating resolutions about independence. On June 7, Richard Henry Lee of Virginia moved "that these United States are and of rights ought to be free and independent states." A committee composed of Thomas Jefferson of Virginia, John Adams of Massachusetts, Benjamin Franklin of Pennsylvania, Roger Sherman of Connecticut, and Robert Livingston of New York was busily drafting a document to justify the inevitable declaration. On July 2, Lee's motion to declare independence from England was formally approved. The famous **Declaration of Independence,** written primarily by Jefferson, was adopted two days later, on July 4.

FIGURE 2.1 EUROPEAN CLAIMS IN NORTH AMERICA

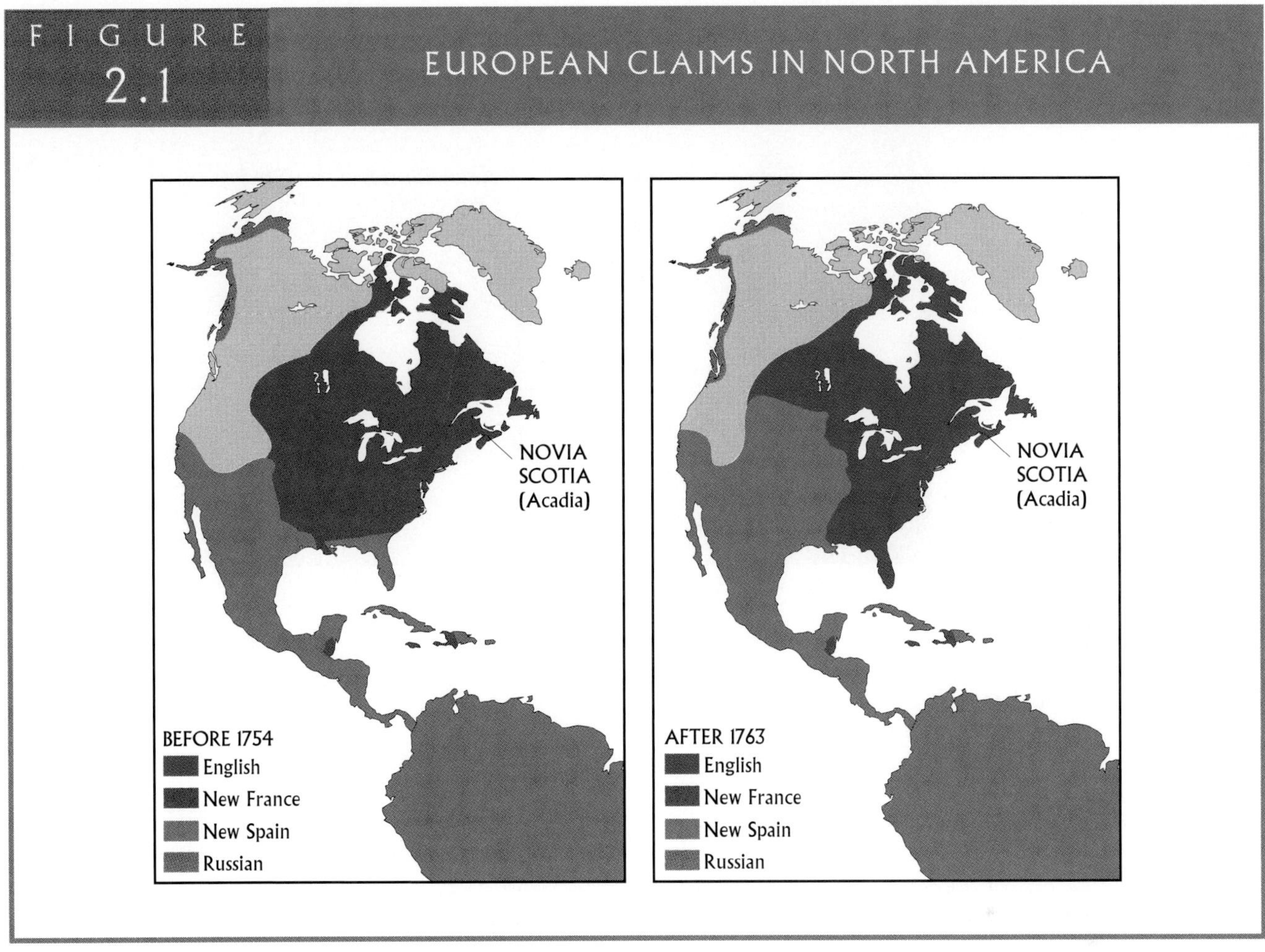

The Declaration of Independence quickly became one of the most widely quoted and revered documents in America. Filled with fine principles and bold language, it can be read as both a political tract and a philosophical treatise. (It is reprinted in the appendix.)

Politically, the Declaration was a polemic, announcing and justifying a revolution. Most of the document—27 of its 32 total paragraphs—listed the ways the King had abused the colonies. George III was accused of all sorts of evil deeds, even though he personally had little to do with Parliament's colonial policies. King George was even blamed for inciting the "merciless Indian savages" to make war on the colonists. The King took the blame because the Convention delegates held that Parliament lacked authority over the colonies.

The Declaration's polemical aspects were important because the colonists needed foreign assistance to take on the most powerful nation in the world. France, which was engaged in a war with Britain, was a prime target for the delegates' diplomacy and eventually provided aid that was critical to the success of the Revolution.

Today, the Declaration of Independence is studied more as a statement of philosophy than as a political polemic. In just a few sentences, Jefferson set forth the American democratic creed, the most important and succinct statement of the philosophy underlying American government—as applicable in the year 2000 as it was in 1776.

THE ENGLISH HERITAGE: THE POWER OF IDEAS

Philosophically, the Jeffersonian pen put on paper ideas that were by then common knowledge on both sides of the Atlantic, especially among those people who wished to challenge the power of kings. Franklin, Jefferson, Madison, Morris, Hamilton, and other intellectual leaders in the colonies were learned and widely read men, familiar with the words of

John Adams (from left), Roger Sherman, Robert R. Livingston, Thomas Jefferson, and Benjamin Franklin submit the Declaration of Independence to Continental Congress President John Hancock. Legend has it that Hancock remarked, "We must be unanimous; there must be no pulling different ways; we must hang together," to which Franklin replied, "We must indeed all hang together, or, most assuredly, we shall hang separately."

English, French, and Scottish political philosophers. These leaders corresponded about the ideas they were reading, quoted philosophers in their debates over the Revolution, and applied those ideas to the new government they formed in the framework of the Constitution.

John Locke was one of the most influential philosophers read by the colonists. His writings, especially *The Second Treatise of Civil Government* (1689), profoundly influenced American political leaders. His work was "the dominant political faith of the American colonies in the second quarter of the eighteenth century. A thousand pulpits thundered with its benevolent principles; a hundred editors filled their pages with its famous slogans."[3]

The foundation upon which Locke built his powerful philosophy was a belief in **natural rights**—rights inherent in human beings, not dependent on governments. Before governments arise, Locke held, people exist in a state of nature, where they are governed only by the laws of nature. Natural law brings natural rights, including life, liberty, and property. Natural law can even justify a challenge to the rule of a tyrannical king, because natural law is superior to human law. Government, Locke argued, must be built on the **consent of the governed;** in other words, the people must agree on who their rulers will be. It should also be a **limited government;** that is, there must be clear restrictions on what rulers can do. Indeed, the sole purpose of government, according to Locke, is to protect natural rights. The idea that certain things were beyond the realm of government contrasted sharply

John Locke, 1637–1704, was an English physician, philosopher, diplomat, and civil servant. Locke wrote *The Second Treatise of Civil Government* (1689), an important source of ideas reflected in both the Declaration of Independence and the Constitution.

with the traditional notion that kings had been divinely granted absolute rights over subjects.

Two limits on government were particularly important to Locke. First, governments must provide standing laws so that people know in advance whether their acts will be acceptable. Second, and Locke was very forceful on this point, "the supreme power cannot take from any man any part of his property without his consent." To Locke, "the preservation of property was the end of government." The sanctity of property was one of the few ideas absent in Jefferson's draft of the Declaration of Independence. Even though Jefferson borrowed from and even paraphrased Lockean ideas, he altered Locke's phrase "life, liberty, and property" to "life, liberty, and the pursuit of happiness." We shall soon see, though, how the Lockean idea of the sanctity of property figured prominently at the Constitutional Convention. James Madison, the most influential member of that body, directly echoed Locke's view that the preservation of property is the purpose of government.

In an extreme case, said Locke, people have a right to revolt against a government that no longer has their consent. Locke anticipated critics' charges that this right would lead to constant civil disturbances. But he stressed that people should not revolt until injustices become deeply felt. The Declaration of Independence accented the same point, emphasizing that "governments long established should not be changed for light and transient causes." But when matters went beyond "patient sufferance," severing these ties was not only inevitable but also necessary.

JEFFERSON'S HANDIWORK: THE AMERICAN CREED

There are some remarkable parallels between Locke's thought and Jefferson's language in the Declaration of Independence (see Table 2.1). Jefferson, like Locke, finessed his way past the issue of how the rebels knew men had rights. Jefferson simply declared that it was "self-evident" that men were equally "endowed by their Creator with certain unalienable rights," including "life, liberty, and the pursuit of happiness." Because it was the purpose of government to "secure" these rights, if a government failed to do so, the people could form a new government.[4]

Locke represented only one element of revolutionary thought from which Jefferson borrowed. In the English countryside, there was also a well-established tradition of opposition to the executive power of the Crown and support for recovering the rights of the people. A native-American republicanism—stressing moral virtue, patriotism, relations based on natural merit, and the equality of independent citizens—intensified the radicalism of this "country" ideology and linked it with older currents of European thought stretching back to antiquity.

It was in the American colonies that the powerful ideas of European political thinkers took root and grew into what Seymour Martin Lipset has termed the "first new nation."[5] With these revolutionary ideas in mind, Jefferson claimed in the Declaration of Independence that people should have primacy over governments, that they should rule instead of be ruled. Moreover, each person was important as an individual, "created equal" and endowed with "unalienable rights." Consent of the governed, not divine rights or tradition, made the exercise of political power legitimate.

No government had ever been based on these principles. Ever since 1776, Americans have been concerned about fulfilling the high aspirations of the Declaration of Independence.

WINNING INDEPENDENCE

The pen may be mightier than the sword, but declaring independence did not win the Revolution—it merely announced its beginning. John Adams wrote to his wife Abigail, "You will think me transported with enthusiasm, but I am not. I am well aware of the toil, blood, and treasure that it will cost us to maintain this Declaration, and support and defend these states." Adams was right. The colonials seemed little match for the finest army in the world, whose size was nearly quadrupled by hired guns from the German state of Hesse and elsewhere. In 1775, the British had 8,500 men stationed in the colonies and had hired nearly 30,000 mercenaries. Initially, the colonists had only 5,000 men in uniform, and their number waxed and waned as the war progressed. How they eventually won is a story best left to history books. How they formed a new government, however, will be explored in the following sections.

THE "CONSERVATIVE" REVOLUTION

Revolutions such as the 1789 French Revolution, the 1917 Russian Revolution, and the 1978–1979 Iranian Revolution produced great societal change—as well as plenty of bloodshed. The American Revolution was different. Although many people lost their lives during the Revolutionary War, the Revolution itself was essentially a conservative movement that did not drastically alter the colonists' way of life. Its primary goal was to restore rights the colonists felt were already theirs as British subjects.

TABLE 2.1 LOCKE AND THE DECLARATION OF INDEPENDENCE: SOME PARALLELS

LOCKE	DECLARATION OF INDEPENDENCE
Natural Rights	
"The state of nature has a law to govern it, which obliges everyone."	"Laws of Nature and Nature's God"
"life, liberty, and property"	"life, liberty, and the pursuit of happiness"
Purpose of Government	
"to preserve himself, his liberty, and property"	"to secure these rights"
Equality	
"men being by nature all free, equal and independent"	"all men are created equal"
Consent of the Governed	
"for when any number of men have, by the consent of every individual, made a community, with a power to act as one body, which is only by the will and determination of the majority"	"Governments are instituted among men, deriving their just powers from the consent of the governed."
Limited Government	
"Absolute arbitrary power, or governing without settled laws, can neither of them consist with the ends of society and government." "As usurpation is the exercise of power which another has a right to, so tyranny is the exercise of power beyond right, which nobody can have a right to."	"The history of the present King of Great Britain is a history of repeated injuries and usurpations."
Right to Revolt	
"The people shall be the judge. . . . Oppression raises ferments and makes men struggle to cast off an uneasy and tyrannical yoke."	"Prudence, indeed, will dictate that Governments long established should not be changed for light and transient causes; and accordingly all experience hath shewn, that mankind are most disposed to suffer, while evils are sufferable, than to right themselves by abolishing the forms to which they are accustomed. But when a long train of abuses and usurpations, pursuing invariably the same Object evinces a design to reduce them under absolute Despotism, it is their right, it is their duty, to throw off such Government."

American colonists did not feel the need for great social, economic, or political upheavals. They "were not oppressed people; they had no crushing imperial shackles to throw off."[6] As a result, the Revolution did not create class conflicts that would split society for generations to come. The colonial leaders' belief that they needed the consent of the governed blessed the new nation with a crucial element of stability—a stability the nation would need.

THE GOVERNMENT THAT FAILED: 1776–1787

The Continental Congress that adopted the Declaration of Independence was only a voluntary association of the states. In 1776, the Congress appointed a committee to draw up a plan for a permanent union of the states. That plan, our first constitution, was the **Articles of Confederation.**[7]

The Articles of Confederation. The Articles established a government dominated by the states. The United States, according to the Articles, was a "league of friendship and perpetual union" among 13 states that were themselves sovereign. The Articles established a national legislature with one house; states could send as many as seven delegates or as few as two, but each state had only one vote. There was no president and no national court, and the powers of the national legislature—the Congress—were strictly limited. Most authority rested with the state legislatures because the new nation's leaders feared a strong central government would become as tyrannical as British rule.

The Articles adopted by Congress in 1777 did not go into effect until 1781, when laggard Maryland finally ratified them, because unanimous consent of the states was needed to put the Articles into operation. In the meantime, the Continental Congress barely survived, lurching from crisis to crisis (as when some of Washington's troops threatened to create a monarchy with him as king unless Congress paid their overdue wages).

Even after the Articles were ratified, many logistical and political problems plagued the Continental Congress. State delegations attended haphazardly. Thomas Jefferson, a delegate to an Annapolis meeting of the Congress, complained as follows to his friend and fellow Virginian James Madison on February 20, 1784.

> We cannot make up a congress at all. There are eight states in town, six of which are represented by two members only. Of these, two members of different states are confined by gout, so that we cannot make . . . a quorum. We have not sat above three days, I believe, in as many weeks. Admonition after admonition has been sent to the states to no effect. We have sent one today. If it fails, it seems as well we should all retire.[8]

The Continental Congress had few powers outside of maintaining an army and navy—and little money to do even that. It had to request money from the states, because it had no power to tax. If states refused to send money (which they often did), Congress did without. In desperation, Congress sold off western lands to speculators, issued securities that sold for less than their face value, or used its own presses to print money that was virtually worthless. Congress also voted to disband the army, despite continued threats from the British and Spanish.

Congress lacked the power to regulate commerce, which inhibited foreign trade and the development of a strong national economy. It did, however, manage to develop sound policies for the management of the western frontiers, passing the Northwest Ordinance of 1787 that encouraged the development of the Great Lakes region.

In general, the weak and ineffective national government could take little independent action. All government power rested in the states. The national government could not compel the states to do anything, and it had no power to deal directly with individual citizens. The weakness of the national government prevented it from dealing with the hard times that faced the new nation. There was one benefit of the Articles, however: When the nation's leaders began to write a new Constitution, they could look at the provisions of the Articles of Confederation and know some of the things they should avoid.

Changes in the States. What was happening in the states was more important than what was happening in the Continental Congress. The most important change was a dramatic increase in democracy and liberty, at least for white males. Many states adopted bills of rights to protect freedoms, abolished religious qualifications for holding office, and liberalized requirements for voting. Expanded political participation brought a new middle class to power.

This middle class included farmers who owned small homesteads rather than manorial landholders—and artisans instead of lawyers. Before the Revolution, almost all members of New York's Assembly were either urban merchants or wealthy landowners. In the 1769 Assembly, for example, 57 percent of the legislators were nonfarmers even though nearly 95 percent of New Yorkers were farmers. But after the Revolution, a major power shift occurred. With expanded voting privileges, farmers and craftworkers became a decisive majority, and the old elite saw its power shrink. The same change happened in other states as power shifted from a handful of wealthy individuals to a more broad-based group (see Table 2.2). After a careful examination of the economic backgrounds of pre- and postrevolutionary legislators, Jackson Turner Main concluded,

> The voters had ceased to confine themselves to an elite, but were selecting instead men like themselves. The tendency to do so had started during the colonial period, especially in the North, and had now increased so dramatically as almost to revolutionize the legislatures.[9]

Democracy was taking hold everywhere.

The structure of government in the states also became more responsive to the people. Power was concentrated in the legislatures, because legislators were considered closer to the voters than governors or judges. Governors were often selected by the legislatures and were kept on a short leash, with brief tenures and limited veto and appointment powers. Legislatures overruled court decisions and criticized judges for unpopular decisions.

The idea of equality was driving change everywhere. Although the Revolutionary War itself did not transform American society, it unleashed the republican tendencies in American life. Americans were in the process of becoming "the most liberal, the most democratic, the most commercially minded, and the most modern people in the world."[10] Members of the old colonial elite found this turn of affairs quite troublesome, because it challenged their hold on power.

Economic Turmoil. After the Revolution, James Madison observed that "the most common and durable source of factions has been the various and unequal division of property."[11] The postrevolutionary legislatures epitomized Madison's argument that economic inequality played an important role in shaping public policy. At the top of the political agenda were economic issues. A postwar depression had left many small farmers unable to pay their debts and threatened them with mortgage foreclosures. Now under control of people more sympathetic to debtors, the state legislatures listened to the demands of small farmers. A few states, notably Rhode Island, demonstrated their support of debtors, passing policies favoring them over creditors. Some printed tons of paper money and passed "force acts" requiring reluctant creditors to accept the almost worthless money. Debtors could thus pay big debts with cheap currency.

TABLE 2.2 POWER SHIFT: ECONOMIC STATUS OF STATE LEGISLATORS BEFORE AND AFTER THE REVOLUTIONARY WAR

After the Revolution, power in the state legislatures shifted from the hands of the wealthy to those with more moderate incomes, and from merchants and lawyers to farmers. This trend was especially evident in the northern states.

	THREE NORTHERN STATES[a]		THREE SOUTHERN STATES[b]	
STATUS OF LEGISLATORS	PREWAR	POSTWAR	PREWAR	POSTWAR
Wealthy	36%	12%	52%	28%
Well-to-do	47%	26%	36%	42%
Moderate	17%	62%	12%	30%
Merchants and lawyers	43%	18%	23%	17%
Farmers	23%	55%	12%	26%

[a]New York, New Jersey, and New Hampshire.
[b]Maryland, Virginia, and South Carolina.
SOURCE: Jackson Turner Main, "Government by the People: The American Revolution and the Democratization of the Legislatures," *The William and Mary Quarterly,* 3rd ser. 23 (July 1966): Table 1. Reprinted by permission.

Shays' Rebellion. Policies favoring debtors over creditors did not please the economic elite who had once controlled nearly all the state legislatures. They were further shaken when, in 1786, a small band of farmers in western Massachusetts rebelled at losing their land to creditors. Led by Revolutionary War Captain Daniel Shays, this rebellion, called **Shays' Rebellion,** was a series of armed attacks on courthouses to prevent judges from foreclosing on farms. Farmers in other states—though never in large numbers—were also unruly. Jefferson called the attack a "little rebellion," but it remained on the minds of the economic elite. They were scared at the thought that people had taken the law into their own hands and violated the property rights of others. Neither Congress nor the state was able to raise a militia to stop Shays and his followers, and a privately paid force was assembled to do the job, which fueled dissatisfaction with the weakness of the Articles of Confederation system.

The Aborted Annapolis Meeting. In September 1786, a handful of continental leaders assembled at Annapolis, Maryland, to discuss problems with the Articles of Confederation and suggest solutions. The assembly was an abortive attempt at reform. Only five states—New York, New Jersey, Delaware, Pennsylvania, and Virginia—were represented at the meeting; the 12 delegates were few enough in number to meet around a dinner table. Called to consider commercial conflicts that had arisen among the states under the Articles of Confederation, the Annapolis delegates decided that a larger meeting and a broader proposal were needed to organize the states. This small and unofficial band of reformers (who held most of their meetings in a local tavern) issued a call for a full-scale meeting of the states in Philadelphia the following May—in retrospect, a rather bold move by so small a group. Their request was granted, however; the Continental Congress called for a meeting of all the states. In May 1787, what we now call the Constitutional Convention got down to business in Philadelphia.

Shays' Rebellion spurred the birth of the Constitution. News of the small rebellion—what we would now call a protest demonstration—quickly spread around the country, and some of the Philadelphia delegates thought a full-fledged revolution would result. The event reaffirmed the framers' belief that the new federal government needed to be a strong one.

MAKING A CONSTITUTION: THE PHILADELPHIA CONVENTION

Representatives from 12 states came to Philadelphia to heed the Continental Congress' call to "take into consideration the situation in the United States." Only Rhode Island, a stronghold of paper-money interests, refused to send delegates. Virginia's Patrick Henry, fearing a centralization of power, also "smelled a rat" in the developments in Philadelphia and did not attend.

The delegates were ordered to meet "for the sole and express purpose of revising the Articles of Confederation." The Philadelphia delegates did not pay much attention to this order, however, because amending the Articles required the unanimous consent of the states, which they knew would be impossible. Thus, the 55 delegates ignored their instructions and began writing what was to become the **U.S. Constitution.**

GENTLEMEN IN PHILADELPHIA

Who were these 55 men? They may not have been demigods, as Jefferson, perhaps sarcastically, called them, but they were certainly a select group of economic and political notables. They were mostly wealthy planters, successful (or once-successful) lawyers and merchants, and men of independent wealth. Many were college graduates, mostly from Princeton (nine alumni), Yale, William and Mary, Harvard, Columbia (then called King's College), and the University of Pennsylvania. Most were coastal residents, rather than residents of the expanding western frontiers, and a significant number were urbanites, rather than part of the primarily rural American population.

PHILOSOPHY INTO ACTION

Both philosophy and politics were prevalent at the Constitutional Convention. The delegates in Philadelphia were an uncommon combination of philosophers and shrewd political architects. The debates moved from high principles on the big issues to self-interest on the small ones.[12] The first two weeks were mainly devoted to general debates about the nature of republican government (government in which ultimate power rests with the voters). After that, very practical and very divisive issues sometimes threatened to dissolve the meeting.

Obviously, 55 men did not share the same political philosophy. Democratic Benjamin Franklin held very different views from aristocratic Alexander Hamilton, who hardly hid his disgust for democracy. Yet, at the core of their ideas, even those of Franklin and Hamilton, existed a common center. The group agreed on questions of human nature, the causes of political conflict, and the object and nature of a republican government.

James Madison, a Virginia lawyer and officeholder, was perhaps the most influential member of the Convention in translating political philosophy into government architecture. He is often called "the father of the Constitution."

A New York delegate to the Convention, Alexander Hamilton favored a strong central government; in fact, he favored an elected king. Hamilton was less influential at the Convention than he would be later as architect of the nation's economic policy.

Views of Human Nature. Reflecting the times in which they lived, the delegates held a cynical view of human nature. People, they thought, were self-interested. Franklin and Hamilton, poles apart philosophically, both voiced this sentiment. Said Franklin, "There are two passions which have a powerful influence on the affairs of men: the love of power and the love of money." Hamilton agreed in his characteristically blunt manner: "Men love power." The men at Philadelphia believed that government should play a key role in checking and containing the natural self-interest of people.[13]

Views of Political Conflict. Of all the words written by and about the delegates, none have been more widely quoted than these by James Madison: "The most common and durable source of factions has been the various and unequal distribution of property." *The distribution of wealth* (property was the main form of wealth in those days) *is the source of political conflict.* "Those who hold and those who are without property," Madison went on, "have ever formed distinct interests in society." Other sources of conflict included religion, views of governing, and attachment to various leaders.[14]

Arising from these sources of conflict are **factions,** as Madison called them (we might call them parties or interest groups). A majority faction might well be composed of the many who have little or no property; the minority faction, of those with property. If unchecked, the delegates thought, one of these factions would eventually tyrannize the other. The majority would try to seize the government to reduce the wealth of the minority; the minority would try to seize the government to secure its own gains. Governments that are run by factions, the founders believed, are prone to instability, tyranny, and even violence. The effects of factions had to be checked.

Views of the Objects of Government. To Gouverneur Morris of Pennsylvania, the preservation of property was the "principal object of government." Morris was outspoken and plainly overlooked some other objects of government, including security from invasion, domestic tranquility, and promotion of the general welfare. Morris' remark typifies the philosophy of many of the delegates. John Locke (who was, remember, the intellectual patron saint of many of the delegates) had said a century before that "The preservation of property is the end of government." Few of these men would have disagreed. Propertyholders themselves, these leaders could not imagine a government that did not make its principal objective an economic one: the preservation of individual rights to acquire and hold wealth. A few (like Morris) were intent on shutting out the propertyless altogether. "Give the votes to people who have no property," he claimed, "and they will sell them to the rich who will be able to buy them."

Views of Government. Human nature, the delegates believed, is avaricious and self-interested. The principal cause of political conflict is economic inequality. Either a majority or a minority faction will be tyrannical if it has too much power. Property must be protected against the tyrannical tendencies of factions. Given this set of beliefs, what sort of government did the delegates believe would work? The delegates answered in different ways, but the message was always the same. Power should be set against power, so that no one faction would overwhelm the others. The secret of good government is "balanced" government. A limited government would have to contain checks on its own power. So long as no faction could seize the whole of government at once, tyranny could be avoided. A complex network of checks, balances, and separation of powers would be required for a balanced government.

Pennsylvania delegate Gouverneur Morris was a man of considerable means and, like Hamilton, an extreme antidemocrat primarily concerned with protecting propertyholders. He was responsible for the style and wording of the Constitution.

THE AGENDA IN PHILADELPHIA

The delegates in Philadelphia could not merely construct a government from ideas. They wanted to design a government that was consistent with their political philosophy, but they also had to meet head-on some of the thorniest issues confronting the United States at the time—issues of equality, the economy, and individual rights.

THE EQUALITY ISSUES

The Declaration of Independence states that all men are created equal; the Constitution, however, is silent on equality. Nevertheless, some of the most important issues on the policy agenda in Philadelphia concerned equality. Three issues occupied more attention than almost any others: whether the states were to be equally represented, what to do about slavery, and whether to ensure political equality.

Equality and Representation of the States. One crucial policy issue was how the new Congress would be constituted. One scheme put before the delegates by William Paterson of New Jersey is usually called the **New Jersey Plan.** It called for each state to be equally represented in the new Congress. The opposing strategy was suggested by Edmund Randolph of Virginia and is usually called the **Virginia Plan.** It called for giving each state representation in Congress on the basis of the state's share of the American population.

The delegates resolved this conflict with a compromise. Devised by Roger Sherman and William Johnson of Connecticut, this compromise has been immortalized as the **Connecticut Compromise.** The solution was to create two houses in Congress. One body, the Senate, would have two members from each state (the New Jersey Plan), and the second body, the House of Representatives, would have representation based on population (the Virginia Plan). The United States Congress is still organized in exactly the same way. Each state has two senators, and its representation in the House is determined by the state's population.

Although the Connecticut Compromise was intended to maximize equality between the states, it actually gives more power to people who live in states with small populations than to those who live in more heavily populated states. Every state has two senators and at least one member of the House, no matter how small its population. To take the most extreme case, Wyoming and California have the same number of votes in the Senate (two), although Wyoming has less than 2 percent of California's population. Thus a citizen of Wyoming has more than *50 times* the representation in the Senate as does a citizen of California.

Because it is the Senate, not the House, that ratifies treaties, confirms presidential nominations, and hears trials of impeachment, citizens in less populated states have a greater say in these key tasks. In addition, the electoral college (which is the body that actually elects the president and is discussed in Chapter 10) gives small states greater weight. If no presidential candidate receives a majority in the electoral college, the final decision is made by the House of Representatives—with each state having one vote. In such a case (which has not occurred since 1824), the votes of citizens of Wyoming would again carry over 50 times as much weight as those of Californians.

Whether representation in the Senate is "fair" is a matter of debate. What is not open to question is that the delegates to the 1787 convention had to accommodate various interests and viewpoints in order to convince all the states to join an untested union.

Some experts have described the conflict as between big and small states (that is, states with large and states with small populations), each presumably looking for a plan that would maximize its representation. The votes in Philadelphia do not support this interpretation. Eight states voted on the New Jersey Plan (Georgia's delegation was split and did not vote), which supposedly favored the small states. In fact, three big states (New York, Maryland, and Connecticut) lined up with two small states (Delaware and, of course, New Jersey) to support equal representation of the states. The two Carolinas, small states at the time, voted against the New Jersey Plan.[15] It was not a sharp cleavage of small versus large. Rather, the vote depended on different views about how to achieve equality of representation, one side favoring equal representation of the states and the other favoring equal representation of people.

When the Constitution was written, many Northern and Southern delegates assumed that slavery, being relatively unprofitable, would soon die out. A single invention—Eli Whitney's cotton gin—made it profitable again. Although Congress did act to control the growth of slavery, the slave economy became entrenched in the South.

Slavery. The second equality issue was slavery. The contradictions between slavery and the sentiments of the Declaration of Independence are obvious, but slavery was legal in every state except Massachusetts. It was concentrated in the South, however, where slave labor was commonplace in agriculture. Some delegates, like Gouverneur Morris, denounced slavery in no uncertain terms. But the convention could not accept Morris' position in the face of powerful Southern opposition led by Charles C. Pinckney of South Carolina. The delegates did agree that Congress could limit future *importing* of slaves (they outlawed it after 1808), but they did not forbid slavery itself. The Constitution, in fact, inclined toward recognizing slavery; it stated that persons legally "held to service or labour" (referring to slaves) who escaped to free states had to be returned to their owners.

Another difficult question about slavery arose at the Convention. How should slaves be counted in determining representation in Congress? Southerners were happy to see slaves counted toward determining their representation in the House of Representatives (though reluctant to count them for apportionment of taxation). Here the result was the famous *three-fifths compromise.* Representation and taxation were to be based on the "number of free persons," plus three-fifths of the number of "all other persons." Everyone, of course, knew who those other persons were.

South Carolina planter and aristocrat Charles Cotesworth Pinckney was an articulate spokesperson for the South and for slavery.

Political Equality. The delegates dodged one other issue on equality. A handful of delegates, led by Franklin, suggested that national elections should require universal manhood suffrage (that is, a vote for all free adult males). This still would have left a

majority of the population disenfranchised, but for those still smarting from Shays' Rebellion, the suggestion was too democratic. Many delegates wanted to put property qualifications on the right to vote. Ultimately, as the debate wound down, they decided to leave the issue to the states. People qualified to vote in state elections could also vote in national elections (see Table 2.3).

THE ECONOMIC ISSUES

The Philadelphia delegates were deeply concerned about the state of the American economy. Economic issues were high on the Constitution writers' policy agenda. People disagreed (in fact, historians still disagree) as to whether the postcolonial economy was in a shambles. Advocates of the Constitution, called Federalists, stressed the economy's "weaknesses, especially in the commercial sector, and Anti-Federalists (those opposed to a strong national government, and thus opposed to a new constitution) countered with charges of exaggeration."[16] The writers of the Constitution, already committed to a strong national government, charged that the economy was indeed in disarray. Specifically, they claimed that the following problems had to be addressed:

- The states had erected tariffs against products from other states.
- Paper money was virtually worthless in some states, but many state governments, which were controlled by debtor classes, forced it on creditors anyway.
- The Continental Congress was having trouble raising money, as the economy went through a recession.

Understanding something about the delegates and their economic interests gives us insight into their views on political economy. They were, by all accounts, the nation's postcolonial economic elite. Some were budding capitalists. Others were creditors whose loans were being wiped out by cheap paper money. Many were merchants who could not even carry on trade with a neighboring state. Virtually all of them thought a strong national government was needed to bring economic stability to the chaotic union of states that existed under the Articles of Confederation.[17]

It is not surprising, then, that the framers of the Constitution would seek to strengthen the economic powers (and thus the scope) of the new national government. One famous historian, Charles A. Beard, claimed that their principal motivation for doing so was to increase their personal wealth. The framers, he said, not only were propertied, upper-class men protecting their interests but also held bonds and invest-

TABLE 2.3 HOW THREE ISSUES OF EQUALITY WERE RESOLVED: A SUMMARY

PROBLEM	SOLUTION
Slavery	
What should be done about slavery?	Basically, nothing. Although Congress was permitted to stop the importing of slaves after 1808, the Constitution is mostly silent on the issue of slavery.
How should slaves be counted for representation in the House of Representatives?	Count each slave as three-fifths of a person.
Equality of the States	
Should states be represented equally (the New Jersey Plan) or in proportion to their population (the Virginia Plan)?	Both, according to the Connecticut Compromise. States have equal representation in the Senate, but representation in the House is proportionate to population.
Political Equality	
Should the right to vote be based on universal manhood suffrage, or should it be very restricted?	Finesse the issue. Let the states decide qualifications for voting.

ments whose value would increase if the Constitution were adopted. The best evidence about the founders' motivations, however, indicates that although they were concerned about protecting property rights, it was in the broad sense of building a strong economy rather than in the narrow sense of increasing their personal wealth.[18]

The delegates made sure that the Constitution clearly spelled out the economic powers of Congress (see Table 2.4). Consistent with the general allocation of power in the Constitution, Congress was to be the chief economic policymaker. It could obtain revenues through taxing and borrowing. These tools, along with the power to appropriate funds, became crucial instruments for influencing the economy (as we will see in Chapter 17). By maintaining sound money and guaranteeing payment for the national debt, Congress was to encourage economic enterprise and investment in the United States. Congress was also given power to build the nation's infrastructure by constructing post offices and roads and to establish standard weights and measures. To protect property rights, Congress was charged with punishing counterfeiters and pirates, ensuring patents and copyrights, and legislating rules for bankruptcy. Equally important (and now a key congressional power, with a wide range of implications for the economy) was Congress' new ability to regulate interstate and foreign commerce.

In addition, the framers prohibited practices in the states that they viewed as inhibiting economic development, such as maintaining individual state monetary systems, placing duties on imports from other states, and interfering with lawfully contracted debts. Moreover, the states were to respect civil judgments and contracts made in other states, and they were to return runaway slaves to their owners. (This last protection of "property" rights is now, of course, defunct as a result of the Thirteenth Amendment, which outlawed slavery.) To help the states, the national government guaranteed them "a republican form of government" to prevent a recurrence of Shays' Rebellion, in which violence, instead of legislation and the courts, was used to resolve commercial disputes.

The Constitution also obligated the new government to repay all the public debts incurred under the Continental Congress and the Articles of Confederation, debts that totaled \$54 million. Although this requirement may seem odd, there was sound economic reason for it. Paying off the debts would ensure from the outset that money would flow

TABLE 2.4 ECONOMICS IN THE CONSTITUTION

Powers of Congress

1. Levy taxes.
2. Pay debts.
3. Borrow money.
4. Coin money and regulate its value.
5. Regulate interstate and foreign commerce.
6. Establish uniform laws of bankruptcy.
7. Punish piracy.
8. Punish counterfeiting.
9. Create standard weights and measures.
10. Establish post offices and post roads.
11. Protect copyrights and patents.

Prohibitions on the States

1. States cannot pass laws impairing the obligations of contract.
2. States cannot coin money or issue paper money.
3. States cannot require payment of debts in paper money.
4. States cannot tax imports or exports from abroad or from other states.
5. States cannot free runaway slaves from other states *(now defunct)*.

Other Key Provisions

1. The new government assumes the national debt contracted under the Articles of Confederation.
2. The Constitution guarantees a republican form of government.
3. The states must respect civil court judgments and contracts made in other states.

into the American economy and would also restore the confidence of investors in the young nation.

Alexander Hamilton, the first secretary of the treasury, stressed the link between a national debt and the emergence of capitalism. "It is a well-known fact," he said, "that in countries in which the national debt is properly funded, and an object of established confidence, it answers most of the purposes of money. Transfers of stock or public debt are the equivalent to payment in money."[19] When shares of the public debt—such as the U.S. savings bonds you may own—can be bought and sold, they constitute a form of capital for investment. Even today, people trade in government debt (in the form of bonds) just as they do in the stocks of corporations. Thus, the Constitution helped to spur a capitalist economy.

THE INDIVIDUAL RIGHTS ISSUES

There was another major item on the Constitutional Convention agenda; the delegates had to design a system that would preserve individual rights. There was no dispute about the importance of safeguarding individualism, and the founders believed that this would be relatively easy. After all, they were constructing a limited government that, by design, could not threaten personal freedoms. In addition, they dispersed power among the branches of the national government and between the national and state governments so that each branch or level could restrain the other. Also, most of the delegates believed that the various states were already doing a sufficient job of protecting individual rights.

As a result, the Constitution says little about personal freedoms. The protections it does offer are as follows:

- It prohibits suspension of the **writ of habeas corpus** (except during invasion or rebellion). Such a writ enables persons detained by authorities to secure an immediate inquiry into the causes of their detention. If no proper explanation is offered, a judge may order their release. (Article I, Section 9)
- It prohibits Congress or the states from passing bills of attainder (which punish people without a judicial trial). (Article I, Section 9)
- It prohibits Congress or the states from passing *ex post facto* laws (which punish people or increase the penalties for acts that were not illegal or not as punishable when committed). (Article I, Section 9)
- It prohibits the imposition of religious qualifications for holding office in the national government. (Article VI)
- It narrowly defines and outlines strict rules of evidence for conviction of treason. To be convicted, one must levy war against the United States or adhere to and aid its enemies during war. Conviction requires confession in open court or the testimony of *two* witnesses to the *same* overt act. The framers of the Constitution would have been executed as traitors if the revolution had failed, and they were therefore sensitive to treason laws. (Article III, Section 3)
- It upholds the right to trial by jury in criminal cases. (Article III, Section 2)

The delegates were content with their document. When it came time to obtain ratification of the Constitution, however, there was widespread criticism of the absence of specific protections of individual rights, such as free expression, and the rights of the accused.

THE MADISONIAN MODEL

The framers believed that human nature was self-interested and that inequalities of wealth were the principal source of political conflict. Regardless, they had no desire to remove the divisions in society by converting private property to common ownership; they also believed that protecting private property was a key purpose of government. Their experience with state governments under the Articles of Confederation reinforced their view that democracy was a threat to property. Many of them felt that the nonwealthy majority—an unruly mob—would tyrannize the wealthy minority if given political power. Thus, the delegates to the Constitutional Convention were faced with the dilemma of reconciling economic inequality with political freedom.

SEPARATION OF POWERS AND CHECKS AND BALANCES

James Madison was the principal architect of the government's final structure, and his work still shapes our policymaking process.[20] He and his colleagues feared both majority and minority factions. Either could take control of the government and use it to their own advantage. Factions of the minority, however, were easy to handle; they could simply be outvoted by the majority. Factions of the majority were harder to handle. If the majority united around some policy issue, such as the redistribution of wealth, they could oppress the minority, violating the latter's basic rights.[21]

As Madison would later explain in the *Federalist Papers,* which advocated the ratification of the Constitution,

> Ambition must be made to counteract ambition. . . . If men were angels, no government would be necessary. If angels were to govern men, neither external nor internal controls would be necessary. In framing a government which is to be administered by men over men, the great difficulty lies in this: you must first enable the government to control the governed; and then in the next place oblige it to control itself.[22]

To prevent the possibility of a tyranny of the majority, Madison proposed the following:

1. Place as much of the government as possible beyond the direct control of the majority.
2. Separate the powers of different institutions.
3. Construct a system of checks and balances.

Madison believed that to thwart tyranny by the majority, it was essential to keep most of the government beyond their power. His plan placed only one element of government, the House of Representatives, within direct control of the votes of the majority. In contrast, senators were to be elected by the state legislatures and the president by special electors; in other words, they would be elected by a small minority, not by the people themselves. Judges were to be nominated by the president (see Figure 2.2). Even if the majority seized control of the House of Representatives, they still could not enact policies without the agreement of the Senate and the president. To further insulate governmental officials from public opinion, judges were given lifetime tenure and senators were given terms of 6 years, with only one-third elected every 2 years, compared with the 2-year election intervals of all members of the House of Representatives.

The Madisonian scheme also provided for a **separation of powers.** Each of the three branches of government—executive, legislative, and judicial—would be relatively independent of one another so that no single branch could control the others. The president, Congress, and the courts were all given independent elements of power. Power was not divided absolutely, however; rather, it was *shared* among the three institutions.

Because powers were not completely separate, each branch required the consent of the others for many of its actions. This created a system of **checks and balances** that reflected Madison's goal of setting power against power to constrain government actions. He reasoned that if one institution was seized by a faction, it still could not damage the whole system. The system of checks and balances was an elaborate and delicate creation. The president checks Congress by holding

FIGURE 2.2 THE CONSTITUTION AND THE ELECTORIAL PROCESS: THE ORIGINAL PLAN

Under Madison's plan, which was incorporated in the Constitution, voters' electoral influence was limited and mostly indirect. Only the House of Representatives was directly elected. Senators and presidents were indirectly elected, and judges were nominated by the president. Over the years, Madison's original model has been substantially democratized. The Seventeenth Amendment (1913) established direct election of senators by popular majorities. Today, the electoral college has become largely a rubber stamp, voting the way the popular majority in each state votes.

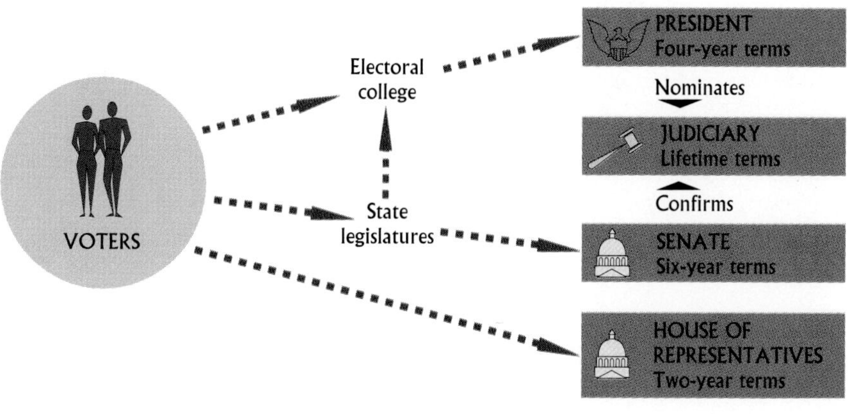

veto power; Congress holds the purse strings of government and must approve presidential appointments.

The courts also figured into the system of checks and balances. Presidents could nominate judges, but their confirmation by the Senate was required. The Supreme Court itself, in *Marbury v. Madison* (1803), asserted its power to check the other branches through judicial review: the right to hold actions of the other two branches unconstitutional. This right, which is not specifically outlined in the Constitution, considerably strengthened the Court's ability to restrain the other branches of government. For a summary of separation of powers and the checks and balances system, see Figure 2.3.

As we will discuss in detail in Chapter 3, the founders also established a federal system of government in which most government activity occurred in the states. They anticipated that this would be an additional check on the national government.

THE CONSTITUTIONAL REPUBLIC

When asked what kind of government the delegates had produced, Benjamin Franklin is said to have replied, "A republic . . . if you can keep it." Franklin, as usual, was correct. Because the founders did not wish to have the people directly make all decisions (as in a town meeting where everyone has one vote),

FIGURE 2.3 SEPARATION OF POWERS AND CHECKS AND BALANCES IN THE CONSTITUTION

The diagram shows how Madison and his fellow Constitution writers used the doctrine of separation of powers to allow the three institutions of government to check and balance one another. Judicial review—the power of courts to hold executive and congressional policies unconstitutional—was not explicit in the Constitution, but was asserted by the Supreme Court under John Marshall in Marbury vs. Madison.

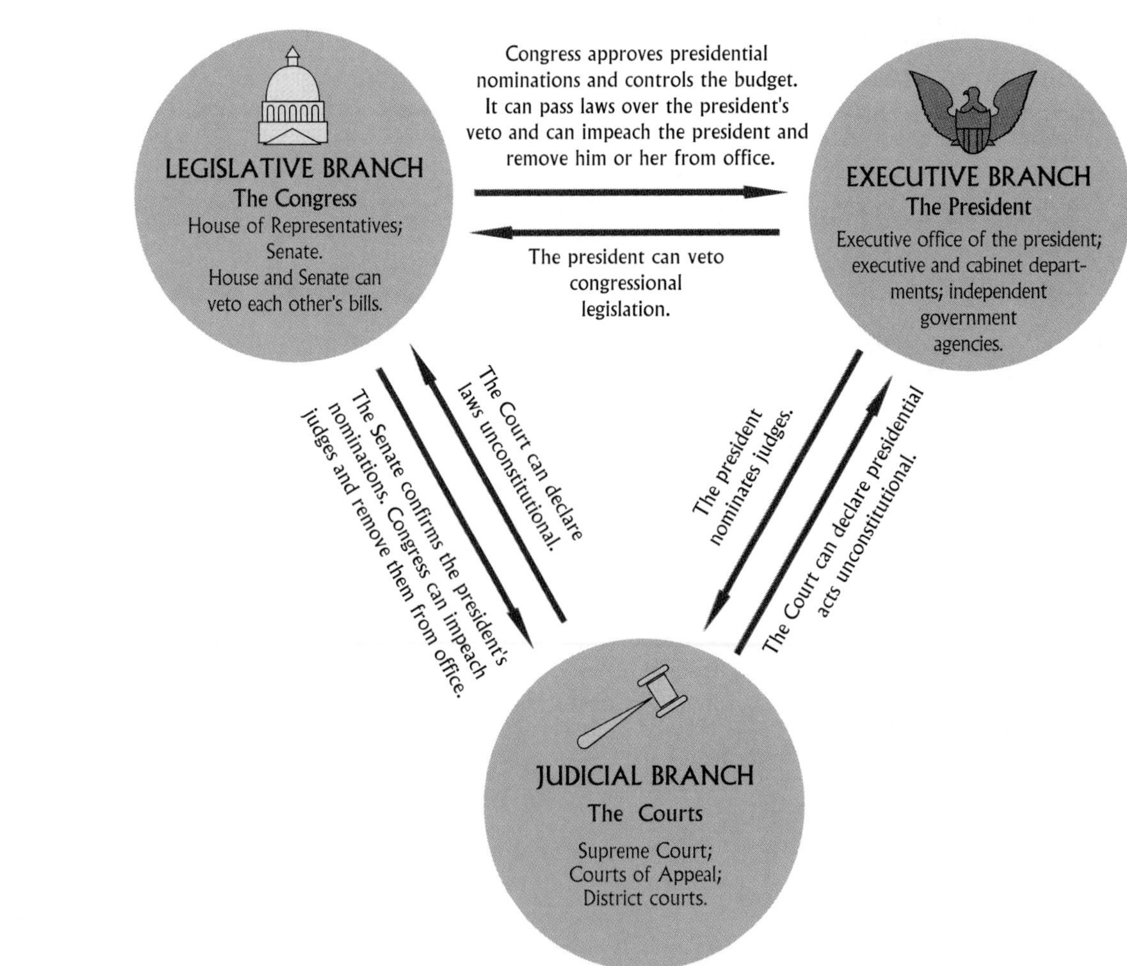

and because even then the country was far too large for such a proposal to be feasible, they did not choose to create a direct democracy. Their solution was to establish a **republic:** a system based on the consent of the governed in which power is exercised by *representatives* of the public. This deliberative democracy required and encouraged reflection and refinement of the public's views through an elaborate decision-making process.

The system of checks and balances and separation of powers has a conservative bias because it favors the status quo. People who desire change must usually have a sizable majority, not just a simple majority of 51 percent. Those opposed to change need only win at one point in the policymaking process—say in obtaining a presidential veto—whereas those who favor change must win every battle along the way. Change usually comes slowly, if at all. As a result, the Madisonian system encourages moderation and compromise and slows change. It is difficult for either a minority or a majority to tyrannize; and both property rights and personal freedoms (with only occasional lapses) have survived.

Franklin was also correct that such a system is not easy to maintain. It requires careful nurturing and balancing of diverse interests. Some critics argue that the policymaking process lacks efficiency, preventing effective responses to pressing matters. We will examine this issue closely throughout *Government in America.*

THE END OF THE BEGINNING

On the 109th day of the meetings, in stifling heat (the windows of the Pennsylvania statehouse were closed to ensure secrecy), the final version of the Constitution was read aloud. Then Dr. Franklin rose with a speech he had written, but the enfeebled Franklin had to ask James Wilson to deliver it. In it, Franklin noted that "there are several parts of this Constitution of which I do not at present approve, but I am not sure that I shall never approve them." He then offered a few political witticisms, defended the handiwork, and concluded by saying, "On the whole, Sir, I cannot help expressing a wish that every member of the Convention who may still have an objection to it, would with me on this occasion, doubt a little of his own infallibility—and make manifest our unanimity, put his name to this instrument."

Nonetheless, Edmund Randolph of Virginia rose to announce apologetically that he did not intend to sign. Gouverneur Morris of Pennsylvania announced his reservations about the compromises but called the document the "best that was to be attained" and said he would "take it with all its faults." Alexander Hamilton of New York again made a plea for unity, but Elbridge Gerry of Massachusetts was adamant in opposition. Taking Franklin's remarks personally, he "could not but view them as levelled against himself and the other gentlemen who meant not to sign." He bluntly predicted that a "civil war may result from the present crisis of the United States."

On Franklin's motion, a vote was taken. Ten states voted yes, and none voted no, but South Carolina's delegates were divided. As the records so quaintly put it, "The Members then proceeded to sign the instrument." Edmund Randolph, Elbridge Gerry, and George Mason of Virginia, however, refused to sign. Franklin then made another short speech, saying that the sun pictured on the chair of convention president George Washington was rising, not setting. Then (quoting the records again) "the Constitution being signed . . . the convention dissolved itself by Adjournment." The members themselves adjourned to a tavern. The experience of the last few hours, when conflict intermingled with consensus, reminded them that implementing this new document would be no small feat.

RATIFYING THE CONSTITUTION

The Constitution did not go into effect once the Constitutional Convention in Philadelphia was over. It had to be ratified by the states. Our awe of the founders sometimes blinds us to the bitter politics of the day. There is no way of determining the public's feelings about the new document, but as John Marshall (who later became Chief Justice) suggested, "It is scarcely to be doubted that *in some of the adopting states, a majority of the people were in opposition.*"[23] The Constitution itself required that only 9 of the 13 states approve the document before it could be implemented, ignoring the requirement that the Articles of Confederation be amended only by unanimous consent.

FEDERALISTS AND ANTI-FEDERALISTS

Throughout the states, a fierce battle erupted between the **Federalists,** who supported the Constitution, and the **Anti-Federalists,** who opposed it. Newspapers were filled with letters and articles, many written under pseudonyms, praising or condemning the document. In praise of the Constitution, three men—James Madison, Alexander Hamilton, and John Jay—wrote a series of articles under the

George Washington presides over the signing of the Constitution. "The business being closed," he wrote, "the members adjourned to the City Tavern, dined together and took cordial leave of each other."

name Publius. These articles, known as the ***Federalist Papers,*** are second only to the Constitution itself in characterizing the framers.

Beginning on October 27, 1787, barely a month after the Convention ended, the *Federalist Papers* began to appear in New York newspapers. Eighty-five were eventually published. They not only defended the Constitution detail by detail but also represented an important statement of political philosophy. (The essays influenced few of the New York delegates, however, who voted to ratify the Constitution only after New York City threatened to secede from the state if they did not.)

Far from being unpatriotic or un-American, the Anti-Federalists sincerely believed that the new government was an enemy of freedom, the very freedom they had just fought a war to ensure. Adopting names like Aggrippa, Cornelius, and Monteczuma, the Anti-Federalists launched bitter, biting, even brilliant attacks on the Philadelphia document. They frankly questioned the motives of the Constitution writers.

One objection was central to the Anti-Federalists' attacks: The new Constitution was a class-based document, intended to ensure that a particular economic elite controlled the public policies of the national government. The following quotations are from three Anti-Federalist critics of the Constitution.

> This government will commence in a moderate aristocracy; it is at present impossible to foresee whether it will, in its operation, produce a monarchy, or a corrupt, oppressive aristocracy. (George Mason)

> Thus, I conceive, a foundation is laid for throwing the whole power of the federal government into the hands of those who are in the mercantile interest; and for the landed, which is the great

52 THE FEDERALIST.

long as it exiſts by a conſtitutional neceſſity for local purpoſes, though it ſhould be in perfect ſubordination to the general authority of the union, it would ſtill be, in fact and in theory, an aſſociation of ſtates, or a confederacy. The propoſed conſtitution, ſo far from implying an abolition of the ſtate governments, makes them conſtituent parts of the national ſovereignty by allowing them a direct repreſentation in the ſenate, and leaves in their poſſeſſion certain excluſive and very important portions of ſovereign power.—This fully correſponds, in every rational import of the terms, with the idea of a federal government.

In the Lycian confederacy, which conſiſted of twenty-three CITIES, or republics, the largeſt were intitled to *three* votes in the COMMON COUNCIL, thoſe of the middle claſs to *two*, and the ſmalleſt to *one*. The COMMON COUNCIL had the appointment of all the judges and magiſtrates of the reſpective CITIES. This was certainly the moſt delicate ſpecies of interference in their internal adminiſtration; for if there be any thing that ſeems excluſively appropriated to the local juriſdictions, it is the appointment of their own officers. Yet Monteſquieu, ſpeaking of this aſſociation, ſays, "Were I to give a model of an excellent "confederate republic, it would be that of Lycia." Thus we perceive that the diſtinctions inſiſted upon were not within the contemplation of this enlightened civilian, and we ſhall be led to conclude, that they are the novel refinements of an erroneous theory.

PUBLIUS.

NUMBER X.

The ſame Subject continued.

AMONG the numerous advantages promiſed by a well conſtructed union, none deſerves to be more accurately developed than its tendency to break and control the violence of faction. The friend of popular

THE FEDERALIST. 53

governments, never finds himſelf ſo much alarmed for their character and fate, as when he contemplates their propenſity to this dangerous vice. He will not fail therefore to ſet a due value on any plan which, without violating the principles to which he is attached, provides a proper cure for it. The inſtability, injuſtice and confuſion introduced into the public councils, have in truth been the mortal diſeaſes under which popular governments have every where periſhed; as they continue to be the favorite and fruitful topics from which the adverſaries to liberty derive their moſt ſpecious declamations. The valuable improvements made by the American conſtitutions on the popular models, both ancient and modern, cannot certainly be too much admired; but it would be an unwarrantable partiality, to contend that they have as effectually obviated the danger on this ſide as was wiſhed and expected. Complaints are every where heard from our moſt conſiderate and virtuous citizens, equally the friends of public and private faith, and of public and perſonal liberty; that our governments are too unſtable; that the public good is diſregarded in the conflicts of rival parties; and that meaſures are too often decided, not according to the rules of juſtice, and the rights of the minor party; but by the ſuperior force of an intereſted and over-bearing majority. However anxiouſly we may wiſh that theſe complaints had no foundation, the evidence of known facts will not permit us to deny that they are in ſome degree true. It will be found indeed, on a candid review of our ſituation, that ſome of the diſtreſſes under which we labor, have been erroneouſly charged on the operation of our governments; but it will be found at the ſame time, that other cauſes will not alone account for many of our heavieſt misfortunes; and particularly, for that prevailing and increaſing diſtruſt of public engagements, and alarm for private rights, which are echoed from one end of the continent to the other. Theſe muſt be chiefly, if not

E 3 wholly,

As an explanation and defense of the Constitution, the *Federalist Papers* were often discussed at dinner parties and debated at countinghouses. Despite today's high literacy rates, it is doubtful that a similar set of documents, so rich in political philosophy, would be so widely read in modern America.

> interest of this country to lie unrepresented, forlorn and without hope. ("Cornelius")
>
> These lawyers, men of learning, and moneyed men . . . expect to get into Congress themselves . . . so they can get all the power and all the money into their own hands. (Amos Singletary of Massachusetts)[24]

Remember that these charges of conspiracy and elitism were being hurled at the likes of Washington, Madison, Franklin, and Hamilton.

The Anti-Federalists had other fears. Not only would the new government be run by a few, but it would erode fundamental liberties. James Lincoln was quoted in the records of the South Carolina ratifying convention as saying that he "would be glad to know why, in this Constitution, there is a total silence with regard to the liberty of the press. Was it forgotten? Impossible! Then it must have been purposely omitted; and with what design, good or bad, I leave the world to judge."

These arguments were persuasive. To allay fears that the Constitution would restrict personal freedoms, the Federalists promised to add amendments to the document specifically protecting individual liberties. They kept their word; James Madison introduced 12 constitutional amendments during the First Congress in 1789. Ten were ratified by the states and took effect in 1791. These first ten amendments to the Constitution, which restrain the national government from limiting personal freedoms, have come to be known as the **Bill of Rights** (see Table 2.5). Another of Madison's original 12 amendments, one dealing with congressional salaries, was ratified 201 years later as the Twenty-seventh Amendment (see the Appendix).

Opponents also feared that the Constitution would weaken the power of the states (which it did). Patrick Henry railed against strengthening the federal government at the expense of the states. "We are come hither," he told his fellow delegates to the Virginia ratifying convention, "to preserve the poor commonwealth of Virginia."[25] Many state political leaders feared that their own power would be diminished as well.

Finally, not everyone wanted the economy to be placed on a more sound foundation. Creditors opposed the issuance of paper money because it would produce inflation and make the money they received as payment on their loans decline in value. Debtors favored paper money, however. Their debts (such as the mortgages on their farms) would remain constant, but if money became more plentiful, it would be easier for them to pay off their debts.

RATIFICATION

Federalists may not have had the support of the majority, but they made up for it in shrewd politicking. They knew that many members of the legislatures of some states were skeptical of the Constitution and that state legislatures were populated with political leaders who would lose power under the Constitution. Thus, the Federalists specified that the Constitution be ratified by special conventions in each of the states—not by state legislatures.

Delaware was the first to approve, on December 7, 1787. Only six months passed before New Hampshire's approval (the ninth) made the Constitution official. Virginia and New York then voted to join the new union. Two states were holdouts: North Carolina and Rhode Island made the promise of the Bill of Rights their price for joining the other states.

With the Constitution ratified, it was time to select officeholders. The framers of the Constitution assumed that George Washington would become the first president of the new government—even giving him the Convention's papers for safekeeping—and they were right. The general was the unanimous choice of the electoral college for president. He took office on April 30, 1789, in New York City, the first national capital. New Englander John Adams became "His Superfluous Excellence," as Franklin called the vice president.

CONSTITUTIONAL CHANGE

"The Constitution," said Jefferson, "belongs to the living and not to the dead." The U.S. Constitution is frequently—and rightly—referred to as a living document. It is constantly being tested and altered.

Generally, constitutional changes are made either by formal amendments or by a number of informal processes. Formal amendments change the letter of the Constitution. There is also an unwritten body of tradition, practice, and procedure that, when altered, may change the spirit of the Constitution. In fact, not all nations, even those that we call democratic, have written constitutions (see "America in Perspective: Democracy *Without* a Constitution?").

THE FORMAL AMENDING PROCESS

The most explicit means of changing the Constitution is through the formal process of amendment. Article V of the Constitution outlines procedures for formal amendment. There are two stages to the amendment process—proposal and ratification—and each stage has two possible avenues (see Figure

TABLE 2.5 THE BILL OF RIGHTS (ARRANGED BY FUNCTION)

Protection of Free Expression	
Amendment 1:	Freedom of speech, press, and assembly Freedom to petition government
Protection of Personal Beliefs	
Amendment 1:	No government establishment of religion Freedom to exercise religion
Protection of Privacy	
Amendment 3:	No forced quartering of troops in homes during peacetime
Amendment 4:	No unreasonable searches and seizures
Protection of Defendants' Rights	
Amendment 5:	Grand-jury indictment required for prosecution of serious crime No second prosecution for the same offense No compulsion to testify against oneself No loss of life, liberty, or property without due process of law
Amendment 6:	Right to a speedy and public trial by a local, impartial jury Right to be informed of charges against oneself Right to legal counsel Right to compel the attendance of favorable witnesses Right to cross-examine witnesses
Amendment 7:	Right to jury trial in civil suit where the value of controversy exceeds $20
Amendment 8:	No excessive bail or fines No cruel and unusual punishments
Protection of Other Rights	
Amendment 2:	Right to bear arms
Amendment 5:	No taking of private property for public use without just compensation
Amendment 9:	Unlisted rights are not necessarily denied
Amendment 10:	Powers not delegated to the national government or denied to the states are reserved for the states or the people

2.4, page 46). An amendment may be proposed either by a two-thirds vote in each house of Congress or by a national convention called by Congress at the request of two-thirds of the state legislatures. An amendment may be ratified either by the legislatures of three-fourths of the states or by special state conventions called in three-fourths of the states. The president has no formal role in amending the Constitution, although the chief executive may influence the success of proposed amendments.

All but one of the successful amendments to the Constitution have been proposed by Congress and ratified by the state legislatures. The exception was the Twenty-first Amendment, which repealed the short-lived Eighteenth Amendment—the prohibition amendment that outlawed the sale and consumption of alcohol. The amendment was ratified by special state conventions rather than by state legislatures. Because proponents of repeal doubted that they could win in Bible-Belt legislatures, they persuaded Congress to require that state conventions be called. Today, some state legislatures are calling for a national convention to amend the Constitution to require a balanced national budget every year. (See "You Are the Policymaker: Should Congress Call a New Constitutional Convention?", page 47)

Unquestionably, formal amendments have made the Constitution more egalitarian and democratic. The emphasis on economic issues in the original document is now balanced by amendments that stress equality

DEMOCRACY *WITHOUT* A CONSTITUTION?

America in Perspective

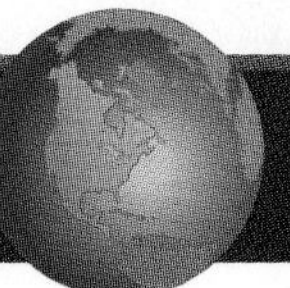

Sometimes it is difficult for Americans to understand that constitutions can be both *written* and *unwritten.* They may be surprised to learn that Great Britain—often called "the cradle of democracy"—has no written constitution at all. The unwritten constitution of Britain is a mixture of acts of Parliament, judicial pronouncements, customs, and conventions about the rules of the political game. A number of documents are British constitutional landmarks, including the Magna Carta (the Great Charter), which King John accepted at Runnymeede in 1215 and which limited the power of the monarch. None of these documents, however, outlines Britain's entire governmental system, as does the U.S. Constitution.

Although in theory the British monarch has the power to overrule laws passed by Parliament (the British legislature), the last time the monarch did so was in 1707, when Queen Anne vetoed the Scottish Militia bill. Today, it is unthinkable that the British monarch would veto an act of Parliament. Thus, in Great Britain, there is no way to argue that an act of Parliament is *unconstitutional,* since there is no written constitution to which one can appeal. If Parliament passes a law, it remains a law.

Nevertheless, Britain is undeniably a democracy. The political system allows free speech, open and free elections, vigorously competing political parties, and all the other characteristics generally associated with democracy. British politicians simply have not had a need to produce a single constitutional document.

Britain has never experienced a sharp break with tradition—as in the American Revolution—forcing politicians to think about the basis of authority and the allocation of power, and then to write down how the country should be governed. As long as there is a basic consensus on how governing should take place, the British system works fine. When such a consensus is lacking, no government, whether it has a written or an unwritten constitution, can endure.

and increase the ability of a popular majority to affect government. The amendments are headed by the Bill of Rights (see Table 2.5), which Chapter 4 will discuss in detail. Later amendments, including the Thirteenth Amendment abolishing slavery, have forbidden various political and social inequalities based on race, gender, and age (these amendments will be discussed in Chapter 5). Other amendments, discussed later in this chapter, have democratized the political system, making it easier for voters to influence the government. Only one existing amendment specifically addresses the economy—the Sixteenth, or "income tax," Amendment. Overall, it is plain that the most important effect of these constitutional amendments has been to expand liberty and equality in the United States.

Some amendments have been proposed but not ratified. The best-known of these in recent years is the **Equal Rights Amendment,** or ERA. First proposed in 1923 by the nephew of suffragist Susan B. Anthony, the ERA had to wait 49 years—until 1972—before Congress passed it and sent it to the states for ratification. The ERA stated simply that "Equality of rights under the law shall not be denied or abridged by the United States or by any State on account of sex."

This seemingly benign amendment sailed through Congress and the first few state legislatures. The Hawaiian legislature, in fact, arranged for Senator Daniel Inouye's office to signal when the Senate passed the ERA so that Hawaii could be the first state to ratify.[26] Public opinion polls showed substantial support for the ERA. Surveys revealed that even people who held traditional views of women's roles still supported the ERA.[27]

Nevertheless, the ERA was not ratified. It failed, in part, because of the system of checks and balances. The ERA had to be approved not by a national majority but by three-fourths of the states. Many conservative Southern states opposed it, thus exercising their veto power despite approval by a majority of Americans.

THE INFORMAL PROCESS OF CONSTITUTIONAL CHANGE

The written document called *The Constitution* was preserved by the members of the Constitutional Convention. They hired Jacob Shallus, a German immigrant in Philadelphia, to write out the Constitution and paid him the handsome sum of $30

FIGURE 2.4

HOW THE CONSTITUTION CAN BE AMENDED

The Constitution sets up two alternative routes for proposing amendments and two for ratifying them. One of the four combinations had been used in every case but one, but there are persistent calls for a constitutional convention to propose some new amendment or another. Amendments to permit prayer in schools, to make abortions unconstitutional, and to require a balanced national budget are recent examples.

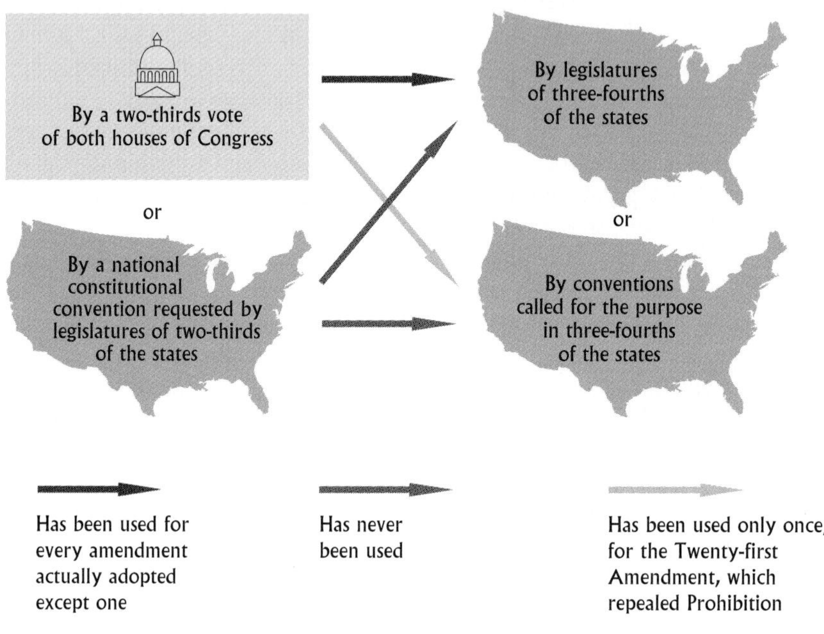

Has been used for every amendment actually adopted except one

Has never been used

Has been used only once, for the Twenty-first Amendment, which repealed Prohibition

to do so. The Convention was disbanding, having finished its work, and needed a rush job. On September 15, 1787, the conventioneers gave Shallus only 40 hours to copy the Constitution itself. Prepared on four pieces of parchment made from lamb or calf skin and written with a quill pen in Shallus' elegant script, the actual document bounced from capital to capital during the early days of the Republic. Today it sits at the National Archives, bathed in helium and under the watchful eye of an electronic camera.

Of course, the written Constitution itself is never changed, even when we pass a constitutional amendment. We do not haul out Shallus' old parchment and then pen in some lines abolishing slavery or creating an income tax; the amendments, too, are deposited in the National Archives. Think for a moment of all the changes in American government that have taken place without altering a word or a letter of the written document. In fact, there is not a word in the Constitution that would lead one to suspect any of the following developments:

- The United States has the world's oldest two-party system, wherein almost every member of Congress and every president since Washington has declared, "I am a Democrat (or Republican, or Federalist, or Whig, or whatever)."
- Abortions through the second trimester of pregnancy when the fetus cannot live outside the mother's womb are legal in the United States.
- Members of the electoral college consider themselves honor bound (and in some places even legally bound) to follow the preference of their state's electorate.
- Proceedings of both the Senate and the House are on TV; TV influences our political agenda and guides our assessments of candidates and issues.
- Government now taxes and spends about one-third of our gross domestic product, an amount the Convention delegates might have found gargantuan.

None of these things is "unconstitutional." The parties emerged, television came to prominence in American life, first technology and then the law permitted abortions—all without having to tinker with the founders' handiwork. These developments could occur because the Constitution changes *informally* as well as *formally.* There are several ways in which the Constitution changes informally: through judicial

You Are the Policymaker

SHOULD CONGRESS CALL A NEW CONSTITUTIONAL CONVENTION?

Since the 1787 Constitutional Convention, Congress has received more than 400 petitions from states requesting constitutional conventions. Most of these have been submitted since 1900. No new constitutional convention has ever been called, because no movement for a convention has obtained applications on a single subject from the required two-thirds of the states.

Calling a constitutional convention would not be an easy task. There are a number of legal questions that would have to be answered before a convention could be held.

- What constitutes a valid call for a convention?
- In what time period must the required two-thirds of the states submit their resolutions? Can a state rescind its own call for a convention?
- Is Congress obligated to call a convention if requested to do so by two-thirds of the states?
- How would delegates be selected and apportioned among the states?
- Would members of Congress be eligible to run for delegate positions?

The biggest issue, however, is what would happen once the convention began. It is not clear that Congress can limit the scope and authority of a constitutional convention to the single amendment for which the convention is called to debate.

Convention opponents fear that a new constitutional convention would go well beyond its ostensible purpose and attempt to rewrite the entire Constitution, undoing the delicate balance of the Madisonian model. The thought of numerous special interest groups clamoring for action on their favorite issues at such a convention dampens the enthusiasm of even those who favor specific changes to the Constitution. Perhaps remembering that the delegates to the 1787 Convention were only supposed to modify the Articles of Confederation, constitutional historian Forrest McDonald predicts that a new constitutional convention "would go berserk."[a]

Proponents of a constitutional convention see things differently. They feel that the only way that certain constitutional amendments—such as requiring a balanced budget, allowing prayers in public schools, or prohibiting abortions—will ever be passed is through the convention mechanism. Congress, they argue, is unwilling or unable to propose such amendments and send them to the states for ratification. Delegates to a new constitutional convention, they believe, would act responsibly and address only the issue for which the convention was called.

As is true for most political and public policy questions, no one knows for sure what would happen. To reach a conclusion requires applying an understanding of both our constitutional system and contemporary American politics. If you favor a constitutional amendment that would require a balanced budget, for example, could you be confident that the convention would not also limit abortion rights, an action you might not support? Would you favor such a convention, despite the risks? What would *you* do?

[a]*Time,* July 6, 1987, 55.

interpretation, through political practice, and as a result of changes in technology and changes in the demands on policymakers.

Judicial Interpretation. Disputes often arise about the meaning of the Constitution. If it is the "supreme law of the land," then someone has to decide how to interpret the Constitution when disputes arise. In 1803, in the famous case of ***Marbury v. Madison,*** the Supreme Court decided it would be the one to resolve differences of opinion (Chapter 16 discusses this case in detail). It claimed for itself the power of **judicial review.** Implied but never explicitly stated in the Constitution,[28] this power gives courts the right to decide whether the actions of the legislative and executive branches of state and national governments are in accord with the Constitution.

Judicial interpretation can profoundly affect how the Constitution is understood, because the Constitution usually means what the Supreme Court says it means. For example, in 1896 the Supreme Court decided that the Constitution allowed racial discrimination despite the presence of the Fourteenth

Amendment. Fifty-eight years later it overruled itself and concluded that segregation by law violated the Constitution. In 1973, the Supreme Court decided that the Constitution protected a woman's right to an abortion during the first two trimesters of pregnancy when the fetus is not viable outside the womb—an issue the founders never imagined. (These cases will be discussed in Chapters 4 and 5.)

Changing Political Practice. Current political practices also change the Constitution—stretching it, shaping it, and giving it new meaning. Probably no changes are more important than those related to parties and presidential elections.

Political parties did not exist as we know them when the Constitution was written. In fact, its authors would have disliked the idea of parties, which encourage factions. Regardless, by 1800 a party system had developed, and it plays a key role in making policy today. American government would be radically different if there were no political parties, even though the Constitution is silent about them.

Changing political practice has also altered the role of the electoral college, which has now been reduced to a clerical one in selecting the president. The writers of the Constitution, eager to avoid giving too much power to the uneducated majority, intended that there be no popular vote for the president; instead, state legislatures or the voters (depending on the state) would select wise electors who would then choose a "distinguished character of continental reputation" (as the *Federalist Papers* put it) to be president. These electors formed the electoral college. Each state would have the same number of electors to vote for the president as it had senators and representatives in Congress.

In 1796, the first election in which George Washington was not a candidate, electors scattered their votes among 13 candidates. By the election of 1800, domestic and foreign policy issues had divided the country into two political parties. To avoid dissipating their support, the parties required electors to pledge in advance to vote for the candidate who won their state's popular vote, leaving electors with a largely clerical function.

Although electors are now rubber stamps for the popular vote, nothing in the Constitution prohibits an elector from voting for any candidate. Every so often, electors have decided to cast votes for their own favorites; some state laws require electors to vote for the candidate chosen by a plurality of their state's citizens, but such laws have never been enforced. The idea that the electoral college would exercise wisdom independent of the majority of people is now a constitutional anachronism, changed not by formal amendment but by political practice.

Technology. The Constitution has also been changed greatly by technology. The mass media now play a role unimaginable in the eighteenth century—questioning governmental policies, supporting candidates, and helping shape citizens' opinions. The bureaucracy has grown in importance with the development of computers, which create new potential for bureaucrats to serve the public (such as writing over 40 million Social Security checks each month)—and, at times, create mischief. Electronic communications and the development of atomic weapons have given the president's role as commander in chief added significance, increasing the power of the president in the constitutional system.

Increasing Demands on Policymakers. The significance of the presidency has also grown as a result of increased demands for new policies. The United States' evolution in the realm of international affairs—from an insignificant country that kept to itself to a superpower with an extraordinary range of international obligations—has concentrated additional power in the hands of the chief executive, who is designated to take the lead in foreign affairs. Similarly, the increased demands of domestic policy have positioned the president in a more prominent role in preparing the federal budget and a legislative program.

The Importance of Flexibility. It is easy to see that the document the framers produced over 200 years ago was not meant to be static, written in stone. Instead, the Constitution's authors created a flexible system of government, one that could adapt to the needs of the times without sacrificing personal freedom. This flexibility has helped ensure the Constitution's—and the nation's—survival. Although the United States is young compared to other Western nations, it has the oldest functioning Constitution. France, which experienced a revolution in 1789, the same year the Constitution was ratified, has had 12 constitutions over the past two centuries. Despite the great diversity of the American population, the enormous size of the country, and the extraordinary changes that have taken place over the nation's history, the U.S. Constitution is still going strong.

THE ELABORATION OF THE CONSTITUTION

The Constitution, even with all 27 amendments, is a short document containing fewer than 8,000 words. It does not prescribe in detail the structure and functioning of the national government. Regarding the judiciary, Congress is told simply to create a court system as it sees fit. The Supreme Court is the only court required

by the Constitution, and even here the number of justices and their qualifications are left up to Congress. Similarly, many of the governing units we have today—such as the executive departments, the various offices in the White House, the independent regulatory commissions, and the committees of Congress, to name only a few examples—are not mentioned at all in the Constitution. The framers allowed future generations to determine their own needs. As muscle grows on the constitutional skeleton, it inevitably gives new shape and purpose to the government.

UNDERSTANDING THE CONSTITUTION

In a nation that prides itself on being "democratic," we must evaluate the Constitution according to democratic standards. Our theme of the scope of government runs throughout this chapter, which focuses on what the national government can and what it cannot do. The following section will examine the Constitution in terms of democracy.

THE CONSTITUTION AND DEMOCRACY

Although the United States is often said to be one of the most democratic societies in the world, the Constitution itself is rarely described as democratic. This is hardly surprising, considering the political philosophies of the men who wrote it. Among eighteenth-century upper-class society, democratic government was generally despised. If democracy was a way of permitting the majority's preference to become policy, the Constitution writers wanted no part of it. The American government was to be a government of the "rich, well-born, and able," as Hamilton said, a government where John Jay's wish that "the people who own the country ought to govern it" would be a reality. Few people today would consider these thoughts democratic.

The Constitution did not, however, create a monarchy or a feudal aristocracy. It created a republic, a representative form of democracy modeled after the Lockean tradition of limited government. Thus, the undemocratic—even antidemocratic—Constitution established a government that permitted substantial movement toward democracy.

One of the central themes of American history is the gradual democratization of the Constitution. What began as a document characterized by numerous restrictions on direct voter participation has slowly become much more democratic. Today, few people share the founders' fear of democracy. The expansion of voting rights has moved the American political system away from the elitist model of democracy and toward the pluralist one.

The Constitution itself offered no guidelines on voter eligibility, leaving it to each state to decide. As a result, only a small percentage of adults could vote; women and slaves were excluded entirely. Five of the 17 constitutional amendments passed since the Bill of Rights have focused on the expansion of the electorate. The Fifteenth Amendment (1870) prohibited discrimination on the basis of race in determining voter eligibility (although it took the Voting Rights Act of 1965, discussed in Chapter 5, to make the amendment effective). The Nineteenth Amendment (1920) gave women the right to vote (although some states had already done so). The Twenty-third Amendment (1961) accorded the residents of Washington, DC, the right to vote in presidential elections. Three years later, the Twenty-fourth Amendment prohibited poll taxes (which discriminated against the poor of all races). Finally, the Twenty-sixth Amendment (1971) lowered the voter eligibility age to eighteen. (See "Since Kennedy: Lowering the Voting Age.")

Not only are more people eligible to vote, but voters also have more officials to elect. The Seventeenth Amendment (1913) provided for direct election of senators. Presidential elections have been fundamentally altered by the development of political parties. By placing the same candidate on the ballot in all the states and requiring members of the electoral college to support the candidate who receives the most votes, parties have increased the probability that the candidate for whom most Americans vote will also receive a majority of the electoral college vote. Although it is possible for the candidate who receives the most popular votes to lose the election (as in 1824 and 1876), this has not happened since 1888. According to the Constitution, the United States selects its president through an electoral

SINCE KENNEDY

Lowering the Voting Age

When John F. Kennedy was elected president in 1960, voting age requirements varied widely among states. In most states, you had to be 21 years old to vote, but if you lived in Georgia or Kentucky, you could vote at 18. In Alaska the voting age was 19, and it was 20 in Hawaii. When Bill Clinton was elected in 1992, the voting age was 18 years old for all Americans.

The catalyst for this change was the war we fought in Vietnam. With young people dying halfway around the globe in a highly controversial war, it only seemed proper that they share the right to vote with those who were sending them to war. As the slogan went, "If you are old enough to die for your country, you are old enough to vote for its officials."

Congress, trying to avoid the usually cumbersome route of amending the Constitution, passed a law lowering the voting age in national, state, and local elections. The Supreme Court ruled, however, that Congress had no authority to set the voting age for state and local elections. Thus, Congress proposed the Twenty-sixth Amendment.

The amendment was proposed on March 23, 1971, and was ratified only five weeks later, on June 30, 1971—the fastest ratification of any amendment. Ratification was swift, in large part, because without the amendment, many states would have been faced with the costly and administratively difficult task of operating separate registration books, ballots, and voting devices for the election of federal officials and the election of state and local officials.

college, but in practice American citizens now directly elect the president. (For more on the electoral college, see Chapter 10.)

Technology has also diminished the separation of the people from those who exercise power. Officeholders communicate directly with the public through television, radio, and targeted mailings. Air travel makes it easy for members of Congress to commute regularly between Washington and their districts. Similarly, public opinion polls, the telephone, and E-mail enable officials to keep apprised of citizens' opinions on important issues. Even though the American population has grown from fewer than 4 million to more than 260 million people since the first census was taken in 1790, the national government has never been closer to those it serves.

THE CONSTITUTION AND THE SCOPE OF GOVERNMENT

The Constitution created political institutions and the rules for politics and policymaking. Many of these rules limit government action. This limiting function is what the Bill of Rights and related provisions in the Constitution are all about. No matter how large the majority, for example, it is unconstitutional to establish a state-supported church.

Most of these limitations are designed primarily to protect liberty and to open the system to a broad range of participants. The potential range of action for the government is actually quite wide. Thus, it is constitutionally permissible, although highly unlikely, for the United States either to abolish Social Security payments to the elderly or to take over ownership of the oil industry or the nation's airlines.

Yet the system of government created by the Constitution has profound implications for what the government does. On the one hand, individualism is reinforced at every turn. The separation of powers and the checks and balances established by the Constitution allow almost all groups some place in the political system where their demands for public policy can be heard. Because many institutions share power, groups can usually find at least one sympathetic ear in government. Even if the president opposes the policies a particular group favors, Congress, the courts, or some other institution can help the group achieve its policy goals.

In the early days of the civil rights movement, for example, African Americans found Congress and the president unsympathetic, so they turned to the Supreme Court. Getting their interests on the political agenda would have been much more difficult if the Court had not had important constitutional power.

On the other hand, the Constitution encourages hyperpluralism. By providing effective access for so many interests, the founders created a system of policymaking in which it is difficult for the government to act. The separation of powers and the system of checks and balances promote the politics of bargaining, compromise, and playing one institution against another. The system of checks and balances implies that one institution is checking another. *Thwarting, blocking,* and *impeding* are synonyms for checking. But if I block you, and you block someone else, and that person blocks me, none of us is going to accomplish anything, and we have gridlock.

Some scholars suggest that so much checking was built into the American political system that effective government is almost impossible. The historian and political scientist James MacGregor Burns has argued that

> We have been too much entranced by the Madisonian model of government. . . . The system of checks and balances and interlocked gears of government . . . requires the consensus of many groups and leaders before the nation can act; . . . we underestimate the extent to which our system was designed for deadlock and inaction.[29]

If the president, Congress, and the courts all pull in different directions on policy, the result may be either no policy at all (gridlock) or an inadequate, makeshift policy. The outcome may be nondecisions when hard decisions are needed. If government cannot respond effectively because its policymaking processes are too fragmented, then its performance will be inadequate. Perhaps the Madisonian model has reduced the ability of government to reach effective policy decisions. Certainly, radical departures from the status quo are atypical in American politics.

SUMMARY

The year 1787 was crucial in building the American nation. The 55 men who met in Philadelphia created a policymaking system that responded to a complex policy agenda. Critical conflicts over equality led to key compromises in the New Jersey and Virginia Plans, the three-fifths compromise on slavery, and the decision to leave the issue of voting rights to the states. There was more consensus, however, about the economy. These merchants, lawyers, and large landowners believed that the American economy was in a shambles, and they intended to make the national government an economic stabilizer. The specificity of the powers assigned to Congress left no doubt that Congress was to forge national economic policy. The delegates knew, too, that the global posture of the fledgling nation was pitifully weak. A strong national government would be better able to ensure its own security and that of the nation.

Madison and his colleagues were less clear about the protection of individual rights. Because they believed that the limited government they had constructed would protect freedom, they said little about individual rights in the Constitution. However, the ratification struggle revealed that protection of personal freedoms was much on the public's mind, so the Bill of Rights was proposed. These first ten amendments to the Constitution, along with the Thirteenth and Fourteenth Amendments, provide Americans with protection from governmental restraints on individual freedoms.

It is important to remember that 1787 was not the only year of nation building. The nation's colonial and revolutionary heritage shaped the meetings in Philadelphia. Budding industrialism in a basically agrarian nation put economic issues on the Philadelphia agenda. What Madison was to call an "unequal division of property" made equality an issue, particularly after Shays' Rebellion. The greatest inequality of all, that between slavery and freedom, was so contentious an issue that it was simply avoided at Philadelphia.

Nor did ratification of the Constitution end the nation-building process. Constitutional change—both formal and informal—continues to shape and alter the letter and the spirit of the Madisonian system.

That system includes separate institutions sharing power, so it results in many checks and balances. Today, some Americans complain that this system has created a government too responsive to too many interests and too fragmented to act. Others praise the way it protects minority views. In Chapter 3, we will look at yet another way in which the Constitution divides governmental power: between the national and the state governments.

KEY TERMS

constitution
Declaration of Independence
natural rights
consent of the governed
limited government
Articles of Confederation
Shays' Rebellion
U.S. Constitution
Connecticut Compromise
writ of habeas corpus
separation of powers
checks and balances
republic
Federalists
Anti-Federalists
Federalist Papers
Bill of Rights
Equal Rights Amendment

factions
New Jersey Plan
Virginia Plan
Marbury v. Madison
judicial review

FOR FURTHER READING

Bailyn, Bernard. *The Ideological Origins of the American Revolution.* Cambridge, MA: Harvard University Press, 1967. A leading work on the ideas that spawned the American Revolution.

Becker, Carl L. *The Declaration of Independence: A Study in the History of Political Ideas.* New York: Random House, 1942. Classic work on the meaning of the Declaration.

Hamilton, Alexander, James Madison, and John Jay. *The Federalist Papers.* 2nd ed. Edited by Roy P. Fairfield. Baltimore: Johns Hopkins University Press, 1981. Key tracts in the campaign for the Constitution and cornerstones of American political thought.

Jensen, Merrill. *The Articles of Confederation.* Madison: University of Wisconsin Press, 1940. Definitive and balanced treatment of the Articles.

Jillson, Calvin C. *Constitution Making: Conflict and Consensus in the Federal Convention of 1787.* New York: Agathon, 1988. Sophisticated analysis of the drafting of the Constitution.

Lipset, Seymour Martin. *The First New Nation.* New York: Basic Books, 1963. Political sociologist Lipset sees the early American experience as one of nation building.

Maier, Pauline. *American Scripture.* New York; Knopf, 1997. Argues the Declaration was the embodiment of the American mind and historical experience.

McDonald, Forrest B. *Novus Ordo Seclorum: The Intellectual Origins of the Constitution.* Lawrence: University Press of Kansas, 1986. Discusses the ideas behind the Constitution.

Morris, Richard B. *The Forging of the Union, 1781–1789.* New York: Harper & Row, 1987. Written to coincide with the bicentennial of the Constitution, this is an excellent history of the document's making.

Rossiter, Clinton. *1787: The Great Convention.* New York: Macmillan, 1966. A well-written study of the making of the Constitution.

Storing, Herbert J. *What the Anti-Federalists Were For.* Chicago: University of Chicago Press, 1981. Analysis of the political views of those opposed to ratification of the Constitution.

Wood, Gordon S. *The Creation of the American Republic.* Chapel Hill: University of North Carolina Press, 1969. In-depth study of American political thought prior to the Constitutional Convention.

Wood, Gordon S. *The Radicalism of the American Revolution.* New York: Vintage, 1993. Shows how American society and politics were thoroughly transformed in the decades following the Revolution.

INTERNET RESOURCES

http://www.law.emory.edu/FEDERAL/
The Declaration of Idependence, the Constitution, and the Federalist Papers. Also allows you to search the Constitution and Federalist Papers using keywords.

http://www.access.gov/congress/senate/constitution/index.html
Allows you to search the Constitution with keywords and find commentary on each part.

http://www.nara.gov.exhall/charters/constitution/confath.html
Biographies of the founders.

http://earlyamerica.com/earlyamerica/milestones/articles/text.html
The Articles of Confederation. Also provides access to a wide range of documents from the founding period.

NOTES

1. Gordon S. Wood, *The Radicalism of the American Revolution* (New York: Vintage, 1993), 4.
2. Garry Wills, *Inventing America: Jefferson's Declaration of Independence* (New York: Doubleday, 1978), 13, 77.
3. Clinton Rossiter, *1787: The Grand Convention* (New York: Macmillan, 1966), 60.
4. On the Lockean influence on the Declaration of Independence, see Carl L. Becker, *The Declaration of Independence: A Study in the History of Political Ideas* (New York: Random House, 1942).
5. Seymour Martin Lipset, *The First New Nation* (New York: Basic Books, 1963).
6. Gordon S. Wood, *The Creation of the American Republic, 1776–1787* (Chapel Hill, NC: University of North Carolina Press, 1969), 3.
7. On the Articles of Confederation, see Merrill Jensen, *The Articles of Confederation* (Madison: University of Wisconsin Press, 1940).

8. Letter from Jefferson to Madison, reprinted in George Bancroft, *The History of the Formation of the Constitution of the United States of America* (New York: Appleton, 1900), 342–343.

9. Jackson Turner Main, "Government by the People: The American Revolution and the Democratization of the Legislatures," *The William and Mary Quarterly,* 3rd ser. 23 (July 1966): 405. Main's article is also the source of the data on New York.

10. Wood, *The Radicalism of the American Revolution,* 6–7.

11. "Federalist #10," in Alexander Hamilton, James Madison, and John Jay, *The Federalist Papers,* 2nd ed. Roy F. Fairfield, ed. (Baltimore: Johns Hopkins University Press, 1981), 18.

12. Calvin C. Jillson and Cecil L. Eubanks, "The Political Structure of Constitution-Making: The Federal Convention of 1787," *American Journal of Political Science* 28 (August 1984): 435–458. See also Calvin C. Jillson, *Constitution Making: Conflict and Consensus in the Federal Convention of 1787* (New York: Agathon, 1988).

13. See Arthur Lovejoy, *Reflections on Human Nature* (Baltimore, MD: Johns Hopkins University Press, 1961), 57–63.

14. "Federalist #10," in Hamilton, Madison, and Jay, *The Federalist Papers.*

15. Paul Eidelberg, *The Philosophy of the American Constitution* (New York: Free Press, 1968), 82.

16. Cecelia M. Kenyon, ed., *The Antifederalists* (Indianapolis, IN: Bobbs-Merrill, 1966), xxxv.

17. Rossiter, *1787.*

18. See Charles A. Beard, *An Economic Interpretation of the Constitution of the United States* (New York: Macmillan, 1913); Robert E. Brown, *Charles Beard and the Constitution* (Princeton, NJ: Princeton University Press, 1956); Forrest B. McDonald, *We the People: The Economic Origins of the Constitution* (Chicago: University of Chicago Press, 1958); and Forrest B. McDonald, *Novus Ordo Seclorum: The Intellectual Origins of the Constitution* (Lawrence: University Press of Kansas, 1986).

19. Alexander Hamilton, "A National Debt Is a Blessing," in *Free Government in the Making,* ed. Alpheas Thomas Mason (New York: Oxford University Press, 1949), 313.

20. A brilliant exposition of the Madisonian model is found in Robert A. Dahl, *A Preface to Democratic Theory* (Chicago: University of Chicago Press, 1956).

21. "Federalist #10," in Hamilton, Madison, and Jay, *The Federalist Papers.*

22. "Federalist #51," in Hamilton, Madison, and Jay, *The Federalist Papers.*

23. Quoted in Beard, *An Economic Interpretation of the Constitution of the United States,* 299. (Italics ours)

24. The three quotations are from Kenyon, *The Antifederalists,* 195, liv, and 1, respectively.

25. Jackson Turner Main, *The Antifederalists* (Chapel Hill: University of North Carolina Press, 1961). For more on the Anti-Federalists, see Herbert J. Storing, *What the Anti-Federalists Were For* (Chicago: University of Chicago Press, 1981).

26. The early attempts at ratification of the ERA are recounted in Janet Boles, *The Politics of the Equal Rights Amendment* (New York: Longman, 1978).

27. Jane J. Mansbridge, *Why We Lost the ERA* (Chicago: University of Chicago Press, 1986).

28. See "Federalist #78," in Hamilton, Madison, and Jay, *The Federalist Papers.*

29. James MacGregor Burns, *The Deadlock of Democracy* (Englewood Cliffs, NJ: Prentice-Hall, 1963), 6.

3 Federalism

In January 1995, the first Republican majority in Congress in four decades took office. The Republicans often referred to themselves as engaged in a "revolution" in public policy, one aimed primarily at restricting the scope of the federal government. They passed bills to give the states more authority over social and environmental programs that have long been in the realm of the federal government. An overhaul of welfare policy was designed to allow states to devise innovative ways to lift people out of poverty, while reducing federal spending and cutting some benefits for the poor. Another bill, passed with an eye toward making it more difficult to enact new environmental protection legislation, prevented the federal government from imposing requirements on states without providing money to pay for them. Congress also repealed national speed limits and made it more difficult for prisoners to challenge the constitutionality of their sentences in federal court or to appeal to federal officials for relief from poor prison conditions.

On the other hand, Republicans found turning to the federal government the most effective way to achieve many of their policy objectives. In an effort to reduce government interference in the marketplace and protect businesses from a patchwork of state requirements more stringent than federal ones, Republicans designated the federal government the sole regulator of products as diverse as mutual funds and agricultural chemicals. They also nullified state laws that had restricted telecommunications competition and set national standards requiring insurers to cover at least 48 hours of hospitalization for mothers and newborns.

To control immigration, Congress required state and local officials to meet new federal antifraud specifications for birth certificates and driver's licenses. And to combat crime, the legislature extended federal criminal penalties to cover crimes such as stalking, domestic terrorist activities, and rape during carjacking. Congress also threatened to cut off federal grants for states that failed to keep criminals behind bars for about 85% of their sentences or to increase arrests of violent criminals.

In addition, the new welfare bill imposed penalties on states that fail to meet new federal targets for placing welfare recipients in jobs. The states must also meet other requirements, such as creating registries to track child-support orders, or face a considerable loss of federal funds. Similarly, a clean drinking water bill required states to study local drinking water sources, map certain watersheds, and publish annual reports on drinking water violations.

Federalism is at the center of important battles over public policy. Republicans—like Democrats—have found that public concerns about issues such as violent crime and reduction of regulations on business have driven even staunch supporters of state control of policy to expand Washington's reach in some areas. Republicans typically use federal power to ease the regulation of business while giving more discretion to states on social and environmental policy, whereas Democrats tend to move in opposite directions. In each case, however, the issue of federalism and of the level of government with responsibility for policy is a crucial political battleground, because the ways in which policymakers answer the questions of how we should be governed (in this case, by the states or by the federal government) and what should be the scope of the national government make an important difference in the policies that are produced by government.

This chapter will explore American federalism, the complex relationships between different levels of government in the United States. We will be especially attentive to our themes of democracy and the scope of government. Does federalism, the vertical division of power, enhance democracy in the United States? Does the additional layer of policymakers make government more responsive to public opinion or merely more complicated? Does it enhance the prospects of a national majority of Americans having their way in public policy? And what are the implications of federalism for the scope of the national government's activities? Why has the national government grown so much in relation to state governments, and has this growth been at the expense of the states?

The relationships between governments at the local, state, and national levels often confuse many Americans. Governmental institutions, it seems, must be able to serve many masters. Neighborhood schools are run by locally elected school boards but also receive state and national funds, and with those funds come state and national rules and regulations. Local airports, sewage systems, pollution control systems, and police departments also receive a mix of local, state, and national funds, so they operate under a complex web of rules and regulations imposed by each level of government.

Sometimes this complex system is almost impossible to understand, especially given the size of the country and the large number of units of government within it. Even the national government has difficulty keeping track of more than $250 billion in federal aid distributed each year to states and cities.[1] In 1972, when the U.S. Treasury Department first sent revenue-sharing checks to 50 states and 38,000 local governments, some 5000 checks were returned, marked "addressee unknown," by the Postal Service and the Tresaury Department. If the Postal Service had trouble keeping up with all the governments in America, pity the poor citizen.

National campaigns for the presidency actually take place in the states; candidates must talk about oil prices in Texas, Social Security benefits in Florida, and federal aid to cities in New York. Here, President Clinton appeals to residents of University City, Missouri, a week before the presidential election.

DEFINING FEDERALISM

Federalism is not the way nations typically organize their governments. It is a rather unusual system for governing, with particular consequences for those who live within it. This section explains the federal system and what difference it makes to Americans living in such a system.

WHAT FEDERALISM IS

Federalism is a way of organizing a nation so that two or more levels of government have formal authority over the same area and people. It is a system of shared power between units of government. For example, the state of California has formal authority over its inhabitants, but the national government can also pass laws and establish policies that affect Californians. Our houses or apartments are subject to the formal authority of both the state and the national governments.

Although federalism is not unique to the United States, it is not a very common method of governing. Only 11 of the 190 or so nations of the world have federal systems. And the countries with federal systems, which include Germany, Mexico, Argentina, Canada, Australia, India, and the United States, share little else. (See "America in Perspective: Why Federalism?")

Most governments in the world today are not federal but **unitary governments,** in which all power resides in the central government. If the British Parliament, for instance, wants to redraw the boundaries of local governments or change their forms, it can (and has). However, if the U.S. Congress wants to abolish Alabama or Oregon, it cannot.

American states are unitary governments with respect to their local governments. Local governments get their authority from the states; they can be created or abolished by the states. States also have the power to make rules for their own local governments. They tell them what their speed limits can be, the way in which they should be organized, how they can tax people, what they can spend money on, and so forth. States, however, receive their authority not from the national government, but *directly* from the Constitution.

There is a third form of governmental structure, a *confederation.* The United States began as such, under the Articles of Confederation. In a confederation, the national government is weak and most or all the power is in the hands of its components—for example, the individual states. Today, confederations are rare except in international organizations such as the United Nations (see Chapter 20).

The workings of the federal system are sometimes called **intergovernmental relations.**[2] This term refers to the entire set of interactions among national, state, and local governments.

WHY FEDERALISM IS SO IMPORTANT

The federal system in America *decentralizes our politics.* Senators are elected as representatives of individual states, not of the entire nation. On election day in November, there are actually 51 presidential elections, one for each state and one for Washington, DC (see Chapter 10). It is even possible—as last happened in 1888—for a candidate who receives the most popular votes in the country to lose the election because of the way the electoral votes are distributed by state.

The federal system decentralizes our politics in more fundamental ways than our electoral system. With more layers of government, more opportunities exist for political participation. With more people wielding power, there are more points of access in government and more opportunities for interests to have their demands for public policies satisfied. With more decisions made in the states, there are fewer sources of conflict at the national level.

As we will see, federalism also enhances judicial power. Dividing government power and responsibilities necessitates umpires to resolve disputes between the two levels of government. In the American system, judges serve as the umpires. Placing prohibitions on the states ensures that issues will arise for the courts to decide.

The federal system not only decentralizes our politics but also *decentralizes our policies.* The history of the

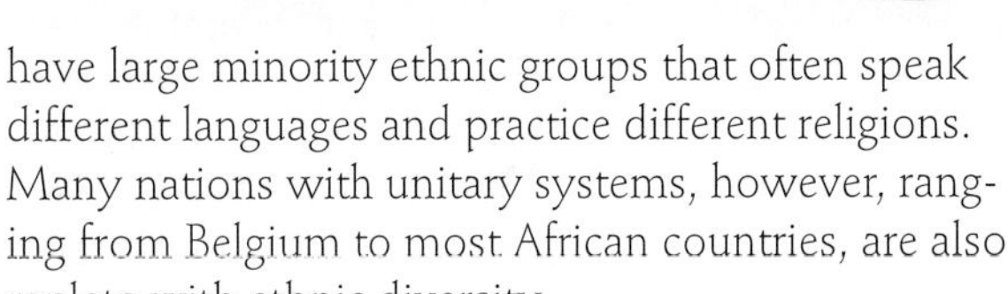

WHY FEDERALISM?

Only 11 countries have federal systems. Trying to determine why these particular nations chose a federal system is an interesting but difficult task. All three North American nations have federal systems, but the trend does not continue in South America, where only two nations have federal systems. Countries large in size—such as Canada and Australia—or large in both size and population—such as India, the United States, Brazil, and Mexico—tend to have federal systems, which decentralize the administration of governmental services. Nevertheless, China and Indonesia—two large countries—have unitary governments, and tiny Malaysia and Switzerland have federal systems.

A nation's diversity may also play a role in the development of a federal system. Brazil, Canada, India, Malaysia, Switzerland, and the United States have large minority ethnic groups that often speak different languages and practice different religions. Many nations with unitary systems, however, ranging from Belgium to most African countries, are also replete with ethnic diversity.

Most federal systems are democracies, although most democracies are not federal systems. Authoritarian regimes generally do not wish to disperse power away from the central government. Both the former Soviet Union and the former Yugoslavia, perhaps reflecting the extraordinary diversity of their populations, had federal systems—of a sort. In both countries, the central government, until recently, retained ultimate power. As democracy swept through these countries, their national governments dissolved and several smaller nations were formed.

NATION	POPULATION	AREA (THOUSAND SQUARE MILES)	DIVERSITY (ETHNIC, LINGUISTIC, AND RELIGIOUS)
Argentina	33,533,256	1,072	Low
Australia	17,827,204	2,966	Low
Austria	7,915,145	32	Low
Brazil	156,664,223	3,286	Medium
Canada	27,769,993	3,852	High
Germany	80,767,591	137	Low
India	903,158,968	1,222	High
Malaysia	18,845,340	127	High
Mexico	90,419,606	762	Low
Switzerland	6,986,621	16	Medium
United States	258,103,721	3,615	Medium

SOURCE: Central Intelligence Agency, *The World Factbook, 1994–95* (Washington, DC: Brassey's, 1994).

federal system demonstrates the tension between the states and the national government about policy: who controls it and what it should be. In the past, people debated whether the states or the national government should regulate the railroads, pass child labor laws, or adopt minimum-wage legislation. Today, people debate whether the states or the national government should regulate abortions, enforce school desegregation, determine speed limits on highways, or tell 18-year-olds they cannot drink alcohol.

Policies about equality, the economy, the environment, and other matters are subject to both the centralizing force of the national government and the dispersing force of the states. The overlapping powers of the two levels of government mean that most of our public policy debates are also debates about federalism.

States are responsible for most public policies dealing with social, family, and moral issues. The Constitution does not give the national government the power to pass laws that *directly* regulate drinking ages, marriage and divorce, or speed limits. These policy prerogatives belong to the states. They become national issues, however, when aggrieved or angry groups take their cases to Congress or the federal courts in an attempt to use the power of the national government to *influence* states or to get federal courts to find a state's policy unconstitutional.

Candy Lightner, for example, a New Jersey mother whose child was killed by a teenage drunken driver, formed Mothers Against Drunk Driving (MADD). This group was the seed from which sprouted hundreds of local MADD chapters, as well as offshoots like Students Against Drunk Driving (SADD). Lightner's lobbyists inundated state capitals to get the drinking age raised. Between 1976 and 1983, 19 states raised their drinking age, typically to age 21.

MADD supporters realized, however, that it was much easier to get a national law passed once than to lobby each of 50 state legislatures separately. Therefore, in 1983, at a press conference on the steps of the Capitol, Lightner and Secretary of Transportation Elizabeth Dole, Senator John Danforth (R-MO), Senator Richard Lugar (R-IN), and Senator Frank Lautenberg (D-NJ, from Lightner's home state) announced their intention to support a nationally standard drinking age. Because they could not pass a bill directly setting the drinking age in the states, however, they proposed using federal highway funds as an incentive for the states to pass their own bills. (See "You Are the Policymaker: Raising the Drinking Age" for more on this case.)

The American states have always been policy innovators.[3] The states overflow with reforms, new ideas,

At a 1983 press conference, Transportation Secretary Elizabeth Dole announced her support of MADD and of congressional legislation to raise minimum drinking ages. Small groups such as MADD, lacking the resources to change policy in 50 states, often attempt to move traditionally local issues onto the national government's policy agenda.

and new policies. From clean air legislation to welfare reform, the states constitute a national laboratory to develop and test public policies and share the results with other states and the national government. Almost every policy the national government has adopted had its beginnings in the states. One or more states pioneered child labor laws, minimum-wage legislation, unemployment compensation, antipollution legislation, civil rights protections, and the income tax. More recently, states have been active in reforming health care, education, and welfare—and the national government is paying close attention to their efforts.

Federalism is an important key to unlocking the secrets of the American political system. Which president is elected, which policy innovations are developed, at what age young men and women can legally drink, and many other issues are profoundly affected by the workings of the federal system.

THE CONSTITUTIONAL BASIS OF FEDERALISM

The word *federalism* is absent from the Constitution, and not much was said about it at the Constitutional Convention. Eighteenth-century Americans had little experience in thinking of themselves as Americans first and state citizens second. In fact, loyalty to state governments was so strong that the Constitution would have been resoundingly defeated had it tried to abolish them. In addition, a central government, working alone, would have had difficulty trying to govern eighteenth-century Americans. The people were too widely dispersed, and the country's transportation and communication systems too primitive, to be governed from a central location.

Thus there was no other practical choice in 1787 but to create a federal system of government. As Chapter 2 explained, the delegates did, however, ensure that the new national government would be stronger, and the state governments weaker, than under the Articles of Confederation.

THE DIVISION OF POWER

The Constitution's writers carefully defined the powers of state and national governments (see Table 3.1, page 60). Although they favored a stronger national government, the framers still made states vital cogs in the machinery of government. The Constitution guaranteed states equal representation in the Senate (and even made this provision unamendable in Article 5). It also made states responsible for both state and national elections—an important power. Further, the Constitution virtually guaranteed the continuation of

RAISING THE DRINKING AGE

You Are the Policymaker

The agony associated with children's deaths caused by drunk drivers is very real. When the drunken driver is a teenager, inexperienced at both driving and drinking, passions heat further. Candy Lightner's MADD had no trouble rousing sentiments against this carnage. No politician wants to be accused of supporting drunks on the road aiming two-ton vehicles at defenseless children.

The most important question about public policy, though, is not whether the problem is real but whether the solution is appropriate. The legislation stemming from the Lightner–Dole–Danforth–Lautenberg press conference was an amendment to the Surface Transportation Act of 1982. The federal government could not legislate drinking ages, so it relied on a carrot-and-stick strategy: Congress would withhold 10 percent of all federal highway aid from states that did not raise their legal drinking age to 21 by 1988. The legislation sailed through Congress (the Senate passed it by a vote of 81 to 16, few Senators presumably wanting their votes construed as tolerating teenage drunken driving). President Reagan—a staunch opponent of federal regulations—signed the legislation in October 1984. By the end of 1989, every state had a legal drinking age of 21.

Popular policies may or may not be wise policies; they may or may not work. Evidence on the impact of state laws that have raised the minimum drinking age is, at best, mixed. Wagenaar studied what happened when Michigan raised its drinking age in the 1970s. He estimated that there were 1,650 fewer accidents in Michigan after it adopted a stiffer drinking-age law. A study by the Wharton School of Economics, though, reached opposite conclusions. It found that changes in the drinking age were not associated with significant changes in either fatalities or accidents. More recent data show that the alcohol-related death rate of drivers 15–24 years old declined from 21.5 per 100,000 persons in 1987 to 14.1 in 1992.

The citizen policy analyst must weigh both values and evidence. How do you weigh the rights of 18- to 20-year-olds to drink against the harm done by teenage drunken driving? What kinds of evidence would you need to be confident that raising the drinking age is effective? How do you isolate the effects of raising the drinking age from the effects of public education about drunken driving, sobriety checkpoints, and prompt license suspension and other stiff penalties for persons who drive while intoxicated? Should any policies in this area be best left to the states individually? What would *you* do about raising the drinking age?

SOURCES: For background information on this issue, see the articles in H. Weschsler, ed., *Minimum Drinking Age Laws* (Lexington, MA: D. C. Heath, 1980). The studies cited are A. C. Wagenaar, *Alcohol, Young Drivers, and Traffic Accidents* (Lexington, MA: D. C. Heath, 1983); Wharton School of Economics, "The Relationship Between Increases in Minimum Purchase Age for Alcoholic Beverages and the Number of Traffic Fatalities," Social Science Working Papers, the Wharton School, University of Pennsylvania, 1985; and "Reduction in Alcohol-Related Traffic Fatalities—United States, 1990–1992, "Centers for Disease Control and Prevention (Atlanta: U.S. Government Printing Office, 1993).

each state; Congress is forbidden to create new states by chopping up old ones, unless a state's legislature approves (an unlikely event).

The Constitution also created obligations of the national government toward the states; it is to protect states against violence and invasion, for example. At times, though, the states find the national government deficient in meeting its obligations. Several states, including California, Texas, New York, and Florida, have sued the national government for failing to control the country's borders. The huge number of illegal aliens entering the country has forced the states to pay for social services and detention.

In Article VI of the Constitution, the framers dealt with what remains a touchy question: In a dispute between the states and the national government, which prevails? The answer that the delegates provided, often referred to as the **supremacy clause,** seems clear enough. They stated that the following three items were the supreme law of the land:

1. the Constitution
2. laws of the national government (when consistent with the Constitution)
3. treaties (which can be made only by the national government)

TABLE 3.1 THE CONSTITUTION'S DISTRIBUTION OF POWERS

SOME POWERS SPECIFICALLY GRANTED BY THE CONSTITUTION

To the National Government	*To Both the National and State Governments*	*To the State Governments*
To coin money To conduct foreign relations To regulate commerce with foreign nations and among states To provide an army and a navy To declare war To establish courts inferior to the Supreme Court To establish post offices To make laws necessary and proper to carry out the foregoing powers	To tax To borrow money To establish courts To make and enforce laws To charter banks and corporations To spend money for the general welfare To take private property for public purposes, with just compensation	To establish local governments To regulate commerce within a state To conduct elections To ratify amendments to the federal Constitution To take measures for public health, safety, and morals To exert powers the Constitution does not delegate to the national government or prohibit the states from using

SOME POWERS SPECIFICALLY DENIED BY THE CONSTITUTION

To the National Government	*To Both the National and State Governments*	*To the State Governments*
To tax articles exported from one state to another To violate the Bill of Rights To change state boundaries	To grant titles of nobility To permit slavery (Thirteenth Amendment) To deny citizens the right to vote because of race, color, or previous servitude (Fifteenth Amendment) To deny citizens the right to vote because of gender (Nineteenth Amendment)	To tax imports or exports To coin money To enter into treaties To impair obligations of contracts To abridge the privileges or immunities of citizens or deny due process and equal protection of the law (Fourteenth Amendment)

Judges in every state were specifically told to obey the U.S. Constitution, even if their state constitutions or state laws directly contradicted it. Today, all state executives, legislators, and judges are bound by oath to support the Constitution.

The national government, however, can operate only within its appropriate sphere. It cannot usurp the states' powers. Thus the question concerns the boundaries of the national government's powers. According to some commentators, the **Tenth Amendment** provides part of the answer. It states that the "powers not delegated to the United States by the Constitution, nor prohibited by it to the states, are reserved to the states respectively, or to the people." To those advocating states' rights, the amendment clearly means that the national government has only those powers specifically assigned to it by the Constitution. The states or people have supreme power over any activity not mentioned there. Despite this interpretation, in 1941 the Supreme Court (in *United States v. Darby*) called the Tenth Amendment a constitutional truism, a mere assertion that the states have independent powers of their own—not a declaration that their powers are superior to those of the national government.

The Court seemed to backtrack on this ruling in favor of national government supremacy in a 1976 case, *National League of Cities v. Usery,* in which it held that extending national minimum-wage and maximum-hours standards to employees of state and local governments was an unconstitutional intrusion of the national government into the domain of the states. In 1985, however (in *Garcia v. San Antonio Metro*), the Court overturned the *National League of Cities* decision. The Court held, in essence, that it was up to Congress, not the courts, to decide which actions of the states should be regulated by the national government. Once again, the Court ruled that the Tenth Amendment did not give states power superior to that of the national government for activities not mentioned in the Constitution.

Occasionally, issues arise in which states challenge the authority of the national government. In the late 1980s, the governors of several states refused to allow their state National Guards to engage in training exercises in Central America. National Guards are state militias, but the Constitution provides that they can be nationalized by the president. In 1990, the Supreme Court reiterated the power of the national government by siding with the president. South Dakota sued the federal government over its efforts to raise states' drinking-age laws and over its efforts to mandate a 55-mph speed limit on highways. The state lost both cases. (In 1995, however, Congress changed the law on speed limits.)

Federal courts can order states to obey the Constitution or federal laws and treaties. However, the *Eleventh Amendment* prohibits individual damage suits against state officials and protects state governments from being sued against their consent by private parties in federal courts. Cases arising under the Fourteenth Amendment (ratified after the Eleventh) are an exception. Suits may also be brought by the federal government against states in federal courts, and by individuals against state officials for injunctions to prohibit future illegal actions.

Recently the Supreme Court has made it easier for citizens to control the behavior of local officials. The Court ruled that a federal law passed in 1871 to protect newly freed slaves permits individuals to sue local governments for damages or seek injunctions against any local official acting in an official capacity who they believe has deprived them of any right secured by the Constitution or by federal law.[4] Such suits are now common in the federal courts.

ESTABLISHING NATIONAL SUPREMACY

Why is it that the federal government has gained power relative to the states? Three key events have largely settled the issue of how national and state powers are related: the *McCulloch v. Maryland* court case, the Civil War, and the civil rights movement.

McCulloch v. Maryland. As early as 1819, the issue of state versus national power came before the Supreme Court in the case of ***McCulloch v. Maryland.*** Here are the facts of the case and the principles it decided.

The new American government had moved quickly on many economic policies. In 1791, it created a national bank. It was not a private bank like today's "First National Bank of Such and Such" but rather a government agency empowered to print money, make loans, and engage in many other banking tasks. A darling of Alexander Hamilton and other Federalists, the bank was hated by those opposed to strengthening the national government's control of the economy. Those opposed—including Thomas Jefferson, farmers, and state legislatures—saw the bank as an instrument of the elite. The First Bank of the United States was allowed to expire, but then the Second Bank was created, fueling a great national debate.

Railing against the "Monster Bank," the state of Maryland passed a law in 1818 taxing the national bank's Baltimore branch $15,000 a year. The Baltimore branch refused to pay, whereupon the state of Maryland sued the cashier, James McCulloch, for payment. When the state courts upheld Maryland's law and its tax, the bank appealed to the U.S. Supreme Court. John Marshall was chief justice when two of the country's ablest lawyers argued the case before the Court.

Daniel Webster argued for the national bank, and Luther Martin, a delegate to the Constitutional Convention, argued for Maryland. Martin maintained that the Constitution was very clear about the powers of Congress (as outlined in Article I of the Constitution). The power to create a national bank was not among them. Thus, Martin concluded, Congress had exceeded its powers, and Maryland had a right to tax the bank. On behalf of the bank, Webster argued for a broader interpretation of the powers of the national government. The Constitution was not meant to stifle congressional powers, he said, but rather to permit Congress to use all means "necessary and proper" to fulfill its responsibilities.

Marshall, never one to sidestep a big decision, wrote his ruling in favor of the bank before the arguments ended—some said before they even began. He and his colleagues set forth two great constitutional principles in their decision. The first was the *supremacy of the national government over the states.* Marshall wrote that "If any one proposition could command the universal assent of mankind, we might expect it to be this—that the government of the United States, though limited in its power, is supreme within its sphere of action." (Note the rhetorical flourish and exaggeration; of course, national supremacy did not command the "universal assent of mankind." Marshall's rhetoric calls to mind the old story about the preacher who wrote in the margin of his sermon, "Weak point—pound the pulpit.") As long as the national government behaved in accordance with the Constitution, said the Court, its policies took precedence over state policies. Accordingly, federal laws or regulations, such as many civil rights acts and rules regulating hazardous substances, water quality, and clean air standards, *preempt* state or local laws or regulations and thus preclude their enforcement.

The Court also held that Congress was behaving consistently with the Constitution when it created the national bank. It was true, Marshall admitted, that Congress had certain **enumerated powers,** specifically listed in Article I, Section 8, of the Constitution. Congress could coin money, regulate its value, impose taxes, and so forth. Creating a bank was not enumerated. But the Constitution added that Congress has the power to "make all laws necessary and proper for carrying into execution the foregoing powers." That, said Marshall, gave Congress certain **implied powers.** It could make economic policy consistent with the Constitution in a number of ways. The other key principle of *McCulloch,* therefore, was that *the national government has certain implied powers that go beyond its enumerated powers.*

Today, the notion of implied powers has become like a rubber band that can be stretched without breaking; the "necessary and proper" clause of the Constitution is often referred to as the **elastic clause.** Especially in the domain of economic policy, hundreds of congressional policies involve powers not specifically mentioned in the Constitution. Federal policies to regulate food and drugs, build interstate highways, protect consumers, try to clean up dirty air and water, and do many other things are all justified as implied powers of Congress.

The Constitution gives Congress the power to regulate interstate and international commerce. American courts have spent many years trying to define commerce. In 1824, the Supreme Court, in deciding the case of ***Gibbons v. Ogden,*** defined commerce very broadly to encompass virtually every form of commercial activity. Today, commerce covers not only the movement of goods, but also radio signals, electricity, telephone messages, the Internet, insurance transactions, and much more.

The Supreme Court's decisions establishing the principles of the federal government's implied powers (*McCulloch v. Maryland*) and a broad definition of interstate commerce (*Gibbons v. Ogden*) created a source of national power as long as Congress employed its power for economic development through subsidies and services for business interests. In the later part of the nineteenth century, however, Congress sought to use these same powers to regulate the economy rather than to promote it. The Court then interpreted the interstate commerce power as giving Congress no constitutional right to regulate local commercial activities such as establishing safe working conditions for laborers or protecting children from working long hours.

Beginning in 1933, the New Deal produced an avalanche of regulatory and social welfare legislation, much of which was voided by the Supreme Court (see Chapter 16). But in 1937 the Court reversed itself and ceased trying to restrict the efforts of the national government to regulate commerce at any level. In 1964, Congress prohibited racial discrimination in places of public accommodation such as restaurants, hotels, and movie theaters on the basis of its power to regulate interstate commerce. Thus, regulating commerce is one of the national government's most important sources of power.

In recent years the Supreme Court has scrutinized the use of the commerce power with a skeptical eye, however. In 1995, it held in *U.S. v. Lopez* that the federal Gun-Free School Zones Act of 1990, which forbid the possession of firearms in public schools, exceeded Congress's constitutional authority to regulate commerce. Guns in a school zone, the majority said, have nothing to do with commerce.

The Supreme Court announced another limitation on the commerce power in 1996. In *Seminole Tribe of Florida v. Florida,* the Court found that the Eleventh Amendment protects state governments from being sued against their consent by private parties in federal courts. Contrary to previous decisions, the Court declared that Congress may not use the interstate commerce power to abrogate states' immunity from such lawsuits. The principal effect of the decision will be to limit suits to enforce rights granted by Congress within its authority under the Commerce Clause (which encompasses much of modern federal regulation).

In yet another recent case with important implications for federalism, the Supreme Court in *Printz v. U.S.* and *Mack v. U.S.* (1997) voided the congressional mandate in the Brady Handgun Violence Prevention Act that the chief law enforcement officer in each local community conduct background checks on prospective gun purchasers. According to the court, "The federal government may neither issue directives requiring the states to address particular problems, nor commend the states' officers, or those of their political subdivision, to administer or enforce a federal regulatory program."

Federalism as the Battleground of the Struggle for Equality. What *McCulloch* pronounced constitutionally, the Civil War (1861–1865) settled militarily. The Civil War is often thought of mainly as a struggle over slavery. It was that, of course, but it was also, and perhaps more important, a struggle between states and the national government. In fact,

Abraham Lincoln announced in his 1861 inaugural address that he would willingly support a constitutional amendment guaranteeing slavery if it would save the Union. Instead, it took a bloody civil war for the national government to assert its power over the Southern states' claim of sovereignty.

A century later, conflict between the states and the national government again erupted over states' rights and national power. Again the policy issue was equality. In 1954, in *Brown v. Board of Education,* the Supreme Court held that school segregation was unconstitutional. Southern politicians responded with what they called "massive resistance" to the decision. When a federal judge ordered the admission of two African-American students to the University of Alabama in 1963, Governor George Wallace literally "stood in the schoolhouse door" to prevent federal marshals and the students from entering the admissions office. (In fact, the confrontation had been elaborately staged by representatives of Deputy Attorney General Nicholas Katzenbach and Wallace; chalk marks were drawn on the sidewalk to show everyone where to stand during the showdown between states' rights and federal power.) Despite Wallace's efforts, the students were admitted, and throughout the 1960s the federal government enacted law after law and policy after policy to end segregation in schools, housing, public accommodations, voting, and jobs. In 1979 (after African Americans began voting in large numbers in Alabama), George Wallace himself said of his stand in the schoolhouse door: "I was wrong. Those days are over and they ought to be over." The conflict between states and the national government over equality issues was decided in favor of the national government. National standards of racial equality prevailed.

In 1963, Alabama Governor George Wallace made a dramatic stand at the University of Alabama to resist integration of the all-white school. Federal marshals won this confrontation, and since then the federal government in general has been able to impose national standards of equal opportunity on the states.

The national government is supreme within its sphere, but the sphere for the states remains a large and important one, as you can see in "Since Kennedy: The Resurgent States."

STATES' OBLIGATIONS TO EACH OTHER

Federalism involves more than relationships between the national government and state and local governments. The states must deal with each other as well, and the Constitution outlines certain obligations that each state has to every other state.

Full Faith and Credit. Suppose that, like millions of other Americans, a person divorces and then remarries. For each marriage this person purchases a marriage license, which registers the marriage with a state. On the honeymoon for the second marriage, the person travels across the country. Is this person married in each state passed through, even though the marriage license is with only one state? Can the person be arrested for bigamy because the divorce occurred in only one state?

The answer, of course, is that a marriage license and a divorce, like a driver's license and a birth certificate, are valid in all states. Article IV of the Constitution requires that states give **full faith and credit** to the public acts, records, and civil judicial proceedings of every other state. This reciprocity is essential to the functioning of society and the economy. Without the full faith and credit clause, people could avoid their obligations, say, to make payments on automobile loans simply by crossing a state boundary. In addition, because contracts between business firms can be enforced across state boundaries, firms incorporated in one state can do business in another.

Usually, the full faith and credit provision in the Constitution poses little controversy. An exception occurred in 1996 when courts in Hawaii recognized same-sex marriages. What would happen in other states that did not recognize Hawaiian marriages between same-sex partners? Congress answered with the Defense of Marriage Act, which permits states to disregard gay marriages, even if they are legal elsewhere in the United States. It remains to be seen whether Congress has the power to make exceptions to the full faith and credit clause.

Extradition. What about criminal penalties? Almost all criminal law is state law. If someone robs a store, steals a car, or commits a murder, the chances are that this person is breaking a state, not a federal, law. The Constitution says that states are required to

SINCE KENNEDY

The Resurgent States

In the early 1960s, Washington, DC, viewed state governments as backward and inept. Some states, especially in the South, needed to be brought into line on national policy such as civil rights. In Washington's view, all state governments needed help.

Things are different now. Whereas Washington faces huge budget deficits and policy gridlock, the states have been dynamic centers of policy innovation. Take the case of health care, for example. States have been a source of innovation in health policy for a decade. Their efforts to provide health care and health insurance for their residents have taken on new importance as the most ambitious federal plans to remake the nation's health care system have fizzled.

Indeed, many state officials suspected all along that they could not count on Washington to solve their problems and moved ahead on their own with innovations that are just now paying dividends. California, Texas, and Florida, for example, have enrolled thousands of people in health insurance alliances that pool the purchasing power of small businesses, enabling them to obtain health care coverage at prices far lower than what they would otherwise pay. Almost every state has passed a law tightening the regulations of health insurance, requiring insurers to sell coverage to small businesses and limiting variation in rates. Several states have expanded Medicaid programs to provide subsidized health insurance to people who would ordinarily be ineligible for Medicaid.

As President Clinton and Congress continue to clash over health care reform, the states are showing that progress is possible. Neither backward nor inept, the states remain a vital part of governing in our federal system.

return a person charged with a crime in another state to that state for trial or imprisonment. This practice is called **extradition.** Although there is no way to force states to comply, they usually are happy to do so, not wishing to harbor criminals and hoping that other states will reciprocate. Thus, a lawbreaker is prevented from avoiding punishment by simply escaping to another state.

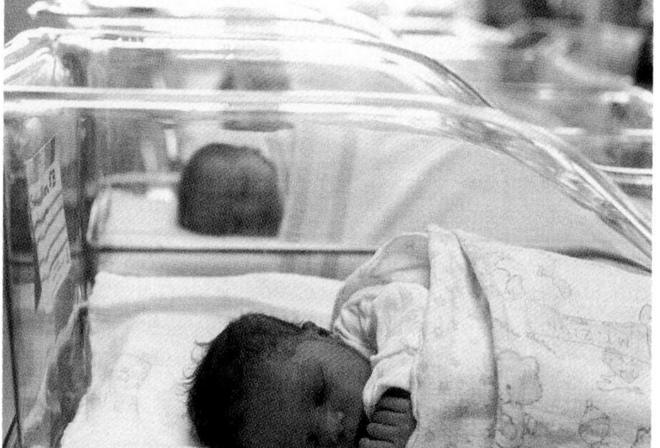

Because of the full faith and credit clause of the Constitution, these babies' birth certificates are valid in every state. They are also entitled to most of the benefits—and subject to most of the obligations—of citizenship in any state they visit, thanks to the privileges and immunities clause.

Privileges and Immunities. The most complicated obligation among the states is the requirement that citizens of each state receive all the **privileges and immunities** of any other state in which they happen to be. The goal of this constitutional provision is to prohibit states from discriminating against citizens of other states. If, for example, a Texan visits California, the Texan will pay the same sales tax and receive the same police protection as residents of California.

There are many exceptions to the privileges and immunities clause, however. Many of you attend public universities. If you are such a student and also reside in the same state as your university, you generally pay a tuition substantially lower than that paid by your fellow students from out of state. Similarly, only residents of a state can vote in state elections. States often attempt to pass the burdens of financing the state government to those outside the state, such as through taxes on minerals mined in the state but consumed elsewhere or special taxes on hotel rooms rented by tourists.

The Supreme Court has never clarified just which privileges a state must make available to all Americans and which privileges can be limited to its own citizens. In general, the more fundamental the rights—such as owning property or receiving police protection—the less likely it is that a state can discriminate against citizens of another state.

INTERGOVERNMENTAL RELATIONS TODAY

American federalism has changed quite a bit over the past two centuries. This section focuses first on the federal system's gradual change from a dual federalism to a cooperative federalism.[5] It then looks at the cornerstone of the relationship between the national government and state governments: federal grants-in-aid. Later, the chapter will explore the relative growth of the national government and state governments.

FROM DUAL TO COOPERATIVE FEDERALISM

One way to understand the changes in American federalism over the past two hundred years is to contrast two types of federalism. The first type is called **dual federalism.** In this kind of federalism, both the national government and the states remain supreme within their own spheres. The states are responsible for some policies, the national government for others. For example, the national government has exclusive control over foreign and military policy, the postal system, and monetary policy. States are exclusively responsible for schools, law enforcement, and road building. In dual federalism, the powers and policy assignments of the layers of government are distinct, as in a layer cake, and proponents of dual federalism believe that the powers of the national government should be interpreted narrowly.

Cooperative federalism began during the Great Depression of the 1930s. In this photo, Works Progress Administration workers, paid by the federal government, build a local road in Tennessee. In subsequent decades, the entire interstate highway system was constructed with a combination of national and state dollars.

Most politicians and political scientists today argue that dual federalism is outdated. They are more likely to describe the current American federal system as one of **cooperative federalism.** Instead of a layer cake, they see American federalism as more like a marble cake, with mingled responsibilities and blurred distinctions between the levels of government. In cooperative federalism, powers and policy assignments are shared between states and the national government.[6] Costs may be shared, with the national government and the states each paying a part. Administration may also be shared, with state and local officials working within federal guidelines. Sometimes even blame is shared when programs do not work well.

Before the national government began to assert its dominance over state governments, the American federal system leaned toward dual federalism. The American system, however, was never neatly separated into purely state and purely national responsibilities. For example, education was usually thought of as being mainly a state and local responsibility, yet even under the Articles of Confederation, Congress set aside land in the Northwest Territory to be used for schools (the first grant-in-aid program). During the Civil War, the national government adopted a policy to create land grant colleges. Important American universities such as Wisconsin, Texas A&M, Illinois, Ohio State, North Carolina State, and Iowa State owe their origins to this national policy.

In the 1950s and 1960s, the national government began supporting public elementary and secondary education. In 1958, Congress passed the National Defense Education Act (largely in response to Soviet success in the space race). The act provided federal grants and loans for college students and financial support for elementary and secondary education in science and foreign languages. In 1965, Congress passed the Elementary and Secondary Education Act, which provided federal aid to numerous schools. Although these policies expanded the national government's role in education, they were not a sharp break with the past.

Today, the federal government's presence is felt in even the tiniest red schoolhouse. Almost all school districts receive some federal assistance. To do so, they must comply with federal rules and regulations. They must, for example, maintain desegregated and nondiscriminatory programs.

Highways are another example of the movement toward cooperative federalism. In an earlier era, states and cities were largely responsible for building roads, although the Constitution does authorize Congress to construct "post roads." In 1956, Congress passed an act creating an interstate highway system. Hundreds of red, white, and blue signs were planted at the beginnings of interstate construction projects. The signs announced that the interstate highway program was a joint federal–state project and specified the cost and sharing of funds. In this as in other areas, the federal system has promoted a partnership between the national and state governments.

Cooperative federalism today rests on several standard operating procedures. For hundreds of programs, cooperative federalism involves

- *Shared costs.* Washington foots part of the bill, but states or cities that want to get their share must pay part of a program's costs. Cities and states can get federal money for airport construction, sewage treatment plants, youth programs, and many other programs, but only if they pay some of the costs.
- *Federal guidelines.* Most federal grants to states and cities come with strings attached. Congress spends billions of dollars to support state highway construction, for example, but to get their share, states must adopt and enforce limits on the drinking age.
- *Shared administration.* State and local officials implement federal policies, but they have administrative powers of their own. The U.S. Department of Labor, for example, gives billions of dollars to states for job retraining, but states have considerable latitude in spending the money.

The cooperation between the national government and state governments is such an established feature of American federalism that it persists even when the two levels of government are in conflict on certain matters. For example, in the 1950s and 1960s, Southern states cooperated well with Washington in building the interstate highway system, while they clashed with the national government over racial integration.

In his first inaugural address, Ronald Reagan argued that the states had primary responsibility for governing in most policy areas, and he promised to "restore the balance between levels of government." Few officials at either the state or the national level agreed with Reagan about ending the national government's role in domestic programs. However, Reagan's opposition to the national government's spending on domestic policies and the huge federal deficits of the 1980s forced a reduction in federal funds for state and local governments and shifted some responsibility for policy back to the states. Despite Reagan's move toward a more dual federalism, most Americans embrace a pragmatic view of governmental responsibilities, seeing the national government as more capable of—and thus responsible for—handling some issues, while they view state and local governments as better at managing others.

FISCAL FEDERALISM

The cornerstone of the national government's relations with state and local governments is **fiscal federalism:** the pattern of spending, taxing, and providing grants in the federal system. Subnational governments can influence the national government through local elections for national officials, but the national government has a powerful source of influence over the states—money. Grants-in-aid are the main instrument the national government uses for both aiding and influencing states and localities.

Despite the constant efforts of the Reagan administration to whittle away aid to states and cities, state and local aid from Washington (including loan subsidies) still amounts to about $250 billion each year. Figure 3.1 illustrates the growth in the amount of money spent on federal grants. Federal aid, covering a wide range of policy areas (see Figure 3.2, page 68), accounts for about one-fourth of all the funds spent by state and local governments and for about 15 percent of all federal government expenditures.[7]

The Federal Grant System: Distributing the Federal Pie. The national government regularly publishes the *Catalogue of Federal Domestic Assistance,* a massive volume listing the federal aid programs available to states, cities, and other local governments. The book lists federal programs that support energy assistance for the aged poor, housing allowances for the poor, drug-abuse services, urban rat-control efforts, community arts programs, state disaster-preparedness programs, and many more.

There are two major types of federal aid for states and localities: categorical grants and block grants. **Categorical grants** are the main source of federal aid to state and local governments. These grants can be used only for one of several hundred specific purposes, or categories, of state and local spending.

Because direct orders from the federal government to the states are rare (an exception is the Equal Opportunity Act of 1982, barring job discrimination by state and local governments), most federal regulation is accomplished in a more indirect manner. Instead of issuing stern edicts that tell citizens or states what they can and cannot do, Congress attaches conditions to the grants that states receive. The federal government has been especially active in appending restrictions to grants since the 1970s.

FIGURE 3.1 FISCAL FEDERALISM: FEDERAL GRANTS TO STATE AND LOCAL GOVERNMENTS

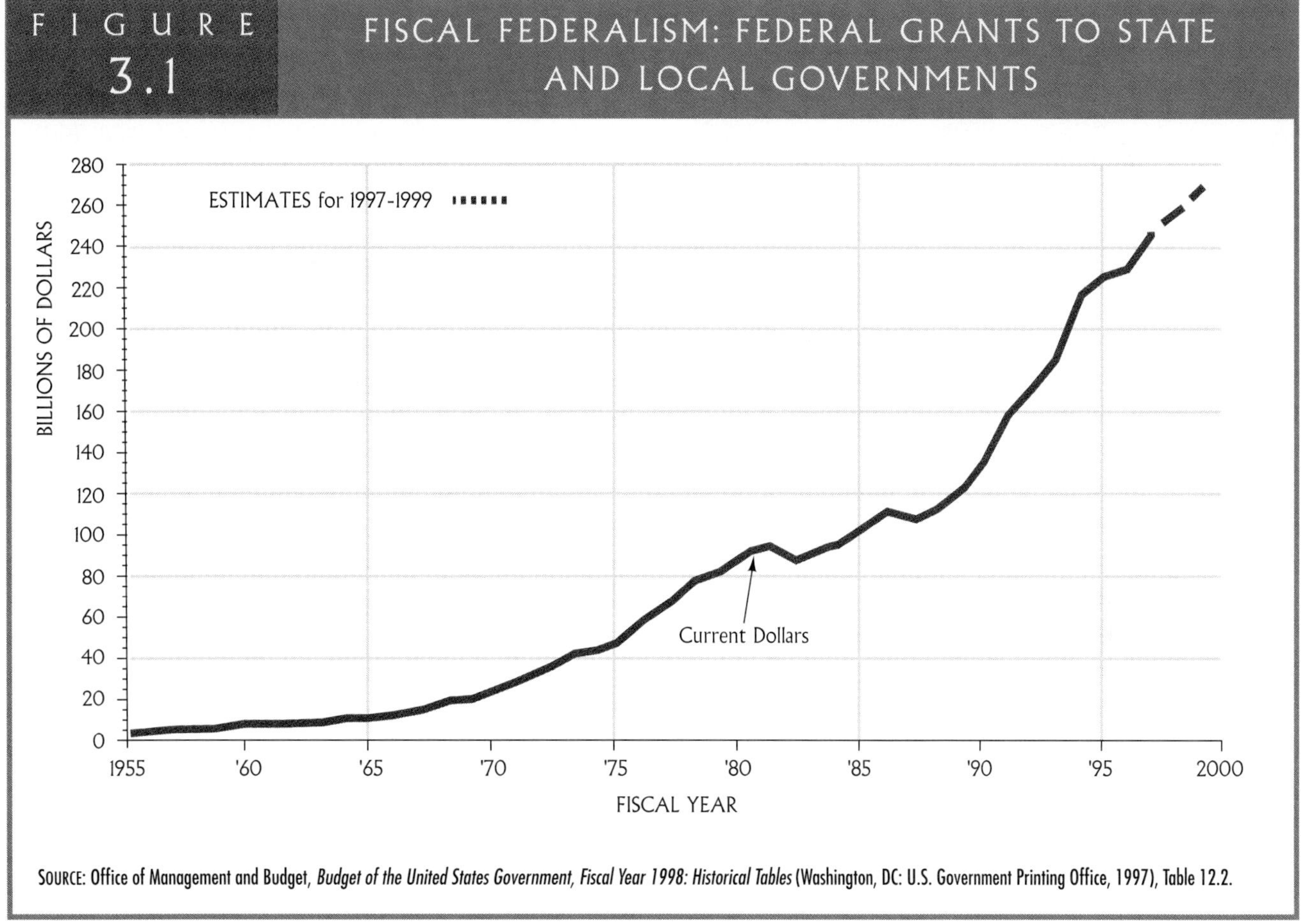

SOURCE: Office of Management and Budget, *Budget of the United States Government, Fiscal Year 1998: Historical Tables* (Washington, DC: U.S. Government Printing Office, 1997), Table 12.2.

One string commonly attached to categorical and other federal grants is a nondiscrimination provision, stating that aid may not be used for purposes that discriminate against minorities, women, or other groups. Another string, a favorite of labor unions, is that federal funds may not support construction projects that pay below the local union wage. Other restrictions may require an environmental impact statement for a federally supported construction project or provisions for community involvement in the planning of the project.

The federal government may also employ *cross-over sanctions* to use federal dollars in one program to influence state and local policy in another, such as when funds are withheld for highway construction unless states raise the drinking age to 21 or establish highway beautification programs.

Cross-cutting requirements occur when a condition on one federal grant is extended to all activities supported by federal funds regardless of their source. The grandfather of these requirements is Title VI of the 1964 Civil Rights Act (see Chapter 5), which bars discrimination in the use of federal funds because of race, color, national origin, gender, or physical disability. For example, if a university discriminates illegally in one program—such as athletics—it may lose the federal aid it receives for all its programs. There are also cross-cutting requirements dealing with environmental protection, historic preservation, contract wage rates, access to government information, the care of experimental animals, the treatment of human subjects in research projects, and a host of other policies.

Sometimes these indirect efforts at regulation are essentially symbolic. Once, a coalition of conservative members of Congress, led by Senator Orrin Hatch (R-UT), got Congress to tack on to some school aid funds a provision forbidding the teaching of "secular humanism," a long-standing right-wing bugaboo referring loosely, and inaccurately, to "godless communism." No one knew exactly what secular humanism was—the bill studiously avoided defining it—but whatever it was, schools would not be eligible for federal funds if they taught it.

There are two types of categorical grants. The most common type is a **project grant.** A project grant is awarded on the basis of competitive applications. National Science Foundation grants obtained by university professors are examples of project grants.

As their name implies, **formula grants** are distributed according to a formula. These formulas vary from grant to grant and may be computed on the basis of

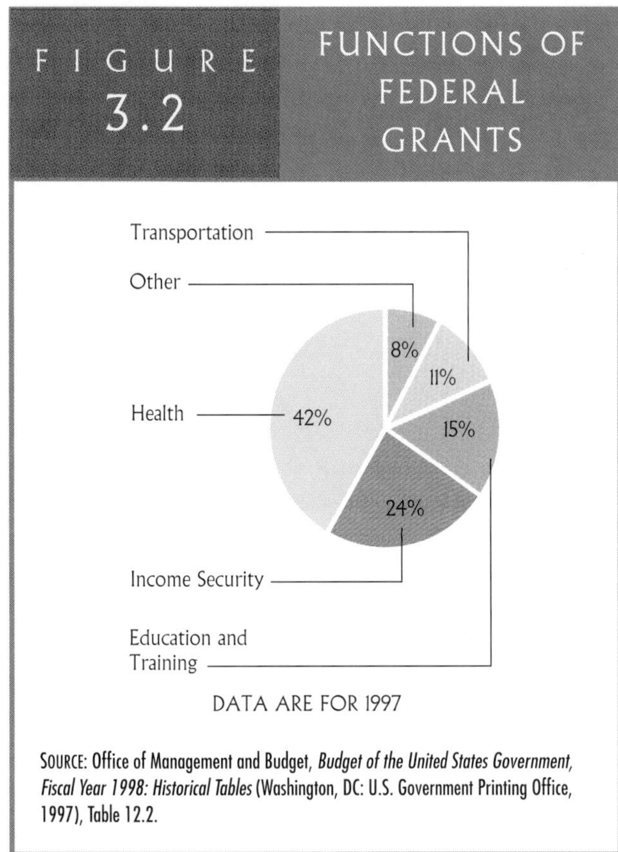

SOURCE: Office of Management and Budget, *Budget of the United States Government, Fiscal Year 1998: Historical Tables* (Washington, DC: U.S. Government Printing Office, 1997), Table 12.2.

population, per capita income, percentage of rural population, or some other factor. A state or local government does not apply for a formula grant; a grant's formula determines how much money the particular government will receive. As a result, Congress is the site of vigorous political battles over the formulas themselves. The most common formula grants are those for Medicaid, child nutrition programs, sewage treatment plant construction, public housing, community development programs, and training and employment programs.

Applications for categorical grants typically arrive in Washington in boxes, not envelopes. Complaints about the cumbersome paperwork and the many strings attached to categorical grants led to the adoption of the other major type of federal aid, **block grants.** These grants are given more or less automatically to states or communities, which then have discretion in deciding how to spend the money. First adopted in 1966, block grants are used to support broad programs in areas like community development and social service. The percentage of federal aid to state and local governments in the form of block grants began increasing in 1995 as the new Republican majority in Congress passed more federal aid in the form of block grants, including grants for welfare programs.

Another response to state and local governmental unhappiness with categorical grants was *revenue sharing.* First proposed by economists in the Johnson administration, revenue sharing became a favorite of the Nixon administration. Under the revenue-sharing program, virtually no strings were attached to federal aid payments; they could be used in almost any policy area. Revenue sharing was helpful to many poor states and localities but never amounted to more than 2 percent of all state and local revenues. In 1987, the program fell victim to the Reagan administration's budgetary axes.

The Scramble for Federal Dollars. With $250 billion in federal grants at stake, most states and many cities have set up full-time staffs in Washington.[8] Their task is to keep track of what money is available and to help their state or city get some of it. There are many Washington organizations of governments—the U.S. Conference of Mayors and the National League of Cities, for example—that act like other interest groups in lobbying Congress. Senators and representatives regularly go to the voters with stories of their influence in securing federal funds for their constituencies. They need continued support at the polls, they say, so that they will rise in seniority and get key posts to help "bring home the bacon."

A general rule of federalism is that the more money there is at stake, the more fervently people will argue

The federal government often uses grants-in-aid as a carrot and stick for the states. For example, aid has been withheld from some cities until police departments have been racially and sexually integrated.

about its distribution. There are some variations in the amount of money that states give to, and get back from, the national government. On the whole, however, federal grant distribution follows the principle of *universalism:* something for everybody. The vigilance of senators and representatives keeps federal aid reasonably well spread among the states. There are not many things in America—not income, access to education, or taxes—more equitably distributed than federal aid to states and cities.

This equality makes good politics, but it also may undermine public policy. Chapter 1 of the 1965 Elementary and Secondary Education Act is the federal government's principal endeavor to assist public schools. The primary intent of Chapter 1 was to give extra help to poor children. Yet the funds are allocated to 95 percent of all the school districts in the country. President Clinton's proposal to concentrate Chapter 1 funds on the poorest students failed when it ran into predictable opposition in Congress.

The Mandate Blues. States and localities are usually pleased to receive aid from the national government, but there are times when they would just as soon not have it. For example, say Congress decides to extend a program administered by the states and funded, in part, by the national government. It passes a law requiring the states to extend the program if they want to keep receiving aid, which most states do. Congress usually (though not always) appropriates some funds to help pay for the new policy, but either way, the states suddenly have to budget more funds for the project just to receive federal grant money.

Medicaid, which provides health care for poor people, is a prime example of a federal grant program that puts states in a difficult situation. Administered by the states, Medicaid receives wide support from both political parties. The national government pays between 50 and 83 percent of the bill, and the states pick up the rest. Since 1984, Congress has moved aggressively to expand Medicaid to specific populations, requiring the states to extend coverage to certain children, pregnant women, and elderly poor. Congress also increased its funding for the program a whopping 146 percent in the 1980s. Increased federal spending for Medicaid means increased spending for the states as well. In 1989, troubled by the drain on their states' budgets, 49 of the 50 governors called for a 2-year moratorium on mandated expansions of Medicaid. In effect, they told Washington to keep its money and leave them alone for a while.

A related problem arises when Congress passes a law creating financial obligations for the states but provides no funds to meet these obligations. For example, in 1990 Congress passed the Americans with Disabilities Act. States were required to make facilities, such as state colleges and universities, accessible to individuals with disabilities but were allocated no funds to implement such a policy. Similarly, the Clean Air Act of 1970 establishes national air quality standards but requires states to administer them and to appropriate funds for their implementation.

In 1995, the newly elected Republican majorities in Congress made limiting unfunded and underfunded mandates on state and local governments a high priority. Congress passed, and President Clinton signed, a law that requires both chambers to take a separate, majority vote in order to pass any bill that would impose unfunded mandates of more than $50 million on state and local governments. The law also requires the Congressional Budget Office to estimate the costs of all bills that impose such mandates. All antidiscrimination legislation and most legislation requiring state and local governments to take various actions in exchange for continued federal funding (such as grants for transportation) are exempt from this procedure.

Federal courts also create unfunded mandates for the states. In recent years, federal judges have issued states orders in areas such as prison construction and management, school desegregation, and facilities in mental health hospitals, sometimes even temporarily taking them over. These court orders often require states to spend funds to meet standards imposed by the judge.

A combination of federal regulatory rules and the lack of resources may also put the states in a bind. The national government requires that a local housing authority build or acquire a new apartment for each one it demolishes. But for years Congress has provided little money for the construction of public housing. As a result, a provision intended to help the poor by ensuring a stable supply of housing actually hurts them because it discourages local governments from demolishing unsafe and inadequate housing.

The federal government may also create financial obligations for the states unintentionally. In 1994, California, New York, Texas, Florida, and other states sued the federal government for reimbursement for the cost of health care, education, prisons, and other public services that the states provide to illegal residents. The states charged that the federal government's failure to control its borders was the source of huge new demands on their treasuries and that Washington, not the states, should pay for the problem.

UNDERSTANDING FEDERALISM

The federal system is central to politics, government, and policy in America. Our themes of democracy and the scope of government are especially helpful in understanding federalism. Federalism has a particularly profound effect on democracy.

FEDERALISM AND DEMOCRACY

The founders established a federal system for several reasons, one of which was to allay the fears of those who believed that a powerful and distant central government would tyrannize the states and limit their voice in government. By decentralizing the political system, federalism was designed to contribute to democracy—or at least to the limited form of democracy supported by the founders. Has it done so?

Advantages for Democracy. Federalism has many implications for democracy. The more levels of government, the more opportunities there are for participation in politics. State governments provide thousands of elected offices for which citizens may vote and/or run.

Adding additional levels of government also contributes to democracy by increasing access to government. Because different citizens and interest groups will have better access to either state-level governments or the national government, the two levels increase the opportunities for government to be responsive to demands for policies. For example, when in the 1950s and 1960s advocates of civil rights found themselves stymied in Southern states, they turned to the national level for help in achieving racial equality. Business interests, on the other hand, have traditionally found state governments to be more responsive to their demands. Organized labor is not well established in some states, but it can usually depend on some sympathetic officials at the national level who will champion its proposals.

Different economic interests are concentrated in different states: oil in Texas, tobacco farming in Virginia, and copper mining in Montana, for example. The federal system allows an interest concentrated in a state to exercise substantial influence in the election of officials, both state and national, from that state. In turn, these officials promote policies advantageous to the interest in both Washington and the state capital. This is a pluralism of interests that James Madison, among others, valued within a large republic.

State and local bases have another advantage. Even if a party loses at the national level, it can rebuild in its areas of strength and develop leaders under its banner at the state and local levels. As a result, losing an election becomes more acceptable, and the peaceful transfer of power is more probable. This was especially important in the early years of the nation before our political norms had become firmly established.

Because the federal system assigns states important responsibilities for public policies, it is possible for the diversity of opinion within the country to be reflected in different public policies among the states. If the citizens of Texas wish to have a death penalty, for example, they can vote for politicians who support it, whereas those in Wisconsin can vote to abolish the death penalty altogether. Similarly, there are large differences in the amounts that states provide for the poor, ranging from $923 per month for a family of three in Alaska to $120 per month in Mississippi (see Table 3.2).

By handling most disputes over policy at the state and local level, federalism also reduces decision making and conflict at the national level. If every issue had to be resolved in Washington, the national government would be overwhelmed.

Disadvantages for Democracy. Despite the advantages, relying on states to supply public services has some drawbacks. States differ in the resources they can devote to services like public education. Thus,

TABLE 3.2 DIVERSITY IN PUBLIC POLICY: STATE WELFARE BENEFITS

Because the American federal system allocates major responsibilities for public policy to the states, policies often vary with the different views of the population in different locations. This table shows that for an issue as emotionally charged as welfare, different states have adopted quite different policies.

	MAX. MONTHLY WELFARE GRANT PER FAMILY OF 3	MAX. INCOME LEVEL BEFORE LOSING ELIGIBILITY FOR WELFARE	
		IN DOLLARS	AS PERCENT OF POVERTY LINE[a]
Alaska	$923	$1,662	123%
Vermont	650	1,095	101
Hawaii	712	1,188	95
Calif.	607	1,215	112
Utah	426	972	90
R.I.	554	951	88
Wis.	517	896	83
N.D.	431	767	71
Montana	425	932	86
Wash.	546	939	87
Minn.	532	918	85
S.D.	430	881	81
N.H.	550	945	87
N.M.	389	704	65
Oregon	460	810	75
N.Y.[b]	577	986	91
Maine	418	950	88
Iowa	426	759	70
Mass.	565	968	89
Conn.	636	1,428	132
Kansas	429	764	71
Mich.[c]	459	809	75
Pa.	421	752	69
Colo.	421	752	69
Wyo.	360	1,005	93
Neb.	364	666	62
Ariz.	347	641	59
Idaho	317	596	55
Okla.	307	581	54
Ohio	341	632	58
Illinois	377	686	63
Va.	240	480	44
W. Va.	253	500	46
Nevada	348	642	59
N.J.	424	785	73
Md.	373	680	63
Ky.	262	909	84
Indiana	288	552	51
Mo.	292	558	52
Florida	303	575	53
Georgia	280	756	70
Del.	338	627	58
N.C.	272	936	87
D.C.	420	750	69
Ark.	204	426	39
S.C.	200	420	39
La.	190	405	37
Texas	188	402	37
Tenn.	185	995	92
Alabama	164	366	34
Miss.	120	672	62

[a]The Federal poverty line is $12,980 for a family of three, except in Alaska and Hawaii.
[b]Figures are for New York City only.
[c]Figures are for Wayne County, which includes Detroit.
(SOURCE: House Ways and Means Committee; Commerce Department)

TABLE 3.3 THE DOWNSIDE OF DIVERSITY: SPENDING ON PUBLIC EDUCATION

The downside of the public policy diversity fostered by federalism is that states are largely dependent on their own resources for providing public services; these resources vary widely from state to state. This table shows the wide variation among the states in the money spent on each child in the public schools.

STATE	DOLLARS PER PUPIL	STATE	DOLLARS PER PUPIL
Alabama	4,458	Montana	5,831
Alaska	9,934	Nebraska	5,384
Arizona	4,252	Nevada	5,126
Arkansas	4,257	New Hampshire	6,127
California	4,731	New jersey	9,860
Colorado	5,500	New Mexico	5,423
Connecticut	8,503	New York	9,448
Delaware	7,172	North Carolina	4,951
District of Columbia	8,211	North Dakota	4,603
Florida	5,717	Ohio	5,620
Georgia	5,396	Oklahoma	4,351
Hawaii	6,159	Oregon	6,250
Idaho	4,330	Pennsylvania	7,196
Illinois	5,259	Rhode Island	7,356
Indiana	6,033	South Carolina	4,931
Iowa	5,560	South Dakota	4,838
Kansas	5,761	Tennessee	4,544
Kentucky	5,611	Texas	5,416
Louisiana	4,705	Utah	3,668
Maine	6,410	Vermont	7,372
Maryland	6,719	Virginia	5,664
Massachusetts	7,341	Washington	5,811
Michigan	6,929	West Virginia	6,521
Minnesota	6,033	Wisconsin	7,001
Mississippi	4,123	Wyoming	6,070
Missouri	4,972		
Average: 1995			5,907

SOURCE: U.S. Department of Commerce, *Statistical Abstract of the United States, 1996* (Washington, DC: U.S. Government Printing Office, 1996), 170.

the quality of education a child receives is heavily dependent on the state in which the child's parents happen to reside. In 1995, New Jersey state and local governments spent an average of $9,860 for each child in the public schools; in Utah the figure was only $3,668 (see Table 3.3).

Diversity in policy can also discourage states from providing services that would otherwise be available. Political scientists have found that generous welfare benefits can strain a state's treasury by attracting poor people from states with lower benefits. As a result, states are deterred from providing generous benefits to those in need. A national program with uniform welfare benefits, however, would provide no incentive for welfare recipients to move to another state in search of higher benefits.[9]

Federalism may also have a negative effect on democracy insofar as local interests are able to thwart national majority support of certain policies. As discussed earlier in this chapter, in the 1960s the states—especially those in the South—became battlegrounds when the national government tried to enforce national civil rights laws and court decisions. Federalism complicated and delayed efforts to end racial discrimination, because state and local governments were responsible for public education and vot-

The People Speak

NATIONAL GOVERNMENT RESPONSIBILITIES

Which level of government should have more responsibility for . . .

	FEDERAL GOVERNMENT	STATE GOVERNMENT
Protecting civil rights	67%	26%
Strengthening the economy	64	24
Protecting the environment	50	38
Improving the health care system	48	41
Providing assistance to the poor	40	44
Reforming welfare	42	46
Providing job training	31	55
Reducing crime	24	68
Improving public education	22	72

The public's views of the national government's responsibilities change as American society changes. The founders did not give much thought to civil rights, environmental protection, or the health care system. Today, Americans frequently turn to Washington for help in dealing with these and other problems, including maintaining a strong economy.

SOURCE: NBC News/*Wall Street Journal* Polls, December 1994 and January 1995.

ing eligibility, for example, and because they had passed most of the laws supporting racial segregation.

Finally, the sheer number of governments in the United States is, at times, as much a burden as a boon to democracy. Program vendors say at baseball games that "you can't tell the players without a scorecard"; unfortunately, scorecards are not available for local governments, where the players are numerous and sometimes seem to be involved in different games. The U.S. Bureau of the Census counts not only people but also governments (see Chapter 21). Its latest count revealed an astonishing 86,743 American governments.

Certainly, almost 87,000 governments ought to be enough for any country. Are there too many? Americans speak eloquently about their state and local governments as grassroots governments, close to the people. (See "The People Speak: National Government Responsibilities") Yet having so many governments makes it difficult to know which governments are doing what. Exercising democratic control over them is even more difficult; voter turnout in local elections is often less than 20 percent.

FEDERALISM AND THE GROWTH OF THE NATIONAL GOVERNMENT

President Ronald Reagan negotiated quotas on imports of Japanese cars in order to give advantages to the American auto industry, raising the price of all automobiles in the process. At the behest of steel companies, President George Bush exercised his authority to continue Reagan's quotas on the amount of steel that could be imported (thereby making steel products more expensive). The first major piece of legislation the Bush administration sent to Congress was a bailout plan for the savings and loan industry, which had gotten into financial trouble through a combination of imprudent loans, declining property values, deregulation of banking, incompetence, and corruption. President Clinton proposed having the Pentagon spend nearly $600 million to fund the development of a U.S. industry in "flat-panel displays" used for laptop computers, video games, and advanced instruments.

In each of these cases and dozens of others, the national government has involved itself (some might say interfered) in the economic marketplace with quotas and subsidies intended to help American businesses. As Chapter 2 explained, the national government took a direct interest in economic affairs from the very founding of the republic. As the United States changed from an agricultural to an industrial nation, new problems arose and with them new demands for governmental action. The national government responded with a national banking system, subsidies for railroads and airlines, and a host of other policies that dramatically increased its role in the economy.

The industrialization of the country raised other issues as well. With the formation of large corporations—Cornelius Vanderbilt's New York Central Railroad and John D. Rockefeller's Standard Oil Company, for example—came the potential for such abuses as monopoly pricing. If there is only one railroad in town, it can charge farmers inflated prices to ship their grain to market. If a single company distributes most of the gasoline in the country, it can set the price at which gasoline sells. Thus, many interests asked the national government to restrain monopolies and to encourage open competition.

There were additional demands on the national government for new public policies. Farming interests sought services such as agricultural research, rural electrification, and price supports. Labor interests wanted the national government to protect their rights to organize and bargain collectively and to help provide safer working conditions, a minimum wage, and pension protection. Along with other groups, labor unions supported a wide range of social welfare policies, from education to health care. As the country became more urbanized, new problems arose in the areas of housing, welfare, the environment, and transportation. In each case, the relevant interest turned to the national government for help.

Why not turn to the state governments instead? In most cases, the answer is simple: A problem or policy requires the authority and resources of the national government. The Constitution forbids states from having independent defense policies. And even if it did not, how many states would want to take on a responsibility that represents more than half of the federal work force and about one-sixth of federal expenditures?

It is constitutionally permissible, but not sensible, for the states to handle a wide range of other issues. It makes little sense for Louisiana to pass strict controls on polluting the Mississippi River if most of the river's pollution occurs upstream, where Louisiana has no jurisdiction. Rhode Island has no incentive to create an energy policy, because no natural energy reserves are located in the state. Similarly, how effectively can a state regulate an international conglomerate such as General Motors? How can each state, acting individually, manage the nation's money supply?

Each state could have its own space program, but it is much more efficient if the states combine their efforts in one national program. The largest category of federal expenditures is that for economic security, including the Social Security program. Although each state could have its own retirement program, how could state governments determine which state should pay for retirees who move to Florida or Arizona? A national program is the only feasible method of ensuring the incomes of the mobile elderly of today's society.

Figure 3.3 on page 75 shows that the national government's share of American governmental expenditures has grown rapidly since 1929 (most of this growth occurred during the Great Depression). Then, the national government spent an amount equal to only 2.5 percent of the size of our economy, our gross domestic product (GDP); today, it spends more than one-fifth of our GDP (this includes grants to states and localities). The proportion of our GDP spent by state and local governments has grown less rapidly than the national government's share. States and localities spent 7.4 percent of our GDP in 1929; they spend 11 percent today (not including federal grants).

Each state could have its own space program, but it is much more efficient for the states to combine their efforts in one national program. The same principle applies to economic security and to a host of other important programs.

Figure 3.3 demonstrates that the states have not been supplanted by the national government; indeed, they carry out virtually all the functions they always have. Instead, with the support of the American people, new responsibilities have been taken on by the national government (see "The People Speak: National Government Responsibilities"). In addition, the national government has added programs to help the states meet their own responsibilities.

SUMMARY

Federalism is a governmental system in which power is shared between a central government and other governments. Federalism is much less common than are the unitary governments typical of most parliamentary democracies. American federal-

FIGURE 3.3 FISCAL FEDERALISM: THE PUBLIC SECTOR AND THE FEDERAL SYSTEM

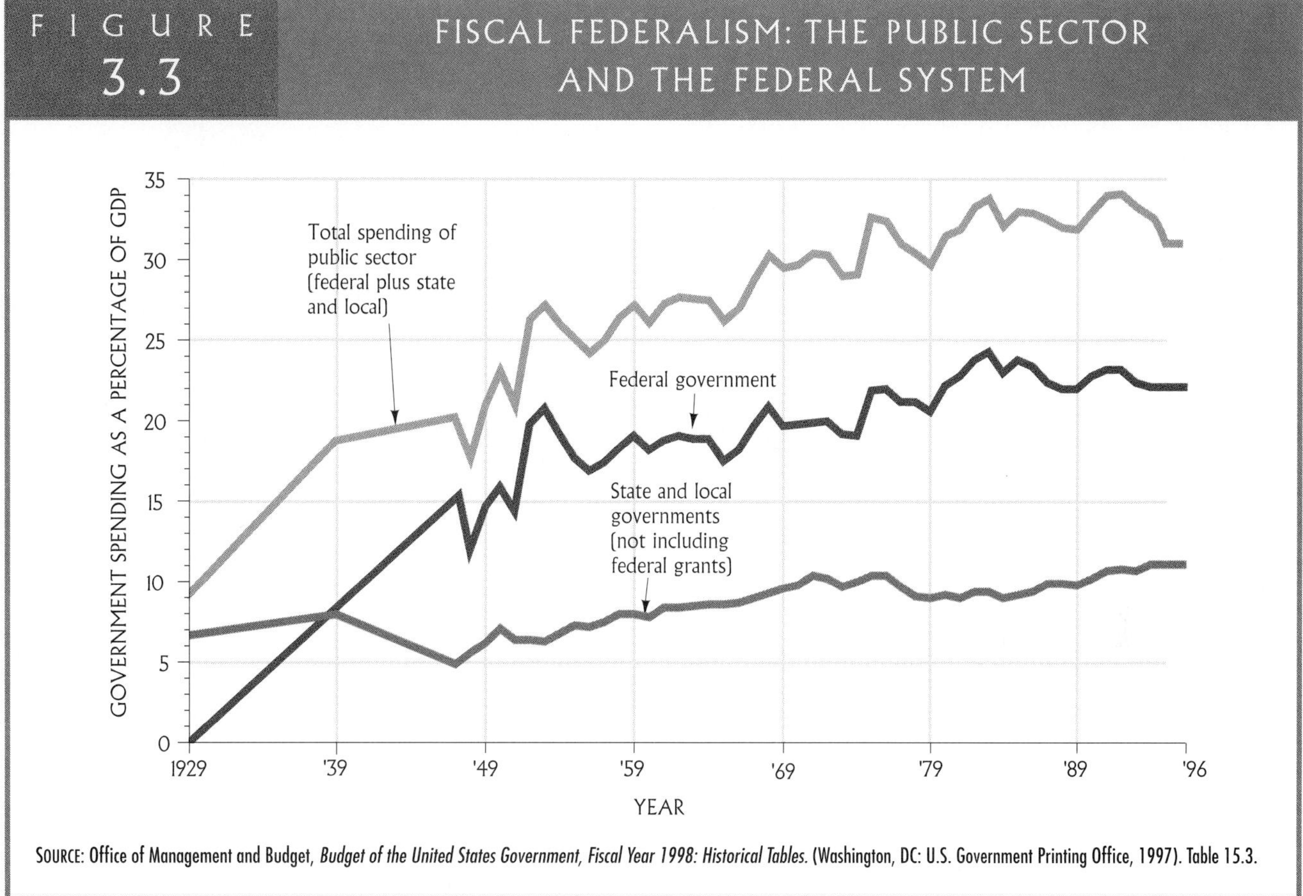

SOURCE: Office of Management and Budget, *Budget of the United States Government, Fiscal Year 1998: Historical Tables.* (Washington, DC: U.S. Government Printing Office, 1997). Table 15.3.

ism consists of 50 state governments joined in an "indestructible union" (as the Supreme Court once called it) under one national government. Today, federal power over the states is indisputable; the Supreme Court case *McCulloch v. Maryland,* the Civil War, and the struggle for equality all helped determine national supremacy. The federal government has recently used its fiscal leverage to discourage teenage drinking in the states.

The United States has moved from a system of dual federalism to one of cooperative federalism, in which the national and state governments share responsibility for public policies. Fiscal federalism is of great help to states. Even after the Reagan Administration reductions, the federal government distributes about $250 billion in federal funds to states and cities each year.

Federalism was instituted largely to enhance democracy in America, and it strengthens democratic government in many ways. At the same time, diverse state policies and the sheer number of local governments cause some problems as well. Demands for new policies and the necessity for national policy on certain issues have contributed to the growth of national government relative to the state governments. Yet the state governments continue to play a central role in governing the lives of Americans.

Although American federalism concerns state power and national power, it is not a concept removed from most Americans' lives. Federalism affects a vast range of social and economic policies. Slavery, school desegregation, abortion, and teenage drinking have all been debated in terms of federalism.

KEY TERMS

federalism
unitary governments
intergovernmental relations
supremacy clause
Tenth Amendment
McCulloch v. Maryland
enumerated powers
implied powers
elastic clause
Gibbons v. Ogden
full faith and credit
extradition
privileges and immunities
dual federalism
cooperative federalism
fiscal federalism
categorical grants
project grant
formula grants
block grants

FOR FURTHER READING

Anton, Thomas. *American Federalism and Public Policy.* Philadelphia: Temple University Press, 1989. An overview of how the national, state, and local governments share responsibility for policies.

Beer, Samuel H. *To Make a Nation: The Rediscovery of American Federalism.* Cambridge, MA: Harvard University Press, 1993. An excellent study of the philosophical bases of American federalism.

Conlan, Timothy J. *New Federalism: Intergovernmental Reform from Nixon to Reagan.* Washington, DC: Brookings Institution, 1988. An analysis of the efforts of Presidents Nixon and Reagan to restructure intergovernmental relations.

Dye, Thomas R. *American Federalism: Competition Among Governments.* Lexington, MA: Lexington Books, 1990. Analyzes competitive federalism, in which states and local governments compete to offer public services at low costs.

Elazar, Daniel J. *American Federalism: A View from the States,* 3rd ed. New York: Harper & Row, 1984. A well-known work surveying federalism from the standpoint of state governments.

Kettl, Donald F. *The Regulation of American Federalism.* Baltimore: Johns Hopkins University Press, 1987. Examines the regulations that the national government imposes on state and local governments.

Peterson, Paul E. *The Price of Federalism.* Washington, DC: Brookings Institution, 1995. A current assessment of the costs and benefits of federalism.

Peterson, Paul, Barry G. Rabe, and Kenneth K. Wong. *When Federalism Works.* Washington, DC: Brookings Institution, 1986. Examines federal grant-in-aid programs and explains why they are implemented better in some areas than in others.

Walker, David B. *The Rebirth of Federalism.* Chatham, NJ: Chatham House, 1995. A history of American federalism and an analysis of its current condition.

Wright, Deil S. *Understanding Intergovernmental Relations,* 3rd ed. Belmont, CA: Brooks/Cole, 1988. A review of the relations among the local, state, and national levels of government.

INTERNET RESOURCES

http://www.gsa.gov/fdac/queryfdac.htm
Allows you to search through the hundreds of federal grants.

http://www.ncs.org/statefed/afipolcy.htm
Information and discussion of issues on federal-state relations.

NOTES

1. Thomas Anton, *Moving Money* (New York: Oxford University Press, 1982).
2. One useful introduction to federalism and intergovernmental relations is Deil S. Wright, *Understanding Intergovernmental Relations,* 3rd ed. (Belmont, CA: Brooks/Cole, 1988). Another is David B. Walker, *The Rebirth of Federalism* (Chatham, NJ: Chatham House, 1995).
3. On the states as innovators, see Jack L. Walker, "The Diffusion of Innovations in the American States," *American Political Science Review* 63 (September 1969): 880–899; Virginia Gray, "Innovation in the States: A Diffusion Study," *American Political Science Review* 67 (December 1973): 1174–1185; and Richard P. Nathan and Fred C. Doolittle, *Reagan and the States* (Princeton, NJ: Princeton University Press, 1987).
4. *Monroe v. Pape,* 1961; *Monell v. New York City Department of Social Welfare,* 1978; *Owen v. Independence,* 1980; *Maine v. Thiboutot,* 1980; *Oklahoma City v. Tuttle,* 1985; *Dennis v. Higgins,* 1991.
5. The transformation from dual to cooperative federalism is described in Walker, *The Rebirth of Federalism,* chap. 4.
6. The classic discussion of cooperative federalism is found in Morton Grodzins, *The American System: A New View of Governments in the United States,* ed. Daniel J. Elazar (Chicago: Rand McNally, 1966).
7. Office of Management and Budget, *Budget of the United States Government, Fiscal Year 1998: Analytical Perspectives* (Washington DC: U.S. Government Printing Office, 1997), table 9.2.
8. On intergovernmental lobbying, see Donald H. Haider, *When Governments Go to Washington* (New York: Free Press, 1974).
9. Paul E. Peterson and Mark Rom, "American Federalism, Welfare Policy, and Residential Choices," *American Political Science Review* 83 (September 1989): 711–728. Some states are now limiting welfare payments to new residents.

Civil Liberties and Public Policy

4

The Bill of Rights—Then and Now

Freedom of Religion

Freedom of Expression

Defendants' Rights

The Right to Privacy

Understanding Civil Liberties

Soldier of Fortune magazine is read by mercenaries, adventurers, and others who live—or imagine living—in the shadowy world of jungle combat, espionage, and murder for hire. A Texas man named Robert Black found an advertisement in *Soldier of Fortune* that read,

> Ex-Marines, '67–'69 Nam Vets, weapons specialist—jungle warfare. Pilot. ME. High-risk assignments. U.S. or overseas.

Black made contact with the man who placed the ad, John Wayne Hearn of Atlanta, and hired Hearn to murder his wife, Sandra Black. Hearn shot and killed her on February 21, 1985. Both Robert Black and John Wayne Hearn were arrested, tried, and sentenced. Hearn received life imprisonment; Black got the death penalty.

Sandra Black's family sued *Soldier of Fortune,* arguing that the advertisement had contributed to her death. The magazine insisted that it could not possibly screen every ad it published and that the First Amendment gave it the right to publish anything it wanted. A federal district court jury ruled in favor of the family and ordered the magazine to pay $1.5 million, but an appeals court reversed this judgment. The higher court found that the magazine had no duty to refrain from publishing ambiguous advertisements that might contribute to some later violation of law. In the meantime, Hearn, who did the killing, is serving time in prison, while Black, who hired him but did not commit the murder, has been executed.

Although it is more exotic than most, the *Soldier of Fortune* case is the sort of complex controversy that shapes American civil liberties. Debates about the right to abortion, the right to bear arms, the rights of criminal defendants, and other similar issues are constantly in the news. Some of these issues arise from conflicting interests. The need to protect society against crime is often in conflict with society's need to protect the rights of people accused of crime. Other conflicts derive from strong differences of opinion about what is ethical, moral, or right. To some Americans, abortion is murder, the taking of a human life. To others, a woman's choice whether to bear a child, free of governmental intrusion, is a fundamental right.

Complex questions about civil liberties require that decisions be made about balancing competing values such as maintaining an open system of expression while protecting individuals from the excesses such a system may produce. As we learned in Chapter 1, civil liberties are essential to democracy. How could we have free elections without free speech, for example? But does it follow that critics of officials should be able to say whatever they want, no matter how untrue? And who should decide the extent of our liberty? Should it be a representative institution such as Congress or a judicial elite such as the Supreme Court?

Other decisions must be made about the role of the government in resolving controversies over civil liberties. Conservatives usually advocate narrowing the scope of government, yet many of them strongly support government-imposed limits on abortion and government-sanctioned prayers in the public schools. They also want government to be less hindered by concern for defendants' rights. Liberals, who typically support a broader scope of government, usually want to limit government's role in prohibiting abortion and encouraging religious activities and to place greater constraints on government's freedom of action in the criminal justice system.

Civil liberties are individual legal and constitutional protections against the government. Americans' civil liberties are set down in the Bill of Rights, but disputes about civil liberties often end up in court. The courts are the arbiters of these liberties, because they determine what the Constitution means in the cases that they decide. The Supreme Court of the United States is the final interpreter of the content and scope of our liberties; this ultimate power to interpret the Constitution accounts for much of the ferocious debate over presidential appointments to the Supreme Court.

At first glance, many questions about civil liberties look easy. The Bill of Rights' guarantee of a free press seems straightforward; either Americans can write what they choose, or they cannot. In the real world of American law, however, these issues are subtle and complex. Throughout this chapter you will find special features entitled "You Are the Judge." Each feature describes an actual case brought before the courts and asks you to evaluate the case and make a judgment about it. Although you do not know as much about the law as a judge, you can apply your sense of fairness and your ethical standards to try to decide these cases. The actual court decisions are collected at the end of the chapter in a feature entitled "The Court Decides" (see p. 107).

An understanding of American civil liberties begins with the Bill of Rights.

THE BILL OF RIGHTS—THEN AND NOW

By the time of the 1787 Convention, all of the state constitutions had bills of rights, some of which survive, intact, to this day. Although the new U.S. Constitution had no bill of rights, the states made it clear that a condition of ratification was the addition of a Bill of Rights. The first ten amendments to the Constitution make up the **Bill of Rights.** They were

Issues of civil liberties present many vexing problems for the courts to resolve. For example, is burning the American flag desecration of a sacred patriotic symbol, or is it an expression of opposition to government policy that is protected by the Constitution?

passed as a group by the First Congress in 1789 and sent to the states for ratification. In 1791, these amendments became part of the Constitution.

The Bill of Rights ensures Americans basic liberties: freedom of speech and religion, protection against arbitrary searches and being held for long periods without trial, and so forth. Because the rest of this chapter will discuss the Bill of Rights, this is a good time for you to read it carefully (see Table 4.1). Pay particular attention to the **First Amendment,** the source of Americans' freedom of religion, speech, press, and assembly. The Bill of Rights was passed when British abuses of the colonists' civil liberties were still a fresh and bitter memory. Newspaper editors had been jailed; citizens had been arrested without cause, detained, and forced to confess at gunpoint or worse. Thus, the first ten amendments enjoyed great popular support.

Today Americans still believe in the Bill of Rights and its commitment to freedom—up to a point. Mark Twain wrote that God gave the American people "the three precious gifts of freedom of speech, freedom of religion, and the prudence never to exercise either of them." Likewise, you have probably heard remarks like "Freedom of the press demands responsibility of the press," "You shouldn't criticize something unless you suggest an alternative," and "Criminals are not entitled to human dignity." These statements reflect the belief that civil liberties sometimes have to yield to other individual or societal values.

Political scientists have discovered that people are devotees of rights in theory but that their support waivers when it comes time to put those rights into practice.[1] For example, Americans in general believe in

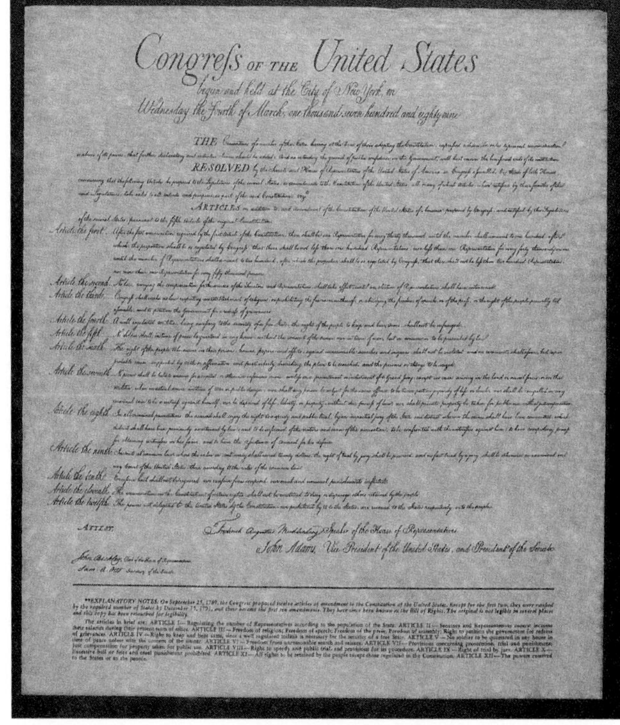

Congress of the United States
begun and held at the City of New-York, on
Wednesday the Fourth of March, one thousand seven hundred and eighty nine

TABLE 4.1 THE BILL OF RIGHTS

(These amendments were passed by Congress on September 25, 1789, and ratified by the states on December 15, 1791.)

Amendment I—Religion, Speech, Assembly, Petition

Congress shall make no law respecting an establishment of religion, or prohibiting the free exercise thereof; or abridging the freedom of speech, or of the press; or the right of the people peaceably to assemble, and to petition the Government for a redress of grievances.

Amendment II—Right to Bear Arms

A well regulated militia, being necessary to the security of a free State, the right of the people to keep and bear arms, shall not be infringed.

Amendment III—Quartering of Soldiers

No Soldier shall, in time of peace be quartered in any house, without the consent of the owner, nor in time of war, but in a manner to be prescribed by law.

Amendment IV—Searches and Seizures

The right of the people to be secure in their persons, houses, papers, and effects, against unreasonable searches and seizures, shall not be violated, and no warrants shall issue, but upon probable cause, supported by oath or affirmation, and particularly describing the place to be searched, and persons or things to be seized.

Amendment V—Grand Juries, Double Jeopardy, Self-Incrimination, Due Process, Eminent Domain

No person shall be held to answer to a capital, or otherwise infamous crime, unless on a presentment or indictment of a Grand Jury, except in cases arising in the land or naval forces, or in the militia, when in actual service in time of war or public danger: nor shall any person be subject for the same offense to be twice put in jeopardy of life or limb; nor shall be compelled in any criminal case to be a witness against himself, nor be deprived of life, liberty, or property, without due process of law; nor shall private property be taken for public use, without just compensation.

Amendment VI—Criminal court Procedures

In all criminal prosecutions, the accused shall enjoy the right to a speedy and public trial, by an impartial jury of the State and district wherein the crime shall have been committed, which district shall have been previously ascertained by law, and to be informed of the nature and cause of the accusation; to be confronted with the witnesses against him; to have compulsory process for obtaining witnesses in his favor, and to have the assistance of counsel for his defense.

Amendment VII—Trial by Jury in Common-Law Cases

In Suits at common law, where the value in controversy shall exceed twenty dollars, the right of trial by jury shall be preserved, and no fact tried by a jury, shall be otherwise reexamined in any Court of the United States.

Amendment VIII—Bails, Fines and Punishment

Excessive bail shall not be required, nor excessive fines imposed, nor cruel and unusual punishments inflicted.

Amendment IX—Rights Retained by the People

The enumeration in the Constitution, of certain rights, shall not be construed to deny or disparage others retained by the people.

Amendment X—Rights Reserved to the States

The powers not delegated to the United States by the Constitution, nor prohibited by it to the States, are reserved to the States respectively, or to the people.

freedom of speech, but many citizens would not let the Ku Klux Klan speak in their neighborhood or allow their public schools to teach about atheism or homosexuality.

THE BILL OF RIGHTS AND THE STATES

Take another look at the First Amendment. Note the first words: "Congress shall make no law . . ." The Bill of Rights was written to restrict the powers of the new national government. In 1791, Americans were comfortable with their state governments; after all, every state constitution had its own bill of rights. Thus, a literal reading of the First Amendment suggests that it does not prohibit a state government from passing a law prohibiting the free exercise of religion, free speech, or freedom of the press.

What happens, however, if a state passes a law violating one of the rights protected by the federal Bill of Rights and the state's constitution does not prohibit this abridgment of freedom? In 1833, the answer to that question was "nothing." A man named Barron brought his legal troubles with the city of Baltimore to the Supreme Court. Complaining that the city had ruined his dry dock business by constructing a wharf, Barron argued that the Fifth Amendment forbade Baltimore from taking his property without just compensation. John Marshall's Court refused to consider Barron's claim. The Bill of Rights, said the Court in ***Barron v. Baltimore,*** restrained only the national government, not states and cities. The city of Baltimore could build a wharf, even if it took business away from Mr. Barron's dry dock.

Almost a century later, however, the Court ruled that a state government must respect some First Amendment rights. The 1925 case ***Gitlow v. New York*** relied not on the First Amendment but on the Fourteenth—the second of three "Civil War Amendments" that ended slavery, gave former slaves legal protection, and ensured their voting rights. Ratified in 1868, the **Fourteenth Amendment** declared the following:

> No state shall make or enforce any law which shall abridge the privileges or immunities of citizens of the United States nor shall any state deprive any person of life, liberty, or property, *without due process of law*; nor deny to any person within its jurisdiction the equal protection of the laws.

In *Gitlow,* the Court announced that freedoms of speech and press "were fundamental personal rights and liberties protected by the due process clause of the Fourteenth Amendment from impairment by the states." In effect, the Court interpreted the Fourteenth Amendment to say that states could not abridge the freedoms of expression protected by the First Amendment. This decision began the development of the **incorporation doctrine** in which the Supreme Court applied to the states rights that are enumerated in the Bill of Rights. However, not everyone agreed that the Fourteenth Amendment incorporated parts of the Bill of Rights into state laws. As recently as 1985, Edwin Meese, who was then attorney general, strongly criticized *Gitlow* and called for "disincorporation" of the Bill of Rights.

After the 1925 *Gitlow* case, only parts of the First Amendment were held binding on the states. Gradually, especially during the 1960s when Earl Warren was Chief Justice, the Supreme Court has applied most of the Bill of Rights to the states (see Table 4.2). "One by one," wrote constitutional scholar Samuel Krislov, "the provisions of the Bill of Rights have been held to apply to the states, not in their own right, but as implicit in the Fourteenth Amendment."[2] Many of the court decisions that empowered the Bill of Rights were controversial, but today the Bill of Rights guarantees individual freedoms against infringement by state and local governments as well as by the national government. Only the Second, Third, and Seventh Amendments, and the grand jury requirement of the Fifth Amendment, have not been applied specifically to the states.

FREEDOM OF RELIGION

The First Amendment makes not one but two statements about religion and government. These statements are commonly referred to as the establishment clause and the free exercise clause. The **establishment clause** states that "Congress shall make no law respecting an establishment of religion." The **free exercise clause** prohibits the abridgment of the citizens' freedom to worship, or not to worship, as they please. Sometimes these freedoms conflict. The government's practice of providing chaplains on military bases is one example of this conflict; some accuse the government of establishing religion in order to ensure that members of the armed forces can freely practice their religion. Usually, however, establishment clause and free exercise clause cases raise different kinds of conflicts.

THE ESTABLISHMENT CLAUSE

Some nations, such as Great Britain, have an established church that is officially supported by the government and recognized as a national institution. A few American colonies had official churches, but the religious persecutions that incited many colonists to move to America discouraged any desire for the First Congress to establish a national church in the United States. Thus, established religion is prohibited by the First Amendment.

It is much less clear, however, what else the first Congress intended to be included in the establishment clause. Some people argued that it meant only that the government could not favor one religion over another. In contrast, Thomas Jefferson argued that the First Amendment created a "wall of separation" between church and state, forbidding not just favoritism but also any support for religion at all. These interpretations continue to provoke argument, especially when religion is mixed with education.

Debate is especially intense over aid to church-related schools and prayers in the public schools.

TABLE 4.2 THE NATIONALIZATION OF THE BILL OF RIGHTS

DATE	AMENDMENT	RIGHT	CASE
1925	First	Freedom of speech	*Gitlow v. New York*
1931	First	Freedom of the press	*Near v. Minnesota*
1937	First	Freedom of assembly	*De Jonge v. Oregon*
1940	First	Free exercise of religion	*Cantwell v. Connecticut*
1947	First	Establishment of religion	*Everson v. Board of Education*
1958	First	Freedom of association	*NAACP v. Alabama*
1963	First	Right to petition government	*NAACP v. Button*
	Second	Right to bear arms	Not Incorporated[a]
	Third	No quartering of soldiers	Not Incorporated[b]
1949	Fourth	No unreasonable searches and seizures	*Wolf v. Colorado*
1961	Fourth	Exclusionary rule	*Mapp v. Ohio*
1897	Fifth	Guarantee of just compensation	*Chicago, Burlington, and Quincy RR v. Chicago*
1964	Fifth	Immunity from self-incrimination	*Mallory v. Hogan*
1969	Fifth	Immunity from double jeopardy	*Benton v. Maryland*
	Fifth	Right to grand jury indictment	Not incorporated
1932	Sixth	Right to counsel in capital cases	*Powell v. Alabama*
1948	Sixth	Right to public trial	*In re Oliver*
1963	Sixth	Right to counsel in felony cases	*Gideon v. Wainwright*
1965	Sixth	Right to confrontation of witnesses	*Pointer v. Texas*
1966	Sixth	Right to impartial jury	*Parker v. Gladden*
1967	Sixth	Right to speedy trial	*Klopfer v. North Carolina*
1967	Sixth	Right to compulsory process for obtaining witnesses	*Washington v. Texas*
1968	Sixth	Right to jury trial for serious crimes	*Duncan v. Louisiana*
1972	Sixth	Right to counsel for all crimes involving jail terms	*Argersinger v. Hamlin*
	Seventh	Right to jury trial in civil cases	Not incorporated
1962	Eighth	Freedom from cruel and unusual punishment	*Robinson v. California*
	Eighth	Freedom from excessive fines or bail	Not Incorporated
1965	Ninth	Right of privacy	*Griswold v. Connecticut*

[a]The Supreme Court has upheld limits on the rights of private citizens to bear arms.
[b]The quartering of soldiers has not occurred under the Constitution.

Proponents of *parochiaid* (short for "aid to parochial schools"), which has existed in various forms since the 1960s, argue that the aid does not favor any particular religion. Opponents claim that the Roman Catholic Church has by far the largest religious school system in the country and gets most of the aid. In ***Lemon v. Kurtzman*** (1971), the Supreme Court declared that aid to church-related schools must

1. Have a secular legislative purpose.
2. Have a primary effect that neither advances nor inhibits religion.
3. Not foster an excessive government "entanglement" with religion.

We examine this issue in "Since Kennedy: Public Support for Religious Schools."

At the same time, the Supreme Court has been opening public schools to religious activities. The Court decided that public universities that let student groups use their facilities must allow student religious groups on campus to use the facilities for religious worship (*Widmar v. Vincent,* 1981). In the 1984 Equal Access Act, Congress made it unlawful for any public high school

SINCE KENNEDY

Public Support for Religious Schools

John F. Kennedy was the first Roman Catholic elected to the presidency. His religion was a major issue in the 1960 presidential campaign and did not disappear once he took office. To make it clear that he was not an agent of the Vatican (yes, there were people who feared he may be just that), Kennedy opposed giving federal aid to parochial schools. It was Protestant Lyndon Baines Johnson who obtained the passage of the first substantial aid to parochial elementary and secondary schools in 1965. He argued that aid went to students, not schools, and thus should go wherever the students were, including parochial schools.

As a result of this federal aid, the Supreme Court has spent considerable time on the issue of aid to religious schools. There is a fine line between aid that is permissible and aid that is not. For instance, the Court has allowed religiously affiliated colleges and universities to use public funds to build buildings, and it has allowed states to lend textbooks to parochial schools. Tax funds may also be used to provide students in parochial schools with textbooks, lunches, transportation to and from school, and standardized testing services. Public funds cannot, however, be used to pay teachers' salaries, buy tape recorders, or provide transportation for students on field trips. The theory underlying these decisions is that it is possible to determine that buildings, textbooks, lunches, school buses, and national tests are not used to support sectarian education. However, determining how teachers handle a subject in class, use equipment, and/or focus a field trip may require complex and constitutionally impermissible regulation of religion. In an important loosening of its constraints on aid to parochial schools, the Supreme Court decided in 1997 in *Agostini v. Felton* that public school systems could send teachers into parochial schools to teach remedial and supplemental classes to needy children.

In the Clinton era, controversy over aid to schools is not limited to Roman Catholic schools or any other single religion. In 1994, the Supreme Court ruled in *Kiryas Joel v. Grumet* that New York state had gone too far in favoring religion when it created a public school district for the benefit of a village of Hasidic Jews.

---

receiving federal funds (almost all of them do) to keep student groups from using school facilities for religious worship if the school opens its facilities for other student meetings; the Court upheld this law in *Westside Community Schools v. Mergens* (1990). Similarly, in *Lamb's Chapel v. Center Moriches Union Free School* (1993) the Court required public schools that rent facilities to organizations to do the same for religious groups. In 1995, the Court held that the University of Virginia was constitutionally required to subsidize a student religious magazine on the same basis as other student publications (*Rosenberger v. University of Virginia*).

The threshold of constitutional acceptability becomes higher when public funds may be used in a more direct way to support education. Thus, school authorities may not permit religious instructors to come into the public school buildings during the school day to provide religious education (*Illinois ex rel McCollum v. Board of Education,* 1948), although they may release students from part of the compulsory school day to receive religious instruction elsewhere (*Zorach v. Clauson,* 1952).

School prayer is more controversial than just about any other religious issue. In 1962 and 1963, the Court aroused the wrath of many Americans by ruling that voluntary recitations of prayers or Bible passages, when done as part of classroom exercises in public schools, violated the establishment clause. ***Engel v. Vitale*** and ***School District of Abington Township, Pennsylvania v. Schempp*** observed that "the place of religion in our society is an exalted one, but in the relationship between man and religion, the State is firmly committed to a position of neutrality." In 1980, the Court also prohibited the posting of the Ten Commandments on the walls of public classrooms (*Stone v. Graham,* 1980).

It is *not* unconstitutional, of course, to pray in public schools. Students may pray silently as much as they wish. What the Constitution forbids is the sponsorship or encouragement of prayer, directly or indirectly, by public school authorities. Thus, in 1992, in *Lee v. Weisman,* the Court ruled that a school-sponsored prayer at a public-school graduation violated the constitutional separation of church and state. Three

Alabama laws—passed in 1978, 1981, and 1982—authorized schools to hold one-minute periods of silence for "meditation or voluntary prayer," but the Court rejected this approach in *Wallace v. Jaffree* (1985) because the state made it clear that the purpose of the statute was to return prayer to the schools. The Court indicated, however, that a less clumsy approach would pass its scrutiny.

Political scientist Kenneth D. Wald observes that the last few years have been marked by great ferment in the relationship between religion and American political life. Religious issues and controversies have assumed much greater importance in political debate than they commanded before.[3] Much of this new importance is due to fundamentalist religious groups that have spurred their members to political action. Many school districts have simply ignored the Supreme Court's ban on school prayer and continue to allow prayers in their classrooms. Some religious groups and many members of Congress, especially conservative Republicans, have pushed for a constitutional amendment permitting prayer in school. The public, as you can see in "The People Speak: Prayer in the Public Schools," remains divided on the issue.

Fundamentalist Christian groups have pressed some state legislatures to mandate the teaching of "creation science"—their alternative to Darwinian theories of evolution—in public schools. Louisiana, for example, passed a Balanced Treatment Act requiring schools that taught Darwinian theory to teach creation science, too. Regardless, the Supreme Court ruled in *Edwards v. Aguillard* (1987) that this law violated the establishment clause. The Court also held (in *Epperson v. Arkansas,* 1968) that states cannot prohibit Darwin's theory of evolution from being taught in the public schools.

Thus, the Supreme Court has struggled with interpreting the establishment clause. In 1984, the Court found that Pawtucket, Rhode Island, could set up a Christmas nativity scene on public property (*Lynch v. Donelly*), along with Santa's house and sleigh, Christmas trees, and other symbols of the Christmas season. Five years later, in *County of Allegheny v. American Civil Liberties Union* (1989), the Court extended the principle to a Hanukkah menorah, placed next to a Christmas tree. The Court concluded that these displays had a secular purpose and provided little or no benefit to religion. At the same time, the Court invalidated an *unadorned* display of the nativity scene in a courthouse because, in this context, the county gave the impression of endorsing the display's religious message.

In the Allegheny County case, the Court said the Constitution does not require complete separation of church and state; it mandates accommodation of all religions and forbids hostility toward any. At the same time, the Constitution forbids government endorsement of religious beliefs. Drawing the line between neutrality toward religion and promotion of it is not easy, and issues regarding the establishment of religion are likely to endure for some time.

The People Speak

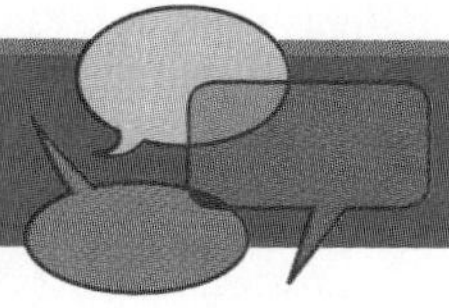

PRAYER IN THE PUBLIC SCHOOLS

Organized prayer in the public schools:

should be permitted:	64%
should not be permitted:	29%

Although the Supreme Court has prohibited organized prayers of any kind in the public schools, many Americans disagree. A majority of the public has never favored the Court's decisions on prayer in school, instead preferring to allow at least a period of voluntary silent prayer. These results demonstrate the Court's important role in protecting minority rights in the face of majority opinion.

SOURCE: *CBS News/New York Times* Poll, December 1994.

THE FREE EXERCISE CLAUSE

The First Amendment also guarantees the free exercise of religion. This guarantee seems simple enough. Whether people hold no religious beliefs, go to church, temple, or mosque, or practice voodoo, they should have the right to practice religion as they choose. The matter is, of course, more complicated. Religions sometimes forbid actions that society thinks are necessary; or, conversely, religions may require actions that society finds disruptive. For example, what if somebody's religion justifies multiple marriages or the use of illegal drugs? Muhammad Ali, the boxing champion, refused induction into the armed services during the Vietnam War because, he said, military service would violate his Muslim faith. Amish parents often refuse to send their children to public schools. Jehovah's Witnesses and Christian Scientists may refuse to accept certain kinds of medical treatment for themselves or their children.

Consistently maintaining that people have an inviolable right to *believe* what they want, the courts have been more cautious about the right to *practice* a belief. What if, the Supreme Court once asked, a person "believed that human sacrifices were a necessary part

The free exercise of religious beliefs sometimes clashes with society's other values or laws, as when the Amish—who prefer to lead simple, traditional lives—refused to send their children to public schools. The Supreme Court eventually held in favor of the Amish, arguing that Amish children, living in such a close-knit community, were unlikely to become dependent on the state.

of religious worship?" In *Employment Division v. Smith* (1990), the Court discarded its previous requirement for a "compelling interest" before a government could even indirectly limit or prohibit religious practices. In *Smith,* the Court decided that state laws interfering with religious practices but not specifically aimed at religion are constitutional. Aside from the specific area of denying people unemployment compensation, as long as a law does not single out and ban religious practices because they are engaged in for religious reasons, or only because of the religious belief they display, a general law may be applied to conduct even if it is religiously inspired. In *Smith,* the state of Oregon was allowed to prosecute persons who used the drug peyote as part of their religious rituals.

Even before this decision, the Supreme Court had never permitted religious freedom to be an excuse for any and all behaviors. The Court had upheld laws and regulations forbidding polygamy, outlawing business activities on Sunday as applied to Orthodox Jews, denying tax exemptions to religious schools that discriminate on the basis of race,[4] building a road through ground sacred to some Native Americans, and even prohibiting a Jewish air force captain from wearing his yarmulke (Congress later intervened to permit military personnel to wear yarmulkes).

The Court did, however, allow Amish parents to take their children out of school after the eighth grade. Reasoning that the Amish community was well established and that its children would not burden the state, *Wisconsin v. Yoder* (1972) held that religious freedom took precedence over compulsory education laws. More broadly, although a state can compel parents to send their children to an accredited school, parents have a right to choose religious schools rather than public schools for their children's education. And a state may not require Jehovah's Witnesses or members of other religions to participate in public school flag-saluting ceremonies. Congress has also ruled and the courts have upheld that people can become conscientious objectors to war on religious grounds. You can examine another free exercise case in "You Are the Judge: The Case of Animal Sacrifices."

In the Religious Freedom Restoration Act of 1993, Congress attempted to overturn the principle the Court articulated in *Smith.* It conferred on all persons the right to perform their religious rituals unless the government can show that the law or regulation in question is narrowly tailored and in pursuit of a "compelling interest." In 1997, however, the Supreme Court in *Boerne v. Flores* declared this act an unconstitutional intrusion by Congress into the states' prerogatives for regulating the health and welfare of citizens.

FREEDOM OF EXPRESSION

A democracy depends on the free expression of ideas. Thoughts that are muffled, speech that is forbidden, and meetings that cannot be held are the enemies of the democratic process. Totalitarian governments know this, which is why they go to enormous trouble to limit expression.

Americans pride themselves on their free and open society. Freedom of conscience is absolute; Americans can *believe* whatever they want to believe. The First Amendment plainly forbids the national government from limiting freedom of *expression*—that is, the right to say or publish what one believes. Is freedom of expression, then, like freedom of conscience, also *absolute*? Supreme Court Justice Hugo Black thought so; he was fond of pointing out that the First Amendment said Congress shall make *no* law. "I read no law abridging to mean no law abridging." In fact, in 1992, the Supreme Court ruled in *R.A.V. v. St. Paul* that legislatures and universities may not single out racial,

THE CASE OF ANIMAL SACRIFICES

You Are The Judge

The church of Lukumi Babalu Aye, in Hialeah, Florida, practiced Santeria, a Caribbean-based mix of African ritual, Voodoo, and Catholicism. Central to Santeria is the ritual sacrifice of animals—at birth, marriage, and death rites, as well as ceremonies to cure the sick and initiate new members.

Offended by these rituals, the city of Hialeah passed ordinances prohibiting animal sacrifices in religious ceremonies. The church challenged the constitutionality of these laws, claiming they violated the free exercise clause of the First Amendment, because the ordinances essentially barred the practice of Santeria. The city, the Santerians claimed, was discriminating against a religious minority. Besides, many other forms of killing animals were legal, including fishing, using animals in medical research, selling lobsters to be boiled alive, and feeding live rats to snakes.

You be the judge: Do the Santerians have a constitutional right to sacrifice animals in their religious rituals? Does the city's interest in protecting animals outweigh the Santerians' requirement for animal sacrifice? For the Court's response, see "The Court Decides" on p. 107.

religious, or sexual insults or threats for prosecution as "hate speech" or "bias crimes."[5]

Yet courts have often ruled that there are instances when speech needs to be controlled, especially when the First Amendment conflicts with other rights. A classic example of impermissible speech was offered in 1919 by Justice Oliver Wendell Holmes: "The most stringent protection of free speech would not protect a man in falsely shouting 'fire' in a theater and causing a panic." The courts have been called upon to decide where to draw the line separating permissible from impermissible speech. In doing so, judges have had to balance freedom of expression against competing values like public order, national security, and the right to a fair trial.

The courts have also had to decide what kinds of activities do and do not constitute *speech* (or press) within the meaning of the First Amendment. Holding a political rally to attack an opposing candidate's stand on important issues gets First Amendment protection. Obscenity and libel, which are also expressions, do not. To make things still more complicated, certain forms of nonverbal speech, such as picketing, are considered symbolic speech and receive First Amendment protection. Other forms of expression, such as fraud and incitement to violence, are considered action rather than speech. Government can limit action more easily than it can limit expression.

The one thing all freedom of expression cases have in common is the question of whether a certain expression receives the protection of the Constitution. The pages that follow examine some of the most important issues that arise in the courts as judges determine the meaning of freedom of speech.

PRIOR RESTRAINT

One principle stands out clearly in the complicated history of freedom of speech laws: Time and time again, the Supreme Court has struck down prior restraint on speech and the press. **Prior restraint** refers to a government's actions that prevent material from being published; in a word, prior restraint is censorship. In the United States, the First Amendment ensures that even if the government frowns on some material, a person's right to publish it is all but inviolable. A typical case involving prior restraint is ***Near v. Minnesota*** (1931). A blunt newspaper editor called local officials a string of names including "grafters" and "Jewish gangsters." The state closed down his business, but the Supreme Court ordered the paper reopened.[6] Of course, the newspaper editor—or anyone else—could later be punished for violating a law or someone's rights *after* publication.

The extent of an individual's or group's freedom from prior restraint does depend in part, however, on who that individual or group is. In 1988, the Supreme Court ruled in *Hazelwood School District v. Kuhlmeier* that a high-school newspaper was not a public forum and could be regulated in "any reasonable manner" by school officials.

Many people would agree that sometimes government should limit individual behavior on the grounds of national security. Few would find it odd or unconstitutional if a newspaper, for example, were hauled into court for publishing troop movement plans during a war. The national government demanded and secured the censorship of a book by former CIA agent Victor Marchetti. It also sued former CIA agent Frank Snepp

THE CASE OF THE PURLOINED PENTAGON PAPERS

You Are the Judge

During the Johnson administration, the Department of Defense had amassed an elaborate secret history of American involvement in the Vietnam War. Hundreds of documents, many of them secret cables, memos, and war plans, were included. Many documented American ineptitude and South Vietnamese duplicity. One former Pentagon official, Daniel Ellsberg, who had become disillusioned with the Vietnam War, managed to retain access to a copy of these Pentagon papers. Hoping that revelations of the Vietnam quagmire would help end American involvement, he decided to leak the Pentagon papers to the *New York Times.*

The Nixon administration pulled out all the stops in its effort to embarrass Ellsberg and prevent publication of the Pentagon papers. Nixon's chief domestic affairs advisor, John Ehrlichman, approved a burglary of Ellsberg's psychiatrist's office, hoping to find damaging information on Ellsberg. (The burglary was bungled, and it eventually led to Ehrlichman's conviction and imprisonment.) In the courts, Nixon administration lawyers sought an injunction against the *Times* that would have ordered it to cease publication of the secret documents. Government lawyers argued that national security was being breeched and that the documents had been stolen from the government by Ellsberg. The *Times* argued that its freedom to publish would be violated if an injunction were granted. In 1971 the case of *New York Times v. United States* was decided by the Supreme Court.

You be the judge: Did the *Times* have a right to publish secret, stolen Department of Defense documents? For the Supreme Court's answer, see "The Court Decides," on page 107.

for failing to have his book about Vietnam, *A Decent Interval,* submitted to the agency for censorship, even though the book revealed no classified information (in 1980, the Supreme Court upheld the government's suit in *U.S. v. Snepp*). Both men had signed agreements allowing the CIA to clear their future writings about the agency.

Nevertheless, the courts are reluctant to issue injunctions prohibiting the publication of material even in the area of national security. The most famous case involving prior restraint and national security involved the publication of stolen Pentagon papers. We examine this case in "You Are the Judge: The Case of the Purloined Pentagon Papers."

FREE SPEECH AND PUBLIC ORDER

Not surprisingly, government has sometimes been a zealous opponent of speech that opposes government policies. In wartime and peacetime, the biggest conflict between press and government has been about the connection between a free press and the need for public order. Wartime often brings censorship. Obviously, sometimes government can and should limit the press (to report troop movements, for example). Critics of the press during the Persian Gulf War complained that press reporting might have helped to pinpoint locations of SCUD missile attacks, knowledge of which could be used to aim future missiles more precisely. Defenders of the freedom of the press complained that never before had the press been as "managed" as in that conflict: Reporters could get to the field only in the company of official Pentagon press representatives—and some who tried other ways of getting there were captured by the Iraqis.

The conflict between free speech and public order is not new. During World War I, Charles T. Schenck, the secretary of the American Socialist Party, distributed thousands of leaflets urging young men to resist the draft. Schenck was charged with impeding the war effort. The Supreme Court upheld his conviction in 1919 (***Schenck v. United States***). Justice Holmes declared that government can limit speech if it provokes a clear and present danger of substantive evils. Only when such danger exists can government restrain speech. It is difficult to say, of course, when speech becomes dangerous rather than simply inconvenient for the government.

The courts confronted the issue of free speech and public order during the 1950s. American anticommunism was a powerful force, and the national government was determined to jail the leaders of the Communist Party. Senator Joseph McCarthy and others in Congress were persecuting people they thought

The prevailing political climate often determines what limits the government will place on free speech. During the early 1950s, Senator Joseph McCarthy's persuasive—if unproven—accusations that many public officials were Communists created an atmosphere in which the courts placed restrictions on freedom of expression—restrictions that would be unacceptable today.

subversive. The government vehicle for persecution was the Smith Act of 1940, which forbade advocating the violent overthrow of the American government. In *Dennis v. United States* (1951), the Supreme Court upheld prison sentences for several Communist party leaders for conspiring to advocate the violent overthrow of the government—even in the absence of evidence that they actually urged people to commit specific acts of violence. Although the activities of this tiny, unpopular group resembled yelling "Fire!" in an empty theater rather than a crowded one, the Court ruled that a Communist takeover was so grave a danger that government could squelch their threat. Free-speech advocates were unable to stem the relentless persecution of the 1950s; the Supreme Court, as in the *Dennis* case, was not willing to protect First Amendment rights at the time.

"The way I see it, the Constitution cuts both ways. The First Amendment gives you the right to say what you want, but the Second Amendment gives me the right to shoot you for it."

Soon the political climate changed, however, and the Court narrowed the interpretation of the Smith Act, making it more difficult to prosecute dissenters. (See "America in Perspective: Civil Liberties in Britain.") In later years, the Court has found that it is permissible to advocate the violent overthrow of the government in the abstract, but not actually to incite anyone to imminent lawless action (*Yates v. U.S.,* 1957; *Brandenburg v. Ohio,* 1969).

The 1960s brought waves of protest that strained and expanded the constitutional meaning of free speech. Among the unrest over political, economic, racial, and social issues, the Vietnam War was the source of the most bitter controversy. Many people saw military service as a duty and war as an issue that government should decide. Others felt that citizens should not be asked to die or pay for conflicts that they felt were unjust. Organized protests on college and university campuses became common. People burned draft cards, seized university buildings, marched, and demonstrated against the Southeast Asian conflict.

Americans today live in relatively less turbulent times, yet many people still engage in public demonstrations. Courts have been quite supportive of the right to protest, pass out leaflets, or gather signatures on petitions—as long as it is done in public places. Campaign literature may even be distributed anonymously (*McIntyre v. Ohio Elections Commission,* 1995).

Constitutional protections diminish once a person steps on private property, like, for example, most shopping centers. *Hudgens v. National Labor Relations Board* (1976) held that federal free-speech guarantees did not apply when a person was on private property. *Pruneyard Shopping Center v. Robins* (1980), however, upheld a state's power to include politicking in shopping centers within its own free-speech guarantee, and in 1994, the Supreme Court ruled that cities cannot bar residents from posting signs on their own property (*City of Ladue v. Gilleo*).

FREE PRESS AND FAIR TRIALS

The Bill of Rights is an inexhaustible source of potential conflicts among different types of freedoms. One is the conflict between a freedom of expression (the right of the press to print what it wants) and a free-

CIVIL LIBERTIES IN BRITAIN

America in Perspective

As discussed in Chapter 2, Great Britain has an unwritten constitution, a set of understood principles that limits governmental power—most of the time. For example, it would be "unconstitutional" to punish someone for an act that is not forbidden by law or for the prime minister to restrict the sovereign's access to government documents (this happened during the brief reign of Edward VIII in the 1930s, before he abdicated to marry the woman he loved). There is no equivalent, however, to the First Amendment to the U.S. Constitution that provides grounds for a lawsuit if someone disapproves of a restriction on freedom of expression. No court in Britain would overturn an act of Parliament for violating someone's freedom of speech.

Freedom of expression is generous in Great Britain, but there are some restrictions there that are unknown, or negligible, in the United States. British libel laws, for instance, are stricter than ours. In November 1988, the government of Prime Minister Margaret Thatcher imposed a restriction that was too much for many British subjects. It forbade the broadcasting of any radio or television interviews with members of the Irish Republican Army or its legal political organization in Northern Ireland. A group of 200 British journalists, judges, and academics issued a plea for an act of Parliament that would guarantee freedom of expression. No such guarantee has been enacted, however. Of course, the Parliament to which they appealed was led by the same government that had imposed the restrictions.

What would happen if the administration tried something similar in the United States? The Pentagon papers case in 1971 has some similarities to Prime Minister Thatcher's gag rule: the U.S. Supreme Court refused to stop the publication of these classified documents, even though the president stated it would harm national security.

The United States has not always been ahead of Britain in permitting free speech and press, however. Remember the imprisonment of American Communists such as Dennis and his associates in the 1950s. When they used the First Amendment to challenge the Smith Act, the Court ruled in favor of the government. Even where written constitutions exist, judges may rely on their own views of political necessity, which are often shared with the legislative and executive branches that developed the civil liberties policies in the first place, to determine the scope of individual rights.

dom at the bar of justice (the right to a fair trial). Journalists, of course, seek the right to cover every trial. The public, they argue, has a right to know. Defense counsels argue that pretrial publicity should not inflame the community—and potential jurors—against their clients. The quantity of press coverage given the trial (and pretrial hearings) of football star O. J. Simpson, accused of murdering his wife and her friend, rivaled that given the Super Bowl, and little of it was sympathetic to Simpson.

Journalists seek full freedom to cover all trials. The public, they argue, has a right to know—although some less credible journalists want to capitalize on the fact that lurid crime stories sell newspapers and attract advertising. When a Nebraska judge issued a gag order forbidding the press to report any details of a particularly gory murder (or even to report the gag order itself), the outraged Nebraska Press Association took the case to the Supreme Court. In *Nebraska Press Association v. Stuart* (1972), the Court sided with the editors and revoked the gag order. In 1978, the Court

Fundamental rights are sometimes in conflict. Press coverage of the murder trial of O. J. Simpson, pictured here with one of his lawyers, made it very difficult to impanel a jury whose members had not reached conclusions about his guilt before the trial began.

reversed a Virginia judge's order to close a murder trial to the public and the press. "The trial of a criminal case," said the Court in *Richmond Newspapers v. Virginia,* "must be open to the public." A pretrial hearing, though, is a different matter. A 1979 case permitted a closed hearing on the grounds that pretrial publicity might compromise the defendant's right to fairness.

Although reporters always want trials to be open to them, they do not always want to open their own files to the courts. Once in a while, a reporter withholds some critical evidence that either the prosecution or the defense wants in a criminal case. Reporters argue that "protecting their sources" should exempt them from revealing notes from confidential sources. More than one reporter has gone to jail for this principle, arguing that they had no obligation to produce evidence that might bear on the guilt or innocence of a defendant.

Some states have passed *shield laws* to protect reporters in these situations. In most states, though, reporters have no more rights than other citizens once a case has come to trial. The Supreme Court has ruled in *Branzburg v. Hayes* (1972) that in the absence of shield laws, the right of a fair trial preempts the reporter's right to protect sources. This issue came to a head in one celebrated case involving the student newspaper at Stanford University. After a violent confrontation with student protestors, the police got a search warrant and marched off to the *Stanford Daily*, which they believed to have pictures of the scene from which they could make arrests. The paper argued that its files were protected by the First Amendment, but the decision in ***Zurcher v.* Stanford Daily** (1976) sided with the police, not the paper.

"*Since you have already been convicted by the media, I imagine we can wrap this up pretty quickly.*"

Drawing by Richter; © 1991 The New Yorker Magazine Inc.

It is one thing to attempt to obtain the press's cooperation in trials and quite another to limit the press's coverage of judicial proceedings. The balance between a free press and a fair trial is not an even one. The Court has *never* upheld a restriction on the press in the interests of a fair trial.

OBSCENITY

In *The Brethren,* a gossipy portrayal of the Supreme Court, Bob Woodward and Scott Armstrong recount the tale of Justice Thurgood Marshall's lunch with some law clerks. Glancing at his watch at about 1:50 P.M., the story goes, Marshall exclaimed, "My God, I almost forgot. It's movie day, we've got to get back."[7] Movie day at the Court was an annual event when movies brought before the Court on obscenity charges were shown in a basement storeroom.

Several justices have boycotted these showings, arguing that obscenity should never be banned and thus that how "dirty" a movie is has no relevance. In 1957, however, the majority held that "obscenity is not within the area of constitutionally protected speech or press" (***Roth v. United States***). The doctrine set forth in this case still prevails. Deciding what is obscene, though, has never been an easy matter. In a line that would haunt him for the rest of his life, Justice Potter Stewart once remarked that although he could not define obscenity, "I know it when I see it." During the Supreme Court's movie day, law clerks echoed Stewart's line, punctuating particularly racy scenes with cries of "That's it! That's it! I know it when I see it." Marshall often led the banter at the screenings. "Well, Harry," he once remarked to Justice Blackmun after a film, "I didn't learn anything. How about you?"

Efforts to define obscenity have perplexed the courts for years. Obviously, public standards vary from time to time, place to place, and person to person. Much of today's MTV would have been banned a decade or two ago. What might be acceptable in Manhattan's Greenwich Village would shock residents of some other areas of the country. Works that some people call obscene might be good entertainment or even great art to others. At one time or another, the works of Aristophanes, those of Mark Twain, and even the "Tarzan" stories of Edgar Rice Burroughs were banned. The state of Georgia banned the acclaimed film *Carnal Knowledge*—a ban the Supreme Court struck down in *Jenkins v. Georgia* (1974).

In 1973, the Court tried to clarify its doctrine by spelling out what could be classified as obscene and thus outside First Amendment protection. The case was ***Miller v. California.*** Former Chief Justice Warren Burger wrote that materials were obscene if

1. The work, taken as a whole, appealed "to a prurient interest in sex."
2. The work showed "patently offensive" sexual conduct that was specifically defined by an obscenity law.
3. The work, taken as a whole, lacked "serious literary, artistic, political, or scientific value."

Decisions regarding whether material was obscene, said the Court, should be based on average people (in other words, juries) applying the contemporary standards of local—not national—communities.

The Court did provide "a few plain examples" of what sort of material might fall within this definition of obscenity. Among these examples were "patently offensive representations of ultimate sexual acts, . . . actual or simulated," "patently offensive representations of masturbation or excretory functions," or "lewd exhibition of the genitals." Cities throughout the country duplicated the language of *Miller* in their obscenity ordinances. The difficulty remains not with deciding what sexual acts or genitals are, but in determining what is *lewd* or *offensive.* Laws must satisfy these qualifying adjectives to prevent communities from banning anatomy texts, for example, as obscene.

Another reason why obscenity convictions can be difficult to obtain is that no nationwide consensus exists that offensive material should be banned—at least not when it is restricted to adults. In many communities the laws are lenient regarding pornography, and prosecutors know that they may not get a jury to convict, even when the disputed material is obscene as defined by *Miller.* Thus, obscene material is widely available in adult bookstores, video stores, and movie theaters.

Regulations aimed at keeping obscene material away from the young, who are considered more vulnerable to its harmful influences, are more popular, and courts have consistently ruled that states may protect children from obscenity. The rating scheme of the Motion Picture Association of America is one example. Equally popular are laws designed to protect the young against pornographic exploitation. It is a violation of federal law to receive sexually explicit photographs of children through the mail, and in 1991 the Supreme Court upheld Ohio's law forbidding the possession of child pornography (*Osborne v. Ohio*).

Despite the Court's best efforts to define obscenity and determine when it can be banned, debate continues. In one famous case, a small New Jersey town with a Biblical name tried to get rid of a nude dancing parlor by using its zoning power to ban all live entertainment. The Court held in *Schad v. Mount Ephraim* (1981) that the measure was too broad and thus unlawful. But the Court upheld an Indiana law banning nude dancing in *Barnes v. Glen Theater, Inc.* (1991). Jacksonville, Florida, tried to ban drive-in movies containing nudity. We will examine the Court's reaction in "You Are the Judge: When Can Obscenity Be Banned? The Case of the Drive-in Theater."

Although the Supreme Court has ruled, in *Roth v. United States,* that obscenity is not protected by the First Amendment, determining just what is obscene has proven difficult. Performances by the rap group 2 Live Crew were banned in Dade Country Florida because of some of their song lyrics.

A recent argument in the obscenity controversy involves the claim of some women's groups that pornography degrades and dehumanizes women, thereby consigning them to inferior status. Legal scholar Catherine MacKinnon claims that "pornography is an . . . industry of rape and battery and sexual harassment."[8] Some cities, at the urging of an unusual alliance of conservative Christians and feminists, have passed antipornography ordinances on the grounds that pornography harms women. So far, however, courts have struck these ordinances down on First Amendment grounds. No such case has reached the Supreme Court—yet.

LIBEL AND SLANDER

Another type of expression not protected by the First Amendment is **libel:** the publication of false statements that are malicious and damage a person's reputation. *Slander* refers to spoken defamation, whereas libel refers to written defamation. Of course, if politicians could collect damages for every untrue thing

You Are The Judge

WHEN CAN OBSCENITY BE BANNED? THE CASE OF THE DRIVE-IN THEATER

Almost everyone concedes that *sometimes* obscenity should be banned by public authorities. One instance might be when a person's right to show pornographic movies clashes with another's right to privacy. Presumably, no one wants hard-core pornography shown in public places where schoolchildren might be passersby. Showing dirty movies in an enclosed theater or in the privacy of your own living room is one thing. Showing them in public is something else. Or is it?

The city of Jacksonville, Florida, wanted to limit the showing of certain kinds of movies at drive-in theaters. Its city council reasoned that drive-ins were public places and that drivers passing by would be involuntarily exposed to movies they might prefer not to see. Some members of the council argued that drivers distracted by steamy scenes might even cause accidents. So the council passed a local ordinance forbidding movies showing nudity (defined in the ordinance as "bare buttocks . . . female bare breasts, or human bare pubic areas") at drive-in theaters. Arrested for violating the ordinance, a Mr. Erznoznik challenged the constitutionality of the ordinance. He claimed that the law was overly broad and banned nudity, not obscenity. The lawyers for the city insisted that the law could be squared with the First Amendment. The government, they claimed, had a responsibility to forbid a "public nuisance," especially one that might cause a traffic hazard.

You be the judge. The issue is whether Jacksonville's ban on nudity in movies at drive-ins went too far or whether it was a constitutional limit on free speech. For the Court's answer, see "The Court Decides" on page 107.

said about them, the right to criticize the government—which the Supreme Court termed "the central meaning of the First Amendment"—would be stifled. No one would dare be critical for fear of making a factual error.

To encourage public debate, the Supreme Court has held in cases such as ***New York Times v. Sullivan*** (1964) that statements about public figures are libelous only if made with malice and reckless disregard for the truth. Public figures have to prove to a jury, in effect, that whoever wrote or said untrue statements about them knew that the statements were untrue and intended to harm them. This standard makes libel cases difficult for public figures to win, because it is difficult to prove that a publication was intentionally malicious.[9]

Private individuals have a lower standard to meet for winning lawsuits for libel. They need show only that statements made about them were defamatory falsehoods and that the author was negligent. Nevertheless,

In the 21st Century

OBSCENITY ON THE WEB

Advances in technology have created a new wrinkle in the obscenity issue. The Internet and the World Wide Web make it easier to distribute obscene material rapidly, and a number of on-line information services have taken advantage of this opportunity. Congress, especially concerned with protecting minors from exposure to pornography, has recently decided that the Internet is not the electronic equivalent of the printing press and thus does not deserve the free-speech protection of the First Amendment. Instead, it regards the Internet as a broadcast medium, subject to government regulation (discussed later in this chapter).

In 1996, Congress passed the Communications Decency Act, banning obscene material and criminalizing the transmission of indecent speech or images to anyone under 18 years of age. The new law made no exception for material that has serious literary, artistic, political, or scientific merit as outlined in *Miller v. California*. In 1997, in *Reno v. ACLU*, the Supreme Court overturned this law as being overly broad and vague and a violation of free speech. Apparently the Supreme Court views the Internet similarly to print media, with similar protections against government regulation.

General William Westmoreland's aborted lawsuit against CBS demonstrates the difficulty public figures have winning libel convictions. Even though Westmoreland (shown here in Vietnam) could show that CBS had knowingly made factual errors, he realized that it would be impossible to prove that the networks had been intentionally malicious, so he dropped the suit in return for a statement from CBS calling him "patriotic."

it is unusual for someone to win a libel case; most people do not wish to publicize critical statements about themselves.

Libel is another freedom of expression issue that involves competing values. If public debate is not free, there can be no democracy. On the other hand, some reputations will be damaged, or at least bruised, in the process. In one widely publicized case, General William Westmoreland, once the commander of American troops in South Vietnam, sued CBS. On January 23, 1982, the network broadcast a documentary called "The Uncounted Enemy." It claimed that American military leaders in Vietnam, including Westmoreland, systematically lied to Washington about their success there to make it appear that the United States was winning the war. All the evidence, including CBS's own internal memoranda, showed that the documentary made errors of fact. Westmoreland sued CBS for libel. Ultimately, the power of the press—in this case, a sloppy, arrogant press—prevailed. Fearing defeat at the trial, Westmoreland settled for a mild apology.[10]

In 1988, the wacky case of *Hustler Magazine v. Falwell* joined the ranks of unusual libel and obscenity trials. *Hustler* editor Larry Flynt had printed a parody of a Campari Liquor ad about various celebrities called "First Time" (in which celebrities related the first time they drank Campari, but with an intentional *double entendre*). When *Hustler* depicted the Reverend Jerry Falwell having had his "first time" in an outhouse with his mother, Falwell sued. He alleged that the ad subjected him to great emotional distress and mental anguish. The case tested the limits to which a publication could go to parody or lampoon a public figure. The Supreme Court ruled that they can go pretty far—all nine justices ruled in favor of the magazine.

SYMBOLIC SPEECH

Freedom of speech, more broadly interpreted, is a guarantee of freedom of expression. In 1965, Mary Beth Tinker and her brother John were suspended from school in Des Moines, Iowa, when they wore black arm bands to protest the Vietnam War. The Supreme Court held in *Tinker v. Des Moines Independent School District* (1969) that the suspension violated the Tinkers' First Amendment rights. The right to freedom of speech, said the Court, went beyond the spoken word.

When Gregory Johnson set a flag on fire at the 1984 Republican National Convention in Dallas to protest nuclear arms buildup, the Supreme Court decided that the state law prohibiting flag desecration violated the First Amendment (***Texas v. Johnson,*** 1989). Burning the flag, the Court said, constituted speech and not just dramatic action.[11] When Massachusetts courts ordered the organizers of the annual St. Patrick's Day parade to include the Irish-American Gay, Lesbian, and Bisexual Group of Boston, the Supreme Court declared that the parade is a form of protected speech and thus that the organizers are free to include whomever they want.

Wearing an arm band and burning a flag are examples of **symbolic speech:** actions that do not consist of speaking or writing but that express an opinion. Court decisions have classified these activities somewhere between pure speech and pure action. The doctrine of symbolic speech is not precise; for example, although burning a flag is protected speech, burning a draft card is not (*U.S. v. O'Brien,* 1968). The relevant cases make it clear, however, that First Amendment rights are not limited by a rigid definition of what constitutes speech.

COMMERCIAL SPEECH

Not all forms of communication receive the full protection of the First Amendment. **Commercial speech,** such as advertising, is restricted far more extensively than expressions of opinion on religious, political, or other matters. The Federal Trade Commission (FTC) decides what kinds of goods may be advertised on radio and television and regulates the content of such advertising. These regulations have responded to changes in social mores and priorities. Thirty years ago, for example, tampons could not be advertised on TV, whereas cigarette commercials were everywhere. Today the situation is just the reverse. The FTC attempts to ensure that advertisers do not make false claims for their products, but "truth" in advertising does not prevent misleading promises. For example, when ads imply that the right mouthwash or deodorant will improve one's love life, that dubious message is perfectly legal.

Nevertheless, commercial speech on the airwaves is regulated in ways that would clearly be impossible in the political or religious realm—even to the point of forcing a manufacturer to say certain words. For example, the makers of Excedrin pain reliever were forced to add the words "on pain other than headache" in their commercials describing tests that supposedly supported the product's superior claims of effectiveness. (The test results were based on the pain experienced after giving birth.)

Although commercial speech is regulated more rigidly than other types of speech, the courts have been broadening its protection under the Constitution. For years, many states had laws that prohibited advertising for professional services—such as legal and engineering services—and for certain products ranging from eyeglasses and prescription drugs to condoms and abortions. Advocates of these laws claimed that they were designed to protect consumers against misleading claims, while critics charged that the laws prevented price competition. In recent years, the courts have struck down many such restrictions as violations of freedom of speech.

REGULATION OF THE PUBLIC AIRWAVES

The Federal Communications Commission (FCC) regulates the content, nature, and very existence of radio and television broadcasting. Although newspapers do not need licenses, radio and television stations do. A licensed station must comply with regulations, including the requirement that they devote a certain percentage of broadcast time to public service, news, children's programming, political candidates, or views other than those its owners support. The rules are more relaxed for cable channels, which can specialize in a particular type of broadcasting, because consumers pay for, and thus have more choice about, the service.

This sort of governmental interference would clearly violate the First Amendment if it were imposed on the print media. For example, the state of Florida passed a law requiring newspapers in the state to provide space for political candidates to reply to newspaper criticisms. The Supreme Court, without hesitation, voided this law (***Miami Herald Publishing Company v. Tornillo,*** 1974). Earlier, in ***Red Lion Broadcasting Company v. Federal Communications Commission*** (1969), the Court upheld similar restrictions on radio and television stations, reasoning that such laws were justified because only a limited number of broadcast frequencies were available.

One FCC rule regulating the content of programs restricts the use of obscene words. Comedian George Carlin has a famous routine called "Seven Words You Can Never Say on Television." A New York City radio station tested Carlin's assertion by airing his routine. The ensuing events proved Carlin right. In *FCC v. Pacifica Foundation* (1978), the Supreme Court upheld the Commission's policy of barring these words from radio or television when children might hear them.

Similarly, in 1992 the FCC fined New York disc jockey Howard Stern $600,000 for indecency. It is especially interesting that if Stern's commentaries had been carried by cable or satellite instead of the airwaves, he could have expressed himself with impunity. Technological change has blurred the line between broadcasting and private communications between individuals. With cable television now in about two-thirds of American homes, the Supreme Court will soon be faced with ruling on the application of free-speech guidelines to cable broadcasting.

FREEDOM OF ASSEMBLY

The last of the great rights guaranteed by the First Amendment is the freedom to "peaceably assemble." This freedom is often neglected alongside the more trumpeted freedoms of speech, press, and religion, yet it is the basis for forming interest groups, political parties, and professional associations, as well as for picketing and protesting.

Right to Assemble. There are two facets of the freedom of assembly. First is the literal right to assemble—that is, to gather together in order to make a statement. This freedom can conflict with other societal values when it disrupts public order, traffic flow, peace and quiet, or bystanders' freedom to go about their business without interference. Within reasonable limits, called *time, place, and manner restrictions,* freedom of assembly includes the rights to parade, picket, and protest. Whatever a group's cause, it has the right to demonstrate, but no group can simply hold a spontaneous demonstration anytime, anywhere, and anyway it chooses. Usually, a group must apply to the local city government for a permit and post a bond of a few hundred dollars—a little like making a security deposit on an apartment. The gov-

THE CASE OF THE NAZIS' MARCH IN SKOKIE

You Are the Judge

Hitler's Nazis slaughtered six million Jews in death camps like Bergen-Belsen, Auschwitz, and Dachau. Many of the survivors migrated to the United States, and many settled in Skokie, Illinois. Skokie, with 80,000 people, is a suburb just north of Chicago. In its heavily Jewish population are thousands of survivors of German concentration camps.

The American Nazi Party was a ragtag group of perhaps 25 to 30 members. Their headquarters was a storefront building on the West Side of Chicago, near an area of an expanding African-American population. Denied a permit to march in an African-American neighborhood of Chicago, the American Nazis announced their intention to march in Skokie in 1977. Skokie's city government required that they post a $300,000 bond to get a parade permit. The Nazis claimed that the high bond was set in order to prevent their march and that it infringed on their freedoms of speech and assembly. The American Civil Liberties Union (ACLU), despite its loathing of the Nazis, defended the Nazis' claim and their right to march. (The ACLU lost half its Illinois membership because it took this position.)

You be the judge: Do Nazis have the right to parade, preach anti-Jewish propaganda, and perhaps provoke violence in a community peopled with survivors of the Holocaust? What rights or obligations does a community have to maintain order? For the Court's response, see "The Court Decides" on page 107.

erning body must grant a permit as long as the group pledges to hold its demonstration at a time and place that allows the police to prevent major disruptions. There are virtually no limitations on the content of a group's message. In one important case, the American Nazi Party applied to the local government to march in the streets of Skokie, Illinois, a Chicago suburb with a sizable Jewish population, including many survivors of Hitler's death camps. You can examine the Court's response in "You Are the Judge: The Case of the Nazis' March in Skokie."

The balance between freedom and order is tested when protest verges on harassment. Protestors lined up outside abortion clinics are now a common sight. Members of groups such as "Operation Rescue" try to shame clients into staying away and may harass them if they do visit a clinic. Rights are in conflict in such cases: A woman seeking to terminate her pregnancy has the right to obtain an abortion; the demonstrators have the right to protest the very existence of the clinic. The courts have acted to restrain these protestors, setting limits on how close they may come to the clinics and upholding damage claims of clients against the protestors. In 1994, Congress passed a law enacting broad new penalties against abortion protestors. Pro-life demonstrators in a Milwaukee suburb paraded outside the home of a physician who was reported to perform abortions. The town board forbade future picketing in residential neighborhoods. In *Frisby v. Schultz* (1988), the Supreme Court agreed that the right of residential privacy was a legitimate local concern and upheld the ordinance.

Right to Associate. The second facet of freedom of assembly is the right to associate with people who share a common interest, including an interest in political change. In a famous case at the height of the civil rights movement, Alabama tried to harass the state chapter of the National Association for the Advancement of Colored People (NAACP) by requiring it to turn over its membership list. The Court found this demand an unconstitutional restriction on freedom of association (***NAACP v. Alabama,*** 1958).

The four freedoms guaranteed by the First Amendment—religion, speech, press, and assembly—are one key part of Americans' civil liberties. When people confront the American legal system as criminal suspects, they also have certain rights under the Constitution. Even convicted criminals are guaranteed some rights, as the following section will discuss.

DEFENDANTS' RIGHTS

The Bill of Rights contains only 44 words that guarantee the freedoms of religion, speech, press, and assembly. Most of the remaining words concern the rights of people accused of crimes. These rights were originally intended to protect the accused in *political*

Louis Farrakhan, the Nation of Islam leader, is a controversial speaker on college campuses because his speeches often contain anti-semitic remarks and have in a few cases led to violence. The Supreme Court has generally upheld the right of any group to assemble peaceably, as long as the group's demonstrations remain on public property.

arrests and trials; British abuse of colonial political leaders was still fresh in the memory of American citizens. Today the protections in the Fourth, Fifth, Sixth, Seventh, and Eighth Amendments are mostly applied in criminal justice cases.

It is useful to think of the stages of the criminal justice system as a series of funnels decreasing in size. Generally speaking, a *crime* is (sometimes) followed by an *arrest,* which is (sometimes) followed by a *prosecution,* which is (sometimes) followed by a *trial,* which (usually) results in a *verdict* of innocence or guilt. The funnels get smaller and smaller, each dripping into the next. Many more crimes occur than are reported; many more crimes are reported than arrests are made (the ratio is about five to one); many more arrests are made than prosecutors prosecute; and many more prosecutions occur than jury trials. In the next few pages, we will move through the criminal justice system, pausing at each stage to see how the Constitution protects the rights of the accused (see Table 4.3).

INTERPRETING DEFENDANTS' RIGHTS

The Bill of Rights sets out a number of civil liberties that American citizens have if they are arrested or brought to court. The Bill of Rights covers every stage of the criminal justice system; at every step, police, prosecutors, and judges must behave in accordance with the Bill of Rights. Any misstep may invalidate a conviction.

The language of the Bill of Rights comes, of course, from the late 1700s. It is often vague. For example, just how speedy is a "speedy trial"? How "cruel and unusual" does a punishment have to be in order to violate the Eighth Amendment? The courts continually must rule on the constitutionality of actions by police, prosecutors, judges, and legislatures—actions that a citizen or group could claim violate certain rights. Defendants' rights, just like those rights protected by the First Amendment, are not well defined in the Bill of Rights.

One thing is clear, however. The Supreme Court's decisions have extended specific provisions of the Bill of Rights—one by one—to the states as part of the general process of incorporation we discussed earlier. Virtually all of the rights discussed in the following sections affect the actions of both the national and state authorities. Just what rights do Americans enjoy in the criminal justice system?

SEARCHES AND SEIZURES

Police cannot arrest a citizen without reason. They need evidence to arrest, and courts need evidence to convict. Before making an arrest, police need what the courts call **probable cause** to believe that someone is guilty of a crime. Often police need to get physical evidence—a car thief's fingerprints, a snatched purse—to use in court. The Fourth Amendment is quite specific in forbidding **unreasonable searches and seizures.** To prevent abuse of police power, the Constitution requires that no court may issue a **search warrant** unless probable cause exists to believe that a crime has occurred or is about to occur. Warrants must specify the area to be searched and the material sought in the police search.

TABLE 4.3 THE BILL OF RIGHTS AND THE STAGES OF THE CRIMINAL JUSTICE SYSTEM

Although our criminal justice system is complex, it can be broken down into stages. The Bill of Rights protects the rights of the accused at every stage. Here are some key constitutional guarantees at various stages of the criminal justice system.

STAGE	PROTECTIONS
1. Evidence gathered	"Unreasonable search and seizure" forbidden (Fourth Amendment)
2. Suspicion cast	Guarantee that "writ of habeas corpus" will not be suspended, forbidding imprisonment without evidence (Article I, Section 9)
3. Arrest made	Self-incrimination forbidden (Fifth Amendment)
	Right to have the "assistance of counsel" (Sixth Amendment)
4. Interrogation held	"Excessive bail" forbidden (Eighth Amendment)
5. Trial held	"Speedy and public trial" by an impartial jury required (Sixth Amendment)
	"Double jeopardy" (being tried twice for the same crime) forbidden (Fifth Amendment)
	Trial by jury required (Article III, Section 2)
	Right to confront witnesses (Sixth Amendment)
6. Punishment imposed	"Cruel and unusual punishment" forbidden (Eighth Amendment)

A warrant is not a constitutional requirement for a reasonable police search, however. Most searches in this country take place without warrants. Such searches are valid if probable cause exists, if the search is necessary to protect an officer's safety, or if the search is limited to material relevant to the suspected crime or within the suspect's immediate control.

Normally, if police find anything in a search, they find what they have probable cause to believe is there. In two cases involving Fourth Amendment issues, authorities used aerial searches to secure the evidence they needed. The first case involved a marijuana grower named Ciraolo. When police, responding to a tip, went to look at his place, it was surrounded by 10-foot fences. The police then rented a private plane, took pictures of the crop, and secured a conviction. Environmental Protection Agency officials took a similar aerial photo of Dow Chemical's Midland, Michigan, plant and located environmental violations. Both Ciraolo and Dow sued, claiming they were the victims of unconstitutional search and seizure. Both lost, however, when their cases came before the Supreme Court. Since then, the Court has also upheld roadside checkpoints in which police randomly examine drivers for signs of intoxication (*Michigan v. Sitz,* 1990).

Ever since 1914, the Supreme Court has used an **exclusionary rule** to weigh evidence in criminal cases. This rule prevents illegally seized evidence from being introduced in court, but until 1961 the rule applied only to the federal government. The Supreme Court broadened the application in the case of a Cleveland woman named Dollree Mapp, who was under suspicion for illegal gambling activities. The police broke into her home looking for a fugitive, and while there, they searched the house and found a cache of obscene materials. Mapp was convicted of possessing them. She appealed her case to the federal courts, claiming that the exclusionary rule should be made a part of the Fourth Amendment. Since the local police had no probable cause to search for obscene materials—only for materials related to gambling—she argued, the evidence should not be used against her. In an important decision (***Mapp v. Ohio,*** 1961), the Supreme Court ruled that the evidence had been seized illegally and the Court reversed Mapp's conviction. Since then, the exclusionary rule has been part of the Fourth Amendment and has been incorporated within the rights that restrict the states, as well as the federal government.

Critics of the exclusionary rule, some of whom sit on the Supreme Court, argue that its strict application may permit guilty persons to go free because of police carelessness or innocent errors. The guilty, they say, should not go free because of a "technicality."

THE CASE OF MS. MONTOYA

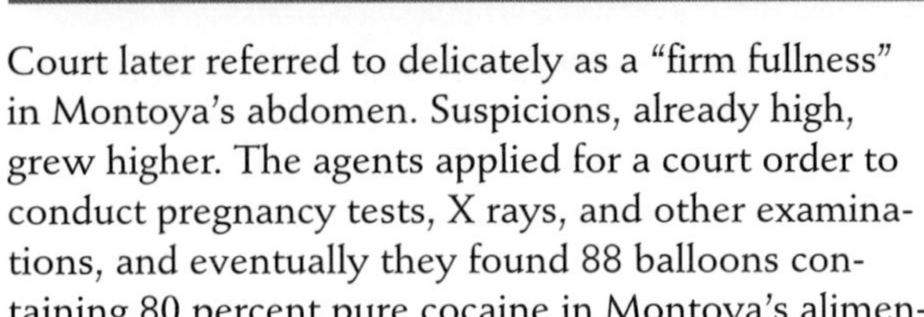

On March 5, 1983, Rose Elviro Montoya de Hernandez arrived at the Los Angeles International Airport on Avianca Flight 080 from Bogotá, Colombia. Her first official encounter was with U.S. Customs Inspector Talamantes, who noticed that she spoke no English. Interestingly, Montoya's passport indicated eight recent quick trips from Bogotá to Los Angeles. She had $5,000 in bills but no billfold or credit cards.

Talamantes and his fellow customs officers were suspicious. Stationed in Los angeles, they were hardly unaware of the fact that Colombia was a major drug supplier. They questioned Montoya, who explained that her husband had a store in Bogotá and that she planned to spend the $5,000 at Kmart and JC Penney, stocking up on items for the store.

The inspector, growing warier and warier, handed Montoya over to female customs inspectors for a search. These agents noticed what the Supreme Court later referred to delicately as a "firm fullness" in Montoya's abdomen. Suspicions, already high, grew higher. The agents applied for a court order to conduct pregnancy tests, X rays, and other examinations, and eventually they found 88 balloons containing 80 percent pure cocaine in Montoya's alimentary canal.

Montoya's lawyer argued that this constituted unreasonable search and seizure and that her arrest and conviction should be set aside. There was, he said, no direct evidence that would have led the officials to suspect cocaine smuggling. The government argued that the arrest had followed from a set of odd facts leading to reasonable suspicion that something was amiss.

You be the judge: Was Montoya's arrest based on a search-and-seizure incident that violated the Fourth Amendment? For the Supreme Court's answer, see "The Court Decides" on p. 107.

Defenders of the exclusionary rule respond that the Constitution is not a technicality. Defendants' rights protect the accused (everyone is supposed to be presumed innocent until proven guilty), not the guilty. You can examine one contemporary search-and-seizure case in "You Are the Judge: The Case of Ms. Montoya."

In the 1980s, the Court made some exceptions to the exclusionary rule. *Nix v. Williams* (1984) allowed the use of illegally obtained evidence when this evidence led police to a discovery that they eventually would have made without it. *United States v. Leon,* decided in the same year, established the good-faith exception to the rule; evidence could be used if the police who seized it mistakenly thought they were operating under a constitutionally valid warrant. In 1995, the Court held that the exclusionary rule does not bar evidence obtained illegally as the result of clerical errors (*Arizona v. Evans*). The Court even allowed evidence illegally obtained from a banker to be used to convict one of his customers (*United States v. Payner,* 1980). The current Supreme Court, with its conservative orientation, may make even more exceptions in the future.

SELF-INCRIMINATION

Suppose that evidence has been gathered and suspicion directed toward a particular person, and the police are ready to make an arrest. In the American system, the burden of proof rests on the police and the prosecutors. Suspects cannot be forced to help with their own conviction by, say, blurting out a confession in the stationhouse. The **Fifth Amendment** forbids forced **self-incrimination,** stating that no person "shall be compelled to be a witness against himself." Whether in a congressional hearing, a courtroom, or a police station, suspects need not provide evidence that can later be used against them. Under law, though, the government may guarantee suspects *immunity*—exemption from prosecution. In return, suspects must testify regarding their own and others' misdeeds.

You have probably seen television shows in which an arrest is made and the arresting officers recite, often from memory, a set of rights to the arrestee. These rights are authentic and originated from a famous court decision—perhaps the most important modern decision in criminal law—involving an Arizona man named Ernesto Miranda.[12]

Miranda was picked up as a prime suspect in the rape and kidnapping of an 18-year-old girl. Selected by the girl from a police lineup, Miranda was questioned for 2 hours. During this time, he was told of neither his constitutional right against self-incrimination nor his right to counsel. In fact, it is unlikely that Miranda had even heard of the Fifth Amendment. He said enough to lead eventually to a conviction. The Supreme Court

THE WIZARD OF ID

reversed his conviction on appeal, however (***Miranda v. Arizona,*** 1966) and also set the following guidelines for police questioning of suspects:

- Suspects must be told that they have a constitutional right to remain silent and may stop answering questions at any time.
- They must be warned that what they say can be used against them in a court of law.
- They must be told that they have a right to have a lawyer present during questioning and that the court will provide an attorney if they cannot afford their own lawyer.

Police departments throughout the country were originally disgruntled by *Miranda.* Officers felt that interrogation was crucial to any investigation. Warning suspects of their rights and letting them call a lawyer were almost certain to silence them. Most departments today, however, seem to take *Miranda* seriously. They usually read a *Miranda* card advising suspects of their rights. Ironically, when Ernesto Miranda himself was murdered, the suspect was read his rights from a *Miranda* card.

In the decades since the *Miranda* decision, the Supreme Court has made a number of exceptions to its requirements. In 1991 in *Arizona v. Fulminante,* for example, the Court held that a coerced confession introduced in a trial does not automatically taint a conviction. If other evidence is enough for a conviction, then the coerced confession is a "harmless error" that does not necessitate a new trial.

The Fifth Amendment prohibits not only coerced confessions but also coerced crimes. If law enforcement officials encourage persons to commit crimes (such as accepting bribes or purchasing illicit drugs) that they otherwise would not commit, convictions for these crimes will be overturned by the courts. For a recent case on this issue, see "You Are the Judge: The Case of the Dirty Old Man."

THE RIGHT TO COUNSEL

One of the most important of the *Miranda* rights is the right to secure counsel. Even lawyers who are taken to court hire another lawyer to represent them. (There is an old saying in the legal profession that a lawyer who defends himself has a fool for a client.) Although the **Sixth Amendment** has always ensured the right to counsel in federal courts, this right was not extended to people tried in state courts until recently. Winning this right for poor defendants was a long fight. Until the 1930s, individuals were tried and sometimes convicted for capital offenses (those in which the death penalty could be imposed) without a lawyer. In 1932, the Supreme Court ordered the states to provide an attorney for indigent (poor) defendants accused of a capital crime (*Powell v. Alabama*).

Ernesto Miranda's overturned conviction compelled law enforcement officials to inform suspects carefully of their constitutional rights.

THE CASE OF THE DIRTY OLD MAN

You Are the Judge

In 1984, Keith Jacobson, a 56-year-old farmer who supported his elderly father in Nebraska, ordered two magazines and a brochure from a California adult bookstore. He expected nude photographs of adult males, but instead found photographs of nude boys. He ordered no other magazines.

Within 3 months the federal law was changed to make the receipt of such materials illegal. Finding his name on the mailing list of the California bookstore, two government agencies repeatedly enticed Jacobson through five fictitious organizations and a bogus pen pal with solicitations for sexually explicit photographs of children. After 26 months of enticement, Jacobson finally ordered a magazine and was arrested for violating the Child Protection Act.

He was convicted of receiving child pornography through the mail, which he undoubtedly did. Jacobson claimed, however, that he had been entrapped into committing the crime.

You be the judge: Was he an innocent victim of police entrapment, or was he a dirty old man seeking child pornography? For the Court's response, see "The Court Decides" on page 107.

Not until 1963 did the Supreme Court extend that right to everyone accused of a felony. In the Florida state prison was a man named Clarence Earl Gideon, convicted of robbing a pool hall.[13] This nickel-and-dime burglary (mostly change from a vending machine) had netted Gideon a 5-year jail term. Because Gideon was too poor to hire a lawyer, he had never been represented by one. Using the prison's law books, he wrote a *pauper's petition* and sent it to the Supreme Court, which reviewed the petition, ordered a hearing, and ruled that defendants in all felony cases had a right to counsel (***Gideon v. Wainwright,*** 1963). Gideon was released, retried (this time with a public defender handling his case), and acquitted.

More than a thousand of Gideon's fellow Florida prisoners, plus thousands more who had been convicted in other states without benefit of counsel, were also released. Subsequently, the Court went a step further than *Gideon* and held that whenever imprisonment could be imposed, a lawyer must be provided for the accused (*Argersinger v. Hamlin,* 1972). Because of the efforts of Clarence Gideon and others, the Supreme Court has universalized this Sixth Amendment right so that today every court is required to appoint a lawyer to represent anyone who does not have the money to hire one.

Clarence Gideon (shown here reading law books in a Florida state prison) fought to obtain a lawyer for himself. His case helped ensure that the Sixth Amendment's guarantee of legal counsel would be incorporated into state law.

TRIAL BY JURY

Television's image of courts and trials is almost as dramatic as its image of detectives and police officers, but myth and reality do not blend well. Highly publicized trials are dramatic, but rare. The murder trial of

O. J. Simpson made headlines for months. Cable News Network even carried much of the pretrial and trial live. But in reality, most cases, even ones in which the evidence is solid, do not go to trial.

If you ever visit a typical American criminal courtroom, you will rarely see a trial complete with judge and jury. In American courts, 90 percent of all cases begin and end with a guilty plea. Most cases are settled through a process called **plea bargaining.** A plea bargain results from an actual bargain struck between a defendant's lawyer and a prosecutor to the effect that a defendant will plead guilty to a lesser crime (or fewer crimes) in exchange for a state's not prosecuting that defendant for a more serious (or additional) crime.

Critics of the plea-bargaining system believe that it permits many criminals to avoid "facing the music"—or as much music as they could face if tried for a more serious offense. The process, however, works to the advantage of both sides; it saves the state the time and money that would otherwise be spent on a trial, and it permits defendants who think they might be convicted of a serious charge to plead guilty to a lesser one.

Whether plea bargaining serves the ends of justice is much debated. To its critics, plea bargaining benefits defendants. David Brereton and Jonathan Casper, studying sentencing patterns in three California counties, discovered that a larger proportion of defendants who went to trial (rather than plea bargained) ended up going to prison, compared with those who pleaded guilty and had no trial. In answer to their question "Does it pay to plead guilty?" these authors give a qualified yes.[14] Good or bad, plea bargaining is here to stay. Only a vast increase in resources devoted to the court system could cope with a trial for every defendant.

For those 300,000 cases per year that actually go to trial, there are many rights available to defendants. The Sixth Amendment ensures the right to a speedy trial by an impartial jury. These days, defendants (those who can afford it, at least) do not leave jury selection to chance. A sophisticated technology of jury selection has developed. Jury consultants—often psychologists or other social scientists putting some of their statistical training to use—develop profiles of jurors likely to be sympathetic or hostile to a defendant. Lawyers for both sides spend hours questioning prospective jurors in a major case.

The Constitution does not specify the size of a jury; in principle, it could be anywhere from one or two people to hundreds or thousands. Tradition in England and America has set jury size at 12, although in petty cases six jurors are sometimes used. Whereas traditionally a jury had to be unanimous in order to convict, the Burger Court eroded those traditions, permitting states to use fewer than 12 jurors and to convict with a less than unanimous vote. Federal courts still employ juries of 12 persons and require unanimous votes for a criminal conviction.

CRUEL AND UNUSUAL PUNISHMENT

Citizens convicted of a crime can expect some punishment ranging from mild to severe, the mildest being some form of probation and the most severe, of course, being the death penalty. The **Eighth Amendment** forbids **cruel and unusual punishment,** although it does not define the phrase. Through the Fourteenth Amendment, this provision of the Bill of Rights applies to the states.

Almost all of the constitutional debate over cruel and unusual punishment has centered on the death penalty. (An exception can be found in "You Are the Judge: When Is Punishment Cruel and Unusual?")

WHEN IS PUNISHMENT CRUEL AND UNUSUAL?

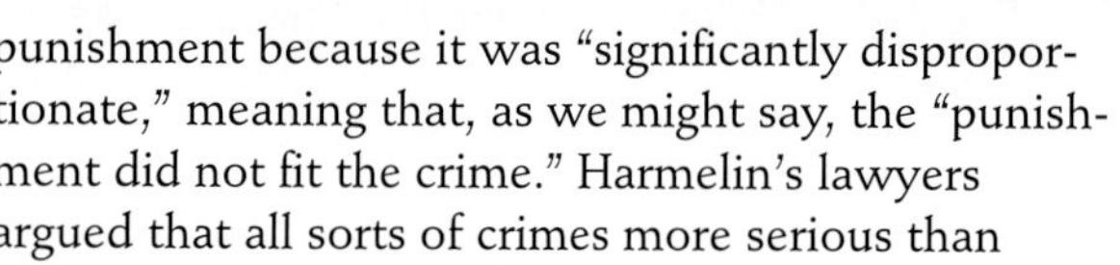

Ronald Harmelin of Detroit was convicted of possessing 672 grams of cocaine (a gram is about one-thirtieth of an ounce). Michigan's mandatory sentencing law required the trial judge to sentence Harmelin, a first-time offender, to life imprisonment without possibility of parole. Harmelin argued that this was cruel and unusual punishment because it was "significantly disproportionate," meaning that, as we might say, the "punishment did not fit the crime." Harmelin's lawyers argued that all sorts of crimes more serious than cocaine possession would net similar sentences.

You be the judge: Was Harmelin's sentence cruel and unusual punishment? For the Supreme Court's answer, see page 107.

Nearly 3,000 people are currently on death row, about a quarter of them in Florida and Texas. In 1968, the Court overturned a death sentence because opponents of the death penalty had been excluded from the jury at sentencing (*Witherspoon v. Illinois*), a factor that stacked the cards, said the Court, in favor of the extreme penalty.

In *Furman v. Georgia* (1972), the Court first confronted the question of whether the death penalty is inherently cruel and unusual punishment. Although *Furman* sent a message, it was a confusing one. Four justices said that the death penalty was not cruel and unusual punishment, yet the Court overturned Georgia's death penalty law because its imposition was "freakish" and "random." Warned by *Furman,* 35 states passed new laws permitting the death penalty. Some states, to prevent arbitrariness in punishment, went to the other extreme, mandating death penalties for some crimes. In *Woodson v. North Carolina* (1976), the Supreme Court ruled against mandatory death penalties.

Since then the Court has come down more clearly on the side of the death penalty. Troy Gregg had murdered two hitchhikers and was awaiting execution in Georgia's state prison. Gregg's attorney argued that the death penalty was cruel and unusual punishment. In ***Gregg v. Georgia*** (1976), the Court disagreed. "Capital punishment," it said, "is an expression of society's outrage at particularly offensive conduct. . . . It is an extreme sanction, suitable to the most extreme of crimes."

A divided Court rebuffed the last major challenge to the death penalty in ***McCleskey v. Kemp*** (1987) when it refused to rule that the penalty violated the equal protection of the law guaranteed by the Fourteenth Amendment. Although social scientists testified that minority defendants and murderers whose victims were white were disproportionately likely to receive death sentences, the Court insisted that this fact did not violate the Fourteenth Amendment, because there was no evidence that juries intended to discriminate on the basis of race. Not everyone is convinced, however. Shortly before retiring from the bench, Justice Harry Blackmun declared that the administration of the death penalty "fails to deliver the fair, consistent and reliable sentences of death required by the Constitution."[15]

Nevertheless, today the death penalty is a part of the American criminal justice system, and nearly 300 persons have been executed since the Court's decision in *Gregg v. Georgia.* In 1989, the Court held that it is constitutionally acceptable to execute even 16- or 17-year-olds and mentally retarded persons. More recently, the Court has made it more difficult for death row prisoners to file habeas corpus petitions that would force legal delays and appeals to stave off their appointed day. The Court has also allowed "victim impact" statements detailing the character of murder victims and their families' suffering to be used against a defendant.

THE RIGHT TO PRIVACY

The members of the First Congress who drafted the Bill of Rights and enshrined American civil liberties would never have imagined that Americans would go to court to argue about wiretapping, surrogate motherhood, abortion, or pornography. New technologies have raised ethical issues unimaginable in the eighteenth century. Today, one of the greatest debates concerning Americans' civil liberties lies in the emerging area of privacy rights.

IS THERE A RIGHT TO PRIVACY?

Nowhere does the Bill of Rights say that Americans have a **right to privacy.** Clearly, however, the First Congress had the concept of privacy in mind when it crafted the first ten amendments. Freedom of religion implies the right to exercise private beliefs; protections against "unreasonable searches and seizures" make persons secure in their homes; private property cannot be seized without "due process of law." In 1928, Justice Brandeis hailed privacy as "the right to be left alone—the most comprehensive of the rights and the most valued by civilized men."

The idea that the Constitution guarantees a right to privacy was first enunciated in a 1965 case involving a Connecticut law forbidding the use of contraceptives. It was a little-used law, but a doctor and family planning specialist were arrested for disseminating birth control devices. The state reluctantly brought them to court, and they were convicted. The Supreme Court, in the case of *Griswold v. Connecticut,* wrestled with the case. Seven justices finally decided that various portions of the Bill of Rights cast "penumbras" (or shadows)—unstated liberties implied by the explicitly stated rights—protecting a right to privacy, including a right to family planning between husband and wife. Supporters of privacy rights argued that this ruling was reasonable enough, for what could be the purpose of the Fourth Amendment, for example, if not to protect privacy? Critics of the ruling—and there were many of them—claimed that the Supreme Court was inventing protections not specified by the Constitution.

The most important application of privacy rights, however, came not in the area of birth control but in the area of abortion. The Supreme Court unleashed a constitutional firestorm in 1973 that has not yet abated.

FIRESTORMS OVER ABORTION

In the summer of 1972, Supreme Court Justice Harry Blackmun returned to Minnesota's famous Mayo Clinic, where he had once served as general counsel. The Clinic lent him a tiny desk in the corner of a librarian's office, where he worked quietly for 2 weeks. His research during this short summer vacation focused on the medical aspects of abortion. Blackmun had been assigned the task of writing the majority opinion in one of the most controversial cases ever to come before the Court. The judge was chronically tardy in his opinion writing; this decision was no exception. Later, back in Washington, Blackmun finished his draft opinion and sent it to his impatient colleagues.

The opinion, in ***Roe v. Wade*** (1973), has been called both radical and temperate. "Jane Roe" was the pseudonym of a Texas woman, Norma McCorvey, who had sought an abortion. She argued that the state law allowing the procedure only to save the life of a mother was unconstitutional. Texas argued that states had the power to regulate moral behavior, including abortions.

Blackmun's decision followed medical authorities in dividing pregnancy into three equal trimesters. *Roe* forbade any state control of abortions during the first trimester; it permitted states to allow regulated abortions, but only to protect the mother's health, in the second trimester; and it allowed the states to ban abortion during the third trimester, except when the mother's life or health was in danger. This decision unleashed a storm of protest. The Court's staff needed extra mailboxes to handle the correspondence, some of which contained death threats.[16] Eventually, states adjusted to the new decision, doctors and hospitals cooperated, and, however awkward the reasoning or controversial the result, the decision governed public policy. Since *Roe v. Wade,* more than 1.5 million legal abortions have been performed annually.

Yet the furor has never subsided. Congress has passed numerous legislative amendments forbidding the use of federal funds for abortions. Many states have passed similar restrictions. Missouri went as far as any other state, forbidding the use of state funds or state employees to perform abortions. A clinic in St. Louis challenged the law as unconstitutional, but in *Webster v. Reproductive Health Services* (1989), the Court upheld the law. It has also upheld laws requiring minors to notify one or both parents or a judge before obtaining an abortion.

In 1991, the conservative Court went even further in upholding restrictions on abortions. In *Rust v. Sullivan,* the Court found that a Department of Health and Human Services ruling—specifying that family planning services receiving federal funds could not provide women any counseling regarding abortion—was constitutional. This decision was greeted by a public outcry that the rule would deny many poor women abortion counseling and limit the First Amendment right of a medical practitioner to counsel a client. On his third day in office, President Clinton lifted the ban on abortion counseling.

In 1992, in ***Planned Parenthood v. Casey,*** the Court changed its standard for evaluating restrictions on abortion from one of "strict scrutiny" of any restraints on a "fundamental right" to one of "undue burden" that permits considerably more regulation. The Court upheld a 24-hour waiting period, a parental or judicial consent requirement for minors, and a requirement that doctors present women with information on the risks of the operation. The Court struck down a provision requiring a married woman to tell her husband of her intent to have an abortion. At the same time, the majority also affirmed their commitment to the basic right of a woman to obtain an abortion.

Americans are deeply divided on the issue of abortion (see "The People Speak: The Abortion Debate"). Polls can be found indicating strong support for a woman's right to choose, whereas other polls indicate strong majorities opposing unlimited abortion. Proponents of choice believe that access to abortion is essential if women are to be fully autonomous human beings. Opponents call themselves pro-life because they believe that the fetus is fully human; therefore, an abortion deprives a fetus of the right to life. These positions are irreconcilable, making abortion a politician's nightmare. Wherever a politician stands on this divisive issue, a large number of voters will be enraged.

Because passions run so strongly on the issue, advocates may take extreme action. Recently, for example, opponents of abortion murdered two physicians who performed abortions in Pensacola, Florida.

Individual rights may also be in conflict as a result of the abortion issue, as when the First Amendment right to protest abortion (which involves the rights to speech and assembly) conflicts with the right to obtain an abortion. In 1994, in *Madsen v. Women's Health Center,* the Supreme Court consolidated the right to abortion established in *Roe* with protection of a woman's right to enter an abortion clinic to exercise that right. Citing the government's interest in preserving order and maintaining women's access to

The People Speak

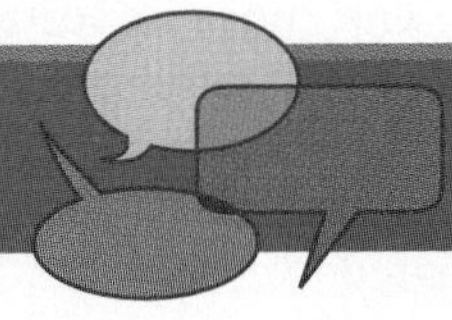

THE ABORTION DEBATE

Which of the following statements most closely describes your personal position on the issue of abortion?

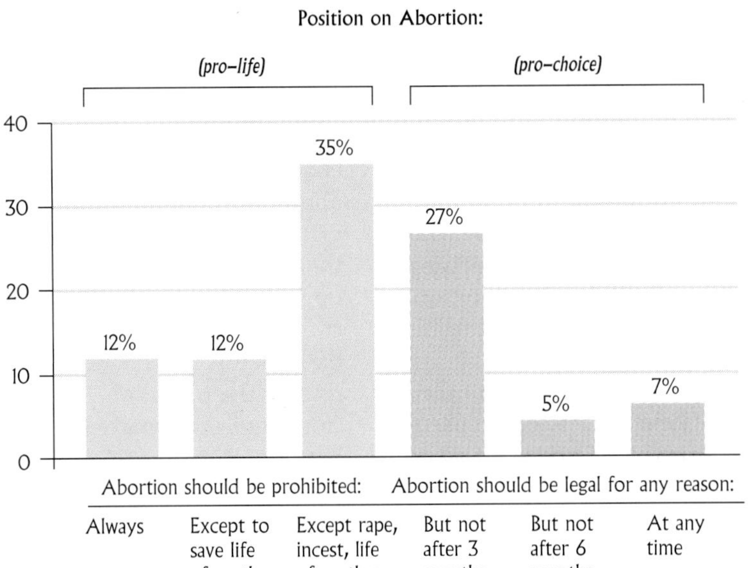

In a few areas of public opinion research do scholars find more divided opinion than on abortion. Some people feel very strongly about the matter, enough so that they are "single-issue voters" unwilling to support any candidate who disagrees with them on abortion. Most take a middle position, one that supports the principle of abortion but that also accepts restrictions on access to abortions.

SOURCE: *The Wirthlin Report,* January 1997, 3.

pregnancy services, the Court upheld a state court's order of a 36-foot buffer zone around a clinic in Melbourne, Florida. In 1997, the Court also upheld a 15-foot buffer zone. In another case, the Court decided that abortion clinics can invoke the federal racketeering law to sue violent anti-abortion protest groups for damages.[17] In 1994, Congress passed the Freedom of Access to Clinic Entrances Act, which makes it a federal crime to intimidate abortion providers or women seeking abortions.

A TIME TO LIVE AND A TIME TO DIE

The idea of rights to live, die, or have children were all but meaningless before the twentieth-century revolution in medicine and biotechnology. Today, medical science can continue certain life functions, especially respiration and blood circulation, in the absence of other vital signs, such as brain activity. State laws struggle to define death. At the same time, *in vitro* fertilization, frozen embryos, and artificial insemination complicate efforts to define birth by separating reproduction from sexual intercourse and the parent–child relationship. Do people have rights to use these new technologies—or refuse to use them? May people make these decisions for their parents or children?

Many of the issues surrounding birth and death were crystallized in two "Baby Doe" cases. Baby Doe was born in Indiana in 1982 with Down syndrome, a genetic defect causing mental retardation. Baby Jane Doe was born in New York in 1983 with spina bifida

Passions sometimes rule in the debate over abortion. Paul Hill went so far as to murder a physician who performed abortions, arguing that he had a right to do so to save the lives of the unborn. The jury did not agree, and Hill was sentenced to death.

(in which the spine fails to close properly), a condition that can cause serious mental and physical defects. Doctors for both babies told the parents that the children would die without surgery. The Indiana parents decided against surgery, at which point the hospital went to court to get permission for it. The hospital's efforts were unsuccessful, and the baby died.

In Baby Jane Doe's case, the parents and the doctors unanimously decided against surgery. However, Lawrence Washburn, an Albany attorney who frequently intervened in lawsuits to prevent abortions, sued the hospital and parents, claiming that their decision constituted discrimination against a disabled person and violated federal law. New York courts upheld the decision of the parents and the hospital. The Justice Department then filed suit, threatening to cut off the $20 to $25 million that the hospital received each year in federal funds if it refused to release its records regarding babies with serious physical disabilities. Eventually, the Supreme Court affirmed parents' rights to make medical decisions for their children.[18] Baby Jane Doe did survive.

Mary Sue Davis and Junior Davis had another kind of conflict over the beginnings of life. At their divorce hearing in Tennessee, they argued about seven fertilized embryos. The embryos had been produced through a new technique known as *in vitro* fertilization, in which sperm and ovum are joined outside a woman's body and frozen for later implantation in the uterus. Mary Sue argued that the embryos were alive and should be released to her. Junior's lawyer argued that life begins at birth; therefore, the embryos were not living things and should be destroyed. The judge gave Mary Sue custody of the embryos, but another judge prohibited her from ever using them.

Similar conflicts led to the famous "Baby M" case in New Jersey. When Elizabeth Stern, a physician, developed health problems that made pregnancy risky, she and her husband William sought help from an agency. Mary Beth Whitehead agreed to become what the press has labeled a "surrogate mother"; she was artificially inseminated with William's sperm in order to bear a child for the Sterns. In March of 1986, Whitehead gave birth to a girl, called Baby M in court records. Whitehead soon decided that she did not want to give up her baby. In 1988, the state Supreme Court gave parental rights to both natural parents: Mary Beth Whitehead and William Stern.

Experts estimate that one in every six American couples who want children will experience difficulty in having them. *In vitro* fertilization and surrogate motherhood are techniques that can compensate for several kinds of fertility problems. As a result, the Davis and Whitehead cases are a foretaste of more legal quandaries to come.

At the other end of the life spectrum is the issue of the right of adults to choose to die—and to receive help in doing so. Most states have legislated against suicide and those who would assist suicide. In *Cruzan v. Director, Missouri Department of Health* (1990) the

One of the most difficult issues facing our high-tech society is whether there is a right to choose to die. Here, Dr. Jack Kervorkian, popularly known as the "suicide doctor," poses with two terminally ill individuals shortly before assisting them in ending their lives. Because not everyone approves of assisted suicide, Dr. Kervorkian spends much of his time in court defending his actions.

Supreme Court recognized a limited constitutional right for patients to refuse unwanted medical treatment, a form of suicide.

What about those who would aid terminally ill patients in ending their lives? Dr. Jack Kervorkian has become a household name as the result of helping terminally ill patients commit suicide and the numerous trials in which he has faced charges for violating the law. So far, jurors have been unwilling to convict him, and two federal courts of appeals have struck down laws prohibiting physician-assisted suicide. In 1997, the Supreme Court ruled in *Vacco v. Quill* and *Washington v. Glucksberg* that there is no constitutional right to physician-assisted suicide and that states may prohibit it if they wish. They may also pass laws legalizing it, so the decision is back in the hands of the state legislatures.

UNDERSTANDING CIVIL LIBERTIES

American government is both democratic and constitutional. America is democratic because it is governed by officials who are elected by the people and who are accountable for their actions. The American government is constitutional because it has a fundamental organic law, the Constitution, that limits the things government may do. By restricting the government, the Constitution limits what the people can empower the government to do. The democratic and constitutional components of government can produce conflicts, but they also reinforce one another.

CIVIL LIBERTIES AND DEMOCRACY

The rights ensured by the First Amendment—the freedoms of speech, press, and assembly—are essential to a democracy. If people are to govern themselves, they need access to all available information and opinions in order to make intelligent, responsible, and accountable decisions. If the right to participate in public life is to be open to all, then Americans—in all their diversity—must have the right to express their opinions.

Individual participation and the expression of ideas are crucial components of democracy, but so is majority rule, which can conflict with individual rights. The majority does not have the freedom to decide that there are some ideas it would rather not hear, although at times, the majority tries to enforce its will upon the minority. The conflict is even sharper in relation to the rights guaranteed by the Fourth, Fifth, Sixth, Seventh, and Eighth Amendments. These rights protect all Americans, but they also make it more difficult to punish criminals. It is easy, though misleading, for the

The Court Decides

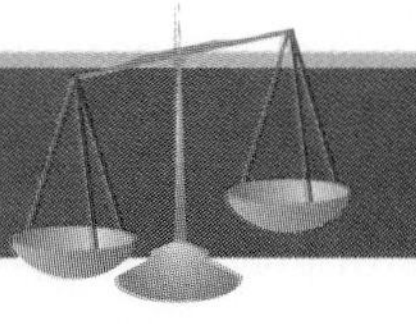

The animal sacrifices case. Answer: In 1993, the Court overturned the Hialeah ordinances that prohibited the use of animal sacrifice in religious ritual. In *Church of the Lukumi Babalu Aye, Inc.* v. *City of Hialeah,* the justices concluded that governments that permit other forms of killing of animals may not then ban sacrifices or ritual killings. In this instance, the Court found no compelling state interest that justified the abridgement of the freedom of religion.

The Pentagon papers case. Answer: In a six-to-three decision, a majority of the justices agreed that the "no prior restraint" rule prohibited prosecution before the papers were published. The justices also made it clear that if the government brought prosecution for theft, the Court might be sympathetic. No such charges were filed.

The drive-in theater case. Answer: In *Erznoznik v. Jacksonville* (1975) the Supreme Court held that Jacksonville's ordinance was unconstitutionally broad. The City Council had gone too far; it could end up banning movies that might not be obscene at all. The ordinance would, said the Court, ban a film "containing a picture of a baby's buttocks, the nude body of a war victim or scenes from a culture where nudity is indigenous." Said Justice Powell for the Court: "Clearly, all nudity cannot be deemed obscene."

The Nazis' march case. Answer: A federal district court ruled that Skokie's ordinance did restrict freedom of assembly and association. No community could use its power to grant parade permits to stifle free expression. In October 1978, in *Collins v. Smith* (Collins was the Nazi leader and Smith was the mayor of Skokie), the Supreme Court let this lower-court decision stand. In fact, the Nazis did not march in Skokie, settling instead for some poorly attended demonstrations in Chicago.

Ms. Montoya's case. Answer: Justice Rehnquist wrote the majority opinion, holding that U.S. Customs agents were well within their constitutional authority to search Montoya. Even though collection of evidence took the better part of 2 days, Justice Rehnquist remarked wryly that "the rudimentary knowledge of the human body which judges possess in common with the rest of mankind tells us that alimentary canal smuggling cannot be detected in the amount of time in which other illegal activities may be investigated through brief . . . stops."

The dirty old man case. Answer: The Court agreed with Jacobson. In *Jacobson v. United States* (1992), it ruled that the government had overstepped the line between setting a trap for the "unwary innocent" and the "unwary criminal" and failed to establish that Jacobson was independently predisposed to commit the crime for which he was arrested. Thus, Jacobson's conviction was overturned.

The cruel and unusual punishment case. Answer: The Court upheld Harmelin's conviction in *Harmelin v. Michigan* (1991), spending many pages to explain that severe punishments were quite commonplace, especially when the Bill of Rights was written. Severity alone does not qualify a punishment as "cruel and unusual." The severity of punishment was up to the legislature of Michigan, which, the justices dryly observed, knew better than they the conditions on the streets of Detroit.

majority to view these guarantees as benefits for criminals at the expense of society.

With some notable exceptions, the United States has done a good job in protecting the rights of diverse interests to express themselves. There is little danger that a political or economic elite will muffle dissent. Similarly, the history of the past four decades is one of increased protections for defendants' rights, and defendants are typically not among the elite. Ultimately, it has been the courts that have decided what constitutional guarantees mean in practice. Although federal judges, appointed for life, are not directly accountable to popular will,[19] it is "elitist" courts that have often protected civil liberties from the excesses of majority rule.

CIVIL LIBERTIES AND THE SCOPE OF GOVERNMENT

Civil liberties in America are both the foundation for and a reflection of our emphasis on individualism. When there is a conflict between an individual or a group attempting to express themselves or worship as they please and an effort by a government to constrain them in some fashion, the individual or group usually wins. If protecting the freedom of an individual or group to express themselves results in inconvenience or even injustice for the public officials they criticize or the populace they wish to reach, so be it. Every nation must choose where to draw the line between freedom and order. In the United States, we generally choose liberty.

When the Constitution was adopted in the 1780s, no government on earth was anywhere near as large or as efficient as the American government is today. European countries had known more than a few despotic monarchs, but no king or emperor had an army powerful enough to repress all free thought. England had persecuted Quakers, dissident Puritans, and Roman Catholics, but members of each of these groups had escaped to North America. A European in disfavor with a king could find protection from a powerful prince.

Today's government is huge and commands vast, powerful technologies. Americans' Social Security numbers, credit cards, drivers' licenses, and school records are all on giant computers to which the government has immediate access. It is virtually impossible to hide from the police, the FBI, the Internal Revenue Service, or any governmental agency. Because Americans can no longer avoid the attention of government, strict limitations on governmental power are essential. The Bill of Rights provides these vital limitations.

Thus, in general, civil liberties limit the scope of government. Yet substantial government efforts are often required to protect the expansion of rights that we have witnessed in this century. Those seeking abortions may need help reaching a clinic; indigent defendants may demand that lawyers be provided them at public expense; advocates of unpopular causes may require police protection; litigants in complex lawsuits over matters of birth or death may rely on judges to resolve their conflicts. It is ironic, but true, that an expansion of freedom may require a simultaneous expansion of government.

SUMMARY

Civil liberties are an individual's protection against the government. The Bill of Rights makes it clear that American government is a constitutional democracy in which individual rights limit government, which is why the Bill of Rights is fundamental to Americans' freedom. Disputes about civil liberties are frequent because the issues involved are complex and divisive. Legislatures and courts are constantly defining in practice what the Bill of Rights guarantees in theory.

In a way, the notion that government can protect people from government is contradictory. Thomas Jefferson wrote in the Declaration of Independence that all men "are endowed by their creator with certain unalienable rights." Jefferson's next "self-evident truth" was that "to secure these rights, governments are instituted among men." People, says Jefferson, do not get their rights from government. Instead, rights precede government, which then gets its power to rule from the people. The Bill of Rights does not give Americans freedom of religion or the right to a fair trial; these amendments merely recognize that these rights exist. People often speak, however, as though rights are things that government gives them.

The First Amendment guarantees freedoms of religion, expression, and assembly. The Bill of Rights also contains protections that are especially important to those accused or convicted of crimes. Together, these rights provide Americans with more liberty than that enjoyed by most other people on earth.

One task that government must perform is to resolve conflicts between rights. Often, First Amendment rights and rights at the bar of justice exist in uneasy tension; a newspaper's right to inform its readers may conflict with a person's right to a fair trial. Today, most of the rights enjoyed under the U.S. Constitution have been extended to the states.

Today's technologies raise key questions about ethics and the Constitution. Although the Constitution does not specifically mention a right to privacy, the Supreme Court found this right implied by several guarantees in the Bill of Rights. The most controversial application of privacy rights has been in abortion cases. And if the right to life is a political and legal issue, so, equally, is the right to die.

KEY TERMS

civil liberties
Bill of Rights
First Amendment
Fourteenth Amendment
incorporation doctrine
establishment clause
free exercise clause
prior restraint
libel
symbolic speech
commercial speech
probable cause
unreasonable searches and seizures
search warrant
exclusionary rule
Fifth Amendment
self-incrimination
Sixth Amendment
plea bargaining
Eighth Amendment
cruel and unusual punishment
right to privacy

KEY CASES

***Barron v. Baltimore* (1833)**
***Gitlow v. New York* (1925)**
***Lemon v. Kurtzman* (1971)**
***Engel v. Vitale* (1962)**
***School District of Abington Township, Pennsylvania v. Schempp* (1963)**
***Near v. Minnesota* (1931)**
***Roth v. United States* (1957)**
***Miller v. California* (1973)**
***New York Times v. Sullivan* (1964)**
***Texas v. Johnson* (1989)**
***Miami Herald Publishing Co. v. Tornillo* (1974)**
***Red Lion Broadcasting Co. v. Federal Communications Commission* (1969)**
***Schenck v. United States* (1919)**
***Zurcher v. Stanford Daily* (1976)**
***NAACP v. Alabama* (1958)**
***Mapp v. Ohio* (1961)**
***Miranda v. Arizona* (1966)**
***Gideon v. Wainwright* (1963)**
***Gregg v. Georgia* (1976)**
***McCleskey v. Kemp* (1987)**
***Roe v. Wade* (1973)**
***Planned Parenthood v. Casey* (1992)**

FOR FURTHER READING

Adler, Renata. *Reckless Disregard.* New York: Knopf, 1986. The story of two monumental conflicts between free press and individual reputations.

Baker, Liva. *Miranda: The Crime, the Law, the Politics.* New York: Atheneum, 1983. An excellent book-length treatment of one of the major criminal cases of our time.

Craig, Barbara Hickson, and David M. O'Brien. *Abortion and American Politics.* Chatham, NJ: Chatham House, 1993. Provides a history of the abortion issue since 1973.

Garrow, David J. *Liberty and Sexuality.* New York: Macmillan, 1994. The most thorough treatment of the development of the law on the right to privacy and abortion.

Levy, Leonard W. *The Emergence of a Free Press.* New York: Oxford University Press, 1985. A major work on the framers' intentions regarding freedom of expression.

Levy, Leonard W. *The Establishment Clause: Religion and the First Amendment.* New York: Macmillan, 1986. The author argues that it is unconstitutional for government to provide aid to any religion.

Lewis, Anthony. *Make No Law: The Sullivan Case and the First Amendment.* New York: Random House, 1991. Very well-written story of the key case regarding American libel law and an excellent case study of a Supreme Court case.

Rosenblatt, Roger. *Life Itself: Abortion in the American Mind.* New York: Random House, 1992. The author seeks to reconcile the clash of absolutes in the abortion controversy with scholarly analysis and interview data.

INTERNET RESOURCES

http://www.fac.org/
Background information and recent news on First Amendment issues.

http://www.eff.org/
Concerned with protecting on-line civil liberties.

http://www.aclu.org/
About the American Civil Liberties Union and connections to many other sites concerned with civil liberties.

http://w3.trib.com/FACT/1st.religion.html
Overview of freedom of religion in the U.S.

http://www.law.cornell.edu/topics/topic2.html#criminal justice
The text of the landmark cases on criminal justice and background material.

http://www.law.cornell.edu/topics/topic2.html#first-amendment
The test of the landmark cases on freedom of religion, speech, press, and assembly and background material.

http://cc.org/
Christian Coalition home page containing background information and discussion of current events.

NOTES

1. James W. Prothro and Charles M. Grigg, "Fundamental Principles of Democracy: Bases of Agreement and Disagreement," *Journal of Politics* 22 (1960): 276–294; John L. Sullivan *et al.,* "The Sources of Political Tolerance: A Multivariate Analysis," *American Political Science Review* 75 (1981): 100–115.

2. Samuel Krislov, *The Supreme Court and Political Freedom* (New York: Free Press, 1968), 81.

3. Kenneth D. Wald, *Religion and Politics in the United States,* 3rd ed. (Chatham, NJ: Chatham House, 1997).

4. *Bob Jones University v. United States,* 1983.
5. However, states may impose longer prison terms on people convicted of "hate crimes" (crimes motivated by racial, religious, or other prejudice) without violating their rights to free speech.
6. See Fred W. Friendly, *Minnesota Rag* (New York: Random House, 1981).
7. Bob Woodward and Scott Armstrong, *The Brethren* (New York: Avon, 1979), 233.
8. Catherine MacKinnon, *Feminism Unmodified* (Cambridge, MA: Harvard University Press, 1987), 198.
9. The story of this case is told in Anthony Lewis, *Make No Law: The Sullivan Case and the First Amendment* (New York: Random House, 1991).
10. Renata Adler, *Reckless Disregard* (New York: Knopf, 1986).
11. After Congress passed the Flag Protection Act of 1989 outlawing desecration of the American flag, the Supreme Court also found the Act an impermissible infringement on free speech in *United States v. Eichman* (1990).
12. On the Miranda case, see Liva Baker, *Miranda: The Crime, the Law, the Politics* (New York: Atheneum, 1983).
13. The story of Gideon is eloquently told by Anthony Lewis, *Gideon's Trumpet* (New York: Random House, 1964).
14. David Brereton and Jonathan D. Casper, "Does It Pay to Plead Guilty? Differential Sentencing and the Function of the Criminal Courts," *Law and Society Review* 16 (1981–1982): 45–70.
15. *Callins v. Callins* (1994).
16. Woodward and Armstrong, *The Brethren,* 271–284.
17. *National Organization for Women v. Scheidler* (1994).
18. *Bowen v. American Hospital Association,* 476 U.S. 610 (1985).
19. Though, as Chapter 16 on the judiciary will show, there is indirect accountability.

Civil Rights and Public Policy

5

On December 1, 1955, a soft-spoken, 42-year-old seamstress named Rosa Parks was riding in the "colored" section of a Montgomery, Alabama, city bus. A white man got on the bus and found that all the seats in the front, which were reserved for whites, were taken. He moved on to the equally crowded colored section. J. F. Blake, the bus driver, then ordered all four passengers in the first row of the colored section to surrender their seats because the law prohibited whites and African Americans from sitting next to or even across from one another.

Three of the African Americans hesitated and then complied with the driver's order. But Rosa Parks said no. The driver threatened to have her arrested, but still she refused to move. He then called the police, and a few minutes later two officers boarded the bus and arrested her.

At this moment the civil rights movement was born. There had been substantial efforts, and some important successes, to use the courts to end racial segregation, but Rosa Parks' refusal to give up her seat sparked opposition to racial discrimination that led to extensive mobilization of African Americans. These individuals employed a wide range of methods to end segregation. A new preacher in town, Martin Luther King, Jr., of Atlanta, organized a boycott of the city buses. He was jailed, his house was bombed, and his wife and infant daughter were almost killed, but neither he nor the African-American community wavered. Finally, the city relented. On December 21, 1956, Rosa Parks boarded a Montgomery city bus for the first time in over a year. She sat near the front.

Americans have never fully come to terms with equality. Most Americans favor equality in the abstract—a politician who advocated inequality would not attract many votes—yet the concrete struggle for equal rights under the Constitution has been our nation's most bitter battle. It pits person against person, as in the case of Rosa Parks and the nameless white rider, and group against group. Those people who enjoy privileged positions in American society have been reluctant to give them up.

Individual liberty is central to democracy. So is a broad notion of equality, such as that implied by the concept of "one person, one vote." Sometimes these values conflict, as when individuals or a majority of the people want to act in a discriminatory fashion. How should we resolve such conflicts between liberty and equality? Can we have a democracy if some citizens do not enjoy basic rights to political participation or employment? On the other hand, how do we remedy past discrimination against minorities and women without violating the principle of rewarding individual merit for white males?

In addition, many people have called on government to act to protect the rights of minorities and women, increasing the scope and power of government in the process. Ironically, this increase in government power is often used to *check* government, as when the federal courts restrict the actions of state legislatures. It is equally ironic that society's collective efforts to use government to protect civil rights are designed not to limit individualism but to enhance it, freeing people from suffering from prejudice. But how far should government go in these efforts? Is an increase in the scope of government to protect some people's rights an unacceptable threat to the rights of yet other citizens?

The struggle for equality revolves around matters of high principle. The phrase "all men are created equal" is at the heart of the American political culture. The rallying call for groups demanding more equality has been **civil rights**, which are policies that extend basic rights to groups historically subject to discrimination. The civil rights umbrella has helped protect many groups from discrimination. Throughout our history, African Americans, women, and other minorities have raised constitutional questions about slavery, segregation, equal pay, and a host of other issues.

The resulting controversies have been fought out in the courts, Congress, and the bureaucracy, but the meaning of *equality* remains as elusive as it is divisive. Today's equality debates center on these key types of inequality in America:

- *Racial discrimination.* Two centuries of discrimination against racial minorities have produced historic Supreme Court and congressional policies that eliminate racial discrimination from the constitutional fabric. Issues such as the appropriate role of affirmative action programs have yet to be resolved, however.
- *Gender discrimination.* The role of women in American society has changed substantially since the 1700s. However, equal rights for women have yet to be constitutionally guaranteed. The Equal Rights Amendment was not ratified, and women continue to press for equality while seeking protection from sexual harassment.
- *Discrimination based on age, disability, sexual preference, and other factors.* As America is "graying," older Americans, too, are demanding a place under the civil rights umbrella. People with disabilities are among the newest claimants for civil rights. Also seeking constitutional protections against discrimination are groups such as gays and lesbians, people with AIDS, and the homeless.

TWO CENTURIES OF STRUGGLE

The struggle for equality in America is older than the government itself and continues today. Slaves sought freedom; free African Americans sought the right to vote; women sought full participation in society; and poor people use "equality" as a rallying cry in their efforts to get better treatment. The fight for equality in America affects everyone. Philosophically, the struggle involves defining the term *equality*. Constitutionally, it involves interpreting laws. Politically, it often involves power.

CONCEPTIONS OF EQUALITY

What does *equality* mean? Jefferson's statement in the Declaration of Independence that "all men are created equal" did not mean that he believed that everybody was exactly alike or that there were no differences among human beings. Jefferson insisted throughout his long life that African Americans were genetically inferior to whites. The Declaration went on to speak, however, of "inalienable rights" to which all were equally entitled. A belief in *equal rights* has often led to a belief in *equality of opportunity;* in other words, everyone should have the same chance. What individuals make of that equal chance depends on their abilities and efforts.

American society does not emphasize *equal results* or *equal rewards;* few Americans argue that everyone should earn the same salary or have the same amount of property. In some other countries, such as the Scandinavian nations, for example, the government uses its taxing power to distribute resources much more nearly equally than in the United States. These countries thus have much less poverty. On the other hand, critics of these more egalitarian countries often complain that emphasis on the equal distribution of resources stifles initiative and limits opportunity.

EARLY AMERICAN VIEWS OF EQUALITY

More than 200 years ago, Virginia lawyer Richard Bland proclaimed, "I am speaking of the rights of a people, rights imply equality." Bland's interpretation of the meaning of the American Revolution was not widely shared. Few colonists were eager to defend slavery, and the delegates to the Constitutional Convention did their best to avoid facing the tension between slavery and the principles of the Declaration of Independence. Women's rights got even less attention than slavery at the Convention. John Adams, for instance, was uncharacteristically hostile to his wife Abigail's feminist opinions. Abigail's claim that "if particular care and attention is not paid to the ladies, we are determined to foment a rebellion" prompted her husband to reply, "I cannot but laugh."[1]

Statements like Bland's were ahead of their times in America but were not unheard of elsewhere. The aspirations of people on this side of the Atlantic were similar to those of people on the other side, such as the French, who were soon to start their own revolution with cries of "liberty, equality, fraternity." Whereas in the French Revolution the king lost his head in the name of equality, in the American Revolution the king lost his colonies in the name of independence.

THE CONSTITUTION AND INEQUALITY

Perhaps the presence of conflicting views of equality in eighteenth-century America explains why the word *equality* does not appear in the original Constitution. In addition, America in 1787 was a place far different from contemporary America, with far different values. The privileged delegates to the Constitutional Convention would have been baffled,

"Well, it all depends. Where are these huddled masses coming from?"

if not appalled, at discussions of equal rights for 12-year-old children, deaf students, gay soldiers, or female road dispatchers. The delegates created a plan for government, not guarantees of individual rights.

Not even the Bill of Rights mentions equality. It does, however, have implications for equality in that it does not limit the scope of its guarantees to specified groups within the society. It does not say, for example, that only whites have freedom from compulsory self-incrimination or that only men are entitled to freedom of speech. The First Amendment guarantees of freedom of expression, in particular, are important because they allow those who are discriminated against to work toward achieving equality. This kind of political activism, for instance, led to the constitutional amendment that enacted a guarantee of equality, the Fourteenth Amendment.

The first and only place in which the idea of equality appears in the Constitution is in the **Fourteenth Amendment,** one of the three amendments passed after the Civil War. (The Thirteenth abolishes slavery, and the Fifteenth extends the right to vote to African Americans.) The Fourteenth Amendment forbids the states from denying to anyone "equal protection of the laws." Those five words represent the only reference to the idea of equality in the entire Constitution, yet within them was enough force to begin ensuring equal rights for all Americans. The full force of the amendment was not felt for nearly 100 years, for it was not until the mid-twentieth century that the Fourteenth Amendment was used as an instrument for unshackling disadvantaged groups. Once dismissed as "the traditional last resort of constitutional arguments," the equal protection clause now has few rivals in generating legal business for the Supreme Court.

But what does **equal protection of the laws** mean? The Fourteenth Amendment does not say that "the states must treat everybody exactly alike" or that "every state must promote equality among all its people." Presumably, it means, as one member of Congress said during the debate on the amendment, "equal protection of life, liberty and property" for all. Thus, a state cannot confiscate an African American's property under the law while letting whites keep theirs, or otherwise give whites privileges denied to African Americans. Some members of Congress interpreted the clause to be a much more lavish protection of rights than this interpretation. But shortly after the amendment was ratified in 1868, the narrow interpretation won out in the courts. In *Strauder v. West Virginia* (1880), the Supreme Court invalidated a law barring African Americans from jury service, but the court refused to extend the amendment to remedy more subtle kinds of discrimination.

Over the last 100 years, however, the equal protection clause has become the vehicle for more expansive constitutional interpretations. The Court has ruled that most classifications that are *reasonable*—that bear a rational relationship to some legitimate governmental purpose—are constitutional. The person who challenges these classifications has the burden of proving that they are arbitrary. Thus, for example, the states can restrict the right to vote to people over the age of 18; age is a reasonable classification and hence a permissible basis for determining who may vote. A classification that is arbitrary—a law singling out, say, people with red hair or blue eyes for inferior treatment—is invalid.

The Court has also ruled that racial and ethnic classifications are *inherently suspect.* These classifications are presumed to be invalid and are upheld only if they serve a "compelling public interest" and there is no other way to accomplish the purpose of the law. In this case, the burden of proof is on the state. Classifications by race and ethnicity may be acceptable if they are made in laws seeking to remedy previous discrimination. However, as we will see in our discussion of affirmative action, the future of such laws is in doubt.

Classifications based on gender fit *somewhere between* these two extremes; they are presumed neither to be constitutional nor to be unconstitutional. A law that discriminates on the basis of gender must bear a substantial relationship to an important legislative purpose. If these three levels of judicial scrutiny (reasonable, inherently suspect, and somewhere in between) appear confusing, indeed they are. Table 5.1 is designed to help you understand the Supreme Court's standards for evaluating the acceptability of classifications.

The African-American struggle for equality paved the way for civil rights movements by women and other minorities. Here, civil rights leaders Ralph Abernathy and Martin Luther King, Jr., join President Lyndon B. Johnson, who signs the landmark Civil Rights Act of 1964 that outlawed many historic forms of discrimination.

TABLE 5.1 SUPREME COURT'S STANDARDS FOR CLASSIFICATIONS UNDER THE EQUAL PROTECTION CLAUSE OF THE FOURTEENTH AMENDMENT

BASIS OF CLASSIFICATION	STANDARD OF REVIEW	APPLYING THE TEST
Race	Inherently suspect (difficult to meet)	Is the classification necessary to accomplish a compelling governmental purpose and the least restrictive way to reach the goal?
Gender	Intermediate standard (moderately difficult to meet)	Does the classification bear a substantial relationship to an important governmental goal?
Others (age, wealth, etc.)	Reasonableness (easy to meet)	Does the classification have a rational relationship to a legitimate governmental goal?

Today the equal protection clause is interpreted expansively enough to forbid racial segregation in the public schools, prohibit job discrimination, reapportion state legislatures, and permit court-ordered busing and affirmative action. Conditions for women and minorities would be radically different if it were not for the "equal protection" clause.[2] The next three sections show how equal protection litigation has worked to the advantage of minorities, women, and other groups seeking protection under the civil rights umbrella.

RACE, THE CONSTITUTION, AND PUBLIC POLICY

Throughout American history, African Americans have been the most visible minority group in the United States. These individuals have blazed the constitutional trail for securing equal rights for all Americans. Three eras delineate African Americans' struggle for equality in America: (1) the era of slavery, from the beginnings of colonization until the end of the Civil War in 1865, (2) the era of reconstruction and resegregation, from roughly the end of the Civil War until 1953, and (3) the era of civil rights, roughly from 1954 to the present.

THE ERA OF SLAVERY

The first African immigrants to America were kidnap victims. Most African Americans lived in slavery for the first 250 years of American settlement. Slaves were the property of their masters. They could be bought and sold, and they could neither vote nor own property. The Southern states, whose plantations required large numbers of unpaid laborers, were primarily the slave states.

During the slavery era, any public policy of the slave states or the federal government had to accommodate the property interests of slave owners. The Supreme Court got into the act, too, along with the legislative and executive branches (see Table 5.2). The boldest decision in defense of slavery was ***Dred Scott v. Sandford*** (1857), wherein Chief Justice Taney bluntly announced that a black man, slave or free, was "chattel" and had no rights under a white man's government and that Congress had no power to ban slavery in the western territories. This decision invalidated the hard-won Missouri Compromise, which allowed Missouri to become a slave state on the condition that northern territories would remain free of slavery. As a result, the *Dred Scott* decision was an important milestone on the road to the Civil War.

The Union victory in the Civil War and the ratification of the **Thirteenth Amendment** ended slavery. The promises implicit in this amendment and the other two Civil War amendments introduced the era of reconstruction and resegregation in which these promises were first honored and then broken.

THE ERA OF RECONSTRUCTION AND RESEGREGATION

After the Civil War ended, Congress imposed strict conditions on the former confederate states before they could be readmitted to the Union. No one who

TABLE 5.2 TOWARD RACIAL EQUALITY: MILESTONES IN THE ERA OF SLAVERY

1600-1865

Slavery takes hold in the South, comes to characterize almost all relations between African Americans and whites, and is constitutionally justified.

1619	Slaves from Africa are brought to Jamestown and sold to planters.
1776	The rebels enlist African Americans in the army to fight the British, after the British offered freedom to slaves who would fight on their side against the rebels.
1787	The Constitution provides for a slave to be counted as three-fifths of a person in representation and taxation and permits Congress to forbid the importation of new slaves after 1808.
1808	Congress prohibits importation of slaves.
1857	The *Dred Scott v. Sandford* decision holds that slaves may not gain freedom by escaping to a free state or territory; it upholds the constitutionality of the slave system.
1865	The Thirteenth Amendment abolishes slavery and involuntary servitude.

had served in secessionist state governments or in the Confederate Army could hold state office; the legislatures had to ratify the new amendments; and the military would govern the states like "conquered provinces" until they could comply with the tough federal plans for reconstruction. Many African-American men held state and federal offices during the 10 years following the war. Some government agencies, such as the Freedmen's Bureau, provided assistance to former slaves who were making the difficult transition to independence.

To ensure his election in 1876, Rutherford Hayes promised to pull the troops out of the South and let the old slave states resume business as usual. The white Southerners lost little time reclaiming power and imposing a code of *Jim Crow laws*, or segregational laws, on African Americans. ("Jim Crow" was the name of a stereotypical African American in a nineteenth-century minstrel song.) These laws relegated African Americans to separate public facilities, separate school systems, and even separate restrooms. Most whites lost interest in helping former slaves. And what the Jim Crow laws mandated in the South was also common practice in the North. In this era, racial segregation affected every part of life, from the cradle to the grave. African Americans were delivered by African-American physicians or midwives and buried in African-American cemeteries.

The Supreme Court provided a constitutional justification for segregation in the 1896 case of ***Plessy v. Ferguson***. The Louisiana legislature required "equal but separate accommodations for the white and colored races" in railroad transportation. Although Homer Plessy was seven-eighths white, he had been arrested for refusing to leave a railway car reserved for whites. The Court upheld the law, saying that segregation in public facilities was not unconstitutional as long as they were substantially equal. In subsequent decisions, the Court paid more attention to the "separate" than to the "equal" part of this principle. For example, Southern states were allowed to maintain high schools and professional schools for whites even when there were no such schools for African Americans. A measure of segregation in both the South and the North existed as late as the 1960s; nearly all of the African-American physicians in the United States were graduates of two medical schools, Howard University in Washington, DC, and Meharry Medical College in Tennessee.

In the era of segregation, housing, schools, and jobs—as well as lesser things like drinking fountains and rest rooms—were, in one way or another, classified as "white" or "colored."

TABLE 5.3 TOWARD RACIAL EQUALITY: MILESTONES IN THE ERA OF RECONSTRUCTION AND RESEGREGATION

1866-1953

Segregation is legally required in the South and sanctioned in the North; lynchings of African Americans occur in the South; beginning of civil rights policy.

1868	The Fourteenth Amendment makes African Americans U.S. citizens and guarantees the "equal protection of the law." This guarantee is widely ignored for nearly a century.
1870	The Fifteenth Amendment forbids racial discrimination in voting, although many states find ways to prevent or discourage African Americans from voting.
1877	End of Reconstruction. African-American gains made in the South (such as antidiscrimination laws) will be reversed as former Confederates return to power. Jim Crow laws flourish, making segregation legal.
1883	In the *Civil Rights Cases* the Supreme Court rules that the Fourteenth Amendment does *not* prohibit discrimination by private businesses and individuals.
1896	The *Plessy v. Ferguson* decision permits "separate but equal" public facilities, providing a constitutional justification for segregation.
1910	The National Association for the Advancement of Colored People (NAACP) is founded by African Americans and whites.
1915	*Guinn v. United States* bans the grandfather clause that had been used to prevent African Americans from voting.
1941	Executive order forbids racial discrimination in defense industries.
1944	The *Smith v. Allwright* decision bans all-white primaries.
1948	President Truman orders the armed forces desegregated.
1950	*Sweatt v. Painter* finds the "separate but equal" formula generally unacceptable in professional schools.

Nevertheless, some progress on the long road to racial equality was made in the first half of the twentieth century. The Supreme Court and the president began to prohibit a few of the most egregious practices of segregation (see Table 5.3), paving the way for a new era of civil rights.

THE ERA OF CIVIL RIGHTS

After searching carefully for the perfect case to challenge legal school segregation, the Legal Defense Fund of the National Association for the Advancement of Colored People (NAACP) selected the case of Linda Brown. An African-American student in Topeka, Kansas, Brown was required by Kansas law to attend a segregated school. In Topeka, the visible signs of education—teacher quality, facilities, and so on—were substantially equal between African-American and white schools. Thus, the NAACP chose the case in order to test the *Plessy v. Ferguson* doctrine of "separate but equal." The Court would be forced to rule directly on whether school segregation was inherently unequal and thereby violated the Fourteenth Amendment's requirement that states guarantee "equal protection of the laws."

Chief Justice Earl Warren had just been appointed by President Eisenhower. So important was the case that the Court had already heard one round of arguments before Warren joined the Court. The justices, after hearing the oral arguments, met in the Supreme Court's Conference Room. Believing that a unanimous decision would have the most impact, the justices negotiated a broad agreement and then determined that Warren himself should write the opinion.

In ***Brown v. Board of Education*** (1954), the Supreme Court set aside its precedent in Plessy and held that school segregation was inherently unconstitutional because it violated the Fourteenth Amendment's guarantee of equal protection. Legal segregation had come to an end.

A year after its decision in Brown, the Court ordered lower courts to proceed with "all deliberate speed" to desegregate public schools. Desegregation began, and proceeded—slowly in the South, however. A few counties threatened to close their public schools; enrollment in private schools by whites soared. In 1957, President Eisenhower had to send troops to desegregate Central High School in Little Rock. In 1969, 15 years after its first ruling that school segregation was unconstitutional and in the face of continued massive resistance, the Supreme Court withdrew its earlier grant of time to school authorities and declared that "Delays in desegregating school systems are no longer tolerable" (*Alexander v. Board of Education*). In 1964, under the Civil Rights Act, Congress prohibited federal aid to schools that remained segregated. Thus, after nearly a generation of modest progress, Southern schools were suddenly integrated (see Figure 5.1).

The Court found that if schools were legally segregated before, authorities had an obligation to overcome past discrimination. This could include the distribution of students and pupils on a racial basis. Some federal judges ordered the busing of students to achieve racially balanced schools, a practice upheld (but not required) by the Supreme Court in *Swann v. Charlotte-Mecklenberg County Schools* (1971).

Not all racial segregation is what is called *de jure* ("by law") segregation. *De facto* ("in reality") segregation results, for example, when children are assigned to schools near their homes, and those homes are in neighborhoods that are racially segregated for social and economic reasons. Sometimes the distinction between *de jure* and *de facto* segregation has been blurred by past official practices. Because minority groups and federal lawyers demonstrated that Northern schools, too, had purposely drawn district lines to promote segregation, school busing came to the North as well. Denver, Boston, and other cities instituted busing for racial balance, just as Southern cities did.

Busing, one of the least popular remedies for discrimination, has been opposed by majorities of both whites and African Americans. In recent years, it has become less prominent as a judicial instrument.

Courts do not have the power to order busing between school districts; thus, school districts that are largely composed of minorities must rely on other means to integrate. Kansas City, Missouri, has spent years and $1.5 billion under federal court orders to attract white students from the city's suburbs, but with limited success. In 1995, in *Missouri v. Jenkins*, the Supreme Court indicated that it would not look favorably on continued federal control of the district.

The civil rights movement organized both African Americans and whites to end the policies and practices of segregation. As we learned earlier, the movement began in 1955 when Rosa Parks, an African-American woman, refused to give up her seat in a Montgomery, Alabama, bus to a white man. This incident prompted a bus boycott led by a local minister, Martin Luther King, Jr., who became the best-known civil rights activist until his assassination in 1968.

Sit-ins, marches, and civil disobedience were key strategies of the civil rights movement, which sought to establish equal opportunities in the political and economic sectors and to end policies that put up barriers between people because of race. The movement's trail was long and sometimes bloody. Its nonviolent marchers were set upon by police dogs in Birmingham, Alabama. Other activists were murdered in Meridian,

On September 25, 1957, troops of the 101st Airborne Division escorted nine African-American children into Central High School in Little Rock, Arkansas. A court had ordered the school's desegregation in response to *Brown v. Board of Education,* but Arkansas Governor Orville Faubus fought the ruling. President Eisenhower used the National Guard to provide continuing protection for the students.

FIGURE 5.1 PERCENTAGE OF BLACK STUDENTS ATTENDING SCHOOL WITH ANY WHITES IN SOUTHERN STATES[a]

Despite the Supreme Court's decision in *Brown v. Board of Education* in 1954, school integration proceeded at a snail's pace in the South for a decade. Most Southern African-American children entering the first grade in 1955 never attended school with white children. Things picked up considerably in the late 1960s, however, when the Supreme Court insisted that obstruction of implementation of its decision in Brown must come to an end.

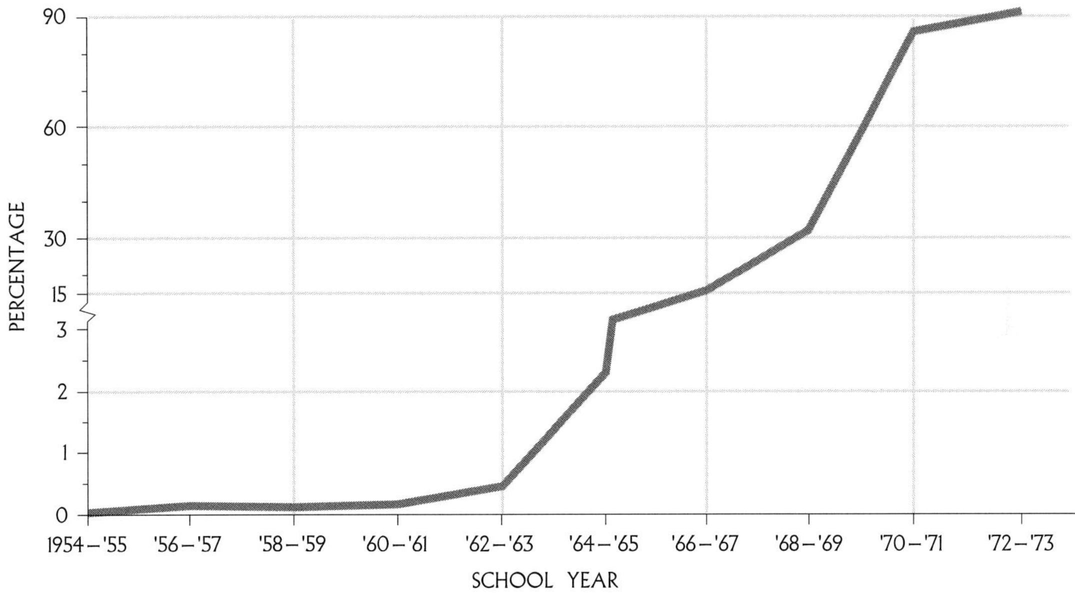

[a]Elementary and secondary students in eleven Southern states, including: Virginia, North Carolina, South Carolina, Georgia, Alabama, Mississippi, Louisiana, Texas, Arkansas, Tennessee, and Florida.

SOURCE: Lawrence Baum, *The Supreme Court*, 5th ed. (Washington, DC: Congressional Quarterly, 1995), 233.

Mississippi, and Selma, Alabama. Fortunately, the goals of the civil rights movement appealed to the national conscience. By the 1970s, overwhelming majorities of white Americans supported racial integration.[3] Today, the principles established in Brown have near universal support.

It was the courts, as much as the national conscience, that put civil rights goals on the nation's policy agenda. *Brown v. Board of Education* was only the beginning of a string of Supreme Court decisions holding various forms of discrimination unconstitutional. Brown and these other cases gave the civil rights movement a momentum that was to grow in the years that followed (see Table 5.4).

As a result of national conscience, the courts, the civil rights movement, and the increased importance of African-American voters, the 1950s and 1960s saw a marked increase in public policies seeking to foster racial equality. These innovations included policies to promote voting rights, access to public accommodations, open housing, and nondiscrimination in many other areas of social and economic life. The **Civil Rights Act of 1964**

- made racial discrimination illegal in hotels, motels, restaurants, and other places of public accommodation
- forbade discrimination in employment on the basis of race, color, national origin, religion, or gender[4]
- created the Equal Employment Opportunity Commission (EEOC) to monitor and enforce protections against job discrimination
- provided for withholding federal grants from state and local governments and other institutions that practiced racial discrimination

TABLE 5.4 TOWARD RACIAL EQUALITY: MILESTONES IN THE ERA OF CIVIL RIGHTS

1954-1997

Integration becomes a widely accepted goal; the civil rights movement grows, followed by urban racial disorders in the 1960s; African-American voting increases; attention shifts to equal results and affirmative action.

1954	*Brown v. Board of Education* holds that segregated schools are inherently unequal and violate the Fourteenth Amendment's equal protection clause.
1955	Martin Luther King, Jr., leads a bus boycott in Montgomery, Alabama.
1957	Federal troops enforce desegregation of a Little Rock, Arkansas, high school.
1963	Civil rights demonstrators numbering 250,000 march on Washington, DC.
1964	Title II of the Civil Rights Act forbids discrimination in public accommodations. Title VI of the Civil Rights Act provides that federal grants and contracts may be withheld from violators. Title VII of the Civil Rights Act forbids discrimination by employers and empowers the Justice Department to sue violators.
	The Twenty-fourth Amendment ends the poll tax in federal elections.
1965	The Voting Rights Act sends federal registrars to Southern states and counties to protect African Americans' right to vote and gives registrars the power to impound ballots in order to enforce the act. Executive order requires companies with federal contracts to take affirmative action to ensure equal opportunity. Riots occur in Watts, California, and other cities and reappear every summer in various cities for the next 5 years.
1966	*Harper v. Virginia* holds that the Fourteenth Amendment forbids making payment of a tax a condition of voting in any election.
1967	Cleveland becomes the first major city to elect an African-American mayor (Carl Stokes).
1968	The *Jones v. Mayer* decision and the Civil Rights Act of 1968 make all racial discrimination in the sale or rental of housing illegal.
1971	The *Swann v. Charlotte-Mecklenberg County Schools* decision approves busing as a means of combating state-enforced segregation.
1978	*California Board of Regents v. Bakke* forbids rigid racial quotas for medical school admissions but does not forbid considering race as a factor when deciding admissions.
1979	*United Steelworkers of America v. Weber* permits an affirmative action program to favor African Americans if the program is designed to remedy past discrimination.
	Dayton Board of Education v. Brinkman upholds school busing to remedy Northern school segregation.
1980	Jesse Jackson becomes the first serious African-American candidate for president.
1984	*Grove City College v. Bell* forbids the federal government from withholding all federal funds from a college that refuses to file forms saying that it does not discriminate. (Only a specific program risked its federal funds.)
1988	Congress rewrites the Civil Rights Act to "overturn" the implications of *Grove City College.*
1991	After 3 years of conflict, Congress enacts the Civil Rights and Women's Equity in Employment Act, which counters the effects of several Supreme Court decisions making it more difficult for workers to bring and win job discrimination suits.
1995	*Adarand Constructors v. Pena* holds that affirmative action programs must undergo strict scrutiny to determine that they are narrowly tailored to serve a compelling governmental interest.

- strengthened voting rights legislation
- authorized the U.S. Justice Department to initiate lawsuits to desegregate public schools and facilities.

The Voting Rights Act of 1965 (discussed below) was the most extensive federal effort to crack century-old barriers to African-American voting in the South. The *Open Housing Act of 1968* took steps to forbid discrimination in the sale or rental of housing.

So many congressional and judicial policies were instituted after 1954 that virtually every type of segregation was attacked by a legislative or judicial policy. By the 1980s, few, if any, forms of racial discrimination were left to legislate against. Efforts for legislation were successful, in part, because by the mid-1960s federal laws effectively protected the right to vote, in fact as well as on paper; members of minority groups thus had some power to hold their legislators accountable.

GETTING AND USING THE RIGHT TO VOTE

When the Constitution was written, no one thought about extending the right to vote to African Americans (most of whom were slaves) or to women. The early Republic limited **suffrage**, the legal right to vote, to a handful of the population—mostly property-holding white males. Only after the Civil War was the right to vote extended, slowly and painfully, to African-American males and then to other minority groups.

The **Fifteenth Amendment**, adopted in 1870, guaranteed African Americans the right to vote—at least in principle. It said, "The right of citizens to vote shall not be abridged by the United States or by any state on account of race, color, or previous condition of servitude." The gap between these constitutional words and their implementation, however, remained wide for a full century. States seemed to outdo one another in developing ingenious methods of circumventing the Fifteenth Amendment.

Oklahoma and other Southern states used a *grandfather clause* to deny African Americans the right to vote. These states required potential voters to complete literacy tests before registering to vote. The grandfather clause, however, exempted persons whose grandfathers were eligible to vote in 1860 from taking these tests. This exemption did not apply, of course, to the grandchildren of slaves and hence assured only illiterate whites of the right to vote. The law was blatantly unfair; it was also unconstitutional, said the Supreme Court in the 1915 decision *Guinn v. United States*.

To exclude African Americans from registering to vote, most Southern states also relied on **poll taxes**, which were small taxes levied on the right to vote that often fell due at a time of year when poor sharecroppers had the least cash on hand. To render African-American votes ineffective, most Southern states also used the **white primary**, a device that permitted political parties in the heavily Democratic South to exclude African Americans from primary elections, thus depriving them of a voice in the most important contests and letting them vote only when it mattered least. The Supreme Court declared white primaries unconstitutional in 1944 in *Smith v. Allwright*.

The Voting Rights Act of 1965 produced a major increase in the number of African Americans registered to vote in Southern states. The ability to vote gave African Americans more political clout: In the 20 years following enactment of the law, more than 2,500 African Americans were elected to state and local offices in that region.

The civil rights movement put suffrage high on its political agenda; one by one, the barriers to African-American voting fell during the 1960s. Poll taxes in federal elections were prohibited by the **Twenty-fourth Amendment**, which was ratified in 1964. Two years later, the Supreme Court voided poll taxes in state elections in *Harper v. Virginia State Board of Elections*.

Many areas in the South employed voter registration tests—requiring literacy or an understanding of the Constitution, for example—in a discriminatory fashion. Voting registrars would declare literate African Americans to be illiterate and thus ineligible to register to vote, while allowing illiterate whites to register. The **Voting Rights Act of 1965** prohibited any government from using voting procedures that denied a person the vote on the basis of race or color and abolished the use of literacy requirements for anyone who had completed the sixth grade. Federal election registrars were sent to areas that had long histories of discrimination, and these same areas had to submit all proposed changes in their voting laws or practices to a federal official for preclearance. As a result of these provisions, hundreds of thousands of African Americans registered in Southern states and counties.

The effects of these efforts were swift and certain, as the civil rights movement turned from protest to politics.[5] When the Voting Rights Act was passed in 1965, only 70 African Americans held public office in the 11 Southern states. By the early 1980s, more than 2,500 African Americans held elected offices in those states, and the number has continued to grow. There are currently more than 8,000 African-American elected officials in the United States.[6]

One direct result of the Voting Rights Act of 1965 was Jesse Jackson's impressive showing in the Southern presidential primaries in 1988. Another was the election of Douglas Wilder, the grandson of slaves, as governor of Virginia. In recent years, the implementation of the Voting Rights Act has become more complex as it has been amended and interpreted to ensure the success of minority candidates (see "Since Kennedy: The Changing Face of Voting Rights").

African Americans are not the only racial group that has suffered legally imposed discrimination. Even before the civil rights struggle, native Americans, Asians, and Hispanics learned how powerless they could become in a society dominated by whites. The civil rights laws for which African Americans fought have benefited members of these groups as well.

OTHER MINORITY GROUPS

Soon African Americans will no longer be the largest minority group in the United States. As we will discuss in Chapter 6, America is heading toward a *minority majority:* a situation in which minority groups will outnumber Caucasians of European descent. Hispanic Americans—chiefly from Mexico, Puerto Rico, and Cuba but also from El Salvador, Honduras, and other countries in Central America—will soon displace African Americans as the largest minority group. Asian Americans are the fastest-growing minority group; their representation in the American population rose from 0.5 percent to 3 percent from 1960 to 1990.

The earliest inhabitants of the continent, the American Indians, are, of course, the oldest minority group. The history of poverty, discrimination, and exploitation experienced by American Indians is a long one. Not until 1924 were American Indians made citizens of the United States, a status that African Americans had achieved a half-century before. Not until 1946 did Congress establish the Indian Claims Act to settle financial disputes arising from lands taken from the American Indians.[7] Today American Indians benefit from the public policy gains won by African Americans—guaranteed access to the polls, to housing, and to jobs. Yet American Indians know, perhaps better than any other group, the significance of the gap between public policy and private realization regarding discrimination.

Asian Americans suffered during World War II when the U.S. government, beset by fears of a Japanese invasion of the Pacific Coast, rounded up more than 100,000 Americans of Japanese descent and herded them into encampments. These internment camps were, critics claimed, America's concentration camps. The Supreme Court, however, in ***Korematsu v. United States*** (1944), upheld the internment as constitutional. Congress has since authorized benefits to the former internees.

Like American Indians and Asian Americans, Hispanic Americans benefit from the nondiscrimination policies originally passed to protect African Americans. Provisions of the Voting Rights Act of 1965 covered San Antonio, Texas, and thereby permitted Hispanic voters to lend weight to the election of Mayor Henry Cisneros. There are now about 5,500 elected Hispanic officials in the United States.[8] (Chapter 6 will discuss in detail these and other groups in the minority majority.)

Social movements tend to beget new social movements; thus, the African-American civil rights movement of the 1960s affected other minorities. American Indians and Hispanics began organizing and became active. American Indian activists such as Dennis Means of the American Indian Movement (AIM), Vine Deloria, and Dee Brown drew attention to the plight of the American Indian tribes. Twenty years later, this movement continues to struggle against the poverty, inferior education, and poor health of many American Indians. Led by Cesar Chavez, the United Farm Workers publicized the plight of migrant workers, a large proportion of whom are Hispanic. Political activity on behalf of women has been so energetic and so far-reaching that a separate section is needed to examine this struggle for equality.

SINCE KENNEDY

The Changing Face of Voting Rights

As Bill Clinton was growing up in the South and John F. Kennedy was serving as president, civil rights was the most hotly debated issue of domestic policy. The debate over voting rights was literally black and white: Were African Americans going to have the right to vote or not? Today, issues of civil rights often fall into much grayer areas.

The Voting Rights Act not only secured the right to vote for African Americans but also ensured that their votes would not be diluted through racial gerrymandering. For example, majority white districts could elect members of a city council in at-large seats and prevent a geographically concentrated minority from electing a minority council member. When Congress amended the Voting Rights Act in 1982, it further insisted that minorities be able to "elect representatives of their choice" when their numbers and configuration permitted. Thus, legislative redistricting was to avoid discriminatory *results* and not just discriminatory *intent.* In 1986, the Supreme Court upheld this principle in *Thornburg v. Gingles.*

Officials in the Justice Department responsible for enforcing the Voting Rights Act and state legislatures that drew new district lines interpreted these actions as a mandate to create minority-majority districts. Consequently, when congressional district boundaries were redrawn following the 1990 census, several states, including Florida, North Carolina, Texas, Illinois, New York, and Louisiana, created odd-shaped districts that were designed to give minority-group voters a numerical majority. Fourteen new U.S. House districts were specifically drawn to help elect African Americans to Congress, and six districts were drawn to elect new Hispanic members (these efforts worked, as we will see in Chapter 12).

However, in 1993, the Supreme Court heard a challenge to a North Carolina congressional district which cut in places no wider than a superhighway, with an African American majority winding snakelike for 160 miles. In its decision in *Shaw v. Reno,* the Court decried the creation of districts based solely on racial composition, as well as the district drawers' abandonment of traditional redistricting standards such as compactness and contiguity. Thus, the Court gave legal standing to challenges to any congressional map with an oddly shaped majority-minority district that may not be defensible on grounds other than race (such as shared community interest or geographical compactness). The next year in *Johnson v. DeGrandy,* the Court ruled that a state legislative redistricting plan does not violate the Voting Rights Act if it does not create the greatest possible number of districts in which minority-group votes would make up a majority.

In 1995 in *Miller v. Johnson,* the Court rejected the efforts of the Department of Justice to achieve the maximum possible number of minority districts. It held that the use of race as a "predominant factor" in drawing district lines should be presumed to be unconstitutional. The next year, in *Bush v. Vera* and *Shaw v. Hunt,* the Supreme Court voided three convoluted districts in Texas and one in North Carolina on the grounds that race had been the primary reason for abandoning compact district lines and that the state legislatures had crossed the line into unconstitutional racial gerrymandering.

Just how lower courts are to determine whether race was a predominant factor in drawing district boundaries is not clear, and we can expect continued litigation concerning this question over the next few years, especially after the census is taken in the year 2000.

WOMEN, THE CONSTITUTION, AND PUBLIC POLICY

Abigail Adams may have been practically alone in her feminist views in the 1770s, but the next century brought significant feminist activity. The first women's rights activists were products of the abolitionist movement, where they often encountered sexist opposition. Two of these women, Lucretia Mott and Elizabeth Cady Stanton, organized a meeting at Seneca Falls in upstate New York. They had much to discuss. Not only were women denied the vote, but they were also subjected to patriarchal family law and denied education and career opportunities. The legal doctrine known as *coverture* deprived married women of any identity separate from that of their husbands;

The growing numbers of Hispanic Americans will soon make them the largest minority group in the United States. Their political power is reflected in the two Hispanic members of President Clinton's first cabinet—Henry Cisneros and Federico Peña—and in the 18 members of the U.S. House of Representatives.

wives could not sign contracts or dispose of property. Divorce law was heavily biased in favor of husbands. Even abused women found it almost impossible to end their marriages; and men had the legal advantage in securing custody of the children.

THE BATTLE FOR THE VOTE

On July 19, 1848, 100 men and women signed the Seneca Falls Declaration of Sentiments and Resolutions. Patterned after the Declaration of Independence, it proclaimed, "The history of mankind is a history of repeated injuries and usurpations on the part of man toward woman, having in direct object the establishment of an absolute tyranny over her." Thus began the movement that would culminate in the ratification of the **Nineteenth Amendment** 72 years later, giving women the vote. Charlotte Woodward, 19 years old in 1848, was the only signer of the Seneca Falls Declaration who lived to vote for the president in 1920.

The battle for women's suffrage was fought mostly in the late nineteenth and early twentieth centuries. Leaders like Stanton and Susan B. Anthony were prominent in the cause, which emphasized the vote but also addressed women's other grievances. The suffragists had considerable success in the states, especially in the Pacific Northwest. Several states allowed women to vote before the constitutional amendment passed. The feminists lobbied, marched, protested, and even engaged in civil disobedience, though not to the extent of their English counterparts.[9]

THE "DOLDRUMS": 1920-1960

Winning the right to vote did not automatically win equal status for women. In fact, the feminist movement seemed to lose rather than gain momentum after winning the vote, perhaps because the vote was about the only goal on which all feminists agreed. There was considerable division within the movement on other priorities.

Many suffragists accepted the traditional model of the family. Fathers were breadwinners, mothers bread bakers. Although most suffragists thought that women should have the opportunity to pursue any occupations they chose, many also believed that women's primary obligations revolved around the roles of wife and mother. Many suffragists had defended the vote as basically an extension of the maternal role into public life, arguing that a new era of public morality would emerge when women could vote. These *social feminists* were in tune with prevailing attitudes.

Public policy toward women continued to be dominated by protectionism rather than by the principle of equality. Laws protected working women from the burdens of overtime work, long hours on the job, and heavy lifting. The fact that these laws also protected male workers from female competition received little attention. State laws tended to reflect—and reinforce—the traditional family roles. These laws concentrated on limiting women's work opportunities outside the home so that they could concentrate on their duties within it. In most states, husbands were legally required to support their families (even after a divorce) and to pay child support, though divorced fathers did not always pay. When a marriage ended, mothers almost always got custody of the children, although husbands had the legal advantage in custody battles. Public policy was designed to preserve traditional motherhood and hence, supporters claimed, to protect the family and the country's moral fabric.[10]

Only a minority of feminists challenged these assumptions. Alice Paul, the author of the original **Equal Rights Amendment** (ERA), was one activist who claimed that the real result of protectionist law was to perpetuate sexual inequality. Simply worded, the ERA reads, "Equality of rights under the law shall not be denied or abridged by the United States or by any state on account of sex." Most people saw the ERA as a threat to the family when it was introduced in Congress in 1923. It gained little support. In fact, women were less likely to support the amendment than men were.

THE SECOND FEMINIST WAVE

The civil rights movement of the 1950s and 1960s attracted many women activists, some of whom also joined student and antiwar movements. These women often met with the same prejudices as had women abolitionists. Betty Friedan's book *The Feminine Mystique*, published in 1963, encouraged many women to question traditional assumptions and to assert their own rights. Groups such as the National Organization for Women (NOW) and the National Women's Political Caucus were organized in the 1960s and 1970s.

Before the advent of the contemporary feminist movement, the Supreme Court upheld virtually any instance of gender-based discrimination. The state and federal governments were free to discriminate against women—and, indeed, men—as they chose. In the 1970s, the Court began to take a closer look at gender discrimination. In ***Reed v. Reed*** (1971), the Court ruled that any "arbitrary" gender-based classification violated the equal protection clause of the Fourteenth Amendment. This was the first time the Court declared any law unconstitutional on the basis of gender discrimination. Five years later, ***Craig v. Boren*** established a "medium scrutiny" standard: Gender discrimination would be presumed to be neither valid nor invalid. Table 5.5 includes important policy milestones on gender equality.

The Supreme Court has struck down many laws and rules for discriminating on the basis of gender. For example, the Court voided laws giving husbands exclusive control over family property in *Kirchberg v. Feenstra*, 1981. The Court also voided employers' rules that denied women equal monthly retirement benefits because they live longer than men (*Arizona Governing Committee for Tax Deferred Annuity and Deferred Compensation Plans v. Norris*, 1983).

In fact, many of the litigants in cases raising constitutional questions about gender discrimination have been men seeking equality with women in their treatment under the law. Thus, the Court has voided laws that

- Provided for alimony payments to women only (*Orr v. Orr*, 1979)
- Closed a state's nursing school to men (*Mississippi v. Hogan*, 1982)
- Set a higher age for drinking for men than for women (*Craig v. Boren*, 1976)
- Set a higher age for reaching legal adult status for men than for women (*Stanton v. Stanton*, 1975)

Men have not always prevailed in their efforts for equal treatment, however. The Court upheld a statutory rape law applying only to men (*Michael M. v. Superior Court*, 1981) and the male-only draft, which we will discuss shortly. The Court also allowed a Florida law giving property tax exemptions only to widows, not to widowers (*Kahn v. Shevin*, 1974).

Contemporary feminists have suffered defeats as well as victories. The ERA was revived when Congress passed it in 1972 and extended the deadline for ratification until 1982. Nevertheless, the ERA was three states short of ratification when time ran out. Paradoxically, the defeat of the ERA had just the opposite effect of that which the 1920 suffrage victory had on feminism. Far from weakening the movement, losing the ERA battle has stimulated vigorous feminist activity. Proponents have vowed to keep reintroducing the amendment in Congress (without success so far) and continue to press hard for state and federal action on women's rights.

WOMEN IN THE WORKPLACE

One reason why feminist activism persists has nothing to do with ideology or other social movements. The family pattern that traditionalists sought to preserve—father at work, mother at home—is becoming a thing of the past. The female civilian labor force amounts to 60 million (as compared to 71 million males), representing 59 percent of adult women. The majority of these women are married. There are also 12 million female-headed households, and about 60 percent of American mothers who have children

TABLE 5.5 TOWARD GENDER EQUALITY: PUBLIC POLICY MILESTONES

1969-1997

1969	Executive order declares that offering equal opportunities for women at every level of federal service is to be national policy and establishes a program for implementing the policy.
1971	In *Reed v. Reed,* the Supreme Court invalidates a state law preferring men to women in court selection of an estate's administrator.
1972	Provisions of Title VII of the Civil Rights Act of 1964 are extended to cover the faculty and professional staffs of colleges and universities.
	The Education Act forbids gender discrimination in public schools (with some exceptions for historically single-gender schools).
	The ERA is proposed by Congress and sent to the states for ratification.
1974	A woman—Ella Grasso of Connecticut—is elected governor for the first time without succeeding her husband to the office.
1975	Congress opens armed services academies to women.
1976	Courts strike down an Oklahoma law setting different legal drinking ages for men and women.
1977	Supreme Court voids arbitrary height and weight requirements for employees in *Dothard v. Rawlinson.*
1978	The deadline for ratification of the ERA is extended.
	Congress passes the Pregnancy Discrimination Act.
1981	The Supreme Court rules that males-only military draft registration is constitutional.
	Sandra Day O'Connor becomes the first woman Supreme Court Justice.
1982	The ERA ratification deadline passes without ratification of the amendment.
1984	Geraldine Ferraro is nominated as the first woman vice-presidential candidate of a major party.
1988	The Supreme Court unanimously upholds a 1984 New York City law aimed primarily at requiring the admission of women to large, private clubs that play an important role in professional life.
1991	After 3 years of conflict, Congress enacts the Civil Rights and Women's Equity in Employment Act, which counters the effects of several Supreme Court decisions making it more difficult for workers to bring and win job discrimination suits.
1992	California becomes the first state to be represented by two female U.S. senators.
1993	Supreme Court in *Harris v. Forklift Systems* lowers the threshold for proving sexual harassment in the workplace.
1994	48 women elected to U.S. House and 8 to the Senate, the most in history.
1996	In *United States v. Virginia et al.,* the Supreme Court declares categorical exclusion of women from state-funded colleges unconstitutional.
1997	Madeline Albright appointed Secretary of State, the first woman to serve in that role.

below school age are in the labor force.[11] As conditions have changed, public opinion and public policy demands have changed, too. Protectionism is not dead. Women still have more duties inside the home than men do, and debates over policies like the "mommy track" (reduced work responsibilities for women workers with children) parental leaves to women reflect this social phenomenon. Demands for equality, however, keep nudging protectionism into the background.

Congress has made some important progress, especially in the area of employment. The Civil Rights Act of 1964 banned gender discrimination in employment. The protection of this law has been expanded several times. For example, in 1972, Congress gave the Equal Employment Opportunity Commission (EEOC) the power to sue employers suspected of illegal discrimination. Title IX of the Education Act of 1972 forbade gender discrimination in federally subsidized education programs, including athletics. The Pregnancy

As women have become more active in politics, they have begun to assume more leadership roles. Here, Dianne Feinstein and Barbara Boxer celebrate their 1992 victories in the U.S. Senate races in California, marking the first time a state has been represented in the Senate by two female senators.

Discrimination Act of 1978 made it illegal for employers to exclude pregnancy and childbirth from their sick leave and health benefits plans (See "You Are the Judge: Are Maternity Leaves a Form of Gender Discrimination?") The Civil Rights and Women's Equity in Employment Act of 1991 shifted the burden of proof in justifying hiring and promotion practices to employers, who must show that employment practices are related to job performance and that they are consistent with "business necessity" (an ambiguous term, however).

The Supreme Court also weighed in against gender discrimination in employment and business activity. In 1977, it voided laws and rules barring women from jobs through arbitrary height and weight requirements (*Dothard v. Rawlinson*). Any such prerequisites must be directly related to the duties required in a particular position. Women have also been protected from being required to take mandatory pregnancy leaves from their jobs (*Cleveland Board of Education v. LaFleur*, 1974) and from being denied a job because of an employer's concern for harming a developing fetus (*United Automobile Workers v. Johnson Controls*, 1991). Many commercial contacts are made in private business and service clubs, which often have excluded women from membership. The Court has upheld state and city laws that prohibit such discrimination.[12]

Education is closely related to employment. Title IX of the Education Act of 1972 forbids gender discrimination in federally subsidized education programs (which include almost all colleges and universities). But what about single-gender schooling? In 1996, in *United States v. Virginia et al.*, the Supreme Court declared that Virginia's categorical exclusion of women from education opportunities at the state-funded Virginia Military Institute (VMI) violated women's rights to equal protection of the law. A few days later, The Citadel, the nation's only other state-supported all-male college, announced that it would also admit women.

Women have made substantial progress in their quest for equality, but more court cases are likely in the future as Congress continues to consider new laws. Three of the most controversial issues that legislators will face are wage discrimination, the role of women in the military, and sexual harassment.

WAGE DISCRIMINATION AND COMPARABLE WORTH

Traditional women's jobs often pay much less than men's jobs that demand comparable skill; a female secretary often earns far less than a male accounts clerk with the same qualifications. Median annual earnings for full-time women workers are only about two-thirds those of men.[13]

In 1983, the Washington state Supreme Court ruled that its state government had discriminated against women for years by denying them equal pay for jobs of **comparable worth.** The U.S. Supreme Court has remained silent so far on the merits of this issue. The executive branch under Ronald Reagan consistently opposed the idea of comparable worth. The late Clarence Pendleton, Reagan's appointee as head of the U.S. Civil Rights Commission, argued that lawsuits based on comparable worth would interfere with the free market for wages by reducing incentives for women to seek higher-paying, traditionally male jobs. Pendleton called comparable worth "the craziest idea since Looney Tunes." Ridicule has not made this serious dispute go away, however.

WOMEN IN THE MILITARY

Military service is another controversial aspect of gender equality. Women have served in every branch of the armed services since World War II. Originally, they served in separate units such as the WACS (Women's Army Corps), the WAVES (Women Accepted for Volunteer Emergency Service in the navy), and the Nurse Corps. The military had a 2 percent quota for women (which was never filled) until the 1970s. Now women are part of the regular service. They make up 11 percent of the armed forces

ARE MATERNITY LEAVES A FORM OF GENDER DISCRIMINATION?

You Are The Judge

In 1982, Lillian Garland gave birth to a baby girl and soon found herself caught in a great legal battle. Her pregnancy was complicated, and she had to take 3 months of unpaid leave from her job as a bank receptionist at the California Federal Savings and Loan Association (Cal Fed). Because California law required employers to grant up to 4 months leave to any "female employee affected by pregnancy, childbirth, or related medical conditions," Ms. Garland anticipated no problems in returning to her job.

She was wrong. Cal Fed had never guaranteed reinstatement to employees who took leaves of absence for reasons other than pregnancy and argued that California law discriminated in favor of pregnant workers by mandating special treatment for them. Ms. Garland won her case at the state level but when Cal Fed appealed to the federal courts, she lost her job and, as a result, her home and custody of her daughter.

By the time the case reached the Supreme Court, feminists had lined up on both sides of the issue. The National Organization for Women sided with Cal Fed, arguing that women-only leaves would "reinforce stereotypes about women's inclinations and abilities" and "deter employers from hiring women of child-bearing age." Other feminists saw these arguments as cowardly capitulation to corporate power and denial of the realities of working women's lives. The Coalition for Reproductive Equality in the Workplace praised the state law because it "in effect equalizes working men and women."

You be the judge: Does requiring employers to grant pregnancy leaves constitute illegal gender discrimination, or does it remove discrimination against women?

Answer: By a vote of six to three, the U.S. Supreme Court ruled that the California law mandating pregnancy leaves did not constitute illegal discrimination in favor of pregnant women. But a week later, the Court ruled that Missouri could deny unemployment compensation to women who left their jobs because of pregnancy, because the state had a "neutral rule" denying compensation to all workers who quit voluntarily.

SOURCE: Judith A. Baer, *Women in American Law* 2nd ed. (New York: Holmes and Meier Publishers, 1996), chap. 3.

(14 percent of the army), and compete directly with men for promotion. Congress opened all of the service academies to women in 1975. Women have done well, including graduating first at the U.S. Naval Academy in Annapolis and serving as First Captain of the Corps of Cadets at West Point.

Two important differences between the treatment of men and that of women persist in military service. Only men must register for the draft when they turn 18. There is no military conscription at present (the United States has had a volunteer force since 1973), but President Jimmy Carter asked Congress to require both men and women to register after the Soviets invaded Afghanistan in 1979. Congress reinstated registration for men only, a policy that was not universally popular. Federal courts ordered registration suspended while several young men filed a suit. They lost. In 1981, the Supreme Court displayed its typical deference to the elected branches in the area of national security; it ruled in *Rostker v. Goldberg* that male-only registration bore a substantial relationship to

In the past few years, women have overcome many obstacles to serving in the military, performing well in a variety of nontraditional roles such as piloting helicopters.

Congress' goal of ensuring combat readiness and was constitutionally acceptable.

Statutes and regulations also prohibit women from serving in combat. A breach exists between policy and practice, however, as the Persian Gulf War showed. Women piloted helicopters at the front and helped to operate antimissile systems; some were taken as prisoners of war. Women are now permitted to serve as combat pilots in the navy and air force and to serve on navy warships. However, they are still not permitted to serve in ground combat units in the army or marines.

These actions have reopened the debate over whether women should serve in combat. Some experts insist that because women, on the average, have less upper-body strength than men, they are inferior warriors. Others argue that men will not be able to fight effectively beside wounded or dying women. Critics of these views point out that some women surpass some men in upper-body strength and that we do not know how well men and women will fight together. This debate is not only a controversy about ability; it also touches on the question of whether engaging in combat is a burden or a privilege. Clearly some women—and some who would deny them combat duty—take the latter view.

SEXUAL HARASSMENT

Whether in the military, on the assembly line, or in the office, women for years have voiced concern about sexual harassment, which, of course, does not affect only women. In 1986, the Supreme Court articulated this broad principle: Sexual harassment that is so pervasive as to create a hostile or abusive work environment is a form of gender discrimination, which is forbidden by the 1964 Civil Rights Act.[14] In 1993, in *Harris v. Forklift Systems*, the Court reinforced its decision. No single factor, the Court said, is required to win a sexual harassment case under Title VII of the 1964 Civil Rights Act. The law is violated when the workplace environment "would reasonably be perceived, and is perceived, as hostile or abusive." Thus, workers are not required to prove that the workplace environment is so hostile as to cause them "severe psychological injury" or that they are unable to perform their jobs. The protection of federal law comes into play before the harassing conduct leads to psychological difficulty.

Sexual harassment can occur anywhere but may be especially prevalent in male-dominated occupations such as the military. A 1991 convention of the Tailhook Association, an organization of naval aviators, made the news after reports surfaced of drunken sailors jamming a hotel hallway and sexually assaulting female guests, including naval officers, as they stepped off the elevator. After the much-criticized initial failure of the navy to identify the officers responsible for the assault, heads rolled, including those of several admirals and the secretary of the navy. In 1996 and 1997, a number of army officers and noncommissioned officers had their careers ended, and some went to prison, for sexual harassment of female soldiers in training situations. Behavior that was once viewed as simply male high jinks is now intolerable.

The push for gender equality is a worldwide phenomenon (see "America in Perspective: Mrs. In-the-Back-of-the-House Goes to Parliament"). Many women are asserting their civil rights for the first time.

NEWLY ACTIVE GROUPS UNDER THE CIVIL RIGHTS UMBRELLA

New activist groups have realized that racial and ethnic minorities and women are not the only Americans who can claim civil rights; policies enacted to protect one or two groups can be applied to others. Four recent entrants into the interest group arena are aging Americans, young Americans, people with disabilities, and homosexuals. All of these groups claim equal rights, as racial minorities and women do, but represent different challenges to mainstream America.

CIVIL RIGHTS AND THE GRAYING OF AMERICA

America is aging rapidly. People in their eighties make up the fastest-growing age group in this country. Aging Americans, the middle-aged as well as the

MRS. IN-THE-BACK-OF-THE-HOUSE GOES TO PARLIAMENT

America in Perspective

In Japan, married women are often supposed to stay at home and clean the house and raise the children. In fact, the Japanese word for wife means "Mrs. In-the-Back-of-the-House." There are even legal incentives to encourage married women to quit full-time jobs, and a married couple is legally required to use the same last name—almost always the husband's.

Such an environment presents immense obstacles for women to overcome in order to transform themselves into a meaningful force in Japanese politics. Women find it difficult to be taken seriously by voters, facing prejudice such as that reflected in one male candidate's taunt, "Women can't do anything. They should just shut up." Many of the women who are elected to Parliament are actresses or other celebrities.

Thus, we should not be surprised that in the Parliament elected in 1996, women composed only 4 percent of the more powerful lower house. (In the United States, as we discuss in Chapter 12, women constitute 9 percent of the Senate and 12 percent of the House.) Most of the women who are elected represent opposition parties and thus have little influence.

Despite these cultural barriers, women in Japan are making progress, however. The number of women in local town and county assemblies has blossomed over the last decade, bringing attention to issues such as environmental and food safety. It remains to be seen whether the base in local government will be sufficient to propel more women into positions of power at the national level.

SOURCE: Sherly WuDunn, "23 Women Break Into a Male Citadel," *New York Times*, October 26, 1996, p. 4.

elderly, have claimed space under the civil rights umbrella. When the Social Security program began in the 1930s, 65 was the retirement age. Although this age was apparently chosen arbitrarily, it soon became the mandatory retirement age for many workers. Although many workers might prefer to retire while they are still healthy and active enough to enjoy leisure, not everyone wants or can afford to do so. Social Security is not, and was never meant to be, an adequate income, and not all workers have good pension plans.

In addition, employers routinely refused to hire people over a certain age. Graduate and professional schools often rejected applicants in their thirties on the grounds that their professions would get fewer years, and thus less return, out of them. This policy had a severe impact on housewives and veterans who wanted to return to school.

As early as 1967, Congress banned some kinds of age discrimination. In 1975, civil rights law denied federal funds to any institution discriminating against people over the age of 40. The Age Discrimination in Employment Act was amended in 1978 to raise the general compulsory retirement age to 70. Now compulsory retirement has been phased out altogether. No one knows what other directions the *gray liberation movement* may take as its members approach the status of a minority majority.

ARE THE YOUNG A DISADVANTAGED GROUP, TOO?

Older Americans are not the only victims of age discrimination. The young, too, have suffered from inferior treatment under the law. The *Hazelwood* case discussed in Chapter 4 provides one example of such treatment. Will there soon be an autonomous children's rights movement? There are obvious difficulties in organizing such a movement, but these do not mean that young people are silent in asserting their rights.

Walter Polovchak of Chicago is one example. In 1980, when Walter was 12, his family emigrated from the Ukraine. His parents, quickly disillusioned, decided to return. Walter, however, wanted to stay in Chicago; he ran away to live with relatives in the area. The law was on his parents' side; so were groups such as the American Civil Liberties Union. Court after court ordered the boy returned to his parents. But what Shakespeare called "the law's delay" was Walter's best ally. When he reached his eighteenth birthday and was no longer answerable to his parents, he was still in Chicago. He remains there today, an American citizen.[15]

In 1992, a precocious 12-year-old boy in Florida went to court and "divorced" his family so that he could be adopted by foster parents. Several similar cases followed, guaranteeing that children's rights will occupy legal scholars for years to come.

CIVIL RIGHTS AND THE PEOPLE WITH DISABILITIES

Many Americans with disabilities have suffered from both direct and indirect discrimination. They have often been denied rehabilitation services (a kind of affirmative action), education, and jobs. Many people with disabilities have been excluded from the work force and isolated without overt discrimination. Throughout most of American history, public and private buildings have been hostile to the blind, deaf, and mobility-impaired. Stairs, buses, telephones, and other necessities of modern life have been designed in ways that keep these individuals out of offices, stores, and restaurants. As one slogan said, "Once, blacks had to ride at the back of the bus. We can't even get on the bus."

The first rehabilitation laws were passed in the late 1920s, mostly to help veterans of World War I. Accessibility laws had to wait another 50 years. The Rehabilitation Act of 1973 (twice vetoed by Richard Nixon as "too costly") added people with disabilities to the list of Americans protected from discrimination. Because the law defines an inaccessible environment as a form of discrimination, wheelchair ramps, grab bars on toilets, and braille signs have become common features of American life. The Education of All Handicapped Children Act of 1975 entitled all children to a free public education appropriate to their needs. The **Americans with Disabilities Act of 1990** strengthened these protections, requiring employers and public facilities to make "reasonable accommodations" and prohibiting employment discrimination against people with disabilities.

Nobody wants to oppose policies beneficial to people with disabilities. After all, people like Helen Keller and Franklin Roosevelt are popular American heroes. Nevertheless, civil rights laws designed to protect the rights of these individuals have met with vehement opposition, and, once passed, with sluggish enforcement. The source of this resistance is the same concern that troubled Nixon: cost. Budgeting for such programs is often short-sighted, however; people often forget that changes allowing people with disabilities to become wage earners, spenders, and taxpayers are a gain, rather than drain, on the economy.

Are people with acquired immune deficiency syndrome (AIDS) entitled to protections? Thus far, no case dealing with AIDS as a disability has reached the Supreme Court. You can be sure, though, that such a case is not far off.

GAY AND LESBIAN RIGHTS

Gay and lesbian activists may face the toughest battle for equality. The reluctance to appear hostile to the aged or to women, which bridles the tongue of many potential opponents, has no apparent equivalent with respect to gay and lesbian Americans.

Moreover, gays and lesbians rarely enjoy even the formal—if often condescending—praise that women,

Americans with disabilities are among the successors to the 1960s civil rights activists. Students at Gallaudet University, the nation's only university exclusively for the deaf, made national news when they opposed the appointment of a president who was not deaf. The students won their fight: The president-elect stepped down, and a deaf president took office in October 1988.

older people, children, and people with disabilities receive. Few positive stereotypes are commonly associated with homosexuality—contrast the feminine virtues attributed to women, the wisdom of the old, the innocence of children, and the courage of people with disabilities—that can counter the impact of the negative stereotyping that gays and lesbians face.

Homophobia—fear and hatred of homosexuals—has many causes; some are very powerful. Some religions, for instance, condemn homosexuality. Such attitudes will probably continue to be characteristic of a large segment of the American public for years to come (see "The People Speak: Discrimination Against Homosexuals").

Even by conservative estimates, several million Americans are homosexual. Whatever their number, they are members of every social stratum and ethnic group. AIDS has had a devastating effect on many groups, including male homosexuals. For some segments of the population, the disease has provided a convenient excuse for the kind of suspicion and outright bigotry that gay people have often encountered. Not only is homosexual activity illegal in some states, but homosexuals often face discrimination in hiring, education, access to public accommodations, and housing.

The People Speak

Discrimination Against Homosexuals

Do you think homosexuals should or should not be hired for each of the following occupations?

	% SAYING "YES"	
	1992	1996
Salesperson	82%	90%
Armed forces	57%	65%
Doctors	53%	69%
High school teachers	47%	60%
Clergy	43%	60%
Elementary school teachers	41%	55%

Homosexuals face opposition to entering many common occupations from a substantial percentage of the American public, but this opposition seems to be decreasing.

SOURCE: Gallup Poll, November 1996

A notorious incident in a New York City bar in 1969 stimulated the growth of the gay rights movement. The Stonewall bar, frequented by gay men, was raided by the police. Violence, arrests, and injury to persons and property resulted. Both gay men and lesbians organized throughout the 1970s and 1980s in an effort to protect their civil rights. During this time, they learned political skills and formed powerful interest groups.

Despite setbacks, including *Bowers v. Hardwick* (1986), which allowed states to ban homosexual relations; rulings permitting the armed forces to exclude homosexuals; and the efforts of some states to prohibit homosexuals from receiving protection against discrimination, gay activists have won important victories. Seven states, including California, and more than a hundred communities have passed laws protecting homosexuals against some forms of discrimination. The state of Hawaii recognizes gay marriages. Most colleges and universities now have gay rights organizations on campus. In 1996, in *Romer v. Evans*, the Supreme Court voided a state constitutional amendment approved by the voters of Colorado that denied homosexuals protection against discrimination. The Court found that the Colorado amendment violated the U.S. Constitution's guarantee of equal protection of the law.

In the summer of 1993, after months of negotiation with the Pentagon and an avalanche of criticism, President Clinton announced a new policy that barred the Pentagon from asking military recruits or service personnel to disclose their sexual orientation. Popularly known as the "don't ask, don't tell" policy, it also reaffirmed the Defense Department's strict prohibition against homosexual conduct. Service members who declare their homosexuality face discharge unless they can prove they will remain celibate, and they are barred from even disclosing to a friend in private conversation that they are gay or bisexual. The new policy also requires commanders to have "credible information" that the policy is being violated before launching an investigation. As you might expect, the policy is currently facing many challenges in the courts.

AFFIRMATIVE ACTION

The public policy paths for women and minorities have not been identical. However, they have converged in the debate about affirmative action to overcome the effects of past discrimination. Some people argue that groups that have suffered invidious discrimination require special efforts to provide them access to education and jobs. **Affirmative action** involves efforts to bring about increased employment, promotion, or admission for members of such groups. The goal is to move beyond *equal opportunity* (in which everyone has the same chance of obtaining good jobs, for example) toward *equal results* (in which different groups have the same percentage of success in obtaining those jobs). This goal might be accomplished through special rules in the public and private sectors that recruit or otherwise give preferential treatment to previously disadvantaged groups. Numerical quotas that ensure that a portion of government contracts, law school admissions, or police department promotions go to minorities and women are the strongest and most controversial form of affirmative action.

The constitutional status of affirmative action has not, however, been clear. New state and federal laws have provided for discrimination *in favor* of these previously disadvantaged groups. Some state governments adopted affirmative action programs to increase minority enrollment, job holding, or promotion. Eventually, the federal government mandated that all state and local governments, as well as each institution receiving aid from or contracting with the federal government, adopt an affirmative action program.

One such program was introduced at the University of California at Davis. Eager to produce more minority physicians for California, the medical school set aside 16 of a total 100 places in the entering class for "disadvantaged groups." One white applicant who did not make the freshman class was Allan Bakke. After receiving his rejection letter from Davis for two straight years, Bakke learned that the mean scores on the Medical College Admissions Test of students admitted under this program were the 46th percentile on verbal tests and the 35th on science tests. Bakke's scores on the same tests were at the 96th and 97th percentiles, respectively. He decided to sue UC-Davis, claiming that it had denied him equal protection of the laws by discriminating against him because of his race.

The result was an important Supreme Court decision in Bakke's favor, ***Regents of the University of California v. Bakke*** (1978).[16] The Court ordered Bakke admitted, holding that the UC-Davis Special Admissions Program did discriminate against him because of his race. Yet the Court refused to order UC-Davis never to use race as a criterion for admission. A university could, said the Court, adopt an "admissions program where race or ethnic background is simply one element—to be weighed fairly against other elements—in the selection process." It could *not*, as UC-Davis Special Admissions Program did, set aside a quota of spots for particular groups.

Although Bakke ended up in medical school, Brian Weber did not get into an apprenticeship program he wanted to enter in Louisiana. In *United Steelworkers of America, AFL-CIO v. Weber* (1979), the Court found that the Kaiser Aluminum Company's special training program, which employed a quota for minorities, was intended to rectify years of past employment discrimination at Kaiser. Thus, said the Court, a voluntary union-and-management-sponsored program to take more African Americans than whites did *not* discriminate against Weber.

Until 1995, the Court was more deferential to Congress than to local government in upholding affirmative action programs. In 1989, in *Richmond v. J.A. Croson Co.*, the Court found a Richmond, Virginia, plan that reserved 30 percent of city subcontracts for minority firms to be unconstitutional. In 1980, on the other hand, the Court upheld a federal rule setting aside 10 percent of all federal construction contracts for minority-owned firms (*Fullilove v. Klutznick*). In 1990, in *Metro Broadcasting Inc. v. Federal Communications Commission*, the Court agreed that Congress may require preferential treatment for minorities to increase their ownership of broadcast licenses. This event marked the first time the Supreme Court upheld a specific affirmative action program that was not devised to remedy past discrimination.

Things changed in 1995, however. In ***Adarand Constructors v. Pena***, the court overturned the decision in *Metro Broadcasting* and cast grave doubt on its holding in *Fullilove*. It held that federal programs that classify people by race, even for an ostensibly benign purpose such as expanding opportunities for members of minorities, should be presumed to be unconstitutional. Such programs must be subject to the most searching judicial inquiry and can survive only if they are "narrowly tailored" to accomplish a "compelling governmental interest." In other words, the Court applied criteria for evaluating affirmative action programs similar to those it applies to other racial classifications, the less benign suspect classifications we discussed earlier in the chapter. These are also the same criteria the Court has applied to state affirmative action programs since 1989. Although *Adarand Constructors v. Pena* did not void federal affirmative action programs in general, it certainly limits their potential impact.

On other matters, the Court has also approved preferential treatment of minorities in promotions (*Local Number 93 v. Cleveland*, 1986, and *United States v. Paradise*, 1987); and it has ordered quotas for minority union memberships (*Local 28 of the Sheet Metal Workers v. EEOC*, 1986). We examine a case of a public employer using affirmative action promotions to counter underrepresentation of women and minorities in the workplace in "You Are the Judge: The Case of the Santa Clara Dispatcher."

THE CASE OF THE SANTA CLARA DISPATCHER

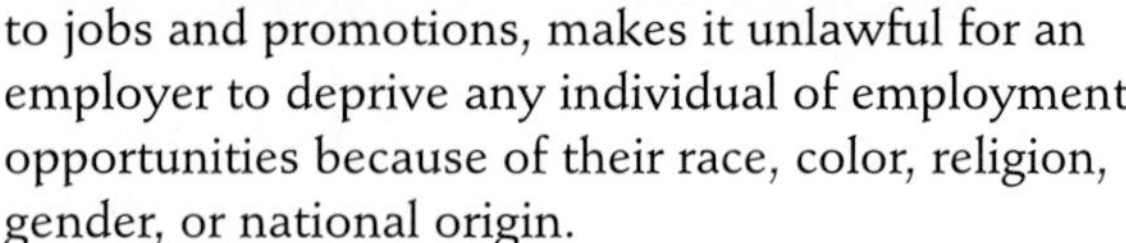

For four years Diane Joyce patched asphalt with a Santa Clara county road crew around San Jose, California, and its suburbs. She applied for a promotion, hoping to work in the less strenuous and better-paid position of dispatcher. Another applicant for the job was Paul Johnson, a white male who had worked for the agency for 13 years.

Like Diane, Paul did well on the exam given to all applicants; in fact, the two scored among the top six applicants, Diane with a score of 73, and Paul with 75. Knowing that Paul's score was a shade better and his work experience longer, the supervisor decided to hire him. The county's affirmative action officers overruled the supervisor, however, and Diane got the job. Paul decided to get a lawyer.

Paul's lawyer argued that Diane's promotion violated Title VII of the Civil Rights Act of 1964. This law, originally passed to guarantee minorities access to jobs and promotions, makes it unlawful for an employer to deprive any individual of employment opportunities because of their race, color, religion, gender, or national origin.

You be the judge: Should Diane Joyce have been promoted?

Answer:

In *Johnson v. Transportation Agency, Santa Clara County* (1987), the Supreme Court held that public employers may use carefully constructed affirmative action promotion plans, designed to remedy specific past discriminations, to counter women's and minorities' underrepresentation in the workplace. Thus, Diane Joyce kept her job. In a stinging dissent, Justice Scalia complained that the Court was "converting [the law] from a guarantee that race or sex will not be a basis for employment determinations, to a guarantee that it often will."

On the other hand, the Court has ruled that affirmative action does not exempt recently hired minorities from traditional work rules specifying the "last hired, first fired" order of layoffs (*Firefighters v. Stotts*, 1984). In 1986, the Court found unconstitutional an effort to give preference to African-American teachers in layoffs, because this policy punished innocent white teachers and the African-American teachers had not been the actual victims of past discrimination (*Wygant v. Jackson Board of Education*).

Not everyone agrees that affirmative action is a wise or fair policy. There is little support from the general public for programs such as those that set aside jobs or employ quotas for members of minority groups (see "The People Speak: Affirmative Action"). Opposition is especially strong when people view affirmative action as *reverse discrimination*—as in the case of individuals like Allan Bakke who are themselves blameless—and less qualified individuals are hired or admitted to educational or training programs.

Critics of reverse discrimination argue that any race or gender discrimination is wrong, even when its purpose is to rectify past injustices rather than to reinforce them. After all, Bakke and Johnson could no more help being white and male than Diane Joyce could help being a woman. Opponents of affirmative action believe that merit is the only fair basis for distributing benefits. Bakke and Johnson found that the rules by which institutions operated had suddenly changed—and they suffered as a result. It is easy to sympathize with them.

In 1996, California voters passed Proposition 209, which banned state affirmative action programs based on race, ethnicity, or gender in public hiring, contracting, and educational admissions. Opponents immediately filed a lawsuit in federal court to block enforcement of the law, claiming that it violated the Fourteenth Amendment. Ultimately, the U.S. Supreme Court will have to resolve the issue, but there is little question that support for Proposition 209 represents a widespread skepticism about affirmative action programs.

On the other hand, the case for affirmative action and reverse discrimination is also persuasive. Proponents of these policies argue that what constitutes merit is highly subjective and can embody prejudices of which the decision maker may be quite unaware. Experts suggest that a man can "look more like" a road dispatcher and thus get a higher rating from interviewers than a woman might. Affirmative action supporters believe that increasing the number of women and minorities in desirable jobs is such an

The People Speak

Affirmative Action

Do you favor or oppose . . . ?

	FAVOR	OPPOSE
Hiring a minority applicant who is *less* qualified than a white applicant, when filling a job in a business that has few minority workers?	12%	85%
Making a certain number of scholarships at public colleges and universities available only to minorities and women?	31	67
Establishing quotas requiring businesses to hire a certain number of minorities and women?	34	64
Establishing quotas requiring schools to admit a certain number of minorities and women as students?	38	58
Requiring a certain percentage of government contracts to be awarded to businesses owned by minorities and women?	48	48
Favoring a well-qualified minority applicant over an *equally* qualified white applicant, when filling a job in a business that has few minority workers?	50	42
Making special efforts at companies to find qualified minorities and women and encouraging them to apply for jobs with that company?	74	24
Providing job training programs for minorities and women to make them qualified for better jobs?	82	17

Although Americans in general support nondiscrimination in employment and education, most Americans oppose "reverse discrimination" programs and quotas that give advantages to women and minorities.

SOURCE: Gallup Poll, March 1995.

important social goal that it should be considered when determining an individual's qualifications. They claim that what white males lose from affirmative action programs are privileges to which they were never entitled in the first place; after all, nobody has the right to be a doctor or a road dispatcher.

UNDERSTANDING CIVIL RIGHTS AND PUBLIC POLICY

The original Constitution is silent on the issue of equality. The only direct reference is in the Fourteenth Amendment, which forbids the states to deny "equal protection of the laws." Those five words have been the basis for major civil rights statutes and scores of judicial rulings protecting the rights of minorities and women. These laws and decisions, granting people new rights, have empowered groups to seek and gain still more victories. The implications of their success for democracy and the scope of government are substantial.

CIVIL RIGHTS AND DEMOCRACY

Equality is a basic principle of democracy. Every citizen has one vote, because democratic government presumes that each person's needs, interests, and preferences are neither any more nor any less important than the needs, interests, and preferences of every other person. Individual liberty is an equally important democratic principle, one that can conflict with equality. Equality and individual liberty often cause democracy to be in conflict with itself.

Equality tends to favor majority rule. Because under simple majority rule everyone's wishes rank equally, the policy outcome that most people prefer seems to be the fairest choice in cases of conflict. What happens, however, if the majority wants to deprive the minority of certain rights? In situations like these, equality threatens individual liberty. Thus, the principle of equality can invite the denial of minority rights, whereas the principle of liberty condemns such action.[17]

Majority rule is not the only threat to liberty. Politically and socially powerful minorities have suppressed majorities as well as other minorities. Women have long outnumbered men in America, about 53 percent to 47 percent. In the era of segregation, African Americans outnumbered whites in many southern states. Inequality persisted, however, because customs that reinforced it were entrenched within the society and because inequality often served the interests of the dominant groups. When slavery and segregation existed in an agrarian economy, whites could get cheap agricultural labor. When men were breadwinners and women were homemakers, married men had a source of cheap domestic labor.

Both African Americans and women made many gains even when they lacked one essential component of democratic power: the vote. They used other rights—such as their First Amendment freedoms—to fight for equality. When Congress protected the right of African Americans to vote in the 1960s, the nature of Southern politics was changed dramatically. The democratic process is a powerful vehicle for disadvantaged groups to press their claims.

CIVIL RIGHTS AND THE SCOPE OF GOVERNMENT

Civil rights laws increase the scope and power of government. These laws tell individuals and institutions that there are things they must do and things they cannot do. Restaurant owners must serve all patrons regardless of race. Professional schools must admit women. Employers must accommodate people with disabilities and make an effort to find minority workers, whether they want to or not. Libertarians and those conservatives who want to reduce the size of government are uneasy with these laws, if not downright hostile to them.

The founders might be greatly perturbed if they knew about all the civil rights laws the government has enacted; these policies do not conform to the eighteenth-century idea of limited government. But the founders would expect the national government to do whatever is necessary to hold the nation together. The Civil War showed that the original Constitution did not adequately deal with issues like slavery that could destroy the society the Constitution's writers had struggled to make secure.

In addition, civil rights, like civil liberties, is an area in which increased government activity in protecting basic rights can lead to greater checks on government by those who benefit from such protections. Remember that much of segregation was *de jure*, established by governments. Moreover, government action in the area of civil rights can be viewed as the protection of individualism. Basic to the notion of civil rights is that individuals are not to be judged according to characteristics they share with a group. Thus, civil rights protect the individual against collective discrimination.

The question of where to draw the line in the government's efforts to protect civil rights has received different answers at different points in American history, but few Americans want to turn back the clock to the days of *Plessy v. Ferguson* and Jim Crow laws or the exclusion of women from the workplace.

SUMMARY

Racial minorities have struggled for equality since the very beginning of the Republic. In the era of slavery, the Supreme Court upheld the practice and denied slaves any rights. After the Civil War and Reconstruction ended, legal segregation was established. For a time, the Supreme Court sanctioned the Jim Crow laws, but in 1954, the *Brown v. Board of Education* case held that *de jure* racial segregation violated equal protection of the laws, which was guaranteed by the Fourteenth Amendment. This event marked the beginning of the era of civil rights. *Brown* inaugurated a movement that succeeded in ending virtually every form of legal discrimination against minorities.

Although feminists have not ignored the courts, the struggle for women's equality has emphasized legislation over litigation. Women won the right to vote in 1920, but the Equal Rights Amendment has not yet been ratified. This defeat did not kill the feminist movement, however. Comparable worth, women's role in the military, sexual harassment, and the balance between work and family are among the many controversial women's issues that are still being debated.

The interests of women and minorities have converged on the issue of affirmative action—that is, policies requiring special efforts on behalf of disadvantaged groups. In the *Bakke* case and in decisions like *Johnson v. Santa Clara,* the Court ruled that affirmative action plans were both legal and constitutional. However, there is substantial opposition to what many see as reverse discrimination.

The civil rights umbrella is a large one. Increasing numbers of groups seek protection for their rights. Older and younger Americans, people with disabilities, and homosexuals have used the laws to ensure their equality. People with AIDS and other chronically ill people may mount battles yet to be fought in the political arena. It is difficult to predict what controversies the twenty-first century will bring, when minority groups will outnumber the current majority.

KEY TERMS

civil rights
Fourteenth Amendment
equal protection of the laws
Thirteenth Amendment
civil rights movement
Civil Rights Act of 1964
Nineteenth Amendment
Equal Rights Amendment
comparable worth
suffrage
Fifteenth Amendment
poll taxes
white primary
Twenty-fourth Amendment
Voting Rights Act of 1965
Americans with Disabilities Act of 1990
affirmative action

KEY CASES

***Dred Scott v. Sandford* (1857)**
***Plessy v. Ferguson* (1896)**
***Brown v. Board of Education* (1954)**
***Korematsu v. United States* (1944)**
***Reed v. Reed* (1971)**
***Craig v. Boren* (1976)**
***Regents of the University of California v. Bakke* (1978)**
***Adarand Constructors v. Pena* (1995)**

FOR FURTHER READING

Baer, Judith A. *Women in the Law: The Struggle Toward Equality from the New Deal to the Present,* 2nd ed. New York: Holmes and Meier, 1996. An excellent analysis of women's changing legal status.

Berger, Raoul. *Government by Judiciary: The Transformation of the Fourteenth Amendment.* Cambridge, MA: Harvard University Press, 1977. Berger is not one who favors use of the Fourteenth Amendment to expand equality.

Berry, Mary F. *Why ERA Failed.* Bloomington: Indiana University Press, 1986. An excellent account of public policies affecting women, with particular attention to the demise of the Equal Rights Amendment.

Brown, Dee. *Bury My Heart at Wounded Knee: An Indian History of the American West.* New York: Holt, Rinehart and Winston, 1970. History from an American Indian perspective.

Bullock, Charles S., III, and Charles M. Lamb. *Implementation of Civil Rights Policy.* Monterey, CA: Brooks/Cole, 1984. Focuses on the difficulty of turning the goals of civil rights policies into reality.

Greenberg, Jack. *Crusader in the Courts.* New York: Basic Books, 1994. The story of litigation in the civil rights era as told by one of the chief participants.

Kluger, Richard. *Simple Justice.* New York: Knopf, 1976. The story of the Brown case.

Mansbridge, Jane. *Why We Lost the ERA.* Chicago: University of Chicago Press, 1986. The politics of women's rights.

McGlen, Nancy, and Karen O'Connor. *Women's Rights: The Struggle for Equality in the Nineteenth and Twentieth Centuries.* New York: Praeger, 1983. A good account of the struggle for equal rights for women.

Verba, Sidney, and Gary R. Orren. *Equality in America: The View from the Top.* Cambridge, MA: Harvard University Press, 1985. An examination of the views of the American elite on equality.

Wilkinson, J. Harvie, III. *From Brown to Bakke.* New York: Oxford University Press, 1979. The political and legal history of civil rights policies between Brown and Bakke.

Woodward, C. Vann. *The Strange Career of Jim Crow,* 2nd ed. New York: Oxford University Press, 1966. Examines the evolution of Jim Crow laws in the South.

INTERNET RESOURCES

http://www.law.cornell.edu/topics/topic2.html#equal_protection
The text of the landmark cases on equal protection and background material.

http://www.law.cornell.edu/topics/topic2.html#civil_rights
The text of the landmark cases on civil rights and background.

http://www.usdoj.gov/crt/

Home page of the Civil Rights Division of the U.S. Department of Justice containing background information and discussion of current events.

http://www.usdoj.crt/ada/adahom1.htm

Home page of the Americans with Disabilities Act in the U.S. Department of Justice containing background information and discussion of current events.

http://www.naacp.org/

Home page of the NAACP containing background information and discussion of current events.

NOTES

1. Bland is quoted in Sidney Verba and Gary R. Orren, *Equality In America: The View from the Top* (Cambridge, MA: Harvard University Press, 1985), 25; The Adams' quotes are from Judith A. Baer, *Equality Under the Constitution: Reclaiming The Fourteenth Amendment* (Ithaca, NY: Cornell University Press, 1983), 44-47.
2. For opposing interpretations of the Fourteenth Amendment, see Baer, *Equality Under The Constitution*, and Raoul Berger, *Government By Judiciary: The Transformation of the Fourteenth Amendment* (Cambridge, MA: Harvard University Press, 1977).
3. D. Garth Taylor, Paul B. Sheatsley, and Andrew M. Greeley, "Attitudes Toward Racial Integration," *Scientific American* 238 (June 1978): 42-49; Richard G. Niemi, John Mueller, and John W. Smith, *Trends in Public Opinion* (Westport, CT: Greenwood Press, 1989), 180.
4. There are a few exceptions. Religious institutions such as schools may use religious standards in employment. Gender, age, and disabilities may be considered in the few cases where such occupational qualifications are absolutely essential to the normal operations of a business or enterprise, as in the case of a men's room attendant.
5. On the implementation of the Voting Rights Act, see Richard Scher and James Button, "Voting Rights Act: Implementation and Impact," in *Implementation Of Civil Rights Policy*, ed. Charles Bullock III and Charles Lamb (Monterey, CA: Brooks/Cole, 1984); Abigail M. Thernstrom, *Whose Votes Count?* (Cambridge, MA: Harvard University Press, 1987); and Chandler Davidson and Bernard Groffman, eds., *Quiet Revolution in the South: The Impact of the Voting Rights Act, 1965-1990* (Princeton, NJ: Princeton University Press, 1994).
6. U.S. Department of Commerce, *Statistical Abstract of the United States, 1996* (Washington, DC: U.S. Government Printing Office, 1996), 284.
7. See Dee Brown, *Bury My Heart at Wounded Knee: An Indian History of the American West* (New York: Holt, Rinehart and Winston, 1970).
8. *Statistical Abstract of the United States, 1996,* 284.
9. See Eleanor Flexner, *Century of Struggle* (New York: Atheneum, 1971).
10. See J. Stanley Lemons, *The Woman Citizen: Social Feminism in the 1920s* (Urbana: University of Illinois Press, 1973).
11. *Statistical Abstract of the United States, 1996,* 58, 393, 399-400.
12. *Roberts v. United States Jaycees,* 1984; *Board of Directors of Rotary International v. Rotary Club of Duarte,* 1987; and *New York State Club Association v. New York,* 1988.
13. *Statistical Abstract of the United States, 1996,* 471.
14. *Meritor Savings Bank v. Vinson.*
15. Walter Polovchak with Kevin Klose, *Freedom's Child* (New York: Random House, 1988).
16. On the affirmative action issues raised by Bakke and other cases, see Allan P. Sindler, *Bakke, De Funis and Minority Admissions* (New York: Longman, 1978).
17. See Barbara S. Gamble, "Putting Civil Rights to a Popular Vote," *American Journal of Political Science* 41 (January 1997): 245-269.

PART TWO

People and Politics

The voice of the people is but an echo. The output of an echo chamber bears an inevitable and invariable relation to the input. As candidates and parties clamor for attention and vie for popular support, the people's verdict can be no more than a selective reflection from among the alternatives and outlooks presented to them.

— *V. O. KEY, POLITICAL SCIENTIST*

Public Opinion and Political Action

In August of 1996, Bob Dole made his big move in pursuit of the presidency, announcing a plan to cut taxes 15 percent across the board if he were elected. Besides putting money into the pocket of every taxpayer, this proposal tapped straight into the fundamental issue of the scope of government. Dole's plan was based on the premise that government was doing too much and that it was time for the government to tighten its belt and pass some of the savings back to the people. No issue could be more fundamental in a democracy, he figured, and if anything could get his stalled campaign moving, this would be it. However, Dole first faced the problem of getting the public to take notice of his plan.

A poll for the PEW Research Center that month asked citizens how much attention they had paid to recent major stories in the news. Only 22 percent said they had paid a great deal of attention to Dole's plan to cut taxes. By comparison, 57 percent reported paying a great deal of attention to the explosion at the Atlanta Olympics, which had occurred the week before.

Public opinion polling has become a major growth industry in recent years. Each of the national evening news broadcasts and almost every major newspaper now commission their own regular polls. Polls are great investments for the media because they provide a timely story that can be billed as exclusive. If there is nothing new in their findings, journalists can always fall back on one sure pattern: the lack of public attention to politics. Whether it's Bob Dole's tax-cut plan, Bill Clinton's signing of major welfare reform legislation, or the Republicans' 1994 "Contract with America," the safest expectation that a public opinion analyst can make is that many people will be unaware of the policy issue.

In a democracy, the people are expected to guide public policy. But do people pay enough attention to public affairs to fulfill their duty as citizens? As we shall see in this chapter, there is much reason to be concerned about the level of public information about politics. This is particularly the case for complex issues that involve the scope of government.

It is common for politicians and columnists to intone the words "the American people..." and then claim their view as that of the citizenry. Yet it would be hard to find a statement about the American people—who they are and what they believe—that is either 100 percent right or 100 percent wrong. The American people are wondrously diverse. There are about 270 million Americans, forming a mosaic of racial, ethnic, and cultural groups. America was founded on the principle of tolerating diversity and individualism, and it remains one of the most diverse countries in the world today. Most Americans view this diversity as one of the most appealing aspects of their society.

Such diversity makes the study of American public opinion especially complex; there are many groups with a great variety of opinions. This is not to say that public opinion would be easy to study even if America were a more homogeneous society; as you will see, the measurement of public opinion involves painstaking interview procedures and careful wording of questions. Further complicating the task is the fact that people are often not well informed about the issues. The least informed are also the least likely to participate in the political process, a phenomenon that creates imbalances in who takes part in political action.

For American government to work efficiently and effectively, the diversity of the American public and its opinions must be faithfully channeled through the political process. This chapter reveals just how difficult a task this is.

THE AMERICAN PEOPLE

One way of looking at the American public is through **demography**—the science of human populations. The most valuable tool for understanding demographic changes in America is the **census**. The U.S. Constitution requires that the government conduct an "actual enumeration" of the population every 10 years.

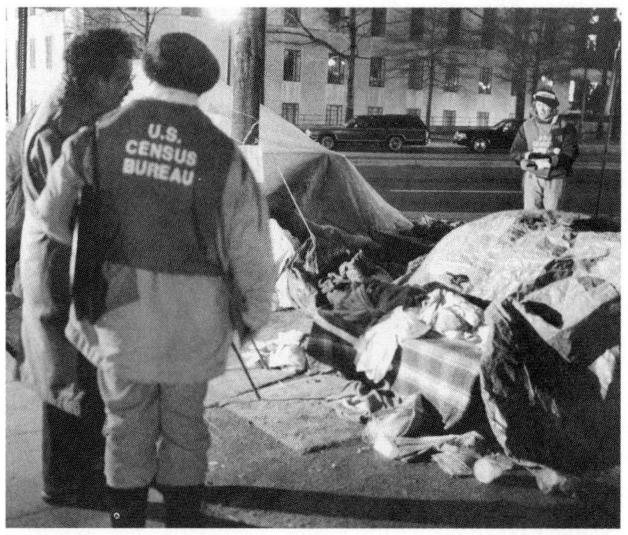

When the Census Bureau was criticized for failing to take into account the hundreds of thousands of Americans who are without homes, it responded in 1990 by sending out employees to attempt to count the homeless in major cities. Here, census takers are shown counting people sleeping in the park just across the street from the White House.

The first such census was conducted in 1790; the most recent was in 1990. Getting a question included on the census form is a highly competitive enterprise, as groups of all different kinds seek to be counted.[1] Once a group can establish its numbers, it can then ask for federal aid in proportion to its size. In 1990, advocates for the disabled won out when the census added a question designed to count people who have difficulty taking care of themselves or getting where they need to go. The census also responded to complaints that the homeless were being left out of the count by sending out in one night 15,000 workers to count them—the final tally came to 228,621.

The next few sections will examine the ways in which the American culture and political system are changing as a result of population changes.

THE IMMIGRANT SOCIETY

The United States has always been a nation of immigrants. As John F. Kennedy said, America is "not merely a nation but a nation of nations." All Americans except Native Americans are either descended from immigrants or are immigrants themselves. Today, federal law allows up to 630,000 new immigrants to be legally admitted to the country every year. This is equivalent to adding a city with the population of Washington, DC, every year. And in recent years, the illegal immigrants have outnumbered the legal immigrants. There have been three great waves of immigration to the United States.

- Before the Civil War, northwestern Europeans (English, Irish, Germans, and Scandinavians) constituted the first wave of immigration.
- After the Civil War, southern and eastern Europeans (Italians, Jews, Poles, Russians, and others) made up the second wave. This immigration reached its high point in the first decade of the twentieth century, with almost all of these immigrants passing through Ellis Island in New York (now a popular museum) as their first stop in the new world.
- In recent decades, a third wave of immigrants has consisted of Hispanics (from Cuba, Puerto Rico, Central America, and Mexico) and Asians (from Vietnam, Korea, the Philippines, and elsewhere). The 1980s saw the second largest number of immigrants of any decade in American history.

Immigrants bring with them their aspirations, as well as their own political beliefs.

Cubans in Miami, who nearly constitute a majority of the city's population, first came to America to escape Castro's Marxist regime and have brought their anti-Communist sentiments with them. Similarly, the Vietnamese came to America after the United States failed to prevent a Communist takeover there. Cubans and Vietnamese are just two recent examples of the many types of immigrants who have come to America over the years to flee an oppressive government. Other examples from previous periods of heavy immigration include the Irish in the first wave and the Russians in the second. Throughout American history, such groups have fostered a great appreciation for individualism in American public policy by their wish to be free of governmental control.

THE AMERICAN MELTING POT

With its long history of immigration, the United States has often been called a **melting pot**. This

In the early twentieth century, millions of European immigrants caught their first glimpse of their new country when they spotted the Statue of Liberty in New York's harbor. They first stepped onto American soil at Ellis Island, which is now a museum dedicated to telling the story of immigration to the United States.

phrase refers to a mixture of cultures, ideas, and peoples. As the third wave of immigration continues, policymakers have begun to speak of a new **minority majority,** by which they mean that America will eventually cease to have a white, generally Anglo-Saxon majority. The 1990 census data found an all-time low in the percentage of non-Hispanic white Americans—just over 75 percent of the population. African Americans made up 12 percent of the population, Hispanics 9 percent, Asians 3 percent, and Native Americans slightly less than 1 percent. Between 1980 and 1990, minority populations grew at a much faster rate than the white population. As you can see in "In the Twenty-first Century: The Coming Minority Majority," the Census Bureau estimates that by the middle of the next century, whites will represent only 52 percent of the population.

Currently, the largest minority group in the country is the African-American population. One in eight Americans is a descendent of reluctant immigrants: Africans who were brought to America by force as slaves. As we saw Chapter 4, a legacy of racism and discrimination has left a higher proportion of the African-American population economically and politically disadvantaged than the white population. About 30 percent of African Americans currently live under the poverty line, compared to about 10 percent of whites.

THE COMING MINORITY MAJORITY

In the 21st Century

On the basis of current birth rates and immigration rates, the Census Bureau estimates that the demographics of the country should change as shown in the accompanying graph. Extend the lines a bit beyond the year 2050, and it is clear that the minority groups will be in the majority nationwide.

Of course, should rates of birth and immigration change, so will these estimates. But already there are 65 congressional districts with a minority majority, about 85 percent of which are represented in the House by an African American, a Hispanic, or an Asian American. These numbers are bound to increase as we move into the twenty-first century.

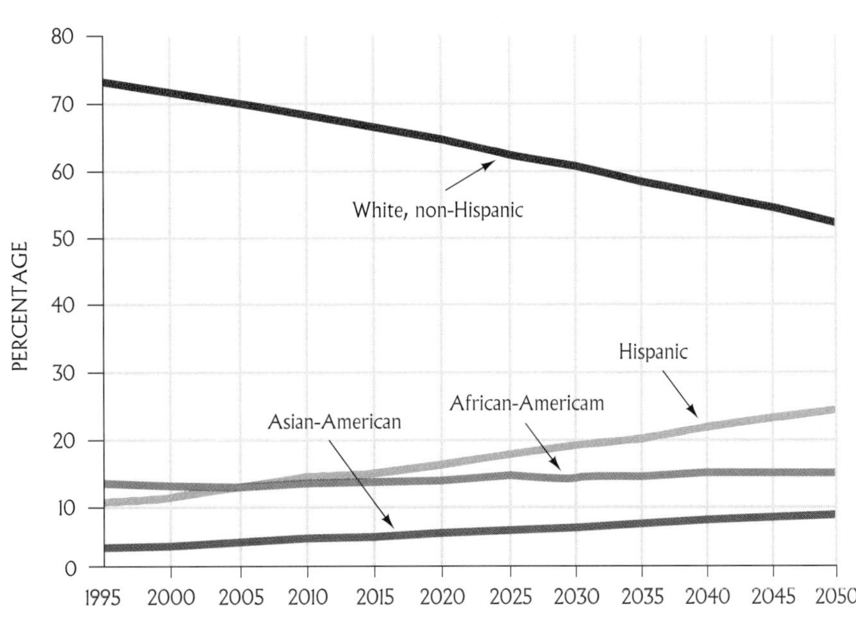

Despite this economic disadvantage, African Americans have recently been exercising a good deal of political power. African Americans have been elected as mayors of many of the country's biggest cities, including Los Angeles, New York, and Chicago. In 1989, Douglas Wilder of Virginia became the nation's first elected African-American governor, and in 1992, Carol Moseley-Braun of Illinois became the first African-American woman to be elected to the U.S. Senate. All told, the number of African-American elected officials increased from 1,469 in 1970 to 7,552 in 1992.[2]

The familiar problems of African Americans sometimes obscure the problems of other minority groups, such as Hispanics (composed largely of Mexicans, Cubans, and Puerto Ricans). If current immigration rates and birthrates persist, sometime early in the twenty-first century, the Hispanic population should outnumber the African-American population. Like African Americans, Hispanics are concentrated in cities. Hispanics are rapidly gaining power in the Southwest, and cities such as San Antonio and Denver have elected mayors of Hispanic heritage. As of 1995, the state legislatures of New Mexico, Texas, Arizona, Colorado, Florida, California, and Connecticut all had at least 5 percent Hispanic representation.

An issue of particular concern to the Hispanic community is what to do about the problem of illegal immigration. The **Simpson-Mazzoli Act,** named after its congressional sponsors, requires that employers document the citizenship of their employees. Whether people are born in Canton, Ohio, or Canton, China, they must prove that they are either citizens or legal immigrants in order to work. Civil and criminal penalties can be assessed against employers who knowingly employ undocumented immigrants. This law has raised concern among leaders of immigrant groups, who worry that employers may simply decline to hire members of such groups rather than take any chances. There has been little evidence of this so far, however. In fact, many believe that the provisions of the Simpson-Mazzoli Act have proved to be inadequate in stopping illegal immigration from Mexico. In 1994, a federal advisory commission recommended the establishment of a computerized data bank to keep track of all people authorized to work in the United States. (See "You Are the Policymaker: Should There Be a National Registry for Work?")

Just north of San Diego, the problem of illegal immigration from Mexico has taken a dangerous turn. Seeking to make their way around a freeway check-point, immigrants sometimes attempt to cross the busy San Diego freeway. After a number of people had been hit by cars, authorities posted signs like these to warn motorists to look out for people crossing the freeway.

Unlike Hispanics who have come to America to escape poverty, the recent influx of Asians has been driven by a new class of professional workers looking for greater opportunity. As Ronald Takaki documents, Asians who have come to America since the 1965 Immigration Act opened the gate to them make up the most highly skilled immigrant group in American history.[3] Indeed, Asian Americans have often been called the superachievers of the minority majority. This is especially true in the case of educational attainment—37 percent of Asian Americans over the age of 25 hold a college degree, almost twice the national average. As a result, their median family income has already surpassed that of non-Hispanic whites.

Whereas Asian Americans are the best off of America's minority groups, by far the worst off is the one indigenous minority, known today as Native Americans. Before Europeans arrived in America, 12 to 15 million Native Americans lived here. War and disease reduced their numbers to a mere 210,000 by 1910. As of the 1990 census, about 1.8 million Americans listed themselves as being of Native American heritage. Statistics show that they are the least healthy, the poorest, and the least educated group in the American melting pot. Only a handful of Native Americans have found wealth, fewer still power. Some tribes have discovered oil or other minerals on their land and used these resources successfully. Most Native Americans, though, remain economically and politically disadvantaged in American society. The 1990 census found that in the Dakotas, site of the largest Sioux reservations, over half of the Native Americans lived below the poverty line.

Americans live in a multicultural and multilingual society. America is becoming a more diverse nation all the time. Yet despite this diversity, there is much agreement among ethnic groups about what truly makes an American. Minority groups have assimilated many basic American values, such as the principle of treating all equally.

The emergence of the minority majority is just one of several major demographic changes that have

SHOULD THERE BE A NATIONAL REGISTRY FOR WORK?

You Are the Policymaker

A recent federal advisory commission headed by the late civil rights activist Barbara Jordan recommended that the federal government establish a computerized registry of the names and Social Security numbers of all citizens and aliens authorized to work in the United States. The proposed registry would include data provided by the Social Security Administration and the Immigration and Naturalization Service. Employers would be required to consult with the registry to check that the Social Security number provided by an applicant was valid and had been issued to someone who could legally work in this country.

Currently, employers must ask for documents to verify that prospective employees either are citizens or are authorized to work in the United States. But phony documents can be obtained easily in many cities near the U.S.-Mexican border. The commission maintained that with the establishment of a computerized work registry, employers would no longer have to ask for such documents and worry about exercising more caution in hiring Hispanics. All they would need to do is to ask for a Social Security number and call the registry to verify the person's eligibility for work. By requiring the same initial check of all potential employees, the commission argued, such a system would reduce the chances of discrimination. Employers would no longer have any reason to ask whether an applicant was an immigrant or to reject all "foreign-looking" applicants for fear of incurring fines if they accepted forged documents.

Opponents of the proposal, such as the American Civil Liberties Union, immediately criticize a national registry as something that could be greatly misused by people in the government. They noted that the proposal comes close to establishing a national identity card. Such a card is an indispensable tool of a totalitarian state, for before a government can begin to control people's lives it must know who they are and where they are, and it must be able to demand proof of their identity whenever it encounters them—applying for work, moving to another address, walking down the street. Many people are fearful that with a national identification system, those with access to the computers could violate the privacy rights of individual citizens.

Assume the role of policymaker. Do you believe that the possible benefits of a computerized work registry outweigh the possible risks of misuse of the information that would be stored?

altered the face of American politics. In addition, the population has been moving and aging.

THE REGIONAL SHIFT

For most of American history, the most populous states have been concentrated north of the Mason-Dixon line and east of the Mississippi River. As you can see in Figure 6.1, though, over the last 50 years, much of America's population growth has been centered in the West and South. In particular, the populations of Florida, California, and Texas have grown rapidly as people moved to the Sunbelt. From 1980 to 1990, the rate of population growth was 33 percent in Florida, 26 percent in California, and 20 percent in Texas. In contrast, there was virtually no population growth at all in so-called "rust belt" states such as Pennsylvania, Ohio, and Michigan.

Demographic changes are associated with political changes. States gain or lose congressional representation as their population changes, and thus power shifts as well. This **reapportionment** process occurs once a decade, after every census. After each census, the 435 seats in the House of Representatives are reallocated to the states on the basis of population changes. Thus, as California has grown throughout this century, its representation in the House has increased from just 7 in 1900 to 52 today. New York, on the other hand, has lost about one-third of its delegation over the last 50 years. The Census Bureau currently projects that reapportionment in 2000 will result in yet another 3 seats for California and a loss of another 2 seats for New York.

THE GRAYING OF AMERICA

One of the three megastates, Florida, has grown in large part as a result of its attractiveness to senior citizens. Nationwide, the fastest-growing age group in America is composed of citizens over 65. Not only are

FIGURE 6.1

SHIFTING POPULATION

These maps paint a population portrait of the United States over the last five decades. The states are drawn to scale on the basis of population. In 1940, the most populous states were concentrated east of the Mississippi River. New York, Pennsylvania, and Illinois stand out. By 1990 the national population picture—and the map—had changed considerably. Today the country's 270 million citizens are scattered more widely, and though large concentrations of population still dominate the East, there has been huge growth on the West Coast, in Texas, and in Florida.

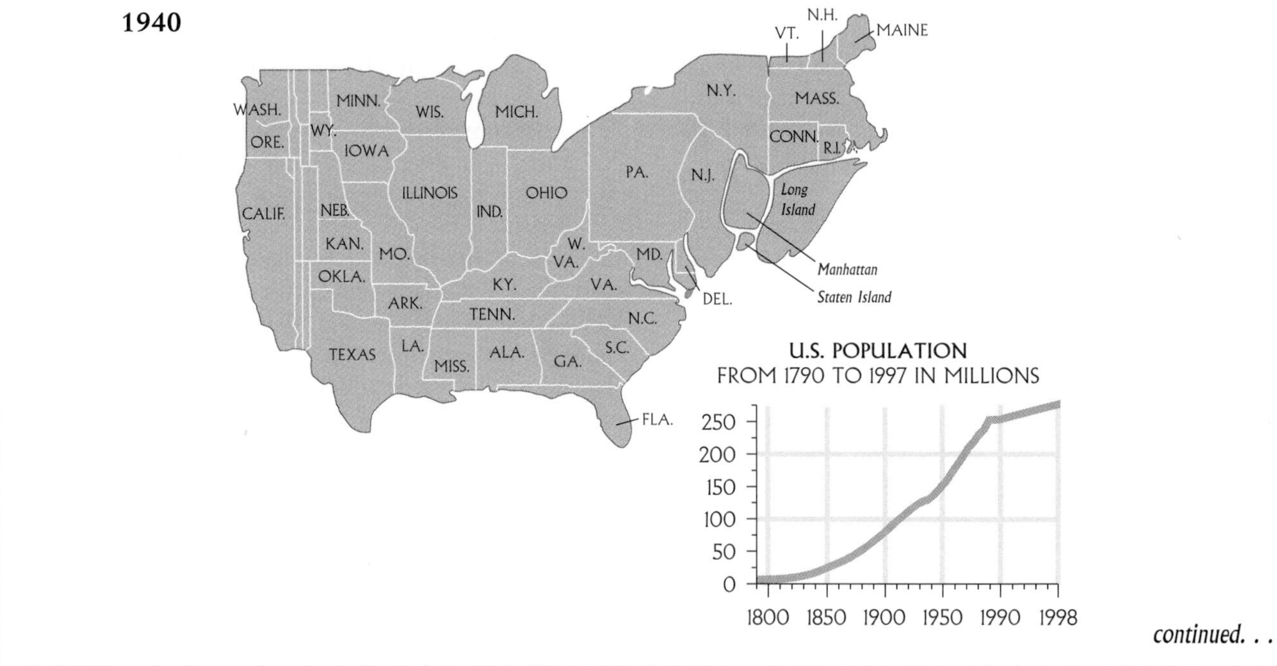

people living longer as a result of medical advances, but the birthrate has dropped substantially. About 60 percent of adult Americans living today grew up in families of four or more children. If the current baby bust continues, this figure will eventually be cut to 30 percent.[4]

By the year 2020, as the post-World War II baby boom generation reaches senior citizen status, there will be just two working Americans for every person over the age of 65. If you think Social Security is being stretched to the limit now, just wait until 2020. The Social Security system, begun under the New Deal, is exceeded only by national defense as America's most costly public policy. The current group of older Americans and those soon to follow can lay claim to roughly $5 trillion guaranteed by Social Security. They also hold title to roughly $1 trillion in public and private pension plans. There is a political message in these numbers: People who have been promised benefits expect to collect them, especially benefits for which they have made monthly contributions. Thus, even Newt Gingrich's budget-cutting policies have so far treated Social Security benefits as sacrosanct.

As the population has aged, new political interests have been mobilized. Once discounted as no longer productive, the aged now claim "gray power."[5] In Florida, the state's senior citizens typically vote against referenda for school taxes, much to the dismay of younger parents. They have managed to secure tax breaks and service benefits for older people from the Florida legislature. Senior citizens have thus discovered an old political dictum: There is strength in numbers. A growing and potent group, the aged have one advantage that no other group has—everyone can anticipate

FIGURE 6.1 SHIFTING POPULATION, *continued. . .*

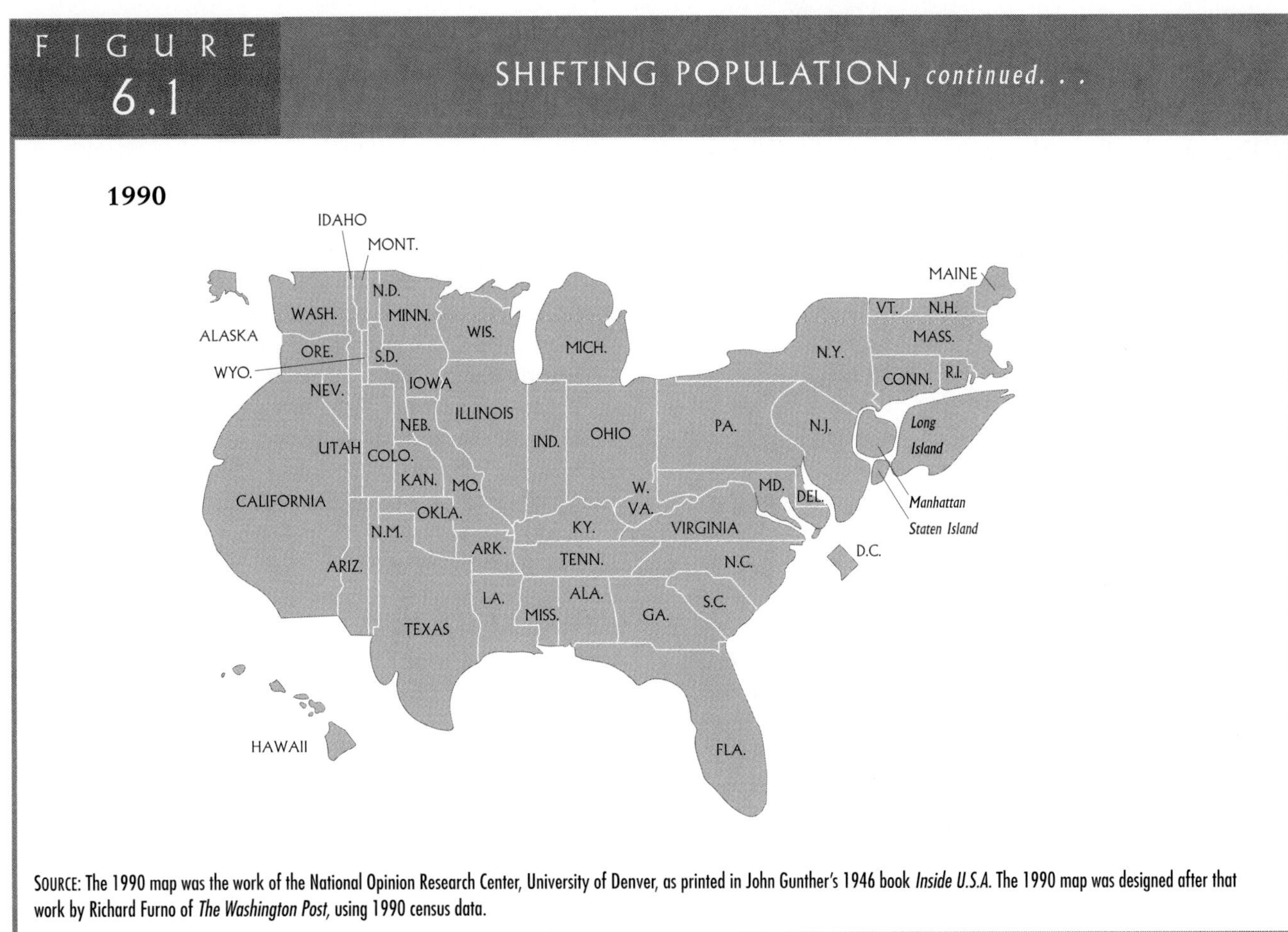

SOURCE: The 1990 map was the work of the National Opinion Research Center, University of Denver, as printed in John Gunther's 1946 book *Inside U.S.A.* The 1990 map was designed after that work by Richard Furno of *The Washington Post,* using 1990 census data.

eventually reaching senior citizen status. The growing demands to care for the elderly will almost certainly become more acute in the decades ahead.

HOW AMERICANS LEARN ABOUT POLITICS: POLITICAL SOCIALIZATION

As the most experienced segment of the population, the elderly have undergone the most political socialization. **Political socialization** is "the process through which an individual acquires his or her particular political orientations—his or her knowledge, feelings, and evaluations regarding his or her political world."[6] As people become more socialized with age, their political orientations grow firmer. It should not be surprising that governments aim their socialization efforts largely at the young, not the old. Authoritarian regimes are particularly concerned with indoctrinating their citizens at an early age. For example, youth groups in the former Soviet Union were organized into the Komsomols, the Young Communist League. Membership in these groups was helpful in gaining admission to college and entering certain occupations. In the Komsomols, Soviet youths were taught their government's view of the advantages of communism (though apparently not well enough to keep the system going). In contrast, socialization is a much more subtle process in the United States.

THE PROCESS OF POLITICAL SOCIALIZATION

Only a small portion of Americans' political learning is formal. Some Americans may take civics or government classes in high school or political science classes in college. In such formal settings, citizens learn some of the nuts and bolts of government—how many senators each state has, what presidents do, and so on. But formal socialization is only the tip of the iceberg. Americans do most of their political learning without teachers or classes.

Informal learning is really much more important than formal, in-class learning about politics. Most informal socialization is almost accidental. Few parents sit down with their children and say, "Johnny, let us tell you why we're Republicans." Words like *pick up, absorb,* and *acquire* perhaps best describe the informal side of socialization.

The agents of socialization are numerous. Among them are the family, the media, and the schools.

The Family. The family's role in socialization is central because of its monopoly on two crucial resources in the early years: time and emotional commitment. The powerful influence of the family is not easily undermined. Most students in an American government class like to think of themselves as independent thinkers, especially when it comes to politics. Yet one can predict how the majority of young people will vote simply by knowing the political leanings of their parents. Table 6.1 shows how well high school seniors and their parents matched up on party affiliation in a classic 1965 study by M. Kent Jennings and Richard Niemi.

As children approach adult status, though, some degree of adolescent rebellion against parents and their beliefs often takes place. Witnessing the outpouring of youthful rebellion in the 1960s, many people thought a generation gap was opening up. Radical youth supposedly condemned their backward-thinking parents. Though such a gap did exist in a few families, the overall evidence for it was slim. When Jennings and Niemi reinterviewed their sample of young adults and their parents 8 years later, in 1973, they still found far more agreement than disagreement across the generational divide. Moving out of the family nest and into adulthood, the offspring did become somewhat less like their parents politically, however.[7] Other socialization agents had apparently exerted influence in the intervening years.

The Mass Media. The mass media are "the new parent" according to many observers. Average grade-school youngsters spend more time each week watching television than they spend at school. And television now displaces parents as the chief source of information as children get older.

Unfortunately, today's generation of young adults is significantly less likely to watch television news than their elders. A recent Times-Mirror study attributed the relative lack of political knowledge of the youth of the 1990s to their media consumption or, more appropriately, to their lack of it.[8] In 1965, Gallup found virtually no difference between age categories in frequency of TV news viewing. By the 1990s, a considerable gap had opened up, though, with older people paying the most attention to the news and young adults the least. If you have ever turned on the TV news and wondered why all the commercials seem to be for Geritol, laxatives, or denture cream, now you know why.

School. Political socialization is as important to a government as it is to an individual. This is one reason why governments (including America's) often use schools to promote loyalty to the country and support for its basic values. In most American schools, the day begins with the Pledge of Allegiance. During the 1988 presidential campaign, George Bush argued

TABLE 6.1 PARENT-CHILD AGREEMENT ON PARTY IDENTIFICATION

In 1965, Jennings and Niemi selected a sample of high school seniors throughout the country and interviewed them as well as one of their parents. Below you will find how closely the two generations matched on party affiliation. The numbers represent the percentage of parent-child pairs that fell into each category. (For example, the 32.6 figure indicates that in 32.6 percent of cases, the parent and child both said they were Democrats.)

CHILDREN	PARENTS		
	DEMOCRAT	INDEPENDENT	REPUBLICAN
Democrat	32.6	7.0	3.4
Independent	13.2	12.7	9.7
Republican	3.6	4.1	13.6
	Agreement = 58.9%	Disagreement = 7.0%	

SOURCE: Adapted from M. Kent Jennings and Richard G. Niemi, *The Political Character of Adolescence* (Princeton, NJ: Princeton University Press, 1973), 39.

that teachers should have to lead students in the Pledge. His opponent, Michael Dukakis, had vetoed a bill to require this in Massachusetts, claiming that it was unconstitutional. Underlying Bush's argument was the assumption that proper socialization in the schools was crucial to the American political system—a position that Dukakis disagreed with more in terms of means than in ends.

Governments throughout the world use schools to attempt to raise children committed to the basic values of the system. For years, American children have been successfully educated about the virtues of capitalism and democracy. In the hands of an unscrupulous government, though, educational socialization can sometimes be a dangerous tool. For example, in Nazi Germany, textbooks were used to justify murderous policies. Consider the following example from a Nazi-era math book:

> If a mental patient costs 4 Reichsmarks a day in maintenance, a cripple 5.50, and a criminal 3.50, and about 50,000 of these people are in our institutions, how much does it cost our state at a daily rate of 4 Reichsmarks—and how many marriage loans of 1,000 Reichsmarks per couple could have been given out instead?[9]

One can only imagine how the constant exposure, in schools, to this kind of thinking warped the minds of some young people growing up in Nazi Germany.

Both authoritarian and democratic governments care that students learn the positive features of their political system, because it helps ensure that youth will grow up to be supportive citizens. David Easton and Jack Dennis have argued that "those children who begin to develop positive feelings toward the political authorities will grow into adults who will be less easily disenchanted with the system than those children who early acquire negative, hostile sentiments."[10] Of course, this is not always the case; well-socialized youths of the 1960s led the opposition to the American regime and the war in Vietnam. It could be argued, however, that even these protesters had been positively shaped by the socialization process, for the goal of most activists was to make the system more democratically responsive rather than to change American government radically.

Today, American educational policy consumes roughly $200 billion a year. Most American schools are public schools, financed by the government; their textbooks are often chosen by the local and state boards, and teachers are certified by the state government. Schooling is perhaps the most obvious intrusion of the government into Americans' socialization. Education exerts a profound influence on a variety of political attitudes and behavior. Better-educated citizens are more likely to vote in elections, they exhibit more knowledge about politics and public policy, and they are more tolerant of opposing (even radical) opinions.

The payoffs of schooling extend beyond better jobs and better pay. Educated citizens also more closely approximate the model of a democratic citizen. A formal civics course may not make much difference, but the whole context of education does. As Albert Einstein once said, "Schools need not preach political doctrine to defend democracy. If they shape men and women capable of critical thought and trained in social attitudes, that is all that is necessary."

POLITICAL LEARNING OVER A LIFETIME

Political learning does not, of course, end when one reaches 18, or even when one graduates from college. Politics is a lifelong activity. Because America is an aging society, it is important to consider the effects of growing older on political learning and behavior.

These children—the faces of the coming minority majority population—suggest the unique problem of American political socialization: transforming people of diverse cultural background and beliefs into participating American citizens.

Aging increases political participation, as well as strength of party attachment. Young adults (those 18 through 25) lack experience with politics, as they do with other things. Because political behavior is to some degree learned behavior, there is some learning yet to do. Political participation rises steadily with age until the infirmities of old age make it harder to participate.[11] Like other attachments, such as religion, party identification grows not so much with "age per se, but rather as a function of the length of time that the individual has felt some generalized preference for a particular party and repetitively voted for it."[12]

Politics, like most other things, is thus a learned behavior. Americans learn to vote, to pick a political party, and to evaluate political events in the world around them. One of the products of all this learning is what is known as public opinion.

WHAT AMERICANS BELIEVE: PUBLIC OPINION AND POLICY

The public holds opinions about many topics. Premarital sex, whether flying saucers exist, the virtues of jogging, and the lengths of women's skirts are all subjects about which people can hold opinions—sometimes strong ones. In the following sections, you will explore a particular kind of **public opinion:** the distribution of the population's beliefs about politics and policy issues. Saying that opinions are distributed among the population implies that there is rarely a single public opinion. If everyone were of one mind about some question, it would not be much of a political issue. Understanding the content and dynamics of public opinion on such issues is important in evaluating the extent to which citizens actually guide policymaking.

MEASURING PUBLIC OPINION

Although public opinion polling is a relatively new science, sophisticated technology is now available for measuring public opinion. Public opinion polling was first developed by a young man named George Gallup, who did some polling for his mother-in-law, a longshot candidate for secretary of state in Iowa in 1932. With the Democratic landslide of that year, Gallup's mother-in-law won a stunning victory, further stimulating his interest in politics. From that little acorn the mighty oak of public opinion polling has grown. The firm that Gallup founded spread throughout the democratic world, and in some languages, *Gallup* is actually the word used for an opinion poll.[13]

It would be prohibitively expensive to ask every citizen his or her opinion on a whole range of issues. Instead, polls rely on a **sample** of the population—a relatively small proportion of people who are chosen as representative of the whole. Herbert Asher draws an analogy to a doctor's blood test to illustrate the principle of sampling.[14] Your doctor does not need to drain a gallon of blood from you to determine whether you have mononucleosis, AIDS, or any other disease. Rather, a small sample of blood will reveal its properties.

In public opinion polling, a sample of about 1,500 to 2,000 people can accurately represent the "universe" of potential voters. The key to the accuracy of opinion polls is the technique of **random sampling,** which operates on the principle that everyone should have an equal probability of being selected. Your chance of being asked to be in the poll should therefore be as good as that of anyone else—rich or poor, African-American or white, young or old, male or female. If the sample is randomly drawn, about 12 percent of those interviewed will be African-American, slightly over 50 percent female, and so forth, matching the population as a whole.

Remember that the science of polling involves estimation; a sample can represent the population with only a certain degree of confidence. The level of confidence is known as the **sampling error,** which depends on the size of the sample. The more people interviewed in a poll, the more confident one can be of the results. A typical poll of about 1,500 to 2,000 respondents has a sampling error of ±3 percent. What this means is that 95 percent of the time the poll results are within 3 percent of what the entire population thinks. If 60 percent of the sample say they approve of the job the president is doing, one can be virtually certain that the true figure is between 57 and 63 percent. There is always a certain amount of risk. Although a sample will produce results far off the mark about 5 percent of the time, the odds are definitely in favor of the pollsters.

In order to be within the margin of error, researchers must follow proper sampling techniques. In perhaps the most infamous survey ever, a 1936 *Literary Digest* poll underestimated the vote for President Franklin Roosevelt by 19 percent, erroneously predicting a big victory for Republican Alf Landon. The well-established magazine suddenly became a laughingstock and soon went out of business. Although the number of responses the magazine obtained for its poll was a staggering 2,376,000, its polling methods were badly flawed. Trying to reach as many people as possible, the magazine drew names from the biggest lists they could find: telephone books and motor vehicle records. In the midst of the Great Depression, the people on these lists were above the average income level (only 40 percent had telephones then; fewer still owned cars) and thus were more likely to vote Republican. The moral of the story is this: Accurate representation, not the number of responses, is the most important feature of a public opinion survey. Indeed, as polling techniques have advanced over the last 50 years, typical sample sizes have been getting smaller, not larger.

The newest computer and telephone technology has made surveying less expensive and more commonplace. Until recently, pollsters needed a national network of interviewers to traipse door-to-door in their localities with a clipboard of questions. Now most polling is done on the telephone with samples selected through **random-digit dialing**. Calls are placed to phone numbers within randomly chosen exchanges (for example, 512-471-xxxx) around the country . In this manner, both listed and unlisted numbers are reached at a cost of about one-fifth that of person-to-person interviewing. There are a couple of disadvantages, however. Seven percent of the population does not have a phone, and people are somewhat less willing to participate over the telephone than in person—it is easier to hang up than to slam the door in someone's face. These are small trade-offs for political candidates running for minor offices, for whom telephone polls are the only affordable method of gauging public opinion.

From its modest beginning with George Gallup's 1932 polls for his mother-in-law in Iowa, polling has become a big business. Public opinion polling is one of those American innovations, like soft drinks and fast-food restaurants, that have spread throughout the world. From Manhattan to Moscow, from Tulsa to Tokyo, people apparently want to know what other people think.

THE ROLE OF POLLS IN AMERICAN DEMOCRACY

Polls help political candidates detect public preferences. Supporters of polling insist that it is a tool for democracy. With it, they say, policymakers can keep in touch with changing opinions on the issues. No longer do politicians have to wait until the next election to see whether the public approves or disapproves of the government's course. If the poll results suddenly turn, then government officials can make corresponding midcourse corrections. Indeed, it was George Gallup's fondest hope that polling could contribute to the democratic process by providing a way for public desires to be heard at times other than elections.

Critics of polling, by contrast, think it makes politicians more concerned with following than leading. Polls might have told the constitutional convention delegates that the Constitution was unpopular or might have told Jefferson that people did not want the Louisiana Purchase. Certainly they would have told William Seward not to buy Alaska, a transaction known widely at the time as "Seward's Folly." Polls may thus discourage bold leadership, like that of Winston Churchill, who once said,

> Nothing is more dangerous than to live in the temperamental atmosphere of a Gallup poll, always taking one's pulse and taking one's temperature. . . . There is only one duty, only one safe course, and that is to try to be right and not to fear to do or say what you believe.[15]

Political scientist Benjamin Ginsberg has even argued that polls weaken democracy.[16] Polls, he says, permit government to think that it has taken public opinion into account when only passive, often ill-informed opinions have been counted. Polls substitute passive attitudes for active expression of opinion. Voting, letter writing, and other political behaviors

Public opinion polls are taken to reveal the distribution of a population's beliefs. The study of American public opinion is especially complex because of the nation's racial, ethnic, and cultural diversity.

take work. Responding to a poll-taker is a lazy way indeed to claim that "my voice has been heard."

Polls can also weaken democracy by distorting the election process. They are often accused of creating a *bandwagon effect.* The wagon carrying the band was the centerpiece of nineteenth-century political parades, and enthusiastic supporters would literally jump on it. Today, the term refers to voters who support a candidate merely because they see that others are doing so. Although only 2 percent of people in a recent CBS/*New York Times* poll claimed that poll results had influenced them, 26 percent said they thought others had been influenced (showing that Americans feel "It's always the other guy who's susceptible"). Beyond this, polls play to the media's interest in the horse race—that is, who's hot and who's not. The issues of recent presidential campaigns have sometimes been drowned out by a steady flood of poll results.

Probably the most widely criticized type of poll is the election-day **exit poll**. For this type of poll, voting places are randomly selected from around the country. Workers are then sent to these places and told to ask every tenth person how they voted. The results are accumulated toward the end of the day, enabling the television networks to project the outcomes of all but very close races before the polls even close. In the presidential elections of 1980, 1984, 1988, and 1996, the networks declared a winner while millions on the West Coast still had hours to vote. Critics have charged that this practice discourages many people from voting and thereby affects the outcome of some state and local races. Although many voters in western states have been outraged by this practice, careful analysis of survey data shows that few voters have actually been influenced by exit-poll results.[17]

Perhaps the most pervasive criticism of polling is that by altering the wording of a question, pollsters can get pretty much the results they want. Sometimes subtle changes in question wording can produce dramatic differences. For example, a month before the start of hostilities against Iraq, the ABC/*Washington Post* poll showed that 63 percent of the public thought we should go to war; but the CBS/*New York Times* poll recorded only 45 percent supporting war. The difference was that the former asked whether the United States should go to war "at some point after January 15 or not," whereas the latter asked whether the "U.S. should start military actions against Iraq, or should the U.S. wait longer to see if the trade embargo and other economic sanctions work."[18] It is therefore important to evaluate carefully how questions are posed when reading public opinion data.

Polling sounds scientific with its talk of random samples and margins of error; it is easy to take results for solid fact. But being an informed consumer of polls requires more than just a nuts-and-bolts knowledge of how they are conducted; you should think about whether the questions are fair and unbiased before making too much of the results. The good—or the harm—that polls do depends on how well the data are collected and how thoughtfully the data are interpreted.

WHAT POLLS REVEAL ABOUT AMERICANS' POLITICAL INFORMATION

Abraham Lincoln spoke stirringly of the inherent wisdom of the American people: "It is true that you may fool all of the people some of the time; and you can even fool some of the people all of the time; but you can't fool all of the people all the time." Obviously, Lincoln recognized the complexity of public opinion.

Thomas Jefferson and Alexander Hamilton had very different views about the wisdom of common people. Jefferson trusted people's good sense and believed that education would enable them to take the tasks of citizenship ever more seriously. Toward that end, he founded the University of Virginia. Hamilton held a contrasting view. His infamous words "Your people, sir, are a great beast" do not reflect confidence in people's capacity for self-government.

If there had been polling data in the early days of the American republic, Hamilton would probably have delighted in throwing some of the results in Jefferson's face. If public opinion analysts agree about anything, it is that the level of public knowledge about politics is dismally low. For example, in the 1996 National Election Study conducted by the University of Michigan, a random sample was asked to identify the position held by some prominent political leaders. The results were as follows:

- 88 percent knew Al Gore was vice president of the United States.
- 66 percent knew Boris Yeltsin was president of Russia.
- 59 percent knew Newt Gingrich was Speaker of the House.
- 10 percent knew William Rehnquist was Chief Justice of the Supreme Court.

With all the results taken into account, the study found that over half of the population failed to identify more than two out of four of these leaders.

No amount of Jeffersonian faith in the wisdom of the common people can erase the fact that Americans are not well informed about politics. Polls have regularly found that less than half of the public can name their representative in the House, much less say how he or she generally votes. Asking most people to explain their opinion on affirmative action, MX missiles, or fiscal policy often elicits blank looks. When trouble flares in a far-off country, polls regularly find that people have no idea where that country is. In fact, surveys show that citizens around the globe lack a basic awareness of the world around them. (See "America in Perspective: Citizens Show Little Knowledge of Geography.")

As Lance Bennett points out, these findings provide "a source of almost bitter humor in light of what the polls tell us about public information on other subjects."[19] He notes that more people know their astrological sign (76 percent) than know the name of their representative in the House. Slogans from TV commercials are better recognized than famous political figures. (For example, 82 percent of the public could identify the toilet tissue that completes the slogan "Please don't squeeze the. . . ," and 79 percent knew which upset-stomach remedy used the jingle "Plop, plop, fizz, fizz. Oh, what a relief it is.") Few people knew George Bush's stand on the capital gains tax, but 75 percent of the public could name the vegetable he did not like (broccoli).

How can Americans, who live in the most information-rich society in the world, be so ill-informed about politics? Some blame the schools. E. D. Hirsch, Jr., criticizes the schools for a failure to teach "cultural literacy."[20] People, he says, often lack the basic contextual knowledge—for example, where Africa is, what the Vietnam War was about, and so forth—necessary to understand and use the information they receive from the news media or from listening to political candidates. Indeed, it has been found that increased levels of education over the last four decades have scarcely raised public knowledge about politics.[21] Despite the apparent glut of information provided by the media, Americans do not remember much about what they are exposed to through the media. (Of course, there are many critics who say that the media fail to provide much meaningful information, a topic that will be discussed in Chapter 7.)

The "paradox of mass politics," says Russell Neuman, is that the American political system works as well as it does given the discomforting lack of public knowledge about politics.[22] Part of the reason for this phenomenon is that people may not know the ins and outs of policy questions or the actors on the political stage, but they know what basic values they want upheld. Sadly, the American public has become increasingly dissatisfied with government over the last three decades, as you can see in "Since Kennedy: The Decline of Trust in Government" (page 155).

When people feel that government is not working according to the values they subscribe to, the sleeping giant of public opinion may be stirred to action. Examining these values is thus of great importance.

WHAT AMERICANS VALUE: POLITICAL IDEOLOGIES

A coherent set of values and beliefs about public policy is a **political ideology.**[23] Liberal ideology, for example, supports a wide scope for the central government, often involving policies that aim to promote equality. Conservative ideology, in contrast, supports a less active scope of government that gives freer reign to the private sector (see Table 6.2, page 156).

DO PEOPLE THINK IN IDEOLOGICAL TERMS?

The authors of the classic study *The American Voter* first looked carefully at the ideological sophistication of the American electorate in the 1950s.[24] They divided the public into four groups, according to ideological sophistication. Their portrait of the American electorate was not flattering. Only 12 percent of the people showed evidence of thinking in ideological terms and thus were classified as *ideologues*. These people could connect their opinions and beliefs with broad policy positions taken by parties or candidates. They might say, for example, that they liked the

America in Perspective

CITIZENS SHOW LITTLE KNOWLEDGE OF GEOGRAPHY

In the spring of 1988, over 12,000 people in 10 nations were asked to identify 16 places on the following world map. The average citizen in the United States could identify barely more than half. Believe it or not, 14 percent of Americans could not even find their own country on the map. Despite years of fighting in Vietnam, 68 percent could not locate this Southeast Asian country. Such lack of basic geographic knowledge is quite common throughout the world. Here is the average score for each of the 10 countries in which the test was administered:

COUNTRY	AVERAGE SCORE	COUNTRY	AVERAGE SCORE
Sweden	11.6	**United States**	**8.6**
West Germany	11.2	Great Britain	8.5
Japan	9.7	Italy	7.6
France	9.3	Mexico	7.4
Canada	9.2	Soviet Union	7.4

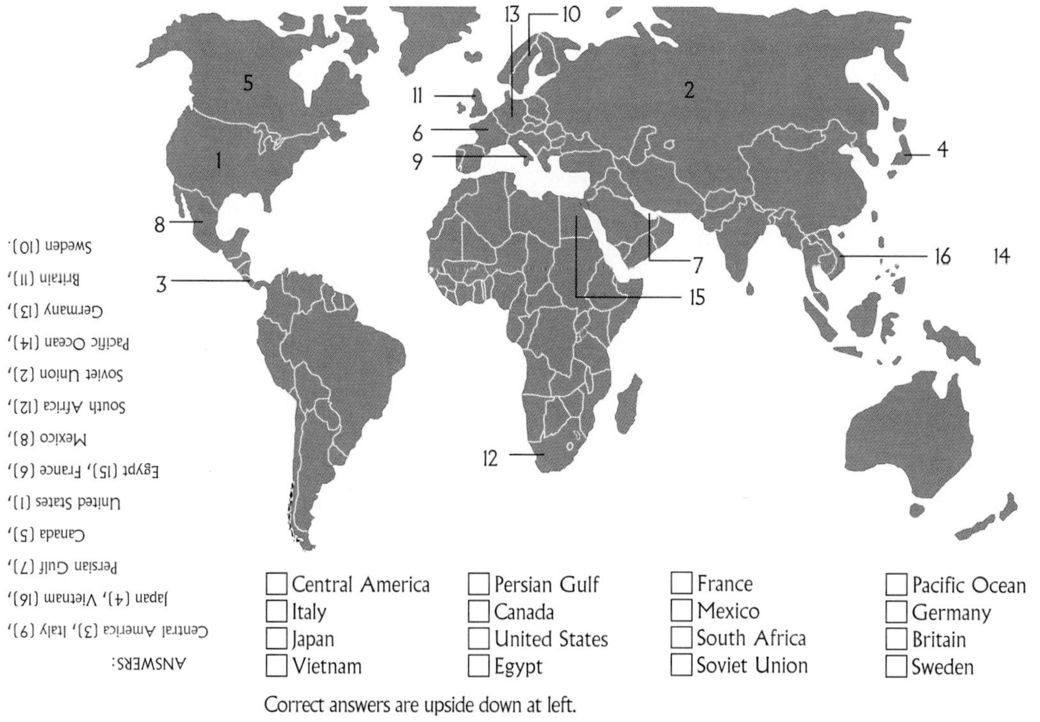

Correct answers are upside down at left.

SOURCE: Warren E. Leary, "Two Superpowers' Citizens Do Badly in Geography," *New York Times*, November 9, 1989, A6.

Democrats because they were more liberal or the Republicans because they favored a smaller government. Forty-two percent of Americans were classified as *group benefits* voters. These people thought of politics mainly in terms of the groups they liked or disliked; for example, "Republicans support small businessmen like me" or "Democrats are the party of the working man." Twenty-four percent of the population were *nature of the times* voters. Their handle on politics was limited to whether the times seemed good or bad to them; they might vaguely link the party in power with the country's fortune or misfortune. Finally, 22 percent of the voters were devoid of any ideological or issue content in their political evaluations. They were called the *no issue content* group. Most of them simply voted routinely for a party or judged the candidates solely by their personalities. Overall, at least during the 1950s, Americans seemed to care little about the differences between liberal and conservative politics.

There has been much debate about whether this portrayal accurately characterizes the public today. Nie,

SINCE KENNEDY

The Decline of Trust in Government

In 1958, a year that marked the worst recession in the United States since the Great Depression of the 1930s, the National Election Studies first asked a national sample the following question: "How much of the time do you think you can trust the government in Washington to do what is right—just about always, most of the time, or only some of the time?" Despite the dismal economic situation, the results revealed that most people had a rather favorable view of the government. Three-quarters of the respondents said that they trusted the government to do the right thing always or mostly. Such was the mood of the country when John Kennedy assumed the presidency 2 years later. A year after Kennedy's death, when this question was next asked of the public, the results were slightly more trusting than in 1958.

Following the 1964 election, however, researchers started to see a precipitous drop in public trust in government, which you can see from the accompanying graph. First Vietnam and then Watergate shook the people's confidence in the federal government. The economic troubles of the Carter years and the Iran hostage crisis helped continue the slide; by 1980, only a quarter of the public thought the government could be trusted most of the time or always. During the Reagan years, public cynicism abated a bit, but by 1994, trust in government had plummeted again to another all-time low.

Having grown up in a time when most people trusted the government most of the time, President Clinton has often shown an awareness that the public mood he is faced with is much different from that when President Kennedy occupied the White House. When asked why he has faced difficulties in getting his proposals enacted into law, one answer he has repeatedly given is that people want the government to take action but just don't trust it to do anything right. His political opponents would challenge any assertions that the public wants to increase the scope of government. However, the data show unequivocally that public confidence in the federal government is only a shadow of what it once was.

Some analysts have noted that a healthy dose of public cynicism helps to keep politicians on their toes. Others, however, note that a democracy is based on the consent of the governed and that a lack of public trust in the government is a reflection of their belief that the system is not serving them well.

SOURCE: 1952-1996 American National Election Studies.

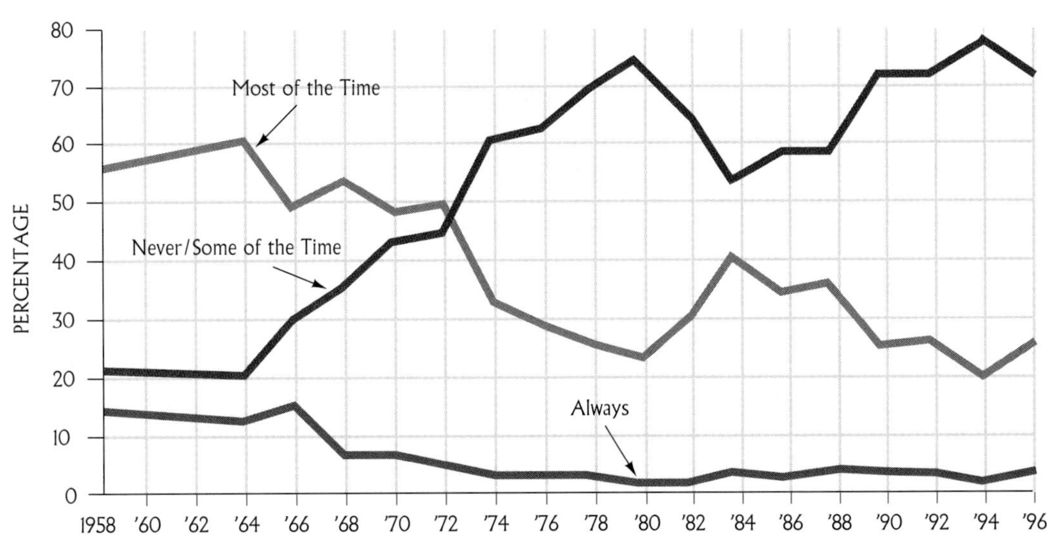

TABLE 6.2 HOW TO TELL A LIBERAL FROM A CONSERVATIVE

Liberal and *conservative*—these labels are thrown around in American politics as though everyone knows what they mean. Most Americans do know that Newt Gingrich isn't a liberal and that Edward Kennedy isn't a conservative, and few could confuse Jesse Helms, the conservative senator from North Carolina, with Jesse Jackson. Here are some of the political beliefs likely to be preferred by liberals and conservatives. This table, to be sure, is oversimplified.

ON FOREIGN POLICY:	LIBERALS	CONSERVATIVES
Military spending	Believe we should spend less	Believe we should maintain peace through strength
Use of force	Less willing to commit troops to action, such as in the Persian Gulf War	More likely to support military intervention around the world
ON SOCIAL POLICY:		
Abortion	Support "freedom of choice"	Support "right to life"
Prayer in schools	Are opposed	Are supportive
Affirmative action	Favor	Oppose
ON ECONOMIC POLICY:		
Scope of government	View government as a regulator in the public interest	Favor free-market solutions
Taxes	Want to tax the rich more	Want to keep taxes low
Spending	Want to spend more on the poor	Want to keep spending low
ON CRIME:		
How to cut crime	Believe we should solve the problems that cause crime	Believe we should stop "coddling criminals"
Defendants' rights	Believe we should guard them carefully	Believe we should stop letting criminals hide behind laws

Verba, and Petrocik took a look at the changing American voter from 1956 to 1972 and argued that voters were more sophisticated in the 1970s than in the 1950s.[25] Others, though, have concluded that people seemed more informed and ideological only because the wording of the questions had changed.[26] If the exact same methods are used to update the analysis of *The American Voter* through more recent elections, one finds some increase in the proportion of ideologues, but the overall picture looks much the same (see Table 6.3).

These findings do not mean that the vast majority of the population does not have a political ideology. Rather, for most people the terms *liberal* and *conservative* are just not as important as they are for the political elite such as politicians, activists, journalists, and the like. Relatively few people have ideologies that organize their political beliefs as clearly as shown in Table 6.2. Thus, the authors of *The American Voter* concluded that to speak of election results as indicating a movement of the public either left (to more liberal policies) or right (to more conservative policies) is not justified because most voters do not think in such terms. Furthermore, those who do are actually the least likely to shift from one election to the next.

The American Voter argued persuasively that Eisenhower's two election victories did not represent

TABLE 6.3 LEVELS OF IDEOLOGICAL CONCEPTUALIZATION (IN PERCENTAGE)[a]

LEVEL	1956	1960	1964	1968	1972	1976	1980	1984	1988
Ideologues	12	19	27	26	22	21	22	22	18
Group benefits	42	31	27	24	27	26	30	27	36
Nature of the times	24	26	20	29	34	30	31	34	25
No issue content	22	23	26	21	17	24	17	17	21

[a]Columns do not always add up to 100% because of rounding.

SOURCES: 1952-1984: Herbert B. Asher, *Presidential Elections and American Politics,* 3rd ed. (Chicago: Dorsey, 1988), Ill; 1988 data supplied by Kathleen Knight of the University of Houston.

a shift in the conservative direction during the 1950s. In the 1980s, the issue of whether public opinion had undergone a major rightward change was once again raised in the wake of the victories of Ronald Reagan, who campaigned vigorously against intrusive government.

PEOPLE LIKED REAGAN BUT NOT HIS POLICIES

Ronald Reagan was clearly the most conservative president since the New Deal. During his 8 years as president, he pressed ahead with a thoroughly conservative agenda that included

- Reduced levels of government spending on programs such as social welfare, education, and job training
- Increased defense spending, including funding for the "Star Wars" program to intercept nuclear weapons before they strike
- Increased American support for groups that claimed to be fighting communism (such as the Nicaraguan Contras)
- Policies to minimize government regulation of business and let the free market reign
- A 25 percent across-the-board reduction in federal income tax rates
- Support for a conservative social agenda, including antiabortion legislation, prayer in schools, and stronger law enforcement
- The appointment of Supreme Court justices to help achieve conservative political and social goals

With Reagan's landslide reelection victory in 1984, some political observers felt that a conservative wildfire had swept the country. Numerous Democratic leaders warned party members not to be left out on a liberal limb. "Don't be the party of more taxing and spending," they cautioned fellow Democrats. In 1992, Bill Clinton followed this advice, saying that his vision for government is "not tax and spend, but invest, educate, innovate, a partnership between government and business."[27]

Despite Reagan's victories throughout the 1980s, scholarly analyses included the common theme that people liked Reagan but not his policies. Indeed, the 1984 National Election Study revealed that although Reagan had the advantage of high approval ratings, on the major policy questions more people felt closer to the stand of Democratic candidate Walter Mondale. By fairly substantial margins, those who expressed opinions disagreed with Reagan's willingness to commit military help to Central America and his desire to spend more on defense. By somewhat smaller margins, people saw Reagan as wanting to cut government services too deeply, not providing enough aid to minorities and women, and being too tough with the Soviet Union.[28] With the exception of a rise in support for military spending during the 1980 campaign, public opinion specialists were unable to document any shift toward conservative attitudes during the 1980s. As Ferguson and Rogers concluded, "If American public opinion drifted anywhere over Reagan's first term, it was toward the left, not the right, just the opposite of the turn in public policy."[29] Asked to assess Reagan's time in office, the 1988 electorate was evenly split on the wisdom of defense increases and was generally unaware and unsupportive of domestic cuts.[30]

If so many people disagreed with Reagan, why was he such a popular president, and why was George Bush able to run successfully on his record in 1988? The answer is simply that many swing voters—those whom *The American Voter* classified as nature of the times voters—care more about results than ideology.[31] The 1980 election was more about voting Carter out of office than voting Reagan into it. In 1984 and 1988, the Republicans had a record of relative peace and prosperity on their side, which was the key to victories for Reagan and Bush. With the economic downturn in 1992, these same swing voters decided that it was time for a change and propelled Bill Clinton into the White House.

In sum, conservatives may have become more visible participants since 1980, but they did not necessarily become more numerous. Just how they—and other Americans—participate in politics is the topic of the next section.

Although Ronald Reagan carried 49 of the 50 states in his 1984 election victory over Walter Mondale, studies showed that more people felt closer to Mondale's stand on the issues than to Reagan's staunch conservatism. It was therefore the results of peace and prosperity that carried Reagan to his landslide win rather than approval of his specific policies.

HOW AMERICANS PARTICIPATE IN POLITICS

In politics, as in many other aspects of life, the squeaky wheel gets the grease. The way citizens "squeak" in politics is to participate. Americans have many avenues of political participation open to them.

- Mrs. Jones of Iowa City goes to a neighbor's living room to attend her local precinct's presidential caucus.
- Tipper Gore, wife of Vice President Al Gore, testifies before a Senate committee to express her view that warning labels should be put on record albums that contain vulgar language.
- Protestors against the massacre in Tiananmen Square gather outside the Chinese embassy in Washington to condemn the Chinese government.
- Parents in Alabama file a lawsuit to oppose textbooks that, in their opinion, promote "secular humanism."
- Mr. Smith, a Social Security recipient, writes to his senator to express his concern about a possible cut in his cost-of-living benefits.
- Over 90 million people vote in a presidential election.

All of these activities are types of political participation. **Political participation** encompasses the many activities in which citizens engage to influence the selection of political leaders or the policies they pursue.[32] Participation can be overt or subtle. The mass protests throughout Eastern Europe in the fall of 1989 represented an avalanche of political participation, yet quietly writing a letter to your congressperson also represents political participation. Political participation can be violent or peaceful, organized or individual, casual or consuming.

Generally, the United States has a culture that values political participation. Citizens express pride in their nation: 87 percent say they are very proud to be Americans.[33] Nevertheless, just 49 percent of adult Americans voted in the presidential election of 1996, and only 39 percent turned out for the 1994 congressional elections. At the local level, the situation is even worse, with elections for city council and school board often drawing less than 10 percent of the eligible voters. (For more on voter turnout and why it is so low, see Chapter 10.)

CONVENTIONAL PARTICIPATION

Although the line is hard to draw, political scientists generally distinguish between two broad types of participation: conventional and unconventional. Conventional participation includes many widely accepted modes of influencing government—voting, trying to persuade others, ringing doorbells for a petition, running for office, and so on. In contrast, unconventional participation includes activities that are often dramatic, such as protesting, civil disobedience, and even violence.

For a few, politics is their lifeblood; they run for office, work regularly in politics, and live for the next election. For others, it is mere drudgery; and for still others, it is a civic obligation. The number of Americans for whom political activity is an important part of their everyday life is minuscule; they number at most in the tens of thousands. To these people, policy questions are as familiar as slogans on TV commercials are to the average citizen. They are the political elites, the gladiators of political conflict—the activists, the party leaders, the interest group leaders, the judges, and the members of Congress. (Part Three will discuss the political elite in detail.)

Yet millions do take part in political activities beyond simply voting. In two comprehensive studies of American political participation conducted by Sidney Verba and his colleagues, samples of Americans were asked in 1967 and 1987 about their role in various kinds of political activities.[34] Included were voting, working in campaigns, contacting government officials, and working on local community issues. As you can see in Figure 6.2, voting is the only aspect of political participation that a majority of the population reported engaging in. At the same time, voting is also the only political activity for which there is evidence of a decline in participation in recent years. Substantial increases in participation can be found on the dimensions of giving money to candidates and contacting public officials, and small increases are evident for all the other activities. Thus, although the decline of voter turnout is a development Americans should rightly be concerned about (see Chapter 10), a broader look at political participation reveals some positive developments for participatory democracy.

Political participation can be as simple as voting or stuffing envelopes for a candidate, or as dramatic as a political protest. Here, demonstrators in San Francisco erect their own "Goddess of Democracy" to show their support for the prodemocracy movement in China.

PROTEST AS PARTICIPATION

Unconventional forms of political participation are missing from the list of activities shown in Figure 6.2. From the Boston Tea Party, to burning draft cards, to demonstrating against abortion, Americans have engaged in countless political protests. **Protest** is a form of political participation designed to achieve policy change through dramatic and unconventional tactics. The media's willingness to cover the unusual can make protest worthwhile, drawing attention to a point of view that many Americans might otherwise never encounter. This is the primary goal of the AIDS activist group appropriately called "ACT-UP," which interrupts political gatherings to draw attention to the need for AIDS research. Indeed, protests today are often orchestrated to provide television cameras with vivid images. Demonstration coordinators steer participants to prearranged staging areas and provide facilities for press coverage.

Throughout American history, individuals and groups have sometimes used **civil disobedience**; that is, they have consciously broken a law that they thought was unjust. In the 1840s, Henry David Thoreau refused to pay his taxes as a protest against the Mexican War and went to jail; he stayed only overnight because his friend Ralph Waldo Emerson paid the taxes. Influenced by India's Mahatma Gandhi, the Reverend Martin Luther King, Jr., won a Nobel Peace Prize for his civil disobedience against segregationist laws in the 1950s and 1960s. His "Letter from a Birmingham Jail" is a classic defense of civil disobedience.[35]

FIGURE 6.2 PERCENTAGE ENGAGING IN VARIOUS KINDS OF POLITICAL PARTICIPATION: 1967 AND 1987

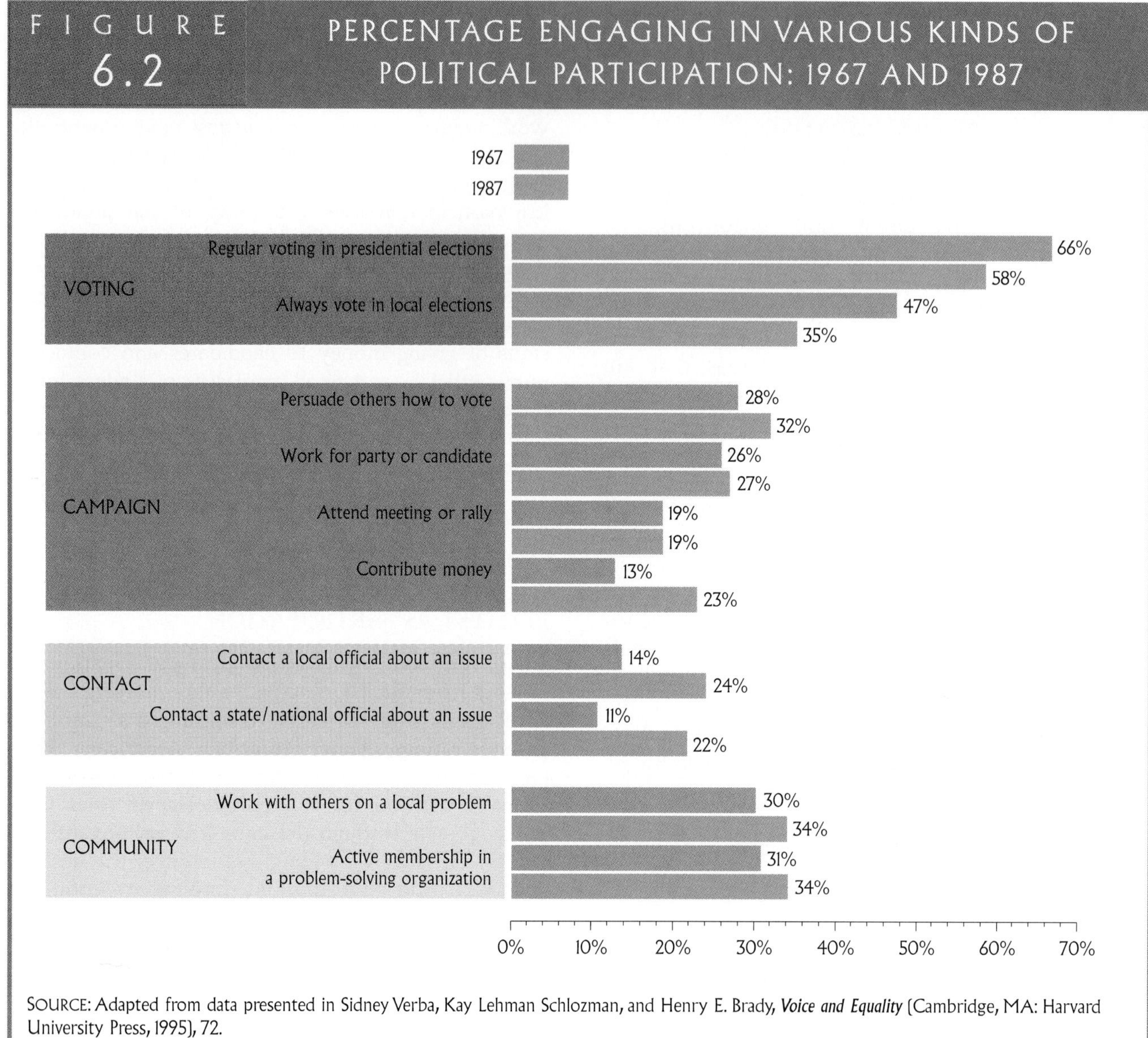

SOURCE: Adapted from data presented in Sidney Verba, Kay Lehman Schlozman, and Henry E. Brady, ***Voice and Equality*** (Cambridge, MA: Harvard University Press, 1995), 72.

Sometimes political participation can be violent. The history of violence in American politics is a long one—not surprising, perhaps, for a nation born in rebellion. The turbulent 1960s included many outbreaks of violence. African-American neighborhoods in American cities were torn by riots. College campuses were sometimes turned into battle zones as protesters against the Vietnam War fought police and National Guard units. At a number of campuses, demonstrations turned violent; students were killed at Kent State and Jackson State in 1970. Although supported by few people, violence has been a means of pressuring the government to change its policies throughout American history.

CLASS, INEQUALITY, AND PARTICIPATION

The rates of political participation are unequal among Americans. Virtually every study of political participation has come to the conclusion that "citizens of higher social economic status participate more in politics. This generalization . . . holds true whether one uses level of education, income, or occupation as the

Unconventional protest techniques are the trademark of ACT-UP, an AIDS-awareness protest group. Here, members of the group are lying down near the White House, defying police orders to disperse. Members of ACT-UP believe that such dramatic protests are necessary to keep the issue of AIDS in the public eye.

Perhaps the best-known image of American political violence from the late-1960s to early-1970s period: A student lies dead on the Kent State campus, one of four killed when members of the Ohio National Guard opened fire on anti-Vietnam War demonstrators.

measure of social status."[36] Theorists who believe that America is ruled by a small, wealthy elite make much of this fact to support their point of view.

The participation differences between African Americans and Hispanics and the national average are no longer enormous, however. For African Americans, participation in 1992 was a mere 10 percentage points below the national average; for Hispanic citizens it was 15 percent. One reason for this smaller-than-expected participation gap is that minorities have a group consciousness that gives them an extra incentive to vote. In fact, when African Americans, Hispanics, and whites of equal income and education are compared, it is the minorities that participate more in politics.[37] In other words, a poor Hispanic or African American is more likely to participate than a poor white. In general, lower rates of political participation among these minority groups are linked with lower socioeconomic status.

People who believe in democracy should be concerned not only about inequalities in participation but also about the low numbers of participants. Those who participate are easy to listen to; nonparticipants are easy to ignore. In a democracy, citizenship carries the promise—and the responsibility—of self-government.

UNDERSTANDING PUBLIC OPINION AND POLITICAL ACTION

Throughout much of the communist world in 1989, people protested for democracy. Many said they wanted their political system to be just like America's, even though they had only a vague idea of how American democracy works. As this chapter has shown, there are many limits on the role Americans play in their political system. The average person, here and elsewhere, is not very well informed about political issues, including the crucial issue of the scope of government.

PUBLIC ATTITUDES TOWARD THE SCOPE OF GOVERNMENT

Central to the ideology of Newt Gingrich and the Republican majority in Congress is the belief that the scope of American government has become too wide-ranging. In this sense, they are true disciples of

Ronald Reagan. According to Reagan, government was not the solution to society's problems—it was the problem. He called for the government to "get off the backs of the American people."

Reagan's rhetoric about an overly intrusive government was reminiscent of the 1964 presidential campaign rhetoric of Barry Goldwater, who lost to Lyndon Johnson in a landslide. Indeed, Reagan first made his mark in politics by giving a televised speech on behalf of the embattled Goldwater campaign. Although the rhetoric was much the same in 1980, public opinion about the scope of government had changed dramatically. In 1964, only 30 percent of the population thought the government was getting too powerful; by 1980, this figure had risen to 50 percent.

For much of the population, however, questions about the scope of government have consistently elicited no opinion at all. Indeed, in 1992, 43 percent of those interviewed said they had not thought about the question. The question of government power is a complex one, but as *Government in America* will continue to stress, it is one of the key controversies in American politics today. Once again, it seems that the public is not nearly so concerned with political issues as would be ideal in a democratic society (see "The People Speak: Public Opinion on the Scope of Government").

Nor does public opinion on different aspects of the same issue exhibit much consistency. Thus, although more people today think the government is too active, a plurality has consistently called for more spending on such programs as education, health care, aid to big cities, protecting the environment, and fighting crime.[38] Many political scientists have looked at these contradictory findings and concluded that Americans are ideological conservatives but operational liberals—meaning that they oppose the idea of big government in principle but favor it in practice. The fact that public opinion is often contradictory in this respect contributes to policy gridlock, because it is hard for politicians to know which aspect of the public's attitudes to respond to.

The People Speak

Public Opinion on the Scope of Government

Some people are afraid the government in Washington is getting too powerful for the good of the country and the individual person. Others feel that the government in Washington is not getting too strong. Do you have an opinion on this or not? (If yes) What is your feeling, do you think the government is getting too powerful or do you think the government is not getting too strong?

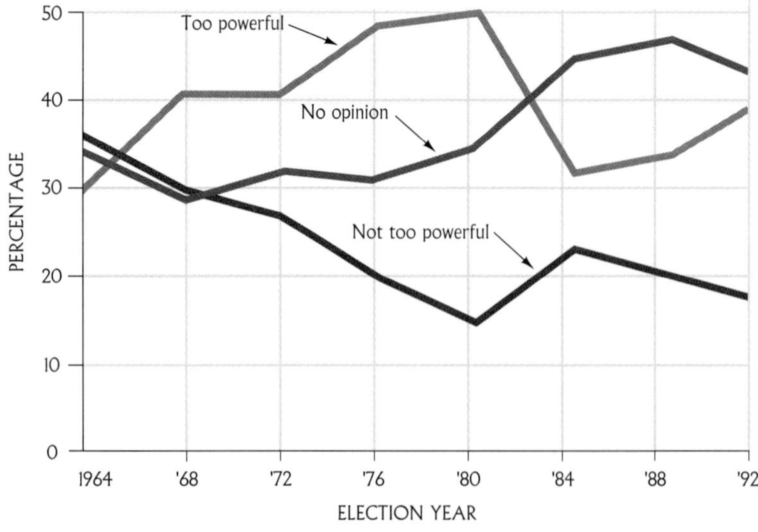

SOURCE: The questions as worded are taken directly from 1964-1992 National Election Studies conducted by the University of Michigan.

DEMOCRACY, PUBLIC OPINION, AND POLITICAL ACTION

Remember, though, that American democracy is representative rather than direct. As *The American Voter* stated many years ago, "The public's explicit task is to decide not what government hall do but rather who shall decide what government shall do."[39] When individuals under communist rule protested for democracy, what they wanted most was the right to have a say in choosing their leaders. Americans can—and often do—take for granted the opportunity to replace our leaders at the next election. Protest is thus directed at making the government listen to specific demands, not overthrowing it. In this sense, it can be said that American citizens have become well socialized to democracy.

If the public's task in democracy is to choose who is to lead, we must still ask whether it can do so wisely. If people know little about where the candidates stand on the issues, how can they make rational choices? Most choose performance criteria over policy criteria. As Morris Fiorina has written, citizens typically have one hard bit of data to go on: "They know what life has been like during the incumbent's administration. They need not know the precise economic or foreign policies of the incumbent administration in order to see or feel the results of those policies."[40] Thus, even if they are only voting according to the nature of the times, their voices are clearly being heard—holding presidents accountable for their actions.

Nonviolent civil disobedience was one of the most effective techniques of the civil rights movement in the American South. Young African Americans sat at "whites only" lunch counters to protest segregation. Photos such as this drew national attention to the injustice of racial discrimination.

SUMMARY

American society is amazingly varied. The ethnic makeup of America is changing to a minority majority. Americans are moving toward warmer parts of the country and growing older as a society. All of these changes have policy consequences. One way of understanding the American people is through demography—the science of population changes. Demography, it is often said, is destiny.

Another way to understand the American people is through examination of public opinion in the United States. What Americans believe—and what they believe they know—is public opinion, the distribution of people's beliefs about politics and policy issues. Polling is one important way of studying public opinion; polls give us a fairly accurate gauge of public opinion on issues, products, and personalities. On the positive side for democracy, polls help keep political leaders in touch with the feelings of their constituents. On the negative side, they help politicians "play to the crowds" instead of providing leadership.

Polls have revealed again and again that the average American has a low level of political knowledge. Far more Americans know their astrological sign than know the names of their representatives in Congress. Ideological thinking is not widespread in the American public, nor are people necessarily consistent in their attitudes. Often they are conservative in principle but liberal in practice; that is, they are against big government but favor more spending on a wide variety of programs. Indeed, many people apparently voted for Reagan even though they disliked his policies.

Acting on one's opinions is political participation. Although Americans live in a participatory culture, their actual level of participation is less than spectacular. In this country, participation is a class-biased activity; certain groups participate more than others. Those who suffer the most inequality sometimes resort to protest as a form of participation. Perhaps the best indicator of how well socialized Americans are to democracy is that protest typically is aimed at getting the attention of the government, not overthrowing it.

KEY TERMS

demography
census
melting pot
minority majority
Simpson-Mazzoli Act
reapportionment
political socialization
public opinion
sample
random sampling
sampling error
random-digit dialing
exit poll
political ideology
political participation
protest
civil disobedience

FOR FURTHER READING

Asher, Herbert. *Polling and the Public: What Every Citizen Should Know,* 3rd ed. Washington, DC: Congressional Quarterly Press, 1995. A highly readable introduction to the perils and possibilities of polling and surveys.

Campbell, Angus, *et al. The American Voter.* New York: Wiley, 1960. The classic study of the American voter, based on data from the 1950s.

Conway, M. Margaret. *Political Participation,* 2nd ed. Washington, DC: Congressional Quarterly Press, 1990. A good review of the literature on political participation.

Delli Carpini, Michael X., and Scott Keeter. *What Americans Know About Politics and Why It Matters.* New Haven: Yale University Press, 1996. The best study of the state of political knowledge in the electorate.

Erikson, Robert S., and Kent L. Tedin. *American Public Opinion,* 5th ed. Boston: Allyn and Bacon, 1995. One of the top textbooks on the subject.

Jennings, M. Kent, and Richard G. Niemi. *Generations and Politics: A Panel Study of Young Adults and Their Parents.* Princeton, N.J.: Princeton University Press, 1981. A highly influential study of the class of 1965, their parents, and how both generations changed over the course of 8 years.

Mayer, William G. *The Changing American Mind.* Ann Arbor: University of Michigan Press, 1993. A comprehensive review of how American public opinion changed between 1960 and 1988, as well as an analysis of the reasons for these changes.

Niemi, Richard G., John Mueller, and Tom W. Smith. *Trends in Public Opinion: A Compendium of Survey Data.* New York: Greenwood Press, 1989. An excellent source of data over time on a wide range of public opinion questions.

Neuman, W. Russell. *The Paradox of Mass Politics: Knowledge and Opinion in the American Electorate.* Cambridge, MA: Harvard University Press, 1986. Neuman addresses the question of how the system works as well as it does given the low level of public information about politics.

Page, Benjamin I., and Robert Y. Shapiro. *The Rational Public: Fifty Years of Trends in Americans' Policy Preferences.* Chicago: University of Chicago Press, 1992. The authors argue that the public, as a collectivity, responds in a reasonable fashion to changing political circumstances and information.

Verba, Sidney, and Norman H. Nie. *Participation in America.* New York: Harper & Row, 1972. A landmark study of American political participation.

Verba, Sidney, Kay Lehman Schlozman, and Henry E. Brady. *Voice and Equality: Civic Voluntarism in American Politics.* Cambridge, MA: Harvard University Press, 1995. A worthy update and extension to *Participation in America.*

INTERNET RESOURCES

www.census.gov
The Census is the best source of information on America's demography. Go to the list of topics to find out the range of materials that are available.

www. gallup.com
The Gallup poll regularly posts reports about their political surveys at this site.

NOTES

1. See Margo Anderson, *The American Census: A Social History* (New Haven, CT: Yale University Press, 1988).
2. *Ibid.,* 399.
3. Ronald T. Takaki, *Strangers from a Different Shore* (Boston: Little, Brown, 1989), chap. 11.
4. Judith Blake, *Family Size and Achievement* (Berkeley, CA: University of California Press, 1989).
5. See Henry J. Pratt, *The Gray Lobby* (Chicago: University of Chicago Press, 1977).
6. Richard Dawson *et al., Political Socialization,* 2nd ed. (Boston: Little, Brown, 1977), 33.
7. See M. Kent Jennings and Richard G. Niemi, *Generations and Politics: A Panel Study of Young Adults and Their Parents* (Princeton, NJ: Princeton University Press, 1981).
8. "The Age of Indifference." Report of the Times Mirror Center for the People and the Press, June 28, 1990.
9. Quoted in Sabine Reichel, *What Did You Do in the War Daddy? Growing Up German* (New York: Hill & Wang, 1989), 113.
10. David Easton and Jack Dennis, *Children in the Political System* (New York: McGraw-Hill, 1969), 106-107.
11. See Raymond E. Wolfinger and Steven J. Rosenstone, *Who Votes* (New Haven, CT: Yale University Press, 1980), chap. 11.
12. Philip E. Converse, *The Dynamics of Party Support* (Beverly Hills: Sage Publications, 1976), 12-13.

13. Jean M. Converse, *Survey Research in the United States: Roots and Emergence, 1890-1960* (Berkeley, CA: University of California Press, 1987), 116. Converse's work is the definitive study on the origins of public opinion sampling.

14. Herbert Asher, *Polling and the Public: What Every Citizen Should Know* (Washington, DC: Congressional Quarterly Press, 1988), 59.

15. Quoted in Norman M. Bradburn and Seymour Sudman, *Polls and Surveys: Understanding What They Tell Us* (San Francisco: Jossey-Bass, 1988), 39-40.

16. See Benjamin Ginsberg, *The Captive Public* (New York: Basic Books, 1986).

17. For a good summary of the evidence, see Seymour Sudman, "Do Exit Polls Influence Voting Behavior?" *Public Opinion Quarterly* 50 (Fall 1986): 331-339.

18. David W. Moore, *the Superpollsters: How They Measure and Manipulate Public Opinion in America* (New York: Four Walls Eight Windows, 1992), 353-354.

19. W. Lance Bennett, *Public Opinion and American Politics* (New York: Harcourt Brace Jovanovich, 1980), 44.

20. E. D. Hirsch, Jr., *Cultural Literacy* (Boston: Houghton Mifflin, 1986).

21. Michael X. Delli Carpini and Scott Keeter, *What Americans Know About Politics and Why It Matters.* New Haven, CT: Yale University Press, 1996, chap. 3.

22. W. Russell Neuman, *The Paradox of Mass Politics: Knowledge and Opinion in the American Electorate* (Cambridge, MA: Harvard University Press, 1986).

23. For a more extended definition, see Robert E. Lane, *Political Ideology* (New York: Free Press, 1962), 13-16.

24. Angus Campbell *et al., The American Voter* (New York: John Wiley, 1960), chap. 10.

25. Norman H. Nie, Sidney Verba, and John R. Petrocik, *The Changing American Voter* (Cambridge, MA: Harvard University Press, 1976), chap. 7.

26. See, for example, John L. Sullivan, James E. Pierson, and George E. Marcus, "Ideological Constraint in the Mass Public: A Methodological Critique and Some New Findings," *American Journal of Political Science* 22 (May 1978): 233-249; and Eric R. A. N. Smith, *The Unchanging American Voter* (Berkeley, CA: University of California Press, 1989).

27. Sar Fritz, "Clinton Rejects Bush's Charges He Is Tax-and-Spend Democrat," *Los Angeles Times,* September 26, 1992, A20.

28. Martin P. Wattenberg, "The Hollow Realignment: Partisan Change in a Candidate-Centered Era," *Public Opinion Quarterly* 51 (Spring 1987): 58-74.

29. Thomas Ferguson and Joel Rogers, *Right Turn* (New York: Hill & Wang, 1986), 28; for a longer-term perspective on the movement of public opinion toward a largely liberal direction, see Benjamin I. Page and Robert Y. Shapiro, *The Rational Public: Fifty Years of Trends in Americans' Policy Preferences* (Chicago: University of Chicago Press, 1992).

30. Martin P. Wattenberg, *The Rise of Candidate-Centered Politics: Presidential Elections of the 1980s.* (Cambridge, MA: Harvard University Press, 1991).

31. This theory is carefully developed in Morris P. Fiorina, *Retrospective Voting in Presidential Elections* (New Haven, CT: Yale University Press, 1981).

32. This definition is a close paraphrase of that in Sidney Verba and Norman H. Nie, *Participation in America* (New York: Harper & Row, 1972), 2.

33. Russell J. Dalton, *Citizen Politics in Western Democracies* (Chatham, NJ: Chatham House, 1988), 237.

34. See Verba and Nie, *Participation in America;* and Sidney Verba, Kay Lehman Schlozman, and Henry E. Brady, *Voice and Equality: Civic Voluntarism in American Politics* (Cambridge, MA: Harvard University Press, 1995).

35. This letter can be found in Juan Williams, *Eyes on the Prize: America's Civil Rights Years, 1954-1965* (New York: Viking, 1987), 187-189.

36. Verba and Nie, *Participation in America,* 125.

37. On African Americans, see Verba and Nie, *Participation in America,* chap. 10; on Hispanics, see Wolfinger and Rosenstone, *Who Votes?,* 92.

38. See the data presented in Richard G. Niemi, John Mueller, and Tom W. Smith, *Trends in Public Opinion: A Compendium of Survey Data* (New York: Greenwood Press, 1989), 77-91.

39. Campbell *et al., The American Voter,* 541.

40. Fiorina, *Retrospective Voting,* 5.

7

The Mass Media and the Political Agenda

In Washington's Smithsonian Museum, the television console used by President Lyndon Johnson in the mid-1960s can be seen on permanent display. Not wanting to miss anything on TV, Johnson asked for three screens to be installed in one console so he could monitor CBS, NBC, and ABC all at the same time. White House technicians rigged up a special remote control for the president, enabling him to switch the audio easily from one network to another. According to many observers, whenever he saw his picture appear, he immediately turned on the audio from that screen to hear what was being said about him.

As a piece of genuine Americana, LBJ's triple TV set symbolizes the tremendous importance that television had assumed in U.S. politics by the mid-1960s. However, Johnson's console looks rather primitive when compared to the TV equipment George Bush used while he was president. In a White House interview with C-SPAN, Bush was asked whether he watched television. He responded as follows:

> Watch quite a bit. I watch the news, and I don't like to tell you this because you'll think I'm into some weird TV freak here, but I have a set upstairs that has five screens on it. And I can sit on my desk and whip ... just punch a button, if I see one off on the corner that moves in to the middle screen, the other one goes to the side, then I can run up and down the dial. So ... and you can record all four going at once while you're watching. I don't quite know how to do that yet.
>
> But I cite this because Barbara accuses me of being too much—not too much—but plugged into TV too often, put it that way.[1]

Although Bush's comments reveal a concern with being portrayed as preoccupied with monitoring television, no one accused him of this. Whereas President Johnson was obsessed with hearing everything said about him on TV, in the hi-tech world of the 1990's, President Bush was compelled to watch TV just to keep up with events.

The rise of television has had a profound impact on the two central questions—*How should we govern?* and *What should government do?*—that we emphasize in this text. As illustrated by the discussion of the TV-viewing habits of Presidents Johnson and Bush, it has brought an immediacy to how we govern. Television has removed the filter of time from events. Whatever the problem or event, it is happening now—live on the TV screen. People thus have more reason than ever to expect immediate governmental responses. However, the Founding Fathers designed a very deliberative governing process, in which problems would be considered by multiple centers of political power and acted upon only after lengthy give and take. Given the difficulties of getting quick action through the American political system, it is no wonder that the public has come to be more dissatisfied with our government in the television age.

In some cases, though, television has set the stage for leaders to take quick action affecting the scope of government. Lyndon Johnson was watching his triple screen TV set when NBC interrupted its airing of "Judgment at Nuremburg" to show film that had just become available of civil rights demonstrators being brutally attacked by police in Selma, Alabama. Sensing the public outrage at this violence and injustice, Johnson soon proposed and pushed through the historic Voting Rights Act of 1965 (see Chapter 5). Similarly, in late-1992, President Bush found his agenda driven by images appearing on his multiple TV screens. This time the scene was from far-off Somalia, where warlords had cut off food to millions of people. The moving scenes of starving children on TV forced Bush's hand and led him to send U.S. troops to Somalia on a humanitarian mission.

In today's technological world, the media—like computers, atomic power, aircraft, and automobiles—are everywhere. The American political system has entered a new period of **high-tech politics**—a politics in which the behavior of citizens and policymakers, as well as the political agenda itself, is increasingly shaped by technology. The **mass media** are a key part of this technology. Television, radio, newspapers, magazines, and other means of popular communication are called *mass media* because they reach and profoundly influence not only the elites but also the masses. This chapter examines media politics, focusing on

- The rise of the modern media in America's advanced technological society
- The making of the news and its presentation through the media
- The biases in the news
- The impact of the media on policymakers and the public

This chapter also reintroduces the concept of the policy agenda, in which the media play an important role.

THE MASS MEDIA TODAY

These days, effectively communicating a message is critical to political success. The key to a successful communication strategy is gaining control over the political agenda, which involves getting one's priorities presented at the top of the daily news. Politicians have learned that one way to guide the media's focus successfully is to limit what they can report on to carefully scripted events. A **media event** is staged primarily for the purpose of being covered. If the media were not there, the event would probably not happen or would have little significance. For example, on the eve of the 1992 New Hampshire primary, Bill and Hillary Clinton went door-to-door in a middle-class neighborhood with TV crews in tow. The few dozen people they met could scarcely have made a difference, but the Clintons were not really there to win votes by personal contact. Rather, the point was to get pictures on TV of the Clintons reaching out to ordinary people. Getting the right image on TV news for just 30 seconds can easily have a greater payoff than a whole day's worth of handshaking. Whereas once a candidate's G.O.T.V. program stood for "Get Out the Vote," today it is more likely to mean "Get on TV."

In addition, a large part of today's so-called 30-second presidency is the slickly produced TV commercial. Approximately 60 percent of presidential campaign spending is now devoted to TV ads. In recent presidential elections, about two-thirds of the prominently aired ads were negative commercials.[2] Many people are worried that the tirade of accusations, innuendoes, and countercharges in political advertising is poisoning the American political process and possibly even contributing to declining turnout.[3] Some would even like the government to use its regulatory power over television to curb negative advertising. (See "You Are the Policymaker: Should Negative Political Ads Be Curbed?")

Yet image making does not stop with the campaign; it is also a critical element in day-to-day governing. Politicians' images in the press are seen as good indicators of their clout. The importance of image is especially evident for presidents, who in recent years have devoted much attention to maintaining a well-honed public image, as shown in the following internal White House memo written by President Nixon.

> When I think of the millions of dollars that go into one lousy 30-second television spot advertising a deodorant, it seems to me unbelievable that we don't do a better job in seeing that Presidential appearances always have the very best professional advice whenever they are to be covered on TV.... The President should never be without the very best professional advice for making a television appearance.[4]

Television enables many more people to see candidates for elected office than would ever be possible in person. In fact, people have become so accustomed to seeing politicians' faces when they speak that giant TV screens are now often used to enable those attending political events to see the speakers' facial expressions.

Few, if any, administrations devoted so much effort and energy to the president's media appearance as did Ronald Reagan's. It has often been said that Reagan played to the media as he had played to the cameras in Hollywood. According to Mark Hertsgaard, news management in the Reagan White House operated on the following seven principles: (1) plan ahead, (2) stay on the offensive, (3) control the flow of information, (4) limit reporters' access to the president, (5) talk about the issues you want to talk about, (6) speak in one voice, and (7) repeat the same message many times.[5]

SHOULD NEGATIVE POLITICAL ADS BE CURBED?

You Are the Policymaker

Democratic Senator Ernest Hollings of South Carolina and former Republican Senator John Danforth of Missouri were fed up with negative TV commercials. Together they introduced a bill in the Senate to use the government's regulatory power over the public airwaves to discourage such commercials. Their proposal, known as the "Clean Campaign Act," is aimed at making candidates voice their charges against an opponent either in person or not at all.

Under provisions of the legislation, candidates are not forbidden to run negative advertisements. Everyone agrees that this would be an infringement of freedom of speech. Thus, the ability of a candidate to run advertisements speaking out personally against an opponent is unaffected by the bill. However, Danforth and Hollings believe that if charges are made not by the candidate but by an ominous-sounding announcer, the government should step in. Their bill requires stations airing such ads to give the opponent free response time.

While this simple provision does not necessarily preclude negative advertising, most agree that it would probably cut it down to a minimum. No one wants to give away free response time to the opposition, and most candidates are likely to be reluctant to attack an opponent in person.

Critics of the bill offer both constitutional and practical political objections. Senator Mitch McConnell (R-KY) states that "its clear purpose is to inhibit political speech. It's not likely to withstand a court test." Senator John McCain (R-AZ) views the bill as a way to make it easier for incumbents to get reelected. Because it would be more difficult to attack an incumbent's record, challengers might find it even harder to win voters' support, argues Senator McCain.

What do you think? Would you support the proposal? To what extent do you believe it would clean up campaigns, limit free speech, or protect incumbents? In short, what are the various trade-offs involved?

SOURCE: "Senators Divide on Proposals to Tame Negative TV Ads," *Congressional Quarterly Weekly Report,* July 22, 1989, 1890.

The task of applying these principles initially fell to Michael Deaver, who occupied the office right outside the Oval Office. Deaver was responsible for advising the president on image making, as former Secretary of the Treasury Donald Regan recalls:

> . . . and image was what he talked about nearly all of the time. It was Deaver who identified the news story of the day at the eight o'clock staff meeting, and coordinated plans for dealing with it, Deaver who created and approved photo opportunities.... He saw—designed—each presidential action as a one-minute or two-minute spot on the evening network news, or a picture on page one of the *Washington Post* or the *New York Times* and conceived every Presidential appearance in terms of camera angles.[6]

To Ronald Reagan, the presidency was often a performance, and aides like Deaver helped to choreograph his public appearances. Perhaps there will never again be a president so concerned with public relations as Reagan, but for a president to ignore the power of image and the media would be perilous. In today's high-tech age, presidents can hardly lead the country if they cannot communicate effectively with it.

THE DEVELOPMENT OF THE MASS MEDIA

Lyndon Johnson was one of two recent American presidents (the other was Richard Nixon) who felt that he was hounded out of office by the press. A year after leaving the White House, Johnson was asked in a televised memoir what had been the biggest change in politics during his long career. "You guys," said Johnson. "All you guys in the media. All of politics has changed because of you. You've broken all the machines and the ties between us in Congress and the city machines. You guys have given us a new kind of politician."[7] True or exaggerated, Johnson's view is a common one: We live in the mass media age.

The Reagan administration carefully—and masterfully—controlled the president's image as presented by the media. To avoid having Reagan give unrehearsed answers, for example, his advisors would place the media at a distance and rev a helicopter engine so that the president could not hear reporters' questions.

When Gennifer Flowers made headlines by saying that she had an affair with Bill Clinton, the Clintons consciously searched for the biggest TV audience they could get to tell their side of the story. When CBS offered to air a 10-minute interview with them on "Sixty Minutes" immediately following the 1992 Super Bowl, the exposure they received made Clinton the best known of the Democratic primary candidates.

It was not always this way, of course. There was virtually no daily press when the First Amendment was written during Washington's presidency. The daily newspaper is largely a product of the late nineteenth century; radio and television have been around only since the first half of the twentieth century. As recently as the presidency of Herbert Hoover (1929–1933), reporters submitted their questions to the president in writing, and he responded in writing—if at all. As Hoover put it, "The President of the United States will not stand and be questioned like a chicken thief by men whose names he does not even know."[8]

Hoover's successor, Franklin D. Roosevelt (1933–1945), practically invented media politics. To Roosevelt, the media were a potential ally. Power radiated from Washington under him, and so did news. Roosevelt promised reporters two **press conferences**—presidential meetings with reporters—a week, and he delivered them. He held about 1,000 press conferences in his 12 years in the White House. Roosevelt was the newsmaker. Stories and leads flowed from the White House like a flood; the United Press news syndicate carried four times as much Washington news under FDR as it had under Hoover.[9] FDR was also the first president to use radio, broadcasting a series of reassuring "fireside chats" to the Depression-ridden nation. Roosevelt's crafty use of radio helped him win four presidential elections. Theodore White tells the story of the time in 1944 when FDR found out that his opponent, Thomas E. Dewey, had purchased 15 minutes of air time on NBC immediately following his own address. Roosevelt spoke for 14 minutes and then left 1 minute silent. Thinking that the network had experienced technical difficulties, many changed their dials before Dewey came on the air.[10]

Another of Roosevelt's talents was knowing how to feed the right story to the right reporter. He used presidential wrath to warn reporters off material he did not want covered, and he chastised news reports he deemed inaccurate. His wrath was rarely invoked, however, and the press revered him, never even reporting to the American public that the President was confined to a wheelchair. The idea that a political leader's private life might be public business was alien to journalists in FDR's day.

This relatively cozy relationship between politicians and the press lasted through the early 1960s. ABC's Sam Donaldson has said that when he first came to Washington in 1961, "many reporters saw themselves as an extension of the government, accepting, with very little skepticism, what government officials told them."[11] The events of the Vietnam War and the Watergate scandal, though, soured the press on government. Today's newspeople work in an environment of cynicism. To them, politicians rarely tell the whole story; the press sees ferreting out the truth as their job. No one epitomized this attitude in the 1980s better than Donaldson, who earned a hard-nosed reputation by regularly shouting unwanted questions at President Reagan. In his book, *Hold On, Mr. President!,* Donaldson wrote,

> If you send me to cover a pie-baking contest on Mother's Day, I'm going to ask dear old Mom whether she used artificial sweetener in violation of the rules, and while she's at it, could I see the receipt for the apples to prove she didn't steal them. I maintain that if Mom has nothing to hide, no harm will have been done. But the questions should be asked.[12]

Many political scientists disagree that no harm comes from such reporting. **Investigative journalism**—the use of detective-like reporting methods to unearth scandals—pits reporters against political leaders. There is evidence that TV's fondness for investigative journalism has contributed to greater public cynicism and negativism about politics.[13] Most analysts would agree that the most important change in media coverage of politics in recent years has been the much greater scrutiny to which politicians are now subjected (see "Since Kennedy: The Rise of the Negative Press").

No longer do the media broach only politics with candidates and incumbents. Here, Barbara Walters obtains a personal interview with George Bush during his presidency.

Scholars distinguish between two kinds of media: the **print media,** which include newspapers and magazines, and the **broadcast media,** which include radio, television, and now the Internet as well. Each has reshaped political communication at different points in American history. The following sections look at their development and their role in the political system.

THE PRINT MEDIA

The first American daily newspaper was printed in Philadelphia in 1783, but such papers did not proliferate until the technological advances of the mid-nineteenth century. The ratification of the First Amendment in 1791, guaranteeing freedom of speech, gave even the earliest American newspapers freedom to print whatever they saw fit. This has given the media a unique ability to display the government's dirty linen, a propensity that continues to distinguish the American press today (see "America in Perspective: The British Media," page 173).

Rapid printing and cheap paper made possible the "penny press," which could be bought for a penny and read at home. In 1841, Horace Greeley's *New York Tribune* was founded, and in 1851 *The New York Times* started up. By the 1840s, the telegraph permitted a primitive "wire service," which relayed news stories from city to city faster than ever before. The Associated Press, founded in 1849, depended heavily on this new technology.

Two newspaper magnates, Joseph Pulitzer and William Randolph Hearst, enlivened journalism around the turn of the century. Between them—Pulitzer operating in New York and Hearst in burgeoning San Francisco—they published stories about high jinks in high places. This was the era of yellow journalism, wherein violence, corruption, wars, and gossip were the main topics. Hearst even sent an artist to cover the Spanish-American conflict in Cuba, telling him, "You furnish the pictures and I'll furnish the war" by arousing American opinion against Spain. On a visit to the United States at that time, young Winston Churchill said that "the essence of American journalism is vulgarity divested of truth."[14]

Newspapers consolidated into **chains** during the early part of the twentieth century. Today's massive media conglomerates (Gannett, Knight-Ridder, and Newhouse are the largest) control newspapers with 78 percent of the nation's daily circulation.[15] Thus, three

SINCE KENNEDY

The Rise of the Negative Press

In his analysis of media coverage of presidential campaigns from 1960 to 1992, Thomas Patterson found that news coverage of presidential candidates has become increasingly less favorable. His coding of *Time* and *Newsweek* stories about the campaigns reveals that favorable references about Kennedy and Nixon outnumbered unfavorable ones by a three-to-one margin. In contrast, there were three negative references regarding Clinton and Bush for every two favorable references. The change in journalistic tone is evident from the types of cover stories that the magazines printed about the candidates in each year. In 1960, *Time* ran basic profile stories simply entitled "Candidate Kennedy" and 'Candidate Nixon." In 1992, its cover stories posed provocative questions such as "Why Voters Don't Trust Clinton" and "Is Bill Clinton for Real?"

Patterson's careful analysis uncovers several aspects of the trend toward more negative media coverage of the candidates over the last three decades. First, he finds that the emphasis of campaign reporting has changed dramatically from "what" to "why." Patterson's content analysis of front-page *New York Times* stories revealed that 30 years ago, over 90 percent of news stories employed a descriptive framework, whereas by 1992 less than 20 percent did so. Second, the type of interpretative story that has become more prominent is hard-biting analysis of political maneuvering and the horse race. Such reporting tends toward unfavorable impressions of the candidates, because the unstated assumption behind much of today's coverage of the issues has shifted from policy statements to campaign controversies. Coverage of such issues as Bill Clinton's marital fidelity, whether he should have participated in antiwar demonstrations while in England, and whether he ever inhaled marijuana are not likely to draw favorable references.

In sum, whereas Kennedy was able to have his words and ideas faithfully reported to the public, Clinton faced a press more concerned with interpreting and analyzing his every move with an eye toward how it would affect the political game. The press maintains that the public is now able to get a complete, accurate, and unvarnished look at the candidates. Critics of the media charge that they overemphasize the controversial aspects of the campaign at the expense of an examination of the major issues. What do you think? Has the change in campaign reporting been for the better or for the worse?

SOURCE: Thomas E. Patterson, *Out of Order* (New York: Knopf, 1993).

of four Americans now read a newspaper owned not by a fearless local editor but by a corporation headquartered elsewhere. Often these chains control television and radio stations as well.

Among the press there is, of course, a pecking order. Almost from the beginning, The *New York Times* was a cut above most newspapers in its influence and impact; it is the nation's "newspaper of record" and now publishes a national edition available almost everywhere in the United States. Its clearest rival in government circles is the *Washington Post,* offering perhaps the best coverage inside Washington and a sprightlier alternative to the *Times*. It now prints a national weekly edition that compiles its most important news analysis and commentary articles of the week. Papers such as the *Chicago Tribune* and the *Los Angeles Times,* as well as those in Atlanta, Boston, and other big cities, are also major national institutions. For most newspapers in medium-sized and small towns, though, the main source of national and world news is the Associated Press wire service, whose stories are reprinted in small newspapers across the country.

Magazines, the other component of the print media, are read avidly by Americans, although the political content of leading magazines is slim. The so-called newsweeklies—mainly *Time, Newsweek,* and *U.S. News and World Report*—rank well behind such popular favorites as the *Reader's Digest, TV Guide,* and *National Geographic*. Although *Time's* circulation is a bit better than that of the *National Enquirer, Playboy* and *People* edge out *Newsweek* in sales competition. Serious magazines of political news and opinion tend to be read by the educated elite; magazines such as the *New Republic,* the *National Review,* and *The Atlantic Monthly* are out-

THE BRITISH MEDIA

America in Perspective

The American media are the freest in the world. They are protected by the First Amendment, which gives legal protection unavailable in most other countries.

Even in democratic nations such as Great Britain, the media do not enjoy the independence of their American counterparts. More **censorship**—government regulation of media content—is permitted in the United Kingdom than in the United States. In Britain, the Official Secrets Act prohibits the media from covering anything the British government wants to stamp secret, and jail terms can be imposed for violating the act. One particularly silly episode involved the publication of *Spycatcher,* a book by Peter Wright, during the 1980s. Wright, a longtime employee of the British Secret Service, claimed that a top official of Her Majesty's Secret Service was in fact a double agent. The British government banned publication of the book and newspaper coverage of it (even of the banning itself). Because *Spycatcher* had already been published in the United States and elsewhere, critics thought it particularly ludicrous to attempt to ban the book in Britain.

British newspapers, like most in Europe, are much more partisan than American newspapers. Whereas American journalists pride themselves on their objectivity, the British papers are fierce partisans of the Conservative or Labour party. By American standards, many British papers are gritty and salacious, some resembling the *National Enquirer.*

On the other hand, the British Broadcasting Company is a publicly owned corporation with a reputation for highbrow news coverage and programming. Ratings are only one factor taken into account in determining the content of what is shown on BBC—quality is highly valued as well. A study comparing election campaign coverage on BBC to that of the American networks found that BBC offered more ample, varied, and substantive coverage. Sound bites were longer on British television, and politicians were more likely to be given a chance to outline their proposals and issue stands during newscasts. To accomplish all of this, the evening news at 9 o'clock was actually extended for 15 minutes during the 3-week election campaign. Thus, BBC takes more care in seeing to the voters' civic education than do the commercial American networks.

SOURCE: The study referred to can be found in Holli A. Semetko *et al., The Formation of Campaign Agendas: A Comparative Analysis of Party and Media Roles in Recent American and British Elections* (Hillsdale, NJ: Lawrence Erlbaum, 1991).

sold by such American favorites as *Hot Rod, Weightwatchers Magazine,* and *Organic Gardening.*

THE BROADCAST MEDIA

Gradually, the broadcast media have displaced the print media as Americans' principal source of news and information, as can be seen from the media milestones displayed in Figure 7.1. By the middle of the 1930s, radio ownership had become almost universal in America, and during World War II, radio went into the news business in earnest. The 1950s and early 1960s were the adolescent years for American television. During those years, the political career of Richard Nixon was made and unmade by television. In 1952, while running as Dwight Eisenhower's vice-presidential candidate, Nixon made a famous speech denying that he took under-the-table gifts and payments. Claiming that his wife, Pat, wore only a "Republican cloth coat," he did admit that one gift he had accepted was his dog Checkers. Noting that his daughters loved the dog, Nixon said that regardless of his political future, they would keep it. His homey appeal brought a flood of sympathetic telegrams to the Republican National Committee, and party leaders had little choice but to leave him on the ticket.

In 1960, Nixon was again on television's center stage, this time in the first televised **presidential debate** against Senator John F. Kennedy. Nixon blamed his poor appearance in the first of the four debates for his narrow defeat in the election. Haggard from a week in the hospital and with his five o'clock shadow and perspiration clearly visible, Nixon looked awful compared to the crisp, clean, attractive Kennedy. The poll results from this debate illustrate the visual power of television in American politics; people listening on the radio gave the edge to Nixon, but those who saw the debate on television thought Kennedy won. Russell

FIGURE 7.1 MEDIA MILESTONES

NEWSPAPERS	
1690	First newspaper published in the colonies; suppressed after first issue
1783	First daily newspaper in the U.S.—*Pennsylvania Evening Post*
1996	Newspapers start to provide campaign coverage on the World Wide Web
TELEGRAPH	
1844	First telegraph message sent
1849	Associated Press (AP) founded to distribute telegraphic news
1963	"Hot Line" established between the White House and the Kremlin
TELEPHONE	
1876	Telephone invented
1878	The first telephone in the White House was installed in the Oval Office—the telephone number was "1"
RADIO	
1903	Radio invented
1920	First commercial radio station (KDKA in Pittsburgh)
1924	First live radio coverage of a nominating convention
1930s	President Franklin D. Roosevelt uses radio for "fireside chats" with the American people
1941–1945	Radio news covers World War II
TELEVISION	
1923	Television invented
1948	First televised nominating conventions
1952	First presidential campaign commercials; Richard Nixon makes the famous "Checkers Speech"
1960	Candidates Kennedy and Nixon hold the first televised presidential debates
1961	President Kennedy holds the first live televised presidential press conference
1960s	Television brings the Vietnam War to American living rooms
1973	Senate Watergate committee holds televised hearings on the Watergate scandal
1979	Founding of C-SPAN to televise House sessions
1986	Founding of C-SPAN 2 to televise Senate Sessions
1991	Initial attack on Iraq televised by CNN as it happened

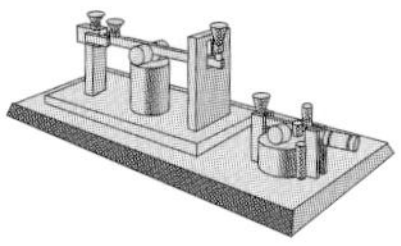

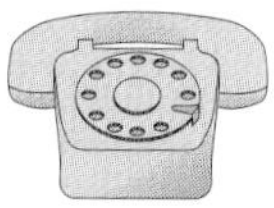

Baker, who covered the event for The *New York Times,* writes in his memoirs that "television replaced newspapers as the most important communications medium in American politics" that very night.[16]

Just as radio had taken the nation to the war in Europe and the Pacific during the 1940s, television took the nation to the war in Vietnam during the 1960s. TV exposed governmental naiveté (some said it was outright lying) about the progress of the war. Napoleon once said that "four hostile newspapers are more to be feared than a thousand bayonets." Lyndon Johnson learned the hard way that three television networks could be even more consequential. Every night, in living color, Americans watched the horrors of war through television. President Johnson soon had two wars on his hands, one in faraway Vietnam and the other at home with antiwar protesters—both covered in detail by the media. In 1968, CBS anchor Walter Cronkite journeyed to Vietnam for a firsthand look at the state of the war. In an extraordinary TV special, Cronkite reported that the war was not being won, nor was it likely to be. Watching from the White House, Johnson sadly remarked that if he had lost Cronkite, he had lost the support of the American people.[17]

With the growth of cable TV, particularly the Cable News Network (CNN), television has recently entered a new era of bringing the news to people—and political leaders—as it happens. President Bush and his aides regularly watched CNN during the Gulf War, as did the Iraqi leadership. Marlin Fitzwater, Bush's press secretary, stated that "CNN has opened up a whole new communications system between governments in terms of immediacy and directness. In many cases it's the first communication we have."[18] A frequent response from U.S. officials to reporters' questions during the Gulf War was "I don't know anymore than what you saw on CNN."[19]

Since 1963, surveys have consistently shown that more people rely on TV for the news than any other medium. Furthermore, by a regular two-to-one margin, people think television reports are more believable than newspaper stories.[20] (Consider the old sayings "Don't believe everything you read" and "I'll believe it when I see it.") Whereas people are predisposed to be skeptical about what they read in a newspaper, with television seeing is believing. As we look toward the twenty-first century, the future seems destined to contain more and more choices regarding what we can see about our government (see "In the Twenty-first Century: Narrowcasting in a 500-Channel Environment").

REPORTING THE NEWS

Regardless of the medium, it cannot be emphasized enough that news reporting is a business in America. Striving for the bottom line—profits—shapes how journalists define what is newsworthy, where they get their information, and how they present it. Because some types of news stories attract more viewers or readers than others, certain biases are inherent in what the American public sees and reads.

DEFINING NEWS

As every journalism student will quickly tell you, news is what is timely and different. It is a man biting a dog, not a dog biting a man. An oft-repeated speech on foreign policy or a well-worn statement on fighting drug abuse is less newsworthy than an odd episode. The public rarely hears about the routine ceremonies at state dinners, but when President Bush threw up all over the Japanese Prime Minister, the world's media jumped on the story. In its search for the unusual, the news media can give the audience a peculiar view of events and policymakers.

Millions of new and different events happen every day; journalists must decide which of them are newsworthy. No one has taken a more careful look at the definition and production of news than Edward J. Epstein, who, given the unique opportunity to observe NBC's news department for a year, wrote *News from Nowhere,* a classic inside account of the TV news business.[21] Epstein found that some important characteristics of the TV news business result from the nature of the viewing audience. In their pursuit of high ratings, news shows are tailored to a fairly low level of audience sophistication. To a large extent, TV networks define news as what is entertaining to the average viewer.

FINDING THE NEWS

Epstein called his book *News from Nowhere* to make the point that the organizational process shapes the news. Of course, news does come from somewhere. Americans' popular image of correspondents or reporters somehow uncovering the news is accurate in some cases, yet a surprising amount of news comes from well-established sources. Most news organizations assign their best reporters to particular **beats**—specific locations from which news often emanates, such as Congress. For example, during the Persian Gulf War, more than 50 percent of the lead stories on the TV newscasts came from the White House, Pentagon, and State Department beats.[22] Numerous studies of both the electronic and the print media have found that journalists rely almost exclusively on such established sources to get their information (see Table 7.1, page 177).

Reporters and their official sources have a symbiotic relationship. Those who make the news depend on the media to spread certain information and ideas to the general public. Sometimes they feed stories to reporters in the form of **trial balloons:** information leaked to see what the political reaction will be. In turn, reporters rely on public officials to keep them in

NARROWCASTING IN A 500-CHANNEL ENVIRONMENT

In the 21st Century

During the last presidential election of the twentieth century, about 60 percent of the American public subscribed to cable television, thereby gaining access to dozens of channels. It is expected that sometime in the twenty-first century, most cable systems will offer 500 channels. How will this explosion of TV channels affect political communication? Our best guess, based on developments with cable TV to date, is that information about politics will be presented in a way that appeals to a rather narrow and specific audience rather than to the public at large.

The first major networks—ABC, NBC, and CBS—adopted the term "broadcasting" in the names of their companies because their signal was being sent out to a broad audience. As long as these networks dominated the industry, each would have to deal with general topics that the public as a whole was concerned with, such as politics and government. But with the development of many channels in recent years, market segmentation has set in. Sports buffs can watch ESPN all day, music buffs can tune to MTV or VH1, history buffs can glue their dial to the History Channel, and so forth. If you are interested in politics, you can channel-surf between C-SPAN, C-SPAN2, CNN, CNN Headline News, and other news stations. Rather than appealing to a general audience, channels such as ESPN, MTV, and C-SPAN focus on a narrow, particular interest. Hence their mission can be termed "narrowcasting," rather than the traditional "broadcasting."

As we look toward the future, the prospects are good for an expansion of the number of channels devoted to politics. Already, C-SPAN has plans to expand from two to five channels. This expansion will enable C-SPAN to cover simultaneously the House and Senate in session, as well as congressional hearings, international events, and events related to business and finance. With the commercial success of CNN, it is likely that other news channels will spring up—each looking for a different market niche, perhaps by openly presenting the news in a proconservative or proliberal fashion. Again, the idea would be to appeal to a relatively small, yet reliable base of viewers rather than to everyone.

If these expectations come to pass, it is clear that political junkies will find more political information readily available on TV than ever before. But with so many channels for so many specific interests, it will also be extremely easy for those who are not much interested in politics to avoid news and public affairs completely. The result could well be a growing inequality of political information, the politically interested becoming more knowledgeable while the rest of the public slips further into political apathy. That's what some scholars fear will happen in the 500-channel TV environment of the twenty-first century.

the know. When reporters feel that their access to information is being impeded, complaints of censorship become widespread. During the Gulf War, reporters' freedom of movement and observation was severely restricted. After the fighting was over, 15 influential news organizations sent a letter to the Secretary of Defense complaining that the rules for reporting the war were designed more to control the news than to facilitate it.[23] Although the signers of the letter vowed not to let this happen again, there is probably little they can do about it. Official sources who have the information usually have the upper hand over those who merely report it.

Despite this dependence on familiar sources, an enterprising reporter occasionally has an opportunity to live up to the image of the crusading truth-seeker. Local reporters Carl Bernstein and Bob Woodward of the *Washington Post* uncovered important evidence in the Watergate case in the early 1970s. Columnists such as Jack Anderson regularly expose the uglier side of government corruption and inefficiency. Such reporting is highly valued among the media elite. Pulitzer prizes typically go to reporters who get exclusive stories through painstaking legwork.

PRESENTING THE NEWS

Once the news has been "found," it has to be neatly compressed into a 30-second news segment or fit in among the advertisements in a newspaper. If you had to pick a single word to describe news coverage by the print and broadcast media, it would be *superficial*. "The name of the game," says former White House press secretary Jody Powell, "is skimming off the

TABLE 7.1 SOURCES FOR NEWSPAPER STORIES

Very little of the news is generated by spontaneous events or a reporter's own analysis. Rather, most stories are drawn from situations over which newsmakers have substantial control. Leon Sigal examined the sources for news stories in the *New York Times* and the *Washington Post,* the nation's two most prestigious newspapers. Listed here are the percentages of news stories drawn from the following sources:

SOURCE	PERCENT
Interviews	24.7
Press conferences	24.5
Press releases	17.5
Official proceedings	7.9
Other nonspontaneous events	4.5
News commentary and editorials	2.3
Leaks	1.5
Nongovernmental proceedings	1.5
Spontaneous events	1.2
Reporter's own analysis	0.9

SOURCE: Leon V. Sigal, *Reporters and Officials: The Organization and Politics of News Reporting* (Lexington, MA: D. C. Heath, 1973), 122.

cream, seizing on the most interesting, controversial, and unusual aspects of an issue."[24] TV news, in particular, is little more than a headline service. Except for the little-watched, but highly regarded "Newshour" on PBS and ABC's late-night "Nightline," analysis of news events rarely lasts more than a minute. Patterson's careful study of campaign coverage (see Chapter 9) found that only skimpy attention was given to the issues during a presidential campaign. Clearly, if coverage of political events during the height of an election campaign is thin, coverage of day-to-day policy questions is even thinner. Issues such as reforming the Medicare system, adjusting how the consumer price index is calculated, and deregulating the communications industry are highly complex and difficult to treat in a short news clip.

Strangely enough, as technology has enabled the media to pass along information with greater speed, news coverage has become less thorough.[25]

Viewers around the world tuned in to CNN to learn of events in the Persian Gulf War. President Bush reportedly told other world leaders, "I learn more from CNN than I do from the CIA."

Bob Woodward (left) and Carl Bernstein, two obscure local reporters for the *Washington Post,* painstakingly uncovered the first details of the Watergate scandal. Watergate signaled a new era in the relationship between journalists and politicians; journalists assumed that politicians had something to hide, and politicians assumed that reporters were out to embarrass them.

Newspapers once routinely reprinted the entire text of important political speeches; now the *New York Times* is virtually the only paper that does so—and even the *Times* has cut back sharply on this practice. In place of speeches, Americans now hear **sound bites** of 15 seconds or less on TV. As you can see in Figure 7.2, the average length of time that a presidential candidate has been given to talk uninterrupted on the TV news has declined precipitously since the late 1960s. Responding to criticism of sound-bite journalism, in 1992 CBS News briefly vowed that it would let a candidate speak for at least 30 seconds at a time. However, CBS found this to be unworkable and soon dropped the threshold to 20 seconds, noting that even this was flexible.[26] In 1996, the average sound bite of a candidate shown talking on the nightly news once again averaged less than 10 seconds.[27]

Even successful politicians sometimes feel frustrated by sound-bite journalism. A year after his election to the presidency, Jimmy Carter told a reporter that

> it's a strange thing that you can go through your campaign for president, and you have a basic theme that you express in a 15- or 20-minute standard speech, . . . but the traveling press—sometimes exceeding 100 people—will never report that speech to the public. The peripheral aspects become the headlines, but the basic essence of what you stand for and what you hope to accomplish is never reported.[28]

Rather than presenting their audience with the whole chicken, the media typically give just a McNugget. Why then should politicians work to build a carefully

crafted case for their point of view when a catchy line will do just as well? As former CBS anchor Walter Cronkite writes, "Naturally, nothing of any significance is going to be said in seven seconds, but this seems to work to the advantage of many politicians. They are not required to say anything of significance, and issues can be avoided rather than confronted."[29]

BIAS IN THE NEWS

Many people believe that the news is biased in favor of one point of view. During the 1996 presidential campaign, Bob Dole often charged that the press was against him. "Annoy the Media—Elect Dole" become one of his favorite lines. The charge that the media have a liberal bias has become a familiar one in American politics, and there is some limited evidence to support it. A lengthy study by the *Los Angeles Times*

FIGURE 7.2 THE INCREDIBLE SHRINKING SOUND BITE

Following is the average length of time a presidential candidate was shown speaking uninterrupted on the evening network news from 1968 to 1996.

1968	1972	1976	1980	1984	1988	1992	1996
43.1 seconds	25.2 seconds	18.2 seconds	12.2 seconds	9.9 seconds	8.9 seconds	8.4 seconds	8.2 seconds

SOURCE: Daniel Hallin, "Sound Bite News: Television Coverage of Elections," *Journal of Communications*, Spring 1992; 1992 and 1996 data from studies by the Center for Media Public Affairs.

in the mid-1980s found that reporters were twice as likely to call themselves liberal as the general public.[30] A 1992 survey of 1,400 journalists found that 44 percent identified themselves as Democrats, compared to just 16 percent who said they were Republicans.[31]

However, there is little reason to believe that journalists' personal attitudes sway their reporting of the news. The vast majority of social science studies have found that reporting is not systematically biased toward a particular ideology or party.[32] Most stories are presented in a "point/counterpoint" format in which two opposing points of view (such as liberal versus conservative) are presented, and the audience is left to draw its own conclusions. A number of factors explain why the news is typically characterized by such political neutrality. Most reporters strongly believe in journalistic objectivity, and those who practice it best are usually rewarded by their editors. In addition, media outlets have a direct financial stake in attracting viewers and subscribers and do not want to lose their broadly based audience by appearing biased—especially when multiple versions of the same story are readily available. It seems paradoxical to say that competition produces uniformity, but this often happens in the news business.

To conclude that the news contains little explicit partisan or ideological bias is not to argue that it does not distort reality in its coverage. Ideally, the news should mirror reality; in practice, there are far too many possible stories for this to be the case. Journalists must choose which stories to cover and to what degree. The overriding bias is toward stories that will draw the largest audience. Surveys show that people are most fascinated by stories with conflict, violence, disaster, or scandal (see "The People Speak: Stories Citizens Have Tuned In and Stories They Have Tuned Out"). Good news is unexciting; bad news has the drama that brings in big audiences.

Conservative Republicans often criticize the media for being biased against them. Studies have indeed shown that TV and newspaper reporters are more likely to be liberals than conservatives. However, there is little evidence that the personal views of reporters influence their coverage.

Television is particularly biased toward stories that generate good pictures. Seeing a **talking head** (a shot of a person's face talking directly to the camera) is boring; viewers will switch channels in search of more interesting visual stimulation. For example, during an unusually contentious and lengthy interview of George Bush by Dan Rather concerning the Iran-Contra scandal, CBS's ratings actually went down as people tired of watching two talking heads argue for an extended period of time.[33] A shot of ambassadors squaring off in a fistfight at the United Nations, on the other hand, will up the ratings. Such a scene was shown three times in one day on CBS in 1973. Not once, though, was the cause of the fight discussed.[34] Network practices like these have led observers such as Lance Bennett to write that "the public is exposed to a world driven into chaos by seemingly arbitrary and mysterious forces."[35]

THE NEWS AND PUBLIC OPINION

How does the threatening, hostile, and corrupt world often depicted by the news media shape what people believe about the American political system? This question is difficult to answer. Studying the effects of the news media on people's opinions and behaviors is a difficult task. One reason is that it is hard to separate the media from other influences. When presidents, legislators, and interest groups—as well as news organizations—are all discussing an issue, it is not easy to isolate the opinion changes that come from political leadership from those that come from the news. Moreover, the effect of one news story on public opinion may be trivial; the cumulative effect of dozens of news stories may be important.

For many years, students of the subject tended to doubt that the media had more than a marginal effect on public opinion. The "minimal effects hypothesis" stemmed from the fact that early scholars were looking for direct impacts—for example, whether the media affected how people voted.[36] When the focus turned to how the media affect *what Americans think about,* more positive results were uncovered. In a series of controlled laboratory experiments, Shanto Iyengar and Donald Kinder subtly manipulated the stories participants saw on the TV news.[37] They found that they could significantly affect the importance people attached to a given problem by splicing a few stories about it into the news over the course of a week. Iyengar and Kinder do not maintain that the networks

The People Speak

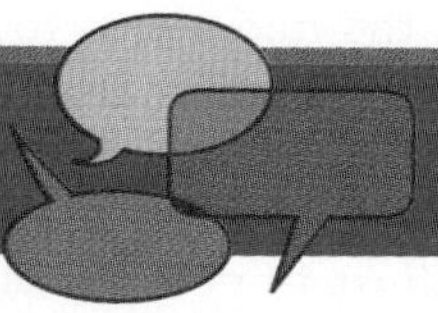

Stories Citizens Have Tuned In and Stories They Have Tuned Out

Since 1986, the monthly survey of the PEW Research Center for the People and the Press has asked Americans how closely they have followed major news stories. As one would expect, stories involving disaster or human drama have drawn more attention than complicated issues of public policy. A representative selection of their findings is presented below. The percentage in each case is the proportion who reported the story "very closely."

Story	Percentage
The explosion of the space shuttle *Challenger*	80%
San Francisco earthquake	73%
Los Angeles riots	70%
Rescue of baby Jessica McClure from a well	69%
Crash of TWA 800	69%
Iraq's invasion of Kuwait	66%
Hurricane Andrew	66%
Explosion during Atlanta Olympics	57%
Supreme Court decision on flag burning	51%
Opening of the Berlin Wall	50%
Introduction of President Clinton's 1993 economic program	49%
Arrest of O. J. Simpson	48%
Nuclear accident at Chermobyl	46%
Attack on ice skater Nancy Kerrigan	45%
Arrest in the Unabomber case	44%
Iran-Contra hearings	33%
Mass suicide of "Heaven's Gate" cult	32%
Passage of the 1994 Crime Bill	30%
1996 New Hampshire primary	22%
Congressional debate over NAFTA	21%
Clinton's veto of the bill to ban "partial-birth" abortions	21%
Congressional repeal of catastrophic health insurance	19%
Nomination of Robert Bork to the Supreme Court	17%
Education summit held by President Bush and the nation's governors	15%
Clinton's cabinet choices for his second term	15%
Passage of the 1996 Communications Deregulation Bill	12%
Discussion and debate about expanding NATO into Eastern Europe	6%

SOURCE: PEW Research Center for the People and the Press.

can make something out of nothing or conceal problems that actually exist. But they do conclude that "what television news does, instead, is alter the priorities Americans attach to a circumscribed set of problems, all of which are plausible contenders for public concern."[38]

This effect has far-reaching consequences. By increasing public attention to specific problems, the media influence the criteria by which the public evaluates political leaders. When unemployment goes up but inflation goes down, does public support for the president increase or decrease? The answer could depend in large part on which story the media emphasize. The fact that the media emphasized the country's slow economic growth in 1992, rather than the good news of low inflation and interest rates, was clearly helpful to Bill Clinton's first campaign for the presidency.

In another study, Page, Shapiro, and Dempsey examined changes in public attitudes about issues over time. They examined public opinion polls on the same issues at two points in time, carefully coding the news coverage of these issues on the networks and in print

during the interim. People's opinions did indeed shift with the tone of the news coverage. The impact of news commentators seemed particularly significant in affecting opinion change. Another source of opinion change was presidential statements, though this varied with the popularity of the president. Not surprisingly, popular presidents were much more effective than unpopular ones in changing people's opinions. In contrast, interest groups seemed to have a negative impact on opinion change, which suggests that interest groups' overt activities on behalf of a certain policy position may in fact *discourage* support for that position. Of all the influences on opinion change that these researchers examined, news commentators had the strongest impact. If Page and his colleagues are correct, the news media today are one of the most potent—perhaps *the* most potent—engines of public opinion change in America.[39]

Much remains unknown about the effects of the media and the news on American political behavior. Enough is known, however, to conclude that the media are a key political institution. The media control much of the technology that in turn controls much of what Americans believe about politics and government. For this reason, it is important to look at the American policy agenda and the media's role in shaping it.

THE POLICY AGENDA AND THE SPECIAL ROLE OF THE MEDIA

Someone who asks you, "What's your agenda?" wants to know something about your priorities. As discussed in Chapter 1, governments also have agendas. John Kingdon defines **policy agenda** as "the list of subjects or problems to which government officials, and people outside of government closely associated with those officials, are paying some serious attention at any given time."[40] Interest groups, political parties, individual politicians, public relations firms, bureaucratic agencies—and, of course, the president and Congress—are all pushing for their priorities to take precedence over others. Health care, education, unemployment, welfare reform—these and scores of other issues compete for attention from the government.

Political activists depend heavily on the media to get their ideas placed high on the governmental agenda. Political activists are often called **policy entrepreneurs**—people who invest their political "capital" in an issue (as an economic entrepreneur invests capital in an idea for making money). Kingdon says that policy entrepreneurs can "be in or out of government, in elected or appointed positions, in interest groups or research organizations."[41] Policy entrepreneurs' arsenal of weapons includes press releases, press conferences, and letter writing; buttonholing reporters and columnists; trading on personal contacts; and, in cases of desperation, resorting to the dramatic. In addition, people in power can use a **leak,** a carefully placed bit of inside information given to a friendly reporter. Leaks benefit both the leaker and the recipient; leakers win points with the press for sharing "secrets," and reporters can print or broadcast exclusive information.

The staging of political events to attract media attention is a political art form. Dictators, revolutionaries, prime ministers, and presidents all play to the cameras. When Henry Kissinger, Nixon's top foreign policy advisor, arranged Nixon's famous trip to China, he was reminded that domestic appearances were as important as foreign policy gains. Meeting with Kissinger and Nixon, White House Chief of Staff Bob Haldeman "saw no sense in making history if television were not there to broadcast it."[42] The three men then had a lengthy discussion of how to obtain plentiful, favorable media coverage. Orchestrated minute by minute, Nixon's 1972 trip to China was perhaps the biggest media event of all time. Chinese officials were cooperative, knowing that good press coverage would help their government establish relations with the United States. They even bought the satellite transmitter the networks needed to broadcast the visit live to America. In the end, Nixon's trip to China was presented to the American public as a TV miniseries. As befits the art form that it was, the trip years later became the subject of a successful opera production.

The media are not always monopolized by political elites; the poor and downtrodden have access to them too. Civil rights groups in the 1960s relied heavily on the media to tell their stories of unjust treatment. Many believe that the introduction of television helped to accelerate the movement by showing Americans—in the North and South alike—just what the situation was.[43] Protest groups have learned that if they can

stage an interesting event that attracts the media's attention, at least their point of view will be heard. Radical activist Saul Alinsky once dramatized the plight of one neighborhood by having its residents collect rats and dump them on the mayor's front lawn. The story was one that local reporters could hardly resist.

Conveying a long-term, positive image via the media is more important, though, than a few dramatic events. Policy entrepreneurs—individuals or groups, in or out of government—depend on good will and good images. Sometimes it helps to hire a public relations firm that specializes in getting a specific message across. Groups, individuals, and even countries have hired public relations firms to improve their image and their ability to peddle their issue positions.[44]

UNDERSTANDING THE MASS MEDIA

The media are so crucial in today's society that they are often referred to as the "fourth branch of government." The media act as key link institutions between the people and the policymakers, having a profound impact on the political policy agenda. Bernard Cohen goes so far as to say that "no major act of the American Congress, no foreign adventure, no act of diplomacy, no great social reform can succeed unless the press prepares the public mind."[45] If Cohen is right, then the growth of government in America would have been impossible without the need for its being established through the media. The following sections will consider the extent to which the media have paved the way for the enlarged scope of government and will also look at how the media have shaped democracy in America.

THE MEDIA AND THE SCOPE OF GOVERNMENT

The watchdog function of the media helps to restrict politicians. Many observers feel that the press is biased against whoever holds office at the moment and that reporters want to expose officeholders in the media. Reporters, they argue, hold disparaging views of most public officials, believing that they are self-serving, hypocritical, lacking in integrity, and preoc-

Richard Nixon's 1972 trip to China was carefully planned for the benefit of the viewing audience back home. The image presented of Nixon as a world statesman and peacemaker boosted his popularity and aided his reelection bid.

cupied with reelection. Thus, it is not surprising that journalists see a need to debunk public officials and their policy proposals.

As every new proposal is met with much skepticism, regular constraints are placed on the scope of what government can do. The watchdog orientation of the press can be characterized as neither liberal nor conservative, but reformist. Reporters often see their job as crusading against foul play and unfairness in government and society. It is when they focus on injustice in society that they inevitably encourage enlarging the scope of government. Once the media identify a problem in society—such as poverty, inadequate medical care for the aged, or poor education for certain children—reporters usually begin to ask what the government is doing about the problem. Could it be acting more effectively to solve the problem? What do people in the White House and the Congress have to say about it? In this way, the media portray government as responsible for handling almost every major problem. Though skeptical of what politicians say and do, the media report on America's social problems in a manner that often also encourages government to take on more and more tasks.

INDIVIDUALISM AND THE MEDIA

More than any other development in the twentieth century, the rise of television broadcasting has reinforced and furthered individualism in the American political process. Candidates are now much more capable of running for office on their own by appealing to people directly through television. Individual voters can see the candidates "up close and personal" for themselves, so they have much less need for political parties or social groups to help them make their decisions.

The American institutional agenda has changed dramatically because television finds it easier to focus on individuals than on groups. Parties have declined, and candidate personality is more important than ever. Congress is difficult to cover on television because there are 535 members, but there is only one president; thus, the presidency has increasingly received more exposure vis-à-vis the Congress. As you can see in Figure 7.3, the president receives almost twice as much coverage as the Congress on the network news, where the notion of equality between the branches is usually not recognized. The Supreme Court, which does not allow TV cameras to cover its proceedings and whose members rarely give interviews, is almost invisible on TV newscasts.

DEMOCRACY AND THE MEDIA

As Ronald Berkman and Laura Kitch remark, "Information is the fuel of democracy."[46] Widespread access to information could be the greatest boon to democracy since the secret ballot, yet most observers think it has fallen far short of this potential. Noting the vast increase in information available through the news media, Berkman and Kitch state that "if the sheer quantity of news produced greater competency in the citizenry, then we would have a society of political masters. Yet, just the opposite is happening."[47] The rise of the "information society" has not brought about the rise of the "informed society." For one thing, complex policy issues are not well

FIGURE 7.3 TIME DEVOTED TO THE THREE BRANCHES OF GOVERNMENT ON NETWORK TELEVISION NEWS

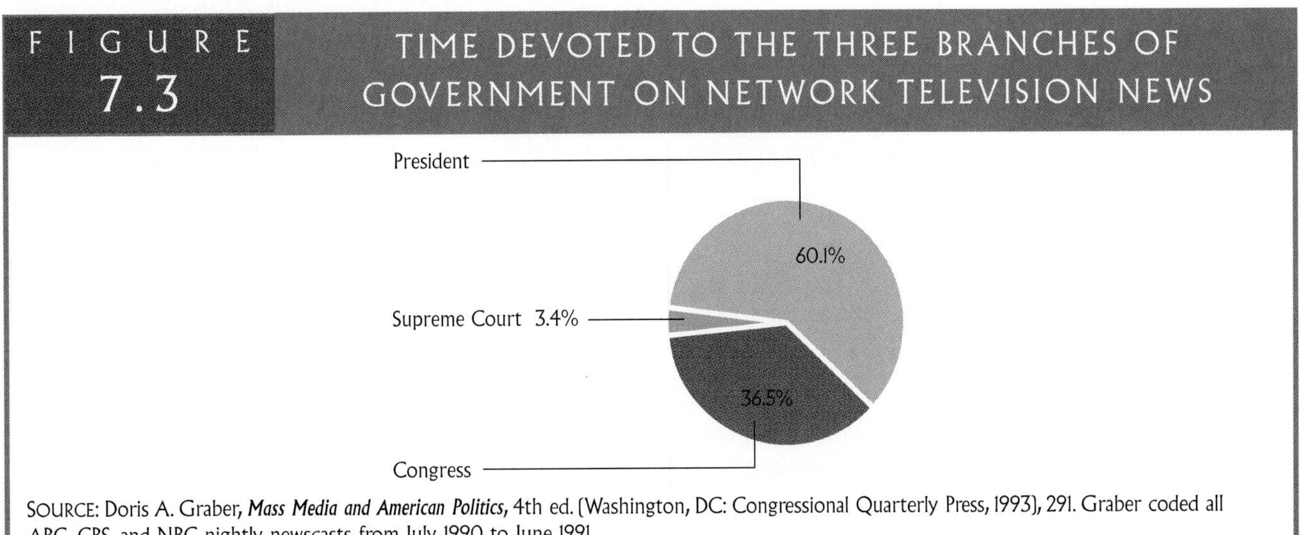

SOURCE: Doris A. Graber, ***Mass Media and American Politics***, 4th ed. (Washington, DC: Congressional Quarterly Press, 1993), 291. Graber coded all ABC, CBS, and NBC nightly newscasts from July 1990 to June 1991.

"What'll it be—entertainment news or entertainment?"

covered in the media. The media do a far more thorough job of covering the "horse race" aspects of politics than they do of covering substantive issues.

Whenever the media are criticized for being superficial, their defense is to say that this is what people want. Network executives remark that if people suddenly started to watch in-depth shows such as PBS's "Newshour," then they would gladly imitate them. If the American people wanted serious coverage of the issues, they would be happy to give it to them. Network executives claim that they are in business to make a profit and that to do so, they must appeal to the maximum number of people. As Matthew Kerbel observes, "the people who bring you the evening news would like it to be informative *and* entertaining, but when these two values collide, the shared orientations of the television news world push the product inexorably toward the latter."[48] It is not their fault if the resulting news coverage is superficial, network executives argue; blame capitalism, or blame the people—most of whom like news to be more entertaining than educational. Thus, if people are not better informed in the high-tech age, it is largely because they do not care to hear about complicated political issues. In this sense, one can say that the people really do rule through the media.

SUMMARY

Plenty of evidence points to the power of the media in American politics. The media are ubiquitous. There is evidence that the news and its presentation are an important—perhaps the most important—shaper of public opinion on political issues. The media are an important ingredient in shaping the policy agenda, and political entrepreneurs carefully use the media for this purpose.

The media can be categorized as the print and the broadcast media. Gradually, the broadcast media have replaced the print media as the principal source of news. The media largely define "news" as people and events out of the ordinary. Because of economic pressures, the media are biased in favor of stories with high drama that will attract people's interest, instead of extended analyses of complex issues. With the media's superficial treatment of important policy issues, it should be no surprise that the incredible amount of information available to Americans today has not visibly increased their political awareness or participation.

KEY TERMS

high-tech politics
mass media
media event
press conferences
investigative journalism
censorship
print media
broadcast media
chains
presidential debate
beats
trial balloons
sound bites
talking head
policy agenda
policy entrepreneurs
leak

FOR FURTHER READING

Epstein, Edward J. *News from Nowhere: Television and the News*. New York: Random House, 1973. Although somewhat dated, this account still provides an excellent view of network news.

Frantzich, Stephen, and John Sullivan. *The C-SPAN Revolution*. Norman: University of Oklahoma Press, 1996. An account of the network for political junkies.

Graber, Doris A. *Mass Media and American Politics,* 5th ed. Washington, DC: Congressional Quarterly Press, 1996. The standard textbook on the subject.

Halberstam, David. *The Powers That Be*. New York: Dell Books, 1979. A massive inquiry into the origins and influence of the *Washington Post, Los Angeles Times,* CBS, and *Time.*

Hertsgaard, Mark. *On Bended Knee: The Press and the Reagan Presidency*. New York: Farrar, Straus & Giroux, 1988. An in-depth look at how the press treated Reagan, and vice versa.

Iyengar, Shanto, and Donald R. Kinder. *News That Matters*. Chicago: University of Chicago Press, 1987.

Two political psychologists show how the media can affect the public agenda.

Jamieson, Kathleen Hall. *Eloquence in an Electronic Age*. New York: Oxford University Press, 1988. A noted communications scholar takes a look at how television has altered political discourse.

Kingdon, John W. *Agendas, Alternatives, and Public Policy,* 2nd ed. New York: HarperCollins, 1995. The best overall study of the formation of the policy agenda.

Neuman, W. Russell, Marion R. Just, and Ann N. Crigler. *Common Knowledge: News and the Construction of Political Meaning*. Chicago: University of Chicago Press, 1992. An interesting study arguing that television is reasonably effective in promoting learning about the issues.

Patterson, Thomas E. *Out of Order*. New York: Knopf, 1993. A highly critical and well-documented examination of how the media covers election campaigns.

Smith, Hedrick, ed. *The Media and the Gulf War: The Press and Democracy in Wartime*. Washington, DC: Seven Locks Press, 1992. A diverse set of readings concerning how the Gulf War was reported.

West, Darrell M. *Air Wars: Television Advertising in Election Campaigns, 1952-1996,* 2nd ed. Washington, DC: Congressional Quarterly Press, 1997. An analysis of how TV campaign ads have evolved over the last four decades and what impact they have had on elections.

INTERNET RESOURCES

www.people-press.org
The PEW Center for the People and the Press regularly surveys people regarding their attitudes toward the media's coverage of politics, and measures which news events people follow most closely.

www.asc.upenn.edu/appc/washington/
The Annenberg Public Policy Center conducts studies that analyze the content of TV coverage of politics, which they post at this site.

NOTES

1. *C-SPAN Update,* January 12, 1992, p. 6.
2. See Darrell M. West, *Air Wars: Television Advertising in Election Campaigns, 1952-1992* (Washington, DC: Congressional Quarterly Press, 1993), 48.
3. Stephen Ansolabehere and Shanto Iyengar, *Going Negative.* New York: Free Press, 1995.
4. December 1, 1969, memo from Nixon to H. R. Haldeman in Bruce Oudes, ed., *From: The President-Richard Nixon's Secret Files* (New York: Harper & Row, 1988), 76-77.
5. Mark Hertsgaard, *On Bended Knee: The Press and the Reagan Presidency* (New York: Farrar, Straus & Giroux, 1988), 34.
6. Donald T. Regan, *For the Record* (New York: Harcourt Brace Jovanovich, 1988), 247-248.
7. The Johnson interview is recounted in David Halberstam, *The Powers That Be* (New York: Dell Books, 1979), 15-16.
8. Quoted in David Brinkley, *Washington Goes to War* (New York: Knopf, 1988), 171.
9. Halberstam, *The Powers That Be,* 19.
10. Theodore H. White, *The Making of the President, 1972* (New York: Atheneum, 1973), 250.
11. Sam Donaldson, *Hold On, Mr. President!* (New York: Random House, 1987), 54.
12. *Ibid.,* 20.
13. See the classic report by Michael J. Robinson, "Public Affairs Television and the Growth of Political Malaise: The Case of 'The Selling of the Pentagon,'" *American Political Science Review* 70 (June 1976): 409-432.
14. William Manchester, *The Last Lion: Winston Churchill, Visions of Glory, 1874-1932* (Boston: Little, Brown, 1984), 225.
15. Doris A. Graber, *Mass Media and American Politics,* 4th ed. (Washington, DC: Congressional Quarterly Press, 1993), 44.
16. Russell Baker, *The Good Times* (New York: William Morrow, 1989), 326.
17. See Walter Cronkite, *A Reporter's Life* (New York: Knopf, 1996), 257-258.
18. Maureen Dowd, "Where Bush Turns for the Latest," *New York Times,* August 11, 1989, A11.
19. Lewis A. Friedland, *Covering the World: International Television News Services* (New York: The Twentieth Century Fund, 1992), 8.
20. See Harold W. Stanley and Richard G. Niemi, *Vital Statistics on American Politics,* 5th ed. (Washington, DC: Congressional Quarterly Press, 1995), 68.
21. Edward J. Epstein, *News from Nowhere: Television and the News* (New York: Random House, 1973).
22. Stephen Ansolabehere, Roy Behr, and Shanto Iyengar, *The Media Game: American Politics in the Television Age* (New York: Macmillan, 1993), 53.
23. This letter can be found in Hedrick Smith, ed., *The Media and the Gulf War: The Press and Democracy in Wartime* (Washington, DC: Seven Locks Press, 1992), 378-380. Smith's book contains an excellent set of readings on media coverage of the war.

24. Jody Powell, "White House Flackery," in Peter Woll, ed., *Debating American Government,* 2nd ed. (Glenview, IL: Scott, Foresman, 1988), 180.
25. This point is well-argued in Kathleen Hall Jamieson, *Eloquence in an Electronic Age* (New York: Oxford University Press, 1988).
26. For a discussion of CBS's failed attempt to lengthen candidate soundbites in 1992, see S. Robert Lichter and Richard E. Noyes, *Good Intentions Make Bad News,* 2nd ed. (Lanham, MD: Rowman & Littlefield, 1996), 246-250.
27. *Ibid.,* 289.
28. Quoted in Austin Ranney, *Channels of Power* (New York: Basic Books, 1983), 116.
29. Walter Cronkite, *A Reporter's Life* (New York: Knopf, 1996), pp. 376-377.
30. William Schneider and I.A. Lewis, "Views on the News," *Public Opinion* 8 (August/September 1985), 6-11.
31. William Glaberson, "More Reporters Leaning Democratic, Study Says," *New York Times,* November 18, 1992, A13.
32. See Michael J. Robinson and Margaret A. Sheehan, *Over the Wire and On TV: CBS and UP in Campaign '80* (New York: Russell Sage Foundation, 1983); and C. Richard Hofstetter, *Bias in the News: Network Television Coverage of the 1972 Election Campaign* (Columbus, OH: Ohio State University Press, 1976).
33. Michael J. Robinson and Margaret Petrella, "Who Won the George Bush-Dan Rather Debate?" *Public Opinion* 10 (March/April 1988), 43.
34. Michael J. Robinson, "Public Affairs Television," 428.
35. W. Lance Bennett, *News: The Politics of Illusion,* 2nd ed. (New York: Longman, 1988), 46.
36. See Paul F. Lazarsfeld *et al., The People's Choice* (New York: Columbia University Press, 1944).
37. Shanto Iyengar and Donald R. Kinder, *News That Matters* (Chicago: University of Chicago Press, 1987).
38. *Ibid.,* 118-119.
39. See Benjamin I. Page, Robert Y. Shapiro, and Glenn R. Dempsey, "What Moves Public Opinion?" *American Political Science Review* 81 (March 1987): 23-44.
40. John W. Kingdon, *Agendas, Alternatives, and Public Policies* (Boston: Little, Brown, 1984), 3.
41. *Ibid.,* 3.
42. Henry A. Kissinger, *White House Years* (Boston: Little, Brown, 1979), 757.
43. See the interview with Richard Valeriani in Juan Williams, *Eyes on the Prize* (New York: Viking, 1987), 270-271.
44. For an interesting study of how hiring a public relations firm can help a nation's TV image, see Jarol B. Manheim and Robert B. Albitton, "Changing National Images: International Public Relations and Media Agenda Setting," *American Political Science Review* 78 (September 1984): 641-657.
45. Bernard Cohen, *The Press and Foreign Policy* (Princeton, NJ: Princeton University Press, 1963), 13.
46. Ronald W. Berkman and Laura W. Kitch, *Politics in the Media Age* (New York: McGraw-Hill, 1986), 311.
47. *Ibid.,* 313.
48. Matthew Robert Kerbel, *Edited for Television: CNN, ABC, and the 1992 Presidential Campaign* (Boulder, CO: Westview Press, 1994), 196.

Political Parties

8

The Meaning of Party

The Party in the Electorate

The Party Organizations: From the Grass Roots to Washington

The Party in Government: Promises and Policy

Party Eras in American History

The Parties Today: Dealignment and Renewal

Understanding Political Parties

In late September of 1994, 367 Republican candidates for the House of Representatives stood on the steps of the U.S. Capitol to sign a document they entitled "Contract with America." This document outlined the reforms the Republicans promised to pass on the first day of the new Congress, as well as ten bills they agreed would be brought to the floor for a vote within the first 100 days of the new Republican-controlled House of Representatives. The contract was the brainchild of Newt Gingrich and Richard Armey, both of whom are former college professors. Gingrich and Armey thought that the Republicans needed a stronger message in 1994 than simply saying they opposed President Clinton's policies. The contract was an attempt to offer the voters a positive program for reshaping American public policy and reforming how Congress works. Without actually knowing much about the individual candidates themselves, voters would know what to expect of the signers of the contract and would be able to hold them accountable for these promises in the future. In this sense, the contract endeavored to make politics user-friendly for the voters.

America's Founding Fathers were more concerned with their fear that political parties could be forums for corruption and national divisiveness than they were with the role that parties could play in making politics user-friendly for ordinary voters. Thomas Jefferson spoke for many when he said, "If I could not go to heaven but with a party, I would not go there at all." In his Farewell Address, George Washington also warned of the dangers of parties.

Today, most observers would agree that political parties have contributed greatly to American democracy. In one of the most frequently—and rightly—quoted observations about American politics, E. E. Schattschneider said that "political parties created democracy ... and democracy is unthinkable save in terms of the parties."[1] Political scientists and politicians alike believe that a strong party system is desirable and bemoan the weakening of American political parties in recent decades. As President Bush once told a meeting of college interns in Washington, "As the strength of our parties erodes, so does the strength of our political system."[2]

The strength of the parties has an impact not only on how we are governed but also on what government does. The major historical developments in the expansion or contraction of the scope of government have generally been accomplished through the implementation of one party's platform. Currently, the Democrats and Republicans differ greatly on the issue of the scope of government. If either party were to gain control of both the presidency and the Congress for an extended period of time, that circumstance would have a profound impact on the scope of government. However, as we shall see in this chapter, the most common pattern in recent years has been for the Congress to be controlled by one party and the White House by the other. This lack of unified party control has largely stifled any major changes in the scope of government in America.

The alternating of power and influence between the two major parties is one of the most important elements in American politics. **Party competition** is the battle between Democrats and Republicans for the control of public offices. Without this competition there would be no choice, and without choice there would be no democracy. Americans have had a choice between two major political parties since the early 1800s, and this two-party system remains intact almost two centuries later.

THE MEANING OF PARTY

William N. Chambers once remarked that "if the beginning of wisdom is to call things by their right name, some attention is due to what we mean by a political party."[3] Almost all definitions of political parties have one thing in common: Parties try to win elections. This is their core function and the key to their definition. By contrast, interest groups do not nominate candidates for office, though they may try to influence elections. For example, no one has ever been elected to Congress as the nominee of the National Rifle Association, though many have received the NRA's endorsement. Thus, Anthony Downs defined a **political party** as a "team of men and women seeking to control the governing apparatus by gaining office in a duly constituted election."[4]

The word *team* is the slippery part of this definition. Party teams may not be so well disciplined and single-minded as teams fielded by top football coaches. Party teams often run every which way (sometimes toward the opposition's goal line) and are difficult to lead. Party leaders often disagree about policy, and between elections the parties seem to all but disappear. So who are the members of these teams? A widely adopted way of thinking about parties in political science is as "three-headed political giants." The three heads are (1) the party-in-the-electorate, (2) the party as an organization, and (3) the party-in-government.[5]

By far the largest component of an American political party is the *party-in-the-electorate*. Unlike many European political parties, American parties do not require dues or membership cards to distinguish members from nonmembers. Americans may register as Democrats, Republicans, Libertarians, or whatever, but

The major parties have different demographic bases of support. Of all social groups, African Americans tend to be the most solidly aligned with one party. Ever since the Civil Rights Act of 1964, they have voted overwhelmingly for Democratic candidates. In 1996, African-American voters cast 84 percent of their votes for Bill Clinton, 12 percent for Bob Dole, and 4 percent for Ross Perot.

registration is not legally binding and is easily changed. To be a member of a party, you need only claim to be a member. If you call yourself a Democrat, you are one—even if you never talk to a party official, never work in a campaign, and often vote for Republicans.

The *party as an organization* has a national office, a full-time staff, rules and bylaws, and budgets. In addition to a national office, each party maintains state and local headquarters. The party organization includes precinct leaders, county chairpersons, state chairpersons, state delegates to the national committee, and officials in the party's Washington office. These are the people who keep the party running between elections and make its rules. From the party's national chairperson to its lowliest precinct captain, the party organization pursues electoral victory.

The *party-in-government* consists of elected officials who call themselves members of the party. Although presidents, members of Congress, governors, and lesser officeholders may share a common party label, they do not always agree on policy. Presidents and governors may have to wheedle and cajole their own party members into voting for their policies. In the United States, it is not uncommon to put personal principle—or ambition—above loyalty to the party's leaders. These leaders are the main spokespersons for the party, however; their words and actions personify the party to millions of Americans. If the party is to translate its promises into policy, the job must be done by the party-in-government.

Political parties are everywhere in American politics—present in the electorate's mind, as an organization, and in government offices—and one of their major tasks is to link the people of the United States to their government and its policies.

TASKS OF THE PARTIES

The road from public opinion to public policy is long and winding. Masses of people cannot raise their voices to government and indicate their policy preferences in unison. If all 270 million Americans spoke at once, all that would be heard is a roar of demands on government that could not possibly be dealt with. In a large democracy, **linkage institutions** translate inputs from the public into outputs from the policymakers. Linkage institutions sift through all the issues, identify the most pressing concerns, and put these onto the governmental agenda. In other words, linkage institutions help ensure that public preferences are heard loud and clear. In the United States, there are four main linkage institutions: parties, elections, interest groups, and the media.

Kay Lawson writes that "parties are seen, both by the members and by others, as agencies for forging links between citizens and policymakers."[6] Here is a checklist of the tasks parties perform, or should perform, if they are to serve as effective linkage institutions.

1. *Parties pick policymakers.* Almost no one above the local level (and often not even there) gets elected to a public office without winning a party's endorsement.[7] A party's endorsement is called a *nomination*. Up until the early twentieth century, American parties chose their candidates with little or no input from the voters. Progressive reformers led the charge for primary elections, in which citizens would have the power to choose nominees for office. The innovation of primary elections spread rapidly, transferring the nominating function from the party organization to the party identifiers.
2. *Parties run campaigns.* Through their national, state, and local organizations, parties coordinate political campaigns. However, recent technology has made it easier for candidates to campaign on their own, without the help of the party organization. For example, Ross Perot received 18.9 percent of the presidential vote in 1992 and 8.5 percent in 1996 with hardly any organizational support at all.
3. *Parties give cues to voters.* Most voters have a **party image** of each party; that is, they know (or think they know) what the Republicans and Democrats stand for. Liberal, conservative, probusiness, prolabor—these are some of the elements of each

party's image. Even in the present era of weakened parties, many voters still rely on a party to give them cues for voting.

4. *Parties articulate policies.* Within the electorate and within the government, each political party advocates specific policy alternatives. For example, the Democratic party has clearly supported abortion rights, and the Republican party has repeatedly called for restrictions on abortion.
5. *Parties coordinate policymaking.* In America's fragmented government, parties are essential for coordination among the branches of government. Virtually all major public officials are also members of a party. When they need support to get something done, the first place they look is to their fellow partisans.

The importance of these tasks makes it easy to see why most political scientists accept Schattschneider's famous assertion that modern democracy is unthinkable without competition between political parties.

PARTIES, VOTERS, AND POLICY: THE DOWNS MODEL

The parties compete, at least in theory, as in a marketplace. A party is in the market for voters; its products are its candidates and policies. Anthony Downs has provided a working model of the relationship among citizens, parties, and policy, employing a rational-choice perspective.[8] **Rational-choice theory** "seeks to explain political processes and outcomes as consequences of purposive behavior. Political actors are assumed to have goals and to pursue those goals sensibly and efficiently."[9] Downs argues that (1) voters want to maximize the chance that policies they favor will be adopted by government and (2) parties want to win office. Thus, in order to win office, the wise party selects policies that are widely favored. Parties and candidates may do all sorts of things to win—kiss babies, call opponents ugly names, even lie and cheat—but in a democracy they will primarily use their accomplishments and policy positions to attract votes. If Party A figures out what the voters want more accurately than does Party B, then Party A should be more successful.

The long history of the American party system has shown that successful parties rarely stray far from the midpoint of public opinion. In the American electorate, a few voters are extremely liberal and a few are extremely conservative, but the majority are in the middle (see Figure 8.1). If Downs is right, then centrist parties will win, and extremist parties will be condemned to footnotes in the history books. Indeed, occasionally a party may misperceive voters' desires or take a risky stand on principle—hoping to persuade voters during the campaign—but in order to survive in a system where the majority opinion is middle-of-the-road, parties must stay near the center.

We frequently hear criticism that there is not much difference between the Democrats and the Republicans. Given the nature of the American political market, however, these two parties have little choice. We would not expect two competing department stores to locate at opposite ends of town when most people live on Main Street. Downs also notes, though, that from a rational-choice perspective, one should expect the parties to differentiate themselves at least somewhat. Just as Chrysler tries to offer something different from and better than General Motors in order to build buyer loyalty, so Democrats and Republicans have to forge different identities to build voter loyalty. More than half of the population currently believes that important differences do exist between the parties. (See "The People Speak: Are There Differences Between the Parties?") When asked what those differences are, respondents most frequently comment that the Republicans favor lower taxes and less domestic spending, whereas Democrats favor more government programs to help the middle class and less advantaged Americans.

THE PARTY IN THE ELECTORATE

In most European nations, being a party member means formally joining a political party. You get a membership card to carry around, you pay dues, and you vote to pick your local party leaders. In America, being a party member takes far less work. There is no formal "membership" in the parties at all. If you believe you are a Democrat or a Republican, then you are a Democrat or a Republican. Thus the party-in-the-electorate consists largely of symbolic images and ideas. For most people the party is a psychological label. They may never go to a party meeting, but they have images of the parties' stances on issues and of which groups the parties generally favor or oppose. Party images give citizens a sense of which party is probusiness or prolabor, which is the party of peace, or which is the better manager of the economy.

Party images help shape people's **party identification,** the self-proclaimed preference for one party or the other. Since 1952, the National Election Study surveys have asked a sample of citizens, "Generally speaking, do you usually think of yourself as a Republican, a Democrat, or an Independent?"

FIGURE 8.1 THE DOWNS MODEL: HOW RATIONAL PARTIES MATCH VOTERS' POLICY PREFERENCES

In 1996, the National Election Study asked a sample of the American electorate to classify themselves on a scale from extremely liberal to extremely conservative. The graph shows how the people located themselves in terms of ideology and how rational (and foolish) parties might reflect these identifications.

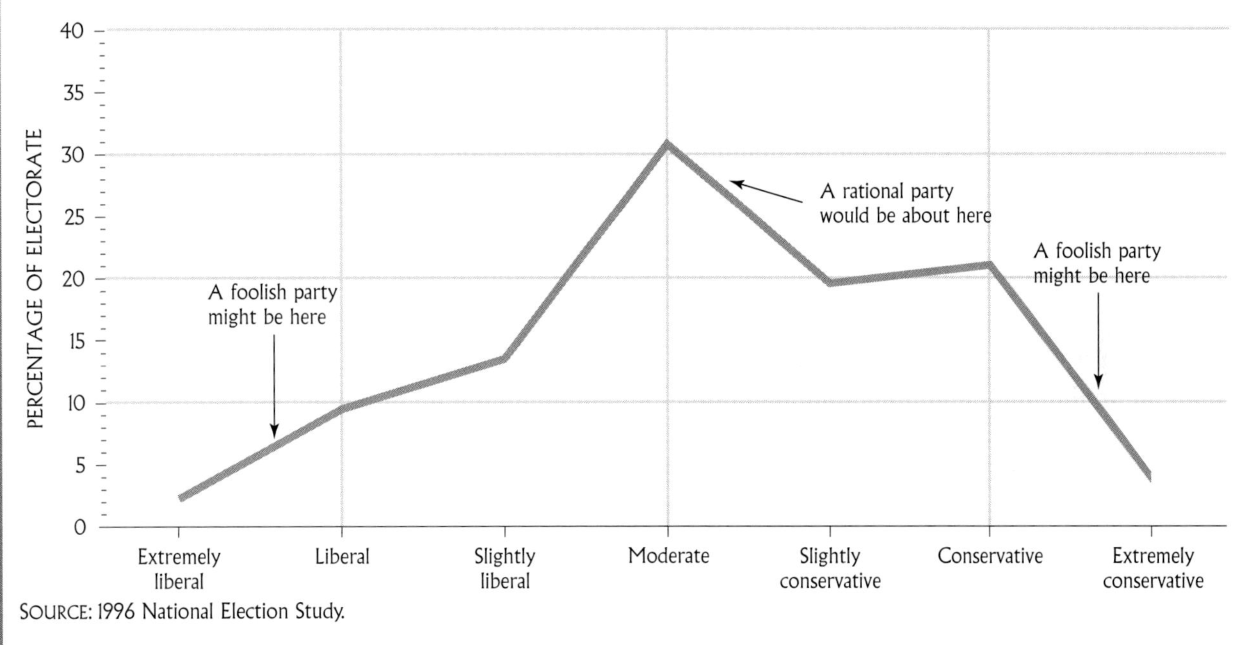

SOURCE: 1996 National Election Study.

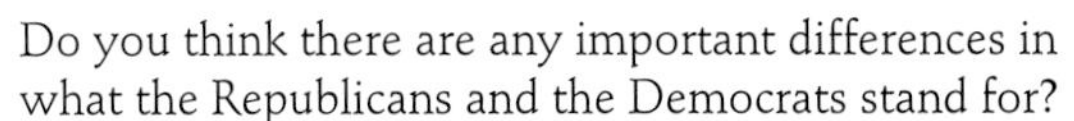

Are There Differences Between the Parties?

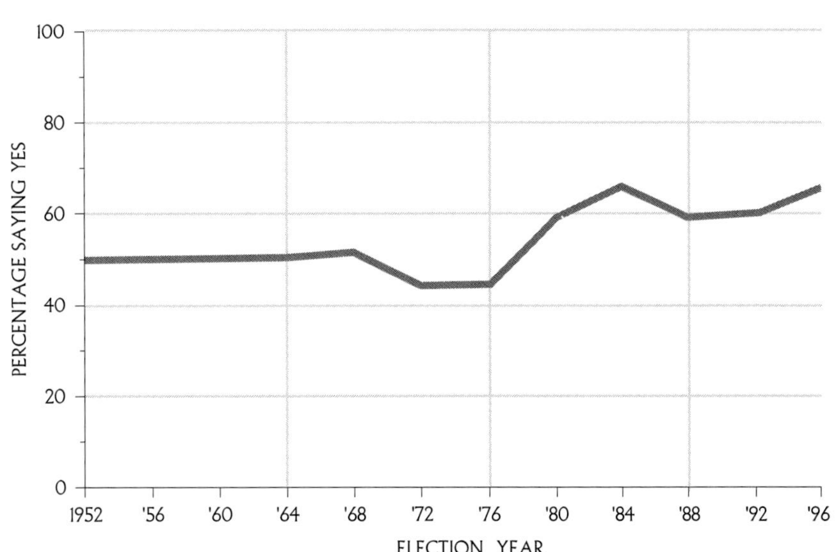

SOURCE: The question as worded is taken directly from the National Election Studies conducted by the University of Michigan.

TABLE 8.1 PARTY IDENTIFICATION IN THE UNITED STATES, 1952–1996[a]

YEAR	DEMOCRATS	INDEPENDENTS	REPUBLICANS
1952	48.6	23.3	28.1
1956	45.3	24.4	30.3
1960	46.4	23.4	30.2
1964	52.2	23.0	24.8
1968	46.0	29.5	24.5
1972	41.0	35.2	23.8
1976	40.2	36.8	23.0
1980	41.7	35.3	23.0
1984	37.7	34.8	27.6
1988	35.7	36.3	28.0
1992	35.8	38.7	25.5
1996	39.3	32.9	27.8

[a]In percentage of people; the small percentage who identify with a minor party, or who cannot answer the question are excluded.

SOURCE: 1952-1996 National Election Studies conducted by the University of Michigan.

Repeatedly asking this question permits political scientists to trace party identification over the past four decades (see Table 8.1). The clearest trend has been *the decline of both parties and resultant upsurge of independence* (mostly at the expense of the Democrats). In 1996, 33 percent of the population called themselves Independents.

Virtually every major social group—Catholics, Jews, poor whites, Southerners, and so on—has moved toward a position of increased independence. The major exception has been African-American voters. A decade of Democratic civil rights policy in the 1960s moved African Americans even more solidly into the Democratic Party. Currently, only about 5 percent of African Americans identify themselves as Republicans.[10]

For many white Americans, though, the abandonment of either party for a nonpartisan stance is well advanced. This abandonment occurred at all age levels in the electorate, but it was most pronounced for younger voters, who have always had the weakest party ties. The baby boom and the lowering of the voting age to 18 contributed to the rising tide of independence during the 1970s. In 1996, 46 percent of those under 30 called themselves Independents.

Not only are there more Independents now, but those who still identify with a party are no longer so loyal in the voting booth. For example, 42 percent of Democrats in 1972 voted for Richard Nixon rather than for their party's nominee, George McGovern. The highest Republican defection rate ever occurred in 1964, when 28 percent abandoned Barry Goldwater's candidacy for that of Lyndon Johnson. In recent years, **ticket-splitting**—voting with one party for one office and with the other for other offices—has reached record proportions.[11] The result of voters failing to make a straight, across-the-board choice between the parties has often been divided party government, at both the federal and state levels.

THE PARTY ORGANIZATIONS: FROM THE GRASS ROOTS TO WASHINGTON

An organizational chart is usually shaped like a pyramid, with those who give orders at the top and those who carry them out at the bottom. In drawing an organizational chart of an American political party, you could put the national committee and national convention of the party at the apex of your pyramid, the state party organizations in the middle, and the thousands of local party organizations at the bottom (see Figure 8.2). When you have finished examining this chart, however, you will have an incomplete picture of an American political party. The president of General Motors is at the top of GM in fact as well as on paper. By contrast, the chairperson of the Democratic or Republican national committee is on top on paper, but not in fact.

FIGURE 8.2 AN ORGANIZATION CHART OF THE AMERICAN POLITICAL PARTY

Here is the way an American political party looks on paper, but remember that real power in the party does not coincide with this neat hierarchical structure.

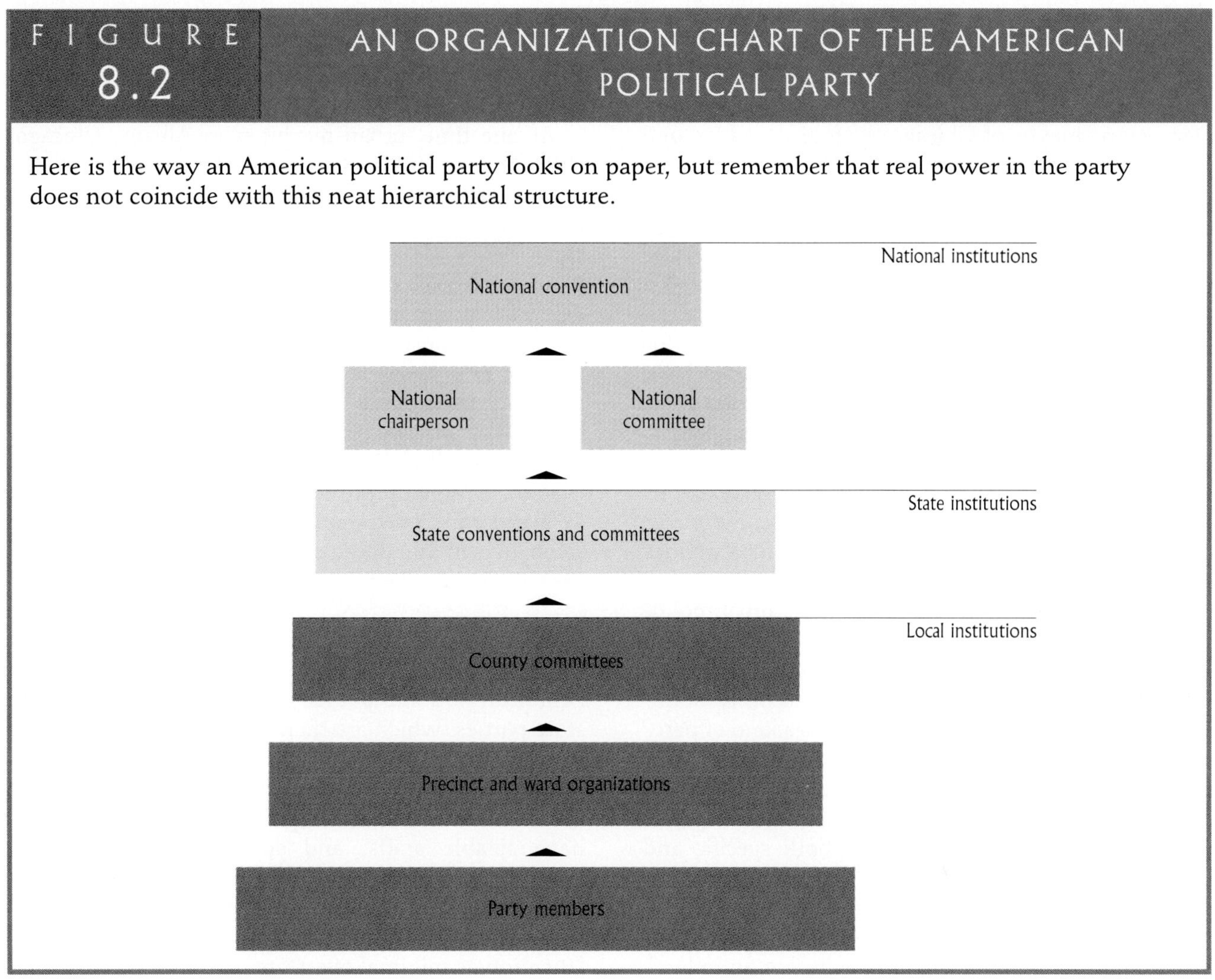

As organizations, American political parties are decentralized and fragmented. As Beck and Sorauf write, party organizations

> lack the hierarchical control and efficiency, the unified setting of priorities and strategy, and the central responsibility we associate with large contemporary organizations. . . . Instead of a continuity of relationships and of operations, the American party organizations feature only improvisatory, elusive, and sporadic structure and activities.[12]

It is no accident that a leading study of national party organizations is called *Politics Without Power.*[13] One can imagine a system in which the national office of a party resolves conflicts among its state and local branches, states the party's position on the issues, and then passes orders down through the hierarchy. One can even imagine a system in which the party leaders have the power to enforce their decisions by offering rewards (campaign funds, advice, appointments) to officeholders who follow the party line and punishing those who do not. Many European parties work just that way, but in America the formal party organizations have little such power. Candidates in the United States can get elected on their own. They do not need the help of the party most of the time, and hence the party organization is relegated to a comparatively limited role.

LOCAL PARTIES: THE DYING URBAN MACHINES

Urban party organizations are also no longer very active, except in a few places. County and city organizations may be the grass roots of the party, but grassroots party volunteers are hard to find, especially if a local party is always in the minority. It takes real perseverance to track down the Republican committeeperson in Chicago, where Democrats win almost every election. Trying to find the Republican headquarters in the eleventh ward—the residence of every Democratic mayor of Chicago for four decades—one industrious researcher reported, "The outside doors to the headquarters are boarded up. . . . There are two alternative entrances, however, if one is persistent enough to discover them; one behind the pin-setting machine in the bowling alley, and another through a tavern."[14]

Obviously, things are not always that bad, even for the minority party. In some cases, both parties have well-oiled precinct, city, and county organizations. They get out the vote, conduct grass-roots campaigns, and help state and local candidates. In some states, such as California, independent reform organizations of amateur politicians are more active than the major parties' organizations. As a rule, however, local politics is no longer a hotbed of party organization.

It was not always this way. Once, the urban political party was the political party organization in America. From the late nineteenth century through the New Deal of the 1930s, scores of cities were dominated by **party machines**. A machine is a kind of party organization very different from the typical fragmented and disorganized political party in America. It can be defined as a "party organization that depends crucially on inducements that are both specific and material."[15] A specific inducement is one that can be given to someone and withheld from someone else; if you get a job as reward for your party work, for instance, someone else cannot have it. For an inducement to be material, it must be monetary or convertible into money, such as a building contract.

Patronage is one of the key inducements used by party machines. A patronage job is one that is given for political reasons rather than for merit or competence alone. In the late nineteenth century, political parties routinely sold some patronage jobs to the highest bidder. Party leaders made no secret of their corruption. Washington newspapers ran ads from wealthy people seeking office offering as much as $1,000 dollars (a substantial sum in those days) for government posts. The parties used some of the money they made selling government positions to buy votes. Much of it, though, went to line the pockets of the politicians themselves. The most notable case was that of Boss Tweed of New York, whose ring reportedly made between $40 million and $200 million from tax receipts, payoffs, and kickbacks. In the spirit of cleaning up government, the civil service system was instituted in the 1880s; it established merit criteria for most government jobs. This reform deprived the parties of the appointment power they had used to reward their friends and financial backers. However, jobs are not the only form of patronage. Machines have been known to give out government contracts in return for handsome campaign contributions.

At one time, urban machines in Albany, Chicago, Philadelphia, Kansas City, and elsewhere depended heavily on ethnic group support. Some of the most fabled machine leaders were Irish politicians, including New York's George Washington Plunkett, Boston's James Michael Curley, and Chicago's Richard J. Daley. Daley's Chicago machine was the last survivor, steamrolling its opposition amid charges of racism and corruption. Even today there are remnants of the Chicago machine, particularly in white and ethnic neighborhoods. The survival of machine politics in Chicago can be traced to its ability to limit the scope of reform legislation. A large proportion of city jobs were classified as "temporary" even though they had been held by the same person for decades, and these positions were exempted from the merit system of hiring.[16]

THE FIFTY STATE PARTY SYSTEMS

American national parties are a loose aggregation of state parties, which are themselves a fluid association of individuals, groups, and local organizations. There are 50 state party systems, and no two are exactly alike. In a few states, the parties are well organized, have sizable staffs, and spend a lot of money. Pennsylvania is one such state. In other states, however, parties are weak. It has been said of the California party system that to describe the parties' "function as minimal overstates the case. . . . The fact is that California has a political party system on paper, and that's about it."[17] California, says Kay Lawson, "has political parties so weak as to be almost nonexistent; it is the birthplace of campaigning by 'hired guns'; and it has been run by special interests for so long that Californians have forgotten what is special about that."[18]

As recently as the early 1960s, half of the state party organizations did not even maintain a permanent headquarters; when the state party elected a new chairperson, the party organization simply shifted its office to his or her hometown.[19] In contrast, almost all state parties today have a physical headquarters, typically in the capital city or the largest city. State party budgets have also increased. In the early 1960s, more than half the parties had an annual budget of less than $50,000. With the development of permanent headquarters, professional staffs, and high-tech equipment, this figure has risen substantially. A 1984 survey found that the average Democratic state party budget was $260,000; the Republican state parties were much better off with an average budget of $795,000.[20]

SHOULD STATE PARTIES MAKE PREPRIMARY ENDORSEMENTS?

You Are the Policymaker

In the 1989 Supreme Court case of *Eu v. San Francisco County Democratic Central Committee,* the law banning official party endorsements during primary elections in California was challenged. The state of California acknowledged that its ban deprived the parties of the right to speak out; however, it argued that it had a compelling interest to do so in order to protect voters from undue influence by party bosses. According to the state, this minor infringement of free speech was necessary to enhance unfettered competition in the primaries.

In its ruling, the court acknowledged that "a state may regulate the flow of information between political associations and their members when necessary to prevent fraud and corruption." The key to its decision was that it was not convinced that voters were unduly influenced by party endorsements. Indeed, it relied in part on the declaration of Professor Malcolm Jewell, a political scientist at the University of Kentucky, whose study concluded that "the party endorsement has little, if any, effect on the way voters cast their vote." The Court also pointed out that the ban on primary endorsements sometimes enabled candidates with views antithetical to those of the party to win nominations. The Grand Dragon of the Ku Klux Klan, for example, was able to win the Democrats' nomination for the House from a San Diego district in 1980. In sum, the Court declared that California's ban on primary endorsements "directly hampers the ability of a party to spread its message and hamstrings voters seeking to inform themselves about the candidates and the campaign issues." Thus it invalidated the law.

Now that the California parties have the right to make endorsements prior to primary elections, they are faced with the question of whether it is wise to do so. Some argue that parties can make candidates pay more attention to the platform by rewarding those who follow it closely with an official endorsement. The very fact that candidates could hope to get an endorsement might lead to greater party unity, even if most voters paid little attention to endorsements. On the other hand, some argue that party endorsements often have a way of backfiring. Many voters prefer a candidate who promises independence of action rather than loyalty to a party. Thus, in some cases it is possible that the party endorsement might end up being a liability rather than an asset. In addition, some argue that the struggle to get the endorsement would add further to factional conflict within a party.

Consider these possible consequences and take on the role of policymaker for the state parties. Would you favor regular use of official endorsements prior to primary elections, or would you save this power for special circumstances only?

SOURCE: *Eu v. San Francisco County Democratic Central Committee,* 109 Supreme Court 1013 (1989).

Clearly, in terms of headquarters and budgets, state parties are better organized than they used to be. Nevertheless, almost any national interest group in Washington will have a richer budget, plusher headquarters, and a bigger staff than even the best state party organization.

STATE PARTIES AS LEGAL ORGANIZATIONS

The states, not the federal government, regulate the parties. State statutes define a party and specify how it is to be organized. Political scientist and Congressman David Price (D-NC) notes that "in no western democracy are parties regulated as closely as in the United States."[21] Price points out that California, where "laws covering party organization and campaign practices cover several hundred pages, is a good example of the lengths to which such regulations can go."[22] California has traditionally been an antiparty state; its complex laws hamstring the parties. One of these laws prevented the parties from making endorsements prior to primary elections, which led to a recent notable Supreme Court case. (See "You Are the Policymaker: Should State Parties Make Preprimary Endorsements?") Other states have less complex regulations than California, but all states set down party law in their statutes.

Sometimes state legislation regarding the parties conflicts with national policy. In 1940, the Supreme Court held that a state could not turn its primary elections over to a party (as a "private organization") in order to prevent African Americans from voting (*United States v. Classic*). More recently, the federal courts have upheld the national parties when national party policy has conflicted with state law. In cases involving Illinois and Wisconsin, the Supreme Court held that the national party convention's rules took precedence over state law governing how delegates to the convention were to be picked.

THE NATIONAL PARTY ORGANIZATIONS

The supreme power within each of the parties is its **national convention**. The convention meets every 4 years, and its main task is to write the party's platform and then nominate its candidates for president and vice president. (Chapter 9 will discuss conventions in detail.) Keeping the party operating between conventions is the job of the **national committee,** composed of representatives from the states and territories. Typically, each state has a national committeeman and a national committeewoman as delegates to the party's national committee. The Democratic committee also includes assorted governors, members of Congress, and other party officials.

Day-to-day activities of the national party are the responsibility of the **national chairperson** of the party. The national party chairperson hires the staff, raises the money, pays the bills, and attends to the daily duties of the party. When the party controls the White House, the chairperson is hand-picked by the president. In the early 1970s, two of the people who served for a while as chair of the Republican Party at the request of President Nixon were Bob Dole and George Bush, both of whom used this position as a means of political advancement. After the 1996 election, President Clinton appointed Governor Roy Romer of Colorado to head the Democratic Party. As the party out of power, the Republicans had a hard-fought campaign among five candidates for the position of national chairperson in 1997. Jim Nicholson, who had been a very active member of the Republican National Committee, emerged as the winner.

THE PARTY IN GOVERNMENT: PROMISES AND POLICY

Which party controls which of America's many elected offices matters because each party and the elected officials who represent it generally try to turn campaign promises into action. As a result, the party that has control over the most government offices will have the most influence in determining who gets what, where, when, and how.

However, because candidates are now less dependent on parties to get nominated and elected, that "control" is much less fixed than it was when President Clinton took political science classes at Georgetown University in the 1960s. Presidents are now less likely to play the role of party leader, and members of Congress are less amenable to being led (see "Since Kennedy: The President as Party Leader").

Voters and coalitions of voters are attracted to different parties largely (though not entirely) by their performance and policies. What parties have done in office and what they promise to do greatly influence who will join their coalition. Sometimes voters suspect that political promises are made to be broken. To be sure, there are notable instances in which politicians have turned—sometimes 180 degrees—from their policy promises. Lyndon Johnson repeatedly promised in the 1964 presidential campaign that he would not "send American boys to do an Asian boy's job" and involve the United States in the Vietnam War, but he did. In the 1980 campaign, Ronald Reagan asserted that he would balance the budget by 1984, yet his administration quickly ran up the largest deficit in American history. Throughout the 1988 campaign George Bush proclaimed, "Read my lips—no new taxes," but he reluctantly changed course 2 years later when pressured on the issue by the Democratic majority in Congress. Bill Clinton promised a tax cut for the middle class during the 1992 campaign, but after he was elected he backed off, saying that first the deficit would have to be substantially reduced.

It is all too easy to forget how often parties and presidents do exactly what they say they will do. For every broken promise, many more are kept. When he first ran for president, Bill Clinton promised to support bills providing for family leave, easing voting registration procedures, and improving gun control—bills that had been vetoed by President Bush. He lobbied hard to get these measures through Congress again and proudly signed them into law once they arrived on his desk. Ronald Reagan promised to step up defense spending and cut back on social welfare expenditures, and within his first year in office he did just that. He promised a major tax cut and provided one. He promised less government regulation and quickly set about deregulating natural gas prices and occupational safety and environmental policies. In sum, the impression that politicians and parties never produce policy out of promises is largely erroneous.

SINCE KENNEDY

The President as Party Leader

In 1963, President Kennedy offered the following remarks to members of the National and State Democratic Committees at the White House:

> Our Founding Fathers did not realize that the basic fact which has made our system work was outside the Constitution. And that was the development of political parties in this country so that the American people would have the means of placing responsibility on one group, that group would have a chance to carry out its program, and the American people would have an opportunity to indicate their dissatisfaction by going to an alternative.
>
> That system has served us well, and there is no greater responsibility in that sense that a President has, as President Truman has pointed out, than he has as leader of a political party, and especially this political party, the oldest in the world, the oldest in our country's history.

It would be hard to imagine President Clinton making such a statement about his role as party leader today. The link between the president and the party has deteriorated substantially in the intervening decades.

When Bill Clinton ran for the presidency in 1992, he rarely made reference to the Democratic Party's majority in Congress. Two years later, his efforts on behalf of Democratic congressional candidates were sharply limited. One Democratic incumbent even said that the only way Clinton would be welcome to campaign in his congressional district would be if he endorsed his opponent. In contrast, John Kennedy often made the point in 1960 that he would be better able to work with the Democratic leadership in Congress than would Richard Nixon. The following midterm elections saw him traveling the country widely to help the party's congressional candidates.

Presidents have always had a tendency to bypass parties on occasion by appealing to the national interest and the people as a whole. However, with the growth of communications technology, such a strategy has become far more feasible and potentially rewarding. Presidents no longer need the party machinery to get their message out; they can go on TV at any time to appeal directly to the American public. Nor do members of Congress feel that they owe any great loyalty to presidents of their own party. As we have seen in this chapter, there has been a notable decline in party-line voting over the last three decades. Few members of Congress these days feel that their reelection is strongly tied to the president's success or failure. Like the president, most congressional candidates can expect to run on their own personal record rather than the party's.

In fact, the parties have done a fairly good job over the years of translating their platform promises into public policy. Gerald Pomper has shown that party platforms are excellent predictors of a party's actual policy performance in office. He tabulated specific pledges in the major parties' platforms from 1944 to 1976. Over that period, the parties made exactly 3,194 specific policy pronouncements. Pomper then looked to see whether the party that won the presidency actually fulfilled its promises. Nearly three-fourths of all promises resulted in policy actions. Others were tried but floundered for one reason or another. Only 10 percent were ignored altogether.[23]

If parties generally do what they say they will, then the party platforms adopted at the national conventions represent blueprints, however vague, for action. Consider what the two major parties promised the voters in 1996 (see Table 8.2, page 198). There is little doubt that the election of Clinton over Dole has directed the government in a course different from the one it would have taken if the outcome had been reversed.

PARTY ERAS IN AMERICAN HISTORY

While studying political parties, remember the following: *America is a two-party system and always has been.* Of course, there are many minor parties around—Libertarians, Socialists, Greens—but they almost never have a chance of winning a major office. In contrast, most democratic nations have more than

TABLE 8.2 PARTY PLATFORMS, 1996

Although few people actually read party platforms, they are one of the best written sources for what the parties believe in. A brief summary of some of the contrasting positions in the Democratic and Republican platforms of 1996 illustrates major differences in beliefs between the two parties.

REPUBLICANS	DEMOCRATS
The Last 4 Years	
Our prestige in the world is declining. Economic growth here at home is anemic. Our society grows more violent and less decent.	The economy is stronger, the deficit is lower, and government is smaller. Education is better, our environment is cleaner, families are healthier, and our streets are safer.
Abortion	
The unborn child has a fundamental individual right to life which cannot be infringed.	The Democratic Party stands behind the right of every woman to choose, consistent with *Roe v. Wade,* and regardless of ability to pay.
The Deficit	
Republicans support a Balanced Budget Amendment to the Constitution phased in over a short period and with appropriate safeguards for national emergencies.	The only deficit left today is interest payments on the debt run up over 12 Republican years before fiscal responsibility returned to the White House.
Health Care	
Our goal is to maintain the quality of America's health care. . . . That means allowing health care providers to respond to consumer demand through consumer choice.	We must take further steps to ensure that Americans have access to quality, affordable health care. We should start by making sure that people get help paying premiums so they do not lose health care while they're looking for a new job.
Taxes	
We support an across-the-board, 15-percent tax cut to marginal tax rates.	America cannot afford to return to the era of something-for-nothing tax cuts. . . . Today's Democratic Party is committed to targeted tax cuts that help working Americans invest in their future.
Defense Spending	
We are the party of peace through strength. We must reverse the decline in what our nation spends for defense.	The Republican desire to spend more money on defense than the Pentagon requests cannot obscure their inability to recognize the challenges of a new era and build the balanced defenses we need to meet them.
Education	
The federal government has no constitutional authority to be involved in school curricula. That is why we will abolish the Department of Education, end federal meddling in our schools and promote family choice at all levels of learning.	Today's Democratic Party will stand firmly against the Republican assault on education. Cutting education as we move into the 21st century would be like cutting defense spending at the height of the Cold War. We must do more to expand educational opportunity.
Illegal Immigration	
Illegal aliens should not receive public benefits other than emergency aid, and those who become parents while illegally in the United States should not be qualified to claim benefits for their offspring.	The mean-spirited effort of the Republicans in Congress to bar the children of illegal immigrants from school is wrong . . . Forcing children onto the streets is an invitation for them to join gangs and turn to crime.

SOURCE: Excerpts from party platforms as posted on the web sites of each organization.

two parties represented in their national legislature. Throughout American history, one party has been the dominant majority party for long periods of time. A majority of voters identify with the party in power; thus this party tends to win a majority of the elections. Political scientists call these periods **party eras**. The majority party does not, of course, win every election; sometimes it suffers from intraparty squabbles (as the Republicans did in 1912) and loses power. Sometimes it nominates a weak candidate, and the opposition cashes in on the majority party's misfortune.

Punctuating these party eras is a **critical election.**[24] A critical election is an electoral earthquake: Fissures appear in each party's coalition, which begins to fracture; new issues appear, dividing the electorate. Each party forms a new coalition—one that endures for years. A critical election period may require more than one election before change is apparent, but in the end, the party system will be transformed.

This process is called **party realignment**—a rare event in American political life that is akin to a political revolution. Realignments are typically associated with a major crisis or trauma in the nation's history. One of the major realignments, when the Republican party emerged, was connected to the Civil War. Another was linked to the Great Depression of the 1930s, when the majority Republicans were displaced by the Democrats. The following sections look more closely at the various party eras in American history.

1796–1824: THE FIRST PARTY SYSTEM

In the *Federalist Papers,* Madison warned strongly against the dangers of "factions," or parties. But New York's Alexander Hamilton, who was one of the coauthors of the *Federalist Papers,* did as much as anyone to inaugurate our party system.[25] Hamilton was the nation's first secretary of the treasury, for which service his picture appears on today's $10 bill. To garner congressional support for his pet policies, particularly a national bank, he needed votes. From this politicking and coalition building came the rudiments of the Federalist Party, America's first political party. The Federalists, though, were also America's shortest-lived major party. After Federalist candidate John Adams was defeated in his reelection bid in 1800, the party quickly faded. The Federalists were poorly organized, and by 1820 they no longer even bothered to offer up a candidate for president. In this early period of American history, most party leaders did not regard themselves as professional politicians. Those who lost often withdrew completely from the political arena. The ideas of a loyal opposition and rotation of power in government had not yet taken hold.[26] Each party wanted to destroy the other party, not just defeat it—and such was the fate of the Federalists.

Aaron Burr dealt a near death-blow to the Federalist Party when he killed its leader, Alexander Hamilton, in this 1804 dual. Burr, then vice president, challenged Hamilton to the duel after the former treasury secretary publicly called him a traitor.

The party that crushed the Federalists was led by Virginians Jefferson, Madison, and Monroe, each of whom was elected president for two terms in succession. They were known as the Democratic-Republicans, or sometimes as the Jeffersonians. The Democratic-Republican Party derived its **coalition**—a set of individuals and groups supporting it—from agrarian interests rather than from the growing number of capitalists, who supported the Federalists. This made the party particularly popular in the largely rural South. As the Federalists disappeared, however, the old Jeffersonian coalition was torn apart by factionalism as it tried to be all things to all people.

1828–1856: JACKSON AND THE DEMOCRATS VERSUS THE WHIGS

More than anyone else, it was General Andrew Jackson who founded the modern American political party. In the election of 1828, he forged a new coalition that included Westerners as well as Southerners, new immigrants as well as settled Americans. Like most successful politicians of his day, Jackson was initially a Democratic-Republican, but soon after his ascension to the presidency his party became known as simply the Democratic Party, which continues to this day. The "Democratic" label was particularly appropriate for Jackson's supporters because their cause was to broaden political opportunity by eliminating many vestiges of elitism and mobilizing the masses.

Whereas Jackson was the charismatic leader, the Democrats' behind-the-scenes architect was Martin Van Buren, who succeeded Jackson as president. Van

Buren's one term in office was relatively undistinguished, but his view of party competition left a lasting mark. He "sought to make Democrats see that their only hope for maintaining the purity of their own principles was to admit the existence of an opposing party."[27] A realist, Van Buren argued that a party could not aspire to pleasing all of the people all of the time. He argued that a governing party needed a loyal opposition to represent parts of society that it could not. This opposition was provided by the Whigs. The Whig party included such notables as Henry Clay and Daniel Webster, but it was able to win the presidency only when it nominated aging but popular military heroes, such as William Henry Harrison (1840) and Zachary Taylor (1848). The Whigs had two distinct wings—Northern industrialists and Southern planters—who were brought together more by the Democratic policies they opposed than by the issues on which they agreed.

1860–1928: THE TWO REPUBLICAN ERAS

In the 1850s, the issue of slavery dominated American politics and split both the Whigs and the Democrats. Slavery, said Senator Sumner, an ardent abolitionist, "is the only subject within the field of national politics which excites any real interest."[28] Congress battled over the extension of slavery to the new states and territories. In *Dred Scott v. Sandford,* the Supreme Court of 1857 held that slaves could not be citizens and that former slaves could not be protected by the Constitution. This decision further sharpened the divisions in public opinion, making civil war increasingly likely.

The Republicans rose in the late 1850s as the antislavery party. Folding in the remnants of several minor parties, the Republicans in 1860 forged a coalition strong enough to elect Abraham Lincoln president and ignite the Civil War. The "War Between the States" was one of those political earthquakes that realigned the parties. Afterward, the Republican Party was in the ascendant for more than 60 years. The Democrats controlled the South, though, and the Republican label remained a dirty word in the old Confederacy.

A second Republican era was initiated with the watershed election of 1896, perhaps the most bitter battle in American electoral history. The Democrats nominated William Jennings Bryan, populist proponent of "free silver" (linking money with silver, which was more plentiful than gold, and thus devaluing money to help debtors). The Republican Party made clear its positions in favor of the gold standard, industrialization, the banks, high tariffs, and the industrial working classes, as well as its positions against the "radical" western farmers and "silverites." "Bryan and his program were greeted by the country's conservatives with something akin to terror."[29] The *New York Tribune* howled that Bryan's Democrats were "in league with the Devil." A staggeringly high turnout put William McKinley in the White House and brought the new working classes and moneyed interests into the Republican fold. Political scientists call the 1896 election a realigning one, because it shifted the party coalitions and entrenched the Republicans for another generation. (For more on the election of 1896, see Chapter 10.)

For the next three decades the Republicans continued as the nation's majority party, until the stock market crashed in 1929. The ensuing Great Depression brought about another fissure in the crust of the American party system.

1932–1964: THE NEW DEAL COALITION

President Herbert Hoover's handling of the Depression turned out to be disastrous for the Republicans. He solemnly pronounced that "economic depression cannot be cured by legislative action." Hoover proved to be "no man on horseback to rescue his suffering people from the storm that enshrouded them in 1929. Salvation—of sorts—came instead from a man in a wheelchair, New York's Governor Franklin D. Roosevelt."[30] Roosevelt handily defeated Hoover in 1932, promising a *New Deal.* In his first 100 days as president, Roosevelt prodded

Political party conventions have changed dramatically as a result of technological progress. When Franklin Roosevelt appeared at the Democratic Convention of 1932, it marked the first time that a nominee's acceptance speech was broadcast live across the nation via radio.

Congress into passing scores of anti-Depression measures. Party realignment began in earnest after the Roosevelt administration got the country moving again. First-time voters flocked into the electorate, pumping new blood into the Democratic ranks and providing much of the margin for Roosevelt's four presidential victories. Immigrant groups in Boston and other cities had been initially attracted to the Democrats by the 1928 campaign of Al Smith, the first Catholic to be nominated by a major party for the presidency.[31] Roosevelt reinforced the partisanship of these groups, and the Democrats forged the **New Deal coalition.**

The basic elements of the New Deal coalition were

- *Urban dwellers.* Big cities such as Chicago and Philadelphia were staunchly Republican before the New Deal realignment; afterward, they were Democratic bastions.
- *Labor unions.* FDR became the first president to support unions enthusiastically, and they returned the favor.
- *Catholics and Jews.* During and after the Roosevelt period, Catholics and Jews were strongly Democratic.
- *The poor.* Though the poor had low turnout rates, their votes went overwhelmingly to the party of Roosevelt and his successors.
- *Southerners.* Ever since the pre-Civil War days, white southerners had been Democratic loyalists. This alignment continued unabated during the New Deal.
- *African Americans.* The Republicans freed the slaves, but under FDR the Democrats attracted the majority of African Americans.
- *Intellectuals.* Small in number, prominent intellectuals provided a wealth of new ideas that fueled the Roosevelt's New Deal policies.

As you can see in Figure 8.3, many of the same groups that supported FDR continue to shape the party coalitions today.

The New Deal coalition made the Democratic Party the clear majority party for decades. Harry S Truman, who succeeded Roosevelt in 1945, promised a Fair Deal. World War II hero and Republican Dwight D. Eisenhower broke the Democrats' grip on power by being elected president twice during the 1950s, but the Democrats regained the presidency in 1960 with the election of John F. Kennedy. His New Frontier was in

FIGURE 8.3 PARTY COALITIONS IN 1996

The two parties continue to draw support from very different social groups, many of which have existed since the New Deal era. This figure shows the percentage of Democrats and Republicans with various characteristics.

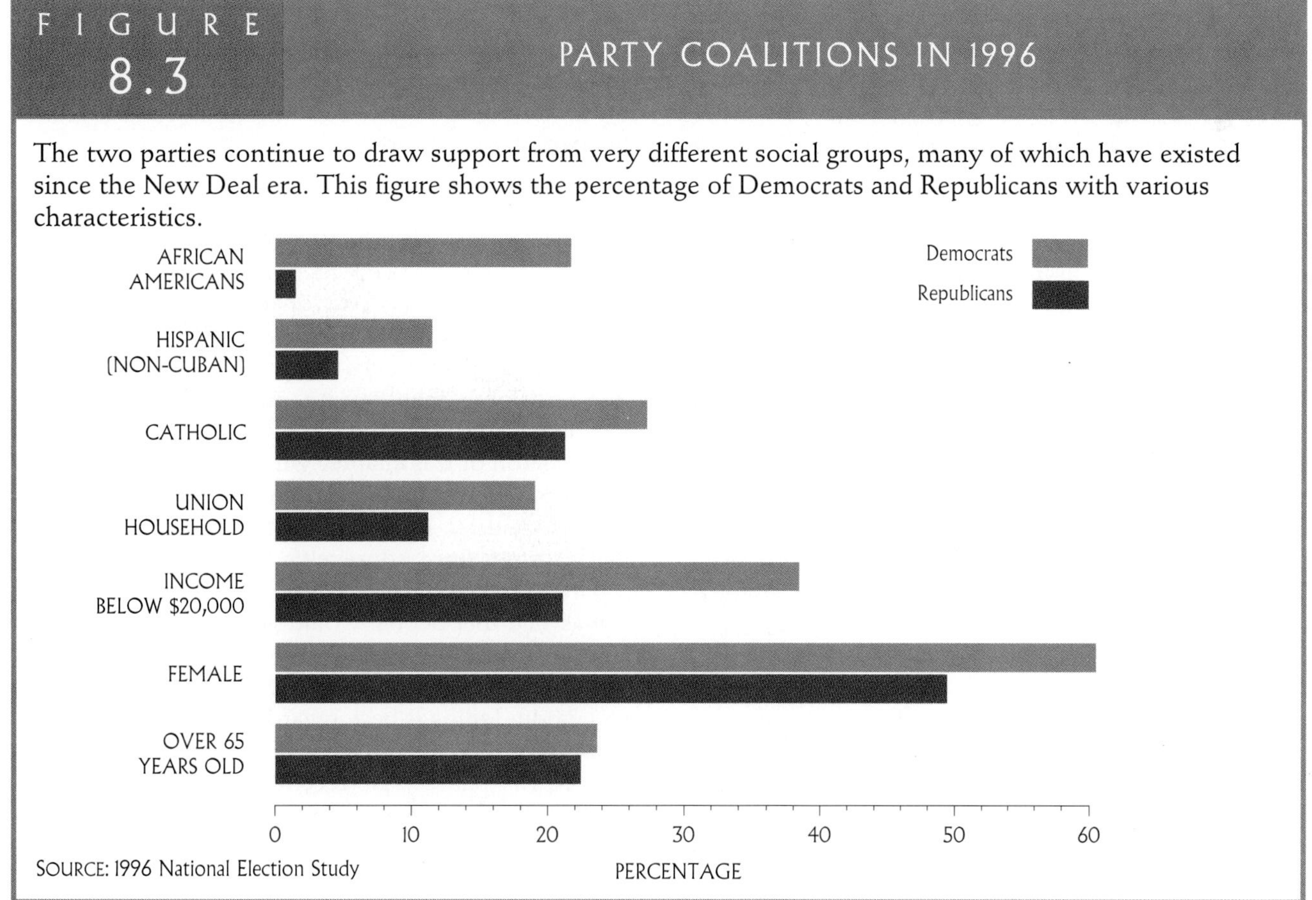

SOURCE: 1996 National Election Study

the New Deal tradition, with platforms and policies designed to help labor, the working classes, and minorities. Lyndon B. Johnson, picked as Kennedy's vice president because he could help win Southern votes, became president upon Kennedy's assassination and was overwhelmingly elected to a term of his own in 1964. Johnson's Great Society programs included a major expansion of government programs to help the poor, the dispossessed, and minorities. His War on Poverty was reminiscent of Roosevelt's activism in dealing with the Depression. Johnson's Vietnam War policies, however, tore the Democratic Party apart in 1968, leaving the door to the presidency wide open for Republican candidate Richard M. Nixon.

1968–PRESENT: THE ERA OF DIVIDED GOVERNMENT

Throughout most of American history, newly elected presidents have routinely swept a wave of their fellow partisans into office with them. For example, the Democrats gained 62 seats in the House when Wilson was elected in 1912 and 97 when FDR was elected in 1932. The first time in the twentieth century that a newly elected president moved into the White House without having his party in control of both houses of Congress was when Nixon won the 1968 election. Nixon's election was not to be an exception, however, but rather the beginning of a common pattern—repeated in the presidential elections won by Reagan and Bush. For a time, it seemed that the normal state of affairs in Washington was to have a Republican president and a Democratic Congress.

Bill Clinton's election in 1992 briefly restored united party government until the Republicans won both houses of Congress in the 1994 elections. After the 1994 elections, Republican leaders were optimistic that they were at last on the verge of a new Republican era in which they would control both the presidency and Congress simultaneously. On the other side, Democratic leaders were hopeful that voters would not like the actions of the new Republican Congress and would restore unified Democratic control of the government. In the end, the ambitions of both sides were frustrated as voters opted to continue divided party government.

With fewer voters attached to the two major parties, it will be difficult for either one to gain a strong enough foothold to maintain simultaneous control of both sides of Pennsylvania Avenue for very long. All told, both houses of Congress and the presidency have been simultaneously controlled by the same party for just 6 of the 30 years from 1969 to 1998.[32] The discrepancy between the patterns of presidential and congressional voting during this era of divided party government is unprecedented in American history.

Divided party government is frequently seen not only at the federal level but at the state level as well. As Morris Fiorina shows, the percentage of states that have unified party control of the governorship and the state legislature has steadily declined for over four decades.[33] Whereas 85 percent of state governments had one party controlling both houses of the legislature and the governorship in 1946, by 1997 this was the case in only 38 percent of the states. Divided government, once an occasional oddity in state capitols, is now commonplace.

THE PARTIES TODAY: DEALIGNMENT AND RENEWAL

The recent pattern of divided government has caused many political scientists to believe that the party system has dealigned rather than realigned. Whereas realignment involves people changing from one party to another, **party dealignment** means that people are gradually moving away from both parties. When your car is realigned, it is adjusted in one direction or another to improve its steering. Imagine if your mechanic were to remove the steering mechanism instead of adjusting it—your car would be useless and ineffective. This is what many scholars fear has been happening to the parties.

There is plenty of evidence that parties have fallen on hard times—the decline of party loyalty, for example, in the electorate. On the other hand, there are also signs of renewal, such as the increase in the regular Washington staff of the national party organizations.[34] Because political parties permeate so many aspects of American politics, there is no simple answer to the question of whether they are undergoing decay or revitalization. Whatever the future of the party system (a later section of this chapter will discuss some differing opinions on this topic), political scientists generally agree that three major changes have occurred in the party system since Roosevelt's New Deal.

First, *party loyalty has declined.* In the parties' heyday, it was said that people would vote for a yellow dog if their party nominated one. Now, more than 90 percent of all Americans insist that "I always vote for the person whom I think is best, regardless of what party they belong to."[35] Rather than reflecting negative attitudes toward the parties, the recent dealignment has been characterized by a growing **party neutrality.**[36] For example, 27 percent of the 1996 National Election

Political conventions today are carefully orchestrated so as to present the best possible image of the ticket on television.

Study respondents answered as follows to a set of four open-ended questions about the parties:

Q. Is there anything in particular that you like about the Democratic party?
A. No.
Q. Is there anything in particular that you don't like about the Democratic party?
A. No.
Q. Is there anything in particular that you like about the Republican party?
A. No.
Q. Is there anything in particular that you don't like about the Republican party?
A. No.

When these questions were first asked in the 1950s, only about 10 percent of respondents answered in this neutral way, generally indicating that they were not very politically knowledgeable. Now, many of those who say nothing about the parties are quite aware of the candidates. Lacking any party anchoring, though, they are easily swayed one way or the other. As a result, they are often referred to as "the floating voters."

Second, *those who do identify with a party are more likely to belong to the party that matches their ideology*. For generations after the Civil War, Southern liberals and conservatives alike allied with the Democrats rather than with the hated party of Lincoln. At the same time, a strong liberal wing of the Republican Party was concentrated in the urban centers of the Northeast. Today, however, conservative Southerners no longer shy away from the Republican label, and liberals hardly feel welcome in the Republican Party. For the most part, people who call themselves conservatives are in the Republican Party, whereas liberals are concentrated in the Democratic Party (see Figure 8.4). The parties, as political scientists like to say, have become ideologically differentiated. Now that Southern conservatives feel comfortable in the Republican column, the Democrats' "Solid South" is a thing of the past. Indeed,

PARTY IDENTIFICATION AND IDEOLOGY: 1996

Although there is a general tendency for the two parties to converge toward the center of the ideological spectrum, the parties need to differentiate themselves somewhat in order to give people incentive to identify with them. As you can see, there is a distinct difference in the ideology of the parties' members. As noted in Chapter 6, however, the terms *liberal* and *conservative* are not very meaningful for a large percentage of the American public. Note that a very common response to the ideology questions is "Haven't thought about it," especially for Independents and Democrats.

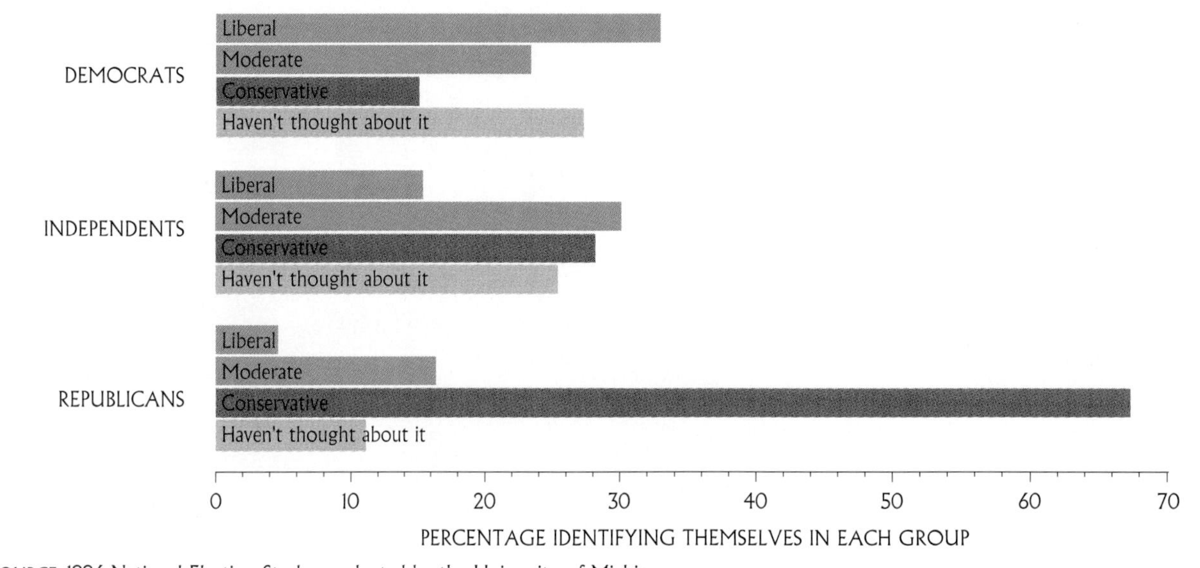

SOURCE: 1996 National Election Study conducted by the University of Michigan.

even with Southerners Clinton and Gore on the ticket, the Democrats were able to win only 4 of the 11 states of the old Confederacy in both 1992 and 1996.

Third, *even though party loyalty has lagged, party organizations have become more energetic and effective*. One reason for this reinvigorated party leadership has been the computerization of campaigns and fund raising. First the Republicans and then the Democrats learned the secrets of high-tech fund raising. The Republican Party could, for example, write a direct-mail letter to every voter over 45 who is registered in a California precinct that voted more than 60 percent for Reagan and who lives in a house costing more than $100,000.[37] As Paul Herrnson documents, "The parties' national, congressional, and senatorial campaign committees are now wealthier, more stable, better organized, and better staffed than ever before."[38]

In sum, the past few years have seen the emergence of what has been called the **split-level party**—a party with a strong, vigorous organization but a weak following on the mass level.[39] Each party, though, has changed in distinctive ways. The following sections give a brief view of each party.

THE DEMOCRATS: ENSURING REPRESENTATION

The most recent restructuring of the Democratic Party began in 1968, the year of the rowdiest national convention ever. As the war in Southeast Asia raged, another war of sorts took place in the streets of Chicago, the Democratic convention city. Demonstrators against the war battled Mayor Richard Daley's Chicago police in what an official report later called a "police riot." Beaten up in the streets and defeated in the convention hall, the antiwar faction won one concession from the party regulars: a special committee to review the party's structure and delegate selection procedures, which they felt had discriminated against them. Minorities, women, youth, and other groups that had been poorly represented in the party leadership also demanded a more open process of conven-

Riots at the 1968 Democratic National Convention led to the creation of the McGovern-Fraser Commission, which established open procedures and affirmative action guidelines for delegate selection. These reforms have made Democratic conventions more representative than Republican conventions.

tion delegate selection. The result was a committee of inquiry, which was chaired first by Senator George McGovern and later by Representative Donald Fraser, who took over when McGovern left the committee to run for president.

The **McGovern-Fraser Commission** brought great changes in the Democratic Party. The commission tried to make conventions more representative; it adopted quotas that required state party organizations to increase the representation and participation of minorities and women. No longer could party leaders hand-pick the convention delegates virtually in secret. All delegate selection procedures were required to be open, so that party leaders had no more clout than college students or anyone else who wanted to participate. By 1972, these rules were in effect. Suddenly, the days of smoke-filled rooms were over; some of those who had protested outside the convention hall in 1968 were now on the inside. Most notably, Mayor Daley's 1972 Chicago delegation was unseated in favor of a more socially representative slate led by the young Jesse Jackson.

Since the McGovern-Fraser Commission, the party has replaced most of its quota requirements with affirmative action guidelines; the one exception is a firm rule that each delegation must be half male and half female. The Democrats have also tried to restore a role for their party leaders. Many thought the reforms went too far, cutting out state and national leaders whose support was needed to win elections. In 1982, another commission chaired by North Carolina's Governor Hunt recommended that a portion of the delegate slots be automatically set aside for party leaders and elected officials. These politicians who are awarded convention seats on the basis of their position are known as **superdelegates**. Superdelegate slots at the convention were designed to restore an element of "peer review" to the process, ensuring participation of the people most familiar with the candidates. It was also thought that these party officials would be more likely than issue enthusiasts to consider the long-term future of the party and would therefore support the most electable candidate.[40]

Finding an electable candidate for the presidency was an elusive task for the Democrats in the two decades during which they continually fiddled with the delegate selection process. In the first five elections after the McGovern-Fraser reforms, the Democrats won only one. Many political analysts believe that the divisiveness of the Democrats' new open procedures hurt their ability to unite for the fall campaign against the Republicans until they stopped fighting about procedures in the 1990s.[41] As Bill Clinton said in March of 1992, "I have always believed that Democrats often forfeit the November election by the nature of primary process, and I've worked very, very hard to keep that from happening this time."[42] Clinton's ability to weather the primary process and unify the Democrats at the party's convention was crucial to his first victory. Similarly, the fact that no Democrat challenged Clinton in the 1996 primaries helped him to get reelected.

THE REPUBLICANS: PUTTING TECHNOLOGY TO USE

In 1968, as the Democratic Party was coming apart at the seams, the Republicans were uniting around former Vice President Richard Nixon as their nominee. Six years later, in 1974, the Republicans faced a political catastrophe when Nixon, who had been resoundingly reelected in 1972, resigned the presidency in the wake of the Watergate scandal (see Chapter 13 for more on Watergate). As often happens when a party is beset by a crisis, friends of the party—in this case, the Republicans—feared for its survival and the survival of the two-party system.

They need not have worried. The Republicans went through very few of the intraparty reforms that so absorbed the Democrats. William Crotty writes that "there was no constituency for reform within the Republican party. Republicans were generally satisfied with their party, the way in which it operated, and what it stood for."[43] Democrats, much more than

The Democratic National Committee meets to consider a new party symbol.

The Republican National Committee meets to consider a new party symbol.

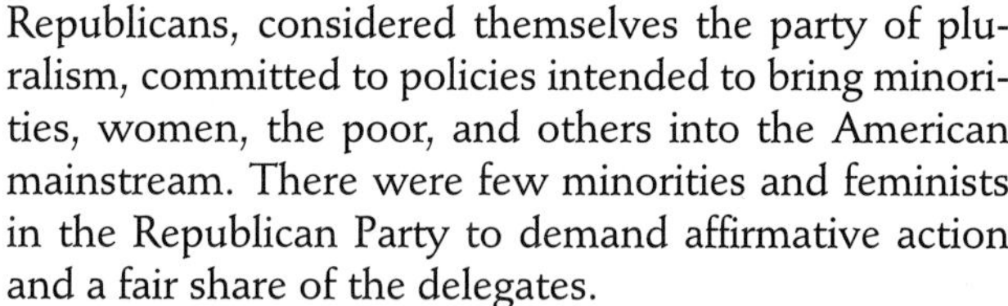

Republicans, considered themselves the party of pluralism, committed to policies intended to bring minorities, women, the poor, and others into the American mainstream. There were few minorities and feminists in the Republican Party to demand affirmative action and a fair share of the delegates.

The Republicans had other work to do—mainly to regenerate their party. They were more concerned with upgrading their organizational machinery than with being balanced by race, gender, age, and ethnicity. After the embarrassment of Watergate, the Republicans turned to former Tennessee Senator Bill Brock to lead them in 1976. Brock wanted the Republican National Committee to provide service to state parties, not to be their watchdog. While the Democrats were making their party more representative, Brock was making the Republican organization more effective and efficient.[44] He pushed for the use of computer technology to adapt the party to the modern age. Computerized lists of potential donors—large and small—gave the Republican Party a great advantage in fund raising, an advantage they still hold today. To help their candidates know what is and what is not working, the Republicans have also made far more use of polling technology than have the Democrats. Democrats are currently catching up with the Republicans' technological sophistication, but Republicans still have an organizational advantage.

THIRD PARTIES: THEIR IMPACT ON AMERICAN POLITICS

The story of American party struggle is primarily the story of two major parties, but **third parties** pop up every year and occasionally attract the public's atten-

Ross Perot challenged the two-party system by running for president in both 1996 and 1992. In 1996, he attempted to institutionalize a third choice by forming the Reform Party as "a party for independent voters."

TABLE 8.3

THE "MAJOR" MINOR PARTIES

ELECTION	PARTY	ITS CLAIM TO FAME
1832	Anti-Masonic Party	As the name implies, this party was opposed to the Masons; it held the first national convention in 1831.
1860	Constitutional Union; Secessionist Democrats	Two of the four parties (together with the Democrats and the Republicans) who ran in the 1860 election.
1892	Populist	Agrarian opponents of banks and railroads; favored "free silver."
1912	Progressive	The "Bull Moose" party, Teddy Roosevelt's splinter from the Republican party; it got 88 electoral votes and cost the Republicans the election.
1948	States' Rights	A walkout by southerners at the Democratic convention led to this Dixiecrat party, whose candidate was Strom Thurmond (SC).
1968	American Independent	The party of segregationist Governor George Wallace of Alabama.
1980	Independent Party	Variously named, this party represented Republican congressman John Anderson's effort to win the presidency.
1992	United We Stand	The volunteer movement that placed Ross Perot's name on the ballot in all 50 states.
1996	Reform Party	Ross Perot's attempt to build a party for independent voters.

tion. American history is strewn with small and now forgotten minor parties: the Free Soil party (a forerunner of the Republican party), the American party (called the "Know Nothings") in 1856, the Jobless party of 1932, the Poor Man's party of 1952, and many others (see Table 8.3).

Third parties come in three basic varieties. First are parties that promote certain causes—either a controversial single issue (prohibition of alcoholic beverages, for example) or an extreme ideological position such as socialism or libertarianism. Second are splinter parties, which are offshoots of a major party. Teddy Roosevelt's Progressives in 1912, Strom Thurmond's States' Righters in 1948, and George Wallace's American Independents in 1968 all claimed they did not get a fair hearing from Republicans or Democrats and thus formed their own new parties. Finally, some third parties are merely an extension of a popular individual with presidential aspirations. Both John Anderson in 1980 and Ross Perot in 1992 and 1996 offered voters who were dissatisfied with the Democratic and Republican nominees another option.

Although third parties almost never win office in the United States, scholars believe they are often quite important.[45] They have brought new groups into the electorate and have served as "safety valves" for popular discontent. The Free Soilers of the 1850s were the first true antislavery party; the Progressives and the Populists put many social reforms on the political agenda. In 1968, George Wallace told his supporters they had the chance to "send a message" to Washington—a message of support for tougher law-and-order measures, which is still being felt to this day. Ross Perot used his saturation of the TV airwaves in 1992 to ensure that the issue of the federal deficit was not ignored in the campaign.

Despite the regular appearance of third parties, the two-party system is firmly entrenched in American politics. Would it make a difference if America had a multiparty system, as so many European countries have? The answer is clearly yes.

TWO PARTIES: SO WHAT?

The most obvious consequence of two-party governance is the moderation of political conflict. If America had many parties, each would have to make a special appeal in order to stand out from the crowd. It is not hard to imagine what a multiparty system might look like in the United States. Quite possibly, African-American groups would form their own party, pressing vigorously for more civil rights legisla-

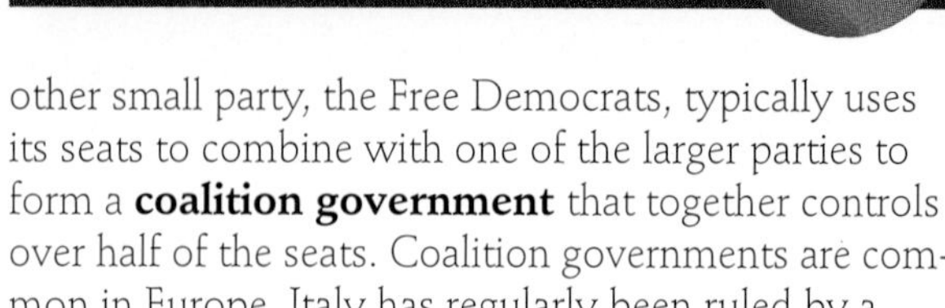

MULTIPARTY SYSTEMS IN OTHER COUNTRIES

One of the major reasons why the United States has only two parties represented in government is structural. America has a **winner-take-all system**, in which whoever gets the most votes wins the election. There are no prizes awarded for second or third place. Suppose there are three parties; one receives 45 percent of the vote, another 40 percent, and the third 15 percent. Though it got less than a majority, the party that finished first is declared the winner. The others are out in the cold. In this way, the American system discourages small parties. Unless a party wins, there is no reward for the votes it gets. Thus, it makes more sense for a small party to form an alliance with one of the major parties than to struggle on its own with little hope. In the example used above, the second- and third-place parties might merge (if they can reach an agreement on policy) to challenge the governing party in the next election.

In a system that employs **proportional representation**, however, such a merger would not be necessary. Under this system, which is used in most European countries, legislative seats are allocated according to each party's percentage of the nationwide vote. If a party wins 15 percent of the vote, then it receives 15 percent of the seats. Even a small party can use its voice in Parliament to be a thorn in the side of the government, standing up strongly for its principles. Such is the role of the Greens in Germany, who are ardent environmentalists. In contrast, Germany's other small party, the Free Democrats, typically uses its seats to combine with one of the larger parties to form a **coalition government** that together controls over half of the seats. Coalition governments are common in Europe. Italy has regularly been ruled by a coalition since the end of World War II, for example.

Even with proportional representation, not every party gets represented in the legislature. To be awarded seats, a party must always achieve a certain percentage of votes, which varies from country to country. Israel has one of the lowest thresholds at 1 percent. This explains why there are always so many parties represented in the Israeli Knesset. The founders of Israel's system wanted to make sure that all points of view were represented, but sometimes this has turned into a nightmare, with small extremist parties holding the balance of power.

Parties have to develop their own unique identities to appeal to voters in a multiparty system. This requires strong stands on the issues, but after the election, compromises must be made to form a coalition government. If an agreement cannot be reached on the major issues, the coalition is in trouble. Sometimes a new coalition can be formed; other times the result is the calling of a new election. In either case, it is clear that proportional representation systems are more fluid than the two-party system in the United States.

tion. Environmentalists could constitute another party, vowing to clean up the rivers, oppose nuclear power, and save the wilderness. America could have religious parties, union-based parties, farmers' parties, and all sorts of others. As in some European countries, there could be half a dozen or more parties represented in Congress (see "America in Perspective: Multiparty Systems in Other Countries").

The American two-party system contributes to political ambiguity. Why should parties risk taking a strong stand on a controversial policy if doing so will only antagonize many voters? Ambiguity is a safe strategy,[46] as extremist candidates Barry Goldwater in 1964 and George McGovern in 1972 found out the hard way. The two-party system thus throttles extreme or unconventional views.

UNDERSTANDING POLITICAL PARTIES

Political parties are considered essential elements of democratic government. Indeed, one of the first steps taken toward democracy in Eastern Europe was the formation of competing political parties to contest elections. After years of one-party totalitarian rule, Eastern Europeans were ecstatic to be able to adopt a multiparty system like those that had proved successful in the West. In contrast, the founding of the world's first party system in the United States was seen as a risky adventure in the then uncharted waters of democracy. Wary of having parties at all, the founders designed a system that has greatly

America's two-party system encourages moderate politics. The presidential candidacies of Democrat George McGovern (left) and Republican Barry Goldwater (far right, with vice-presidential candidate William Miller) demonstrated the perils of controversy. McGovern, an extreme liberal, lost to Richard Nixon by a landslide in 1972; Goldwater, an ultraconservative, was crushed by Lyndon Johnson in 1964.

restrained their political role to this day. Whether American parties should continue to be so loosely organized is at the heart of today's debate about their role in American democracy.

DEMOCRACY AND RESPONSIBLE PARTY GOVERNMENT

Ideally, in a democracy candidates should say what they mean to do if elected and, once they are elected, should be able to do what they promised. Critics of the American party system lament that this is all too often not the case and have called for a "more responsible two-party system."[47] Advocates of the **responsible party model** believe the parties should meet the following conditions:

1. Parties must present distinct, comprehensive programs for governing the nation.
2. Each party's candidates must be committed to its program and have the internal cohesion and discipline to carry out its program.
3. The majority party must implement its programs, and the minority party must state what it would do if it were in power.
4. The majority party must accept responsibility for the performance of the government.

A two-party system operating under these conditions would make it easier to convert party promises into governmental policy. A party's officeholders would have firm control of the government, so they would be collectively, rather than individually, responsible for their actions. Voters would therefore know whom to blame for what the government does and does not accomplish.

As this chapter has shown, American political parties fall far short of these conditions. They are too decentralized to take a single national position and then enforce it. Most candidates are self-selected, gaining their nomination by their own efforts rather than the party's. Virtually anyone can vote in party primaries; thus, parties do not have control over those who run under their labels. In 1991, for example, a former grand wizard of the Ku Klux Klan, David Duke, became the Republican nominee for Governor of Louisiana despite denunciations from President Bush, who ultimately said he preferred the Democratic nominee. Had Duke won the election, the Republican Party would have been powerless to control his actions in office.

In America's loosely organized party system, there simply is no mechanism for a party to discipline officeholders and thereby ensure cohesion in policymaking. As David Mayhew writes, "Unlike most politicians elsewhere, American ones at both legislative and exec-

Distributed by King Features Syndicate

utive levels have managed to navigate the last two centuries of history without becoming minions of party leaders."[48] Thus, it is rare to find congressional votes in which over 90 percent of Democrats vote in opposition to over 90 percent of Republicans. Indeed, Mayhew's analysis of historic legislation from 1946 to 1990 failed to uncover a single case in which a major law was passed by such a clearly partisan vote.[49]

Not everyone thinks that America's decentralized parties are a problem, however. Critics of the responsible party model argue that the complexity and diversity of American society are too great to be captured by such a simple model of party politics. Local differences need an outlet for expression, they say. One cannot expect Texas Democrats always to want to vote in line with New York Democrats. In the view of those opposed to the responsible party model, America's decentralized parties are appropriate for the type of limited government the founders sought to create and most Americans wish to maintain.[50]

America's decentralized political parties have little control over candidates, as shown by the Senate nomination of Oliver North, who figured prominently in the Iran-Contra scandal. North obtained the Republican nomination in Virginia despite being denounced by the state's senior Republican Senator, John Warner, as well as by former Presidents Reagan and Bush.

INDIVIDUALISM AND GRIDLOCK

The Founding Fathers were very concerned that political parties would trample on the rights of individuals. They wanted to preserve individual freedom of action by various elected officials. With America's weak party system, this has certainly been the case. Individual members of Congress and other elected officials have great freedom to act as they see fit rather than toeing the party line.

One frequently cited consequence of this allowance for individualism, however, is gridlock in American policymaking. The lack of a strong party structure makes it easier for politicians to pass the buck than bite the bullet. In particular, the divided government of the Reagan-Bush era allowed Republican leaders to blame budget deficits on congressional unwillingness to cut social programs, while Democratic leaders put the blame on what they viewed as the president's excessive military spending. With neither party really in charge and each pointing a finger at the other, it is no wonder that little was done to resolve the budget deficit. With the situation reversed in 1995-1996, the new Republican majority in Congress found their agenda frustrated by a Democratic president. Although both sides agreed on the importance of passing a plan to balance the budget, the two sides could not reach an agreement, and at two points during the budget controversy, unprecedented shutdowns of parts of the federal government occurred.

When one party has simultaneous control of the executive and legislative branches, there is much less open conflict. Nevertheless, the party in control typically has a hard time maintaining sufficient unity to accomplish major changes. When President Clinton had the chance to work with Democratic majorities in the House and Senate in 1993 and 1994, he found it hard to get the support he needed from his fellow Democrats. Gridlock was clearly evident on such issues as health care, campaign finance reform, and welfare reform during the first two years of the Clinton presidency.

AMERICAN POLITICAL PARTIES AND THE SCOPE OF GOVERNMENT

The lack of disciplined and cohesive European-style parties in America goes a long way to explain why the scope of governmental activity is less in the United States than in other established democracies. The absence of a national health care system in America provides a perfect example. In Britain, the Labour Party had long proposed such a system, and after it won the 1945 election, all of its members of Parliament voted to enact national health care into law. On the other side of the Atlantic, President Truman also proposed a national health care bill in the first presidential election after War World II. But even though he won the election and had majorities of his own party in both houses of Congress, his proposal never got very far. The weak party structure in the United States allowed many congressional Democrats to oppose Truman's health care proposal. Over four decades later, President Clinton again proposed a system of universal health care and had a Democratic-controlled Congress to work with. His experience in 1994 was much the same as Truman's; the Clinton health care bill never even came up for a vote in Congress because of the President's inability to get enough members of his own party to go along with him. Thus, substantially increasing the scope of government in America is not something that can be accomplished through the disciplined actions of one party's members, as is the case in other democracies.

In addition, because no single party in the United States can ever be said to have firm control over the government, the hard choices necessary to cut back on existing government spending are rarely addressed. A disciplined and cohesive governing party would have the power to say no to various demands on the government. In contrast, America's loose party structure makes it possible for individual politicians to focus their efforts on getting more from the government for their own constituents.

IS THE PARTY OVER?

The key problem of American political parties today is this: The parties are low-tech institutions in a high-tech political era. Political columnist David Broder once wrote that "a growing danger to the prospects for responsible party government is the technological revolution that has affected campaigning in the past decade."[51] The party, through its door-to-door canvassers, still makes house calls, yet more and more political communication is not face-to-face but rather through the mass media.[52] The technology of campaigning—television, polls, computers, political consultants, media specialists, and the like—is available for hire to candidates who can afford it. Why should candidates rely on the parties for what they can buy for themselves?

No longer are parties the main source of political information, attention, and affection. The party of today has rivals that appeal to voters and politicians alike, the biggest of which is the media. With the advent of television, voters no longer need the party to find out what the candidates are like and what they stand for. The interest group is another party rival. As Chapter 11 will discuss, the power of interest groups has grown enormously in recent years. Interest groups, not the parties, pioneered much of the technology of modern politics, including mass mailings and sophisticated fund raising.

The People Speak

Are Political Parties Obsolete?

Regardless of your opinion of the Republican Party and the Democratic Party, do you think those two parties have become obsolete or do you think the Republican Party and the Democratic Party are still necessary?

Obsolete	31%
Necessary	61%
Only Democrats Necessary	1%
Only Republicans Necessary	0%
Don't Know	7%

SOURCE: The question as worded is taken directly from a CBS/*New York Times* Poll, June 1992.

The parties have clearly been having a tough time of late, but there are indications that they are beginning to adapt to the high-tech age. Although the old city machines are largely extinct, state and national party organizations have become more visible and active than ever. More people are calling themselves Independents and splitting their tickets, but the majority still identify with a party, and this percentage seems to have stabilized. As you can see in "The People Speak: Are Political Parties Obsolete?" the majority of the public still believes parties are necessary.

For a time, some political scientists were concerned that parties were on the verge of disappearing from the political scene. A more realistic view is that parties will continue to play an important, but significantly diminished, role in American politics. Leon Epstein sees the situation as one in which the parties have become "frayed." He concludes that the parties will "survive and even moderately prosper in a society evidently unreceptive to strong parties and yet unready, and probably unable, to abandon parties altogether."[53]

SUMMARY

Even though political parties are one of Americans' least beloved institutions, political scientists see them as a key linkage between policymakers and the people. Parties are pervasive in politics; for each party there is a *party-in-the-electorate,* a *party organization,* and a *party-in-government.* Political parties affect policy through their platforms. Despite much cynicism about party platforms, they are taken seriously when their candidates are elected.

America has a two-party system. This fact is of fundamental importance in understanding American politics. The ups and downs of the two parties constitute party competition. In the past, one party or the other has dominated the government for long periods of time. These periods were punctuated by critical elections, in which party coalitions underwent realignment. Since 1968, however, American government has experienced a unique period of party dealignment. Although parties are currently weaker at the mass level, they are stronger and richer than ever in terms of national and state organization. Some would have them be far more centralized and cohesive, following the responsible party model. The loose structure of American parties allows politicians to avoid collective responsibility, a state of affairs that facilitates big government. Although the party system is certainly not about to disappear, it remains to be seen whether it can fully adapt itself to the high-tech age.

KEY TERMS

party competition
political party
linkage institutions
party image
rational-choice theory
party identification
ticket-splitting
party machines
patronage
national convention
national committee
national chairperson
party eras
critical election
party realignment
coalition
New Deal coalition
party dealignment
party neutrality
split-level party
McGovern-Fraser Commission
superdelegates
third parties
winner-take-all system
proportional representation
coalition government
responsible party model

FOR FURTHER READING

Beck, Paul Allen. *Party Politics in America,* 8th ed. New York: Longman, 1996. The standard textbook on political parties.

Black, Earl, and Merle Black. *Politics and Society in the South.* Cambridge, MA: Harvard University Press, 1987. An excellent examination of the transformation of party politics in the South.

Black, Gordon S., and Benjamin D. Black. *The Politics of American Discontent: How a New Party Can Make Democracy Work Again*. New York: Wiley, 1994. An indictment of the two-party system that calls for the formation of a third party.

Cox, Gary W., and Samuel Kernell, eds. *The Politics of Divided Government*. Boulder, CO: Westview Press, 1991. A set of readings that addresses both the causes and the consequences of divided party government.

Downs, Anthony. *An Economic Theory of Democracy*. New York: Harper & Row, 1957. An extremely influential theoretical work that applies rational-choice theory to party politics.

Epstein, Leon. *Political Parties in the American Mold*. Madison: University of Wisconsin Press, 1986. Epstein demonstrates the remarkable persistence of both parties during a century of profound social change.

Green, John C., and Daniel M. Shea. *The State of the Parties,* 2nd ed. Lanham, MD: Rowman & Littlefield, 1996. A diverse set of articles on numerous aspects of party politics, with an emphasis on how well the party system is working.

Herrnson, Paul S. *Party Campaigning in the 1980s*. Cambridge, MA: Harvard University Press, 1988. An analysis of the role that parties play in congressional elections, arguing that they are in the process of making a comeback.

Klinkner, Philip A. *The Losing Parties: Out-Party National Committees, 1956-1993*. New Haven, CT: Yale University Press, 1994. A study that shows how the two parties have generally responded differently to presidential defeat, the Republicans emphasizing organization and the Democrats focusing on party procedures.

Maisel, L. Sandy, ed. *The Parties Respond: Changes in the American Parties and Campaigns,* 2nd ed. Boulder, CO: Westview Press, 1994. A good collection of readings on how parties have adapted to changes in the political system.

Rosenstone, Steven, Roy Behr, and Edward Lazarus. *Third Parties in America,* 2nd ed. Princeton, NJ: Princeton University Press, 1996. An analytical study of why third parties appear when they do and what effect they have.

Sabato, Larry. *The Party's Just Begun: Shaping Political Parties for America's Future*. Glenview, IL: Scott, Foresman/Little, Brown, 1988. A spirited prescription for strengthening the parties.

Sundquist, James L. *Dynamics of the Party System,* rev. ed. Washington, DC: Brookings Institution, 1983. One of the best books ever on the major realignments in American history.

Wattenberg, Martin P. *The Decline of American Political Parties, 1952-1994*. Cambridge, MA: Harvard University Press, 1996. An account of the decline of parties-in-the-electorate.

White, John Kenneth, and Jerome M. Mileur. *Challenges to Party Government*. Carbondale, IL: Southern Illinois University Press, 1992. A collection of essays that examines the responsible party model from the perspective of politics in the 1990s.

INTERNET RESOURCES

www.rnc.org
The official site of the Republican National Committee.

www.democrats.org
The Democratic Party online.

NOTES

1. E. E. Schattschneider, *Party Government* (New York: Farrar and Rinehart, 1942), 1.
2. James Gerstenzang, "Bush Campaign Reforms Seek Curbs on PACs," *Los Angeles Times,* June 30, 1989, 23.
3. William N. Chambers, "Party Development and the American Mainstream," in William N. Chambers and Walter Dean Burnham, *The American Party Systems,* 2nd ed. (New York: Oxford University Press, 1967), 5.
4. Anthony Downs, *An Economic Theory of Democracy* (New York: Harper & Row, 1957).
5. Paul Allen Beck and Frank J. Sorauf, *Party Politics in America,* 7th ed. (New York: HarperCollins, 1992), 11.
6. Kay Lawson, ed., *Political Parties and Linkage: A Comparative Perspective* (New Haven, CT: Yale University Press, 1980), 3.
7. The major exception to this rule is nominations for the one-house state legislature in Nebraska, which is officially nonpartisan. In addition, Bernard Sanders has represented Vermont in the House as an Independent since 1990, and in 1994 Angus King was elected governor of Maine as an Independent.
8. Downs, *Economic Theory.*
9. Morris P. Fiorina, *Congress: Keystone of the Washington Establishment,* 2nd ed. (New Haven, CT: Yale University Press, 1989), 101.

10. See Katherine Tate, *From Protest to Politics: The New Black Voters in American Elections* (Cambridge, MA: Harvard University Press, 1993).

11. Wattenberg, *The Decline,* chap. 10.

12. Beck and Sorauf, *Party Politics in America,* 7th ed., 112.

13. Cornelius Cotter and Bernard C. Hennessey, *Politics Without Power* (New York: Atherton, 1964).

14. Milton Rakove, *Don't Make No Waves, Don't Back No Losers* (Bloomington: Indiana University Press, 1975), 167.

15. Edward C. Banfield and James Q. Wilson, *City Politics* (Cambridge, MA: Harvard University Press and the M.I.T. Press, 1963), 115.

16. Gerald M. Pomper, *Passions and Interests: Political Party Concepts of American Democracy* (Lawrence: University of Kansas Press, 1992), 74.

17. Terry Christensen and Larry N. Gerston, *The California Connection* (Boston: Little, Brown, 1984), 37.

18. Kay Lawson, "California: The Uncertainties of Reform," in *Party Renewal in America,* chap. 8.

19. John F. Bibby *et al.,* "Parties in State Politics," in Virginia Gray, Herbert Jacob, and Kenneth Vines, eds., *Politics in the American States,* 4th ed. (Boston: Little, Brown, 1983), 76-79.

20. John F. Bibby, *Politics, Parties, and Elections in America,* 2nd ed. (Chicago: Nelson-Hall, 1992), 102.

21. Price, *Bringing Back the Parties,* 124.

22. *Ibid.,* 124.

23. Gerald M. Pomper, *Elections in America* (New York: Longman, 1980), 161. Another study of presidential promises from Kennedy through Reagan also reaches the conclusion that campaign pledges are taken seriously. See Jeff Fishel, *Presidents and Promises* (Washington, DC: Congressional Quarterly Press, 1985).

24. The term is from V. O. Key. The standard source on critical elections is Walter Dean Burnham, *Critical Elections and the Mainsprings of American Politics* (New York: Norton, 1970).

25. On the origins of the American party system, see William N. Chambers, *Political Parties in a New Nation* (New York: Oxford University Press, 1963).

26. See Richard Hofstader, *The Idea of a Party System: The Rise of Legitimate Opposition in the United States, 1780-1840* (Berkeley: University of California Press, 1969).

27. James W. Ceaser, *Presidential Selection: Theory and Development* (Princeton, NJ: Princeton University Press, 1979), 130.

28. Quoted in James L. Sundquist, *Dynamics of the Party System,* rev. ed. (Washington, DC: Brookings Institution, 1983), 88. Sundquist's book is an excellent account of realignments in American party history.

29. *Ibid.,* 1955.

30. David M. Kennedy, "The Changing Image of the New Deal," *Atlantic Monthly.* (January 1985): 90.

31. On Boston, see Gerald H. Gamm, *The Making of New Deal Democrats: Voting Behavior and Realignment in Boston, 1920-1940* (Chicago: University of Chicago Press, 1989).

32. For a good collection of readings on the causes and consequences of divided party government, see Gary W. Cox and Samuel Kernell, eds., *The Politics of Divided Government* (Boulder, CO: Westview, 1991).

33. See Morris P. Fiorina, *Divided Government* (New York: Macmillan, 1992).

34. See Paul S. Herrnson, "American Political Parties After Three Decades of Growth and Change," in Gillian Peele *et al., Developments in American Politics 2* (New York: Macmillan, 1994).

35. Larry Sabato, *The Party's Just Begun: Shaping Political Parties for America's Future* (Glenview, IL: Scott, Foresman/Little, Brown, 1988), 133.

36. Martin P. Wattenberg, *The Decline of American Political Parties, 1952-1992* (Cambridge, MA: Harvard University Press, 1994).

37. Xandra Kayden and Eddie Mahe, Jr., *The Party Goes On: The Persistence of the Two-Party System in the United States* (New York: Basic Books, 1985), 80.

38. Paul S. Herrnson, *Party Campaigning in the 1980s* (Cambridge, MA: Harvard University Press, 1988), 121.

39. Denise Baer and David Bositis, *Elite Cadres and Party Coalitions: Representing the Public in Party Politics* (Westport, CT: Greenwood Press, 1988).

40. See David E. Price, *Bringing Back the Parties* (Washington, DC: Congressional Quarterly Press, 1984), 201-205.

41. See Martin P. Wattenberg, *The Rise of Candidate-Centered Politics: Presidential Elections of the 1980s* (Cambridge, MA: Harvard University Press, 1991), chap. 3.

42. Robert Shogan, "Clinton's Last Hurdle Gone, Experts Say," *Los Angeles Times,* March 20, 1992, A1.

43. William Crotty, "Party Reforms and Party Adaptability," in Eric M. Uslaner, ed., *American Political Parties: A Reader* (Itasca, IL: F.E. Peacock, 1993), 282.

44. On the Republican reforms, see John Bibby, "Party Renewal in the National Republican Party," in Gerald M. Pomper, ed., *Party Renewal in America* (New York: Praeger, 1980), 102-115.

45. Steven J. Rosenstone, Roy L. Behr, and Edward H. Lazarus, *Third Parties in America* (Princeton, NJ: Princeton University Press, 1984).

46. For discussion of political ambiguity as a strategy, see Kenneth A. Shepsle, "The Strategy of Ambiguity: Uncertainty and Electoral Competition," *American Political Science Review* 66 (June 1972): 555-68; and Benjamin I. Page, *Choices and Echoes in Presidential Elections* (Chicago: University of Chicago Press, 1978), chap. 6.

47. The classic statement on responsible parties can be found in "Toward a More Responsible Two-Party System: A Report of the Committee on Political Parties, American Political Science Association," *American Political Science Review* 44 (1950): supplement, number 3, part 2.

48. David R. Mayhew, *Divided We Govern: Party Control, Lawmaking, and Investigations, 1946-1990* (New Haven: Yale University Press, 1991), 199.

49. *Ibid.,* 126.

50. See Evron M. Kirkpatrick, "Toward a More Responsible Party System: Political Science, Policy Science, or Pseudo-Science?" *American Political Science Review* 65 (1971): 965-990.

51. David S. Broder, *The Party's Over* (New York: Harper & Row, 1972), 236.

52. Banfield and Wilson were among the first to note the impact of technology on parties when they ascribed to television the weakening of the importance of a precinct captain's visits: "The precinct captain who visits in the evening interrupts a television program and must either stay and watch in silence or else excuse himself quickly and move on." See their *City Politics,* 122.

53. Leon Epstein, *Political Parties in the American Mold* (Madison: University of Wisconsin Press, 1986), 346.

9 Nominations and Campaigns

Campaigning for any major office has become a massive undertaking in today's political world. Consider Bill Clinton's grueling five-state schedule for March 6, 1992:

- The campaigning begins in Houston, Texas, with a morning tour of a combined court, police station, and detention center.
- Around lunchtime Clinton's plane departs for Tampa, Florida, where he will spend 4 hours speaking to a crowd of senior citizens and taping an interview for the MacNeil-Lehrer Newshour.
- For dinner Clinton flies to Columbia, South Carolina, where he stays just long enough to give a quick stump speech.
- The next stop is Nashville, Tennessee, where he receives an endorsement from the state's governor and then holds a news conference to respond to a new attack from one of his opponents.
- Finally, Clinton arrives late in the evening in Baton Rouge, Louisiana, where he can get a little sleep before he is to go out jogging in the morning with students from LSU.[1]

It is often said that the presidency is the most difficult job in the world, but getting elected to it may well be tougher. It is arguable that the long campaign for the presidency puts candidates under more continuous stress than they could ever face in the White House.

The current American style of long and arduous campaigns has evolved from the belief of reformers that the cure for the problems of democracy is more democracy. Whether this approach is helpful or harmful to democracy is a question that arouses much debate with respect to American political campaigns. Some scholars believe it is important that presidential candidates go through a long and difficult trial by fire. Others, however, worry that the system makes it difficult for politicians with other responsibilities—such as sitting governors and senior senators—to take a run at the White House. This chapter will give you a better understanding of the pros and cons of having a nomination and campaign process that is so open and democratic.

The consequences for the scope of government are also debatable. Anthony King argues that American politicians do too little governing because they are always "running scared," in today's perpetual campaign.[2] From King's perspective, the campaign process does not allow politicians the luxury of trying out solutions to policy problems that might not be immediately popular but would work well in the long run. The scope of government thus stays pretty much as is, given that politicians are usually too concerned with the next election to risk fundamental change. Of course, many analysts would argue that having officeholders constantly worrying about public opinion is good for democracy and that changes in the scope of government shouldn't be undertaken without extensive public consultation. What's not debatable, however, is that today's nomination and campaign process provides much opportunity for interaction between the public and candidates for office.

With about half a million elected officials in this country, someone, somewhere, is always running for office. One of the campaigns is for the world's most powerful office: the presidency of the United States. This chapter will focus mainly on the presidential election. On some topics that are broadly generalizable, such as money and campaigning, we will include examples from congressional races as well. In Chapter 12 we will specifically discuss the congressional election process.

Campaigns in American politics can be divided into two stages: first, nominations, and second, campaigns between the two nominees. The prize for a nomination campaign is garnering a party's nod as its candidate; the prize for an election campaign is winning an office. This chapter discusses what happens up to the election day. Chapter 10 then turns to how people decide whether to vote and whom to vote for.

THE NOMINATION GAME

A **nomination** is a party's official endorsement of a candidate for office. Anyone can play the nomination game, but few have any serious chance of victory. Generally, success in the nomination game requires money, media attention, and momentum. **Campaign strategy** is the way in which candidates attempt to manipulate each of these elements to achieve the nomination.

A campaign, whether for a nomination or the election, is often unpredictable. Even with name recognition, money, and political savvy, a major blunder can change the political complexion virtually overnight, especially when the press pounces on it. In 1968, George Romney's promising campaign for the Republican nomination fell apart soon after he returned from a trip to Vietnam and said that he had been "brainwashed" about the war. After all, who would want a president who admitted to having been brainwashed? Four years later, Edmund Muskie decided to attack a harsh newspaper report about his wife. When he broke down emotionally during his denunciation of the newspaper's publisher, his front-running campaign for the Democratic nomination soon collapsed. In 1987, Gary Hart responded to questions about his alleged womanizing by challenging reporters to follow him around. When two reporters from the *Miami Herald* staked out his condominium

Most Americans feel that presidential campaigns are far too long. Candidates often begin their quest for votes more than a year before the Iowa Caucus. Here, publisher Steve Forbes shakes hands with caucus goers prior to the February 1996 Iowa Caucuses. Lacking support, Forbes later withdrew from the campaign.

In the 1972 New Hampshire primary, front-runner Edmund Muskie lost ground in the campaign when he gave this emotional speech denouncing a local newspaper report about his wife. Reporters wrote that he had broken down in tears; Muskie said he was merely wiping snow from his eyes. In any case, the image of a candidate who couldn't control his emotions negatively affected the Muskie campaign.

and observed actress Donna Rice go in with Hart and apparently spend the night, the resulting media firestorm forced Hart to drop out of the presidential race.

Conscious choices and slips of the tongue help determine outcomes of the nomination and election games. One thing, though, is certain: A candidate must first win a nomination to get a chance at election.

DECIDING TO RUN

Believe it or not, not every politician wants to run for president. One reason for this is that campaigns have become more physically and emotionally taxing than ever. As former Speaker of the House Thomas Foley once said, "I know of any number of people who I think would make good presidents, even great presidents, who are deterred from running by the torture candidates are obliged to put themselves through."[3] This factor clearly discouraged Colin Powell, among others, from running in 1996. To run for president, a person needs what Walter Mondale once called a "fire in the belly." Remarking on his 1984 bid for the presidency, Mondale said, "For four years, that's all I did. I mean, all I did. That's all you think about. That's all you talk about. . . . That's your leisure. That's your luxury. . . . I told someone, 'The question is not whether I can get elected. The question is whether I can be elected and not be nuts when I get there.' "[4]

In Britain, campaigns are limited by law to 5 weeks (see "America in Perspective: Choosing Party Leaders in Great Britain"). In contrast, American campaigns seem endless; a presidential candidacy needs to be either announced or kept as an open secret for at least a year before the election. In the winter of 1995, it was already clear to most observers that Bob Dole, Phil Gramm, Pete Wilson, Richard Lugar, Arlen Specter, Pat Buchanan, and Lamar Alexander were already laying the groundwork for a shot at the Republican presidential nomination for 1996. By the end of 1995, over $60 million had already been spent by the Republican candidates.

Political scientists David Rohde and John Aldrich emphasize that presidential candidates need to be risk takers.[5] Presidential candidates need sufficient self-confidence to put everything on the line in hopes of reaching America's highest political office. Those who aspire to the presidency also need an electoral base from which to begin. Rarely in American history has a

America in Perspective

CHOOSING PARTY LEADERS IN GREAT BRITAIN

The short length of campaigns in Britain is only one of many major differences between the way in which British prime ministers and American presidents are chosen. The process of selecting each party's candidate for the top slot is particularly different. Anthony King, one of Britain's foremost political scientists, offers the following general observations about how British candidates for prime minister were chosen prior to the 1979 campaign, the year that Margaret Thatcher first came to power.

1. "The winners had entered politics at an early age and had served for a considerable number of years in Parliament before becoming their party's leader." Each had "served in a number of different national-level offices."
2. "The candidates were assessed and voted upon exclusively by their fellow politicians." The process of electing the leader was "entirely a party process."
3. "The leadership campaigns involved very little wear and tear on the part of the candidates and their families."
4. "The leadership campaigns cost next to nothing" (less than the equivalent of $10,000 all told).

Compared to other countries around the world, the British process for selecting party leaders is typical; it is the American system that is unique.

SOURCE: Anthony King, "How Not to Select Presidential Candidates: A View from Europe," in Robert E. DiClerico, ed., *Analyzing the Presidency,* 2nd ed. (Guilford, CT: Dushkin, 1990), 9-10.

Democratic or Republican candidate for the presidency been taken seriously as a presidential contender without first holding a key political office; most of the exceptions have been famous generals, such as Dwight Eisenhower in 1952. Three offices—U.S. senator, U.S. representative, and state governor—have provided the electoral base for about 80 percent of the major candidates since 1972.[6] Of the major Republican candidates in 1996, all but magazine heir Steve Forbes and journalist Pat Buchanan had held one or more of these offices.

Having an electoral base is a first step, but the road to the convention is long and full of stumbling blocks. From the convention, held in the summer of election years, only one candidate will emerge as each party's nominee.

COMPETING FOR DELEGATES

In some ways, the nomination game is tougher than the general election game; it whittles a large number of players down to two. The goal of the nomination game is to win the majority of delegates' support at the **national party convention.**

There are 50 different roads to the national convention, one through each state. From February through June of the election year, the individual state parties busily choose their delegates to the national convention via either caucuses or primaries. Candidates try to ensure that delegates committed to them are chosen.

The Caucus Road. Before primaries existed, all state parties selected their delegates to the national convention in a meeting of state party leaders called a **caucus**. Sometimes one or two party "bosses" ran the caucus show, often the governor of the state or the mayor of its largest city. Such state party leaders could control who went to the convention and how the state's delegates voted once they got there. They were the kingmakers of presidential politics who met in smoke-filled rooms at the convention to cut deals and form coalitions.

Today's caucuses are different from those of the past. In the dozen states that still have them, caucuses are now open to all voters who are registered with the party. Iowa traditionally holds the earliest caucus, and an obscure former Georgia governor named Jimmy Carter took his first big presidential step by winning there in 1976. George Bush also made his first big step into the national scene with an upset victory over Ronald Reagan in Iowa in 1980. In 1988, Jesse Jackson leaped to the front of the Democratic pack with a surprise victory in the Michigan caucuses.

Televised debates have become a regular part of presidential primaries. Here, all six announced candidates for the 1992 Democratic nomination are shown participating in a TV forum. During one particularly intense part of the 1992 campaign, the Democratic candidates took part in debates in Colorado, Georgia, and Maryland—all within a period of 30 hours.

Caucuses usually are organized like a pyramid. Small, neighborhood, precinct-level caucuses are held initially—often meeting in a church, an American Legion hall, or even someone's home. At this level, delegates are chosen, on the basis of their preference for a certain candidate, to attend county caucuses and then congressional district caucuses, where delegates are again chosen to go to a higher level—a state convention. At the state convention, which usually occurs months after the precinct caucuses, delegates are finally chosen to go to the national convention. Thus, the Iowa precinct caucuses are only the first step in a long process for selecting the state's delegates. Nevertheless, this arena is the first test of the candidates' vote-getting ability; hence it often becomes a full-blown media extravaganza.[7] In the winter of 1996, the Republican candidates and the national media once again descended on the state of Iowa. Pat Buchanan's strong second-place finish behind Bob Dole in Iowa surprised almost everyone and catapulted him into the national media spotlight.

The Presidential Primary Road. Today, most of the delegates to the Democratic and Republican conventions are selected in **presidential primaries,** in which voters in a state go to the polls and vote for a candidate or delegates pledged to that candidate. The presidential primary was promoted around the turn of the century by reformers who wanted to take nominations out of the hands of the party bosses. The reformers wanted to let the people vote for the candidate of their choice and then bind the delegates to vote for that candidate at the national convention. In 1912, the first presidential primaries were held in 13 states. A half a century later, when John Kennedy sought the presidency, primaries still played a rather small role in the process. Since the McGovern-Fraser Commission Reforms were implemented in 1972, as discussed in the previous chapter, victories in the primaries have become essential to winning a party's presidential nomination (see "Since Kennedy: The Rise of Presidential Primaries").

Few developments have transformed American politics as much as the proliferation of presidential primaries. Presidential election watcher Theodore White calls the primaries the "classic example of the triumph of goodwill over common sense." Says White,

> An entirely new breed of professionals has grown up, voyaging like Gauleiters from state to state, specializing in get-out-the-vote techniques, cross sectionings, media, ethnic breakdowns, and other specialties. . . . Most of all, delegates, who were supposed to be free to vote by their own common sense and conscience, have become for the most part anonymous faces, collected as background for the television cameras, sacks of potatoes packaged in primaries, divorced from party roots, and from the officials who rule states and nation.[8]

The primary season begins during the winter in New Hampshire, where license plates boldly state, "Live free or die." (One can only guess what the prison inmates of New Hampshire must think while making these plates.) Like the Iowa caucuses, the importance of the New Hampshire primary is not the number of delegates or how representative the state is (if there is a representative American state, New Hampshire is certainly not it), but rather that it is always first. At this early stage, the campaign is not for delegates, but for images—candidates want the rest of the country to see them as frontrunners. The frenzy of political activity in this small state is given lavish attention in the national press. During the week of the primary, half the portable satellite dishes in the country can be found in Manchester, New Hampshire, and the networks move their anchors and top reporters to the scene to broadcast the nightly news. In 1992, 23 percent of TV coverage of the nomination races was devoted to the New Hampshire primary.

Other state primaries follow New Hampshire's. State laws determine when primaries are held, and

SINCE KENNEDY

The Rise of Presidential Primaries

One of the greatest changes in American politics from the Kennedy era to the present has been the way presidential nominees are chosen. What was once a relatively straightforward task conducted largely out of public view has been turned into a long and tortuous media circus. In the 1960s, the nomination battle was a test of a candidate's ability to build support among a small cadre of party leaders; in the 1990s, building popularity among primary and caucus voters throughout the 50 states has become the key test. The process has thus moved from smoke-filled rooms to rooms filled with the bright lights of ever-present television cameras.

More than that of any candidate before 1960, Kennedy's campaign was boosted by primary victories. Yet his decision to enter seven primaries was seen at the time as an indication of weakness. The conventional wisdom of 1960 held that primary losses would ruin a campaign, whereas victories might hardly matter. However, Kennedy believed that only by showing his popularity with the voters could he convince the party leaders that he was electable—especially since many doubted whether a Catholic could ever win the presidency. Kennedy's victory over Hubert Humphrey in West Virginia, an overwhelmingly Protestant state, won him not so much delegates but rather key endorsements from such crucial party leaders as Mayor Daley of Chicago and Governor DiSalle of Ohio.

Unlike the primary contests of 1960, those of 1992 were crucial because the overwhelming majority of delegates were chosen through this route. With roughly three-quarters of the delegates now chosen in primaries, these elections have become the main road to both the Democratic and the Republican nominations. In contrast to the primary marathon that Bill Clinton had to run in, only two primary contests drew any attention in 1960. All told, Kennedy's primary victories (mostly in uncontested races, such as in New Hampshire), produced just 18 percent of the delegates he needed for the nomination. Had the party leaders turned against him, Kennedy could clearly have been denied the party's nomination by someone who had bypassed the primaries. Indeed, 8 years later, Democratic party leaders selected Hubert Humphrey as their candidate even though he had not entered a single primary. Today, such a nomination would be unthinkable.

each state party sets up its own rules for how delegates are allocated. Even the experts are often confused by the variety of different procedures used from state to state. One thing is certain, though: Week after week, the primaries serve as elimination contests. The politicians, the press, and the public all love a winner. Candidates who fail to win in the early primaries get labeled as losers and typically drop out of the race. Usually they have little choice: losing quickly inhibits a candidate's ability to raise the money necessary to win in other states. As one veteran fund raiser put it, "People don't lose campaigns. They run out of money and can't get their planes in the air. That's the reality."[10]

In the 1980 delegate chase, a commonly used football term became established in the language of American politics. After George Bush scored a surprise victory over Ronald Reagan in Iowa, he proudly claimed to possess "the big mo"—momentum. Actually, Bush had only a little "mo" and quickly fell victim to a decisive Reagan victory in New Hampshire. But the term neatly describes what candidates for the nomination are after. Primaries and caucuses are more than an endurance contest, though they are certainly that; they are also proving grounds. Week after week, the challenge is to do better than expected. To get "mo" going, candidates have to beat people they were not expected to beat, collect margins above predictions, and—above all else—never lose to people they were expected to trounce. Momentum is good to have, but it is no guarantee of victory, because candidates with a strong base sometimes bounce back. Political scientist Larry Bartels found that "substantive political appeal may overwhelm the impact of momentum, as it did for Reagan against Bush and for Mondale against Hart."[11]

Evaluating the Primary and Caucus System. The primaries and the caucuses are here to stay. That

reality does not mean, however, that political scientists or commentators are particularly happy with the system. Criticisms of this marathon campaign are numerous; here are a few of the most important:

- *Disproportionate attention goes to the early caucuses and primaries.* Take a look at Figure 9.1, which shows how critics think America's media-dominated campaigns are distorted by early primaries and caucuses. Neither New Hampshire nor Iowa is particularly representative of the national electorate. Both are rural; both have only small minority populations; and neither is at the center of the political mainstream. Whereas Iowa is more liberal than the nation as a whole, New Hampshire is the reverse. Although Iowa and New Hampshire are not always "make or break" contests, they play a key—and a disproportionate—role in building momentum, generating money, and garnering media attention.
- *States that vote late in the process are often irrelevant.* At one time, it was considered advantageous for a state to choose its delegates late so that it could play a decisive role. But with so much attention being paid to the early contests, more states have moved their contests up in the calendar in order to capitalize on the media attention. This **frontloading** of the process resulted in 67 percent of the Republican delegates for 1996 being chosen within a month of the New Hampshire primary. States that voted in the last 12 weeks of the 1996 nomination race, such as Pennsylvania and New Jersey, were of no consequence. Bob Dole had already wrapped up the nomination by the time their turn came around.
- *Prominent politicians find it difficult to take time out from their duties to run.* Running for the presidency has become a full-time job. The governor of big state or a member of the congressional leadership is likely to find the task of balancing the demands of a presidential race and political office to be quite tricky. One 1988 candidate who did not let his official responsibilities keep him from running for president was Massachusetts Governor Michael Dukakis. In an extraordinary apology to the state, Dukakis said he underestimated the demands of running for the presidency and managing the state simultaneously. "Trying to do two jobs at the same time was more difficult and more grueling than I expected," he said.[12]
- *Money plays too big a role in the caucuses and primaries.* Momentum means money—getting more of it than your opponents. Many people think that money plays too large a role in American presidential elections. (This topic will be discussed in detail shortly.) Candidates who drop out early in the process often lament that their inability to raise money left them without a chance to compete.
- *Participation in primaries and caucuses is low and unrepresentative.* Although about 50 percent of the population votes in the November presidential election, only about 20 percent casts ballots in presidential primaries. Participation in caucus states is much smaller, because a person must usually devote several hours to attending a caucus. Except for Iowa, where media attention usually boosts the participation, only about 5 percent of registered voters typically show up for caucuses. Moreover, voters in primaries and caucuses are hardly representative of voters at large; they tend to be better educated and more affluent.
- *Primaries and caucuses exaggerate regional factors in decision making.* In 1988, Southern states, feeling that Northern states such as New Hampshire and Iowa had disproportionate influence in the choice of the Democratic nominee, created **Super Tuesday** by moving all their primaries to the same day in early March. No longer could conservative Democrats be ignored, said Southern Democrat leaders. Although the hope of Southern Democrats did not materialize in 1988, in 1992 the Clinton campaign was given a big boost by big wins on Super Tuesday.
- *The system gives too much power to the media.* Critics contend that the media have replaced the party bosses as the new kingmakers. Deciding who has momentum at any given moment, the press readily labels candidates as winners and losers.

FIGURE 9.1 THE INFLATED IMPORTANCE OF IOWA AND NEW HAMPSHIRE IN THE PRESIDENTIAL NOMINATION PROCESS

In 1984, 34 percent of all TV news stories about the nomination campaigns were focused on Iowa and New Hampshire, even though these two small states selected only about 2 percent of the convention delegates. Here are the 50 states drawn to scale in terms of the media attention their primaries and caucuses received in 1984, according to an analysis of coverage by the *New York Times.* A similar analysis of the 1996 Republican primaries would undoubtedly reveal much the same pattern, as once again Iowa and New Hampshire received far more coverage than the states that voted after them.

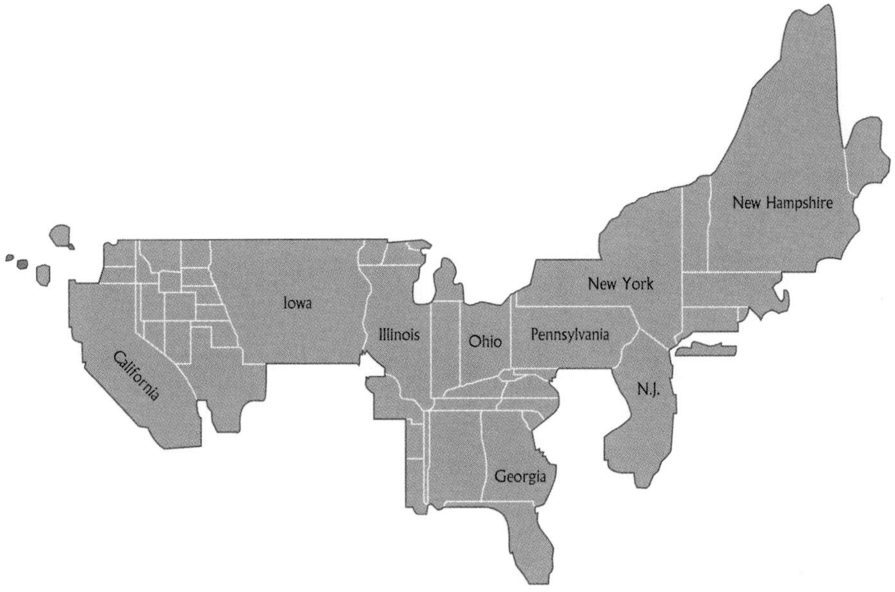

SOURCE: William C. Adams, "As New Hampshire Goes. . . ," in Gary R. Orren and Nelson W. Polsby, eds., *Media and Momentum* (Chatham, NJ: Chatham House, 1987), 43.

Is this, critics ask, the best way to pick a president? Critics answer their own question with a strong "No" and have come up with a number of reform proposals (see "You Are the Policymaker: National and Regional Presidential Primary Proposals").

Nevertheless, the current system has powerful defenders—most notably the candidates themselves. For example, George Bush wrote in his 1987 autobiography that

> our presidential selection process may be pressurized, chaotic, sometimes even unfair; but I disagree with critics who think that it needs a massive overhaul—especially those who argue that television, because it can reach millions, makes it unnecessary for a candidate to travel the country "retailing" his campaign message.
>
> For all its flaws, the virtue of the present system is that it brings presidential candidates—as well as Presidents—out of the insulated politics of television and electronic computers into contact with the flesh-and-blood world.[13]

Even candidates who finish well back in the pack usually support the process. Senator Paul Simon, who won only his home state in 1988, argues that it is best to start the race in small states where people can meet the candidates face to face and where "a candidate of limited means has a chance."[14] He adds that the people of Iowa and New Hampshire, recognizing their important role in the process, "make their commitments with considerably more caution and care than do most citizens in other states."[16] Interior Secretary Bruce Babbitt, who got great press coverage but few votes in 1988, defends the length of the nomination race. He argues that "it has to be long, to allow us to surface national leadership outside of a parliamentary system. Congress does not automatically produce national

NATIONAL AND REGIONAL PRESIDENTIAL PRIMARY PROPOSALS

You Are the Policymaker

The idea of holding a **national primary** to select party nominees has been discussed virtually ever since state primaries were introduced. In 1913, President Woodrow Wilson proposed it in his first message to Congress. Since then over 250 proposals for a national presidential primary have been introduced in Congress. These proposals do not lack public support; opinion polls have consistently shown that a substantial majority of Democrats, Republicans, and Independents alike favor such reform.

According to its proponents, a national primary would bring directness and simplicity to the process for the voters as well as the candidates. The length of the campaign would be shortened, and no longer would votes in one state have more political impact than votes in another. The concentration of media coverage on this one event, say its advocates, would increase not only political interest in the nomination decision but also public understanding of the issues involved.

A national primary would not be so simple, respond the critics. Because Americans would not want a candidate nominated with 25 percent of the vote from among a field of six candidates, in most primaries a runoff election between the top two finishers in each party would have to be held. So much for making the campaign simpler, national primary critics note. Each voter would have to vote three times for president—twice in the primaries and once in November.

Another common criticism of a national primary is that only well-established politicians would have a shot at breaking through in such a system. Big money and big attention from the national media would become more crucial than ever. Obscure candidates, such as Jimmy Carter in 1976, would never have a chance. Do Americans, however, really want politicians without an established reputation to become president?

Perhaps more feasible than a national primary is holding a series of **regional primaries** in which, say, states in the eastern time zone would vote one week, those in the central time zone the next, and so on. This would impose a more rational structure and cut down on candidate travel. No longer would candidates be faced with campaigning simultaneously in primaries at opposite ends of the country. (In 1984, Gary Hart complained that his wife got to campaign in California while he was stuck in New Jersey; he won California but was trounced in New Jersey for this remark.)

The major problem with the regional primary proposal, however, is the advantage gained by whichever region goes first. For example, if the western states were the first to vote, any candidate from California would have a clear edge in building momentum. Although most of the proposed plans call for the order of the regions to be determined by lottery, this would not erase the fact that regional advantages would surely be created from year to year.

Put yourself in the role of policymaker. Do the advantages of the national primary or of the regional primary proposal outweigh the disadvantages? Would either represent an improvement over the current system? Keep in mind that there are almost always unintended consequences associated with reforms.

---

leadership."[16] It is important to enable new national leaders to emerge, says Babbitt, and the current American system facilitates this.

Obviously, some of the candidates would like to see changes, but as long as most candidates and citizens support the process in general, major reform is unlikely. For the foreseeable future, states will continue to select delegates in primaries and caucuses who will attend the national conventions, where the nominees are formally chosen.

THE CONVENTION SEND-OFF

At one time party conventions provided great drama. Great speeches were given, dark-horse candidates suddenly appeared, and numerous ballots were held as candidates jockeyed to win the nomination. It took the Democrats 46 ballots in 1912, 44 in 1920, and a record 103 in 1924 to nominate their presidential standard bearer. Multiballot conventions died out in 1952, however, with the advent of television.

Nevertheless, television did not immediately put an end to drama at the conventions. In fact, for a while it helped to create it. In 1964, NBC's John Chancellor was arrested for standing in the aisles while reporting from the floor of the Republican Convention. His producers promised him bail, and as he was escorted off the floor, he signed off saying, "This is John Chancellor reporting under custody and now returning you to the anchor booth." Four years later it was protesters in the streets of Chicago who were being arrested at the Democratic Convention. The networks shifted back and forth from scenes of violence in the streets to the bitter debate and occasional scuffles inside the convention hall. In 1972, the Democrats were at it again, this time extending their debates late into the night, causing nominee George McGovern to give his acceptance speech at three in the morning. Some delegates took pity on the overworked TV anchors, holding up signs like "Free Walter Cronkite," who then anchored CBS's coverage.

Today, though, the drama has largely been drained from the conventions, because the winner is a foregone conclusion. No longer can a powerful governor shift a whole block of votes at the last minute. Delegates selected in primaries and open caucuses have known preferences. The last time there was any doubt about who would win at the convention was in 1976, when Ford barely edged out Reagan for the Republican nomination. The parties have also learned that it is not in their best interest to provide high drama. The raucous conventions held by the Republicans in 1964 and the Democrats in 1968 and 1972 captured the public's attention, but they also exposed such divisiveness that the parties were unable to unite for the fall campaign.

Despite a strong effort by his supporters at the 1924 Democratic National Convention, Alfred E. Smith eventually withdrew after 95 ballots, and John W. Davis received the nomination after a record 103 ballots. Davis subsequently lost the presidential election to Republican Calvin Coolidge. Today's conventions lack such drama, because the parties strictly control the proceedings to present a unified image.

Without such drama, the networks have substantially scaled back the number of hours of coverage substantially in recent years, as you can see in Figure 9.2. Even with the condensed TV coverage, the Nielsen ratings have fallen to abysmal levels.[17] For example, when George Bush and Dan Quayle delivered their speeches at the 1992 Republican Convention, NBC and ABC each got a rating of 7.0, and CBS trailed with 5.7. By comparison, CBS scored a whopping 29.3 rating with its 1992 season-opener of "Murphy Brown," during which the fictional reporter gave her response to Quayle's criticism of her lifestyle choice.

One can hardly blame people for tuning out the conventions, though, when little news is made at them. Today's conventions are carefully scripted to present the party in its best light. Delegates are no longer there to argue for their causes but merely to support their candidate. The parties carefully orchestrate a massive send-off for the presidential and vice-presidential candidates. The party's leaders are there in force, as are many of its most important followers—people whose input will be critical during the campaign. Thus, although conventions are no longer very interesting, they are a significant rallying point for the parties.

The conventions are also important in developing the party's policy positions and in promoting political representation. In the past, conventions were essentially an assembly of state-party and local-party leaders, gathered together to bargain over the selection of the party's ticket. Almost all delegates were white, male, and over 40. Lately, party reformers, especially among the Democrats, have worked hard to make the conventions far more demographically representative. Meeting in an oversized, overstuffed convention hall in a major city, a national convention is a short-lived affair. The highlight of the first day is usually the keynote speech, in which a dynamic speaker recalls party heroes, condemns the opposition party, and touts the nominee apparent.

The second day centers on the party platform—the party's statement of its goals and policies for the next 4 years. The platform is drafted prior to the convention by a committee whose members are chosen in rough

FIGURE 9.2 THE DECLINING COVERAGE OF CONVENTIONS ON NETWORK TV

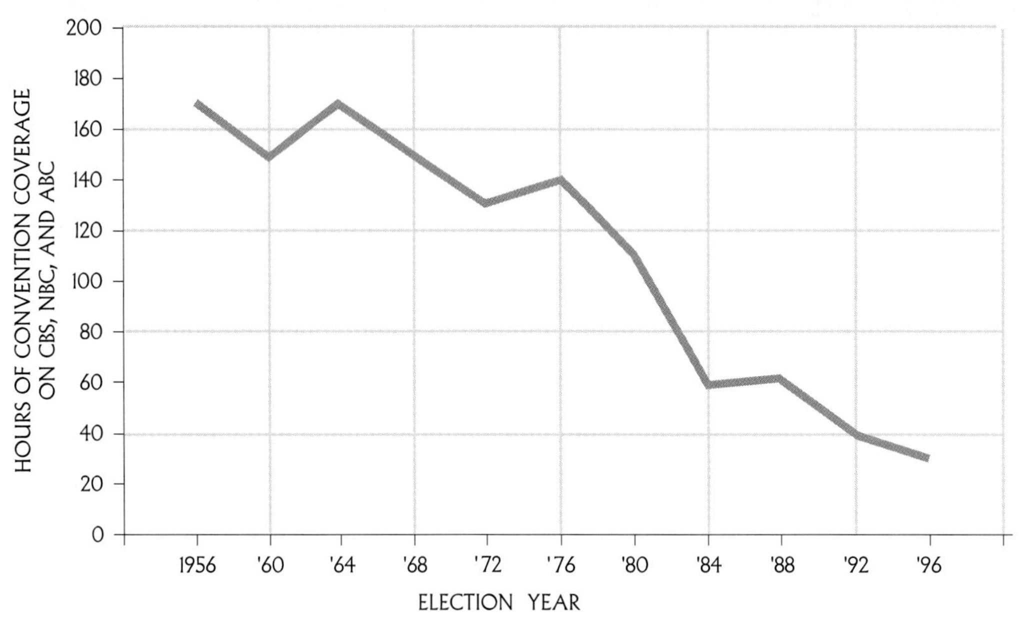

HOURS OF CONVENTION COVERAGE ON CBS, NBC, AND ABC

0, 20, 40, 60, 80, 100, 120, 140, 160, 180, 200

ELECTION YEAR

1956, '60, '64, '68, '72, '76, '80, '84, '88, '92, '96

SOURCE: For 1956-1984, calculated from data reported in Byron E. Schafer, *Bifurcated Politics: Evolution and Reform in the National Party Convention* (Cambridge, MA: Harvard University Press, 1988), 274; updated by the authors for 1988 through 1996.

proportion to each candidate's strength. Any time over 20 percent of the delegates to the platform committee disagree with the majority, they can bring an alternative minority plank to the convention floor for debate. In former times, contests over the platform were key tests of candidates' strength before the actual nomination. Now they serve mostly as a way for the minority factions in the party to make sure that their voices are heard. In 1992 and 1996, some pro-choice Republicans tried in vain to force a vote on the solidly anti-abortion plank in the GOP platform. Fearing the negative publicity the party would incur by showing open disagreement on this emotionally charged issue, Republican leaders such as California's pro-choice Governor Pete Wilson worked hard to dissuade delegates from forcing such a confrontation.

The third day of the convention is devoted to formally nominating a candidate for president. One of each candidate's eminent supporters gives a speech extolling the candidate's virtues; a string of seconding speeches then follow. Demonstrations erupt as if spontaneous, though in reality they are carefully planned. Toward the end of the evening, balloting begins as states announce their votes ("Florida, the sunshine state, casts all its votes for . . ."). After all the votes are counted, the evening's last demonstration celebrates the long-anticipated nomination.

The vice-presidential nominee is chosen by roll call vote on the convention's final day, though custom dictates that delegates simply vote for whomever the presidential nominee recommends. The vice-presidential candidate then comes to the podium to make a brief acceptance speech. This speech is followed by the grand finale—the presidential candidate's acceptance speech, in which the battle lines for the coming campaign are drawn. Afterward, all the party leaders come out to congratulate the party's ticket, raise their hands, and bid the delegates farewell.

THE CAMPAIGN GAME

Once nominated, candidates concentrate on campaigning for the general election. These days, the word *campaign* is part of the American political vocabulary, but it was not always so. The term was originally a military one: Generals mounted campaigns, using their scarce resources to achieve strategic objectives. Political campaigns proceed in a similar fashion—resources are scarce, expenditures in the presidential race are limited by federal law, and both have to be timed and targeted. A candidate's time and energy are also finite. Choices must be made concerning where to go and how long to spend at each stop.

Campaigns involve more than organization and leadership. Artistry also enters the picture, for campaigns deal in images. The campaign is the canvas on which political strategists try to paint portraits of leadership, competence, caring, and other images Americans value in presidents. Campaigning today is an art and a science, heavily dependent—like much else in American politics—on technology.

THE HIGH-TECH CAMPAIGN

The new machines of politics have changed the way campaigns are run. During the first half of the twentieth century, candidates and their entourage piled onto a campaign train and tried to speak to as many people as time, energy, and money would allow. Voters journeyed from miles around to see a presidential whistle-stop tour go by and to hear a few words in person from the candidate. Today, television is the most prevalent means used by candidates to reach voters. Thomas Patterson stresses that "today's presidential campaign is essentially a mass media campaign. . . . It is no exaggeration to say that, for the majority of voters, the campaign has little reality apart from its media version."[18] Most of the money spent on presidential campaigns these days is spent on the media, and little of consequence occurs outside the media's ever-present gaze. Technology has made it possible for candidates to speak directly to the American people in the comfort of their living rooms. At the grass-roots level, some candidates now distribute 10-minute videotapes of themselves rather than the old-fashioned political pamphlet. During the 1992 New Hampshire primary, the Clinton campaign passed out over 25,000 videotapes detailing his economic plan.[19]

In writing a party platform, disagreements between various factions of the party often become evident. In 1992 and 1996, Ann Stone led a movement of Republican women in favor of a pro-choice plank on abortion. Although Ann Stone drew a fair amount of media attention, she was unsuccessful in getting the Republican Convention to consider changing its pro-life platform.

In this high-tech age, things have changed since President Dwight Eisenhower first used a TelePrompTer (a machine used to magnify a speech so that the speaker does not have to look down at his or her text) and found it totally confusing. He grumbled in front of a national television audience, "How does this damned thing work, anyway?" The computer revolution has now overtaken political campaigns. At the end of the first presidential debate in 1996, Bob Dole encouraged viewers to go to his site on the World Wide Web for more information on his issue stands. Both the Dole and the Clinton web sites received millions of "hits" during the campaign, and no doubt this form of communication will play an increasingly important role in the campaigns of the twenty-first century.

Technology has changed the way campaigns are run and the way candidates attempt to reach the people. Senator Edward Kennedy was one of the first in the Senate to have his own home page on the World Wide Web.

Perhaps the most important use of computer technology in campaigns thus far has been the use of targeted mailings to prospective supporters. The technique of **direct mail** involves locating potential supporters by sending information and a request for money to huge lists of people who have supported candidates of similar views in the past. Conservative fund raiser Richard Viguerie pioneered the mass-mailing list, including in his computerized list the names and addresses of hundreds of thousands of contributors to conservative causes. The accumulation of mailing lists enables a candidate to pick almost any issue, be it helping the homeless, opposing abortion, aiding Israel, or anything else, and write to a list of people concerned about it. R. Kenneth Godwin estimates that direct mail now induces over 14 million persons a year to give contributions totaling about $1 billion to various candidates and political causes.[20] The high-tech campaign is no longer a luxury. Candidates *must* use the media and computer technology just to be competitive.

ORGANIZING THE CAMPAIGN

In every campaign, there is too much to do and too little time to do it. Every candidate must prepare for nightly banquets and endless handshaking. More important, to organize their campaigns effectively, candidates must do the following:

- *Line up a campaign manager*. Some candidates try to run their own campaign, but they usually end up regretting it. A professional campaign manager can keep the candidate from getting bogged down in organizational details. This person also bears the day-to-day responsibility for keeping the campaign square on its message. James Carville, Clinton's 1992 campaign manager, will probably be best remembered for the large sign in his office reading "It's the economy, stupid!"—an admonition to all in the campaign never to veer far from this central theme.
- *Get a fund raiser*. Money, as this chapter will soon discuss in detail, is an important key to election victory.
- *Get a campaign counsel*. With all the current federal regulation of campaign financing, legal assistance is essential to ensure compliance with the laws.
- *Hire media and campaign consultants*. Candidates have more important things to do with their time than plan ad campaigns, contract for buttons and bumper stickers, and buy TV time and newspaper space. Professionals can get them the most exposure for their money.
- *Assemble a campaign staff*. It is desirable to hire as many professionals as the campaign budget allows, but it is also important to get a coordinator of volunteers to ensure that envelopes are licked, doorbells rung, and other small but vital tasks addressed.
- *Plan the logistics*. A modern presidential campaign involves jetting around the country at an incredible pace. Good advance people handle the complicated details of candidate scheduling and see to it that events are well publicized and well attended.
- *Get a research staff and policy advisors*. Candidates have little time to master the complex issues reporters will ask about. Policy advisors—often distinguished academics—feed them the information they need to keep up with events.
- *Hire a pollster*. There are dozens of professional polling firms that do opinion research to tell candidates how the voters view them and what is on the voters' minds.
- *Get a good press secretary*. Candidates running for major office have reporters dogging them every step of the way. The reporters need news, and a good press secretary can help them make their deadlines with stories that the campaign would like to see reported.

Most of these tasks cost money. Campaigns are not cheap, and the role of money in campaigns is a controversial one.

MONEY AND CAMPAIGNING

There is no doubt that campaigns are expensive and, in America's high-tech political arena, growing more so. As California Treasurer Jesse Unruh used to say,

"Money is the mother's milk of politics." Candidates need money to build a campaign organization and to get their message out. Many people and groups who want certain things from the government are all too willing to give it; thus, there is the common perception that money buys votes and influence. The following sections take a close look at the role of money in campaigns.

The Maze of Campaign Finance Reforms. As the costs of campaigning skyrocketed with the growth of television, and as the Watergate scandal exposed large, illegal campaign contributions, momentum developed in the early 1970s for campaign financing reform. Several public interest lobbies (see Chapter 11), notably Common Cause and the National Committee for an Effective Congress, led the drive. In 1974, Congress passed the **Federal Election Campaign Act**. It had two main goals: tightening reporting requirements for contributions and limiting overall expenditures. In essence, here is what the act, with subsequent amendments, did:

- *It created the **Federal Election Commission (FEC)**.* A bipartisan body, the six-member FEC administers the campaign finance laws and enforces compliance with their requirements.
- *It provided public financing for presidential primaries and general elections.* Presidential candidates who raise $5,000 on their own in at least 20 states can get individual contributions of up to $250 matched by the federal treasury. For the general election, each party nominee gets a fixed amount of money to cover all campaign expenses.
- *It limited presidential campaign spending.* If presidential candidates accept federal support at any stage, they agree to limit their campaign expenditures to an amount prescribed by federal law.
- *It required disclosure.* Regardless of whether they accept any federal funding, all candidates for federal office must file periodic reports with the FEC, listing who contributed and how the money was spent.
- *It limited contributions.* Scandalized to find out that wealthy individuals such as J. Willard Marriott had contributed a million dollars to the 1972 Nixon campaign, Congress limited individual contributions to presidential and congressional candidates to $1,000.

Although the campaign reforms were generally welcomed by both parties, the constitutionality of the Act was challenged in the 1976 case of *Buckley v. Valeo.* In this case, the Supreme Court struck down, as a violation of free speech, the portion of the Act that had limited the amount individuals could contribute to their own campaigns. This aspect of the Court ruling made it possible for Ross Perot to spend over $50 million of his own fortune on his independent presidential candidacy in 1992 and for oil tycoon Michael Huffington to spend over $25 million in unsuccessful pursuit of a California Senate seat in 1994. All told, congressional candidates threw in $57 million of their personal funds to help out their campaigns in 1996.

Another loophole in the financing limits was opened in 1979 with an amendment to the original act that made it easier for political parties to raise money for voter registration drives and the distribution of campaign material (buttons, pamphlets, yard signs, and so forth) at the grass-roots level. Money raised for such purposes is known as **soft money** and is not subject to any contribution limits. In 1996, an unprecedented amount of money flowed into the coffers of the national parties through this loophole. Republicans raised $141 million in soft money, and the Democrats were only a bit behind with $122 million. These totals were about twice the levels raised during the 1992 election and were over ten times those raised in 1980, when the soft-money donations were first allowed. Critics of soft money point to a number of instances in which individuals who have given over $100,000 have been appointed as ambassadors, and they emphasize that companies such as Philip Morris and Amway have had their policy concerns heard loud and clear by making multimillion-dollar soft-money donations.

Overall, there is little doubt that campaign spending reforms have made campaigns more open and honest. Small donors are encouraged, and the rich are restricted—at least in terms of the money they can give directly to a candidate. All contribution and expenditure records are now open for all to examine, and FEC auditors try to make sure that the regulations are enforced. As Frank Sorauf writes, the detailed FEC reports have "become a wonder of the democratic political world. Nowhere else do scholars and journalists find so much information about the funding of campaigns, and the openness of Americans about the flow of money stuns many other nationals accustomed to silence and secrecy about such traditionally private matters."[21]

The Proliferation of PACs. The campaign reforms also encouraged the spread of **political action committees,** generally known as **PACs**. Before the 1974 reforms, corporations were technically forbidden to donate money to political campaigns, but many wrote big checks anyway. Unions could make indirect contributions, although limits were set on how they could aid candidates and political parties. The

Partly in response to disclosures that individuals such as W. Clement Stone (shown here) had contributed more than $1 million to the Nixon reelection campaign, the 1974 Federal Election Campaign Act placed strict limits on the amount a person can contribute to candidates for national office. The act also provides government funding for presidential candidates and limits their spending.

1974 reforms created a new, more open way for interest groups such as business and labor to contribute to campaigns. Any interest group, large or small, can now get into the act by forming its own PAC to directly channel contributions of up to $5,000 per candidate in both the primary and the general election. *Buckley v. Valeo* extended the right of free speech to PACs, and they can now spend unlimited amounts indirectly—that is, if such activities are not coordinated with the campaign.

PACs have proliferated in recent years. The FEC counted 4,079 PACs in 1996. These PACs contributed $192 million to congressional candidates for the 1996 campaign. Many believe that this has led to a system of open graft.[22] Few developments since the Watergate crisis have generated so much cynicism about government as the explosive growth of PACs over the last 20 years.

A PAC is formed when a business association, or some other interest group, decides to contribute to candidates that it believes will be favorable toward its goals. The group registers as a PAC with the FEC and then puts money into the PAC coffers. The PAC can collect money from stockholders, members, and other interested parties. It then donates the money to candidates, often after careful research on their issue stands and past voting records. One very important ground rule prevails: All expenditures must be meticulously accounted for to the FEC. If PACs are corrupting democracy, at least they are doing so openly.

Candidates need PACs because high-tech campaigning is expensive. Tightly contested races for the House of Representatives can cost over a million dollars; every Senate incumbent running for reelection in 1994 raised at least this much. PACs play a major role in paying for expensive campaigns. Thus there emerges a symbiotic relationship between the PACs and the candidates: Candidates need money, which they insist can be used without compromising their integrity; PACs want access to officeholders, which they insist can be gained without buying votes. Justin Dart of Dart Industries, a close friend of former President Reagan, remarks of his PAC that "talking to politicians is fine, but with a little money, they hear you better."[23]

An abundance of PACs are around to help out the candidates. There are big PACs, such as the Realtors Political Action Committee and the American Medical Association Political Action Committee. There are little ones, too, representing smaller industries or business associations: EggPAC, FishPAC, FurPAC, LardPAC, and—for the beer distributors, SixPAC.[24] Table 9.1 lists the business, labor, and ideological PACs that gave the most money to congressional candidates in 1996 and shows which party each favored.

Critics of the PAC system worry that all this money leads to PAC control over what the winners do once in office. Archibald Cox and Fred Wertheimer of Common Cause write that the role of PACs in campaign finance "is robbing our nation of its democratic ideals and giving us a government of leaders beholden to the monied interests who make their election possible."[25] On some issues, it seems clear that PAC money has made a difference. The Federal Trade Commission, for example, once passed a regulation requiring that car dealers list known mechanical defects on the window stickers of used cars. The National Association of Automobile Dealers quickly became the fourth largest donor in the 1980 congressional elections, contributing just over a million dollars to candidates of both parties. Soon afterward, 216 representatives co-sponsored a House resolution nullifying the FTC regulation. Of

TABLE 9.1

THE BIG-SPENDING PACS

According to an analysis of Federal Election Commission data by the Center for Responsive Politics, here are the largest business, labor, and ideological/single-issue PAC contributors to congressional candidates for the 1995-1996 election cycle.

	AMOUNT CONTRIBUTED	PERCENTAGE GIVEN TO DEMOCRATS
BUSINESS		
Association of Trial Lawyers of America	$1,579,975	87
National Auto Dealers Association	1,563,175	17
American Medical Association	1,503,780	21
United Parcel Service	1,320,031	36
National Association of Home Builders	1,196,549	83
LABOR		
Teamsters Union	2,064,210	96
International Brotherhood of Electrical Workers	1,531,700	98
United Auto Workers	1,486,775	99
Laborers' International Union	1,410,450	89
International Association of Machinists and Aerospace Workers	1,396,375	99
IDEOLOGICAL/SINGLE-ISSUE		
National Rifle Association	981,768	19
National Committee for an Effective Congress	656,380	99
National Committee to Preserve Medicare and Social Security	417,050	72
Human Rights Campaign	399,000	86
Campaign America (Dan Quayle's leadership PAC)	313,333	0

SOURCE: Center for Responsive Politics study archived at http://www.crp.org.

these House members, 186 had been aided by the auto dealers' PAC.[26]

It is questionable, however, whether such examples are the exception or the rule. Most PACs give money to candidates who agree with them in the first place. For instance, the anti-abortion PACs will not waste their money supporting outspokenly pro-choice candidates. Frank Sorauf's careful review of the subject concludes that "there simply are no data in the systematic studies that would support the popular assertions about the 'buying' of the Congress or about any other massive influence of money on the legislative process."[27]

The impact of PAC money on presidents is even more doubtful. Presidential campaigns, of course, are partly subsidized by the public and so are less dependent upon PACs. Moreover, presidents have well-articulated positions on most important issues. A small contribution from any one PAC is not likely to turn a presidential candidate's head.

To summarize, money matters in campaigns. Because it matters during campaigns, it sometimes also matters during legislative votes. Although scare stories about the proliferation of PACs may be exaggerated, campaign finance is an old issue that is not likely to go away as long as campaigns continue to be so expensive.

Are Campaigns Too Expensive? Every 4 years, Americans spend over $2 billion on national, state, and local elections. This seems like a tremendous amount of money. Yet American elections cost, per person, about as much as a dinner at a relatively inexpensive restaurant.

What bothers politicians most about the rising costs of high-tech campaigning is that fund raising has come to take up so much of their time. Former Florida Governor Reuben Askew pulled out of a Senate race he was favored to win for this very reason. "Something is seriously wrong with our system when many candidates for the Senate need to spend 75 percent of their time raising money," Askew said.[28] Many officeholders feel that the need for continuous fund raising distracts them from their jobs as legislators.

Public financing of congressional campaigns would take care of this problem. Some lawmakers support some sort of public financing reform; however, it will be very difficult to get Congress to consent to equal financing for the people who will challenge them for their seats. Incumbents will not readily give up the advantage they have in raising money.

Does Money Buy Victory? Money is, of course, absolutely crucial to electoral victory; important offices are rarely won these days by candidates without a substantial campaign war chest. One of the last of the nonspending breed was Senator William Proxmire of Wisconsin, who recently retired. He was succeeded by wealthy businessman Herbert Kohl, who funded his multimillion-dollar campaign entirely out of his own pocket. As Kohl said, he was so rich that at least no one had to worry about his being bought by special interests.

Perhaps the most basic complaint about money and politics is that there may be a direct link between dollars spent and votes received. Few have done more to dispel this charge than political scientist Gary Jacobson. His research has shown that "the more incumbents spend, the worse they do."[29] This fact is not as odd as it at first sounds. It simply means that incumbents who face a tough opponent must raise more money to meet the challenge. When a challenger is not a serious threat, as they all too often are not, incumbents can afford to campaign cheaply. As you can see in Table 9.2, Democratic House incumbents who won with over 70 percent of the vote in 1994 had little to worry about because their Republican opponents were so poorly funded. In contrast, the Democrats who lost their seats raised great sums of money in their struggle to beat back a set of well-funded opponents.

More important than having "more" money is having "enough" money. Herbert Alexander calls this "the doctrine of sufficiency." As he writes, "Enough money must be spent to get a message across to compete effectively but outspending one's opponent is not always necessary—even an incumbent with a massive ratio of higher spending."[30] One case in point is that of Paul Wellstone, a previously obscure political science professor, who beat an incumbent senator in 1990 despite being outspent by eight to one. Another example is the 1994 California Senate race, in which incumbent Democrat Dianne Feinstein prevailed even though she was outspent two to one by Republican challenger Michael Huffington.

THE MEDIA AND THE CAMPAIGN

Money matters, and so does media attention. Media coverage is determined by two factors: (1) how candidates use their advertising budget and (2) the "free" attention they get as newsmakers. The first, obviously, is relatively easy to control; the second is more difficult but not impossible. Almost every logistical decision in a campaign—where to eat breakfast, whom to include on the rostrum, when to announce a major policy proposal—is calculated according to its intended media impact. Years ago (say, in the election of 1896), the biggest item in a campaign budget might have been renting a railroad train. Today the major item is unquestionably television advertising. About half the total budget for a presidential or senatorial campaign will be used for television advertising.

TABLE 9.2 1994 CAMPAIGN SPENDING BY DEMOCRATIC HOUSE INCUMBENTS AND REPUBLICAN CHALLENGERS[a]

	AVERAGE CAMPAIGN SPENDING BY:	
	DEMOCRATIC INCUMBENT	REPUBLICAN CHALLENGER
Democrat won with over 70% of the vote	$373,524	$23,881
Democrat won with between 60 and 70% of the vote	$455,136	$109,542
Democrat won with less than 60% of the vote	$693,973	$268,203
Democrat lost	$943,588	$612,588

[a]by Democratic Vote Percentage

SOURCE: Authors' analysis of 1994 election returns and Federal Election Commission Report of campaign spending.

The Supreme Court has ruled that to limit how much a person can spend on his or her own campaign would be an infringement on one's freedom of speech. Thus, wealthy individuals such as California's Michael Huffington (shown here campaigning for the senate with his family) are able to dip into their own pockets to finance their campaigns.

No candidate for a major office can do without what political scientist Dan Nimmo calls "the political persuaders."[31] A new profession of political consultants has emerged, and for the right price, they can turn a disorganized campaign into a well-run, high-tech operation. They can do it all—polling or hiring the pollster, molding a candidate's image, advising a candidate on his or her spouse's role, handling campaign logistics, managing payrolls, and so forth. Incumbents as well as challengers turn to professional consultants for such help.

All this concern with public relations worries some observers of American politics. They fear a new era of politics in which the slick slogan and the image salesperson will dominate—an era when Madison Avenue will be more influential than Main Street. Most political scientists, however, are concluding that such fears are overblown. Research has shown that campaign advertising can be a source of information about issues as well as about images. Thomas Patterson and Robert McClure examined the information contained in TV advertising and found that viewers learned more about candidates' stands on the issues from watching their ads than from watching the nightly news. Most news coverage stresses where the candidates went, how big their crowds were, and other campaign details. Only rarely do the networks delve into where the candidates stand on the issues. In contrast, political ads typically address issues.[32] Perhaps there is less conflict between issues and images than there appears to be on the surface. The candidates' positions are also a crucial part of their images. Getting those positions across to voters is as important as persuading them that a candidate is honest, competent, and a leader.

Candidates attempt to manipulate their images through advertising and image building, but they have less control over the other aspect of the media, news coverage. To be sure, most campaigns have press aides who feed "canned" news releases to reporters. Still, the media largely determine for themselves what is happening in a campaign. Campaign coverage seems to be a constant interplay between hard news about what candidates say and do and the human interest angle, which most journalists think sells newspapers or interests television viewers.

Apparently, news organizations believe that policy issues are of less interest to voters than the campaign itself. The result is that news coverage is disproportionately devoted to campaign strategies, speculation about what will happen next, poll results, and other aspects of the campaign game. Patterson tabulated the amount of media attention to the campaign itself and the amount of attention to such substantive issues as the economy in the 1976 presidential race. Examining several newspapers and news magazines as well as television network news, he found that attention to the "game" far exceeded attention to substance.[33] Once a candidate has taken a policy position and it has been reported, it becomes old news. The latest poll showing Smith ahead of Jones is thus more newsworthy in the eyes of the media. Republican media consultant Roger Ailes calls this his "orchestra pit" theory of American politics: "If you have two guys on stage and one guy says, 'I have a solution to the Middle East problem,' and the other guy falls in the orchestra pit, who do you think is going to be on the evening news?"[34]

The media follow a presidential nominee almost everywhere during the campaign. Here, a crowd of photographers focus their lenses on Bob Dole as he heads toward the Senate chamber to give his farewell speech.

THE IMPACT OF CAMPAIGNS

Politicians are great believers in campaigns. Almost all of them figure that a good campaign is the key to victory. Many political scientists, however, question their importance. Reviewing the evidence, Dan Nimmo concluded, "Political campaigns are less crucial in elections than most politicians believe."[35] For years, researchers studying campaigns have stressed that campaigns have three effects on voters: **reinforcement, activation,** and **conversion**. Campaigns can reinforce voters' preferences for candidates; they can activate voters, getting them to contribute money or ring doorbells as opposed to merely voting; and they can convert, changing voters' minds.

Four decades of research on political campaigns lead to a single message: Campaigns mostly reinforce and activate; only rarely do they convert. The evidence on the impact of campaigns points clearly to the conclusion that the best-laid plans of campaign managers change very few votes. Given the millions of dollars spent on political campaigns, it may be surprising to find that they do not have a great effect. Several factors tend to weaken campaigns' impact on voters:

- Most people pay relatively little attention to campaigns in the first place. People have a remarkable capacity for **selective perception**—paying most attention to things they already agree with and interpreting events according to their own predispositions.
- Factors such as party identification—though less important than they used to be—still influence voting behavior regardless of what happens in the campaign.
- Incumbents start with a substantial advantage in terms of name recognition and an established track record.

Such findings do not mean, of course, that campaigns never change voters' minds or that converting a small percentage is unimportant. In tight races, a good campaign can make the difference between winning and losing.

UNDERSTANDING NOMINATIONS AND CAMPAIGNS

Throughout the history of American politics, election campaigns have become longer and longer as the system has become increasingly open to public participation. Reformers in the nineteenth and twentieth centuries held that the solution to democratic problems was more democracy—or as John Lennon sang, "Power to the people." In principle, more democracy always sounds better than less, but it is not such a simple issue in practice.

ARE NOMINATIONS AND CAMPAIGNS TOO DEMOCRATIC?

If American campaigns are judged solely by how open they are, then certainly the American system must be viewed favorably. In other countries, the process of leadership nomination occurs within a relatively small circle of party elites. Thus, politicians must work their way up through an apprenticeship system. In contrast, America has an entrepreneurial system in which the people play a crucial role at every stage from nomination to election. In this way, party outsiders can get elected in a way virtually unknown beyond the United States. By appealing directly to the people, a candidate can emerge from obscurity to win the White House, as Jimmy Carter did. In this sense, the chance to win high office is open to almost everyone.

There is a price to be paid for all this openness, however. The process of selecting American leaders is a convoluted one that has little downtime before it revs up all over again. Some analysts have even called the American electoral process "the permanent campaign."[36] Many wonder whether people would pay more attention to politics if it did not ask so much of them. Given so much democratic opportunity, many citizens are simply overwhelmed by the process and stay on the sidelines. Similarly, the burdens of the modern campaign can discourage good candidates from throwing their hats into the ring. One of the most worrisome burdens that candidates must face is amassing a sufficient campaign war chest. The system may be open, but it requires a lot of fund raising to be able to take one's case to the people.

Today's campaigns clearly promote individualism in American politics. The current system of running for office has been labeled by Wattenberg the "candidate-centered age."[37] It allows for politicians to decide on their own to run, to raise their own campaign funds, to build their own personal organizations, and to make promises about how they specifically will act in office. The American campaign game is one of individual candidates, by individual candidates, and for individual candidates.

DO BIG CAMPAIGNS LEAD TO AN INCREASED SCOPE OF GOVERNMENT?

Today's big campaigns involve much more communication between candidates and voters than America's founders ever could have imagined. In their view, the

The American political system allows citizens a voice at almost every point of the election process, unlike many countries where a political elite controls the nomination process. Jimmy Carter, for example, here with his wife Rosalynn, won the 1976 presidential election by appealing directly to the people rather than coming up through the party ranks.

presidency was to be an office responsible for seeing to the public interest as a whole. They wished to avoid "a contest in which the candidates would have to pose as 'friends' of the people or make specific policy commitments."[38] Thus, the founders would probably be horrified by the modern practice in which candidates make numerous promises during nomination and election campaigns.

States are the key battlegrounds of presidential campaigns, and candidates must tailor their appeals to the particular interests of each major state. When in Iowa, for instance, candidates typically promise to keep agricultural subsidies high; in New York, to help big cities with federal programs; in Texas, to help the oil and gas industry. To secure votes from each region of the country, candidates end up supporting a variety of local interests. Promises mount as the campaign goes on, and these promises usually add up to new government programs and money. The way modern campaigns are conducted is thus one of many reasons why politicians usually find it easier to promise, at least, that government will do more. Furthermore, with their finger constantly to the wind assessing all the different political cross-currents, it is hard for politicians to promise that the scope of government will be limited through specific cuts.

SUMMARY

In this age of high-tech politics, campaigns have become more media-oriented and far more expensive. There are really two campaigns of importance in presidential (and other) contests: the campaign for nomination and the campaign for election.

There are two ways by which delegates are selected to the national party conventions: state caucuses and primaries. The first caucus is traditionally held in Iowa, the first primary in New Hampshire. These two small, atypical American states have disproportionate power in determining who will be nominated and thus become president. This influence stems from the massive media attention devoted to these early contests and the momentum generated by winning them.

Money matters in political campaigns. As the costs of campaigning have increased, it has become all the more essential to amass large campaign war chests. Although federal campaign finance reform in the 1970s lessened the impact of big contributors, it also allowed the proliferation of PACs. Some observers believe that PACs have created a system of legal graft in campaigning; others feel that the evidence for this view is relatively weak.

In general, politicians tend to overestimate the impact of campaigns; political scientists have found that campaigning serves primarily to reinforce citizens' views rather than to convert them. American election campaigns are easily the most open and democratic in the world—some say too open. They are also extraordinarily long, leading politicians to make many promises that contribute to big government.

KEY TERMS

nomination
campaign strategy
national party convention
caucus
presidential primaries
frontloading
Federal Election Campaign Act
Federal Election Commission (FEC)
soft money
political action committees (PACs)

Super Tuesday
national primary
regional primaries
direct mail
reinforcement
activation
conversion
selective perception

FOR FURTHER READING

Bartels, Larry M. *Presidential Primaries and the Dynamics of Public Choice*. Princeton, NJ: Princeton University Press, 1988. The best recent book on voters' choices in the nominating season.

Brown, Clifford W., Jr., Lynda W. Powell, and Clyde Wilcox. *Serious Money: Fundraising and Contributing in Presidential Nomination Campaigns*. New York: Cambridge University Press, 1995. A unique look into who contributes to presidential campaigns and why.

Fenno, Richard F. *The Presidential Odyssey of John Glenn*. Washington, DC: Congressional Quarterly Press, 1990. A marvelous case study of a failed presidential campaign.

King, Anthony. *Running Scared*. New York: Free Press, 1997. King argues that American politicians campaign too much and govern too little.

Mayer, William G., ed. *In Pursuit of the White House: How We Choose Our Presidential Nominees*. Chatham, NJ: Chatham House, 1996. A good set of current readings on the presidential nomination process.

Orren, Gary R., and Nelson W. Polsby, eds. *Media and Momentum*. Chatham, NJ: Chatham House, 1987. The story of the exaggerated impact of New Hampshire on our presidential selection process.

Patterson, Thomas E. *Out of Order*. New York: Knopf, 1993. A good review of the role of the media in elections.

Royer, Charles T., ed. *Campaign for President: The Managers Look at '92*. Hollis, NH: Hollis Publishing Co., 1994. The campaign managers for all the 1992 presidential candidates gather at Harvard to discuss their experiences in the primaries and the general election.

Shafer, Byron E. *Bifurcated Politics: Evolution and Reform in the National Party Convention*. Cambridge, MA: Harvard University Press, 1988. The story of how conventions have been transformed from important decision-making bodies to TV sideshows.

Sorauf, Frank J. *Inside Campaign Finance: Myths and Realities*. New Haven, CT: Yale University Press, 1992. A definitive work on the impact of money on elections—an impact that Sorauf thinks is often exaggerated.

Winebrenner, Hugh. *The Iowa Precinct Caucuses: The Making of a Media Event*. Ames, IA: Iowa State University Press, 1987. A highly critical view of the Iowa caucuses from one of the state's leading political analysts.

INTERNET RESOURCES

www.fec.gov
The Federal Election Commission's reports on campaign spending can be found at this site.

www.camelect.com
Campaigns and Elections magazine posts some of its articles here.

NOTES

1. See "Campaign Calendar: 5 States in a Day," *New York Times,* March 9, 1992, A11.
2. Anthony King, *Running Scared* (New York: Free Press, 1997).
3. R. W. Apple, Jr., "Foley Assesses Presidential Elections and Tells Why He Wouldn't Run," *New York Times,* November 4, 1988, A12.
4. Paul Taylor, "Is This Any Way to Pick a President?" *Washington Post National Weekly Edition,* April 13, 1987, 6.
5. The Rohde theory is explained in his "Risk-Bearing and Progressive Ambition: The Case of the U.S. House of Representatives," *American Journal of Political Science* 23 (February 1979): 1-26. The Aldrich adaptation of the theory to the presidency appears in his *Before the Convention* (Chicago: University of Chicago Press, 1980), chap. 2.
6. Paul R. Abramson, John H. Aldrich, and David W. Rohde, *Change and Continuity in the 1992 Elections* (Washington, DC: Congressional Quarterly Press, 1994), 20.
7. See Hugh Winebrenner, *The Iowa Precinct Caucuses: The Making of a Media Event* (Ames, IA: Iowa State University Press, 1987).
8. Theodore White, *America in Search of Itself: The Making of the President 1956-1980* (New York: Harper & Row, 1982), 285.
9. Harold W. Stanley and Richard G. Niemi, *Vital Statistics on American Politics,* 4th ed. (Washington, DC: Congressional Quarterly Press, 1994), 61. The same research also showed that New Hampshire received just 1 percent of the TV coverage during the general election—a figure roughly proportionate to its population size.

10. Robert Farmer, quoted in Clifford W. Brown, Jr., Lynda W. Powell, and Clyde Wilcox, *Serious Money: Fundraising and Contributing in Presidential Nomination Campaigns* (New York: Cambridge University Press, 1995), 1.

11. Larry M. Bartels, *Presidential Primaries and the Dynamics of Public Choice* (Princeton, NJ: Princeton University Press, 1988), 269.

12. "Dukakis Says Campaign Damage a Surprise," *New York Times,* January 18, 1990, A15.

13. George Bush, *Looking Forward* (New York: Doubleday, 1987), 208.

14. Paul Simon, *Winners and Losers: The 1988 Race for the Presidency—One Candidate's Perspective* (New York: Continuum, 1989), 112.

15. *Ibid.,* 113.

16. Bruce Babbitt, "Bruce Babbitt's View from the Wayside," *Washington Post National Weekly Edition,* February 29, 1988, 24.

17. See Martin P. Wattenberg, "When You Can't Beat Them, Join Them: Shaping the Presidential Nominating Process to the Television Age," *Polity* 21 (Spring 1989): 587-597.

18. Thomas E. Patterson, *The Mass Media Election* (New York: Praeger, 1980), 3.

19. Charles T. Royer, *Campaign for President: The Managers Look at '92* (Hollis, NH: Hollis Publishing Co., 1994), 77.

20. R. Kenneth Godwin, *One Billion Dollars of Influence: The Direct Marketing of Politics* (Chatham, NJ: Chatham House, 1988), 2.

21. Frank J. Sorauf, *Inside Campaign Finance: Myths and Realities* (New Haven, CT: Yale University Press, 1992), 229.

22. See, for example, Brooks Jackson, *Honest Graft: Big Money and the American Political Process* (New York: Knopf, 1988).

23. Quoted in Jeffrey Berry, *The Interest Group Society* (Boston: Little, Brown, 1984), 162.

24. *Ibid.,* 162-163.

25. Archibald Cox and Fred Wertheimer, "The Choice Is Clear: It's People vs. the PACs," in Peter Woll, ed., *Debating American Government,* 2nd ed. (Glenview, IL: Scott, Foresman, 1988), 125.

26. This is discussed in Berry, *The Interest Group Society,* 172.

27. Frank J. Sorauf, *Money in American Elections* (Glenview, IL: Scott, Foresman, 1988), 312.

28. Dexter Filkins, "The Only Issue Is Money," *Washington Post National Weekly Edition,* June 13, 1988, 28.

29. Gary C. Jacobson, "The Effects of Campaign Spending in Congressional Elections," *American Political Science Review* 72 (June 1978): 469. For an updated analysis of this argument, see Gary C. Jacobson, "The Effects of Campaign Spending in House Elections: New Evidence for Old Arguments," *American Journal of Political Science* 34 (May 1990): 334-362.

30. Herbert E. Alexander, *Financing Politics: Money, Elections, and Political Reform,* 4th ed. (Washington, DC: Congressional Quarterly Press, 1992), 96.

31. Dan Nimmo, *The Political Persuaders: The Techniques of Modern Campaigning* (Englewood Cliffs, NJ: Prentice-Hall, 1970).

32. Thomas E. Patterson and Robert D. McClure, *The Unseeing Eye* (New York: Putman, 1976).

33. Patterson, *Mass Media Election,* 22-25. For a more recent study that shows similar results, see S. Robert Lichter and Richard E. Noyes, *Good Intentions Make Bad News,* 2nd ed. (Lanham, MD: Rowman & Littlefield, 1996).

34. David R. Runkel, ed., *Campaign for President: The Managers Look at '88* (Dover, MA: Auburn, 1989), 136.

35. Nimmo, *The Political Persuaders,* 5.

36. Sidney Blumenthal, *The Permanent Campaign* (New York: Simon & Schuster, 1982).

37. See Martin P. Wattenberg, *The Rise of Candidate-Centered Politics: Presidential Elections of the 1980s* (Cambridge, MA: Harvard University Press, 1991).

38. James W. Ceaser, *Presidential Selection: Theory and Development* (Princeton, NJ: Princeton University Press, 1979), 83.

10 Elections and Voting Behavior

How American Elections Work

A Tale of Three Elections

Whether to Vote: A Citizen's First Choice

How Americans Vote: Explaining Citizens' Decisions

The Last Battle: The Electoral College

Understanding Elections and Voting Behavior

One of the most memorable moments in the history of presidential debates occurred during the second debate of 1992 when a young woman asked the candidates the following question: "How has the national debt personally affected each of your lives, and if it hasn't how can you honestly find a cure for the economic problems of the common people if you have no experience in what is ailing them?" Ross Perot answered first, saying the nation's red ink is what led him to run for president and endure disruptions of his family life and business. George Bush then started to answer the question by saying that the debt affects everyone, at which point the young woman quickly interjected that her question was how the debt has affected *you personally*. Bush appeared to be thrown off guard by this question and in a short exchange with her, said, "I'm not sure I get it." He then went on to argue that just because you haven't been hit by a truck doesn't mean that you don't know how it feels. When it was Bill Clinton's turn to answer, he walked right toward the questioner and said the debt had affected him in much the same way it had her. He pointed out that when a local company went out of business, he, as the governor of a small state, would know many of those who had lost their jobs. Clinton then went on to argue that Republican economic policies were responsible for the large deficit and ailing economy.

In the postdebate analysis, the media focused on this portion of the debate more than any other, commenting particularly on how Bush seemed out of touch because he was at first unable to make sense of the question. After Bush's defeat, some commentators pointed to this as the moment when Bush lost any chance of reelection.

If only interpreting elections were really as simple as the above story suggests. One of the most astute observers of American politics, journalist Walter Lippman, once remarked,

> We call an election an expression of the popular will. But is it? We go into a polling booth and mark a cross on a piece of paper for one of two, or perhaps three or four names. Have we expressed our thoughts on the public policy of the United States? Presumably we have a number of thoughts on this and that with many buts and ifs and ors. Surely the cross on a piece of paper does not express them.[1]

This chapter will discuss the numerous aspects of American elections that make it difficult for elections to be a faithful mechanism for expressing the public's desires concerning what government should do. The fact that only about half of the eligible electorate participates is one such factor. And those who do go to the polls often have to choose from candidates who obscure the issues. Even on an issue as fundamental as the scope of government, it has not always been crystal clear what the candidates would do if they were elected.

Elections serve two important functions in American society. They *socialize* and *institutionalize* political activity, making it possible for most political participation to be channeled through the electoral process rather than bubbling up through demonstrations, riots, or revolutions. Elections provide *regular access to political power,* so that leaders can be replaced without being overthrown. As we will see shortly, the presidential election of 1800 was the first transition of power between parties accomplished by voters' ballots in the history of the world. One set of leaders left office, and another set assumed control peacefully—all because of an election. This orderly transition was possible because the election had **legitimacy** in the eyes of the American people; that is, the election was almost universally accepted as a fair and free method of selecting political leaders. Furthermore, by choosing who is to lead the country, the people—if they make their choices carefully—can also guide the policy direction of the government.

This chapter will give you some perspective on how elections function in the American system, as well as how voters generally behave—both in terms of their decisions on whether or not to vote and in terms of how those who do vote make their choices. The focus here is primarily on presidential elections; Chapter 12 will examine congressional elections in detail.

HOW AMERICAN ELECTIONS WORK

Unlike most other democracies, the United States has three kinds of elections: those that select party nominees, those that select officeholders from among the nominees, and those in which voters engage in making or ratifying legislation. Typically, elections in other countries perform only one of these three functions: selecting officeholders.

Elections held for the purpose of picking party nominees are called **primaries.** Although Americans are most familiar with presidential primaries (as discussed in Chapter 9), most states also use primaries to select party nominees for congressional and state offices. These state primaries are called **direct primaries,** because party nominees are chosen directly by the people. In contrast, presidential primaries are indirect; they choose only delegates to go to a national convention.

Also virtually unique to the United States is a system of state-level elections that permits voters to enact legislation directly. Twenty-three states allow voters to put proposed legislation on the ballot via an **initiative petition**. All that is usually required is that signatures be gathered in numbers equaling 10 percent of the voters in the previous election. In this way, citizens can force a decision on an issue on which state legislatures have failed to act. The most famous example is California's Proposition 13, which in 1978 put a limit on the rise in property taxes in California. Eighteen years and 196 propositions later, California voters passed Proposition 209, a measure intended to end affirmative action programs in the state. Probably the most widely voted on type of initiative in recent years has been proposals to limit the terms of legislators. A number of states have adopted initiatives that limit the number of terms its state legislators can serve in office.

Another example of a provision for direct legislation is the **referendum**, whereby voters are given the chance to approve or disapprove some legislative act or constitutional amendment. Many states require school bonds and other bonds to be approved by referendum. For example, California voters in 1994 voted down a bond act to provide $1 billion for intercity rail transit programs.

Primaries, initiative petitions, and referenda have all been reforms of the American election system. Today's American election system permits all adult citizens to play a role in the electoral drama, but some futurists believe that participation could be broadened if technology were used more effectively. (See "In the Twenty-first Century: Registration and Voting By E-mail?") Indeed, the history of American elections has been profoundly influenced by technological advancements.

One recent referendum that has drawn national attention is California's vote on Proposition 209, which has ended affirmative action programs in the state. Here, opponents make their point of view clear.

A TALE OF THREE ELECTIONS

Times change, and so do elections. Modern campaigns are slick, high-tech affairs. Imagine John Adams and Thomas Jefferson standing under bright TV lights, adjusting their wigs, and waiting for the "Presidential Debate of 1800" to begin. Or think of Abraham Lincoln securing the nomination and then lining up an ad agency and a professional pollster. Early twentieth-century candidates such as Woodrow Wilson and Franklin Roosevelt did not have network exit polls to report their victories before the polls even closed in the West; they had to wait for the returns to come in slowly. A glance at three American elections—1800, 1896, and 1996—will give you a good idea of how elections have changed over nearly two centuries.

1800: THE FIRST ELECTORAL TRANSITION OF POWER

By current standards, the 1800 election was not much of an election at all. There were no primaries, no nominating conventions, no candidate speeches, and no entourage of reporters. Both incumbent President John Adams and challenger Thomas Jefferson were nominated by their parties' elected representatives in Congress—Federalists for Adams and Democratic-Republicans for Jefferson. Once nominated, the candidates sat back and let their state and local organizations promote their cause. Communication and travel were too slow for candidates to get their message across themselves. Besides, campaigning was considered beneath the dignity of contenders for the presidential office.

At that time, however, newspapers were little concerned with dignity, or for that matter with honesty. Most were rabidly partisan and did all they could to run down the opposition's candidate. Jefferson was regularly denounced as a Bible-burning atheist, the father of mulatto children, and a mad scientist. Adams, on the other hand, was said to be a monarchist "whose grand object was to destroy every man who differed from his opinions."[2]

The focus of the campaign was not on voters but rather on the state legislatures, which were responsible for choosing members of the electoral college. When the dust settled, the Jeffersonians had won a slim victory in terms of electoral votes; however, they had also

REGISTRATION AND VOTING BY E-MAIL?

In the 21st Century

Although modern technology is widely available, Americans have not harnessed much of it to improve democracy. Though most precincts now use computer punch cards to record votes, the high-tech age has not yet made much of an impact on the voting process. There is good reason to expect that this state of affairs will change in the twenty-first century.

First, the development of the personal computer and the World Wide Web is likely to be used to facilitate the process of voter registration. Already, one can go to the web site of the Federal Election Commission (http://www.fec.gov) and download the "National Mail Voter Registration Form." Twenty-two states currently accept copies of this application printed from the computer image, signed by the applicant, and mailed in the old-fashioned way. It does not seem too fanciful to imagine, as e-mail becomes ever more popular and "snail mail" fades into a method reserved for packages, the entire voter registration process will be conducted electronically in most cases. In an age where personal computers in the home will be as common as television sets are today, this would clearly make registering to vote more user-friendly.

If people can register by computer, the next step naturally is voting by e-mail. A growing trend in the Pacific Coast states has been voting by mail. In early 1996, Oregon even conducted a special election for a U.S. Senate seat entirely through the mail. Again, as e-mail takes the place of regular mail, why not have people cast their votes through cyberspace? It would be less costly for the state, as well as easier for the average citizen, assuming that computer literacy reaches near universal proportions sometime in the future. The major concerns, of course, would be ensuring that no one votes more than once and preserving the confidentiality of the vote. These security concerns are currently being worked on by some of the world's top computer programmers, as commercial enterprises look toward using the Internet to conduct business. If the technology can be perfected to allow trillions of dollars of business to be conducted via the Internet, then it seems reasonable that any obstacles to its use in the voting process can be overcome as well.

Whether such possible developments will improve democracy in America is debatable. Although making voting more user-friendly should encourage turnout, people will still have to be interested enough in the elections of the future to send in their e-mail ballots. In fact, if old-style polling places are relegated to the history books and everyone votes electronically in the convenience of their own homes, the sense of community on election day may be lost. This loss could lead to even lower turnout. Whether the benefits outweigh the potential costs will be something for the citizens of the twenty-first century to eventually decide.

committed a troubling error. In the original constitutional system, each elector cast two ballots; the top vote-getter was named president, and the runner-up became vice president.[3] In 1796, Jefferson had become Adams' vice president by virtue of finishing second. Not wanting Adams to be his vice president, Jefferson made sure that all his electors also voted for his vice-presidential choice, Aaron Burr of New York. The problem was that when each and every one of them did so, Jefferson and Burr ended up tied for first. This meant that the Federalist-controlled House of Representatives would have to decide between the two Democratic-Republican candidates. Burr saw the chance to steal the presidency from Jefferson by cutting a deal with the Federalists, but his efforts failed. After 35 indecisive ballots in the House, the Federalists finally threw their support to Jefferson. On March 4, 1801, the transition from Adams to Jefferson marked the first peaceful transfer of power between parties via the electoral process in history.

1896: A BITTER FIGHT OVER ECONOMIC INTERESTS

Nearly a century later, the election of 1896 was largely fought over economics. By then, national nominating conventions had become well established, and Republicans, meeting in St. Louis for their convention, had a clear front-runner—former Congressman William McKinley. The Republicans' major issues were support for the gold standard and high tariffs. The gold standard linked money to this

scarce precious metal so that debtors never got a break from inflation. Tariffs protected capitalists and their workers from foreign competition. After piling up a commanding majority on the first ballot at St. Louis, McKinley sat back to see what the upcoming Democratic convention would do.

The Democrats met in Chicago's sticky July heat. They had an issue—unlimited coinage of silver—but no clear front-runner. Their incumbent president, Grover Cleveland, was blamed for the 1893 depression, and a resolution praising the Cleveland administration was hooted down. The high point of the Chicago convention was a speech by young William Jennings Bryan of Nebraska, whose "Cross of Gold" speech proclaimed the virtues of the silver rather than the gold standard. "You shall not crucify mankind on a cross of gold," he concluded, and went on to win the nomination on the fifth ballot.

The flamboyant Bryan broke with tradition and took to the stump in person. He gave 600 speeches as his campaign train traveled through 26 states, logging 18,000 miles. Debtors and silver miners were especially attracted to Bryan's pitch for cheap silver money. In contrast, the serene McKinley was advised to sit home in Ohio and run a front-porch campaign. He did, and he managed to label the Democrats as the party of depression ("In God We Trust, with Bryan We Bust").

Bryan won the oratory, but McKinley won the election. Eastern manufacturers contributed a small fortune to the Republicans. A few manufacturers even told their workers not to report back to work if Bryan won. Only white Southerners, Westerners in the silver-producing states, and rural debtors lined up behind the Democrats. The Republicans won overwhelmingly in the industrial Northeast and Midwest and became firmly entrenched as the nation's majority party for the next several decades. As Walter Dean Burnham writes, Bryan's effort to create a coalition of the dispossessed created, instead, the most enduringly sectional political alignment in American history—an alignment in which the agrarian South and West supported the Democrats but were typically outnumbered by Republican voters in the industrially advanced Northeast and Midwest.[4]

William Jennings Bryan was the Democratic Party's standard bearer at the turn of the century. Eastern industrialists, fearing Bryan's powerful speeches and populist politics, used their financial clout to help William McKinley defeat "The Boy Orator of the Platte" (thus named after a river in his native Nebraska) in the 1896 and 1900 presidential elections.

McKinley triumphed by a margin of 271 to 176 in the electoral college. Nearly 80 percent of the eligible electorate voted in one of the highest turnouts ever.

THE 1996 ELECTION: BUILDING A BRIDGE TO THE TWENTY-FIRST CENTURY

The last presidential election of the twentieth century failed either to excite the voters or to resolve any key issue. Indeed, one of the biggest stories to come out of the long campaign was the lack of citizen engagement. Ratings for the political conventions and televised debates were the lowest ever recorded, and turnout fell below 50 percent despite the fact that the Motor Voter Act made registering to vote much easier.

One of the most often cited reasons for the low level of voter involvement was that the campaign was too negative, though it was certainly less so than the bitter campaigns of 1800 or 1896. Unlike these nineteenth-century campaigns, however, in 1996 it was the candidates themselves and not their supporters who were hurling charges and epithets back and forth. As late as 1948, both Harry Truman and Thomas Dewey went through the entire presidential campaign without once mentioning the other's name.[5] Although Bob Dole often compared his uphill struggle to Harry Truman's in 1948, his strategy differed in that it relied on strong attacks on his opponent. Indeed, over the last 3 weeks of the campaign, his principal theme was that Bill Clinton was ethically unfit to serve as president, given all the scandals within his administration. As Dole said at one point, "A President should be a source of inspi-

President Clinton, his wife Hillary, Vice President Al Gore, and his wife Tipper greet supporters during the 1996 election night celebration in Little Rock, Arkansas.

ration. And this President is a source of cynicism. He has led an Administration without a compass and without a core. We deserve an ethical White House."

In addition to being a referendum on the incumbent, presidential elections are also a referendum on the state of the nation. Thus, Bob Dole was faced with the task of convincing the electorate that the country was on the wrong track. The 73-year-old former senator put his case as follows during his acceptance speech at the Republican Convention: "Age has its advantages. Let me be the bridge to an America that only the unknowing call myth. Let me be the bridge to a time of tranquillity, faith, and confidence in action. To those who say it was never so, that America has not been better, I say, you're wrong, and I know, because I was there."

In his speech accepting the Democratic nomination, President Clinton responded directly by stating, "We do not need to build a bridge to the past—we need to build a bridge to the future. . . . Let us resolve to build that bridge to the 21st century, to meet our challenges and protect our values." During his speeches, Clinton stressed that this bridge needed to be built while protecting Medicare, Medicaid, education, and the environment. He continually argued that Republican budget proposals would seriously weaken the federal government's efforts in these areas. Thus, Clinton became the advocate of a status quo, moderate approach in 1996. With the economic news looking more and more favorable, his stay-the-course message resonated well.

The most dramatic proposal for change during the campaign was Dole's call for a 15 percent across-the-board tax cut. Dole argued that the American people could better spend this money than the government could. "It's your money" was one of his favorite lines. Shouldn't the government, rather than the people, have to tighten its belt? he asked. In response, the Clinton campaign argued that such "a risky tax scheme" would "blow a hole in the deficit" and cause sharp cutbacks in popular government programs. In sum, Dole proposed a clear reduction in the scope of government, whereas Clinton defended the existing scope of government activities.

While Clinton and Dole debated the crucial theme of the scope of government, Ross Perot played the typical role of third-party candidates by raising issues neglected by the major parties. As the candidate of the newly formed Reform Party, Perot emphasized aspects of the political process that he argued needed revamping. He proposed campaign financing reform, lobbying reform, immigration reform, and reform in a host of other areas. Of these, he clearly struck gold with campaign financing when a rash of stories about irregularities in the fund raising of both major parties made the news in the closing days of the campaign. Not only was this issue suddenly something that voters cared about, but it also was an issue that Perot had unique credibility on. Just as the major parties had taken up Perot's priority issue of the budget deficit soon after 1992, so it seemed that campaign financing would be something the parties would be compelled to deal with after the 1996 election.

With three major candidates in the race, the popular vote in 1996 was unusually split. Ross Perot's percentage of the vote fell from 19 percent in 1992 to 9 percent in 1996, but he nevertheless became the first third-party candidate ever to win over 5 percent of the vote twice. Bob Dole's 41 percent enabled him to carry only 19 states. It was Bill Clinton's 49 percent of the vote that carried the day, translating into victories in states yielding 379 out of 538 electoral college votes (see Figure 10.1). However, this victory was tarnished by Clinton's failure to win a majority of the vote, as well as by the fact that he became the first Democrat ever elected president while the Republicans won control of Congress.

In 1996, as in all election years, voters faced two key choices: whether to vote and, if they chose to do so, how to vote. The following sections will investigate how voters make these choices.

WHETHER TO VOTE: A CITIZEN'S FIRST CHOICE

Nearly two centuries of American electoral history include greatly expanded **suffrage**—the right to vote. In the election of 1800, only property-owning white males over the age of 21 were typically allowed to

FIGURE 10.1 THE ELECTORAL COLLEGE RESULTS FOR 1996

The following map shows the number of delegates each state has in the electoral college and which states were carried by Bill Clinton (green) and Bob Dole (rose) in 1996.

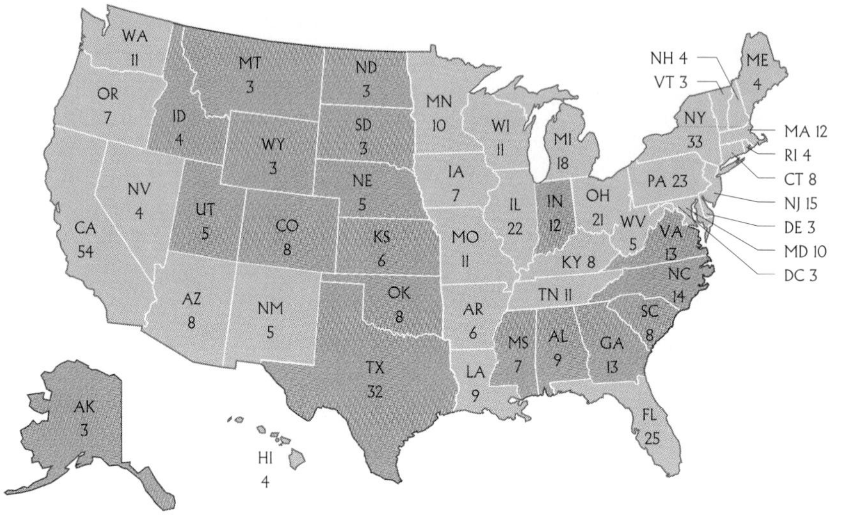

vote. Now this right is guaranteed to all individuals over the age of 18—male or female, white or nonwhite, rich or poor. (For these developments, particularly as they affect women and minorities, see Chapter 5.)

Ironically, as the right to vote has been extended, proportionately fewer of those eligible have chosen to exercise that right. In the past hundred years, the 80 percent turnout in the 1896 election was the high point of electoral participation. In 1996, only 49 percent of the adult population voted in the presidential election (see Figure 10.2).

One of the reasons for low American voter turnout has been the burdensome process of voter registration. In some states, voter registration tables can be set up anywhere by volunteers who have taken a state course in registration procedures.

WHO VOTES AND WHO STAYS HOME?

When just over half the population votes, the necessity of studying nonvoters takes on added importance. The classic study of nonvoting in American elections was done by Raymond Wolfinger and Steven Rosenstone.[6] Several conclusions emerged from their research:

- *Voting increases with education.* People with higher-than-average educational levels have a higher rate of voting than people with lower educational achievement. Among all factors affecting turnout, this one is the most important.
- *Young people have the lowest turnout rate.* In 1994, the Census Bureau found that only 20 percent of people under the age of 25 voted. As people age, their likelihood of voting increases until the infirmities of old age make it difficult for them to get to the polls.
- *Whites vote with greater frequency than members of minority groups.* African Americans and Hispanics are underrepresented among voters relative to their share of the population, but this

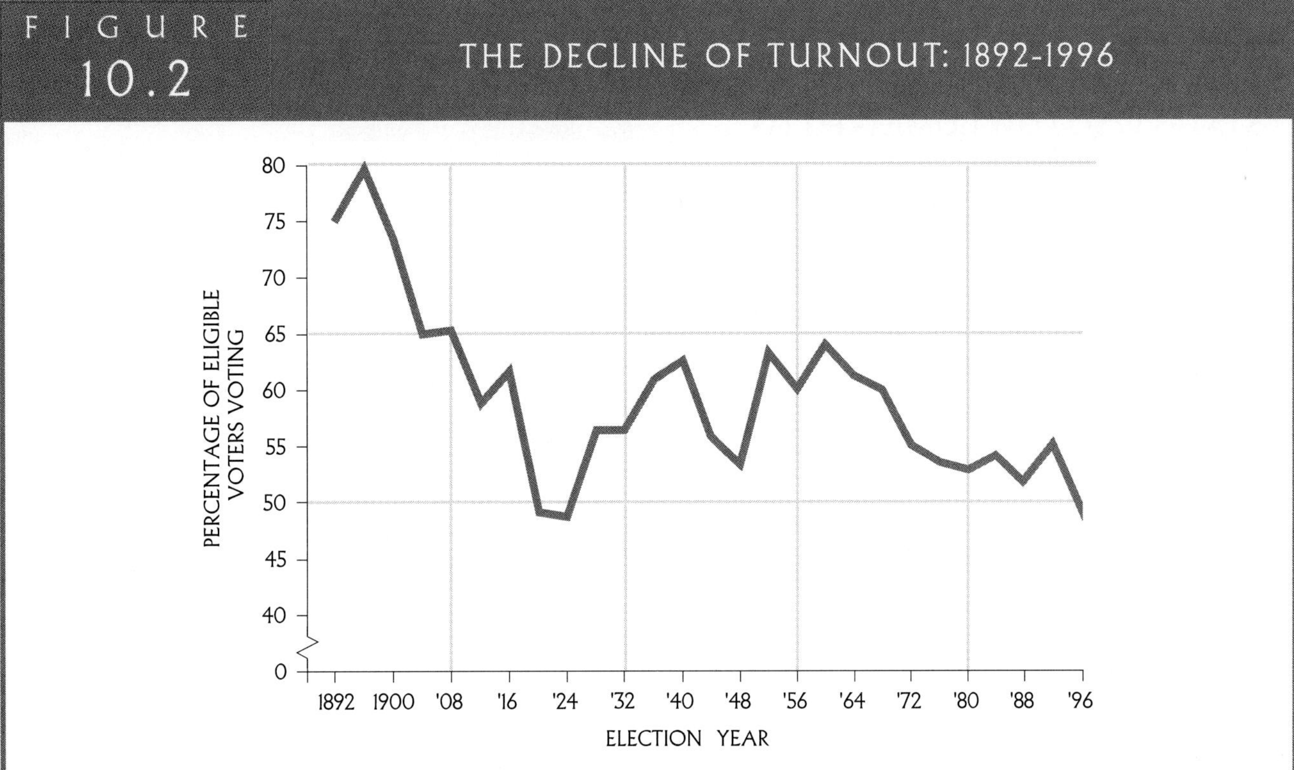

SOURCES: For data up to 1968, ***Historical Statistics of the United States*** (Washington DC: Government Printing Office, 1975), part 2, 1071. For 1972-1988, *Statistical Abstract of the United States,* 1990 (Washington, DC: Government Printing Office, 1990), 264. 1992 and 1996 data are from news reports.

underrepresentation can be attributed to their generally low level of education and income. African Americans and other minority groups with high levels of income and education have a higher turnout rate than whites with comparable socioeconomic status.

- *Southerners are less likely to vote than Northerners.* Although the 1965 Voting Rights Act forced the South to make it easier for its citizens (particularly African Americans) to vote, the historical legacy of low participation remains.
- *Government employees are heavy participators in the electoral process.* Having something at stake (their jobs and the future of the programs they work on) and being in a position to know more about government spur government workers to high levels of participation.
- *Voting is only weakly related to gender.* In an earlier period, many women were discouraged from voting, but today women actually participate in elections at a slightly higher rate than men.

These differences in turnout rates are cumulative. Possessing several of these traits (say, being well educated, middle-aged, and a government worker) adds significantly to one's likelihood of voting. Conversely, being young, poorly educated, and southern is likely to add up to a very low probability of voting.

As Wolfinger and Rosenstone point out, the best predictor of whether a person will vote is whether that person is registered. America's unique registration system is partly to blame for Americans' being significantly less likely to go to the polls than citizens of other democratic nations (see "America in Perspective: Why Turnout in the United States Is So Low Compared to Other Countries").

THE REGISTRATION SYSTEM

A century ago politicians used to say, "Vote early and often." Cases such as West Virginia's 159,000 votes being cast by 147,000 eligible voters in 1888 were not that unusual. Largely to prevent corruption associated with stuffing ballot boxes, states adopted **voter registration** around the turn of the century. And requiring citizens to register in advance of election day made elections much less susceptible to unethical influences.

Registration procedures currently differ greatly from state to state. States in the upper Great Plains and the

WHY TURNOUT IN THE UNITED STATES IS SO LOW COMPARED TO OTHER COUNTRIES

America in Perspective

Despite living in a culture that encourages participation, Americans have a woefully low turnout rate compared to other democracies. Here are some figures on voting rates in the United States and other industrial nations:

Australia, 1996	93%
South Africa, 1994	87%
New Zealand, 1996	86%
Czech Republic, 1992	84%
Italy, 1996	83%
Austria, 1995	83%
Greece, 1993	82%
Finland, 1994	82%
Israel, 1996	80%
Germany, 1994	79%
Spain, 1996	78%
Taiwan, 1996	76%
Albania, 1996	75%
Norway, 1993	75%
South Korea, 1992	72%
Great Britain, 1997	71%
France, 1997	71%
Russia, 1996	69%
Ireland, 1992	69%
Estonia, 1992	68%
Poland, 1995	67%
Canada, 1997	67%
Bulgaria, 1997	62%
Japan, 1996	60%
United States, 1996	**49%**
Switzerland, 1995	42%

There are several reasons given for Americans' abysmally low turnout rate. Probably the reason most often cited is the unique American requirement of voter registration. The governments of other democracies take the responsibility of seeing to it that all of their eligible citizens are on the voting lists. In America, the responsibility for registration lies solely with the individual.

A second difference between the United States and other countries is that the American government asks citizens to vote far more often. Whereas the typical European voter may be called upon to cast two or three ballots in a 4-year period, many Americans are faced with a dozen or more separate elections in the space of 4 years. Furthermore, Americans are expected to vote for a much wider range of political offices. With 1 elected official for every 442 citizens and elections held somewhere virtually every week, it is no wonder that it is so difficult to get Americans to the polls. It is probably no coincidence that the one European country that has a comparable turnout rate—Switzerland—has also overwhelmed its citizens with voting opportunities, typically asking people to vote three times every year.

Finally, the stimulus to vote is not so high in the United States because the choice offered Americans is not so great as in other countries. This is because the United States stands virtually alone in the democratic world in lacking a major left-wing socialist party. When European voters go to the polls, they are deciding on whether their country will be run by parties with socialist goals or by conservative (and in some cases religious) parties. The consequences of their vote for redistribution of income and the scope of government are far greater than the ordinary American voter can conceive of.

SOURCE: For turnout figures around the world, see the various election reports in recent issues of *Electoral Studies*.

Northwest make it easiest to register: Voters can sign up at many everyday locations (such as supermarkets), and no elaborate procedures are used. In sparsely populated North Dakota there is no registration at all, and in Minnesota, Wisconsin, Wyoming, Idaho, and Maine, voters can register on election day. It is probably no coincidence that these states all ranked near the top in voting turnout in 1996 (see Table 10.1). Prior to 1996, some states—particularly in the South—had burdensome registration procedures. As a result of the 1993 **Motor Voter Act,** these no longer exist. The act required states to permit people to register at the same time they apply for driver's licenses. Whereas less than 70 percent of all eligible voters are currently registered, nearly 90 percent of this group have driver's licenses. The Motor Voter Act made voter registration easier by allowing eligible voters simply to check a box on their driver's license application or renewal form. Nevertheless, its impact on turnout

TABLE 10.1 TURNOUT IN 1996: STATE BY STATE

STATE	VOTERS (IN %)	STATE	VOTERS (IN %)
Maine	65	Oklahoma	50
Minnesota	64	Delaware	50
Montana	63	Pennsylvania	49
South Dakota	61	Illinois	49
Wyoming	60	Indiana	49
Vermont	59	Alabama	48
Idaho	58	Florida	48
New Hampshire	58	Arkansas	48
Iowa	58	Kentucky	47
Oregon	58	Tennessee	47
Wisconsin	57	Virginia	47
Louisiana	57	Maryland	47
Kansas	57	New York	47
Alaska	57	North Carolina	46
North Dakota	56	Mississippi	46
Nebraska	56	New Mexico	46
Connecticut	56	West Virginia	45
Massachusetts	55	Arizona	45
Washington	55	Georgia	43
Missouri	54	California	43
Ohio	54	District of Columbia	43
Michigan	54	Texas	42
Colorado	53	Hawaii	41
Rhode Island	52	South Carolina	41
New Jersey	51	Nevada	39
Utah	50		

SOURCE: Calculated by the authors on the basis of election results and U.S. Census estimates of the voting-age population in each state.

was limited in the first election in which it was in effect. The percentage of the population that was registered increased, but turnout was still significantly lower than in 1992.

Ruy Teixeira notes that turnout has steadily declined in the United States since 1960, even though registration procedures have actually been made easier. For example, many states have enacted postal registration and have permitted deputy registrars to go out and register people rather than have the people come to them. Thus, in recent decades, those who have been registered have shown less propensity to actually vote. Teixeira traces the drop in turnout to a decline in Americans' social and political connectedness. A younger, single, and less church-going electorate has resulted in voters who are less socially tied to their political communities. Furthermore, political withdrawal has resulted from declines in partisanship, in political interest, and in the belief that government is responsive, according to Teixeira's research.[7]

A POLICY APPROACH TO DECIDING WHETHER TO VOTE

Realistically, when over 95 million people vote in a presidential election, as they did in 1996, the chance that one vote will affect the outcome is very, very slight. Once in a while, of course, an election is decided by a handful of votes. In 1948, Lyndon Johnson won a race for the U.S. Senate by a total of 87 votes—very suspicious votes—earning him the nickname "Landslide Lyndon."[8] In 1960, John

Kennedy carried the state of Hawaii by a mere 115 votes. It is more likely, however, that you will be struck by lightning during your lifetime than that you will participate in an election decided by a single vote.

Not only does your vote probably not make much difference to the outcome, but voting is somewhat costly. You have to spend some of your valuable time becoming informed, making up your mind, and getting to the polls. If you carefully calculate your time and energy, you might rationally decide that the costs of voting outweigh the benefits.

Economist Anthony Downs, in his model of democracy, tries to explain why a rational person would ever bother to vote. He argues that rational people vote if they believe that the policies of one party will bring more benefits than the policies of the other party.[9] Thus, people who see **policy differences** between the parties are more likely to join the ranks of voters. If you are an environmentalist and you expect the Democrats to pass more environmental legislation than the Republicans, then you have an additional incentive to go to the polls. On the other hand, if you are truly indifferent—that is, if you see no difference whatsoever between the two parties—you may rationally decide to abstain. You may also abstain if you believe that the Democrats' proenvironmental platform is balanced by Republican policies, such as those to control inflation. Even if you are indifferent about the outcome you may decide to vote anyway, simply to support democratic government. In this case, you are impelled to vote by a sense of **civic duty.**

Why, then, is there so much inequality in voting, with the rich and the well educated participating more than the poor and the less educated? First, in nearly every election and on nearly every issue, members of the upper socioeconomic class are more likely than members of the lower class to recognize and understand policy differences. In particular, higher education trains a person to see the impact of policy decisions and the nuances of party platforms. Second, upper-class people score higher on **political efficacy**—the belief that ordinary people can influence the government. In other words, people with low socioeconomic status turn out less because they are more likely to think their votes do not really matter. Third, the poor and less educated find the bureaucratic hurdles of the registration process especially difficult. It might not seem much of a chore for you to register to vote after having gone through course registration at your school, but for those not fortunate enough to go to college, it does not seem so easy. In 1994, the Census Bureau found that 73 percent of college-educated persons were registered to vote as compared to 54 percent among those who had not gone to college.

"You mean, like, wow, we can actually get rid of, you know, incumbents with this whatchamacallit?"

Until some of the factors that inhibit voting—such as registration and low efficacy levels—change dramatically, it is likely that American elections will continue to be decided by only about half of the eligible voters. The following sections will discuss how voters make their decisions.

HOW AMERICANS VOTE: EXPLAINING CITIZENS' DECISIONS

Here is a common explanation of how Americans vote—an explanation favored by journalists and politicians: Americans vote because they agree more with the policy views of Candidate A than with those of Candidate B. Of course, the candidates have invested a lot of time and have gone to a lot of trouble to get those views implanted in the public mind. Because citizens vote for the candidate whose policy promises they favor, many journalists and politicians say that the election winner has a mandate from the people to carry out the promised policies. This idea is sometimes called the **mandate theory of elections.**

Politicians, of course, are attracted to the mandate theory. It lets them justify what they want to do by claiming public support for their policies. As President

Clinton said during the final presidential debate in 1992, "That's why I am trying to be so specific in this campaign—to have a mandate, if elected, so the Congress will know what the American people have voted for."

Political scientists, however, think little of the mandate theory of elections.[10] Whereas victorious politicians are eager to proclaim "the people have spoken," political scientists know that "the people" rarely vote a certain way for the same reasons. Instead, political scientists focus on three major elements of voters' decisions: (1) voters' party identification, (2) voters' evaluation of the candidates, and (3) the match between voters' policy positions and those of the candidates and parties—a factor termed *policy voting.*

PARTY IDENTIFICATION

Party identifications are crucial for many voters because they provide a regular perspective through which voters can view the political world. "Presumably," say Niemi and Weisberg, "people choose to identify with a party with which they generally agree.... As a result they need not concern themselves with every issue that comes along, but can generally rely on their party identification to guide them."[11] Parties tend to rely on groups that lean heavily in their favor to form their basic coalition. Even before an election campaign begins, Republicans usually assume they will not receive much support from African Americans, Jews, and Hispanic Americans. Democrats have an uphill struggle attracting groups that are staunchly Republican in their leanings, such as conservative evangelical Christians and upper-income voters. Even so, as you can see in "Since Kennedy: Changing Patterns in Voting Behavior," there have been substantial changes in how various groups have voted for president over the last three decades.

With the emergence of television and candidate-centered politics, the hold of the party on the voter eroded substantially during the 1960s and 1970s and then stabilized at a new and lower level during the 1980s.[12] In the 1950s, scholars identified party affiliation as the best single predictor of a voter's decision. It was said that many Southern Democrats would vote for a yellow dog if their party nominated one. "My party—right or wrong" was the motto that typified strong party identifiers. Today, voting along party lines is less common, particularly in elections for the House of Representatives, where incumbency is now paramount (see Chapter 12). Many voters now feel that they no longer need the parties to guide their choices, given that modern technology makes it possible for them to evaluate and make their own decisions about the candidates. Thus, American voters have become increasingly individualistic. Voting choices have become largely a matter of individual choice, and many voters are up for grabs in each election (the so-called "floating voters"). In such an individualistic political environment, the characteristics of each candidate for office play an important role.

CANDIDATE EVALUATIONS: HOW AMERICANS SEE THE CANDIDATES

All candidates try to present a favorable personal image. Using laboratory experiments, political psychologists Shawn Rosenberg and Patrick McCafferty showed that it is possible to manipulate a candidate's appearance in a way that affects voters' choices. Holding a candidate's issue stands and party identification constant, they found that when good pictures are substituted for bad ones, a candidate's vote-getting ability is significantly increased. Although a laboratory setting may not be representative of the real world, Rosenberg and McCafferty conclude that "with appropriate pretesting and adequate control over a candidate's public appearance, a campaign consultant should be able to significantly manipulate the image projected to the voting public."[13]

To do so, a consultant would need to know what sort of candidate images voters are most attuned to. Research by Miller, Wattenberg, and Malanchuk shows that the three most important dimensions of candidate image are integrity, reliability, and competence.[14] In 1976, Jimmy Carter told Americans, "I will never lie to you." Even going down to defeat in 1980, Carter was seen as a man of great integrity. Therefore, it obviously takes more than honesty to win. A candidate must also be seen as dependable and decisive—traits that Miller, Wattenberg, and Malanchuk label as "reliability." When George Bush broke his "no new taxes" pledge prior to the 1992 campaign, his image of reliability clearly suffered. The personal traits most often mentioned by voters, though, involve competence. In 1988, Michael Dukakis proudly proclaimed that the major election issue was not ideology but competence. Ironically, the majority of voters were more impressed with Bush's wide experience in office than with Dukakis' lawyer-like precision.

Such evaluations of candidate personality are sometimes seen as superficial and irrational judgments. Miller and his colleagues disagree with this interpretation, arguing that "candidate assessments actually concentrate on instrumental concerns about the manner in

SINCE KENNEDY

Changing Patterns in Voting Behavior

Although group voting patterns are one of the most stable aspects of American elections from year to year, over the course of several decades a variety of changes can usually be found. Some of the demographic characteristics that most distinguished Kennedy voters from Nixon voters in 1960 are of far less relevance to voting behavior now. In particular, as you can see from the accompanying table, the divide between Protestants and Catholics has dwindled dramatically, and union membership is slightly less associated with voting Democratic than it once was. On the other hand, race and income were more closely related to voting behavior in 1996 than in 1960. Clinton clearly drew more support from African Americans and lower-income voters than did Kennedy. Interestingly, voting patterns by gender and age have reversed in the years from Kennedy's election to Clinton's. Despite all the talk of Kennedy as a handsome candidate, women were actually less likely than men to support him, because the Republicans were viewed as the party of peace; by the 1990s, the Democrats' stands for increased social services and less defense spending had given them the advantage in winning the women's vote. Another advantage that the Democrats now enjoy is with elderly voters. Whereas the senior citizens of 1960 had been socialized during an era when the Republicans were the dominant party, today's elderly came of age during the New Deal. As these voters die, the Democrats will need to do well with new voters in order to compensate for the loss of one of their most reliable groups of supporters.

	KENNEDY	NIXON	CLINTON	DOLE	PEROT
Protestant	36	63	49	43	7
Catholic	83	17	55	37	7
Jewish	89	11	92	4	4
White	48	52	48	42	8
African-American	71	29	96	1	2
Male	52	48	46	44	9
Female	47	53	59	33	6
18-34	52	48	54	33	10
35-64	50	49	51	40	7
65+	39	60	56	38	5
Lowest income third	45	54	67	23	8
Middle income third	55	45	53	38	7
Upper income third	48	52	44	47	7
Union	63	37	66	22	9
Non-union	44	56	50	42	7

SOURCE: 1960 and 1996 National Election Surveys.

which a candidate would conduct governmental affairs.[15] If a candidate is too incompetent to carry out policy promises, or too dishonest for those promises to be trusted, it makes perfect sense for a voter to pay more attention to personality than to policies. Interestingly, Miller and his colleagues find that college-educated voters are actually the most likely to view the candidates in terms of their personal attributes. They argue that better-educated voters are able to make important issue-oriented inferences from these attributes (for example, that a candidate who is unreliable may not be the right person to be the commander-in-chief of the armed forces).

POLICY VOTING

Policy voting occurs when people base their choices in an election on their own issue preferences. True policy voting can take place only when several conditions are met. First, voters must have a clear view of their own policy positions. Second, voters must know where the candidates stand on policy issues. Third, they must actually cast a vote for the candidate whose policy positions coincide with their own.

Given these conditions, policy voting is not always easy—even for the educated voter. One recurrent problem is that candidates often decide that the best way to handle a controversial issue is to cloud their positions in rhetoric. For example, in 1968 both major party candidates—Nixon and Humphrey—were deliberately ambiguous about what they would do to end the Vietnam War. Their ambiguity made it extremely difficult for voters to cast their ballots according to how they felt about the war.

The media may not be of much help, either, because they typically focus more on the "horse race" aspects of the campaign than on the policy stands of the candidates. Voters thus often have to work fairly hard just to be well enough informed to engage in policy voting. In the view of some analysts, the public would be better informed about policy stands if the candidates were given free air time for a series of nights to discuss their opposing views. (See "You Are the Policymaker: Should the Networks Have to Provide Free Air Time to Presidential Candidates?"). In the early days of voting research, the evidence seemed clear: Voters rarely voted on policies, preferring to rely on party identification or candidate evaluations to make up their minds. In the 1950s, the authors of *The American Voter* stressed that only a small percentage of the American electorate relied on issues to decide their votes.[16] *The Changing American Voter* challenged this claim, however, arguing that voters in more recent years had become more sophisticated about issues and better able to use policy positions to assess candidates.[17]

Although it is questionable whether today's voters are more sophisticated about issues (see Chapter 6), policy voting has become somewhat easier than in the past; today's candidates are regularly forced to take clear stands to appeal to their own party's primary voters. As late as 1968, it was still possible to win a nomination by dealing with the party bosses; now candidates must appeal first to the issue-oriented activists in the primaries. No longer can a candidate get a party's nomination without taking stands on the major issues of the day, as both Humphrey and Nixon did in 1968 when they equivocated on how to handle the Vietnam War. Thus, what has changed is not the voters but the electoral process that once discouraged policy voting by greatly blurring differences between the candidates.

Party voting, candidate evaluation, and policy voting all play a role in elections. The impact of each may vary from one election to another, but they are the main factors that affect voter decisions. In presidential elections, once voters make their decisions, it is not just a simple matter of counting the ballots to see who has won the most support nationwide. Rather, the complicated process of determining electoral college votes begins.

THE LAST BATTLE: THE ELECTORAL COLLEGE

It is the **electoral college**, not the popular vote, that actually determines the president of the United States. The electoral college is a unique American

SHOULD THE NETWORKS HAVE TO PROVIDE FREE AIR TIME TO PRESIDENTIAL CANDIDATES?

You Are the Policymaker

In 1996, a group of prominent political and media figures proposed the idea of a series of free prime-time television appearances for presidential candidates to address the issues. The Coalition for Free Air Time called upon the networks to turn over 2 to 5 minutes a night to the candidates in the month before the presidential election. Furthermore, the Coalition suggested that these segments should be "road blocked"—shown simultaneously on all networks, PBS, and interested cable stations so that people watching prime-time entertainment would be sure to see the candidates. The coalition hoped that this format would promote a nightly dialogue on the issues, with candidates making news with their replies to each other's previous segments. The only requirement would be that the candidates look straight into the camera and talk. There would be no manipulation of images or unseen narrators—just candidates making their case directly to the biggest potential audience every night.

Most of the networks did eventually grant the candidates some free time, but the approach was a scattershot one. The segments varied from 1 to 2½ minutes, and each network chose a different time to broadcast them. A survey done by the Annenberg School of Communication immediately after the election found that only 22 percent of registered voters even knew that the free-time effort existed. Virtually everyone involved was disappointed with the results.

Many observers believe that the experience of 1996 demonstrated the necessity of adopting a common format and time for all networks in 2000, and some even advocate using the government's regulatory powers to force the networks to adopt this approach. Others point to the poor ratings of the televised debates as an example of the ineffectiveness of roadblocking political dialogue when the public just isn't much interested. You be the policymaker. Is this an experiment that the government should mandate in future presidential elections?

institution, created by the Constitution. The American Bar Association once called it "archaic, undemocratic, complex, ambiguous, indirect, and dangerous."[18] Many (though certainly not all) political scientists oppose its continued use, as do most voters.

Because the founders wanted the president to be selected by the nation's elite, not directly by the people, they created the electoral college, a body of electors who are charged solely with the task of voting for the president and vice president. Since 1828, though, political practice has been that electors vote for the candidate who won their state's popular vote. Occasionally, though, electors exercise the right to vote their conscience, as did one West Virginia elector in 1988 who voted for Bentsen for president and Dukakis for vice president. Here is how the electoral college system works today:

- Each state, according to the Constitution, has as many electoral votes as it has U.S. senators and representatives.[19] The state parties select slates of electors, positions they use as a reward for faithful service to the party.
- Except for Maine and Nebraska, each state has a winner-take-all system.[20] Electors vote as a bloc for the winner, whether the winner got 35 percent or 95 percent of the popular vote.
- Electors meet in their states in December, following the November election, and then mail their votes to the vice president (who is also president of the Senate). The vote is counted when the new congressional session opens in January and is reported by the vice president. Thus, Al Gore had the duty of announcing Bill Clinton's reelection in early 1997.
- If no candidate receives an electoral college majority, then the election is thrown into the House of Representatives, which must choose from among the top three electoral vote winners. A significant aspect of the balloting in the House is that each state delegation has one vote, thus giving the single representative from Wyoming an equal say with the 52 representatives from California.

The electoral college is important to the presidential election for two reasons. First, it introduces a bias into the campaign and electoral process. Provided that the election is not thrown into the House, it gives extra clout to big states, especially those where the race is thought to be close. The winner-take-all rule means that winning big states such California, New York, Texas, and Ohio is more important than piling up big leads in small states (see Figure 10.1). Furthermore, big states are likely to have big cities (New York has New York City, Texas has Houston, California has Los Angeles, Illinois has Chicago, and so on). Thus, the big-state bias produces an urban bias in the electoral college.

The electoral college attracts special attention when the prospect looms either that the election will be thrown into the House or that the electoral college result may not reflect the popular vote. Only twice has the election been decided by the House—in 1800, as discussed earlier, and in 1824. Not since 1888, when Cleveland lost to Harrison, has the winner of the popular vote lost in the electoral college. In almost every close election, however, a few changes here and there have the potential to produce an incompatible result. In 1976, a shift of just 6,000 votes in Ohio and 4,000 votes in Hawaii would have given Ford the election even though Carter would still have led by a substantial margin in the popular vote. Until either a popular-vote winner is denied election or a decision is again thrown into the House by the presence of a third-party candidate such as Ross Perot, reform of the electoral college is unlikely. On this issue, most politicians abide by the old adage, "If it ain't broke, don't fix it." Whether the American electoral system as a whole is compatible with democratic theory is a broader question to which this chapter now turns.

UNDERSTANDING ELECTIONS AND VOTING BEHAVIOR

According to democratic theory, elections accomplish two tasks. First, and most obviously, they *select the policymakers*. Second, elections are supposed to help *shape public policy*. Whether elections in fact make the government pay attention to what the people think is at the center of debate concerning how well democracy works in America. (See "The People Speak: Do Elections Make Government Listen?") In the hypothetical world of rational-choice theory and the Downs model (see Chapter 8), elections do in fact guide public policy; however, over a generation of social science research on this question has produced mixed findings. It is more accurate to describe the connection between elections and public policy as a two-way street: elections affect public policy to some degree, and public policy decisions somewhat affect electoral outcomes.

DEMOCRACY AND ELECTIONS

There will probably never be a definitive answer to the question of how much elections affect public policy, for it is a somewhat subjective matter. The broad contours of the answer, however, seem reasonably clear: *The greater the policy differences between the candi-*

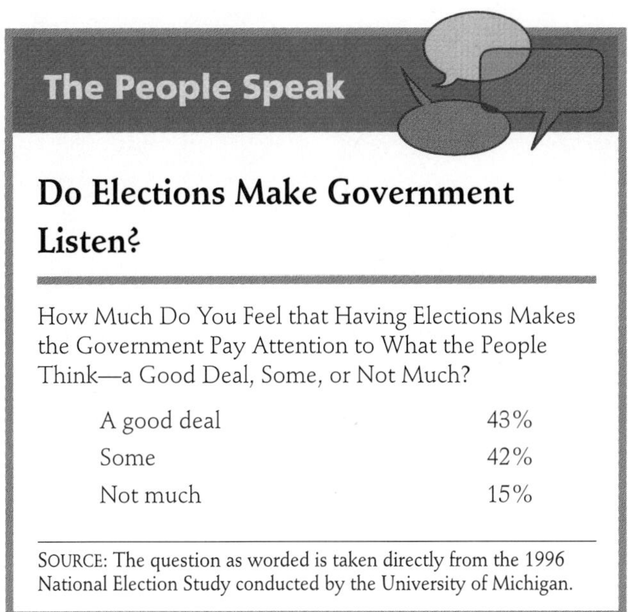

The People Speak

Do Elections Make Government Listen?

How Much Do You Feel that Having Elections Makes the Government Pay Attention to What the People Think—a Good Deal, Some, or Not Much?

A good deal	43%
Some	42%
Not much	15%

SOURCE: The question as worded is taken directly from the 1996 National Election Study conducted by the University of Michigan.

"And here with us this evening, to skirt the issues, are Senator Tom Kirkland and Congressman Alan Sullivan."

dates, the more likely voters will be able to steer government policies by their choices.

Of course, the candidates do not always help to clarify the issues. One result is that the policy stands are often shaped by what Benjamin Page once called "the art of ambiguity," in which "presidential candidates are skilled at appearing to say much while actually saying little."[21] Learning how to sidestep controversial questions and hedge answers is indeed part of becoming a professional politician, as you can observe at most every presidential press conference. As long as politicians can take refuge in ambiguity (and the skimpy coverage of issues in the media does little to make them clarify their policy stands), the possibility of democratic control of policy is lessened. As with policy voting, if citizens cannot see the policy differences between candidates, then they can hardly express their own beliefs by voting for one instead of the other.

When individual candidates do offer a plain choice to the voters (what 1964 Republican nominee Barry Goldwater once called "a choice, not an echo"), voters are better able to guide the government's policy direction. Ronald Reagan followed in Goldwater's footsteps in the 1980s by making clear his intention to cut the growth of domestic spending, reduce taxes, and build up American military capability. Once elected, he proceeded to do much of what he said he would, demonstrating that elections can sometimes dramatically affect public policy.

If elections affect policies, then policies can also affect elections. Most policies have consequences for the well-being of certain groups or the society as a whole. Those who feel better off as a result of certain policies are likely to support candidates who pledge to continue those policies, whereas those who feel worse off are inclined to support opposition candidates. This is known as the theory of **retrospective voting,**[22] in which voters essentially ask the simple question "What have you done for me lately?" Incumbents who provide desired results are rewarded; those who fail to do so are not reelected.

Nothing makes incumbent politicians more nervous than the state of the economy. When the economy takes a downturn, the call to "throw the rascals out" usually sweeps the nation. In presidential elections, people unhappy with the state of the economy tend to blame the incumbent. Republican Herbert Hoover was in office when the stock market crash of 1929 sparked the Great Depression. Hoover became so unpopular that the shantytowns occupied by unemployed people were called "Hoovervilles" and the apples they sold were called "Hoover apples." Hoover and his fellow Republicans were crushed by Franklin Roosevelt in the 1932 elections. Sixty years later, Democrats were still hitting the Republicans with the memory of Hoover, calling Bush a modern-day Hoover who had spent all his energy on foreign policy while the American economy was sinking.

Clearly, elections affect policy, but public policy—especially the perception of economic policy impacts—can affect elections. Once in office, politicians use fiscal policy to keep the American economy running on an even keel. (Chapter 17 considers how they try to do this.) If economic troubles mount, voters point their fingers at incumbent policymakers, and those fingers

Economic conditions can have a profound effect on election outcomes. In 1932, voters expressed their despair over the Great Depression by electing Franklin Roosevelt in a landslide over Herbert Hoover. Here, an unemployed man sells "Hoover apples" in front of the capitol.

are more likely to pull the lever for the challengers on election day. As V. O. Key once wrote, "The only really effective weapon of popular control in a democratic regime is the capacity of the electorate to throw a party from power."[23]

ELECTIONS AND THE SCOPE OF GOVERNMENT

Although the threat of electoral punishment constrains policymakers, it also helps to increase generalized support for government and its powers. Because voters know that the government can be replaced at the next election, they are much more likely to feel that it will be responsive to their needs. Furthermore, when people have the power to dole out electoral reward and punishment, they are more likely to see government as their servant instead of their master. As Benjamin Ginsberg writes, "Democratic elections help to persuade citizens that expansion of the state's powers represents an increase in the state's capacity to serve them."[24]

The final chapter of any presidential campaign is the swearing in of the winner at noon on the following January 20th. Here, Chief Justice Rehnquist administers the oath to Bill Clinton as Hillary Clinton holds the Bible.

Therefore, rather than wishing to be protected from the state, citizens in a democracy often seek to benefit from it. It is no coincidence that "individuals who believe they can influence the government's actions are also more likely to believe, in turn, that the government should have more power."[25] Voters like to feel that they are sending a message to the government to accomplish something. It should thus be no surprise that as democracy has spread, government has come to do more and more, and its scope has grown.

SUMMARY

This chapter has examined the final act in the electoral drama. Once the parties have made their nominations and the campaign has concluded, voters take center stage. Elections have changed dramatically since 1800, when Adams ran against Jefferson. By 1896, it was acceptable for candidates to campaign in person, and William Jennings Bryan did so with a vengeance. At that time suffrage—the right to vote—was still limited mostly to white males. Now the democratization of elections has made suffrage available to all American citizens over the age of 18.

Voters make two basic decisions at election time. The first is whether to vote. Americans' right to vote is well established, but in order to do so, citizens must go through the registration process. America's unique registration system is one major reason why turnout in American elections is much lower than in most other democracies. The 1996 election was another in a long string of low-turnout elections. Second, those who choose to vote must decide for whom to cast their ballots. Over a generation of research on voting behavior has helped political scientists understand the dominant role played by three factors in voters' choices: party identification, candidate evaluations, and policy positions.

Elections are the centerpiece of democracy. Few questions are more important in understanding American government than this: Do elections matter? Under the right conditions, elections can influence public policy, and policy outcomes can influence elections. Elections also legitimize the power of the state, thereby making it easier to expand the scope of the government.

KEY TERMS

legitimacy
primaries
direct primaries
initiative petition
referendum
suffrage
voter registration
Motor Voter Act
policy differences
civic duty
political efficacy
mandate theory of elections
policy voting
electoral college
retrospective voting

FOR FURTHER READING

Abramson, Paul R., John H. Aldrich, and David W. Rhode. *Change and Continuity in the 1992 Elections.* Washington, DC: Congressional Quarterly Press, 1994. A good overview of voting behavior in the 1992 elections, which also focuses on recent historical trends.

Campbell, Angus, *et al. The American Voter.* New York: John Wiley, 1960. This classic study of the American electorate in the 1950s has shaped scholarly approaches to the subject ever since.

Ginsberg, Benjamin. *Consequences of Consent.* Reading, MA: Addison-Wesley, 1982. Emphasizes that elections are a means both for the people to control the government and for the government to control the people.

Kelley, Stanley G., Jr. *Interpreting Elections.* Princeton, NJ: Princeton University Press, 1983. Presents a theory of "the simple act of voting."

McCormick, Richard P. *The Presidential Game.* New York: Oxford University Press, 1982. An interesting historical look at the origins of presidential politics.

Nie, Norman H., Sidney Verba, and John R. Petrocik. *The Changing American Voter.* Cambridge, MA: Harvard University Press, 1976. Challenges some of the assumptions of Campbell *et al.*'s *The American Voter.*

Niemi, Richard G., and Herbert F. Weisberg, eds. *Controversies in Voting Behavior,* 3rd ed. Washington, DC: Congressional Quarterly Press, 1993. An excellent set of readings on some of the most hotly debated facets of voting.

Polsby, Nelson W., and Aaron Wildavsky. *Presidential Elections,* 9th ed. Chatham, NJ: Chatham House, 1996. The classic text on the subject.

Pomer, Gerald M., *et al. The Election of 1996: Reports and Interpretations.* Chatham, NJ: Chatham House, 1997. A good collection of readings on a variety of aspects of the 1996 campaign.

Teixeira, Ruy A. *The Disappearing American Voter.* Washington, DC: Brookings Institution, 1992. A good review of the reasons for declining voter turnout, as well as what can be done about it.

Wolfinger, Raymond E., and Steven J. Rosenstone. *Who Votes?* New Haven, CT: Yale University Press, 1980. A classic quantitative study of who turns out and why.

INTERNET RESOURCES

www.umich.edu/~nes
The National Election Studies are a standard source of survey data about voting behavior. One can find information about these studies, as well as some of the results from them, at this site.

www.census.gov/population/www/socdemo/voting.html
The Census Bureau's studies of registration and turnout can be found at this address.

NOTES

1. Quoted in Stanley G. Kelley, Jr., *Interpreting Elections* (Princeton, NJ: Princeton University Press, 1983), 3-4.
2. Morton Grodzins, "Political Parties and the Crisis of Succession in the United States: The Case of 1800." In Joseph LaPalombara and Myron Weiner, eds., *Political Parties and Political Development* (Princeton, NJ: Princeton University Press, 1966), 319.
3. In 1804, the Twelfth Amendment to the Constitution changed the procedure to the one we know today, in which each elector votes separately for president and vice president.

4. Walter Dean Burnham, *The Current Crisis in American Politics* (New York: Oxford University Press, 1982), 48.
5. David McCullough, *Truman* (New York: Simon & Schuster, 1992), 670.
6. Raymond E. Wolfinger and Steven J. Rosenstone, *Who Votes?* (New Haven, CT: Yale University Press, 1980).
7. Ruy Teixeira, *The Disappearing American Voter* (Washington, DC: Brookings Institution, 1992), , chap. 2.
8. For a gripping account of Johnson's manipulations to win this election, see Robert A. Caro, *The Years of Lyndon Johnson: Means of Ascent* (New York: Knopf, 1990).
9. Anthony Downs, *An Economic Theory of Democracy* (New York: Harper & Row, 1957), chap. 14.
10. See George C. Edwards III, *At the Margins* (New Haven, CT: Yale University Press, 1989), chap. 8.
11. Richard G. Niemi and Herbert F. Weisberg, eds., *Controversies in Voting Behavior,* 2nd ed. (Washington, DC: Congressional Quarterly Press, 1984), 164-165.
12. See Martin P. Wattenberg, *The Decline of American Political Parties,* 1952-1988 (Cambridge, MA: Harvard University Press, 1990).
13. Shawn W. Rosenberg with Patrick McCafferty, "Image and Voter Preference," *Public Opinion Quarterly* 51 (Spring 1987): 44.
14. Arthur H. Miller, Martin P. Wattenberg, and Oksana Malanchuk, "Schematic Assessments of Presidential Candidates," *American Political Science Review* 80 (1986): 521-540.
15. *Ibid.,* 536.
16. Angus Campbell *et al., The American Voter* (New York: John Wiley, 1960) chap. 6.
17. Norman H. Nie, Sidney Verba, and John R. Petrocik, *The Changing American Voter* (Cambridge, MA: Harvard University Press, 1976).
18. American Bar Association, *Electing the President* (Chicago: ABA, 1967), 3.
19. The Twenty-third Amendment (1961) permits the District of Columbia to have three electors, even though it has no representatives in Congress.
20. In both Maine and Nebraska, an elector is allocated for every congressional district won, and whoever wins the state as a whole wins the two electors allotted to the state for its senators.
21. Benjamin Page, *Choices and Echoes in American Presidential Elections* (Chicago: University of Chicago Press, 1978), 153.
22. See Morris P. Fiorina, *Retrospective Voting in American National Elections* (New Haven, CT: Yale University Press, 1981).
23. V. O. Key, *The Responsible Electorate* (New York: Random House, 1966), 76.
24. Benjamin Ginsberg, *Consequences of Consent* (Reading, MA: Addison-Wesley, 1982), 194.
25. *Ibid.,* 198.

Interest Groups

11

The Role and Reputation of Interest Groups

Theories of Interest Group Politics

What Makes an Interest Group Successful?

The Interest Group Explosion

How Groups Try to Shape Policy

Types of Interest Groups

Understanding Interest Groups

One of the most successful lobbies in Washington during the 1980s was that of the savings and loan industry. The members of this industry wanted more freedom from federal regulators to run their business and make investments as they saw fit. In the deregulatory climate of the Reagan years, they were quite successful in this goal. The result was that while some S & Ls profited, many others undertook risky investments that lost money. The government had to take over many failed savings and loans and use taxpayer dollars to pay back depositors.

Probably the most famous case of S & L failure is that of Lincoln Savings and Loan, headed by Charles Keating. When federal regulators threatened to take over Lincoln, Keating turned to five U.S. senators to intervene on his behalf. Not surprisingly, the five politicians he called upon for help (John McCain, John Glenn, Alan Cranston, Donald Riegle, and Dennis DeConcini) had all been recipients of very large political contributions from Keating. The five senators met twice as a group for over 2 hours with the head of the Federal Home Loan Bank Board, pressuring him to drop his plan to shut down the financially ailing business. When five senators get together, bureaucrats usually listen. Lincoln was allowed to stay in business for 2 more years, accumulating more and more debt, until it was finally closed with a staggering $2.5 billion deficit.

When the story of the senators' involvement broke, all five contended that whatever they did on Keating's behalf was no different from inquiries that members of Congress routinely make on behalf of constituents. Senator McCain, for example, compared his actions to helping a little old lady who did not get her Social Security check. Other senators involved noted that they were concerned by the possibility that thousands of their constituents could lose their jobs if Lincoln were closed.

Many critics took a more cynical view of the senators' actions, however, calling the case a prime example of how special interests' campaign contributions taint congressional action. They argued that Keating's situation was a regulatory matter in which the goal should have been the integrity of the savings and loan system, not the protection of constituents. They viewed the fact that Keating had made such large contributions to the senators as clear evidence that influence had been bought and sold. It is doubtful that the senators would have gone to such lengths for Keating—perhaps even given him the time of day—without the contributions.

The worst and oldest stereotype of a lobbyist is of someone who bribes a lawmaker to get a favorable policy decision. In contrast, Charles Keating's leverage with the five senators was obtained by open and legal means. Indeed, as this chapter will show, the problems of honest lobbying now appear to outweigh the traditional problems of dishonest lobbying.

By making the system so openly democratic, the means have been created for an incredible array of interests to be heard loud and clear in Washington. Some critics believe that the basic problem is that there are too many interest groups making demands on the government; others feel that the real problem is that the moneyed interests get a disproportionate share of access and influence. Those who are concerned that the system is too democratic often argue that the result is the frustration of any proposals for changing the existing scope of government. For those most concerned with the domination of the well-off interest groups, the scope of government that results is inevitably seen as helping the rich get richer. Nevertheless, there are scholars who believe that the interest group system is working pretty much as the Founders intended. James Madison argued in *The Federalist No. 10* that the sphere of influence must be extended to ensure democracy. As this chapter will show, we are further along toward this goal than ever before.

Our nation's capital has become a hub of interest group activity. On any given day, it is possible to observe pressure groups in action in many forums. In the morning, you could attend congressional hearings in which you are sure to see interest groups testifying for and against proposed legislation. At the Supreme Court, you might stop in to watch a public interest lawyer arguing for strict enforcement of environmental regulations. Take a break for lunch at a nice Washington restaurant, and you may see a lobbyist entertaining a member of Congress.

You could spend the afternoon in any department of the executive branch (such as commerce, labor, or the interior), where you might catch bureaucrats working out rules and regulations with friendly—or sometimes unfriendly—representatives of the interests they are charged with overseeing. You could stroll past the impressive headquarters of the National Rifle Association, the AFL-CIO, or the American Association of Retired Persons to get a sense of the size of some of the major lobbying organizations. To see some lobbying done on college students' behalf, you might drop by One Dupont Circle, where all the higher education groups have their offices. These groups lobby for student loans and scholarships, as well as for aid to educational institutions. At dinner time, if you are able to finagle an invitation to a Georgetown cocktail party, you may see lobbyists trying to get the ear of government officials—both elected and unelected.

All of this lobbying activity poses an interesting paradox: Although turnout in elections has declined since 1960, participation in interest groups has mushroomed. As Kay Schlozman and John Tierney write, "Recent decades have witnessed an expansion of astonishing proportions in the involvement of private organizations in Washington politics."[1] This chapter will explore the factors behind the interest group explosion, how these groups enter the policymaking process, and what they get out of it.

THE ROLE AND REPUTATION OF INTEREST GROUPS

All Americans have some interests they want represented. Organizing to promote these interests is an essential part of democracy. The right to organize groups is protected by the Constitution, which guarantees people the right "peaceably to assemble, and to petition the Government for a redress of grievances." This important First Amendment right has been carefully defended by the Supreme Court. The freedom to organize is as fundamental to democratic government as freedom of speech and freedom of the press.

DEFINING INTEREST GROUPS

The term *interest group* seems simple enough to define. Interest refers to a policy goal; a group is a combination of people. An **interest group,** therefore, is an organization of people with similar policy goals who enter the political process to try to achieve those aims. Whatever their goals—outlawing abortion or ensuring the right to one, regulating tax loopholes or creating new ones—interest groups pursue them in many arenas. Every branch of government is fair game; every level of government, local to federal, is a possible target. A policy battle lost in Congress may be turned around when it comes to bureaucratic implementation or to the judicial process.

This multiplicity of policy arenas helps distinguish interest groups from political parties. Parties fight their battles through the electoral process; they run candidates for public office. Interest groups may support candidates for office, but American interest groups do not run their own slate of candidates, as in some other countries (see "America in Perspective: Interest Groups as Parties in Other Democracies"). In other words, no serious candidate is ever listed on the ballot as a candidate of the National Rifle Association or Common Cause. It may be well known that a candidate is actively supported by a particular group, but that candidate faces the voters as a Democrat or a Republican.

Another key difference between parties and interest groups is that *interest groups are often policy specialists, whereas parties are policy generalists.* Most interest groups have a handful of key policies to push: A farm group cares little about the status of urban transit; an environmental group has its hands full bringing polluters into court without worrying about the minimum wage. Unlike political parties, these groups do not face the constraint imposed by trying to appeal to everyone.

All candidates for public office seek to obtain the votes of various interest groups. Here, President Clinton greets automobile workers to show his support of unions.

WHY INTEREST GROUPS GET BAD PRESS

Despite their importance to democratic government, interest groups traditionally have received bad press in America. The authors of the *Federalist Papers* thought interest groups were no better than political parties, which they also disliked. Madison's derogatory term *faction* was general enough to include both parties and interest groups.

Today, Americans' image of interest groups is no more favorable. As one lobbyist writes "My mother has never introduced me to her friends as 'My son, the lobbyist. . . . I can't say I blame her. Being a lobbyist has long been synonymous in the minds of many Americans with being a glorified pimp."[2] On a slow news day, editorial cartoonists can always depict lobbyists skulking around in the congressional hallways, their pockets stuffed with money, just waiting to funnel it to a legislator's wallet. Comedians reinforce the stereotype with lines such as Jay Leno's suggestion that the Home Shopping Network should merge with C-SPAN for those who want the convenience of buying a politician in the privacy of their own home.

Defenders of the interest group system counter that the relationship between public officials and lobbyists is probably more free of out-and-out bribery than ever before in American history. The principal method of

INTEREST GROUPS AS PARTIES IN OTHER DEMOCRACIES

In many countries with multiparty systems, interest groups form their own political parties to push for their demands. With proportional representation systems (see Chapter 8), all it takes is between 1 and 5 percent of the vote, depending on the country, for a narrowly based party to win seats in the national legislature. Although special interest groups usually cannot win very many seats, their impact can be large if their votes are crucial in obtaining a majority in the Parliament.

In many of the Scandinavian countries, for example, farmers' parties have long been in existence. Typically, the farmers' party has received between 10 and 20 percent of the vote in nations such as Sweden and Finland. For a conservative, nonsocialist government to be formed, their support is often critical. Therefore, any conservative government in these countries will be quite responsive to agrarian interests. If you are troubled by the fact that American agricultural policy is heavily influenced by congressional representatives from farm states, imagine a situation where key officeholders owe their election exclusively to this single economic interest.

Many new interest groups in Europe have formed parties not on the basis of shared economic interests, such as labor or agriculture, but rather on the basis of shared values. In particular, Green parties have sprung up throughout Western Europe to represent the concerns of environmentalists. Imagine having two dozen members of the American Congress insist on discussing the environmental impact of every decision. These members might not often win, but they would certainly draw more attention to the issue of environmental protection. This is the situation in countries such as Germany where the Greens have won enough votes to enter the national legislature.

controlling dishonest lobbying has been through disclosure laws, which have been tightened substantially over the past two decades. Lobbyists are required to identify themselves, whom they represent, and their legislative interests. PACs must keep complete records of where they get their money and how they spend it. Members of Congress are required to file regular, detailed financial statements, which makes it difficult to hide ill-gotten income.

For every scandal that makes the headlines, hundreds of honest transactions between Congress and interest groups take place. There is little doubt that honest lobbying outpaces dishonest lobbying by a wide margin. However, many political scientists now believe that open and legal lobbying (such as the Lincoln Savings case) poses greater problems for democracy than illegal lobbying activities.

"YOU'LL LIKE THEM... THEIR SPECIAL INTEREST IS GIVING AWAY MORE MONEY THAN OTHER SPECIAL INTEREST GROUPS!"

THEORIES OF INTEREST GROUP POLITICS

Understanding the debate over whether honest lobbying—and interest groups in general—create problems for government in America requires an examination of three important theories, which were introduced in Chapter 1. **Pluralist theory** argues that interest group activity brings representation to all. According to pluralists, groups compete and counterbalance one another in the political marketplace. In contrast, **elite theory** argues that a few groups (primarily the wealthy) have most of the power. Finally, **hyperpluralist theory** asserts that too many groups are getting too much of what they want, resulting in a government policy that is often contradictory and lacking in direction. The following sections will examine each of these three theories with respect to interest groups.

PLURALISM AND GROUP THEORY

Pluralist theory rests its case on the many centers of power in the American political system. Pluralists consider the extensive organization of competing groups evidence that influence is widely dispersed among them. They believe that groups win some and lose some but that no group wins or loses all the time. A considerable body of writings by pluralist theorists offers a *group theory of politics,* which contains several essential arguments.[3]

- *Groups provide a key link between people and government.* All legitimate interests in the political system can get a hearing from government once they are organized.
- *Groups compete.* Labor, business, farmers, consumers, environmentalists, and other interests constantly make claims on one another.
- *No one group is likely to become too dominant.* When one group throws its weight around too much, its opponents are likely to intensify their organization and thus restore balance to the system. For every action, there is a reaction.
- *Groups usually play by the "rules of the game."* In the United States group politics is a fair fight, with few groups lying, cheating, stealing, or engaging in violence to get their way.
- *Groups weak in one resource can use another.* Big business may have money on its side, but labor has numbers. All legitimate groups are able to affect public policy by one means or another.

Pluralists would never deny that some groups are stronger than others or that competing interests do not always get an equal hearing. Still, they can point to many cases in which a potential group organized itself and, once organized, affected policy decisions. African Americans, women, and consumers are all groups who were long ignored by government officials but who, once organized, redirected the course of public policy. In sum, pluralists argue that lobbying is open to all and is therefore not to be regarded as a problem.

ELITES AND THE DENIAL OF PLURALISM

Whereas pluralists are impressed by the vast number of organized interests, elitists are impressed by how insignificant most of them are. Real power, elitists say, is held by relatively few people, key groups, and institutions. They maintain that the government is run by a few big interests looking out for themselves—a view that the majority of the public has agreed with for the last two decades (see "The People Speak: Perceptions of the Dominance of Big Interests").

Elitists critique pluralist theory by pointing to the concentration of power in a few hands. Where pluralists find dispersion of power, elitists find interlocking and concentrated power centers. About one-third of top institutional positions—corporate boards, foundation boards, university trusteeships, and so on—are occupied by people who hold more than one such position.[4] Elitists see the rise of mighty multinational corporations as further tightening the control of corporate elites. A prime example is America's giant oil companies. Robert Engler has tried to show that government has always bent over backward to maintain high profits for the oil industry.[5] When they come up against the power of these multinational corporations, consumer interests are readily pushed aside, according to elitists.

In sum, the elitist view of the interest group system makes the following points:

- The fact that there are numerous groups proves nothing, because groups are extremely unequal in power.
- Awesome power is held by the largest corporations.
- The power of a few is fortified by an extensive system of interlocking directorates.
- Other groups may win many minor policy battles, but the corporate elites prevail when it comes to the big decisions.

Thus, even honest lobbying is a problem, say elite theorists, because it benefits the few at the expense of the many.

HYPERPLURALISM AND INTEREST GROUP LIBERALISM

Hyperpluralists, also critical of pluralism, argue that the pluralist system is out of control. Theodore Lowi coined the phrase *interest group liberalism* to refer to the government's excessive deference to groups. Interest group liberalism holds that virtually all pressure group demands are legitimate and that the job of the government is to advance them all.[6]

In an effort to please and appease every interest, agencies proliferate, conflicting regulations expand, programs multiply, and, of course, the budget skyrockets. If environmentalists want clean air, government imposes clean-air rules; if businesses complain that

The People Speak

Perceptions of the Dominance of Big Interests

Would you say the government is pretty much run by a few big interests looking out for themselves or that it is run for the benefit of all the people?

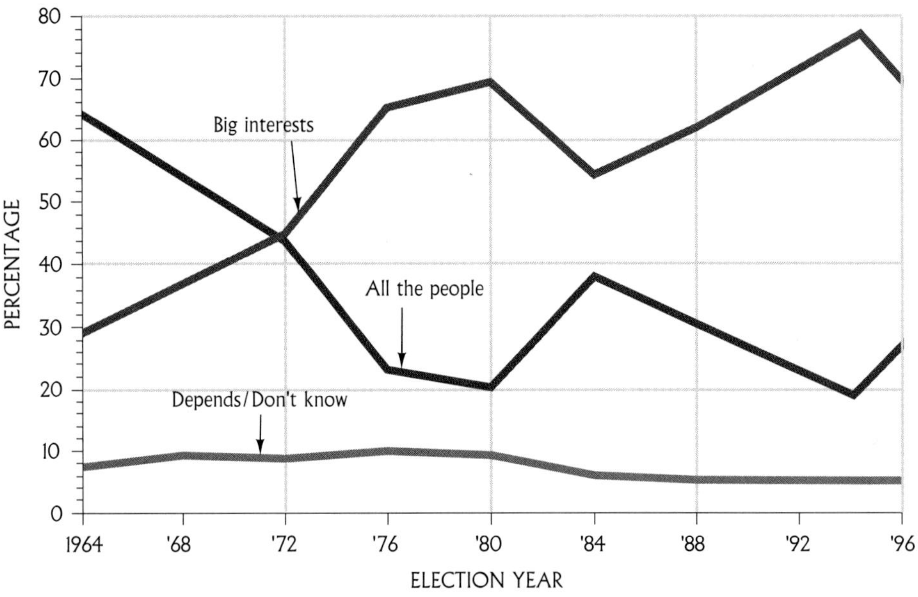

SOURCE: The question as worded is taken directly from National Election Studies conducted by the University of Michigan.

cleaning up pollution is expensive, government gives them a tax write-off for pollution control equipment. If the direct-mail industry wants cheap rates, government gives it to them; if people complain about junk mail, the postal service gives them a way to take their names off mailing lists. If cancer researchers convince the government to launch an antismoking campaign, tobacco sales may drop; if they do, government will subsidize tobacco farmers to ease their loss.[7]

Interest group liberalism is promoted by the network of **subgovernments** in the American political system. These subgovernments, which are also known as iron triangles, are composed of key interest group leaders interested in policy X, the government agency in charge of administering policy X, and the members of congressional committees and subcommittees handling policy X.

All the elements composing subgovernments have the same goal: protecting their self-interest. The network of subgovernments in the agricultural policy area of tobacco is an excellent example. Tobacco interest groups include the Tobacco Institute, the Retail Tobacco Distributors of America, and the tobacco growers. Various agencies in the Department of Agriculture administer tobacco programs, and they depend on the tobacco industry's clout in Congress to help keep their agency budgets safe from cuts. Finally, most of the members of the House Tobacco Subcommittee are from tobacco-growing regions. All of these elements want to protect the interests of tobacco farmers. Similar subgovernments of group-agency-committee ties exist in scores of other policy areas.

Hyperpluralists' major criticism of the interest group system is that relations between groups and the government have become too cozy. Hard choices about national policy are rarely made. Instead of making choices between X and Y, the government pretends there is no need at all to choose and tries to favor them both. It is a perfect script for policy gridlock. In short, the hyperpluralist position on group politics is that

- Groups have become too powerful in the political process as government tries to aid every conceivable interest.
- Interest group liberalism is aggravated by numerous subgovernments—comfortable relationships among a government agency, the interest group it deals with, and congressional subcommittees.
- Trying to please every group results in contradictory and confusing policy.

Ironically, the recent interest group explosion is seen by some scholars as weakening the power of subgovernments. As Morris Fiorina writes, "A world of active public interest groups, jealous business competitors, and packs of budding investigative reporters is less hospitable to subgovernment politics than a world lacking in them."[8] With so many more interest groups to satisfy, and with many of them competing against one another, a cozy relationship between groups and the government is plainly more difficult to sustain.

WHAT MAKES AN INTEREST GROUP SUCCESSFUL?

Many factors affect the success of an interest group. Among these factors are the size of the group (the smaller the better), its intensity, and its financial resources. It is somewhat counterintuitive to learn that small groups are actually more likely to get their way than large groups. Thus, considerable space will be devoted here to explaining this surprising finding. The discussion will then turn to some of the other, less surprising factors.

THE SURPRISING INEFFECTIVENESS OF LARGE GROUPS

In one of the most oft-quoted statements concerning interest groups, E. E. Schattschneider wrote that "pressure politics is essentially the politics of small groups. . . . Pressure tactics are not remarkably successful in mobilizing general interests."[9] There are perfectly good reasons why consumer groups are less effective than producer groups, patients are less effective than doctors, and energy conservationists less effective than oil companies: Small groups have organizational advantages over large groups.

To shed light on this point, it is important to distinguish between a potential and an actual group. A **potential group** is composed of all people who might be group members because they share some common interest.[10] In contrast, an **actual group** is composed of those in the potential group who choose to join. Groups vary enormously in the degree to which they enroll their potential membership. Consumer organizations are minuscule when compared with the total number of consumers, which is almost every American. Some organizations, however, do very well in organizing virtually all of their potential members. The U.S. League of Savings Institutions, the Tobacco Institute, and the Air Transport Association include a good portion of their potential members. Compared with consumers, these groups are tightly organized.

Economist Mancur Olson explains this phenomenon in *The Logic of Collective Action.*[11] Olson points out that all groups, unlike individuals, are in the business of providing collective goods. A **collective good** is something of value, such as clean air, that cannot be withheld from a potential group member. When the AFL-CIO wins a higher minimum wage, all low-paid workers benefit, regardless of whether they are members of the union. In other words, members of the potential group share in benefits that members of the actual group work to secure. If this is the case, an obvious and difficult problem results: Why should potential members work for something if they can get it free? Why join the group, pay dues, and work hard for a goal when a person can benefit from the group's activity without doing anything at all? A perfectly rational response is thus to sit back and let other people do the work. This is commonly known as the **free-rider problem.**

The bigger the group, the more serious the free-rider problem. That is the gist of **Olson's law of large groups:** "The larger the group, the further it will fall short of providing an optimal amount of a collective good."[12] Small groups thus have an organizational advantage over large ones. In a small group, members' shares of the collective good may be great enough that they will try to secure it. The old saying that "everyone can make a difference" is much more credible in the case of a small group. In the largest groups, however, each member can expect to get only a tiny share of the policy gains. Weighing the costs of participation against the relatively small benefits, the temptation is always to "let somebody else do it." Therefore, as Olson argues, the larger the potential group, the less likely potential members are to contribute.

This distinct advantage of small groups helps explain why public interest groups have a hard time making ends meet. Consumer groups and environmentalists claim to seek "public interest" goals, but the

Hyperpluralist theorists often point to the government's contradictory tobacco-related policies as an example of interest group liberalism. Former Surgeon General C. Everett Koop (left), for example, led a high-profile campaign against smoking, whereas North Carolina Senator Jesse Helms has long worked to keep subsidies to tobacco farmers high.

gains they win are usually spread thin over millions of people. In contrast, the lobbying costs and benefits for business are concentrated. Suppose, for example, that consumer advocates take the airlines to court over charges of price fixing and force the airlines to return $10 million to consumers in the form of lower prices. This $10 million settlement is spread over 270 million Americans—about four cents per person (actually, the benefit is a little higher if one divides only by the number of people who use airlines). The $10 million airline loss is shared by 60 carriers at over $165,000 apiece. One can quickly see which side will be better organized in such a struggle.

In sum, Olson's law of large groups explains why small interest groups are generally more effective. The power of business in the American political system is thus due to more than just money, as proponents of elite theory would have us believe. Besides their financial strength, wealthy corporations also enjoy an inherent size advantage. Because there are a limited number of multinational corporations, these businesses have an easier time organizing themselves for political action than larger potential groups, such as consumers. Once well organized, large groups may be very effective, but it is much harder for them to get together in the first place.

The primary way for large potential groups to overcome Olson's law is to provide attractive benefits for only those who join the organization. **Selective benefits** are goods that a group can restrict to those who pay their yearly dues, such as information publications, travel discounts, and group insurance rates. The American Association of Retired Persons (AARP) has built up a membership list of 33 million senior citizens by offering a variety of selective benefits, as shown in Figure 11.1. Similarly, Consumers Union gains most of its members not because of its efforts on behalf of product safety but by offering the selective benefit of receiving *Consumer Reports*, a monthly magazine that rates the reliability, safety, and cost-effectiveness of products.

INTENSITY

Another way a large potential group may be mobilized is through an issue that people feel intensely about, such as abortion. Intensity is a psychological advantage that can be enjoyed by small and large groups alike. When a group shows that it cares deeply about an issue, politicians are more likely to listen; many votes may be won or lost on a single issue. The rise of single-issue groups has been one of the most dramatic political developments in recent years.

A **single-issue group** can be defined as a group that has a narrow interest, dislikes compromise, and single-mindedly pursues its goal. Anti-Vietnam War activists may have formed the first modern single-issue group.

FIGURE 11.1 WHY THE AARP'S 33 MILLION MEMBERS SAY THEY JOINED

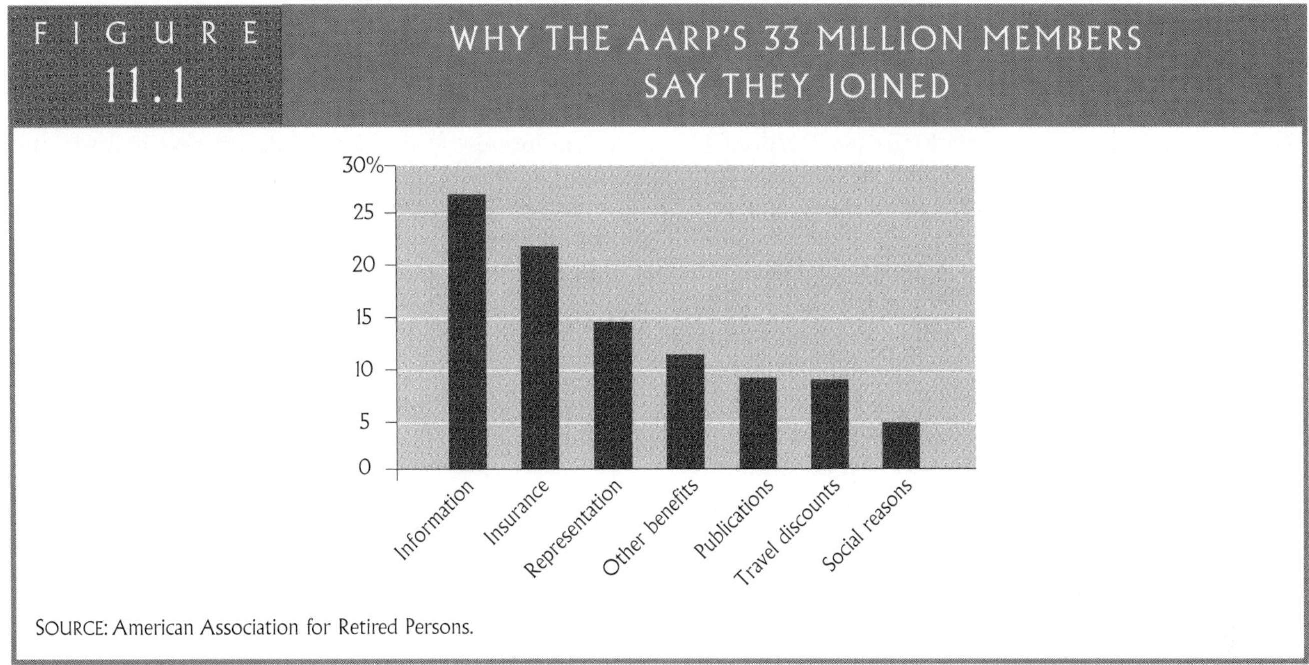

SOURCE: American Association for Retired Persons.

Opponents of nuclear power plants, gun control, and abortion are some of the many such groups that exist today. All these groups deal with issues that evoke the strong emotions characteristic of single-interest groups.

Perhaps the most emotional issue of recent times has been that of abortion. The 1973 Supreme Court ruling in *Roe v. Wade,* upholding the right of a woman to secure an abortion during the first trimester of pregnancy, spurred a wave of group formation. Opponents quickly labeled this court decision legalized murder and formed such organizations as the National Right to Life Committee. As befits the intensity of the issue, their activities have not been limited to conventional means of political participation. Protesting—often in the form of blocking entrances to abortion clinics—has

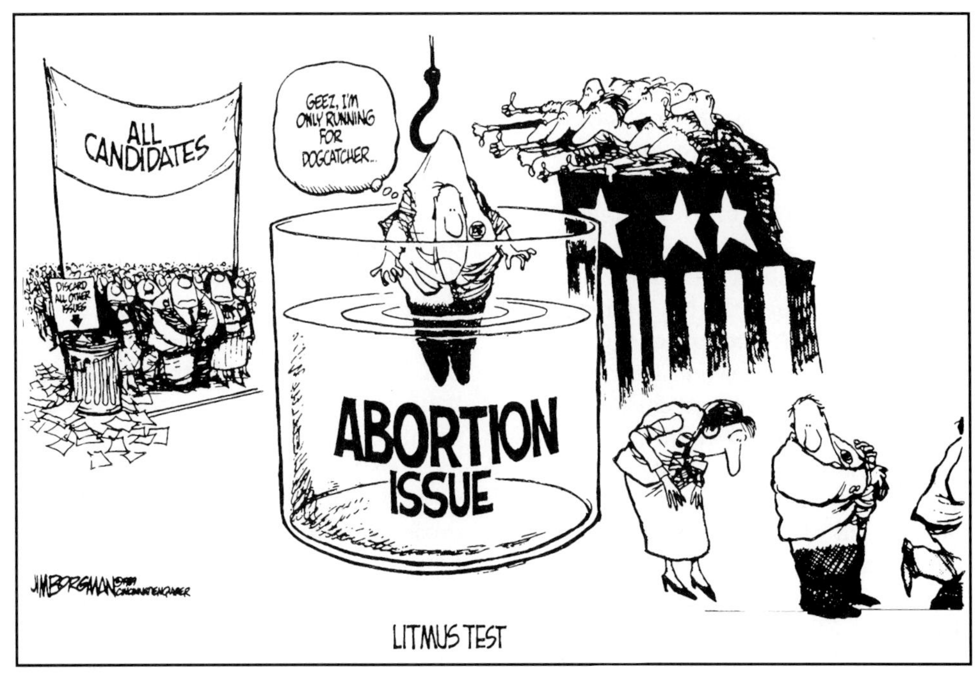

now become a common practice for anti-abortion activists. Pro-choice activists have organized as well, forming groups such as the National Abortion Rights Action League. Since the 1989 *Webster v. Reproductive Health Services* case allowed states greater freedom to restrict abortions, the pro-choice side has become better mobilized than ever before. Like the anti-abortion activists, their position is clear, is not subject to compromise, and influences their vote. Regardless of which side candidates for political office are on, they will be taking heat on the abortion issue for years to come.

FINANCIAL RESOURCES

One of the major indictments of the American interest group system is that it is biased toward the wealthy. When he was majority leader in the Senate, Bob Dole once remarked that he had never been approached by a Poor People's PAC. There is no doubt that money talks in the American political system, and those who have it get heard. A big campaign contribution may ensure a phone call, a meeting, or even a direct *quid pro quo*. When Lincoln Savings and Loan chairman Charles Keating was asked whether the $1.3 million he had funneled into the campaigns of five U.S. Senators had anything to do with these Senators later meeting with federal regulators on his behalf, he candidly responded, "I certainly hope so."

Critics charge that PACs, as the source of so much money in today's expensive high-tech campaigns, distort the governmental process in favor of those who can raise the most money. Representative Jim Leach of Iowa believes that "it's a myth to think they [the PACs] don't want something in return."[13] They may want to be remembered only on one or two crucial votes or with an occasional intervention with government agencies, but multiply this by the thousands of special interests that are organized today and the worst fears of the hyperpluralists could be realized—a government that constantly yields to every organized special interest.

It is important to emphasize, however, that even on some of the most important issues, the big interests do not always win. The best recent example of this is the Tax Reform Act of 1986. In *Showdown at Gucci Gulch,* two reporters from the *Wall Street Journal* chronicle the improbable victory of sweeping tax reform.[14] In this case, a large group of well-organized, highly paid (and thus Gucci-clad) lobbyists were unable to preserve many of their most prized tax loopholes. One of the heroes of the book, Senator Packwood of Oregon, was Congress' top PAC recipient during the tax reform struggle; he had raked in $992,000 for his reelection campaign. As chair of the Senate Finance Committee, however, Packwood ultimately turned against the hordes of lobbyists trying to get his ear on behalf of various loopholes. The only way to deal with the tax loophole problem, he concluded, was to go virtually cold turkey by eliminating all but a very few. "There is special interest after special interest that is hit in this bill," Packwood gloated, pointing out that many of them contributed to his campaign. In the end, passage of the reform bill offered "encouraging proof that moneyed interests could not always buy their way to success in Congress."[15]

THE INTEREST GROUP EXPLOSION

The number of interest groups in the United States has been increasing rapidly over the last several decades. Although no one has ever compiled a *Who's Who* of interest groups, the closest thing is the annual *Encyclopedia of Associations.*[16] As of 1993, the *Encyclopedia* listed approximately 23,000 organizations, up more than 50 percent since 1980 and almost 400 percent since 1955.[17]

There are many reasons for this explosion in the number of groups. Certainly one of the major factors has been the development of sophisticated technology. Andrew McFarland observes that

> technological innovations have made the coordination of constituents' activities and efforts of lobbyists much easier. Many lobbyists, for example, have available computerized lists of names and phone numbers of group members that can be easily arranged by congressional district or state. Address labels can be printed automatically or members can be called by WATS line from a group's headquarters.[18]

Technology has also made it easier for groups back on Main Street to make their voices immediately heard in Washington. A well-organized interest group can deluge members of Congress with tens of thousands of faxes and electronic mail messages in a matter of hours. Technology did not create interest group politics, but it surely made the process much easier.

The interests of many groups are primarily economic. The trade, commercial, and business section of the *Encyclopedia* lists thousands of groups, beginning with organizations of accountants and ending with those of wholesale distributors. Between these two types of organizations, one can find such groups as the American Cricket Growers Association and the National Frozen Food Association.

It seems that there is now an organized group for every conceivable interest. Indeed, the growth rate of

TABLE 11.1 PERCENTAGE OF GROUPS USING VARIOUS LOBBYING TECHNIQUES

TECHNIQUE	PERCENTAGE
Testifying at hearings	99
Contacting government officials directly to present a point of view	98
Engaging in informal contacts with officials—at conventions, over lunch, etc.	95
Presenting research results or technical information	92
Sending letters to members of an organization to inform them about its activities	92
Entering into coalitions with other organizations	90
Attempting to shape the implementation of policies	89
Talking with people from the press and the media	86
Consulting with government officials to plan legislative strategy	85
Helping to draft legislation	85
Inspiring letter-writing or telegram campaigns	84
Shaping the government's agenda by raising new issues and calling attention to previously ignored problems	84
Mounting grass-roots lobbying efforts	80
Having influential constituents contact their congressperson's office	80
Helping to draft regulations, rules, or guidelines	78
Serving on advisory commissions and boards	76
Alerting members of Congress to the effects of a bill on their districts	75
Filing lawsuits or otherwise engaging in litigation	72
Making financial contributions to electoral campaigns	58
Doing favors for officials who need assistance	56
Attempting to influence appointments to public office	53
Publicizing candidates' voting records	44
Engaging in direct-mail fund raising	44
Running advertisements in the media about issues	31
Contributing work or personnel to electoral campaigns	24
Making public endorsements of candidates for office	22
Engaging in protests or demonstrations	20

SOURCE: Kay L. Schlozman and John T. Tierney, *Organized Interests and American Democracy* (New York: Harper & Row, 1986).

interest groups has been astounding. Jack Walker studied 564 groups listed in the *Washington Information Directory* and tried to trace their origins and expansion.[19] He found that 80 percent of the groups originated from occupational, industrial, or professional memberships. Interestingly, half of the groups he studied were established after World War II. Walker also found a gravitation of groups to Washington, DC. In 1960, only 66 percent of the groups in his study were headquartered in the nation's capital; today, over 90 percent are located there. Very few occupations or industries now go without an organized group to represent them in Washington. Even lobbyists themselves now have lobbies to represent their profession, such as the American League of Lobbyists.

HOW GROUPS TRY TO SHAPE POLICY

No interest group has enough staff, money, or time to do everything possible to achieve its policy goals. Interest groups must therefore choose from a variety of tactics. Table 11.1 illustrates the range and frequency of tactics employed by a sample of interest groups. The three traditional strategies are lobbying, electioneering, and litigation. In addition, groups have recently developed a variety of sophisticated techniques to appeal to the public for widespread support. These four general strategies are the topic of the next four sections.

LOBBYING

The term **lobbying** comes from the place where petitioners used to collar legislators. In the early years of politics in Washington, members of Congress had no offices and typically stayed in boarding houses or hotels while Congress was in session. A person could not call them up on the phone or make an appointment with their secretary; the only sure way of getting in touch with them was to wait in the lobby where they were staying, so as to catch them either coming in or going out. These people were dubbed *lobbyists* because they spent so much of their time waiting in lobbies.

Of course, merely loitering in a lobby does not make one a lobbyist; there must be a particular reason for such action. Lester Milbrath has offered a more precise definition of the practice. He writes that lobbying is a "communication, by someone other than a citizen acting on his or her own behalf, directed to a governmental decision-maker with the hope of influencing his or her decision."[20] Lobbyists, in other words, are political persuaders who represent organized groups. They normally work in Washington, handling groups' legislative business. Oftentimes, they are former legislators themselves.

There are two basic types of lobbyists. Members of the first type are regular, paid employees of a corporation, union, or association. They may hold a title such as vice president for government relations, but everyone knows that their office is in Washington for a reason, even if the company headquarters is in Houston. The second type of lobbyists is available for hire on a temporary basis. One group may be too small to afford a full-time lobbyist; another may have a unique, but temporary, need for access to Congress or the executive branch. Several thousand Washingtonians are available as "lobbyists for hire."

Although lobbyists are primarily out to influence members of Congress, it is important to remember that they can be of help to them as well. Ornstein and Elder list four important ways in which lobbyists can help a member of Congress.[21]

- *They are an important source of information.* Members of Congress have to concern themselves with many policy areas; lobbyists can confine themselves to only one area and can thus provide specialized expertise.
- *They can help politicians with political strategy for getting legislation through.* Lobbyists are politically savvy people, and they can be useful consultants. When he served as White House Chief of Staff, Leon Panetta regularly convened a small group of Washington lobbyists to discuss how the administration should present its proposals.[22]
- *They can help formulate campaign strategy and get the group's members behind a politician's reelection campaign.*
- *They are a source of ideas and innovations.* Lobbyists cannot introduce bills, but they can peddle their ideas to politicians eager to attach their name to an idea that will bring them political credit.

Like anything else, lobbying can be done crudely or gracefully. Lobbyists can sometimes be heavy-handed. They can threaten or cajole a legislator, implying that electoral defeat is a certain result of not "going along." They can even make it clear that money flows to the reelection coffers of those who cooperate. It is often difficult to tell the difference between lobbying as a shady business and lobbying as a strictly professional representation of legitimate interests.

For years, the National Rifle Association has successfully lobbied against gun control policies, arguing that the Constitution guarantees all citizens the right to bear arms. In addition to intense lobbying and electioneering, the NRA uses advertisements such as this one to build popular support with which to pressure policymakers.

Political scientists disagree about the effectiveness of lobbying. Much evidence suggests that lobbyists' power over policy is often exaggerated. A classic 1950s study of the influence of groups on foreign-trade policy started with the hypothesis that when major business lobbies spoke, Congress listened—and acted accordingly.[23] Instead, the study found groups involved in trade policy to be ineffective, understaffed, and underfinanced. Usually the lobbyists were too disorganized to be effective. Members of Congress often had to pressure the interest groups to actively support legislation that would be in their own interest. Similarly, Milbrath concluded his own analysis of lobbying by arguing that "there is relatively little influence or power in lobbying per se."[24] Lobbyists are most effective as information sources, he claims, and are relatively ineffectual in winning over legislators.

Plenty of other evidence, however, suggests that sometimes lobbying can persuade legislators to support a certain policy. The National Rifle Association, which for years kept major gun control policies off the congressional agenda, has long been one of Washington's most effective lobbying groups. In a more specific example, intensive lobbying by the nation's most wealthy senior citizens—enraged by the tax burden imposed on them by the Catastrophic Health Care Act—led Congress to repeal the act only a year after it was passed.

Nailing down the specific effects of lobbying is difficult, partly because it is hard to isolate its effects from other influences. Lobbying clearly works best on people already committed to the lobbyist's policy position. Thus, like campaigning, lobbying is directed primarily toward activating and reinforcing one's supporters. For example, anti-abortion lobbyists would not think of approaching California's Barbara Boxer to attempt to convert her to their position, because Boxer clearly supports the pro-choice movement. If Senator Boxer is lobbied by anyone on the abortion issue, it will be by the pro-choice faction, urging her not to compromise with the opposition.

ELECTIONEERING

Because lobbying works best with those already on the same side, getting the right people into office and keeping them there is also a key strategy of interest groups. Many groups therefore get involved in **electioneering**—aiding candidates financially and getting group members out to support them. Pressure group involvement in campaigns is nothing new. In the election of 1896 (see Chapter 10), silver-mining interests poured millions into the losing presidential campaign of William Jennings Bryan, who advocated unlimited coinage of silver.

Recently, **political action committees (PACs)** have provided a means for groups to participate in electioneering more than ever before. The number of PACs exploded from 608 in 1974 to 4,079 in 1996 (see Figure 11.2). No major interest group seeking to exert influence on the electoral process these days can pass up the opportunity to funnel money honestly and openly into the campaign coffers of its supporters. As campaign costs have risen, PACs have come along to help pay the bill. In recent years, nearly half of the candidates running for reelection to the House of Representatives have received the majority of their campaign funds from PACs. Furthermore, this advantage was not enjoyed by their challengers. PACs gave a whopping $133 million to House incumbents during the 1995-1996 election cycle, compared to a mere $28 million to the challengers.

Why does PAC money go so overwhelmingly to incumbents? The answer is that PAC contributions are basically investments for the future, and incumbents are the most likely to return the investment. However, sometimes PACs like to play it safe; an examination of seven hotly contested Senate races in 1988 showed that 274 PACs guaranteed that their investments were risk free by contributing to both Democratic and Republican candidates for the same seat.[25]

Only a handful of candidates have resisted the lure of PAC money in recent years. One candidate described his experiences trying to get on the PAC bandwagon. When Democrat Steve Sovern ran for the House from Iowa's Second District, he made the now common pilgrimage to Washington to meet with potential contributors. "I found myself in line with candidates from all over," he reported. Each PAC had eager candidates fill out a multiple-choice questionnaire on issues important to the PAC. Candidates who shared the same concerns and views and who looked like winners got the money. Sovern later reported that "the process made me sick." After his defeat, he orga-

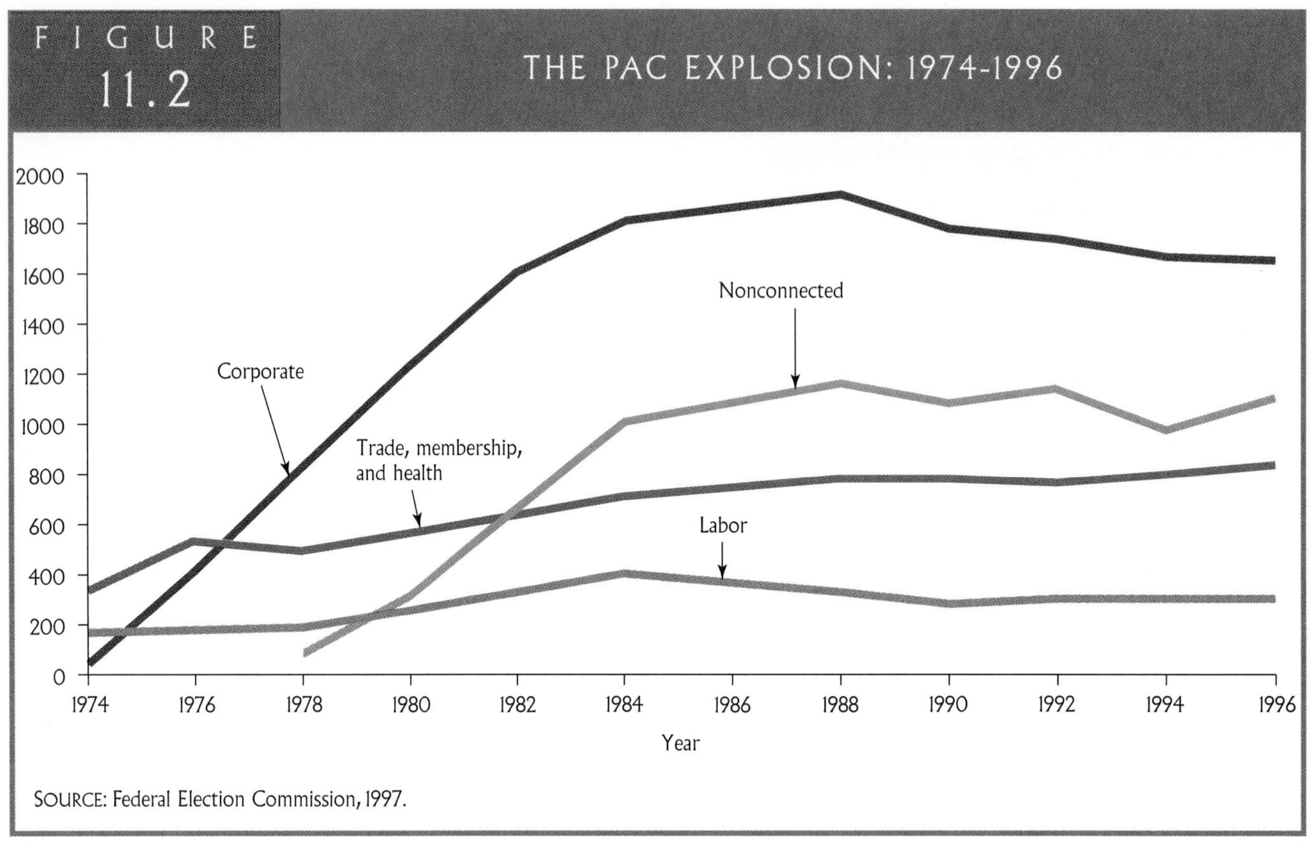

SOURCE: Federal Election Commission, 1997.

nized his own PAC called LASTPAC (for Let the American System Triumph), which urged candidates to shun PAC campaign contributions.[26] The grandparent of public interest lobbies, Common Cause, is also waging a public campaign against PACs.

LITIGATION

If interest groups fail in Congress or get only a vague piece of legislation, the next step is to go to court in the hope of getting specific rulings. Karen Orren has linked much of the success of environmental interest groups to their use of lawsuits. "Frustrated in Congress," she wrote, "they have made an end run to the courts, where they have skillfully exploited and magnified limited legislative gains."[27] Environmental legislation, such as the Clean Air Act, typically includes written provisions allowing ordinary citizens to sue for enforcement. As a result, every federal agency involved in environmental regulation now has hundreds of suits pending against it at any given time. These suits may not halt environmentally troublesome practices, but the constant threat of a lawsuit increases the likelihood that businesses will consider the environmental impact of what they do.

Perhaps the most famous interest group victories in court were by civil rights groups in the 1950s. While civil rights bills remained stalled in Congress, these groups won major victories in court cases concerning school desegregation, equal housing, and labor market equality. More recently, consumer groups have used suits against businesses and federal agencies as a means of enforcing consumer regulations. As long as law schools keep producing lawyers, groups will fight for their interests in court. Indeed, the increase in the proportion of lawyers licensed to practice in Washington has been phenomenal over the last several decades (see Figure 11.3).

One tactic that lawyers employ to make the views of interest groups heard by the judiciary is the filing of ***amicus curiae*** ("friend of the court") **briefs**. *Amicus* briefs consist of written arguments submitted to the courts in support of one side of a case. Through these written depositions, a group states its collective position as well as how its own welfare will be affected by the outcome of the case. Numerous groups may file *amicus* briefs in highly publicized and emotionally charged cases. For example, in the case of *Regents of the University of California v. Bakke* (see Chapter 5), which challenged affirmative action programs as reverse discrimination, over a hundred different groups filed *ami-*

FIGURE 11.3 WASHINGTON LAWYERS

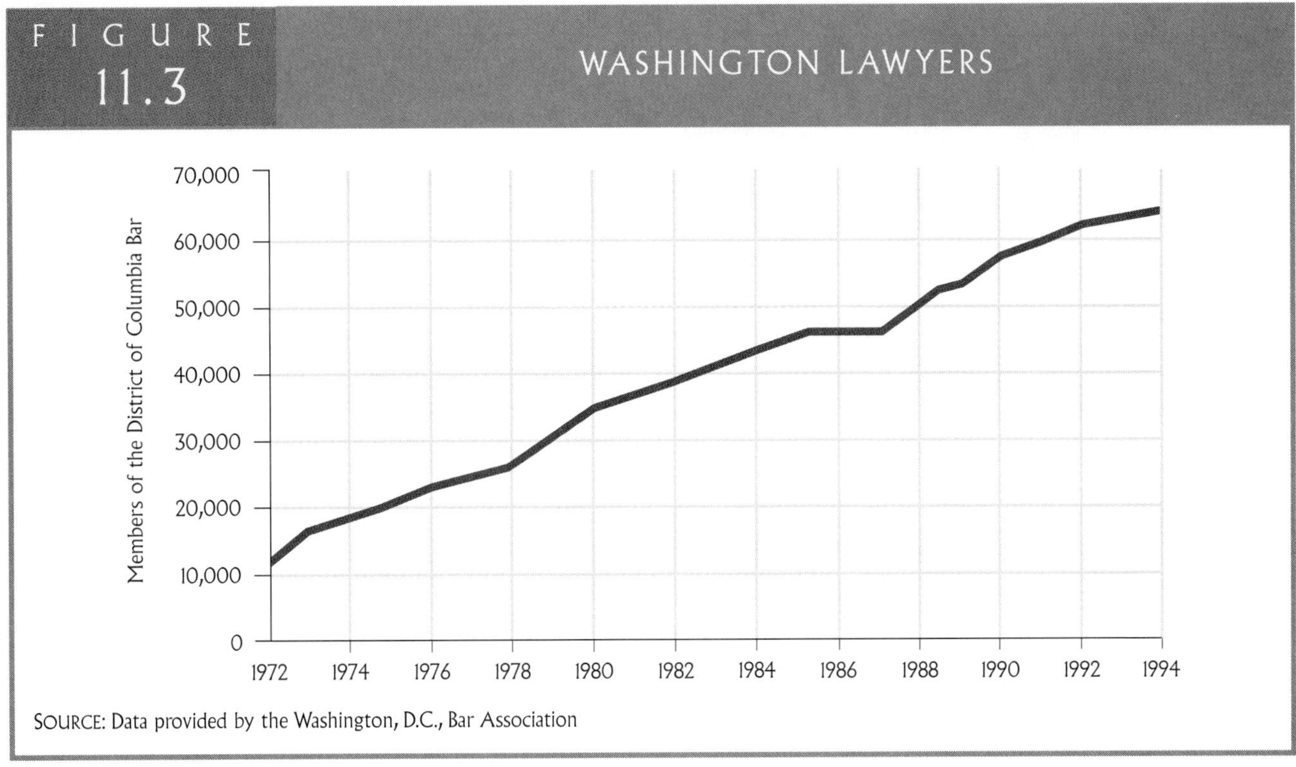

SOURCE: Data provided by the Washington, D.C., Bar Association

cus briefs. A study of participation in *amicus* briefs by Caldeira and Wright found that the Supreme Court has been accessible to a wide array of organized interests, in terms of deciding both which cases to hear and how to rule.[28]

A more direct judicial strategy employed by interest groups is the filing of a **class action lawsuit,** which enables a group of similarly situated plaintiffs to combine similar grievances into a single suit. For instance, flight attendants won a class action suit against the airline industry's regulation that all stewardesses be unmarried. As one lawyer who specializes in such cases states, "The class action is the greatest, most effective legal engine to remedy mass wrongs."[29]

GOING PUBLIC

Groups are also interested in the opinions of the public. Because public opinion ultimately makes its way to policymakers, interest groups carefully cultivate their public image. Interest groups market not only their stand on issues but also their reputations. Business interests want people to see them as "what made America great," not as wealthy Americans trying to ensure large profits. The Teamsters Union likes to be known as a united organization of hard-working men and women, not as an organization often influenced by organized crime. Farmers cultivate the image of a sturdy family working to put bread on the table, not the huge agribusinesses that have largely replaced family farms. In this way, many groups try to create a reservoir of goodwill with the public.

The practice of interest groups' appealing to the public for support has a long tradition in American politics. In 1908, AT&T launched a major magazine advertising campaign to convince people of the need for a telephone monopoly. Similarly, after President Truman proposed a system of national health insurance in 1948, the American Medical Association spent millions of dollars on ads attacking "socialized medicine." In 1994, the Health Insurance Association of America ran a $15 million nationally televised ad campaign criticizing President Clinton's health care package, which many analysts believe lessened public support for the reform bill. So many groups placed advertisements regarding the Clinton health care reform package and so much money was spent (over $100 million), that many observers compared this activity to a national electoral campaign.

Lately, more and more organizations have undertaken expensive public relations (PR) efforts. Soft sell and reasoned analysis—even presenting both sides of the issues—are the hallmark of this new era of public relations. Caterpillar, the manufacturer of massive earth-moving and strip-mining machinery, inundated *National Geographic* and other magazines with balanced ads presenting both sides of environmental

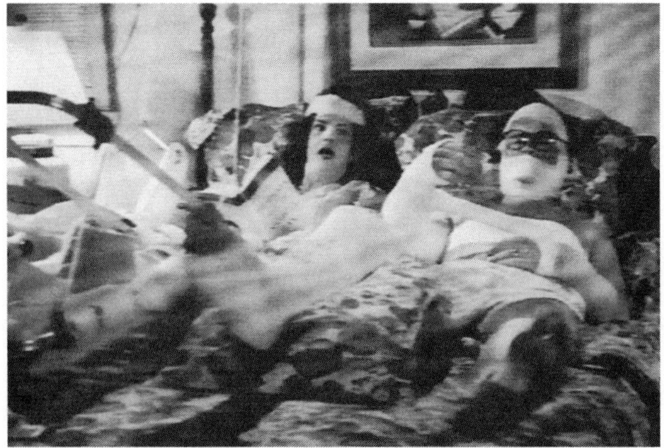

Interest groups spent over $50 million appealing to public opinion during the debate over health care in 1994. The health insurance industry's "Harry and Louise" ads opposing national health care even drew a counter ad from the Democratic National Committee. Here, Harry and Louise are shown after Harry has lost his job. The couple is bemoaning the financial toll of their illnesses now that they are uninsured.

issues, such as strip-mining. Mobil Oil runs the most visible corporate PR effort to influence the public with its regular op-ed style ads in the *New York Times* and other major publications. These ads typically address issues that affect the oil industry and big business in general. One time Mobil even ran an ad entitled "Why Do We Buy This Space?" It answered "that business needs voices in the media, the same way labor unions, consumers, and other groups in our society do."[30] No one knows just how effective these image-molding efforts are, but many groups seem to believe firmly that advertising pays off.

TYPES OF INTEREST GROUPS

Whether they are lobbying, electioneering, litigating, or appealing to the public, interest groups are omnipresent in the American political system. As with other aspects of American politics and policymaking, political scientists loosely categorize interest groups into clusters. Some deal mainly with economic issues, others with issues of energy and the environment, and still others with equality issues.

Of course, not all groups are easily pigeonholed into these three policy arenas. Public interest groups such as Common Cause and ideological groups such as the Americans for Democratic Action involve themselves in a whole range of issues. Even groups that have a prevailing interest in one policy area do not always confine their activities to that area. The American Petroleum Institute and the American Mining Conference, for example, have a great influence on economic as well as energy issues. Still, the Pharmaceutical Manufacturers are not likely to spend their valuable resources lobbying for or against environmental bills or school busing policies. The classifications discussed in the following sections are made on the assumption that most groups concern themselves with a limited range of issues.

ECONOMIC INTERESTS

All economic interests are ultimately concerned with wages, prices, and profits. In the American economy, government does not determine these directly. Only on rare occasions has the government imposed wage and price controls. These have usually been during wartime, although the Nixon administration briefly used wage and price controls to combat inflation. More commonly, public policy in America has economic effects through regulations, tax advantages, subsidies and contracts, and international trade policy.

Business, labor, and farmers all fret over the impact of government regulations. Even a minor change in government regulatory policy can cost industries a great deal or bring increased profits. Tax policies also affect the livelihood of individuals and firms. How the tax code is written determines whether people and producers pay a lot or a little of their incomes to the government. Because government often provides subsidies to farmers, small businesses, railroads, minority businesses, and others, every economic group wants to get its share of direct aid and government contracts. In this era of economic global interdependence, all groups worry about import quotas, tariffs (fees imposed on imports), and the soundness of the American dollar. In short, business executives, factory workers, and farmers seek to influence government because regulations, taxes, subsidies, and international economic policy all affect their economic livelihoods. The following sections discuss the impact of some of the major organized interests in the economic policy arena.

Labor. Labor has more affiliated members than any other interest group except the American Association for Retired Persons. Fourteen million workers are members of unions belonging to the AFL-CIO—itself a union of unions. Several million others are members of non-AFL-CIO unions, such as the National Education Association, which represents schoolteachers.

Like labor unions everywhere, American unions press for policies to ensure better working conditions and higher wages. Recognizing that many workers

Strikes are among labor unions' most powerful weapons. This recent strike by Caterpillar workers lasted 5 months. In addition to the usual salary demands, the strikers wanted written assurances limiting the company's ability to replace older workers.

would like to enjoy union benefits without actually joining a union and paying dues, unions have fought hard to establish the **union shop,** which requires new employees to join the union representing them. In contrast, business groups have supported **right-to-work laws,** which outlaw union membership as a condition of employment. They argue that such laws deny a basic freedom—namely, the right not to belong to a group. In 1947, the biggest blow ever to the American labor movement occurred when Congress passed the Taft-Hartley Act, permitting states to adopt right-to-work laws (known as "slave labor laws" within the AFL-CIO). Most of the states that have right-to-work laws are in the South, which traditionally has had the lowest percentage of unionized workers.

The American labor movement reached its peak in 1956, when 33 percent of the nonagricultural work force belonged to a union; since then, the percentage has declined to about 16 percent. One factor behind this decline is that low wages in other countries have diminished the American job market in a number of key manufacturing areas. Steel, once made by American workers, is now made more cheaply in Korea and imported to the United States. The United Auto Workers has found its clout greatly reduced as Detroit has faced heavy competition from Japanese automakers. Some political scientists, however, believe labor's problems result from more than the decline of blue-collar industries. Paul Johnson argues that the most important reason for the decline in union membership is the problems unions have had in convincing today's workers that they will benefit from unionization. In particular, Johnson argues that this task has become more difficult in recent years because of the efforts of employers to make nonunion jobs satisfying.[31] Whatever the reason, it is clear that labor unions no longer have the ability that they once enjoyed to shape public policy (see "Since Kennedy: The Decline of Labor's Policy Clout").

Agriculture. Though it was once the occupation of the majority of Americans, only 3 percent now make their living in farming. The family farm has given way to massive agribusinesses, often heavily involved with exports. To the vast majority who have never lived on a farm, the tangled policies of acreage controls, price supports, and import quotas are mysterious and confusing. To agribusinesses and the few family farmers still around, however, government policies are often more important than the whims of nature.

There are several broad-based agricultural groups, such as the American Farm Bureau Federation. But equally important are the commodity associations formed of peanut farmers, potato growers, dairy farmers, and other producers. The U.S. Department of Agriculture and the agricultural subcommittees in Congress are organized along commodity lines, such as dairy or wheat. As mentioned earlier in this chapter, this organizational system leads to very cordial relations between the policymakers, the bureaucrats, and the interest groups—promoting classic examples of what hyperpluralists call subgovernments.

Business. If the elite theorists are correct, however, and there is an American power elite, it surely must be dominated by leaders of the biggest banks, insurance companies, and multinational corporations. Elitists' views may or may not be exaggerated, but business is certainly well organized for political action. Schlozman and Tierney report that 70 percent of all interest group organizations that have a Washington presence represent business.[32] Furthermore, business PACs have increased more

SINCE KENNEDY

The Decline of Labor's Policy Clout

Perhaps no issue has illustrated the diminished ability of labor to exercise influence over public policy better than the debate over the North American Free Trade Act (NAFTA) in 1993. In the past, when labor decided to throw all its lobbying efforts against a proposal, it could be sure that its clout on Capitol Hill would persuade most Democrats to support its position. One Democrat who wasn't persuaded by labor's fierce opposition to NAFTA, however, was President Clinton. He supported the trade act, even though he could have easily justified opposing it on the grounds that it had been negotiated by President Bush and would result in the loss of hundreds of thousands of American blue-collar jobs to Mexico. However, Clinton agreed with Bush that NAFTA would benefit the U.S. economy more than it would hurt it by opening Mexican markets to American businesses. Despite the intensive lobbying effort of organized labor on Capitol Hill, the administration won a close bipartisan vote ratifying the agreement.

The open warfare between labor and a Democratic administration over NAFTA illustrates the declining influence of big labor within the Democratic Party. Labor is still a major Democratic constituency, and it surely prefers President Clinton to his Republican predecessors. But Clinton's agenda and labor's agenda are hardly one and the same. Organized labor can no longer expect to reap huge gains when the Democrats are in office or to be protected from policies that may hurt their members.

In contrast, the domestic policy agenda of the Kennedy administration and that of organized labor shared a great deal in common in the early 1960s. Whereas President Clinton received just one-fifth of his votes from people in labor union households, President Kennedy received a third of his votes from labor. Thus, Kennedy felt he owed much to organized labor, and his policy initiatives drew heavily from the AFL-CIO's legislative program. The minimum wage was raised to $1.25 an hour and was extended to cover employees in the hotel, restaurant, and laundry trades for the first time ever. Salaries of federal employees were also raised, and their right to organize was recognized by an executive order of President Kennedy. The Manpower Development and Training Act provided for the training of unskilled workers and the retraining of selected skilled workers for the new skills that industrial change demanded. Millions of dollars were appropriated for public works in distressed areas, and the Area Redevelopment Act provided funds to help move industries into these locales. In addition, two major pieces of legislation that were passed after Kennedy's death—the Civil Rights Act of 1964 and Medicare—were strongly supported by labor unions.

dramatically than any other category of PACs, as shown in Figure 11.2. Most large firms, such as AT&T and Ford, now have offices in Washington that monitor legislative activity. Two umbrella organizations, the National Association of Manufacturers (NAM) and the Chamber of Commerce, include most corporations and businesses and speak for them when general business interests are at stake.

Different business interests compete on many specific issues, however. Trucking and construction companies want more highways, but railroads do not. An increase in international trade will help some businesses expand their markets, but others may be hurt by foreign competition. Business interests are generally unified when it comes to promoting greater profits but are often fragmented when policy choices have to be made.

The hundreds of trade and product associations are far less visible than the NAM and the Chamber of Commerce, but they are at least as important in pursuing policy goals for their members. These associations fight regulations that would reduce their profits and seek preferential tax treatment as well as government subsidies and contracts. America's complex schedules of tariffs are monuments to the activities of the trade associations. Although they are the least visible of Washington lobbies, their successes are measured in amendments won, regulations rewritten, and exceptions made. It is not only American trade associations that are concerned with these policies, but foreign corporations and governments as well. The practice of foreign economic interests' hiring influential former governmental officials to lobby on their behalf has recently led to a number of reform proposals (see "You

Earth Day was first held in 1970. Its mood was one of protest, as speakers demanded that the government take stronger action to protect the environment. By the 1990s, the tone of the now annual Earth Day had changed from protest to celebration.

Are the Policymaker: Restricting Lobbying for Foreign Interests", page 276).

Consumers and Public Interest Lobbies. Pluralist theory holds that for virtually every interest in society, there is an organized group. But what about the interests of all of us—the buying public? Today over 2,000 organized groups are championing various causes or ideas "in the public interest."[33] These **public interest lobbies** are organizations that seek "a collective good, the achievement of which will not selectively and materially benefit the membership or activists of the organization."[34] If products are made safer by the lobbying of consumer protection groups, it is not the members of such groups alone that benefit. Rather, everyone should be better off, regardless of whether they joined in the lobbying.

Many public interest groups claim to speak for those who cannot speak for themselves. Animal rights groups, for example, protest against what they see as cruel practices used by fur trappers and try to discourage people from buying fur coats.

If ever a lobbying effort was spurred by a single person, it was the consumer movement. At first, Ralph Nader took on American business almost single-handedly in the name of consumerism. He was propelled to national prominence by his book *Unsafe at Any Speed,* which attacked General Motors' Corvair as a mechanically deficient and dangerous automobile. General Motors made the mistake of hiring a private detective to dig into Nader's background and follow him around, hoping that there might be some dirt they could uncover that would discredit him. No one who knew the ascetic Nader would ever have expected to find anything of the kind. Nader eventually learned about the investigation, sued General Motors for invasion of privacy, and won a hefty damage settlement in court. He used the proceeds to launch the first major consumer group in Washington.

Consumer groups have won many legislative victories in recent years. In 1973, Congress responded to consumer advocacy by creating the Consumer Product Safety Commission. Congress authorized it to regulate all consumer products and even gave it the power to ban particularly dangerous ones, bearing in mind that household products are responsible for 30,000 deaths annually. Among the products the commission has investigated are children's sleepwear (some of which contained a carcinogen), hot tubs, and lawn mowers.

Consumer groups are not the only ones that claim to be public interest groups. Groups speaking for those who cannot speak for themselves seek to protect children, animals, and the mentally ill; good-government groups such as Common Cause push for openness and fairness in government; religious groups like the Christian Coalition crusade for the protection of ethical and moral standards in American society; and environmental groups seek to preserve ecological balance.

ENERGY AND ENVIRONMENTAL INTERESTS

Among the newest political interest groups are the environmentalists. A handful, such as the Sierra Club and the Audubon Society, have been around since the nineteenth century, but many others trace their origins to the first Earth Day, April 22, 1970. On that day, ecology-minded people marched on Washington and other places to symbolize their support for environmental protection. Twenty years later, one estimate pegged the number of environmental groups at over 10,000 and their combined revenues at $2.9 billion—demonstrating "how widely and deeply green values had permeated the society."[35]

RESTRICTING LOBBYING FOR FOREIGN INTERESTS

You Are the Policymaker

In the 1992 campaign, H. Ross Perot frequently called for restrictions on government officials leaving public service to lobby on behalf of foreign corporations and governments. Perhaps the most influential study of this practice has been produced by Pat Choate, who was Ross Perot's running mate in 1996. Choate details how a revolving door exists by which American trade negotiators switch sides after a short period of government service to become lobbyists for foreign concerns. In particular, Choate maintains that the Japanese have acquired great influence over U.S. trade policy by building a network of high-priced lobbyists. These former government officials turned lobbyists are extremely valuable to foreign interests, given their contacts in high places, their knowledge of the American political process, and (in some cases) their inside information regarding the American trade negotiating position.

Choate believes that foreign lobbying clearly poses a threat to America's ability to compete in a global economy. He suggests that several steps be taken to restrict and more carefully monitor lobbying by foreign interests. First, he recommends that officials such as the cabinet secretaries, members of Congress, and those in charge of U.S. trade negotiations be banned for life from working as foreign lobbyists. Second, he proposes that the current "cooling off" period (which restricts federal officials from lobbying or advising on trade matters for 1 year) be extended to at least 5 years. Third, he advocates closing the loopholes in the Foreign Agents Registration Act of 1938 so that all those who represent foreign clients will be required to provide full disclosure to the Justice Department. And finally, he argues that a flat prohibition should be placed on foreign contributions to American political campaigns.

After the attention drawn by Perot to the matter of foreign lobbying, in 1993 the Congress began serious deliberation regarding this issue. Many members felt that something had to be done, but a number of objections were raised on constitutional and policy grounds. Here are a few reservations you should take into account as you decide what should be done:

- Would such restrictions be an infringement on the right to petition the government, as guaranteed by the U.S. Consitutution?
- Do foreigners operating in the United States not have the same constitutional rights as American citizens?
- Will these reforms lead to retaliation by foreign governments against U.S. companies operating abroad?
- Could these restrictions be so strict that they would prevent former government officials from providing assistance to foreigners that would further American interests? For example, might they prevent former officials from advising the first post-Castro Cuban government about reestablishing trade ties with the United States?

SOURCE: Pat Choate, *Agents of Influence: How Japan Manipulates America's Political and Economic System* (New York: Simon & Schuster, 1990).

Environmental groups have promoted pollution-control policies, wilderness protection, and population control. Perhaps more significant, however, is what they have opposed. Their hit list has included strip-mining, supersonic aircraft, the Alaskan oil pipeline, offshore oil drilling, and nuclear power plants. On these and other issues, environmentalists have exerted a great deal of influence on Congress and state legislatures.

The concerns of environmentalists often come into direct conflict with energy goals. Environmentalists insist that, in the long run, energy supplies can be ensured without harming the environment or risking radiation exposure from nuclear power plants. On the issue of nuclear power plants, their arguments have had a profound impact on public policy. No new nuclear power plants have been approved since 1977, and many that had been in the works were canceled.[36] Short-term energy needs, however, have won out over environmental concerns in many other cases. Energy producers argue that environmentalists oppose nearly every new energy project. Given that there is no sign of a major drop in energy demands, they argue that some limited risks have to be taken. What is worse, they ask, an occasional oil spill off the shore of Alaska or long lines every day at the gas pumps? Thus, despite the opposition of environmentalists, Congress subsidized the massive trans-Alaskan pipeline, which a consortium of companies use to transport oil from Alaska's North Slope. Similarly, the strip-mining of coal continues despite constant objections from environmentalists. Group politics intensifies with the clash of two public interests, such as environmental protection and an ensured supply of energy.

EQUALITY INTERESTS

The Fourteenth Amendment guarantees equal protection under the law. American history, though, shows that this is easier said than done. Two sets of interest groups, representing minorities and women, have made equal rights their main policy goal. Chapter 5 reviewed the long history of the civil rights movement; this section is concerned with its policy goals and organizational base.

Equality at the polls, in housing, on the job, in education, and in all other facets of American life has long been the dominant goal of African-American groups. The oldest and largest of these groups is the National Association for the Advancement of Colored People (NAACP). It argued and won the monumental *Brown v. Board of Education* case in 1954. In that decision, the Supreme Court held that segregated schools were unconstitutional. The NAACP and other civil rights groups have also lobbied and pressed court cases to forbid discrimination in voting, employment, and housing. Although they have won many victories in principle, equality in practice has been much slower in coming. Today, civil rights groups continue to push for more effective affirmative action programs to ensure that minority groups are given educational and employment opportunities. In recent years, the NAACP's main vehicle has been the Fair Share program, which negotiates agreements with national and regional businesses to increase minority hiring and the use of minority contractors. Affirmative action is not so emotionally charged an issue as desegregation, but it too has been controversial.

When the NAACP was just starting up, suffragists were in the streets and legislative lobbies were demanding women's right to vote. The Nineteenth Amendment, ratified in 1920, guaranteed women the vote, but other guarantees of equal protection remained absent from the Constitution. More recently, women's rights groups, such as the National Organization for Women (NOW), have lobbied for an end to gender discrimination. Their primary goal has been the passage of the Equal Rights Amendment (ERA), which states that "equality of rights under the law shall not be abridged on account of sex."

In the first month after the ERA was approved by Congress in 1972, it was overwhelmingly ratified by 15 states. Even Texas and Kansas, fairly conservative states, voted decisively for the ERA in the first year. The quiet consensual politics of the ERA ratification process soon came to a boisterous end, however, when Phyllis Schlafly, a conservative activist from Alton, Illinois, began a highly visible STOP ERA movement. She and her followers argued the ERA would destroy the integrity of the family, require communal bathrooms, lead to women in combat, and eliminate legal protections that women already had. Their emotional appeal was just enough to stop the ERA 3 states short of the 38 necessary for ratification.

Though the ERA seems dead for the moment, NOW remains committed to enacting the protection that the amendment would have constitutionally guaranteed

Interest groups often clash on issues, as when Phyllis Schlafly's Eagle Forum battled NOW and other women's groups over ratification of the ERA. Here, Schlafly addresses a STOP ERA rally in the rotunda of the Illinois state capitol; her well-publicized efforts helped defeat pro-ERA forces in her home state.

by advocating the enactment of many individual statutes. As is often the case with interest group politics, issues are rarely settled once and for all; rather, they shift to different policy arenas.

Like other public interest groups, the Children's Defense Fund works against Olson's law of large groups; that is, it is easier to organize a small group with clear economic goals than it is to organize a large potential group with broader goals.

UNDERSTANDING INTEREST GROUPS

The problem of interest groups in America today remains much the same as Madison defined it over 200 years ago. A free society must allow for the representation of all groups that seek to influence political decision making. Yet groups are usually more concerned with their own self-interest than with the needs of society as a whole, and for democracy to work well, it is important that they not be allowed to assume a dominant position.

INTEREST GROUPS AND DEMOCRACY

James Madison's solution to the problems posed by interest groups was to create a wide-open system in which many groups would be able to participate. In such an extended sphere of influence, according to Madison, groups with opposing interests would counterbalance one another. Pluralist theorists believe that a rough approximation of the public interest emerges from this competition.

With the tremendous growth of interest group politics in recent years, some observers feel that Madison may at last have gotten his wish. For every group with an interest, there now seems to be a competing group to watch over it—not to mention public interest lobbies to watch over them all. Robert Salisbury argues that "the growth in the number, variety, and sophistication of interest groups represented in Washington" has transformed policymaking such that it "is not dominated so often by a relatively small number of powerful interest groups as it may once have been."[37] Paradoxically, Salisbury concludes that the increase in lobbying activity has resulted in less clout overall for interest groups—and better democracy.

Elite theorists clearly disagree with this conclusion and point to the proliferation of business PACs as evidence of more interest group corruption in American politics than ever. A democratic process requires a free and open exchange of ideas in which candidates and voters should be able to hear one another out, but PACs—the source of so much money in elections—distort the process. Elite theorists particularly note that wealthier interests are greatly advantaged by the PAC system. Business PACs have become the dominant force in the fund-raising game. Furthermore, the richest 3 percent of PACs account for over half of the campaign contributions from such groups.[38]

PACs can sometimes link money to politics at the highest levels. The old party machines may have bought votes in the voting booth; the new PACs are accused of buying votes in legislatures. Technology, especially television, makes American elections expensive; candidates need money to pay for high-tech campaigns, and PACs are able to supply that money. In return, they ask only to be remembered when their interests are clearly at stake.

Hyperpluralist theorists maintain that whenever a major interest group objects strongly to proposed legislation, policymakers will bend over backward to try to accommodate it. With the formation of so many groups in recent years, and with so many of them having influence in Washington, hyperpluralists argue that it has been increasingly difficult to accomplish major policy change in Washington. Thus, hyperpluralist theory offers a powerful explanation for the policy gridlock evident in American politics today.

INTEREST GROUPS AND THE SCOPE OF GOVERNMENT

Though individualistic, Americans are also very associational. As Alexis de Tocqueville wrote in the 1830s, "Americans of all ages, all conditions, and all dispositions constantly form associations."[39] This is not at all contradictory. By joining a number of political associations, Americans are able to politicize a variety of aspects of their own individualism. The multiplicity of the American interest group structure and the openness of American politics to inputs from interest groups allow individuals many channels for political participation and thus facilitate representation of individual interests.

Though individualism is most often treated in this book as being responsible for the relatively small scope of American government, when it works its way through interest group politics, the result is just the opposite. Individual interest groups fight to sustain government programs that are important to them, thereby making it hard for politicians ever to reduce the scope of government. Both President Carter and President Reagan remarked at the end of their time in office that their attempts to cut waste in federal spending had been frustrated by interest groups. In his farewell address, Carter "suggested that the reason he had so much difficulty in dealing with Congress was the fragmentation of power and decision making that was exploited by interest groups."[40] Similarly, Reagan remarked a month before leaving office that "special interest groups, bolstered by campaign contributions, pressure lawmakers into creating and defending spending programs."[41] Above all, most special interest groups strive to maintain established programs that benefit them.

However, one can also argue that the growth in the scope of government in recent decades accounts for a good portion of the proliferation of interest groups. The more areas in which the federal government has become involved, the more interest groups have developed to attempt to influence policy. As William Lunch notes, "a great part of the increase was occasioned by the new government responsibility for civil rights, environmental protection, and greater public health and safety."[42] For example, once the government got actively involved in protecting the environment, many groups sprung up to lobby for strong standards and enforcement. Given the tremendous effects of environmental regulations on many industries, it should come as no surprise that these industries also organized to ensure that their interests were taken into account. As Salisbury writes, many groups have "come to Washington out of need and dependence rather than because they have influence."[43] He argues that interest groups spend much of their time merely monitoring policy developments in order to alert their membership and develop reactive strategies.

SUMMARY

This chapter's discussion of group politics has familiarized you with the vast array of interest groups in American politics—all vying for policies they prefer. Pluralists see groups as the most important way people can have their policy preferences represented in government. Hyperpluralists, though, fear that too many groups are getting too much of what they want, skillfully working the many subgovernments in the American system. Elite theorists believe that a few wealthy individuals and multinational corporations exert control over the major decisions regarding distribution of goods and services.

A number of factors influence a group's success in achieving its policy goals. Most surprising is that small groups have an organizational advantage over large groups. Large groups often fall victim to the free-rider problem, which is explained by Olson's law of large groups. Both large and small groups can benefit from the intensity of their members' beliefs. Money always helps lubricate the wheels of power, though it is hardly a sure-fire guarantee of success.

Interest groups can choose from among four basic strategies to maximize their effectiveness. Lobbying is one well-known group strategy. Although the evidence on its influence is mixed, it is clear that lobbyists are most effective with those legislators already sympathetic to their side. Thus, electioneering becomes critical because it helps put supportive people in office. Often today, groups operate in the judicial as well as the legislative process, using litigation in the courts when lobbying fails or is not enough. Many also find it important to project a good image, employing public relations techniques to present themselves in the most favorable light.

This chapter also examined some of the major kinds of interest groups, particularly those concerned with economic, equality, and energy and environmental policy. Public interest lobbies claim to be different from other interest groups, representing, they say, an important aspect of the public interest. Recently there has been a rapid growth of single-interest groups, which focus narrowly on one issue and are not inclined to compromise.

The problem of controlling interest groups remains as crucial to democracy today as it was in Madison's time. Some scholars believe that the growth of interest groups has worked to divide political influence just as Madison hoped it would. Other scholars point to the PAC system as the new way in which special interests corrupt American democracy.

KEY TERMS

interest group
pluralist theory
elite theory
hyperpluralist theory
selective benefits
single-issue group
lobbying
electioneering

subgovernments
potential group
actual group
collective good
free-rider problem
Olson's law of large groups
political action committees (PACs)
***amicus curiae* briefs**
class action lawsuits
union shop
right-to-work laws
public interest lobbies

FOR FURTHER READING

Berry, Jeffrey M. *The Interest Group Society,* 3rd ed. New York: Longman, 1997. One of the best contemporary textbooks on interest groups.

Birnbaum, Jeffrey H., and Alan S. Murray. *Showdown at Gucci Gulch: Lawmakers, Lobbyists, and the Unlikely Triumph of Tax Reform.* New York: Vintage, 1987. A fascinating account of how the 1986 tax reform bill passed over the objections of the Gucci-clad lobbyists.

Cigler, Allan J., and Burdett A. Loomis, eds. *Interest Group Politics,* 4th ed. Washington, DC: Congressional Quarterly Press, 1995. An excellent collection of original articles on the modern interest group system.

Dye, Thomas R. *Who's Running America?* 6th ed. Englewood Cliffs, NJ: Prentice-Hall, 1995. A good summary of the elitist view of interest groups.

Godwin, R. Kenneth. *One Billion Dollars of Influence.* Chatham, NJ: Chatham House, 1988. An interesting look at the direct marketing of politics via direct mail.

Lowi, Theodore J. *The End of Liberalism,* 2nd ed. New York: Norton, 1979. A critique of the role of subgovernments and the excessive deference to interest groups in the American political system.

McFarland, Andrew S. *Common Cause: Lobbying in the Public Interest.* Chatham, NJ: Chatham House, 1984. A study of the major public interest lobby.

Olson, Mancur. *The Logic of Collective Action.* Cambridge, MA: Harvard University Press, 1965. Develops an economic theory of groups, showing how the cards are stacked against larger groups.

Rauch, Jonathan. *Demosclerosis: The Silent Killer of American Government.* New York: Random House, 1994. A good recent treatment of hyperpluralism in American politics.

Schlozman, Kay L., and John T. Tierney. *Organized Interests and American Democracy.* New York: Harper & Row, 1986. Survey results from a sample of Washington lobbyists are used to draw a portrait of the interest group system.

Walker, Jack L. *Mobilizing Interest Groups in America: Patrons, Professions and Social Movements.* Ann Arbor: University of Michigan Press, 1991. An important collection of essays on the formation and activities of interest groups.

INTERNET RESOURCES

www.aarp.org
The official site of the American Association of Retired Persons.

www.aflcio.org
The nation's largest labor association, the AFL-CIO, posts material at this site.

www.nea.org
The site of the National Education Association.

NOTES

1. Kay L. Schlozman and John T. Tierney, *Organized Interests and American Democracy* (New York: Harper & Row, 1986), 1.
2. Quoted in Schlozman and Tierney, *Organized Interests,* 261-262.
3. The classic work is David B. Truman, *The Governmental Process,* 2nd ed. (New York: Knopf, 1971).
4. Thomas R. Dye, *Who's Running America?,* 5th ed. (Englewood Cliffs, NJ: Prentice-Hall, 1990), 170.
5. Robert Engler, *The Brotherhood of Oil* (Chicago: University of Chicago Press, 1977).
6. Theodore J. Lowi, *The End of Liberalism,* 2nd ed. (New York: Norton, 1979).
7. See Lee Fritschler, *Smoking and Politics: Policy Making and the Federal Bureaucracy* (Englewood Cliffs, NJ: Prentice-Hall, 1983).
8. Morris P. Fiorina, *Congress: Keystone of the Washington Establishment,* 2nd ed. (New Haven, CT: Yale University Press, 1989), 122.
9. E. E. Schattschneider, *The Semisovereign People* (New York: Holt, Rinehart & Winston, 1960), 35.
10. Truman, *The Governmental Process,* 2nd ed., 511.
11. Mancur Olson, *The Logic of Collective Action* (Cambridge, MA: Harvard University Press, 1965), especially 9-36.
12. *Ibid.,* 35.
13. "Taking an Ax to the PACs," *Time,* August 20, 1984, p. 27.
14. Jeffrey H. Birnbaum and Alan S. Murray, *Showdown at Gucci Gulch: Lawmakers, Lobbyists, and the Unlikely Triumph of Tax Reform* (New York: Vintage, 1987).
15. *Ibid.,* 235.

16. Dennis Akey, ed., *Encyclopedia of Associations,* 1993, 27th ed. (Detroit: Gale Research Company, 1992).
17. Jonathan Rauch, *Demosclerosis: The Silent Killer of American Government* (New York: Random House, 1994), 39.
18. Andrew S. McFarland, *Common Cause: Lobbying in the Public Interest* (Chatham, NJ: Chatham House, 1984), 1.
19. Jack L. Walker, "The Origins and Maintenance of Interest Groups in America," *American Political Science Review* 77 (June 1983): 390-406.
20. Lester W. Milbrath, *The Washington Lobbyists* (Chicago: Rand McNally, 1963), 8.
21. Norman Ornstein and Shirley Elder, *Interest Groups, Lobbying, and Policymaking* (Washington, DC: Congressional Quarterly Press, 1978), 59-60.
22. Peter H. Stone, "Friends, After All," *National Journal,* October 22, 1994, 2440.
23. Raymond A. Bauer, Ithiel de Sola Pool, and Lewis A. Dexter, *American Business and Public Policy* (New York: Atherton, 1963).
24. Milbrath, *The Washington Lobbyists,* 354.
25. "No Risk Investments," *Common Cause News,* May 9, 1989.
26. The Sovern story is told in "Taking an Ax to PACs," *Time,* August 20, 1984, 27.
27. Karen Orren, "Standing to Sue: Interest Group Conflict in Federal Courts," *American Political Science Review* 70 (September 1976): 724.
28. Gregory A. Caldeira and John R. Wright, "*Amici Curiae* Before the Supreme Court: Who Participates, When, and How Much," *Journal of Politics* 52 (August 1990): 782-804.
29. Ronald J. Hrebenar and Ruth K. Scott, *Interest Group Politics in America,* 2nd ed. (Englewood Cliffs, NJ: Prentice-Hall, 1990), 201.
30. Quoted in Jeffrey M. Berry, *The Interest Group Society,* 2nd ed. (Glenview, IL: Scott, Foresman, 1989), 103.
31. Paul Edward Johnson, "Organized Labor in an Era of Blue-Collar Decline," in Allan J. Cigler and Burdett A. Loomis, eds., *Interest Group Politics,* 3rd ed. (Washington, DC: Congressional Quarterly Press, 1991), 33-62.
32. Schlozman and Tierney, *Organized Interests,* 68.
33. H. R. Mahood, *Interest Group Politics in America: A New Intensity* (Englewood Cliffs, NJ: Prentice-Hall, 1990), 162.
34. Jeffrey M. Berry, *Lobbying for the People* (Princeton, NJ: Princeton University Press, 1977), 7.
35. Christopher J. Bosso, "The Color of Money: Environmental Groups and the Pathologies of Fund Raising," in Allan J. Cigler and Burdett A. Loomis, *Interest Group Politics,* 4th ed. (Washington, DC: Congressional Quarterly Press, 1995), 102.
36. For an interesting analysis of how changes in the regulatory environment, congressional oversight, and public opinion altered the debate on nuclear power, see Frank R. Baumgartner and Bryan D. Jones, *Agendas and Instability in American Politics* (Chicago: University of Chicago Press, 1993).
37. Robert H. Salisbury, "The Paradox of Interest Groups in Washington—More Groups, Less Clout," in Anthony King, ed., *The New American Political System,* 2nd version. (Washington, DC: American Enterprise Institute, 1990), 204.
38. Paul S. Herrnson, *Congressional Elections: Campaigning at Home and in Washington* (Washington, DC: Congressional Quarterly Press, 1995), 108.
39. Alexis de Tocqueville, *Democracy in America,* vol. 2 (New York: Vintage, 1945), 114.
40. Hrebenar and Scott, *Interest Group Politics in America,* 2nd ed., 234.
41. Steven V. Roberts, "Angered President Blames Others for the Huge Deficit," *New York Times,* December 14, 1988, A16.
42. William M. Lunch, *The Nationalization of American Politics* (Berkeley: University of California Press, 1987), 206.
43. Salisbury, "The Paradox of Interest Groups," 229.

PART THREE

The Policymakers

Government is itself an art, one of the subtlest of the arts. It is the art of making men live together in peace with reasonable happiness.

— *Felix Frankfurter, Supreme Court Justice*

12 Congress

David Boren of Oklahoma decided to quit. He was a senior U.S. senator in good health and could look forward to years of prominence in making public policy. Yet he chose to leave office in mid-term to become president of the University of Oklahoma. In 1996, a record number of his colleagues decided to follow Boren's example and voluntarily retire from the Senate. They had had enough.

To most Americans, however, the job of U.S. senator seems rather glamorous. What citizens do not see is the 14-hour days spent dashing from one meeting to the next, the continuous travel between Washington and constituencies, the lack of time for reflection or exchange of ideas, the partisan rancor that permeates Congress, and—perhaps most important of all—the feeling that Congress is making little headway in solving the country's problems.

It is ironic that such frustrations exist in a body that each member puts blood, sweat, tears, and a great deal of money into joining. Yet it is difficult to get anything done. The movement of legislation through the congressional labyrinth has never been more complicated. Power is fragmented within Congress, and members of Congress can be, and often are, fiercely independent. Former Senate Majority Leader Howard Baker declared that moving the Senate is like "trying to push a wet noodle."

And then there is the president. Often the majority in Congress and the chief executive are of different political parties, as is the case in 1997-1998. Even if a bill passes Congress, it may be vetoed at the other end of Pennsylvania Avenue. Lack of agreement between the two branches may even lead to a shut down of the government, as happened during the battle over the 1996 budget.

"So," many senators and representatives ask themselves, "what is the point of serving? The public holds us in low regard, the pundits criticize us continuously, and we get little done. Isn't it better to be doing something else?"

The discontent with Congress among its own members is ironic. The framers of the Constitution conceived of the legislature as the center of policymaking in America. The great disputes over public policy were to be resolved there, not in the White House or the Supreme Court. Although the prominence of Congress has ebbed and flowed over the course of American history, in recent years Congress has been the true center of power in Washington.

Congress is not only our central policymaking branch, but is also our principal *representative* branch. As such, it lies at the heart of American democracy. How does Congress combine its roles of representing constituents *and* making effective public policy? Not very well, according to many critics. Some argue that Congress is too responsive to constituents and, especially, to organized interests and is thus unable to make difficult choices regarding public policy. Conversely, others argue that Congress is too insulated from ordinary citizens. Many critics even support efforts to force members of Congress to retire after serving just a few terms.

Other critics focus on Congress as the source of the expansion of government. If Congress is responsive to a multitude of interests and those interests desire government policies to aid them in some way, does the nature of Congress predispose it to continually increasing the size of the public sector? In addition, do the benefits of servicing constituents provide an incentive for members of Congress to tolerate—even to expand—an already big government?

Congress's tasks become more difficult each year. On any day a representative or senator can be required to make a sensible judgment about nuclear missiles, nuclear waste dumps, abortion, trade competition with Japan, the enormous federal deficit, the soaring costs of Social Security and Medicare, and countless other issues. President Clinton's 1993 health care reform proposal was 1,342 pages long and weighed 6 pounds. Just finding time to think about these issues—much less debate them—has become increasingly difficult.

Whether the job is frustrating or not, there is no shortage of men and women running for congressional office. The following sections will introduce you to these people.

THE REPRESENTATIVES AND SENATORS

Being a member of Congress is a difficult and unusual job. A person must be willing to spend considerable time, trouble, and money to obtain a crowded office on Capitol Hill. To nineteenth-century humorist Artemus Ward, such a quest was inexplicable: "It's easy to see why a man goes to the poorhouse or the penitentiary. It's because he can't help it. But why he should voluntarily go live in Washington is beyond my comprehension."

THE JOB

Hard work is perhaps the most prominent characteristic of a congressperson's job. Representatives and senators deeply resent common beliefs that they are overpaid, underworked, corrupt, and ineffective. Members have even commissioned their own time-and-motion studies of their efficiency to demonstrate that they do work hard (see Table 12.1). For example, the typical representative is a member of about six committees and subcommittees; a senator is a member of about ten. The laws of physics notwithstanding, members are often scheduled to be in two places at the same time.

TABLE 12.1 A REPRESENTATIVE'S "AVERAGE DAY"

ACTIVITY	AVERAGE TIME
In the House chamber	*Total 2:53 hours*
In committee/subcommittee work	
Hearings	26 minutes
Business	9 minutes
Markups	42 minutes
Other	7 minutes
	Total 1:24 hours
In office	
With constituents	17 minutes
With organized groups	9 minutes
With others	20 minutes
With staff aides	53 minutes
With other representatives	5 minutes
Answering mail	46 minutes
Preparing legislation, speeches	12 minutes
Reading	11 minutes
On the telephone	26 minutes
	Total 3:19 hours
In other Washington locations	
With constituents at the Capitol	9 minutes
At events	33 minutes
With leadership	3 minutes
With other representatives	11 minutes
With informal groups	8 minutes
In party meetings	5 minutes
Personal time	28 minutes
Other	25 minutes
	Total 2:02 hours
Other	*Total 1:40 hours*
Total average representative's day	*11:18 hours*

SOURCE: U.S. House of Representatives, Commission on Administrative Review, *Administrative Reorganization and Legislative Management* (95th Congress, 1st session, 1977, H. Doc. 95-232): 18-19.

There are attractions to the job, however. First and foremost is power. Members of Congress make key decisions about important matters of public policy. In addition, the salary and the perks that go with the job make it tolerable. Members of Congress receive the following:

- A salary of $133,644, high by most Americans' standards, but well below that of hundreds of corporate presidents who earn several times as much
- Generous retirement benefits
- Office space in Washington and in their constituencies, usually cramped with staffers
- A substantial congressional staff who serve individual members, committees, and party leaders

- Handsome travel allowances to see their constituents each year, plus opportunities to travel at low fares or even free to foreign nations on congressional inquiries (what critics call "junkets")
- Franking privileges—the free use of the mail system to communicate with constituents, and machines that duplicate a member's signature in real ink (it will even smear if a constituent should test its authenticity)
- Plenty of small privileges, such as free flowers from the National Botanical Gardens, research services from the Library of Congress, and exercise rooms and pools

Despite their gains in recent congressional elections, women are the most underrepresented demographic group in Congress. Here, 8 female senators of both parties celebrate their success.

Despite the salaries, the perquisites, and the thousands of staff members, Congress is relatively inexpensive. Per citizen, what Americans spend annually on running the nation's legislature is about the cost of a hamburger, fries, and cola at a favorite fast-food franchise.

THE MEMBERS

There are 535 members of Congress. An even hundred, two from each state, are members of the Senate. The other 435 are members of the House of Representatives. The Constitution specifies only that members of the House must be at least 25 years old and must have been American citizens for 7 years; senators must be at least 30 and must have been American citizens for 9 years. In addition, all members of Congress must be residents of the states from which they are elected.

Members of Congress are not typical or average Americans, however. Elite theorists are quick to point out that members come largely from occupations with high status and usually have substantial incomes. Although calling the Senate a "millionaire's club" is an exaggeration, the proportion of millionaires and near-millionaires is much higher in Congress than in an average crowd of 535 people. A glance at a collective portrait of the Congress, such as that in Table 12.2, reveals what an atypical collection of Americans it is. Business and law are the dominant prior occupations; other elite occupations such as academia are also well represented.

Law attracts persons interested in politics and provides the flexibility (and often the financial support of a law firm) to wage election campaigns. In addition, many positions in government in which aspiring members of Congress can make their marks, such as district attorney, are reserved for lawyers.

Nine percent (or 37 voting members) of the House are African American (compared with about 12 percent of the total population), and most (but not all) of these representatives have been elected from overwhelmingly African-American constituencies. No state is predominantly African American, and there is only 1 African American in the Senate. There are 18 Hispanics in the House and none in the Senate. In terms of numbers, however, women are the most underrepresented group; more than half of the population is female, but only 9 senators and 51 voting representatives are female (the representative from Washington, DC, does not vote).

How important are the personal characteristics of members of Congress? Because power in Congress is highly decentralized, the backgrounds of representatives and senators can be important if they influence how issues are prioritized and how officials vote on these issues. Can a group of predominantly white, upper-middle-class, middle-aged Protestant males adequately represent a much more diverse population?[1] On the other hand, would a group of more typical citizens be more effective in making major policy decisions?

Obviously, members of Congress cannot claim *descriptive* representation—that is, representing constituents by mirroring their personal, politically relevant characteristics. They may, however, engage in *substantive* representation—representing the interests of groups.[2] For example, members of Congress with a background of wealth and privilege, such as Senator Edward Kennedy, can be champions of the interests of the poor. Moreover, most members of Congress have lived for many years in the constituencies they represent and share the beliefs and attitudes of at least a large proportion of their constituents. If they do not share such perspectives, they may find it difficult to keep their seats. The next sections will examine just

TABLE 12.2 A PORTRAIT OF THE 105TH CONGRESS: SOME STATISTICS

CHARACTERISTIC	HOUSE (435 TOTAL)	SENATE (100 TOTAL)
Party		
Democrat	207	45
Republican	227	55
Independent	1	—
Sex		
Men	384	91
Women	51	9
Race		
Asian	3	2
African American	37	1
Hispanic	18	0
White and other	377	97
Average Age	52 years	58 years
Religion		
Protestant	274	62
Roman Catholic	127	24
Jewish	25	10
Other and unspecified	9	4
Prior Occupation[a]		
Law	172	53
Business and banking	181	33
Education	74	13
Public service/politics	100	26
Agriculture	22	8
Journalism	12	9
Real estate	23	5

[a]Some members specify more than one occupation.

SOURCE: *Congressional Quarterly Weekly Report,* January 4, 1997, 27-30.

how members of Congress obtain their positions in the first place.

CONGRESSIONAL ELECTIONS

Congressional elections are wearing, expensive,[3] and, as you will see, generally foregone conclusions—yet the role of politician is the most universal one in Congress. Men and women may run for Congress to forge new policy initiatives, but they also run because they are politicians, they enjoy politics, and they consider a position in Congress near the top of their chosen profession. Even if they dislike politics, without reelection they will not be around long enough to shape policy.

WHO WINS?

Everyone in Congress is a politician, and politicians continually have their eyes on the next election. The players in the congressional election game are the incumbents and the challengers.

FIGURE 12.1 THE INCUMBENCY FACTOR IN CONGRESSIONAL ELECTIONS

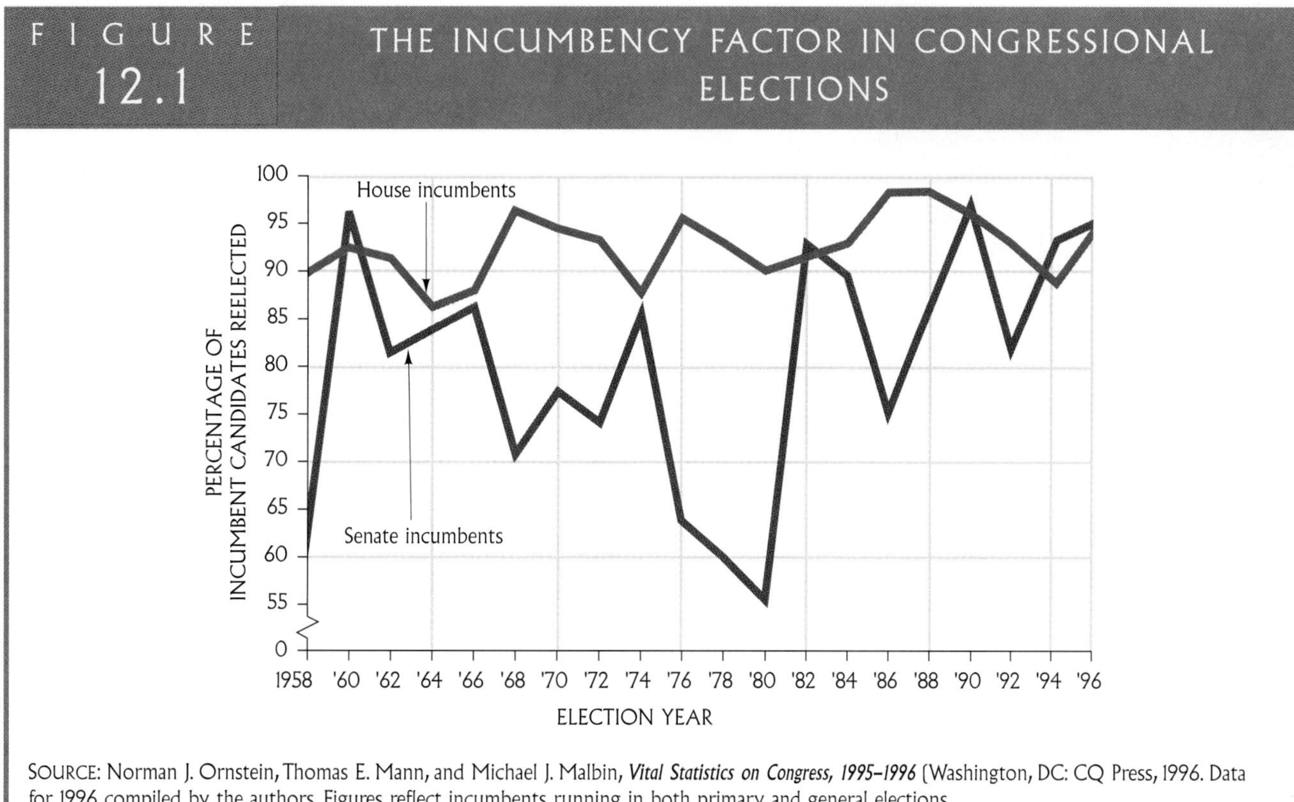

SOURCE: Norman J. Ornstein, Thomas E. Mann, and Michael J. Malbin, *Vital Statistics on Congress, 1995–1996* (Washington, DC: CQ Press, 1996. Data for 1996 compiled by the authors. Figures reflect incumbents running in both primary and general elections.

Incumbents are individuals who already hold office. Sometime during each term, the incumbent must decide whether to run again or to retire voluntarily. Most decide to run for reelection. They enter their party's primary, almost always emerge victorious (two incumbents lost in 1996), and typically win in the November general election, too. Indeed, the most important fact about congressional elections is this: *Incumbents usually win.*

Thus, the key to ensuring an opponent's defeat is not having more money than the opponent, although that helps. It is not being more photogenic, although that helps, too. The best thing a candidate can have going for him or her is simply to be the incumbent (see Figure 12.1). Even in a year of great political upheaval such as 1994, in which the Republicans gained 8 seats in the Senate and 53 seats in the House, 92 percent of incumbent senators and 89 percent of incumbent representatives won their bids for reelection.

Not only do more than 90 percent of the incumbents seeking reelection win, but most of them win with more than 60 percent of the vote. Perhaps most astonishing of all is the fact that even when challengers' positions on the issues are closer to the voters' positions, incumbents still tend to win.[4]

The picture for the Senate is a little different. Even though senators still have a good chance of beating back a challenge, the odds are often not as handsome as for House incumbents; senators typically win by narrower margins.

One reason for the greater competition in the Senate is that an entire state is almost always more diverse than a congressional district and thus provides a larger base for opposition to an incumbent. At the same time, senators have less personal contact with their constituencies, which on average are nearly ten times larger than those of members of the House of Representatives. Senators also receive more coverage in the media than representatives do and are more likely to be held accountable on controversial issues. Moreover, senators tend to draw more visible challengers, such as governors or members of the House, who are already known to voters and who have substantial financial backing—a factor that lessens the advantages of incumbency. Many of these challengers, as you might expect, know that the Senate is a stepping stone to national prominence and sometimes even the presidency.

Despite their success at reelection, incumbents often feel quite vulnerable. As Thomas Mann put it, members of Congress perceive themselves as "unsafe

Members of Congress who do not share their constituents' economic and social backgrounds can nonetheless represent their concerns. Senator Edward Kennedy, for example, born into one of America's wealthiest families, has championed the poor and underprivileged throughout his career. Here, Kennedy speaks to flood victims in West Virginia.

at any margin."[5] Thus, they have been raising and spending more campaign funds, sending more mail to their constituents, visiting their states and districts more often, and staffing more local offices than ever before.[6] They realize that with the decline of partisan loyalty in the electorate, they bear more of the burden of obtaining votes.

THE ADVANTAGES OF INCUMBENTS

There are several possible explanations for the success of incumbents. One is that voters know how their elected representatives vote on important policy issues and agree with their stands, sending them back to Washington to keep up the good work. This, however, is usually not the case. In fact, voters are rather oblivious to how their senators and representatives actually vote.[7] As one expert put it, "Mass public knowledge of congressional candidates declines precipitously once we move beyond simple recognition, generalized feelings, and incumbent job ratings."[8]

Another possibility is that voter assessments of presidential candidates influence their voting for Congress. Most stories of presidential "coattails" (so called because other candidates were said to ride into office by clinging to presidential coattails), however, seem to be just stories.[9] Bill Clinton ran *behind* almost every winning Democrat in Congress in both 1992 and 1996. Nor do members of Congress gain or lose very much from the ups and downs of the economy.[10]

What accounts for the success of congressional incumbents? Members of Congress engage in three primary activities that increase the probability of their reelection: advertising, credit claiming, and position taking.[11]

Advertising. For members of Congress, advertising means much more than placing ads in the newspapers and on television. Most congressional advertising takes place between elections in the form of contact with constituents. The goal is *visibility*.

Members of Congress work hard to get themselves known in their constituencies. As Table 12.3 demonstrates, they usually succeed. Not surprisingly, members concentrate on staying visible. Trips home are frequent. In a typical week, members spend time in their home districts.[12]

Credit Claiming. Congresspersons also engage in credit claiming, which involves personal and district service. One member told Richard Fenno about the image he tried to cultivate in his constituency:

> [I have] a very high recognition factor. And of all the things said about me, none of them said, "He's a conservative or a liberal," or "He votes this way on such and such an issue." None of that at all. There were two things said. One, "He works hard." Two, "He works for us." Nothing more than that. So we made it our theme, "O'Connor gets things done"; and we emphasized the dams, the highways, the buildings, the casework.[13]

Morris Fiorina has stressed this close link between service and success.[14] Members of Congress, he says, *can* go to the voters and stress their policymaking record. They *can* make promises about their stands on new policy issues on the agenda. The problem with facing the voters on one's record—past, present, and future—is that policy positions make enemies as well as friends. A member of Congress' vote for reducing government spending may win some friends, but it will make enemies of voters who happen to link that vote with service cutbacks. Besides, a congressperson can almost never show that he or she alone was responsible for a major policy. Being only one of 435 members of the House or of 100 senators, a person can hardly promise to end inflation, cut taxes, or achieve equal rights for women single-handedly.

One thing, though, always wins friends and almost never makes enemies: *servicing the constituency*. There are two ways in which members of Congress can service their constituencies: through casework and through the pork barrel. **Casework** is helping constituents as individuals—cutting through some bureau-

TABLE 12.3 CONTACT WITH MEMBERS OF THE HOUSE OF REPRESENTATIVES

Members of Congress have high levels of contact with their constituents, giving them a substantial advantage in visibility relative to their election challengers. This contact is the result of a sustained effort and not simply a product of advertisements during an election campaign. It is continuous attention to constituents that brings visibility.

TYPE OF CONTACT	INCUMBENTS	CHALLENGERS
Received mail from	49%	18%
Saw on television	54%	27%
Read something about	49%	23%
Heard on radio	26%	13%
Met personally	11%	3%
Saw at meeting	9%	2%
Talked to staff	10%	3%

SOURCE: 1994 National Election Study.

cratic red tape to give people what they think they have a right to get. The **pork barrel** is the mighty list of federal projects, grants, and contracts available to cities, businesses, colleges, and institutions.

Do you have trouble getting your check from the Social Security Administration on time? Call your congressperson; he or she can cut red tape. Do you have trouble getting federal bureaucrats to respond to Pottsville's request for federal construction money? Call your congressperson. Representatives and senators can single-handedly take credit for each of these favors. Fiorina put it like this:

> Even committee chairmen have a difficult time claiming credit for a piece of major legislation, let alone a rank-and-file congressman. Ah, but casework, and the pork barrel. In dealing with the bureaucracy, the congressman is not merely one vote in 435. Rather he is a nonpartisan power, someone whose phone calls snap an office to attention. He is not kept on hold. The constituent who receives aid believes that his congressman and his congressman alone got results. Similarly, congressmen find it easy to claim credit for federal projects awarded in their districts. The congressman may have instigated the project in the first place, issued regular progress reports, and ultimately announced the award through his office. Maybe he can't claim credit for the 1965 Voting Rights Act, but he can take credit for Littletown's spanking new sewage treatment plant.[15]

Representative Silvio Conte used a pig nose and ears to protest pork barrel spending—until he wanted multimillion dollar federal grants for his Massachusetts district. Because credit claiming is so important to reelection, members of Congress rarely pass up the opportunity to increase federal spending in their state or district.

Getting things done for the folks back home often gets an incumbent the chance to serve them again.

As a result of the advantages of incumbency in advertising and credit claiming, incumbents, especially in the House, are usually much better known and have a more favorable public image than do their opponents.[16] Shrewd use of the resources available to incumbents may give them an advantage, but congressional elections are not determined solely by casework and pork barrel.[17] Other factors play a role as well.

Position Taking. Members of Congress must also engage in position taking on matters of public policy when they vote on issues and when they respond to constituents' questions about where they stand on issues. You have seen that in establishing their public images, members of Congress emphasize their personal qualities as experienced, hard-working, trustworthy representatives who have served their constituencies—an image often devoid of partisan or programmatic content. Nevertheless, all members must take policy stands, and the positions they take may affect the outcome of an election, especially if the issues are on matters salient to voters and the candidates' stands differ from those of a majority of their constituents. This is especially true in elections for the Senate, in which issues are likely to play a greater role than in House elections.

Weak Opponents. Another advantage for incumbents is that they are likely to face weak opponents. Confronted with the advantages of incumbency, potentially effective opponents are often unlikely to risk challenging members of the House.[18] Those individuals who do run are usually not well known or well qualified and lack both experience and organizational and financial backing.[19] The lack of adequate campaign funds is a special burden, because challengers need money to become as well known to voters as incumbents are from their advertising and credit claiming.[20]

THE ROLE OF PARTY IDENTIFICATION

At the base of every electoral coalition are the members of the candidate's party in the constituency. Although party loyalty at the voting booth is not so strong as it was a generation ago, it is still a good predictor of voting behavior. In the 1996 congressional elections, for example, nearly 90 percent of voters who identified with a party voted for the House candidates of their party.[21] Most members of Congress represent constituencies in which their party is in the majority.

DEFEATING INCUMBENTS

In light of the advantages of incumbents, it is reasonable to ask why anyone challenges them at all. One of the main reasons is simply that challengers are often naive about their chances of winning. Not blessed with money for expensive polls, they rely on friends and local party leaders, who often tell them what they want to hear. Sometimes they do get some unexpected help; incumbents almost have to beat themselves, and some do.

An incumbent tarnished by scandal or corruption becomes instantly vulnerable. Clearly, voters do take out their anger at the polls. For example, representatives who bounced large numbers of checks at the House bank were much more likely to lose their seats in the 1992 elections than their more fiscally responsible colleagues.[22] In a close election, negative publicity can turn victory into defeat.[23]

Incumbents may also be redistricted out of their familiar turfs. After each federal census, Congress reapportions its membership. States that have gained significantly in population will be given more seats; states that have lost substantial population will lose one or more of their seats. The state legislatures must then redraw their states' district lines; one incumbent may be moved into another's district, where the two must battle for one seat. A state party majority is more likely to move into a single district two of the opposition party's representatives than two of its own.

Finally, major political tidal waves occasionally roll across the country, leaving defeated incumbents in their wake. One such wave occurred in 1994, when the public mood turned especially sour and voters took out their frustration on Democratic incumbents, defeating 34 in the House and 2 in the Senate.

MONEY IN CONGRESSIONAL ELECTIONS

When an incumbent is not running for reelection and the seat is open, there is greater likelihood of competition. If the party balance in a constituency is such that either party has a chance of winning, each side may offer a strong candidate—each with enough money to establish name recognition among the voters. Most of the turnover in the membership of Congress results from vacated seats, particularly in the House.

It costs a great deal more money to elect a Congress than to elect a president. In 1996 Bill Clinton, Bob Dole, and Ross Perot together spent about $200 million on their presidential campaigns. The 1996 general election Senate races alone cost at least $220 million, and House candidates spent another $406 million. In addition, the two political parties spent another $66 million on behalf of their candidates. Thus, the cost of congressional elections in the 1995-1996 election cycle—for those who made it to the general election—was $692 million!

In the 1996 Senate elections, the average winner spent over $4.7 million. In the 1996 House elections,

TABLE 12.4

SPENDING IN CONGRESSIONAL ELECTIONS, 1996

A typical major-party candidate who wins the general election for a House seat spends about $660,000 on the campaign; Senate candidates spend more than five times as much. Incumbents, especially in House elections, have a considerable advantage over their opponents, which, of course, is one reason why incumbents do so well. The real spending contest, though, is in districts where the seat is open. When there is no incumbent and each party feels it has a chance to win, the spending is much greater than when a challenger faces an incumbent.

HOUSE	AVERAGE EXPENDITURE	SENATE	AVERAGE EXPENDITURE
Incumbent	$645,000	Incumbent	$4,156,000
Challenger	$247,000	Challenger	$2,530,000
Open seat	$603,000	Open seat	$3,138,000

SOURCE: Federal Election Commission, 1996, 1997.

the average winning candidate spent more than $673,000. An example of spending in congressional elections can be found in Table 12.4.

Aside from the fact that candidates spend enormous sums on campaigns for Congress, it is important to ask where this money comes from and what it buys. Although most of the money spent in congressional elections comes from individuals, 29 percent (about $192 million) of the funds raised by candidates for Congress in 1996 came from the 4,079 Political Action Committees (PACs) (see Chapters 5, 9, and 11). Critics of PACs offer plenty of complaints about the present system of campaign finance. Why, they ask, is money spent to pay the campaign costs of a candidate already heavily favored to win? In 1994, incumbents in both houses got $131 million from PACs, challengers received $26 million, and $34 million went to candidates for open seats. Even more interesting is that PACs often make contributions *after* the election. Congressional candidates elected in 1994, for example, received nearly $600,000 from just business-related PACs in the 2 months following the election. Much of this money came from groups that had supported the representatives' opponents during the election.[24]

There is a continuous debate in America today on whether PACs "buy" votes in Congress. (See "You Are the Policymaker: Should We Do Away with PACs?") Although this question remains unresolved, everyone agrees that at the very least, PACs seek *access* to policymakers. Thus, they give most of their money to incumbents, who are likely to win anyway; when they support someone who loses, they quickly make amends and contribute to the winner. PACs want to keep the lines of communication open and create a receptive atmosphere in which to be heard. Because each PAC is limited to an expenditure of $5,000 per candidate (most give less), a single PAC can at most account for only a small percentage of a winner's total spending. If one PAC does not contribute to a candidate, there are lots more PACs from which to seek funds.

Some organized interests circumvent the limitations on contributions, however, and create or contribute to several PACs. This tactic may increase their leverage with those to whom they contribute. As we saw in Chapter 11, in the late 1980s one tycoon, Charles Keating, managed to contribute $1.3 million to the campaigns of five senators. These senators then interceded with the Federal Home Loan Bank Board to avoid (for a while, at least) enforcement of banking regulations on Keating's savings and loan. Many people saw a connection between the campaign contributions and the senators' actions.

Aside from the question of whether money buys influence, what does it buy the candidates who spend it? In 1996, Guy Millner spent more than $9 million for a Senate seat in Georgia and still lost. In 1994, Californian Michael Huffington spent nearly $30 million—most of it his own money—which was about three times the expenditures of his rival, Senator Dianne Feinstein, and still lost. Oliver North spent about $20 million in the much smaller state of Virginia, and he lost as well. Obviously, spending a lot of money in a campaign is no guarantee of success.

SHOULD WE DO AWAY WITH PACS?

You Are the Policymaker

The effect of PAC campaign contributions on congressional votes has become a perennial issue on Capitol Hill. Critics of PACs, including Common Cause, are convinced that PACs are not trying to elect senators and representatives but trying to influence them. As a result, critics call for the elimination of PACs.

Critics are fond of suggesting links between donations and congressional votes. For example, in November 1983, the 250 House members who voted to retain dairy price supports had received $1.7 million—about $6,800 each—from a dairy PAC. Most critics fear the worst; Gregg Easterbrook summarizes his argument this way: "Money can buy individual congressmen's votes on a bill, or distort congressmen's thinking on an issue—normally all an interest group needs to achieve its ends."

However, others argue that connection is not causation. Most senators and representatives, they say, are firm in their conviction that their decisions are not affected by PAC contributions. Many political scientists are also skeptical of the influence of PACs. There is little systematic evidence that contributions affect outcomes on voting in Congress.

PACs usually contribute to those who already agree with them or to those who are likely to win (or who have already won). In addition, because national organizations are dependent on local units for raising money, Washington lobbyists must be responsive to the desires of local contributors. Thus, funds often go to candidates that the lobbyists feel are undeserving, which weakens their bargaining power. Moreover, PACs are not "outside" interests; they usually contribute to or lobby members of Congress from districts or states to which they have geographic ties.

Of course, PACs may influence voting in Congress by reinforcing members in their views and activating some to work on behalf of the interests PACs represent, rather than by converting ("buying") those opposed to the interests' goals. Such influence is less dramatic than conversion, but it can be crucial to legislative success.

President Bush called for banning business, labor, and trade association PACs—the source of most of the millions that PACs give congressional candidates. Less concerned about selling their votes than losing their seats, members of Congress did not support the president. They also could not agree to President Clinton's proposal to limit the amount that PACs could give to a congressional candidate.

Whatever *your* conclusion about PACs, keep Bo Pilgrim in mind. In July 1989, Lonnie (Bo) Pilgrim, a millionaire chicken farmer with interests in legislation, visited the chamber of the Texas state Senate and handed several senators checks for $10,000—with blanks for them to fill in their names.

SOURCES: Easterbrook's quote is from his "What's Wrong with Congress?" *Atlantic Monthly*, December 1984, 70. Other information is from John R. Wright, "PACs, Contributions, and Roll Calls," *American Political Science Review* 79 (June 1985): 400-414; Janet M. Grenzke, "PACs and the Congressional Supermarket: The Currency Is Complex," *American Journal of Political Science* 33 (February 1989): 1-24; John R. Wright, "PAC Contributions, Lobbying, and Representation," *Journal of Politics* 51 (August 1989): 713-729; Richard L. Hall and Frank W. Wayman, "Buying Time: Moneyed Interests and the Mobilization of Bias in Congressional Committees," *American Political Science Review* 84 (September 1990), 797-820; and John R. Wright, "Contributions, Lobbying, and Committee Voting in the U.S. House of Representatives," *American Political Science Review* 84 (June 1990), 417-438.

Money is important for challengers, however. The more they spend, the more votes they receive. Money buys them name recognition and a chance to be heard. Incumbents, by contrast, already have high levels of recognition among their constituents and benefit less from campaign spending; what matters most is how much their opponents spend. Challengers have to raise a lot of money if they hope to succeed in defeating an incumbent, but they usually are substantially outspent by incumbents.[25] In contests for open seats, the candidate who spends the most usually wins.

STABILITY AND CHANGE

Because incumbents usually win reelection, there is some stability in the membership of Congress. This provides the opportunity for representatives and senators to gain some expertise in dealing with complex questions of public policy. At the same time, it also may insulate them from the winds of political change. Safe seats make it more difficult for citizens to "send a message to Washington" with their votes. Particularly in the House, it takes a large shift in votes to affect the outcomes of most elections.

To increase turnover in the membership of Congress, some reformers have proposed *term limitations* for representatives and senators.[26] Most such proposals would restrict members of Congress to 6 or 12 consecutive years in office. Twenty-three states have enacted term limitations for members of their state legislatures.

Opponents of term limitations object to the loss of experienced legislators and of the American people's ability to vote for whomever they please. In addition, they add, there is plenty of new blood in the legislature: At the beginning of the 105th Congress (1997), more than half the members of the House and 40 percent of the senators had no more than 4 years' experience in their chambers. Moreover, recent research indicates that the movement of party fortunes in the House follows the movement of citizen preferences for public policy.[27]

Proponents of term limits suffered two setbacks in 1995 when Congress failed to pass a constitutional amendment on term limitations (it also failed in 1997), and when the Supreme Court, in *U.S. Term Limits, Inc. et al. v. Thornton et al.*, decided that state-imposed term limits on members of Congress were unconstitutional. In the meantime, most people seem comfortable with their *own* representatives and senators and appear content to reelect them again and again.

HOW CONGRESS IS ORGANIZED TO MAKE POLICY

Of all the senators' and representatives' roles, making policy is toughest. Congress is a collection of generalists trying to make policy on specialized topics. Members are short of time and of expertise as well. As amateurs in almost every subject, they are surrounded by people who know (or claim to know) more than they do—lobbyists, agency administrators, even their own staffs. Even if they had time to study all the issues thoroughly, making wise national policy would be difficult. If economists disagree about policies to fight unemployment, how are legislators to know which policies may work better than others?

Thus, when ringing bells announce a roll-call vote, representatives or senators rush into the chamber from their offices or from a hearing—often unsure of what is being voted on. Frequently, "uncertain of their position, members of Congress will seek out one or two people who serve on the committee which considered and reported the bill, in whose judgment they have confidence."[28]

The Founders gave Congress' organization just a hint of specialization when they split it into the House and the Senate. The complexity of today's issues require much more specialization. Congress tries to cope with these demands through its elaborate committee system, as we discuss in the following sections.

AMERICAN BICAMERALISM

A **bicameral legislature** is a legislature divided into two houses. The U.S. Congress is bicameral, as is every American state legislature except Nebraska's, which has one house (unicameral). As we learned in Chapter 2, the Connecticut Compromise at the Constitutional Convention created a bicameral Congress. Each state is guaranteed 2 senators, and its number of representatives is determined by the population of the state (California has 52 representatives; Alaska, Delaware, Montana, North Dakota, South Dakota, Vermont, and Wyoming have just 1 each). By creating a bicameral Congress, the Constitution set up yet another check and balance. No bill can be passed unless both House and Senate agree on it; each body can thus veto the policies of the other. Some of the basic differences between the two houses are shown in Table 12.5.

The House. More than four times larger than the Senate, the House is also more institutionalized—that is, more centralized, more hierarchical, and less anarchic.[29] Party loyalty to leadership and party-line voting are more common in the House than in the Senate. Partly because there are more members, leaders in the House do more leading than leaders in the Senate. First-term House members are more likely to be seen and not heard, and they have less power than senior representatives.[30]

Both the House and the Senate set their own agendas. Both use committees, which we will examine shortly, to winnow down the thousands of bills introduced. One institution unique to the House, however, plays a key role in agenda setting: the **House Rules Committee**. This committee reviews most bills coming from a House committee before they go to the full House. Performing a traffic cop function, the committee gives each bill a "rule," which schedules the bill on

TABLE 12.5 HOUSE VERSUS SENATE: SOME KEY DIFFERENCES

CHARACTERISTIC	HOUSE OF REPRESENTATIVES	SENATE
Constitutional powers	Must initiate all revenue bills; must pass all articles of impeachment	Must give "advice and consent" to many presidential nominations; must approve treaties; tries impeached officials
Membership	435 members	100 members
Term of office	2 years	6 years
Centralization of power	More centralized; stronger leadership	Less centralized; weaker leadership
Political prestige	Less prestige	More prestige
Role in policy	More influential on budget; more specialized	More influential on foreign affairs; less specialized
Turnover	Small	Moderate
Role of seniority	More important in determining power	Less important in determining power

the calendar, allots time for debate, and sometimes even specifies what kind of amendments may be offered. The Rules Committee is generally responsive to the House leadership, in part because the Speaker of the House now appoints the committee's members.

The Senate. The Constitution's framers thought the Senate would protect elite interests against the tendencies of the House to protect the masses. Thus, to the House they gave the power of initiating all revenue bills and of impeaching officials; to the Senate they gave the responsibility for ratifying all treaties, for confirming important presidential nominations (including nominations to the Supreme Court), and for trying impeached officials. Experience has shown that when the same party controls each chamber, the Senate is just as liberal as, and perhaps more liberal than, the House.[31] The real differences between the bodies lie in the Senate's organization and decentralized power.

Smaller than the House, the Senate is also less disciplined and less centralized. Today's senators are more nearly equal in power than representatives are. They are also more nearly equal in power than senators have been in the past. Even incoming senators sometimes get top committee assignments; they may even become chairs of key subcommittees. In 1981, the Senate had 16 newcomers, none of them eager to take a back seat to old-timers. For example, in 1981 Dan Quayle, who would become vice president 8 years later, was elected to the Senate from Indiana and made his mark chairing a subcommittee handling a key bill on job training.

Committees and the party leadership are important in determining the Senate's legislative agenda, just as they are in the House. Party leaders do for Senate scheduling what the Rules Committee does in the House. One phenomenon unique to the Senate is the **filibuster**. In the House, debate can be ended by a simple majority vote. Priding itself on freedom of discussion, the Senate in the past permitted unlimited debate on a bill. But if debate is unlimited, opponents of a bill may try to talk it to death; Strom Thurmond of South Carolina once held forth for a full 24 hours. Yielding at times to a fresh voice, filibusterers can tie up the legislative agenda until proponents decide to give up their battle. Filibusters were once a favorite device of Southern senators to prevent civil rights legislation, but today they are commonly used by opponents of all types of legislation (see "Since Kennedy: The Dramatic Growth of the Filibuster").[32] Sixty members present and voting can halt a filibuster by voting for *cloture* on debate, but many senators are reluctant to vote for cloture for fear of setting a precedent to be used against them when *they* want to filibuster.

CONGRESSIONAL LEADERSHIP

Leading 100 senators or 435 representatives in Congress—each jealous of his or her own power and responsible to no higher power than the con-

SINCE KENNEDY

The Dramatic Growth of the Filibuster

A Senate filibuster is one of the most unusual tactics in American politics. At its core it raises profound questions about American democracy, because it is used by a minority, sometimes a minority of one, to defeat a majority. The Founders considered numerous schemes for requiring supermajorities to pass legislation, but, as we learned in Chapter 2, they rejected them except in a few matters such as convictions for impeachment, ratifying treaties, and amending the Constitution.

Senators have done what the Founders would not do, however, and created rules that allow minorities to stop clear majorities from passing legislation. The filibuster was never used until 1841, and in John F. Kennedy's time, 120 years later, the filibuster was reserved for matters of grave importance. There was a mutual understanding that a bill could be "filibustered" three times, and usually senators availed themselves of only one such opportunity.

Things have changed dramatically since the early 1960s. More than half of all filibusters have occurred since 1975, and during the presidency of Bill Clinton filibusters have become the weapon of first resort on even the most trivial matters. By the end of 1994, each senator knew that he or she had at least six opportunities to filibuster a single bill and that these opportunities could be used one after another. In addition, the tactical uses of a filibuster have expanded. A senator might threaten to filibuster an unrelated measure in order to gain concessions on a bill he or she opposes.

You might reasonably ask, "If the minority is blocking the majority, why doesn't the majority change the rules to prevent filibusters?" The answer is twofold. First, changing the rules requires 67 votes. It is always difficult to obtain the agreement of two-thirds of the Senate on a controversial matter. Second, every senator knows that he or she might be in the minority on an issue at some time. A filibuster gives senators who are in the minority a powerful weapon for defending their (or their constituencies') interests.

In the meantime, Americans complain about gridlock in Congress. Nevertheless, the Senate has decided that it is more concerned with allowing senators to block legislation they oppose than in expediting the passage of legislation a majority favors.

stituency—is no easy task. "Few members of the House, fewer still in the Senate," Robert Peabody once wrote, "consider themselves followers."[33] Chapter 8 discussed the party-in-government. Much of the leadership in Congress is really party leadership. There are a few formal posts whose occupants are chosen by nonparty procedures, but those who have the real power in the congressional hierarchy are those whose party put them there (see Table 12.6).

The House. Chief among leadership positions in the House of Representatives is the **Speaker of the House**. This is the only legislative office mandated by the Constitution. In practice, the majority party does the choosing. Before each Congress begins, the majority party presents its candidate for Speaker, who—because this person attracts the unanimous support of the majority party—turns out to be a shoo-in. Typically, the Speaker is a senior member of the party. Newt Gingrich of Georgia was elected Speaker in 1995. The Speaker is also two heartbeats away from the presidency, being second in line (after the vice president) to succeed a president who resigns, dies in office, or is impeached.

Years ago, the Speaker was king of the congressional mountain. Autocrats such as "Uncle Joe Cannon" and "Czar Reed" ran the House like a fiefdom. A great revolt in 1910 whittled down the Speaker's powers and gave some of them to committees, but six decades later, members of the House restored some of the Speaker's powers. Today the Speaker of the House has some important formal powers. The Speaker

- Presides over the House when it is in session.
- Plays a major role in making committee assignments, which are coveted by all members to ensure their electoral advantage.
- Appoints or plays a key role in appointing the party's legislative leaders and the party leadership staff.
- Exercises substantial control over which bills get assigned to which committees.

TABLE 12.6 PARTY LEADERS IN THE 105TH CONGRESS

HOUSE	SENATE
Speaker: Newt Gingrich (R-GA)	Majority Leader: Trent Lott (R-MS)
Majority Leader: Richard Armey (R-TX)	Majority Whip: Don Nickles (R-OK)
Majority Whip: Tom DeLay (R-TX)	
Minority Leader: Richard Gephardt (D-MO)	Minority Leader: Thomas Daschle (D-SD)
Minority Whip: David Bonior (D-MI)	Minority Whip: Wendell Ford (D-KY)

In addition, the Speaker has a great deal of informal clout inside and outside Congress. When the Speaker's party differs from the president's party, as it frequently does, the Speaker is often a national spokesperson for the party. The bank of microphones in front of the Speaker of the House is a commonplace feature of the evening news. A good Speaker also knows the members well—including their past improprieties, the ambitions they harbor, and the pressures on them.

Leadership in the House, however, is not a one-person show. The Speaker's principal partisan ally is the **majority leader**—a job that has been the main stepping stone to the Speaker's role. The majority leader is responsible for scheduling bills in the House. More important, the majority leader is responsible for rounding up votes on behalf of the party's position on legislation. Working with the majority leader are the party's **whips**, who carry the word to party troops, counting votes beforehand and leaning on waverers whose votes are crucial to a bill. Party whips also report the views and complaints of the party rank-and-file back to the leadership.

The minority party is also organized, poised to take over the Speakership and other key posts if it should win a majority in the House. The Republicans had been the minority party in the House for 40 years before 1995, although they had a president to look to for leadership for much of that period. Now the Democrats are experiencing minority status, led by the **minority leader**, Richard Gephardt of Missouri.

The Senate. The Constitution makes the vice president of the United States the president of the Senate; this is the vice president's only constitutionally defined job. But even the mighty Lyndon Johnson, who had been the Senate majority leader before becoming vice president, found himself an outsider when he returned as the Senate's president. Vice presidents usually slight their senatorial chores, leaving power in the Senate to party leaders. Senators typically return the favor, ignoring vice presidents except in the rare case when their vote can break a tie.

Thus, the Senate majority leader—aided by the majority whips—is a party's workhorse, corralling votes, scheduling the floor action, and influencing committee assignments. The majority leader's counterpart in the opposition, the minority leader, has similar responsibilities. Power is widely dispersed in the contemporary Senate; it no longer lies in the hands of a few key members of Congress who are insulated from the public. Therefore, party leaders must appeal broadly for support, often speaking to the country, directly or indirectly, over television.

Congressional Leadership in Perspective. Despite their stature and power, congressional leaders are not in strong positions to move their troops. Both houses of Congress are highly decentralized and rarely show an inclination for major changes in the way they operate. Leaders are elected by their fellow party members and must remain responsive to them. Except in the most egregious cases (which rarely arise), leaders cannot punish those who do not support the party's stand, and no one expects members to vote against their constituents' interests. Senator Robert Dole nicely summed up the leader's situation when he once dubbed himself the "Majority Pleader."

Nevertheless, party leadership, at least in the House, has been more effective in recent years. As the party contingents have become more homogeneous, there has been more policy agreement within the parties and thus more party unity in voting on the floor. Increased agreement has made it easier for the Speaker to exercise his prerogatives regarding the assignment of bills and members to committees, the rules by which legislation is brought to the floor, and the use of an

Speaker of the House Newt Gingrich of Georgia is known for his conservative politics and confrontational style. Minority Leader Richard Gephardt leads the Democrats in the House. Trent Lott of Mississippi is the Senate Majority Leader, which makes him the most powerful member of that body. Nevertheless, in the decentralized power structure in the upper chamber, even he must stump for support.

expanded whip system—all developments that have enabled the parties to advance an agenda that reflects party preferences.[34] Following the Republican takeover of Congress in 1995, Speaker Newt Gingrich began centralizing power and exercising vigorous legislative leadership.

THE COMMITTEES AND SUBCOMMITTEES

Will Rogers, the famous Oklahoma humorist, once remarked that "outside of traffic, there is nothing that has held this country back as much as committees." Members of the Senate and the House would apparently disagree. Most of the real work of Congress goes on in committees. In fact, South Carolina Senator Ernest Hollings once remarked that so little is done on the Senate floor that a senator could run naked through the chamber and no one would notice. Most senators would be handling committee business. Committees dominate congressional policymaking in all its stages, although they usually attract little attention.

Committees regularly hold hearings to investigate problems and possible wrongdoing and to oversee the executive branch. Most of all, *they control the congressional agenda and guide legislation* from its introduction to its send-off to the president for his signature. Committees can be grouped into four types, of which the first is by far the most important.

1. **Standing committees** are formed to handle bills in different policy areas (see Table 12.7). Each house of Congress has its own standing committees; members do not belong to a committee in the other house. In the 105th Congress, the typical representative served on two committees and four subcommittees, whereas the smaller number of senators averaged three committees and seven subcommittees each.
2. **Joint committees** exist in a few policy areas, such as the economy and taxation; their membership is drawn from both the Senate and the House.
3. **Conference committees** are formed when the Senate and the House pass a particular bill in different forms. Appointed by the party leadership, a conference committee consists of members of each house chosen to iron out Senate and House differences and report back having forged a compromise bill.
4. **Select committees** are appointed for a specific purpose. The Senate select committee that investigated Watergate is a well-known example.

The Committees at Work: Legislation and Oversight. With more than 11,000 bills submitted by members every 2 years, some winnowing is essential. Every bill goes to a committee, which then has virtually the power of life and death over it. Usually only bills that obtain a favorable committee report are considered by the whole House or Senate.

New bills sent to a committee typically go directly to a subcommittee, which can hold hearings on the bill. Sizable committee and subcommittee staffs conduct research, line up witnesses for hearings, and write

TABLE 12.7 STANDING COMMITTEES IN THE SENATE AND IN THE HOUSE

SENATE COMMITTEES	HOUSE COMMITTEES
Agriculture, Nutrition, and Forestry	Agriculture
Appropriations	Appropriations
Armed Services	Banking and Financial Services
Banking, Housing, and Urban Affairs	Budget
Budget	Commerce
Commerce, Science, and Transportation	Economic and Educational Opportunities
Energy and Natural Resources	Government Reform and Oversight
Environment and Public Works	House Oversight
Finance	International Relations
Foreign Relations	Judiciary
Governmental Affairs	National Security
Judiciary	Resources
Labor and Human Resources	Rules
Rules and Administration	Science
Small Business	Small Business
Veterans' Affairs	Standards of Official Conduct
	Transportation and Infrastructure
	Veterans' Affairs
	Ways and Means

and rewrite bills. Committees and their subcommittees report on proposed legislation; these reports are typically bound in beige or green covers and are available from the Government Printing Office. A committee's most important output, however, is the "marked up" (rewritten) bill itself, submitted to the full House or Senate for debate and voting.

The work of committees does not stop when the bill leaves the committee room. Members of the committee usually serve as "floor managers" of the bill, helping party leaders hustle votes for it. They are also the "cue givers" to whom other members turn for advice. When the Senate and House pass different versions of the same bill, some committee members serve on the conference committee.

The committees and subcommittees do not leave the scene even after legislation is passed. They stay busy in legislative **oversight,** the process of monitoring the bureaucracy and its administration of policy. Oversight is handled mainly through hearings. When an agency wants a bigger budget, the use of its present budget is reviewed. Even if no budgetary issues are involved, members of committees constantly monitor how a law is being implemented. Agency heads and even cabinet secretaries testify, bringing graphs, charts, and data on the progress they have made and the problems they face. Committee staffs and committee members grill agency heads about particular problems. For example, a member may ask a Small Business Administration official why constituents who are applying for loans get a runaround. On another committee, officials charged with listing endangered species may defend the gray wolf against a member of Congress whose sheep-ranching constituents are not fond of wolves. Oversight, one of the checks Congress can exercise on the executive branch, gives Congress the power to pressure agencies and, in extreme cases, cut their budgets in order to secure compliance with congressional wishes, even congressional whims.[35]

Occasionally, congressional oversight rivets the nation's attention. One such example occurred in 1973 when the Senate established the Select Committee on Campaign Activities to investigate the misdeeds and duplicity of the 1972 presidential campaign, otherwise known as the Watergate scandal. This action was followed the next year by the House Judiciary Committee's hearings on the impeachment of President Nixon for his conduct in attempting to cover

Most of Congress' work takes place—and most of its members' power is wielded—in the standing committees and their numerous subcommittees. Here, the Senate Armed Services Committee is holding hearings on the issue of gays in the military.

up the scandal. Shortly after the Judiciary Committee recommended three articles of impeachment, the president resigned.

More recently, a special joint committee was established in 1987 to investigate what became known as the Iran-Contra affair, a term that refers to the secret sale of arms to Iran (for which President Reagan hoped to obtain the release of American hostages held in the Middle East) and the diversion of some of the funds from these sales to the Contras fighting the Sandinista government in Nicaragua (in the face of congressional prohibition of such aid). Many people thought the hearings, especially the testimony of Lieutenant Colonel Oliver North, made for great spy-novel-like entertainment but did little to illuminate the issues involved in the matter.

Congress keeps tabs on more routine activities of the executive branch through its committee staff members. These members have specialized expertise in the fields and agencies that their committees oversee and maintain an extensive network of formal and informal contacts with the bureaucracy. By reading the voluminous reports that Congress requires of the executive and by receiving information from numerous sources—agencies, complaining citizens, members of Congress and their personal staff, state and local officials, interest groups, and professional organizations—staff members can keep track of the implementation of public policy.[36]

Members of Congress have many competing responsibilities, and there are few political payoffs for carefully watching a government agency to see whether it is implementing policy properly. It is difficult to go to voters and say, "Vote for me. I oversaw the routine handling of road building." Because of this lack of incentives, problems may be overlooked until it is too late to do much about them. A major scandal involving the Department of Housing and Urban Development's administration of housing programs during the Reagan presidency was not uncovered until 1989, after Reagan had left office. Taxpayers could have saved well over $100 billion if Congress had insisted that the agencies regulating the savings and loan industry enforce their regulations more rigorously.

Nevertheless, Congress *did* substantially increase its oversight activities in the 1970s and 1980s. As the size and complexity of the national government grew in the 1960s, and after numerous charges that the executive branch had become too powerful (especially in response to the widespread belief that Presidents Johnson and Nixon had abused their power), Congress responded with more oversight. The tight budgets of recent years have provided additional incentives for oversight, as members of Congress have sought to protect programs they favor from budget cuts and to get more value for the tax dollars spent on them. As the publicity value of receiving credit for controlling governmental spending has increased, so has the number of representatives and senators interested in oversight.[37]

Getting on a Committee. One of the first worries for an incoming member of Congress (after paying off campaign debts) is getting on the right committee. Although it is not always easy to figure out what the right committee is, it is fairly easy to recognize some wrong committees. The Iowa newcomer does not want to get stuck on the Banking, Housing, and Urban Affairs Committee; the Brooklyn freshman would like to avoid Agriculture. Members seek committees that will help them achieve three goals: reelection, influence in Congress, and the opportunity to make policy in areas they think are important.[38]

Just after their election, new members write to the party's congressional leaders and members of their state delegation, indicating their committee preferences. Every committee includes members from both parties, but a majority of each committee's members, as well as its chair, come from the majority party. Each party in each house has a slightly different way of picking its committee members. Party leaders almost always play a key role.

Those who have supported the leadership are favored in the committee selection process, but generally the parties try to grant members' requests for committee assignments whenever possible. They want their members to please their constituents (being on the right committee should help them play their role of constituency representative more effectively) and to develop expertise in an area of policy. The parties also try to apportion the influence that comes with committee membership among the state delegations, in order to accord representation to diverse components of the party.[39]

Getting Ahead on the Committee: Chairs and the Seniority System. If committees are the most important influencers of the congressional agenda, **committee chairs** are the most important influencers of the committee agenda. They play dominant—though no longer monopolistic—roles in scheduling hearings, hiring staff, appointing subcommittees, and managing committee bills when they are brought before the full house.

Until the 1970s, there was a simple rule for picking committee chairs: the **seniority system**. If committee members had served on their committee longest and their party controlled the chamber, they got to be chairs—whatever their party loyalty, mental state, or competence. This system gave a decisive edge to members from "safe" districts. They were least likely to be challenged for reelection and most likely to achieve seniority. In the Democratic Party, most safe districts were in the South; as a result, Southern politicians exercised power beyond their numbers. They chaired many committees, often dominating them. The South has become a two-party region, however, and electoral losses, aging, and mortality have taken their toll on Southern committee chairs.

Woodrow Wilson, a political scientist before he became a politician, once said that the government of the United States was really government by the chairs of the standing committees of Congress. So powerful were the chairs for most of the twentieth century that they could bully members or bottle up legislation at any time—and with almost certain knowledge that they would be chairs for the rest of their electoral life. But in the 1970s, Congress faced a revolt of its younger members. Both parties in both branches permitted members to vote on committee chairs; in 1975, the House Democrats dumped four chairs with 154 years of seniority among them.

Today seniority remains the *general rule* for selecting chairs, but there are exceptions. For example, ailing Jamie Whitten of Mississippi was stripped of his Appropriations Committee gavel in 1992. When his successor, William Natcher of Kentucky, died in 1994, David Obey of Wisconsin became chair, although he was not the most senior Democrat on the committee. The Republicans skipped over several senior representatives when they named the House committee chairs in 1995.

These and other reforms discussed later in this chapter have somewhat reduced the clout of the chairs from that of a generation ago. Chairs are far less able to mold the decision-making processes of their committees.[40] Yet there are disadvantages to decentralizing committee power. Richard Fenno, a veteran congressional observer, once remarked that the "performance of Congress as an institution is very largely the performance of its committees" but that the committee system is the "epitome of fragmentation and decentralization."[41] The more that power is dispersed, the more difficult it is to make coherent policy.

CAUCUSES: THE INFORMAL ORGANIZATION OF CONGRESS

Although the formal organization of Congress consists of its party leadership and its committee structures, the informal organization of the House and Senate is also important. The informal networks of trust and mutual interest can spring from numerous sources. Friendship, ideology, and geography are long-standing sources of informal organization.

Lately, these traditional informal groupings have been dominated by a growing number of caucuses. In this context, a **caucus** is a grouping of members of Congress who share some interest or characteristic. In the 105th Congress, there are about 130 of these caucuses, most of them containing members from both parties, and some containing members from both the House and the Senate. The goal of all caucuses is to promote the interests around which they are formed.

Within Congress they press for committees to hold hearings, they push particular legislation, and they pull together votes on bills they favor. They are somewhat like interest groups, but with a difference: their members are members of Congress, not petitioners to Congress on the outside looking in. Thus caucuses—interest groups within Congress—are nicely situated to pack more punch than interest groups outside Congress.

Some, such as the Black Caucus, the Congresswomen's Caucus, and the Hispanic Caucus, are based on the characteristics of their members. Others, such as the Sunbelt Caucus and the Northeast-Midwest Congressional Coalition, are based on regional groupings. Still others, such as the Moderate/Conservative Democrats, are ideological groupings. And still others, such as the Steel, Travel and Tourism, Coal, and Mushroom caucuses, are based on some economic interest that is important to a set of constituencies. (Yes, there really is a Mushroom Caucus; it is composed of members interested in protecting the interests of mushroom growers.)

This explosion of informal groups in Congress has made the representation of interests in Congress a more direct process. The caucuses proceed on the assumption that no one is a more effective lobbyist than a senator or representative.

As with other interest groups, the caucuses must proceed within the legislative process, following a bill from its introduction to its approval. The next sections will discuss this process, which is often termed "labyrinthine" to reflect the fact that getting a bill through Congress is very much like navigating a difficult, intricate maze.

The proliferation of congressional caucuses gives members of Congress an informal, yet powerful, means of shaping the policy agenda. Composed of legislative insiders who share similar concerns, the caucuses—such as the Black Caucus pictured here—exert a much greater influence on policymaking than most citizen-based interest groups can.

THE CONGRESSIONAL PROCESS

Chapter 7 described the government's agenda. Congress' agenda is, of course, a crowded one—about 5,500 bills are introduced annually. A **bill** is a proposed law, drafted in precise, legal language. Anyone—even you or I—can draft a bill. The White House and interest groups are common sources of polished bills. However, only members of the House or the Senate can formally submit a bill for consideration. The traditional route for a bill as it works its way through the legislative labyrinth is depicted in Figure 12.2. Most bills are quietly killed off early in the process. Some are introduced mostly as a favor to a group or a constituent; others are private bills, granting citizenship to a constituent or paying a settlement to a person whose car was demolished by a Postal Service truck. Still other bills may alter the course of the nation.

Congress is typically a reactive and cumbersome decision-making body. Rules are piled upon rules, and procedures upon procedures.[42] Moreover, reforms in the 1970s (which we discuss later in the chapter) decentralized the internal distribution of power in Congress, making legislating more difficult. The polarized political climate of 1980s also exacerbated the problems of legislating. Party leaders sought ways to cope with these problems, and what Barbara Sinclair has termed *unorthodox lawmaking* has become common in the congressional process, especially for the most significant legislation.[43]

In both chambers party leaders involve themselves in the legislative process on major legislation earlier and more deeply, using special procedures to aid the passage of legislation. Bills are often referred to several committees at the same time, bringing more interests to bear on an issue but complicating the process of passing legislation. Since committee leaders cannot always negotiate compromises *among* committees, party leaders have accepted this responsibility, often negotiating compromises and making adjustments in bills after a committee or committees report legislation. On the other hand, committees may be bypassed altogether when party leaders form special task forces for high-priority legislation.

In the House, special rules from the Rules Committee have become powerful tools for controlling floor consideration of bills and sometimes for shaping the outcomes of votes. Often party leaders from each chamber negotiate among themselves

FIGURE 12.2

HOW A BILL BECOMES A LAW

Many bills travel full circle, coming first from the White House as part of the presidential agenda, then returning to the president at the end of the process. In the interim, there are two parallel processes in the Senate and House, starting with committee action. If a committee gives a bill a favorable report, the whole chamber considers it. When it is passed in different versions by the two chambers, a conference committee drafts a single compromise bill.

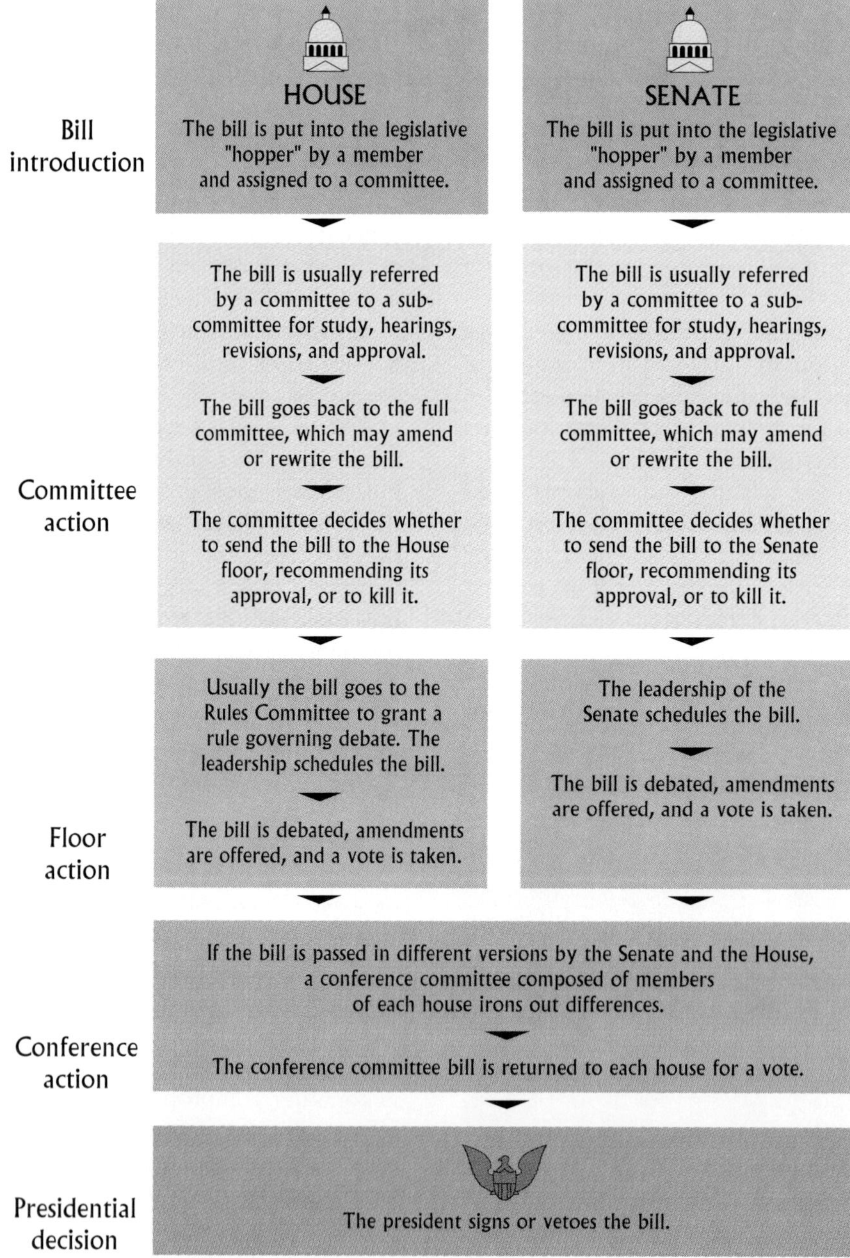

instead of creating conference committees. Sometimes, special "summits" between the legislative and executive branches are employed to obtain agreement on the passage of legislation. Party leaders also use *omnibus* legislation that addresses numerous and perhaps unrelated subjects, issues, and programs to create winning coalitions.

These new procedures are generally under control of party leaders in the House, but in the Senate, leaders have less leverage and *individual* senators have retained great opportunities for influence (such as using the filibuster). As a result, it is more difficult to pass legislation in the Senate.

There are, of course, countless influences on this legislative process. Presidents, parties, constituents, interest groups, the congressional and committee leadership structure—these influences and more offer members cues for their decision making. We will now examine a few of the major influences, starting with the president.

PRESIDENTS AND CONGRESS: PARTNERS AND PROTAGONISTS

Political scientists sometimes call the president the *chief legislator*, a phrase that might have appalled the Constitution writers, with their insistence on separation of powers. Presidents do, however, help create the congressional agenda. They are also their own best lobbyists.

Presidents have their own legislative agenda, based in part on their party's platform and their electoral coalition. Their task is to persuade Congress that their agenda should also be Congress' agenda. Lyndon Johnson once claimed (with perhaps a touch of that famous Johnsonian overstatement), "If an issue is not included on the presidential agenda, it is almost impossible—short of crisis—to get the Congress to focus on it."[44]

Presidents have many resources with which to influence Congress. (The next chapter will examine presidential leadership.) They may try to influence members directly—calling up wavering members and telling them that the country's future hinges on this one vote, for example—but they do not do this often. If presidents were to pick just one key bill and spend 10 minutes on the telephone with each of the 535 members of Congress, they would spend 89 hours chatting with them. Instead, presidents wisely leave most White House lobbying to the congressional liaison office and work mainly through regular meetings with the party's leaders in the House and Senate.

It seems a wonder that presidents, even with all their power and prestige, can push and wheedle anything through the cavernous congressional process. The president must usually win at least ten times to hope for final passage: (1) in one House subcommittee, (2) in the full House committee, (3) in the House Rules Committee to move to the floor, (4) on the House floor, (5) in one Senate subcommittee, (6) in the full Senate committee, (7) on the Senate floor, (8) in the House-Senate conference committee to work out the differences between the two bills, (9) back to the House floor for final passage, and (10) back to the Senate floor for final passage.

As one scholar put it, presidential leadership of Congress is *at the margins*.[45] In general, successful presidential leadership of Congress has not been the result of the dominant chief executive of political folklore who reshapes the contours of the political landscape to pave the way for change. Rather than creating the conditions for important shifts in public policy, the effective American leader is the less heroic *facilitator* who works at the margins of coalition building to recognize and exploit opportunities presented by a favorable configuration of political forces.

Presidents are only one of many claimants for the attention of Congress, especially on domestic policy. As we will show in the next chapter, popular presidents and presidents with a large majority of their party in each house of Congress have a good chance of getting their way. Yet, as Figure 12.3 shows, presidents often lose. Ronald Reagan was considered a strong chief executive, and budgeting was one of his principal tools for affecting public policy. Yet the budgets he proposed to Congress were typically pronounced DOA, dead on arrival. Members of Congress truly compose an independent branch.

PARTY, CONSTITUENCY, AND IDEOLOGY

Presidents come and go; the parties linger on. Presidents do not determine a congressional member's electoral fortunes; constituents do. Where presidents are less influential, on domestic policies especially, party and constituency are more important.

Party Influence. On some issues, members of the parties stick together like a marching band. They are most cohesive when Congress is electing its official leaders. A vote for Speaker of the House is a straight party-line vote, with every Democrat on one side and every Republican on the other. On other issues, however, the party coalition may come unglued. Votes on civil rights policies, for example, have revealed deep divisions within each party. Figure 12.4 (see page 307) shows the percentage of times a majority of Democrats were opposed by a majority of Republicans.

Differences between the parties are sharpest on questions of social welfare and economic policy.[46]

FIGURE 12.3 PRESIDENTIAL SUCCESS ON VOTES IN CONGRESS

Presidential success rates for influencing congressional votes vary widely among presidents and within a president's tenure in office. Presidents are usually most successful early in their tenures and when their party has a majority in one or both houses of Congress. Regardless, in almost any year the president will lose on many issues. Congress considers the president's views when it makes decisions, but when it disagrees with the White House, which it often does, it does not hesitate to go in its own direction.

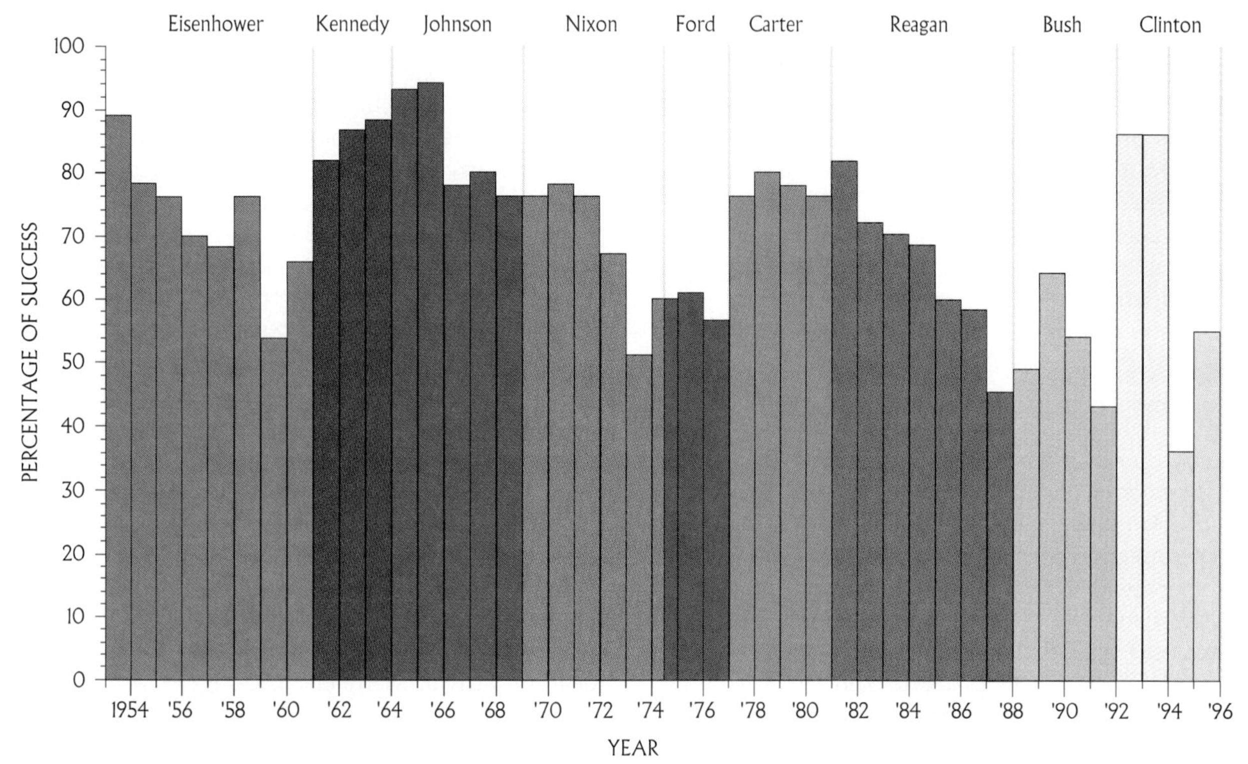

SOURCE: Independent calculation of ***Congressional Quarterly*** data. See George C. Edwards III *At the Margins: Presidential Leadership of Congress* (New Haven, CT: Yale University Press, 1989), Table 2.1.

When voting on labor issues, Democrats traditionally cling together, leaning toward the side of the unions, whereas Republicans almost always vote with business. On social welfare issues—poverty, unemployment aid, help to the cities—Democrats are more generous than Republicans. This split between the parties should not be too surprising if you recall the party coalitions described in Chapter 8. Once in office, party members favor their electoral coalitions.

Party leaders in Congress help "whip" their members into line. Their power to do so is limited, of course. They cannot drum a recalcitrant member out of the party. Leaders have plenty of influence, however, including some say about committee posts, the power to boost a member's pet projects, and the subtle but significant influence of information to which a member is not privy.

Recently the parties, especially the Republicans, have been a growing source of money for congressional campaigns. The congressional campaign committees have energized both parties, helping to recruit candidates, running seminars in campaign skills, and conducting polls. Equally important, the congressional campaign committees today have money to hand out to promising candidates. The parties can thus have an impact on the kinds of people who sit in Congress on either side of the aisle.

Constituency versus Ideology. Members of Congress are representatives; their constituents expect them to

FIGURE 12.4

PARTY UNITY VOTES IN CONGRESS[a]

In democracies with parliamentary systems such as Great Britain, almost all votes are party-line votes. Parties, as Chapter 8 showed, are considerably weaker in the United States. Party affiliation is a rallying point for representatives and senators and does influence their votes, yet in a typical year, a majority of Democrats and Republicans oppose each other only half the time. Members of both parties often end up deserting their colleagues and voting against the party line. In recent years, partisanship has been stronger in the House than in the Senate.

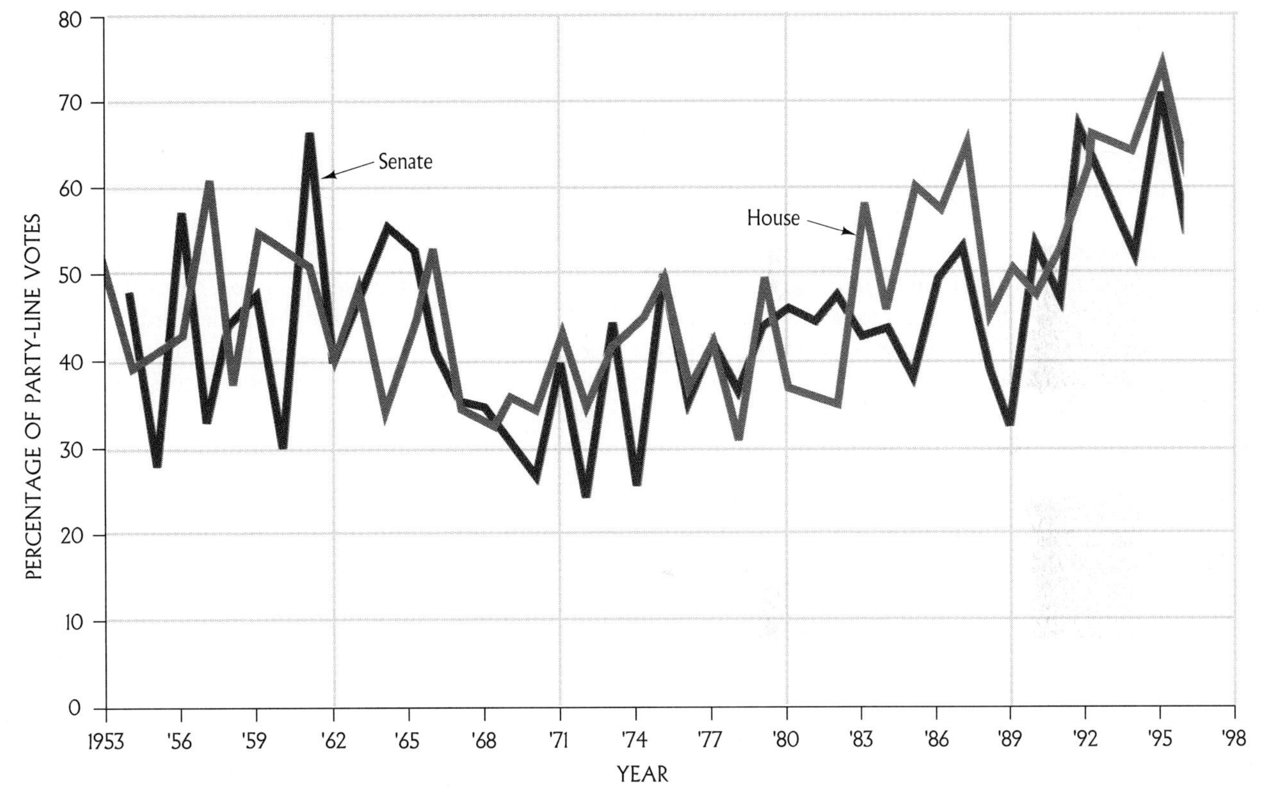

[a]Data indicate the percentage of all recorded votes on which a majority of voting Democrats opposed a majority of voting Republicans.

SOURCE: Independent calculation of Congressional Quarterly data.

represent their interests in Washington. In 1714, Anthony Henry, a member of the British Parliament, received a letter from some of his constituents asking him to vote against an excise tax. He is reputed to have replied in part:

> Gentlemen: I have received your letter about the excise, and I am surprised at your insolence in writing to me at all. . . .
>
> . . . may God's curse light upon you all, and may it make your homes as open and as free to the excise officers as your wives and daughters have always been to me while I have represented your rascally constituency.[47]

Needless to say, notions of representation have changed since Henry's time.

Sometimes representation requires a balancing act, however. If some representatives favor more defense spending but suspect that their constituents do not, what are they to do? The English politician and philosopher Edmund Burke favored the concept of legislators as *trustees*, using their best judgment to make policy in the interests of the people. Others prefer the concept of representatives as *instructed delegates,* mirroring the preferences of their constituents. Actually, members of Congress are *politicos,* adopting both trustee and instructed delegate roles as they strive to be both representatives and policymakers.[48] (See "The People Speak: Delegates or Trustees?")

The best way constituents can influence congressional voting is also simple: Elect a representative or senator who agrees with their views. John Sullivan and Robert O'Connor discovered that congressional candidates tend to take policy positions different from each other's. Moreover, the winners generally vote on roll calls as they said they would.[49] If voters use their good sense to elect candidates who share their policy positions, then constituents *can* influence congressional policy.

If voters miss their chance and elect someone out of step with their thinking, it may be difficult to influence that person's votes. It is difficult even for well-intentioned legislators to know what people want. Some pay careful attention to their mail, but the mail is a notoriously unreliable indicator of people's thinking; individuals with extreme opinions on an issue are more likely to write than those with moderate views. Some members send questionnaires to constituents, but the answers they receive are unreliable because few people respond. Some try public opinion polling, but it is expensive if professionally done and unreliable if not.

Defeating an incumbent is no easy task. Even legislators whose votes conflict with the views of their constituents tend to be reelected. Most citizens have trouble recalling the names of their congressional representatives (at election time in 1994, only 28 percent of the public could name their representatives in the House),[50] let alone keeping up with their representatives' voting records. According to one expert. "Probably less than a third of all constituents can recognize who their representatives are and what policy positions they have generally taken—and even that third tends not to evaluate incumbents on the basis of policy."[51] A National Election Study found that only 11 percent of the people even claimed to remember a particular vote of their representative.

On some controversial issues, however, legislators ignore constituent opinion at great peril. For years, Southern members of Congress would not have dared to vote for a civil rights law. Lately, representatives and senators have been concerned about the many new single-issue groups. Such groups care little about a member's overall record; to them, a vote on one issue—gun control, abortion, the ERA—is all that counts. Ready to pounce on one wrong vote and pour money into an opponent's campaign, these new forces in constituency politics make every legislator nervous.

Nevertheless, most issues remain obscure. On such issues legislators can safely ignore constituency opinion. On a typical issue, the prime determinant of a congressional member's vote is personal ideology. On issues where ideological divisions are sharp and constituency preferences and knowledge are likely to be weak, such as defense and foreign policy, ideology is virtually the only determinant of voting.[52] As ideological divisions weaken and constituency preferences strengthen, members are more likely to deviate from their own position and adopt those of their constituencies. Thus, when they have differences of opinion with their constituencies, members of Congress consider constituency preferences but are not controlled by them.[53]

The People Speak

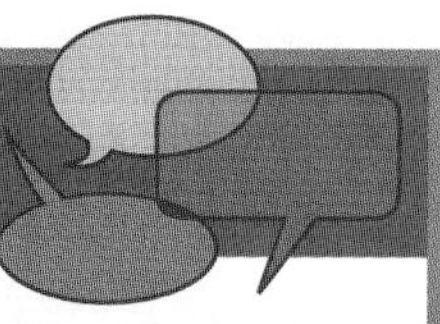

If a Member of Congress Thinks a Bill is in the Best Interest of the Country, But a Majority of the People He or She Represents Are Against It, Should the Member of Congress Vote for the Bill or Vote Against It?

Vote for it	34%
Vote against it	59%

Many members of Congress act as trustees, but most of their constituents want them to act as delegates.

SOURCE: The question as worded is taken directly from a CBS News/*New York Times* Poll, May 1987.

LOBBYISTS AND INTEREST GROUPS

The nation's capital is crawling with lawyers, lobbyists, registered foreign agents, public relations consultants, and others—more than 14,000 individuals representing nearly 12,000 organizations at last count—all seeking to influence Congress.[54] Several dozen groups are concerned with the single issue of protecting Alaska's environment; the bigger the issue, the more lobbyists are involved in it. Any group interested in influencing national policymaking, and that includes almost everyone, either hires Washington lobbyists or sends its own. Washington lobbyists can be a formidable group.

Lobbyists have a dismal image, one worsened by periodic scandals in which someone seeking to influence Congress presents huge amounts of cash to senators and representatives. No one knows how much lobbyists spend to influence legislation, but it undoubtedly runs into the billions (recall the $1.3 million

Lobbyists have never been held in high esteem by the public, and they have come under especially harsh criticism in recent years. Nevertheless, lobbyists play an important role in the legislative process.

"Mr. Speaker, will the gentleman from Small Firearms yield the floor to the gentleman from Big Tobacco?"

Charles Keating alone gave to five senators to encourage them to intercede with the Federal Home Loan Bank Board). Such stories give lobbyists a bad name, no doubt often deserved. But lobbyists have a job to do—namely, to represent the interests of their organizations. Lobbyists, some of them former members of Congress, can provide legislators with crucial information and often with assurances of financial aid in the next campaign.

Lobbyists do not hold all the high cards in their dealings with Congress; congressional representatives hold some trump cards of their own. The easiest way to frustrate lobbyists is to ignore them. Lobbyists usually make little headway with their opponents anyway: The lobbyist for General Motors arguing against automobile pollution controls would not have much influence with a legislator concerned about air pollution. Members of Congress can make life uncomfortable for lobbyists, too. They can embarrass them, expose heavy-handed tactics, and spread the word among an organization's members that it is being poorly represented in Washington. Last but not least, Congress *can* regulate lobbyists.

In 1995, Congress passed a law requiring anyone hired to lobby members of Congress, congressional staff members, White House officials, and federal agencies to report what issues they were seeking to influence, how much they were spending on the effort, and the identities of their clients. This law was designed to close loopholes in a 1946 law that had allowed most lobbyists to avoid registering and had permitted those who did to disclose only limited information about their activities. Congress also placed severe restrictions on the gifts, meals, and expense-paid travel that public officials may accept from lobbyists. In theory, these reporting requirements and restrictions will not only prevent shady deals between lobbyists and members of Congress but also curb the influence of special interests. Nevertheless, interest groups are thriving; indirect, grass-roots lobbying—such as computerized mailings to encourage citizens to pressure their representatives on an issue—has grown also.

There are many forces that affect senators and representatives as they decide how to vote on a bill. After his exhaustive study of influences on congressional decision making, John Kingdon concluded that none was important enough to suggest that congresspeople vote as they do because of that one influence.[55] The process is as complex for individual legislators as it is for those who want to influence their votes.

UNDERSTANDING CONGRESS

Congress is a complex institution. Its members want to make sound national policy, but they also want to return to Washington after the next election. How do these sometimes conflicting desires affect American democracy and the scope of American government? This section will address that question.

CONGRESS AND DEMOCRACY

In a large nation, the success of democratic government depends on the quality of representation. In a tiny decision-making body, people can cast their own votes, but Americans could hardly hold a national referendum on every policy issue on the government agenda. Instead, Americans delegate decision-making power to representatives. If Congress is a successful democratic institution, it will have to be a successful representative institution.

Certainly, some aspects of Congress make it very *un*representative. Its members are an American elite (see "America in Perspective: The Russian Duma: A Reformer's Paradise"). Its leadership is chosen by its own members, not by any vote of the American people. Voters have little direct influence over the individuals who chair key committees or lead congressional parties. Voters in just a single constituency control the fate of committee chairs and party leaders. Voters in the other 434 House districts and the other 49 states have no real say, for example, about who chairs a committee considering new forms of energy, a committee considering defense buildups, or a committee making economic policy.

Nevertheless, the evidence in this chapter demonstrates that Congress *does* try to listen to the American people. Whom voters elect makes a difference in how congressional votes turn out; which party is in power affects policies. Linkage institutions actually link voters to policymakers. Perhaps Congress could do a better job at representation than it does, but there are many obstacles to improved representation. Legislators find it hard to know what constituents want. Groups may keep important issues off the legislative agenda. Members may spend so much time servicing their constituencies that they have little time left to represent those constituencies in the policymaking process.

Members of Congress are responsive to the people, if the people make clear what they want. For example, in response to popular demands, Congress established a program in 1988 to shield the elderly against the catastrophic costs associated with acute illness. In 1989, in response to complaints from the elderly about higher Medicare premiums, Congress abolished most of what it had created the previous year.

REFORMING CONGRESS

Reformers have tried to promote a more open, democratic Congress. To a large degree, they have succeeded. Looking at Congress in the 1950s, one could say that it was like a stepladder. The members

America in Perspective

THE RUSSIAN DUMA: A REFORMER'S PARADISE

The next time you grow exasperated at Congress, just remember the Russian Duma, the 450-member lower house of Parliament. In the anything-goes world of the Duma, there are no rules of sexual conduct, no sensitivities about political correctness, and no ethics investigations. Sergie Semyonov is the deputy chair of the committee on women, families, and youth. His expertise in the area seems to be a result of living with three women. Recently, he proposed a bill to legalize polygamy, arguing that he had "the money and energy to keep all my women fully satisfied."

But Mr. Semyonov is positively chivalrous compared to the ultranationalist leader of his party, Vladimir V. Zhirinovsky. Mr. Zhirinovsky got into a fistfight on the floor of the Duma and punched another deputy—a woman—in the face. He later claimed he was fending off her sexual advances!

Parliamentary immunity attracts candidates who face criminal charges and want to escape prosecution by becoming legislators. They should feel right at home. There are no financial scandals in the Duma, because no one even tries to hide their conflicts of interest. Graft and corruption are blatant, and there is no way to trace illicit money, no oversight committees, no paper trail for prosecutors to follow, and no watchdog press to hold lawmakers accountable.

Sexual harassment seems to have replaced the work ethic as a norm of behavior. Often the deputies simply do not show up at all, even for key votes. In several instances, all the leaders were absent, leaving Communist party leader Anatoly Lukyanov, who supported the 1991 coup against Mikhail Gorbachev, in charge. There is one saving grace for the Russian people, however. The newest Russian constitution has stripped the Duma of most of its power.

SOURCE: Alesasandra Stanley, "Russia's Gross National Legislature," *New York Times,* January 19, 1997. sec. 4, p. 3.

advanced one rung at a time toward the heights of power with each reelection. At the top was real power in Congress. Committee chairs were automatically selected by seniority. Their power on the committee was unquestioned. Bills disappeared forever into chairs' "vest pockets" if those chairs did not like them. The chairs alone created subcommittees, picked their members, and routed bills to them. If committees controlled bills from the cradle to the grave, the chairs were both midwives and undertakers. At the bottom of the ladder, the norm of apprenticeship—"be seen and not heard"—prevailed. The standing Washington line about seniority was this: "Son, the longer you're here, the more you'll come to appreciate the seniority system." The system was democratic—one person, one vote—when the roll call came, but it was not democratic when the bill itself was shaped, shelved, or sunk.

Cable television's live coverage of Congress has further democratized the legislative process by letting Americans see their representatives at work. Here, the U.S. House of Representatives is shown at the opening of the 104th Congress.

Democratization. The waves of congressional reform in the 1960s and especially the 1970s changed this political atmosphere. Lyndon Johnson started the reform ball rolling during his majority leadership with the "Johnson rule," which gave each senator a seat on at least one key committee. This reform allowed junior members more room at the top.

By the 1970s the reform movement, bent on democratizing Congress, picked up speed.[56] Reformers tried to create more democracy by spreading power around. First to go was the automatic and often autocratic dominance of the most senior members as committee chairs. Instead, chairs were elected by the majority party, and some of the most objectionable chairs were dropped. The chairs' power was also reduced by the proliferation of subcommittees, which widened the distribution of authority, visibility, and resources in both chambers. Subcommittees became the new centers of power in Congress.

Not only the formal reforms of Congress but also the proliferation of informal caucuses tended to decentralize power in Congress. Burdett Loomis remarks that "the proliferation of caucuses illustrates the shoring up of particularistic forces in Congress. . . . And while members decry the increase in single-issue politics, they have only to consider their own behavior."[57]

Partially in response to the problems of decentralized power in the House, the Republicans passed prominent reforms when they took control in 1995. Committee chairs were allowed to choose the chairs of subcommittees on their committees and to hire all the committee and subcommittee staff. Some subcommittees were simply eliminated. At the same time, both committee and subcommittee chairs were limited to three consecutive 2-year terms as chair (Senate Republicans also adopted this rule), and committee chairs lost the power to cast proxy votes for those committee members not in attendance. Members were prohibited from using appropriations for their office allowances to fund the various caucuses. The Speaker also put the committees on short leashes, giving them instructions regarding the legislation they were to report and a timetable for reporting it. In a few instances, the leadership bypassed committees by setting up separate task forces to prepare legislation.

By 1997, however, the leadership backed off. Weakened by his low ratings in the polls, Speaker Newt Gingrich gave committee chairs greater leeway to set their committee's agenda and promised to allow legislation to be first fashioned by committees. At the moment, both the Speaker and the committee chairs are stronger than they were in the 1980s. How this will affect the quality of public policy remains to be seen.

Representativeness versus Effectiveness. The central legislative dilemma for Congress is combining the faithful representation of constituents with the making of effective public policy. Supporters see Congress as a forum in which many interests compete for a spot on the policy agenda and over the form of a particular policy—which is just as the founders intended it to be.

Critics charge that Congress is responsive to so many interests that policy is as uncoordinated, fragmented, and decentralized as Congress itself. Interest groups grow on committees and subcommittees like barnacles on a boat. After a while, these groups develop intimacy and influence with "their" committee. Committee decisions usually carry the day on the roll-call vote. Thus, the committee system links congressional policymaking to a multiplicity of interests, rather than to a majority's preferences.

In addition, some observers believe Congress is too representative—so much so that it is incapable of taking decisive action to deal with difficult problems. The agricultural committees busily tend to the interests of tobacco farmers, while committees on health and welfare spend millions for lung cancer research. One committee wrestles with domestic unemployment while another makes tax policy encouraging businesses to open new plants out of the country. One reason why government cannot balance the budget, critics say, is that Congress is protecting the interests of too many people. As long as each interest tries to preserve the status quo, bold reforms cannot be enacted.

On the other hand, defenders of Congress point out that, thanks to its being decentralized, there is no oligarchy in control to prevent the legislature from taking comprehensive action. In fact, Congress has enacted the huge tax cut of 1981, the comprehensive (and complicated) tax reform of 1986, and various bills structuring the budgetary process designed to balance the budget.[58]

There is no simple solution to Congress' dilemma. It tries to be both a representative and an objective policymaking institution. As long as this is true, it is unlikely that Congress will please all its critics.

"Listen, pal! I didn't spend seven million bucks to get here so I could yield the floor to you."

Drawing by Dana Fardon: ©1987 *The New Yorker Magazine.*

CONGRESS AND THE SCOPE OF GOVERNMENT

If Congress is responsive to a multitude of interests and those interests desire government policies to aid them in some way, does the nature of Congress predispose it to continually increasing the scope of the public sector? And do the benefits of servicing constituents provide an incentive for members of Congress to tolerate, even to expand, an already big government? The more policies there are, the more potential ways members can help their constituencies. The more bureaucracies there are, the more red tape members can help cut. Big government helps members of Congress get reelected and even gives them good reason to support making it bigger.

Members of Congress vigorously protect the interests of their constituents. At the same time, there are many members who agree with Ronald Reagan that government is not the answer to problems but rather *is* the problem. These individuals make careers out of fighting against government programs (although these same senators and representatives typically support programs aimed at aiding *their* constituents).

Americans have contradictory preferences regarding public policy. As we have noted in previous chapters, they want to balance the budget and pay low taxes, but they also support most government programs. Congress does not impose programs on a reluctant public; instead, it responds to the public's demands for them.

SUMMARY

According to the Constitution, members of Congress are the government's policymakers, but legislative policymaker is only one of the roles of members of Congress. They are also politicians, and politicians always keep one eye on the next election. Success in congressional elections may be determined as much by constituency service—casework and the pork barrel—as by policymaking. Senators and representatives have become so skilled at constituency service that incumbents have a big edge over challengers, making it more difficult to bring about major changes in the makeup, and thus the policies, of Congress.

The structure of Congress is so complex that it seems remarkable that legislation gets passed at all. Its bicameral division means that bills have two sets of committee hurdles to clear. Because recent reforms have decentralized power, the job of leading Congress is more difficult than ever.

Presidents try hard to influence Congress, and parties and elections can also shape legislators' choices. The impact of these factors clearly differs from one policy area to another. Party impacts are clearest on issues for which the party's coalitions are clearest, especially social welfare and economic issues. Constituencies influence policy mostly by the initial choice of a representative. Members of Congress do pay attention to voters, particularly on visible issues, but most issues do not interest voters. On these less visible issues other factors, such as lobbyists and members' individual ideologies, influence policy decisions.

Congress clearly has some undemocratic and unrepresentative features. Its members are hardly average Americans. Even so, they pay attention to popular preferences, when they can figure out what they are. People inside and outside the institution, however, think that Congress is ineffective. Its objective policymaking decisions and representative functions sometimes conflict, yet from time to time Congress does show that it can deal with major issues in a comprehensive fashion. Many members of Congress have incentives to increase the scope of the federal government, but these incentives are provided by the people who put those representatives in office.

KEY TERMS

incumbents
casework
pork barrel
bicameral legislature
House Rules Committee
filibuster
Speaker of the House
majority leader
whips
minority leader
standing committees
joint committees
conference committees
select committees
oversight
committee chairs
seniority system
caucus
bill

FOR FURTHER READING

Aberbach, Joel D. *Keeping a Watchful Eye*. Washington, DC: Brookings Institution, 1990. A thorough study of congressional oversight of the executive branch.

Bernstein, Robert A. *Elections, Representation, and Congressional Voting Behavior*. Englewood Cliffs, NJ: Prentice-Hall, 1989. Examines the issue of constituency control over members of Congress.

Deering, Christopher J., and Steven S. Smith. *Committees in Congress*, 3rd ed. Washington, DC: Congressional Quarterly Press, 1997. A thorough overview of the complex committee structure in the House and Senate.

Dodd, Lawrence C., and Bruce I. Oppenheimer. *Congress Reconsidered*, 6th ed. Washington, DC: Congressional Quarterly, 1997). Excellent essays covering many aspects of Congress.

Fenno, Richard F., Jr. *Home Style*. Boston: Little, Brown, 1978. How members of Congress mend fences and stay in political touch with the folks back home.

Fiorina, Morris P. *Congress: Keystone of the Washington Establishment*, 2nd ed. New Haven, CT: Yale University Press, 1989. Argues that members of Congress are self-serving in serving their constituents, ensuring their reelection but harming the national interest.

Jacobson, Gary C. *The Politics of Congressional Elections*, 4th ed. New York: Longman, 1997. An excellent review of congressional elections.

Kingdon, John W. *Congressmen's Voting Decisions*, 3rd ed. Ann Arbor: University of Michigan Press, 1989. A thorough and insightful study of congressional voting decisions.

Loomis, Burdett. *The New American Politician*. New York: Basic Books, 1988. Focuses on how a new generation of political entrepreneurs has come to dominate Congress.

Mayhew, David R. *Congress: The Electoral Connection*. New Haven, CT: Yale University Press, 1974. An analysis of Congress based on the premise that the principal motivation of congressional behavior is reelection.

INTERNET RESOURCES

http://voter.cq.com
Congressional Quarterly's online service providing news about Congress and your own senators and representatives as well as a reference library.

http://www.house.gov/
The official House Web Site, containing information on the organization, operations, schedule, and activities of the House and its committees, and links to the offices of members and committees. Enables you to directly contact your representative.

http://www.senate.gov/
The official Senate Web Site, with information and links similar to those for the House.

http://Thomas.loc.gov/
Information on the activities of Congress, the status and text of legislation, the *Congressional Record*, committee reports, and historical documents.

http://www.rollcall.com
Roll Call, the online version of the Capitol Hill newspaper.

http://www.fec.gov/
Federal Election Commission data on campaign expenditures.

NOTES

1. There is some evidence that women state legislators in states with the highest percentage of female representatives are more likely than men to introduce and pass legislation dealing with women, children, and families. See Sue Thomas, "The Impact of Women on State Legislative Policies," *Journal of Politics* 53 (November 1991): 958-976. See also Arturo Vega and Juanita M. Firestone, "The Effects of Gender on Congressional Behavior and the Substantive Representation of Women," *Legislative Studies Quarterly* 20 (May 1995): 213-222.
2. On various views of representation, see Hanna Pitkin, *The Concept of Representation* (Berkeley, CA: University of California Press, 1967).
3. An excellent review of the costs of congressional campaigns and the uses to which money is put in them is Edie N. Goldenberg and Michael W. Traugott, *Campaigning for Congress* (Washington, DC: Congressional Quarterly Press, 1984).
4. John L. Sullivan and Eric Uslaner, "Congressional Behavior and Electoral Marginality," *American Journal of Political Science* 22 (August 1978): 536-553.
5. Thomas Mann, *Unsafe at Any Margin* (Washington, DC: American Enterprise Institute, 1978).
6. Glenn R. Parker, *Homeward Bound* (Pittsburgh, PA: University of Pittsburgh Press, 1986); and John R. Johannes, *To Serve the People* (Lincoln, NB: University of Nebraska Press, 1984).
7. Actually, only about 17 percent of the population can make an accurate guess about how their representatives have voted on any issue in Congress. See Patricia Hurley and Kim Q. Hill, "The Prospects for Issue Voting in Contemporary Congressional Elections," *American Politics Quarterly* 8 (October 1980): 446.
8. Mann, *Unsafe at Any Margin*, 37.
9. That presidential elections and congressional elections are not closely related is an argument made in Lyn Ragsdale, "The Fiction of Congressional Elections as Presidential Events," *American Politics Quarterly* 8 (October 1980): 375-398. For evidence that voters' views of the president affect their voting for senators, see Lonna Rae Atkeson and Randall W. Partin, "Economic and Referendum Voting: A Comparison of Gubernatorial and Senatorial Elections," *American Political Science Review* 89 (March 1995): 99-107.
10. John R. Owens and Edward C. Olson, "Economic Fluctuations and Congressional Elections," *American Journal of Political Science* 24 (August 1980): 469-493; Benjamin Radcliff, "Solving a Puzzle: Aggregate Analysis and Economic Voting Revisited," *Journal of Politics* 50 (May 1988): 440-458; Robert S. Erikson, "Economic Conditions and the Congressional Vote: A Review of the Macrolevel Evidence," *American Journal of Political Science* 34 (May 1990): 373-399; James E. Campbell, *The Presidential Pulse of Congressional Elections* (Lexington, KY: University Press of Kentucky, 1993), 119; and Gary C. Jacobson, "Does the Economy Matter in Midterm Elections?" *American Journal of Political Science* 34 (May 1990): 400-404.
11. David R. Mayhew, *Congress: The Electoral Connection* (New Haven, CT: Yale University Press, 1974).
12. Richard F. Fenno, Jr., *Home Style* (Boston: Little, Brown, 1978), 32.
13. *Ibid.,* 106-107.
14. The "service spells success" argument is made in Morris P. Fiorina, *Congress: Keystone of the Washington Establishment*, 2nd ed. (New Haven, CT: Yale University Press, 1989); and, with a slightly different emphasis, in Glenn R. Parker, "The Advantages of Incumbency in Congressional Elections," *American Politics Quarterly* 8 (October 1980): 449-461.
15. Fiorina, *Congress: Keystone of the Washington Establishment*, 43.
16. Gary C. Jacobson, *The Politics of Congressional Elections*, 4th ed. (New York: Longman, 1997), 108-116.
17. See, for example, Paul Feldman and James Jondrow, "Congressional Elections and Local Federal Spending," *American Journal of Political Science* 28 (February 1984): 147-163; Glenn R. Parker and Suzanne L. Parker, "The Correlates and Effects of Attention to District by U.S. House Members," *Legislative Studies Quarterly* 10 (May 1985): 223-242; and John C. McAdams and John R. Johannes, "Congressmen, Perquisites, and Elections," *Journal of Politics* 50 (May 1988): 412-439.
18. On strategies of challengers, see Gary C. Jacobson and Samuel Kernell, *Strategy and Choice in Congressional Elections*, 2nd ed. (New Haven, CT: Yale University Press, 1983); and Gary C. Jacobson, "Strategic Politicians and the Dynamics of U.S. House Elections, 1946-1986," *American Political Science Review* 83 (September 1989): 773-794. See also Steven D. Levitt and Catherine D. Wolfram, "Decomposing the Sources of Incumbency Advantage in the U.S. House," *Legislative Studies Quarterly* 22 (February 1997): 45-60.
19. See Gary C. Jacobson, *Money in Congressional Elections* (New Haven, CT: Yale University Press, 1980).
20. On the importance of challenger quality and financing, see Alan I. Abramowitz, "Explaining Senate Election Outcomes," *American Political Science Review* 82 (June

1988): 385-403; and Donald Philip Green and Jonathan S. Krasno, "Salvation for the Spendthrift Incumbent," *American Journal of Political Science* 32 (November 1988): 884-907.

21. Voter News Service exit polls, 1996.

22. Gary C. Jacobson and Michael A. Dimock, "Checking Out: The Effects of Bank Overdrafts on the 1992 House Elections," *American Journal of Political Science* 38 (August 1994): 601-624. See also "Checks and Choices: The House Bank Scandal's Impact on Voters in 1992," *Journal of Politics* 57 (November 1995): 1143-1159; and Carl McCurley and Jeffrey J. Mondak, "Inspected by #1184063113: The Influence of Incumbents' Competence and Integrity in U.S. House Elections," *American Journal of Political Science* 39 (November 1995): 864-885.

23. John G. Peters and Susan Welch, "The Effects of Corruption on Voting Behavior in Congressional Elections," *American Political Science Review* 74 (September 1980): 697-708; and Susan Welch and John R. Hibbing, "The Effects of Charges of Corruption on Voting Behavior in Congressional Elections, 1982-1990," *Journal of Politics* 59 (February 1997): 226-239.

24. Federal Election Commission, 1995.

25. Jacobson, *The Politics of Congressional Elections*, 38-43, 104-106. See also Gary C. Jacobson, "The Effects of Campaign Spending in House Elections: New Evidence for Old Arguments," *American Journal of Political Science* 34 (May 1990): 334-362; and Christopher Kenny and Michael McBurnett, "An Individual-Level Multiequation Model of Expenditure Effects in Contested House Elections," *American Political Science Review* 88 (September 1994): 699-707.

26. On term limits, see Gerald Benjamin and Michael J. Malbin, eds., *Limiting Legislative Terms* (Washington, DC: Congressional Quarterly Press, 1992).

27. Suzanna De Boef and James A. Stimson, "The Dynamic Structure of Congressional Elections," *Journal of Politics* 57 (August 1995): 630-648.

28. So says former House Speaker Jim Wright, in *You and Your Congressman* (New York: Putnam, 1976), 190. See also Donald R. Matthews and James Stimson, *Yeas and Nays: Normal Decision-Making in the House of Representatives* (New York: Wiley, 1975); and John L. Sullivan *et al.*, "The Dimensions of Cue-Taking in the House of Representatives: Variations by Issue Area," *Journal of Politics* 55 (November 1993): 975-997.

29. Nelson W. Polsby *et al.*, "Institutionalization of the House of Representatives," *American Political Science Review* 62 (1968): 144-168.

30. John R. Hibbing, "Contours of the Modern Congressional Career," *American Political Science Review* 85 (June 1991): 405-428.

31. See Bernard Grofman, Robert Griffin, and Amihai Glazer, "Is the Senate More Liberal than the House? Another Look," *Legislative Studies Quarterly* 16 (May 1991): 281-296.

32. See Sarah A. Binder and Steven S. Smith, *Politics or Principle? Filibustering in the United States Senate* (Washington, DC: Brookings Institution, 1997).

33. Robert L. Peabody, *Leadership in Congress* (Boston: Little, Brown, 1976), 4.

34. On the increasing importance of party leadership in the House, see David W. Rohde, *Parties and Leaders in the Postreform House* (Chicago: University of Chicago Press, 1991); Barbara Sinclair, "The Emergence of Strong Leadership in the 1980s House of Representatives," *Journal of Politics* 54 (August 1992): 657-684; and Gary W. Cox and Matthew D. McCubbins, *Legislative Leviathan* (Berkeley, CA: University of California Press, 1993).

35. For more on congressional oversight, see Christopher H. Foreman, Jr., *Signals From the Hill* (New Haven, CT: Yale University Press, 1988); and Diana Evans, "Congressional Oversight and the Diversity of Members' Goals," *Political Science Quarterly* 109 (No. 4, 1994): 669-687.

36. Joel D. Aberbach, *Keeping a Watchful Eye: The Politics of Congressional Oversight* (Washington, DC: Brookings Institution, 1990).

37. Aberbach, *Keeping a Watchful Eye*.

38. Richard F. Fenno, Jr., *Congressmen in Committees* (Boston: Little, Brown, 1973), 1.

39. Useful studies of committee assignments include Kenneth Shepsle, *The Giant Jigsaw Puzzle* (Chicago: University of Chicago Press, 1978); and Cox and McCubbins, *Legislative Leviathan*, chapters 1, 7, and 8.

40. See Christopher J. Deering and Steven S. Smith, *Committees in Congress*, 3rd ed. (Washington, DC: Congressional Quarterly Press, 1997).

41. Richard F. Fenno, Jr., "If, as Ralph Nader Says, Congress Is the 'Broken Branch,' How Come We Love Our Congressmen So Much?" in *Congress in Change*, ed. Norman Ornstein (New York: Praeger, 1975), 282.

42. For a thorough discussion of recent rule changes and the impact of procedures, see Steven S. Smith, *Call to Order: Floor Politics in the House and Senate* (Washington, DC: Brookings Institution, 1989).

43. Barbara Sinclair, *Unorthodox Lawmaking* (Washington, DC: Congressional Quarterly Press, 1997).

44. Quoted in Doris Kearns, *Lyndon Johnson and the American Dream* (New York: New American Library, 1976), 146.

45. George C. Edwards III, *At the Margins: Presidential Leadership of Congress* (New Haven, CT: Yale University Press, 1989).

46. Aage Clausen, *How Congressmen Decide: A Policy Focus* (New York: St. Martin's, 1973).

47. Quoted in Peter G. Richards, *Honourable Members* (London: Faber and Faber, 1959), 157.

48. See Roger H. Davidson, *The Role of the Congressman* (New York: Pegasus, 1969); and Thomas E. Cavanaugh, "Role Orientations of House Members:

The Process of Representation" (paper delivered at the annual meeting of the American Political Science Association, Washington, DC, August 1979).

49. John L. Sullivan and Robert E. O'Connor, "Electoral Choice and Popular Control of Public Policy: The Case of the 1966 House Elections," *American Political Science Review* 66 (December 1972): 1256-1268.

50. *New York Times*/CBS News Poll cited in "Voters Disgusted with Politicians as Election Nears," *New York Times*, November 13, 1994, A10.

51. Robert A. Bernstein, *Elections, Representation, and Congressional Voting Behavior* (Englewood Cliffs, NJ: Prentice-Hall, 1989), 99.

52. But Larry M. Bartels found that members of Congress were responsive to constituency opinion in supporting the Reagan defense buildup. See "Constituency Opinion and Congressional Policy Making: The Reagan Defense Buildup," *American Political Science Review* 85 (June 1991): 457-474.

53. On the importance of ideology, see Bernstein, *Elections, Representation, and Congressional Voting Behavior.*

54. *Washington Representatives 1997* (Washington, DC: Columbia Books, 1997.

55. John W. Kingdon, *Congressmen's Voting Decisions*, 3rd ed. (Ann Arbor: University of Michigan Press, 1989), 242.

56. For more on congressional reform, see Leroy N. Rieselbach, *Congressional Reform* (Washington, DC: Congressional Quarterly Press, 1986).

57. Burdett Loomis, "Congressional Caucuses and the Politics of Representation," in *Congress Reconsidered*, 2nd ed., Lawrence C. Dodd and Bruce I. Oppenheimer, eds. (Washington, DC: Congressional Quarterly Press, 1981).

58. See M. Darrell West, *Congress and Economic Policymaking* (Pittsburgh: University of Pittsburgh Press, 1987).

The Presidency

13

- The Presidents
- Presidential Powers
- Running the Government: The Chief Executive
- Presidential Leadership of Congress: The Politics of Shared Powers
- The President and National Security Policy
- Power from the People: The Public Presidency
- The President and the Press
- Understanding the American Presidency

On January 20, 1997, Bill Clinton stood before the chief justice of the Supreme Court on the steps of the Capitol to take the oath of office for the second time. Things had certainly changed since he took the oath for the first time four years earlier. He had struggled in the public opinion polls, going 3 years without averaging even 50 percent approval. Congress had failed to pass many of his major initiatives, including health care reform, and now both houses of Congress were in the hands of the opposition party. Winning a contested vote in the legislature was going to be difficult. He had experienced a critical press almost from the beginning of his term, and his wife, Hillary Rodham Clinton, was the focus of investigations about investments they had made when he was governor of Arkansas. There was going to be little time to reflect on his presidential legacy. He knew he faced four more years of constantly campaigning to pass legislation and obtain the public's support.

Powerful, strong, leader of the free world, commander in chief—these are common images of the American president. The president epitomizes American government. The only place in the world where television networks assign a permanent camera crew is the White House. The presidency is power—at least according to popular myth.

In this presidency-as-powerhouse myth, presidents are the government's command center. Problems are brought to their desk, they decide on the right courses of action, they issue orders, and an army of aides and bureaucrats carries out their commands.

As Bill Clinton and all other presidents soon discover, nothing could be further from the truth. The main reason why presidents have trouble getting things done is that other policymakers with whom they deal have their own agendas, their own interests, and their own sources of power. Presidents operate in an environment filled with checks and balances and competing centers of power. As one presidential aide put it, "Every time you turn around people resist you."[1] Congress is beholden not to the president but to the individual constituencies of its members. Cabinet members often push their departmental interests and their constituencies (the Department of Agriculture has farmers as its constituency, for example). Rarely can presidents rely on unwavering support from their party, the public, or even their own appointees.

As the pivotal leader in American politics, the president is the subject of unending political analysis and speculation. A perennial question focuses on presidential power. World history is replete with examples of leaders who have exceeded the prescribed boundaries of their power. Can the presidency become too powerful and thus pose a threat to democracy? Or is the Madisonian system strong enough to check any such tendencies? On the other hand, is the president *strong enough* to stand up to the diverse interests in the United States? Does the president have enough power to govern on behalf of the majority?

A second question regarding democratic leaders is the nature of their relationship with the public and its consequences for public policy. The president and vice president are the only officials elected by the entire nation. In their efforts to obtain public support from the broad spectrum of interests in the public, are presidents natural advocates of an expansion of government? Do they promise more than they should in order to please the voters? As they face the frustrations of governing, do presidents seek to centralize authority in the federal government, where they have greater influence, while reducing that of the states? Does the chief executive seek more power through increasing the role of government?

Since not everyone bends easily to even the most persuasive president, the president must be a *leader*. As Richard Neustadt has argued, presidential power is the power to *persuade*, not to command.[2] To accomplish policy goals, the president must get other people—important people—to do things they otherwise would not do. To be effective, the president must have highly developed *political skills* to mobilize influence, manage conflict, negotiate, and fashion compromises. This chapter will examine presidential leadership, but first, you will meet some of the presidents themselves.

THE PRESIDENTS

The presidency is an institution composed of the roles presidents must play, the powers at their disposal, and the large bureaucracy at their command. It is also a highly personal office. The personality of the individual serving as president makes a difference.

GREAT EXPECTATIONS

When President Clinton took the oath of office, he faced many daunting tasks. Perhaps the most difficult was living up to the expectations of the American people. Americans expect the chief executive to ensure peace, prosperity, and security.[3] As President Carter remarked, "The President is . . . held to be responsible for the state of the economy . . . and for the inconveniences, or disappointments, or the concerns of the American people."[4] Americans want a good life, and they look to the president to provide it.

Americans are of two minds about the presidency. On the one hand, they want to believe in a powerful president, one who can do good. They look back longingly on the great presidents of the first American century—Washington, Jefferson, Lincoln—and some in the second century as well, especially Franklin D. Roosevelt and John F. Kennedy.

On the other hand, Americans do not like a concentration of power. Although presidential responsibilities have increased substantially in the past few decades, there has been no corresponding increase in presidential resources to meet these new expectations. Americans are basically individualistic and skeptical of authority. According to Samuel Huntington, "The distinctive aspect of the American Creed is its antigovernment character. Opposition to power, and suspicion of government as the most dangerous embodiment of power, are the central themes of American political thought."[5] Throughout *Government in America,* you have seen the American political culture's strong belief in limited government, liberty, individualism, equality, and democracy. These values generate a distrust of strong leadership, authority, and the public sector in general.

Because Americans' expectations of the presidency are so high, who serves as president is doubly important. Just who are the people who have occupied the Oval Office?

WHO THEY ARE

When Warren G. Harding, one of the least illustrious American presidents, was in office, Clarence Darrow remarked, "When I was a boy, I was told that anybody could become president. Now I'm beginning to believe it." The Constitution simply states that the president must be a natural-born citizen at least 35 years old and must have resided in the United States for at least 14 years. In fact, all American presidents have been white, male, and (except for John Kennedy) Protestant. In other ways, however, the recent collection of presidents suggests considerable variety. Since World War II, the White House has been home to a Missouri haberdasher, a war hero, a Boston Irish politician, a small-town Texas boy who grew up to become the biggest wheeler-dealer in the Senate, a California lawyer described by his enemies as "Tricky Dick" and by his friends as a misunderstood master of national leadership, a former Rose Bowl player who

'Okay, bring in the new guy . . .'

TABLE 13.1 RECENT PRESIDENTS

Harry S Truman (1945-1953) was a Democrat from Missouri. A haberdasher by trade, Truman worked his way up through the political machine in Kansas City to become a U.S. senator from Missouri. Tapped by Roosevelt to be his vice-presidential running mate in 1944, Truman had barely taken office when FDR died. Truman had to decide whether to drop atomic bombs on Japan (he ordered them dropped) and then presided over the trying times of postwar recovery and the beginning of the Cold War. A man of strong opinions, Truman often shot from the lip. Never popular while in office (partly because FDR was a hard act to follow), his stature seemed to grow once he retired to Independence, Missouri.

Dwight D. Eisenhower (1953-1961), a Republican, was born in Texas and reared in Kansas. Though "Ike" had been the commander of Allied Forces in Europe during World War II, he never voted until he became the Republican nominee in 1952. He presided over the relatively tranquil 1950s, offering to the public a grandfatherly image of dependable conservatism and cool crisis management. His public standing remained high, and he crushed the Democratic nominee, Adlai Stevenson, in the 1952 and 1956 presidential elections. Ike made Richard Nixon his vice president but never his friend; he even declined to invite Nixon inside his house at Gettysburg, Pennsylvania.

John F. Kennedy (1961-1963) was a Democrat from Massachusetts. JFK is remembered most for his leadership style; his elegant wife, Jackie; and his tragic assassination in Dallas, Texas, on November 22, 1963. Kennedy was a senator before he ran for president in 1960. Handsome, virile, and graceful, he touted culture and made *charisma* a household word. Kennedy's legislative record was not enviable, but his popularity with the public was impressive. His presidency began in the 1960s era of liberal domestic policies and staunchly anti-Communist foreign policies.

Lyndon B. Johnson (1963-1969) was a Democrat from Texas. As Senate majority leader, Lyndon Johnson was one of the most skilled politicians ever to walk the Capitol corridors. In private he was simultaneously charming, cunning, and coercive. After the culture and charisma of the Kennedy years, LBJ's public image seemed coarse and he was easily ridiculed. Johnson was frustrated that he, unlike Kennedy, somehow lacked the "right background" to mix with the Harvard-educated elite. Nonetheless, he tackled the presidency with energy, launching the War on Poverty at home and escalating the Vietnam War abroad. The latter caused the unmaking of his presidency. In March 1968 he announced that he would neither seek nor accept renomination.

Richard M. Nixon (1969-1974), a Republican, was from California and later New York. Eisenhower's vice president, Nixon was a natural candidate for the Republicans in 1960 but lost that presidential race to John F. Kennedy. Trying again in 1968, Nixon edged out Democrat Hubert Humphrey and the American Independent party's George Wallace. Most interested in foreign policy, Nixon wound down the Vietnam War and established American links with China. Running for reelection in 1972, he crushed George McGovern. During that campaign, though, the Watergate break-in started the beginning of the end of the Nixon presidency. After the House Judiciary Committee voted to recommend his impeachment for high crimes and misdemeanors, Nixon resigned on August 9, 1974.

Gerald R. Ford (1974-1977) was a Republican from Michigan. Ford spent his political career in the House of Representatives before becoming president. He was "the accidental president," becoming vice president when Spiro T. Agnew left office under a cloud of scandal and later becoming president when the same thing happened to Nixon. Though cartoonists depicted Ford as none too intelligent, Ford reestablished respect for a Watergate-tainted presidency. Ford's pardon of Nixon caused him to slip in the polls, and, he maintained, cost him reelection.

Jimmy Carter (1977-1981) was a Democrat from Georgia. Carter, who had been a naval officer, a peanut warehouser, and a governor, surprised the nation by first winning the Democratic nomination in 1976 and then defeating the incumbent president, Gerald Ford. "If I had to choose one politician to sit at the Pearly Gates and pass judgment on my soul," wrote Carter's ex-speech writer James Fallows in the *Atlantic,* "Jimmy Carter

TABLE 13.1 RECENT PRESIDENTS Continued...

would be the one." But Carter also, claimed Fallows, lacked the sophistication, the ability to communicate his goals, and the passion necessary to be an effective leader. Once in office, Carter demonstrated that being a Washington outsider may help get one elected but makes it hard to influence the Washington community. Carter was defeated in his bid for reelection by Ronald Reagan.

Ronald W. Reagan (1981-1989) was a Republican from California. Born in Illinois, Reagan moved to California and pursued a show-business career, becoming an actor of middling stature. His presidency of the Screen Actors' Guild brought him into politics. As governor of California, he was ideologically conservative but more liberal in his policies than opponents had feared. As president, he managed to convey genial affability, using power with poise. Resoundingly reelected in 1984, his principal goals were to pare domestic spending and boost defense spending while coping with massive deficits.

George H. W. Bush (1989-1993) was a Republican from Texas. The son of a prominent New England family, Bush moved to Texas and made his fortune in the oil business. After a short tenure in Congress, he held a series of prominent jobs, including head of the Central Intelligence Agency, ambassador to the United Nations, ambassador to China, and vice president for 8 years under Ronald Reagan. His presidency was marked by the success of the Gulf War but also by a stagnant economy that ultimately cost him reelection.

Bill Clinton (1993-) is a Democrat from Arkansas. A Rhodes Scholar and long-time governor, he helped move the Democratic party toward the center of the political spectrum. Despite a flood of attacks on his character, he beat George Bush in 1992 by asking the American people to support change and reject the legacy of Ronald Reagan.

had spent his entire political career in the House of Representatives, a former governor who had been a Georgia peanut wholesaler, an actor who was also a former governor of California, a CIA chief and ambassador who was the son of a U.S. senator, and an ambitious governor from a small state (see Table 13.1).

All manner of men have occupied the Oval Office. Thomas Jefferson was a scientist and scholar who assembled dinosaur bones when presidential business was slack. Woodrow Wilson, the only political scientist ever to become president, combined a Presbyterian moral fervor and righteousness with a professor's intimidating style of leadership and speech making. His successor, Warren G. Harding, became president because Republican leaders thought he looked like one. Poker was his pastime. Out of his element in the job, Harding is almost everyone's choice as the worst American president. His speech making, said opponent William G. McAdoo, sounded "like an army of pompous phrases marching across the landscape in search of an idea." Harding's friends stole the government blind, prompting his brief assessment of the presidency: "God, what a job!"

In this potpourri of personalities, James David Barber has identified some patterns in an effort to understand how presidents perform. He suggests that one can examine presidents by looking at their *presidential character*.[6] Presidents, he claims, vary in their *activity* or *passivity* toward the job. Some, like Lyndon Johnson, throw themselves into the job with great vigor and work furiously at being president; others, like Calvin Coolidge (who sometimes slept 11 hours at night), do not. Presidents also vary in their *positive* or *negative* response to politics. Some, like Franklin Roosevelt and John Kennedy, claim to love politics and enjoy the job of being president; others, like Richard Nixon, feel that duty impels their performance and have a grim, self-sacrificial attitude toward the job.

Barber argues that presidents who are both active and negative—presidents like Lyndon Johnson and Richard Nixon (see Table 13.2)—are prone to tragedy. When such presidents experience certain kinds of stress, he says, their psychological needs cause them to persist in failed policies.

Not all presidential scholars agree with Barber's typology of presidential character. Garry Wills describes Barber's analysis as an example of the "games academics play."[7] Some criticize the categories in which Barber placed the presidents. Some scholars believe, for example, that Eisenhower was not "pas-

TABLE 13.2 BARBER'S CLASSIFICATION OF PRESIDENTS' CHARACTER

ACTIVE-POSITIVE	ACTIVE-NEGATIVE	PASSIVE-POSITIVE	PASSIVE-NEGATIVE
F. Roosevelt	Hoover	Taft	Coolidge
Truman	Wilson	Harding	Eisenhower
Kennedy	Johnson	Reagan	
Ford	Nixon		
Carter			
Bush			

SOURCE: James David Barber, *The Presidential Character,* 4th ed. (Englewood Cliffs, NJ: Prentice-Hall, 1992).

sive" at all.[8] Others feel that such categories are uninformative. Kennedy, Carter, Ford, and Bush all fall into the "active-positive" category, but there are great differences in their performances as president. There are many opinions, but no single answer to the question of what makes a successful president.

HOW THEY GOT THERE

No one is born to be the future president of the United States in the way that someone is born to be the future king or queen of England. Regardless of their background or character, all presidents must come to the job through one of two basic routes.

Elections: The Normal Road to the White House. Most presidents take a familiar journey to 1600 Pennsylvania Avenue: They run for president through the electoral process, which is described in Chapters 9 and 10. Once in office, presidents are guaranteed a 4-year term by the Constitution, but the **Twenty-second Amendment,** passed in 1951, limits them to two such terms.

Only 11 of the 41 presidents before Bill Clinton have actually served two or more full terms in the White House: Washington, Jefferson, Madison, Monroe, Jackson, Grant, Cleveland (whose terms were not consecutive), Wilson, Franklin Roosevelt, Eisenhower, and Reagan. A few decided against a second term ("Silent Cal" Coolidge said simply, "I do not choose to run"). Five other presidents (Polk, Pierce, Buchanan, Hayes, and Lyndon Johnson) also threw in the towel at the end of one full term. Seven others (both of the Adamses, Van Buren, Taft, Hoover, Carter, and Bush) thought they had earned a second term, but the voters disagreed.

The Vice Presidency: Another Road to the White House. For more than 10 percent of American history, the presidency has actually been occupied by an individual not elected to the office. About one in five presidents got the job not through the normal road of elections, but because they were vice president when the incumbent president either died or (in Nixon's case) resigned (see Table 13.3). In the twentieth century, almost one-third (5 of 16) of those who occupied the office were "accidental presidents." The most accidental of all was Gerald Ford, who did not run for either the vice presidency or the presidency before taking office. Ford was nominated vice president by President Nixon when Vice President Spiro Agnew resigned; he then assumed the presidency when Nixon himself resigned.

Richard Nixon was the only American President ever to resign his office. Nixon decided to resign rather than face impeachment for his role in the Watergate scandal, a series of illegal wiretaps, break-ins, and cover-ups.

TABLE 13.3 INCOMPLETE PRESIDENTIAL TERMS

PRESIDENT	TERM	SUCCEEDED BY
William Henry Harrison	March 4, 1841-April 4, 1841	John Tyler
Zachary Taylor	March 5, 1849-July 9, 1850	Millard Fillmore
Abraham Lincoln	March 4, 1865-April 15, 1865[a]	Andrew Johnson
James A. Garfield	March 4, 1881-September 19, 1881	Chester A. Arthur
William McKinley	March 4, 1901-September 14, 1901[a]	Theodore Roosevelt
Warren G. Harding	March 4, 1921-August 2, 1923	Calvin Coolidge
Franklin D. Roosevelt	January 20, 1945-April 12, 1945[b]	Harry S. Truman
John F. Kennedy	January 20, 1961-November 22, 1963	Lyndon B. Johnson
Richard M. Nixon	January 20, 1973-August 9, 1974[a]	Gerald R. Ford

[a]Second term. [b]Fourth term.

Neither politicians nor political scientists have paid much attention to the vice presidency. Once the choice of a party's "second team" was an afterthought; now it is often an effort to placate some important symbolic constituency. Southerner Jimmy Carter selected a well-known liberal, Walter Mondale, as his running mate, and Ronald Reagan chose his chief rival, George Bush, in part to please Republican moderates.

Vice presidents have rarely enjoyed the job. John Nance Garner of Texas, one of Franklin Roosevelt's vice presidents, declared that the job was "not worth a warm bucket of spit." Some have performed so poorly as to have been an embarrassment to the president. After Woodrow Wilson's debilitating stroke, almost everyone agreed that Vice President Thomas Marshall—a man who shirked all responsibility, including cabinet meetings—would be a disaster as acting president. Spiro Agnew, Richard Nixon's first vice president, had to resign and was convicted of evading taxes (on bribes he had accepted).

Once in office, vice presidents find that their main job is waiting. Constitutionally, they are assigned the minor tasks of presiding over the Senate and voting in case of a tie among the senators. As George Bush put it when he was vice president, "the buck doesn't stop here." Recent presidents, though, have taken their vice presidents more seriously, involving them in policy discussions and important diplomacy.[9]

Jimmy Carter and Ronald Reagan, both Washington outsiders, chose vice presidents who had substantial Washington experience: Walter Mondale and George Bush. To become intimates of the president, both had to be completely loyal, losing their political independence in the process. Vice President Bush, for example, was accused of knowing more about the Iran-Contra affair than he admitted, but he steadfastly refused to reveal his discussions with President Reagan on the matter.

When his turn came to choose a vice president, Bush selected Senator Dan Quayle of Indiana, considered by many a political lightweight. Quayle met regularly with the president, represented him in discussions with the leaders of numerous countries, chaired a prominent effort to decrease government regulation, and raised funds for Republican candidates. Albert Gore, Bill Clinton's choice for vice president, is a Washington insider and plays a prominent role in the administration.

Impeachment and Succession. Getting rid of a discredited president before the end of a term is not easy. The Constitution prescribes the process through **impeachment**, which is roughly the political equivalent of an indictment in criminal law. The House of Representatives may, by majority vote, impeach the president for "Treason, Bribery, or other high Crimes and Misdemeanors." Once the House votes for impeachment, the case goes to the Senate, which tries the accused president, with the chief justice of the Supreme Court presiding. By a two-thirds vote, the Senate may convict and remove the president from office.

Only once has a president been impeached: Andrew Johnson, Lincoln's successor, was impeached by the House in 1868 on charges stemming from his disagreement with radical Republicans. He narrowly escaped conviction. Richard Nixon came as close to impeachment as any president since then. On July 31, 1974, the

SHOULD NIXON HAVE BEEN IMPEACHED?

You Are the Policymaker

If a novelist had invented Watergate, it would have made a fascinating but not very believable story. As reality, it forced the resignation of the president who was elected by what was then the largest popular majority in American history—Richard M. Nixon.

Dozens of events and decisions produced the Watergate affair. Many centered on Nixon's 1972 reelection campaign. His campaign manager, former Attorney General John Mitchell, hired a man named G. Gordon Liddy as counsel to the Committee to Reelect the President (CREEP). Liddy did little lawyering at CREEP, but he did develop an expensive "counter-intelligence" program.

On January 2, 1972, Liddy presented his multimillion-dollar plan to Mitchell, who later described the plan as including "mugging squads, kidnapping teams, prostitutes to compromise the opposition, and electronic surveillance." He ordered Liddy to scale down the program.

One offshoot of Liddy's plan was to plant a wiretap at the headquarters of the Democratic National Committee (DNC) in Washington's Watergate complex. On June 17, 1972, five men were caught inside the DNC headquarters with burglary tools, bugging devices, and a stack of one hundred dollar bills. Their links to CREEP soon became known, and Liddy himself was arrested. Nixon's press secretary, Ron Ziegler, dismissed the incident as a "third-rate burglary," and Nixon assured the press that the White House had no involvement whatsoever in the bungled break-in.

To this day, no one has demonstrated that Nixon had prior knowledge of the break-in. But within hours after the arrests, paper shredders at the White House and CREEP were destroying documents that might link the burglars to the White House. CREEP and White House officials pressured Nixon's personal lawyer, Herbert Kalmbach, to collect funds quietly to "support the families" of the accused. Anthony Ulasewicz, a former New York police officer working for the White House, later regaled the Watergate Committee with stories of leaving money in paper bags to be picked up and delivered to the accused burglars. *Washington Post* reporters Robert Woodward and Carl Bernstein began an investigation that eventually tracked the Watergate break-in and its cover-up to the very door of the Oval Office.

As the trail got closer, Nixon's aides resigned one by one. Chief of Staff Bob Haldeman, domestic-policy advisor John Ehrlichman, and others were writing their resignations and ringing up their lawyers simultaneously. On May 17, 1973, hearings of the Senate Select Committee on Campaign Activities opened, chaired by Senator Sam Ervin (D-NC). Nixon's former White House counsel, John Dean, claimed that Nixon had known more than he was admitting and had played fast and loose with the truth about White House involvement. Haldeman and Ehrlichman defended the president.

One White House functionary, Alexander Butterfield, broke the news that Nixon had a secret taping system that recorded every conversation in the Oval Office. The battle for control of the tapes began. The Ervin committee demanded access to the tapes. Courts trying the Watergate defendants subpoenaed them. Nixon asserted that executive privilege permitted him to refuse to disclose them. Finally, the Supreme Court, in *United States v. Nixon* (1974), ruled that Nixon had to hand over the tapes to courts trying the Watergate burglars. The tapes confirmed that Nixon *had* been involved in the cover-up (a felony) and had been lying to the American people.

As the Watergate cover-up unraveled, more became known about what John Mitchell called "the White House horrors." Nixon's White House aides and CREEP officials had sponsored the burglary of the office of a psychiatrist treating Daniel Ellsberg, an opponent of the Vietnam War who had leaked classified documents to the press; they had audited the administration's opponents' income tax records, had tapped phones illegally, had collected campaign contributions (preferably cash) in return for specific favors, and had manipulated Nixon's own tax returns.

The House launched impeachment hearings in 1974. On July 31, 1974, the Judiciary Committee recommended Nixon's impeachment. Facing almost

continued. . .

Should Nixon Have Been Impeached, continued. . .

certain impeachment by the House and probable conviction by the Senate, Nixon resigned 10 days later. Shortly after assuming the presidency, Gerald Ford pardoned Nixon, arguing that years of trials and appeals would aggravate bitterness over Watergate. Most of Nixon's aides were not so lucky—many were convicted and served prison sentences.

Nevertheless, to this day there are some, perhaps many, who believe that Richard Nixon was unfairly hounded from office. They claim he and his aides really did nothing that was uncommon in American politics. His only problem, they contend, is that he got caught. Should Nixon have lost his presidency? If *you* had been a member of the House in 1974, would you have voted to impeach the president?

House Judiciary Committee voted to recommend his impeachment to the full House as a result of the **Watergate** scandal. Nixon escaped a certain vote for impeachment by resigning. (See "You Are the Policymaker: Should Nixon Have Been Impeached?")

Constitutional amendments cover one other important problem concerning the presidential term: presidential disability and succession. Several times a president has become disabled, incapable of carrying out the job for weeks or even months at a time. After Woodrow Wilson suffered a stroke, his wife became virtual acting president. The **Twenty-fifth Amendment** (1967) clarified some of the Constitution's vagueness about disability. The Amendment permits the vice president to become acting president if the vice president and the president's cabinet determine that the president is disabled or if the president declares his own disability, and it outlines how a recuperated president can reclaim the Oval Office. Other laws specify the order of presidential succession—from the vice president, to the Speaker of the House, to the president *pro tempore* of the Senate, and down through the cabinet.

The Twenty-fifth Amendment also created a means for selecting a new vice president when the office becomes vacant (a frequent occurrence). The president nominates a new vice president, who assumes the office when both houses of Congress approve the nomination.

PRESIDENTIAL POWERS

The contemporary presidency hardly resembles the one the Constitution framers designed in 1787. The executive office they conceived had more limited authority, fewer responsibilities, and much less organizational structure than today's presidency. The founders feared both anarchy and monarchy. They wanted an independent executive but disagreed about both the form the office should take and the powers it should exercise. In the end, they created an executive unlike any the world had ever seen.[10] (See "America in Perspective: What a Difference a Border Makes.")

At first some delegates proposed a plural executive—dividing responsibility for various areas of power or functioning as a committee. Others felt that governing a large nation required a single president with significant powers. James Wilson, a delegate from Pennsylvania, argued that only a single individual could combine the necessary characteristics of "energy, dispatch, and responsibility." Critics immediately responded that such an executive would be dangerous—"the fetus of monarchy," claimed Edmund Randolph. Wilson carried the day, aided by the fact that virtually everyone assumed that the first president would be George Washington, the person the delegates most trusted not to abuse power.

CONSTITUTIONAL POWERS

When it came to detailing the executive's power, the delegates to the Constitutional Convention turned for inspiration to the constitutions of New York and New Jersey, states with strong governors. Couching the description of presidential powers in the language of two state constitutions made it more palatable to the delegates, who adopted most of it with little debate.

The Constitution says remarkably little about presidential power. The discussion of the presidency begins with these general words: "The executive power shall be vested in a president of the United States of America." It goes on to list just a few powers (see Table 13.4, page 327). The framers' invention fit nicely within the Madisonian system of shared power and checks and balances. There is little that presidents can do on their own, and they share executive, legislative, and judicial power with the other branches of government.

WHAT A DIFFERENCE A BORDER MAKES

America in Perspective

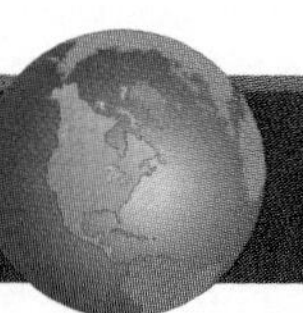

Mexico's Constitution resembles the American Constitution in many important ways. It provides for the separation of power among three branches of government, legal opposition parties, and independent, organized interest groups. Under such a system one might anticipate that Mexican presidents would face a necessity to persuade similar to that of chief executives in the United States. Such an assumption would be incorrect, however, because the Mexican government is characterized by a strong centralization of power in the hands of presidents and their parties, a structure that might make American presidents envious indeed.

Mexican presidents enjoy a wide range of constitutionally invested and *de facto* authority. Neither the judicial nor the legislative branch is independent of their control. The decisions of the highest court in Mexico generally follow the policy of the executive, and the legislative branch is equally compliant. The two houses of the legislature are often regarded as a rubber stamp for presidential policy. In addition, presidents can appoint or dismiss all but a few public officeholders, including judges.

Immunity from criticism in the press has eroded in the past decades, but criticism is still discouraged by a state monopoly on the supply of newsprint paper. The government also controls the bulk of paid advertisements in many publications, and it uses its discretion to discourage critics. Presidents have also silenced criticism through government-orchestrated hostile takeovers of newspapers. Television is virtually monopolized by a private firm with close working relations with the governing party.

It is easy to imagine American presidents wishing they were south of the border in Mexico. Despite what seemed to be an era of reform, the essential powers of the Mexican president are still intact.

SOURCE: Wayne A. Cornelius and Ann L. Craig, "Politics in Mexico," in Gabriel A. Almond and G. Bingham Powell, Jr., eds., *Comparative Politics Today: A World View,* 5th ed. (New York: HarperCollins, 1992), 475-478.

Institutional balance was essential to the convention delegates, who had in mind the abuses of past executives combined with the excesses of state legislatures (discussed in Chapter 2). The problem was how to preserve the balance without jeopardizing the independence of the separate branches or impeding the lawful exercise of their authority. The framers resolved this problem by checking those powers that they believed to be most dangerous, the ones that historically had been subject to the greatest abuse (for example, they gave Congress the power to declare war and approve treaties and presidential appointments), while protecting the general spheres of authority from encroachment (the executive, for instance, was given a qualified veto).

Presidential responsibility was also encouraged by provisions for reelection and a short term of office. For those executives who flagrantly abused their authority, impeachment was the ultimate recourse.

THE EXPANSION OF POWER

Today there is more to presidential power than the Constitution alone suggests, and that power is derived from many sources. Chapter 2 showed that the role of the president changed as America increased in prominence on the world stage and that technology has also reshaped the presidency. George Washington's ragtag militias (mostly disbanded by the time the first commander in chief took command) are of a much different order than the mighty nuclear arsenal that today's president commands.

Presidents themselves have taken the initiative in developing new roles for the office. In fact, many presidents have enlarged the power of the presidency by expanding the president's responsibilities and political resources. Thomas Jefferson was the first leader of a mass political party. Andrew Jackson presented himself as the direct representative of the people. Lincoln mobilized the country for war, whereas Theodore Roosevelt mobilized the public behind his policies. He and Woodrow Wilson set precedents for presidents to serve as world leaders; Wilson and Franklin D. Roosevelt developed the role of the president as manager of the economy. The following sections will explore the relationship between the president's responsibilities and resources by examining how contemporary presidents try to lead the nation.

TABLE 13.4 CONSTITUTIONAL POWERS OF THE PRESIDENT

National Security Powers

Serve as commander in chief of the armed forces
Make treaties with other nations, subject to the agreement of two-thirds of the Senate
Nominate ambassadors, with the agreement of a majority of the Senate
Receive ambassadors of other nations, thereby conferring diplomatic recognition on other governments

Legislative Powers

Present information on the state of the union to Congress
Recommend legislation to Congress
Convene both houses of Congress on extraordinary occasions
Adjourn Congress if the House and Senate cannot agree on adjournment
Veto legislation (Congress may overrule with two-thirds vote of each house)

Administrative Powers

"Take care that the laws be faithfully executed"
Nominate officials as provided for by Congress and with the agreement of a majority of the Senate
Request written opinions of administrative officials
Fill administrative vacancies during congressional recesses

Judicial Powers

Grant reprieves and pardons for federal offenses (except impeachment)
Nominate federal judges, who are confirmed by a majority of the Senate

RUNNING THE GOVERNMENT: THE CHIEF EXECUTIVE

Although the president is often called the "chief executive," it is easy to forget that one of the president's most important roles is presiding over the administration of government. This role does not receive the same publicity as appealing to the public for support for policy initiatives, dealing with Congress, or negotiating with foreign powers, but it is of great importance nevertheless.

We see in Table 13.4 that the Constitution exhorts the president to "take care that the laws be faithfully executed." In the early days of the republic, this clerical-sounding function was fairly easy. Today, the sprawling federal bureaucracy spends more than $1.6 trillion a year and numbers more than 4.5 million civilian and military employees. Running such a large organization would be a full-time job for even the most talented of executives, yet it is only one of the president's many jobs.

One of the resources for controlling this bureaucracy is the presidential power to appoint top-level administrators. New presidents have about three hundred of these high-level positions available for appointment—cabinet and subcabinet jobs, agency heads, and other non-civil service posts—plus 2,000 lesser jobs. Since passage of the Budgeting and Accounting Act of 1921, presidents have had one other important executive tool: the power to recommend agency budgets to Congress.

The vastness of the executive branch, the complexity of public policy, and the desire to accomplish their policy goals have led presidents in recent years to pay even closer attention to appointing officials who will be responsive to the president's policies. Presidents have also taken more interest in the regulations issued by agencies. This trend toward centralizing decision making in the White House pleases those who feel the bureaucracy should be more responsive to elected officials. On the other hand, it dismays those who believe that increased politicization of policymaking will undermine the "neutral competence" of professional bureaucrats and may encourage them to follow the policy preferences of the president rather than the intent of laws as passed by Congress.

Chapter 15 on the bureaucracy explores the president's role as chief executive further. This chapter will focus on how presidents go about organizing and

Members of the president's cabinet are important for both the power they exercise and the status they symbolize. President Clinton promised to form a cabinet that was representative of America's diversity. Pictured here is Secretary of Energy Frederico Peña, an Hispanic.

using the parts of the executive branch most under their control—the cabinet, the Executive Office of the President, and the White House staff.

THE CABINET

Although the Constitution does not mention the group of presidential advisors known as the **cabinet**, every president has had one. The cabinet is too large and too diverse, and its members are too concerned with representing the interests of their departments, for it to serve as a collective board of directors, however. The major decisions remain in the president's hands. Legend has it that Abraham Lincoln asked his cabinet to vote on an issue, and the result was unanimity in opposition to his view. He announced the decision as "seven nays and one aye, the ayes have it."

George Washington's cabinet was small, consisting of just three secretaries (state, treasury, and war) and the attorney general. Presidents since Washington have increased the size of the cabinet by requesting that new executive departments be established. These requests must be approved by Congress, which creates the department. Today 13 secretaries and the attorney general head executive departments and constitute the cabinet (see Table 13.5). In addition, presidents may designate other officials (the ambassador to the United Nations is a common choice) as cabinet members.[11]

Even in his "official family," the president is subject to the constitutional system of checks and balances, however. President Bush met resistance when he nominated John Tower, a former senator, to be secretary of defense. After a bitter debate, Tower was rejected by the Senate, handing the president a serious defeat. President Clinton's first nominee to serve as attorney general, Zoe Baird, had to withdraw from consideration after she came under fire from senators of both parties for hiring an illegal alien as her baby sitter and failing to pay Social Security taxes for her employee.

THE EXECUTIVE OFFICE

Next to the White House sits an ornate building called the EOB, or Executive Office Building. It houses a collection of offices and organizations loosely grouped into the Executive Office of the President.[12] Some of these offices (such as the Council of Economic Advisors) are created by legislation, and some are organized essentially by the president. Starting small in 1939, when it was established by President Roosevelt, the Executive Office has grown with the rest of government. In the Executive Office are housed three major policymaking bodies—the National Security Council, the Council of Economic Advisors, and the Office of Management and Budget—along with several other units that serve the president (see Figure 13.1, page 330).

The **National Security Council (NSC)** is the committee that links the president's key foreign and military policy advisors. Its formal members include the president, vice president, and secretaries of state and defense, but its informal membership is broader. The president's special assistant for national security affairs plays a major role in the NSC. The occupant of this post has responsibility for running the council's staff. This assistant and the staff provide the president with information and policy recommendations on national security, aid the president in national security crisis management, coordinate agency and departmental activities bearing on national security, and monitor the implementation of national security policy.

TABLE 13.5

THE CABINET DEPARTMENTS

DEPARTMENT	FUNCTION
The Department of State	Founded in 1789, responsible for making foreign policy, including treaty negotiations
The Department of Treasury	The government's banker, founded in 1789
The Department of Defense	Created in 1947 by consolidating the former Departments of the Army and the Navy
The Department of Justice	Created in 1870 to serve as the government's attorney, headed by the attorney general
The Department of the Interior	Created in 1849, manages the nation's natural resources, including wildlife and public lands
The Department of Agriculture	Created in 1862, administers farm and food stamp programs and aids farmers
The Department of Commerce	Created in 1903 as the Department of Commerce and Labor, aids businesses and conducts the U.S. census
The Department of Labor	Separated from the Department of Commerce in 1913, runs programs and aids labor in various ways
The Department of Health and Human Services	Runs health and welfare programs; created as the Department of Health, Education, and Welfare in 1953; it lost its education function in 1979 and Social Security in 1995
The Department of Housing and Urban Development	Created in 1966, responsible for urban and housing programs
The Department of Transportation	Created in 1966, responsible for mass transportation and highway programs
The Department of Energy	Created in 1977, responsible for energy policy and research, including atomic energy
The Department of Education	Created in 1979, responsible for the federal government's education programs
The Department of Veterans Affairs	Created in 1988, responsible for programs aiding veterans

The **Council of Economic Advisors (CEA)** has three members, each appointed by the president, who advise him on economic policy. They prepare the *Annual Report of the Council of Economic Advisors* and help the president make policy on inflation, unemployment, and other economic matters.

The **Office of Management and Budget (OMB)** grew out of the Bureau of the Budget (BOB) created in 1921. The OMB is composed of a handful of political appointees and more than 600 career officials, many of whom are highly skilled professionals. Its major responsibility is to prepare the president's budget (discussed in Chapter 14). President Nixon revamped the BOB in 1970 in an attempt to make it a managerial as well as a budgetary agency, changing its name in the process to stress its managerial functions.

Because each presidential appointee and department will have its own agenda, presidents need a clearinghouse—the OMB. Presidents use the OMB to review legislative proposals from the cabinet and other executive agencies so that they can determine whether they want an agency to propose these initiatives to Congress. The OMB assesses the proposals' budgetary implications and advises presidents on the proposals' consistency with their overall program. The OMB also plays an important role in reviewing regulations proposed by departments and agencies.

Though presidents find that the Executive Office is smaller and more manageable than the cabinet depart-

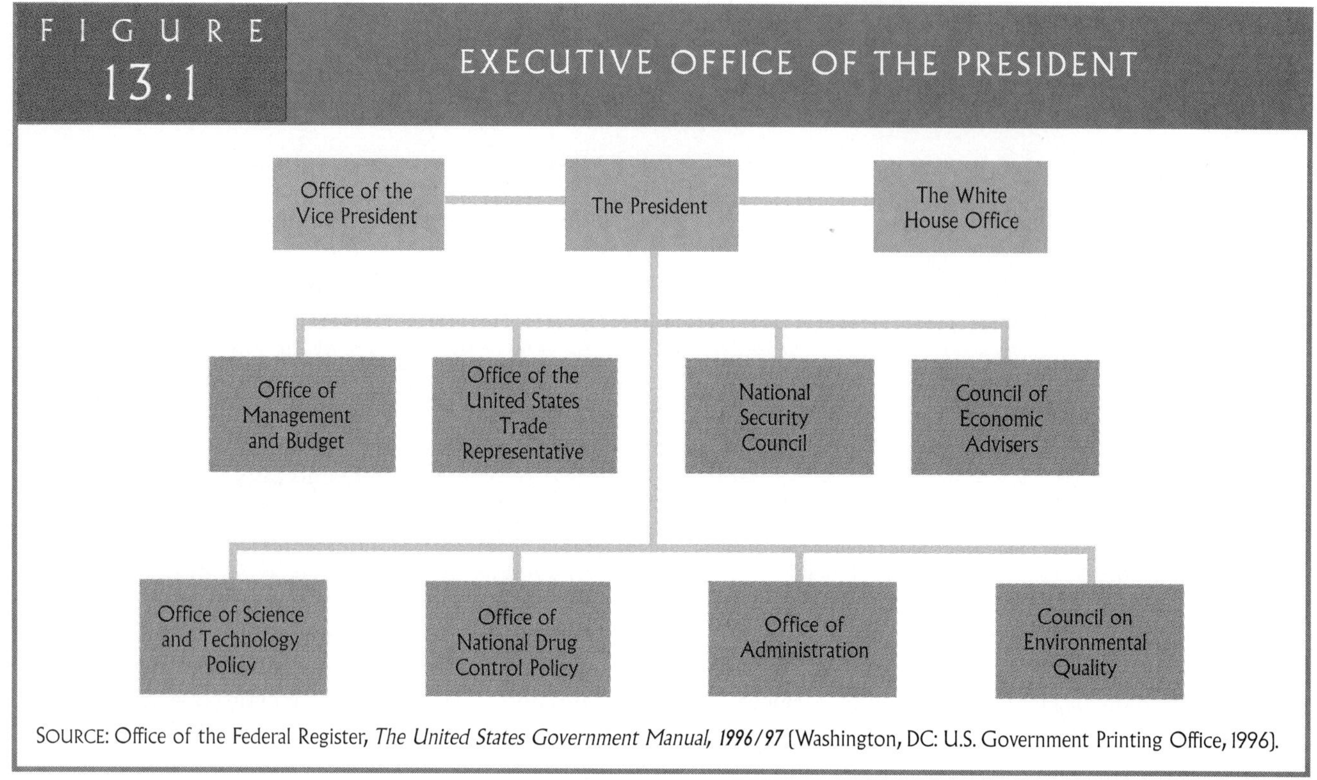

SOURCE: Office of the Federal Register, *The United States Government Manual, 1996/97* (Washington, DC: U.S. Government Printing Office, 1996).

ments, it is still filled with people performing jobs required by law. There is, however, one part of the presidential system that presidents can truly call their own: the White House staff.

THE WHITE HOUSE STAFF

Before Franklin D. Roosevelt, the president's personal staff resources were minimal. Thomas Jefferson was served by only one messenger and one secretary. A hundred years later the president's staff had grown only to 13, including clerks and secretaries. Woodrow Wilson was in the habit of typing his own letters. As recently as the 1920s, the entire budget for the White House staff was no more than $80,000.

The White House staff consists of the key aides that the president sees daily: the chief of staff, congressional liaison people, a press secretary, a national security assistant, and a few other administrative and political assistants. Today, there are about 600 people at work on the White House staff—many of whom the president rarely sees—who provide the chief executive with a wide variety of services ranging from making advance travel preparations to answering the avalanche of letters received each year (see Figure 13.2).

The top aides in the White House hierarchy are people who owe total loyalty to the president, and the president turns to them for advice on the most serious or mundane matters of governance. Good staff people are self-effacing, working only for the boss and shunning the limelight. The 1939 report of the Brownlow Committee, which served as the basis for the development of the modern White House staff, argued that presidential assistants should have a "passion for anonymity." So important are their roles, though, that the names of top White House aides quickly become well known. Woodrow Wilson's Colonel Edward M. House, Franklin D. Roosevelt's Harry Hopkins, Richard Nixon's Henry Kissinger, and George Bush's John Sununu, for example, did much to shape domestic and global policy.

Presidents rely heavily on their staffs for information, policy options, and analysis. Different presidents have different relationships with their staffs. They all organize the White House to serve their own political and policy needs and their own decision-making style. Most presidents end up choosing some form of *hierarchical* organization with a chief of staff at the top, whose job it is to see that everyone else is doing his or her job and that the president's time and interests are protected. A few presidents, such as John F. Kennedy, have employed a *wheel-and-spokes* system of White House management in which many aides had equal status and were balanced against one another in the process of decision making.[13] In all systems, White House aides are central in the policy-making process—

FIGURE 13.2 PRINCIPAL OFFICES IN THE WHITE HOUSE

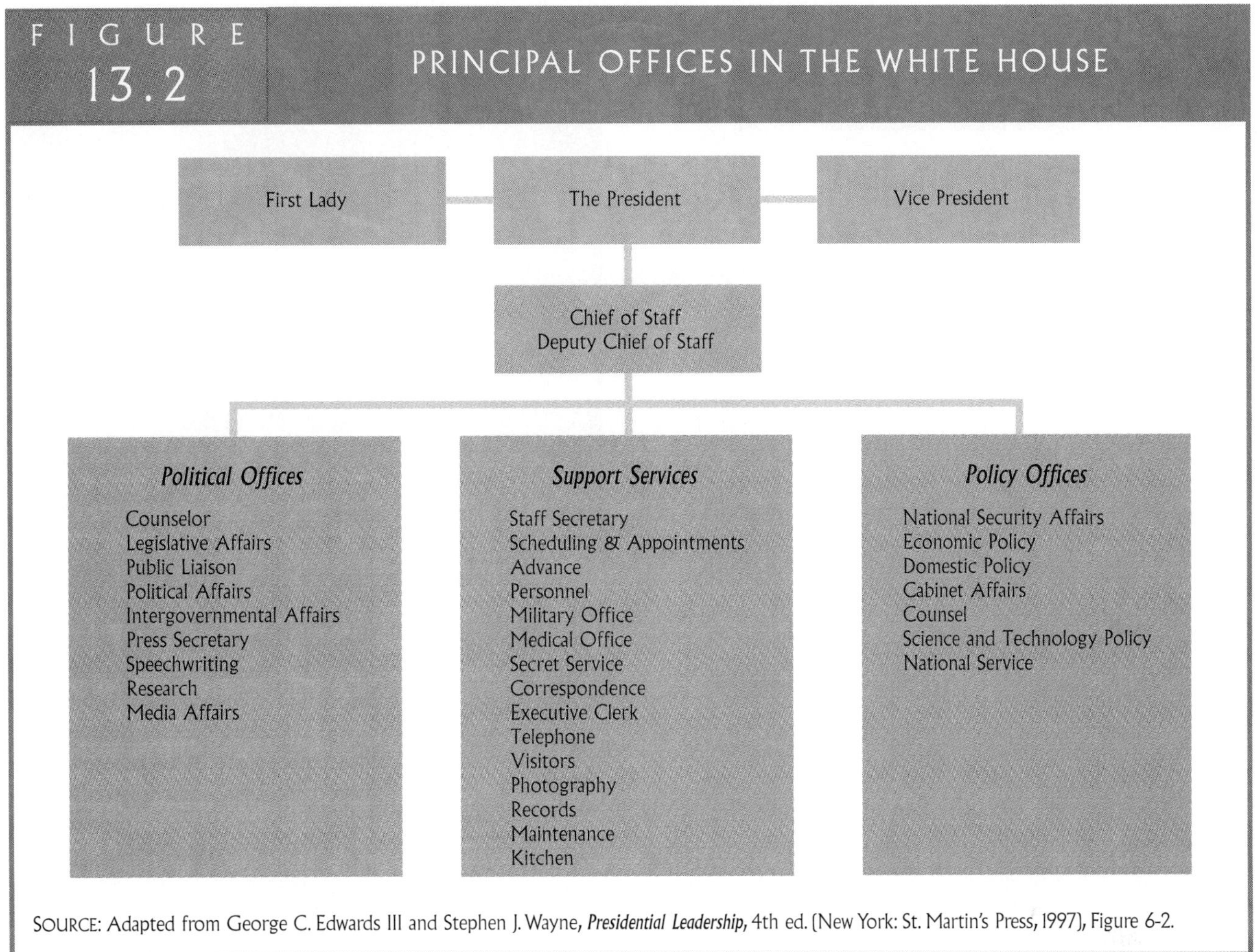

SOURCE: Adapted from George C. Edwards III and Stephen J. Wayne, ***Presidential Leadership***, 4th ed. (New York: St. Martin's Press, 1997), Figure 6-2.

fashioning options, negotiating agreements, writing presidential statements, controlling paperwork, molding legislative details, and generally giving the president their opinions on most matters.

No presidential management styles contrasted more sharply than those of Presidents Carter and Reagan. Carter was a detail man, pouring endlessly over memoranda and facts. President Reagan was the consummate delegator. So adept at dispersing authority was Reagan that his advisors—the news media often called them his "handlers"—periodically felt it necessary to have the president insist that "I am the boss" in media interviews.

George Bush's operating style fell between the extremes of his two immediate predecessors. He consulted widely both within and outside of government, and he insisted on letting others' views reach him unfiltered by his staff. He was considerably more accessible than Reagan and devoted more energy to decision making. At the same time, he liked to delegate responsibility to his subordinates and took little initiative in domestic policy.

President Clinton, like Carter, immerses himself in the details of policy. He has run an open White House, dealing directly with a large number of aides and reading countless policy memoranda. His emphasis on deliberation and his fluid staffing system have generated criticism that his White House is "indecisive" and "chaotic."

Despite presidents' reliance on their staffs, it is the president who sets the tone for the White House. Although it is common to blame presidential advisors for mistakes made in the White House, it is the president's responsibility to demand that staff members analyze a full range of options and their probable consequences before they offer the president their advice. If the chief executive does not demand quality staff work, then the work is less likely to be done, and disaster or embarrassment may follow.

Presidents not only have responsibility for running the executive branch; they must also deal intensively with the legislative branch. These dealings are the topic of the following section.

PRESIDENTIAL LEADERSHIP OF CONGRESS: THE POLITICS OF SHARED POWERS

Near the top of any presidential job description would be "working with Congress." Because the American system of separation of powers is actually one of *shared* powers, presidents can rarely operate independently of Congress. If presidents are to succeed in leaving their stamp on public policy, much of their time in office must be devoted to leading the legislature to support presidential initiatives.

White House staff members play a key role in presidential decision making. Here, Erskine Bowles, White House Chief of Staff, meets with President Clinton.

CHIEF LEGISLATOR

Nowhere does the Constitution use the phrase *chief legislator*; it is strictly a phrase invented by textbook writers to emphasize the executive's importance in the legislative process. The Constitution does require that the president give a State of the Union address to Congress and instructs the president to bring other matters to Congress' attention "from time to time." In fact, as we noted in Chapter 12, the president plays a major role in shaping the congressional agenda.

The Constitution also gives the president power to **veto** congressional legislation. Once Congress passes a bill, the president may (1) sign it, making it law; (2) veto it, sending it back to Congress with the reasons for rejecting it; or (3) let it become law after 10 working days by not doing anything. Congress can pass a vetoed law, however, if two-thirds of each house vote to override the president. At one point in the lawmaking process the president has the last word, however: if Congress adjourns within 10 days after submitting a bill, the president can simply let it die by neither signing nor vetoing it. This process is called a **pocket veto.** Table 13.6 shows how frequently recent presidents used the veto.

The presidential veto is usually effective; only about 4 percent of all vetoed bills have been overridden by Congress since the nation's founding. Thus, even the threat of a presidential veto can be an effective tool for persuading Congress to give more weight to the presi-

TABLE 13.6 PRESIDENTIAL VETOES

PRESIDENT	REGULAR VETOES	VETOES OVERRIDDEN	PERCENTAGE OF VETOES OVERRIDDEN	POCKET VETOES	TOTAL VETOES
Eisenhower	73	2	3	108	181
Kennedy	12	0	0	9	21
Johnson	16	0	0	14	30
Nixon	26	7	27	17	43
Ford	48	12	25	18	66
Carter	13	2	15	18	31
Reagan	39	9	23	39	78
Bush	31	1	3	15	46
Clinton*	17	1	6	0	17

*First Term.

dent's views. On the other hand, the veto is a blunt instrument. Presidents must accept or reject bills in their entirety; they cannot veto only the parts they do not like (most governors have a line item veto that allows them to veto particular portions of a bill). As a result, the White House often must accept provisions of a bill it opposes in order to obtain provisions that it desires. For example, in 1987, Congress passed the entire discretionary budget of the federal government in one bill (called an "omnibus" bill). President Reagan had to accept the whole package or lose appropriations for the entire government.

In 1996, Congress passed a law granting the president authority to propose rescinding funds in appropriations bills and tax provisions that apply to only a few people. The president has 5 days following his signing of tax or spending bills to propose rescissions, and the only way such provisions can become law is that Congress passes them as separate bills, which would then be subject to a presidential veto. The law was immediately challenged in the courts as being an unconstitutional grant of power to the president, but the Supreme Court refused to hear the case in 1997. So, for the time being, the law will give the president much greater leverage in negotiating with Congress over spending bills, but it also will place more responsibility on the White House for cutting wasteful, though popular, spending.

The presidential veto is an inherently negative resource. It is most useful for preventing legislation. Much of the time, however, presidents are more interested in passing their own legislation. To do so, they must marshall their political resources to obtain positive support for their programs. Presidents' three most useful resources are their party leadership, public support, and their own legislative skills.

PARTY LEADERSHIP

No matter what other resources presidents may have at their disposal, they remain highly dependent on their party to move their legislative programs. Representatives and senators of the president's party usually form the nucleus of coalitions supporting presidential proposals and provide considerably more support than do members of the opposition party. Thus, party leadership in Congress is every president's principal task when countering the natural tendencies toward conflict between the executive and legislative branches that are inherent in the American government's system of checks and balances.[14]

The Bonds of Party. For most senators and representatives, being in the same political party as the president creates a psychological bond. Personal loyalties or emotional commitments to their party and their party leader, a desire to avoid embarrassing "their" administration and thus hurting their chances for reelection, and a basic distrust of the opposition party—these inclinations produce support for the White House. Members of the same party also agree on many matters of public policy, and they are often supported by similar electoral coalitions, reinforcing the pull of party ties.

If presidents could rely on their fellow party members to vote for whatever the White House sent up to Capitol Hill, presidential leadership of Congress would be rather easy. All presidents would have to do is make sure members of their party showed up to vote. If their party had the majority, presidents would always win. If their party was in the minority, presidents would only have to concentrate on converting a few members of the other party.

Slippage in Party Support. Things are not so simple, however. Despite the pull of party ties, all presidents experience substantial slippage in the support of their party in Congress. Presidents can count on their own party members for support no more than two-thirds of the time, even on key votes. Presidents are thus forced to be active in party leadership and to devote their efforts to conversion as much as to mobilization of members of their party.

The primary obstacle to party unity is the lack of consensus on policies among party members, especially in the Democratic Party. Jimmy Carter, a Democrat, remarked, "I learned the hard way that there was no party loyalty or discipline when a complicated or controversial issue was at stake—none."[15]

This diversity of views often reflects the diversity of constituencies represented by party members. The frequent defection of Southern Democrats from Democratic presidents (such defectors are called "boll weevils") has been one of the most prominent features of American politics. When constituency opinion and the president's proposals conflict, members of Congress are more likely to vote with their constituents, whom they rely on for reelection. If the president is not popular in their constituencies, congressional party members may avoid identifying too closely with the White House.

Leading the Party. The president has some assets as party leader, including congressional party leaders, services and amenities for party members, and campaign aid. Each asset is of limited utility, however.

The president's relationship with party leaders in Congress is a delicate one. Although the leaders are predisposed to support presidential policies and typically work closely with the White House, they are free

Presidents frequently face opposition party majorities in Congress and must seek the opposition's support to pass their policies. Here, President Clinton, a Democrat, meets with House Speaker Newt Gingrich, and Senate majority leader Trent Lott, both Republicans.

to oppose the president or lend only symbolic support; some party leaders may be ineffective themselves. Moreover, party leaders are not in a position to reward or discipline members of Congress on the basis of presidential support.

To create goodwill with congressional party members, the White House provides them with many amenities, ranging from photographs with the president to rides on Air Force One. Although this arrangement is to the president's advantage and may earn the benefit of the doubt on some policy initiatives, party members consider it their right to receive benefits from the White House and as a result are unlikely to be especially responsive to the president.

Just as the president can offer a carrot, so, too, can the president wield a stick in the form of withholding favors, although this is rarely done. Despite the resources available to the president, if party members wish to oppose the White House, there is little the president can do to stop them. The parties are highly decentralized, as we saw in Chapter 8. National party leaders do not control those aspects of politics that are of vital concern to members of Congress—nominations and elections. Members of Congress are largely self-recruited, gain their party's nomination by their own efforts and not the party's, and provide most of the money and organizational support needed for their elections. Presidents can do little to influence the results of these activities.

One way for the president to improve the chances of obtaining support in Congress is to increase the number of fellow party members in the legislature. The phenomenon of **presidential coattails** occurs when voters cast their ballots for congressional candi-

TABLE 13.7 CONGRESSIONAL GAINS OR LOSSES FOR THE PRESIDENT'S PARTY IN PRESIDENTIAL ELECTION YEARS

Presidents cannot rely on their coattails to carry into office senators and representatives of their party to help pass White House legislative programs. The president's party typically gains few, if any, seats when the president wins election. For instance, the Democrats lost seats in the House and gained none in the Senate when President Clinton was elected in 1992.

YEAR	PRESIDENT	HOUSE	SENATE
1952	Eisenhower	+22	+1
1956	Eisenhower	−2	−1
1960	Kennedy	−22	−2
1964	Johnson	+37	+1
1968	Nixon	+5	+6
1972	Nixon	+12	−2
1976	Carter	+1	0
1980	Reagan	+34	+12
1984	Reagan	+14	−2
1988	Bush	−3	−1
1992	Clinton	−10	0
1996	Clinton	+9	−2

TABLE 13.8 CONGRESSIONAL GAINS OR LOSSES FOR THE PRESIDENT'S PARTY IN MIDTERM ELECTION YEARS

The president's party typically *loses* seats in midterm elections. Thus, presidents cannot be certain of helping to elect members of their party once in office.

YEAR	PRESIDENT	HOUSE	SENATE
1954	Eisenhower	−18	−1
1958	Eisenhower	−47	−13
1962	Kennedy	−4	+3
1966	Johnson	−47	−4
1970	Nixon	−12	+2
1974	Ford	−47	−5
1978	Carter	−15	−3
1982	Reagan	−26	0
1986	Reagan	−5	−8
1990	Bush	−9	−1
1994	Clinton	−52	−8

dates of the president's party because those candidates support the president. Most recent studies show a diminishing connection between presidential and congressional voting, however, and few races are determined by presidential coattails.[16] The change in party balance that usually emerges when the electoral dust has settled is strikingly small. In the 12 presidential elections between 1952 and 1996, the party of the winning presidential candidate gained an average of eight seats (out of 435) per election in the House. In the Senate the opposition party actually gained seats in six of the elections (1956, 1960, 1972, 1984, 1988, and 1996), and there was no change in 1976 and 1992. The net gain for the president's party in the Senate averaged only one seat per election (see Table 13.7).

What about midterm elections—those held between presidential elections? Can the president depend on increasing the number of fellow party members in Congress then? Actually, the picture is even more bleak than during presidential elections. As you can see in Table 13.8, the president's party typically *loses* seats in these elections. In 1986, the Republicans lost eight seats in the Senate, depriving President Reagan of a majority. In 1994, the Democrats lost eight Senate seats and 52 House seats, losing control of both houses in the process.[17]

To add to these party leadership burdens, the president's party often lacks a majority in one or both houses of Congress. Between 1953 and 1998 there have been 26 years in which Republican presidents faced a Democratic House of Representatives and 20 years in which they encountered a Democratic Senate. Since 1995, President Clinton has faced both a House and a Senate with Republican majorities.

As a result of election returns and the lack of dependable party support, the president usually has to solicit help from the opposition party. The opposition is generally not fertile ground for seeking support. Nevertheless, even a few votes may be enough to give the president the required majority.

PUBLIC SUPPORT

One of the president's most important resources for leading Congress is public support. Presidents who enjoy the backing of the public have an easier time influencing Congress. Said one top aide to Ronald Reagan, "Everything here is built on the idea that the president's success depends on grassroots support."[18] Presidents with low approval ratings in the polls find it difficult to influence Congress. As one of President Carter's aides put it, "No president whose popularity is as low as this president's has much clout on the Hill."[19] Members of Congress and others in Washington closely watch two indicators of public support for the president: approval in the polls and mandates in presidential elections.

Public Approval. Members of Congress anticipate the public's reactions to their support for or opposition to presidents and their policies. They may choose to be close to or independent of the White House—depending on the president's standing with the public—to increase their chances for reelection.

Representatives and senators may also use the president's standing in the polls as an indicator of presidential ability to mobilize public opinion against presidential opponents.

Public approval also makes other leadership resources more efficacious. If the president is high in the public's esteem, the president's party is more likely to be responsive, the public is more easily moved, and legislative skills become more effective. Thus, public approval is the political resource that has the most potential to turn a stalemate between the president and Congress into a situation supportive of the president's legislative proposals.

Public approval operates mostly in the background and sets the limits of what Congress will do for or to the president. Widespread support gives the president leeway and weakens resistance to presidential policies. It provides a cover for members of Congress to cast votes to which their constituents might otherwise object. They can defend their votes as support for the president rather than support for a certain policy alone.

Lack of public support strengthens the resolve of those inclined to oppose the president and narrows the range in which presidential policies receive the benefit of the doubt. In addition, low ratings in the polls may create incentives to attack the president, further eroding an already weakened position. For example, after the arms sales to Iran and the diversion of funds to the Contras became a *cause celebre* in late 1986, it became more acceptable in Congress and in the press to raise questions about Ronald Reagan's capacities as president. Disillusionment is a difficult force for the White House to combat.

The impact of public approval or disapproval on the support the president receives in Congress is important, but it occurs at the margins of the effort to build coalitions behind proposed policies. No matter how low presidential standing dips, the president still receives support from a substantial number of senators and representatives. Similarly, no matter how high approval levels climb, a significant portion of Congress will still oppose certain presidential policies. Members of Congress are unlikely to vote against the clear interests of their constituencies or the firm tenets of their ideology out of deference to a widely supported chief executive. Public approval gives the president leverage, not control.[20]

In addition, presidents cannot depend on having the approval of the public, and it is not a resource over which they have much control, as we will see later. Once again, it is clear that presidents' leadership resources do not allow them to dominate Congress.

Mandates. The results of presidential elections are another indicator of public opinion regarding presidents. An electoral mandate—the perception that the voters strongly support the president's character and policies—can be a powerful symbol in American politics. It accords added legitimacy and credibility to the newly elected president's proposals. Moreover, concerns for both representation and political survival encourage members of Congress to support new presidents if they feel the people have spoken.

More important, mandates change the premises of decisions. Following the 1932 election, the essential question became *how* government should act to fight the Depression rather than *whether* it should act. Similarly, following the 1964 election, the dominant question in Congress was not whether to pass new social programs but how many social programs to pass and how much to increase spending. In 1981, the tables were turned; Ronald Reagan's victory placed a stigma on big government and exalted the unregulated marketplace and large defense efforts. Reagan had won a major victory even before the first congressional vote.

Although presidential elections can structure choices for Congress, merely winning an election does not provide presidents with a mandate. Every election produces a winner, but mandates are much less common. Even large electoral victories, such as Richard Nixon's in 1972 and Ronald Reagan's in 1984, carry no guarantee that Congress will interpret the results as mandates from the people to support the president's programs, especially if the voters also elect majorities in Congress from the other party (of course, the winner may *claim* a mandate anyway).[21]

LEGISLATIVE SKILLS

Presidential legislative skills come in a variety of forms, including bargaining, making personal appeals, consulting with Congress, setting priorities, exploiting "honeymoon" periods, and structuring congressional votes. Of these skills, bargaining receives perhaps the most attention from commentators on the presidency, and by examining it, one can learn much about the role that a president's legislative skills play in leading Congress.

There is no question that many bargains occur and that they occur in numerous forms. Reagan's budget director David Stockman recalled that "the last 10 or 20 percent of the votes needed for a majority of both houses on the 1981 tax cut had to be bought, period." The concessions for members of Congress included special breaks for oil-lease holders, real estate tax shelters, and generous loopholes that virtually eliminated the corporate income tax. "The hogs were really feeding," declared Stockman. "The greed level, the level of opportunities, just got out of control."[22]

Presidents influence the legislative agenda more than any other political figure. One of Ronald Reagan's chief legislative skills was the ability to communicate his policy priorities effectively to Congress and the public. No matter what a president's skills are, however, the "chief legislator," as the president is often called, can rarely exercise complete control over the agenda.

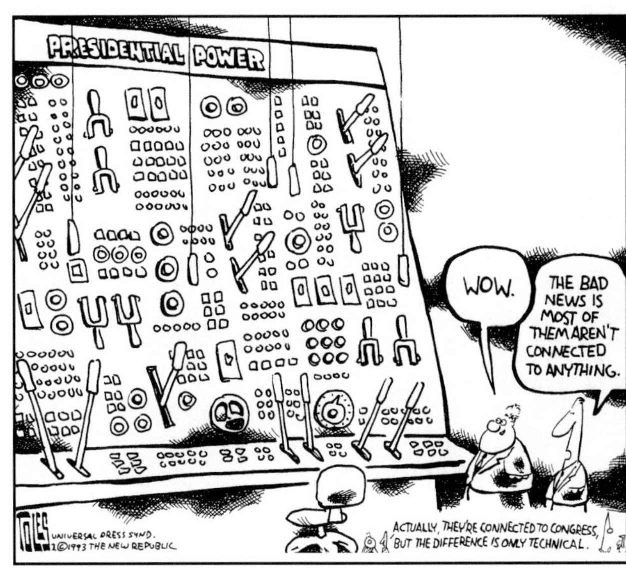

Nevertheless, bargaining, in the form of trading support on two or more policies or providing specific benefits for representatives and senators, occurs less often and plays a less critical role in the creation of presidential coalitions in Congress than one might think. For obvious reasons, the White House does not want to encourage the type of bargaining Stockman describes, and there is a scarcity of resources with which to bargain, especially in an era of large budget deficits (discussed in Chapter 14).

Moreover, the president does not have to bargain with every member of Congress to receive support. On controversial issues on which bargaining may be useful, the president usually starts with a sizable core of party supporters and may add to this group those of the opposition party who provide support on ideological or policy grounds. Others may support the president because of relevant constituency interests or strong public approval. The president needs to bargain only if this coalition does not provide a majority (two-thirds on treaties and one-third on veto overrides).

Presidents may improve their chances of success in Congress by making certain strategic moves. It is wise, for example, for a new president to be ready to send legislation to the Hill early during the first year in office in order to exploit the "honeymoon" atmosphere that typically characterizes this period. Obviously, this is a one-shot opportunity.

An important aspect of presidential legislative strategy can be establishing priorities among legislative proposals. The goal of this effort is to set Congress' agenda. If presidents are unable to focus the attention of Congress on their priority programs, these programs may become lost in the complex and overloaded legislative process. Setting priorities is also important because presidents and their staffs can lobby effectively for only a few bills at a time. Moreover, each president's political capital is inevitably limited, and it is sensible to focus on a limited range of personally important issues; otherwise, this precious resource might be wasted.

In 1981 Ronald Reagan followed both of these strategies, moving fast and setting priorities. He had great success—obtaining passage of a large tax cut, a substantial increase in defense expenditures, and sizable decreases in the rate of spending for domestic policies. George Bush, in contrast, did not enter the White House geared for legislative action and did little to articulate his priorities. With a large budget deficit, few legislative goals, and the opposition in the majority in both the House and Senate, he did not feel it necessary or useful to focus his energies on Congress. From the outset Bush seemed destined to make his mark on foreign policy, where the president has more latitude to maneuver.

Within a month after taking office, President Clinton presented Congress with an ambitious agenda, including tax increases and both spending cuts and increases. A major health care reform bill and the North American Free Trade Agreement followed later in the year. The president lacked the political capital to pass much of his agenda, however, and some of the most important proposals fell prey to Republican opposition. By failing to focus on his priorities, Clinton spent his political capital on matters of less importance. Although he engaged in an endless campaign of

Presidents find the role of legislative leader a challenging one. Often they must compromise with opponents in Congress, as President Bill Clinton did in 1996 when he signed the welfare reform bill.

public appearances and congressional meetings to build support for his legislation, in the end he met with substantial disappointment and was rebuffed by the voters in the 1994 midterm elections as the Republicans captured both houses of Congress.

The president is the nation's key agenda builder; what the administration wants strongly influences the parameters of Washington debate. John Kingdon's careful study of the Washington agenda found that "no other single actor in the political system has quite the capability of the president to set agendas."[23] There are limits to what the president can do, however.

By his second year in office, Ronald Reagan's honeymoon with Congress was over, and he had lost control of the legislative agenda. Although the White House can put off dealing with many national issues at the beginning of a new president's term in order to focus on its highest-priority legislation, it cannot do so indefinitely. Eventually it must make decisions about a wide range of matters. Soon the legislative agenda is full and more policies are in the pipeline, as the administration attempts to satisfy its constituents and responds to unanticipated or simply overlooked problems. Moreover, Congress is quite capable of setting its own agenda, providing competition for the president's proposals.

In general, presidential legislative skills must compete—as presidential public support does—with other, more stable factors that affect voting in Congress: party, ideology, personal views and commitments on specific policies, constituency interests, and so on. By the time a president tries to exercise influence on a vote, most members of Congress have made up their minds on the basis of these other factors.

After accounting for the status of the president's party in Congress and standing with the public, systematic studies have found that presidents known for their legislative skills (such as Lyndon Johnson) are no more successful in winning votes, even close ones, or obtaining congressional support than those considered less adept at dealing with Congress (such as Jimmy Carter).[24] The president's legislative skills are not at the core of presidential leadership of Congress. Even skilled presidents cannot reshape the contours of the political landscape and *create* opportunities for change. They can, however, recognize favorable configurations of political forces—such as existed in 1933, 1965, and 1981—and effectively exploit them to embark on major shifts in public policy.

Perhaps the most important role of presidents—and their heaviest burden—is their responsibility for national security. Dealing with Congress is only one of the many challenges presidents face in the realm of defense and foreign policy.

THE PRESIDENT AND NATIONAL SECURITY POLICY

Constitutionally, the president has the leading role in American defense and foreign policy (often termed *national security* policy). Such matters are of obvious importance to the country (they involve issues ranging from foreign trade to war and peace) and occupy much of the president's time. There are several dimensions to the president's national security responsibilities, including negotiating with other nations, commanding the armed forces, managing crises, waging war, and obtaining the necessary support in Congress.

CHIEF DIPLOMAT

The Constitution allocates certain powers in the realm of national security that are exclusive to the executive. The president alone extends diplomatic recognition to foreign governments—as Jimmy Carter did on December 14, 1978, when he announced the exchange of ambassadors with the People's Republic of China and the downgrading of the U.S. Embassy in Taiwan. The president can also terminate relations with other nations, as Carter did with Iran after Americans were taken hostage in Tehran.

The president also has the sole power to negotiate treaties with other nations, although the Constitution requires the Senate to approve them by a two-thirds vote. Sometimes presidents win and sometimes they lose when presenting a treaty to the Senate. After

Presidents usually conduct diplomatic relations through envoys, but occasionally they engage in personal diplomacy. Here, President Clinton meets with PLO Chairman Yasir Arafat, Jordan's King Hussein, and Prime Minister Benjamin Netanyahu of Israel.

In 1950, President Harry Truman fulfilled his role as commander in chief by pinning a distinguished service medal on the shirt of General Douglas MacArthur, who was commanding American troops in Korea. The following year, Truman exercised his powers by dismissing MacArthur for disobeying orders—an unpopular decision given MacArthur's fame as a World War II hero.

extensive lobbying, Jimmy Carter persuaded the Senate to approve a treaty returning the Panama Canal to Panama (over objections such as those of one senator who declared, "We stole it fair and square"). Carter was not so lucky when he presented the SALT II treaty on arms control; it never even made it to a vote on the Senate floor.

In addition to treaties, presidents also negotiate *executive agreements* with the heads of foreign governments. However, executive agreements do not require Senate ratification (although they are supposed to be reported to Congress). Most executive agreements are routine and deal with noncontroversial subjects such as food deliveries or customs enforcement, but some, such as the Vietnam peace agreement and the SALT I agreement limiting offensive nuclear weapons, implement important and controversial policies.

Occasionally presidential diplomacy involves more than negotiating on behalf of the United States. Theodore Roosevelt won the Nobel Peace Prize for his role in settling the war between Japan and Russia. One of Jimmy Carter's greatest achievements was forging a peace treaty between Egypt and Israel. For 13 days he mediated negotiations between the leaders of both countries at his presidential retreat, Camp David.

As the leader of the Western world, the president must try to lead America's allies on matters of both economics and defense. This is not an easy task, given the natural independence of sovereign nations; the reduced status of the United States as an economic power relative to other countries, such as Japan and Germany; and the many competing influences on policymaking in other nations. As in domestic policymaking, the president must rely principally on persuasion to lead.

COMMANDER IN CHIEF

Because the Constitution's framers wanted civilian control of the military, they made the president the commander in chief of the armed forces. President George Washington actually led troops to crush the Whiskey Rebellion in 1794. Today, presidents do not take the task quite so literally, but their military decisions have changed the course of history. Harry Truman personally selected the target and the date for dropping atomic bombs on Japan to end World War II. Two decades later, Lyndon Johnson selected targets for bombing missions in North Vietnam. Richard Nixon made the decision to invade Cambodia in 1970. Bill Clinton joined the ranks of presidents exerting their prerogatives as commander in chief when he sent American troops to occupy Haiti, keep the peace in Bosnia, prevent an invasion of Kuwait, and bomb Iraq.

When the Constitution was written, the United States did not have—nor did anyone expect it to have—a large standing or permanent army. Today the president is commander in chief of more than 1.5 million uniformed men and women. In his farewell address, George Washington warned against "entangling alliances," but today America has commitments to defend nations across the globe. Even more important, the president commands a vast nuclear arsenal. Never more than a few steps from the president is "the football," a macabre briefcase with the codes needed to unleash nuclear war. The Constitution, of course, states that only Congress has the power to declare war, but it is unreasonable to believe that Congress can convene, debate, and vote on a declaration of war in the case of a nuclear attack. The House and Senate chambers would be gone—*literally* gone—before the conclusion of a debate.

WAR POWERS

Perhaps no issue of executive-legislative relations generates more controversy than the continuing dispute over war powers. Though charged by the Constitution with declaring war and voting on the military budget, Congress long ago accepted that presidents make short-term military commitments of troops or naval vessels. In recent decades, however, presidents have paid even less attention to constitutional details; for example, Congress never declared war during the conflicts in either Korea or Vietnam.

In 1973 Congress passed (over President Nixon's veto) the **War Powers Resolution**. As a reaction to disillusionment about American fighting in Vietnam and Cambodia, the law was intended to give Congress a greater voice in the introduction of American troops into hostilities. It required presidents to consult with Congress, whenever possible, before using military force, and it mandated the withdrawal of forces after 60 days unless Congress declared war or granted an extension. Congress could at any time pass a concurrent resolution (which could not be vetoed) ending American participation in hostilities.

The War Powers Resolution cannot be regarded as a success for Congress, however. All presidents serving since 1973 have deemed the law an unconstitutional infringement on their powers, and there is reason to believe the Supreme Court would consider the law's use of the **legislative veto** (the ability of Congress to pass a resolution to override a presidential decision) to end American involvement in fighting to be a violation of the doctrine of separation of powers. Presidents have largely ignored the law and sent troops into hostilities, sometimes with heavy loss of life, without effectually consulting with Congress. The legislature has found it difficult to challenge the president, especially when American troops were endangered, and the courts have been reluctant to hear a congressional challenge on what would be construed as a political, rather than a legal, issue.[25]

Following numerous precedents, George Bush took an expansive view of his powers as commander in chief. On his own authority, he ordered the invasion of Panama in 1989 and moved half a million troops to Saudi Arabia to liberate Kuwait after its invasion by Iraq in 1990.

Matters came to a head in January 1991. President Bush had given President Saddam Hussein of Iraq until January 15 to pull out of Kuwait. At that point, President Bush threatened to move the Iraqis out by force. Debate raged over the president's power to act unilaterally to engage in war. A constitutional crisis was averted when Congress passed (on a divided vote) a resolution on January 12 authorizing the president to use force against Iraq.

In a sweeping assertion of presidential authority, Bill Clinton moved toward military intervention in Haiti and essentially dared Congress to try to stop him (see "The People Speak" on this page). Congress did nothing but complain to block military action, even though a majority of members of both parties clearly opposed an invasion. In the end, an invasion (as opposed to a more peaceful "intervention") was avoided, but Congress was unlikely to have cut off funds for such an operation had it occurred.

Questions continue to be raised about the relevance of America's 200-year-old constitutional mechanisms for engaging in war. Some observers are concerned that modern technology, by allowing the president to engage in conflicts so quickly that opposing points of view do not receive proper consideration, thereby undermines the separation of powers. Others stress the importance of the commander in chief's having the

The People Speak

Do You Think President Clinton Should Have First Gotten Approval from Congress Before Sending U.S. Troops to Haiti, or Don't You Think So?

Should have gotten approval	62%
Don't think so	35%
No Opinion	3%

There has been much controversy over the issue of who should be able to commit the United States to war, but the public overwhelmingly believes Congress should be involved in the decision.

SOURCE: Gallup/CNN/*USA Today* Poll, September 1994.

flexibility to meet America's global responsibilities and combat international terrorism without the hindrance of congressional checks and balances. All agree that the change in the nature of warfare brought about by nuclear weapons inevitably delegates to the president the ultimate decision to use them.

CRISIS MANAGER

The president's roles as chief diplomat and commander in chief are related to another presidential responsibility: crisis management. A **crisis** is a sudden, unpredictable, and potentially dangerous event. Most crises occur in the realm of foreign policy. They often involve hot tempers and high risks; quick judgments must be made on the basis of sketchy information. Be it American hostages held in Iran or the discovery of Soviet missiles in Cuba, a crisis challenges the president to make difficult decisions. Crises are rarely the president's doing, but handled incorrectly, they can be the president's undoing.

Early in American history there were fewer immediate crises. By the time officials were aware of a problem, it often had resolved itself. Communications could take weeks or even months to reach Washington. Similarly, officials' decisions often took weeks or months to reach those who were to implement them. The most famous land battle of the War of 1812, the Battle of New Orleans, was fought *after* the United States had signed a peace treaty with Great Britain. Word of the treaty did not reach the battlefield; thus, General Andrew Jackson won a victory for the United States that contributed nothing toward ending the war, although it did help put him in the White House as the seventh president.

With modern communications, however, the president can instantly monitor events almost anywhere. Moreover, because situations develop more rapidly today, there is a premium on rapid action, secrecy, constant management, consistent judgment, and expert advice. Congress usually moves slowly (one might say deliberatively), and it is large (making it difficult to keep secrets), decentralized (requiring continual compromising), and composed of generalists. As a result, the president—who can come to quick and consistent decisions, confine information to a small group, carefully oversee developments, and call upon experts in the executive branch—has become more prominent in handling crises.

WORKING WITH CONGRESS

As America begins its third century under the Constitution, presidents might wish the framers had been less concerned with checks and balances in the area of national security. In recent years, Congress has challenged presidents on all fronts, including foreign aid; arms sales; the development, procurement, and deployment of weapon systems; the negotiation and interpretation of treaties; the selection of diplomats; and the continuation of nuclear testing.

Congress has a central constitutional role in making national security policy, although this role is often misunderstood. The allocation of responsibilities for such matters is based on the founders' apprehensions about the concentration of power and the subsequent potential for its abuse. They divided the powers of supply and command, for example, in order to thwart adventurism in national security affairs. Congress can thus refuse to provide the necessary authorizations and appropriations for presidential actions, whereas the chief executive can refuse to act (for example, by not sending troops into battle at the behest of the legislature).

Despite the constitutional role of Congress, the president is the driving force behind national security policy, providing energy and direction. Congress is well organized to deliberate openly on the discrete components of policy, but it is not well designed to take the lead on national security matters. Its role has typically been overseeing the executive rather than initiating policy. Congress frequently originates proposals for domestic policy, but it is less involved in national security policy.[26]

The president has a more prominent role in foreign affairs as the country's sole representative in dealing with other nations and as commander in chief of the armed forces (functions that effectively preclude a wide range of congressional diplomatic and military initiatives). In addition, the nature of national security issues may make the failure to integrate the elements of policy more costly than in domestic policy. Thus, members of Congress typically prefer to encourage, criticize, or support the president rather than to initiate their own national security policy. If leadership occurs, it is usually centered in the White House.

Commentators on the presidency often refer to the "two presidencies"—one for domestic policy and the other for national security policy.[27] By this phrase they mean that the president has more success in leading Congress on matters of national security than on matters of domestic policy. The typical member of Congress, however, supports the president on national security roll call votes only slightly more than half the time. There is a significant gap between what the president requests and what members of Congress are willing to give. Certainly the legislature does not accord the president automatic support on national security policy.[28]

Nevertheless, presidents do end up obtaining much, often most, of what they request from Congress on national security issues. Some of the support they receive is the result of agreement on policy, but presidential leadership also plays an important role. That role is not one in which presidents simply bend the legislature to their will, however; rather, they lead by persuasion.

Presidents need resources to persuade others to support their policies. As we noted earlier, an important presidential asset can be the support of the American people. The following sections will take a closer look at how the White House tries to increase and use public support.

POWER FROM THE PEOPLE: THE PUBLIC PRESIDENCY

"Public sentiment is everything. With public sentiment nothing can fail; without it nothing can succeed." These words, spoken by Abraham Lincoln, pose what is perhaps the greatest challenge to any president—to obtain and maintain the public's support. Because presidents are rarely in a position to command others to comply with their wishes, they must rely on persuasion. *Public support is perhaps the greatest source of influence a president has,* for it is difficult for other power holders in a democracy to deny the legitimate demands of a president who has popular backing.

GOING PUBLIC

Presidents are not passive followers of public opinion. The White House is a virtual whirlwind of public relations activity.[29] John Kennedy, the first "television president," considerably bettered the rate of public appearances held by his predecessors. Kennedy's successors, with the notable exception of Richard Nixon, have been even more active in making public appearances. Indeed, they have averaged more than one appearance every weekday of the year. Bill Clinton is a tireless campaigner who invests enormous time and energy in attempting to sell his programs to the public.

Often the president's appearances are staged purely to get the public's attention. When George Bush introduced his clean-air bill, he flew to Idaho to use the eye-catching Grand Tetons as a backdrop. He announced his support for a constitutional amendment to prohibit flag burning in front of the Iwo Jima Memorial in Arlington National Cemetery. In cases such as these, the president could have simply made an announcement, but the need for public support drives the White House to employ public relations techniques similar to those used to publicize commercial products.

Presidents often use commercial public relations techniques to win support for their policy initiatives. President Bush, for example, used the spectacular backdrop of the Grand Tetons to gain public approval for renewal and strengthening of the Clean Air Act.

In many democracies, the jobs of head of state and head of government are occupied by different people. For example, the queen is head of state in England, but she holds little power in government and politics. In America, these roles are fused. As head of state, the president is America's ceremonial leader and symbol of government. Trivial but time-consuming activities—tossing out the first baseball of the season, lighting the White House Christmas tree, meeting some extraordinary Boy or Girl Scout—are part of the ceremonial function of the presidency. Meeting foreign heads of state, receiving ambassadors' credentials, and making global goodwill tours represent the international side of this role. Presidents rarely shirk these duties, even when they are not inherently important. Ceremonial activities give them an important symbolic aura and a great deal of favorable press coverage, contributing to their efforts to build public support.

PRESIDENTIAL APPROVAL

Much of the energy the White House devotes to public relations is aimed at increasing the president's public approval. The reason is simple: The higher the president stands in the polls, the easier it is to persuade others to support presidential initiatives.

Because of the connection between public support and presidential influence, the president's standing in the polls is monitored closely by the press, members of Congress, and others in the Washington political community. "President watching" is a favorite American pastime. For years, the Gallup Poll has asked Americans this question: "Do you approve or disapprove of the way John Kennedy, Bill Clinton, or whoever is handling his job as president?" You can see the results in Figure 13.3.

Presidents frequently do not have widespread public support, often failing to win even majority approval. Figure 13.4 shows the average approval levels of recent presidents. Presidents Nixon, Ford, and Carter did not even receive approval from 50 percent of the public on the average. Ronald Reagan, a "popular" president, had only a 52 percent approval level. For 3 years, George Bush enjoyed much higher levels of approval on the average than his predecessors. In his fourth year, however, his ratings dropped below the 40 percent mark. For most of his tenure in office, President Clinton has struggled to rise above the 50 percent mark.

Presidential approval is the product of many factors.[30] At the base of presidential evaluations is the predisposition of many people to support the president. Political party identification provides the basic underpinning of approval or disapproval and mediates the impact of other factors. On average, those who identify with the president's party give approval nearly 40 percentage points higher than that expressed by those who identify with the opposition party. In other words, Democrats love Democratic presidents, and Republicans are equally fond of GOP chief executives. Moreover, partisans are not inclined to approve presidents of the other party. Presidents also usually benefit from a "honeymoon" with the American people after taking office. Predispositions provide the foundations of presidential approval and furnish it with a basic stability.

Some observers believe that "honeymoons" are fleeting phenomena in which the public affords new

FIGURE 13.3

AVERAGE YEARLY PRESIDENTIAL APPROVAL

For years the Gallup Poll has asked Americans, "Do you approve or disapprove of the way ____ is handling his job as president?" Here you can track the percentage approving of presidential performance from Eisenhower to Clinton. Notice that most presidents seem to be most popular when they first enter office; later on, their popularity often erodes. Bill Clinton is an exception.

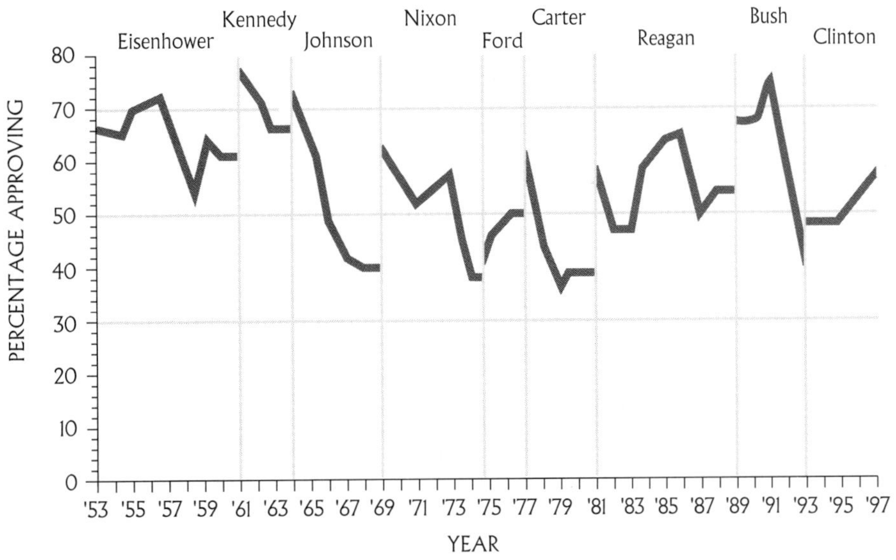

SOURCE: George C. Edwards III, *Presidential Approval* (Baltimore: Johns Hopkins University Press, 1990); updated by the authors.

FIGURE 13.4 AVERAGE PRESIDENTIAL APPROVAL FOR ENTIRE TERMS IN OFFICE

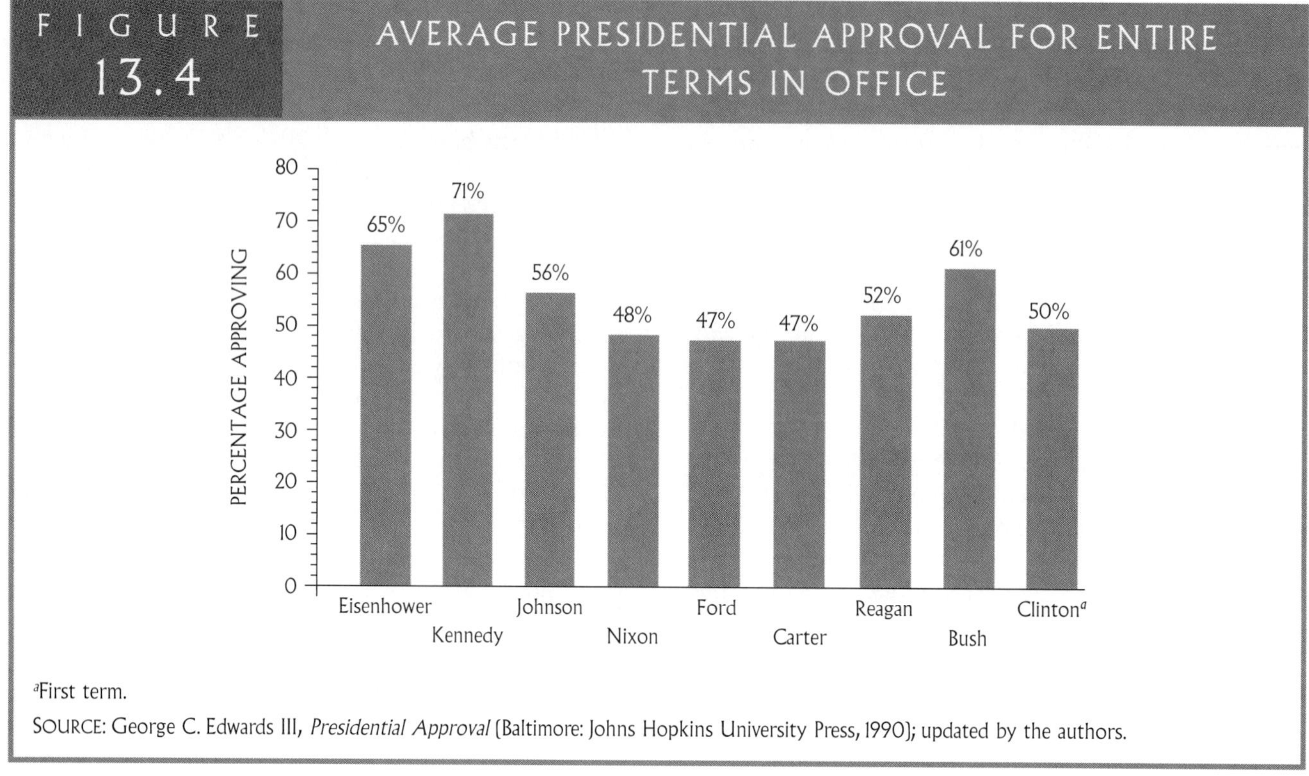

[a]First term.

SOURCE: George C. Edwards III, *Presidential Approval* (Baltimore: Johns Hopkins University Press, 1990); updated by the authors.

occupants of the White House only a short grace period before they begin their inevitable descent in the polls. You can see in Figure 13.3 that declines do take place, but they are neither inevitable nor swift. Throughout his two terms in office, Ronald Reagan experienced considerable volatility in his relations with the public, but his record certainly does not indicate that the loss of public support is inexorable or that support cannot be revived and maintained. George Bush obtained more public support in his third year in office than in his first two years, and Bill Clinton enjoyed more approval in his fourth year in office than in any of his first three.

Changes in approval levels appear to reflect the public's evaluation of how the president is handling policy areas such as the economy, war, and foreign affairs. Different policies are salient to the public at different times. For example, if communism is collapsing, then foreign policy is likely to dominate the news and be on the minds of Americans. If the economy turns sour, then people are going to be concerned about unemployment.

Contrary to the conventional wisdom, citizens seem to focus on the president's efforts and stands on issues rather than on personality ("popularity") or simply how presidential policies affect them (the "pocketbook"). Job-related personal characteristics of the president, such as integrity and leadership skills, also play an important role in influencing presidential approval.

Sometimes public approval of the president takes sudden jumps. One popular explanation for these surges of support is "rally events," which John Mueller defined as events that are related to international relations, directly involve the United States and particularly the president, and are specific, dramatic, and sharply focused.[31] A classic example is the 18-percentage-point rise in President Bush's approval ratings immediately after the fighting began in the Gulf War in 1991. Such occurrences are unusual and isolated events, however; they have little enduring impact on a president's public approval. President Bush, for example, dropped precipitously in the polls and lost his bid for reelection in 1992.

The criteria on which the public evaluates presidents—such as the way they are handling the economy, where they stand on complex issues, and whether they are "strong" leaders—are open to many interpretations. The modern White House makes extraordinary efforts to control the context in which presidents appear in public and the way they are portrayed by the press, to try to influence how the public views them. The fact that presidents are frequently low in the polls anyway is persuasive testimony to the limits of presidential leadership of the public. As one student of the public presidency

put it, "The supply of popular support rests on opinion dynamics over which the president may exert little direct control." [32]

POLICY SUPPORT

Commentators on the presidency often refer to it as a "bully pulpit," implying that presidents can persuade or even mobilize the public to support their policies if only they are skilled-enough communicators. Certainly presidents often do attempt to obtain public support for their policies with speeches over radio and television and speeches to large groups.[33] All presidents since Truman have had media advice from experts on lighting, makeup, stage settings, camera angles, clothing, pacing of delivery, and other facets of making speeches.

Despite this aid and despite the experience that politicians have in speaking, presidential speeches designed to lead public opinion have typically been rather unimpressive. In the modern era only Franklin D. Roosevelt, John Kennedy, Ronald Reagan, and Bill Clinton could be considered especially effective speakers. The rest were not, and they also tended not to look good under the glare of hot lights and the unflattering gaze of television cameras. Partly because of his limitations as a public speaker, President Bush waited until he had been in office for over 7 months before making his first nationally televised address.

Moreover, the public is not always receptive to the president's message. Chapter 6 showed that Americans are not especially interested in politics and government; thus, it is not easy to get their attention. Citizens also have predispositions about public policy (however ill-informed) that act as screens for presidential messages. In the absence of national crises, most people are unreceptive to political appeals.[34]

John Kennedy was the first president to use public appearances regularly to seek popular backing for his policies. Despite his popularity and skills as a communicator, Kennedy was often frustrated in his attempts to win widespread support for his administration's "New Frontier" policies.

The public may misperceive or ignore even the most basic facts regarding presidential policy. For example, at the end of October 1994, 59 percent of the public thought the economy was still in recession (although it was growing so fast that the Federal Reserve Board was taking strong action to cool it off), only 34 percent knew the deficit had decreased since Clinton became president (it had decreased substantially), and 65 percent thought taxes on the middle class had increased during that period (income taxes had been raised for less than 2 percent of the public).[35] Partly as a consequence of these misconceptions, the president was frustrated repeatedly in his efforts to obtain public support for his policy initiatives.[36]

Ronald Reagan, sometimes called the "Great Communicator," was certainly interested in policy change and went to unprecedented lengths to influence public opinion on behalf of such policies as deregulation, decreases in spending on domestic policy, and increases in the defense budget. Nevertheless, support for regulatory programs and spending on health care, welfare, urban problems, education, environmental protection, and aid to minorities increased, not decreased, during Reagan's tenure. Support for increased defense expenditures was decidedly lower when he left office than when he was inaugurated.[37]

MOBILIZING THE PUBLIC

Sometimes merely changing public opinion is not sufficient, and the president wants the public to communicate its views directly to Congress. Mobilization of the public may be the ultimate weapon in the president's arsenal of resources with which to influence Congress. When the people speak, especially when they speak clearly, Congress listens.

Mobilizing the public involves overcoming formidable barriers and accepting substantial risks. It entails the double burden of obtaining both opinion support and political action from a generally inattentive and apathetic public. If the president tries to mobilize the public and fails, the lack of response speaks clearly to members of Congress.

Perhaps the most notable recent example of the president's mobilization of public opinion to pressure Congress is Ronald Reagan's effort to obtain passage of his tax-cut bill in 1981. Shortly before the crucial vote in the House, the president made a televised plea for support of his tax-cut proposals and asked the people to let their representatives in Congress know how they felt. Evidently Reagan's plea worked; thousands of phone calls, letters, and telegrams poured into congressional offices. On the morning of the vote, Speaker Tip O'Neill declared, "We are experiencing a telephone blitz like this nation has never seen. It's had a devastating effect."[38] The president easily carried the day.

The Reagan administration's effort at mobilizing the public on behalf of the 1981 tax cut is significant not only because of the success of presidential leadership but also because it appears to be an anomaly. In the remainder of Reagan's tenure, the president went repeatedly to the people regarding a wide range of policies, including the budget, aid to the Contras in Nicaragua, and defense expenditures. Despite high levels of approval for much of that time, Reagan was never again able to arouse many in his audience to communicate their support of his policies to Congress. Substantial tax cuts hold more appeal to the public than most other issues.

THE PRESIDENT AND THE PRESS

Despite all their efforts to lead public opinion, presidents do not directly reach the American people on a day-to-day basis. It is the mass media that provide people with most of what they know about chief executives and their policies. The media also interpret and analyze presidential activities, even the president's direct appeals to the public. The press is thus the principal intermediary between the president and the public, and relations with the press are an important aspect of the president's efforts to lead public opinion.

No matter who is in the White House or who reports on presidential activities, presidents and the press tend to be in conflict. George Washington complained that the "calumnies" against his administration were "outrages of common decency." Thomas Jefferson once declared that "nothing in a newspaper is to be believed." Presidents are inherently policy advocates. They want to control the amount and timing of information about their administration, whereas the press want all the information that exists without delay. As long as their goals are different, presidents and the media are likely to be adversaries.

Because of the importance of the press to the president, the White House monitors the media closely.

The president's press secretary is the primary channel through which the White House communicates with the media. Here, President Clinton's press secretary, Mike McCurry, holds one of his daily press briefings.

Some presidents have installed special televisions so that they can watch the news on all the networks at once; Lyndon Johnson even had news tickers from AP, UPI, and Reuters in the Oval Office. The White House also goes to great lengths to encourage the media to project a positive image of the president's activities and policies. About one-third of the high-level White House staff members are directly involved in media relations and policy of one type or another, and most staff members are involved at some time in trying to influence the media's portrayal of the president.

The person who most often deals directly with the press is the president's *press secretary*, who serves as a conduit of information from the White House to the press. Press secretaries conduct daily press briefings, giving prepared announcements and answering questions. They and their staff also arrange private interviews with White House officials (often done on a background basis, in which the reporter may not attribute remarks to the person being interviewed), photo opportunities, and travel arrangements for reporters when the president leaves Washington.

The best-known direct interaction between the president and the press is the presidential press conference. Presidents since Eisenhower have typically met with the press about twice a month (the exceptions were Nixon and Reagan, who averaged a press conference only about every 2 months). George Bush often met with the press in informal sessions, but he rarely held prime-time, televised press conferences. Bill Clinton took office with an antagonistic attitude to the national media and planned to bypass it rather than use it as part of his political strategy. He waited 2 months before holding his first formal news conference and 5 months before he held one in prime-time viewing hours in the evening. After a rocky start in his press relations, the president made himself somewhat more accessible to the national press.

Despite their visibility, press conferences are not very useful means of eliciting information. Presidents and their staffs can anticipate most of the questions that will be asked and prepare answers to them ahead of time, reducing the spontaneity of the sessions. Moreover, the large size and public nature of press conferences reduce the candor with which the president responds to questions.

Most of the news coverage of the White House comes under the heading "body watch." In other words, reporters focus on the most visible layer of the president's personal and official activities and provide the public with step-by-step accounts. They are interested in what presidents are going to do, how their actions will affect others, how they view policies and individuals, and how they present themselves, rather than in the substance of policies or the fundamental processes operating in the executive branch. ABC White House correspondent Sam Donaldson tells of covering a meeting of Western leaders on the island of Guadeloupe. It was a slow news day, so Donaldson did a story on the roasting of the pig the leaders would be eating that night, including "an exclusive look at the oven in which the pig would be roasted."[39] Because there are daily deadlines to meet and television reporters must squeeze their stories into sound bites measured in seconds, not minutes, there is little time for reflection, analysis, or comprehensive coverage.

Bias is the most politically charged issue in relations between the president and the press. A large number of studies have concluded that the news media, including the television networks and major newspapers, are not biased *systematically* toward a particular person, party, or ideology, as measured in the amount or favorability of coverage.[40]

To conclude that the news contains little explicitly partisan or ideological bias is not to argue that the news does not distort reality in its coverage of the president. As the following excerpt from Jimmy Carter's diary regarding a visit to a U.S. Army base in Panama in 1978 illustrates, "objective" reporting can be misleading.

> I told the Army troops that I was in the Navy for 11 years, and they booed. I told them that we depended on the Army to keep the Canal open, and they cheered. Later, the news reports said that there were boos and cheers during my speech.[41]

We learned in Chapter 7 that the news is fundamentally superficial and oversimplified and is often overblown, all of which provides the public with a distorted view of, among other things, presidential activities, statements, policies, and options. We have also seen that the press prefers to frame the news in themes, which both simplify complex issues and events and provide continuity of persons, institutions, and issues. Once these themes are established, the press tends to maintain them in subsequent stories. Of necessity, themes emphasize some information at the expense of other data, often determining what information is most relevant to news coverage and the context in which it is presented.

Once a stereotype of President Ford as a "bumbler" was established, every stumble was magnified as the press emphasized behavior that fit the mold. He was repeatedly forced to defend his intelligence, and many of his acts and statements were reported as efforts to "act" presidential. Once Ford was typecast, his image was repeatedly reinforced and was very difficult to overcome.[42]

News coverage of the presidency often tends to emphasize the negative (even if the negative stories are presented in a seemingly neutral manner),[43] and over the past 20 years journalists have become more active in setting a negative tone for their stories.[44] In the 1980 election campaign, the press portrayed President Carter as mean and Ronald Reagan as imprecise rather than Carter as precise and Reagan as pleasant. The emphasis, in other words, was on the candidates' negative qualities. George Bush received extraordinarily negative press during the 1992 election campaign, and the television networks' portrayal of the economy, for which Bush was blamed, got worse as the economy actually improved to a robust rate of growth![45] President Clinton has received mostly negative coverage during his tenure in office, with a ratio of negative to positive comments on network television of about 2 to 1.[46]

White House reporters are always looking to expose conflicts of interest and other shady behavior of public officials. In addition, many of their inquiries revolve around the question "Is the president up to the job?" Reporters who are confined in the White House all day may attempt to make up for their lack of investigative reporting with sarcastic and accusatory questioning. Moreover, the desire to keep the public interested and the need for continuous coverage may create in the press a subconscious bias against the presidency that leads to critical stories.

On the other hand, the president has certain advantages in dealing with the press. He is typically portrayed with an aura of dignity and treated with deference.[47] According to Sam Donaldson, who was generally considered an aggressive White House reporter, "For every truly tough question I've put to officials, I've asked a dozen that were about as tough as Grandma's apple dumplings."[48] Thus, when he left after serving as President Reagan's press secretary for 6 years, Larry Speakes told reporters they had given the Reagan administration "a fair shake."[49]

Remember that the White House can largely control the environment in which the president meets the press—even going so far as to have the Marine helicopters revved as Ronald Reagan approached them so that he could not hear reporters' questions and give unrehearsed responses.

UNDERSTANDING THE AMERICAN PRESIDENCY

Because the presidency is the single most important office in American politics, there has always been concern about whether the president is a threat to democracy. The importance of the president has raised similar concerns for the scope of government in America.

THE PRESIDENCY AND DEMOCRACY

From the time the Constitution was written, there has been a fear that the presidency would degenerate into a monarchy or a dictatorship. Even America's greatest presidents have heightened these fears at times. Despite George Washington's well-deserved reputation for peacefully relinquishing power, he also had certain regal tendencies that fanned the suspicions of the Jeffersonians. Abraham Lincoln, for all his humility, exercised extraordinary powers at the outbreak of the Civil War. Since that time, political commentators have alternated between extolling and fearing a strong presidency (see "Since Kennedy: Perspectives on Presidential Power").

Concerns over presidential power are generally closely related to policy views. Those who oppose the president's policies are the most likely to be concerned about *too much* presidential power. As you have seen, however, aside from acting outside the law and the Constitution, there is little prospect that the presidency will be a threat to democracy. The Madisonian system of checks and balances remains intact.

This system is especially evident in an era characterized by divided government—government in which the president is of one party and a majority in each house of Congress is of the other party. Some observers are concerned that there is too much checking and balancing and too little capacity to act on pressing national challenges. More potentially important legislation fails to pass under divided government than when one party controls both the presidency and Congress.[50] However, major policy change *is* possible under a divided government. One author found that major change is just as likely to occur when the parties share control as when one party holds both the presidency and a majority in each house of Congress.[51]

THE PRESIDENCY AND THE SCOPE OF GOVERNMENT

The president is the central leader in American politics, and some of the most noteworthy presidents in the twentieth century (including Theodore Roosevelt, Woodrow Wilson, and Franklin Roosevelt) have successfully advocated substantial increases in the role of the national government. Supporting an increased role for government is not inherent in the presidency, however; leadership can move in many directions.

All six of the presidents since Lyndon Johnson have championed constraints on government and limits on spending, especially in domestic policy. It is often said

SINCE KENNEDY

Perspectives on Presidential Power

During the 1950s and 1960s it was fashionable for political scientists, historians, and commentators to favor a powerful presidency. Historians rated presidents from strong to weak—and there was no question that "strong" meant good and "weak" meant bad. Political scientists waxed eloquent about the presidency as the epitome of democratic government.*

By the 1970s, many felt differently. The Vietnam War was unpopular. Lyndon Johnson and the war made people reassess the role of presidential power, and Richard Nixon and the Watergate scandal doubled public distrust. Presidential duplicity was revealed in the Pentagon papers, a series of secret documents slipped to the press by Daniel Ellsberg. Nixon's "enemies list" and his avowed goal to "screw our enemies" by illegally auditing their taxes, tapping their phones, and using "surreptitious entry" (a euphemism for burglary) asserted that presidents considered themselves above the law. Nixon's lawyers argued solemnly to the Supreme Court and Congress that the presidency has "inherent powers" permitting presidents to order acts that otherwise would be illegal. Nixon protected himself with an umbrella defense of executive privilege, claiming that he did not need to provide evidence to Congress or the courts.

Early defenders of a strong presidency made sharp turnabouts in their position. In his book *The Imperial Presidency,* historian Arthur Schlesinger, an aide of John Kennedy's, argued that the presidency had become too powerful for the nation's own good.** (Critics pointed out that Schlesinger did not seem to feel that way when he worked in the White House.) Whereas an older generation of scholars had written glowing accounts of the presidency, a newer generation wrote about "The Swelling of the Presidency" and "Making the Presidency Safe for Democracy."***

The Nixon era was followed by the presidencies of Gerald Ford and Jimmy Carter, whom many critics saw as weak leaders and failures. Ford himself spoke out in 1980, claiming that Carter's weakness had created an "imperiled" presidency. In the 1980s, Ronald Reagan experienced short periods of great influence and longer periods of frustration as the American political system settled back into its characteristic mode of stalemate and incremental policymaking. The Iran-Contra affair kept concern about a tyrannical presidency alive, while, in most instances, Reagan's inability to impose his will on Congress evoked a desire on the part of some people (mostly conservatives) for a stronger presidency. Both of Reagan's successors, George Bush and Bill Clinton, found it difficult to get things done.

*A good example is Clinton Rossiter, *The American Presidency,* rev. ed. (New York: Harcourt, 1960).

**Arthur Schlesinger, *The Imperial Presidency* (Boston: Houghton Mifflin, 1973).

***The titles of chaps. 5 and 11 in Thomas E. Cronin, *The State of the Presidency,* 2nd ed. (Boston: Little, Brown, 1980).

that the American people are ideologically conservative and operationally liberal. For most of the past generation, it has been their will to choose presidents who reflected their ideology and a Congress that represented their appetite for public service. It has been the president more often than Congress who has said "no" to government growth.

SUMMARY

This chapter has focused on the president and the presidency. Americans expect a lot from presidents—perhaps too much. The myth of the president as a powerhouse clouds Americans' image of presidential reality. Presidents mainly have the power to persuade, not to impose their will.

Presidents do not work alone. Gone are the days when the presidency meant the president plus a few aides and advisors. The cabinet, the Executive Office of the President, and the White House staff all assist today's presidents. These services come at a price, however, and presidents must organize their subordinates effectively for decision making and policy execution.

Although presidential leadership of Congress is central to all administrations, it often proves frustrating. Presidents rely on their party, the public, and their own legislative skills to persuade Congress to support their policies, but most of the time their efforts are at the margins of coalition building. Rarely are presidents in a position to create—through their own leadership—

opportunities for major changes in public policy. They may, however, use their skills to exploit favorable political conditions to bring about policy change.

Some of the president's most important responsibilities fall in the area of national security. As chief diplomat and commander in chief of the armed forces, the president is the country's crisis manager. Still, disputes with Congress over war powers and presidential discretion in foreign affairs demonstrate that even in regard to national security, the president operates within the Madisonian system of checks and balances.

Because presidents are dependent on others to accomplish their goals, their greatest challenge is to obtain support. Public opinion can be an important resource for presidential persuasion, and the White House works hard to influence the public. Public approval of presidents and their policies is often elusive, however; the public does not reliably respond to presidential leadership. The press is the principal intermediary between the president and the public, and relations with the press present yet another challenge to the White House's efforts to lead public opinion.

KEY TERMS

Twenty-second Amendment
impeachment
Watergate
Twenty-fifth Amendment
cabinet
National Security Council (NSC)
Council of Economic Advisors (CEA)
Office of Management and Budget (OMB)
veto
pocket veto
presidential coattails
War Powers Resolution
legislative veto
crisis

FOR FURTHER READING

Barber, James David. *The Presidential Character*, 4th ed. Englewood Cliffs, NJ: Prentice-Hall, 1992. Provocative work predicting performance in the White House.

Burke, John P. *The Institutional Presidency*. Baltimore, MD: Johns Hopkins University Press, 1992. Examines White House organization and presidential advising.

Burke, John P., and Fred I. Greenstein. *How Presidents Test Reality*. New York: Russell Sage Foundation, 1989. Excellent work on presidential decision making.

Edwards, George C., III. *At the Margins: Presidential Leadership of Congress*. New Haven, CT: Yale University Press, 1989. Examines the president's efforts to lead Congress and explains their limitations.

Edwards, George C., III. *Presidential Approval*. Baltimore, MD: Johns Hopkins University Press, 1990. The relationship between the president and public opinion in the White House's pursuit of popular support.

Fisher, Louis. *Constitutional Conflicts Between Congress and the President*, 4th ed. revised. Lawrence, KS: University Press of Kansas, 1997. Presents the constitutional dimensions of the separation of powers.

Grossman, Michael Baruch, and Martha Joynt Kumar. *Portraying the President: The White House and the News Media*. Baltimore, MD: Johns Hopkins University Press, 1981. A comprehensive study of presidential relations with the press.

Hart, John. *The Presidential Branch*, 2nd ed. Chatham, NJ: Chatham House, 1995. Discusses the Executive Office of the President and the White House staff.

Nathan, Richard P. *The Administrative Presidency*. New York: Wiley, 1983. The president's role in managing the bureaucracy.

Neustadt, Richard E. *Presidential Power and the Modern Presidents*. New York: Free Press, 1990. The most influential book on the American presidency; argues that presidential power is the power to persuade.

Pfiffner, James P. *The Strategic Presidency*, 2nd ed. Lawrence: University Press of Kansas, 1996. Organizing the presidency.

INTERNET RESOURCES

http://www.whitehouse.gov/
Presidential speeches, documents, schedule, and radio addresses, federal statistics, and White House press releases and briefings.

http://www1.whitehouse.gov/WH/EOP/html/EOP_org.html
The Executive Office of the President.

http://www.sunsite.unc.edu/lia/president/
Presidents and presidential libraries.

http2.sils.umich.edu/FordLibrary/
A day in the life of President Ford.

http://www.nara.gov/nara/fedreg/ec/
Electoral College.

http://www.nara.gov/education/teaching/watergate/
Watergate.

NOTES

1. Quoted in Thomas E. Cronin, *The State of the Presidency*, 2nd ed. (Boston: Little, Brown, 1980), 223.
2. Richard E. Neustadt, *Presidential Power and the Modern Presidents* (New York: Free Press, 1990).
3. On the public's expectations of the president, see George C. Edwards III, *The Public Presidency* (New York: St. Martin's Press, 1983), chap. 5.
4. Office of the White House Press Secretary, *Remarks of the President at a Meeting with Non-Washington Editors and Broadcasters*, September 21, 1979, 12.
5. Samuel P. Huntington, *American Politics: The Promises of Disharmony* (Cambridge, MA: Belknap, 1981), 33.
6. James David Barber, *The Presidential Character*, 4th ed. (Englewood Cliffs, NJ: Prentice-Hall, 1992).
7. Garry Wills, *The Kennedy Imprisonment* (Boston: Atlantic-Little, Brown, 1982), 186. See also Alexander George, "Assessing Presidential Character," *World Politics* 26 (January 1974): 10-30.
8. On Eisenhower as a leader, see Fred I. Greenstein, *The Hidden-Hand Presidency* (New York: Basic Books, 1982).
9. See Paul C. Light, *Vice Presidential Power* (Baltimore, MD: Johns Hopkins University Press, 1984).
10. On the creation of the presidency, see Donald L. Robertson, *"To the Best of My Ability"* (New York: Norton, 1987); and Thomas E. Cronin, ed., *Inventing the American Presidency* (Lawrence, KS: University Press of Kansas, 1989).
11. For a study of the backgrounds of cabinet members, see Jeffrey E. Cohen, *The Politics of the U.S. Cabinet* (Pittsburgh, PA: University of Pittsburgh Press, 1988).
12. For background on the Executive Office, see John Hart, *The Presidential Branch*, 2nd ed. (Chatham, NJ: Chatham House, 1995).
13. Two useful books on the history and functions of the White House staff are Hart, *The Presidential Branch*; and Bradley H. Patterson, Jr., *The Ring of Power* (New York: Basic Books, 1988).
14. For a discussion of presidential party leadership in Congress, see George C. Edwards III, *At the Margins: Presidential Leadership of Congress* (New Haven, CT: Yale University Press, 1989), chaps. 3-5.
15. Jimmy Carter, *Keeping Faith* (New York: Bantam, 1982), 80.
16. For a review of these studies and an analysis showing the limited impact of presidential coattails on congressional election outcomes, see Edwards, *The Public Presidency*, 83-93.
17. For evidence of the impact of the president's campaigning in midterm elections, see Jeffrey E. Cohen, Michael A. Krassa, and John A. Hamman, "The Impact of Presidential Campaigning on Midterm U.S. Senate Elections," *American Political Science Review* 85 (March 1991): 165-178. On the president's effect on presidential elections more broadly, see James E. Campbell, *The Presidential Pulse of Congressional Elections* (Lexington, KY: University Press of Kentucky, 1993).
18. Quoted in Sidney Blumenthal, "Marketing the President," *New York Times Magazine*, September 13, 1981, 110.
19. Quoted in "Slings and Arrows," *Newsweek*, July 31, 1978, 20.
20. Edwards, *At the Margins*, chaps. 6-7.
21. For an analysis of the factors that affect perceptions of mandates, see Edwards, *At the Margins*, chap. 8.
22. David Stockman, *The Triumph of Politics* (New York: Harper & Row, 1986), 251-265; and William Greider, "The Education of David Stockman," *Atlantic*, December 1981, 51.
23. John Kingdon, *Agendas, Alternatives, and Public Policies* (Boston: Little, Brown, 1984), 25. On presidential agenda setting, see Paul C. Light, *The President's Agenda* (Baltimore, MD: Johns Hopkins University Press, 1983).
24. Edwards, *At the Margins*, chaps. 9-10; and Jon R. Bond and Richard Fleisher, *The President in the Legislative Arena* (Chicago: University of Chicago Press, 1990), chap. 8.
25. For an analysis of war powers and other issues related to separation of powers, see Louis Fisher, *Constitutional Conflicts Between Congress and the President,* 4th ed. rev.(Lawrence, KS: University Press of Kansas, 1997) and Louis Fisher, *Presidential War Power* (Lawrence, KS: University Press of Kansas, 1995).
26. See Barbara Hinckley, *Less than Meets the Eye* (Chicago: University of Chicago Press, 1994).
27. The phrase was originated by Aaron Wildavsky in "The Two Presidencies," *TransAction* 4 (December 1966): 7-14. He later determined that the two presidencies applied mostly to the 1950s. See Duane M. Oldfield and Aaron Wildavsky, "Reconsidering the Two Presidencies," in Steven A. Shull, ed., *The Two Presidencies: A Quarter Century Assessment* (Chicago: Nelson-Hall, 1991), 181-190.
28. Edwards, *At the Margins*, chap. 4.
29. See William W. Lammers, "Presidential Attention-Focusing Activities," Doris A. Graber, ed., in *The President and the Public* (Philadelphia: ISHI, 1982), 145-171; and Samuel Kernell, *Going Public*, 2nd ed. (Washington, DC: Congressional Quarterly Press, 1992), chap. 4.
30. Edwards, *The Public Presidency*, chap. 6; and George C. Edwards III, *Presidential Approval* (Baltimore, MD: Johns Hopkins University Press, 1990).
31. Mueller also included the inaugural period of a president's term as a rally event. See John E. Mueller, *War, Presidents and Public Opinion* (New York: Wiley, 1973), 208-213.
32. Kernell, *Going Public*, 148.
33. See Jeffrey K. Tulis, *The Rhetorical Presidency* (Princeton, NJ: Princeton University Press, 1987), on presidents' efforts to build policy support.

34. For a discussion of the social flow of information, see Robert Huckfeldt and John Sprague, "Networks in Context: The Social Flow of Political Information," *American Political Science Review* 81 (December 1987): 1197-1216.

35. *Newsweek* Poll, October 28-30, 1994, cited in "The Problem with the President," *Newsweek*, November 7, 1994, p. 42.

36. George C. Edwards III, "Frustration and Folly: Bill Clinton and the Public Presidency," in Colin Campbell and Bert A. Rockman, eds., *The Clinton Presidency: First Appraisals* (Chatham, NJ: Chatham House, 1995).

37. Useful comparisons over Reagan's tenure can be found in William G. Mayer, *The Changing American Mind* (Ann Arbor, MI: University of Michigan Press, 1992); Benjamin I. Page and Robert Y. Shapiro, *The Rational Public* (Chicago: University of Chicago Press, 1992); and James A. Stimson, *Public Opinion in America: Moods, Cycles, and Swings* (Boulder, CO: Westview, 1991).

38. Quoted in "Tax Cut Passed by Solid Margin in House, Senate," *Congressional Quarterly Weekly Report*, August 1, 1981, 1374.

39. Sam Donaldson, *Hold On, Mr. President!* (New York: Random House, 1987), 196-197.

40. Two of the leading studies are found in Michael J. Robinson and Margaret A. Sheehan, *Over the Wire and on TV* (New York: Russell Sage Foundation, 1983); and Daniel C. Hallin, "The Media, the War in Vietnam, and Political Support," *Journal of Politics* 46 (February 1984): 2-24.

41. Carter, *Keeping Faith*, 179-180.

42. See Mark J. Rozell, *The Press and the Ford Presidency* (Ann Arbor, MI: University of Michigan Press, 1992).

43. Graber, *Mass Media and American Politics*, 227. On the 1992 presidential campaign, see "Clinton's the One," *Media Monitor*, 6 (November 1992): 3-5.

44. Thomas E. Patterson, *Out of Order* (New York: Knopf, 1993), chap. 3.

45. Patterson, *Out of Order*, 113.

46. *Media Monitor*, May/June 1995, pp. 2-5; Thomas E. Patterson, "Legitimate Beef: The Presidency and a Carnivorous Press," *Media Studies Journal* (Spring 1994): 21-26. But see Andras Szanto, "In Our Opinion . . .: Editorial Page Views of Clinton's First Year," *Media Studies Journal* (Spring 1994): 97-105.

47. Michael Baruch Grossman and Martha Joynt Kumar, *Portraying the President: The White House and the News Media* (Baltimore, MD: Johns Hopkins University Press, 1981), chaps. 10-11.

48. Donaldson, *Hold On, Mr. President!*, 237-238.

49. Quoted in Eleanor Randolph, "Speakes Aims Final Salvo at White House Practices," *Washington Post*, January 31, 1987, A3.

50. George C. Edwards III, Andrew Barrett, and Jeffrey S. Peake, "The Legislative Impact of Divided Government," *American Journal of Political Science* 41 (April 1997): 545-563.

51. David R. Mayhew, *Divided We Govern* (New Haven, CT: Yale University Press, 1991).

14

The Congress, the President, and the Budget: The Politics of Taxing and Spending

The Government's Sources of Revenue

Federal Expenditures

The Budgetary Process

Understanding Budgeting

For years, the dominant issue of public policy at the national level has not been whether it is good for the government to spend money to feed the poor, provide health care for the elderly, or clean up the environment. Most people support such policies. Instead, the central political issue has been how much to spend on such policies and how to pay for them.

Making tough decisions can be dangerous, however. In 1985, Republican senators took the lead with a reform that was designed to balance the budget. In the 1986 congressional elections, Republicans lost control of the Senate. In 1990, President George Bush bit the bullet of reversing his pledge not to raise taxes and agreed to a budget deal with the congressional Democrats that succeeded in reducing the deficit and limiting spending. In 1992, he lost his bid for reelection.

In 1993, President Clinton followed the precedent of his predecessor and reversed his promise to lower taxes with a program of higher taxes and spending constraints. In the 1994 elections, Republicans won majorities in both houses of Congress—the first time they had done so since 1952. Many of the Republicans had signed a "Contract with America," a party platform containing pledges to enact major changes in public policy. At the core of the "contract" were promises to cut taxes, balance the budget, and reform programs that gave citizens entitlements to certain benefits such as welfare. A 2-year political battle ensued between President Clinton, who vigorously opposed the scope of the contract's proposals, and congressional Republicans. In the end, little changed, and each side vowed to take its case to the American people in the 1996 elections.

The public—which typically seeks a balanced budget, little or no cut in government programs, and tax relief—split its decision. The Democrats won the presidency, but Republicans won both houses of Congress—the only time that had *ever* happened. It is not surprising, then, that the battle of the budget remains at the center of American politics.

Two questions are central to public policy: Who bears the burdens of paying for government? Who receives the benefits? Some observers are concerned that democracy poses a danger to budgeting. Do politicians seek to "buy" votes by spending public funds on things voters will like—and will remember on election day? Or is spending the result of demands made on government services by the many segments of American society? In addition, does the public choose to "soak the rich" with taxes that redistribute income? And why haven't we been able to balance the budget? Is it a lack of resolve or competence among policymakers? Or is it the result of a lack of consensus among Americans on policy? Do Americans want to spend but not pay higher taxes and, as we would expect in a democracy, end up with red ink as a result?

Budgets are central to our theme of the scope of government. Indeed, for many programs, budgeting *is* policy. The amount of money spent on a program determines how many people are served, how well they are served, or how much of something (weapons, vaccines, and so on) the government can purchase. The bigger the budget, the bigger the government. But is the growth of the government's budget inevitable? Or are the battles over the allocation of scarce public resources actually a *constraint* on government?

The Constitution allocates various tasks to both the president and Congress, but it generally leaves to each branch the decision of whether to exercise its power to perform a certain task. There is an exception, however. Every year the president and Congress *must* appropriate funds. If they fail to do so, the government will come to a standstill. The army will be idled, Social Security offices will have to close, and food stamps will not be distributed to the poor.

During the 1980s and 1990s, the national government has run up large annual budget deficits. A budget **deficit** occurs when **expenditures** exceed **revenues** in a fiscal year. In other words, the national government spends more money than it receives in taxes. As a result, the total national debt rose sharply during the 1980s, increasing from less than $1 trillion to about $5.5 trillion by the year 1998. About 15 percent of all current budget expenditures go to paying just the *interest* on this debt.

With the national government awash in red ink, the president and Congress have been caught in a budgetary squeeze: Americans want them to balance the budget, maintain or increase the level of government spending on most policies, and keep taxes low. As a result, the president and Congress are preoccupied with budgeting, trying to cope with these contradictory demands.

In this chapter you will learn how the president and Congress produce a budget, making decisions on both taxes and expenditures. In short, you will look at how government manages its money—which is, of course, really *your* money.

THE GOVERNMENT'S SOURCES OF REVENUE

"Taxes," said the late Supreme Court Justice Oliver Wendell Holmes, Jr., "are what we pay for civilization." Despite his assertion that "I like to pay taxes," most taxpayers throughout history would not agree. The art of taxation, said Jean-Baptiste Colbert, Louis XIV's finance minister, is in "so plucking the goose as to procure the largest quantity of feathers with the least possible amount of squealing."[1] You can see in Figure 14.1 where the federal government has been getting its feathers. Only a small share comes from excise taxes (for example, those on gasoline) and other sources; the three major sources of federal revenues are the personal and corporate income tax, social insurance taxes, and borrowing.

INCOME TAX

Bleary-eyed, millions of American taxpayers struggle to the Post Office before midnight every April 15 to mail their income tax forms. Individuals are required to pay the government a portion of the money they earn; this portion is an **income tax**. Although the government briefly adopted an income tax during the Civil War, the first peacetime income tax was enacted in 1894. Even though the tax was only 2 percent of income earned beyond the then magnificent sum of $4,000, a lawyer opposing it called the tax the first step of a "communist march." The Supreme Court wasted little time in declaring the tax unconstitutional in *Pollock v. Farmer's Loan and Trust Co.* (1895).

In 1913, the **Sixteenth Amendment** was added to the Constitution, explicitly permitting Congress to levy an income tax. Congress was already receiving income tax revenue before the amendment was ratified, however, and the *Internal Revenue Service* was established to collect it. Today the IRS receives about 120 million individual tax returns each year. Each return is scrutinized by people or computers. In addition, the IRS audits in greater detail more than a million tax returns, investigates thousands of suspected criminal violations of the tax laws, and annually prosecutes and secures the conviction of thousands of errant taxpayers or nonpayers.[2]

Corporations, like individuals, pay income taxes. Although corporate taxes once yielded more revenues than individual income taxes, this is no longer true. Today corporate taxes yield about 12 cents of every federal revenue dollar, compared with 44 cents from individual income taxes.

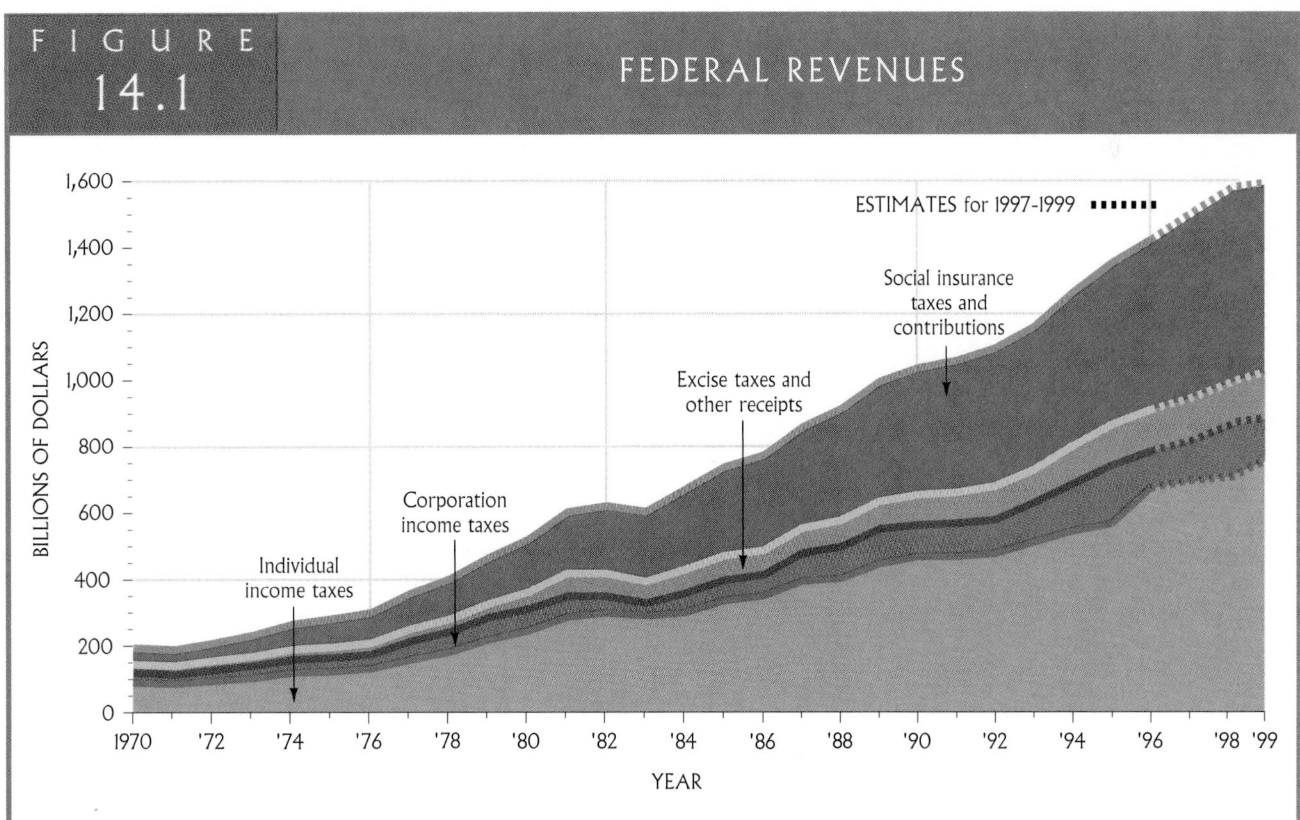

SOURCE: *Budget of the United States Government, Fiscal Year 1998: Historical Tables* (Washington, DC: U.S. Government Printing Office, 1997) Table 2.1.

SOCIAL INSURANCE TAXES

Social Security taxes come from both employers and employees. Money is deducted from employees' paychecks and matched by their employers. Unlike other taxes, these payments do not go into the government's general money fund but are earmarked for a specific purpose: the Social Security Trust Fund that pays benefits to the elderly, the disabled, the widowed, and the unemployed.

Social Security taxes have grown faster than any other source of federal revenue, and they will surely grow even more. In 1957, these taxes made up a mere 12 percent of federal revenues; today they account for about one-third. In 1997, employees and employers each paid a Social Security tax equal to 6.2 percent of the first $65,400 of earnings, and for Medicare they paid another 1.45 percent on all earnings.

BORROWING

Like families and firms, the federal government may borrow money to make ends meet. When families and firms need money, they go to their neighborhood bank, savings and loan association, or moneylender. When the federal government wants to borrow money, the Treasury Department sells bonds, guaranteeing to pay interest to the bondholder. Citizens, corporations, mutual funds, and other financial institutions can all purchase these bonds; there is always a lively market for government bonds.

Today the **federal debt**—all of the money borrowed over the years that is still outstanding—is nearing $6 trillion (see Figure 14.2). Fifteen percent of all federal expenditures go to paying interest on this debt rather than being allocated for current policies. Yesterday's consumption of public policies is at the expense of

FIGURE 14.2 TOTAL NATIONAL DEBT

The national debt mushroomed in the 1980s. One principal cause of this huge increase was the loss of revenue resulting from the huge tax cut proposed by President Reagan in 1981. The large increase in defense expenditures in the early years of the Reagan administration was another contributing factor.

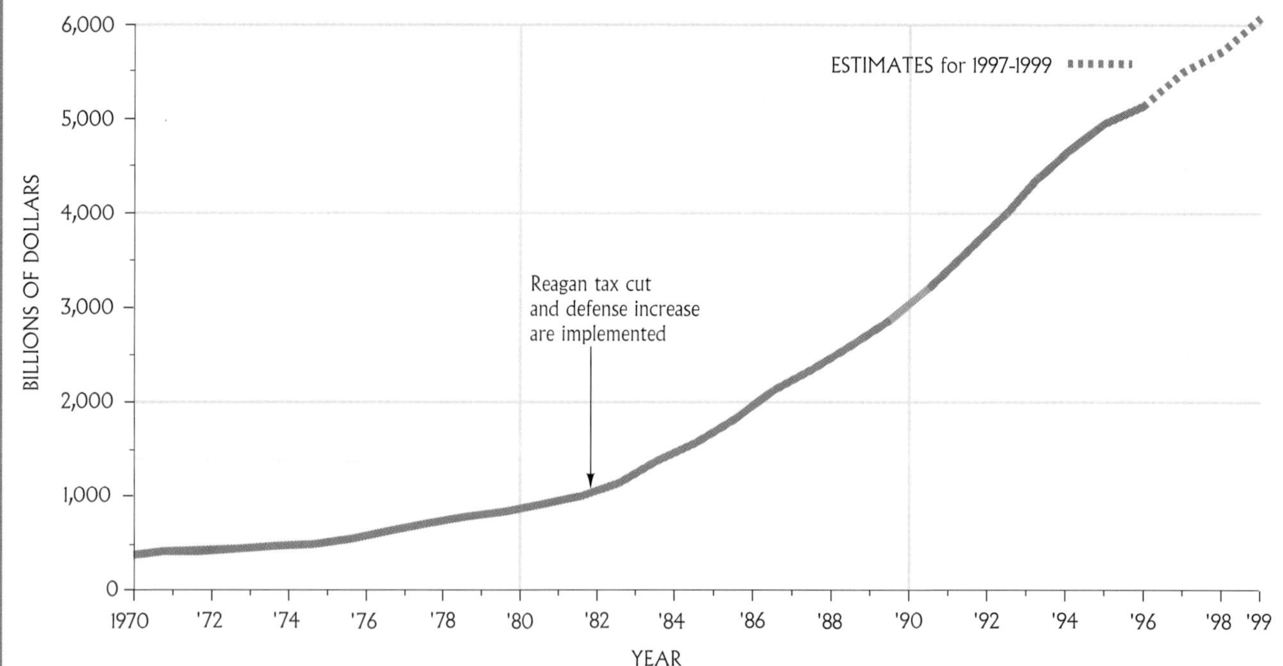

SOURCE: *Budget of the United States Government, Fiscal Year 1998: Historical Tables* (Washington, DC: U.S. Government Printing Office, 1997), Table 7.1.

tomorrow's taxpayers, because borrowing money shifts the burden of repayment to future taxpayers who will have to service the debt and pay the principal.

Government borrowing also crowds out private borrowers, both individuals and businesses, from the loan marketplace. (For instance, your local bank may know that you are a low-risk borrower, but it thinks the federal government is an even lower risk.) A substantial percentage of all the net private savings in the country goes to the federal government. The American government is also dependent on foreign investors, including other governments, to fund its debt—not a favorable position for a superpower. Most economists believe that this competition to borrow money increases interest rates and makes it more difficult for businesses to invest in capital expenditures (such as new plants and equipment) that produce economic growth.

Aside from its impact on private borrowing, the federal debt raises additional concerns. Every dollar that the government borrows today will cost taxpayers many more dollars in interest over the next 30 years. Government is borrowing not so much for its capital needs (as individuals and firms do when they buy a house or build a factory) as for its day-to-day expenses. Most families wisely do not borrow money for their food and clothing, yet the government is largely borrowing money for its farm subsidies, its military pensions, and its aid to states and cities.

Most observers are concerned about the national debt.[3] The perceived perils of gigantic deficits have led to calls for a **balanced budget amendment**. This proposed amendment to the Constitution would require Congress to balance peacetime federal budgets. Only a supermajority (larger than a simple majority) vote in both houses of Congress could authorize a specific expenditure beyond the government's expected revenues.[4] Opponents argue that it is difficult to estimate both expenditures and revenues more than a year ahead (if the economy performs worse than expected, for example, revenues go down and expenditures go up). And both Congress and the president could circumvent the intent of the amendment by adjusting economic assumptions or even changing the dates of the fiscal year.

Sometimes we hear politicians complain that because families and businesses and even state and local governments balance their budgets, the federal government ought to be able to do the same. Such statements reflect a fundamental misunderstanding of budgeting, however. Most families do *not* balance their budgets. They use credit cards to give themselves instant loans, and they go to the bank to borrow money to purchase automobiles, boats, and, most important, homes. The mortgages on their homes are debts they owe for most of their lives.

Because budgetary policy is so important, decisionmakers may be reluctant to compromise. In 1995-1996, the inability of the president and Congress to reach agreement led to the shutdown of the federal government.

Unlike state and local governments and private businesses, the federal government does not have a *capital budget*, a budget for expenditures on items that will serve for the long term, such as equipment, roads, and buildings. Thus, for example, when airlines purchase new airplanes or when school districts build new schools, they do not pay for them out of current income. Instead, they borrow money, often through issuing bonds. These debts do not count against the operating budget. When the federal government purchases new jets for the air force or new buildings for medical research, however, these purchases are counted as current expenditures and run up the deficit.

Despite its borrowing habits, most of the government's income still comes from taxes. Few government policies provoke more heated discussion than taxation.

TAXES AND PUBLIC POLICY

No government policy affects as many Americans as tax policy. In addition to raising revenues to finance its services, the government can use taxes to make citizens' incomes more nearly or less nearly equal, to encourage or discourage growth in the economy, and to promote specific interests. Whereas in Chapters 17 and 18 you will see how taxes affect economic and equality issues, the following sections will focus on how tax policies can promote the interests of particular groups or encourage specific activities.

Tax Loopholes. No discussion of taxes goes very far before the subject of tax loopholes comes up. Difficult to define, a *tax loophole* is presumably a tax break or tax benefit. The IRS Code, which specifies what income is subject to taxation, is riddled with exemptions, deductions, and special cases. Jimmy Carter, campaigning for the presidency, called the American tax system a "national disgrace" because of its special treatment of favored taxpayers. Some taxpayers, he stressed, get advantages from the tax code that are not available to everyone. Businesspeople, he complained, could deduct costly "three-martini lunches" as business expenses, whereas ordinary workers, carrying a sandwich and coffee in a thermos to work, cannot write off their lunch expenses.

In 1975, Texas computer magnate and 1992 and 1996 presidential candidate H. Ross Perot hired a former Internal Revenue Service commissioner to aid him in changing the tax code. The proposed change would have saved Perot $15 million. The amendment passed through the House Ways and Means Committee (billionaire Perot was reported to be a generous contributor to the campaign chests of several members) but was killed on the House floor when the press reported that only Perot would benefit from this provision.[5]

Tax loopholes may offend Americans' sense of fair play, but they cost the treasury relatively little. Loopholes are actually only one type of tax expenditure.

Tax Expenditures. What does cost the federal budget a substantial sum is the system of **tax expenditures**, defined by the 1974 Budget Act as "revenue losses attributable to provisions of the federal tax laws which allow a special exemption, exclusion, or deduction." These expenditures represent the difference between what the government actually collects in taxes and what it would have collected without special exemptions. Thus, tax expenditures amount to subsidies for different activities. For example:

- The government *could* send checks for billions of dollars to charities. Instead, it permits some taxpayers to deduct their contributions to charities from their income, thus encouraging charitable contributions.
- The government *could* give cash to families with the desire and financial means to buy a home. Instead, it permits homeowners to deduct from their income the billions of dollars they collectively pay each year in mortgage interest.
- The government *could* write a check to all businesses that invest in new plants and equipment. It does not do so, but it does allow such businesses to deduct these expenses from their taxes at a more rapid rate than they deduct other expenses. In effect, the owners of these businesses, including stockholders, get a subsidy that is unavailable to owners of other businesses.

Tax expenditures are among the most obscure aspects of a generally obscure budgetary process, partly because they receive no regular review by Congress—a great advantage for those who benefit from a tax expenditure. Few ordinary citizens seem to realize their scope; you can see the magnitude of tax expenditures in Table 14.1. On the whole, tax expenditures benefit middle- and upper-income taxpayers and corporations. Poorer people, who tend not to own homes, can take little advantage of provisions that permit homeowners to deduct mortgage interest payments. Likewise, poorer people in general can take less advantage of a deduction for charitable expenses.

To some, tax expenditures such as business-related deductions, tuition tax credits, and capital gains tax rates are loopholes. To others, they are public policy choices that support a social activity worth subsidizing. Either way, they amount to the same thing: revenues that the government loses because certain items are exempted from normal taxation or are taxed at lower rates. The Office of Management and Budget (OMB) estimates that the total tax expenditures in the late-1990s equal about one-third of the total receipts of the federal government.

Tax Reduction. The annual rite of spring—the preparation of individual tax returns—is invariably accompanied by calls for tax reform and, frequently, tax reduction. Early in his administration, President Reagan proposed a massive tax-cut bill. Standing in the way of tax cuts is never easy, and in July 1981, Congress passed Reagan's tax-cutting proposal. Over a 3-year period, the federal tax bills of Americans were reduced 25 percent, corporate income taxes were also reduced, new tax incentives were provided for personal savings and corporate investment, and taxes were *indexed* to the cost of living. These tax cuts meant that, beginning in 1985, government no longer received a larger share of income when inflation pushed incomes into higher brackets while the tax rates stayed the same. (This is important because people with high incomes also pay a higher *percentage* of their incomes in taxes.)

Families with high incomes saved many thousands of dollars on taxes, but those at the lower end of the income ladder saw little change in their tax burden because social insurance and excise taxes (which fall disproportionately on these people) rose during the same period. Many blamed the massive deficits of the 1980s and 1990s at least partially on the 1981 tax cuts,

TABLE 14.1 TAX EXPENDITURES: THE MONEY GOVERNMENT DOES NOT COLLECT

Tax expenditures are essentially monies that government could collect but does not because they are exempted from taxation. The Office of Management and Budget estimated that the total tax expenditures in 1998 would be more than $500 billion—about a third of the total federal receipts. Individuals receive most of the tax expenditures, and corporations get the rest. Here are some of the largest tax expenditures and their cost to the treasury:

TAX EXPENDITURE	MAIN BENEFICIARY	COST
Exclusion of company-paid benefits	Families	$76 billion
Exclusion of company contributions to pension funds	Families	$56 billion
Deduction of mortgage interest on owner-occupied houses	Families	$52 billion
Deductions for state and local taxes	Families	$48 billion
Step-up basis of capital gains at death	Families	$32 billion
Accelerated depreciation	Corporations	$29 billion
Deductions for charitable contributions	Families and corporations	$22 billion
Exclusion of Social Security benefits	Families	$18 billion
Exclusion for interest earned on state and local government bonds	Families	$16 billion
Deferral of capital gains on home sales	Families	$15 billion

In other words, government could easily close its budget deficit by taxing things it does not currently tax, such as Social Security benefits, pension fund contributions, charitable contributions, and the like. You can easily figure out, though, that these are not popular items to tax, and doing so would evoke strong opposition from powerful interest groups.

SOURCE: *Budget of the United States Government, Fiscal Year 1997: Analytical Perspectives* (Washington, DC: U.S. Government Printing Office, 1996), Table 5-3.

President Reagan signs the Tax Reform Act of 1986, passed with the backing of congressional leaders and administration officials. The legislation—the most wide-ranging reform of federal tax policy since the Sixteenth Amendment legalized income taxes in 1913—was implemented despite the protests of numerous interest groups that did not want to lose their tax deductions.

as government continued to spend but reduced its revenues. The appropriate level of taxation remains one of the most vexing problems in American politics. (See "America in Perspective: How Much Is Too Much?")

Tax Reform. Gripes about taxes are at least as old in America as the Boston Tea Party. When President Reagan first revealed his massive tax simplification plan in 1985—with its proposals to eliminate many tax deductions and tax expenditures—it was met with howls of protest. The insurance industry, for example, launched a $6 million advertising campaign to save the tax deductions for fringe benefits (much of which are in the form of life and health insurance) that employers set aside for employees. A pitched battle raged between tax reformers and interest groups determined to hold on to their tax benefits.

For once, however, a tax reform plan was not derailed. Democrats, including the powerful chair of the House Ways and Means Committee, Dan Rostenkowski, were enthusiastic about tax reform.

HOW MUCH IS TOO MUCH?

America in Perspective

No one likes to pay taxes, and it is common for Americans—and citizens all over the world—to complain that taxes are too high. The figures in the accompanying graph show that the national, state, and local governments in the United States tax a smaller percentage of the resources of the country than do those in almost all other democracies with developed economies. The Scandinavian countries of Sweden, Norway, and Denmark take half of the wealth of the country in taxes each year.

Comparatively, citizens in the United States have a rather light tax burden. Naturally, tax levels are related to the level of public services that governments provide. If you compare this graph with "America in Perspective: How Big Is Too Big?" (page 363), you will see that the big taxers are also the big spenders.

TOTAL TAX REVENUES OF GOVERNMENT AS A PERCENTAGE OF THE GROSS DOMESTIC PRODUCT

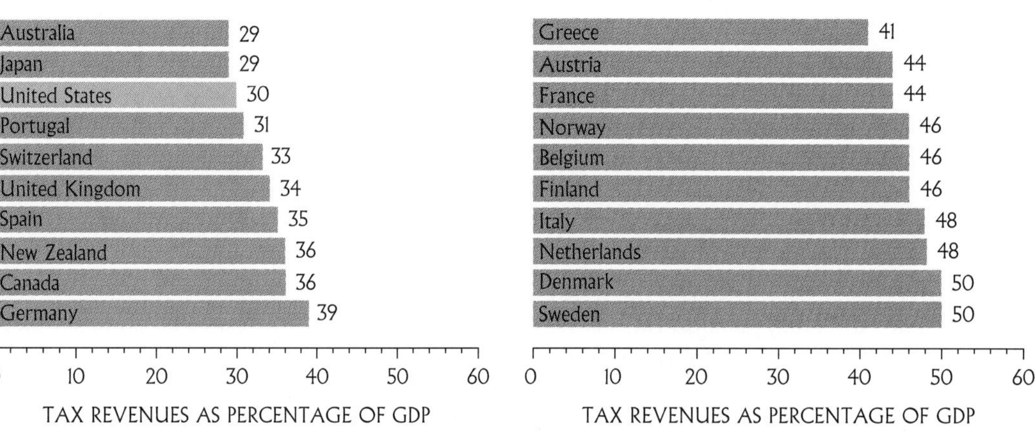

SOURCE: U.S. Department of Commerce, ***Statistical Abstract of the United States 1996*** (Washington, DC: Government Printing Office, 1996), 840.

They also did not want the Republicans to get all the credit for reform. In fact, the president actually had more problems obtaining the support of those in his own party and had to make an unusual trip to Capitol Hill to plead with House Republicans to support the tax bill after its initial defeat when it came to the floor.

The Senate posed an even bigger problem, because the bill was loaded with special tax treatments for a wide variety of groups. While the president was on a trip abroad, the Finance Committee met behind closed doors and emerged with a bill similar in spirit to the bill supported by the president and the House. The *Tax Reform Act of 1986* was one of the most sweeping alterations in federal tax policy history. It eliminated or reduced the value of many tax deductions, removed several million low-income individuals from the tax rolls, and reduced the 15 separate tax brackets to just two generally lower rates (28 percent and 15 percent). In 1990, a third bracket of 31 percent was added for those with high incomes (see "The People Speak: Taxes and Equity").

In 1993, Congress agreed to President Clinton's proposal to raise the income tax rate to 36 percent for families with incomes over $140,000 and add an additional surcharge of 3.6 percent to those families with incomes over $250,000. Congress also increased the top corporate income tax and an energy tax that would be paid by all but those with low incomes.

FEDERAL EXPENDITURES

In 1932, when President Franklin D. Roosevelt took office in the midst of the Great Depression, the federal government was spending just over $3 billion a year. Today, that sum would get the federal government through less than a day. Program costs once

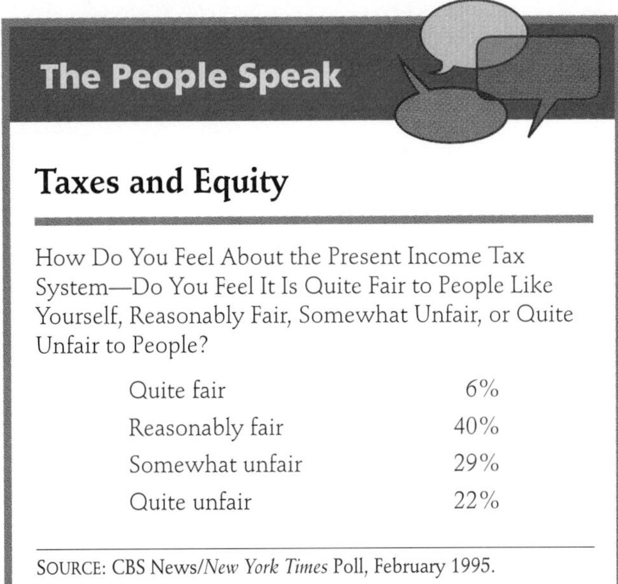

Taxes and Equity

How Do You Feel About the Present Income Tax System—Do You Feel It Is Quite Fair to People Like Yourself, Reasonably Fair, Somewhat Unfair, or Quite Unfair to People?

Quite fair	6%
Reasonably fair	40%
Somewhat unfair	29%
Quite unfair	22%

SOURCE: CBS News/*New York Times* Poll, February 1995.

measured in the millions are now measured in billions. Comparisons over time are a little misleading, of course, because they do not account for changes in the value of the dollar. You can see in Figure 14.3 how the federal budget has grown in actual dollars.

Figure 14.3 makes two interesting points. First, the policies and programs on which the government spends money change over time. Second, expenditures keep rising. Thus, the following sections explore three important questions: Why are government budgets so big? Where does the money go? Why is it difficult to control federal expenditures?

BIG GOVERNMENTS, BIG BUDGETS

One answer to the question of why budgets are so large is simple: Big budgets are necessary to pay for big governments. Among the most important changes of the twentieth century is the rise of large governments.[6] Actually, as you can see in "America in Perspective: How Big Is Too Big?" (page 363), among Western nations, America has one of the *smallest* public sectors relative to the size of the gross domestic product (GDP). Nevertheless, it is difficult to characterize the national government, with a budget of more than $1.7 trillion per year, as anything but large—some critics would say enormous.

As with other Western nations, the growth of government in the United States has been dramatic. Political scientist E. E. Schattschneider took a look backward at government growth:

> The beginnings were almost unbelievably small. In 1792 the federal government . . . resembled the present government in about the way Henry Ford's old bicycle repair shop resembles the modern Ford Motor Company. President Washington made his budget on a single sheet of paper. Jefferson ran his Department of Foreign Affairs with a staff of six writing clerks. The government issued three patents in 1790. As late as 1822 the government spent $1000 for the improvement of rivers and harbors and President Monroe vetoed a $9000 appropriation for the repair of the Cumberland Road.[7]

This relatively tiny government was, said Schattschneider, the "grain of mustard seed" from which today's huge government has grown. American governments—national, state, and local—spend an amount equal to one-third of the gross domestic product. Expenditures of the national government alone equal over 20 percent of the GDP.

No one, of course, knows for sure exactly why government has grown so rapidly in all the Western democracies. William Berry and David Lowery launched a major assault on the question, but their findings were mixed. Overall, however, they found the most support for the view that the public sector expands principally in response to changes in the public's preferences and in economic and social conditions that affect the public's level of demand for government activity.[8] This is why the rise of big government has been strongly resistant to reversal: citizens like government services. Even Ronald Reagan, a strong leader with an antigovernment orientation, succeeded only in slowing the growth of government, not in actually trimming its size. When he left office, the federal government employed more people and spent more money than when he was inaugurated.

Two conditions associated with government growth in America are the rise of the national security state and the rise of the social service state. The following sections will examine these phenomena briefly.

THE RISE AND DECLINE OF THE NATIONAL SECURITY STATE

A generation ago, the most expensive part of the federal budget was not its social services but its military budget. Before World War II, the United States customarily disbanded a large part of its military forces at the end of a war. After World War II, however, the "cold war" with the Soviet Union resulted in a permanent military establishment and expensive military technol-

FIGURE 14.3 FEDERAL EXPENDITURES

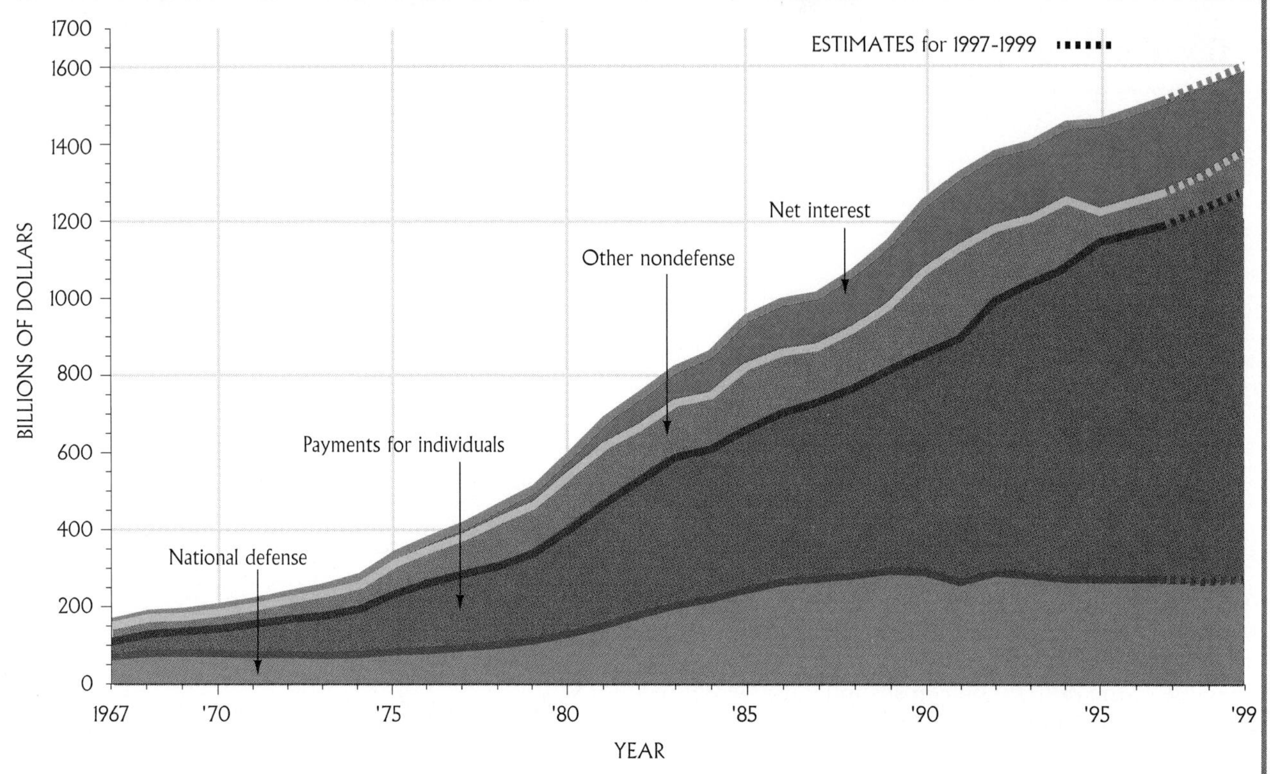

ESTIMATES for 1997-1999

BILLIONS OF DOLLARS: 0, 200, 400, 600, 800, 1000, 1200, 1400, 1600, 1700

YEAR: 1967, '70, '75, '80, '85, '90, '95, '99

Net interest

Other nondefense

Payments for individuals

National defense

SOURCE: *Budget of the United States Government, Fiscal Year 1998: Historical Tables* (Washington, DC: U.S. Government Printing Office, 1997), Table 6.1.

ogy. Fueling the military machine greatly increased the cost of government. It was President Eisenhower—not some liberal antimilitary activist—who coined the phrase *military industrial complex* to characterize the close relationship between the military hierarchy and the defense industry that supplies its hardware needs.

The Air Force unveiled its new Stealth Bomber in 1989. The plane's unusual shape allows it to fly undetected by enemy radar, but such technology costs money—over $1 billion per plane. These huge expenditures contributed to substantial increases in the defense budget in the 1980's.

In the 1950s and early 1960s, spending for past, present, and future wars amounted to more than half the federal budget. The Department of Defense got the majority of federal dollars. Liberals complained that government was shortchanging the poor while lining the pockets of defense contractors. Things soon changed, however. Over a decade and a half, from the mid-1960s to the early 1980s, defense expenditures crept downward in real dollars while social welfare expenditures more than doubled.

Although President Reagan proposed scrapping scores of domestic programs in his annual budget requests, he also urged Congress to increase the defense budget substantially. Throughout his entire second term, Congress balked, however, and in the 1990s, defense expenditures have decreased in response to the lessening tensions in Europe (discussed in Chapter 20). The budget of the Department of Defense, once the driving force in the expansion of the federal budget, now constitutes only about one-sixth of all federal expenditures (see Figure 14.4, page 364).

HOW BIG IS TOO BIG?

America in Perspective

When one hears about trillion-dollar federal budgets and budget deficits that may run $200 billion in a single year, it's easy to think of "big government." The figures in the accompanying graph, however, show that the national, state, and local governments in the United States actually spend a smaller percentage of their country's resources than those in most other democracies with developed economies. All the major Western democracies devote a considerably larger share of their wealth to government services, with Sweden spending two out of every three dollars in the economy on government programs. Compared with these countries, the United States has a rather modest public sector.

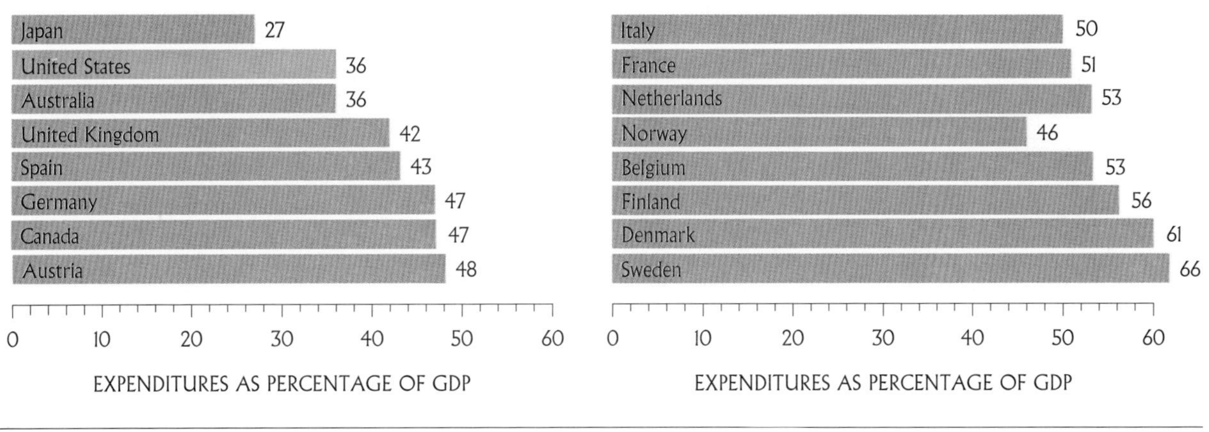

SOURCE: *OECD, 1997, pp. 44-45.*

Payrolls and pensions for the 2.2 million Pentagon employees, the 900,000 reservists, the 1.7 million people who receive military retirement pay, and the more than one million veterans who receive pensions constitute a large component of the defense budget. So do the research, development, and *procurement* (purchasing) of military hardware. The costs of procurement are high, even though total military expenditures have declined as a percentage of American GDP since the end of World War II. The cost of advanced technology makes any weapon, fighter plane, or component more expensive than its predecessors. Moreover, cost overruns are common. The American fleet of Stealth bombers will cost several times the original estimate—over a *billion* dollars each. According to former Secretary of the Air Force Edward C. Aldridge, "Whatever it costs, it's worth it."[9] Many critics of such expensive military hardware disagree.

THE RISE OF THE SOCIAL SERVICE STATE

The biggest slice of the budget pie, once reserved for defense, now belongs to *income security* expenditures, a bundle of policies extending direct and indirect aid to the elderly, the poor, and the needy. In 1935, during the Great Depression and the administration of President Franklin D. Roosevelt, Congress passed the **Social Security Act**. The act was intended to provide a minimal level of sustenance to older Americans, saving them from poverty.

In January 1940, the treasurer of the United States sent the nation's first Social Security check to Ida Fuller of Brattleboro, Vermont, in the amount of $22.54. An early entrant into the fledgling Social Security program, Fuller had contributed less than the amount of her first check to the system. By the time she died in December 1974 at the age of 100, she had collected $20,944.42 from the Social Security Administration. These days, 43 million Americans receive payments from the Social Security system each month. The typical retired worker received about $750 a month in 1998.

In the 1950s, disability insurance became a part of the Social Security program; thus, workers who had not retired but who were disabled could also collect benefits. In 1965, **Medicare**, which provides both hospital and physician coverage to the elderly, was added to the system. Although most Social Security checks go to retired workers, many also go to the disabled, to

FIGURE 14.4 TRENDS IN DEFENSE SPENDING

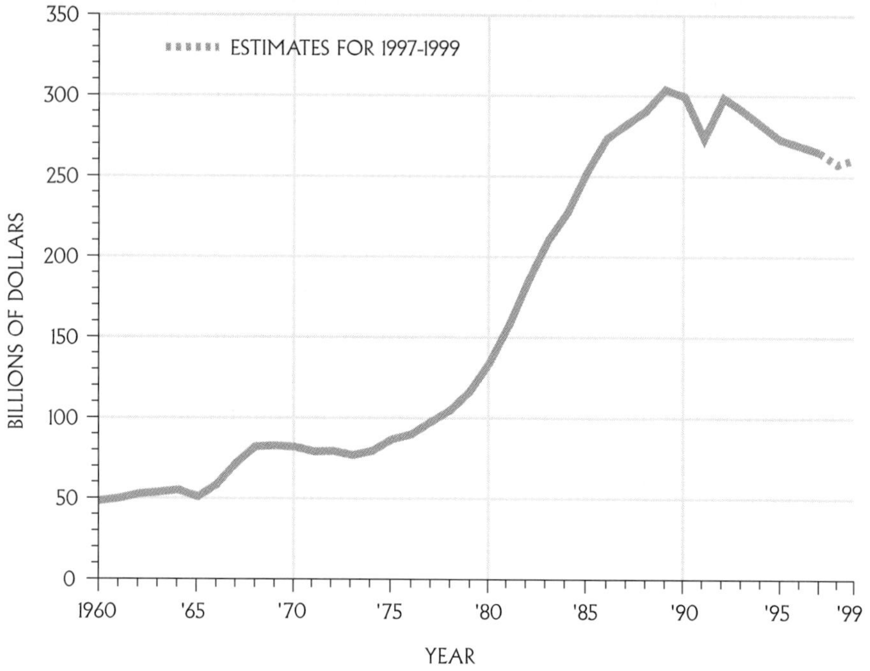

SOURCE: *Budget of the United States Government, Fiscal Year 1998: Historical Tables* (Washington, DC: U.S. Government Printing Office, 1997), Table 3.1.

Medicare patients, and to nonelderly spouses of workers who have died.

Social Security is less an insurance program than a kind of intergenerational contract. Essentially, money is taken from the working members of the population and spent on the retired members. Today, however, demographic and economic realities threaten to dilute this intergenerational bargain. In 1940, the entire Social Security system was financed with a 3 percent tax on payrolls; by 1990, the tax was in excess of 15 percent. In 1945, 50 workers paid taxes to support each Social Security beneficiary. In 1990, about three workers supported each beneficiary. By the year 2040, when today's young college students will be getting their Social Security checks, only two workers will be supporting each beneficiary.

Not surprisingly, the Social Security program faced a problem as the 1980s began. As Paul Light candidly described the problem: "It was going broke fast. More money was going out in benefits than was coming in . . . . At the height of the crisis, social security was spending about $3000 more per minute than it was taking in."[10] And that was only the short-term problem. The aging population added more people to the Social Security rolls annually; once there, people

Lyndon Johnson's "Great Society" initiatives in the mid-1960s greatly expanded America's social services network, adding Medicare and Medicaid to the Social Security system and creating many new programs designed to aid the poor. Here, LBJ campaigns during the 1964 presidential election.

tended to stay on the rolls because life expectancies were increasing. Building automatic escalators for taxes became a congressional necessity.

Social Security is the largest social policy of the federal government (Social Security and Medicare account for about one-third of the federal budget). However, other social service expenditures paralleled the upward growth of income security. In health, education, job training, and many other areas, the rise of the social service state has also contributed to America's growing budget. No brief list could do justice to the range of government social programs, which provide funds for the aged, businesses run by minority entrepreneurs, consumer education, drug rehabilitation, environmental education, food subsidies for the poor, guaranteed loans to college students, housing allowances for the poor, inspections of hospitals, and so on. Liberals often favor these programs to assist individuals and groups in society; conservatives see them as a drain on the federal treasury. In any event, they cost money—a lot of it (see "Since Kennedy: Trends in Social Service Spending").

The rise of the social service state and that of the national security state are linked with much of American governmental growth since the end of World War II. Although American social services expanded less than similar services in Western European nations, for most of the post-war period American military expenditures expanded more rapidly. Together, these factors help explain why the budget is the center of attention in American government today. Why is it so difficult to bring this increasing federal budget under control?

INCREMENTALISM

Sometimes political scientists use the term *incrementalism* to describe the spending and appropriations process. **Incrementalism** means simply that the best predictor of this year's budget is last year's budget plus a little bit more (an increment). According to Aaron Wildavsky, "The largest determining factor of the size and content of this year's budget is last year's. Most of each budget is a product of previous decisions."[11] Incremental budgeting has several features:

- Very little attention is focused on the budgetary base—the amounts agencies have had over the previous years.

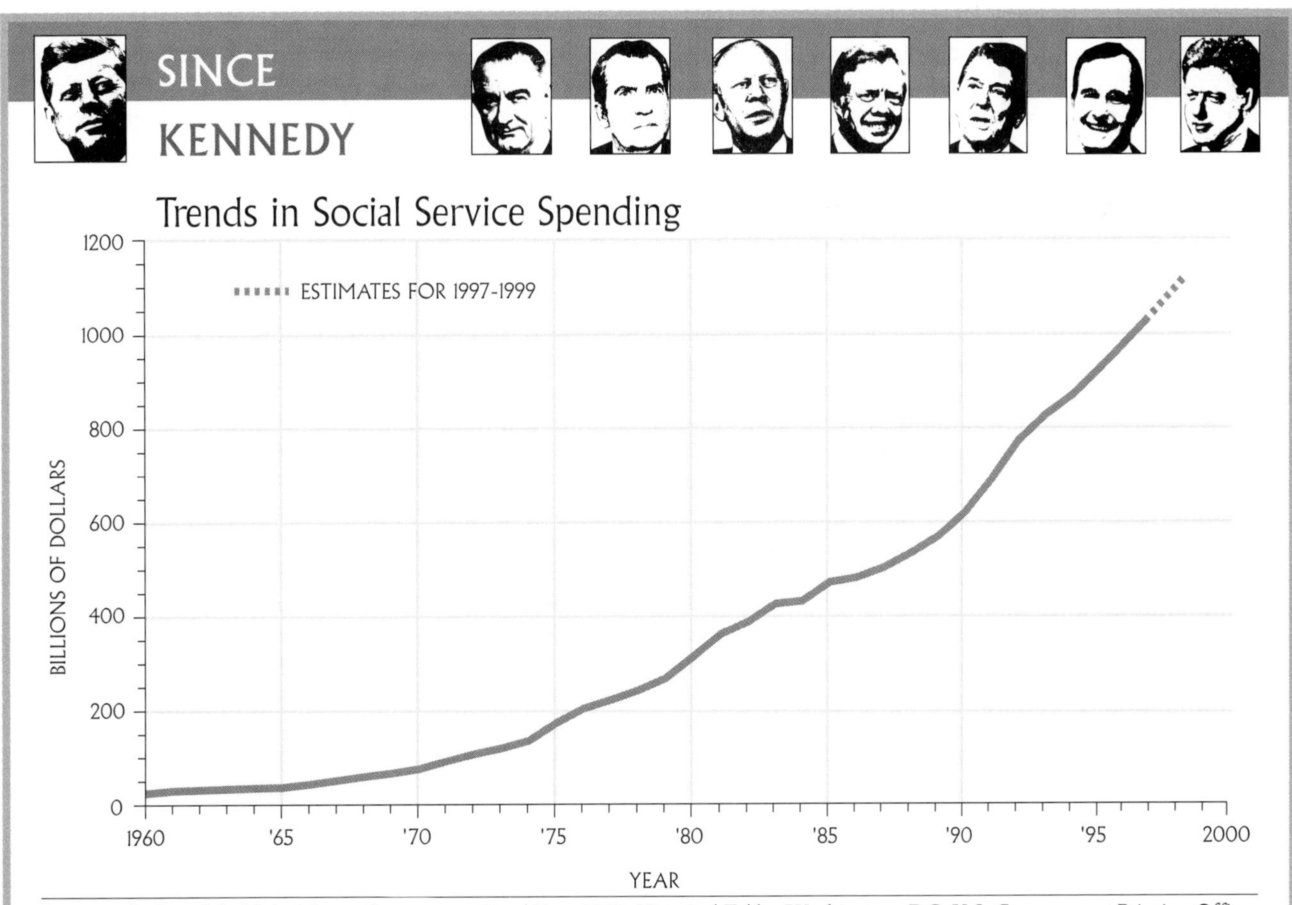

SOURCE: *Budget of the United States Government, Fiscal Year 1998: Historical Tables* (Washington, DC: U.S. Government Printing Office, 1997), Table 3.1.

- Usually, agencies can safely assume they will get at least the budget they had the previous year.
- Most of the debate and most of the attention of the budgetary process are focused on the proposed increment.
- The budget for any given agency tends to grow by a little bit every year.

This picture of the federal budget is one of constant, slow growth. Expenditures mandated by an existing law or obligation (such as Social Security) are particularly likely to follow a neat pattern of increase.[12] There are exceptions, however. Paul Schulman observed that budgets for the National Aeronautics and Space Administration (NASA) were hardly incremental; they initially rose as fast as a NASA rocket but later plummeted to a fraction of their former size.[13] Incrementalism may be a general tendency of the budget, but it does not fully describe all budgetary politics.

Because so much of the budgetary process looks incremental, there is a never-ending call for budgetary reform. The idea is always to make it easier to compare programs so that the "most deserving" ones can be supported and the "wasteful" ones cut. Lyndon Johnson tried to impose *Program Planning Budgeting Systems* (PPBS) on the whole government. Under this system, agencies must budget programs and demonstrate that the programs' goals are being achieved. The congressional reforms of 1974 (discussed below) were Congress' effort to make budgeting more rational. Jimmy Carter brought *zero-based budgeting* (ZBB) to Washington—an idea that he had used as the governor of Georgia. ZBB requires agencies making budget requests to assume that their base is zero and then justify any additional funding needs above zero, a very difficult task. When the Department of Agriculture experimented with ZBB, it found a big increase in its budgetary workload, with little change in the results.[14]

The budgetary process, like all aspects of government, is affected by relevant interests. It is these interests that make it difficult to pare the budget. In addition, the budget is too big to review from scratch each year, even for the most systematic and conscientious members of Congress. The federal budget is a massive document, detailing annual outlays larger than all countries' economies except those of the United States, Japan, and Russia. At the rate of one account per minute, eight hours per day, it would take over a year to reflect upon its nearly 200,000 accounts! And there is yet another reason why federal spending is hard to control: Much of it has become "uncontrollable."

"UNCONTROLLABLE" EXPENDITURES

At first glance, it is hard to see how one could call the federal budget uncontrollable. After all, Congress has the constitutional authority to budget—to add or subtract money from an agency. Indeed, Presidents Reagan, Bush, and Clinton proposed and Congress adopted some proposals to cut the growth of government spending. How, then, can one speak of an uncontrollable budget?

Consider for a moment what we might call the "allowance theory" of the budget. In this theory, a government budget works rather like an allowance. Mom and Dad hand over to Mary Jean and Tommy a monthly allowance, say $10 each, with the stern admonition, "Make that last to the end of the month because that's all we're giving you until then." In the allowance model of the budget, Congress plays this parental role; the agencies play the roles of Mary Jean and Tommy. Congress thus allocates a lump sum—say, $5.2 billion—and instructs agencies to meet their payrolls and other expenses throughout the fiscal year. When most Americans think of the government's budget, they envision the budget as a kind of allowance to the agencies.

About two-thirds of the government's budget, however, does not work this way at all. Vast expenditures are determined not by how much Congress appropriates to an agency, but by *how many eligible beneficiaries* there are for some particular program. **Uncontrollable expenditures** result from policies that make some group automatically eligible for some benefit. Thus, an expenditure is classified as uncontrollable if it is mandated under current law or by a previous obligation. Congress writes the eligibility rules; the number of people eligible and their level of guaranteed benefits determine how much Congress must spend. The Social Security Administration, for example, does not merely provide benefits on a first-come, first-served basis until the money runs out. Many expenditures are uncontrollable because Congress has in effect obligated itself to pay *X* level of benefits to *Y* number of recipients. Such policies are called **entitlements**. Each year, Congress' bill is a straightforward function of the *X* level of benefits times the *Y* beneficiaries.

The biggest uncontrollable expenditure of all is the Social Security system, including Medicare, which costs nearly $600 billion per year. Eligible individuals automatically receive Social Security payments. Of course, Congress can, if it desires, cut the benefits or tighten eligibility restrictions. Doing so, however, would provoke a monumental outcry from millions of elderly voters. Other items—veterans aid, agricultural subsidies, military pensions, civil service workers' retirement benefits, interest on the national debt—are uncontrollable expenditures also. Government cannot decide this year, for example, that it will not pay the interest on the federal debt, or that it will chop the pensions earned by former military personnel in half.

Altogether, the federal budget document itself estimates that fully two-thirds of the federal budget is uncontrollable—that is, Congress *can* control such expenditures, but only by changing a law or altering existing benefit levels. To control the uncontrollables, Congress can cut benefits, decrease the growth of benefits, or reduce the number of beneficiaries. You can see why neither would be a popular strategy for an elected Congress (see "You Are the Policymaker: Balancing the Budget").

In 1995 and 1996, the Republican majorities in Congress attempted to reduce the growth of Medicare benefits and to change programs, including Medicaid and welfare, from entitlements into block grants to the states. President Clinton was willing to accept substantial changes only in welfare benefits. Parts of the federal government closed down twice because of lack of funds, but the stalemate continued and the most significant Republican proposals have yet to be adopted.

THE BUDGETARY PROCESS

Budgets are produced through a long and complex process that starts and ends with the president and has the Congress squarely in the middle. Because budgets are so important to almost all other policies, the budgetary process is the center of political battles in Washington and involves nearly everyone in government. This section examines the process and the politics through which the president and Congress produce a budget.

Everyone has a basic understanding of budgeting. Public budgets are superficially like personal budgets. Aaron Wildavsky has remarked that a budget is a document that "contains words and figures that propose expenditures for certain objects and purposes." There is more to public budgets than bookkeeping, however, because such a **budget** is a policy document allocating burdens (taxes) and benefits (expenditures). Thus, "budgeting is concerned with translating financial resources into human purposes. A budget therefore may also be characterized as a series of goals with price tags attached."[15]

BALANCING THE BUDGET

You Are the Policymaker

You have seen that over the last generation the national government has run budget deficits of unprecedented size and that the national debt has ballooned. Moreover, public opinion polls have found that Americans believe the deficit to be a serious problem.

You have also seen that two-thirds of the federal budget is "uncontrollable," mostly composed of expenditures that have widespread public support, such as payments to individuals under Social Security.

Thus, here is a situation you would face as a budget decision maker: According to the OMB, in fiscal year 1998 the national government will have revenues (including Social Security taxes) of about $1,567 trillion. Mandatory expenditures for domestic policy (entitlements and other prior obligations) total about $899 billion. Nondiscretionary payments on the national debt will cost another $250 billion. National defense and international programs will cost an additional $279 billion. That leaves you with just $149 billion to spend and still balance the budget. The president's proposals for discretionary domestic policy programs will take $268 billion, however. If you spend this amount you will run a deficit of $119 billion—and you will not even have had a chance to fund any significant new programs.

What would *you* do? Would you drastically reduce defense expenditures further? Or would you leave them alone and close down the entire rest of the government, including programs for space and science, transportation and public works, economic subsidies and development, education and social services, health research and services, and law enforcement and other core functions of government—programs that also have broad public support? Perhaps you would show great political courage and seek a tax increase to pay for these programs. What *would* you do?

FIGURE 14.5 THE FEDERAL GOVERNMENT DOLLAR (FISCAL YEAR 1998 ESTIMATE)

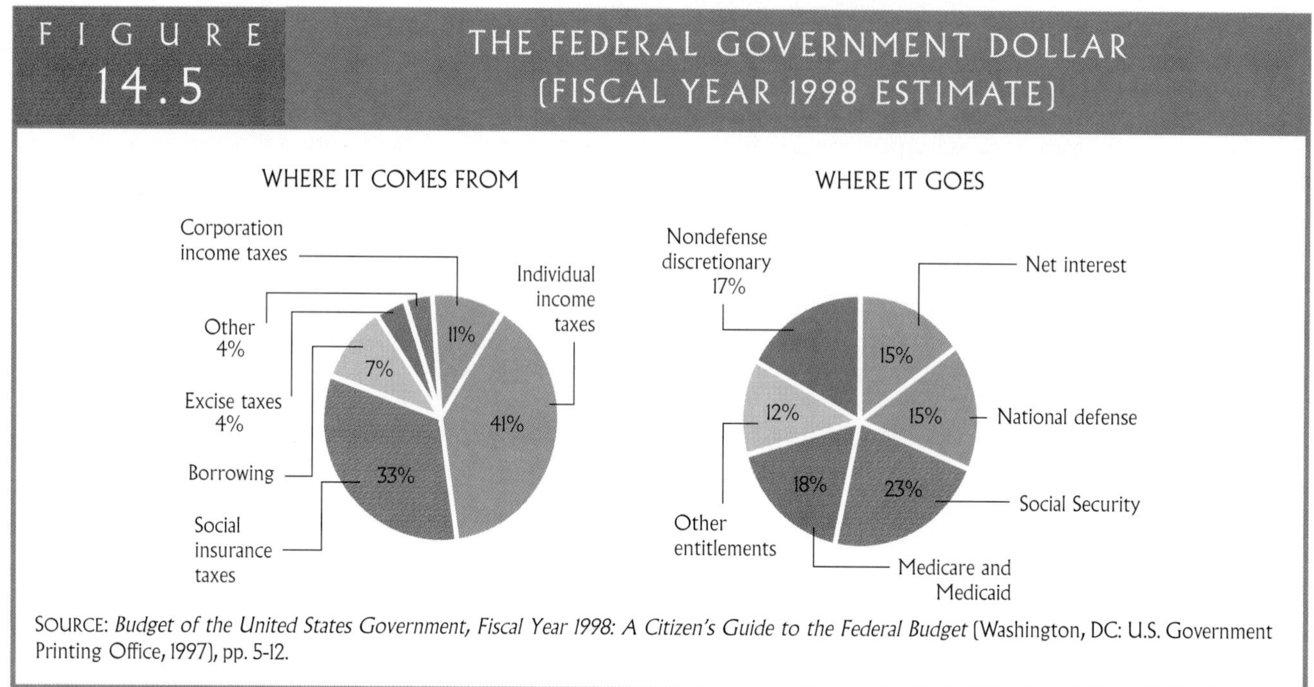

SOURCE: *Budget of the United States Government, Fiscal Year 1998: A Citizen's Guide to the Federal Budget* (Washington, DC: U.S. Government Printing Office, 1997), pp. 5-12.

Figure 14.5 gives a quick overview of the federal budget. It offers a simplified picture of the two sides of the budgetary coin, revenues and expenditures. The distribution of the government's budget is the outcome of a very complex budgetary process. Nestled inside the tax and expenditures figures are thousands of policy choices, each prompting plenty of politics.

BUDGETARY POLITICS

Public budgets are the supreme example of Harold Lasswell's definition of politics as "who gets what, when, and how." Budget battles are fought over contending interests, ideologies, programs, and agencies.

Stakes and Strategies. Every political actor has a stake in the budget. Mayors want to keep federal grants-in-aid flowing in; defense contractors like a big defense budget; scientists like the National Science Foundation to be given a large budget. Agencies within the government also work to protect their interests. Individual members of Congress act as policy entrepreneurs for new ideas (which cost money) and support constituent benefits (which also do not come free). Presidents try to use budgets to manage the economy and leave their imprint on Congress' policy agenda.

Think of budgetary politics as resembling a game in which players choose among strategies.[16] Agencies pushing their budgetary needs to the president and Congress, for instance, try to link the benefits of their program to a senator's or representative's electoral needs.[17] Almost invariably, agencies pad their requests a bit, hoping that the almost inevitable cuts will be bearable. President John Adams justified this now common budgetary gambit by saying to his cabinet, "If some superfluity not be given Congress to lop off, they will cut into the very flesh of the public necessities." Interest groups try to identify their favorite programs with the national interest. Mayors tell Congress not how much they like to receive federal aid but how crucial cities are to national survival. Farmers stress not that they like federal aid but that feeding a hungry nation and world is the main task of American agriculture. All the players have their own strategies in the game of budgetary politics, and in the pluralistic politics of budget making, there are plenty of players.

The Players. Deciding how to carve up more than one-fifth of the GDP is a process likely to attract plenty of interest—from those formally required to participate in the budgeting process as well as those whose stakes are too big to ignore it. Here are the main actors in the budgetary process:

- *The interest groups.* No lobbyist worth his or her pay would ignore the budget. Lobbying for a group's needs takes place in the agencies, with presidents (if the lobbyist has access to them), and before congressional committees. A smart agency head will be sure to involve interest groups in defending the agency's budget request.

- *The agencies.* Convinced of the importance of their mission, the heads of agencies almost always push for higher budget requests. They send their requests to the Office of Management and Budget and later get a chance to present themselves before congressional committees as well.
- *The Office of Management and Budget (OMB).* The OMB is responsible to the president, its boss, but no president has the time to understand and make decisions about the billions of dollars in the budget—parceled out to hundreds of agencies, some of which the chief executive has probably never heard. The director and staff of the OMB have considerable independence from the president, which makes them major actors in the annual budget process.
- *The president.* The president makes the final decisions on what to propose to Congress. In early February, the president unveils the proposed budget; the president then spends many a day trying to ensure that Congress will stick close to the recommendations.
- *The Tax Committees in Congress.* The government cannot spend money it does not have. The **House Ways and Means Committee** and the **Senate Finance Committee** write the tax codes, subject to the approval of Congress as a whole.
- *The Budget Committees and the Congressional Budget Office (CBO).* The CBO—which is the congressional equivalent of the OMB—and its parent committees, the Senate and House Budget Committees, set the parameters of the congressional budget process through examining revenues and expenditures in the aggregate and proposing resolutions to bind Congress within certain limits.
- *The subject-matter committees.* Committees of Congress write new laws, which require new expenditures. Committee members may use hearings either to publicize the accomplishments of their pet agencies, thus supporting larger budgets for them, or to question agency heads about waste or overspending.
- *The Appropriations Committees and their subcommittees.* The Appropriations Committee in each house decides who gets what. These committees take new or old policies coming from the subject-matter committees and decide how much to spend. Appropriations subcommittees hold hearings on specific agency requests.
- *The Congress as a whole.* The Constitution requires that Congress as a whole approve taxes and appropriations, and senators and representatives alike have a strong interest in delivering federal dollars to their constituents. A dam here, a military base there, and a job-training program somewhere else—these are items that members look for in the budget.
- *The General Accounting Office (GAO).* Congress' role does not end when it has passed the budget. The GAO works as Congress' eyes and ears, auditing, monitoring, and evaluating what agencies are doing with their budgets.

Budgeting involves a cast of thousands. However, their roles are carefully scripted and their time on stage is limited, because budget making is both repetitive (the same things must be done each year) and sequential (actions must occur in the proper order and more or less on time). The budget cycle begins in the executive branch a full 19 months before the fiscal year begins.

THE PRESIDENT'S BUDGET

Until 1921, the various agencies of the executive branch sent their budget requests to the secretary of the treasury, who in turn forwarded them to the Congress. Presidents played a limited role in proposing the budget; sometimes they played no role at all. Agencies basically peddled their own budget requests to Congress. In 1921 Congress, concerned about retiring the debt the country had accumulated during World War I, passed the Budget and Accounting Act, which required presidents to propose an executive budget to Congress, and created the Bureau of the Budget to help them. In the 1970s, President Nixon reorganized the Bureau of the Budget and gave it a new name, the Office of Management and Budget (OMB). The OMB, whose director is a presidential appointee requiring Senate approval, now supervises preparation of the federal budget and advises the president on budgetary matters.

It takes a long time to prepare a presidential budget.[18] By law, the president must submit a budget by the first Monday in February. The process begins almost a year before (see Table 14.2), when the OMB communicates with each agency, sounding out its requests and tentatively issuing guidelines. By the summer, the president has decided on overall policies and priorities and has established general targets for the budget. These are then communicated to the agencies.

The budget makers now get down to details. During the fall, the agencies submit formal, detailed estimates for their budgets, zealously pushing their needs to the OMB. Budget analysts at the OMB pare, investigate, weigh, and meet on agency requests. Typically, the agency heads ask for hefty increases; sometimes they threaten to go directly to the president if their priorities are not met by the OMB. As the Washington winter

TABLE 14.2 THE PRESIDENT'S BUDGET: AN APPROXIMATE SCHEDULE

Spring	
Budget policy developed	The OMB presents to the president an analysis of the economic situation, and they discuss the budgetary outlook and policies. The OMB then gives guidelines to the agencies, which in turn review current programs and submit to the OMB their projections of budgetary needs for the coming year. The OMB reviews these projections and prepares recommendations to the president on final policy, programs, and budget levels. The president establishes guidelines and targets.
Summer	
Agency estimates submitted	The OMB conveys the president's decisions to the agencies and advises and assists them in preparing their budgets.
Fall	
Estimates reviewed	The agencies submit to the OMB formal budget estimates for the coming fiscal year, along with projections for future years. The OMB holds hearings, reviews its assessment of the economy, and prepares budget recommendations for the president. The president reviews these recommendations and decides on the agencies' budgets and overall budgetary policy. The OMB advises the agencies of these decisions.
Winter	
President's budget determined and submitted	The agencies revise their estimates to conform with the president's decisions. The OMB once again reviews the economy and then drafts the president's budget message and prepares the budget document. The president revises and approves the budget message and transmits the budget document to Congress.

sets in, the budget document is readied for final presidential approval. There is usually some last-minute juggling—agencies may be asked to change their estimates to conform with the president's decisions, or cabinet members may make a last-ditch effort to bypass the OMB and convince the president to increase their funds. With only days—or hours—left before the submission deadline, the budget document is rushed to the printers. Then the president sends it to Capitol Hill. The next steps are up to Congress.

CONGRESS AND THE BUDGET

According to the Constitution, all federal appropriations must be authorized by Congress. Thus, Congress always holds one extremely powerful trump card in national policymaking: the power of the purse.[19] It is Congress that decides how to spend more than $1.7 trillion each year.

Reforming the Process. For years Congress budgeted in a piecemeal fashion. Each agency request was handled by a subcommittee of the House and Senate Appropriations Committees; then all these appropriations were added to produce a total budget. People never quite knew what the budget's bottom line would be until all the individual bills were totaled up. What Congress spent had little to do with any overall judgment of how much it should spend.

The **Congressional Budget and Impoundment Control Act of 1974** was designed to reform the congressional budgetary process. Its supporters hoped that it would also make Congress less dependent on the president's budget and more able to set and meet its own budgetary goals. Here is what the act established:

- *A fixed budget calendar.* For each step in the budgetary process there is an established completion date. In the past, Congress sometimes

TABLE 14.3 THE CONGRESSIONAL BUDGET PROCESS: TARGETS AND TIMETABLES

DATE	ACTION TO BE COMPLETED
First Monday in February	Congress receives the president's budget.
February 15	The CBO submits a budget report to the House and Senate Budget Committees, including an analysis of the president's budget.
February 25	Other committees submit reports on outlays and revenues to Budget Committees in each house.
April 1	Budget committees report concurrent resolution on the budget, which sets a total for budget outlays, an estimate of expenditures for major budget categories, and the recommended level of revenues. This resolution acts as an agenda for the remainder of the budgetary process.
April 15	Congress completes action on concurrent resolution on the budget.
May 15	Annual appropriations bills may be considered in the House.
June 10	House Appropriations Committee reports last annual appropriations bill.
June 15	Congress completes action on reconciliation legislation, bringing budget totals into conformity with established ceilings.
June 30	House completes action on annual appropriation bills.
October 1	The new fiscal year begins.

SOURCE: Howard E. Shuman, *Politics and the Budget,* 3rd ed. (Englewood Cliffs, NJ: Prentice-Hall, 1992), 67.

failed to appropriate money to agencies until after the fiscal year was over, leaving agencies drifting for months with no firm budget. Now there is a timetable mandated by law, which has been amended several times (see Table 14.3).

- *A Budget Committee in each house.* These two committees are supposed to recommend target figures to Congress for the total budget size by April 1 of each year. By April 15, Congress is to agree on the *total* size of the budget, which guides the Appropriations Committees in juggling figures for individual agencies.
- *A Congressional Budget Office.* The Congressional Budget Office (CBO) advises Congress on the probable consequences of its budget decisions, forecasts revenues, and is a counterweight to the president's OMB.

The new budgeting system was supposed to force Congress to consider the budget (both projected expenditures and projected revenues) as a whole, rather than in bits and pieces as it had done before. An important part of the process of establishing a budget is to set lim-

Every year the president must submit a budget to Congress. Although Congress often does not follow the president's budgetary priorities, the president's budget provides the foundation for the budgetary process.

its on expenditures on the basis of revenue projections—a step that is supposed to be done through a **budget resolution**. Thus, in April of each year, both houses are expected to agree on a budget resolution—thereby binding Congress to a total expenditure level that should form the bottom line of all federal spending for all programs. Only then is Congress supposed to begin acting on the individual appropriations.

In terms of a family budget, Family A might decide to budget by adding up all its needs and wants and calling that its budget. Such a strategy almost guarantees overspending the family income. Family B, though, might begin by looking first at its revenue and then trying to bring its total expenditures into line with its revenue before dealing with its individual expenditure decisions. With its 1974 reforms, Congress was trying to force itself to behave more like Family B than Family A.

Like the president's budget proposal, the congressional budget resolution often requests that certain changes be made in law, primarily to achieve savings incorporated into the spending totals and thus meet the budget resolution. These changes are legislated in two separate ways.

First is budget **reconciliation**, which revises program authorizations to achieve required savings; it frequently also includes tax or other revenue adjustments. Usually reconciliation comes near the end of the budgetary process. However, in an attempt to strike while his political standing was high and to overcome the opposition of special interests and the parochialism and power of congressional committees, President Reagan in 1981 successfully proposed using an extremely complex reconciliation bill to reduce the budget by approximately $40 billion. Reagan thought that he could obtain substantial cuts only if he lumped them all together in one bill in which everyone lost something. The preparation of the bill was so hurried that few members of Congress could give it serious consideration; in fact, the name and telephone number of Rita Seymour, a CBO staffer, were even inadvertently included in one amendment.

The second way that laws are changed to meet the budget resolution (or to create or change programs for other reasons) involves more narrowly drawn legislation. An **authorization bill** is an act of Congress that establishes a discretionary government program or an entitlement, or that continues or changes such programs. Authorizations specify program goals and, for discretionary programs, set the maximum amount that they may spend. For entitlement programs, an authorization sets or changes eligibility standards and benefits that must be provided by the program. Authorizations may be for 1 year, or they may run for a specified or indefinite number of years.

An additional measure, termed an **appropriations bill**, must be passed actually to fund programs established by authorization bills. The appropriations bills usually cover 1 year and cannot exceed the amount of money authorized for a program, but they may appropriate less than was authorized.

The Success of the 1974 Reforms. Have these reforms worked? If *worked* means that Congress has brought its spending into line with its revenues, then the reforms have been an almost total failure. Congressional budgets have been in the red every year since the 1974 amendments. In fact, the red ink has grown from a puddle to an ocean (see Figure 14.6). Presidents have made matters worse, submitting budget proposals that contain large deficits.

In addition, Congress has often failed to meet its own budgetary timetable. There has been too much conflict over the budget for the system to work according to design. Moreover, in many instances Congress has not been able to reach agreement and pass appropriations bills at all and has instead resorted to **continuing resolutions**—laws that allow agencies to spend at the previous year's level. Sometimes, as in 1986 and 1987, appropriations bills have been lumped together in one enormous and complex bill (rather than in the 13 separate appropriations bills that are supposed to pass), precluding adequate review by individual members of Congress and forcing the president either to accept unwanted provisions or to veto the funding for the entire government. These omnibus bills in 1986 and 1987 also became magnets for unrelated and controversial pieces of legislation that could not pass on their own.

On the other hand, the 1974 reforms have helped Congress view the entire budget early in the process; now Congress can at least see the forest as well as the trees. The problem, as you will see, is not so much the procedure as disagreement over how scarce resources should be spent—or whether they should be spent at all.

More Reforms. By 1985 Congress was desperate. President Reagan refused to consider tax increases to pay for federal spending and continued to submit budgets that contained huge deficits. In response to growing frustration at its inability to reduce annual budget deficits substantially, Congress enacted the Balanced Budget and Emergency Deficit Control Act, better known as *Gramm-Rudman-Hollings* after its co-sponsors, Senators Phil Gramm (R) of Texas, Warren Rudman (R) of New Hampshire, and Ernest Hollings (D) of South Carolina.

This legislation, as it was amended in 1987, mandated maximum allowable deficit levels for each year

FIGURE 14.6

ANNUAL FEDERAL DEFICITS

Yearly deficits mushroomed during the Reagan administration (1981-1988), despite the president's oft-repeated commitment to a balanced budget. The size of the deficit has been reduced during the Clinton administration but remains large in historical terms. The budget is scheduled to be balanced in 2002.

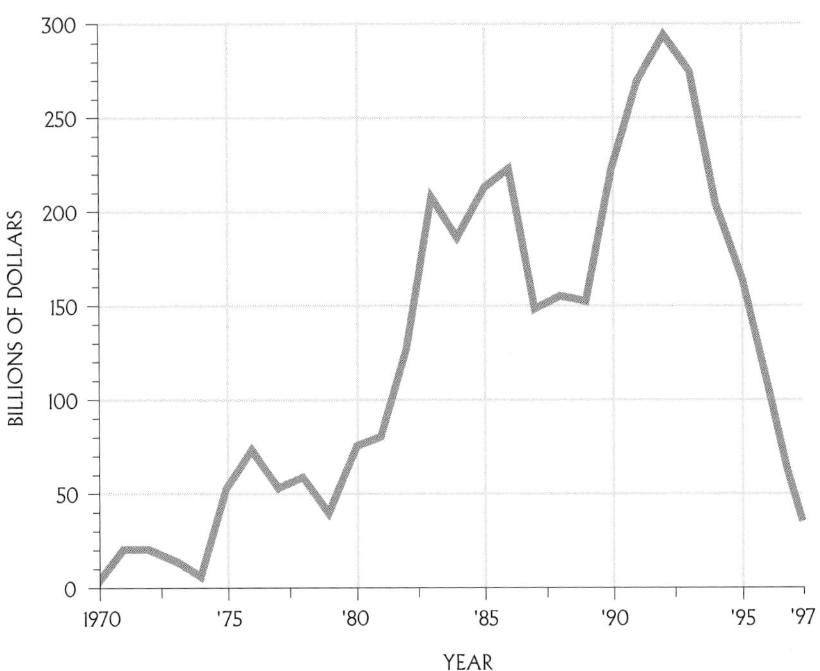

SOURCE: *Budget of the United States Government, Fiscal Year 1998: Historical Tables* (Washington, DC: U.S. Government Printing Office, 1997), Table 1.1.

until 1993, when the budget was supposed to be in balance. If Congress failed to meet the deficit goals, automatic across-the-board spending cuts, called *sequestrations*, were to be ordered by the president (a number of programs, including Social Security and interest on the national debt, were exempt from this process).

Gramm-Rudman-Hollings was clearly an indelicate, unthinking approach to budgeting; no one liked the arbitrary nature of the automatic budget cuts, half of which were to come from defense and half from domestic programs. Even Senator Rudman described it as "a bad idea whose time has come." In the absence of consensus on spending priorities, Congress believed it had no other way to force itself to reduce the deficit. Success was elusive, however, as you can see in Figure 14.6.

Near the end of 1990, Congress abandoned Gramm-Rudman-Hollings and approved a major change in budgeting policy. It decided to shift the focus on future savings from controlling the size of the deficit, which was the trigger for sequestration under Gramm-Rudman-Hollings, to controlling increases in spending. Thus, the sheer size of the deficit would not matter.

Discretionary spending was divided into three categories: domestic, defense, and international. Any new spending in any of these categories had to be offset by decreases elsewhere within the category. Violations of these strictures would lead to across-the-board sequestration within the affected category. Spending for entitlement programs such as Medicare was placed on a "pay-as-you-go" basis, requiring that any expansion be paid for by a corresponding entitlement cut or revenue increase. Similarly, any tax cut was to be paid for by a compensating tax increase or entitlement cut.

President Clinton presented his first budget to Congress in 1993. After the dust cleared following a highly partisan legislative battle, the president and Congress had made a significant decrease in the deficit. There was a single cap for all discretionary spending (rather than one for each of the three components), imposing a hard freeze on appropriations, yet there was little prospect of balancing the budget in the foreseeable future.

The results of the 1994 congressional elections once again altered the budgetary game. In 1995, the new Republican majorities in each house were determined to balance the budget within 7 years, arguing for substantial cuts in the rate of growth of popular entitlement programs such as Medicaid and the outright elimination of many other programs. Most Democrats strongly opposed these proposals. The president agreed with the goal of balancing the budget—but on his terms—and took his case to the voters in 1996. The outcome, as we have seen, was divided government.

In 1997, the president and Congress agreed to a budget that was to be in balance—by 2002. Each political party claimed victory, but the path to a balanced budget was eased by the booming economy, which produced more tax revenues than either side had anticipated. Whether the agreement will stick in the face of an economic downturn remains to be seen.

UNDERSTANDING BUDGETING

Citizens and politicians alike fret about whether government is too big. President Bush was elected by claiming that government has too many hands in Americans' pockets. He promised not to raise taxes to pay for more government spending. Of course, not everyone agrees that the national government is too large (even Bush had backtracked on his "no new taxes" pledge by 1990 and was defeated by the more activist Bill Clinton in 1992). There is agreement on the centrality of budgeting to modern government and politics, however. Exploring the themes of democracy and the scope of government will help you to understand the federal budgeting process.

DEMOCRACY AND BUDGETING

Almost all democracies have seen a substantial growth in government in the twentieth century. One explanation for this growth is that politicians spend money to "buy" votes. They do not buy votes in the sense that a corrupt political machine pays voters to vote for its candidates; rather, policymakers spend public money on things voters will like—and will remember on election day. As you saw in Chapter 12, members of Congress have incentives to make government grow; they use both constituency services and pork barrel policies to deliver benefits to the folks back home, and government grows as a result.

Economists Allen Meltzer and Scott Richard have argued that government grows in a democracy because of the equality of suffrage. They maintain that in the private sector people's incomes are unequal, whereas in the political arena power is much more equally distributed. Each voter has one vote. Parties must appeal to a majority of the voters. Hence, claim Meltzer and Richard, poorer voters will always use their votes to support public policies that redistribute benefits from the rich to the poor. Even if such voters cannot win in the marketplace, they can use the electoral process to their advantage. As Meltzer and Richard summarize, "Government continues to grow because there is a decisive difference between the political process and the market process. The market process produces a distribution of income that is less equal than the distribution of votes. Consequently, those with the lowest income use the political process to increase their income."[20] Many politicians willingly cooperate with the desire of the working-class voters to expand their benefits, because voters return the favor at election time. Not surprisingly, the most rapidly growing expenditures are items such as Social Security, Medicaid, Medicare, and social welfare programs, which benefit the poor more than the rich.

One often thinks that elites, particularly corporate elites, oppose big government. In recent years, however, Lockheed and Chrysler Corporation have appealed to the government for large bailouts when times got rough. Corporations support a big government that offers them contracts, subsidies, and other benefits. A $100 billion procurement budget at the Department of Defense benefits defense contractors, their workers, and their shareholders.

Low-income and wealthy voters alike have voted for parties and politicians who promised them benefits. When the air is foul, Americans expect government to help clean it up. When Americans get old, they expect a Social Security check. In a democracy, what people want affects what government does. Citizens are not helpless victims of big government and its big taxes; they are at least co-conspirators.

Government also grows by responding to groups and their demands. The parade of PACs is one example of groups asking government for assistance. From agricultural lobbies supporting loans, to zoologists pressing for aid from the National Science Foundation, groups seek to expand their favorite part of the budget. They are aided by committees and government agencies that work to fund projects favored by supportive groups (see the discussion on iron triangles in Chapter 15).

You have also seen, however, that some politicians compete for votes by promising *not* to spend money. After all, Ronald Reagan did not win election to the presidency twice by promising to raise taxes and provide more services, nor did the Republicans who took control of Congress in 1995. No country has a more

Public opinion is a key element in the budgeting process, affecting all players. Occasionally, the public has a direct role in budget making, as when the citizens of California voted on Proposition 13, a referendum proposing strict limits to local property taxes. Despite protests against the proposed legislation—many citizens argued that tax limits would restrict many government services—the proposition was passed.

open political system than the United States, but as the "America in Perspective" features in this chapter demonstrate, Americans have chosen to tax less and spend less on public services than almost all other democracies with developed economies. The size of government budgets varies widely among democratic nations. Thus, democracy may encourage government spending, but it does not compel it.

One of the most common criticisms of government is its failure to balance the budget. Public officials are often criticized for lacking the will to deal with the problem, yet it is not lack of resolve that prevents a solution to enormous budget deficits. Instead, it is a lack of consensus on policy. Americans want to spend but not pay taxes and, being a democracy, this is exactly what the government does. The inevitable result is red ink.

THE BUDGET AND THE SCOPE OF GOVERNMENT

One of this text's themes, the scope of government, has pervaded this chapter. The reason is obvious—in many ways, the budget *is* the scope of government. The bigger the budget, the bigger the government.

The budgetary process can also limit government. One could accurately characterize policymaking in the American government since 1980 as the "politics of scarcity"—scarcity of funds, that is. Thus, the budget can be a force for reining in the government as well as for expanding its role.[21] President Clinton came into office hoping to make new investments in education, worker training, and the country's physical infrastructure, such as roads and bridges. He soon found, however, that there was no money to fund new programs.

The president was reduced to speaking loudly and carrying a small budgetary stick in other policy areas as well. Because there was not enough money in the budget to pay for health care reform, he had to accept a reduced benefits package and advocate the politically difficult option of forcing employers to pay for their employees' health insurance. Welfare reform faced a similar obstacle. America's large budget deficit is as much a constraint on government as it is evidence of a burgeoning public sector.

SUMMARY

When the federal government's budget consumes one-fifth of America's gross domestic product, it demands close attention. The government's biggest revenue source remains the income tax, but the Social Security tax is becoming increasingly important. Lately, much of the government's budget has been financed through borrowing. Annual deficits exceeding $100 billion—and sometimes reaching nearly $300 billion—have boosted the federal debt to about $6 trillion by the end of the century.

In all Western democracies, government budgets have grown during the twentieth century. In the United States, government spending has also experienced significant change. Defense spending dominated the 1950s; social services spending has dominated the 1990s. President Reagan, for one, wanted to reverse this balance by increasing military expenditures and cutting domestic ones. Nonetheless, much of the American budget consists of "uncontrollable" expenditures that are extremely difficult to pare. Many of these expenditures are associated with Social Security payments and with grants-in-aid.

Budget making is complex, with many actors playing many roles. The president sets the budgetary agenda, whereas Congress and its committees approve the budget itself.

Some critics believe that democracy turns politics into a bidding war for votes, increasing the size of the budget in the process. In the United States, however, many candidates campaign on *not* spending money or increasing taxes. Although larger budgets mean larger government, the budget, at least in times of substantial deficits such as those the United States has experienced in the past decade, can also serve as a constraint on further government growth.

KEY TERMS

deficit
expenditures
revenues
income tax
Sixteenth Amendment
federal debt
balanced budget amendment
tax expenditures
Social Security Act
Medicare
incrementalism
continuing resolutions
uncontrollable expenditures
entitlements
budget
House Ways and Means Committee
Senate Finance Committee
Congressional Budget and Impoundment Control Act of 1974
Congressional Budget Office (CBO)
budget resolution
reconciliation
authorization bill
appropriations bill

FOR FURTHER READING

Bennett, Linda L. M., and Stephen Earl Bennett. *Living with Leviathan*. Lawrence, KS: University Press of Kansas, 1990. Examines Americans' coming to terms with big government and their expectations of government largesse.

Berry, William D., and David Lowery. *Understanding United States Government Growth*. New York: Praeger, 1987. An empirical analysis of the causes of the growth of government in the period since World War II.

King, Ronald F. *Money, Taxes, and Politics*. New Haven, CT: Yale University Press, 1993. Explains why democratically elected officials approve tax policies that make rich people richer.

Light, Paul. *Artful Work: The Politics of Social Security Reform*. New York: Random House, 1985. A case study of the perennial crisis of Social Security and what has been done about it.

Schick, Allen. *The Federal Budget*. Washington, DC: Brookings Institution, 1995. A useful "hands on" view of the federal budgeting.

Schuman, Howard E. *Politics and the Budget*, 3rd ed. Englewood Cliffs, NJ: Prentice-Hall, 1992. An excellent primer on the entire budgetary process.

Wildavsky, Aaron, and Naomi Caiden *The New Politics of the Budgetary Process*, 3rd ed. New York: Longman, 1997. The standard work on the budgetary process.

INTERNET RESOURCES

http://www.access.gpo.gov/su_docs/budget/index.html
The current and recent Economic Reports to the President and the budgets for the federal government.

NOTES

1. Quoted in Gerald Carson, *The Golden Egg: The Personal Income Tax, Where It Came From, How It Grew* (Boston: Houghton Mifflin, 1977), 12.
2. Statistics on the number of returns and audits come from the U.S. Department of Commerce, *Statistical Abstract of the United States, 1996* (Washington, DC: U.S. Government Printing Office, 1996), 342.
3. An exception is Robert Eisner, who argues that if the government counted its debt as families and business firms do—that is, by balancing assets against liabilities—the government would be in pretty good shape. See *How Real Is the Federal Deficit?* (New York: Free Press, 1986).
4. On the balanced budget amendment, see Aaron Wildavsky, *How to Limit Government Spending* (Berkeley, CA: University of California Press, 1980).
5. Carson, *The Golden Egg*, 181-182.
6. For some perspectives on the rise of government expenditures, see David Cameron, "The Expansion of the Public Economy: A Comparative Analysis," *American Political Science Review* 72 (December 1978): 1243-1261; and William D. Berry and David Lowery, *Understanding United States Government Growth* (New York: Praeger, 1987).
7. E. E. Schattschneider, *Two Hundred Million Americans in Search of a Government* (New York: Holt, Rinehart and Winston, 1969), 29-30.
8. Berry and Lowery, *Understanding United States Government Growth*.
9. Richard Halloran, "Cost Estimate of Stealth Bombers Increased 16% by the Air Force," *New York Times*, December 17, 1988, 10.

10. Paul Light, *Artful Work: The Politics of Social Security Reform* (New York: HarperCollins, 1992), 82.

11. Aaron Wildavsky and Naomi Caiden, *The New Politics of the Budgetary Process*, 3rd ed. (New York: Longman, 1997), 45.

12. John R. Gist, *Mandatory Expenditures and the Defense Sector* (Beverly Hills, CA: Russell Sage Foundation, 1974).

13. Paul R. Schulman, "Nonincremental Policymaking: Notes Toward an Alternative Paradigm," *American Political Science Review* 69 (December 1975): 1354-1370.

14. Wildavsky and Caiden, *The New Politics of the Budgetary Process*, 270-273.

15. *Ibid.*, 2.

16. A good description of budgetary strategies is in Wildavsky and Caiden, *The New Politics of the Budgetary Process*, chap. 3.

17. For a discussion of the ways in which bureaucracies manipulate benefits to gain advantage with members of Congress, see Douglas Arnold, *Congress and the Bureaucracy* (New Haven, CT: Yale University Press, 1979); and the articles in Barry S. Rundquist, ed., *Political Benefits* (Lexington, MA: D.C. Heath, 1980).

18. A good review of the formation of the executive budget is Howard E. Schuman, *Politics and the Budget*, 3rd ed. (Englewood Cliffs, NJ: Prentice-Hall, 1992), chap. 2.

19. An important work on congressional budget making is Wildavsky and Caiden, *The New Politics of the Budgetary Process*,

20. Allen Meltzer and Scott F. Richard, "Why the Government Grows (and Grows) in a Democracy," *The Public Interest* 52 (Summer 1978): 117.

21. See James D. Savage, *Balanced Budgets and American Politics* (Ithaca, NY: Cornell University Press, 1988) for a study of the influence the principle of budget balancing has had on politics and public policy from the earliest days of U.S. history.

15 The Federal Bureaucracy

Americans are taken hostage in the Middle East. The president orders the army to send its special Delta Force to rescue them. A new spy satellite is needed to monitor rapidly changing events in Eastern Europe. The president orders the National Aeronautics and Space Administration (NASA) to place such a satellite in orbit. Forest fires ravage Yellowstone National Park. The president orders the Forest Service to put them out. An epidemic breaks out among those exposed to certain chemicals used in the Vietnam War. The president orders the Department of Veterans Affairs to treat the victims in its hospitals.

To whom does the president turn when action is needed? The answer is simple: to bureaucrats. Soldiers, scientists, forest rangers, and physicians may have little in common except that they are all bureaucrats, working in government organizations and performing specialized tasks to implement public policy.

Bureaucrats do much more than simply follow orders. They possess crucial information and expertise that make them partners with the president and Congress in decision making about public policy. Who knows more than bureaucrats about Social Security recipients or the military capabilities of China? Moreover, because of their expertise, bureaucrats inevitably have discretion in carrying out policy decisions.

Bureaucratic power extends to every corner of American economic and social life, yet bureaucracies are scarcely hinted at in the Constitution. Each bureaucratic agency is created by Congress, which sets its budget and writes the policies it administers. Most agencies are responsible to the president, whose constitutional responsibility to "take care that the laws shall be faithfully executed" sheds only a dim light on the problems of managing so large a government. How to manage and control bureaucracies is a central problem of democratic government.

Reining in the power of bureaucracies is also a common theme in debates over the scope of government in America. Some political commentators see the bureaucracy as the prime example of a federal government growing out of control. They view the bureaucracy as acquisitive, constantly seeking to expand its size, budgets, and authority while being entwined in red tape and spewing forth senseless regulations. Others see the bureaucracy as laboring valiantly against great odds to fulfill the missions elected officials have assigned it. Where does the truth lie? The answer is less obvious than you may think. Clearly, bureaucracies require closer examination.

THE BUREAUCRATS

Bureaucrats are typically much less visible than the president or members of Congress. As a result, Americans usually know little about them. This section will examine some myths about bureaucrats and explain who they are and how they got their jobs.

SOME BUREAUCRATIC MYTHS AND REALITIES

Bureaucrat-baiting is a popular American pastime. George Wallace, former Alabama governor and frequent presidential hopeful, warmed up his crowds with a line about "pointy-headed Washington bureaucrats who can't even park their bicycles straight." Even successful presidential candidates climbed aboard the antibureaucracy bandwagon. Jimmy Carter complained about America's "complicated and confused and overlapping and wasteful" bureaucracies; Gerald Ford complained about the "dead weight" of bureaucracies; and Ronald Reagan insisted that bureaucrats "overregulated" the American economy, causing a decline in productivity.

Any object of such unpopularity will spawn plenty of myths. The following are some of the most prevalent myths about bureaucracy:

- *Americans dislike bureaucrats.* Despite the rhetoric about bureaucracies, Americans are generally satisfied with bureaucrats and the treatment they get from them. Americans may dislike bureaucracies, but they like individual bureaucrats. Surveys have found that two-thirds or more of those who have had encounters with a bureaucracy evaluate these encounters positively. In most instances, bureaucrats are described as helpful, efficient, fair, courteous, and working to serve their clients' interests.[1]
- *Bureaucracies are growing bigger each year.* This myth is half true and half false. The number of government employees has been expanding, but not the number of *federal* employees. Almost all the growth in the number of public employees has occurred in state and local governments. The 14 million state and local public employees far outnumber the fewer than 3 million civilian federal government employees (see Figure 15.1). As a percentage of America's total work force, *federal* government employment has been shrinking, not growing; it now accounts for about 3 percent of all civilian jobs. Of course, many state and local employees work on programs that are federally funded, and the federal government hires many private contractors to provide goods and services ranging from hot meals to weapons systems.

FIGURE 15.1 GROWTH IN GOVERNMENT EMPLOYEES

The number of government employees has grown rapidly since 1950. The real growth, however, has been in the state and local sector, with its millions of teachers, police officers, and other service deliverers. Many state and local employees and programs, though, are supported by federal grants-in-aid. (Note that the figures for federal employment do not include military personnel.)

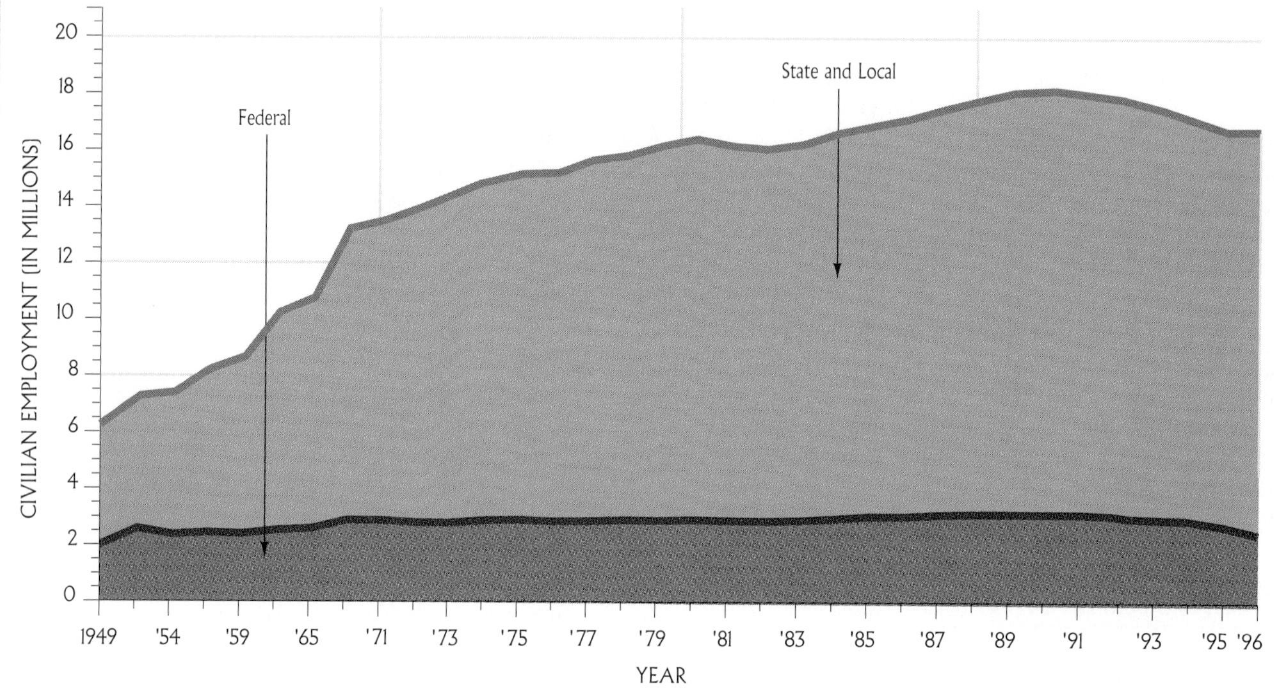

SOURCE: *Budget of the United States Government, Fiscal Year 1998: Historical Tables* (Washington, DC: U.S. Government Printing Office, 1997), Table 17-5.

- *Most federal bureaucrats work in Washington, DC.* Only about 7 percent of 3 million federal civilian employees work in Washington, DC. California leads the nation in federal employees, with 295,000. Texas has 176,000, New York 145,000. Nearly 100,000 federal employees work in foreign countries and American territories.[2] You can see where federal bureaucrats work by looking in your local phone book under "U.S. Government." You will probably find, among many others, listings for the local offices of the Postal Service, the Social Security Administration, the FBI, the Department of Agriculture's county agents, recruiters for the armed services, air traffic controllers, and, of course, the Internal Revenue Service.
- *Bureaucracies are ineffective, inefficient, and always mired in red tape.* No words describing bureaucratic behavior are better known than "red tape."[3] Bureaucracy, however, is simply a way of organizing people to perform work. General Motors, a college or university, the U.S. Army, the Department of Health and Human Services, and the Roman Catholic Church are all bureaucracies. Bureaucracies are a little like referees: When they work well, no one gives them much credit, but when they work poorly, everyone calls them unfair or incompetent or inefficient. Bureaucracies may be inefficient at times, but no one has found a substitute for them; and no one has yet demonstrated that government bureaucracies are more or less inefficient, ineffective, or mired in red tape than private bureaucracies.[4]

Anyone who looks with disdain on American bureaucracies should contemplate life without them.

Despite all the carping about bureaucracies, the vast majority of tasks carried out by governments at all levels are noncontroversial. Bureaucrats deliver mail, test milk, clean streets, issue Social Security and student loan checks, run national parks, and perform other routine governmental tasks in a perfectly acceptable manner. Most of the people who work for cities, states, and the national government are typical Americans, the sort who are likely to be your neighbors.

A plurality of all federal civilian employees work for just a few of the agencies (see Table 15.1). The Department of Defense employs about one-fourth of federal *civilian* workers in addition to the 1.5 million men and women in uniform. Altogether, the DOD (Washington's abbreviation for the Department of Defense) makes up more than half of the federal bureaucracy. Clearly, most federal bureaucrats serve in one way or another in the area of national defense.

The Postal Service accounts for an additional quarter of the federal civilian employees, and the various health professions constitute nearly 10 percent (one in three doctors, for example, works for the government). The Department of Veterans Affairs, clearly related to national defense, has more than 220,000 employees. All other functions of government are handled by the remaining 20 percent of federal employees.

WHO THEY ARE AND HOW THEY GOT THERE

Because there are nearly 3 million civilian bureaucrats (17 million if we include state and local public employees), it is hard to imagine a statistically typical bureaucrat. Bureaucrats are male and female, all races and religions, well paid and not so well paid. Like other institutions, the federal government has been

TABLE 15.1 FEDERAL CIVILIAN EMPLOYMENT

EXECUTIVE DEPARTMENTS	NUMBER OF EMPLOYEES[a]
Agriculture	101,700
Commerce	34,900
Defense (military functions)	760,000
Education	4,600
Energy	18,200
Health and Human Services	57,600
Housing and Urban Development	11,400
Interior	70,600
Justice	113,300
Labor	16,600
State	23,200
Transportation	64,000
Treasury	148,300
Veterans Affairs	215,500
LARGER INDEPENDENT AGENCIES	
Corps of Engineers	27,100
Environmental Protection Agency	17,500
General Services Administration	14,900
National Aeronautics and Space Administration	20,700
Social Security Administration	65,600
Tennessee Valley Authority	15,700
U.S. Information Agency	7,000
U.S. Postal Service	834,143

[a]Figures are for 1997.

SOURCE: *Budget of the United States Government, Fiscal Year 1998: Analytical Perspectives* (Washington, DC: U.S. Government Printing Office, 1997), Tables 10-1, 10-3.

under pressure to expand its hiring of women and minorities. Congress has ordered federal agencies to make special efforts to recruit and promote previously disadvantaged groups, but women and nonwhites still cluster at the lower ranks. As a whole, however, the permanent bureaucracy is more broadly representative of the American people than are legislators, judges, or presidential appointees in the executive branch[5] (see Figure 15.2).

The diversity of bureaucratic jobs mirrors the diversity of private-sector jobs, including occupations literally ranging from A to Z. Working for government are accountants, bakers, census analysts, defense procurement specialists, electricians, foreign service officers, guards in federal prisons, home economists, Indian Affairs agents, judges, kitchen workers, lawyers, missile technologists, narcotics agents, ophthalmologists, postal carriers, quarantine specialists, radiologists, stenographers, truck drivers, underwater demolition experts, virologists, wardens, X-ray technicians, youth counselors, and zoologists (see Table 15.2).

Civil Service: From Patronage to Protection. Until roughly 100 years ago, a person got a job with the government through the patronage system. **Patronage** is a hiring and promotion system based on knowing the right people. Working in a congressional campaign, making large donations, and having the right connections helped people secure jobs with the government. Nineteenth-century presidents staffed the government with their friends and allies. Scores of office seekers would swarm over the White House after Inauguration Day. It is said that during a bout with malaria, Lincoln told an aide to "send in the office seekers" because he finally had something to give them all.

It was a disappointed office seeker named Charles Guiteau who helped end this "spoils system" ("to the victor belong the spoils") of federal appointments in 1881. Frustrated because President James A. Garfield would not give him a job, Guiteau shot and killed Garfield. The so-called Prince of Patronage himself, Vice President Chester A. Arthur, then became president. Arthur, who had been collector of the customs for New York—a patronage-rich post—surprised his critics by encouraging passage of the **Pendleton Civil Service Act** (1883), which created the federal Civil Service. Today, most federal agencies are covered by some sort of civil service system.

All **civil service** systems are based on merit and the desire to create a nonpartisan government service. The **merit principle**—using entrance exams and promotion ratings to reward qualified individuals—is intended to produce an administration of people with talent and skill. Creating a nonpartisan civil service means insulating government workers from the risk of being fired when a new party comes to power. At the same time, the **Hatch Act**, originally passed in 1939 and amended most recently in 1993, prohibits civil service employees from actively participating in partisan politics while on duty. (While off duty they may engage in political activities, but they cannot run for partisan elective offices or solicit contributions from

FIGURE 15.2 CHARACTERISTICS OF FEDERAL CIVILIAN EMPLOYEES[a]

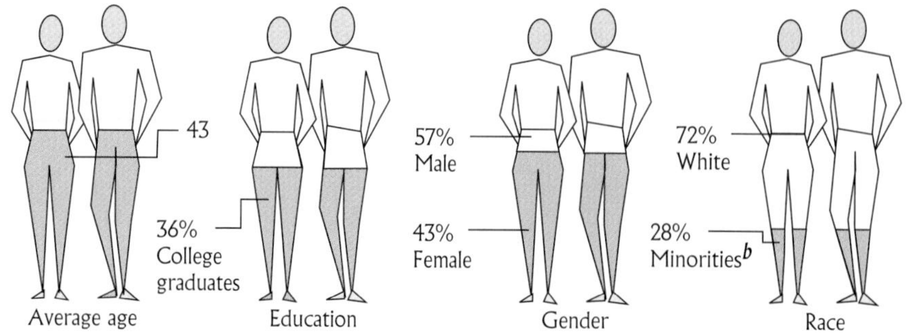

[a] Does not include postal workers.
[b] Includes African Americans, Orientals, Native Americans, and Hispanics.

Source: Office of Personnel Management, *Federal Civilian Workforce Statistics, Employment and Trends as of November 1992* (Washington, DC: U.S. Government Printing Office, 1993), 78.

TABLE 15.2 FULL-TIME CIVILIAN WHITE-COLLAR EMPLOYEES OF THE FEDERAL GOVERNMENT

SELECTED OCCUPATIONAL CATEGORIES	NUMBER OF EMPLOYEES
General administrative, clerical, and office services	437,158
Engineering and architecture	166,867
Medical, dental, and public health	154,491
Accounting and budget	147,999
Business and industry	103,401
Legal and kindred	79,834
Investigation	78,411
Biological sciences	66,188
Social science, psychology, and welfare	65,109
Personnel management and industrial relations	51,765
Supply	44,791
Physical sciences	43,578
Transportation	43,571
Education	34,244
Information and the arts	21,579
Equipment, facilities, and service	16,036
Quality assurance	15,618
Mathematics and statistics	15,206
Library and archives	9,794
Copyright, patent, and trademark	2,710
Veterinary medical science	2,540

SOURCE: U.S. Office of Personnel Management, *Occupations of Federal White-Collar and Blue-Collar Workers, Federal Civilian Workforce Statistics, as of September 1993* (Washington, DC: U.S. Government Printing Office, 1993), Table 2.

the public. Employees with sensitive positions, such as those in the national security area, may not engage in political activities even while off duty.)

The **Office of Personnel Management (OPM)** is in charge of hiring for most federal agencies. Its director is appointed by the president and confirmed by the Senate. The OPM has elaborate rules about hiring, promotion, working conditions, and firing. Usually, to get a civil service job, candidates must first take a test. If they pass, their names are sent to agencies when jobs requiring their particular skills open up. For each position that is open, the OPM will send three names to the agency. Except under unusual circumstances, the agency must hire one of these three individuals. (This process is called the "rule of three.") Each job is assigned a **GS (General Schedule) rating** ranging from GS 1 to GS 18. Salaries are keyed to rating and experience. At the very top of the civil service system are about 9000 members of the **Senior Executive Service,** the "cream of the crop" of the federal employees. These executives earn high salaries and may be moved from one agency to another as leadership needs change.

Once hired, and after a probationary period, civil servants are protected—overprotected, critics claim—by the civil service system. Ensuring a nonpartisan civil service requires that workers have protection from dismissals that are politically motivated. Protecting all workers against political firings may also protect a few from dismissal for good cause. Firing incompetents is hard work. Recently, the government managed to fire only 314 employees for poor performance and another 2700 for misconduct, about 0.001 percent of civilian federal workers. According to Civil Service regulations, the right of appeal must be exhausted before one's paycheck stops. Appeals can consume weeks, months, or even years. More than one agency has decided to tolerate incompetents, assigning them trivial or no duties, rather than invest its resources in the nearly hopeless task of discharging them. Firing incompetent female, minority, or older workers may be even more difficult than dislodging incompetent young or middle-aged white males. These groups not only have the usual Civil Service protections but also can resort to antidiscrimination statutes to appeal their dismissals.

The Other Route to Federal Jobs: Recruiting from the Plum Book. As an incoming administration celebrates its victory and prepares to take control of the government, Congress publishes the *plum book,* which lists top federal jobs (that is, "plums") available for direct presidential appointment, often with Senate confirmation. Hugh Heclo has estimated that there are about 300 of these top policymaking posts (mostly cabinet secretaries, undersecretaries, assistant secretaries, and bureau chiefs) and a few thousand lesser positions.[6]

All incoming presidents launch a nationwide talent search for qualified personnel. Presidents seek individuals who combine executive talent, political skills, and sympathy for policy positions similar to those of the administration. Often, the president tries to include men and women, whites and nonwhites, people from different regions, and party members who represent different interests (although few recent presidents have appointed as high a percentage of middle-aged white males as did Ronald Reagan). Some positions, especially ambassadorships, go to large campaign contributors. A few of these appointees will be civil servants, temporarily elevated to a "political" status; most, though, will be political appointees, "in-and-outers" who stay for a while and then leave.[7]

Once in office, these administrative policymakers constitute what Heclo has called a "government of strangers." Their most important trait is their transience. The average assistant secretary or undersecretary lasts about 22 months.[8] Few top officials stay long enough to know their own subordinates well, much less people in other agencies. Administrative routines, budget cycles, and legal complexities are often new to them. To these new political executives, the possibilities of power may seem endless. Nevertheless, although plum book appointees may have the outward signs of power, many of them find it challenging to exercise real control over much of what their subordinates do and have difficulty leaving their mark on policy. They soon learn that they are dependent on senior civil servants, who know more, have been there longer, and will outlast them.

WHAT THEY DO: SOME THEORIES OF BUREAUCRACY

Bureaucracies govern modern states, but governmental bureaucracies are not the only type of bureaucracy. Perhaps the oldest is the hierarchical governance of the Roman Catholic Church. Bureaucracies also run American armies, corporations, schools, and almost every other social, political, and economic institution. The following sections explain three prominent theories of bureaucracy.

The Weberian Model. Most people have confronted a bureaucracy only to be told, "Perhaps Mrs. Smith could help you; your problem is really under her jurisdiction," or "You'll have to talk to the supervisor, because I am only enforcing our rules."

The classic conception of bureaucracy was advanced by the German sociologist Max Weber, who stressed that the bureaucracy was a "rational" way for a modern society to conduct its business.[9] According to Weber, a **bureaucracy** depends on certain elements:

It has a *hierarchical authority structure,* in which power flows from the top down and responsibility from the bottom up; it uses *task specialization,* so that experts instead of amateurs perform technical jobs; and it develops extensive *rules,* which may seem nit-picking at times, but which allow similar cases to be handled similarly instead of capriciously. Bureaucracies operate on the *merit principle,* in which entrance and promotion are awarded on the basis of demonstrated abilities rather than on "who you know." Bureaucracies behave with *impersonality* so that all of their clients are treated impartially. Weber's classic prototype of the bureaucratic organization depicts the bureaucracy as a well-organized machine with plenty of working, but hierarchical, parts.

The Acquisitive, Monopolistic Bureaucracy. When agency heads sit before congressional committees to discuss their budgetary needs, they rarely (unless under overwhelming pressure from the White House) testify that the agency needs a *lower* budget.

The neat, Weberian model is only one way of thinking about bureaucracies. Other, more contemporary writers have seen bureaucracies as essentially "acquisitive," busily maximizing their budgets and expanding their powers.[10] Conservative economist William Niskanen, once a member of President Reagan's Council of Economic Advisors, believes that bureaucracies are like private corporations in seeking goals,[11] except that private corporations seek to maximize their *profits* whereas governmental bureaucracies seek to maximize their *budgets.* Bureaucratic administrators are committed to the "products" they "sell"—national security, schooling, public health, higher education, police protection—and their piece of the government's total budget pie is a good measure of how highly their product is valued. Moreover, all administrators take more professional pride in running a large, well-staffed agency than a puny one. For these reasons, insists Niskanen, bureaucracies are themselves largely responsible for the growth of modern governments.[12] Bureaucracies may even couple with Congress in an unholy alliance to expand big government (see the discussion of Fiorina's theory in Chapter 12 and "The People Speak: Bureaucracy and Governmental Waste").

Not only can bureaucracies be acquisitive; they also can be monopolistic. In the private sector, a monopoly, being the sole supplier of some key good, is free from competition. It can afford to exact high prices and behave inefficiently. Public bureaucracies are typically monopolies, too. As a general rule, there is no alternative to the local fire department or water supply system; certainly, there is no alternative to the national defense system. Only well-to-do people really have an

The People Speak

Bureaucracy and Governmental Waste

Do You Think People in the Government Waste a Lot of the Money We Pay in Taxes, Waste Some of It, or Don't Waste Very Much of It?

	1964	1968	1972	1984	1988	1992	1996
A lot	47%	59%	66%	65%	64%	68%	60%
Some	44%	34%	30%	29%	34%	30%	38%
Not very much	6%	4%	2%	4%	3%	2%	2%

SOURCE: The question as worded is taken directly from National Election Studies.

alternative to the local school system, the Social Security system, or government-run Medicare for the elderly. Some of Americans' complaints about bureaucracies are really complaints about bureaucratic monopoly. No matter how the bureaucracies behave, they will not lose their clients; there is no competitive pressure to force them to improve service or provide services more efficiently.[13]

Many conservative—and even liberal—critics of bureaucracy have favored *privatizing* some bureaucratic services to cut back on their monolithic and monopolistic power.[14] Local garbage collection or fire protection, for example, could be (and sometimes is) contracted out to private companies. Governments might thus accept the best service at the lowest price.[15]

Garbage Cans and Bureaucracies. One Washington official, lobbying for some policy changes in the nation's capital, told John Kingdon,

> I can trace the path of ideas. But my personal theory is that people plant seeds every day. There are a lot of ideas around . . . . The real question is, which of these ideas will catch hold? When you plant a seed, you need rain, soil, and luck.[16]

Both the Weberian model and the model of the acquisitive, monopolistic bureaucracy make bureaucracies sound calculating and purposive. Another view of bureaucracy, though, makes them sound ambling and groping, affected by chance. Cohen, March, and Olsen suggest that the typical organization is a "loose collection of ideas, rather than a coherent structure."[17] As likely as not, they say, organizations operate by trial and error. Far from being tightly controlled, they are typically loosely run. For most organizations, technological certainty is low. It is rarely clear that one policy will work and another fail. Lots of ideas may be floating around any organization. Faced with a particular problem, members of the organization may pull one of these ideas from the "garbage can" of ideas and latch onto it. Organizations are not necessarily trying to find solutions to problems; *just as often, solutions are in search of problems.* The police department gets a new computer and then discovers how many tasks it has that need computerizing. Kingdon's careful study of governmental agenda building found much to recommend the "garbage can" model of policymaking.[18]

Each of these perspectives offers a different view of the American bureaucracy. None of them is completely right. Consider each of them as you examine the organization and functions of bureaucracies in modern America.

HOW BUREAUCRACIES ARE ORGANIZED

A complete organizational chart of the American federal government would be big enough to occupy a large wall. You could pore over this chart, trace the lines of responsibility and authority, and see how government is organized—at least on paper. A very simplified organizational chart of the executive branch appears in Figure 15.3. A much easier way to look at how the federal executive branch is organized is to group agencies into four basic types: cabinet departments, regulatory agencies, government corporations, and independent executive agencies.

THE CABINET DEPARTMENTS

Each of the cabinet departments is headed by a secretary (except the Department of Justice, which is headed by the attorney general) chosen by the president and approved by the Senate. Reporting to the secretary are undersecretaries, deputy undersecretaries, and assistant secretaries. Each department manages specific policy areas (see the list in Table 13.5, page 329), and each has its own budget and its own staff.

Each department has a unique mission and is organized somewhat differently. The Department of the Interior, a well-established and traditional department, is portrayed in Figure 15.4 (see page 388). The real work of a department is done in the bureaus, which divide the work into more specialized areas (a bureau is sometimes called a *service, office, administration,* or other name).

Until the 1970s, the largest cabinet department was the Department of Defense. From then until 1995, the Department of Health and Human Services (HHS) was the largest federal department in dollars spent (although the Department of Defense still had more employees). The Social Security Administration became an independent agency in 1995, spending one-third of the federal budget on the massive programs of Social Security and Medicare.

Sometimes status as a cabinet department can be controversial. For several years, Republicans have been trying to disband the Departments of Education, Energy, and Commerce.

THE REGULATORY AGENCIES

Each **independent regulatory agency** has responsibility for some sector of the economy, making and enforcing rules designed to protect the public interest. The independent regulatory agencies also judge disputes over these rules. Their powers are so far-reaching that they are sometimes called "the fourth branch of government."[19] They are also sometimes called the alphabet soup of American government, because most such agencies are known in Washington by their initials. Here are some of these independent regulatory agencies:

- *FRB (the Federal Reserve Board),* charged with governing banks and, even more important, regulating the supply of money and thus interest rates
- *NLRB (the National Labor Relations Board),* created to regulate labor-management relations
- *FCC (the Federal Communications Commission),* charged with licensing radio and TV stations and regulating their programming in the public interest, as well as with regulating interstate long-distance telephone rates, cable television, and the Internet
- *FTC (the Federal Trade Commission),* intended to regulate business practices and control monopolistic behavior, and now involved in policing the accuracy of advertising
- *SEC (the Securities and Exchange Commission),* created to police the stock market

Each of these independent regulatory agencies is governed by a small commission, usually with five to ten members appointed by the president and confirmed by the Senate for fixed terms. Unlike cabinet officers and members of the president's staff, regulatory commission members cannot be fired by the pres-

FIGURE 15.3

ORGANIZATION OF THE EXECUTIVE BRANCH

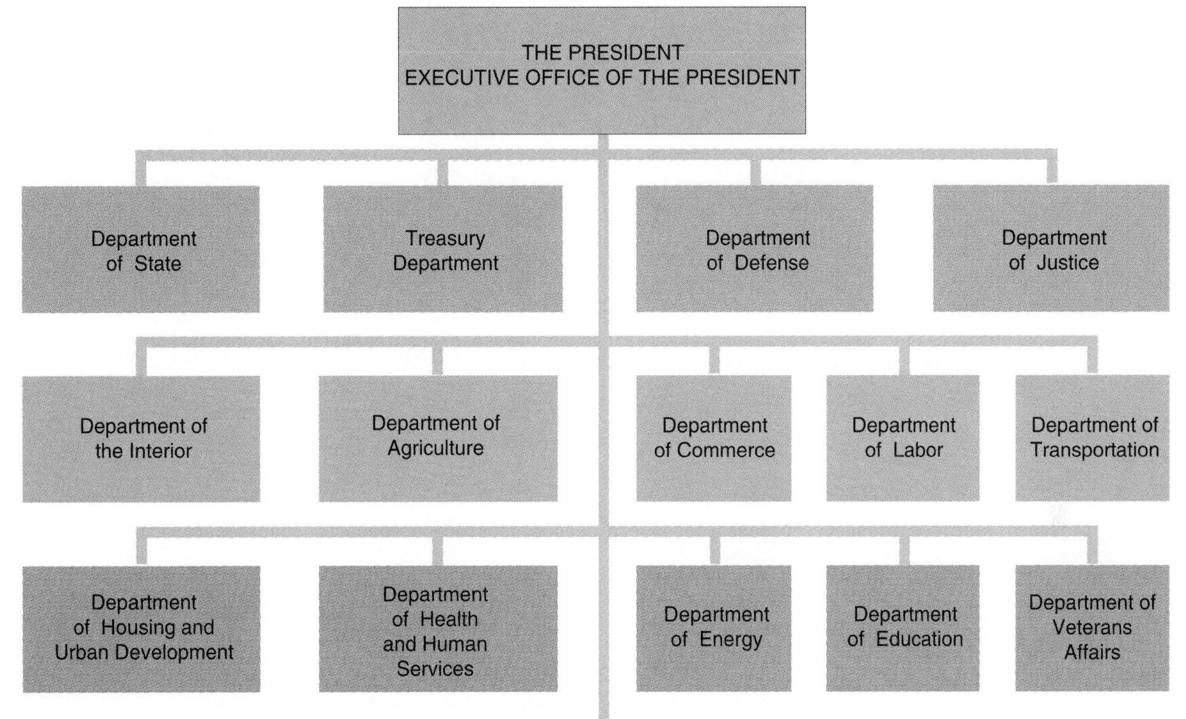

INDEPENDENT ESTABLISHMENTS AND GOVERNMENT CORPORATIONS

African Development Foundation
Central Intelligence Agency
Commodity Futures Trading Commission
Consumer Product Safety Commission
Corporation for National and Community Service
Defense Nuclear Facilities Safety Board
Environmental Protection Agency
Equal Employment Opportunity Commission
Export-Import Bank of the U.S.
Farm Credit Administration
Federal Communications Commission
Federal Deposit Insurance Corporation
Federal Election Commission
Federal Emergency Management Agency
Federal Housing Finance Board
Federal Labor Relations Authority
Federal Maritime Commission
Federal Mediation and Conciliation Service
Federal Mine Safety and Health Review Commission
Federal Reserve System
Federal Retirement Thrift Investment Board
Federal Trade Commission
General Services Administration
Inter-American Foundation
Interstate Commerce Commission
Merit Systems Protection Board
National Aeronautics and Space Administration
National Archives and Records Administration
National Capital Planning Commission
National Credit Union Administration
National Foundation on the Arts and Humanities
National Labor Relations Board
National Mediation Board
National Railroad Passenger Corporation (Amtrak)
National Science Foundation
National Transportation Safety Board
Nuclear Regulatory Commission
Occupational Safety and Health Review Commission
Office of Government Ethics
Office of Personnel Management
Office of Special Counsel
Panama Canal Commission
Peace Corps
Pension Benefit Guaranty Corporation
Postal Rate Commission
Railroad Retirement Board
Resolution Trust Corporation
Securities and Exchange Commission
Selective Service System
Small Business Administration
Social Security Administration
Tennessee Valley Authority
Trade and Development Agency
U.S. Arms Control and Disarmament Agency
U.S. Commission on Civil Rights
U.S. information Agency
U.S. International Development Cooperation Agency
U.S. International Trade Commission
U.S. Postal Service

SOURCE: Office of the Federal Register, *United States Government Manual 1997-98* (Washington, DC: U.S. Government Printing Office, 1997), 22.

FIGURE 15.4 ORGANIZATION OF THE DEPARTMENT OF THE INTERIOR

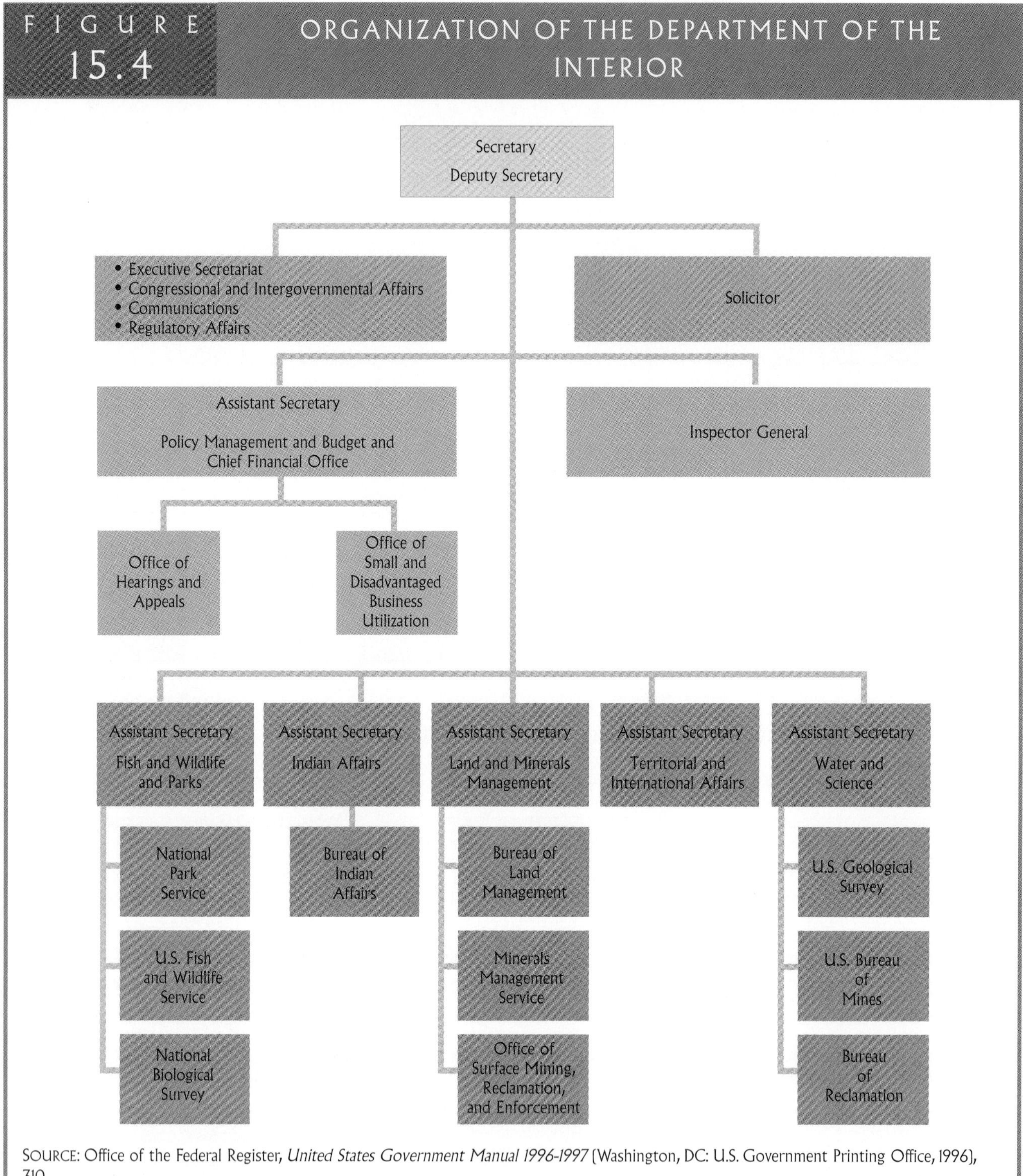

SOURCE: Office of the Federal Register, *United States Government Manual 1996-1997* (Washington, DC: U.S. Government Printing Office, 1996), 310.

ident. The Supreme Court made this ruling after President Franklin Roosevelt fired a man named Humphrey from the Federal Trade Commission. Humphrey died shortly afterward, but his angry executors sued for back pay, and the Court held that presidents could not fire members of regulatory agencies without just cause (*Humphrey's Executor v. United States,* 1935).

Interest groups consider the rule making by independent regulatory agencies (and, of course, their membership) very important. The FCC can deny a multimillion-dollar TV station a license renewal—a power that certainly sparks the interest of the National Association of Broadcasters. The FTC regulates business practices—a power that prompts both business and consumers to pay careful attention to its activities and membership.

Interest groups are so concerned with these regulatory bodies that some critics point to the "capture" of the regulators by the regulatees.[20] It is common for members of commissions to be drawn from the ranks of the regulated. Sometimes, too, members of commissions or staffs of these agencies move on to jobs in the very industries they were regulating. Some lawyers among them use contacts and information gleaned at the agency when they represent clients before their former employers at the agency. A later section of this chapter will discuss the bureaucracy's relationship with interest groups.

THE GOVERNMENT CORPORATIONS

The federal government also has a handful of **government corporations.** These are not exactly like private corporations in which you can buy stock and collect dividends, but they *are* like private corporations—and different from other parts of the government—in two ways. First, they provide a service that *could be* handled by the private sector. Second, they typically charge for their services, though often at cheaper rates than the consumer would pay a private-sector producer.

The granddaddy of the government corporations is the Tennessee Valley Authority (TVA), which, at least until recently, provided inexpensive electricity to millions of Americans in Tennessee, Kentucky, Alabama, and neighboring states. Through Comsat—a modern-day government corporation that sells timesharing on NASA satellites—you can rent time on a space satellite for radio communications. Even the Post Office, one of the original cabinet departments (first headed by Benjamin Franklin), has become a government corporation: the U.S. Postal Service.

Occasionally the government has taken over a "sick industry" and turned it into a government corporation. Amtrak, the railroad passenger service, is one example. Congress grumbles about Amtrak's multibillion-dollar subsidy (although some critics point out that billions of dollars in federal highway funds also constitute something of a subsidy for the auto industry), but members of Congress have only reluctantly agreed to let Amtrak shed its most unprofitable runs.

The Environmental Protection Agency is the federal government's largest independent regulatory agency, overseeing the administration of all environmental legislation. Here, EPA workers clean up hazardous waste.

In an effort to make the agency financially independent as well as more responsive to consumers, Congress, in 1970, transformed the Post Office Department into the U.S. Postal Service, the government's largest corporation. The agency has improved its fiscal performance (partly as a result of increased postal rates), although it is now subject to direct competition from private businesses that offer parcel and overnight mail services.

THE INDEPENDENT EXECUTIVE AGENCIES

The **independent executive agencies** are essentially all the rest of the government—not cabinet departments, not regulatory commissions, and not government corporations. Their administrators are typically appointed by the president and serve at his will. To name and describe these scores of bureaus would be tedious, but they are listed in the current issue of the *United States Government Manual.* The following are a few of the biggest independent executive agencies (in size of budget):

- *General Services Administration (GSA),* the government's landlord, which handles buildings, supplies, and purchasing
- *National Science Foundation (NSF),* which supports scientific research
- *National Aeronautics and Space Administration (NASA),* the agency that takes Americans to the moon and points beyond

BUREAUCRACIES AS IMPLEMENTORS

In modern government, bureaucracies are essentially *implementors* of policy. They take congressional, presidential, and sometimes even judicial pronouncements and develop procedures and rules for implementing policy goals. They also manage the routines of government, from delivering mail to collecting taxes to training troops. The following sections will focus more closely on this crucial function of governing.

WHAT IMPLEMENTATION MEANS

Public policies are rarely self-executing. One of the few policies that administers itself is the president's decision to "recognize" a foreign government. It is entirely the chief executive's prerogative to do so, and once it is done, diplomatic relations with the country are thereby established.

Most policies, however, are not self-executing. Congress typically announces the goals of a policy in broad terms, sets up an administrative apparatus, and leaves the bureaucracy the task of working out the details of the program; in other words, the bureaucracy is left to implement the program. **Policy implementation** is the stage of policymaking between the establishment of a policy (such as the passage of a legislative act, the issuing of an executive order, the handing down of a judicial decision, or the promulgation of a regulatory rule) and the consequences of the policy for the people whom it affects.[21] To paraphrase loosely a famous line about war from German General Karl von Clausewitz: "Implementation is the continuation of policymaking by other means."[22] At a minimum, implementation includes three elements:

1. Creation of a new agency or assignment of a new responsibility to an old agency
2. Translation of policy goals into operational rules; development of guidelines for the program or policy
3. Coordination of resources and personnel to achieve the intended goals[23]

WHY THE BEST-LAID PLANS SOMETIMES FLUNK THE IMPLEMENTATION TEST

There is a famous line from the Scottish poet Robert Burns: "The best laid schemes o'mice and men/Gang aft a-gley [often go awry]." So, too, with the best intended public policies. Policies that people expect to work often fail. Martha Derthick told the sad tale of a "new towns" program in which the government was to sell surplus property to groups that were helping to expand urban housing. In fact, little property was sold and few houses were built.[24] High expectations followed by dashed hopes is the all-too-common fate of well-intended public policies.

Program Design. Implementation can break down for several reasons. One is faulty program design. "It is impossible," said Eugene Bardach, "to implement well a policy or program that is defective in its basic theoretical conception." Consider, he suggested, the following hypothetical example:

> If Congress were to establish an agency charged with squaring the circle with compass and straight edge—a task mathematicians have long ago shown is impossible—we could envision an agency coming into being, hiring a vast number of consultants, commissioning studies, reporting that progress was being made, while at the same time urging in their appropriations request for the coming year that the Congress augment the agency's budget.[25]

And the circle would remain round.[26]

Lack of Clarity. Congress is fond of stating a broad policy goal in legislation and then leaving implementation up to the bureaucracies. Members of Congress can thus escape messy details, and place blame for the implementation decisions elsewhere.

One such policy was the controversial Title IX of the Education Amendments of 1972,[27] which said: "No person in the United States shall, on the basis of sex, be excluded from participation in, be denied the benefits of, or be subjected to discrimination under any education program or activity receiving federal financial assistance." Because almost every college and university receives some federal financial assistance, almost all were thereby forbidden to discriminate on the basis of gender. Interest groups supporting women's athletics convinced Congress to include a provision about college athletics as well. So Section 844 reads,

> The Secretary of [HEW then, today of Education] shall prepare and publish . . . proposed regulations implementing the provisions of Title IX . . . relating to prohibition of sex discrimination in Federally assisted education programs *which shall include with respect to intercollegiate athletic activities reasonable provisions considering the nature of the particular sports* [italics added].

Just what does this section mean? Supporters of women's athletics thought it meant that discrimination against women's sports was also prohibited. Some, with good reason, looked forward to seeing women's sports on an equal footing with men's. One member of the House-Senate Conference Committee proposed language specifically exempting "revenue-producing athletics" (meaning men's football and basketball) from the prohibition. The committee rejected this suggestion, but to colleges and universities with big-time athletic programs, and to some alumni, the vague Section 844 called for equality in golf and swimming, not men's football and basketball programs, which could continue to have the lion's share of athletic budgets.

Joseph Califano, President Carter's secretary of HEW, was the man in the middle on this tricky problem. His staff developed a "policy interpretation" of the legislation, which he announced in December 1978. HEW's interpretation of the 100 or so words of Section 844 of Title IX numbered 30 pages. The interpretation recognized that football was "unique" among college sports. If football was unique, then the interpretation implied (but did not directly say) that male-dominated football programs could continue to outspend women's athletic programs.

Supporters of equal budgets for male and female athletics were outraged. Charlotte West of the Association for Intercollegiate Athletics for Women called HEW's interpretation "a multitude of imprecise and confusing explanations, exceptions, and caveats." Even the football-oriented National Collegiate Athletic Association was wary of the interpretation. One of its lawyers allowed, "They are trying to be fair. The question is how successful they are." A 100-word section in a congressional statute, which prompted a 30-page interpretation by the bureaucracy, in turn prompted scores of court suits. The courts have had to rule on such matters as whether Title IX requires that exactly equivalent dollar amounts be spent on women's and men's athletics. Litigation continues to this day.

Bureaucracies are often asked to implement unclear laws. When Congress decided to prohibit sexual discrimination in college athletics, for example, it left to bureaucrats the task of creating guidelines that would end discrimination while addressing the diverse needs of different sports. It took years—and several lawsuits—to establish the law's meaning.

The complex case of implementing Title IX for intercollegiate athletics contains an important lesson: Policy problems that Congress cannot resolve are not likely to be resolved easily by bureaucracies.

Bureaucrats receive not only unclear orders but also contradictory ones. James Q. Wilson points out that the Immigration and Naturalization Service is supposed to keep out illegal immigrants but let in necessary agricultural workers; to screen carefully foreigners seeking to enter the country but facilitate the entry of foreign tourists; and to find and expel illegal aliens but not break up families, impose hardships, violate civil rights, or deprive employers of low-paid workers. "No organization can accomplish all of these goals well, especially when advocates of each have the power to mount newspaper and congressional investigations of the agency's 'failures.'"[28]

Lack of Resources. As noted earlier, bureaucracies are often perceived as bloated. The important issue, however, is not the size of the bureaucracy in the abstract but whether it is the appropriate size to do the job it has been assigned to do. Often, as big as a bureaucracy may seem in the aggregate, it frequently lacks the staff—along with the necessary training, funding, supplies, and equipment—to carry out the tasks it has been assigned. Recently, for example, the news has been filled with complaints such as the following:

- A shortage of staff causes delays in testing new drugs to combat AIDS.
- Because of lack of funding, the popular Head Start program serves fewer than half the children who are theoretically eligible to participate.
- The Immigration and Naturalization Service lacks the resources even to identify, much less deport, more than 10 percent of the 200,000 convicted criminal aliens in the United States. It also lacks the personnel to open letters containing checks for application fees.
- The Department of Education's lack of sufficient auditors prevented it from detecting fraud in the federal government's student aid programs.
- In their inspections of facilities handling and storing hazardous wastes, inadequately trained inspectors for the Environmental Protection Agency were found to be overlooking more than half of the serious violations.
- Some observers fear that the lack of financing to maintain the national parks will lead to permanent deterioration of such treasured American vacation spots as Yosemite and Yellowstone.
- The Federal Aviation Agency lacks the proper personnel and equipment to direct the nation's air traffic safely.
- Drug runners had more and faster ships and planes for smuggling drugs into the country than government agents who were trying to catch them.
- The Internal Revenue Service lacks the appropriate computer systems to integrate the dozens of data bases that contain the information necessary to collect the $1.4 trillion in taxes that finance the federal government.

Agencies may also lack the *authority* necessary to meet their responsibilities. For example, many observers believe that the Federal Drug Administration (FDA) lacks adequate powers to protect the public from dangerous drugs such as the sleeping pill Halcion and the sedative Versed. The FDA does no testing of its own and must rely entirely on the test results submitted by manufacturers. Yet it lacks the subpoena power to obtain documents from drug companies when its suspicions are aroused regarding the withholding of data about adverse drug reactions or fraudulent representation of test results. It often lacks access to potentially damaging company documents that have been involved in private product-liability cases.

Administrative Routine. For most bureaucrats, administration is a routine matter most of the time. They follow **standard operating procedures,** better known as SOPs, to help them make numerous everyday decisions. Such rules save time. If a Social Security caseworker had to invent a new rule for every potential client and have it cleared at higher levels, few clients would be served. Thus, detailed manuals are written to cover as many particular situations as officials can anticipate. The regulations elaborating the Internal Revenue Code compose the bible of an IRS agent; similarly, a customs agent has binders filled with rules and regulations about what can and what cannot be brought into the United States free of duty.

SOPs also bring uniformity to complex organizations. Justice is better served when rules are applied uniformly, as in the implementation of welfare policies that distribute benefits to the needy or in the levying of fines for underpayment of taxes. Uniformity also makes personnel interchangeable. Soldiers, for example, can be transferred to any spot in the world and still find out how to do their job by referring to the appropriate manual.

Routines, then, are essential to bureaucracy. Yet they sometimes become frustrating to citizens, who term them "red tape" when they do not seem appropriate to a situation. SOPs then become obstacles to action. Presidents have had many plans thwarted by SOPs. In an October 1983 terrorist attack on their barracks outside Beirut, Lebanon, 241 Marines were killed while they slept. A presidential commission appointed to examine the causes of the tragedy concluded that, among other factors contributing to the disaster, the Marines in the peacekeeping force were "not trained, organized, staffed or supported to deal effectively with the terrorist threat."[29] In other words, they had not altered their SOPs regarding security, which is basic to any military unit, to meet the unique challenges of a terrorist attack.

Problems with SOPs are nothing new. They certainly frustrated Franklin D. Roosevelt:

> The Treasury is so . . . ingrained in its practices that I find it impossible to get the action and results I want . . . . But the Treasury is not to be compared with the State Department. You should go through the experience of trying to get any changes in the thinking, policy, and action of the career diplomats . . . . But both put together are nothing as compared to the Na-a-vy . . . . To change anything in the Na-a-a-vy is like punching a feather bed. You punch it with your right and you punch it with your left until you are finally exhausted, and then you find the damn bed just as it was before you started punching.[30]

Administrators' Dispositions. Paradoxically, bureaucrats operate not only within the confines of routines, but often with considerable discretion to behave independently. **Administrative discretion** is the authority of administrative actors to select among various responses to a given problem.[31] Discretion is greatest when rules do not fit a particular case, and this is often the case—even in agencies with elaborate rules and regulations.

Although the income tax code is massive and detailed, the IRS wields vast discretion because of the complexity of the U.S. economy and the multitude of tax situations it produces. The IRS agent must be "armed against the machinations, not of the average citizen, but of the cleverest adversary the best law schools can produce."[32] Here are a few examples:

- Congress and the IRS code say that medical expenses above a certain percentage of income are deductible, but how about the expenses of a vasectomy? (The IRS said yes.)
- A girl who had been ordered to take strenuous exercise under the supervision of a doctor was enrolled by her father in $8,436 worth of ballet lessons. Was it deductible? (The IRS said no.)
- Congress and the IRS code say that business expenses are deductible, but can an airline flight attendant deduct the cost of uniforms? (The IRS said yes.)
- Are taxi expenses incurred in visiting your stockbroker a deductible expense? (The IRS said yes.)

Some administrators exercise more discretion than others. Michael Lipsky coined the phrase **street-level bureaucrats** to refer to those bureaucrats who are in constant contact with the public (often a hostile one) and have considerable discretion; they include police officers, welfare workers, and lower-court judges.[33] No amount of rules, not even the thousands of pages of IRS rules, will eliminate the need for bureaucratic discretion on some policies.

Because bureaucrats will inevitably exercise discretion, it is important to understand how they use it. Ultimately, how they use discretion depends on their dispositions about the policies and rules they administer. Although bureaucrats may be indifferent to the implementation of many policies, other policies will conflict with their views or their personal or organizational interests. When people are asked to execute orders with which they do not agree, slippage is likely to occur between policy decisions and performance. A great deal of mischief may occur as well.

On one occasion, President Nixon ordered Secretary of Defense Melvin Laird to bomb a hideaway of the Palestine Liberation Organization, a move Laird opposed. According to the secretary, "We had bad weather for forty-eight hours. The Secretary of Defense can always find a reason not to do something."[34] Thus, the president's order was stalled for days and eventually rescinded.

Controlling the exercise of discretion is a difficult task. It is not easy to fire bureaucrats in the Civil Service, and removing appointed officials may be politically embarrassing to the president, especially if those officials have strong support in Congress and among

Bureaucrats typically apply thousands of pages of rules in the performance of routine tasks, but many of them—especially street-level bureaucrats—must exercise administrative discretion as well. This border patrol officer, for example, must decide whom he will search carefully and whom he will let pass with a quick check.

interest groups. In the private sector, leaders of organizations provide incentives such as pay raises to encourage employees to perform their tasks in a certain way. In the public sector, however, special bonuses are rare, and pay raises tend to be small and across-the-board. Moreover, there is not necessarily room at the top for qualified bureaucrats. Unlike a typical private business, a government agency cannot expand just because it is performing a service effectively and efficiently.

In the absence of positive and negative incentives, the government relies heavily on rules to limit the discretion of implementors. As Vice President Al Gore put it in a report issued by the National Performance Review,

> Because we don't want politicians' families, friends, and supporters placed in "no-show" jobs, we have more than 100,000 pages of personnel rules and regulations defining in exquisite detail how to hire, promote, or fire federal employees. Because we don't want employees or private companies profiteering from federal contracts, we create procurement processes that require endless signatures and long months to buy almost anything. Because we don't want agencies using tax dollars for any unapproved purpose, we dictate precisely how much they can spend on everything from telephones to travel.[35]

Often these rules end up creating new obstacles to effective and efficient governing, however. As U.S. forces were streaming toward the Persian Gulf in the fall of 1990 to liberate Kuwait from Iraq, the air force placed an emergency order for 6000 Motorola commercial radio receivers. But Motorola refused to do business with the air force because of a government requirement that the company set up separate accounting and cost-control systems to fill the order. The only way the U.S. Air Force could acquire the much-needed receivers was for Japan to buy them and donate them to the United States!

Fragmentation. Sometimes responsibility for a policy is dispersed among several units within the bureaucracy. The federal government has more than 150 training and employment programs spread across 14 departments, agencies, and commissions. In the field of welfare, more than 100 federal human services programs are administered by ten different departments and agencies. The Department of Health and Human Services has responsibility for basic welfare grants to families; the Department of Housing and Urban Development provides housing assistance; the Department of Agriculture runs the Food Stamp program; and the Department of Labor administers training programs and provides assistance in obtaining employment.

This diffusion of responsibility makes the coordination of policies both time-consuming and difficult. For years, efforts to control the flow of illicit drugs into the country have been hindered by lack of cooperation among the Drug Enforcement Administration in the Department of Justice, the Customs Service in the Treasury Department, the State Department, and other relevant agencies.

Sometimes those who are supposed to comply with a law receive contradictory signals from different agencies. The regulation of hazardous wastes, such as the radioactive waste produced by the nuclear power industry, is one of the major concerns of the Environmental Protection Agency and a matter of paramount importance to the public. The Department of Energy, however, has routinely paid all the fines its contractors have received for violating laws designed to protect the environment, and it has even paid the legal fees the contractors incurred while defending themselves against the fines. The Energy Department has also given generous bonuses to its contractors even while they were being fined by the EPA. Such contradictory policies obviously undermine efforts to limit pollution of the environment.

If fragmentation is a problem, why not reorganize the government? The answer lies in hyperpluralism and the decentralization of power. Congressional committees recognize that they would lose jurisdiction over agencies if these agencies were merged with others. Interest groups (such as the nuclear power industry) do not want to give up the close relationships they have developed with "their" agencies. Agencies themselves do not want to be submerged within a broader bureaucratic unit. All these forces fight reorganization, and they usually win.[36] President Clinton's proposal to merge the Drug Enforcement Agency and the Customs Service met with immediate opposition from the agencies and their congressional allies. Pursuing the merger became too costly for the president, who had to focus on higher-priority issues. He faced the same problem and came to the same decision with a proposal to merge the Export-Import Bank of the United States, which provides low-cost financing for American exporters; the Overseas Private Investment Corporation, which provides political-risk insurance to companies trading or investing overseas; and the Trade and Development Agency, which develops feasibility studies of overseas markets for exports and investment in emerging markets.

A CASE STUDY: THE VOTING RIGHTS ACT OF 1965

Policy implementation does not always work. Even when a policy is controversial, however, implementation can be effective if goals are clear and there are adequate means to achieve them.

In 1965, Congress, responding to generations of discrimination against prospective African-American voters in the South, passed the Voting Rights Act. The act singled out six states in the Deep South in which the number of registered African-American voters was minuscule. Congress ordered the Justice Department to send federal registrars to each county in those states to register qualified voters. Congress outlawed literacy tests and other tests previously used to discriminate against African-American registrants. The government promised stiff penalties for those who interfered with the work of federal registrars.

Congress charged the attorney general with implementing the Voting Rights Act. He acted quickly and dispatched hundreds of registrars—some protected by U.S. marshals—to Southern counties. Within seven and a half months after passage of the Act, more than 300,000 new African-American voters were on the rolls. The proportion of the Southern African-American population registered to vote increased from 43 percent in 1964 to 66 percent in 1970, partly (though not entirely) because of the Voting Rights Act.[37]

The Voting Rights Act of 1965 was successfully implemented because its goal was clear: to register African Americans to vote in Southern counties where their voting rights had been denied for years. This federal registrar, like hundreds of others working for the Department of Justice, helped bring the vote to some 300,000 African Americans in less than a year.

The Voting Rights Act was a successful case of implementation by any standard, but not because it was popular with everyone. Southern representatives and senators were outraged by it, and a filibuster delayed its passage in the Senate. It was successful because its goal was clear (to register large numbers of African-American voters); its implementation was straightforward (sending out people to register them); and the authority of the implementors was clear (they had the support of the attorney general and even U.S. marshals) and concentrated in the Justice Department, which was disposed to implementing the law vigorously.

BUREAUCRACIES AS REGULATORS

Government **regulation** is the use of governmental authority to control or change some practice in the private sector. All sorts of activities are subject to government regulation. Regulations by government pervade Americans' everyday lives and the lives of businesses, universities, hospitals, and other institutions. Federal regulations now fill more than 200 volumes. Regulation is the most controversial role of the bureaucracies, yet Congress gives them broad mandates to regulate activities as diverse as interest rates, the location of nuclear power plants, and food additives.

REGULATION IN THE ECONOMY AND IN EVERYDAY LIFE

The notion that the American economy is largely a "free enterprise" system, unfettered by government intervention, is about as up-to-date as a shiny new Model T Ford. You can begin to understand the sweeping scope of governmental regulation by examining how the automobile industry is regulated.

- Buying stock and selling stock in an automobile corporation are regulated by the Securities and Exchange Commission.
- Relations between the workers and managers of the company come under the scrutiny of the National Labor Relations Board.
- Affirmative action in hiring workers is mandated and administered by the Department of Labor and the Equal Employment Opportunity Commission, because automakers are major government contractors.
- Pollution-control, energy-saving, and safety devices are required by the Environmental

Protection Agency, the National Highway Traffic Safety Administration, and the Department of Transportation.
- Unfair advertising and deceptive consumer practices in marketing cars come under the watchful eye of the Federal Trade Commission.

A Full Day of Regulation. Everyday life itself is the subject of bureaucratic regulation. Almost all bureaucratic agencies—not merely the ones called independent regulatory agencies—are in the regulatory business. Consider a typical factory worker (we'll name him John Smith) working in the city of Chicago and living with his wife Joan Smith and their three young children in suburban Mount Prospect, Illinois. Both at work and at home, federal regulations affect John's life. He is awakened at 5:30 A.M. by his clock radio, set to a country music station licensed to operate by the Federal Communications Commission. For breakfast he has cereal, which has passed inspection by the Food and Drug Administration, as has the lunch Joan packs for him. The processed meat in his sandwich is packed under the supervision of the Food Safety and Quality Service of the U.S. Department of Agriculture.

John takes the train to work, buying a quick cup of coffee before the journey. The caffeine in his coffee, the FDA has warned, has caused birth defects in laboratory animals, and there is discussion in Washington about regulating it. Paying his fare (regulated by the state government), he hops aboard and shortly arrives at work, a small firm that makes refrigeration equipment for the food industry.

At home, Joan Smith is preparing breakfast for the children. The price of the milk she serves is affected by the dairy price supports regulated by the Agricultural Stabilization and Conservation Service. As the children play, she takes note of the toys they use, wanting to avoid any that could be dangerous. A Washington agency, the Consumer Product Safety Commission, also takes note of children's toys, regulating their manufacture and sale. The lawn mower, the appliances, the microwave oven, and numerous other items around the Smith house are also regulated by the Consumer Product Safety Commission.

Setting out for the grocery store and the bank, Joan encounters even more government regulations. The car has seat belts mandated by the National Highway Traffic Safety Administration, and its gas mileage is certified by the Department of Transportation. It happens that the car's pollution-control devices are now in need of service, because they do not meet the requirements of the Environmental Protection Agency. The bank at which Joan deposits money and writes a check is among the most heavily regulated institutions she encounters in her daily life. Her passbook savings rate is regulated by the Depository Institutions Deregulation Committee, and her account is insured by the Federal Deposit Insurance Commission.

Meanwhile, John Smith is at work assembling food-processing machinery. He and his fellow workers are members of the International Association of Machinists. Their negotiations with the firm are held under rules laid down by the National Labor Relations Board. Not long ago, the firm was visited by inspectors from the Occupational Safety and Health Administration, a federal agency charged with ensuring worker safety. OSHA inspectors noted several violations and forwarded a letter recommending safety changes to the head of the firm. Arriving home, John has a beer before dinner. It was made in a brewery carefully supervised by the Bureau of Alcohol, Tobacco, and Firearms, and when it was sold, federal and state taxes were collected.

After dinner (almost all the food served has been transported by the regulated trucking industry), the children are sent to bed. An hour or so of television, broadcast on regulated airwaves, is followed by bedtime for the Smiths. A switch will turn off the electric lights, whose rates are regulated by the Illinois Commerce Commission and the Federal Regulatory Commission.[38]

REGULATION: HOW IT GREW, HOW IT WORKS

From the beginnings of the American republic until 1887, the federal government made almost no regulatory policies; the little regulation produced was handled by state and local authorities. Even the minimal

Most government regulation is clearly in the public interest. For example, the U.S. Department of Agriculture is charged with regulating the quality of meat products, a task it was given after novelist Upton Sinclair exposed the meat-packaging industry's unsanitary conditions at the turn of the century.

regulatory powers of state and local governments were much disputed. In 1877, the Supreme Court upheld the right of government to regulate the business operations of a firm. The case, *Munn v. Illinois,* involved the right of the state of Illinois to regulate the charges and services of a Chicago warehouse. During this time, farmers were seething about alleged overcharging by railroads, grain elevator companies, and other business firms. In 1887—a decade after *Munn*—Congress created the first regulatory agency, the Interstate Commerce Commission (ICC), and charged it with regulating the railroads, their prices, and their services to farmers; the ICC thus set the precedent for regulatory policymaking.

As regulators, bureaucratic agencies typically operate with a large grant of power from Congress, which may detail goals to be achieved but permits the agencies to sketch out the regulatory means. In 1935, for example, Congress created the National Labor Relations Board to control "unfair labor practices," but the NLRB had to play a major role in defining "fair" and "unfair." Most agencies charged with regulation must first develop a set of rules, often called *guidelines.* The appropriate agency may specify how much food coloring it will permit in a hot dog, how many contaminants it will allow an industry to dump into a stream, how much radiation from a nuclear reactor is too much, and so forth. Guidelines are developed in consultation with, and sometimes with the agreement of, the people or industries being regulated.

Opponents of government regulation contend that the rapid increase in the number and scope of environmental regulations during the past two decades has stifled economic growth. Others argue that such regulations are essential to protect the nation's air, land, and water—and the people who use them.

Next, the agency must apply and enforce its rules and guidelines, either in court or through its own administrative procedures. Sometimes it waits for complaints to come to it, as the Equal Employment Opportunity Commission does; sometimes it sends inspectors into the field, as the Occupational Safety and Health Administration does; and sometimes it requires application for a permit or license to demonstrate performance consistent with congressional goals and agency rules, as the Federal Communications Commission does. Often government agencies take violators to court, hoping to secure a judgment and fine against an offender. (See "You Are the Policymaker: How Should We Regulate?") Whatever strategy Congress permits a regulating agency to use, all regulation contains these elements: (1) *a grant of power and set of directions from Congress,* (2) *a set of rules and guidelines* by the regulatory agency itself, and (3) *some means of enforcing compliance* with congressional goals and agency regulations.

Government regulation of the American economy and society has, of course, grown in recent decades. The budgets of regulatory agencies, their level of employment, and the number of rules they issue are all increasing—and did so even during the Reagan administration. As we have seen, few niches in American society are *not* affected by regulation. Not surprisingly, this situation has led to charges that government is overdoing it.

TOWARD DEREGULATION

Deregulation is currently a fashionable term in Washington and elsewhere.[39] The idea behind deregulation is that the number and complexity of regulatory policies have made regulation too complex and burdensome. To critics, the problem with regulation is that it raises prices, distorts market forces, and—worst of all—does not work. Here are some of the accusations against the regulatory system:

- *It raises prices.* If the producer is faced with expensive regulations, the cost will inevitably be

HOW SHOULD WE REGULATE?

You Are the Policymaker

Almost every regulatory policy was created to achieve some desirable social goal. When more than 10,000 people are killed annually in industrial accidents, who would disagree with the goal of a safer workplace? Who would dissent from greater highway safety, when more than 50,000 die each year in automobile accidents? Who would disagree with policies to promote equality in hiring, when the history of opportunities for women and minorities is one of discrimination? Who would disagree with policies to reduce industrial pollution, when pollution threatens health and lives? However, there may be more than one way to achieve these—and many other—desirable social goals.

Charles L. Schultze, chair of President Carter's Council of Economic Advisors, is—like Murray L. Weidenbaum, who held the same position under President Reagan—a critic of the current state of federal regulation. Schultze reviewed the regulatory activities of the Environmental Protection Agency and the Occupational Safety and Health Administration. Neither agency's policies, he concluded, had worked very well. He described the existing system as **command-and-control policy:** The government tells business how to reach certain goals, checks that these commands are followed, and punishes offenders. Schultze prefers an **incentive system.** He argues that instead of telling construction businesses how their ladders must be constructed, measuring the ladders, and charging a small fine for violators, it would be more efficient and effective to levy a high tax on firms with excessive worker injuries. Instead of trying to develop standards for 62,000 pollution sources, as the EPA now does, it would be easier and more effective to levy a high tax on those who cause pollution. The government could even provide incentives in the form of rewards for such socially valuable behavior as developing technology to reduce pollution. Incentives, Schultze argues, use marketlike strategies to regulate industry. They are, he claims, more effective and efficient than command-and-control regulation.

Not everyone is as keen on the use of incentives as Schultze. Defenders of the command-and-control system of regulation compare the present system to preventive medicine; it is designed to minimize pollution or workplace accidents before they become too severe. Defenders of the system argue, too, that penalties for excessive pollution or excessive workplace accidents would be imposed only after substantial damage had been done. They also add that if taxes on pollution or unsafe work environments were merely externalized (that is, passed along to the consumer as higher prices), they would not be much of a deterrent. Moreover, it would take a large bureaucracy to monitor carefully the level of pollution discharged, and it would require a complex calculation to determine the level of tax necessary to encourage businesses not to pollute.

The issue of the manner of regulation is a complex one. What would *you* do?

SOURCES: Charles L. Schultze, *The Public Use of the Private Interest* (Washington, DC: Brookings Institution, 1977); and Steven Kelman, *What Price Incentives? Economists and the Environment* (Boston: Auburn House, 1981).

passed on to the consumer in the form of higher prices.

- *It hurts America's competitive position abroad.* Other nations may have fewer regulations on pollution, worker safety, and other business practices than the United States. Thus, American products may cost more in the international marketplace, undermining sales in other countries.
- *It does not always work well.* Tales of failed regulatory policies are numerous. Regulations may be difficult or cumbersome to enforce. Critics charge that regulations sometimes do not achieve the results that Congress intended and maintain that they simply create massive regulatory bureaucracies.

President Reagan's conservative political philosophy was opposed to much government regulation, but even before the Reagan administration, sentiment favoring deregulation was building in the Washington community. Even liberals sometimes joined the anti-regulation chorus; for example, Senator Edward

Kennedy of Massachusetts pushed for airline deregulation. Indeed, the airline industry pressed for deregulation, too, and in 1978 the Civil Aeronautics Board (CAB) began to deregulate airline prices and airline routes. In 1984, the CAB formally disbanded; it even brought in a military bugler to play taps at its last meeting.

Not everyone, however, believes that deregulation is in the nation's best interest.[40] For example, critics point to severe environmental damage resulting from lax enforcement of environmental protection standards during the Reagan administration. Similarly, many observers attribute at least a substantial portion of the blame for the enormously expensive bailout of the savings and loan industry to deregulation in the 1980s. Many people now argue for more regulation of savings and loans institutions.

In addition, many regulations have proved beneficial to Americans. As a result of government regulations, we breathe cleaner air,[41] we have lower levels of lead in our blood, miners are safer at work,[42] seacoasts have been preserved,[43] and children are more likely to survive infancy.[44]

UNDERSTANDING BUREAUCRACIES

You have looked at bureaucracies as implementors and regulators. In performing each of these functions, bureaucracies are making public policy, not just administering someone else's decisions. The fact that bureaucrats, who are not elected, compose most of the government raises fundamental issues about who controls governing and what the bureaucracy's role should be.

BUREAUCRACY AND DEMOCRACY

Bureaucracies constitute one of America's two unelected policymaking institutions (courts are the other). In democratic theory, popular control of government depends on elections, but we could not possibly elect the nearly 5 million federal civilian and military employees, or even the few thousand top men and women, though they spend more than $1.7 trillion of the American GDP. Furthermore, the fact that voters do not elect civil servants does not mean that bureaucracies cannot respond to and represent the public's interests. Figure 15.2 showed that bureaucrats are actually more representative of the public than presidents or members of Congress. Much depends on whether bureaucracies are effectively controlled by the policymakers that citizens do elect—the president and Congress.[45]

Presidents Try to Control the Bureaucracy. Chapter 13 looked at some of the frustrations presidents endure in trying to control the government they are elected to run. Presidents try hard—not always with success—to impose their policy preferences on agencies (see "America in Perspective: Influencing Independent Agencies"). The following are some of their methods of doing this:

- *Appoint the right people to head the agency.* Normally, presidents control the appointments of agency heads and subheads. Putting their people in charge is one good way for presidents to influence agency policy,[46] yet even this has its problems. President Reagan's efforts to whittle the powers of the Environmental Protection Agency led to his appointment of controversial Anne Gorsuch to head the agency. Gorsuch had previously supported policies contrary to the goals of the EPA. When Gorsuch attempted to implement her policies, legal squabbles with Congress and political controversy ensued, ultimately leading to her resignation. To patch up the damage Gorsuch had done to his reputation, Reagan named a moderate and seasoned administrator, William Ruckelshaus, to run the agency. Ironically, Ruckelshaus demanded, and got, more freedom from the White House than Gorsuch had sought.
- *Issue orders.* Presidents can issue **executive orders** to agencies. Sometimes presidential aides simply pass the word that "the President was wondering if . . . ." These messages usually suffice, although agency heads are reluctant to run afoul of Congress or the press on the basis of a broad presidential hint.
- *Tinker with an agency's budget.* The Office of Management and Budget is the president's own final authority on any agency's budget. The OMB's threats to cut here or add there will usually get an agency's attention. Each agency, however, has its constituents within and outside of Congress, and Congress, not the president, does the appropriating.
- *Reorganize an agency.* Although President Reagan promised, proposed, and pressured to abolish the Department of Energy and the Department of Education, he never succeeded—largely because each department was in the hands of an entrenched bureaucracy backed by elements in Congress and strong constituent groups.

INFLUENCING INDEPENDENT AGENCIES

America in Perspective

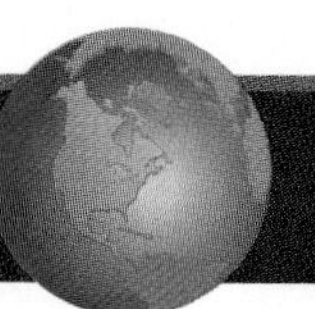

We often think of the president as head of the executive branch, but we also have learned that there are agencies, such as the Federal Reserve Board, that are very powerful and are generally free from the chief executive's direction. This often leaves presidents frustrated, as when they wish the Federal Reserve Board to lower interest rates to stimulate the economy. There are even more autonomous agencies in Latin America, however—agencies removed from the direct control of the president and the legislature.

Why would Latin American governments create agencies they cannot control? The primary reason is to protect a new agency providing a new service from changes in policy made by future decision makers. Those who create an agency fear that its policies will be undone by a new administration or legislature, so they make it autonomous.

These agencies often have their own sources of revenue and thus can increase their budgets without going through the public and controversial process of government budget debates. They are also freer from legislative oversight and formal presidential controls than are regular agencies, and conflict over their programs is less visible. Expenditures for autonomous agencies also allow the government to engage in creative financing, because when these agencies contract debt, it does not count against the central government's debt (which is substantial in Latin America).

Autonomy is decidedly a mixed blessing, however. Creative financing is not necessarily good for a nation, nor is the difficulty policymakers have in consolidating bureaucracies and increasing their efficiency. The lack of traditional means of influence also makes it difficult to alter the priorities of agencies, such as shifting the emphasis from building roads to building apartments.

SOURCES: Michelle M. Taylor, "When Are Juridicially Autonomous Agencies Responsive to Elected Officials? A Simulation Based on the Costa Rican Case," *Journal of Politics* 57 (November 1995): 1070-1092; and Gene E. Bigler and Enrique Viloria, "State Enterprises and the Decentralized Public Administration," in John D. Martz and David J. Myers, eds., *Venezuela, the Democratic Experience,* rev. ed. (New York: Praeger, 1986).

Reorganizing an agency is hard to do if it is a large and strong one, and reorganizing often is not worth the trouble if it is a small and weak one.

Congress Tries to Control the Bureaucracy. Congress exhibits a paradoxical relationship with the bureaucracies. On the one hand (as we have seen), members of Congress may find a big bureaucracy congenial.[47] Big government provides services to constituents. Moreover, when Congress lacks the answers to policy problems, it hopes the bureaucracies will find them. Unable itself, for example, to resolve the touchy issue of equality in intercollegiate athletics, Congress passed the ball to HEW. Unable to decide how to make workplaces safer, Congress produced OSHA. As you saw in Chapter 12, Congress is increasingly the problem-identifying branch of government, setting the bureaucratic agenda but letting the agencies decide how to implement the goals it sets.

On the other hand, Congress has found it hard to control the government it helped create. There are several measures Congress can take to oversee the bureaucracy:

- *Influence the appointment of agency heads.* Even when senatorial approval of a presidential appointment is not required, members of Congress are not shy in offering their ideas about who should and who should not be running the agencies. When congressional approval is required, members are doubly influential. Committee hearings on proposed appointments are almost guaranteed to produce lively debates if some members find the nominee's probable orientations unpalatable.
- *Tinker with an agency's budget.* With the congressional power of the purse comes a mighty weapon for controlling bureaucratic behavior. At the same time, Congress knows that agencies perform services that its constituents demand.

Too much budget cutting may make an agency more responsive, at the price of losing an interest group's support for a reelection campaign.
- *Hold hearings.* Committees and subcommittees can hold periodic hearings as part of their oversight job. Flagrant agency abuses of congressional intent can be paraded in front of the press, but responsibility for oversight typically goes to the very committee that created a program; the committee thus has some stake in showing the agency in a favorable light.
- *Rewrite the legislation or make it more detailed.* Every statute is filled with instructions to its administrators. To limit bureaucratic discretion and make its instructions clearer, Congress can write new or more detailed legislation. Still, even voluminous detail (as you saw in the case of the IRS) can never eliminate discretion.

Through these and other devices, Congress tries to keep bureaucracies under its control. Never entirely successful, Congress faces a constant battle to limit and channel the vast powers that it delegated to the bureaucracy in the first place.

Sometimes these efforts are detrimental to bureaucratic performance. The explosion of legislative subcommittees has greatly increased Congress's oversight activities. Numerous subcommittees may review the actions of a single agency. A half-dozen or more subcommittees may review the activities of the Department of Energy, the Department of Agriculture, or the Department of Commerce. Different committees may send different signals to the same agency. One may press for stricter enforcement, another for more exemptions. As the oversight process has become more vigorous, it has also become more fragmented, thus limiting the effectiveness of the bureaucracies.

Former FBI Director J. Edgar Hoover is an example of a powerful bureaucrat who worked outside the law. Hoover took over the new agency in 1924 and, after consolidating his power following World War II, began collecting information on presidents, members of Congress, and, later, liberal groups and civil rights leaders. Partly because they were afraid of what he might have in his files, elected officials were unwilling to control Hoover, who did not relinquish power until his death in 1972.

Iron Triangles and Issue Networks. There is one other crucial explanation for the difficulty presidents and Congress face in controlling bureaucracies: Agencies have strong ties to interest groups on the one hand and to congressional committees and subcommittees on the other. You learned in Chapter 11 that bureaucracies often enjoy cozy relationships with interest groups and with committees or subcommittees of Congress. When agencies, groups, and committees all depend on one another and are in close, frequent contact, they form what are sometimes called *iron triangles* or *subgovernments.* These triads have advantages on all sides (see Figure 15.5).

There are plenty of examples of subgovernments at work. A subcommittee on aging, senior citizens' interest groups, and the Social Security Administration are likely to agree on the need for more Social Security benefits. Richard Rettig has recounted how an alliance slowly jelled around the issue of fighting cancer. It rested on three pillars: cancer researchers, agencies within the National Institutes of Health, and members of congressional health subcommittees.[48]

When these iron triangles shape policies for senior citizens or cancer or tobacco or any other interest, each policy is made independently of the others, sometimes even in contradiction to other policies. Moreover, the iron triangles' decisions tend to bind larger institutions, such as Congress and the White House. Congress often defers to the decisions of committees and subcommittees, especially on less visible issues. The White House may be too busy wrestling with global concerns to fret over agricultural issues or cancer. Emboldened by this lack of involvement, subgovernments flourish and add a strong decentralizing and fragmenting element to the policymaking process.

Hugh Heclo points out that the system of subgovernments is now overlaid with an amorphous system of *issue networks.* There is more widespread participation in bureaucratic policymaking, and many of the participants have technical policy expertise and are drawn to issues because of intellectual or emotional commitments rather than material interests. Those

FIGURE 15.5 IRON TRIANGLES: ONE EXAMPLE

Iron triangles—composed of bureaucratic agencies, interest groups, and congressional committees or subcommittees—have dominated some areas of domestic policymaking by combining internal consensus with a virtual monopoly on information in their area. The tobacco triangle is one example; there are dozens more. Iron triangles are characterized by mutual dependency, in which each element provides key services, information, or policy for the others. The arrows indicate some of these mutually helpful relationships. In recent years, a number of well-established iron triangles, including the tobacco triangle, have been broken up.

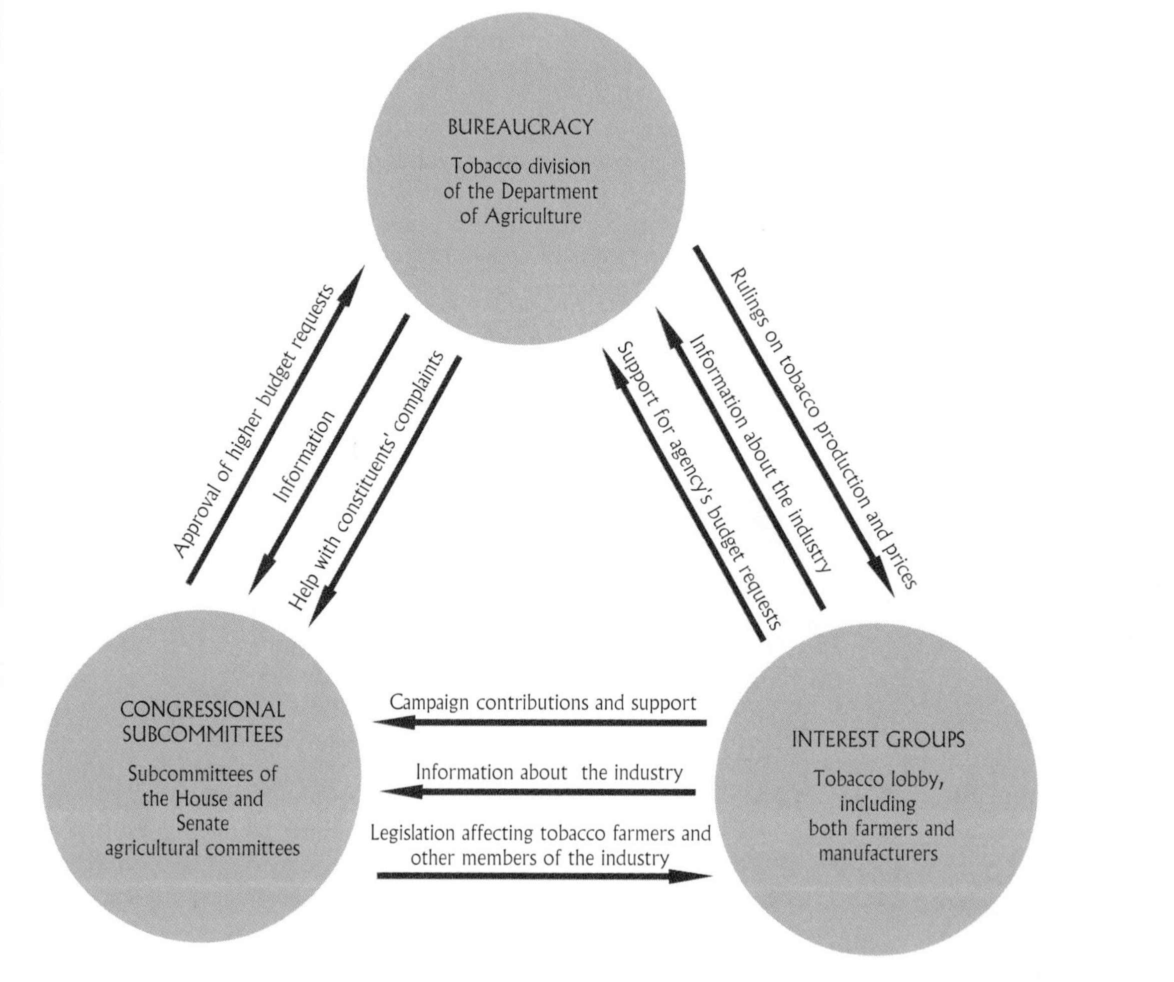

concerned with environmental protection, for example, have challenged formerly closed subgovernments on numerous fronts (see Chapter 19). This opening of the policymaking process complicates the calculations and decreases the predictability of those involved in the stable and relatively narrow relationships of subgovernments.[49]

Although subgovernments are often able to dominate policymaking for decades, they are not indestructible.[50] For example, the subgovernment pictured in Figure 15.5 long dominated smoking and tobacco policy, focusing on crop subsidies to tobacco farmers. But increasingly, these policies have come under fire from health authorities, who were not involved in tobacco policymaking in earlier years. Similarly, pesticide policy, once dominated by chemical companies and agricultural interests, is no longer considered separately from environmental and health concerns. An espe-

SINCE KENNEDY

The Death of an Iron Triangle

During the 1940s and 1950s, Americans were convinced that the technology that had ended World War II could also serve peaceful purposes. Nuclear scientists spoke enthusiastically about harnessing the atom to achieve all sorts of goals, eventually making electricity so inexpensive that it would be "too cheap to meter." Through the miracle of atoms, they explained, poverty and hunger could be eliminated and standards of living raised across the globe. In the heady atmosphere of the postwar years, optimism in progress through science was the rule, and the federal government encouraged the development of nuclear power through a powerful iron triangle.

A special congressional joint committee, the Joint Committee on Atomic Energy, was established and given complete control over questions of nuclear power in Congress. A new executive agency, the Atomic Energy Commission (AEC), was created, and together with the private companies that built the nuclear power plants and the electrical utilities that wanted to operate them, they formed a powerful subgovernment. America built more nuclear power plants than any other country in the world, and American technology was exported overseas to dozens of nations.

Nuclear power today—after the accidents at Three Mile Island and Chernobyl and the various cost overruns associated with the industry—bears almost no resemblance to that of the early 1960s when the iron triangle was at its peak. What happened? The experts lost control. When questions arose concerning the safety of the plants being built and when opponents were able to get local officials to question the policies publicly, the issue grew into a major political debate of the late-1960s, associated with the growth of environmentalism. Two of the most powerful legs of the iron triangle were destroyed. The Joint Committee on Atomic Energy was disbanded; a variety of congressional committees now claim some jurisdiction over nuclear power questions. Similarly, the AEC was replaced by two new agencies: the Nuclear Regulatory Commission and the Department of Energy.

The nuclear power industry has been devastated: No new nuclear power plants have been built in the United States since 1978, and almost all those under construction at that time have been abandoned at huge financial loss. Environmental interest groups have grown so much since the 1950s that issues once ignored no longer can be glossed over. In sum, the wave of environmental concern that developed in the late 1960s swept away one of the most powerful iron triangles in recent American history.

SOURCE: Frank R. Baumgartner and Bryan D. Jones, *Agendas and Instability in American Politics* (Chicago: University of Chicago Press, 1993).

cially vivid example of the death of an iron triangle is the case of nuclear power (see "Since Kennedy: The Death of an Iron Triangle").

BUREAUCRACY AND THE SCOPE OF GOVERNMENT

To many, the huge American bureaucracy is the prime example of a federal government's growing out of control. As this chapter discussed earlier, some observers view the bureaucracy as acquisitive, constantly seeking to expand its size, budgets, and authority. Much of the political rhetoric against big government also adopts this line of argument, along with complaints about red tape, senseless regulations, and the like. It is easy to take pot shots at a faceless bureaucracy that usually cannot respond.

One should keep in mind, however, that the federal bureaucracy has not grown over the past two generations, as Figure 15.1 illustrates. Indeed, if one considers the fact that the population of the country has grown significantly over this period, then the federal bureaucracy has actually *shrunk* in size relative to the population it serves.

Originally, the federal bureaucracy had the modest role of promoting the economy, defending the country, managing foreign affairs, providing justice, and delivering the mail. Its role gradually expanded to include providing services to farmers, businesses, and workers. The discussion of federalism in Chapter 3 showed that as the economy and the society of the United States changed, additional demands were made on government. Government—and the bureaucracy—are now expected to play an active role in dealing with social and economic problems. Thus, a good case can be made that the bureaucracy is actually too *small* for many of the tasks currently assigned to it, tasks ranging from the control of illicit drugs to protection of the environment.

In addition, it is important to remember that when the president and Congress have chosen to deregulate certain areas of the economy or cut taxes, the bureaucracy could not and did not prevent them from doing so. The question of what and how much the federal government should do—and thus how big the bureaucracy should be—is answered primarily at the polls and in Congress, the White House, and the courts—not by "faceless bureaucrats."

SUMMARY

Americans rarely congratulate someone for being a good bureaucrat. Unsung, taunted by cartoonists, and maligned by columnists, bureaucrats are the scapegoats of American politics. Americans may call presidents great and reelect members of Congress, but almost no one praises bureaucrats. Those who compose the bureaucracy, however, perform most of the vital services provided by the federal government.

Bureaucrats shape policy as administrators, as implementors, and as regulators. In this chapter you examined who bureaucrats are, how they got their positions, and what they do. Today, most bureaucrats working for the federal government get their jobs through the Civil Service system, although a few at the very top are appointed by the president.

In general, there are four types of bureaucracies: the cabinet departments, the regulatory agencies, the government corporations, and the independent executive agencies.

As policymakers, bureaucrats play three key roles. First, they are policy implementors, translating legislative policy goals into programs. Policy implementation does not always work well, and when it does not, bureaucrats usually take the blame, whether they deserve it or not. Second, bureaucrats administer public policy. Much of administration involves a prescribed routine, but nearly all bureaucrats still have some discretion. Third, bureaucrats are regulators. Congress increasingly delegates large amounts of power to bureaucratic agencies and expects them to develop rules and regulations. Scarcely a nook or cranny of American society or the American economy escapes the long reach of bureaucratic regulation.

Although bureaucrats are not elected, bureaucracies are not necessarily undemocratic. It is essential that bureaucracies be controlled by elected decision makers, but presidential or congressional control over bureaucracies is difficult. Bureaus have strong support from interest groups—a factor that contributes to pluralism because interest groups try to forge common links with bureaucracies and congressional committees. These subgovernments tend to decentralize policymaking, thereby contributing to hyperpluralism.

KEY TERMS

patronage
Pendleton Civil Service Act
civil service
merit principle
Hatch Act
Office of Personnel Management (OPM)
GS (General Schedule) rating
Senior Executive Service
bureaucracy
independent regulatory agency
government corporations
independent executive agencies
policy implementation
standard operating procedures
administrative discretion
street-level bureaucrats
regulation
command-and-control policy
incentive system
deregulation
executive orders

FOR FURTHER READING

Arnold, Peri E. *Making the Managerial Presidency.* Princeton, NJ: Princeton University Press, 1986. A careful examination of efforts to reorganize the federal bureaucracy.

Derthick, Martha, and Paul J. Quirk. *The Politics of Deregulation.* Washington, DC: Brookings Institution, 1985. Explains why advocates of deregulation prevailed over the special interests that benefited from regulation.

Edwards, George C., III. *Implementing Public Policy.* Washington, DC: Congressional Quarterly Press, 1980. A good review of the issues involved in implementation.

Goodsell, Charles T. *The Case for Bureaucracy,* 3rd ed. Chatham, NJ: Chatham House, 1993. A strong case on behalf of the effectiveness of bureaucracy.

Gormley, William T., Jr. *Taming the Bureaucracy.* Princeton, NJ: Princeton University Press, 1989. Examines remedies for controlling bureaucracies.

Heclo, Hugh M. *Government of Strangers: Executive Powers in Washington.* Washington, DC: Brookings Institution, 1977. A study of the top executives of the federal government, who constitute (says the author) a "government of strangers."

Kerwin, Cornelius M. *Rulemaking: How Government Agencies Write Law and Make Policy.* Washington, DC: Congressional Quarterly Press, 1994. Explains how agencies write regulations to implement laws.

Osborne, David, and Ted Gaebler. *Reinventing Government.* Reading, MA: Addison-Wesley, 1992. Simplistic but important view of making government more entrepreneurial and responsive to citizens.

Peterson, Paul, Barry G. Rabe, and Kenneth K. Wong. *When Federalism Works.* Washington, DC: Brookings Institution, 1986. Examines federal grant-in-aid programs and explains why they are implemented better in some areas than in others.

Pressman, Jeffrey, and Aaron Wildavsky. *Implementation,* 3rd ed. Berkeley, CA: University of California Press, 1984. The classic—and often witty—study of implementation.

Rourke, Francis E. *Bureaucratic Power in National Policymaking,* 4th ed. Boston: Little, Brown, 1986. Classic work on bureaucratic politics.

Savas, E. S. *Privatization: The Key to Better Government.* Chatham, NJ: Chatham House, 1987. A conservative economist's argument that many public services performed by bureaucracies would be better handled by the private sector.

Wilson, James Q. *Bureaucracy.* New York: Basic Books, 1989. Presents a "bottom up" approach to understanding how bureaucrats, managers, and executives decide what to do.

INTERNET RESOURCES

http://www.npr.gov/
National Performance Review.

http://www.access.gpo.gov/nara/nara001.html
U.S. *Government Manual* providing information on the organization of the U.S. government.

http://www.access.gpo.gov/nara/fedreg/fedreg.html
The *Federal Register*, providing information on U.S. laws and regulations.

http://www1.whitehouse.gov/WH/Cabinet/html/cabinet_links.html
Federal cabinet departments.

http://www1.whitehouse.gov/Independent_Agencies/html/independent_links.html
Federal independent agencies and commissions.

http://www.govexec.com/
Government Executive magazine.

NOTES

1. See Charles T. Goodsell, *The Case for Bureaucracy,* 3rd ed. (Chatham, NJ: Chatham House, 1993), chap. 2. See also Daniel Katz *et al., Bureaucratic Encounters* (Ann Arbor: Institute for Social Research, University of Michigan, 1975).
2. U.S. Department of Commerce, *Statistical Abstract of the United States, 1996* (Washington, DC: U.S. Government Printing Office, 1996), 346-347.
3. See Herbert Kaufman, *Red Tape* (Washington, DC: Brookings Institution, 1977).
4. See Goodsell, *The Case for Bureaucracy,* 61-69.
5. *Ibid.,* chap. 5.
6. Hugh M. Heclo, *A Government of Strangers: Executive Politics in Washington* (Washington, DC: Brookings Institution, 1977), 94.
7. On the transient nature of presidential appointees, see G. Calvin Mackenzie, ed., *The In-and-Outers* (Baltimore, MD: Johns Hopkins University Press, 1987).
8. *Ibid.,* 103.
9. H. H. Gerth and C. Wright Mills, *From Max Weber: Essays in Sociology* (New York: Oxford University Press, 1958), chap. 8.
10. See Anthony Downs, *Inside Bureaucracy* (Boston: Little, Brown, 1967).
11. William Niskanen, *Bureaucracy and Representative Government* (Chicago: Aldine-Atherton, 1971).
12. For critiques of the Niskanen perspective, see Gary J. Miller and Terry M. Moe, "Bureaucrats, Legislators, and the Size of Government," *American Political Science Review* 77 (June 1983): 297-322; William D. Berry and David Lowery, *Understanding United States Government Growth* (New York: Praeger, 1987); Patrick Dunleavy, *Democracy, Bureaucracy and Public Choice: Economic Explanations in Political Science* (Englewood Cliffs, NJ: Prentice-Hall, 1991); and Andre Blais and Stephane Dion, eds., *The Budget-Maximizing Bureaucrat: Appraisals and Evidence* (Pittsburgh: University of Pittsburgh Press, 1991).
13. See Vincent Ostrom, *The Intellectual Crisis in American Public Administration* (University, AL: University of Alabama Press, 1973).
14. See, for example, E. S. Savas, *Privatization: The Key to Better Government* (Chatham, NJ: Chatham House, 1987).
15. See Donald F. Kettl, *Sharing Power: Public Governance and Private Markets* (Washington, DC: Brookings Institution, 1993) on contracting with private firms to provide public services. Kettl, and others, fear that privatizing public services separates public officials from citizens and places discretionary authority in the operation of public programs in the hands of third-party, private implementors. Critics also are skeptical that there will be sufficient competition among contractors to furnish efficiently most of the services provided by the federal government.

16. John Kingdon, *Agendas, Alternatives, and Public Policies* (Boston: Little, Brown, 1984), 81.

17. Michael Cohen, James March, and Johan Olsen, "A Garbage Can Model of Organizational Choice," *Administrative Science Quarterly* 17 (March 1972): 1.

18. Kingdon, *Agendas, Alternatives, and Public Policies,* 88-94.

19. On the independent regulatory agencies, see the classic work by Marver Bernstein, *Regulating Business by Independent Commission* (Princeton, NJ: Princeton University Press, 1955). See also, on regulation, James Q. Wilson, ed., *The Politics of Regulation* (New York: Basic Books, 1980); and A. Lee Fritschler and Bernard H. Ross, *Business Regulation and Government Decision-Making* (Cambridge, MA: Winthrop, 1980).

20. Bernstein, *Regulating Business,* 90. For a partial test of the capture theory that finds the theory not altogether accurate, see John P. Plumlee and Kenneth J. Meier, "Capture and Rigidity in Regulatory Administration," in *The Policy Cycle,* ed. Judith May and Aaron Wildavsky (Beverly Hills, CA: Russell Sage Foundation, 1978). Another critique of the capture theory is Paul J. Quirk, *Industry Influence in Federal Regulatory Agencies* (Princeton, NJ: Princeton University Press, 1981).

21. George C. Edwards III, *Implementing Public Policy* (Washington, DC: Congressional Quarterly Press, 1980), 1.

22. Eugene Bardach, *The Implementation Game* (Cambridge, MA: The M.I.T. Press, 1977), 85; and Robert L. Lineberry, *American Public Policy: What Government Does and What Difference It Makes* (New York: Harper & Row, 1977), 71. Clausewitz called war "the continuation of politics by other means."

23. Lineberry, *American Public Policy,* 70-71.

24. Martha Derthick, *New Towns In-Town* (Washington, DC: The Urban Institute Press, 1972).

25. Bardach, *The Implementation Game,* 250-251.

26. A good discussion of how policymakers ignored the administrative capacity of one important agency when assigning it new responsibilities can be found in Martha Derthick, *Agency Under Stress* (Washington, DC: Brookings Institution, 1990).

27. The implementation of the athletics policy is well documented in two articles by Cheryl M. Fields in the *Chronicle of Higher Education,* December 11 and 18, 1978, on which this account relies.

28. James Q. Wilson, *Bureaucracy* (New York: Basic Books, 1989), 158.

29. *Report of the DOD Commission on Beirut International Airport Terrorist Act, October 23, 1983,* December 20, 1983, 133.

30. Quoted in M. S. Eccles, *Beckoning Frontiers* (New York: Knopf, 1951), 336.

31. On administrative discretion, see Gary S. Bryner, *Bureaucratic Discretion* (New York: Pergamon Press, 1987).

32. Gerald Carson, *The Golden Egg* (Boston: Houghton Mifflin, 1977), 10. The examples given in this paragraph are from Carson.

33. Michael Lipsky, *Street-Level Bureaucracy* (New York: Russell Sage Foundation, 1980).

34. Quoted in Seymour Hersh, *The Price of Power: Kissinger in the Nixon White House* (New York: Summit, 1983), 235-236.

35. Albert Gore, *From Red Tape to Results: Creating a Government That Works Better and Costs Less* (New York: Times Books, 1993), 11.

36. For a careful analysis of efforts to reorganize the federal bureaucracy, see Peri E. Arnold, *Making the Managerial Presidency* (Princeton, NJ: Princeton University Press, 1986).

37. On the implementation and impact of the Voting Rights Act, see Charles S. Bullock III and Harrell R. Rodgers, Jr., *Law and Social Change: Civil Rights Laws and Their Consequences* (New York: McGraw-Hill, 1972), chap. 2; Richard Scher and James Button, "Voting Rights Act: Implementation and Impact," in *Implementation of Civil Rights Policy,* ed. C. S. Bullock and C. M. Lamb (Monterey, CA: Brooks/Cole, 1984), chap. 2; and Abigail M. Thernstrom, *Whose Votes Count?* (Cambridge, MA: Harvard University Press, 1987).

38. Based on a more elaborate account by James Worsham, "A Typical Day Is Full of Rules," *Chicago Tribune,* July 12, 1981, 1ff, with updating by the authors.

39. See Martha Derthick and Paul J. Quirk, *The Politics of Deregulation* (Washington, DC: Brookings Institution, 1985).

40. See, for example, Susan J. Tolchin and Martin J. Tolchin, *Dismantling America: The Rush to Deregulate* (New York: Oxford University Press, 1983).

41. Evan J. Ringquist, "Does Regulation Matter? Evaluating the Effects of State Air Pollution Control Programs," *Journal of Politics* 55 (November 1993): 1022-1045.

42. Michael Lewis-Beck and John Alford, "Can Government Regulate Safety? The Coal Mine Example," *American Political Science Review* 74 (September 1980): 745-756.

43. Paul Sabatier and Dan Mazmanian, *Can Regulation Work? Implementation of the 1972 California Coastal Initiative* (New York: Plenum, 1983).

44. Gary Copeland and Kenneth J. Meier, "Gaining Ground: The Impact of Medicaid and WIC on Infant Mortality," *American Politics Quarterly* 15 (April 1987): 254-273.

45. See B. Dan Wood and Richard W. Waterman, *Bureaucratic Dynamics: The Role of Bureaucracy in a Democracy* (Boulder, CO: Westview, 1994).

46. A good work on this point is Richard P. Nathan, *The Administrative Presidency* (New York: Wiley, 1983).

47. Morris Fiorina, *Congress: Keystone of the Washington Establishment,* 2nd ed. (New Haven, CT: Yale University Press, 1989).

48. Richard A. Rettig, *Cancer Crusade* (Princeton, NJ: Princeton University Press, 1977).

49. Hugh M. Heclo, "Issue Networks and the Executive Establishment," in *The New American Political System,* ed. Anthony King (Washington, DC: American Enterprise Institute, 1978), 87-124. See also William P. Browne and Won K. Paik, "Beyond the Domain: Recasting Network Politics in the Postreform Congress," *American Journal of Political Science* 37 (November 1993): 1054-1078; and John P. Heinz, Edward O. Laumann, Robert L. Nelson, and Robert L. Salisbury, *The Hollow Core: Private Interests in National Policy Making* (Cambridge, MA: Harvard University Press), 1993.

50. Frank R. Baumgartner and Bryan D. Jones, *Agendas and Instability in American Politics* (Chicago: University of Chicago Press, 1993)

16 The Federal Courts

Let us say that you are involved in a lawsuit regarding the application of an affirmative action policy in your college or university. A trial is held in a federal district court. After the trial, a verdict is rendered and you lose. Not content to accept this decision, you appeal to the court of appeals. Once again, you lose. Now you have only two options left: to accept the decision or to appeal to the U.S. Supreme Court. You decide to appeal, and of the thousands of petitions for hearings presented to the Court each year, yours is one of a few dozen the Court selects.

On the day of the oral argument (there are no trials in the Supreme Court), you walk up the steep steps of the Supreme Court building, the impressive "Marble Palace" with the motto "Equal Justice under Law" engraved over its imposing columns. The Court's surroundings and procedures suggest the nineteenth century. The justices, clothed in black robes, take their seats at the bench in front of a red velvet curtain. Behind the bench there are still spittoons, one for each justice. (Today, the spittoons are used as wastebaskets.)

Your case, like most of the cases the Court selects for oral arguments, is scheduled for about an hour. Lawyers arguing before the Court often wear frock coats and striped trousers. They find a goose quill pen on their desk, bought by the Court from a Virginia supplier. (They may take it with them as a memento of their day in court.) As is the norm, each side is allotted 30 minutes to present its case. The justices may, and do, interrupt the lawyers with questions. When the time is up, a discreet red light goes on at your lawyer's lectern, and she immediately stops talking.

That is the end of the hearing, but not the end of the process. You have asked the Court to overrule a policy established by your state legislature. As the Court considers doing so, it recognizes that its decision will become precedent for all such policies across the nation. Months will go by, as the justices deliberate and negotiate an opinion, before the Court announces its decision. If you win, it will take many more months for your university, aided by lower courts, to interpret the decision and implement it.

The scope of the Supreme Court's power is great, extending even to overruling the decisions of elected officials. Despite the trappings of tradition and majesty, however, the Court does not reach its decisions in a political vacuum. Instead, it works in a context of political influences and considerations, a circumstance that raises important questions about the role of the judiciary in the U.S. political system.

The federal courts pose a special challenge to American democracy. Although it is common for state judges to be elected in one fashion or another, federal judges, as we will learn, are *appointed* to their positions—for life. The framers of the Constitution purposefully insulated federal judges from the influence of public opinion. How can we reconcile powerful courts populated by unelected judges with American democracy? Do they pose a threat to majority rule? Or do the federal courts actually function to protect the rights of minorities and thus maintain the type of open system necessary for democracy to flourish?

The power of the federal courts also raises the issue of the appropriate scope of judicial power in our society. Federal courts are frequently in the thick of policymaking on issues ranging from affirmative action and abortion to physician-assisted suicide and the financing of public schools. Numerous critics argue that judges should not be actively involved in determining public policy. Instead, the critics say, judges should focus on the settlement of routine disputes and leave the determination of policy to elected officials. On the other hand, advocates of a more aggressive role for the courts emphasize that judicial decisions have often met pressing needs—especially needs of those who are politically or economically weak—left unmet by the normal processes of policymaking. We have already seen the leading role that the federal courts played in ending the legal sanctioning of racist practices in the United States. To evaluate these arguments, we must first understand the nature of our judicial system.

However impressive the Supreme Court may be, only the tiniest fraction of American judicial policy is made there. To be sure, the Court decides a handful of key issues each year. Some will shape people's lives, perhaps even decide issues of life and death. In addition to the Supreme Court, there are 12 federal courts of appeal, 91 federal district courts, and thousands of state and local courts. It is in these less august courts that most of America's legal business is transacted. This chapter will focus on federal courts and the judges who serve on them—the men and women in black robes who are important policymakers in the American political system.

THE NATURE OF THE JUDICIAL SYSTEM

The judicial system in the United States is, at least in principle, an adversarial one in which the courts provide an arena for two parties to bring their conflict before an impartial arbiter (a judge). The system is based on the theory that justice will emerge out of the struggle between two contending points of view. In reality, most cases never go to trial because they are settled by agreements reached out of court.

There are two basic kinds of cases: criminal law cases and civil law cases. In a *criminal law* case, an individual is charged by the government with violating a specific law. The offense may be harmful to an individual or to society as a whole, but in either case it warrants punishment, such as imprisonment or a fine. In a *civil law* case, there is no charge of criminality—no charge that a law has been violated. Such a case involves a dispute between two parties (one of whom, of course, may be the government itself) and defines relationships between them. Civil law consists of both statutes and common law (the accumulation of judicial decisions).

Just as it is important not to confuse criminal and civil law, it is important not to confuse state and federal courts. The vast majority of all criminal and civil cases involve state law and are tried in state courts. Criminal cases such as burglary and civil cases such as divorce normally begin and end in the state, not the federal, courts.

PARTICIPANTS IN THE JUDICIAL SYSTEM

The serenity and majesty of the U.S. Supreme Court are a far cry from the grimy urban courts where strings of defendants are bused from the local jails for their day—often only a few minutes—in court. Yet every case has certain components in common, including litigants, attorneys, and judges. Sometimes organized groups are also directly involved. Judges are the policymakers of the American judicial system, and we examine them extensively in later sections of this chapter. Here we will discuss the other regular participants in the judicial process.

Most litigation is heard in state and local courts presided over by judges such as Lance Ito. Ito came to national attention when he presided over the murder trial of O. J. Simpson.

Litigants. Federal judges are restricted by the Constitution to deciding *"cases or controversies"*—that is, actual disputes rather than hypothetical ones. Judges do not issue advisory opinions on what they think (in the abstract) may be the meaning or constitutionality of a law. The judiciary is essentially passive, dependent on others to take the initiative.

Thus, two parties must bring a case to the court before it may be heard. Every case is a dispute between a *plaintiff* and a *defendant* in which the former brings some charge against the latter. Sometimes the plaintiff is the government, which may bring a charge against an individual or a corporation. The government may charge the defendant with the brutal murder of Jones or charge the XYZ Corporation with illegal trade practices. All cases are identified with the name of the plaintiff first and the defendant second, for example, *State v. Smith* or *Anderson v. Baker.* The task of the judge or judges is to apply the law to the case, determining whether the plaintiff or the defendant is legally correct. In many (but not all) cases, a *jury,* a group of citizens (usually 12), is responsible for determining the success of a lawsuit.

Litigants end up in court for a variety of reasons. Some are reluctant participants—the defendant in a criminal case, for example. Others are eager for their day in court. For some, the courts can be a potent weapon in the search for a preferred policy. For example, in the 1960s, atheist Madelyn Murray O'Hair was an enthusiastic litigant, always ready to take the government to court for promoting religion.

Not everyone can challenge a law, however. Litigants must have what is called **standing to sue;** that is, they must have serious interest in a case, which is typically determined by whether they have sustained or are in immediate danger of sustaining a direct and substantial injury from another party or an action of government. Except in cases pertaining to governmental support for religion, merely being a taxpayer and being opposed to a law do not provide the standing necessary to challenge that law in court. Nevertheless, Congress and the Supreme Court have liberalized the rules for standing, making it somewhat easier for citizens to challenge governmental and corporate actions in court.

In recent years, the concept of standing to sue has been broadened. **Class action suits** permit a small number of people to sue on behalf of all other people similarly situated. These suits may be useful in cases as varied as civil rights, in which a few persons seek an end to discriminatory practices on behalf of all who might be discriminated against, and environmental protection, in which a few persons may sue a polluting industry on behalf of all who are affected by the air or water the industry pollutes. Following an explosion of such cases, the Supreme Court in 1974 began making it more difficult to file class action suits.

Conflicts must not only arise from actual cases between litigants with standing in court, but they must also be **justiciable disputes**—issues that are capable of being settled by legal methods. Thus, one would not go to court to determine whether Congress should fund the Strategic Defense Initiative (SDI), for the matter could not be resolved through legal methods or knowledge.

Groups. Because they recognize the courts' ability to shape policy, interest groups often seek out litigants whose cases seem particularly strong. Few groups have been more successful in finding good cases and good litigants than the National Association for the Advancement of Colored People, which selected the school board of Topeka, Kansas, and a young schoolgirl named Linda Brown as the litigants in *Brown v. Board of Education.* NAACP legal counsel Thurgood Marshall (later a Supreme Court justice) believed that Topeka represented a stronger case than other school districts in the United States in the effort to end the policy of "separate but equal"—meaning racially segregated—public education, because the city provided segregated facilities that were otherwise genuinely equal. Thus, the courts could not resolve the case simply by insisting that expenditures for schools for white and African-American children be equalized.

Sometimes people find themselves involved in extraordinary court decisions. Linda Brown was a plaintiff in *Brown v. Board of Education,* a key civil rights case in which the Supreme Court overturned its earlier *Plessy v. Ferguson* ruling that had legalized segregation.

The American Civil Liberties Union is another interest group that is always seeking cases and litigants to support in its defense of civil liberties. One ACLU attorney, stressing that principle took priority over a particular client, even admitted that the ACLU's clients are often "pretty scurvy little creatures . . . . It's the principle that we're going to be able to use these people for that's important."[1] (For an example, review the case in Chapter 4 of the Nazis who tried to march in Skokie, Illinois.)

Attorneys. Lawyers have become another indispensable actor in the judicial system. Law is one of the nation's fastest-growing professions. The United States counted about 100,000 lawyers in 1960 but has about 750,000 today—1 for every 360 Americans. Lawyers busily translate policies into legal language and then enforce them or challenge them.

Once lawyers were primarily available to the rich. Today, public interest law firms can sometimes handle legal problems of the poor and middle classes. The federally funded Legal Services Corporation employs lawyers to serve the legal needs of the poor, although the Reagan administration made drastic cuts in legal aid. Some employers and unions now provide legal insurance, which works like medical insurance. Members with legal needs—for a divorce, a consumer complaint, or whatever—can secure legal aid through prepaid plans. As a result, more people than ever before can take their problems to the courts.

The audience for the judicial drama is a large and attentive one that includes interest groups, the press (a close observer of the judicial process, especially of its more sensational aspects), and the public, who often have very strong opinions about how the process works. All these participants—plaintiffs, defendants, lawyers, interest groups, and others—play a role in the judicial drama, even though many of their activities take place outside the courtroom. How these participants arrive in the courtroom and which court they go to reflect the structure of the court system.

THE STRUCTURE OF THE FEDERAL JUDICIAL SYSTEM

The Constitution is vague about the structure of the federal court system. Aside from specifying that there will be a Supreme Court, the Constitution left it to

Congress' discretion to establish lower federal courts of general jurisdiction. In the Judiciary Act of 1789, Congress created these *constitutional courts,* and although the system has been altered over the years, America has never been without them. The current organization of the federal court system is displayed in Figure 16.1.

Congress has also established *legislative courts* for specialized purposes. These courts include the Court of Military Appeals, the Court of Claims, the Court of International Trade, and the Tax Court. They are staffed by judges who have fixed terms of office and who lack the protections of judges on constitutional courts against removal or salary reductions. The following sections, however, will focus on the courts of general jurisdiction.

First, we must understand another difference among courts. Courts with **original jurisdiction** are those in which a case is heard first, usually in a trial. These are the courts that determine the facts about a case, whether it is a criminal charge or a civil suit. The great majority of judicial business is transacted in courts of original jurisdiction. More than 90 percent of court cases begin and end in the court of original jurisdiction.

Lawyers can sometimes appeal an adverse decision to a higher court for another decision. Courts with **appellate jurisdiction** hear cases brought to them on appeal from a lower court. Appellate courts do not review the factual record, only the legal issues involved. At the state level, the appellate process normally ends with the state's highest court of appeal, which is usually called the state supreme court. Appeals from a state high court can be taken only to the U.S. Supreme Court.

DISTRICT COURTS

The entry point for most litigation in the federal courts is one of the 91 **district courts,** at least one of which is located in each state, in addition to one in Washington, DC, and one in Puerto Rico (there are also 3 somewhat different territorial courts for Guam, the Virgin Islands, and the Northern Mariana Islands). The district courts are courts of original jurisdiction; they hear no appeals. They are the only federal courts in which trials are held and in which juries may be empaneled. The 649 district court judges usually preside over cases alone, but certain rare cases require that 3 judges constitute the court. Each district court has between 2 and 28 judges, depending on the amount of judicial work within its territory.

The jurisdiction of the district courts extends to

- Federal crimes
- Civil suits under federal law
- Civil suits between citizens of different states where the amount in question exceeds $50,000
- Supervision of bankruptcy proceedings
- Review of the actions of some federal administrative agencies

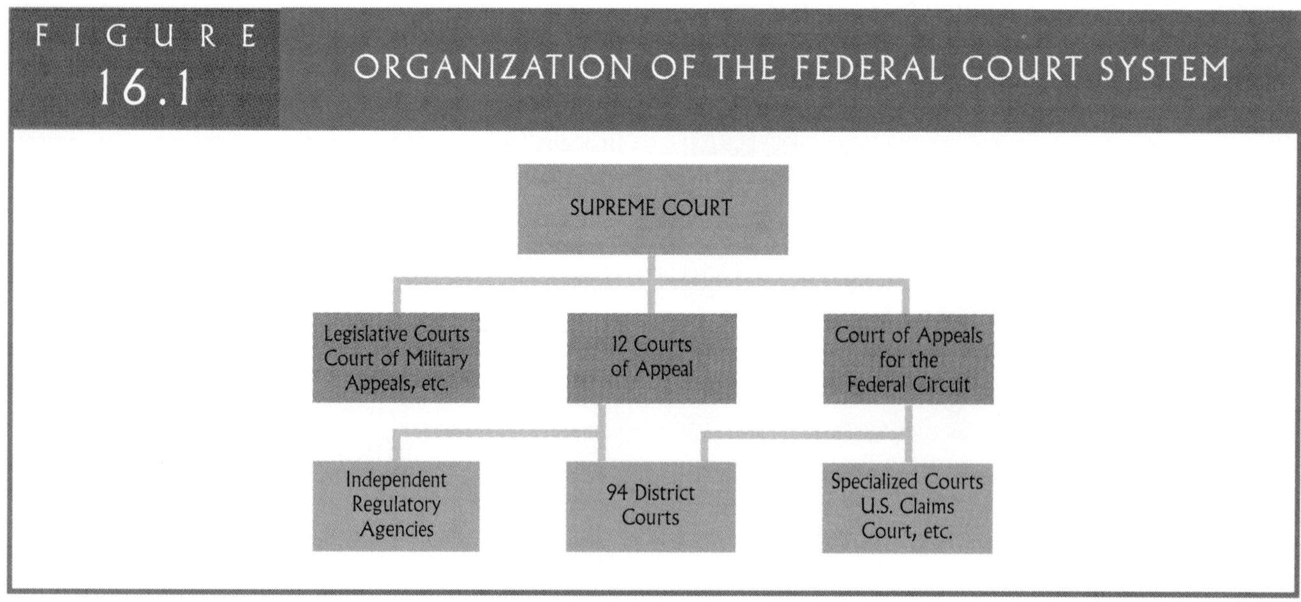

- Admiralty and maritime law cases
- Supervision of the naturalization of aliens

It is important to remember that about 98 percent of all the criminal cases in the United States are heard in state and local court systems, not in the federal courts. Moreover, only a small percentage of the persons convicted of federal crimes in the federal district courts actually have a trial. Most enter guilty pleas as part of a bargain to receive lighter punishment.

Most civil suits in the United States are also handled in state and local courts. The vast majority of civil cases that commence in the federal courts are settled out of court. Only about 5 percent of the more than 200,000 civil cases resolved each year are decided by trials.

Diversity of citizenship cases involve civil suits between citizens of different states (such as a citizen of California suing a citizen of Texas) or suits in which one of the parties is a citizen of a foreign nation and the matter in question exceeds $50,000. Congress established this jurisdiction to protect against the possible bias of a state court in favor of a citizen from that state. In these cases, federal judges are to apply the appropriate state laws.

District judges are assisted by an elaborate supporting cast. In addition to clerks, bailiffs, law clerks, stenographers, court reporters, and probation officers, U.S. marshals are assigned to each district to protect the judicial process and to serve the writs that the judges issue. Federal magistrates, appointed to 8-year terms, issue warrants for arrest, determine whether to hold arrested persons for action by a grand jury, and set bail. They also hear motions subject to review by their district judge and, with the consent of both parties in civil cases and of defendants in petty criminal cases, preside over some trials. As the workload for district judges increases, magistrates are becoming essential components of the federal judicial system.

Another important player at the district court level is the U.S. attorney. Each of the 91 regular districts has a U.S. attorney who is nominated by the president and confirmed by the Senate and who serves at the discretion of the president (U.S. attorneys do not have lifetime appointments). These attorneys and their staffs prosecute violations of federal law and represent the U.S. government in civil cases.

Most of the cases handled in the district courts are routine, and few result in policy innovations. Usually district court judges do not even publish their decisions. Although most federal litigation ends at this level, a large percentage of those cases that district court judges actually decide (as opposed to those settled out of court or by guilty pleas in criminal matters) are appealed by the losers. A distinguishing feature of the American legal system is the relative ease of appeals and the long time it may take to reach final resolution on an issue.

COURTS OF APPEAL

The U.S. **courts of appeal** are appellate courts empowered to review all final decisions of district courts, except in rare instances in which the law provides for direct review by the Supreme Court (injunctive orders of special three-judge district courts and certain decisions holding acts of Congress unconstitutional). Courts of appeal also have authority to review and enforce orders of many federal regulatory agencies, such as the Securities and Exchange Commission and the National Labor Relations Board. About 90 percent of the more than 40,000 cases heard in the courts of appeal each year come from the district courts.

The United States is divided into 12 judicial circuits, including one for the District of Columbia (see Figure 16.2). Each circuit serves at least 2 states and has between 6 and 28 permanent circuit judgeships (179 in all), depending on the amount of judicial work in the circuit. Each court of appeal normally hears cases in panels consisting of three judges, but each may sit *en banc* (with all judges present) in particularly important cases. Decisions in either arrangement are made by majority vote of the participating judges.

There is also a special appeals court called the U.S. Court of Appeals for the Federal Circuit. Composed of 12 judges, it was established by Congress in 1982 to hear appeals in specialized cases, such as those regarding patents, claims against the United States, and international trade.

The courts of appeal focus on correcting errors of procedure and law that occurred in the original proceedings of legal cases. These courts hold no trials and hear no testimony. Their decisions set precedent for all the courts and agencies within their jurisdictions.

THE SUPREME COURT

Sitting at the pinnacle of the American judicial system is the U.S. **Supreme Court.** The Court does much more for the American political system than decide discrete cases. Among its most important functions are resolving conflicts among the states and maintaining national supremacy in the law. The Supreme Court also plays an important role in ensuring uniformity in the interpretation of national laws. For example, in 1984 Congress created a federal sentencing

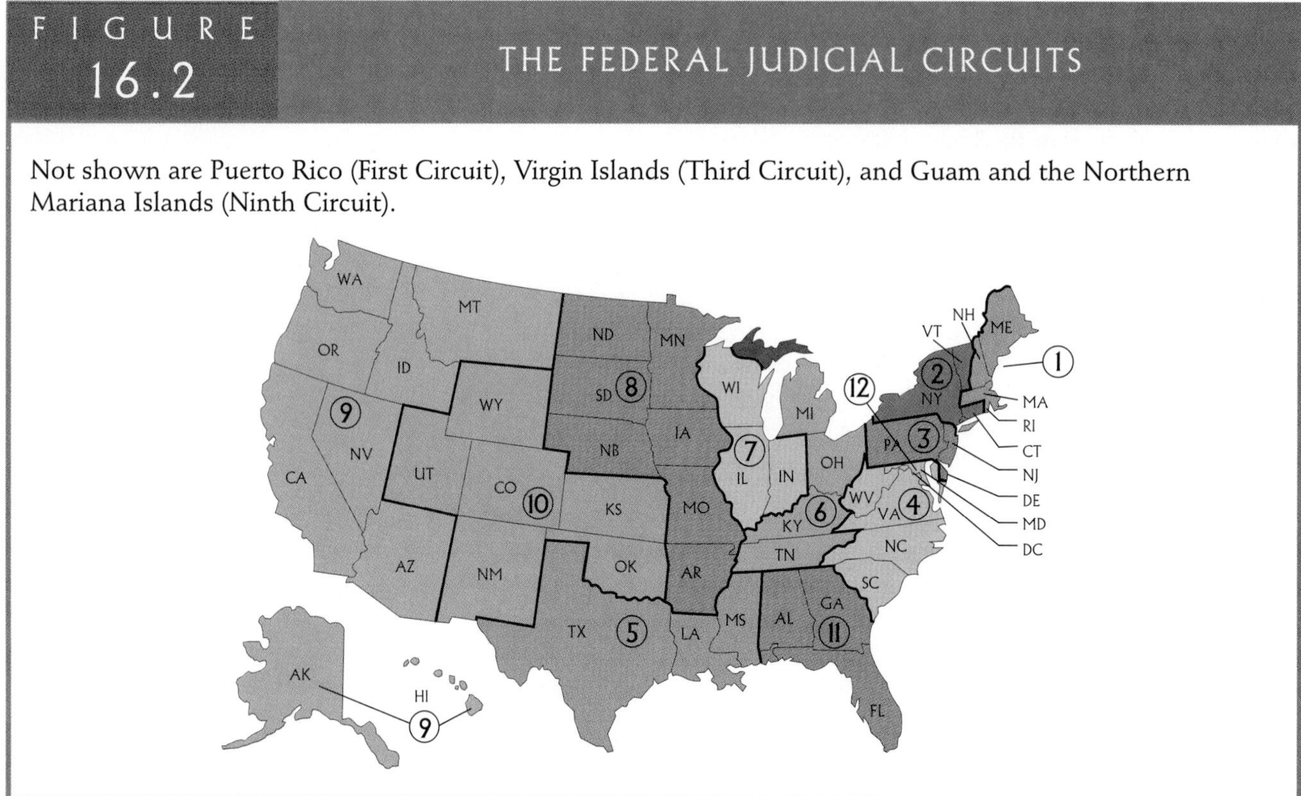

FIGURE 16.2 THE FEDERAL JUDICIAL CIRCUITS

Not shown are Puerto Rico (First Circuit), Virgin Islands (Third Circuit), and Guam and the Northern Mariana Islands (Ninth Circuit).

commission to write guidelines aimed at reducing the wide disparities in punishment for similar crimes tried in federal courts. By 1989, more than 150 federal district judges had declared the law unconstitutional, and another 115 had ruled it valid. Only the Supreme Court could resolve this inconsistency in the administration of justice, which it did when it upheld the law.

There are nine justices on the Supreme Court: eight associates and one chief justice (see Table 16.1). The Constitution does not require this number, however, and there have been as few as six justices and as many as ten. The size of the Supreme Court was altered many times between 1801 and 1869. In 1866, Congress reduced the size of the Court from ten to eight members so that President Andrew Johnson could not nominate new justices to fill two vacancies. When Ulysses S. Grant took office, Congress increased the number of justices to nine, because it had confidence that he would nominate members to its liking. Since then, the number of justices has remained stable.

All nine justices sit together to hear cases and make decisions. But they must first decide which cases to hear. A familiar battle cry for losers in litigation in lower courts is "I'll appeal this all the way to the Supreme Court!" In reality, this is most unlikely to happen. Unlike other federal courts, the Supreme Court controls its own agenda (it decides what cases it will hear).

You can see in Figure 16.3 that the Court does have an original jurisdiction, yet very few cases arise under it, as Table 16.2 (page 416) illustrates. Almost all the business of the Court comes from the appellate process, and cases may be appealed from both federal and state courts. In the latter instance, however, a "substantial federal question" must be involved. In deference to the states, cases from state courts are heard in the Supreme Court only if they involve federal law, and then only after the petitioner has exhausted all the potential remedies in the state court system. Cases from state courts cannot be appealed to any other federal court.

The Court will not try to settle matters of state law or determine guilt or innocence in state criminal proceedings. To obtain a hearing in the Supreme Court, a defendant convicted in a state court might demonstrate, for example, that the trial was not fair as required by the Bill of Rights, which was extended to cover state court proceedings by the due process clause of the Fourteenth Amendment. The majority of cases heard by the Supreme Court come from the lower federal courts.

TABLE 16.1 CHIEF JUSTICES OF THE U.S. SUPREME COURT

CHIEF JUSTICE	NOMINATING PRESIDENT	YEARS OF SERVICE
John Jay	Washington	1789-1795
John Rutledge	Washington	1795[a]
Oliver Ellsworth	Washington	1796-1800
John Marshall	Adams	1801-1835
Roger B. Taney	Jackson	1836-1864
Salmon P. Chase	Lincoln	1864-1873
Morrison R. Waite	Grant	1874-1888
Melville W. Fuller	Cleveland	1888-1910
Edward D. White	Taft	1910-1921
William Howard Taft	Harding	1921-1930
Charles Evans Hughes	Hoover	1930-1941
Harlan Fiske Stone	F. Roosevelt	1941-1946
Fred M. Vinson	Truman	1946-1953
Earl Warren	Eisenhower	1953-1969
Warren E. Burger	Nixon	1969-1986
William H. Rehnquist	Reagan	1986-present

[a]Not confirmed by the Senate.

FIGURE 16.3 THE ORGANIZATION AND JURISDICTION OF THE COURTS

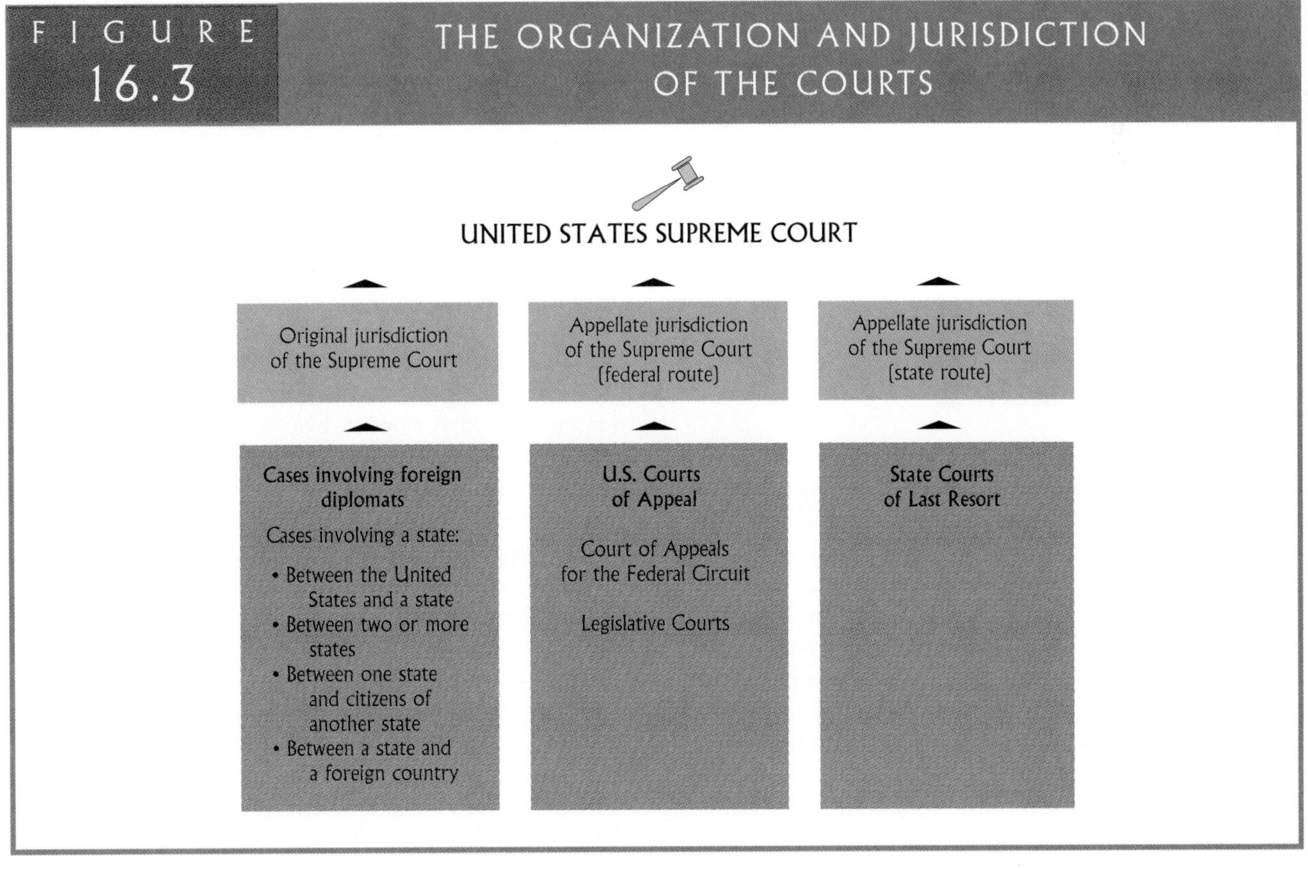

TABLE 16.2 FULL OPINIONS IN THE SUPREME COURT'S 1995–1996 TERM

TYPE OF CASE	NUMBER OF CASES
Original jurisdiction	1
Civil actions from lower federal courts	50
Federal criminal and *habeas corpus* cases	17
Civil actions from state courts	8
State criminal cases	3
TOTAL	79

SOURCE: "The Supreme Court, 1995 Term: The Statistics," *Harvard Law Review* 109 (November 1996): 373-376.

The central participants in the judicial system are, of course, the judges. Once on the bench, they must draw on their backgrounds and beliefs to guide their decision making. Some, for example, will be more supportive of abortion or of prayer in the public schools than others. Because presidents and others involved in the appointment process know perfectly well that judges are not neutral automatons who methodically and literally interpret the law, they work diligently to place candidates sympathetic to presidential policies on the bench. Who are the men and women who serve as federal judges and justices (only members of the Supreme Court are called justices; all others are called judges), and how did they obtain their positions?

THE POLITICS OF JUDICIAL SELECTION

Appointing a federal judge or a Supreme Court justice is a president's chance to leave an enduring mark on the American legal system. Guaranteed by the Constitution the right to serve "during good behavior," federal judges and justices enjoy, for all practical purposes, lifetime positions. They may be removed only by conviction of impeachment, which has occurred a mere seven times in two centuries under the Constitution. No Supreme Court justice has ever been removed from office, although one, Samuel Chase, was tried but not convicted by the Senate in 1805. Nor can members of the federal judiciary have their salaries reduced, a stipulation that further insulates them from political pressures.

Although the president nominates persons to fill judicial slots, the Senate must confirm each nomination by majority vote. Because the judiciary is a coequal branch, the upper house of the legislature sees no reason to be especially deferential to the executive's recommendations. Thus, the president's discretion, because of the Senate's role, is actually less important than it appears.

THE LOWER COURTS

The customary manner in which the Senate disposes of state-level federal judicial nominations is through **senatorial courtesy.** Under this unwritten tradition (which began under George Washington in 1789), nominations for lower-court positions are not confirmed when opposed by a senator of the president's party from the state in which the nominee is to serve (all states have at least one federal district court). In the case of judges for courts of appeal, nominees are not confirmed if opposed by a senator of the president's party from the state of the nominee's residence.

To invoke the right of senatorial courtesy, the relevant senator usually simply states a general reason for opposition. Other senators then honor their colleague's views and oppose the nomination, regardless of their personal evaluations of the candidate's merits.

Because of the strength of this informal practice, presidents usually check carefully with the relevant senator or senators ahead of time so that they will avoid making a nomination that will fail to be confirmed. In many instances, this is tantamount to giving the power of nomination to these senators. Typically, when there is a vacancy for a federal district judgeship, the one or two senators of the president's party from the state where the judge will serve suggest one or more names to the attorney general and the president. If neither senator is of the president's party, then the party's state congresspersons or other state party leaders may make suggestions.

The Department of Justice and the Federal Bureau of Investigation next conduct competency and background checks on these persons, and the president usually selects a nominee from those who survive the screening process. It is difficult for the president to reject the recommendation of the party's senator in favor of someone else if the person recommended clears the hurdles of professional standing and integrity. Thus, the Constitution is often turned on its head, and the Senate ends up making nominations, which the president then approves.

Others have input in judicial selection as well. The Department of Justice may ask sitting judges, usually federal judges, to evaluate prospective nominees. Sitting judges may also initiate recommendations to advance or retard someone's chances of being nominated. In addition, candidates for the nomination are often active on their own behalf. They have to alert the relevant parties that they desire the position and may orchestrate a campaign of support. As one appellate judge observed, "People don't just get judgeships without seeking them. Anybody who thinks judicial office seeks the man is mistaken. There's not a man on the court who didn't do what he thought needed to be done."[2]

The president usually has more influence in the selection of judges to the federal courts of appeal than to federal district courts. The decisions of appellate courts are generally more significant than those of lower courts, so the president naturally takes a greater interest in appointing people to these courts. At the same time, individual senators are in a weaker position to determine who the nominee will be, because the jurisdiction of an appeals court encompasses several states. Although custom and pragmatic politics require that these judgeships be apportioned among the states in a circuit, the president has some discretion in doing this and therefore has a greater role in recruiting appellate judges than in recruiting district court judges. Even here, however, senators of the president's party from the state in which the candidate resides may be able to veto a nomination.

THE SUPREME COURT

The president is vitally interested in the Supreme Court because of the importance of its work and will generally be intimately involved in recruiting potential justices. Nominations to the Court may be a president's most important legacy to the nation.

A president cannot have much impact on the Court unless there are vacancies to fill. Although on the average there has been an opening on the Supreme Court every two years, there is a substantial variance around this mean.[3] Franklin D. Roosevelt had to wait 5 years before he could nominate a justice; in the meantime, he was faced with a Court that found much of his New Deal legislation unconstitutional. More recently, Jimmy Carter was never able to nominate a justice. Indeed, between 1972 and 1984, there were only two vacancies on the Court. Nevertheless, Richard Nixon was able to nominate four justices in his first 3 years in office, and Ronald Reagan had the opportunity to add three new members.

When the chief justice's position is vacant, the president may nominate either someone already on the Court or someone from outside to fill the position. Usually presidents choose the latter course to widen their range of options, but if they decide to elevate a sitting associate justice—as President Reagan did with William Rehnquist in 1986—the nominee must go through a new confirmation hearing by the Senate Judiciary Committee.

The president operates under fewer constraints in nominating persons to serve on the Supreme Court than in naming persons to be judges in the lower courts. Although many of the same actors are present in the case of Supreme Court nominations, their influence is typically quite different. The president usually relies on the attorney general and the Department of Justice to identify and screen candidates for the Court. Sitting justices often try to influence the nominations of their future colleagues, but presidents feel little obligation to follow their advice.

Senators also play a lesser role in the recruitment of Supreme Court justices than in the selection of lower-court judges. No senator can claim that the jurisdiction of the Court falls within the realm of his or her special expertise, interest, or sphere of influence. Thus, presidents typically consult with senators from the state of residence of a nominee after they have decided whom to select. At this point, senators are unlikely to oppose a nomination, because they like having their state receive the honor and are well aware that the president can simply select someone from another state.

Candidates for nomination usually keep a low profile. Little can be accomplished through aggressive politicking, and because of the Court's standing, actively pursuing the position might offend those who play important roles in selecting nominees. The American Bar Association's Standing Committee on the Federal Judiciary has played a varied but typically modest role at the Supreme Court level. Presidents have not generally been willing to allow the committee to prescreen candidates before their nominations are announced.

Through 1997, there have been 148 nominations to the Supreme Court, and 108 persons have served on the Court. Four people were nominated and confirmed twice, 8 declined appointment or died before beginning service on the Court, and 28 failed to secure Senate confirmation. Thus, presidents have failed 20 percent of the time to appoint the nominees of their choice to the Court—a percentage much higher than that for any other federal position.

Thus, although home-state senators do not play prominent roles in the selection process for the Court, the Senate as a whole does. Through its Judiciary Committee, it may probe a nominee's judicial philosophy in great detail.

Seven nominees have failed to receive Senate confirmation in this century (see Table 16.3). Six of these have occurred since the presidency of John F. Kennedy (see "Since Kennedy: Contentious Nominations to the Supreme Court").

Nominations are most likely to run into trouble under certain conditions. Presidents whose parties are in the minority in the Senate or who make a nomination at the end of their terms face a greatly increased probability of substantial opposition. Equally important, opponents of a nomination usually must be able to question a nominee's competence or ethics in order to defeat a nomination. Opposition based on a nominee's ideology is generally not considered a valid reason to vote against confirmation, as the case of Chief Justice William Rehnquist, who was strongly opposed by liberals, illustrates. Questions of the legal competence and ethics of nominees must usually be raised by their opponents in order to attract moderate senators to their side and to make ideological protests seem less partisan.

THE BACKGROUNDS OF JUDGES AND JUSTICES

What is the result of this complex process of judicial recruitment? What kind of people are selected? The Constitution sets no special requirements for judges or justices, but most observers conclude that the federal judiciary is composed of a distinguished group of men and women. Competence and ethical behavior are important to presidents for reasons beyond merely obtaining Senate confirmation of their judicial nominees. Skilled and honorable judges and justices reflect well on the president and are likely to do so for many years. Moreover, these individuals are more effective representatives of the president's views.

Although the criteria of competence and character screen out some possible candidates, there is still a wide field from which to choose. Other characteristics then play prominent roles.

The judges serving on the federal district and circuit courts are not a representative sample of the American people (see Table 16.4, page 421). They are all lawyers (although this is not a constitutional requirement), and they are overwhelmingly white males. Jimmy Carter appointed 40 women, 37 African Americans, and 16 Hispanics to the federal bench, more than all previous presidents combined. Ronald Reagan did not continue this trend, although he was the first to appoint a woman to the Supreme Court. His administration placed a higher priority on screening candidates on the

TABLE 16.3 TWENTIETH-CENTURY SENATE REJECTIONS OF SUPREME COURT NOMINEES

NOMINEE	YEAR	PRESIDENT
John J. Parker	1930	Hoover
Abe Fortas[a]	1968	Johnson
Homer Thornberry[b]	1968	Johnson
Clement F. Haynsworth, Jr.	1969	Nixon
G. Harrold Carswell	1970	Nixon
Robert H. Bork	1987	Reagan
Douglas H. Ginsburg[a]	1987	Reagan

[a]Nomination withdrawn. Fortas was serving on the Court as an associate justice and was nominated to be chief justice.
[b]The Senate took no action on Thornberry's nomination.

SINCE KENNEDY

Contentious Nominations to the Supreme Court

For most of the twentieth century, Supreme Court nominations were routine affairs. Only one nominee failed to win confirmation in the first two-thirds of the century. But the 1960s were tumultuous times and bred ideological conflict. Although John F. Kennedy had no trouble with his two nominations to the Court—Byron White and Arthur Goldberg—his successor, Lyndon Johnson, was not so fortunate. Johnson had to withdraw his nomination of Abe Fortas (already serving on the Court) to serve as Chief Justice; therefore, the Senate never voted on Homer Thornberry, Johnson's nominee to replace Fortas as an associate justice. Richard Nixon, the next president, had two nominees rejected in a row after bruising battles in the Senate.

The most recent failed nominations occurred in 1987. President Reagan nominated Robert H. Bork to fill the vacancy created by the resignation of Justice Lewis Powell. Bork testified before the Senate Judiciary Committee for 23 hours. A wide range of interest groups entered the fray, mostly in opposition to the nominee, and in the end, following a bitter floor debate, the Senate rejected the president's nomination by a vote of 42 to 58.

Six days after the Senate vote on Bork, the president nominated Judge Douglas H. Ginsburg to the high court. Just nine days later, however, Ginsburg withdrew his nomination after disclosures that he had used marijuana while a law professor at Harvard.

In June 1991, at the end of the Supreme Court's term, Associate Justice Thurgood Marshall announced his retirement from the Court. Shortly thereafter, President Bush announced his nomination of another African American, federal appeals judge Clarence Thomas, to replace Marshall on the Court. Thomas was a conservative, so this decision was consistent with the Bush administration's emphasis on placing conservative judges on the federal bench.

The president claimed that he was not employing quotas when he chose another African American to replace the only African American ever to sit on the Supreme Court. Not everyone believed him, but liberals were placed in a dilemma. On the one hand, they favored a minority group member serving on the nation's highest court. On the other hand, Thomas was unlikely to vote the same way as Thurgood Marshall had voted. Instead, Thomas presented the prospect of strengthening the conservative trend in the Court's decisions. In the end, this ambivalence inhibited spirited opposition to Thomas, who was circumspect about his judicial philosophy in his appearances before the Senate Judiciary Committee. The committee sent his nomination to the Senate floor on a split vote.

Just as the Senate was about to vote on the nomination, however, charges of sexual harassment leveled against Thomas by University of Oklahoma law professor Anita Hill were made public. Hearings were reopened on the charges in response to criticism that the Senate was sexist for not seriously considering them in the first place. For several days, citizens sat transfixed before their television sets as Professor Hill calmly and graphically described her recollections of Thomas' behavior. Thomas then emphatically denied any such behavior and charged the Senate with racism for raising the issue. Ultimately, public opinion polls showed that most people believed Thomas, and he was confirmed in a 52-48 vote—the closest vote on a Supreme Court nomination in more than a century.

The Senate's treatment of President Clinton's two nominees (as of 1997) harks back to the Kennedy era. Neither Ruth Bader Ginsburg nor Stephen Breyer caused much controversy. Whether the days of deference to the president have returned, however, remains to be seen, especially now that the Republicans have a majority in the upper chamber.

basis of ideology than on screening them in terms of ascriptive characteristics. George Bush continued to place conservatives on the bench, but he was much more likely to appoint women and minorities than was Reagan. Bill Clinton has nominated Democrats, who are more liberal than the nominees of Reagan and Bush, and a large percentage of them have been women and minorities.

Federal judges have typically held office as a judge or prosecutor, and often they have been involved in partisan politics. This involvement is generally what brings them to the attention of senators and the Department of Justice when they seek nominees for judgeships. As former U.S. Attorney General and Circuit Court Judge Griffin Bell once remarked, "For me, becoming a federal judge wasn't very difficult. I

In 1991, after 2 weeks of riveting hearings in which he was charged with sexual harassment, the Senate narrowly confirmed the nomination of Clarence Thomas to the Supreme Court. Historically, about one-fifth of those nominated to the Court have failed to obtain confirmation.

managed John F. Kennedy's presidential campaign in Georgia. Two of my oldest and closest friends were senators from Georgia. And I was campaign manager and special unpaid counsel for the governor."[4]

Like their colleagues on the lower federal courts, Supreme Court justices share characteristics that are quite unlike those of the typical American and that qualify them as an elite group. All have been lawyers, and all but four (Thurgood Marshall, nominated in 1967; Sandra Day O'Connor, nominated in 1981; Clarence Thomas, nominated in 1991; and Ruth Bader Ginsburg, nominated in 1993) have been white males. Most have been in their fifties and sixties when they took office, from the upper-middle or upper class, and Protestants.[5]

Race and gender have become more salient criteria in recent years. In the 1980 presidential campaign, Ronald Reagan promised to appoint a woman to the first vacancy on the Court if he were elected. President Bush chose to replace the first African-American justice, Thurgood Marshall, with another African American, Clarence Thomas. Women and minorities may serve on all federal courts more frequently in the future because of increased opportunity for legal edu-

Most members of the federal judiciary have had backgrounds atypical of most Americans. Thurgood Marshall was the first African American to sit on the Supreme Court, and Sandra Day O'Connor is the first woman. All previous members of the Court were white males, most of them from the upper-middle or upper class.

TABLE 16.4 BACKGROUNDS OF RECENT FEDERAL DISTRICT AND APPEALS COURT JUDGES

CHARACTERISTIC	APPEALS COURT				DISTRICT COURT			
	CLINTON[a]	BUSH	REAGAN	CARTER	CLINTON[a]	BUSH	REAGAN	CARTER
Total number of nominees	29	37	78	56	169	148	290	202
Occupation (%)								
Politics/government	3	11	6	5	11	11	13	4
Judiciary	59	60	55	47	44	42	37	40
Large law firm	17	16	13	11	17	26	18	14
Moderate-size firm	10	11	10	16	17	15	19	20
Solo or small firm	—	—	1	5	8	5	10	14
Professor of law	10	3	13	14	2	1	2	3
Other	—	—	1	2	1	1	1	1
Experience (%)								
Judicial	69	62	60	54	50	47	47	55
Prosecutorial	38	30	28	32	38	39	44	39
Neither one	21	32	35	38	31	32	28	28
Party (%)								
Democrat	86	5	—	82	91	5	5	93
Republican	3	89	97	7	2	89	93	4
Independent	10	5	1	11	7	6	2	3
Past party activism (%)	48	70	69	73	54	61	59	61
Ethnicity or race (%)								
White	72	89	97	79	72	90	92	79
African American	14	5	1	16	20	7	2	14
Hispanic	10	5	1	4	7	4	5	7
Asian	3	—	—	2	1	—	1	1
Gender (%)								
Male	69	81	95	80	70	80	92	86
Female	31	19	5	20	30	20	8	14
Average age	51	49	50	52	49	48	49	50

[a]First term.

SOURCE: Sheldon Goldman and Elliot Slotnick, "Clinton's First Term Judiciary: Many Bridges to Cross," *Judicature* 80 (No. 6, 1997), pp. 261, 269..

cation and decreased prejudice against their judicial activity, as well as because of their increasing political clout.

Geography was once a prominent criterion for selection to the Court, but it is no longer very important. Presidents do like to spread the slots around, however, as when Richard Nixon decided that he wanted to nominate a Southerner. At various times there have been what some have termed a "Jewish seat" and a "Catholic seat" on the Court, but these guidelines are not binding on the president. For example, after a half-century of having a Jewish justice, the Court did not have one from 1969 to 1993.

Typically, justices have held high administrative or judicial positions before moving to the Supreme Court (see Table 16.5). Most have had some experience as a judge, often at the appellate level, and many have worked for the Department of Justice. Some have held elective office, and a few have had no government service but have been distinguished attorneys. The fact that many justices, including some of the most distinguished ones, have not had previous judicial experience may seem surprising, but the unique work of the Court renders this background much less important than it might be for other appellate courts.

Partisanship is another important influence on the selection of judges and justices. Only 13 of 108 members of the Supreme Court have been nominated by presidents of a different party. Moreover, many of the 13 exceptions were actually close to the president in

TABLE 16.5 SUPREME COURT JUSTICES, 1997

NAME	YEAR OF BIRTH	PREVIOUS POSITION	NOMINATING PRESIDENT	YEAR OF APPOINTMENT
William H. Rehnquist[a]	1924	Assistant U.S. Attorney General	Nixon	1971
John Paul Stevens	1920	U.S. Court of Appeals	Ford	1975
Sandra Day O'Connor	1930	State Court of Appeals	Reagan	1981
Antonin Scalia	1936	U.S. Court of Appeals	Reagan	1986
Anthony M. Kennedy	1936	U.S. Court of Appeals	Reagan	1988
David H. Souter	1939	U.S. Court of Appeals	Bush	1990
Clarence Thomas	1948	U.S. Court of Appeals	Bush	1991
Ruth Bader Ginsburg	1933	U.S. Court of Appeals	Clinton	1993
Stephen G. Breyer	1938	U.S. Court of Appeals	Clinton	1994

[a]William Rehnquist was promoted from associate justice to Chief Justice by President Reagan in 1986.

ideology, as was the case in Richard Nixon's appointment of Lewis Powell. Herbert Hoover's nomination of Benjamin Cardozo seems to be one of the few cases in which partisanship was completely dominated by merit as a criterion for selection. Usually more than 90 percent of presidents' judicial nominations are of members of their own parties.

The role of partisanship is really not surprising. Most of a president's acquaintances are made through the party, and there is usually a certain congruity between party and political views. Most judges and justices have at one time been active partisans—an experience that gave them visibility and helped them obtain the positions from which they moved to the courts.

Judgeships are also considered very prestigious patronage plums. Indeed, the decisions of Congress to create new judgeships, and thus new positions for party members, are closely related to whether the majority party in Congress is the same as the party of the president. Members of the majority party in the legislature want to avoid providing an opposition party president with new positions to fill with their opponents.

Ideology is as important as partisanship in the selection of judges and justices. Presidents want to appoint to the federal bench people who share their views. In effect, all presidents try to "pack" the courts. They want more than "justice"; they want policies with which they agree. Presidential aides survey candidates' decisions (if they have served on a lower court),[6] speeches, political stands, writings, and other expressions of opinion. They also glean information from people who know the candidates well. Although it is considered improper to question judicial candidates about upcoming court cases, it is appropriate to discuss broader questions of political and judicial philosophy. The Reagan administration was especially concerned about such matters and had each potential nominee fill out a lengthy questionnaire and be interviewed by a special committee in the Department of Justice. Like its predecessor, the Bush administration was attentive to appointing conservative judges.

Members of the federal bench also play the game of politics, of course, and may try to time their retirements so that a president with compatible views will choose their successors. This is one reason why justices remain on the Supreme Court for so long, even when they are clearly infirm. William Howard Taft, a rigid conservative, even feared that a successor would be named by Herbert Hoover, a more moderate conservative.[7]

Presidents are typically pleased with the performance of their nominees to the Supreme Court and through them have slowed or reversed trends in the Court's decisions. Franklin D. Roosevelt's nominees substantially liberalized the Court, whereas Richard Nixon's turned it in a conservative direction.

Nevertheless, it is not always easy to predict the policy inclinations of candidates, and presidents have been disappointed in their nominees about one-fourth of the time. President Eisenhower, for example, was displeased with the liberal decisions of both Earl Warren and William Brennan. Once, when asked whether he had made any mistakes as president, he replied, "Yes, two, and they are both sitting on the

Supreme Court."[8] Richard Nixon was certainly disappointed when Warren Burger, whom he had nominated as chief justice, wrote the Court's decision calling for immediate desegregation of the nation's schools shortly after his confirmation. This turn of events did little for the president's "Southern strategy." Burger also wrote the Court's opinion in *United States v. Nixon,* which forced the president to release the Watergate tapes. Nixon's resignation soon followed.

Thus, presidents influence policy through the values of their judicial nominees, but this impact is limited by numerous legal and "extra-legal" factors beyond the chief executive's control. As Harry Truman put it, "Packing the Supreme Court can't be done . . . . I've tried it and it won't work . . . . Whenever you put a man on the Supreme Court, he ceases to be your friend. I'm sure of that."[9]

There is no doubt that various women's, racial, ethnic, and religious groups desire to have their members appointed to the federal bench. At the very least, judgeships have symbolic importance for them.[10] Thus, presidents face many of the same pressures for representativeness in selecting judges that they experience in naming their cabinet.

What is less clear is what policy differences result when presidents nominate persons with different backgrounds to the bench. The number of female and minority group judges is too few and their service too recent to serve as a sound basis for generalizations about their decisions. Many members of each party have been appointed, of course, and it appears that Republican judges in general are somewhat more conservative than Democratic judges. Former prosecutors serving on the Supreme Court have tended to be less sympathetic toward defendants' rights than other justices. It seems that background does make some difference,[11] yet for reasons that we will examine in the following sections, on many issues, party affiliation and other characteristics bring no more predictability to the courts than they do to Congress.

THE COURTS AS POLICYMAKERS

"Judicial decision making," a former Supreme Court law clerk wrote in the *Harvard Law Review,* "involves, at bottom, a choice between competing values by fallible, pragmatic, and at times nonrational men and women in a highly complex process in a very human setting."[12] This is an apt description of policymaking on the Supreme Court and on other courts, too. The next sections will look at how courts make policy, paying particular attention to the role of the U.S. Supreme Court; although it is not the only court involved in policymaking and policy interpretation, its decisions have the widest implications for policy.

ACCEPTING CASES

Deciding what to decide about is the first step in all policymaking. Courts of original jurisdiction cannot very easily refuse to consider a case; appeals courts, including the U.S. Supreme Court, have much more control over their agendas. The approximately 7,000 cases submitted annually to the U.S. Supreme Court must be read, culled, and sifted. Every Wednesday afternoon and every Friday morning, the nine justices meet in conference. With them in the conference room sit some 25 carts, each wheeled in from the office of one of the nine justices, and each filled with petitions, briefs, memoranda, and every item the justices are likely to need during their discussions. These meetings operate under the strictest secrecy; only the justices themselves attend.

At these weekly conferences two important matters are hammered out. First is an agenda: the justices consider the chief justice's "discuss list" and decide which cases they want to discuss. Because few of the justices can take the time to read materials on every case submitted to the Court, most rely heavily on their law clerks (each justice has up to four) to screen each case. If four justices agree to grant review of a case, it can be scheduled for oral argument or decided on the basis of the written record already on file with the Court.

The most common way for the Court to put a case on its docket is by issuing to a lower federal or state court a *writ of certiorari,* a formal document that calls up a case. Until 1988, some cases—principally those in which federal laws had been found unconstitutional, in which federal courts had concluded that state laws violated the federal Constitution, or in which state laws had been upheld in state courts despite claims that they violated federal law or the Constitution—were technically supposed to be heard by the Court "on appeal." In reality, however, the Court always exercised broad discretion over hearing these and other cases.

Cases that involve major issues—especially civil liberties, conflict between different lower courts on the interpretation of federal law, or disagreement between a majority of the Supreme Court and lower-court decisions—are likely to be selected by the Court.[13]

Because getting into the Supreme Court is half the battle, it is important to remember this chapter's earlier discussion of standing to sue (litigants must have serious interest in a case, having sustained or being in immediate danger of sustaining a direct and substantial injury from another party or an action of government)—a criterion the Court often uses to decide whether to hear a case. In addition, the Court has used other means to avoid deciding cases that are too politically "hot" to handle or that divide the Court too sharply.[14]

Another important influence on the Supreme Court is the **solicitor general.**[15] As a presidential appointee and the third-ranking official in the Department of Justice, the solicitor general is in charge of the appellate court litigation of the federal government. The solicitor general and a staff of about two dozen experienced attorneys have four key functions: (1) to decide whether to appeal cases the government has lost in the lower courts, (2) to review and modify the briefs presented in government appeals, (3) to represent the government before the Supreme Court, and (4) to submit a brief on behalf of a litigant in a case in which the government is not directly involved. Unlike attorneys for private parties, the solicitors general are careful to seek Court review only of important cases. By avoiding frivolous appeals and displaying a high degree of competence, they typically earn the confidence of the Court, which in turn grants review of a large percentage of the cases for which they seek it.

Ultimately, the Supreme Court decides very few cases. In recent years, the Court has made fewer than 100 formal written decisions per year in which their opinions could serve as precedent and thus as the basis of guidance for lower courts. In a few dozen additional cases, the Court reaches a *per curiam decision*—that is, a decision without explanation. Such decisions resolve the immediate case but have no value as precedent because the Court does not offer reasoning that would guide lower courts in future decisions.[16]

MAKING DECISIONS

The second task of the justices' weekly conferences is to discuss cases actually accepted and argued before the Court. Beginning the first Monday in October and lasting until June, the Court hears oral arguments in 2-week cycles: 2 weeks of courtroom arguments followed by 2 weeks of reflecting on cases and writing opinions about them.

Before the justices enter the courtroom to hear the lawyers for each side present their arguments, they have received elaborately prepared written briefs from each party to the case. They have also probably received several other briefs from parties (often groups) who are interested in the outcome of the case but are not formal litigants. These ***amicus curiae*** ("friend of the court") **briefs** may, in an attempt to influence the Court's decision, raise additional points of view and present information not contained in the briefs of the attorneys for the official parties to the case. In controversial cases, there may be many such briefs submitted to the Court; 58 were presented in the landmark *Bakke* case on affirmative action (discussed in Chapter 5).

Amicus curiae briefs have another important role: The government, under the direction of the solicitor general, may submit them in cases in which it has an interest. For instance, a case between two parties may involve the question of the constitutionality of a federal law. The federal government naturally wants to have its voice heard on such matters, even if it is not formally a party to the case. These briefs are also a means to urge the Court to change established doctrine. For example, the Reagan administration frequently submitted *amicus curiae* briefs to the Court to try to change the law dealing with defendants' rights.

In most instances, the attorneys for each side have only a half-hour to address the Court. During this time they summarize their briefs, emphasizing their most compelling points. The justices may listen attentively, interrupt with penetrating or helpful questions, request information, talk to one another, read (presumably briefs), or simply gaze at the ceiling. After 25 minutes, a white light comes on at the lectern from which the lawyer is speaking, and 5 minutes later a red light signals the end of that lawyer's presentation, even if he or she is in midsentence. Oral argument is over.[17]

Back in the conference room, the Chief Justice, who presides over the Court, raises a particular case and invites discussion, turning first to the senior associate

Here, William H. Rehnquist, Chief Justice of the Supreme Court, prepares a written opinion.

justice. Discussion can range from perfunctory to profound and from courteous to caustic. If the votes are not clear from the individual discussions, the chief justice may ask each justice to vote. Once a tentative vote has been reached, it is necessary to write an **opinion,** a statement of the legal reasoning behind the decision.

Opinion writing is no mere formality. In fact, the content of an opinion may be as important as the decision itself. Broad and bold opinions have far-reaching implications for future cases; narrowly drawn opinions may have little impact beyond the case being decided. Tradition in the Supreme Court requires that the chief justice, if in the majority, write the opinion or assign it to another justice in the majority. The chief justice often writes the opinion in landmark cases, as Earl Warren did in *Brown v. Board of Education* and Warren Burger did in *U.S. v. Nixon.* If the chief justice is part of the minority, the opinion is assigned by the senior associate justice in the majority. Drafts are then circulated among the majority, suggestions are made, and negotiations are conducted among the justices.[18] Votes can be gained or lost by the content of the opinion. An opinion that proves unacceptable to a clear majority is reworked and redrafted.

Justices are free to write their own opinions, to join in other opinions, or to associate themselves with part of one opinion and part of another. *Dissenting opinions* are those written by justices opposed to all or part of the majority's decision. *Concurring opinions* are those written not only to support a majority decision but also to stress a different constitutional or legal basis for the judgment. When the opinions are written and the final vote is taken, the decision is announced. At least six justices must participate in a case, and decisions are made by majority vote. If there is a tie (because of a vacancy on the Court or because a justice chooses not

"Do you ever have one of those days when everything seems un-Constitutional?"

to participate), the decision of the lower court from which the case came is sustained. Five votes in agreement on the reasoning underlying an opinion are necessary for the logic to serve as precedent for judges of lower courts.

The vast majority of cases that reach the courts are settled on the principle of ***stare decisis*** ("let the decision stand"), meaning that an earlier decision should hold for the case being considered. All courts rely heavily on **precedent**—the way similar cases were handled in the past—as a guide to current decisions. Lower courts, of course, are expected to follow the precedents of higher courts in their decision making. If the Supreme Court, for example, rules in favor of the right to abortion under certain conditions, it has established a precedent that lower courts are expected to follow. Lower courts have much less discretion than the Supreme Court.

The Supreme Court is in a position to overrule its own precedents, and it has done so dozens of times.[19] One of the most famous of such instances occurred with *Brown v. Board of Education* (1954) (see Chapter 5), in which the court overruled *Plessy v. Ferguson* (1896) and found that segregation in the public schools violated the Constitution.

What happens when precedents are unclear? This is especially a problem for the Supreme Court, which is more likely than other courts to handle cases at the forefront of the law. Precedent is typically less firmly established on these matters. Moreover, the justices are often asked to apply to concrete situations the vague phrases of the Constitution ("due process of law," "equal protection," "unreasonable searches and seizures") or vague statutes passed by Congress. This ambiguity provides leeway for the justices to disagree (only about one-third of the cases in which full opinions are handed down are decided unanimously) and for their values to influence their judgment.

As a result, it is often easy to identify consistent patterns in the decisions of justices. For example, if there is division on the Court (indicating that precedent is not clear) and you can identify a conservative side to the issue at hand, it is likely that Chief Justice William Rehnquist will be on that side. Ruth Bader Ginsburg may very well be voting on the other side of the issue. Liberalism and conservatism have several dimensions, including freedom, equality, and economic regulation. The point is that policy preferences do matter in judicial decision making, especially on the nation's highest court[20] (see "You Are the Policymaker: The Debate Over Original Intentions").

Once a decision is announced, copies of it are conveyed to the press as the decision is being formally announced in open court. Media coverage of the court

THE DEBATE OVER ORIGINAL INTENTIONS

You Are the Policymaker

The most contentious issue involving the courts is the role of judicial discretion. According to Christopher Wolfe, the difficulty is this: "The Constitution itself nowhere specifies a particular set of rules by which it is to be interpreted. Where does one go, then, in order to discover the proper way to interpret the Constitution?"

Some have argued for a jurisprudence of **original intent** (sometimes referred to as *strict constructionism*). This view holds that judges and justices should determine the intent of the framers of the Constitution regarding a particular matter and decide cases in line with that intent. Such a view is popular with conservatives, such as Ronald Reagan's close advisor and attorney general, Edwin Meese. Advocates of strict constructionism view it as a means of constraining the exercise of judicial discretion, which they see as the foundation of the liberal decisions of the past four decades, especially on matters of civil liberties, civil rights, and defendants' rights (discussed in Chapters 4 and 5).

They also see following original intent as the only basis of interpretation consistent with democracy. Judges, they argue, should not dress up constitutional interpretations with *their* views on "contemporary needs," "today's conditions," or "what is right." It is the job of legislators, not judges, to make such judgments.

Other jurists, such as former Justice William Brennan, disagree. They maintain that what appears to be deference to the intentions of the framers is simply a cover for making conservative decisions. Opponents of original intent assert that the Constitution is subject to multiple meanings by thoughtful people in different ages. Judges will differ in time and place about what they think the Constitution means. Thus, basing decisions on original intent is not likely to have much affect on judicial discretion.

In addition, Brennan and his supporters contend that the Constitution is not like a paint-by-numbers kit. Trying to reconstruct or guess the framers' intentions is very difficult. Recent key cases before the Supreme Court have concerned issues, such as school busing, abortions, and wire tapping, that the framers could not have imagined; there were no public schools or buses, no contraceptives or modern abortion techniques, and certainly no electronic surveillance equipment or telephones in 1787. Not long ago the Supreme Court was asked to rule on the case of a female tourist from Colombia whose stomach, filled with more than eighty small balloons of cocaine, had been pumped by the authorities. She claimed it was an "unreasonable search and seizure," but was it a violation of the intent of the framers, who had never heard of "coke" and could not imagine a stomach pump?

As you have seen, the founders embraced general principles, not specific solutions, when they wrote the Constitution. They frequently lacked discrete, discoverable intent. Moreover, there is often no record of their intentions, nor is it clear whose intentions should count—those of the writers of the Constitution, those of the more than sixteen hundred members who attended the ratifying conventions, or those of the voters who sent them there. This problem grows more complex when you consider the amendments to the Constitution, which involve thousands of additional "framers."

Others point out that it is not even clear that the framers expected that their "original intent" should guide others' interpretations of their document. Historian Jack N. Rakove points out that there is little historical evidence that the framers believed their intentions should guide later interpretations of the Constitution. In fact, there is some evidence for believing that Madison—the key delegate—left the Constitutional Convention bitterly disappointed with the results, and wrote as much to his friend Jefferson. What if Madison had one set of intentions but—like anyone working in a committee—got a different set of results?

Thus the lines are drawn. On one side is the argument that any deviation from following the original intentions of the Constitution framers is a deviation from principle, leaving unelected judges to impose their views on the American people. If judges do not follow original intentions, then on what do they base their decisions?

On the other side are those who believe that it is often impossible to discern the views of the framers,

continued. . .

The Debate Over Original Intentions continued. . .

and that there is no good reason to be constrained by the views of the eighteenth century, which reflect a more limited conception of constitutional rights. In order to cope with current needs, they argue, it is necessary to adapt the principles in the Constitution to the demands of each era.

The choice here is at the very heart of the judicial process. If you were a justice sitting on the Supreme Court and were asked to interpret the meaning of the Constitution, what would *you* do?

SOURCES: Christopher Wolfe, *The Rise of Modern Judicial Review* (New York: Basic Books, 1986), 17. Wolfe is a strong critic of the rise of judicial activism and the lack of adherence to the original-intent criteria of judicial review. For further arguments in favor of original intent, see Raoul Berger, *Government by Judiciary: The Transformation of the Fourteenth Amendment* (Cambridge, MA: Harvard University Press, 1977). For views in favor of judicial activism, see Traciel V. Reid, A Critique of Interpretivism and Its Claimed Influence upon Judicial Decision Making," *American Politics Quarterly* 16 (July 1988); 329-356; and Jack N. Rakove, "Mr. Meese, Meet Mr. Madison," *Atlantic Monthly*, December 1986, 79.

remains primitive—short and shallow. Doris Graber reports that "much court reporting, even at the Supreme Court level, is imprecise and sometimes even wrong."[21] More important to the legal community, the decisions are bound weekly and made available to every law library and lawyer in the United States. There is, of course, an air of finality to the public announcement of a decision. In fact, however, even Supreme Court decisions are not self-implementing; they are actually "remands" to lower courts, instructing them to act in accordance with the Court's decisions.

IMPLEMENTING COURT DECISIONS

Reacting bitterly to one of Chief Justice Marshall's decisions, President Jackson is said to have grumbled: "John Marshall has made his decision; now let him enforce it." Court decisions carry legal, even moral, authority, but courts must rely on other units of government to enforce their decisions. **Judicial implementation** refers to how and whether court decisions are translated into actual policy, affecting the behavior of others.

You should think of any judicial decision as the end of one process—the litigation process—and the beginning of another process—the process of judicial implementation. Sometimes delay and foot-dragging follow even decisive court decisions. There is, for example, the story of the tortured efforts of a young African American named Virgil Hawkins to get himself admitted to the University of Florida Law School. Hawkins' efforts began in 1949, when he first applied for admission, and ended unsuccessfully in 1958, after a decade of court decisions. Despite a 1956 order from the U.S. Supreme Court to admit Hawkins, continued legal skirmishing produced a 1958 decision by a U.S. district court in Florida ordering the admission of nonwhites but upholding the denial of admission to Hawkins himself. Other courts and other institutions of government can be roadblocks in the way of judicial implementation.

Charles Johnson and Bradley Canon suggest that implementation of court decisions involves several elements.[22] First, there is an *interpreting population,* heavily composed of lawyers and judges. They must correctly understand and reflect the intent of the original decision in their subsequent actions. Usually lower-court judges do follow the Supreme Court, but sometimes they circumvent higher-court decisions to satisfy their own policy interests.[23]

Second, there is an *implementing population.* Suppose the Supreme Court held (as it did) that prayers organized by school officials in the public schools are

Virgil Hawkins' unsuccessful struggle to attend the all-white University of Florida Law School illustrates how judicial implementation can affect the impact of court decisions. The Supreme Court ordered the school to admit Hawkins in 1956, but the school and state refused to implement the ruling, continuing to appeal the case. Two years later a Florida district court again denied admission to Hawkins, although it did order the school's desegregation.

unconstitutional. The implementing population (school boards and school administrators) must then actually abandon prayers. Police departments, hospitals, corporations, government agencies—all may be part of the implementing population. With so many implementors, many of whom may disagree with a decision, there is plenty of room for "slippage" between what the Supreme Court decided and what actually occurs. Judicial decisions are more likely to be smoothly implemented if implementation is concentrated in the hands of a few highly visible officials, such as the president or state legislators.

Third, every decision involves a *consumer population.* The potential "consumers" of an abortion decision are those who want abortions (and those who oppose them); the consumers of the *Miranda* decision (see Chapter 4) are criminal defendants and their attorneys. The consumer population must be aware of its newfound rights and stand up for them.

Congress and presidents can also help or hinder judicial implementation. The Supreme Court held in 1954 that segregated schools were "inherently unconstitutional" and the next year ordered public schools desegregated with "all deliberate speed." President Eisenhower refused to state clearly that Americans should comply with this famous decision in *Brown v. Board of Education.* Congress was not much help either; only a decade later, in the wake of the civil rights movement discussed in Chapter 5, did it pass legislation denying federal aid to segregated schools. Different presidents have different commitments to a particular judicial policy. After years of court and presidential decisions supporting busing to end racial segregation, the Reagan administration in December 1984 went before the Supreme Court and argued against school busing in a case in Norfolk, Virginia.

The fate and effect of a Supreme Court decision are complex and unpredictable. The implementation of any court decision involves many actors besides the justices, and the justices have no way of ensuring that their decisions and policies will be implemented. Courts have made major changes in public policies, however, not because their decisions are automatically implemented, but because the courts both reflect and help to determine the national policy agenda.[24]

THE COURTS AND THE POLICY AGENDA

Even though American courts and judges work largely alone and in isolation from daily contact with other political institutions, you have seen that they do play a key role in shaping the policy agenda. Like all policymakers, however, the courts are choice-takers. Confronted with controversial policies, they make controversial decisions that leave some people winners and others losers. The courts have made policy about slavery and segregation, about corporate power and capital punishment, and about dozens of other controversial matters.

A HISTORICAL REVIEW

Until the Civil War, the dominant questions before the Court concerned the strength and legitimacy of the federal government and slavery. These issues of nation-building were resolved in favor of the supremacy of the national government. From the Civil War until 1937, questions of the relationship between the federal government and the economy predominated. During this period, the Court restricted the power of the federal government to regulate the economy. From 1938 to the present, the paramount issues before the Court have concerned personal liberty and social and political equality. In this era, the Court has enlarged the scope of personal freedom and civil rights and has removed many of the constitutional restraints on the regulation of the economy.

Few justices played a more important role in making the Court a significant national agenda-setter than John Marshall, chief justice from 1801 to 1835. His successors have continued not only to respond to the political agenda but also to shape discussion and debate about it.

John Marshall and the Growth of Judicial Review. Scarcely was the government housed in its new capital when Federalists and Democrats clashed over the courts. In the election of 1800, Democrat Thomas Jefferson had beaten Federalist John Adams. Determined to leave at least the judiciary in trusted hands, Adams tried to fill it with Federalists. He is alleged to have stayed at his desk until nine o'clock signing commissions on his last night in the White House (March 3, 1801).

In the midst of this flurry, Adams appointed William Marbury to the minor post of justice of the peace in the District of Columbia. In the rush of last-minute business, however, Secretary of State John Marshall failed to deliver commissions to Marbury and 16 others. He left the commissions to be delivered by the incoming secretary of state, James Madison.

Madison and Jefferson were furious at Adams' actions and refused to deliver the commissions. Marbury and three others in the same situation sued

John Marshall, chief justice from 1801 to 1835, established the Supreme Court's power of judicial review in the 1803 case *Marbury v. Madison.* In their ruling on the case, Marshall and his associates declared that the Court had the power to determine the constitutionality of congressional actions.

Madison, asking the Supreme Court to issue a **writ of mandamus** ordering Madison to give them their commissions. They took their case directly to the Supreme Court under the Judiciary Act of 1789, which gave the Court original jurisdiction in such matters.

The new chief justice was none other than Adams' former secretary of state and arch-Federalist John Marshall, himself one of the "midnight appointments" (he took his seat on the Court barely three weeks before Adams' term ended). Marshall and his Federalist colleagues were in a spot. Threats of impeachment came from Jeffersonians fearful that the Court would vote for Marbury. Moreover, if the Court ordered Madison to deliver the commissions, he was likely to ignore it, thereby risking ridicule for the nation's highest court over a minor issue. Marshall had no means of compelling Madison to act.

The Court could also deny Marbury's claim. Taking that option, however, would concede the issue to the Jeffersonians and give the appearance of retreat in the face of opposition, thereby reducing the power of the Court.

Marshall devised a shrewd solution to the case of ***Marbury v. Madison.*** In February 1803, he delivered the unanimous opinion of the Court. First, Marshall and his colleagues argued that Madison was wrong to withhold Marbury's commission. The Court also found, however, that the Judiciary Act of 1789, under which Marbury had brought suit, contradicted the plain words of the Constitution about the Court's original jurisdiction. Thus, Marshall dismissed Marbury's claim, saying that the Court, according to the Constitution, had no power to require that the commission be delivered.

Conceding a small battle over Marbury's commission (he did not get it), Marshall won a much larger war, asserting for the courts the power to determine what is and what is not constitutional. As Marshall wrote, "An act of the legislature repugnant to the Constitution is void," and "it is emphatically the province of the judicial department to say what the law is." Thus, the chief justice established the power of **judicial review,** the power of the courts to hold acts of Congress, and by implication the executive, in violation of the Constitution.

Marbury v. Madison was part of a skirmish between the Federalists on the Court and the Democratic-controlled Congress. Partly, for example, to rein in the Supreme Court, the Jeffersonian Congress in 1801 abolished the lower federal appeals courts and made the Supreme Court judges return to the unpleasant task of "riding circuit"—serving as lower-court judges around the country. This was a bit of studied harassment of the Court by its enemies.

After *Marbury,* angry members of Congress, together with other Jeffersonians, claimed that Marshall was a "usurper of power," setting himself above Congress and the president. This view, however, was unfair. State courts, before and after the Constitution, had declared acts of their legislatures unconstitutional. In the *Federalist Papers,* Alexander Hamilton had expressly assumed the power of the federal courts to review legislation, and the federal courts had actually done so. *Marbury* was not even the first case of striking down an act of Congress; a lower federal court had done so in 1792, and the Supreme Court itself had approved a law after a constitutional review in 1796. Marshall was neither inventing nor imagining his right to review laws for their constitutionality.

The case also illustrates that the courts must be politically astute in exercising their power over the other branches. By in effect reducing its *own* power—the authority to hear cases such as Marbury's under its original jurisdiction—the Court was able to assert the right of judicial review in a fashion that the other branches could not easily rebuke.

More than any other power of the courts, judicial review has embroiled them in policy controversy. Before the Civil War the Supreme Court, headed by Chief Justice Roger Taney, held the Missouri Compromise unconstitutional because it restricted slavery in the territories. The decision was one of many steps along the road to the Civil War. After the Civil War, the Court was again active, this time using judicial review to strike down dozens of state and federal laws curbing the growing might of business corporations.

The "Nine Old Men." Never was the Court so controversial as during the New Deal. At President Roosevelt's urging, Congress passed dozens of laws designed to end the Depression. The Court, though, was dominated by conservatives—most nominated by Republican presidents—who viewed federal intervention in the economy as unconstitutional and tantamount to socialism.

The Supreme Court began to dismantle New Deal policies one by one. One of the string of anti-Depression measures was the National Recovery Act. Although it was never particularly popular, the Court sealed its doom in *Schechter Poultry Corporation v. United States* (1935), declaring the Act unconstitutional because it regulated purely local business that did not affect interstate commerce.

Incensed, Roosevelt in 1937 proposed what critics called a "court-packing plan." Noting that the average age of the Court was over seventy, Roosevelt railed against those "nine old men." Because Congress can set the number of justices, he proposed that Congress expand the size of the Court, a move that would have allowed him to appoint additional justices sympathetic to the New Deal. Congress objected and never passed the plan. Indeed, it became irrelevant when two justices, Chief Justice Charles Evans Hughes and Associate Justice Owen Roberts, began switching their votes in favor of New Deal legislation. (One wit called it the "switch in time that saved nine.") Shortly thereafter Associate Justice William Van Devanter retired, and Roosevelt got to make the first of his many appointments to the Court.

The Warren Court. Few eras of the Supreme Court have been as active in shaping public policy as that of the Warren Court (1953-1969) presided over by Chief Justice Earl Warren. Scarcely had President Eisenhower appointed Warren when the Court faced the issue of school segregation. In 1954, it held that laws requiring segregation of the public schools were

The Warren Court's controversial decisions on desegregation, criminal defendants' rights, and voting reapportionment led to calls for Chief Justice Earl Warren's impeachment. Critics argued that the unelected justices were making policy decisions that were the responsibility of elected officials. Here, demonstrators protest Court rulings that expanded defendants' rights.

unconstitutional. Later it expanded the rights of criminal defendants, extending the right to counsel and protections against unreasonable search and seizure and self-incrimination (see Chapter 4 and "You Are the Policymaker: The Rule of Law Versus Individual Justice"). It ordered states to reapportion both their legislatures and their congressional districts according to the principle of one person, one vote, and it prohibited organized prayer in public schools. So active was the Warren Court that right-wing groups, fearing that it was remaking the country, posted billboards all over the United States urging Congress to "Impeach Earl Warren." [25]

The Burger Court. Warren's retirement in 1969 gave President Richard Nixon his hoped-for opportunity to appoint a "strict constructionist"—that is, one who interprets the Constitution narrowly—as chief justice. He chose Minnesotan Warren E. Burger, then a conservative judge on the District of Columbia Court of Appeals. As Nixon hoped, the Burger Court turned out to be more conservative than the liberal Warren Court. It narrowed defendants' rights, though it did not overturn the fundamental contours of the *Miranda* decision. The conservative Burger Court, however, also wrote the abortion decision in *Roe v. Wade,* required school busing in certain cases to eliminate historic segregation, and upheld affirmative action programs in the *Weber* case (see Chapter

THE RULE OF LAW VERSUS INDIVIDUAL JUSTICE

You Are the Policymaker

Ernesto Miranda, a 23-year-old eighth grade dropout and ex-convict who had a police record extending back 10 years and a dishonorable discharge from the army, was arrested in Phoenix and identified by two women as the man who robbed one at knifepoint and kidnapped and raped the other. He made a confession in his own handwriting, noting that he was doing so voluntarily and with full knowledge of his legal rights.

At his trial, the police officers who obtained Miranda's confession testified that they had not informed him of his right to counsel and that no counsel was present during the confession. Over the objections of Miranda's lawyer, the judge admitted the confession into evidence, and Miranda was found guilty of kidnapping and rape. In a separate trial, he was found guilty of armed robbery.

Following an unsuccessful appeal to the Arizona Supreme Court, the U.S. Supreme Court agreed to review Miranda's case in 1966. The issue before the justices was whether the confession of a poorly educated, mentally abnormal, indigent defendant who had not been told of his right to counsel, and who had confessed in police custody without a lawyer present to represent him, was admissible as evidence in court.

The dilemma was a difficult one to resolve. There was every reason to believe that Miranda was guilty, and if the Court ruled that his confession was not admissible, it was possible that he might not be convicted in a new trial and would thus go free. Such a result was hard to reconcile with the concept of justice in a criminal trial. On the other hand, there was a question of the rule of law, in which accused persons—any persons—have rights, including that of counsel and against self-incrimination. What should the Court do in such a case?

As you learned in Chapter 4, the Supreme Court decided not to allow Miranda's confession as evidence and specified procedures the police must use when questioning persons accused of crimes. Miranda was retried and convicted once again. He was later killed in a barroom fight. The Supreme Court was criticized severely for its decision, and it became an issue in the 1968 presidential election when Richard Nixon promised to nominate justices who would weigh the trade-offs involved in such cases differently, giving more weight to concerns for punishing the guilty. If you had to choose, what would *you* do?

5). One of the most notable decisions of the Burger Court weighed against Burger's appointer, Richard Nixon. At the height of the Watergate scandal (see Chapter 13), the Supreme Court was called upon to decide whether Nixon had to turn his White House tapes over to the courts. It unanimously ordered him to do so in ***United States v. Nixon*** (1974), thus hastening the president's resignation.

The Rehnquist Court. In the late-1990s, the conservative nominees of Republican presidents, led by Chief Justice William Rehnquist, composed a clear Supreme Court majority. One justice, Harry Blackmun, even took the extraordinary step of speaking out publicly, declaring that the Supreme Court was "moving to the right . . . where it wants to go, by hook or by crook."[26] Needless to say, others saw the trend in the Court's decisions in a more positive light.[27]

However one evaluates the Court's current direction, the Rehnquist Court has not created a revolution in constitutional law. Instead, as discussed in Chapters 4 and 5, it has been slowly chipping away at liberal decisions such as those regarding defendants' rights, abortion, and affirmative action. Although its protection of the First Amendment rights of free speech and free press remains robust, the Court no longer sees itself as the special protector of individual liberties and civil rights for minorities. Instead, it has typically deferred to the will of the majority and the rules of the government. Most professional Supreme Court watchers expect this trend to continue, unless Bill Clinton is able to place several justices of a more liberal bent on the Court.

UNDERSTANDING THE COURTS

Powerful courts are unusual; few nations have them. The power of American judges raises questions about the compatibility of unelected courts with a democracy and about the appropriate role for the judiciary in policymaking.

THE COURTS AND DEMOCRACY

Announcing his retirement in 1981, Justice Potter Stewart made a few remarks to the handful of reporters present. Embedded in his brief statement was this observation: "It seems to me that there's nothing more antithetical to the idea of what a good judge should be than to think it has something to do with representative democracy." He meant that judges should not be subject to the whims of popular majorities. In a nation that insists so strongly that it is democratic, where do the courts fit in?

In some ways, the courts are not a very democratic institution. Federal judges are not elected and are almost impossible to remove. Indeed, their social backgrounds probably make the courts the most elite-dominated policymaking institution. If democracy requires that key policymakers always be elected or be continually responsible to those who are, then the courts diverge sharply from the requirements of democratic government.

As you saw in Chapter 2, the Constitution's framers wanted it that way. Chief Justice Rehnquist, a judicial conservative, put the case as follows: "A mere change in public opinion since the adoption of the Constitution, unaccompanied by a constitutional amendment, should not change the meaning of the Constitution. A merely temporary majoritarian groundswell should not abrogate some individual liberty protected by the Constitution."[28]

The courts are not entirely independent of popular preferences, however. Turn-of-the-century Chicago humorist Finley Peter Dunne had his Irish saloonkeeper character "Mr. Dooley" quip that "th' Supreme Court follows th' iliction returns." Many years later, political scientists have found that the Court is normally in line with popular majorities.[29] Even when the Court seems out of step with other policymakers, it eventually swings around to join the policy consensus, as it did in the New Deal. A study of the period from 1937 to 1980 found that only on the issue of prayers in the public schools was the Court clearly out of line with public opinion.[30]

Despite the fact that the Supreme Court sits in a "marble palace," it is not so insulated from the normal forms of politics as one might think. The two sides in the abortion debate flooded the Court with mail, targeted it with advertisements and protests, and bombarded it with 78 *amicus curiae* briefs in the *Webster v. Reproductive Health Services* case. Members of the Supreme Court are unlikely to cave in to interest group pressures, but they are aware of the public's concern about issues, and this awareness becomes part of their consciousness as they decide cases. Political scientists have found that the Court is more likely to hear cases for which interest groups have filed *amicus curiae* briefs.[31]

Courts can also promote pluralism. When groups go to court, they use litigation to achieve their policy objectives.[32] Both civil rights groups and environmentalists, for example, have blazed a path to show how interest groups can effectively use the courts to achieve their policy goals. The legal wizard of the NAACP's litigation strategy, Thurgood Marshall, not only won most of his cases but also won for himself a seat on the Supreme Court. Almost every major policy decision these days ends up in court. Chances are good that some judge can be found who will rule in an interest group's favor. On the other hand, agencies and businesses commonly find themselves ordered by different courts to do opposite things. The habit of always turning to the courts as a last resort can add to policy delay, deadlock, and inconsistency (see "America in Perspective: Courts and Culture").

WHAT COURTS SHOULD DO: THE SCOPE OF JUDICIAL POWER

The courts, Alexander Hamilton wrote in *The Federalist Papers,* "will be least in capacity to annoy or injure" the people and their liberties.[33] Throughout American history, critics of judicial power have disagreed. They see the courts as too powerful for their own—or the nation's—good. Yesterday's critics focused on John Marshall's "usurpations" of power, on the proslavery decision in *Dred Scott,* or on the efforts of the "nine old men" to kill off Franklin D. Roosevelt's New Deal legislation. Today's critics are never short of arguments to show that courts go too far in making policy.

Courts make policy on both large and small issues. Recently, courts have made policies on major issues involving school busing, abortion, affirmative action, nuclear power, and other key issues. In other cases around the country, courts have

- Ordered the city of Mobile, Alabama, to change its form of government because it was alleged to have discriminated against minorities (the Supreme Court overturned this decision)

COURTS AND CULTURE

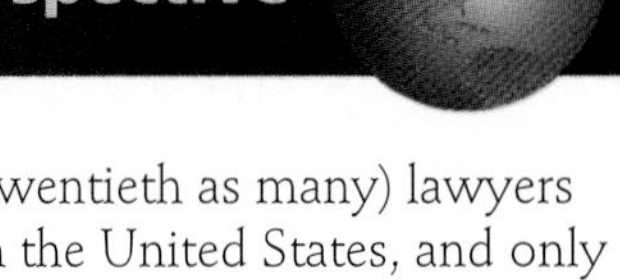

The Japanese and Americans have many things in common. Both live in nations that are modern industrial giants with robust economies and complex societies. The role of the law and the judiciary in the daily life of the people of Japan is quite different from that in the United States, however.

The role of the courts in Japan is influenced by the prevailing attitude toward law and the court system. The Japanese typically find adversary proceedings distasteful and will resort to going to court only when all the preferred traditional forms of informal mediation and negotiation have failed. Most people prefer to settle disputes through a compromise agreement arrived at with the mediation of friends, relatives, or influential persons, rather than engage in litigation in courts.

The Japanese have traditionally preferred amicable and harmonious social relations, relations that would be jeopardized by clear-cut court decisions based on the assertion of individuals' legal rights and on the assignment of moral fault. They prefer to de-emphasize conflict and the existence of disputes and to seek compromise solutions. The Japanese are also less likely to desire others to apply the universalistic standards that characterize the law. Instead, they favor participating in the settlement of disputes, applying their personal criteria for reconciling differences.

This attitude toward litigation is reflected in the small number of practicing lawyers in Japan. There are far fewer (about one-twentieth as many) lawyers per capita in Japan than in the United States, and only about one-fourth as many civil suits per capita come to court in Japan as in the United States.

All is not well in the land of the rising sun, however. Some of the functions performed by American lawyers are handled in Japan by legal specialists and by graduates of law faculties who have knowledge of the law but who are not professionally trained as lawyers. Moreover, the increased tempo of life in modern Japan has brought greater use of courts and legal procedures, especially in commercial matters.

There is also more involved here than just the cultural preferences of potential litigants. The Japanese government has deliberately restricted access to the courts through a formidable system of procedural barriers. In addition, the number of courts and lawyers is purposely kept small to encourage Japanese citizens to resolve their differences in other forums.

SOURCES: Bradley M. Richardson and Scott C. Flanagan, ***Politics in Japan*** (Boston: Little, Brown, 1984), 59-60; Marc Galanter, "Reading the Landscape of Disputes: What We Know and Don't Know (and Think We Know) About Our Allegedly Contentious and Litigious Society," ***UCLA Law Review*** 31 (October 1983): 51-59; and Louis D. Hayes, ***Introduction to Japanese Politics*** (New York: Paragon House, 1992), 66-68.

- Closed some prisons and ordered other states to expand their prison capacities
- Eliminated high school diplomas as a requirement for a fire fighter's job
- Decided that Mexican-American children have a constitutional right to a bilingual education[34]

There are strong disagreements about the appropriateness of allowing the courts to have a policymaking role. Many scholars and judges favor a policy of **judicial restraint,** in which judges adhere closely to precedent and play minimal policymaking roles, leaving policy decisions strictly to the legislatures. These observers stress that the federal courts, composed of unelected judges, are the least democratic branch of government and question the qualifications of judges for making policy decisions and balancing interests. Advocates of judicial restraint believe that decisions such as those on abortion and prayer in public schools go well beyond the "referee" role they feel is appropriate for courts in a democracy.

On the other side are proponents of **judicial activism,** in which judges make bolder policy decisions, even charting new constitutional ground with a particular decision. Advocates of judicial activism emphasize that the courts may alleviate pressing needs—especially needs of those who are politically or economically weak—left unmet by the majoritarian political process.

It is important not to confuse judicial activism or restraint with liberalism or conservatism. In Table 16.6, you can see the varying levels of the Supreme Court's use of judicial review to void laws passed by Congress in different eras. The table shows that in the early years of the New Deal, judicial activists were conservatives. During the tenure of Earl Warren as chief justice (1953-1969), activists made liberal decisions. It is interesting to note that the tenure of the

TABLE 16.6 SUPREME COURT RULINGS IN WHICH FEDERAL STATUTES HAVE BEEN FOUND UNCONSTITUTIONAL

PERIOD	STATUTES VOIDED[a]
1798-1864	2
1864-1910	33 (34)[b]
1910-1930	24
1930-1936	14
1936-1953	3
1953-1969	25
1969-1986	35
1986-present	17
TOTAL	153

[a]In whole or in part.

[b]An 1883 decision in the ***Civil Rights Cases*** consolidated five different cases into one opinion declaring one act of Congress void. In 1895, ***Pollock v. Farmers Loan and Trust Co.*** was heard twice, with the same result both times.

SOURCE: Adapted from Henry J. Abraham, *The Judicial Process,* 6th ed. (New York: Oxford University Press, 1993), 273. Updated by authors.

conservative Chief Justice Warren Burger (1969-1986) and several conservative nominees of Republican presidents marked the most active use of judicial review in the nation's history.

The problem remains of reconciling the American democratic heritage with an active policymaking role for the judiciary. The federal courts have developed a doctrine of **political questions** as a means to avoid deciding some cases, principally those that involve conflicts between the president and Congress. The courts have shown no willingness, for example, to settle disputes regarding the War Powers Resolution (see Chapter 13).

"Call it 'legislating from the bench,' if you will, but on this occasion I should like to repeal the First Amendment."

Similarly, judges typically attempt, whenever possible, to avoid deciding a case on the basis of the Constitution, preferring less contentious "technical" grounds. They also employ issues of jurisdiction, mootness (whether a case presents an issue of contention), standing, ripeness (whether the issues of a case are clear enough and evolved enough to serve as the basis of a decision), and other conditions to avoid adjudication of some politically charged cases. The Supreme Court refused to decide, for example, whether it was legal to carry out the war in Vietnam without an explicit declaration of war from Congress.

Thus, as you saw in the discussion of *Marbury v. Madison,* from the earliest days of the republic, federal judges have been politically astute in their efforts to maintain the legitimacy of the judiciary and to conserve their resources. (Remember, judges are typically recruited from political backgrounds.) They have tried not to take on too many politically controversial issues at one time. They have also been much more likely to find state laws (more than 1,000) than to find federal laws (approximately 150, as shown in Table 16.6) unconstitutional.

Another factor that increases the acceptability of activist courts is the ability to overturn their decisions. First, the president and the Senate determine who sits

Interest groups often use the judicial system to pursue their policy goals, forcing the courts to rule on important social issues. Some Hispanic parents, for example, have successfully sued local school districts to compel them to offer bilingual education.

on the federal bench. Second, Congress, with or without the president's urging, can begin the process of amending the Constitution to overcome a constitutional decision of the Supreme Court. Although this process does not occur rapidly, it is a safety valve. The Eleventh Amendment in 1798 reversed the decision in *Chisolm v. Georgia,* which permitted an individual to sue a state in federal court; the Fourteenth Amendment in 1868 reversed the decision in *Dred Scott v. Sanford,* which held African Americans not to be citizens of the United States; the Sixteenth Amendment in 1913 reversed the decision in *Pollock v. Farmer's Loan and Trust Co.,* which prohibited a federal income tax; and the Twenty-sixth Amendment in 1971 reversed part of *Oregon v. Mitchell,* which voided a congressional act according 18- to 20-year-olds the right to vote in state elections.

Even more drastic options are available as well. In 1801, the Federalists, just before leaving office, created a tier of circuit courts and populated them with Federalist judges; the Jeffersonian Democrats took over the reins of power and promptly abolished the entire level of courts. In 1869, the Radical Republicans in Congress altered the appellate jurisdiction of the Supreme Court to prevent it from hearing a case (*Ex parte McCardle*) that concerned the Reconstruction Acts. This kind of alteration has never recurred, although Congress did threaten to employ the method in the 1950s regarding some matters of civil liberties.

Finally, if the issue is one of **statutory construction,** in which a court interprets an act of Congress, then the legislature routinely passes legislation that clarifies existing laws and, in effect, overturns the courts.[35] In 1984, for example, the Supreme Court ruled in *Grove City College v. Bell* that when an institution receives federal aid, only the program or activity that actually gets the aid, not the entire institution, is covered by four federal civil rights laws. In 1988 Congress passed a law specifying that the entire institution is affected. Thus, the description of the judiciary as the "ultimate

Today's Supreme Court: from the left, Clarence Thomas, Antonin Scalia, Sandra Day O'Connor, Anthony M. Kennedy, David H. Souter, Stephen G. Breyer, John Paul Stevens, Chief Justice William H. Rehnquist, and Ruth Bader Ginsburg.

arbiter of the Constitution" is hyperbolic; all the branches of government help define and shape the Constitution.

SUMMARY

The American judicial system is complex. Sitting at the pinnacle of the judicial system is the Supreme Court, but its importance is often exaggerated. Most judicial policymaking and enforcement of laws take place in the state courts and the lower federal courts.

Throughout American political history, courts have shaped public policy about the economy, liberty, equality, and, most recently, ecology. In the economic arena, until the time of Franklin D. Roosevelt, courts traditionally favored corporations, especially when government tried to regulate them. Since the New Deal, however, the courts have been more tolerant of government regulation of business, shifting much of their policymaking attention to issues of liberty and equality. From *Dred Scott* to *Plessy* to *Brown,* the Supreme Court has moved from a role of reinforcing discriminatory policy toward racial minorities to a role of shaping new policies for protecting civil rights. Most recently, environmental groups have used the courts to achieve their policy goals.

A critical view of the courts claims that they are too powerful for the nation's own good and are rather ineffective policymakers besides. Throughout American history, however, judges have been important agenda-setters in the political system. Many of the most important political questions make their way into the courts at one time or another. The judiciary is an alternative point of access for those seeking to obtain public policy decisions to their liking, especially those who are not advantaged in the majoritarian political process.

Once in court, litigants face judges whose discretion in decision making is typically limited by precedent. Nevertheless, on questions that raise novel issues (as do many of the most important questions that reach the Supreme Court), the law is less firmly established. Here there is more leeway and judges become more purely political players, balancing different interests and linked to the rest of the political system by their own policy preferences and the politics of their selection.

KEY TERMS

standing to sue
class action suits
justiciable disputes
stare decisis
precedent
original intent
original jurisdiction
appellate jurisdiction
district courts
courts of appeal
Supreme Court
senatorial courtesy
solicitor general
***amicus curiae* briefs**
opinion
judicial implementation
writ of mandamus
Marbury v. Madison
United States v. Nixon
judicial review
judicial restraint
judicial activism
political questions
statutory construction

FOR FURTHER READING

Abraham, Henry J. *Justices and Presidents: A Political History of Appointments to the Supreme Court,* 3rd ed. New York: Oxford University Press, 1992. A readable history of the relationships between presidents and the justices they appointed.

Baum, Lawrence. *The Supreme Court,* 5th ed. Washington, DC: Congressional Quarterly Press, 1995. An excellent work on the operations and impact of the Court.

Ely, John Hart. *Democracy and Distrust.* Cambridge, MA: Harvard University Press, 1980. An appraisal of judicial review and an effort to create a balanced justification for the role of the courts in policymaking.

Epstein, Lee, and Joseph F. Kobylka. *The Supreme Court and Legal Change.* Chapel Hill, NC: University of North Carolina Press, 1992. Examines how interest groups propelled issues regarding abortion and the death penalty to the Supreme Court, and how the way they framed their legal arguments affected outcomes on these issues.

Gates, John B., and Charles A. Johnson, eds. *The American Courts: A Critical Assessment.* Washington, DC: Congressional Quarterly Press, 1991. Useful essays covering many aspects of judicial politics.

Horowitz, Donald. *The Courts and Social Policy.* Washington, DC: Brookings Institution, 1977. A critical assessment of the courts' role in social issues.

Howard, J. Woodford, Jr. *Courts of Appeals in the Federal Judicial System.* Princeton, NJ: Princeton University Press, 1981. A leading work on the federal courts of appeal.

Jacob, Herbert. *Law and Politics in the United States,* 2nd ed. Boston: HarperCollins, 1995. An introduction to the American legal system with an emphasis on linkages to the political arena.

Johnson, Charles A., and Bradley C. Canon. *Judicial Policies: Implementation and Impact.* Washington, DC:

Congressional Quarterly Press, 1984. One of the best overviews of judicial policy implementation.

O'Brien, David M. *Storm Center,* 3rd ed. New York: Norton, 1993. An overview of the Supreme Court's role in American politics.

Rowland, C.K., and Robert A. Carp. *Politics and Judgment in Federal District Courts.* Lawrence, KS: University Press of Kansas, 1996. An important work on the operations of the federal district courts.

Woodward, Bob, and Scott Armstrong. *The Brethren.* New York: Simon & Schuster, 1979. A gossipy "insider's" portrayal of the Supreme Court.

INTERNET RESOURCES

http://supct.law.cornell.edu/supct/index.html
Decisions of the Supreme Court, background, schedule, and rules of the Court, and background of the justices serving on the Court.

http://oyez.at.nwu.edu/oyez/html
Hear oral arguments before the Supreme Court.

http://www.courttv.com/cases/
Decide actual cases before the courts, then compare your decisions to those of the judges.

http://www.uscourts.gov/
Explains the organization, operation, and administration of federal courts.

http://www.nara.gov/education/teaching/conissues/separat.html
FDR's court packing plan.

NOTES

1. Quoted in Lawrence C. Baum, *The Supreme Court,* 4th ed. (Washington, DC: Congressional Quarterly Press, 1992), 72.

2. Quoted in J. Woodford Howard, Jr., *Courts of Appeals in the Federal Judicial System: A Study of the Second, Fifth, and District of Columbia Circuits* (Princeton, NJ: Princeton University Press, 1981), 101.

3. See Gary King, "Presidential Appointments to the Supreme Court: Adding Systematic Explanation to Probabilistic Description," *American Politics Quarterly* 15 (July 1987): 373-386.

4. Quoted in Nina Totenberg, "Will Judges Be Chosen Rationally?" *Judicature* 60 (August/September 1976): 93.

5. See John Schmidhauser, *Judges and Justices: The Federal Appellate Judiciary* (Boston: Little, Brown, 1978).

6. One study found, however, that judicial experience is not related to the congruence of presidential preferences and the justices' decisions on racial equality cases. See John Gates and Jeffrey Cohen, "Presidents, Supreme Court Justices, and Racial Equality Cases: 1954-1984," *Political Behavior* 10 (No. 1, 1988): 22-35.

7. On the importance of ideology and partisanship considerations in judicial retirement and resignation decisions, see Deborah J. Barrow and Gary Zuk, "An Institutional Analysis of Turnover in the Lower Federal Courts, 1900-1987," *Journal of Politics* 52 (May 1990): 457-476.

8. Quoted in Henry J. Abraham, *Justices and Presidents: A Political History of Appointments to the Supreme Court,* 3rd ed. (New York: Oxford University Press, 1992), 266.

9. *Ibid.,* 70.

10. See, for example, the important role that African-American support played in the confirmation of Clarence Thomas even though he was likely to vote against the wishes of leading civil rights organizations. L. Marvin Overby, Beth M. Henschen, Julie Walsh, and Michael H. Strauss, "Courting Constituents: An Analysis of the Senate Confirmation Vote on Justice Clarence Thomas," *American Political Science Review* 86 (December 1992): 997-1003.

11. On the impact of the background of members of the judiciary, see Robert A. Carp and C. K. Rowland, *Policymaking and Politics in the Federal District Courts* (Knoxville, TN: University of Tennessee Press, 1983); Thomas G. Walker and Deborah J. Barrow, "The Diversification of the Federal Bench: Policy and Process Ramifications," *Journal of Politics* 47 (May 1985): 596-617; and C. Neal Tate, "Personal Attribute Models of the Voting Behavior of United States Supreme Court Justices: Liberalism in Civil Liberties and Economics Decisions, 1946-1978," *American Political Science Review* 75 (June 1981): 355-367.

12. Quoted in Nina Totenberg, "Behind the Marble, Beneath the Robes," *New York Times Magazine,* March 16, 1975, 37.

13. H. W. Perry, Jr., *Deciding to Decide: Agenda Setting in the United States Supreme Court* (Cambridge, MA: Harvard University Press, 1991); Doris Marie Provine, *Case Selection in the United States Supreme Court* (Chicago: University of Chicago Press, 1980); and Stuart H. Teger and Douglas Kosinski, "The Cue Theory of Supreme Court Certiorari Jurisdiction: A Reconsideration," *Journal of Politics* 42 (August 1980): 834-846.

14. Sidney Ulmer, "The Supreme Court's Certiorari Decisions: Conflict as a Predictive Variable," *American Political Science Review* (December 1984): 901-911.

15. See Rebecca Mae Salokar, *The Solicitor General* (Philadelphia: Temple University Press, 1992).

16. Each year, data on Supreme Court decisions can be found in the November issue of the *Harvard Law Review.*

17. A useful look at attorneys practicing before the Supreme Court is Kevin McGuire, *The Supreme Court Bar: Legal Elites in the Washington Community* (Charlottesville, VA: University Press of Virginia, 1993).

18. See, for example, Forrest Maltzman and Paul J. Wahlbeck, "Strategic Policy Considerations and Voting Fluidity on the Burger Court," *American Political Science Review* 90 (September 1996): 581-592.

19. A. P. Blaustein and A. H. Field, "Overruling Opinions in the Supreme Court," *Michigan Law Review* 57, no. 2 (1957): 151.

20. See, for example, David W. Rohde and Harold J. Spaeth, *Supreme Court Decision Making* (San Francisco: W.H. Freeman, 1976); Jeffrey A. Segal and Albert O. Cover, "Ideological Values and the Votes of U.S. Supreme Court Justices," *American Political Science Review* 83 (June 1989): 557-566; Tracey E. George and Lee Epstein, "On the Nature of Supreme Court Decision Making," *American Political Science Review* 86 (June 1992): 323-337; and Jeffrey A. Segal and Harold J. Spaeth, "The Influence of *Stare Decisis* on the Votes of United States Supreme Court Justices," *American Journal of Political Science* 40 (November 1996): 971-1003.

21. Doris Graber, *Mass Media and American Politics,* 4th ed. (Washington, DC: Congressional Quarterly Press, 1993), 329.

22. Charles A. Johnson and Bradley C. Canon, *Judicial Policies: Implementation and Impact* (Washington, DC: Congressional Quarterly Press, 1984), chap. 1. See also James F. Spriggs II, "The Supreme Court and Federal Administrative Agencies: A Resource-Based Theory and Analysis of Judicial Impact," *American Journal of Political Science* 40 (November 1996): 1122-1151.

23. See Richard L. Pacelle, Jr., and Lawrence Baum, "Supreme Court Authority in the Judiciary," *American Politics Quarterly* 20 (April 1992): 169-191; and Donald R. Songer, Jeffrey A. Segal, and Charles M. Cameron, "The Hierarchy of Justice: Testing a Principal-Agent Model of Supreme Court-Circuit Court Interactions," *American Journal of Political Science* 38 (August 1994): 673-696.

24. However, see Gerald N. Rosenberg, *The Hollow Hope: Can Courts Bring About Social Change?* (Chicago: University of Chicago Press, 1991), who questions that the courts have brought about much social change.

25. For an excellent overview of the Warren period by former Watergate special prosecutor and Harvard law professor Archibald Cox, see *The Warren Court* (Cambridge, MA: Harvard University Press, 1968).

26. *Washington Post Weekly Review,* October 1, 1984, 33.

27. On the Rehnquist Court, see David G. Savage, *Turning Right: The Making of the Rehnquist Supreme Court* (New York: Wiley, 1992).

28. William Rehnquist, "The Notion of a Living Constitution," in *Views from the Bench,* ed. Mark W. Cannon and David M. O'Brien (Chatham, NJ: Chatham House, 1985), 129.

29. Richard Funston, "The Supreme Court and Critical Elections," *American Political Science Review* 69 (1975): 810; John B. Gates, *The Supreme Court and Partisan Realignment* (Boulder, CO: Westview, 1992); Thomas R. Marshall, "Public Opinion, Representation, and the Modern Supreme Court," *American Politics Quarterly* 16 (July 1988): 296-316; William Mishler and Reginald S. Sheehan, "The Supreme Court as a Countermajoritarian Institution? The Impact of Public Opinion on Supreme Court Decisions," *American Political Science Review* 87 (March 1993): 87-101; William Mishler and Reginald S. Sheehan, "Public Opinion, the Attitudinal Model, and Supreme Court Decision Making: A Micro-Analytic Perspective," *Journal of Politics* 58 (February 1996): 169-200; and Roy B. Flemming and B. Dan Wood, "The Public and the Supreme Court: Individual Justice Responsiveness to American Policy Moods," *American Journal of Political Science* 41 (April 1997): 468-498.

30. David G. Barnum, "The Supreme Court and Public Opinion: Judicial Decision Making in the Post-New Deal Period," *Journal of Politics* 47 (May 1985): 652-662.

31. Gregory A. Caldeira and John R. Wright, "Organized Interests and Agenda Setting in the U.S. Supreme Court," *American Political Science Review* 82 (December 1988): 1109-1128.

32. On group use of the litigation process, see Karen Orren, "Standing to Sue: Interest Group Conflict in the Federal Courts," *American Political Science Review* 70 (September 1976): 723-742; Karen O'Connor and Lee Epstein, "The Rise of Conservative Interest Group Litigation," *Journal of Politics* 45 (May 1983): 479-489; and Lee Epstein and C. K. Rowland, "Debunking the Myth of Interest Group Invincibility in the Courts," *American Political Science Review* 85 (March 1991): 205-217.

33. "Federalist No. 78" in Hamilton, Madison, and Jay, *The Federalist Papers.*

34. These and other examples of judicial activism are reported in a critical assessment of judicial intervention by Donald Horowitz, *The Courts and Social Policy* (Washington, DC. Brookings Institution, 1977).

35. William N. Eskridge, "Overriding Supreme Court Statutory Interpretation Decisions," *Yale Law Journal* 101 (1991): 331-455; and Joseph Ignagni and James Meernik, "Explaining Congressional Attempts to Reverse Supreme Court Decisions," *Political Research Quarterly* 10 (June 1994): 353-372. See also R. Chep Melnick, *Between the Lines: Interpreting Welfare Rights* (Washington, DC: Brookings Institution, 1994).

PART FOUR

Policies

Politics is who gets what, when, and how.

— *HAROLD LASSWELL, POLITICAL SCIENTIST*

17

Economic Policymaking

- Government and the Economy
- Government's Instruments for Controlling the Economy
- Obstacles to Controlling the Economy
- Arenas of Economic Policymaking
- Understanding Economic Policymaking

Shortly after the 1996 election, a commission of economists appointed by the Senate Finance Committee issued a much anticipated report concerning the accuracy of the government's techniques for measuring inflation. Led by former Bush economic advisor Michael Boskin, they concluded that the government had been overestimating inflation by approximately 1.1 percent in recent years, costing it billions of dollars in inflated payments to Social Security recipients, retired government employees, and military veterans.

Boskin's commission pointed to three technical problems with the current methods of estimating inflation. First, the current methods do not take into account quality improvements in products—such as computers and VCRs—that give consumers more value for their money. Second, the government fails to account for the ability of consumers to substitute one buying choice for another when the price of a particular item rises. (Thus, the cost of living may not go up if beef, say, becomes more expensive, because many people will just eat more chicken.) Third, people also react to rising prices by buying more goods at discount stores. Currently, the government assumes that the difference in price charged by retail and discount stores is equivalent to the value of the extra service given to retail store customers. The Boskin Commission argued against this view.

Although these points may seem like minor technicalities, they could add up to big money if they were put into practice. The estimates are that these adjustments could save the federal government about $500 billion over the next decade. Such savings would go a long way toward the elusive goal of balancing the budget. Yet, despite the obvious benefits offered by the commission's recommendations, politicians on both sides of the aisle approached them with the utmost of caution. In economic policymaking, even a slight policy change can invoke the wrath of powerful interests that fear ending up worse off. Hence, with so much money on the line, no one in political life wanted to stick his or her neck out too soon for fear of the reaction from these groups.

In America's democratic system, economic policymaking involves far more than just implementing the best technical advice that economists can offer. Policymakers certainly want to take into account the best principles of economics, but they also must be concerned with the probable impact of their decisions on who gets what. In the case of the Boskin Commission's report, implementing the recommendations clearly would bring changes that would adversely impact many people—in terms of both reduced benefits and higher taxes.

The most visible group that would lose out is the 45 million Social Security recipients. If the principles laid out by the Boskin commission report had been in effect over the past dozen years, the typical Social Security beneficiary would now be receiving over $1000 less annually than currently is the case. It therefore should come as no surprise that the American Association of Retired Persons immediately started to mobilize against any change in the way inflation is measured.

The scope of the government's policy on how to measure inflation, however, extends well beyond the public sector. Many regular financial transactions in the private sector depend on the government's annual estimate of inflation in order to make yearly cost-of-living adjustments. For example, many divorce agreements include escalator clauses for child support. Labor union contracts sometimes include cost-of-living raises pegged to changes in the government's estimate of inflation. In areas with rent control, localities often use the government's measurement of inflation to calculate the maximum allowable rent increases.

And finally, the widest impact of the Boskin Commission's recommendations would be felt through the tax system. Taxes are adjusted in a variety of ways to protect taxpayers from the effects of inflation. A lower inflation rate would mean almost everyone would pay more taxes than they would have paid if no change had been made.

In sum, although the Boskin Commission might present its proposals as technical matters for economists to decide, the reality is that they could have far-reaching consequences for almost everyone. Proposals such as these are the heart of economic policymaking. As you will see, even in America's free-enterprise economy, the government has some limited tools to affect economic behavior, and hence who gets what. How government goes about this important task is the subject of this chapter.

Americans are accustomed to seeing politics and economics as two quite different subjects. Robert Reich, the Clinton administration's first secretary of labor, has written that

> Americans tend to divide the dimensions of our national life into two broad realms. The first is the realm of government and politics. The second is the realm of business and economics.... The choice is falsely posed. In advanced industrial nations like the United States, drawing such sharp distinctions between government and the market has ceased to be useful.[1]

The view that politics and economics are closely linked is neither new nor unique. Indeed, both James

Madison, the architect of the Constitution, and Karl Marx, the founder of communist theory, argued that economic conflict was at the root of politics. This chapter asserts that politics and economics are powerful, intertwined forces shaping public policies—and public lives.

GOVERNMENT AND THE ECONOMY

Economic problems create social problems. Thus, the most sensitive part of a voter's anatomy is the pocketbook. When the economy goes sour, the cry of "throw the rascals out" reverberates throughout the country; too much unemployment or inflation can increase unemployment among politicians. One major reason why George Bush failed to keep his job in 1992 was that so many Americans had lost theirs (see Figure 17.1).

Measuring how many and what types of workers are unemployed is one of the major jobs of the Bureau of Labor Statistics (BLS) in the Department of Labor. To carry out this task, the BLS conducts a random survey of the population every month. Unlike most of the surveys discussed in this book, the sample size is not a mere one or two thousand, but rather a massive 50,000 households. Therefore, policymakers can be assured that any change of over one-tenth of 1 percent is more than could possibly be attributed to sampling error. No one questions using a survey to determine the **unemployment rate,** but recently the survey questions were redesigned to correct what many felt was a bias in how women who were not currently working outside the home were interviewed. In the traditional BLS survey, interviewers were able to assume that

FIGURE 17.1 UNEMPLOYMENT: JOBLESSNESS IN AMERICA, 1960-1996

The United States has always experienced some joblessness. Each 1 percent in the unemployment rate represents more than a million people out of work. Unemployment falls especially heavily upon minorities, who typically suffer unemployment rates two or three times higher than whites. Unemployment, like any other measure of a policy problem, is partly a matter of definition. The unemployment rate would be higher if it included what the Bureau of Labor Statistics calls "discouraged workers," people who have become so frustrated that they have stopped actively seeking employment. On the other hand, if the unemployment rate included only those who were unemployed long enough to cause them severe hardship, the number would be much lower, because most people are out of work only a short time.

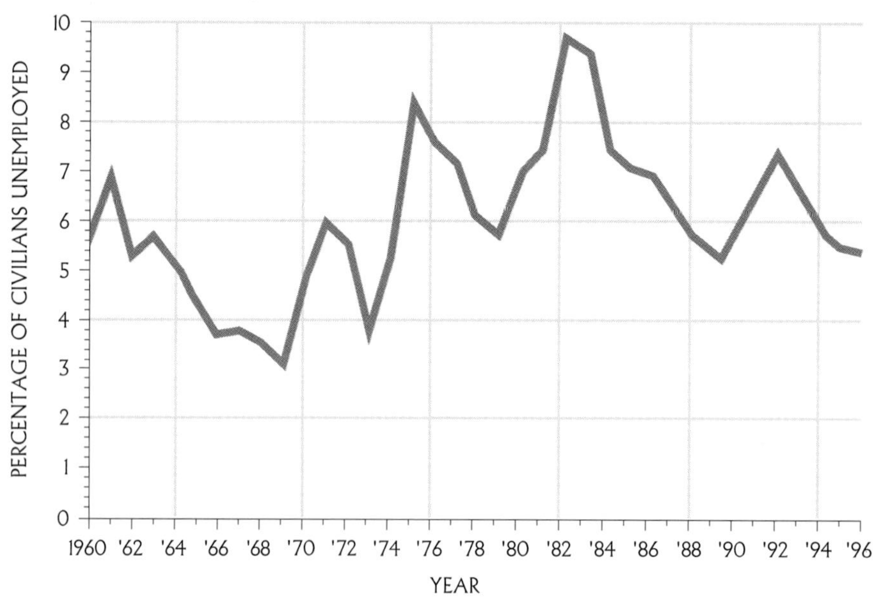

SOURCE: *Economic Report of the President, 1997* (Washington, DC: U.S. Government Printing Office, 1997).

women who were at home were out of the work force, when in fact some had recently been laid off. Under the new method of interviewing, which began in late 1993, respondents are asked a series of specific yes-or-no questions to determine whether they are working or looking for work.[2]

The effects of unemployment are clear. One careful analysis found that a 1 percent increase in the unemployment rate was associated with

- A 4.1 percent increase in the suicide rate
- A 3.4 percent increase in admissions to state mental hospitals
- A 5.7 percent increase in the homicide rate
- A 1.9 percent increase in deaths from cirrhosis of the liver (usually associated with alcoholism)[3]

Of course, unemployment's effects are probably more subtle than statistical analyses suggest. It is unlikely that people who lose their jobs suddenly become suicidal or alcoholics. It is likely, however, that adverse economic conditions are significantly associated with complex social problems.

The problem of inflation is the other half of policymakers' regular economic concern. For decades the government has also kept tabs on inflation via the **consumer price index (CPI),** which measures the change in the cost of buying a fixed basket of good and services. On a regular basis, the prices of 95,000 items from 22,000 stores are surveyed, as well as the cost of 35,000 rental units. As discussed at the beginning of this chapter, many economists and politicians believe that methods for calculating the CPI need to be revised in order to avoid overestimating inflation.

Unlike unemployment, inflation hurts some but actually benefits others. Some groups are especially hard hit, such as those who live on fixed incomes: Their rent and grocery costs go up, but their income does not. In contrast, people whose salary increases are tied to the CPI but whose mortgage payments are fixed may find that inflation actually increases their buying power. As David Piachaud puts it, "Inflation acts neither as Robin Hood nor as Robber Baron: Neither the poor nor the rich are affected in a uniform way."[4] In any case, few people welcome the economic uncertainty generated by high inflation (see Figure 17.2).

ELECTIONS AND THE ECONOMY

People who are unemployed, worried about the prospect of being unemployed, or struggling with runaway inflation have an outlet to express some of their dissatisfaction—the polling booth. Ample evidence indicates that voters pay attention to economic trends in making up their minds on election day, taking into consideration not just their own financial situation but the economic condition of the nation as well. In a careful analysis of two decades of election study data, Roderick Kiewiet finds that voters who experience unemployment in their family are more likely to support Democratic candidates.[5] And it is not only a voter's personal experience with unemployment that benefits the Democrats; employed voters who feel that joblessness is a serious national problem lean strongly to the Democratic Party. Concern over inflation, on the other hand, has had less impact on voter choices, according to Kiewiet. Perceptions of Nixon's forceful handling of the problem did help him win reelection in 1972, whereas spiraling inflation in 1980 certainly contributed to Carter's defeat. These cases, however, are exceptions to the general rule that most of the time people are not sufficiently affected by inflation for it to influence their vote.

POLITICAL PARTIES AND THE ECONOMY

Because voters are sensitive to economic conditions, the parties must pay close attention to those conditions when selecting their policies. Some years ago, Nobel laureate Paul Samuelson articulated a common belief about the two parties in the United States. "We tend to get our recessions during Republican administrations," he remarked. "The Democrats," he continued, "are willing to run with some inflation; the Republicans are not."[6] This observation leads to an interesting hypothesis about party behavior: Republicans are willing to risk higher unemployment and recession, whereas Democrats are willing to tolerate high inflation. Douglas Hibbs investigated this hypothesis as part of his influential analysis of economic policy in 20 advanced industrialized democracies. His general conclusion was that economic policies "pursued by left-wing and right-wing governments are broadly in accordance with the objective economic interests and subjective preferences of their class-defined core political constituencies."[7]

Parties thus behave very much the way voters expect them to. In the United States, the Democratic coalition is made up heavily of groups who worry the most about unemployment—union members, minorities, and the poor. This characteristic gives the Democratic Party a special incentive to pursue policies designed to lower unemployment. On the other hand, the Republican coalition rests more heavily on a base of people who are most concerned about steady prices for their goods and services—business owners, managers, and professional people. Therefore, Republican administrations have taken stronger action to keep

FIGURE 17.2

INFLATION: INCREASES IN THE COST OF LIVING, 1960-1996

Inflation was low in the 1960s, but it began to roar in the 1970s, partly as a consequence of the huge increases in energy prices resulting from the Arab oil embargo that began in 1973. Between 1967 and the end of 1978, the cost of living doubled. Throughout the late 1970s, the cost of medical care, housing, energy, and almost everything else soared. Prices were escalating so fast that the average family's real income (its income after the effects of inflation had been discounted) was actually decreasing. Inflation has cooled, however, since the recession of 1982, permitting real wages to catch up to their former levels.

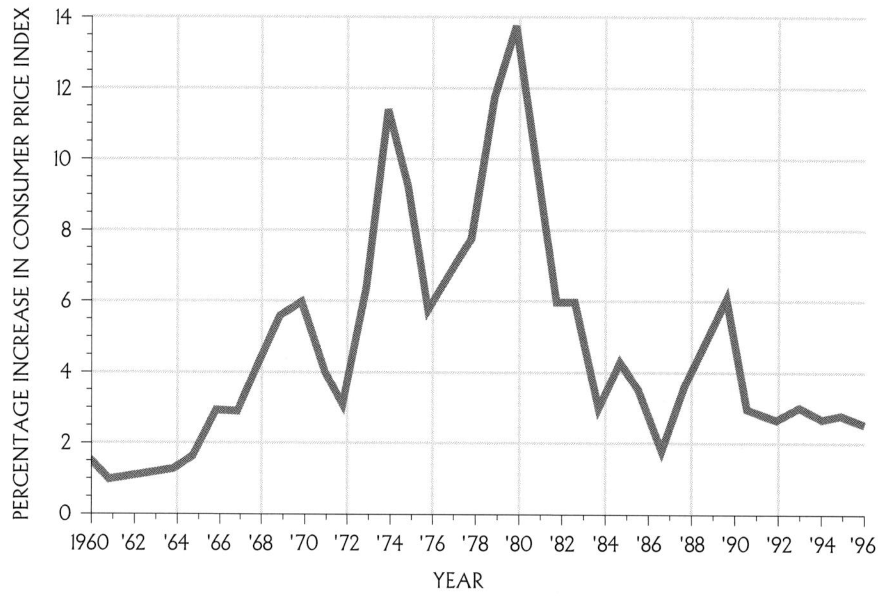

SOURCE: *Economic Report of the President,* 1997 (Washington, DC: U.S. Government Printing Office, 1997).

inflation down, even at the risk of greater unemployment. George Bush could indeed point to a low inflation rate of just 2.9 percent in 1992, but Bill Clinton was able to criticize the Bush economic record by pointing to the rise in unemployment to 7.4 percent.

Politicians and parties exert enormous effort to control the economy. The impact of government on the economic system is substantial, but it is also sharply limited by a basic commitment to a free-enterprise system. Before we examine the obstacles American government faces in guiding the economy, the following sections will introduce the economic tools it does possess.

GOVERNMENT'S INSTRUMENTS FOR CONTROLLING THE ECONOMY

The time when government could ignore economic problems, confidently asserting that the private marketplace could handle them, has long passed, if it ever really existed. Especially since the Great Depression and the New Deal, government has been actively involved in steering the economy. When the stock market crash of 1929 sent unemployment soaring, President Herbert Hoover clung to the **laissez-faire** principle that government should not meddle with the economy. In the next presidential election, Hoover was handed a crushing defeat by Franklin D. Roosevelt, whose New Deal experimented with dozens of new federal policies to put the economy back on track.

Since the New Deal, policymakers have regularly sought to control the economy. The American political economy offers two important tools to guide the economy: monetary policy and fiscal policy.

MONETARY POLICY AND THE FED

One way the government can influence the overall operation of the economy is through **monetary policy**—that is, manipulation of the supply of money

Unemployment is one of the most important problems with which economic policymakers must deal. An unemployment rate of 7 percent may not seem so bad, but to the person who is without a job, it seems more like 100 percent. Politicians are particularly attuned to the problem of unemployment, for when too many voters are concerned about losing their jobs, elected officials tend to lose theirs.

and credit in private hands. An economic theory called **monetarism** holds that the supply of money is the key to the nation's economic health. Monetarists believe that having too much cash and credit in circulation generates inflation. Essentially, they advise holding the growth in money supply to the rise in the real (in other words, after inflation) gross domestic product. Politicians worry constantly about the money supply because it affects the rate of interest their constituents have to pay for home loans, new cars, starting up new businesses, and so on.

The main agency for making monetary policy is "the Fed," whose formal title is the Board of Governors of the **Federal Reserve System.** Created by Congress in 1913 to regulate the lending practices of banks and thus the money supply, the Federal Reserve System is intended to be formally beyond the control of the president and Congress. Its seven-member Board of Governors—appointed by the president and confirmed by the Senate—is expected to do its job without regard to partisan politics. Accordingly, members of the Fed are given 14-year terms designed to insulate them from political pressures.

The Fed has three basic instruments for controlling the money supply. First, the Fed sets discount rates for the money that banks borrow from the Federal Reserve banks. If the Fed raises this rate, banks will have to pass their increased costs along to the customers. Thus, fewer people will want to take out loans, and less money will be in circulation. Second, the Fed sets reserve requirements that determine the amount of money that banks must keep in reserve at all times. When the Fed increases this requirement, banks have less money to lend out and therefore charge their customers more for it. And third, the Fed can exercise control over the money supply by buying and selling government securities in the market, thereby either expanding or contracting the money supply. Whereas raising the costs of borrowing money increases the risk of unemployment and recession, making more money available to borrow increases the risk of inflation.

In sum, the amount of money available, interest rates, inflation, and the availability of jobs are all affected either directly or indirectly by the complicated financial dealings of the Fed. The Fed can profoundly influence the state of the economy; it is no wonder that it attracts the attention of politicians. When the Fed, under the leadership of Paul Volker, decided to tighten the money supply in late 1979 in order to control inflation, interest rates soared. President Carter, already suffering from what he termed "a crisis of confidence," saw his popularity rating fall to nearly the same level as the prime interest rate (about 20 percent). The resulting deep recession helped Reagan win office in 1980 but also made the early years of his presidency difficult until the economic recovery took hold in 1983.

With so much riding on its decisions, presidents quite naturally try to persuade the Fed to pursue policies in line with presidential plans for the country. In 1995, for example, White House aides pressed Fed chairman Alan Greenspan to keep interest rates low, lest he not be reappointed by President Clinton. Greenspan did indeed lead the Fed to hold the line on interest rates, thus adding more evidence to the general finding that the Fed is responsive to the White House, though not usually to the extent of trying to influence election outcomes.[8] Nevertheless, even the chief executive can be left frustrated by the politically insulated decisions of the Fed. Some have called for more openness in its decision-making process, whereas others have proposed more direct political control of the Fed through shorter terms for its Board of Governors.

Alan Greenspan, chair of the Federal Reserve Board, prepares to brief the Senate Banking Committee. The Fed controls the supply of money to individuals and businesses, thus wielding enormous influence over interest rates, inflation, and unemployment—an influence that draws the close attention of Congress and the president.

John Maynard Keynes' influential economic theories encouraged the use of government spending to stimulate the economy during down periods.

FISCAL POLICY: KEYNESIAN VERSUS SUPPLY-SIDE ECONOMICS

How much the government runs in the red (being in the black hardly seems plausible these days) is another factor in determining the nation's economic health. **Fiscal policy** describes the impact of the federal budget—taxing, spending, and borrowing—on the economy. Unlike monetary policy, fiscal policy is shaped mostly by the Congress and the president. The use of fiscal policy to stimulate the economy is most often associated with advocates of big intrusive government.

On the side of an activist government with a large scope is **Keynesian economic theory,** named after English economist John Maynard Keynes. Soon after the 1936 publication of his landmark book *The General Theory of Employment, Interest, and Money,* Keynesianism became the dominant economic philosophy in America. This theory emphasized that government spending could help the economy weather its normal ups and downs, even if it meant running in the red. Keynes argued that government could spend its way out of the Depression by stimulating the economy through an infusion of money from government programs. If businesses were not able to expand, it would be up to the government to pick up the slack, he claimed. If there were no jobs available for people, the government should create some—building roads, dams, houses, or whatever seemed most appropriate. The key would be to get money back in the consumers' pockets, for if only a few have money to buy goods, then little will be produced. Thus, the government's job would be to increase the demand when necessary; the supply would take care of itself.

So dominant was Keynesian thinking in government policymaking that Democrats and Republicans alike adhered to its basic tenets—that is, until the Reagan administration. Reagan's economic gurus proposed a radically different theory based on the premise that the key task for government economic policy is to stimulate the supply of goods, not their demand.[9] Thus, this theory has been labeled **supply-side economics.** To supply-siders, big government soaked up too much of the gross domestic product; by taxing too heavily, spending too freely, and regulating too tightly, government curtailed economic growth. Supply-side economists argued that incentives to invest, work harder, and save could be increased by cutting back on the scope of government, especially tax rates. Economist Arthur Laffer proposed (legend says he did so on the back of a cocktail napkin) a curve suggesting that the more government taxed, the less people worked, and thus the smaller the government's tax revenues. Cut the taxes, Laffer reasoned, and people would work harder and thereby stimulate the economy by producing a greater supply of goods. In its most extreme form, this theory held that by taking a smaller percentage of people's income, the government would actually get more total revenue as production increased.

Faced with the worst economic downturn since the Depression of the 1930s, Reagan and the supply-siders believed that cutting taxes would pull business out of its doldrums. During his first administration, Reagan fought for and won massive tax cuts, from which the wealthiest Americans profited the most. One cannot emphasize enough how this approach differed from the established Keynesian model. Rather than public works programs to stimulate demand, Americans got tax cuts to stimulate supply; rather than a fiscal policy that promoted bigger government, Americans got a policy that tried, but ultimately failed, to reduce the scope of government. Whichever fiscal approach politicians favor, one formerly controversial issue is now agreed upon: It is the government's responsibility to use fiscal policy to try to control the economy. But like controlling the weather, this is much easier said than done.

OBSTACLES TO CONTROLLING THE ECONOMY

Some scholars argue that politicians manipulate the economy for short-run advantage to win elections. Edward Tufte writes, "When you think economics, think elections; when you think elections, think economics."[10] Tufte concluded that real disposable income (after taxes and inflation) tended to increase more at election time than at other times. In addition, transfer payments, such as Social Security and veterans' benefits, seemed more likely to increase just prior to an election.

A neat trick if you can do it, this ability of politicians to control economic conditions precisely in order to facilitate their reelection. There are some missing links in the argument, however. For starters, most of the evidence is circumstantial; no one has shown that decisions to influence the economy at election time have been made on a regular basis.

Controlling unemployment and inflation with precision is like stopping on an economic dime. All the instruments for controlling the economy have one aspect in common: They are difficult to use. To begin with, even economists do not understand the workings of the economy well enough to understand always why the economy fluctuates as it does. For example, the best economic minds in the country have been unable to explain why economic growth since 1973 has been so anemic compared to growth in previous eras (see "Since Kennedy: Theories on the Economic Slowdown").

Politicians sometimes proclaim that they have the solution to bringing economic prosperity. But even when such optimists have the ability to implement their programs, most policies must be decided upon a year or more before they will have their full impact on the economy. The president's budget, for example, is prepared many months in advance of its enactment into law. In addition, benefits such as Social Security are now indexed—that is, they go up automatically as the cost of living increases. Thus, it is hard to know what the economy will be like when the government's money is actually spent.

The American capitalist system imposes an additional restraint on controlling the economy. Because the private sector is much larger than the public sector, it dominates the economy. An increase in the price of raw materials or in the wages of union workers can offset a host of government efforts to control inflation. Also, in our increasingly interdependent world, the activities of other nations can throw a monkey wrench in the government's economic plans. Such a jolt

SINCE KENNEDY

Theories on the Economic Slowdown

The Kennedy years were a time of great economic optimism, and with good reason. During the period from 1946 to 1973, the average annual growth rate for the nation's economy was 2.8 percent—enough to double living standards in about a generation. Thus, when John Kennedy talked about "getting the country moving again" he was alluding to the temporary slowdown in the late 1950s. In contrast, when politicians today talk about reinvigorating the economy, they are often referring to the decades-long recent period of weak economic growth. Since 1973, the nation's productivity has risen about 1 percent a year on average. At this rate, it will take about 80 years to double the country's standard of living.

The search for the explanation of the productivity slowdown since 1973 is the preeminent question for scholars of the American economy. Unfortunately, there is nothing approaching a consensus. In his recent book on economics and policymaking, Paul Krugman outlines three major theories regarding the poor performance of the economy over the past two decades. He classifies these theories as technological, social, and political.

The technological explanation asserts that innovations in manufacturing, such as the assembly line, drove the post-World War II boom but that by the early 1970s, these technologies had been fully developed. This theory holds that recent inventions, such as the personal computer, will have to make major contributions toward increasing productivity in order to get the economy growing at a fast pace again.

The sociological explanation focuses on the tremendous changes in American society beginning in the 1960s. The nuclear family grew less common as divorce became more widely accepted and practiced. In addition, the rise of single mothers among minority populations led to a growing underclass that could make little contribution to economic growth. Among all groups, educational standards fell, as evidenced by the long-term decline in SAT scores. Thus, the sociological approach holds that a return to family values and a focus on better education will be required to restore the economy back to its pre-1973 pace.

Finally, the political explanation blames the government for getting in the way of worker productivity. It is no coincidence, according to this theory, that the economic slowdown occurred shortly after the number of government regulations on business started to skyrocket. It is widely accepted, for example, that regulations to control pollution reduced the productivity of some businesses, though analysts disagree on how much of an effect they have had. Besides regulations, increased taxes to pay for the Great Society programs siphoned off money needed to stimulate new business investments, according to this line of thinking. Therefore, proponents of this political theory believe that the answer to the productivity slowdown is to get the government off people's backs.

These three theories are not mutually exclusive. Perhaps each of them explains part of why the American economy has been moving in slow motion since 1973. In any case, it seems unlikely that we will really know what is responsible for this period of weak economic growth as long as we remain mired in it.

Source: Paul Krugman, *Peddling Prosperity: Economic Sense and Nonsense in the Age of Diminished Expectations.* New York: Norton, 1994, chap. 2.

occurred twice in the 1970s when OPEC oil price increases sent inflationary shock waves throughout the American economy.

Fiscal policy is also hindered by the budgetary process. As you saw in Chapter 14, most of the budget expenditures for any year are "uncontrollable." Given that most spending is already mandated by law, it is very difficult to make substantial cuts. Coordinating economic policymaking is equally difficult. The president and Congress both have central roles, but they may not see eye to eye on taxes or spending, and neither may agree with the independent-minded Fed on the money supply. Like the rest of policymaking in the United States, the power to make economic policy is decentralized.

ARENAS OF ECONOMIC POLICYMAKING

When the government spends one-third of America's gross domestic product and regulates much of the other two-thirds, its policies will surely provoke

Many factors limit the American government's ability to control the economy. The 1973 OPEC oil embargo (in response to America's support of Israel in the Yom Kippur War) and the 1979 Iranian revolution led to increased oil prices, gas lines, inflation, and economic recession.

much debate. Liberals tend to favor active government involvement in the economy in order to smooth out the unavoidable inequality of a capitalist system. Conservatives maintain that the most productive economy is one in which the government exercises a hands-off policy of minimal regulation.

Liberal or conservative, most interest groups seek benefits, protection from unemployment, or safeguards against harmful business practices. Business, consumers, and labor are three of the major actors in, and objects of, government economic policy. The following sections examine the role of each in economic policymaking.

BUSINESS AND PUBLIC POLICY: SUBSIDIES AMID REGULATIONS

The corporation has long stood at the center of the American economy. Every year, *Fortune* magazine publishes a listing of the Fortune 500, the 500 largest industrial corporations in the United States. Their leaders are the giants of American business, controlling assets in the hundreds of billions of dollars. To elite theorists, they represent "monopoly capital," a concentration of wealth sufficient to shape both America's and the world's economy.[11] Indeed, the concentration of resources among the top 100 corporations has been increasing since 1950 (see Figure 17.3). Corporate giants have also internationalized in the postwar period. Some **transnational corporations,** businesses with vast holdings in many countries, are bigger than most governments.

The Changing Face of Corporate Capitalism. "A better idea." "We try harder." These are the types of slogans one would like to think describe prospering corporations. Providing innovative new products or better service is a way not only to make a good profit but also to contribute to economic growth. No doubt it always will be.

Since the early 1980s, a new form of entrepreneurship has flourished—merger mania. Billions have been spent by conglomerates buying up and buying out other companies. Completed corporate mergers amounted to a whopping $200 billion in 1986 compared to just $30 billion 6 years earlier.[12] The history of this textbook is just one of many

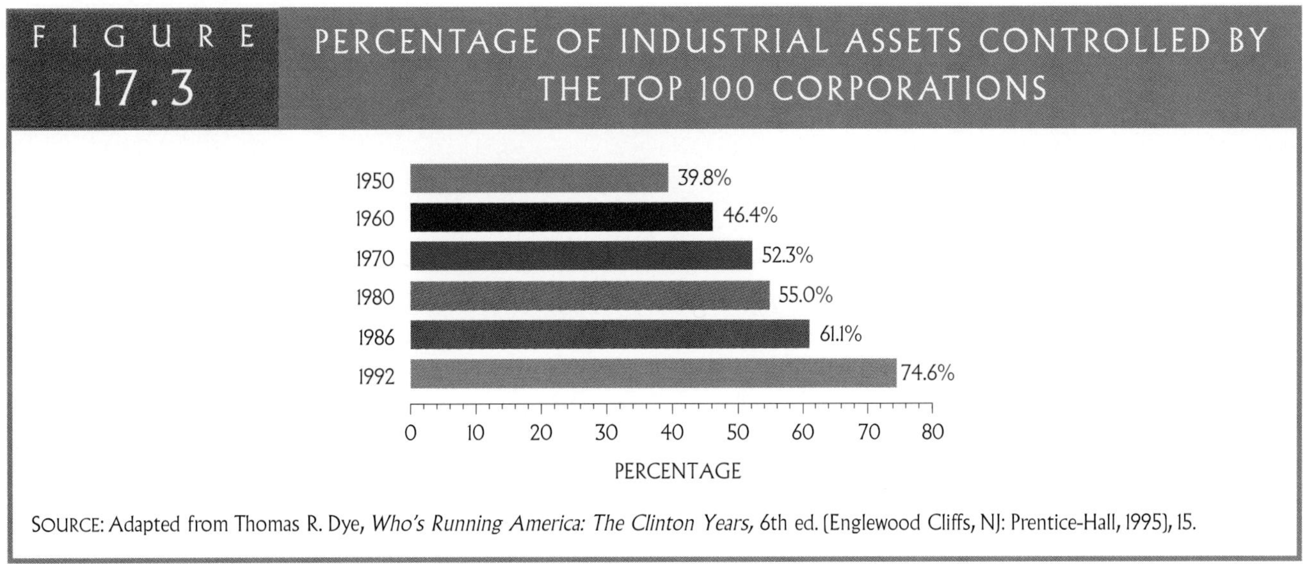

SOURCE: Adapted from Thomas R. Dye, *Who's Running America: The Clinton Years,* 6th ed. (Englewood Cliffs, NJ: Prentice-Hall, 1995), 15.

examples. The book was originally published by Little, Brown. Then, Little, Brown's textbook division was taken over by Scott, Foresman, which in turn was taken over by HarperCollins. Now, as you can see, the book is being published by Addison Wesley Longman, Inc., which bought the textbook division of HarperCollins Inc.

Interestingly, mergers need not even be completed for corporate raiders to make a bundle. Millions, even hundreds of millions, in profits can be made by merely *threatening* to buy another company. "Greenmailers," as they are called, buy a substantial proportion of stock in Corporation X and then publicize their desire to secure controlling interest in the company. As their newly acquired stock soars in value, they have the opportunity to take a windfall profit by selling out, which many of them do. Robert Reich has labeled this highly risky business "paper entrepreneurialism." He and others criticize it as producing no products and no new jobs. "Paper entrepreneurs," Reich insists, "provide nothing of tangible use.... Resources circulate endlessly among giant corporations, investment bankers, and their lawyers, but little new is produced."[13] Business leaders respond that the fear of corporate takeovers keeps management constantly on its toes, providing better products and services.

Another popular argument in favor of the increased concentration of corporate assets is that it strengthens the American economy against foreign competition from giant Japanese and European firms. Certainly, competition from abroad has not helped American corporations. Foreign products now account for about one-fifth of all American consumption, and American workers have suffered from this trend. As you can see in Table 17.1, America's share of the global market for high-tech products has slipped somewhat over the last few decades.

American technological inventions have revolutionized the world economy. Yet American companies have been unable to keep up with Japanese competition in the production of many high-tech products. For example, Japanese companies such as Matsushita (shown here) make virtually all the television sets currently sold in the United States.

To ensure that America will be competitive in important high-tech industries in the future, some analysts, including several of President Clinton's top economic advisers, believe that the government should have an aggressive **industrial policy.** As Charles Schultze writes, the central concept of industrial policy is that government should identify strategic industries "and foster their growth through such measures as tariffs and quotas to keep out foreign competition, subsidies to assist exports, and support for large R&D measures."[14] The problem, as Schultze points out, is identifying what industries are to receive this sort of special treatment. In America's pork barrel political system, it is questionable whether such decisions could be sufficiently separated from political pressures to be effective.[15] Still, advocates of industrial policy point out that the Japanese have been successful with

TABLE 17.1 AMERICA'S FALLING SHARE OF THE WORLDWIDE MARKET FOR HIGH-TECH GOODS (IN PERCENTS)

	1965	1975	1985	1990
United States	27.5	24.5	24.2	23.1
Japan	7.2	11.6	19.4	17.1
Germany (West)	16.9	16.8	14.8	15.3
France	7.3	8.4	7.9	8.4
Great Britain	12.0	9.6	9.2	9.1

SOURCE: Derek Bok, *The State of the Nation* (Cambridge, MA: Harvard University Press, 1996), p. 50.

such a policy and that America needs something along these lines in order to stay competitive.[16]

An increasing number of Americans believe that the greatest threat to national security comes not from any military power but rather from the economic power of Japan. When the Japanese make highly visible purchases such as New York's Rockefeller Center and baseball's Seattle Mariners, concern about foreign domination rises throughout the country. For example, Representative Doug Applegate of Ohio rose on the House floor in 1989 to say,

> Mr. Speaker, the Berlin Wall is coming down, but the Bamboo Wall is getting taller, and it is getting stronger. Japan is beating us in American Monopoly. They are buying America out, they are shutting us out. . . . We should be mad as hell, and we should be getting back to what America used to be, and that is: No. 1.[17]

As you can see in "The People Speak" on this page, the majority of the American public does not view Japanese investment positively.

It is important, however, to keep in mind that although foreign investment in the United States is growing, it still remains below that in most other economic powers. A recent study showed that 9 percent of American manufacturing assets were owned by foreign companies compared to 14 percent in Great Britain and 17 percent in West Germany.[18] Former Secretary of Labor Robert Reich argues that criticism of foreign investment is misplaced. He writes that a foreign company that "contracts with Americans to solve or identify complex problems helps Americans far more than does an American-owned firm that contracts with foreigners to do the same."[19]

The People Speak

Do You Think the Increase in Japanese Investment in the United States Poses a Threat to American Economic Independence or Is It a Development that Will Strengthen the American Economy?

Threat to U.S. independence	62%
Strengthen economy	25%
Don't know	13%

SOURCE: The question as worded is taken directly from a November 1991 *New York Times*/CBS News poll.

Regulating Business. Government regulation of business is at least as old as the first antitrust act, the Sherman Act of 1890. The purpose of **antitrust policy** is to ensure competition and prevent monopoly (control of a market by one company). Antitrust legislation permits the Justice Department to sue in federal court to break up companies that control too large a share of the market. It also generally prevents restraints on trade or limitations on competition, such as price fixing.[20]

Because they are usually lengthy and expensive, antitrust suits are more often threatened than carried out. Some have lasted decades and cost millions of corporate and federal dollars. The recent Justice Department suits against AT&T and IBM illustrate this. After seven years, an out-of-court settlement with AT&T resulted in its agreement to sell 22 local operating organizations—the Bell companies. A 13-year effort to break up IBM was deemed without merit by the attorney general's office, and the case was dropped. In both cases, though, because of the upheaval of the industries involved, the eventual result was increased competition.

Antitrust policy is hardly the only way business is regulated; Chapter 15 reviewed a variety of regulatory policies affecting businesses. Business owners and managers, especially in small businesses, complain constantly about regulation, but before they complain too much, they should remember some of the benefits they get from government.

Benefiting Business. Government has not always been just a silent partner in American business. In a few cases—namely, Chrysler, Lockheed, and the nation's railroads—government loans or buyouts have made government an actual partner or owner in corporate America. When a crucial industry falls on hard times, it usually looks to the government for help in the form of subsidies, tax breaks, or loan guarantees.

Throughout economic booms and busts, the Department of Commerce serves as a veritable storehouse of assistance for business. It collects data on products and markets through the Census Bureau, helps businesses export their wares, and protects inventions through the Patent Office. The Small Business Administration is the government's counselor, advisor, and loan maker to small businesses. Several agencies fund research that is valued by businesses involved with natural resources, transportation, electronics and computers, and health. In fact, the federal government is the principal source of research and development funding in the United States.

Calvin Coolidge's saying that "the business of America is business" rings particularly true when Republican administrations are in office, but some would argue that it applies almost all the time. One of the reasons why official Washington is so hospitable to business interests is that industry lobbyists in Washington are well organized and well funded (see Chapter 11). Businesses organized for lobbying have been around for years; consumer groups, by contrast, are a relatively new arrival on the economic policy stage.

Budget cuts made during the 1980s left many independent regulatory agencies open to criticism from the consumer groups they were created to protect. Here, demonstrators protest FDA delays in testing and approving experimental drugs for AIDS patients.

CONSUMER POLICY: THE RISE OF THE CONSUMER LOBBY

Years ago the governing economic principle of consumerism was "let the buyer beware." With a few exceptions, public policy ignored consumers and their interests. The first major consumer protection policy in the United States was the Food and Drug Act of 1906, which prohibited the interstate transportation of dangerous or impure foods and drugs. Today, the **Food and Drug Administration (FDA)** has broad regulatory powers over the manufacturing, contents, marketing, and labeling of food and drugs. It is the FDA's responsibility to ascertain the safety and effectiveness of new drugs before approving them for marketing in the United States.

One recent criticism of the FDA is that funding cuts have left it overburdened and seriously understaffed. Thus, although federal laws stipulate that new drug applications be completed in 6 months, the average review now takes 31 months. For instance, the agency's inability to approve quickly experimental drugs for the treatment of AIDS has incited public outcry, bringing on strong protests from gay activists and AIDS patients. By 1992, the problem at the FDA had become so severe that pharmaceutical companies agreed to pay fees that would be used by the FDA to hire 600 new examiners and thereby speed up the process. It may seem ironic that businesses are paying for their own regulation by the government, but ultimately, the costs will be passed on to the consumer.

Consumerism was a sleeping political giant until the 1960s, when it was awakened by self-proclaimed consumer activists such as Ralph Nader. Uncovering clear cases of unsafe products and false advertising, these activists argued that it was the government's responsibility to be a watchdog on behalf of the consumer. As they garnered broad public support, the 1960s and 1970s saw a flood of consumer protection legislation. Created in 1972 by the Product Safety Act, the Consumer Product Safety Commission (CPSC) has broad powers to ban hazardous products from the market. Today the CPSC regulates the safety of items ranging from toys to lawn mowers.

The **Federal Trade Commission (FTC),** traditionally responsible for regulating trade practices, also jumped into the business of consumer protection in the 1960s and 1970s, becoming a defender of consumer interests in truth in advertising. For example, the FTC ordered Carter's Liver Pills to drop "liver" from its name because the pills have no medical effect on the liver. It made new rules about product labeling, exaggerated product claims, and the use of celebrities in advertising. In 1968, Congress made the FTC the administrator of the new Consumer Credit Protection Act. This act stipulates that whenever you borrow money, even if only by using a credit card, you must receive a form stating the exact amount of interest you must pay. Through such forms and other means, the FTC enforces truth in lending.

LABOR AND GOVERNMENT

Perhaps the biggest change in economic policymaking has been the virtual about-face in public policy toward labor unions over the past century. Throughout most of the nineteenth century and well into the twentieth, the federal government allied with business elites to squelch labor unions. The courts interpreted the antitrust laws as applying to unions as well as to businesses. Until the Clayton Antitrust Act of 1914 exempted unions from antitrust laws, the mighty arm of the federal government was busier busting unions than squelching trusts. Government lent its hand to enforcing "yellow dog contracts"—contracts that forced workers to agree not to join a union as a condition of employment.

The major turnabout in government policy toward labor took place during the New Deal. In 1935 Congress passed the **National Labor Relations Act,** often called the Wagner Act after its sponsor, Senator Robert Wagner of New York. The Wagner Act guaranteed workers the right of **collective bargaining**—the right to have labor union representatives negotiate with management to determine working conditions. It also set rules to protect unions and organizers. For example, under the Wagner Act, an employer cannot fire or discriminate against a worker who advocates unionizing.

After World War II, a series of strikes and a new Republican majority in Congress tilted federal policy somewhat back in the direction of management. The **Taft-Hartley Act** of 1947 continued to guarantee unions the right of collective bargaining, but it prohibited various unfair practices by unions as well. The Act also gave the president power to halt major strikes by seeking a court injunction for an eighty-day "cooling off" period. Most important, section 14B of the law permitted states to adopt what union opponents call **right-to-work laws.** Such laws forbid labor contracts from requiring workers to join unions to hold their jobs. The effect of right-to-work laws is to subject unions to the free-rider problem (see Chapter 11); workers can enjoy the benefits of union negotiations without contributing dues to support the union. Later public policies focused on union corruption. Stirred by revelations of the mismanagement of funds, racketeering, and violence by some unions, Congress tried to crack down by passing the Labor-Management Reporting and Disclosure Act, called the Landrum-Griffin Act, in 1959. The Act enabled union members to exercise more control over their leaders and forbade ex-convicts from serving as union officials for 5 years after their release.

Unions have had two notable successes over the years, which have become staples of the American economy. First, partly as the result of successful union lobbying, the government provides unemployment compensation—paid for by workers and employers—to cushion the blows of unemployment. Second, since the New Deal, the government has guaranteed a minimum wage, setting a floor on the hourly wages earned by employees. Recently, President Clinton signed into law a substantial increase in the minimum wage. (See "You Are the Policymaker: Should the Minimum Wage Be Raised?")

SHOULD THE MINIMUM WAGE BE RAISED?

You Are the Policymaker

In the summer of 1996, President Clinton and the Republican leaders in Congress clashed over a proposal to raise the minimum wage from $4.25 to $5.15 an hour over a period of 2 years. Clinton insisted that a person could not live on $4.25 an hour, pointing out that 40 hours of work at this pay rate would leave one's income below the poverty line. He also argued that because of inflation, the purchasing power of the minimum wage was near a 40-year low. Secretary of Labor Robert Reich estimated at least 11 million workers would benefit from an increase in the minimum wage to $5.15. Furthermore, he stressed the point that nearly two-thirds of minimum-wage workers are adults and more than one-third are the sole breadwinners in their families.

Reaction to the president's proposal from both the left and the right was critical. The AFL-CIO said that they would welcome any increase in the minimum wage but that in their view it should be raised to $5.75 rather than $5.15. Such an increase would restore the minimum wage to what it was originally pegged at: one-half of the average hourly salary.

Republican congressional leaders were skeptical of any increase at all, promising a fair hearing and nothing more. Many Republicans expressed concern that increasing the minimum wage could end up destroying jobs, particularly for minority teenagers. They argued that businesses that can afford to pay people above the minimum wage already do so to attract the best people they can. Raising the minimum wage might mean that businesses that are barely making ends meet would no longer be profitable, and the employees who earn a minimum-wage salary with them would be out of work.

Clinton won in the end, and his proposal to raise the minimum wage to $5.15 was approved by Congress. What do you think? Do you think the minimum wage needed to be raised to ensure that hard work pays, or did increasing the minimum wage risk the elimination of too many jobs?

UNDERSTANDING ECONOMIC POLICYMAKING

The minimum wage and unemployment compensation are just two of many economic policies that contradict Karl Marx' assumptions of how a capitalist system inevitably exploits ordinary workers. Looking at mid-nineteenth-century business practices, Marx saw an economic system in which working conditions were long, hard, and miserable. Most workers barely managed to earn a meager livelihood while the rich got richer off their labor. In a completely free economic system, there was no way to compel the owners of the factories to treat the workers better. Exploitation would continue, and even get worse, Marx felt. His radical solution was for the state to assume all power over the economy in a revolution of the proletariat. In the communist system envisioned by Marx, all the means of production would be owned by the state—in which each citizen would be an equal shareholder. In practice, however, the state-run economy of the Soviet Union did not provide the necessary incentives to get people to work productively (see "America in Perspective: The Soviet Economic Morass").

In America, however, solutions to many of the problems of a free-enterprise economy were achieved through the democratic process. A large part of this effort involved expanding the scope of government, which conservatives would like to see at least partially diminished in today's economy.

DEMOCRACY AND ECONOMIC POLICYMAKING

As the voting power of the ordinary worker grew, so did the potential for government regulation of the worst ravages of the capitalist system. Political pressure grew for action to restrict unfair business practices and protect individual rights. Over time, the state assumed responsibility for setting the age at which one could work, determining the normal work week, establishing standards for safety on the job, protecting pension funds, and many other aspects of economic life. Just as the right of free speech is not interpreted so as to allow someone to shout "fire" in a crowded movie theater, so the right to free enterprise is no longer interpreted as giving businesses the right to employ 10-year-olds or to force employees to work in unsafe conditions. It is now generally agreed that such practices should be forbidden by the government. Through the ballot box, Americans essentially decided to give up certain economic freedoms for the good of society as a whole.

In New York, circa 1890, this Bohemian cigar maker and his family worked 17 hours a day, 7 days a week, for 13 cents an hour. As American workers have slowly gained more political power, they have demanded government action to improve working conditions.

It would be a vast exaggeration, however, to say that democracy regularly facilitates an economic policy that looks after general rather than specific interests. As you have seen throughout this text, the decentralized American political system often works against efficiency in government. In particular, groups that may be adversely affected by an economic policy have many avenues through which they can work to block it. Therefore, one of the consequences of democracy for economic policymaking is that it is difficult to make decisions that hurt particular groups or that involve short-term pain for long-term gain. Of course, this is the way most Americans presumably want it to be.

ECONOMIC POLICYMAKING AND THE SCOPE OF GOVERNMENT

What liberals and conservatives disagree about most when it comes to economic policymaking is the scope of government involvement in the economy. In general, liberals look to the writings of economists such as John Maynard Keynes and Robert Solow, whose work offers justification for an expanded role of government in stimulating the economy during times of recession. Conservatives, on the other hand, rely on Friedrich Hayek's influential theories on the free market and on Milton Friedman's arguments against government intervention. Whereas liberals focus on the imperfections of the market and what government can do about them, conservatives focus on the imperfections of government. For example, liberals often

THE SOVIET ECONOMIC MORASS

What went wrong with the Soviet economy? The simplest answer is that having the national government make all the decisions on what to produce proved to be impractical and inefficient. Or as Mikhail Gorbachev, who tried to reform the system, once said, "It is an illusion to think that everything can be foreseen from the center within the framework of such a huge economy as ours."

The communist economic system depended on the wisdom of central planners in Moscow to decide what was in the people's best interest to produce, as well as what the appropriate prices would be. Thus, the Soviet economy was a *command* economy. Annual national production quotas were drawn up for everything from tractors to tennis shoes, typically without any consideration of how much people wanted the specific goods. Each individual plant was then assigned the task of meeting a specific percentage of the national quota. Rather than a measure of success that was customer satisfaction and profit, the goal was merely to churn out the goods.

Quality was thereby regularly sacrificed for quantity, which often produced disastrous results. Tens of thousands of tractors would come off the assembly lines, but few spare parts would be made available. Millions of pairs of shoes were left on the shelves of stores because their sizes did not match the population's. Television sets were so shoddily made that they regularly blew up in people's living rooms, becoming the leading cause of household fires in the Soviet Union.

With an emphasis on production rather than profit, Soviet workers were given little incentive to make quality job #1. Absenteeism from the job was high, and morale was low. A favorite saying of the workers became "They pretend to pay us and we pretend to work." About the only incentive people had at the workplace was to steal. Many workers reportedly made up for their poor pay by pilfering goods at their plant. The common saying was "What belongs to everyone, belongs to no one, so why shouldn't it be mine?"

America in Perspective

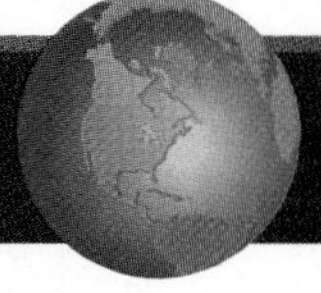

The inefficiency of the command economy can perhaps best be illustrated by a joke about a rare Soviet who managed to save enough money to buy a new car. Entering the car dealership, the customer soon finds he has no choice of model or color. But anxious to have any car at all, he accepts this lack of choice and just asks when he can pick his new car up. The salesman looks in his datebook and answers that he can have it 10 years from today, exactly. The customer then looks in his datebook and inquires whether that would be in the morning or the afternoon. Stunned by this question, the salesman asks why it should matter. The customer responds, "Well, I see the plumber has promised to finally come over that morning."

SOURCE: Hedrick Smith, ***The New Russians*** (New York: Random House, 1990), chaps. 10–12.

The state-run economy of the former Soviet Union was so inefficient that there were shortages of virtually everything. Standing in line for goods in short supply became an integral part of every citizen's life, often consuming several hours a day.

propose job training programs for unskilled workers, whereas conservatives argue that businesses can create new jobs and prepare people for them if government will just stay out of the way.

It should be noted that the disagreement about the scope of government in economic policymaking is one concerning the means rather than the ends. This could recently be seen in the contrast between the reactions of President Clinton and Republican congressional leaders regarding how to deal with the baseball strike in 1995. As spring training loomed with no resolution of the strike, the president called representatives of the players and owners into the Oval Office to try to save the baseball season. When he failed to broker an agreement, he called upon Congress to pass legislation authorizing him to intervene and compel both sides to accept binding arbitration. Republican leaders Dole and Gingrich responded that they believed it would be unwise for the government to interfere in any labor dispute not related to national security. In their view, the processes of the free market would just have to be relied on to work out the problem. At the same time, both Dole and Gingrich stated emphatically that they—like the President and every other baseball fan—wanted to see the strike resolved as soon as possible.

SUMMARY

In the United States, the political and economic sectors are closely intermingled. Although politicians have strong feelings about the economy and pay close attention to it, only scattered evidence indicates that they can successfully manipulate the economic situation at election time. The two parties do have different economic policies, particularly with respect to unemployment and inflation; Democrats try to curb unemployment more than Republicans, though they risk inflation in so doing, and Republicans are generally more concerned with controlling inflation. Two major instruments are available to government for managing the economy: monetary and fiscal policy. Democrats lean more toward Keynesian economics, which holds that government must stimulate greater demand, when necessary, with bigger government such as federal job programs. In contrast, many Republicans advocate supply-side economics, which calls for smaller government, such as tax cuts, to increase the incentive to produce more goods.

Through public policy, government also regulates various sectors of the economy. It regulates business and offers some protection to consumers and to labor. Through the democratic process, some of the unjust aspects of a capitalist economy—which have caused revolutions in other countries—have been curbed in the United States.

KEY TERMS

unemployment rate
consumer price index (CPI)
laissez-faire
monetary policy
monetarism
Federal Reserve System
fiscal policy
Keynesian economic theory
supply-side economics
transnational corporations
industrial policy
antitrust policy
Food and Drug Administration (FDA)
Federal Trade Commission (FTC)
National Labor Relations Act
collective bargaining
Taft-Hartley Act
right-to-work laws

FOR FURTHER READING

Carson, Robert B. *Economic Issues Today: Alternative Approaches,* 5th ed. New York: St. Martin's, 1991. Examines 16 separate economic policy questions from the conservative, liberal, and radical viewpoints.

Gilder, George. *Wealth and Poverty.* New York: Basic Books, 1981. A supply-sider's bible.

Grieder, William. *Secrets of the Temple: How the Federal Reserve Runs the Country.* New York: Simon & Schuster, 1987. A book that demystifies the Fed.

Kiewiet, D. Roderick. *Macroeconomics and Micropolitics.* Chicago: University of Chicago Press, 1983. A good study of the electoral effects of economic issues.

Krugman, Paul. *Peddling Prosperity: Economic Sense and Nonsense in the Age of Diminished Expectations.* New York: Norton, 1994. A top economist traces how various economic theories have affected policymaking over the last two decades of declining American economic growth.

Reich, Robert B. *The Work of Nations: Preparing Ourselves for 21st Century Capitalism.* New York: Knopf, 1991. Argues that education, communications, and transportation facilities are crucial to a country's economic success in our increasingly interdependent world.

Schultze, Charles L. *Memos to the President: A Guide Through Macroeconomics for the Busy Policymaker.* Washington, DC: Brookings Institution, 1992. A set of very readable memos explaining what politicians need to know about how the American economy works.

Stein, Herbert. *Presidential Economics,* 3rd ed. Washington, DC: American Enterprise Institute, 1994. The making of economic policy from FDR to Clinton.

Tufte, Edward R. *Political Control of the Economy.* Princeton, NJ: Princeton University Press, 1978. A bold argument that politicians manipulate the economy to their electoral advantage.

Weidenbaum, Murray L. *Business, Government, and the Public,* 4th ed. Englewood Cliffs, NJ: Prentice-Hall, 1990. An excellent text on how the private and public sectors interact.

INTERNET RESOURCES

www.whitehouse.gov/esbr.html
Official economic statistics are regularly posted at this site.

www.bog.frb.fed.us
The site for information about the activities of the Federal Reserve Board.

NOTES

1. Robert B. Reich, *The Next American Frontier* (New York: Penguin Books. 1983), 4-5.
2. Robert D. Hershey, Jr., "Jobless Rate Underestimated, U.S. Says, Citing Survey Bias," *New York Times,* November 17, 1993, A1.
3. M. Harvey Brenner, *Estimating the Social Costs of National Economic Policy: Implications for Mental and Physical Health, and Criminal Aggression* (Washington, DC: Government Printing Office, 1976).
4. David Piachaud, "Inflation and the Income Distribution," in Fred Hirsch and John H. Goldthorpe, eds., *The Political Economy of Inflation* (Cambridge, MA: Harvard University Press, 1978), 115.
5. D. Roderick Kiewiet, *Macroeconomics and Micropolitics: The Electoral Effects of Economic Issues* (Chicago: University of Chicago Press, 1983).
6. Quoted in Douglas Hibbs, "Political Parties and Macroeconomic Policy," *American Political Science Review* 71 (December 1977): 1467.
7. *Ibid.,* 1468.
8. See William Grieder, *Secrets of the Temple: How the Federal Reserve Runs the Country* (New York: Simon & Schuster, 1987); Nathaniel Beck, "Elections and the Fed: Is There a Political Monetary Cycle?" *American Journal of Political Science* 31 (February 1987): 194-216; and Nathaniel Beck, "Presidential Influence on the Federal Reserve in the 1970s," *American Journal of Political Science* 26 (August 1982): 415-445.
9. One supply-side theory can be found in George Gilder, *Wealth and Poverty* (New York: Basic Books, 1981).
10. Edward R. Tufte, *Political Control of the Economy* (Princeton, NJ: Princeton University Press, 1978), 65.
11. The argument that the American economy is dominated by "monopoly capital" is common among Marxist economists. See, for example, James O'Connor, *The Fiscal Crisis of the State* (New York: St. Martin's, 1973).
12. Murray L. Weidenbaum, *Business, Government, and the Public,* 4th ed. (Englewood Cliffs, NJ: Prentice-Hall, 1990), 458.
13. Reich, *The Next American Frontier,* 57.
14. Charles L. Schultze, *Memos to the President: A Guide Through Macroeconomics for the Busy Policymaker* (Washington, DC: Brookings Institution, 1992), 320.
15. For some examples of the problems of pork barrel politics when the government tries to get involved in high-tech ventures, see Linda R. Cohen and Roger G. Noll, *The Technology Pork Barrel* (Washington, DC: Brookings Institution, 1991).
16. For a good analysis of the development of industrial policy in Japan, see Chalmers A. Johnson, *MITI and the Japanese Miracle* (Stanford: Stanford University Press, 1982).
17. Quoted in David S. Broder, "Way Short of the Mark," *Washington Post Weekly,* December 4-10, 1989, 4.
18. Tom Redburn, "Difference Between 'Us' and 'Them' Blurs in a Global Economy," *Los Angeles Times,* August 8, 1989, part IV, page 1.
19. Robert B. Reich, *The Work of Nations: Preparing Ourselves for 21st Century Capitalism* (New York: Knopf, 1991), 154.
20. For a good review of the history of antitrust issues, see Marc Allen Eisner, *Antitrust and the Triumph of Economics: Institutions, Expertise, and Policy Change* (Chapel Hill: University of North Carolina Press, 1991).

18 Social Welfare Policymaking

When Newt Gingrich became Speaker of the House, one of his highest priorities for the first Republican-controlled Congress in 40 years was to undertake a major reform of the welfare system. Referring to the welfare programs instituted under Lyndon Johnson's Great Society program, Gingrich said, "They are a disaster. They ruin the poor, they create a culture of poverty and a culture of violence which is destructive of this civilization, and they have to be replaced thoroughly from the ground up."[1] When asked how poor mothers were to take care of their children without governmental assistance, he suggested that a return to orphanages might be a good thing. Indeed, the "Personal Responsibility Act" proposed in the Republicans' "Contract With America" offered money to the states to set up orphanages if they chose to do so.

Defenders of the social welfare system were outraged at Gingrich's remarks. George Stephanopolous, a senior advisor to President Clinton, suggested that perhaps all Republican members of Congress should be mailed a copy of *Oliver Twist* to remind them what the heyday of orphanages was like. Many liberals argued that although there is no doubt some waste in welfare programs, the country is better off with them than it was before they were instituted. Surely, they contended, a government rich enough to build the military weapons that have made America the world's only superpower can afford to give aid and comfort to its least fortunate citizens.

In August of 1996, the critics of the welfare system prevailed and ended America's 60-year-old policy of guaranteeing support to the poor. After vetoing two previous versions of welfare reform passed by Congress, President Clinton signed a welfare reform bill that received almost unanimous backing among congressional Republicans but was opposed by half of congressional Democrats. The major provisions of this bill were as follows: (1) Each state would receive a *fixed* amount of money to run its own welfare programs. (2) People on welfare would have to find work within 2 years or lose all their benefits. (3) A lifetime maximum of 5 years on welfare was set. Opponents of the bill expressed fears that these changes would push at least a million innocent children into poverty; proponents countered by asserting that millions would be lifted out of the culture of dependency and given the incentive to make something of their lives. For the foreseeable future, assessing which side proves to be right will be a key question in social welfare policymaking.

The controversy over welfare reform illustrates key concepts with regard to our themes of democracy and the scope of government. With regard to democracy, it was notable how little input there was from the people who would be most directly affected by any policy change. People who were dependent on welfare did not have the resources to form political action committees or hire lobbyists to ensure that key legislators heard from them. Furthermore, politicians worried little about upsetting lower-income citizens just prior to an election, because their turnout rates are consistently low (see Chapter 10). This is not to say that the welfare reform bill was necessarily bad for the poor—just that policy decisions were made with much less input from them than is the case with policies affecting powerful interest groups, such as the elderly.

With regard to the scope of government, the welfare reform debate illustrates divergent views about what the federal government should do. Advocates of the reform maintain that decisions on how to design and implement welfare policy are best left to the states and localities. In their view, having Washington bureaucrats decide on eligibility criteria makes for a very inflexible and wasteful process. The new reform has even made it possible for the administration of welfare programs to be contracted out to private firms, who many believe would be more efficient than governments ever could be. On the other side of the issue, critics of the reform worry that states and counties would now have an incentive to be as stingy as possible with welfare benefits in order to encourage poor people to move somewhere else in search of assistance. Such critics also believe that day-to-day management of welfare programs is the proper role of the government, not of private industry. As with so many other public policies, there are those who believe the government should do more and those who believe the government only makes things worse.

The United States is a diverse nation whose citizens and groups achieve different levels of material success. The fact that such differences exist in American democracy, however, raises important political questions: What are the economic differences among Americans? Why do they exist? Are they acceptable? What roles should the government and the private sector play in helping those who are less fortunate? What are the most effective government policies? What groups in America support and oppose these policies, and why?

The answers Americans provide to these questions determine the nation's approach to social welfare policies. **Social welfare policies** attempt to provide assistance and support to specific groups in society. Some benefits may be provided regardless of financial need and are termed *entitlements*. For example, even billionaire Ross Perot is entitled to Medicare benefits simply by being over 65 years old. Other benefits, such as Food Stamps and unemployment payments, are provided selectively to those in particular need and who meet specific eligibility criteria. These benefits are termed *means-tested*.

Who gets these benefits, what level of support is provided, and who is eligible to receive them are issues that must be resolved by the political system. How America resolves these issues depends on how its leaders, political parties, interest groups, and citizens view the nature and distribution of poverty, the role of government, and the effectiveness of various social welfare programs. This chapter places these issues in a broader context. It explores the problems of social welfare in American society and discusses the options that citizens face in attempting to deal with this very important and controversial policy area.

INCOME, POVERTY, AND PUBLIC POLICY

Americans are a rich people. Once, the United States had the highest per capita income on earth. Today, it ranks seventh behind five small European nations and Japan. Even so, Americans do extremely well, given their relatively low cost of living and low taxes in comparison with other nations. Only tiny Luxembourg ranks ahead of the United States in terms of purchasing power.

In 1995, the Census Bureau reported that the median American family income was $34,074. In this land of plenty, however, there is still a great deal of poverty. The following sections look more closely at who is getting what in America today.

Poverty in America is concentrated among a few groups. More than one-third of single-parent, female-headed families, for example, live below the poverty line.

WHO'S GETTING WHAT?

The novelist F. Scott Fitzgerald once said to his friend Ernest Hemingway, "The rich are different from you and me." "Yes," replied Hemingway, "they have more money." In fact, the distribution of income across segments of the American population is quite uneven. The concept of **income distribution** describes the share of national income earned by various groups in the United States.

Thomas B. Edsall remarks that "the distribution of income and wealth in a democratic country goes to the heart of its political ethic, defining the basic contours of a nation's sense of justice and equality."[2] The range of American incomes is vast indeed. You can see in Table 18.1 how income in America has been distributed in recent decades. During the 1960s and 1970s, there was relatively little change in the distribution of income in America. The 1980s and 1990s, however, have been a period in which the old adage "the rich get richer and the poor get poorer" applies. As Republican political analyst Kevin Phillips writes, these times have been a "triumph of upper America—an ostentatious celebration of wealth, the political ascendancy of the richest third of the population and a glorification of capitalism, free markets and finance."[3]

This situation, where one group believes it is doing less well in relation to another reference group, is called **relative deprivation**. Harrison, Tilly, and Bluestone remark that "it now seems fairly clear that both family incomes and individual wages and salaries are being distributed more and more unequally among the working people of the United States. . . . The sense of relative deprivation, of frustrated expectations, of falling behind, of being badly paid—this is becoming the common experience of a growing number of Americans."[4]

Although the words *income* and *wealth* might seem similar, they are not the same thing. **Income** is the amount of money collected between any two points in time (say, a week or a year); **wealth** is the amount already owned, including stocks, bonds, bank accounts, cars, houses, and so forth. Studies of wealth display even more inequality than those of income: The top 1 percent of the wealth-holders currently possess about 37 percent of all American wealth. The assets held by the wealthiest 1 percent of Americans actually exceed the net worth of those in the bottom 90 percent.

You can see from Table 18.1 that many of the poor have recently been losing ground, relatively speaking,

TABLE 18.1 WHO GETS WHAT? INCOME SHARES OF AMERICAN HOUSEHOLDS

INCOME QUINTILE	1960	1970	1980	1990	1994
Lowest fifth	4.9	5.5	5.1	4.6	4.2
Second fifth	11.8	12.0	11.6	10.8	10.0
Third fifth	17.6	17.4	17.5	16.6	15.7
Fourth fifth	23.6	23.5	24.3	23.8	23.3
Highest fifth	42.0	41.6	41.6	44.3	46.9

SOURCE: U.S. Census Bureau.

to higher-income groups. This fact would be less painful if all groups were increasing their wealth, with the poor increasing at a slightly lower rate. The problem is that many of the poor have been losing ground in absolute terms as well. Between 1979 and 1995, the poorest fifth of the population saw their real incomes decline by 9 percent while the richest fifth enjoyed a gain of 26 percent.

WHO'S AT THE BOTTOM? POVERTY IN AMERICA

Counting the poor may seem easy, but it is not. First one needs to define poverty. Compared with most people in India, poor Americans seem almost prosperous. Russia is a poor country by American standards, but it is not afflicted with the poverty of rural Mexico. Mexico City may look poor to an American visitor, but millions come there from the Mexican countryside seeking prosperity—relatively speaking.

To count the poor, the U.S. Bureau of the Census has established the **poverty line,** which takes into account what a family would need to spend to maintain an "austere" standard of living. This official statistic was designed by Mollie Orshansky during the 1960s. She observed that a family barely managing to make ends meet spent roughly one-third of its money on food. She then took the cost of the Department of Agriculture's subsistence diet and multiplied it by three to set the poverty level. For 1995, the Census Bureau defined a family of four as falling below the poverty level if it had an annual income below $15,569 and found that 13.8 percent of all Americans were living in poverty.

A careful, decade-long study of 5,000 American families showed that poverty may be even more extensive than the poverty line suggests.[5] In this representative sample of American families, almost one-third were below the poverty level at least once during the decade, which suggests that as many as 70 million Americans live so close to the poverty line that some crisis could push them into poverty.

Although the poor are a varied group, poverty is more common among some groups—African Americans, Hispanics, young people, and inner-city residents—than among others. Figure 18.1 reports the

Estimates vary, but most experts believe that around a million Americans—like this man across the street from the White House—are homeless. Cuts to government programs that funded low-income housing and unemployment benefits, in addition to the deinstitutionalization of the mentally ill, forced thousands of people out into the streets during the 1980s.

FIGURE 18.1 POVERTY RATES FOR PERSONS WITH SELECTED CHARACTERISTICS: 1995

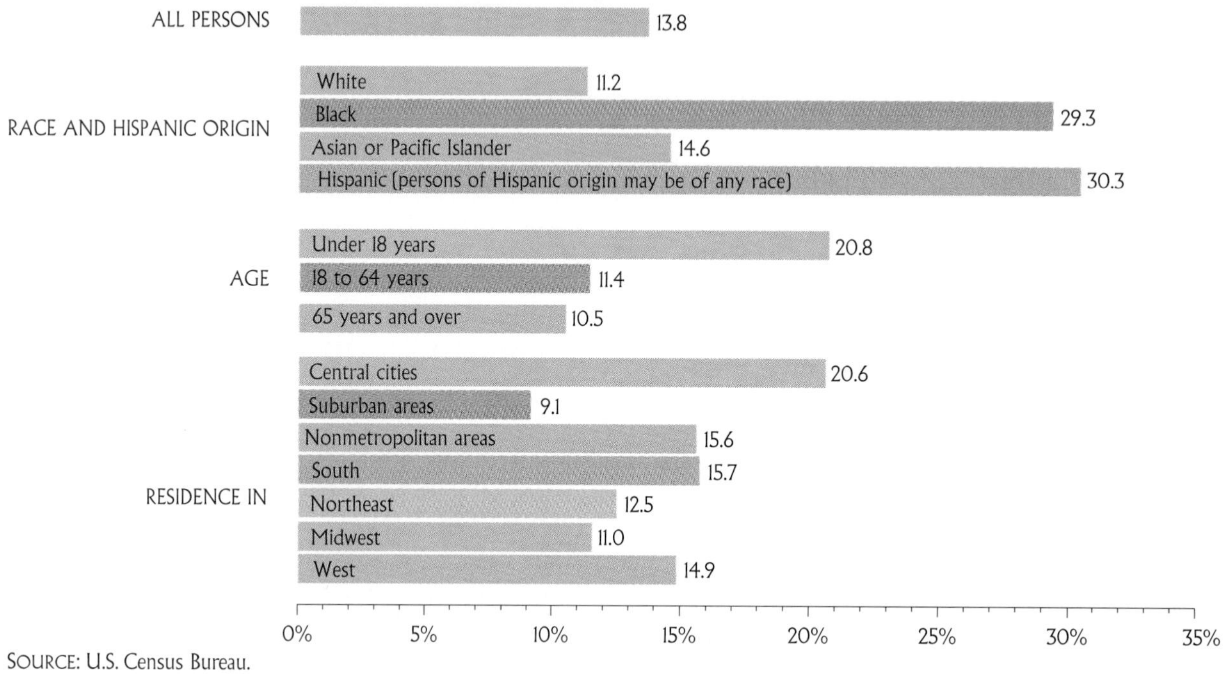

		Percent
ALL PERSONS		13.8
RACE AND HISPANIC ORIGIN	White	11.2
	Black	29.3
	Asian or Pacific Islander	14.6
	Hispanic (persons of Hispanic origin may be of any race)	30.3
AGE	Under 18 years	20.8
	18 to 64 years	11.4
	65 years and over	10.5
RESIDENCE IN	Central cities	20.6
	Suburban areas	9.1
	Nonmetropolitan areas	15.6
	South	15.7
	Northeast	12.5
	Midwest	11.0
	West	14.9

0% 5% 10% 15% 20% 25% 30% 35%

SOURCE: U.S. Census Bureau.

characteristics of persons in America living below the poverty line.

THE NATURE OF WEALTH AND POVERTY

Politicians' views on who are poor and why affect their approaches to solving the problems of poverty. People's understanding of the causes of poverty will direct and limit what they believe government can and should do about it. As you can see in "The People Speak: The Public's Perceptions of Welfare," most Americans say the government has a responsibility to take care of the poor but at the same time blame the poor for a lack of effort. A comprehensive study of public opinion about social welfare programs by Fay Lomax Cook and Edith Barrett finds that support for public assistance programs depends a great deal on the images of those who receive aid. They write that "when recipients are seen as being in need, as wanting to be independent, and as not being at fault for their condition, support will be forthcoming."[6] Thus,

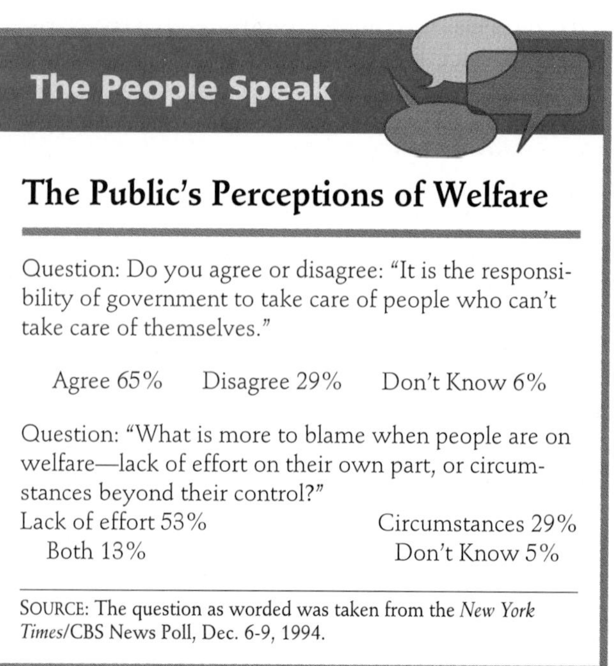
The People Speak

The Public's Perceptions of Welfare

Question: Do you agree or disagree: "It is the responsibility of government to take care of people who can't take care of themselves."

Agree 65%   Disagree 29%   Don't Know 6%

Question: "What is more to blame when people are on welfare—lack of effort on their own part, or circumstances beyond their control?"

Lack of effort 53%   Circumstances 29%

Both 13%   Don't Know 5%

SOURCE: The question as worded was taken from the *New York Times*/CBS News Poll, Dec. 6-9, 1994.

understanding the debate regarding the causes of poverty is crucial to understanding the political debate over welfare programs.

IS THERE A CULTURE OF POVERTY?

Conservatives and liberals in America tend to disagree on the reasons why some people are rich and others are poor. In general, conservatives tend to believe that individual characteristics, attitudes, and values are the primary factors that affect economic status. The poor, many conservatives argue, possess a **culture of poverty**—negative attitudes and values toward work, family, and success that condemn them to lower levels of accomplishment. This argument holds that the poor are present-oriented, lack self-control, exhibit poor work habits, lack positive aspirations, and have weak family structures and relationships.

Liberals take strong exception to these culture-of-poverty assertions. They argue that some people face more hostile environments than others. These negative environments include racial discrimination, social and cultural customs, and educational limits. People are poor, these critics argue, not because of particular characteristics or values, but rather because of external barriers to their success.[7]

The conservative argument elicits hypotheses that can be carefully tested against hard data. If the conservatives are right, social scientists should observe the presence of long-term welfare status among America's poor. In addition, a set of values and attitudes—a culture of poverty—should also be observable among the poor. The facts do not support either of these assertions, however. Examination of the welfare rolls over time indicates that most beneficiaries are not long-term recipients. A 1994 survey of recipients of Aid to Families with Dependent Children (AFDC) found that the majority of families had received benefits for less than 2 years and that only 20 percent had been on the welfare rolls for over 5 years.[8]

As for the existence of a particular set of negative attitudes that characterize a dependent, helpless poor, most researchers cannot find it. For example, in Greg Duncan's 10-year study of the economic life of American families, he found no distinctive set of attitudes—no culture of poverty—distinguishing the poor from the nonpoor. Instead, it was more commonly some crisis, such as losing a job or getting a divorce, that accounted for movement below the poverty line.[9]

Recently, much attention has focused on the **urban underclass**—the poorest of the poor in America. They constitute a large percentage of the Americans afflicted by homelessness, crime, drugs, alcoholism, unwanted pregnancies, and other endemic social problems. The problems of the urban underclass may stem not from possessing a unique value system but from the lack of any value system at all. As William Kelso argues, it is crucial to keep in mind that the "underclass began to grow in the late 1960s, when traditional socializing agents broke down and the commitment of many of the poor to social norms began to weaken."[10]

HOW PUBLIC POLICY AFFECTS INCOME

To eradicate poverty, some people believe the government should ensure that everyone has a minimal level of income. Income is determined by many factors. Some people work hard; others are lazy. Some live in regions where opportunities are plentiful; others reside in areas of scarcity and decline. Some people have wealthy parents who ensure that the best education is available to them; others do not have this advantage. Many of these conditions are clearly not subject to governmental control. The government does, however, spend one out of every three dollars in the American economy, so it has a major impact on its citizens' wealth and income. In particular, there are two principal ways in which government can affect a person's income: Government can manipulate incomes through its taxing powers, and government can affect income through its expenditure policies.

Taxation. "Nothing," said Benjamin Franklin, "is certain in life but death and taxes." In general, there

In January 1995, Newt Gingrich suggested tax credits for laptop computers as a way to help the urban underclass compete in the information age.

are three types of taxes; each can affect citizens' incomes in a different way. A **progressive tax** takes a bigger bite from the incomes of the rich than from those of the poor; an example is charging millionaires 50 percent of their income and the poor 5 percent of theirs. Second, if the government takes the same percentage from everyone, rich and poor alike, it is levying a **proportional tax**. And finally, a **regressive tax** takes a higher percentage from those at lower income levels than from the well-to-do.

Rarely are taxes overtly regressive, but some taxes are regressive in effect. Consider state sales taxes, for example. States typically raise more than half of their tax revenues from sales taxes. Poor families usually spend a larger *proportion* of their income on items subject to state sales tax—such as gasoline, fast food, and so forth. Thus, poor families pay a higher percentage of their incomes in state sales taxes than well-to-do families.

Taxes, therefore, can affect the distribution of income in three ways. (1) Progressive taxes can make the poor better off and the rich worse off. (2) Proportional taxes can have no net effect on income. (3) Regressive taxes can make the rich richer and the poor poorer. The best evidence indicates that regressive state and local taxes are counterbalanced by more progressive federal taxes. The overall impact of taxes in America is thus proportional—neither regressive nor progressive.

At the national level, the wealthy are paying a good deal of the income taxes used to support many government policies, including poverty-related social welfare programs. In 1991, for example, taxpayers making over $100,000 made up about 3 percent of total taxpayers but paid about 36 percent of total income taxes. At the same time, taxpayers making under $22,000 made up 54 percent of taxpayers and paid about 7 percent of total income taxes that year.[11] This is not to imply that all are paying their proper share or that the current income tax structure is completely equitable.

Government Expenditures. Another important way in which the government can affect a person's income is through its spending policies. Government can affect the income a citizen receives by a simple act: It can write you a check. Literally billions of government checks are written every year, mostly to Social Security beneficiaries and retired government employees. Government can also give an "in-kind payment," something with cash value that is not cash itself. (Food stamps are one example; a low-interest loan for college education is another.) All these benefits from government are called **transfer payments;** they transfer money from the general treasury to those in specific need.

It is clear that many are better off after these transfers than before—particularly the elderly, whose poverty rate declined from 35 percent in 1959 to 11 percent in 1995 primarily because of Social Security payments and Medicare. Many of the poor have been raised above the poverty line by these cash and in-kind transfers. In spite of these marginal improvements rel-

The United States is a wealthy nation but one that also has tremendous inequality in wealth. In many parts of the country, affluent suburban neighborhoods can be found less than 10 miles away from poverty-stricken areas.

ative to poverty status, however, there is little evidence that transfer programs have significantly redistributed income in America or reduced income inequality.

A careful (and complicated) study of government's impact on income equality has been conducted by Morgan Reynolds and Eugene Smolensky. They estimated the effect of government expenditures in various categories (schooling, highways, defense, policing, and so forth) on individual incomes. Looking at three points in time—1950, 1960, and 1970—they concluded that government spending had done little to make incomes more nearly equal. Despite massive government commitments to social programs during this period, income inequality had hardly been affected by public policy.[12]

Clearly, income inequality is common in industrialized societies and is not likely to be substantially reversed in the United States. However, although income inequality is recognized as a problem in America, there is no widespread approval of income redistribution aimed at reducing this inequality. Americans tend to favor equal opportunity over equal outcomes and to reject redistribution policies that would substantially reduce income inequality by government action.

SOCIAL WELFARE PROGRAMS

Although social welfare programs have not ended poverty or reduced income inequality in America, many would argue that these programs were never intended to accomplish such ambitious goals. It is true, however, that these programs have produced substantial improvements in the day-to-day living conditions of many Americans.

Crime, drugs, and poverty are a part of life for the urban underclass. Slogans like "just say no," which assume that addictions and other problems can be changed by a simple change in attitude, seem meaningless in the face of hostile urban environments such as this one.

ENTITLEMENT AND POVERTY PROGRAMS

Programs such as Social Security and Medicare have substantially improved older Americans' quality of life. Medicaid, food stamps, and housing and family assistance programs have also kept many American families from despair and homelessness. Table 18.2 summarizes these programs.

Entitlement programs such as Social Security and Medicare are the largest and most expensive social welfare programs in America. In 1992, 26 percent of American families received Social Security payments and 24 percent received Medicare benefits, whereas only 9 percent received food stamps and 4 percent Aid to Families with Dependent Children (AFDC). Social Security and Medicare have had a positive effect on the health and income of older Americans. The elderly are receiving more and better medical treatment as a result of Medicare, and Social Security payments keep many senior citizens out of poverty.

Means-tested programs aimed specifically at the poor, such as Medicaid and food stamps, are funded at much lower levels than non-means-tested entitlement programs for the elderly. Medicaid, the medical assistance program for the poor, spent about $70 billion in 1994, and many of these expenditures went to the elderly poor for nursing home care and supplemental medical expenses. Levels of annual spending for Food Stamps and AFDC are both currently at slightly more than $20 billion.

Even though the expenditures for all these poverty programs are substantially less than those provided for entitlement programs, they have raised many of the poor above the official poverty line. These programs help a lot of poor Americans escape some of the ravages of poverty.

SOCIAL WELFARE POLICY ELSEWHERE

The United States is not the only nation that provides social welfare benefits to its citizens. In fact, most industrial nations not only provide such benefits but are usually more generous with them than the U.S. government. One example can be seen in "America in Perspective: Maternity Leave Policies in Seven Countries" (see page 467).

Other national governments and their citizens often take quite a different approach to the problems of poverty and social welfare from that of the United States. In Great Britain and many other European countries, comprehensive medical services are provided through a National Health Service. In Sweden, nursing homes that cost about $200 a day are provided

TABLE 18.2 THE MAJOR SOCIAL WELFARE PROGRAMS

SOCIAL INSURANCE PROGRAMS	PUBLIC ASSISTANCE PROGRAMS
Old Age, Survivors, and Disability Insurance (OASDI)[a] Monthly payments to retired or disabled people and to surviving members of their families. Paid for by a payroll tax on employees and employers. Popularly called *Social Security.*	*Food Stamps*[b] Coupons that can be used to buy food. Given to people whose income is below a certain level. Paid for out of general federal revenues.
Medicare[a] Part A: Federal government pays for part of the cost of hospital care for retired and disabled people covered by Social Security. Paid for by payroll taxes on employees and employers. Part B: Voluntary program of medical insurance (pays physicians) for persons 65 or over and disabled Social Security beneficiaries who pay the premiums.	*Aid to Families with Dependent Children (AFDC)*[b] Payments to families with children, either one-parent families or, in some states, two-parent families where the breadwinner is unemployed. Paid for partly by states and partly by the federal government.
	Supplemental Security Income (SSI)[b] Cash payments to aged, blind, or disabled people whose income is below a certain amount. Paid for by general federal revenues.
Medicaid[b] Provides medical and hospital aid to the poor through federally assisted state health programs. Need is the only criterion; if you are poor, you qualify.	*Unemployment Insurance (UI)*[a] Weekly payments to workers who have been laid off and cannot find work. Benefits and requirements determined by states. Paid for by taxes on employers.

[a]No means test (a means test is a required demonstration of need based on income and assets).
[b]Means test.

to citizens in need for a mere $12 charge, and in Norway, workers who suffer from a long-term illness are paid their full salary (up to $27,500) by the government for a year.

Americans tend to see poverty and social welfare needs as individual rather than governmental concerns, whereas European nations tend to support greater governmental responsibility for these problems. Also, Europeans often have a more positive attitude toward government, whereas Americans are more likely to distrust government action in areas such as social welfare policy.

Nations also differ in how universal or selective they make their social welfare payments. Some nations, such as Switzerland and Australia, focus attention on selective benefits that are targeted at people with specific needs. Other nations, such as those in Scandinavia, tend to favor universal benefits that go to large categories of the population without regard to demonstrated need. America has both types of programs; Social Security and Medicare programs are universal; poverty programs are selective.

Taxes commensurate with the benefits of social policy are common in Western European nations, where taxes far exceed those in the United States (see Chapter 14). Japan is the only nation with a developed economy that spends a smaller proportion of its gross domestic product on social policies than does the United States, in part because in Japan, the family's traditional role of supporting the elderly is still commonplace.

THE EVOLUTION OF AMERICA'S SOCIAL WELFARE PROGRAMS

For centuries, societies considered family welfare a private, not a public, concern. Children were to be nurtured by their parents and, in turn, to nurture them in their old age. When children cast off their parents or when parents let their children go hungry, significant social pressure was often enough to make people accept their proper family responsibilities.

MATERNITY LEAVE POLICIES IN SEVEN COUNTRIES

America in Perspective

One of the first bills passed under the Clinton Administration was the Family and Medical Leave Act. This law requires employers with 50 or more employees to provide workers with up to 12 weeks of unpaid leave for the birth or adoption of a child or the illness of a close family member. To qualify, a person must have worked for the employer for at least a year and worked at least 1,250 hours during that year. However, an employer can deny unpaid leave to a worker who is among the company's top 10 percent in salary and whose leave would result in "substantial and grievous economic injury" to the business.

President Clinton hailed the Family and Medical Leave Act as a landmark piece of legislation, whereas the majority of Republicans denounced it as yet another example of intrusive government. In comparison to a number of other advanced industrial democracies, though, the provisions it offers for maternity leave are relatively meager. As you can see in the chart below, it is common elsewhere in the world for the government to pay women a substantial part of their salary after they have had a child. Furthermore, in most of these countries, the paid leave that women receive lasts longer than the unpaid leave that the U.S. government has only recently mandated.

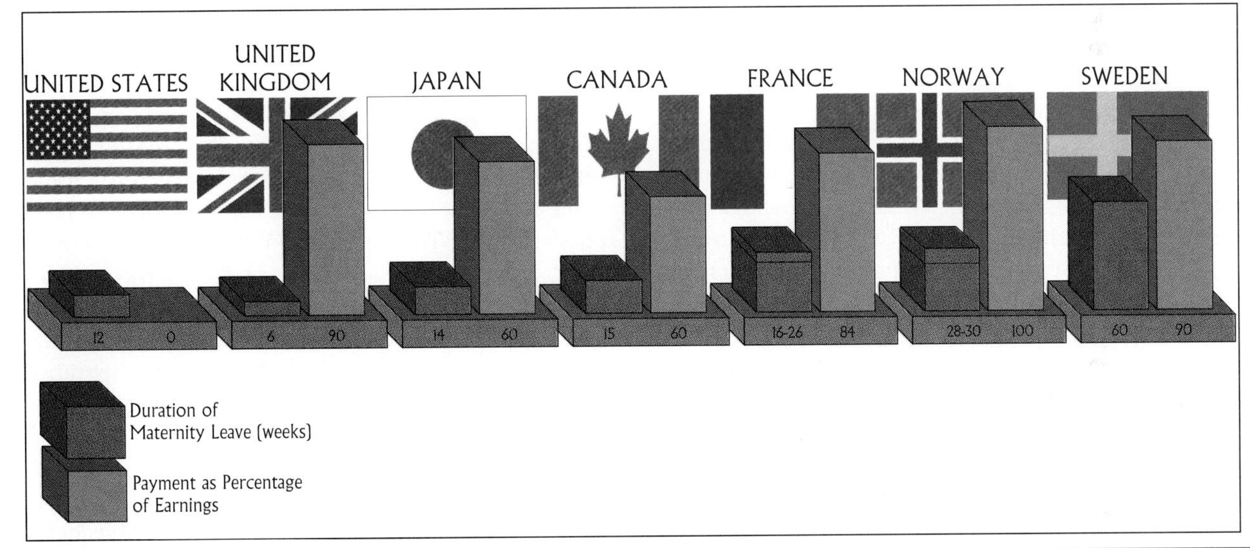

SOURCE: *The Sydney Morning Herald,* June 3, 1994, p. 13.

There was a time, in other words, when an implied contract existed between one generation and the next.

After the turn of the century, however, America and other industrialized societies recognized the breakdown in these family-based support networks. With the growth of large, depersonalized cities and the requirements of the urban workplace, the old ways of thinking about the problems of the elderly and the poor seemed inadequate. The government was impelled to take a more active role in social welfare support. As with other major policy changes in America, these changes in the patterns of government support for the needy were incremental in nature, with key breakthroughs in policy direction coming at times of particular societal need or crisis. A major change in how Americans viewed government's role in providing social welfare came during the Great Depression.

THE NEW DEAL AND THE ELDERLY

After the onset of the Great Depression in 1929, many Americans began to think that governments must do more to protect their citizens against the vicissitudes of economic downturns. Families would not always have the resources to look after one another as they would like. External circumstances far beyond the control of individuals or their families began to be seen as major contributors to short- and long-term poverty and need. In 1935, the federal government responded to this change by passing one of the most significant pieces of social welfare legislation of all time—the Social Security Act. This act brought government into the equation of one generation's obligations to another. Never would middle-class family choices be quite the same. Adults could put their own children, instead of their parents, first. Later, in 1965, when the federal government adopted Medicare, adults were freed even more from paying for their own parents' expenses. Thus the post-1965 generation of adults was the first to be substantially free of the ancient obligation of caring for its parents as well as its children. "Substantially free" does not, of course, mean that millions of Americans have not dutifully filled in gaps left by Social Security or Medicare. The burden, though, is no longer theirs alone, for government benefits provide a crucial cushion.

The costs were shifted but not reduced; what citizens had paid out of their pocket they now paid for in taxes. First Social Security and then Medicare became the most rapidly increasing parts of the federal budget. Today, Americans over the age of 80 make up the fastest-growing age group. Americans spend 13 percent of their nation's gross domestic product on medical care. Every year, a larger part of that cost goes to aiding older Americans. In the 1980s, for the first time, the United States spent more of its public dollars on the aged than on the young. As you can see in "Since Kennedy: Poverty Rates for the Young and the Old," throughout the 1960s, the poverty rate was higher for the elderly than for children, but now it is substantially lower.

No event has shaped American social welfare policy more than the Great Depression. Franklin Roosevelt's administration initiated hundreds of New Deal programs in its efforts to help citizens like these jobless men. Government spending on social welfare has continued to grow, even during the Reagan administration.

To illustrate intergenerational equality issues, economist Robert Kuttner offers a comparison of the government policies affecting a male born in 1921 and a woman born in 1961.[13] The male worker born in 1921 saw government help his family through the Great Depression of the 1930s. Chances are he fought in World War II and then returned home to find government helping him with a GI Bill loan to buy a house or get an education. He enjoyed a rise in his real income during the 1950s and 1960s and probably saw government initiate a whole raft of projects to benefit people just like him. Government built a new interstate highway system; it expanded the public schools; it expanded its protection for him on the job. Furthermore, the government did all these things while keeping his taxes relatively low.

Now consider the young woman born in 1961. As she entered the world of work, says Kuttner, "the role of government as provider looms much smaller, and government as taxer looms much larger."[14] Because take-home income has not kept pace with inflation since the early 1970s, her taxes are higher than her parents' taxes. Whereas in 1944 they paid 3 percent of their earnings to support their elders through Social Security, she pays more than 15 percent of her earnings for that purpose. She grew up in a house whose mortgage was subsidized by the Veterans Administration or some other federal loan program; today, although she wants to buy a house, she cannot afford one. Federal housing subsidies are now quite limited. In 1949, the average 30-year-old could buy a house with 14 percent of his or her income; today the comparable figure is about three times as much.

The issue posed by problems of intergenerational equality is this: Who should get what share of public policy benefits and at what costs? This complex, emerging debate about social policy may, in the future, pit different age groups against one another.

PRESIDENT JOHNSON AND THE GREAT SOCIETY

In the 1960s, America experienced an outpouring of federal programs to help the poor and the elderly, to create economic opportunities for those at the lower rungs of the economic ladder, and to reduce discrimination against minorities. Many of these programs were established during the presidency of Lyndon B. Johnson (1963-1969), whose administration coined the term "The Great Society" for these policy initiatives. Johnson was a policy entrepreneur, initiating

SINCE KENNEDY

Poverty Rates for the Young and the Old

In the 1960s, the number of senior citizens living in poverty was a national scandal. Today, the poverty rate among elderly Americans is slightly below the national average, thanks in large part to a variety of social welfare programs. Unfortunately, although poverty rates for children also declined substantially in the 1960s, since then the poverty rate for America's children has been creeping upward. In 1974, the Census Bureau for the first time reported higher poverty levels for children than for senior citizens. Those under the age of 18 are currently almost twice as likely to live in poverty as people who are over 65. The living conditions of young people in minority groups are particularly bad. In 1992, 47 percent of African Americans and 40 percent of Hispanics under the age of 18 were living in poverty.

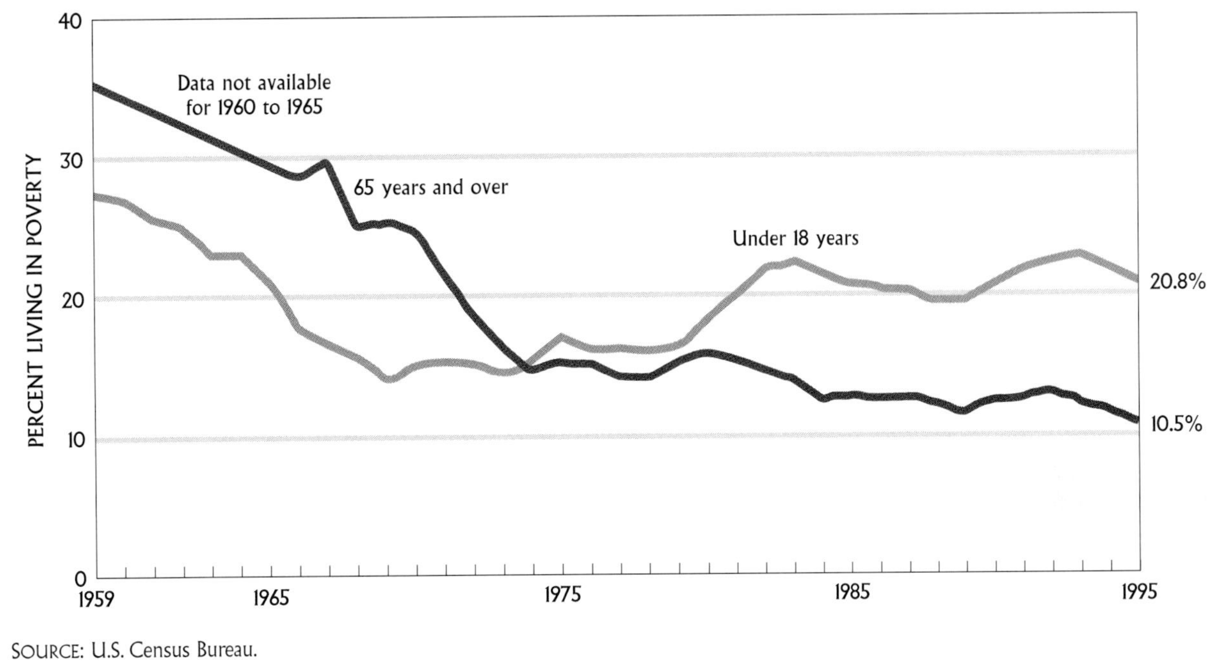

SOURCE: U.S. Census Bureau.

antipoverty programs, community development programs, Medicare, school-aid schemes, job-retraining programs, and a host of other public programs. During this period, government revenues were still growing and budget deficits were low. Although the Vietnam War eventually drained funds from Johnson's Great Society, many of the programs Ronald Reagan later railed against were set in place during the Johnson period. Richard Nixon, Johnson's Republican successor, carried on and even expanded many of them, as did Presidents Ford and Carter.

Political scientist John Kingdon has argued that problem areas reach the political agenda through a convergence of "streams." Problems get identified and brought into the open, policies get identified with problem solutions, and changes in public opinion, political leadership, and other factors in the political environment create a window of opportunity for action.[15] The entitlement and poverty programs that made up the Great Society had quite different streams. The entitlement programs, aimed primarily at the elderly, had strong political support. The elderly were a growing political constituency that was important to both political parties. Demographic trends showed an expanding elderly population, and medical advances were increasing health options and demands for care. Public opinion supported paying greater attention to the elderly.

In 1965, President Lyndon Johnson signed Medicare legislation into law. This program, which helps older Americans with their medical expenses, was first proposed more than a decade earlier by former President Harry Truman (right), who was invited to the signing.

Advocates of greater spending for poverty programs had a more difficult time. Many people believed that poverty was closely tied to race issues, and the worst aspects of racial discrimination and segregation were still quite fresh in their minds. In addition, the ability of the poor and their supporters to form strong political bases from which to demand government help was limited. Compared to the elderly, poor people were less organized, were less powerful, and had lower turnout rates at the polls. On the positive side, minorities and the poor were becoming a more important constituency in the Democratic Party, which was beginning to pay more attention to the electoral demands of these groups. The growth of the civil rights movement, the increasing media coverage of poverty and discrimination, and the outbreak of urban violence created a climate of opinion that supported paying more attention to the problems of poverty.

Perhaps the most important element for the success of both program types, however, was strong presidential leadership. Making important changes in social welfare programs usually requires strong presidential commitment, and this was provided by President Johnson. He made these programs a centerpiece of his administration and worked to rally the Congress, public opinion, and major interest groups behind him. It is impossible to overestimate the role of political leadership, particularly by the president, in building the public and political coalitions needed to support new program initiatives in the area of social welfare policy. It was the active leadership of a subsequent president, Ronald Reagan, that helped build coalitions to move American social welfare programs in a different direction.

Drawing by Dana Fardon; ©1992 The New Yorker Magazine, Inc

PRESIDENT REAGAN AND LIMITS TO THE GREAT SOCIETY

Unlike Presidents Nixon, Ford, and Carter—who largely accepted and even expanded some portions of the programs initiated by Johnson—President Reagan took a very different approach. Again, the streams surrounding social welfare policy in his administration had changed substantially from those present for the preceding presidents. Public support for some welfare programs was eroding, particularly among members of the traditional Democratic coalition. It was possible, therefore, for Republicans to make some headway into the Democratic Party's constituency by taking a more restrictive stand on social welfare programs.

In addition, the growing demands of defense spending and entitlement programs for the elderly had increased government deficits and threatened to stifle economic growth. The working class and the middle and upper-income groups were seeing their incomes threatened and were looking for places to cut government expenditures. One thing that had not changed was the vulnerability of the poor. Their group bases of support were still smaller than those of the elderly. The poor were limited to the Democratic Party, which was becoming more divided on support for poverty and social welfare programs, and the poor's representation in the interest group system was as weak as ever. The elderly still had bipartisan support and strong electoral and interest group bases.

Just as in the Johnson era, the major actor was the president. In this case, President Reagan chose to target poverty programs as one major way to cut government spending. This action was consistent with his own ideological beliefs in less government and more self-sufficiency. The president set the tone, rallied public opinion, and worked to create congressional coalitions to support these efforts.

The Omnibus Budget Reconciliation Act (OBRA) of 1981 initiated many of the cuts President Reagan had sought. For example, OBRA included substantial cuts (estimated to be about 14 percent) in the AFDC program. These cuts resulted in an AFDC caseload reduction of about 12 percent, with many who remained on the rolls receiving lower benefits.[16]

In this and subsequent policy battles, Democratic leaders in Congress worked to limit these cuts. The growth rates of many programs were reduced, benefits were slashed, program burdens were shifted to the states, and many previously eligible recipients were removed from the rolls. Still, the basic outlines of the original programs persisted throughout the Reagan and Bush administrations.

THE FUTURE OF SOCIAL WELFARE POLICY

More and more, political campaigns and congressional debates have focused on the social welfare policy programs initiated in the Johnson period and modified or expanded during subsequent administrations. Although President Reagan was not successful in dismantling the Great Society programs, he was able to focus more attention on these programs and to set the stage for continuing debate. The major question remains: What should government do in the area of social welfare policy?

The major point of disagreement is over the extent to which social welfare programs work. Discussion is heated over whether these programs help or hurt the poor, ameliorate or exacerbate poverty, provide a safety net for the needy or encourage dependence and failure.

In the late 1970s, Americans witnessed burgeoning government deficits, rising inflation, and further disintegration of the family. Many believed that the programs implemented in the Great Society had contributed to these problems. This skepticism led a number of Americans to question the appropriateness of increased government activity in the social policy arena and to consider cutting these programs.

A major study underwritten by the conservative Manhattan Institute and conducted by Charles Murray seemed to provide the budget cutters with the ammunition needed to begin dismantling the social programs of earlier years.[17] Murray's book argued that the social programs of the Great Society and later administrations not only failed to curb the advance of poverty but actually made the situation worse. The problem, Murray maintained, was that these public policies discouraged the poor from solving their problems. Murray contended that the programs made it profitable to be poor and victimized, thus encouraging the poor to stay that way. For example, Murray pointed out that poor couples could obtain more benefits if they weren't married; thus most would not marry, a decision that leads to further disintegration of the family. Another criticism is that welfare rules discourage poor people from saving money, as you can see in "You Are the Policymaker: Should Welfare Mothers Be Allowed to Save for Their Children's Education?"

Many scholars, however, have strongly criticized Murray's arguments and the program cuts emanating from them. Directly challenging Murray's assertions, political scientist Arnold Vedlitz has argued that "the conservatives exaggerate both the expectations and intentions of the programs and denigrate their accomplishments. . . . The reality of these programs is that they were never designed to end poverty, presidential rhetoric to the contrary."[18] In a separate challenge to Murray's position, economists David Ellwood and Lawrence Summers showed not only that spending for the poor was relatively limited in these programs but also that economic growth and recessions were responsible for much of the movement into and out of poverty during the post-1965 period.[19] Scholars such as Ellwood and Summers are much more likely to conclude that the Great Society programs contributed to easing the shocks to the American economic and social system caused by international oil crises, deindustrialization of the American economy, and increased foreign economic competition. Their position is that the poor would have been much worse off were it not for LBJ's safety net programs.

For those looking for the "right" answer, the evidence is clearly mixed. Scholars disagree on how beneficial the programs were and are. Although the preponderance of the evidence seems to support the notion that the programs provided some assistance, one can still ask whether more could have been accomplished with other programs or other approaches. What is the correct path for Americans to take if they wish to help the poor? One's answer depends on one's judgment as to the real causes of poverty, but a thorough and fair examination of the nature of poverty in America will show that it is a complex phenomenon, with many antecedents. Poverty raises no simple problems and yields to no simple policy solutions.

UNDERSTANDING SOCIAL WELFARE POLICY

Discussing and debating social welfare policies are very difficult tasks in a capitalist, democratic political system such as the United States. Americans struggle

SHOULD WELFARE MOTHERS BE ALLOWED TO SAVE FOR THEIR CHILDREN'S EDUCATION?

You Are the Policymaker

Sandra Rosado of New Haven, Connecticut, had known poverty most of her young life, but she was determined to go to college. The oldest of eight children, she saved every dollar she could from her part-time job after school at a neighborhood community center. As one might expect, Sandra's mother was very proud of her. Sandra seemed well on her way to providing for herself rather than ending up on welfare like her mother.

When state officials became aware of Sandra's college savings, however, it soon became a bureaucratic nightmare for the Rosado family. For years the family had received welfare support from the Aid to Families with Dependent Children (AFDC) program. But because of Sandra's $4,900 bank account, welfare officials told them they were no longer eligible for AFDC (federal law stipulates that recipients must not have liquid assets of over $1,000). Without the means to support her eight children, Mrs. Rosado asked whether there wasn't some way to get around this problem. The easiest way, she was told, was simply for Sandra to spend the money immediately. Thus, rather than spending her money on a college education, Sandra ended up buying clothes, jewelry, shoes, and perfume.

The case of Sandra Rosado presents a difficult problem for policymakers. The rationale for the AFDC rule concerning assets is that the government should not be supporting people who have the means to support themselves. But to discourage poor people from saving for things like a college education only makes it more likely that they will continue indefinitely on the public dole. Critics thus charge that the AFDC rule is counterproductive in that it punishes welfare recipients when they exercise personal initiative and responsibility. They propose that welfare families be allowed to set up special bank accounts to be used only for educational purposes.

Sandra Rosado

Assume the role of the policymaker. Should people on AFDC be allowed to save money for purposes such as education, which will help them break their dependency on welfare? When you ponder this question, consider how a working-class family living from paycheck to paycheck might feel knowing that its tax dollars are going to support people with money in the bank. In addition to trying to provide the right incentives to people on welfare, there are also questions of fairness to all citizens involved in such a policy decision.

SOURCE: Constance L. Hays, "Girl's Plan to Save for College Runs Afoul of Welfare Rules," *New York Times,* May 15, 1992, p. A1.

to balance individual merit and the rewards of initiative with the reality of systemic inequalities and the need to provide support to many. Citizens disagree on how much government can or should do to even out the competition and protect those who are less able to compete. In short, Americans seek to retain a commitment to both competition and compassion. Sorting out the proper balance of these values is at the heart of policy disagreements about social welfare programs.

DEMOCRACY AND SOCIAL WELFARE

There are no easy answers to the problems that social welfare policies create for a democratic society. There is evidence of people in great need and evidence that, although much has been and can be accomplished, the results of social welfare programs may be limited and the costs astronomical. The demand for action from some is met by the call for restraint from others.

In a democracy, competing demands are resolved by government decisionmakers, but decisionmakers do not act in a vacuum. They are aligned with and pay allegiance to various groups in society. These groups include members of their legislative constituencies, members of their electoral coalitions, and members of their political party. Many of these groups provide the financial assistance that the decisionmakers need to seek and retain political office.

In the social welfare policy arena, the competing groups are often quite unequal in terms of political resources. For example, the elderly are relatively well organized and often have the resources needed to wield significant influence in support of their programs. In the pressure cooker of legislative decision making, the elderly can turn up the heat. As a result, they are usually successful in protecting and expanding their programs. For the poor, however, influencing political decisions is more difficult. They vote less and lack strong, focused organizations and money.

Although government benefits are difficult to obtain, especially for the poor, the nature of democratic politics makes it difficult to withdraw them once they are established. Policymaking in the United States is very incremental in nature. Once put in place, policies develop a life of their own. They engage supporters in the public, in Congress, in the bureaucracy, and among key interest groups.

Tremendous pressures come from these supporters to keep or expand programs and to preserve them from elimination. These pressures persist even when the size and costs of programs seem to have grown beyond anything anyone might have originally envisioned. Despite a succession of presidents who have talked about the need for cuts in welfare, government now spends a larger share of the gross domestic product on social welfare policies than it did during the Johnson administration in the 1960s. Although the pressures to hold down program expansion and growth are present, inertia, in addition to the demands of various interest groups, makes it very difficult to slow the rate of growth of social welfare programs.

SOCIAL WELFARE POLICY AND THE SCOPE OF GOVERNMENT

Past democratic conflicts and compromises in the social welfare policy area have given Americans a huge social welfare bureaucracy at all levels of government. Tens of thousands of government employees at federal, state, and local levels process requests for service, evaluate eligibility, authorize payments, and monitor for efficiency, fraud, and abuse. This expenditure of money and energy is not necessarily wasteful. These activities and these employees are, for the most part, providing useful and cost-efficient services. It is true that some portion of the social welfare dollar goes into management and oversight, thereby limiting the amount that directly reaches the recipient. At the same time, many argue that expenditures for management and oversight activities are necessary because they make sure that the correct amount is delivered to the appropriate beneficiary under the proper program guidelines.

Large government programs, whether in the area of national defense or social welfare, require large organizations to administer them. The appropriate way to evaluate these administrative systems is not to focus on their scope or expense alone but rather to weigh these factors against the conduct of their mission, the goals and accomplishments of their programs, and the extent to which private, nongovernmental entities

could realistically be depended on to help. Clearly, these are questions on which well-intentioned people can come to quite different conclusions.

These are just some of the important social policy questions that Americans will face in the coming years. How we as citizens answer them may have a great deal to do with our quality of life in the twenty-first century.

SUMMARY

You have seen in this chapter that government action and inaction can play a major role in affecting the social welfare status of many poor and elderly Americans. Entitlement programs such as Social Security and Medicare have significantly improved the lot of the elderly, but these very costly programs threaten to grow ever larger and more expensive. Programs aimed more specifically at the poor cost less (and perhaps have accomplished less), but they seem likely to remain objects of political controversy for many years to come.

You have also learned about the nature of wealth and poverty and have discovered that ideas about the causes of poverty are closely related to decisions on what to do about it. Some believe that poverty results from problems within the individual—creating a culture of poverty—whereas others have shown that legal, social, and economic environments may be the most important correlates of poverty status. Individuals' ideas about the causes of poverty are closely associated with the social welfare policies they support and their view of society's responsibilities to the poor.

Social welfare programs, like other government policies, evolve slowly over time. Although there have been important watershed events and policies, such as Social Security in 1935 and the Great Society in the late 1960s, much of the growth and change in American social welfare policies has been incremental in nature, building on past policies, adding a little here, taking a little there.

As we approach the year 2000, Americans will have to struggle over the future directions and financial commitments for social welfare policy. The issues are already well developed and include considerations of the appropriate scope of government and the effectiveness, costs, and fairness of various programs.

With limited financial resources and a growing national debt, choices will be even more difficult to make in the future. Should the government continue spending for the elderly at current levels and rates of increase? As the economy continues to become more technologically sophisticated, how will Americans use their human capital to serve the nation best? Can the United States afford to have a large and essentially nonproductive underclass?

KEY TERMS

social welfare policies
income distribution
relative deprivation
income
wealth
poverty line
culture of poverty
urban underclass
progressive tax
proportional tax
regressive tax
transfer payments

FOR FURTHER READING

Bane, Mary Jo, and David Ellwood, *Welfare Realities: From Rhetoric to Reform.* Cambridge, MA: Harvard University Press, 1994. An overview, by two key participants in the current debate, of some of the key issues related to welfare reform.

Cook, Fay Lomax, and Edith J. Barrett. *Support for the American Welfare State.* New York: Columbia University Press, 1992. A comprehensive review of public opinion about social welfare programs that argues that there is widespread public support for the programs of the Great Society.

Handler, Joel F. *The Poverty of Welfare Reform.* New Haven, CT: Yale University Press, 1995. Handler explodes numerous myths regarding the welfare system and presents evidence that past attempts to reform welfare have proved both ineffective and misguided.

Jencks, Christopher. *Rethinking Social Policy.* Cambridge, MA: Harvard University Press, 1992. A good collection of essays on race, poverty, and the urban underclass.

Kelso, William A. *Poverty and the Underclass: Changing Perceptions of the Poor in America.* New York: New York University Press, 1994. An excellent analysis of the supporting evidence for numerous approaches to dealing with poverty.

Murray, Charles. *Losing Ground: American Social Policy, 1950-1980.* New York: Basic Books, 1984. A conservative's argument that social policies have not worked but actually have made things worse.

Obey, David, and Paul Sarbanes, eds. *The Changing American Economy.* New York: Basil Blackwell, 1986.

Co-chairs of the Joint Economic Committee of Congress, Obey and Sarbanes have brought together a useful selection of articles on the economy and equality.

Olasky, Marvin. *The Tragedy of Human Compassion*. Washington, DC: Regnery, 1992. Newt Gingrich highly recommends this book, which argues that entitlement programs have hurt the poor by driving out aid from private charities that in the past promoted personal responsibility.

Patterson, James T. *America's Struggle Against Poverty, 1900-1994*. Cambridge, MA: Harvard University Press, 1994. A good review of the history of governmental programs to combat poverty.

Phillips, Kevin. *The Politics of Rich and Poor: Wealth and the American Electorate in the Reagan Aftermath*. New York: Random House, 1990. A best-selling book about the redistribution of power and wealth during the 1980s: who got it, who lost it, and through what policies.

Vedlitz, Arnold. *Conservative Mythology and Public Policy in America*. New York: Praeger, 1988. A good counterweight to Murray.

Wilson, William J. *The Truly Disadvantaged: The Inner City, the Underclass, and Public Policy*. Chicago: University of Chicago Press, 1987. The story of the poorest of the poor.

INTERNET RESOURCE

www.census.gov/hhes/www/poverty.html
The Census bureau makes available at this address reports about poverty.

NOTES

1. "Remarks by Rep. Newt Gingrich," in Ed Gillespie and Bob Schellhas, eds., *Contract With America* (New York: Random House, 1994), 189.
2. Thomas B. Edsall, *The New Politics of Inequality* (New York: Norton, 1984), 18.
3. Kevin Phillips, *The Politics of Rich and Poor: Wealth and the American Electorate in the Reagan Aftermath* (New York: Random House, 1990), xvii.
4. Bennet Harrison, Chris Tilly, and Barry Bluestone, "Rising Inequality" in David Obey and Paul Sarbanes, eds., *The Changing American Economy* (New York: Basil Blackwell, 1986), 123.
5. Greg J. Duncan and James N. Morgan, eds., *Five Thousand American Families* (Ann Arbor: University of Michigan Institute for Social Research).
6. Fay Lomax Cook and Edith J. Barrett, *Support for the American Welfare State* (New York: Columbia University Press, 1992), 212.
7. For a discussion of the nature of wealth and poverty in American society, see Arnold Vedlitz, *Conservative Mythology and Public Policy in America* (New York: Praeger, 1988), chaps. 2 and 3.
8. "Welfare Booby Traps," *Newsweek*, December 12, 1994, 34.
9. Duncan and Morgan, *Five Thousand American Families*.
10. William A. Kelso, *Poverty and the Underclass: Changing Perceptions of the Poor in America* (New York: New York University Press, 1994), 170.
11. *Statistical Abstract of the United States, 1994* (Washington, DC: U.S. Government Printing Office, 1994), 343.
12. Morgan Reynolds and Eugene Smolensky, *Public Expenditures, Taxes, and the Distribution of Income* (New York: Academic Press, 1977).
13. Robert Kuttner, "Renewing Opportunity," in *The Changing American Economy*, 138-141.
14. *Ibid.*, 138.
15. John Kingdon, *Agendas, Alternatives, and Public Policies* (Boston: Little, Brown, 1984).
16. For a more detailed discussion of the impact of OBRA on cuts in social welfare programs, see Tom Joe and Cheryl Rogers, *By the Few for the Few: The Reagan Welfare Legacy* (Lexington, MA: Lexington Books, 1985), chap. 7.
17. Charles Murray, *Losing Ground: American Social Policy, 1950-1980* (New York: Basic Books, 1984).
18. Arnold Vedlitz, *Conservative Mythology*, chap. 6.
19. David T. Ellwood and Lawrence H. Summers, "Is Welfare Really the Problem?" *Public Interest* 83 (Spring 1986): 57-78.

19 Policymaking for Health, Energy, and the Environment

The pace of technological change is dizzying. Just over a century separates the production of the first typewriter and the production of the first word processor; about three decades divide the discovery of the proton from the explosion of atomic bombs; only 15 years separate the invention of the jet airplane from the first spacecraft; and just 8 years passed between the time of the first patenting of a microorganism to the first patenting of an animal.

The increasing speed of technological advance creates special problems for government and for policymakers. New issues must be dealt with, posing both practical and moral problems for the political system. When medical researchers develop new techniques for prolonging life, everyone is pleased. Many of these new technologies, however, are amazingly expensive, and their cost has transformed the American medical system. The rapid growth of the American economy during the twentieth century has brought energy and pollution problems to the forefront of politics. Complex issues of energy—for example, choosing between nuclear power and coal as a source of electricity or between offshore oil drilling and dependence on foreign sources of oil—have created political problems during the last three decades. At the same time, Americans have become increasingly sensitive to the quality of the environment, but they find it difficult to determine who should pay to clean up toxic wastes and to make trade-offs between protecting an endangered species and saving jobs.

Technological development has posed new challenges to American democracy. How does the general public affect government decisions on such technically complex issues as determining standards for clean air and regulating pesticides? Does the complexity of such issues give special interests an advantage in the policymaking process? How can citizens compete with the wealth and expertise of organized interests in a battle over health care policy? How can elected officials make decisions about storing nuclear waste when no one wants it near them?

Technological change has also altered Americans' expectations regarding the scope of government. Demands for solutions to problems such as providing access to health care and controlling pollution have greatly expanded the scope of government policies. What *should* the role of government be in ensuring access to health care for all citizens? If energy supplies are scarce and lines at gas stations are long, should government intervene in the marketplace to ration gasoline? Should we go to war to ensure a plentiful supply of petroleum products? Should government impose restrictions on activities in the private sector in order to protect the environment?

Technology has brought important changes to the lives of Americans (see Table 19.1), and the quickened pace of change has made policymaking more complex. This chapter examines public policy and policymaking in three related areas that are important to all Americans and that have been profoundly affected by technological developments: health, energy, and the environment.

HEALTH CARE POLICY

There are few things more important to people than their health. It is often said that Americans enjoy the best health care in the world. But do they also enjoy the best health? And just how much are Americans paying for their health care? Does everyone have access to the miracles of medical technology? And what role does government play in the financing, delivery, and regulation of health care? How does it make policy regarding health care?

THE HEALTH OF AMERICANS

Although Americans are generally healthy (which is to be expected given the country's wealth), health care statistics show that they still lag behind other countries in some key health care categories (see Table 19.2). Americans are *not* the healthiest people in the world.

The average American has a life expectancy of 76 years—a high number, but not the highest in the world. Despite advances in medical technology, the average American does not live as long as the average Canadian. This difference *may* be due in part to lifestyle differences among adults. But what about the *infant mortality rate*—the proportion of babies who do not survive their first year of life—a common indicator of a nation's health? As Table 19.2 shows, the chances in the United States of a baby dying in the first year of life are 50 percent higher than those of a baby born in Japan.[1] Indeed, the United States ranks only nineteenth among the world's nations in infant mortality. The health care system in the United States may be part of the explanation.

THE COST OF HEALTH CARE

The United States spends a higher proportion of its wealth on health care than any other country. Health is one of the largest single components of America's economy, accounting for *one-seventh* (more than 14 percent) of the gross domestic product. Canada,

TABLE 19.1 LIFE IN THE FAST LANE: TECHNOLOGICAL CHANGE IN THE TWENTIETH CENTURY

TECHNOLOGY	1900	1950	2000
Best means of transportation	Horse, train	Automobile	Airplane, automobile
Electricity	Little or none	Nearly universal	Nearly universal
Telephones	Invented, not widespread	Widespread among middle-income families	Nearly universal
Mass communication	Word of mouth or newspapers	Radio	Television, computer
Written communication	Mail, books, some magazines	Newspapers, books, magazines	Newspapers, books, magazines, satellite, computer networks
Most powerful weapons of war	Howitzers, cannons, rifles	Atomic bombs	Hydrogen bombs
Political campaigns	By train	By radio, public rallies	By television, computers, direct mail
"Last frontier" of human exploration	North and South Poles being "discovered"	Most of world explored; some discussion of space	Genes, outer space
Recent advance in medicine	Aspirin first marketed in 1899	Vaccinations against polio and other human scourges nearly ready	Transplants of human organs
Recent advance in biology	Darwinian theory gaining acceptance	Early ideas about DNA and human heritability discussed	Genetic engineering, animal patents
Recent advance in physics	Einstein working on his second paper on relativity	Ability to produce weapons even more destructive than the atomic bomb	Experiments in superconductivity, discovery of subatomic particles

TABLE 19.2 COMPARING AMERICA'S HEALTH: LIFE EXPECTANCY AND INFANT MORTALITY RATES IN SELECTED COUNTRIES

COUNTRY	LIFE EXPECTANCY	INFANT MORTALITY RATE (DEATHS PER 1,000 BIRTHS)
United States	**76.0**	**6.7**
Germany	76.0	6.0
Britain	76.4	6.4
Switzerland	77.6	5.4
Italy	78.1	6.9
France	78.4	6.2
Canada	79.1	6.1
Japan	79.6	4.4

SOURCE: U.S. Bureau of the Census, *Statistical Abstract of the United States, 1996* (Washington, DC: U.S. Government Printing Office, 1996), 831-832.

France, and Germany provide universal health care coverage for their citizens but spend only 8 to 10 percent of their GDPs on health care, and Britain, Japan, and Spain spend only 6 to 7 percent for universal coverage.[2]

As we saw in Chapter 14, 19 cents of every federal tax dollar goes for health care; the cost of every car built in the United States includes $700 for workers' health insurance. The costs of health care are a major obstacle to balancing the federal budget and to investing in the economy. As President Clinton said shortly before taking office, "If I could wave a magic wand tomorrow and do one thing for this economy, I would bring health costs in line with inflation . . . because . . . that would free more money for people to invest in the plants and the production and the jobs of the future."[3]

Americans spend about *$1 trillion* a year on health care, and health care costs are increasing rapidly. Why are health care expenditures in the United States so enormous? There are many reasons. American health providers have overbuilt medical care facilities (34 percent of all hospital beds are vacant on any given day),[4] and doctors and hospitals have few incentives to be more efficient. New technologies, drugs, and procedures often add to the cost of health care by addressing previously untreatable conditions or by providing better, but more expensive, care. Much of the money that Americans pay for health care goes to services like organ transplants, kidney dialysis, and other treatments that are not widely available outside the United States. These treatments also cost a lot.

Because insurance companies and government programs pay for most health care expenses, most patients have no reason to ask for cheaper care—they do not face the full financial consequences of their care. The providers of health care, such as physicians, are also insulated from competing with each other to offer less expensive care. In fact, with the rise in medical malpractice suits, doctors may be ordering extra tests, however expensive they may be, to ensure that they cannot be sued—an approach that is sometimes called "defensive medicine." Such practices drive up the costs of medical care for everyone. As doctors are hit with higher and higher costs for insurance against malpractice suits, they increase their fees to pay their premiums. Because insurance companies pay the bills, patients do not protest. However, increased costs associated with medical care are making insurance rates skyrocket.

How can one explain the contradiction between the high costs that Americans pay for health care—the highest costs in the world—and the fact that Americans are not the world's healthiest people? One explanation can be found in the way the American health care industry organizes itself.

ACCESS TO HEALTH CARE

Inequalities in health and health care are a serious problem in America. Americans spend large amounts of money on health, and the world's highest-quality care is available to some citizens. Nevertheless, many poor and working Americans are relegated to an inferior health care system, because access to health insurance is not universal in the United States as it is in many countries.[5]

Most Americans have health insurance, but about 41 million people—15 percent of the public—are without health insurance coverage for the entire year.[6] Millions of others are without health insurance for shorter periods.[7] Most of the uninsured are under 65, because nearly everyone 65 and older participates in Medicare. Another 36 million individuals without private health insurance receive health care benefits from Medicaid, which helps those with very low incomes. Yet many Americans simply go without proper health care. A national poll found that 39 percent of Americans reported not seeing a doctor for a medical problem because it would have cost too much.[8]

Getting and keeping health insurance are often linked to having a job, especially a high-paying job.[9] Often, the lack of health insurance is associated with short periods of unemployment. Nevertheless, the majority of the nation's uninsured are full-time workers (and their families), most of whom work for companies with 100 or fewer employees and earn low

Many Americans lack access to health care. President Clinton, appearing here at a rally in Minneapolis, has made improved health care a centerpiece of his administration.

wages. Their employers have to pay more for health insurance do than larger companies, mostly because health risks and marketing and administrative costs cannot be spread as broadly. Thus, many small companies find providing health insurance too costly.[10]

Access to health insurance in the United States is also closely tied to race and income. Thirty-three percent of Hispanics and 21 percent of African Americans lack health insurance for the entire year, but only 14 percent of whites do. Thirty percent of the poor lack health insurance, despite the existence of Medicaid and Medicare.[11]

Discrepancies in access to health care are reflected in the health of different groups. Whites have an average life expectancy 7 years longer than that of African Americans. For African-American males, life expectancy is 8 years less than for white males and is lower than the averages in many Eastern European and less developed countries. Not all of this difference can be explained by variances in lifestyles and nutrition. Similarly, infant mortality rates among those with good insurance plans and a family doctor are very low. For those without insurance, the statistics are disturbing. African-American infant mortality is over twice as high as that for whites.[12]

For Americans who lack health insurance, having the most up-to-date research and equipment available is less important than having access to a family doctor or someone to administer prenatal and neonatal care. These people receive less health care, they do not see health care professionals regularly, and when they do, they typically receive poorer-quality care than individuals with insurance. They also run the risk of financial ruin in paying for health care.

Tremendous advances have been made in the technology available to keep premature babies alive, but many pregnant women, especially in the nation's inner cities, lack the care that will ensure that their babies will be born healthy. Instead of having a family doctor (few doctors practice in poor neighborhoods), many of the nation's poor go only to hospital emergency rooms. Prenatal care is an important component in reducing health risks during the first year of life, but prenatal care is not available to all. Often, the availability of family doctors and routine hospital services are more important in determining the quality of a nation's health care than the most current medical and research equipment.

Even among those who have insurance, coverage is often incomplete. Especially for those with low-paying jobs, health insurance may not cover all of their health needs. About 20 million Americans have inadequate insurance and receive less and poorer-quality health care than those with more comprehensive insurance. These individuals often postpone treatment until illnesses worsen and require more expensive emergency treatment.[13]

THE ROLE OF GOVERNMENT IN HEALTH CARE

Medical care in the United States differs from that in most other democracies in one important way: the role that the government plays. The United States has the most thoroughly privatized medical care system in the developed world. Forty-seven percent of the country's total health bill is paid for by government sources, whereas the average for all industrialized countries is about 75 percent (see Figure 19.1). The government also subsidizes employer-provided health insurance with tax breaks worth about $76 billion per year, the benefits of which go disproportionately to affluent, highly paid workers.

Forty-seven percent amounts to much more than most Americans realize. Many hospitals are connected to public universities, and much medical research is financed through the **National Institutes of Health (NIH)**, for example. Further, the federal government pays for much of the nation's medical bill through the Medicare program for the elderly, the Medicaid program for the poor, and health care for veterans. One of three doctors in the United States works for the federal government, and nearly all the rest receive payments from it. The government thus plays an important health care role in America, though less so than in other countries.

Who pays for the rest of Americans' health care? Private insurance companies cover about one-third, and Americans pay one-fifth of their health care costs out of their own pockets (see Figure 19.2, page 482). Americans often think that insurance companies pay most health care costs, but in fact the government is more heavily involved than the private insurance industry.

Harry S Truman was the first president to call for **national health insurance,** a compulsory insurance program to finance all Americans' medical care. The idea was strongly opposed by the American Medical Association, the largest physicians' interest group, which called this program *socialized medicine.* Although every other industrial nation in the world has adopted some form of national health insurance, the United States remains the exception.

Nonetheless, in 1965 Congress recognized the special problems of elderly Americans by adopting **Medicare.** Medicare is part of the Social Security system and covers 39 million people. Part A of Medicare provides hospitalization insurance and short-term nursing care; Part B, which is voluntary, permits older Americans to purchase inexpensive coverage for doc-

FIGURE 19.1 GOVERNMENT SPENDING AS A PERCENT OF TOTAL HEALTH SPENDING IN SELECTED DEMOCRACIES

As in many other areas of the economy, the role of government is smaller in the United States than in comparable countries. The United States lacks national health insurance or a national health service to provide health care directly to those who need it. Still, the government accounts for over 47 percent of all money spent on health care in this country—a sizable percentage. In fact, the government is the largest single source of health care dollars, providing more funds than even private insurance companies.

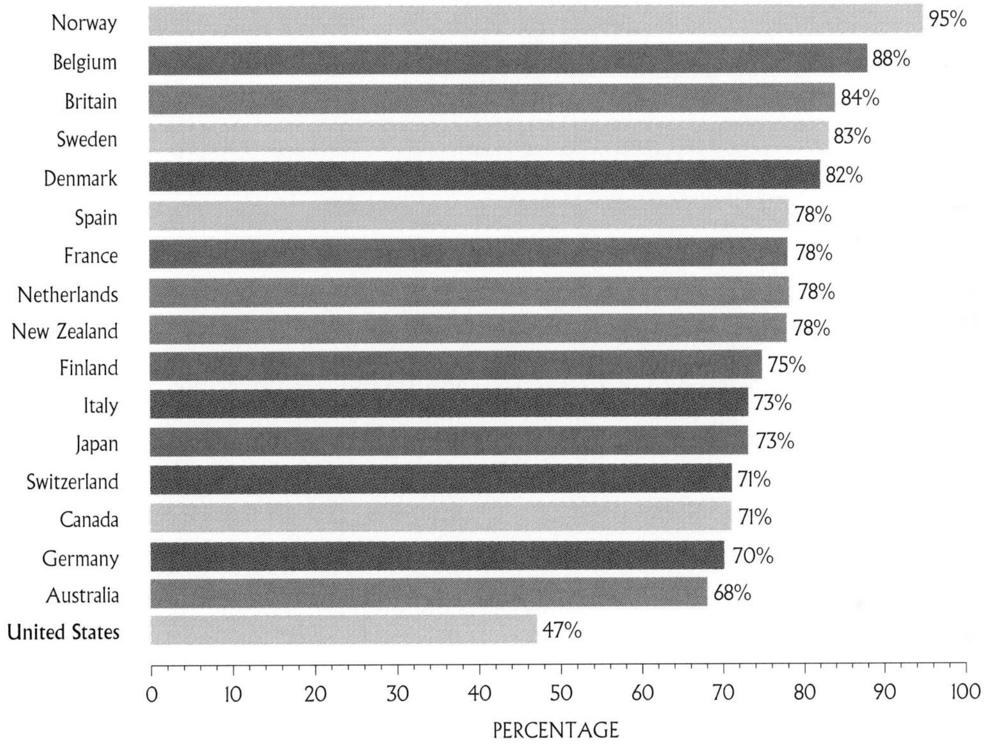

SOURCE: U.S. Bureau of the Census, *Statistical Abstract of the United States, 1996* (Washington, DC: U.S. Government Printing Office, 1996), 834.

tor fees and other nonhospital medical expenses. Because the number of older Americans grows rapidly—and because the cost of medical care is growing just as fast (Medicare cost about $207 billion in 1998)—the funding of health care for the elderly is one of the country's most pressing public policy issues.

Not to be confused with Medicare is **Medicaid,** a program that is designed to provide health care for the poor and serves about 35 million people. Like other public assistance programs, Medicaid is funded by both the states and the national government (in 1998, the federal government alone spent $106 billion on Medicaid). Unlike Medicare, which goes to elderly Americans regardless of their income, Medicaid is a means-tested program. Only those who make less than a certain amount of money are eligible to receive Medicaid. Debates arise about the formulas for determining eligibility, because people with low-paying jobs often are not eligible, whereas those on welfare may qualify. Thus, because of the loss of health benefits and the high cost of purchasing them privately, it may not pay to take a low-wage service job. Obviously, however, the government does not want to encourage people *not* to work.

Government in America plays an important role in health care, even if it is less involved than in other countries. One way to explain the uneven access to health care in the United States is to look at the makers of health care policy.

POLICYMAKING FOR HEALTH CARE

The cost of medical care in a high-tech age raises issues people do not usually like to discuss, much less debate

FIGURE 19.2 WHO PAYS MEDICAL COSTS? GOVERNMENT VERSUS PRIVATE SOURCES

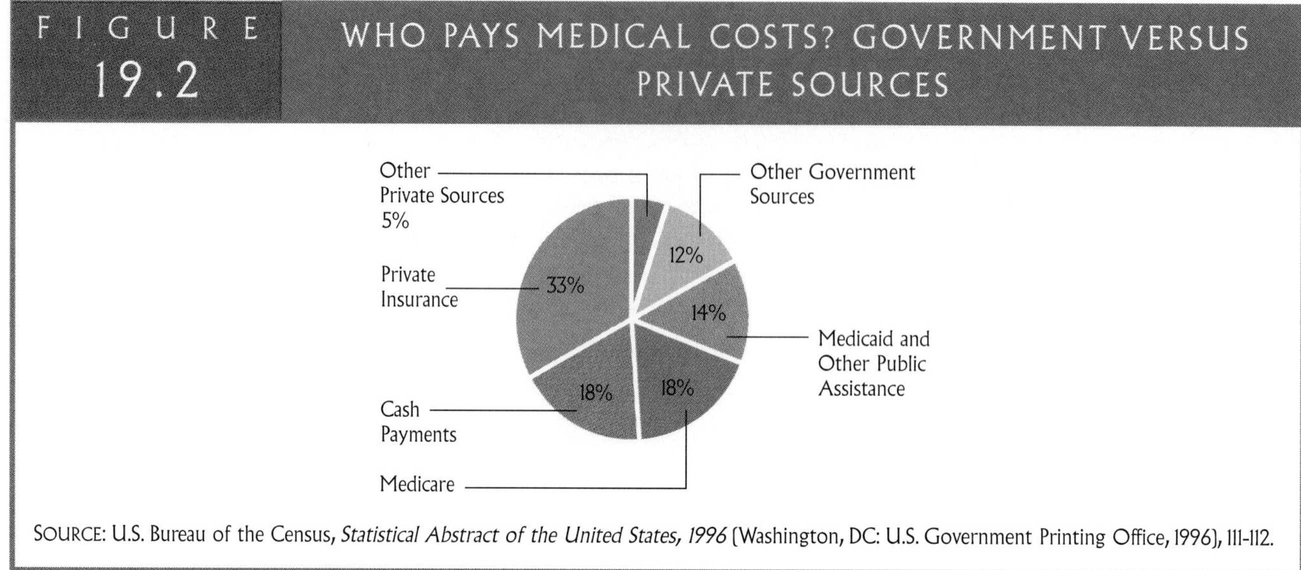

SOURCE: U.S. Bureau of the Census, *Statistical Abstract of the United States, 1996* (Washington, DC: U.S. Government Printing Office, 1996), 111-112.

as public policy problems. Death is one such issue; today, 90 percent of all Americans die either in hospitals or in nursing homes, most of them funded and regulated by the government. Like it or not, health care is a governmental problem in the United States.

One of the reasons why the United States emphasizes expensive and high-tech solutions to complicated health problems is that traditionally, no single institution has paid medical bills. With a mixture of government funds, private insurance, and out-of-pocket payments, no one is solely responsible for health care costs, and no one has primary responsibility for controlling them. In countries with national health care systems (or national health insurance), government policymakers have focused more on ensuring equality of care and on containing costs, especially administrative costs. In the United States, equality of care and cost containment have taken a back seat to technological advance. At times, competition among urban hospitals to provide the most advanced care has led to duplication of expensive equipment and thus higher health costs. Thus, Americans have high-tech, expensive, and unequal care.

Many lifesaving procedures are extremely expensive, so allocating their use involves complicated questions of public policy. Dollars spent on expensive procedures to save a few lives cannot be spent on other, equally pressing health needs. Thus, when the government allows Medicare payments for certain procedures, less money is available for rural hospitals, for health clinics in poor areas of the nation's cities, or for other problems. Oregon has taken the lead on the issue of rationing health care, trying to set priorities for medical treatments under the Medicaid program, which is funded by both the state and the national government.

One reason for uneven government and private health care policies involves the representation of interests. Powerful lobbying organizations representing hospitals, doctors, and the elderly want Medicare to pay for the latest techniques. Politicians hardly feel comfortable denying these lifesaving measures to those who may have voted them into office. On the other hand, many groups are unrepresented in government. Their health needs may not be met simply because no well-organized groups are insisting that the government meet them.

The elderly are now one of the most powerful voting and lobbying forces in American politics. Health care policy that favors the elderly is one of the results of this interest group activity. The American Association of Retired Persons (AARP) has grown from about 150,000 members in 1959 to more than 32 million in 1996, making it the largest voluntary association in the world.[14] This single group now can claim to represent 1 American in 8 and speaks with authority on all questions associated with the elderly. The political power of the elderly was obvious to members of Congress in 1989 when older people objected to the Social Security surtax designed to pay for new catastrophic illness coverage. Congress was forced to repeal the tax after the "gray lobby" flexed its muscles.

For workers in low-paying service jobs that do not include health insurance, and for those who are unemployed and cannot afford private health insurance, there is no organization capable of exerting such influence in government. Because many of these people do

Health care policymaking involves difficult ethical issues. For example, should limited federal funds be spent on the expensive, unproven, but potentially lifesaving artificial heart technology shown here? Or should public money be devoted to less dramatic medical procedures that could help many more Americans?

not vote, the bias in representation is even greater. The groups that enjoy good health care coverage in the United States are largely those that are well organized to influence the government.

One group that is increasingly active in health care policymaking is business. Conflict between the government (which pays many medical bills) and private employers (who pay much of the insurance premiums for their employees) is increasing. Each side wants the other to assume more of the health care burden. For example, the government is saving money by forcing patients to exhaust their private insurance before allowing government programs to begin making payments. As the government reduces its payments in such ways, doctors and hospitals pass on their costs to those patients with private insurance. As private insurance rates increase, employers complain that they are paying inflated premiums for their workers to cover the costs of those who cannot pay or whose insurance provides only partial reimbursement for medical care. Employers then may attempt to reduce their burden by cutting out benefits that are covered by government programs.

Business groups are increasingly calling for relief in the health care field. For example, they complain that their foreign competitors avoid the high costs of private insurance premiums because governments, rather than employers, cover health insurance costs in many other countries. At the same time, employers defend the $76 billion tax break, or subsidy, that they receive for providing health insurance to their employees. Yet such insurance has high administrative costs, ties workers to a specific job rather than encouraging labor mobility, and continues to insulate people from the consequences of their health care costs.[15]

Insurance companies are also major players in health care policymaking. They have been making it more difficult for doctors and hospitals to pass along the costs of others' unpaid bills to them, causing a cost crunch for some institutions, including inner-city hospitals and trauma centers that serve the poor. In addition, the health insurance industry has a huge stake in the outcome of the debate on national health insurance. A program funded and run by the national government would leave insurance companies without a function. Thus, they are fighting to be seen as a viable alternative.

President Clinton made health care reform the centerpiece of his first administration. His 5-pound, 1,342-page Health Security Act proposal was an effort to deal with the two great problems of health care policy: costs and access. The difficulties the president faced with this proposal reveal much about the challenge of reforming health care in America.

The president's main concern was guaranteeing health care coverage for all Americans. This would particularly have benefited the 15 percent or so of the people without any health insurance, but it would also have extended coverage for millions of others with inadequate health insurance.

Paying for the plan would have necessitated either broad-based taxes, which were politically unpalatable, or a requirement that employers provide health insurance for their employees or pay a premium into a public fund (which would also cover Medicaid and Medicare recipients). The president chose the employer insurance option, but the small business community was adamantly opposed to bearing the cost of providing health insurance. The president also proposed raising taxes on cigarettes, which angered the tobacco industry, and imposing a small tax on certain large companies.

To contain health care costs, the administration would have required states to set up large consumer groups called "health alliances" to collect premiums, bargain with health plans, and handle payments. Most companies would have had to buy coverage through an alliance. The proposal would also have limited the annual increase in the price of health insurance premiums and cap government spending for Medicare (threatening the elderly) and Medicaid.

Because the White House reform plan for health care was bureaucratic and complicated, it was easy for opponents to label it a government takeover of the health care system. An aggressive advertising campaign mounted by opponents characterized the president's plan as being expensive and experimental, as providing lower-quality and rationed care, and as killing jobs.

In addition, the middle class felt its health care threatened. Gallup polls found that the public saw Clinton's health care reform proposal as a typical Democratic social welfare program—one that helps the poor, hurts the middle class, and creates bigger government. In the end, people were more worried about what would happen if health care reform passed than about losing their health insurance: Too much government was a bigger concern than too little health insurance.[16] After a long and tortuous battle, the plan died in Congress.

As Congress wrangles over the government's role in health care, private market forces are transforming the country's health care system dramatically. A majority of privately insured Americans are enrolled in managed-care plans that limit the choice of doctors and treatments. Insurers choose health maintenance organizations (HMOs) or restricted physician lists for the provision of care, negotiate with physician groups and hospitals on fees and costs, and try to monitor most aspects of care to control unnecessary use. At least three-fourths of all doctors have signed contracts, covering at least some of their patients, to cut their fees and accept oversight of their medical decisions. These measures are designed to contain the costs of health care, but they have done nothing to ease the plight of those without health insurance. In addition, they have raised new questions about how quality care can be preserved.

Health care will be an important public policy problem for some time to come. There are likely to be increasing calls for more government regulation of the costs of health care and some attempt to help those who fall through the cracks of the American health care system. Health care is only one area where increasing technology has significantly affected American public policy; such impacts are also clear in the area of energy.

ENERGY POLICY

Modern American society depends on the availability of abundant energy. Producing the amounts of energy necessary to retain Americans' standard of living and accustomed patterns of life is increasingly difficult, however. Government is constantly involved in battles concerning what forms of energy the country should be producing, and from what sources.

The federal government shapes energy policies in dozens of ways. For one thing, it owns much of the land from which energy comes. In California, for example, about half the land is owned by government. David Davis, a political scientist who specializes in the subject, emphasizes that energy politics is fragmented.[17] Whereas some energy sources (such as nuclear power) are tightly regulated by the government, others (such as coal) are left mostly to the free market.

AMERICA'S ENERGY PROFILE

Once Americans used wood, animals, water, and people power for energy. Today 85 percent of the nation's energy comes from coal, oil, and natural gas.[18] Americans search continually for new and more efficient sources of energy, both to increase supplies and to reduce pollution. Much of the research on new energy sources and efficiencies comes from the government in Washington.

Oil, which accounts for half the energy Americans use, is one of nature's **nonrenewable resources.** Some resources, such as the wind and solar energy, are renewable; that is, using them once does not reduce the amount left to be used in the future. These things are constantly renewed by nature. Oil, coal, and other common sources of energy, however, are not renewable.

More than half of the world's recoverable reserves of oil lie in the Middle East; Saudi Arabia alone controls much of this resource. States such as Texas, Oklahoma, Louisiana, and Alaska produce considerable amounts of oil within the United States, but not enough to meet the country's needs. America imports about 50 percent of its annual consumption of oil from other countries, particularly from the Middle East. The United States is not so dependent on foreign sources of oil as many European countries, like France or Italy, which have virtually no oil of their own, or like Japan, which also imports all of its oil. On the other hand, America's dependence on foreign oil is growing greater every year.

Oil has made its mark on political history; by any measure, it is the world's biggest business. Many believe it fuels wars in the Middle East, and few would question that guaranteeing oil supplies—not liberating Kuwait or deterring Saddam Hussein—was the primary reason for Operation Desert Storm in 1991. Oil, as much as anything else, is at the root of decades of tension between Iran and the United States.[19] Domestically, when fingers are pointed at a corporate or political elite, the names of oil companies soon come up.

Coal, not oil, is America's most abundant fuel. An estimated 90 percent of the country's energy resources are in coal deposits—enough to last hundreds of years. Coal, however, accounts for only about 22 percent of the energy Americans use.[20] Although coal may be the nation's most abundant fuel, unfortunately it is also the dirtiest. It is responsible for the "black lung" health hazard to coal miners and for the soot-blackened cities of the Northeast. Acid rain is traced to the burning of coal to produce electricity. Coal may be abundant, but most Americans do not want to rely on it exclusively for their energy needs.

The most controversial energy source is nuclear power. During the 1940s and 1950s, Americans were convinced that the technology that had ended World War II could be made to serve peaceful purposes. Nuclear scientists spoke enthusiastically about harnessing the atom to produce electricity that would be "too cheap to meter." At one time, more nuclear power plants were built in the United States than any other country in the world, and American technology was exported overseas to dozens of nations.

After the accidents at Three Mile Island and Chernobyl and the cost overruns associated with the industry, nuclear power today bears almost no resemblance to the optimistic images it conjured up in the 1950s and early 1960s. The wave of environmental concern that developed in the late 1960s devastated the nuclear power industry.[21] The United States has not initiated any new nuclear power plants since 1978, and nearly all those under construction at that time have been abandoned with huge financial losses.

POLICYMAKING FOR ENERGY ISSUES

Energy issues involve a number of different actors, from local governments (which often own municipal power companies) to the states, the federal government, and outside interests. These issues often pit environmentalists against energy producers and even pit different levels of government against each other. For example, many local power companies are owned by cities but are regulated by states and the federal government. Federalism plays an important role in energy issues.

Energy issues continually present thorny problems for policymakers to resolve. For example, there are a number of ways to produce electricity. The United States generates about 56 percent of its electricity by burning coal. About 13 percent comes from either natural gas or petroleum. Nuclear power represents about 22 percent of electrical production, hydroelectric power about 9 percent. All other forms of energy—including solar, wind, wood, and geothermal power—account for only about 0.5 percent of America's electrical capacity.[22]

Each source of electricity creates problems. Coal is abundant but filthy. It contributes to global warming, smog, and acid rain, and it causes health problems for miners. Natural gas and petroleum are somewhat cleaner (though they too contribute to global warming), but neither is renewable, and petroleum imports inevitably lead to oil spills. Nuclear power produces radioactive waste, and hydroelectric power plants flood large areas of land. And conserving wasted energy requires either regulation or the investment of scarce financial resources. None of these forms of electricity generation is perfect, but Americans want their lights to come on when they flip a switch. Policymakers must decide what mix of energy sources to use (see "America in Perspective: Comparing Sources of Electricity").

Recently, policymakers have shown more interest in conservation, renewable energy supplies, and alternative fuels. The 1992 energy bill, for example—the closest thing the United States has to a comprehensive national energy strategy—encourages the development of renewable energy sources and alternative "clean" fuels (such as methane and natural gas), mandates efficiency standards for buildings and home appliances, and encourages state utilities to reward conservation. The bill left many issues open, but it showed a new appreciation for the role that newer

COMPARING SOURCES OF ELECTRICITY

America in Perspective

Every country must decide what mix of energy sources to use to meet its electricity needs. These decisions are based on the availability of natural resources and on the mobilization of political interests. Hydroelectric power is generally inexpensive and poses few environmental problems, especially when fast-flowing rivers or waterfalls already exist. Countries are limited by nature in the extent to which they can exploit this resource, however. Italy, for example, has many dams in the northern alpine regions. Most countries face a choice between conventional sources of electricity (essentially coal or oil) and nuclear power. France has virtually eliminated conventional sources. In the United States, over 70 percent of the country's electricity comes from conventional sources.

How did the French do it? In 1973, the Arab oil embargo hit France much harder than the United States, because France imported over 95 percent of its oil. National leaders decided to adopt an ambitious plan to build 55 new nuclear reactors. Ten years later, over 60 percent of the nation's electricity came from nuclear power. Frank Baumgartner, a political scientist who has studied this decision, says that France's nuclear program was implemented successfully because participation is strictly limited to technical experts. Opportunities for nuclear power opponents to intervene in administrative hearings, to initiate court cases, or to obstruct the process in any way are limited by law. The national legislature has not played an important role, in contrast to the active role that the U.S. Congress has sometimes played in nuclear power regulation. Similarly, the courts have not intervened as they have in other countries. (One of Napoleon's legacies is that the executive branch is rarely subject to independent judicial review.) Local governments in France are not in a position to oppose national government decisions, either (another Napoleonic legacy). Finally, regulatory procedures are designed in such a way as to limit the opportunity for nongovernmental officials to participate; in other words, no environmental impact statements.

"The most fundamental difference between French and U.S. policymaking concerning nuclear power," explains Baumgartner, "is the great authority of the high civil service to make decisions virtually in secret and without any public debate over the merits of its choices, which are always portrayed as simply the technical and neutral implementation of decisions made by the elected officials." The complicated institutional structures and open participation requirements of American policymaking would have made France's massive implementation of nuclear power impossible.

SOURCE: Frank R. Baumgartner, *Conflict and Rhetoric in French Policymaking* (Pittsburgh: University of Pittsburgh Press, 1989).

energy sources (and conservation) can play in improving the environment and reducing the United States' dependence on energy imports. The bill's passage also suggested that renewable and alternative energy sources, as well as conservation, are increasingly seen as compatible with continued economic growth.

Still, despite considerable media attention to the newer fuels—solar energy, windmills, geothermal power, and the like—their contribution to America's energy supply is likely to remain small for the foreseeable future, and the United States is likely to continue to lag behind its chief economic competitors in energy efficiency. Unless the costs of fuel once again skyrocket (as oil prices did in the 1970s), and unless policymakers substantially widen the scope of the 1992 energy plan, significant investment either in conservation or in the new fuels is unlikely.

The trade-offs between nuclear and other forms of energy emphasize many of the problems of politics in a high-tech age. Environmentalists dislike nuclear power because of radiation leaks in the mining, transportation, and use of atomic fuel; because of the enormous problem of nuclear waste disposal; and because of the inherent difficulty of regulating such complex technology. Defenders of nuclear energy argue that burning coal to generate electricity continues to blacken miners' lungs, causes acid rain that defoliates forests and kills lakes, adds to global warming, and creates other problems. Discussing energy policy in the United States, therefore, almost automatically means discussing environmental policy as well.[23]

ENVIRONMENTAL POLICY

One might think that such a cherished national treasure as the natural environment would be above politics. After all, public opinion analyst Louis Harris reported that "the American people's desire to battle pollution is one of the most overwhelming and clearest we have ever recorded in our twenty-five years of surveying public opinion."[24] As you have learned throughout this text, however, politics infuses itself into all public decisions—even measures to control air and water pollution. Issues of pollution affect political choices through their impact on business, economic growth, and jobs.

ECONOMIC GROWTH AND THE ENVIRONMENT

Environmental controls figure prominently in the debate about local and state economic development. As you saw in Chapter 3, the federal system puts the states in competition for economic advantage. Millions of dollars are spent by states and cities pushing for large investments, such as a billion-dollar GM Saturn plant. New business is a boon to the local and state economies as well as to the political fortunes of their politicians. Business elites can often argue that stringent pollution-control laws will drive businesses away by driving up their costs. On the other hand, states with lax pollution enforcement may find their citizens unhappy, and those businesses that move to their area may find employees unwilling to come along. Thus, state competition does not always work against pollution standards. In fact, sometimes states compete with each other to enforce tighter pollution and land use controls. In the process, they sometimes realize substantial direct savings as well.[25]

This dying forest on Mount Mitchell in North Carolina shows the devastating effects of acid rain, which is formed when tall smokestacks at coal-burning plants belch pollution high into the atmosphere. Much of the acid rain caused by American industries actually falls in Canada; officials there estimate that more than 2000 lakes have "died" as a result of acid rain.

Inevitably, business and government battle over the impact of pollution control on economic development. This is one of the trade-offs policymakers often face: Will tougher pollution legislation drive away commerce and industry? No one, of course, knows for sure.[26] Many states are betting that they will not. California, which has the most stringent antipollution laws in the country, still attracts thousands of businesses every year. It may be costly to enforce pollution legislation, but states can save money by reducing health risks to residents. In addition, many new industries are in the service sector of the economy rather than the industrial sector, and these new businesses often do not want to locate in areas where environmental enforcement is lax.

Concern for the environment and concern about economic development can overlap in complex ways. The fledgling **Environmental Protection Agency (EPA),** created in 1970, has had to deal with industrial pollution, among other things. Congress required that the EPA set standards for "ambient air"—standards about just how clean the air had to be. States and localities were required to take policy actions to bring air cleanliness up to standards set by the EPA. Naturally, environmentalists insisted that *higher* standards be adopted for those areas with *cleaner* air. It would be silly, said environmentalists, to set standards so low in clean-air San Antonio that industries and autos might pollute it to the level of dirty-air Gary, Indiana.

In 1977 Congress wrote some amendments to the Clean Air Act, formally requiring the "nondegradation" standard. A community could not, insisted the policy, permit "degradation" of its air quality, whether it started out with pristine air or the foulest air in the country. Suppose you wanted to locate a new plant in a community that had little pollution. You could not, said the law, worsen air quality there, even if the air was still better than that in 99 percent of the rest of the country. Thus, you would have to install expensive "scrubbers" if you used coal and other expensive pollution abatement techniques if you did not.

The results of these amendments were predictable. Industries were discouraged from relocating in clean-air environments, mostly in the Sunbelt, because of the cost of doing so. Robert Crandall carefully analyzed the supporters of this clean-air amendment. Not surprisingly, they hailed mostly from urban, industrialized areas of the Northeast—the areas likely, without a nondegradation policy, to lose industry to the Sunbelt.[27] No doubt each vote was motivated by a sincere environmental concern. Still, environmental concern can often be mixed with an equal measure of self-interest.

PUBLIC CONCERN ABOUT THE ENVIRONMENT

Concern for the environment has increased greatly in the United States since the 1950s, when few environmental groups were around. Since then, growth in membership for many of the most important groups has been measured in the millions. Following the passage of important legislation in the early 1970s, these groups have gained important victories, and many of their goals are now part of the political mainstream.

Americans today are much more concerned about the environment than they were when President Reagan came to office in 1981. Steadily increasing percentages of Americans are willing to see the government spend money to clean up and protect the environment. As you can see in "The People Speak" on this page, the great majority of people favor strong government action to protect the environment and strict regulations against polluters.

ENVIRONMENTAL POLICIES IN AMERICA

The centerpiece of federal environmental policy is the **National Environmental Policy Act (NEPA)**, passed in 1969.[28] This law requires both government and private agencies to complete **environmental impact statements (EIS).** Every time an agency proposes to undertake a policy that is potentially disruptive to the natural environment, it must file an EIS with the Environmental Protection Agency, detailing possible effects of the policy. Big dams and small post offices, major port construction and minor road widening—proposals for all these projects must include an EIS.

Strictly speaking, an environmental impact statement is merely a procedural requirement. "In theory," says William Ophuls, "an agency can report that a proposed activity will cause the sky to fall . . . and still proceed with the project once it has satisfied the procedural requirements of the act."[29] In practice, the filing of impact statements alerts environmentalists to proposed projects. Environmentalists can then take agencies to court for violating the Act's procedural requirements if the agencies file incomplete or inaccurate impact statements. Because environmental impacts are usually so complicated and difficult to predict, it is relatively easy to argue that the statements are either incomplete or inaccurate in some way. Agencies have often abandoned proposed projects to avoid prolonged court battles with environmental groups.

The law does not give the environmental groups the right to stop any environmentally unsound activities, but it does give them the opportunity to delay construction so much that agencies simply give up. Chances are that many of the biggest public works projects of the past century—including the Hoover Dam, Kennedy Airport, Cape Canaveral's space facility, and most Tennessee Valley Authority projects—would not have survived the environmental scrutiny to which they would have been subject had they been undertaken after the NEPA was enacted. In any case, the NEPA has been an effective tool in preventing environmental despoliation.

Another landmark piece of legislation affecting the environment is the **Clean Air Act of 1970.** It charges the Department of Transportation (DOT) with the responsibility of reducing automobile emissions. For years after the Act's passage, fierce battles raged between the automakers and the DOT about how stringent the requirements had to be. Automakers claimed it was impossible to meet DOT standards; the DOT claimed that automakers were deliberately dragging their feet in the hope that Congress would delay or weaken the requirements. In fact, Congress did weaken them, again and again. Still, the smaller size of American cars, the use of unleaded gasoline, and the lower gas consumption of new cars are all due in large part to DOT regulations. In 1990 Congress passed a reauthorization of the Clean Air Act, which significantly increased the controls on cars, oil refineries, chemical plants, and coal-fired utility plants. This bill

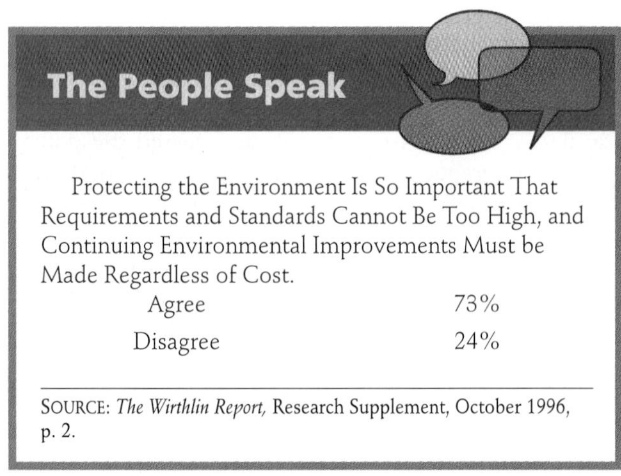
The People Speak

Protecting the Environment Is So Important That Requirements and Standards Cannot Be Too High, and Continuing Environmental Improvements Must be Made Regardless of Cost.

Agree	73%
Disagree	24%

SOURCE: *The Wirthlin Report,* Research Supplement, October 1996, p. 2.

DETERMINING STANDARDS FOR CLEAN AIR

You Are the Policymaker

As Congress considers standards for industry to rid the air of toxic substances, there are many complicated trade-offs. In the 1970 Clean Air Act, Congress ordered the Environmental Protection Agency to list all air pollutants likely to cause an increase in death or serious illness. Then the EPA was to have 1 year to set limits on emissions in order to protect public health. Twenty years later the EPA had set standards for only 7 toxins. More than 200 others had been identified as candidates for regulation. Why is it so difficult to set limits on air pollution?

One reason is the scope of the problem. In 1987, the EPA estimated the amount of toxins belched out by American factories to be 2.7 billion pounds. Then they reported that their estimate might be low; the actual figure might be two to five times higher. People had not realized the scope of the emissions problem until the EPA report. Once the scope became clear, pressure for quick government action increased. Environmentalists, who had claimed that the problem was worse than the government estimated, were reinforced in their perceptions, giving them greater clout in Congress.

Another reason for delay is the complicated nature of the evidence. For example, many of the toxic emissions that come from factory smoke are known to cause cancer in high doses, but there is debate about their effects in smaller doses. How much of each toxin is required to give someone cancer is not well known. Some people argue that the EPA should enforce a *zero-emissions policy*. Such a policy would allow no emissions of those toxins that are known to cause cancer in any quantity. This might be safe, but it would be likely to close down whole segments of industry, devastating local and state economies. Thus, setting the precise standards is a tricky exercise in balancing economic costs with the health of the population.

Another problem for policymakers is where to put the first priority for action. Although some emissions come from large chemical plants, automobile factories, and the like, many others come from millions of small sources, such as cars, dry cleaners, wood stoves, and gas stations. The EPA estimates that such local sources cause up to three-quarters of all the cancers in some urban areas.

If you were involved in determining standards for clean air, how would you set standards for emissions of toxins? With a zero-emissions policy, or some less strict standard? How high should the emissions levels be for each of the toxins you would have to regulate? Would you think it best to focus government enforcement activities on cleaning up the relatively small number of large industrial polluters or on regulating the large number of small polluters? These are a few of the questions you would face as a policymaker trying to address the diverse problems that arise in the area of clean-air legislation.

SOURCE: George Hager, "Clean-Air Package, Part One: Toxic Air Pollutants," *Congressional Quarterly*, April 22, 1989, 888-889. Much of this example is based on his article.

was the strongest step forward in the fight to clean the air since the bill's original passage 20 years earlier (see "You Are the Policymaker: Determining Standards for Clean Air").

Congress acted to control pollution of the nation's lakes and rivers with the **Water Pollution Control Act of 1972.** This was enacted in reaction to the tremendous pollution of northeastern rivers and the Great Lakes. Since its passage, water quality has improved dramatically.

As we have noted, the agency charged with administering these laws is the *Environmental Protection Agency (EPA)*. Created in 1970, it is now the nation's largest federal regulatory agency. The EPA has a wide-ranging mission; in addition to enforcing the NEPA, the Clean Air Act, and the Water Pollution Control Act, it is charged with administering policies that deal with toxic wastes such as dangerous chemicals.

In addition to protecting air and water, environmental policy literally aims to keep some parts of the environment intact. One component of the environment that has received special attention is wilderness—those areas that are largely untouched by human activities. Ever since the founding of the National Park system in 1916, the United States has been a world leader in wilderness preservation.

Perhaps the most consistently successful environmental campaigns in the postwar era have been those aimed at preserving such wild lands.[30] Still, only about 4 percent of the United States is now designated as wilderness, and half of that is in Alaska. In addition, wilderness areas—with the biological, recreational, and symbolic values they embody—are coming under increasing pressure from those who stress the economic benefits lost by keeping them intact.

Preserving wilderness areas indirectly helps protect another part of the larger environment: wildlife. National policy protects wildlife in other, more direct ways as well. The **Endangered Species Act of 1973,** for example, created an endangered species protection program in the U.S. Fish and Wildlife Service. More important, the law required the government to protect actively each of the hundreds of species listed as endangered—regardless of the economic effect on the surrounding towns or region. Later, during the Reagan administration, the act was amended to allow exceptions in cases of overriding national or regional interest. A cabinet-level committee, quickly labeled "The God Squad," was established to decide such cases. As EPA Chief William Reilly explained, "The God Squad is a group of people, of which I am a minor divinity, which has the power to blow away a species."[31] The God Squad has granted few exemptions to the Endangered Species Act so far, but because endangered species are increasingly threatened by expanding human populations and growing economic demands, it is likely to be called on more frequently in coming years to exercise its "divine" powers.

Recently an intense fight over protecting endangered species centered on the northern spotted owl, a bird that prospers in the large, centuries-old trees of the Pacific Northwest. Environmentalists wanted areas of old-growth, publicly owned timber declared off limits to lumber companies in order to protect the habitat of the owl. Timber industry spokespersons contended that environmentalists were not concerned so much with the owl but merely wanted to prohibit harvesting of the country's few remaining virgin forests. They complained about "the wine and cheese and brie crowd that was trying to park-ify the national forests" and predicted an epidemic of foreclosures and a crippling recession in the timber-cutting areas.

The greatest concentration of spotted owls is in Oregon, the nation's top timber-producing state. Since cutting in the virgin forests was substantially curtailed in 1991, Oregon has enjoyed its lowest unemployment rate in a generation, and the average wage has risen as the state has gained thousands of high-tech jobs and high technology has surpassed timber as the leading source of jobs in the Beaver State. Instead of using 300-year-old trees from public lands to make 2-by-4's, mills are relying on wood from privately owned tree farms.

The story of the spotted owl has a happy ending. Whether the United States can avoid trade-offs between protecting the environment and economic prosperity in other cases remains to be seen.

DEALING WITH TOXIC WASTES

Long before the environmental movement was born, polluters created problems that we are still trying to solve. During the 1940s and 1950s, for example, before government oversight of toxic substances was as stringent as it is now, Hooker Chemical Company dumped toxic wastes near the shores of the Love Canal in New York. Then in 1953, the company generously donated a 16-acre plot next to the canal to build a school. Thereafter, tons of chemicals, some in rotting barrels, were discovered, and children and adults were found later to have developed liver, kidney, and other health problems. With the company out of business, with the level of contamination so great, and with the identification of a huge number of other toxic waste dumps, popular outcry led to action from Washington.

In 1980, Congress reacted to increased pressure to deal with toxic waste by establishing a **Superfund,** created by taxing chemical products. The law established that those who polluted the land were responsible for paying for cleaning it up. A controversial retroactive liability provision holds companies liable even for legal dumping prior to 1980. The law also contains strict provisions for joint and several liability, under which the government can hold a single party liable for cleaning up an entire site that had received waste from many sources.

Dealing with toxic waste is an expensive and time-consuming process. Here, contaminated soil is treated in a toxic waste dump.

The Comprehensive Environmental Response, Compensation, and Liability Act, the formal name of the Superfund law, has virtually eliminated haphazard dumping of toxic wastes, but it has been less successful in cleaning up existing waste. Instead, the law has led to endless rounds of litigation. Large companies facing multimillion-dollar cleanup bills have tried to recover some of their costs by suing small businesses that had contributed to the hazardous waste. They have also been embroiled in protracted court fights with their insurers over whether policies written in the early 1980s cover Superfund-related costs.[32]

The federal government spends more than $11 billion annually to restore lands spoiled by chemical and radioactive wastes, about $2 billion of which comes from the Superfund. This is the fastest-growing segment of the nation's environmental budget. The average cleanup takes 10 years, and its cost has reached nearly $30 million. The EPA says that about 350 sites have been cleaned and that the most dangerous compounds have been removed from 3,300 more. Just 279 of the 1,296 sites on the EPA's Priority List have been cleaned up; 64 of these are now so pristine that they have been taken off the list.

The EPA has found it more difficult to clean up toxic waste sites than it had hoped; workers find that the damage at some sites is so serious that they may never be cleaned satisfactorily. The effort is also hampered by the sheer number of sites requiring attention—more than 30,000—and by the limits of technology for cleaning up toxic compounds. Moreover, as it investigates more and more sites, the EPA finds that there are many more dangerous sites than it estimated. Equally troublesome, there is no consensus on how clean a contaminated site has to become. In most cases, the EPA has chosen the strictest—and most expensive—standards, whether the site is to be used for a factory or a playground.

In the meantime, a series of governmental policies has been implemented to prevent future Love Canals by the more carefully monitoring and regulating of the use and disposal of hazardous wastes. Regulations mandated by the Resource Conservation and Recovery Act of 1977, for example, require "cradle-to-grave" tracking of many toxic chemicals, specify how these chemicals are to be handled while in use or in transit, and prescribe certain disposal techniques.[33]

Another serious environmental challenge is the disposal of nuclear wastes, such as that from nuclear reactors and the production of nuclear weapons. These wastes must be isolated for 10,000 years! We need to protect from radioactive materials not only ourselves but also the people of a distant future. It is not surprising that no state is eager to have a storage area for nuclear wastes within its boundaries. There can be little doubt that cleaning up wastes left by private businesses (and by some government operations, such as the production of nuclear weapons) is going to take decades and cost billions of dollars.

MAKING ENVIRONMENTAL POLICY

Nobody is against cleaning up the environment. The issue becomes a political question only because environmental concerns often conflict with equally legitimate concerns about foreign trade, economic growth, and jobs. Those who generate pollution do so in their efforts to make cars, to produce electricity, and to provide food and the consumer products that Americans take for granted. On federally owned land, including national parks and forests, there has long been a policy of multiple use whereby mining, lumbering, and grazing leases are awarded to private companies or ranchers at very low cost. Often the industries supported by these arrangements are important sources of jobs to otherwise depressed areas, and they may also lessen the country's dependence on foreign sources of oil and minerals.

Massive battles pitting lumbering interests against national and local environmental groups have raged in Alaska, where exports of lumber products to Japan provide jobs, but decimate large parts of the Tongass National Forest. Similarly, harvesting old-growth timber on public lands has caused great concern in Oregon and Washington. In the Northwest and Alaska, environmentalists have complained that some of the few remaining large tracts of virgin forest, with trees hundreds of years old, are being felled by logging companies operating under generous lease agreements with the U.S. government, which owns the lands. Oil exploration on public lands and off shore in coastal waters also brings the goals of environmental protection and economic growth into conflict. The spill of the *Exxon Valdez* off the coast of Alaska demonstrated the environmental risks of oil exploration.

One of the biggest changes in environmental policymaking in recent years is the increasing presence of new sectors of society as they join interest groups to complain about pollution and to press for government action. Once, only a few conservation groups actively attempted to conserve public lands or oppose potentially damaging projects. Pollution was mostly seen as an inevitable product of economic growth; because Americans wanted jobs, they accepted the pollution that accompanied the businesses.

The 1960s and 1970s saw an explosion in the size and number of environmental interest groups. For example, The National Wildlife Federation has nearly 4.5 million members; Greenpeace USA, the World Wildlife Fund, and the Conservation Foundation have more than a million members each; and the Sierra Club, the Clean Water Action Project, the Nature Conservancy, and the National Audubon Society have more than a half-million members each. In addition, there are numerous other environmental groups—ranging from the Wilderness Society to the Citizens' Clearinghouse for Hazardous Waste. Obviously, American environmental interest groups discovered much untapped interest in the early 1970s.

As old groups evolved into active political organizations and as new groups formed and grew, the nature of environmental policymaking changed. At first many politicians viewed these new lobbyists with skepticism. Over time, however, the environmental movement has made its way into the halls of government. Now politicians of both parties seek the support of environmental groups as they enter the electoral season. Issues that were once considered only from the point of view of jobs and economic growth are now much more controversial.

Yet support for environmental policy cannot be taken for granted, despite the public opinion surveys discussed earlier in this chapter. The very success of the environmental movement in passing laws designed to protect public health and to preserve or restore the ecosystem has spawned a backlash against vigorous protection of the environment. These opponents demand evidence that policies are accomplishing their goals and insist that Congress and the bureaucracy subject regulations to cost-benefit analysis to determine that they do not cost more than the benefits they create. Opponents of strict environmental protection laws argue that the effects of environmental regulations on employment, economic growth, and international competitiveness must be part of the policymaking equation. Others, especially ranchers, miners, farmers, and the timber industry, demand inexpensive access to public land and the right to use their own property as they wish or else be compensated by government for being prohibited from doing so.

In the early 1980s, government scientists argued that exposure to asbestos could cause thousands of cancer deaths. Because asbestos was used as insulation in schools and public buildings, parents reacted with alarm. In 1985, Congress approved a sweeping law that led cities and states to spend between $15 billion and $20 billion to remove asbestos from public buildings. But in 1990, EPA officials admitted that ripping out the asbestos had been an expensive mistake; the removal often sent tiny asbestos fibers into the air. Now, except in cases where the asbestos is damaged or crumbling, the government's official advice is: Don't touch it. Such examples continue to fuel the call for a more cautious approach to environmental protection.

In March of 1989, the *Exxon Valdez* ran aground off the southern coast of Alaska, spilling 11 million gallons of crude oil. Despite a $2 billion cleanup effort, the oil killed thousands of fish and animals and ruined miles of shoreline. No other single oil spill has drawn so much public attention to the environmental dangers of America's reliance on oil as an energy source.

Widening opposition to potentially hazardous industrial facilities (such as toxic or nuclear waste dumps) has further complicated environmental policymaking in recent years. Local groups have often successfully organized resistance to planned development, rallying behind the cry "Not In My Back Yard!"[34] The so-called NIMBY phenomenon highlights another difficult dilemma in environmental policy: How can government equitably distribute the costs associated with society's seemingly endless demand for new technologies, some of which turn out to be environmentally threatening? If, for example, we are to use nuclear power to keep our lights on, the waste it produces must go in someone's back yard. But whose?

For all of these reasons, then, government policies designed to clean up the environment are sure to be controversial, to be expensive, and to be debated for years to come.

UNDERSTANDING HEALTH, ENERGY, AND ENVIRONMENTAL POLICY

Technologically complex issues such as health, energy, and the environment pose many special problems in a democracy. These issues are difficult to understand when discussed in the experts' terms, but most Americans do not want to leave them to "experts" to decide. This section discusses how democracies handle technological issues and then considers the impact of these issues on the scope of government.

"I'm rather fortunate. I have no parents, so Medicare is no problem, and I have no children, so the environment is no problem."

Drawing by Handelsman ©1995 *The New Yorker Magazine*, Inc

DEMOCRACY AND HEALTH, ENERGY, AND ENVIRONMENTAL POLICY

Very few Americans actually understand how a nuclear power plant operates. And most do not know how to perform a heart operation. Does such ignorance mean that citizens should not be allowed to participate in the public policy debates concerning complex technologies? High-tech issues, more than any others, strain the limits of public participation in a democracy. Further, the issues associated with high technology are often so complex that many different levels of government—local, state, and national—become heavily involved. Whether it be the new ethical issues raised by machines and devices that can keep patients alive indefinitely—respirators, artificial kidneys, and the like—or whether it be the threats to public safety inherent in an accident at a nuclear power plant, governments are constantly called on to make decisions that involve tremendously complex technologies. Maintaining the right balance between public participation and technological competence is not an easy task.

High-technology issues make it especially difficult to include the public in a reasoned political debate. Often groups of specialists are the only ones who seem qualified to make decisions (and these specialists may have "special interest" in the issues on which they pass expert judgment). Still, in the United States, dramatic change has occurred. Environmental groups that once focused only on dramatic statements or loud protests now have their own staffs of scientists. Because knowledge is important in a highly complex debate, they have procured the resources to develop that knowledge. No longer are major public issues such as environmental pollution debated in the absence of well-informed groups looking out for the public interest.

Policymaking for technological issues seems to rely heavily on group representation. Individual citizens are unlikely to have the information or the resources to participate meaningfully because of the complexity of the debates. Interest groups—associations of professionals and citizens—play an active role in making the complicated decisions that will affect all Americans for generations.

THE SCOPE OF GOVERNMENT AND HEALTH, ENERGY, AND ENVIRONMENTAL POLICY

Americans do not hesitate to call for government to play a greater role in high-technology issues, and the scope of the federal government has grown in response to these demands. Medicare for the aged, Medicaid for the poor, and tax subsidies for employer-provided health insurance are large, expensive public policies. Further efforts to reform health care, such as President Clinton's proposals, will only increase the government's role. So will responses to health crises like the AIDS epidemic.

Similarly, in the past three decades, concerns for environmental protection have placed additional demands on the federal government (see "Since Kennedy: The Revolution in Environmental Protection"). Americans like to think that nuclear power plants are inspected by federal officials to ensure safety. As the plants grow older, citizens might want

Citizen action is a powerful force even on highly technical issues such as nuclear power. Here, protesters oppose the nuclear power plant in Shoreham, New Hampshire.

more, not fewer, people working in this federal agency. When the *Exxon Valdez* spilled millions of gallons of oil into the waters off Alaska, no one complained about the use of the Coast Guard in coordinating the cleanup.

At the same time, important forces rein in the federal government. One of the principal reasons why President Clinton's health care proposal failed to pass Congress in 1994 was the public's fear of too much government regulation of health care. The Republicans who took over Congress in 1995 are demanding that future health, safety, and environmental regulations be subjected to rigorous standards of evaluation. Thus, there is a tension between demands for government services and protections and a concern about the government's providing those services and protections.

SINCE KENNEDY

The Revolution in Environmental Protection

When John F. Kennedy took office, environmental protection policy was not a prominent feature of federal policy. It focused largely on the establishment of parks. Things soon changed, however. Beginning in the last year of Kennedy's tenure, Congress passed numerous bills that firmly established protection of the environment as one of the principal responsibilities of the federal government.

MAJOR ENVIRONMENTAL PROTECTION LAWS

1963	Clean Air Act
1964	Wilderness Act
1965	Highway Beautification Act
	Water Quality Act
1967	Air Quality Act
1968	Wild and Scenic Rivers Act
1969	National Environmental Policy Act
	Endangered Species Conservation Act
1970	Clean Air Act Amendments
	Water Quality Improvement Act
1972	Federal Water Pollution Control Act
	Marine Mammal Protection Act
	Marine Protection, Research, and Sanctuaries Act
	Coastal Zone Management Act
	Federal Environmental Pesticide Control Act
	Noise Control Act
1973	Endangered Species Act
1974	Safe Drinking Water Act
1976	Federal Land Policy and Management Act
	National Forest Management Act
	Resource Conservation and Recovery Act
	Toxic Substances and Control Act
1977	Clean Air Act Amendments
	Clean Water Act
	Surface Mining Control and Reclamation Act
1978	Outer Continental Shelf Lands Act Amendments
1980	Comprehensive Environmental Response, Compensation, and Liability Act
	Alaska National Interest Lands Conservation Act
1984	Hazardous and Solid Waste Amendments
1986	Safe Drinking Water Act Amendments
	Superfund Amendments and Reauthorization Act
1987	Water Quality Act
1988	Endangered Species Act Reauthorization
	Federal Insecticide, Fungicide, and Rodenticide Act Amendments
1990	Clean Air Act Reauthorization
1994	California Desert Protection Act
	Marine Mammal Protection Act Reauthorization
1996	Safe Drinking Water Act Amendments
	Overhaul of Pesticide Regulations
1997	Higher Standards for Clean Air

SUMMARY

Americans live in an age driven by technology. Like so much in human history, technology brings its blessings and its curses. In particular, there are three areas in which technology meets public policy: health, energy, and the environment. Americans at the end of the twentieth century can do much to control birth, death, and the genetics of life itself. Today scientists patent mice; tomorrow they may patent strains of human genetic material. Energy researchers now look for superconductive materials to enhance the efficiency of the present energy system.

Health care already makes up one-seventh of America's GDP, and with increased technology, its costs will almost certainly continue to rise. The government has chosen to accept patents on new life-forms and to invest in these new technologies. These advances have improved health care, but tremendous problems also plague health care in America, including inadequate insurance coverage (or no coverage at all) for many people and ever-increasing costs for even routine medical attention. Health is an area of striking contrasts in America and of monumental policy problems.

America also faces important energy problems. Of all the different ways to produce energy, none is perfect. Coal, the country's most abundant resource, is also the dirtiest source of energy, causing many environmental and health problems. Nuclear power, once seen as a solution to the nation's energy needs, is at a virtual standstill because of the massive public fear of exposure to radioactivity, the high costs of the technology, and inconsistency in design and management. Oil has been at the center of many national and international crises, from the Persian Gulf War to the *Exxon Valdez* spill.

Finally, Americans are increasingly concerned with the environment. Environmental issues will continue to cause the government to become involved in many aspects of daily life, and they often pit citizens' groups against important economic interests. The government has become very active in ensuring the quality of America's air, land, and water.

In all three of these public policy areas, government is, and will continue to be, at the center of public debate. Decisions made in Washington, in state capitals, and in international negotiations will affect all Americans in terms of health care, energy use, the nature of the environment, and the quality of life in general. Furthermore, governmental activities can be expected to grow, rather than to decrease, in each of these areas. Finally, citizen participation has profoundly influenced governmental decisions in these areas. Voting and organizing interest group campaigns will continue to be important means of influencing government decisions.

KEY TERMS

National Institutes of Health (NIH)
national health insurance
Medicare
Medicaid
nonrenewable resources
Environmental Protection Agency (EPA)
National Environmental Policy Act (NEPA)
environmental impact statement (EIS)
Clean Air Act of 1970
Water Pollution Control Act of 1972
Endangered Species Act of 1973
Superfund

FOR FURTHER READING

Davis, David. *Energy Politics,* 4th ed. New York: St. Martin's Press, 1993. A useful overview of the multiple dimensions of energy policy and politics.

Easterbrook, Gregg. *A Moment on the Earth: The Coming Age of Environmental Optimism.* New York: Viking, 1995. Stresses the successes of environmental protection.

Ginzberg, Eli, ed. *Critical Issues in U.S. Health Reform.* Boulder, CO: Westview, 1994.

Gore, Albert. *Earth in the Balance: Ecology and the Human Spirit.* Boston: Houghton Mifflin, 1992. The vice president presents a manifesto for protecting the environment.

Landy, Marc K., Marc J. Roberts, and Stephen R. Thomas. *The Environmental Protection Agency,* expanded edition. New York: Oxford University Press, 1994. A critical evaluation of the EPA.

Marmor, Theodore R. *Understanding Health Care Reform.* New Haven, CT: Yale University Press, 1994. A thorough discussion of the central issues of health care reform by a leading expert on health policy.

McCormick, John. *Reclaiming Paradise: The Global Environmental Movement.* Bloomington: Indiana University Press, 1989. A discussion of the origins and the explosive growth of the environmental movement worldwide.

Nelkin, Dorothy, ed. *Controversy: The Politics of Technical Decisions.* Ithaca, NY: Cornell University

Press, 1979. Nelkin discusses the problems of high-tech decisionmaking, presenting a number of interesting case studies.

Schrepfer, Susan R. *The Fight to Save the Redwoods.* Madison: University of Wisconsin Press, 1983. Schrepfer provides a readable history of the environmental movement during most of the current century.

Switzer, Jacqueline Vaughn. *Environmental Politics—Domestic and Global Dimensions.* New York: St. Martin's Press, 1994. A good overview of the politics of environmental policy.

Vig, Norman J., and Michael E. Kraft, eds. *Environmental Policy in the 1990s,* 2nd ed. Washington, DC: Congressional Quarterly Press, 1994. Useful articles on a range of environmental policy issues.

Weart, Spencer. *Nuclear Fear: A History of Images.* Cambridge, MA: Harvard University Press, 1988. Weart traces the popular understanding of the atom over the past century and shows how far from reality have been both the claims and the fears of this new technology.

Wilson, Edward O. *The Diversity of Life.* Cambridge, MA: Belknap Press, 1992. The dean of American biologists argues that human beings are in danger of precipitating a biological disaster, diminishing the world's biodiversity.

Winner, Langdon. *The Whale and the Reactor.* Chicago: University of Chicago Press, 1986. Winner discusses the dilemmas of living in a high-tech society.

INTERNET RESOURCES

http://www.census.gov:80/stat_abstract/
The *Statistical Abstract of the United States.*

http://www.census.gov/
Home page for the Census Bureau, where you can search for statistics on health and other policy issues.

NOTES

1. U.S. Bureau of the Census, *Statistical Abstract of the United States, 1996* (Washington, DC: U.S. Government Printing Office, 1996), 831-832.
2. U.S. Bureau of the Census, *Statistical Abstract of the United States, 1996,* 834.
3. Quoted in Richard L. Berke, "Clinton Warns That Economy May Still Be Bad," *New York Times,* December 8, 1992, A13.
4. U.S. Bureau of the Census, *Statistical Abstract of the United States, 1996,* 127.
5. See Laurene A. Craig, *Health of Nations,* 2nd ed. (Washington, DC: Congressional Quarterly Press, 1993) for a discussion of health care in other developed countries.
6. U.S. Bureau of the Census, *Current Population Reports: Health Insurance Coverage: 1995,* September 1996, 1.
7. U.S. Bureau of the Census, *Current Population Reports: Who Loses Coverage and for How Long?* May 1996, 1.
8. CBS News/*New York Times* Poll, reported in *The American Enterprise,* March/April 1992, 87.
9. U.S. Bureau of the Census, *Current Population Reports: Health Insurance Coverage: 1995,* 2-3.
10. Julie Kosterlitz, "A Sick System," *National Journal,* February 15, 1992, 380.
11. U.S. Bureau of the Census, *Current Population Reports: Health Insurance Coverage: 1995,* 1-3.
12. U.S. Bureau of the Census, *Statistical Abstract of the United States, 1996,* 89, 93, 831-832.
13. Kosterlitz, "A Sick System," 376.
14. See the *Encyclopedia of Associations, 1997,* Vol. 1, Part 2 (Detroit: Gale Research, Inc. , 1997), 1278.
15. Edgar K. Browning and Jacqueline M. Browning, *Public Finance and the Price System,* 4th ed. (New York: Macmillan, 1994), 185-188.
16. Polls of August 8-9, 1994, and August 15-16, 1994.
17. David Davis, *Energy Politics,* 4th ed. (New York: St. Martin's Press, 1993).
18. U.S. Bureau of the Census, *Statistical Abstract of the United States, 1996,* 578.
19. James A. Bill, *The Eagle and the Lion: The Tragedy of American-Iranian Relations* (New Haven, CT: Yale University Press, 1988).
20. U.S. Bureau of the Census, *Statistical Abstract of the United States, 1996,* 578.
21. Frank R. Baumgartner and Bryan D. Jones, *Agendas and Instability in American Politics* (Chicago: University of Chicago Press, 1993).
22. U.S. Bureau of the Census, *Statistical Abstract of the United States, 1996,* 590.
23. See John L. Campbell, *Collapse of an Industry: Nuclear Power and the Contradictions of U.S. Policy* (Ithaca, NY: Cornell University Press, 1988).
24. Louis Harris, *Washington Post,* January 15, 1982.
25. Jonathan Walters, "Land Use Laws and Hard Times," *Governing,* 6 (October 1992): 25.
26. J. Clarence Davies, "Environmental Institutions and the Reagan Administration," in Norman J. Vig and

Michael E. Kraft, eds., *Environmental Policy in the 1980s* (Washington, DC: Congressional Quarterly Press, 1984), 150; and Edwin R. Clark III, "Reaganomics and the Environment," in Vig and Kraft, eds., *Environmental Policy in the 1980s,* 348-349.

27. Robert Crandall, *Controlling Industrial Pollution* (Washington, DC: Brookings Institution, 1983).

28. For a legislative and administrative discussion and evaluation of the NEPA, see Richard A. Loroff, *A National Policy for the Environment: NEPA and Its Aftermath* (Bloomington: Indiana University Press, 1976).

29. William Ophuls, *Ecology and the Politics of Scarcity* (San Francisco: Freeman, 1977), 177.

30. Samuel Hays, *Beauty, Health, Permanence* (New York: Cambridge University Press, 1987), 99.

31. Charles P. Alexander, "On the Defensive," *Time,* June 15, 1992, 35.

32. On implementing the Superfund law, see Thomas W. Church and Robert T. Nakamura, *Cleaning Up the Mess: Implementation Strategies in Superfund* (Washington, D.C.: Brookings Institution, 1993).

33. Steven Cohen, "Defusing the Toxic Time Bomb: Federal Hazardous Waste Programs," in Vig and Kraft, eds., *Environmental Policy in the 1980s,* 273-291; and Kent Portney, *Controversial Issues in Environmental Policy* (Beverly Hills, CA: Sage Publications, 1992), chap. 5.

34. Denis J. Brion, *Essential Industry and the NIMBY Phenomenon* (New York: Quorum Books, 1991); Charles Piller, *The Fail-Safe Society* (New York: Basic Books, 1991); Daniel Mazmanian and David Morell, "The 'NIMBY' Syndrome: Facility Siting and the Failure of Democratic Discourse," in Vig and Kraft, eds., *Environmental Policy in the 1990s* (Washington, DC: Congressional Quarterly Press, 1990), chap. 6.

20 Foreign and Defense Policymaking

American Foreign Policy: Methods and Actors

American Foreign Policy: An Overview

The Politics of Defense Policy

The New Global Agenda

Understanding Foreign and Defense Policymaking

In 1987, President Ronald Reagan stood before the historic Brandenburg Gate in a divided Berlin and challenged President Gorbachev of the Soviet Union to tear down the Berlin Wall. Five years later, on June 17, 1992, Boris Yeltsin addressed a joint session of the U.S. Congress. When the burly, silver-haired president of the new Russian republic entered the House chamber, members of Congress greeted him with chants of "Bo-ris, Boris" and hailed him with numerous standing ovations.

Between these two events the world had changed fundamentally. As Yeltsin proclaimed to thunderous applause,

> The idol of communism, which spread everywhere social strife, animosity and unparalleled brutality, which instilled fear in humanity, has collapsed . . . . I am here to assure you that we will not let it rise again in our land.

The cold war that had been waged for two generations had ended, and the West, led by the United States, had won.

There was not much time to rejoice, however. The end of one set of challenges raised another to prominence. Now that communism is no longer the principal threat to the security of the United States, what should our foreign policy goals be? What should be the role of the world's only remaining superpower? What should we do with our huge defense establishment, which had just undergone an enormous increase in the 1980s?

The need to answer the question of the appropriate role of the national government in foreign and defense policy is more important, and perhaps more difficult, than ever. How should we deal with our former adversaries? Yeltsin's visit to the United States was not motivated primarily by a desire simply to bury the cold war. He also signed an unprecedented arms control agreement with President Bush, discussed mutually beneficial trade, and sought aid for his ailing economy. At the same time, many of the former Communist nations of Eastern and Central Europe exhibited a frightening tendency to self-destruct in civil wars. In 1996, President Clinton proclaimed that "[t]here are times when only America can make the difference between war and peace, between freedom and repression, between hope and fear." Should the United States get involved in trying to end civil wars and the breakdown of political authority that results from the surfacing of long-suppressed ethnic, religious, and sectional conflicts?

And just how should we decide about national security policy? Should the American people delegate discretion in this area to officials who seem more at home with complex and even exotic issues of defense and foreign policy? Or should they and their representatives fully participate in the democratic policymaking process, just as they do in domestic policy? And can the public or its representatives in Congress or in interest groups have much influence on the elites who often deal in secrecy in national security policy?

The end of the cold war has not lessened the importance of defense and foreign policy. New and complex challenges have emerged to replace the conflict with communism, and most of these are not traceable to a malevolent enemy who can be contained or defeated.

AMERICAN FOREIGN POLICY: METHODS AND ACTORS

Foreign policy is like domestic policy in that it involves making choices—but the choices involved are about relations with the rest of the world. Because the president is the main force behind foreign policy, every morning the White House receives a highly confidential intelligence briefing that might cover monetary transactions in Tokyo, last night's events in some trouble spot on the globe, or Fidel Castro's health. The briefing is part of the massive informational arsenal the president uses to manage American foreign policy.

The instruments of foreign policy are, however, different from those of domestic policy. Foreign policies depend ultimately on three types of tools: military, economic, and diplomatic. Among the oldest instruments of foreign policy are war and the threat of war. German General Karl von Clausewitz once called war a "continuation of politics by other means." As we learned in Chapter 13, the United States has been involved in only a few full-scale wars. It has often employed force to influence actions in other countries, however. Most of this influence has been close to home, in Latin America, as you can see in Table 20.1.

In recent years, the United States has also used force in limited ways to prevent the toppling of the democratic government of the Philippines, rescue our embassy in Somalia, rescue stranded foreigners and protect our embassy in Liberia, and launch a missile attack on Baghdad in retaliation for an effort to assassinate former President Bush. The United States has also employed military forces recently for humanitarian relief operations in Iraq, Somalia, Bangladesh, Russia, and Bosnia.

Today, economic instruments are becoming weapons almost as potent as those of war. The control of oil can be as important as the control of guns. Trade regulations, tariff policies, and monetary policies are other economic instruments of foreign policy. A number of recent studies have called attention to the

TABLE 20.1 U.S. INCURSIONS IN LATIN AMERICA SINCE 1900

YEAR	COUNTRY	YEAR	COUNTRY
1903	Panama	1961	Cuba
1914-1917	Mexico	1965	Dominican Republic
1915-1934	Haiti	1983	Grenada
1916-1924	Dominican Republic	1989	Panama
1926-1933	Nicaragua	1994	Haiti
1954	Guatemala		

importance of a country's economic vitality to its long-term national security.[1]

Diplomacy is the quietest instrument. It often evokes images of ambassadors at chic cocktail parties, but the diplomatic game is played for high stakes. Sometimes national leaders meet in summit talks. More often, less prominent negotiators work out treaties covering all kinds of national contracts, from economic relations to the aid of stranded tourists.

ACTORS ON THE WORLD STAGE

If all the world's a stage, then there are more actors on it than ever before. More than 125 nations have emerged since 1945—nearly two dozen in the 1990s alone. Once foreign relations were almost exclusively transactions among nations in which military, economic, or diplomatic methods were used to achieve foreign policy goals. Nations remain the main actors in international politics, but today's world stage is more crowded.

Most of the challenges in international relations, ranging from peacekeeping and controlling weapons of mass destruction to protecting the environment and maintaining stable trade and financial networks, require the cooperation of many nations. Thus, it is not surprising that **international organizations** play an increasingly important role on the world stage.

The best-known international organization is the **United Nations (UN).** Housed in a magnificent skyscraper in New York City, the UN was created in 1945. Its members agree to renounce war and respect certain human and economic freedoms. The UN General Assembly is composed of about 185 member nations. Each nation has one vote. Although not legally binding, General Assembly resolutions can achieve a measure of collective legitimization when a broad international consensus is formed on some matter concerning relations among states.

It is the Security Council, however, that is the seat of real power in the UN. Five of its 15 members (the United States, Great Britain, China, France, and Russia) are permanent members; the others are chosen from session to session by the General Assembly. Each permanent member has a veto over Security Council decisions, including any decisions that would commit the UN to a military peacekeeping operation. The Secretariat is the executive arm of the UN and directs the administration of UN programs. Composed of 14,000 international civil servants, it is headed by the secretary general. In addition to its peacekeeping function, the UN runs a number of programs focused on economic development and on health, education, and welfare.

The UN has been especially active in peacekeeping in recent years. In 1990, the UN Security Council backed resolutions authorizing an embargo on the shipment of goods to or from Iraq in an attempt to force its withdrawal from Kuwait. Later, it authorized the use of force to compel Iraq to withdraw. In 1992, the UN assisted famine relief in Somalia. More recently, it supported the return of the democratically elected president of Haiti and has been active, with only modest success, in trying to end the civil war in Bosnia-Herzegovina. Often, it is the United States that plays the critical role in implementing UN policies. Although President Clinton envisioned an expanded role for UN peacekeeping operations at the beginning of his term, he later concluded that the UN is often not capable of making and keeping peace, particularly when hostilities among parties still exist. He also backtracked on his willingness to place American troops under foreign commanders, always a controversial policy.

The UN is only one of many international organizations. The International Monetary Fund, for example, helps regulate the chaotic world of international finance; the World Bank finances development projects in new nations; and the International Postal Union helps get the mail from one country to another.

Regional organizations have proliferated in the post-World War II era. These are organizations of several nations bound by a treaty, often for military reasons. The **North Atlantic Treaty Organization (NATO)** was created in 1949. Its members—the United States, Canada, most Western European nations, and Turkey—agreed to combine military forces and to treat a war against one as a war against all. More than a million NATO troops (including about 325,000 Americans) were spread from West Germany to Portugal. They faced troops from the *Warsaw Pact*—the regional security community of the Soviet Union and its Eastern European allies. The Warsaw Pact has been dissolved, however, and the role of NATO has changed dramatically as the cold war has thawed. In 1997, Poland, Hungary, and the Czech Republic, former members of the Warsaw Pact, were admitted into NATO.

Regional organizations can be economic rather than military. The **European Union (EU)** is an economic alliance of the major Western European nations. The EU coordinates monetary, trade, immigration, and labor policies so that its members have become one economic unit, just as the 50 United States are an economic unit. Other economic federations exist in Latin America and Africa, but none is as unified as the EU.

Chapter 17 discussed the potent *multinational corporations,* or MNCs. Today more than one-third of the world's industrial output comes from these corporations.[2] Sometimes more powerful (and often much wealthier) than the governments under which they operate, MNCs have voiced strong opinions about governments, taxes, and business regulations. They have even linked forces with agencies such as the Central Intelligence Agency (CIA) to overturn governments they disliked. In the 1970s, for example, several of these corporations worked with the CIA to "destabilize" the democratically elected Marxist government in Chile; Chile's military overthrew the government in 1973. Even when they are not so heavy-handed, MNCs are forces to be reckoned with in nearly all nations.

Groups are also actors on the global stage. Churches and labor unions have long had international interests and activities. Today, environmental and wildlife groups such as Greenpeace have also proliferated. Ecological interests are active in international as well as in national politics. Groups interested in protecting human rights, such as Amnesty International, have also grown. Not all groups, however, are committed to saving whales, oceans, or even people. Some are committed to the overthrow of particular governments and operate as terrorists around the world. Airplane hijackings, assassinations, bombings, and similar terrorist attacks have made the world a more unsettled place. Conflicts within a nation or region thus spill over into world politics.

Finally, *individuals* are international actors. The recent explosion of tourism sends Americans everywhere and brings to America legions of tourists from Japan, Europe, and the less developed world. Tourism creates its own costs and benefits and thus always affects the international economic system. Tourism may enhance friendship and understanding among nations. However, more tourists traveling out of the country than arriving in the country can create problems with a country's balance of payments (discussed later in this chapter). In addition to tourists, growing numbers of students are going to and coming from other nations; they are carriers of ideas and ideologies. So are immigrants and refugees, who also place new demands on public services.

Just as there are more actors on the global stage than in the past, there are also more American decision makers involved in foreign policy problems.

THE POLICYMAKERS

The president, you know from Chapter 13, is the main force behind foreign policy. As chief diplomat, the president negotiates treaties; as commander in chief of the armed forces, the president deploys American troops abroad.

Presidents do not act alone in foreign policy; they are aided (and sometimes thwarted) by a huge national security bureaucracy. In addition, they must contend with the views and desires of Congress, which also wields considerable clout in the foreign policy arena—sometimes doing so in opposition to a president. The following sections examine the diplomatic and defense sides of the vast foreign policy and national security bureaucracy and the role of Congress in foreign and defense policy.

The Diplomats. The State Department is the foreign policy arm of the U.S. government. As the department's chief, the **secretary of state** (Thomas Jefferson was the first) has traditionally been the key advisor to the president on foreign policy matters. In over 300 overseas posts from Albania to Zimbabwe, the State Department staffs U.S. embassies and consulates, representing the interests of Americans. Once a dignified and genteel profession, diplomacy is becoming an increasingly dangerous job. The November 1979 seizure of the American embassy in Tehran is an extreme example of the hostilities that diplomats can face.

The secretary of state is typically the president's chief foreign policy advisor, presiding over a global bureaucracy of diplomats. Here, Madeleine Albright meets with Chinese Minister of Foreign Affairs and Vice Premier Qian Qichen at Diaoyutai, the state guesthouse in Beijing.

The 23,000 people working in the State Department are organized into functional areas (such as economic and business affairs and human rights and humanitarian affairs) and area specialties (a section on Middle Eastern affairs, one on European affairs, and so on), each nation being handled by a "country desk." The political appointees who occupy the top positions in the department and the highly select members of the Foreign Service are heavily involved in formulating and executing American foreign policy.

Many recent presidents have found the State Department too bureaucratic and intransigent. Even its colloquial name "Foggy Bottom," taken from the part of Washington where it is located, conjures up less than an image of cooperation. Some recent presidents have bypassed institutional arrangements for foreign policy decision making and have instead established more personal systems for receiving policy advice. Presidents Nixon and Carter, for example, relied more heavily on their special assistants for national security affairs (Henry Kissinger and Zbigniew Brzezinski, respectively) than on their secretaries of state. Foreign policy was thus centered in the White House and was often disconnected from what was occurring in the State Department. Critics, however, charged that this situation led to split-level government and chronic discontinuity in foreign policy.[3] President Reagan, by contrast, relied less on his assistants for national security affairs (six different men filled the job in 8 years) and more on his Secretary of State George Schultz, who was a powerful player. George Bush continued this pattern, appointing his closest friend, James Baker, as secretary of state. President Clinton has also relied heavily on his secretaries of state, Warren Christopher and Madeleine Albright.

The National Security Establishment. Foreign policy and military policy are closely linked. Thus, the Department of Defense is a key foreign policy actor. Often called "the Pentagon" after the five-sided building in which it is located, the Defense Department was created after World War II. The U.S. Army, Navy, and Air Force were collected into one giant department, although they have never been thoroughly integrated and continue to plan and operate largely independently of one another. Recent reforms, made law under the Goldwater-Nichols Defense Reorganization Act of 1986, have increased interservice cooperation and centralization of the military hierarchy. The **secretary of defense** manages a budget larger than that of most nations and is the president's main civilian advisor on national defense matters.

The commanding officers of all of the services, along with a chair, constitute the **Joint Chiefs of Staff.** American military leaders are sometimes portrayed as aggressive hawks in policymaking, presumably eager to crush some small nation with a show of American force. Richard Betts carefully examined the Joint Chiefs' advice to the president in many crises and found the Joint Chiefs to be no more likely than civilian advisors to push an aggressive military policy. (The most hawkish advice, incidentally, came from the admirals. The most dovish advice came from the army generals and the Marine Corps.[4]) On several occasions during the Reagan administration, the president's uniformed advisors cautioned against aggressive actions—

The senior U.S. military officer is the chair of the Joint Chiefs of Staff. Here the current chair, General Henry Shelton.

including the use of military force—favored by the State Department. The military was similarly conservative regarding the use of force against Iraq in 1991[5] and intervention in the civil wars in Eastern Europe. Steeped in the mythology of generals like George Patton and Curtis LeMay, many Americans would be surprised at the cautious attitudes of America's top military leaders today.

American foreign and military policies are supposed to be coordinated. The *National Security Council (NSC)* was formed in 1947 for this purpose. The NSC is composed of the president, the vice president, the secretary of defense, and the secretary of state. The NSC staff is managed by the president's national security assistant—a position that first gained public prominence with the flamboyant, globe-trotting Henry Kissinger during President Nixon's first term.

Despite the coordinating role assigned to the NSC, conflict within the foreign policy establishment remains common. The NSC staff has sometimes competed with, rather than integrated, policy advice from cabinet departments—particularly State and Defense. It has also become involved in covert operations. A scandal erupted in November 1986 when NSC staff was found to be involved in a secret operation to sell battlefield missiles to Iran in return for Iranian help in gaining the release of hostages held by Iranian-backed terrorists in Lebanon. Some of the money from the sale was funneled secretly to anti-Communist rebels (called *Contras*) fighting the Nicaraguan government, despite a congressional ban on such aid.

The scandal, termed the Iran-Contra affair, resulted in the resignation of the president's assistant for national security affairs, Vice Admiral John Poindexter, and the sacking of a number of lower-level NSC officials, including Lieutenant Colonel Oliver North. North went from obscurity to national prominence overnight as he described his involvement in the affair before a televised congressional inquiry in 1987. Both Poindexter and North were subsequently convicted of felony charges related to the diversion of funds and misleading Congress, but their convictions were overturned because their testimony before Congress, given under conditions of immunity, was judged to have been used against them in court.

No discussion of the institutional structures of foreign policy would be complete without mention of the **Central Intelligence Agency (CIA).** "The Company," as the CIA is known to insiders, was created after World War II to coordinate American information- and data-gathering intelligence activities abroad and to collect, analyze, and evaluate its own intelligence. Technically, its budget and staff are secret; estimates put them at $3 billion and about 19,000 people.

The CIA plays a vital role in providing information and analyses necessary for effective development and implementation of national security policy. And most of its activities are uncontroversial, because the bulk of the material it collects and analyzes comes from readily available sources such as government reports and newspapers.

One way the CIA collects information, however, is by espionage. Most people accept the necessity of this form of information collection, at least when it is directed against foreign adversaries. However, in the 1970s it was discovered that at times the agency had also engaged in wiretaps, interception of mail, and the infiltration of interest groups—in the United States. These actions violated the CIA's charter, and revelations of spying on Americans who disagreed with the foreign policy of the administration badly damaged the agency's morale and external political support.

The CIA also has a long history of involvement in other nations' internal affairs. After the end of World War II, when Eastern European nations had fallen under Moscow's shadow and Western European nations were teetering, the CIA provided aid to anti-Communist parties in Italy and West Germany. It was no less busy in the developing countries, where, for example, it nurtured coups in Iran in 1953 and in Guatemala in 1954. The CIA has also trained and supported armies—the most notable, of course, in Vietnam. It subsidized Communist defectors, often in an extravagant style. In the 1980s, a major controversy surrounded the CIA's activity in Central America, where the Sandinistas overthrew Nicaraguan dictator Anastasio Somoza in 1979. Shortly thereafter, the dominant Marxist regime developed close ties with the Soviet Union and Cuba and embarked on a massive military buildup. Determined to undermine the regime, the Reagan administration aggressively supported assistance to anti-Sandinista rebels. Congressional inquiries suggested that the CIA, under Director William Casey, was quietly involved in covert operations to assist the Contra rebels.[6] Director Casey died in 1987, while his agency and the NSC staff were under intense congressional and public scrutiny for involvement in the Iran-Contra affair.

Reconciling covert activities with the principles of open democratic government remains a challenge for public officials. With the end of the cold war, there is less pressure for covert activities and a climate more conducive to conventional intelligence gathering. Currently, Congress requires the CIA to inform relevant congressional committees promptly of current and anticipated covert operations. In the meantime, there is substantial debate on the role of the CIA in the post-Cold War era.

There are numerous other components of America's intelligence community. For example, the National Reconnaissance Office uses imagery satellites to monitor missile sites and other military activities around the world, and the National Security Agency is on the cutting edge of electronic eavesdropping capabilities.

After World War II, these military and foreign policy institutions steadily grew. As the American role on the world stage grew, so did the importance of these institutions as foreign policy instruments.

Congress. Chapters 12 and 13 discussed how the U.S. Congress shares with the president constitutional authority over foreign and defense policy. Congress has sole authority, for example, to declare war, raise and organize the armed forces, and appropriate funds for national security activities. The Senate determines whether treaties will be ratified and ambassadorial and cabinet nominations confirmed. The "power of the purse" (discussed in Chapter 14) and responsibilities for oversight of the executive branch give Congress considerable clout, and each year senators and representatives carefully examine defense budget authorizations.[7]

Congress' important constitutional role in foreign and defense policy is sometimes misunderstood. It is a common mistake among some journalists, executive officials, and even members of Congress to believe that the Constitution vests foreign policy decisions solely in the president. Sometimes this erroneous view leads to perverse results, such as the Iran-Contra affair that dominated the news in late 1986 and much of 1987. Officials at high levels in the executive branch "sought to protect the president's 'exclusive' prerogative by lying to Congress, to allies, to the public, and to one another." Louis Fisher suggests that such actions undermined the "mutual trust and close coordination by the two branches that are essential attributes in building a foreign policy that ensures continuity and stability."[8]

AMERICAN FOREIGN POLICY: AN OVERVIEW

Throughout most of its history, the United States followed a foreign policy course called **isolationism.** This policy, articulated by George Washington in his Farewell Address, directed the country to stay out of other nations' conflicts, particularly European wars. The famous Monroe Doctrine, enunciated by President James Monroe, reaffirmed America's inattention to Europe's problems but warned European nations to stay out of Latin America. The United States—believing that its own political backyard included Central and South America—did not hesitate to send marines, gunboats, or both to intervene in South American and Caribbean affairs. When European nations were at war, however, Americans relished their distance from the conflicts. So it was until World War I (1914-1918).

In the wake of World War I, President Woodrow Wilson urged the United States to join the League of Nations. The U.S. Senate refused to ratify the League of Nations treaty, indicating that the country was not ready to abandon the long-standing American habit of isolationism. It was World War II that dealt a deathblow to American isolationism. At a conference in San Francisco in 1945, a charter for the United Nations was signed. The United States was an original signatory and soon donated land to house the United Nations permanently in New York City.

THE COLD WAR

At the end of World War II, Germany and Japan were vanquished and much of Europe was strewn with rubble. The United States was unquestionably the dominant world power, both economically and militarily. It not only had helped to bring the war to an end but also had inaugurated a new era in warfare by dropping the first atomic bombs on Japan in August 1945. Because only the United States possessed nuclear weapons, Americans looked forward to an era of peace secured by their nuclear umbrella.

After World War II, the United States forged strong alliances with the nations of Western Europe. To help them rebuild their economies, the United States poured billions of dollars into war-ravaged European nations through an aid package known as the Marshall Plan—named after its architect, Secretary of State George C. Marshall. A military alliance was also forged; the creation of NATO in 1949 affirmed the mutual military interests of the United States and Western Europe, and NATO remains a cornerstone of American foreign and defense policy.

Containment and Korea. Although many Americans also expected cooperative relations with their wartime ally, the Soviet Union, they soon abandoned these hopes. There is still much dispute about how the cold war between the United States and the Soviet Union started.[9] Even before World War II ended, some American policymakers feared that their Soviet allies were intent on spreading communism not only to their neighbors but everywhere. All of Eastern Europe fell under Soviet domination as World War II ended. In 1946, Winston Churchill warned that the Russians had sealed off Eastern Europe with an "iron curtain."

Communist support of a revolt in Greece in 1946 compounded fears of Soviet aggression. Writing in *Foreign Affairs* in 1947, foreign policy strategist George

F. Kennan proposed a policy of "containment."[10] His **containment doctrine** called for the United States to isolate the Soviet Union—to "contain" its advances and resist its encroachments—by peaceful means if possible, but with force if necessary. When economic problems forced Great Britain to decrease its support of Greece, the United States stepped in with the Truman Doctrine of helping other nations oppose communism. The Soviet Union's own response was the Berlin Blockade of 1948-1949, in which it closed off land access to West Berlin (which was surrounded by Communist East Germany). The United States and its allies broke the blockade by airlifting food, fuel, and other necessities to the people of the beleaguered city.

The fall of China to Mao Zedong's Communist-led forces in 1949 seemed to confirm American fears that communism was a cancer spreading over the "free world." In the same year, the Soviet Union exploded its first atomic bomb. The invasion of pro-American South Korea by Communist North Korea in 1950 further fueled American fears. Believing that the Korean invasion was linked with Soviet imperialism, President Truman said bluntly, "We've got to stop the Russians now" and sent American troops to Korea under United Nations auspices. The Korean War was a chance to put containment into practice. Involving China as well as North Korea, the war dragged on until July 27, 1953.

The 1950s were the height of the **cold war**; though hostilities never quite erupted into armed battle, the United States and the Soviet Union were often on the brink of war. John Foster Dulles, secretary of state under Eisenhower, even proclaimed a policy of "brinkmanship," in which the United States was to be prepared to use nuclear weapons in order to *deter* the Soviet Union and Communist China from taking aggressive actions.

Fear of communism affected domestic as well as foreign policy. Those who subscribed to **McCarthyism** assumed that international communism was conspiratorial, insidious, bent on world domination, and infiltrating American government and cultural institutions. Named after Senator Joseph McCarthy—who with flimsy evidence accused scores of prominent Americans and State Department officials of being Communists—McCarthyism flowered during the Korean War. Domestic policy in general was deeply affected by the cold war and by anti-Communist fears. A burgeoning defense budget during the Korean War and later in the 1950s was another result of the cold war.

The Swelling of the Pentagon. The cold war ensured that military needs and massive national security expenditures would remain fixtures in the American economy. As early as 1947, aircraft manufacturers noted that the decline of military procurement after World War II would injure the industry; to avert dislocation, they launched a campaign to sell planes to the U.S. Air Force.[11] Thus were forged some of the first links between policymakers' perceptions of the Soviet threat and corporations' awareness of potential profits from military hardware. Generals and admirals believed that they needed weapons systems, and private industry was happy to supply them for a profit. Defense expenditures grew to be the largest component of the federal budget in the 1950s, consuming $13 of every $100 of the gross domestic product (GDP) by 1954. Large parts of this defense budget were spent on weapons supplied by giant companies such as Westinghouse, RCA, Western Electric, and General Motors.

The interests shared by the armed services and defense contractors produced what some call a *military-industrial complex.* The phrase was coined not by a left-wing critic of the military but by President Dwight D. Eisenhower, himself a former general. Elite theorists especially pointed to this tight alliance between business and government. Economist Seymour Melman wrote about *pentagon capitalism,* linking the military's drive to expand with the profit motives of private industry.[12] As the defense budget grew, so did the profits of aircraft producers and other defense contractors.

In the 1950s, the Soviet Union and the United States engaged in an **arms race.** One side's weaponry goaded the other side to procure yet more weaponry, as one missile led to another. By the 1960s, the result of the arms race was a point of *mutual assured destruction (MAD),* in which each side could annihilate the other, even after absorbing a surprise attack. Later sections of this chapter will examine efforts to control the arms race.

The Vietnam War. Even though it reached its peak during the 1960s, American involvement in Vietnam began much earlier. The Korean War and the 1949 victory of Mao Zedong's Communist forces in China fixed the government's attention on Asian communism. In 1950, while the Korean War raged and just after the fall of Chiang Kai-shek in China, President Truman decided to aid the French effort to retain France's colonial possessions in Southeast Asia.[13]

During the early 1950s, the Viet Minh—the Vietnamese Communist forces—began to receive military aid from the new Communist government in China. In 1954, the French were defeated by the Viet Minh, led by Ho Chi Minh, in a battle at Dien Bien Phu. U.S. Defense Department officials considered, but then decided against, using atomic weapons to support the French cause at Dien Bien Phu. On May 7, 1954, the Viet Minh raised their flag at Dien Bien Phu. The

In 1963, President John Kennedy looked over the Berlin Wall, which the Soviet Union had built to separate Communist East Berlin from the western sectors of the city. The wall stood as the most palpable symbol of the cold war for almost 30 years until it was torn down in 1989.

next morning, peace talks among the participants and other major powers began in Geneva, Switzerland.

Though a party to the resultant agreements, the United States never accepted the Geneva agreement to hold national elections in Vietnam in 1956. Instead, it began supporting one non-Communist leader after another in South Vietnam, each seemingly more committed than the last to defeating Ho Chi Minh's forces in the north.

Vietnam first became an election-year issue in 1964. President Lyndon B. Johnson, who had succeeded John F. Kennedy, was seeking his first full term. His Republican opponent, Arizona Senator Barry Goldwater, was a foreign policy hard-liner. Beginning with Truman's administration, the United States had sent military "advisors" to South Vietnam—which was in the midst of a civil war spurred by the Viet Cong (also known as the National Liberation Front), who sought reunification of South Vietnam with Communist North Vietnam. During the 1964 campaign, Johnson promised that he would not "send American boys to do an Asian boy's job" of defending the pro-American regime in South Vietnam. Goldwater advocated tough action in Vietnam; he promised to send American troops if necessary and even defoliate the jungles with chemicals so that the Viet Cong guerrillas would have no place to hide.

There was a standing joke among Johnson's opponents after his victory in 1964: "They told me that if I voted for Goldwater, we'd have half a million American troops in Vietnam in four years. I did, and we do." Unable to contain the forces of the Viet Cong and North Vietnam with American advisors, Johnson sent in American troops—more than 500,000 at the peak of the undeclared war. He dropped more bombs on Communist North Vietnam than the United States had dropped on Germany in all of World War II. American troops and massive firepower failed to contain the North Vietnamese, however. At home, widespread protests against the war contributed to Johnson's decisions not to run for reelection in 1968 and to begin peace negotiations.

The new Nixon administration prosecuted the war vigorously, in Cambodia as well as in Vietnam, but also worked to negotiate a peace treaty with the Viet Cong and North Vietnam. A peace treaty was signed in 1973, but no one expected it to hold. South Vietnam's capital, Saigon, finally fell to the North Vietnamese army in 1975. South and North Vietnam were reunited into a single nation, and Saigon was renamed Ho Chi Minh City, in honor of the late leader of Communist North Vietnam.

Looking back on the Vietnam War, few Americans think it was worthwhile. It divided the nation and made citizens painfully aware of the ability of the government to lie to them—and (perhaps worse) to itself. It reminded Americans that even a "great power" cannot prevail in a protracted military conflict against a determined enemy unless there is a clear objective and unless the national will is sufficiently committed to expend vast resources on the task.

THE ERA OF DÉTENTE

Even while the Vietnam War was being waged, Richard Nixon—a veteran fighter of the cold war—supported a new policy that came to be called *détente.* The term was popularized by Nixon's national secu-

The Vietnam War Memorial is one of Washington, DC's most moving sights. Often called "The Wall," the memorial lists the names of more than 58,000 Americans killed during the Vietnam War.

rity assistant and later secretary of state, Henry Kissinger.

Détente represented a slow transformation from "conflict thinking" to cooperative thinking in foreign policy strategy. It sought a relaxation of tensions between the superpowers, coupled with firm guarantees of mutual security. The policy assumed that the United States and the Soviet Union had no long-range, irrevocable sources of conflict; that both had an interest in peace and world stability; and that a nuclear war was—and should be—unthinkable. Thus, foreign policy battles between the United States and the Soviet Union were to be waged with diplomatic, economic, and propaganda weapons; the threat of force was downplayed.

One major initiative emerging from détente was the *Strategic Arms Limitation Talks (SALT)*. These talks represented a mutual effort by the United States and the Soviet Union to limit the growth of their nuclear capabilities, with each power maintaining sufficient nuclear weapons to deter a surprise attack by the other. The first SALT accord was signed by Nixon in 1972 and was followed by negotiations for a second agreement, SALT II. After 6 years of laborious negotiations, the agreement was finally signed and sent to the Senate by President Carter in 1979. The Soviet invasion of Afghanistan that year caused Carter to withdraw the treaty from Senate consideration, however, even though both he and Ronald Reagan insisted that they would be committed to the agreement's arms limitations: Neither country could have more than 2,250 strategic nuclear missile launchers, and other nuclear weaponry restrictions applied to both sides.

The United States applied the philosophy of détente to the People's Republic of China as well as to the Soviet Union. After the fall of pro-American Chiang Kai-shek in 1949, the United States had refused to extend diplomatic recognition to the world's most populous nation, recognizing instead Chiang's government-in-exile on the nearby island of Taiwan. As a senator in the early 1950s, Richard Nixon had been an implacable foe of "Red China," even suggesting that the Democratic administration had traitorously "lost" China. Nevertheless, two decades later it was this same Richard Nixon who, as president, first visited the People's Republic and sent an American mission there. President Jimmy Carter extended formal diplomatic recognition to China in November 1978. Since then, cultural and economic ties between the United States and China have increased greatly.

Not everyone favored détente, however. Few people saw more threats from the Soviet Union than did Ronald Reagan, who called it the "Evil Empire." He viewed the Soviet invasion of Afghanistan in 1979 as typical Russian aggression that, if unchecked, could only grow more common. He hailed anti-Communist governments everywhere and pledged to increase American defense spending.

THE REAGAN REARMAMENT

From the mid-1950s to 1981 (with the exception of the Vietnam War), the defense budget had generally been declining as a percentage of both the total federal budget and the GDP. In 1955, during the Eisenhower administration, the government was spending 61 percent of its budget for defense purposes, or about 10 percent of the GDP (the total value of all the goods and services produced annually by the United States). By the time President Reagan took office in 1981, less than 25 percent of the federal budget and 5.2 percent of the GDP were devoted to defense expenditures. These figures reflected a substantial cut indeed, though it came about more because levels of social spending had increased than because military spending had declined. Still, Republican Richard Nixon used to boast that he was the first president in recent history who committed more of the national budget to social services than to military expenditures.

During his campaign for the presidency, Reagan argued that "we cannot negotiate arms control agreements that will slow down the Soviet military buildup as long as we let the Soviets move ahead of us in every category of armaments." America faced, said Reagan, a "window of vulnerability" because the Soviet Union was galloping ahead of the United States in military spending.

As president, Reagan was determined to reverse the trend of diminishing defense spending and proposed the largest peacetime defense spending increase in American history: a 5-year defense buildup costing $1.5 trillion. The early days of the Reagan administration were the most critical in this defense spending buildup. The news came down to the Pentagon rank-and-file quickly: President Carter's last budget had proposed a large increase in defense spending, and the Reagan administration would add $32 billion on top of that. Defense officials were ordered to find places to spend more money.[14] These heady days for the Pentagon lasted only through the first term of Reagan's presidency, however. In his second term, concern over huge budget deficits brought defense spending to a standstill. After taking inflation into account, Congress appropriated no increase in defense spending at all from 1985 to 1988.

In 1983 President Reagan added another element to his defense policy—a new plan for defense against missiles. He called it the **Strategic Defense Initiative (SDI)**; critics quickly renamed it "Star Wars." Reagan's plans for SDI proposed creating a global umbrella in space, wherein computers would scan the skies and use various high-tech devices to destroy invading missiles. The administration proposed a research program that would have cost tens of billions of dollars over the next decade.

In the face of an onslaught of criticism regarding the feasibility of SDI, its proponents have reduced their expectations about the size and capabilities of any defensive shield that could be erected over the next generation. Talk of a smaller system—capable of protecting against an accidental launch of a few missiles or against a threat by some third country with nuclear weapons—has replaced the dream of an impenetrable umbrella over the United States capable of defeating a massive Soviet nuclear strike.

Beginning in 1989, communism in the Soviet Union and in Eastern Europe suddenly began to crumble. The end of the cold war between East and West reduced the threat of nuclear war between the superpowers, but it also left a host of difficult new national security issues in its wake. Here, soldiers remove a bust of Vladimir Lenin, the founder of Soviet communism, from a Moscow military school.

THE FINAL THAW IN THE COLD WAR

On May 12, 1989, in a commencement address at Texas A&M University, President Bush announced a new era in American foreign policy. He termed this era one "beyond containment"; the United States' goal would be more than simply containing Soviet expansionism. Bush declared that it was time to seek the integration of the Soviet Union into the community of nations.

The cold war ended as few had anticipated—spontaneously. Suddenly, the elusive objective of 40 years of post-World War II U.S. foreign policy—freedom and self-determination for Eastern Europeans and Soviet peoples and the reduction of the military threat from the East—occurred. Forces of change sparked by Soviet leader Mikhail Gorbachev led to a staggering wave of upheaval that shattered Communist regimes and the postwar barriers between Eastern and Western Europe. The Berlin Wall, the most prominent symbol of oppression in Eastern Europe, came tumbling down, and East and West Germany formed a unified, democratic republic. The former Soviet Union split into 15

DEFENDING HUMAN RIGHTS

You Are the Policymaker

Americans sat riveted to their television screens for several weeks in May and June of 1989 as they watched Chinese students and workers in Beijing's Tiananmen Square protest on behalf of greater democracy. This was heady stuff for the world's most populous country, apparently emerging from two generations of totalitarian rule.

For a time it looked as though China's rulers would accommodate demands for reform. On the night of June 3, however, the army violently crushed the democracy movement, killing hundreds—perhaps thousands—of protestors and beginning a wave of executions, arrests, and repression.

Westerners were shocked at the bloodshed and widely condemned the Chinese government. Regardless, in July and December 1989, President Bush sent his national security advisor Brent Scowcroft and Deputy Secretary of State Lawrence Eagleburger to meet secretly with Chinese leaders. Bush also lifted economic sanctions against China. The president claimed he was not normalizing relations with China, but many political leaders criticized him for moral capitulation to the hard-line Communist leaders.

The president asked, "How else should nuclear powers deal with each other?" and pointed out that the United States maintains relations with many countries that have even more egregious records of human rights violations than China. In addition, Bush argued that keeping the lines of communication open would increase his ability to encourage the Chinese leaders to moderate their repression.

His critics responded, "How can you deal with immoral leaders who slaughter their own people for nonviolently advocating rights that Americans cherish? Is there no place for morality in international relations?"

If you were president, what would *you* have done?

separate nations, and non-Communist governments formed in most of them. Poland, Czechoslovakia (splitting into the Czech Republic and Slovakia), and Hungary established democratic governments, and reformers overthrew the old-line Communist leaders in Bulgaria and Rumania.

Events were unfolding so fast and in so many places at once that no one was quite sure how to deal with them. President Bush declared, "Every morning I receive an intelligence briefing, and I receive the best information available to any world leader today. And yet, the morning news is often overtaken by the news that very same evening."[15]

In 1989, reform seemed on the verge of occurring in China as well as in Eastern Europe. That spring in Tiananmen Square, the central meeting place in Beijing, thousands of students held protests on behalf of democratization. Finally, the aging Chinese leaders could tolerate challenges to their rule no longer, and they forcibly—and brutally—evacuated the square, crushing some protestors under armored tanks. It is still not clear how many students were killed and how many others arrested, but the reform movement received a serious setback. This suppression of efforts to develop democracy sent a chill through what had been a warming relationship between the United States and the People's Republic of China (see "You Are the Policymaker: Defending Human Rights").

Despite its risks and uncertainties, the cold war was characterized by a stable and predictable set of relations among the great powers. Now international relations have entered an era of improvisation as nations struggle to come up with creative responses to changes in the global balance of power.

Almost everyone agrees that today's more cooperative, albeit more complicated, international environment portends an overhaul of the American national security infrastructure. Armed forces and alliances, defense industries, and budgets built up since World War II are being reassessed in light of the recent cold war thaw.

THE POLITICS OF DEFENSE POLICY

The politics of national defense involves high stakes—the nation's security, for example. Domestic political concerns, budgetary limitations, and ideology all influence decisions on the structure of defense

SINCE KENNEDY

Trends in Defense Spending

John F. Kennedy took office in 1961 at the height of the Cold War. National defense was the dominant public policy for the U.S. government; it accounted for half of all the money ("outlays") the government spent that year. Things have changed dramatically since then, however. Although defense spending continued to increase until the 1990s, spending on other policies increased even more. As a result, defense spending is now only about one-sixth of the budget. Still, at nearly $270 billion per year, it remains a significant sum, one over which battles continue to be fought in Congress.

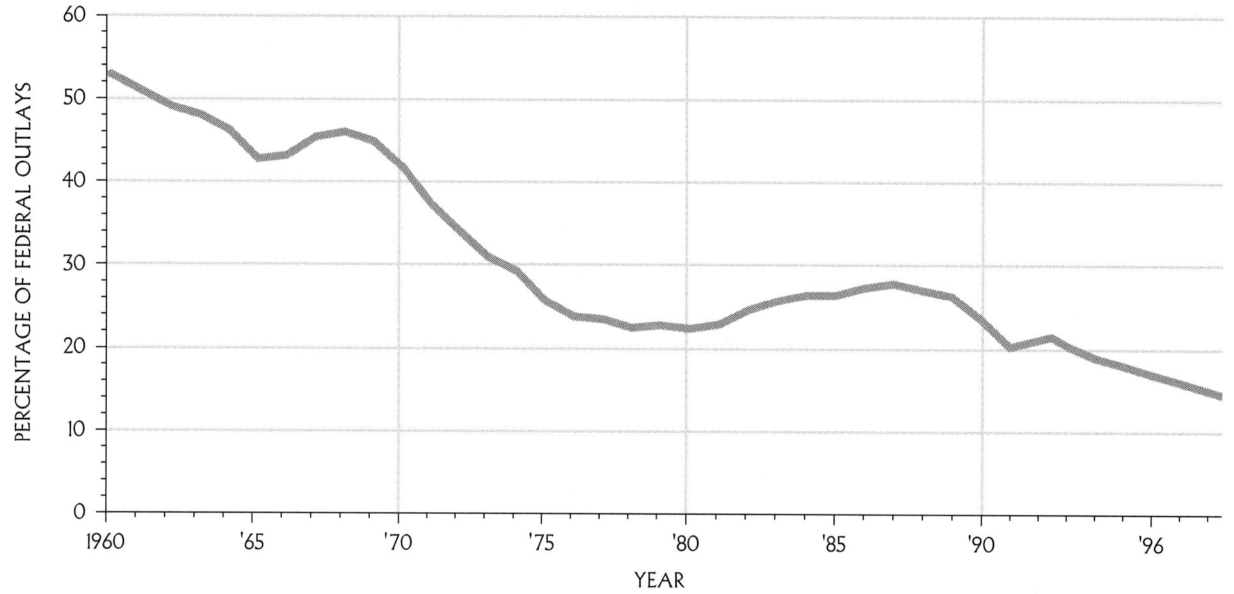

SOURCE: Office of Management and Budget, *Budget of the United States Government, Fiscal Year 1998: Historical Tables* (Washington, DC: U.S. Government Printing Office, 1997), Table 3.1.

policy and negotiations with allies and adversaries. All public policies include budgets, people, and equipment. In the realm of national defense, these elements are especially critical because of the size of the budget and the bureaucracy, as well as the destructive potential of modern weapons.

At the core of defense policy is a judgment about what the United States will defend. The central assumption of the current American defense policy is that the United States requires forces and equipment sufficient to fight two nearly simultaneous major regional conflicts. For example, our goal is to be ready to fight potential aggression by a remilitarized Iraq against Kuwait and Saudi Arabia *and* aggression by North Korea against South Korea. A large military infrastructure is necessary to meet the two-war goal.

DEFENSE SPENDING

Defense spending now makes up about one-sixth of the federal budget. Although this is much smaller than in earlier years (see "Since Kennedy: Trends in Defense Spending"), vast sums of money (as we saw in Chapter 14) and fundamental questions of public policy are still involved. Some scholars have argued that America faces a trade-off between defense spending and social spending. A nation, they claim, must choose between guns and butter, and more guns mean less butter. Evidence supporting the existence of such a trade-off is mixed, however. In general, defense and domestic policy expenditures appear to be independent of each other.[16] Ronald Reagan's efforts to increase military budgets while cutting back on domestic policy expenditures seem to have stemmed more from his own ideology than from any inevitable choice between the two.

Defense spending is a thorny political issue, entangled with ideological disputes. Conservatives fight deep cuts in defense spending, pointing out that many nations retain potent military capability and insisting that America maintain its readiness at a high level. They refer to the Gulf War to prove that wars on a significant scale are still possible. In addition, they attribute the collapse of communism in Eastern and Central Europe to Western toughness and the massive increase in defense spending that occurred in the early 1980s. When the Soviet Union saw that it could not outspend the United States, they argue, it finally decided not to continue to allocate so much of its scarce resources to defense and to loosen its grip on Eastern Europe.

Liberals, on the other hand, maintain that the Pentagon wastes money and that the United States buys too many guns and too little butter. The most crucial aspect of national defense, they argue, is a strong economy, which is based on investments in "human capital" such as health and education. The erosion of the Communist Party's authority was well under way when Gorbachev rose to power, liberals insist; it accelerated as *glasnost* (the Russian term for the new openness of society) made the party's failures a matter of public ridicule and as democratization freed new forces to challenge the existing order. They contend that Gorbachev and his fellow reformers were responding primarily to internal, not external, pressures. Inadequacies and defects at the core of the Soviet economy—the inertia, wastefulness, and corruption inherent in the system—were the driving forces that brought change to the Soviet Union, not American defense spending.

In addition, scholars such as Paul Kennedy and David Calleo envision a new world order different from the bipolar dominance of the United States and the Soviet Union.[17] Kennedy warns of the historical dangers of "imperial overstretch," suggesting that great empires in a stage of relative economic decline vis-à-vis emerging powers accelerate their decline by clinging to vast military commitments.

Whatever its cause, the lessening of East-West tensions has given momentum to significant reductions in defense spending, what some call the *peace dividend.* Some conservatives favor cutting defense spending in order to decrease the budget deficit, whereas liberals want to allocate the funds to expand domestic programs.

Changing spending patterns is not easy, however. For example, dozens of military hardware acorns planted during the lush years of the early 1980s are now maturing into mighty, expensive oaks. And when the assembly lines at weapons plants close down, submarine designers, welders, and others lose their jobs. These programs become political footballs as candidates compete over promises to keep weapons systems such as the *Seawolf* submarine or the Osprey helicopter in production. Ideology plays a crucial role in the basic decisions members of Congress make regarding defense spending, but once these decisions are made, liberal as well as conservative representatives and senators fight hard to help constituencies win and keep defense contracts.[18]

Nevertheless, defense spending is decreasing as weapons systems are canceled, procurement is slowed, and the size of the armed forces is reduced.

PERSONNEL

The structure of America's defense has been based on a large standing military force and a battery of strategic nuclear weapons. The United States has nearly 1.5 million men and women on active duty and nearly 900,000 million in the National Guard and Reserves (see Table 20.2). About 300,000 active-duty troops are deployed abroad, mostly in Europe and South Korea.[19] This is a very costly enterprise and one that frequently evokes calls to bring the troops home. Many observers believe that America's allies, especially prosperous nations such as Japan and Germany, should bear a greater share of common defense costs.

WEAPONS

To deter an aggressor's attack, the United States has relied on a triad of nuclear weapons: ground-based intercontinental ballistic missiles (ICBMs), submarine-launched ballistic missiles (SLBMs), and strategic bombers. Both the United States and Russia have thousands of large nuclear warheads. These weapons, like troops, are costly (each Stealth bomber costs over a billion dollars), and they pose obvious dangers to human survival.

The rapid drive toward democracy in Eastern Europe, combined with Moscow's economic stagnation and the Pentagon's budgetary squeeze, pushed arms reduction inexorably onto the two superpowers' discussion agenda. Substantial progress has been made to end the arms race and what was known as "the balance of terror."

During the May 1988 Moscow summit meeting, President Reagan and Mikhail Gorbachev exchanged ratified copies of a new treaty eliminating *intermediate-*

The *Trident* submarine is one of the U.S. Navy's most sophisticated weapons. A key component of America's nuclear weapons triad, the Trident can launch missiles from the ocean's depths, where it is virtually invisible and invulnerable to enemy attack. Like most weapons systems, however, the submarines cost hundreds of millions of dollars more than planned.

TABLE 20.2 SIZE OF THE ARMED FORCES

BRANCH	PERSONNEL[a]
Army	495,000
Navy	390,802
Air Force	371,577
Marines	174,000
SUBTOTAL	1,431,379
Reserves	891,618
TOTAL	2,322,997

[a]1997 estimates

SOURCES: Office of Management and Budget, *Budget of the United States Government, Fiscal Year 1998: Appendix* (Washington, DC: U.S. Government Printing Office, 1997).

President Reagan and Soviet President Mikhail Gorbachev begin their 1988 summit meeting in Moscow. The two presidents later signed a treaty eliminating intermediate-range nuclear missiles from Europe. The INF treaty marked the first time an American president had agreed to reduce current levels of nuclear weapons.

range nuclear forces (INF). Reagan, who had built his reputation on fervid anti-Communism and had denounced earlier arms control efforts (such as Jimmy Carter's SALT II agreement), became the first American president to sign a treaty to reduce current levels of nuclear weapons. Under the terms of the INF treaty, more than 2,500 nuclear weapons with ranges between 300 and 3,400 miles were to be destroyed.

Superpower relations continued to improve at a dizzying pace, accelerated by the dissolution of the Soviet Union. On November 19, 1990, the leaders of 22 countries signed a treaty reducing conventional armed forces in Europe. The treaty slashed forces in Europe by 40 percent—the Soviet Union was called on to remove the most troops. A related change occurred in 1991 as the Warsaw Pact, the military alliance tying Eastern Europe to the Soviet Union, was dissolved.

On July 31, 1991, shortly before Soviet hard-liners attempted to remove President Gorbachev and other reformers from power in a coup, he and President Bush signed the *Strategic Arms Reduction Treaty (START)*—after 9 years of negotiations. The treaty had the distinction of being the first accord mandating the elimination of strategic nuclear weaponry. (The Intermediate-Range Nuclear Forces pact banned a whole class of shorter-flying nuclear arms.)

The significance of these changes was soon overshadowed by other events, however, as the democratization of Eastern Europe, the restructuring of the Soviet Union, and the deterioration of the Soviet economy substantially diminished both Russia's inclination and potential to threaten the interests of the United States and its allies. President Bush broke ground with his decision in the fall of 1991 to dismantle unilaterally some U.S. nuclear weapons, enticing President Gorbachev to follow suit shortly afterward. In January 1993, Presidents Bush and Yeltsin signed an agreement

(START II) to cut the U.S. and Russian (including those of Ukraine, Belarus, and Kazakhstan) nuclear arsenals to a total of no more than 6,500 weapons by the year 2003—less than one-third of the 20,000 long-range nuclear weapons the two possessed at the time. Large, accurate ICBMs with multiple warheads or MIRVs were banned altogether. The 3,500 strategic nuclear weapons that the United States is allowed under this agreement would be the smallest stockpile this country has possessed since the Kennedy administration of the early 1960s.

Nuclear weapons are the most destructive in America's arsenal, but they are by no means the only ones. Jet fighters, aircraft carriers, and even tanks are extraordinarily complex and equally costly. The perception that space-age technology helped win the Gulf War in "100 hours" with few American casualties, in addition to the fact that producing expensive weapons provides jobs for American workers, means that high-tech weapons systems will continue to play an important role in America's defense posture.

Although progress has been made on reducing tensions between East and West, other international matters clamor for attention. Even the mightiest nation can be mired in intractable issues.

The People Speak

Which of the following is a critical threat to the vital interests of the United States in the next ten years?

Possibility of unfriendly countries becoming nuclear powers	72%
International terrorism	69%
Economic competition from Japan	62%
Development of China as a world power	57%
Military power of Russia	32%

By the 1990s, views of threats to U.S. vital interests had changed substantially from previous decades. The public was twice as likely to be concerned about economic competition from Japan as about a military threat from Russia.

SOURCE: Chicago Council on Foreign Relations Poll, October 1994.

THE NEW GLOBAL AGENDA

The global agenda is changing rapidly. As military competition with the East has diminished, economic competition with the world has increased. The gap between domestic and foreign policy is increasingly obscure. Dealing with allies such as Japan and Germany on trade and finance is as crucial as negotiating arms reductions with Russia. Maintaining access to petroleum in the Middle East is more crucial than ever, and determining policy regarding the global environment has taken on new prominence.

Regardless of the standards one uses for measurement, the United States is the world's mightiest military power. Its very strength seems to belie an essential weakness, however. Events on the world stage often appear to counter the American script. In the long and controversial Vietnam War, 500,000 American troops were not enough. U.S. economic vulnerability has increased. Oil supply lines depend on a precarious Middle Eastern peace and on the safe passage of huge tankers through a sliver of water called the Strait of Hormuz. We sometimes appear to be losing the highly publicized "war on drugs" to an international network of wealthy drug lords called *narco-traficantes.* Perhaps most important of all, our economy is increasingly dependent on international trade, placing us at the mercy of interest rates in Germany and restrictive markets in Japan and China.

Public opinion polls find that in the post-cold war era, Americans are more likely to perceive threats to their security from the economic competition of allies than from military rivalry with old adversaries (see "The People Speak" on this page). In addition, it is terrorists and the *potential* of weaker, less developed countries to become adversaries that concern us now.

THE DECREASING ROLE OF MILITARY POWER

One explanation for America's tribulations is that the nation's supposed strong suit—military might—is no longer the primary instrument of foreign policy. Robert Keohane and Joseph Nye, in describing the diminishing role of military force in contemporary international politics, say that among the developed nations, "the perceived margin of safety has widened: fears of attack in general have declined, and fears of attacks by one another are virtually nonexistent."[20]

Today military power is losing much of its utility in resolving many international issues. "Force," argue Keohane and Nye, "is often not an appropriate way of achieving other goals (such as economic and ecological welfare) that are becoming more important" in world affairs.[21] Economic conflicts do not readily yield to nuclear weapons. America cannot persuade Arab nations to sell it cheap oil by bombing them, nor can it prop up the textile industry's position in world trade by resorting to military might. The United States is long on firepower at the very time when firepower is decreasing in its utility as an instrument of foreign policy.

Conflict among large powers, the threat of nuclear war, and the possibility of conventional war have certainly not disappeared, but grafted onto them are new issues. Former Secretary of State Henry Kissinger described the new era eloquently:

> The traditional agenda of international affairs—the balance among major powers, the security of nations—no longer defines our perils or our possibilities. Now we are entering a new era. Old international patterns are crumbling; old slogans are uninstructive. The world has become interdependent in economics, in communications, in human aspirations.[22]

Harvard political scientist Stanley Hoffman likened the United States' plight to that of Jonathan Swift's Gulliver, the traveler seized and bound by the tiny Lilliputians.[23] For Americans, as for Gulliver, merely being big and powerful is no guarantee of dominance. Time after time and place after place, so it seems, the American Gulliver is frustrated by the Lilliputians. Nowhere does Gulliver confront more problems than in the troubled Middle East (see in "In the Twenty-First Century: The Middle East").

THE INTERNATIONAL ECONOMY

Once upon a time, nations took pains to isolate themselves from the world. They erected high tariff barriers to fend off foreign products and amassed large armies to defend their borders against intruders. Times have changed. One key word describes today's international economy: **interdependency.** When two people are independent, they can go about their business without fearing each other's actions. In a time of interdependency, actions reverberate and affect other people's economic lifelines. The health of the American economy depends increasingly on the prosperity of its trading partners and on the smooth flow of trade and finance across borders.

International Trade. Since the end of World War II, trade among nations has grown rapidly. Exports and imports have increased tenfold since 1970 alone (see Figure 20.1, page 517). Among the largest U.S. exporters are grain farmers, producers of computer hardware and software, aircraft manufacturers, movie makers, heavy construction companies, and purveyors of accounting and consulting services. The spending of foreign tourists bolsters the U.S. travel, hotel, and recreation industries. American colleges and universities derive a significant portion of their revenue from educating foreign students. The globalization of finances has been even more dramatic than the growth of trade. Worldwide computer and communications networks link financial markets in all parts of the globe instantaneously, making it easier to move capital across national boundaries but also increasing the probability that a steep decline in the Japanese stock market will send prices plummeting on Wall Street.

Coping with foreign economic issues is becoming just as difficult, and increasingly just as important, as coping with domestic ones. In a simpler time, the main instrument of international economic policy was the **tariff,** a special tax added to the cost of imported goods. Tariffs are intended to raise the price of imported goods and thereby protect American businesses and workers from foreign competition. Tariff making, though, is a game everyone can play. High U.S. tariffs encourage other nations to respond with high tariffs on American products. The high tariffs that the government enacted early in the Great Depression (and that some say aggravated this economic crisis) were the last of their kind. Since that time, the world economy has moved from a period of high tariffs and protectionism to one of lower tariffs and freer trade.

However, nontariff barriers such as quotas, subsidies, and quality specifications for imported products are common means of limiting imports. The United States places quotas on the amount of steel that can be imported and negotiates voluntary limits on the importation of Japanese automobiles. Such policies do save American jobs, but they also raise the price of the steel and automobiles that Americans use. American and European subsidies for agricultural products have been an obstacle to negotiating tariff reductions.

Recently, substantial progress has been made in lowering barriers to trade. In 1992, President Bush signed the *North American Free Trade Agreement (NAFTA)* with Canada and Mexico, which would eventually eliminate most tariffs among North American countries. In 1993, after a heated battle, President Clinton obtained congressional passage of the legislation implementing the agreement.

President Clinton submitted an even more important agreement to Congress in 1994. The *General Agreement on Tariffs and Trade (GATT)* is the mechanism by which most of the world's nations negotiate widespread trade agreements. In 1994, 117 nations agreed to (1) reduce tariffs 38 percent for developed countries; (2) eliminate certain nontariff barriers and subsidies; (3)

THE MIDDLE EAST

In the 21st Century

The Middle East is a great triangle of civilization, roughly bounded by Iran on the east, Egypt on the south, and Turkey on the north (see the accompanying map). It has been a place of turbulence for at least a millennium. Until World War II, the United States could safely ignore the region because much of it, including Palestine, was under British rule. In 1948, after World War II, the United Nations created the state of Israel, intended as a homeland for Jews who survived the scourge of fascism. However, returning the Jews to their historic homeland involved displacing Palestinians from theirs. Spawning dozens of organizations committed to the destruction of Israel—the Palestinian Liberation Organization (PLO) is merely the best known—the Palestinians have created a major impediment to Middle Eastern peace. Four times since its founding, Israel has gone to war with its Arab neighbors. Each time the United States has been Israel's key supporter and arms supplier.

During the 1970s, the American commitment to Israel, long supported by the American Jewish community, had to confront the new reality of Arab oil. Though repeatedly beaten by Israeli military power, Arab nations had an economic weapon Israel could not match—one on which American dependence grew annually. An oil embargo by the Arab members of the **Organization of Petroleum Exporting Countries (OPEC)** in the winter of 1973-1974 brought home to the United States the reality of economic power in world politics. If it did nothing else, the embargo persuaded Washington that peace between Israel and its Arab neighbors would have to be a primary foreign policy goal of the United States.

After he launched a war against Israel in 1973 and demonstrated yet again the costs of the Arab-Israeli conflict, Egyptian President Anwar Sadat proposed a peace initiative that culminated in a peace treaty between Egypt and Israel in 1979. Negotiations were facilitated by the efforts of President Carter, who arranged a week of meetings at Camp David between Sadat and Israeli Prime Minister Menachem Begin. Henry Kissinger, to whom Sadat gave the pen he had used in signing the Camp David accords, remarked, "It is a new world now." Euphoria and exuberance in Washington, Cairo, and Jerusalem only temporarily overshadowed backlash in the Arab world, however. Sadat was praised in Washington and Jerusalem but scorned in Arab capitals. Even the more moderate Arab nations cut off diplomatic relations and aid to Egypt. OPEC quickly announced a series of staggering increases in oil prices. Significantly, President Carter, immediately after bidding farewell to Sadat and Begin, went to work on the task of finding a new energy policy. Two years after signing the treaty, Sadat was assassinated in Egypt by a band of militant Moslem fundamentalists.

Israel itself was never fully supportive of the framework of the 1979 treaty. To protect its borders from the PLO, Israel invaded Lebanon in the summer of 1982—an action that led to bloody attacks on refugee camps in Beirut. The United States, Britain, and Italy agreed to send troops to Lebanon to separate the warring factions there. A year later, nearly 250 American Marines were killed in a terrorist attack. President Reagan moved the remaining troops offshore and later nearly eliminated an American presence in Lebanon.

Energy and religion are the volatile ingredients of Middle Eastern politics. Both Arab and Israeli governments now confront the threat of Islamic fundamentalism, particularly in Iran. Indeed, Iranian fundamentalists dominated the news and the policy agenda in the United States after taking Americans hostage in the U.S. embassy in November 1979. They were not released until noon on January 20, 1981—the minute Jimmy Carter left office. A war between Iran and Iraq for most of the 1980s drained both countries and spilled over into the Persian Gulf, where in 1987 the U.S. Navy was sent to protect shipping in that vital corridor.

Then in August 1990, Iraq invaded Kuwait, a small country that produces about 10 percent of the world's oil. President Bush sent U.S. troops to the Persian Gulf, initially in small numbers, to defend neighboring Saudi Arabia, which produces another 20 percent of the world's oil. (Kuwait and Saudi Arabia also possess about half the world's proven oil reserves.) The United Nations Security Council supported an economic embargo against Iraq and set a deadline of January 15, 1991, for Iraq to pull out of Kuwait or face war. In the meantime, the United States and its allies were pouring troops into Saudi Arabia (more than half a million from the United States alone). The deadline passed without action

The Middle East (continued)

from Baghdad, and on the evening of January 16, the allies launched the most massive coordinated air attack in history. After five and a half weeks of bombing, the United States and its allies launched a ground attack that defeated Iraq in 100 hours.

Kuwait was liberated. The speed of the victory and the low level of allied casualties were undeniably impressive. Yet Saddam Hussein remained in power in Baghdad, and the Middle East remained an unstable powder keg high on the agenda of U.S. policymakers.

There was reason for optimism, however. U.S. success in the Gulf War increased its credibility in the Middle East, especially among Israel's traditional foes. In addition, the PLO and Jordan sided with Iraq, thereby losing the financial support of Saudi Arabia and Kuwait. The result was new incentives for negotiations, leading to an agreement in 1993 for Palestinian self-rule in Gaza and Jericho and further negotiations on expanding self-rule to most of the West Bank. In 1994, Israel also signed a peace accord with Jordan.

Trouble erupted again, however. Israeli Prime Minister Yitzhak Rabin was assassinated by an Israeli student angry at Rabin's concessions to the Palestinians. In 1996, Benjamin Netanyahu was elected prime minister and adopted a more hard-line position than had Rabin. This provoked a violent Arab reaction and set back the peace process. As we approach the twenty-first century, tensions remain high in the Middle East. The one safe prediction seems to be that the United States will continue to be frustrated as it attempts to broker a peace between conflicting cultures, each with important leverage in the international arena.

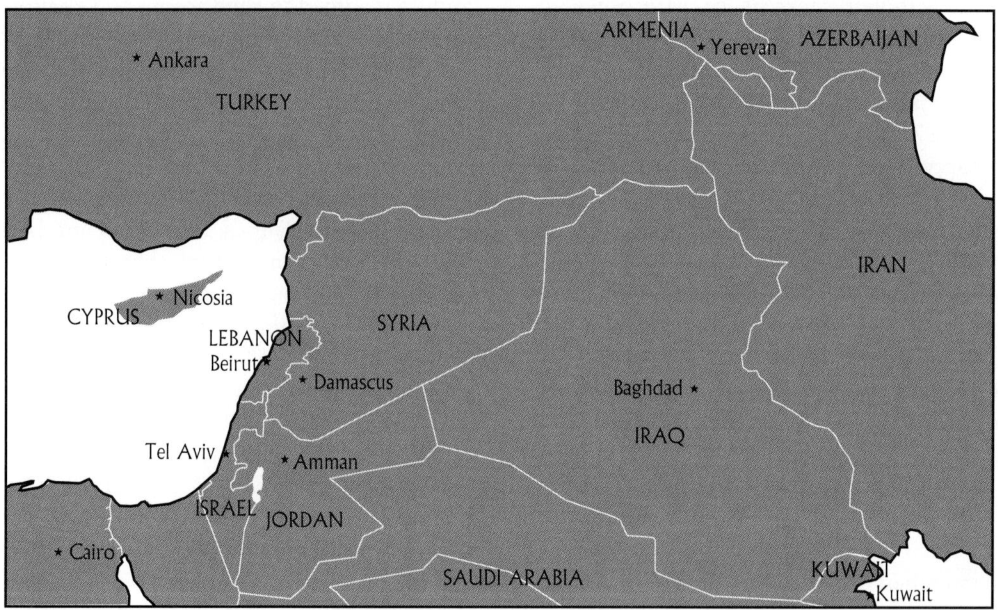

broaden GATT principles to areas such as trade in services, investment, and intellectual property rights; and (4) apply more effective disciplines to agricultural trade. The GATT also included a charter to create a World Trade Organization (WTO) that would act as the arbiter of international trade disputes. In its last action, the 103rd Congress passed the legislation necessary to implement this agreement.

A persistent issue for the president is opening up foreign markets for U.S. goods and services. The White House is especially eager to open Japanese markets in areas such as automobiles, auto parts, telecommunications, insurance, and medical equipment. The United States lacks the influence to *demand* that these markets be opened, however. If we refuse to trade with another nation, that nation will deny *our* exports access to its markets, and United States consumers will lose access to its products. In addition, thousands of Americans now work in foreign-owned companies in the United States, such as Japanese automobile assembly plants. Although foreign investments and the creation of jobs are good for the United States, a by-product is that Americans have a stake in averting a trade crisis with investing nations. Those benefiting from Japanese

FIGURE 20.1 EXPORTS AND IMPORTS

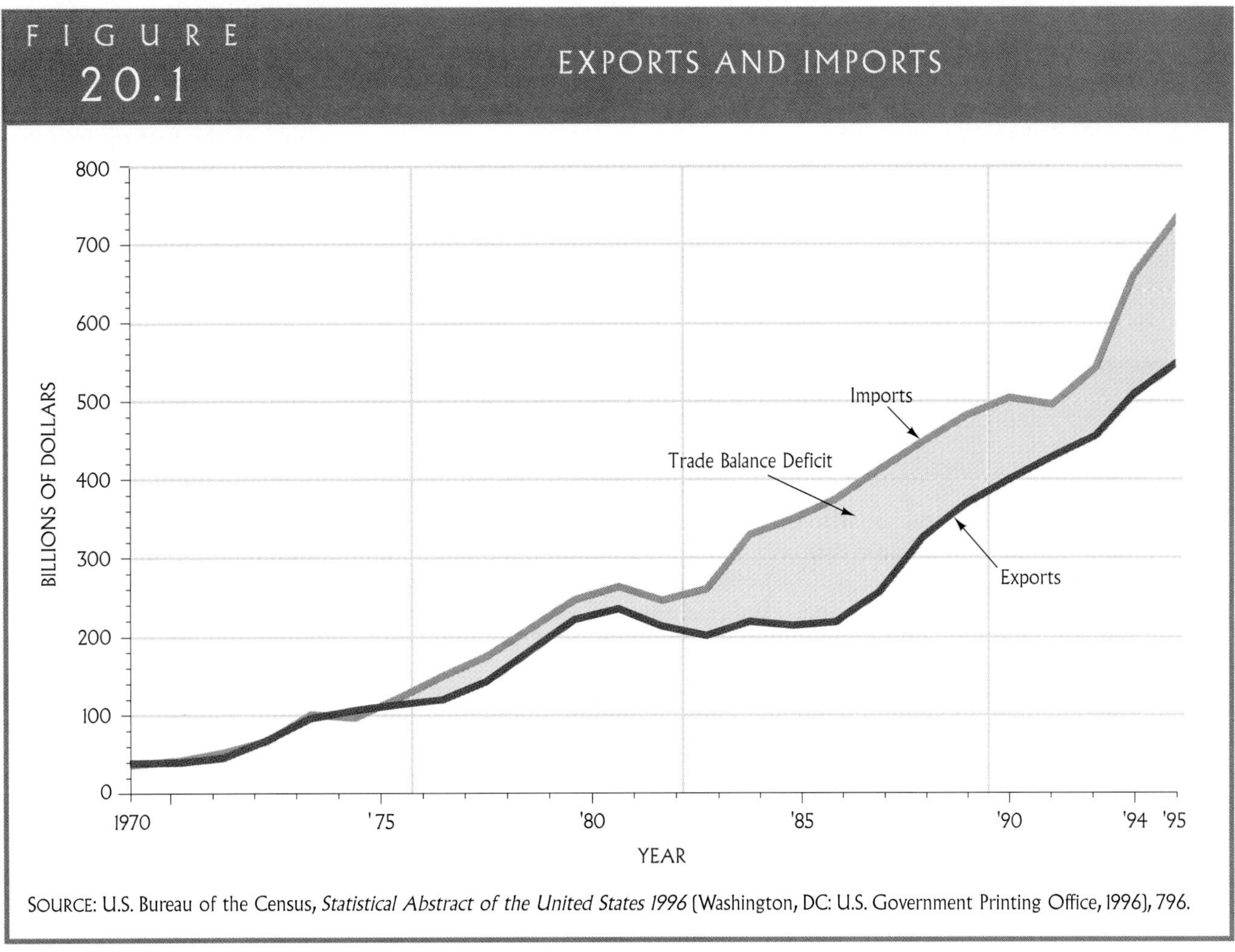

SOURCE: U.S. Bureau of the Census, *Statistical Abstract of the United States 1996* (Washington, DC: U.S. Government Printing Office, 1996), 796.

investments, for example, may flock to Tokyo's side on some important issues.

Balance of Trade. Foreign products are not free. When citizens pay for them, they send dollars out of the country. When an oil tanker arrives in Houston, dollars travel to Saudi Arabia. If other nations do not buy as many American products as Americans do of theirs, then the United States is paying out more than it is taking in. If the United States puts military bases in Germany, the money that soldiers spend for a night on the town goes into German pockets. When American tourists spend their dollars abroad, they, too, carry American dollars away. All these instances combine to upset the **balance of trade**: the ratio of what a country pays for imports to what it earns from exports. When a country imports more than it exports, it has a balance-of-trade *deficit.* Year after recent year, the American balance of trade has been preceded by a minus sign. The deficit for merchandise was $167 billion in 1996.

The excess of imports over exports decreases the dollar's buying power against the mark, yen, pound, and other currencies, making Americans pay more for goods that they buy from other nations. This decline in the value of the dollar, however, also makes American products cheaper abroad, thereby increasing our exports. Since the late 1980s, the United States has experienced an export boom that has given us a balance-of-trade surplus with Western Europe. Exports account for more than 10 percent of the GDP, and 5 percent of all civilian employment in the United States is related to manufacturing exports. So is a substantial amount of white-collar employment—in the area of financial services, for example. The U.S. trade deficit with Japan and other Asian countries has also declined, but much more slowly.

A poor balance of trade also exacerbates unemployment. Not only dollars but also jobs are flowing abroad. Because labor is cheaper in Mexico, Taiwan, Malaysia, and South Korea, products made there can be priced lower than American-made products (see Figure 20.2). Sometimes American firms have shut down their domestic operations and relocated in countries where labor costs are lower. The AFL-CIO claims that hundreds of thousands of American jobs have been lost to foreign competition. Under a special act guaranteeing compensation to American workers who lose their jobs to foreign competition, the Department of Labor has aided thousands of workers. The Labor Department, however, would be the first to note that short-term aid is no substitute for a long-term job.

Even so, a cheaper dollar also makes the cost of American labor more competitive. In response to this and to criticism about the balance of trade, more for-

FIGURE 20.2 THE GLOBAL CONNECTION AND A PERSONAL COMPUTER

The industry standard in personal computers is the IBM PC. The different parts of the PC are made around the world as shown below; note that only a small fraction of the manufactured parts are made in the United States. Does this have implications for American foreign policy? You bet it does. "Foreign sourcing" costs Americans jobs. Foreign economic policies must try to cope with this problem by making American products more desirable abroad.

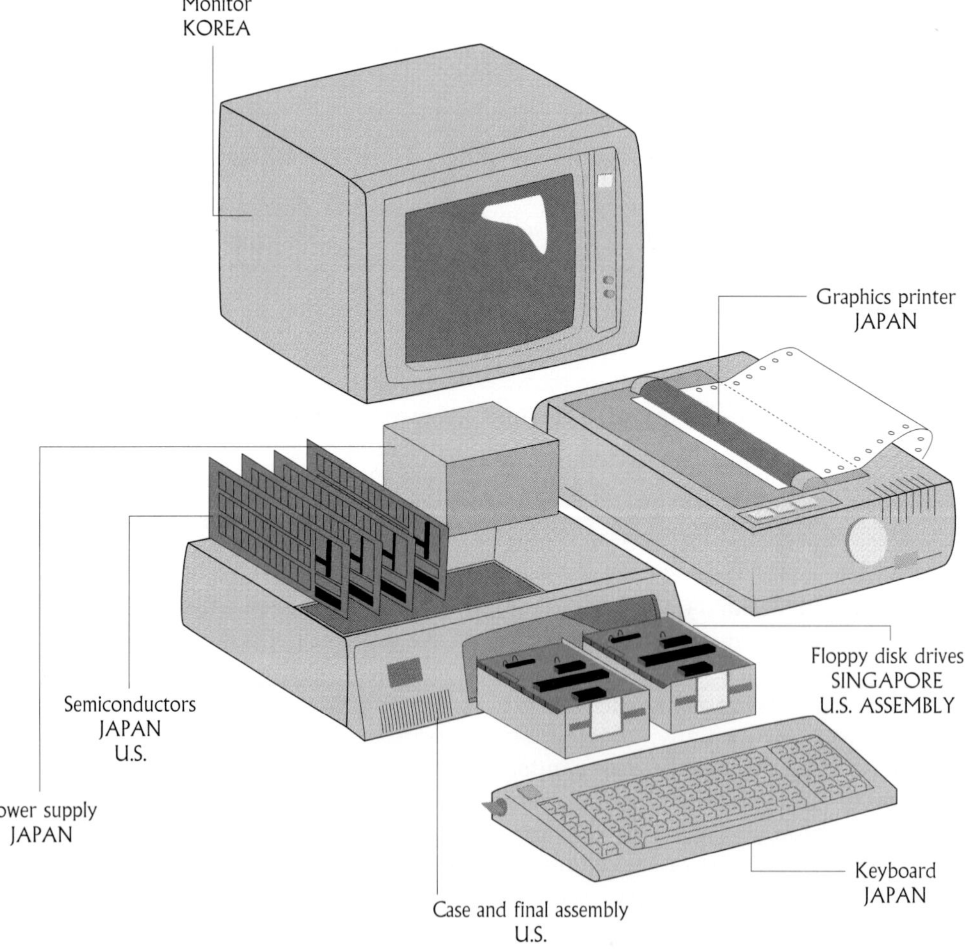

SOURCE: Reprinted from the March 11, 1985, issue of *Business Week* by special permission. Copyright ©1985 by McGraw-Hill, Inc.

eign-owned companies are building factories in the United States—just as American companies have plants around the globe. Thus, many Hondas are made in the United States, and parts for some cars manufactured by General Motors are made abroad. The web of interdependency has become so tangled that it is increasingly difficult to define "imports."

In addition, the stability of the U.S. economy and the low value of the dollar have made the United States attractive to foreign investors, who buy everything from major motion picture studios to Rockefeller Center. Although advantages accrue to the United States when investors pour money into the country, some fear that both profits and control will move outside our borders.

INTERNATIONAL INEQUALITY AND FOREIGN AID

A major transformation in the international system over the past two decades has been the addition of North-South conflict to the old rivalries between East and West. Whereas the cold war meant continuous conflict between the Soviet Union and the West, world politics today includes a growing conflict between rich and poor nations—the rich nations primarily being concentrated in the Northern hemisphere, the poor nations in the Southern hemisphere. (You can see some differences among nations in Table 20.3.)

The old expression "the rich get richer and the poor get poorer" describes fairly accurately the inequalities among nations today. The income gap between rich, industrialized nations and poor, less developed nations is widening rather than narrowing. One reason for the widening gap is suggested by a modern-day twist on the old line about rich and poor: "The rich get richer and the poor get children." While birthrates in the developed nations are leveling off, those in the poorer nations often outpace increases in these countries' gross domestic products. If a nation's GDP increases 3 percent but its birthrate increases 5 percent, the nation has to divide 3 percent more money among 5 percent more people.

Less developed countries have responded to their poverty by borrowing money, and international banks have been willing participants in this debt dependency.

TABLE 20.3 RICH NATIONS, POOR NATIONS

NATION	POPULATION (MILLIONS)	BIRTH RATE	LIFE EXPECTANCY AT BIRTH (YEARS)	GROSS DOMESTIC PRODUCT (PER CAPITA $)
Low-income				
Ethiopia	57.2	46.1	46.9	91
Bangladesh	123.1	30.5	55.9	206
Indonesia	206.6	23.7	61.6	838
Pakistan	129.3	36.2	58.5	399
China	1,210.0	17.0	69.6	1,860
Middle-income				
Algeria	29.2	28.5	68.3	1,452
Malaysia	20.2	26.2	69.8	3,483
Colombia	36.8	21.3	72.8	1,753
High-income				
United States	265.6	14.8	76.0	25,810
Japan	125.5	10.2	79.6	37,000
France	58.0	10.9	78.4	22,760

SOURCE: Central Intelligence Agency, *The World Factbook 1994-95* (Washington, DC: Brassey's, 1994). U.S. Bureau of the Census, *Statistical Abstract of the United States 1996* (Washington, DC: Government Printing Office, 1996), 827-829, 831-832, 835.

Nations unable to pay the installments could simply refinance their debt, though naturally at ever-higher interest rates. Viewed from any perspective, the foreign debts of these governments are truly staggering, often amounting to large percentages of their gross domestic products. In 1994, the United States had to provide massive loan guarantees for Mexico to avoid a Mexican default on its foreign debt. This would have resulted in a deep depression in the Mexican economy, drying up a huge market for U.S. exports, causing massive losses for U.S. investors in Mexican bonds, and propelling thousands of illegal aliens across the U.S. border. Mexico, unlike most countries, repaid its loan ahead of schedule.

There is another complication to the issue of international inequality. Not only are there wide gaps between rich and poor nations (international inequality), but there are also big gaps between the rich and poor within less developed countries (intranational inequality). Every nation has income inequality. The poorer the nation, though, the wider the gap between rich and poor.[24] The poor in a poor country are doubly disadvantaged; their economic system produces little wealth, and a minority of elites receives most of the wealth that is produced.

Given that American policy has done little to alter income distribution at home, it is perhaps surprising to discover that American foreign policy has attempted to eliminate international inequalities. Less developed nations have claimed at various conferences that the developed nations have exploited their resources. Such nations have thus passed resolutions calling for a redistribution of the world's wealth. These requests have never received much sympathy in Washington.

Nevertheless, presidents of each party have pressed for aid to nations in the developing world. Aside from simple humanitarian concern for those who are suffering, presidents have wanted to stabilize nations that were friendly to the United States or that possessed supplies of vital raw materials. Sometimes aid has been given in the form of grants, but often it has taken the form of credits and loan guarantees to purchase American goods, loans at favorable interest rates, and forgiveness of previous loans. At other times, the United States has awarded preferential trade agreements for the sale of foreign goods.

A substantial percentage of foreign aid is in the form of military assistance and is targeted to a few countries the United States considers to be of vital strategic significance: Israel, Egypt, Turkey, and Greece have received the bulk of such assistance in recent years. Foreign aid programs have also assisted with agricultural modernization, irrigation, and population control. Food for Peace programs have subsidized the sale of American agricultural products to poor countries (and simultaneously given an economic boost to American farmers). Peace Corps volunteers have fanned out over the globe to provide medical care and other services in less developed nations.

Nevertheless, foreign aid has never been very popular with Americans. Lacking a constituency, the president's foreign aid requests are typically cut by Congress, which appropriated less than $12 billion for foreign aid in fiscal year 1998. Moreover, many people believe that the provision of economic aid to other nations serves only to further enrich the few without helping the many within a poor nation. Although the United States donates more total aid than almost any other country, it devotes a smaller share of its GDP to foreign economic development than any other developed nation (see "America in Perspective: Ranking Largess").

Since the thaw in the cold war, the nations of Central and Eastern Europe, including Russia, have sought aid from the West. Some leaders in the United States have argued that failure to support the formerly Communist nations of the Soviet Union would prove costly in the long run if democracy in these countries failed because of severe economic dislocations resulting from the transition to market economies. Yet many complain bitterly that we need to spend our resources at home rather than abroad. The United States has given some aid to Russia, Poland, and a few of their neighbors, but much less than they requested.

THE GLOBAL CONNECTION, ENERGY, AND THE ENVIRONMENT

In an interdependent world, issues of economics and trade share the foreign policy stage with military and diplomatic issues. Issues of energy and the international environment are also important.

Nothing symbolizes the global connection of energy and the environment as succinctly as the massive oceangoing oil tankers. In 1946, the largest oil tanker was a mere 18,000 tons. Today the biggest tankers are 326,000 tons, and bigger ones are being designed. These tankers have made it possible to import half of the oil Americans now use, but they have also despoiled fisheries and beaches when they have spilled their contents.

Growing Energy Dependency. Most, though not all, of these tankers are sailing from nations of the **Organization of Petroleum Exporting Countries (OPEC)**—the organization that first made headlines in 1973 when it responded to American support of

America in Perspective

RANKING LARGESS

The United States is the second largest donor of foreign aid, but it ranks lower than other industrialized nations in the percentage of its gross domestic product (GDP) that it spends on economic development aid for helping needy nations.

COUNTRY	TOTAL AID (IN MILLIONS)	PERCENTAGE OF GDP
Norway	$1,137	1.05
Denmark	1,446	1.03
Sweden	1,819	.96
Netherlands	2,517	.76
France	8,466	.64
Canada	2,250	.43
Switzerland	982	.36
Australia	1,091	.35

COUNTRY	TOTAL AID (IN MILLIONS)	PERCENTAGE OF GNP
Germany	6,818	.34
Austria	665	.33
Belgium	726	.32
Finland	290	.31
United Kingdom	3,197	.31
Japan	13,239	.29
Italy	2,705	.27
New Zealand	110	.24
United States	**9,927**	**.15**

SOURCE: Organization for Economic Cooperation and Development. Data are for 1995.

Israel in the short Yom Kippur War by embargoing oil shipments to the United States and Western European nations.

Energy transfers show convincingly that world politics is a politics of growing dependency. The less developed nations have long depended on more industrialized nations. Recently the industrialized nations have discovered the meaning of dependency, especially in the context of their growing need for sources of imported energy. Americans are less dependent on imported oil than most nations. Most European countries import almost 100 percent of their oil. Japan, for example, does not produce a single barrel of its own oil. Most of the less developed nations also depend on oil imports, but they have fewer resources to pay the new oil barons than do the United States, Europe, and Japan.

Fortunately for the U.S. economy, the era of scarce oil in the 1970s and early 1980s was followed by an oil glut. Prices sank as supplies increased; nations and businesses depending on oil income suffered a severe recession (as did oil-producing states such as Texas, Oklahoma, and Louisiana); oil millionaires went bankrupt; and discipline within the OPEC cartel crumbled. This abundance, of course, was a great boon to users of energy. Speed limits on U.S. highways, which had been reduced in the 1970s to save energy, were raised in 1996.

Circumstances may again restrict the availability of oil, however. And the United States is vulnerable, because it now imports half of the oil it uses (see Figure 20.3). Our willingness to go to war with Iraq to defend Kuwait and Saudi Arabia was based in large part on the huge oil reserves beneath the desert sands of these two countries.

Environment and the World Commons. The oceans traveled by the supertankers are an important part of the world commons (areas shared by everyone). When a supertanker spills its oil on the beaches, it makes environmental headlines. Supertankers are hardly the only ecological problem in the world commons, however.

Almost every nation faces environmental problems at least as severe as those facing America. A nation's political ideology seems unrelated to its level of environmental despoliation. The formerly Communist nations of Central and Eastern Europe certainly rank among the worst offenders. The explosion of a nuclear reactor at Chernobyl contaminated a vast area not only within the U.S.S.R. but in other European nations as well. Germany has poured as many chemicals into the Rhine as Americans have poured into their rivers. Underdeveloped nations almost always favor economic growth at the expense of ecological sensitivity. Environmentalists have cautioned less developed nations to think ecologically, but in places where economic development means the difference between starvation and salvation, most ecological pleas go unheard.

FIGURE 20.3 AMERICAN DEPENDENCE ON FOREIGN OIL

Dependency on imported oil decreased in the early 1980s, but by 1995 it had increased to more than half of the oil in the United States.

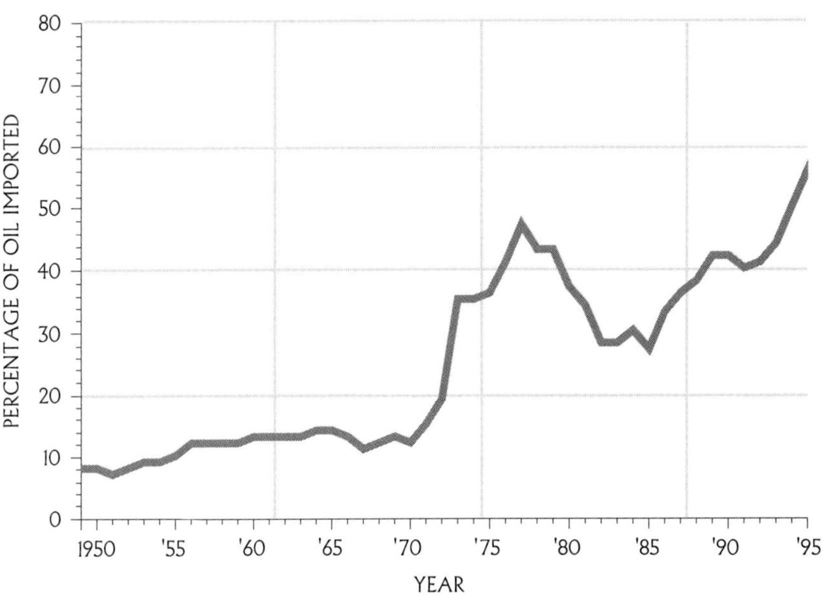

SOURCE: Energy Information Administration, *Monthly Energy Review* (Washington, DC: U.S. Government Printing Office, various years).

Global issues of environment and energy have crept slowly onto the nation's policy agenda. Recent concerns about the effects of fluorocarbons, found in many household products, on the earth's ozone layer have generated international studies and diplomatic discussions. Americans have bargained with other nations to restrict overfishing of some of the world's fishing areas; they have pressured the Japanese to eliminate whaling; they have shown their concern about pollution in the Rhine and the deforestation of the tropical rain forests.

Issues closer to home, however, are often harder to preach about. In 1992, President Bush refused to sign an international agreement on environmental protection, arguing that it would cost the United States jobs and that it failed to protect patent rights in newly developing industries. President Clinton has not agreed to follow a specific timetable to reduce the threat of global warming (the U.S. produces a fifth of the world's greenhouse gases). The Canadian government has become gravely concerned about acid rain, which afflicts the eastern half of its country (and the United States, as well). Rain containing more than ten times the normal acidity falls on lakes in the northeastern United States and Canada. On the pH scale—a measure of acidity in which 7 represents neutral—the Adirondack lakes in northeastern New York consistently measure 5 (vinegar measures 3). Acid rain, which originates from emissions in the United States, has soured some goodwill between Americans and their Canadian neighbors, but global issues of the world commons have yet to become a major issue of U.S. foreign policy.

UNDERSTANDING FOREIGN AND DEFENSE POLICYMAKING

Foreign and defense policy are perhaps the most exotic arenas of public policy, dealing with issues and nations that are often far from America's shores. Nevertheless, the themes that have guided your understanding of American politics throughout *Government in America*—democracy and the scope of government—can also shed light on the topic of international relations.

FOREIGN AND DEFENSE POLICYMAKING AND DEMOCRACY

To some commentators, democracy has little to do with the international relations of the United States. Because domestic issues are closer to their daily lives and easier to understand, Americans are usually more interested in domestic policy than in foreign policy. This preference would seem to give public officials more discretion in making foreign policy. In addition, some say, those with the discretion are elites in the State Department and unelected military officers in the Pentagon.

There is little evidence, however, that policies at odds with the wishes of the American people can be sustained; civilian control of the military is unquestionable. When the American people hold strong opinions regarding international relations—as when they first supported and later opposed the war in Vietnam—they find policymakers are usually responsive. In fact, studies have found that well-established democracies rarely go to war against one another.[25]

In addition, the system of separation of powers discussed so often in *Government in America* plays a crucial role in foreign as well as domestic policy. You saw in Chapter 12 that Congress has a central role in matters of international relations. Whether treaties are ratified, defense budgets appropriated, weapons systems authorized, or foreign aid awarded is ultimately at the discretion of the Congress—the government's most representative policymaking body. Congressional elections are rarely determined by specific issues such as the proper funding for the Strategic Defense Initiative, but public demands for and objections to policies are likely to be heard in Washington.

When it comes to the increasingly important arena of American international economic policy, pluralism is pervasive. Agencies and members of Congress, as well as their constituents, all pursue their own policy goals. For example, the Treasury Department and the Federal Reserve Board worry about the negative balance of trade, and the Department of Defense spends billions in other countries to maintain American troops abroad. The Departments of Agriculture and Commerce and their constituents—farmers and businesspeople—want to peddle American products abroad and generally favor freer trade. The Department of Labor and the unions worry that the nation may export not only products but also jobs to other countries where labor costs are low. Jewish citizens closely monitor U.S. policy toward Israel, whereas Greek Americans seek to limit military aid to Turkey, Greece's ancient rival. Even foreign governments hire lobbying firms and join in the political fray.

Public opinion plays an important part in American foreign and defense policy; as with other issues, policymakers are reluctant to make unpopular decisions. Worldwide demonstrations against the arms race are responsible, in part, for the recent willingness of American and Russian policymakers to negotiate reductions in conventional and nuclear arms.

FOREIGN AND DEFENSE POLICYMAKING AND THE SCOPE OF GOVERNMENT

America's global connections as a superpower have many implications for how active the national government is in the realm of foreign policy and national defense. Treaty obligations to defend allies around the world, the nation's economic interests in an interdependent global economy, and pressing new questions on the global agenda—ranging from illicit drugs to environmental protection—guarantee that the national government will be active in international relations.

You have seen that national defense consumes about one-sixth of the federal government's budget and requires about 2.2 million civilian and military employees for the Department of Defense. Even though the United States has improved relations with Eastern and Central Europe, the United States will remain a superpower and continue to have interests to defend around the world. As long as these interests remain, the scope of American government in foreign and defense policy will be substantial.

SUMMARY

The world—its politics and its economics—intrudes on Americans more each year. This chapter examined America's global connections and the contours of its foreign policy.

The cold war began shortly after World War II, when the containment doctrine became the basis of American foreign policy. The cold war led to actual wars in Korea and Vietnam when the United States tried to contain Communist advances. With containment came a massive buildup of the military apparatus, resulting in what some people called the *military-industrial* complex. Gradually, containment has been balanced by détente and then friendship with many of our former adversaries. This trend has accelerated with the democratization of Central and Eastern Europe and the dissolution of the Soviet Union. Nevertheless, the United States maintains an enormous defense capability. Still, both foreign and defense policy are undergoing substantial reevaluation in response to the cold war thaw that began in 1989.

Although the Unites States has great military power, many of the issues facing the world today are not military issues. Interconnected issues of equality, economics, energy, and the environment have become important. The international economic system pulls the United States deeper and deeper into the world's problems as global interdependency and its own vulnerability become more apparent.

KEY TERMS

foreign policy
international organizations
United Nations (UN)
North Atlantic Treaty Organization (NATO)
Central Intelligence Agency (CIA)
isolationism
containment doctrine
cold war
McCarthyism
arms race
European Union (EU)
secretary of state
secretary of defense
Joint Chiefs of Staff
détente
Strategic Defense Initiative (SDI)
Organization of Petroleum Exporting Countries (OPEC)
interdependency
tariff
balance of trade

FOR FURTHER READING

Calleo, David. *Beyond American Hegemony.* New York: Basic Books, 1987. An important study of America's role as a world power in an age of increasing economic interdependency and competition.

Hilsman, Rogers. *The Politics of Policymaking in Defense and Foreign Affairs.* Englewood Cliffs, NJ: Prentice-Hall, 1987. An insightful analysis of how the American political system copes with defense and foreign policy problems.

Huntington, Samuel P. *The Clash of Civilizations and the Remaking of World Order.* Simon & Schuster, 1996. Argues that civilizational identities built on religious empires of the past will be the source of international turmoil in the next century.

Kagan, Donald. *On the Origins of War and the Preservation of Peace.* New York: Doubleday, 1995. Provides insights gleaned from studying the origins of great wars.

Kennedy, Paul. *The Rise and Fall of the Great Powers.* New York: Random House, 1987. A provocative historical analysis of the interconnections between relative economic strength and military power.

Lieber, Robert J., ed. *Eagle Adrift: American Foreign Policy at the End of the Century.* New York: Longman, 1997. An excellent collection of articles on U.S. foreign policy in the post-cold war era.

Lindsay, James M. *Congress and the Politics of U.S. Foreign Policy.* Baltimore, MD: Johns Hopkins University Press, 1994. A useful discussion of the role of Congress in setting U.S. foreign policy.

Mueller, John. *Retreat from Doomsday: The Obsolescence of Major War.* New York: Basic Books, 1989. An insightful rethinking of defense policy.

Nye, Joseph S. *Bound to Lead.* New York: Basic Books, 1990. Argues that America is not in decline, but that American power faces serious challenges in an increasingly interdependent world.

Yergin, Daniel. *Shattered Peace: The Origins of the Cold War and the National Security State.* Boston: Houghton Mifflin, 1977. An excellent political history of the early years of the cold war and containment.

INTERNET RESOURCES

http://www.state.gov/
Information about the Department of State and current foreign policy issues.

http://www.dtic.dla.mil/defenselink/
Information about the Department of Defense and current issues in national security policy.

http://portal.research.bell-labs.com/cgi-wald/dbaccess/411
CIA World Factbook.

http://www.oecdwash.org/
Organization for Economic Cooperation and Development (OECD) provides a wealth of economic information on the world's nations.

http://www.nato.int/
Background and activities of NATO.

NOTES

1. See, for example, Paul Kennedy, *The Rise and Fall of the Great Powers* (New York: Random House, 1987).
2. Raymond Vernon, *Storm over the Multinationals: The Real Issues* (Cambridge, MA: Harvard University Press, 1977).
3. I. M. Destler, "National Security Management: What Presidents Have Wrought," *Political Science Quarterly* 95 (Winter 1980-1981): 573-588.
4. Richard Betts, *Soldiers, Statesmen, and Cold War Crises* (Cambridge, MA: Harvard University Press, 1977), 216, table A.
5. For more on decision making regarding the Gulf War, see Bob Woodward, *The Commanders* (New York: Simon & Schuster, 1991).
6. See Bob Woodward, *Veil: The Secret Wars of the CIA, 1981-1987* (New York: Simon & Schuster, 1987).
7. A good study of the role of Congress in setting U.S. foreign policy is James M. Lindsay, *Congress and the Politics of U.S. Foreign Policy* (Baltimore, MD: Johns Hopkins University Press, 1994). Congress' role in the defense budget process is discussed in Ralph G. Carter, "Budgeting for Defense," in Paul E. Peterson, ed., *The President, Congress, and the Making of Foreign Policy* (Norman, OK: University of Oklahoma Press, 1994).
8. Louis Fisher, "Executive-Legislative Relations in Foreign Policy" (paper presented at the United States-Mexico Comparative Constitutional Law Conference, Mexico City, June 17, 1988), 1.
9. An excellent treatment of the origins of the cold war is Daniel Yergin, *Shattered Peace: The Origins of the Cold War and the National Security State* (Boston: Houghton Mifflin, 1977).
10. The article was titled "Sources of Soviet Conduct" and appeared in *Foreign Affairs* (July 1947), under the pseudonym *X*.
11. Yergin, *Shattered Peace,* 268.
12. Seymour Melman, *Pentagon Capitalism: The Political Economy of War* (New York: McGraw-Hill, 1970).
13. Stanley Karnow, *Vietnam: A History* (New York: Penguin Books, 1983), 43. Karnow's book is one of the best of many excellent books on Vietnam. See also Frances FitzGerald, *Fire in the Lake* (Boston: Little, Brown, 1972); and David Halberstam, *The Best and the Brightest* (New York: Random House, 1972).
14. Nicholas Lemann, "The Peacetime War," *Atlantic Monthly,* October 1984, 72.
15. Quoted in Andrew Rosenthal, "Striking a Defensive Tone, Bush Sees Virtue in Caution," *New York Times,* February 8, 1990, A10.
16. See, for example, Bruce Russett, "Defense Expenditures and National Well-Being," *American Political Science Review* 76 (December 1982): 767-777; William K. Domke, Richard C. Eichenberg, and Catherine M. Kelleher, "The Illusion of Choice: Defense and Welfare in Advanced Industrial Democracies, 1948-78," *American Political Science Review* 77 (March 1983): 19-35; and Alex Mintz, "Guns Versus Butter: A Disaggregated Analysis," *American Political Science Review* 83 (December 1989): 1285-1296.
17. Kennedy, *The Rise and Fall of the Great Powers*; and David Calleo, *Beyond American Hegemony: The Future of the Western Alliance* (New York: Basic Books, 1987). For a different view, see Joseph S. Nye, *Bound to Lead* (New York: Basic Books, 1990).
18. On the importance of ideology, see studies discussed in Robert A. Bernstein, *Elections, Representation, and Congressional Voting Behavior* (Englewood Cliffs, NJ: 1989), 70-76.
19. U.S. Department of Commerce, *Statistical Abstract of the United States, 1996* (Washington, DC: U.S. Government Printing Office, 1996), 359.
20. Robert O. Keohane and Joseph S. Nye, *Power and Interdependence,* 2nd ed. (New York: HarperCollins, 1989), 27.
21. *Ibid.,* 27-28.
22. *Ibid.,* 3.
23. Stanley Hoffman, *Gulliver's Troubles, or the Setting of American Foreign Policy* (New York: McGraw-Hill, 1968).
24. Michael Don Ward, *The Political Economy of Distribution: Equality Versus Inequality* (New York: Elsevier, 1978), 44.
25. See Bruce M. Russett, *Controlling the Sword* (Cambridge, MA: Harvard University Press, 1990), chap. 5; Thomas Hartley and Bruce M. Russett, "Public Opinion and the Common Defense: Who Governs Military Spending in the United States?" *American Political Science Review* 86 (December 1992): 905-915; and Bruce M. Russett, *Grasping the Democratic Peace* (Princeton, NJ: Princeton University Press, 1993).

21

The New Importance of State and Local Government

- State Constitutions
- State Legislatures
- Governors and the Executive Branch
- State Court Systems
- Local Governments
- State and Local Finance Policy
- Understanding State and Local Governments

When the owners of the Chicago White Sox baseball club announced in 1985 that Comiskey Park, their venerable old stadium in Chicago's Bridgeport neighborhood, would need to be replaced, a public policy debate on the scope of government began. The 75-year-old ballpark was becoming structurally unsound, and the owners planned to move the team to a new site very soon. The White Sox owners had secured an option on land in suburban Addison, west of Chicago, and considered building a new stadium there. In 1986, however, a majority of voters in an Addison referendum registered their opposition to major league baseball in their community.

The next year, the White Sox owners suggested the team be moved to another state where tax dollars were available to build a new stadium for the franchise. However, both Governor James Thompson and Mayor Harold Washington vowed to fight to keep the White Sox in the state and in Chicago. Eventually they convinced the Illinois General Assembly to pass a bill creating a new local government, the Illinois Sports Facilities Authority (ISFA), to build and operate a publicly financed stadium for the White Sox. In 1988, the state legislature appropriated $150 million for New Comiskey Park to be built across the street from the existing site on Chicago's south side.

In effect, Illinois lawmakers—at the urging of the governor, a big-city mayor, and many business and sports interests—not only declared baseball to be an activity in the public interest that warranted the expenditure of taxpayers' money to build a stadium and improve the surrounding infrastructure, but also permitted use of eminent domain powers to take quickly private properties in the stadium area that would be needed for construction sites. Property owners and area tenants organized the South Armour Square Neighborhood Coalition to fight the Sports Authority's efforts to take their property. Ultimately, the interest group lost to the ISFA, and residents had to relocate. Homeowners received a $25,000 bonus on top of fair market value for their homes, and renters received a $4,500 relocation bonus and a 1-year monthly rent supplement. The new stadium opened in 1991.

A responsible democracy is apparent in the example of suburban voters rejecting the development of a sports facility in their city. But is it democratic when residents of another Chicago community are not afforded the same voice? How democratic is a process that awards millions of dollars in tax revenues to a private corporation? Should the elected representatives of a state's population be entrusted with the power of the purse if it means spending public funds on baseball? Is popular sovereignty being circumvented when democratic governments at the local level are permitted to take private property for promotion of a baseball stadium? Is the financial settlement to stadium neighbors a mark of successful interest group action? In general, would the public agree that a sports facility is a good venture for government?

The building of New Comiskey Park raises a number of questions fundamental to a democracy that has powers "reserved" to state and local governments. What should be the proper scope of state and local governments? Should either a state or a city be in the business of running a sports stadium? For that matter, are state governments expected to chase after corporations and offer them incentives to do business in their states? Or should one state government sit idly by while another state attempts to capture one of its premier business activities? Should such activities be beyond the scope of the public sector? Are they better left in the hands of private businesses?

As the American democratic state grew both in population and in territory, governments closer to the people became necessary links between public policymakers and citizens. Not long ago, however, some political observers predicted that state governments would cease to exist in the near future—if they were not already gone.[1] Not only were these assessments wrong, but through a process of reform, modernization, and intergovernmental change since the 1960s, state and local governments have become more vital to our democratic system than ever. In this chapter, we discuss the patterns of subnational politics, the processes that state and local governments engage in, and the behavior of their officials.

Recently, states and localities have assumed new and costly responsibilities in areas such as welfare, health, education, and corrections. States and localities have also gained importance as federal policymakers have confronted budgetary limits. And policymakers have recognized the virtues of grass-roots democracy—of giving decision-making power to governments closer to the people.

Both Democrats and Republicans have begun to place new emphasis on state and local government. Bill Clinton's program of reinventing government has sought to allow states and localities greater freedom to experiment to find more effective and more economical ways of providing public services. The new welfare legislation approved in 1996 dramatically changed federal welfare programs and imposed requirements that state and local governments get people off welfare and into the work force. The new Republican majorities that took control of Congress in 1995 showed a similar, if not greater, respect for the prerogatives of state and local governments. The Republicans sought to reduce the number of categorical grant programs, in which the federal government defines program purposes quite narrowly and attaches numerous federal "strings" and conditions to the aid provided. In their place, the Republicans have sought to substitute broader block grants that would give subnational governments greater freedom in deciding what programs to support. In an effort to deregulate the federal system, both the Congress and the president in 1995 agreed to legislation to reduce future unfunded mandates, which we discussed in Chapter 3.[2] Yet environmental activists, defenders of school lunch programs, and advocates for children and the poor all generally oppose these changes. They doubt whether important programs would be protected if authority over them were transferred to the individual states and localities.

State and local governments have not always enjoyed a favorable image in the federal system. Although some critics may continue to see state and local governments as unduly influenced by elite interests, there has been a clear resurgence of the states since the 1960s. The states have modernized their governing structures and improved their capacity to solve important social problems.[3] Whatever their shortcomings, there can be little doubt that state and local governments are vastly improved and are more democratic governing institutions today than they were a generation ago.

New and costly responsibilities have forced state governments to trim their budgets. Here, protestors express their concern about state health care cuts at a recent demonstration in New York City.

STATE CONSTITUTIONS

Each state is governed by a separate and unique state constitution that spells out basic rules of the political game for that particular state. State constitutions are subordinate to the U.S. Constitution and the laws of the United States, but they take precedence over state law. Although the U.S. Constitution is a relatively brief document of 8,700 words that provides a framework for the operation of the national government, states have tended to write considerably longer and much more detailed constitutions. Alabama has the longest (220,000 words), followed by Texas (80,806) and Oklahoma (68,800). In contrast, Vermont's constitution, adopted in 1793, is a model of brevity with only 6,880 words.

What is behind these lengthy state constitutions? One reason for longer constitutions is that states have tended to establish the parameters for an active state government; therefore, much of what a state does or can do is found in its constitution rather than in state laws. Does length make a better constitution? Probably not. Most state constitutions are burdened with details that attempt to spell out government authority or fit the constitution to the state's political culture. It has long been argued that powerful interest groups have encouraged lengthy constitutions in order to protect their interests. And in one-party states, the lack of effective opposition seems to lead to more protection for programs in the constitution.[4] Longer constitutions also help limit too much governmental interference with our valued individualism.

THE NATURE OF STATE CONSTITUTIONS

A review of state constitutions reveals many common provisions:

- Separation of powers. State constitutions usually reflect the U.S. Constitution's separation of legislative, executive, and judicial functions. Because of unsatisfactory experiences with strong colonial governors, most states have made legislative powers superior to those of the executive.
- Legislative powers. Like the U.S. Congress, all states (except Nebraska) have a bicameral legislature with an upper and lower chamber. Constitutions typically define the length of legislative sessions. Most states, including populous ones such as California, Illinois, and New York, provide for annual legislative sessions. A few states—Arkansas, Kentucky, Montana, Nevada, North Dakota, Oregon, and Texas—have

legislatures that meet in regular session only every other year. (These states' legislatures have been forced to meet annually in special sessions to respond to unusual state financial problems in the past decade.)

- Executive powers. Many state constitutions divide important administrative powers between an elected governor and separately elected officers (for example, the state treasurer) and boards (for example, state university boards of regents). Governors have historically been given weaker powers than those of legislatures to ensure that the executive does not become dominant in state policymaking.
- Judicial powers. The state judicial system is typically established as a hierarchical system, similar to the federal court system, with a series of trial courts, an appellate level, and a court of last resort.
- Local governments. All state constitutions establish the powers and organization of local governments. These governments are considered subdivisions of state government. Many constitutions delegate responsibilities to local governments; establish taxing, spending, and debt limits; and specify the relationship between local governments and the parent state government.
- Taxation and finance. All state constitutions have articles on taxation and finance that normally limit government tax options and spending powers. Many of these provisions have been added to constitutions as a result of taxpayer distrust of legislatures. Most state constitutions also restrict the amount of debt that state and local governments can incur; many are required to have a balanced budget.
- Bill of Rights. Every state constitution has a bill of rights that protects freedoms of speech, press, religion, and assembly. Nearly every state has duplicated the U.S. Constitution in this regard.

Each state's constitution is also unique in its length and provisions. Each was written with a somewhat different set of philosophical principles in mind. Some are modern documents; others retain century-old ideas. The differences that can be found in these state documents are also a reflection of the diversity—social, economic, geographic, historic, and political—among the states.[5]

AMENDING STATE CONSTITUTIONS

Periodically, states consider changes to the rules of the political game. Most avoid the politically difficult process of writing a new constitution. Massachusetts, for example, is governed by a constitution written in 1780. California, New York, Texas, and Wisconsin are among states that have nineteenth-century constitutions. Although a few states have attempted to prepare more modern constitutions, such as Georgia's 1982 constitution, most states have adapted their governing documents to the late twentieth century by periodically approving amendments.

State constitutions may be amended through a two-step process of proposal and ratification. The most common method is the **legislative proposal** (permitted in all 50 states). Typically, this process requires a constitutional proposal to be approved by a vote of two-thirds of the legislature. The proposal is then submitted to state voters, who may ratify it by a simple majority vote. In 1995, out of 202 legislative proposals for constitutional amendment, 151 (75 percent) were approved by states' voters.[6]

A second amending method expressly permitted in 41 state constitutions (and probably legal in the others) is the calling of a constitutional convention. This usually requires the legislature to hold a referendum to obtain voter approval for a convention. If voters approve, convention delegates are appointed, act, and ultimately submit proposed amendments to the electorate for final approval. Only one state has used this method in the 1990s.

THE DEBATE OVER DIRECT DEMOCRACY

California is a good example of a state that has made wide use of the **popular initiative**— a direct-democracy method to amend its constitution. This process, which is available to citizens in 18 states,[7] permits proposed amendments to be placed directly before voters (bypassing the legislature) when enough signatures are obtained on petitions. (Mississippi is the most recent state to permit this method of amendment.) Limited alterations are permitted under this method. In 1996, California voters overwhelmingly passed Proposition 209, which is intended to end affirmative action programs for women and minorities in education and public employment.

The constitutional initiative is one of the tools of direct democracy that sought to place increased power directly with the people. The constitutional initiative and the other tools of direct democracy have their roots in the Progressive Era (1890-1920), when reformers in such states as California saw that the state legislatures were corrupted by professional political party politicians who were controlled by railroads and other powerful interests.

The Progressive Era reforms went beyond new procedures for amending the constitution. The reformers also sought constitutional provisions that would give the populace more influence in the day-to-day workings of government. Under a legislative *initiative,* the people could directly author and vote on legislation, bypassing the legislature entirely. Under the *referendum,* the people would approve or reject measures submitted to them by the legislature. Under a *recall,* voters could gather enough signatures, through a petition, to call a special election to decide whether a representative should continue in office. Under a *direct primary,* the voters themselves, not political party officials, would select a party's candidates for office in the next election.

The initiative process gives citizens the power to bypass recalcitrant state legislatures. Voters have been able to use the initiative to enact changes that elected representatives would otherwise ignore. Particularly in the western states, where the initiative device is quite popular, citizen initiatives have been used to pass new environmental laws, reduce state and local taxing and spending, and limit the terms of public officials. In 1996, more than 90 measures were on ballots in 20 states following a direct-democracy petition process by citizens.[8]

California is a state known for its citizen-initiated policies. In 1994, Proposition 187 was passed by voters in this state to limit social services for illegal immigrants.

Direct democracy today has not worked exactly as the reformers envisioned. In particular, there is considerable debate over the desirability of rewriting and adding constitutional provisions through citizen-initiated amendments. The process of amending the state constitution by direct vote also suffers from numerous disadvantages. Proposed constitutional amendments are often poorly drafted. They may contain ambiguous or contradictory provisions. As a result, such amendments may produce new problems, leading to lawsuits and court interpretation and eventually requiring corrective action. It is also unclear to what extent the initiative process empowers citizens or merely gives new tools to better-financed, more privileged interest groups. In larger states, special interests can pay professional firms to gather the required number of signatures. Monied interests also have the advantage in mounting expensive television advertising campaigns that can frame an issue for voters. These ads can present voters with a biased or incomplete set of facts on an issue they would otherwise know little about. For example, in states where constitutional change was required to permit casino gambling (such as New Jersey) or a state lottery (such as California), the gambling industry spent lavishly on advertisements that exaggerated the benefits of introducing gambling in the state. In initiative and referendum campaigns, complex public policy questions too often are reduced to simplistic sloganeering. As Ann O'M. Bowman and Richard C. Kearney ask,

> (I)s the initiative process appropriate for resolving tough public problems? Seldom are issues so simple that a yes-or-no ballot question can adequately reflect appropriate options and alternatives. A legislative setting, in contrast, fosters the negotiation and compromise that produce workable solutions. Legislatures are deliberative bodies, not instant problem solvers.[9]

STATE LEGISLATURES

Today's state legislatures are generally effective, modern institutions for state policymaking by the people's representatives. State legislatures are often easy targets for criticism from those who believe that "professional politicians"—who are usually not held in high regard—have taken up residence in the statehouse. Although state legislatures and legislators who serve in them have a history of poor performance, the modern state legislature has typically earned good marks.

Samuel C. Patterson, a leading scholar of legislatures, has found these state lawmaking bodies very effective, having become professional bodies with full-time, well-paid legislators and good staff support.[10] Many have become quite highly professionalized as more and more legislators acquire expertise by serving several terms, during which they are paid on a full-time basis, in a legislature that meets annually and has developed a complex system of committees and staff organizations.

STATE LEGISLATIVE ELECTIONS

How democratic and representative of society are U.S. legislative bodies? An examination of the politicians who serve in the 50 state legislatures shows that they are more diverse in the 1990s than they were just a decade ago but that they remain a rather homogeneous group that does not necessarily mirror the characteristics of their constituents. As political scientist Thomas R. Dye has observed, ". . . state legislators are generally selected from the better-educated, more prestigiously employed, middle-class segments of the population."[11] Indeed, businesspeople, lawyers, and other professionals dominate state legislatures. Unlike members of Congress, state legislators normally continue to work in their professions or businesses because state legislatures are typically part-time institutions. About three-fourths of legislators have a college education. Twenty years ago, less than 5 percent of state legislators were women and only about 3 percent were African Americans. Today, the number of female candidates for state legislative seats is increasing, and slightly more than one-fifth of state legislators are women. The number of racial and ethnic minority group members serving in state legislatures has also increased, though it remains less than 10 percent; Southern states have a somewhat higher proportion of minority members than Northern legislatures.[12]

Throughout much of the twentieth century, state legislatures were horribly malapportioned, giving greater representation to rural areas than their population warranted. Following a succession of U.S. Supreme Court decisions in the mid-1960s, state legislative districts were redrawn to adhere to the principle of "one person, one vote."[13] The changes that have occurred in state legislatures as a result of these Supreme Court actions are highlighted in "Since Kennedy: The Transformation of State Legislatures."

Most states elect legislators from single-member districts. But about one-fourth of state representatives and a small number of state senators are still chosen from multimember districts. In these districts, which are larger than typical single-member districts, voters elect several representatives to the state legislature rather than just one. Many populous states used this method of representation for legislative redistricting because it often was easier to construct one larger district than two or three small ones. For example, the Texas House of Representatives used this method for counties with more than one representative until 1975, and Illinois had 59 multimember districts in operation until 1982.

Getting elected to a state legislature is normally a two-step process of nomination and election. The primary election—a political party nomination process—is used in most state legislative elections, although it is often seemingly unnecessary. In a state legislative primary, as many as half of state legislators are unopposed for renomination. Many states, especially in the South, require a candidate to receive a majority vote in the primary in order to be nominated. Runoff elections are held between the top two vote-getters when no candidate receives a majority. This requirement, which is used in such large states as Texas, ensures that the nominee has the support of a majority of party voters. Louisiana is unique; it holds a single, nonpartisan election for all legislators and conducts a runoff only when no candidate receives a clear majority.

The pattern of wins and losses in general elections over time in a state strongly influences competition in primaries. The eminent political scientist V. O. Key observed that the most competition in a primary occurs in a party's safe districts—those it tends to win in the general election. Some competition occurs in marginal districts, in which either party has a chance to win the general election. Little or no competition is found in a primary of the party that consistently has lost the general election in a district.[14] Few would-be challengers will invest time and money in obtaining a nomination for an election they cannot win.

The level of competition in general elections has declined over time. One-party states, especially in the South, often have races with no (or only token) opposition in the general election. But even very competitive states, including California, New York, and Wisconsin, have held state legislative elections in which as many as 60 percent of the candidates lack serious opposition.[15]

LEGISLATIVE TURNOVER AND TERM LIMITS

The elections of 1996 brought significant change to state legislatures, reversing some gains made by Republicans in the 1994 elections. For example, the 1996 elections gave the Democrats 8 more state legislative chambers for the 1997 legislative term. Table 21.1 (see page 533) shows how party control of state governments looked in 1997. Significant changes

SINCE KENNEDY

The Transformation of State Legislatures

Representation in state legislatures has historically been done by geographic areas or districts. Earlier in this century, most state legislators represented rural areas—where the population resided. When John F. Kennedy was president in the early 1960s, the population of this country was overwhelmingly urban, but state legislatures continued to be dominated by rural politicians. The main reason for the underrepresentation of urban areas was that districts were often constructed on the basis of an existing jurisdictional boundary, such as the county, regardless of how many people actually lived in the county. This meant that in most states, rural counties of a few hundred residents and urban counties with hundreds of thousands of residents all had the same level of representation.

In 1962, the U.S. Supreme Court ruled that the lower chamber of the Tennessee state legislature had to be reapportioned periodically on the basis of population. This landmark decision in *Baker* v. *Carr* established the principle of "one person, one vote" in drawing up districts for state houses in all states. Two years later, the court ruled in *Reynolds* v. *Simms* that state senates must also be apportioned in this fashion.

These cases dramatically changed the face of state legislatures. Gone was the rural dominance of these chambers. In its place arrived new representatives of central cities and metropolitan areas. Urban problems became the focus of more activist state legislatures.

Periodic reapportionment following the decennial censuses has further changed legislatures. In 1995, one finds that large states such as New York and California have legislatures that are younger, better educated, and are more racially and ethnically diverse. And today's continuing migration of citizens to the suburbs has resulted in new voting power for suburban metropolitan interests and a decline in the power of central cities in state capitols. These changes are the result of guaranteeing fair representation in state legislatures.

occurred in states such as California, Michigan, and Illinois, where Democrats recaptured state house chambers that had been lost to the Republicans in their 1994 victories. Democrats control the legislatures in 20 states; Republicans have control in 17, and 12 states have divided or split party control in 1997.

Aside from the issue of party changes in the legislatures is the phenomenon of state legislative turnover. Recent history has shown that in any 10-year period, about 75 percent of state legislative seats are turned over. Thus, significant change in persons holding state legislative office is the norm in states. During the 1980s, New York had the lowest percent of changes in its senate (38 percent), followed by Michigan (50 percent). Mississippi and West Virginia had the highest turnover in their upper chambers: 94 percent. On the House side, Arkansas and Illinois have had the lowest turnover with 49 percent, whereas Washington and West Virginia have had 90 percent turnovers during this decade.[16]

Voters have been attempting to limit legislators' terms in office through formal restrictions on the number of terms a member may serve. Increasingly, voters appear to support the argument that professional, career-oriented legislators become so entrenched and difficult to unseat that they lose touch with their constituents and instead pander to special interests. This sentiment is reflected in the fact that in 1997, Nevada became the twenty-first state to institute legislator term limits since 1990. The number of terms permitted varies from state to state. For example, California limits its assembly members to 6 years and its senators to 8 years in office, Colorado legislators are limited to 8 (consecutive) years, and Oklahoma legislators may serve up to 12 years.[17]

WHAT DO LEGISLATURES DO?

The job of a state legislator is not identical to that of a member of Congress, but similar responsibilities can be found in both types of legislatures. A review of common tasks of state legislatures reveals a number of roles typically performed in Congress:

- Making laws is the legal function of state legislatures. It involves processing more than 250,000 bills that are introduced by legislators in the 50 states each year and passing about 30 percent of them into law.[18]

TABLE 21.1 PARTY AFFILIATIONS—GOVERNORS, SENATE, AND HOUSE

STATE BY STATE

THE BALANCE OF POWER

State	Governor	State Senate	State House
Ala.	Republican	Democratic	Democratic
Alaska	Democratic	Republican	Republican
Ariz.	Republican	Republican	Republican
Ark.	Republican	Democratic	Democratic
Calif.	Republican	Democratic	Democratic
Colo.	Democratic	Republican	Republican
Conn.	Republican	Democratic	Democratic
Del.	Democratic	Democratic	Republican
Fla.	Democratic	Republican	Republican
Ga.	Democratic	Democratic	Democratic
Hawaii	Democratic	Democratic	Democratic
Idaho	Republican	Republican	Republican
Ill.	Republican	Republican	Democratic
Ind.	Democratic	Republican	Split
Iowa	Republican	Republican	Republican
Kan.	Republican	Republican	Republican
Ky.	Democratic	Democratic	Democratic
La.	Republican	Democratic	Democratic
Me.	Independent	Democratic	Democratic
Md.	Democratic	Democratic	Democratic
Mass.	Republican	Democratic	Democratic
Mich.	Republican	Republican	Democratic
Minn.	Republican	Democratic	Democratic
Miss.	Republican	Democratic	Democratic
Mo.	Democratic	Democratic	Democratic
Mont.	Republican	Republican	Republican
Neb.	Democratic	Unicameral/nonpartisan	
Nev.	Democratic	Republican	Democratic
N.H.	Democratic	Republican	Republican
N.J.	Republican	Republican	Republican
N.M.	Republican	Democratic	Democratic
N.Y.	Republican	Republican	Democratic
N.C.	Democratic	Democratic	Republican
N.D.	Republican	Republican	Republican
Ohio	Republican	Republican	Republican
Okla.	Republican	Democratic	Democratic
Ore.	Democratic	Republican	Split
Pa.	Republican	Republican	Republican
R.I.	Republican	Democratic	Democratic
S.C.	Republican	Democratic	Republican
S.D.	Republican	Republican	Republican
Tenn.	Republican	Democratic	Democratic
Tex.	Republican	Republican	Democratic
Utah	Republican	Republican	Republican
Vt.	Democratic	Democratic	Democratic
Va.	Republican	Split	Democratic
Wash.	Democratic	Republican	Republican
W.Va.	Republican	Democratic	Democratic
Wis.	Republican	Democratic	Republican
Wyo.	Republican	Republican	Republican

Legend: Democratic; Republican; Independent; Split

SOURCE: Council of State Governments.

- Appropriating money is one of the most important functions of legislatures. A state budget must be passed to authorize spending and collecting revenues for state programs.
- Overseeing the executive branch is part of the normal "checks and balances" built into state constitutions. This activity is often performed by legislative committees and subcommittees as they go about the process of authorizing agency programs or approving budgets. In addition, more than half of the states have passed so-called "sunset laws" that require regular legislative evaluation of on-going state programs and the agencies that operate these programs. Sunset laws are designed to reduce the size of state governments by eliminating unneeded agencies.
- Approving the governor's appointments is a process related to oversight. Similar to the appointments of the national government, the governor nominates individuals to positions in the cabinet, various governing boards and commissions, and, in some states, the judiciary. One or both houses of the legislature hold hearings on nominations, and legislators ultimately vote on whether to approve the nominations.
- Serving constituents is an essential component of legislative activity and a function closely tied to democracy. From performing casework, to resolving constituent problems, to acting as a liaison between citizens and government agencies, to proposing legislation to benefit local interests—legislators have been shown to spend considerable time on service to their constituents. Not surprisingly, many legislators engage in this activity as part of their continuing efforts to be reelected.

The U.S. Constitution also assigns some responsibilities to states that are carried out by the legislatures, such as ratifying proposed amendments to the Constitution and redrawing congressional districts after each census and reapportionment. Like the national government, state governments—through their legislatures—adhere to the principle of individualism. We do not want our state representatives to interfere with our personal freedoms. For this reason, many state constitutions limit the actions of state leaders.

We cannot overlook what may be the most important informal role of state legislatures: managing public policy conflicts in their state. Legislators are expected to represent constituent interests, advance statewide interests, and act as agents of fiscal responsibility in the state—much like members of Congress. To do so, they must balance competing demands, debate wide-ranging issues, and then make decisions to resolve the inevitable conflict that surrounds public policymaking.

HOW LEGISLATURES ARE ORGANIZED TO MAKE POLICY

As we saw in Chapter 12, all state legislatures except Nebraska's are organized as bicameral legislatures: two separate chambers to consider policy proposals. In a bicameral legislature, each house has its own leadership positions, committees, and rules of procedure. Policymaking demands of state legislatures normally dictate that they conduct business nearly year round. Today, nine states—California, Illinois, Massachusetts, Michigan, New Jersey, New York, Ohio, Pennsylvania, and Wisconsin—have full-time legislatures that meet for long sessions each year and have staff who receive high salaries and perform their jobs professionally.[19] Indeed, most state legislatures have become more professionalized over the past 30 years, providing their members with enhanced resources and the capacity to be better legislators.

Legislative salaries and staff assistance are generally a reflection not only of greater professionalism but also of what state voters think is important to have in their state. For example, states such as Arkansas, Kentucky, Montana, Oregon, and Texas still hold regular sessions of the state legislature only every other year. States that want more professionalism will promote full-time, career-oriented legislators; those that want a "citizen-legislature" are more likely to support briefer sessions, smaller salaries, and term limits.

Each state legislature has a set of leaders in both chambers of state legislatures, leaders who are often selected along party lines. Leadership posts and the committee system are controlled by the majority political party in that house. The majority and minority parties both have floor leaders, and committees and subcommittees all have chairpersons drawn from the majority party. Among these leadership posts, the speaker of the assembly or house is most important, because this individual is typically both head of the chamber and leader of the majority party in the lower house. Senate leaders are typically less well known in their states and beyond, probably because of limits placed on their powers. In 26 states, the office is held by the lieutenant governor, a member of the executive branch, who is given formal—but limited—powers over the senate's actions.[20] In a few states, such as Texas, the lieutenant governor is actually a force to be reckoned with in state politics because of the extensive legislative role assigned to that post.

Legislative leaders must make the legislative system work by managing conflict and producing public policy. Most of the work of policymaking is done by an extensive array of committees and subcommittees that operate like congressional committees; they are the true workhorses of the policymaking process. Committee chairs and members often become experts on the policy matters assigned to their committees. As such, they are sources of legislative information and guidance for other legislators when a vote is to be held on policy in their area.

From introduction to final passage, every bill undergoes a process of hearings by committees and subcommittees, calendar scheduling, floor debate, amendments, two or three floor votes, conference committees, and final votes before going to the governor for action. Research has shown that when deciding how to vote on a bill, legislators are influenced by at least six agents:

- Their party and party leaders, who mobilize support for legislation
- Committees, which guide members on bills deserving support
- Staff, who advise legislators on the pros and cons of supporting a bill
- Lobbyists, who educate legislators on private interest groups' views on a bill
- The governor, who initiates most legislation and can veto unwelcome bills
- Constituents, whose opinions legislators consider before most votes[21]

Thus, the democratic process is alive in state legislative policymaking. The legislative job is becoming more demanding, however, as states seek solutions to complex problems in this era of fiscal constraints and growing citizen demands. Because most legislation originates in the governor's office, we will examine the executive branch next.

GOVERNORS AND THE EXECUTIVE BRANCH

The governor is the chief executive of state government and the best-known state public official. The public looks to the governor for leadership, assurance, conflict resolution, and policy initiatives. If administering public policy is the governor's main constitutional responsibility, then promoting democracy—through attending to constituents, championing citizen initiatives, and assuring voters that problems of the state are manageable—is the governor's primary responsibility to the public. For these reasons, no state politician is more in the public eye than its **governor.**

ELECTING GOVERNORS

In November 1996, Washington state voters chose Gary Locke, the son of Chinese immigrants, as their governor. Locke became the first Asian American ever to be elected governor of one of the 48 contiguous states. Modern governors are a different breed from the politicians who commonly led their states earlier in this century. Today's governor is more likely to be bright, experienced, and capable of managing the diverse problems of a state. In addition to being better educated than their predecessors, recent governors have often had previous experience as a state-wide elected official or have held a federal elective position, such as U.S. senator or representative. A sample of recent governors' previous jobs shows that California's Pete Wilson was a U.S. senator, Mel Carnahan of Missouri was lieutenant governor, and Stephen Merrill of New Hampshire and Jim Edgar of Illinois were state-wide elected officials. New Hampshire governor Jeanne Shaheen is one of the few governors who moved up from the state legislature. Shaheen and New Jersey's Christine Whitman were the only women to hold the governor's post in 1997.

Campaigning for governor is a consuming and expensive process. Candidates must have the time, stamina, and money to enable them to endure the lengthy process of securing their party's nomination and winning the general election. The costs of running for the governorship have risen to an exceedingly high level, with candidates spending over $50 million in California and Texas, for example. In a few small states, it may still be possible to wage a gubernatorial campaign for about $1 million.

In 1996, Washington state voters elected Gary Locke, the first Asian American governor of one of the 48 Contiguous states.

Incumbents possess a decided edge in gubernatorial elections; about three-fourths win reelection. But the mid-1990s also saw many prominent incumbents lose their posts, including Mario Cuomo of New York and Ann Richards of Texas, both of whom lost bids for reelection to less-experienced campaigners and politicians. Not all governors are permitted to seek reelection, however. The trend has been to extend the governor's term of office from 2 to 4 years and limit the number of terms that can be served.

With few exceptions, governors are male, white lawyers who are married. Virginia's Douglas Wilder, who could serve only one term because of state term limits, became the first elected African-American governor in 1989. Only 2 women held the top post in their states in 1997. In rare instances, Independents have been able to win a gubernatorial election, such as Alaska's Walter Hickel. In 1997, 32 Republicans, 17 Democrats and 1 Independent were occupying the governorships in the United States (see Table 21.1).

THE JOB OF GOVERNOR

Like our presidents, governors are expected to wear many hats in their jobs—sometimes fulfilling constitutionally assigned duties, sometimes performing political tasks. But the powers of governors are not always commensurate with citizens' expectations. State constitutions often accord only weak powers to governors, frequently dividing executive powers among many different administrative actors and agencies. Modernization in state governments has resulted in enhanced powers for governors by greatly reducing the number of independently elected officials and independent boards and commissions in the state executive. Changes have established clearer lines of accountability and enhanced the governor's appointment, reorganization, and budgetary powers. The states also generally raised the salaries of governors and increased their term of service from 2 to 4 years. Nevertheless, executive power in the states remains fragmented.

How powerful are the nation's governors? Political scientist Thad Beyle has devoted considerable attention to this subject. On the basis of an analysis of gubernatorial powers outlined in state constitutions, prescribed in statutes, and expanded by direct-democracy actions of the voters, he classifies governors' institutional powers into four categories. Table 21.2 shows the relative power of each state's governor assessed in terms of the governor's ability to stay in office, make major appointments, prepare the state budget, veto legislation, and direct political party agendas. Nine states' governors—those in Hawaii, Iowa, Maryland, New Jersey, New York, Ohio, Pennsylvania, Tennessee, and West Virginia—have very strong powers. Another 21 governors enjoy strong executive powers. Seventeen states accord their governors moderate powers. The remaining states—North Carolina, South Carolina, and Vermont—give only weak powers to governors.[22]

In most states, the governor's power is further diminished by extensive civil service and merit system employment policies. These systems seek to professionalize administration and to safeguard programs against politicization. Civil service or merit system rules require that the majority of state jobs be awarded competitively on the basis of qualifications; jobs cannot simply be given to a governor's friends and political allies. Administrators protected by civil service status cannot be fired without cause. But such protections also insulate the bureaucracy from gubernatorial control, even when the governor has legitimate policy concerns or questions about an agency's performance.

Limits on executive powers are consistent with the principle of individualism and limited government. Most of the restraints on gubernatorial power are established in state constitutions. Powers given to the governor vary from state to state, but all governors have the constitutional or legal responsibility to fulfill several key roles:

- *Chief executive.* The governor is responsible for administration or implementation of many state government programs, newly passed legislation, and assorted regulations. Governors typically prepare the state budget for submission to and approval by the legislature. Because a large number of other executive branch officials are also elected in most states (such as the attorney general, secretary of state, and state treasurer), a governor's control over policy administration is somewhat diminished. Texas and California, for instance, have very fragmented executive systems based on a fear of concentrated power. In addition, many states have civil service employment policies that require most state jobs to be competitively awarded to the most qualified job candidate rather than to a political friend of the governor. These limit a governor's power over behavior of state employees.
- *Chief of state.* In this role, the governor serves largely as the symbolic political head of the state. When meeting with the president, other governors, or heads of federal agencies, the governor is acting as the political leader of the people of that state. The governor is also acting as chief of state when conducting any kind of intergovernmental affairs with local officials, other states, or the national government. The

TABLE 21.2 INSTITUTIONAL POWERS OF THE GOVERNORS

VERY STRONG	STRONG	MODERATE	WEAK
Hawaii	Alaska	Alabama	North Carolina
Iowa	Arizona	California	South Carolina
Maryland	Arkansas	Colorado	Vermont
New Jersey	Connecticut	Florida	
New York	Delaware	Georgia	
Ohio	Illinois	Idaho	
Pennsylvania	Kansas	Indiana	
Tennessee	Kentucky	Maine	
West Virginia	Louisiana	Massachusetts	
	Michigan	Mississippi	
	Minnesota	Nevada	
	Missouri	New Hampshire	
	Montana	Oklahoma	
	Nebraska	Texas	
	New Mexico	Virginia	
	North Dakota	Washington	
	Oregon	Wyoming	
	Rhode Island		
	South Dakota		
	Utah		
	Wisconsin		

SOURCE: Thad Beyle, "Governors: The Middlemen and Women in Our Political System," Chapter 6 in Gray and Jacobs, *Politics in the American States,* Table 6-17, 237.

governor of Arkansas assumed this role in 1997 when he called for immediate federal assistance to help the state recover from a dramatic series of deadly tornadoes that hit the state.

- *Chief legislator.* Like the president, governors are the primary initiators of public policy. Governors typically announce their legislative agenda at the beginning of the legislative session, often during an annual "State of the State" address. Support for a governor's proposals tends to be higher among legislators whose districts voted heavily for the governor in the last election.
- *Veto authority.* Governors perform a check on the state legislature through their executive veto (except in North Carolina), which usually may be overridden with a supermajority vote of legislators. Unlike the president, 43 governors have a line-item veto that permits vetoing or amending portions of a budget bill or language in legislation that has been approved by the legislature. A governor may also call the legislature into special session, a tool quite often used in states such as Texas where the legislature meets in regular session only once every 2 years for a limited schedule.

To enhance their influence, governors can combine "personal power" with their formal institutional powers.[23] A governor's real power depends more on character, leadership style, and persuasive abilities than on the formal prerogatives of the office. Building public support is an increasingly important part of the policy persuasion process. Public relations and media experts have become part of many governors' staffs. These aides distribute stories and media "feeds" to local newspapers and TV and radio stations. However, newspapers and television rarely find it worth their while to devote much coverage to news in the state capitol. Network news focuses on national stories; local televised news and the print press focus on local and human interest stories. People are generally more interested in what is happening in their own community than in state affairs. Press coverage of state politics is intermittent at best, focusing on only the most salient controversies and such predictable events as the governor's State of the State address.

OTHER EXECUTIVE OFFICERS

Governors must work with an array of other executive branch officials in conducting the affairs of state government. At various times, these officials who are elected to head branches of state government assist and oppose the chief executive. State voters choose a **lieutenant governor** in 43 states. The governor and lieutenant governor are elected together in 24 states. In states where the governor and lieutenant governor are chosen in separate elections, it is possible for the two top state executives to be members of different political parties, and real battles between them can ensue. For example, in the 1970s, Missouri's governor was unable to leave the state for fear that the lieutenant governor—as acting governor—would make a major appointment in his absence. Most lieutenant governors have few formal duties aside from presiding over the state senate and being in the succession path for governor.

Major executive positions in other states (and the number of states electing each position) include attorney general (43), treasurer (38), secretary of state (36), auditor (25), and comptroller, agricultural commissioner and commissioners for land, labor, mines, and utilities, among others.[24] So many executives and additional boards are running state governments that many politicians and scholars have called for reorganized state governments with fewer independent executives. Every state has undertaken some kind of reorganization of the executive branch in the last decade. However, research shows that the benefits expected of reorganized state governments are not always achieved. Such reorganization seldom results in cost saving and efficiency—issues often touted by proponents of reorganization.[25] Although state residents may value smaller governments, at times they also prefer many democratically elected officials that add to the size of state executive branches.

STATE COURT SYSTEMS

States have separate courts from the federal court system discussed in Chapter 16. The organization of the states' courts reflects two major influences: (1) the model of organization set by the federal courts and (2) the judicial preferences of each state's citizens as manifested in state constitutions and statutes. State courts are very important to the administration of justice in our society and are more involved in administrating justice than is the federal judiciary. Recent data show that state courts have 100 times the number of trials and hear 5 times more appeals than federal courts.[26] In addition, state court workloads have been increasing in both criminal and civil cases, forcing states to experiment with alternatives to trial courts: mediation, arbitration, and plea bargaining, among others. The volume of cases heard by state courts is significant, but courts are also policymaking bodies. Particularly when the highest court in the state rules on a case, judges are more than just interpreting the law; they are often making policy in the same fashion as the U.S. Supreme Court.

The organization of state courts is most often a three-tier system, with trial courts at the local level, an intermediate set of courts of appeal, and a court of last resort (see Figure 21.1). These courts have jurisdiction for both civil and criminal cases.

TRIAL COURTS

The local courts in each state are usually established for county-size areas and are the setting for most trials. These courts are known by a variety of labels—district courts, circuit courts, superior courts, and (in the case of New York) supreme courts. Judges assigned to these trial courts often work in only one county and specialize in criminal, juvenile, or civil litigation. A single judge presides over each case, and citizens are called upon to serve as jurors and members of grand jury panels.

At the trial court level, the facts of a case are considered, along with due process required for the accused under the Constitution. The number of cases tried in these state courts is affected by the size of the population and by socioeconomic and legal factors. The types of cases that have increased in number most significantly in recent years have been felonies and civil disputes.

APPELLATE COURTS

Our system of justice guarantees the right to appeal trial court decisions, so in 37 states, defendants and litigants who are unhappy with the decision at the trial court level may appeal this decision to an intermediate court of appeal (in other states, the court of last resort hears appeals). States organize their appeals courts on a regional basis in which judges work together in panels of three or more, with a majority deciding each case. No witnesses are called

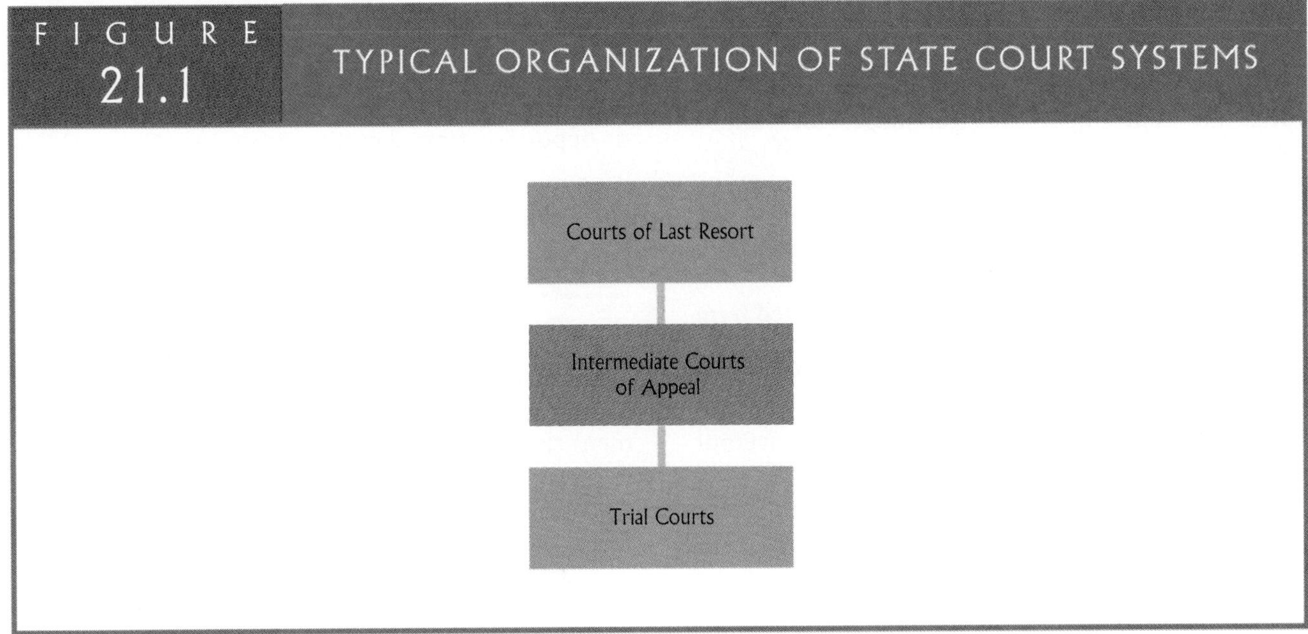

before appellate courts, and juries are not used. Instead, judges read briefs and hear arguments prepared by lawyers that address whether the law was appropriately applied at the trial court level and whether due process of law was followed. The job of judges at this level is not to determine the facts of a case but to interpret the laws and the state or national constitution, if necessary, as they apply to the case. The workload of the intermediate courts of appeal has also increased in recent years, primarily because of mandatory appeals, also called "appeals of right," which are cases that must be heard and decided by appellate courts on the basis of merit.

Twelve states, all with small populations, do not have intermediate courts of appeal,[27] so the appellate work in these states falls to the "court of last resort." Every state has a court of last resort, usually called the supreme court, that is the final appellate level within a state. This court has appellate jurisdiction for both civil and criminal cases, except in Oklahoma and Texas, which both have two top courts—one for civil appeals and one for criminal matters. The number of justices sitting on these courts ranges from five to nine, and each is headed by a chief justice.

The workload of these courts is largely driven by population; larger states have more appeals to handle. Also, states without intermediate courts have courts of last resort with busier workloads. Research has shown that the U.S. Supreme Court has increased the workload of states' appeals courts by limiting access to federal courts, thereby encouraging states to decide more cases on the basis of state constitutions.[28]

Supreme court decisions have a profound affect on state policy. These courts are often called on to practice judicial review of actions of the state legislature and the executive branch, to interpret laws and the state constitution, and to make judicial policy. In deciding cases, many state supreme courts often attempt to follow a role of judicial self-restraint, deferring to the policy wishes of state legislators—representatives elected for the express purpose of policymaking. In other states, the supreme courts have leaned more toward judicial activism, as justices have shown a greater willingness to engage in judicial policymaking in order to produce a more fair and equitable political system. Recently, state supreme courts have exhibited a new wave of liberal activism, expanding the legal rights of people who have suffered personal injury and protecting other individual rights and civil liberties.[29] The belief among supreme court justices who received their legal education in the 1960s that they should play an active role in protecting rights is reflected in Utah Supreme Court Justice Christine Durham's views:

> [M]ost of us who sit on state supreme courts, and most of the lawyers who appear before us, were educated during a generation of expansivist, creative, and enormously "generative" thinking on the subject of the federal constitution and in the context of civil liberties. We saw in the Warren Court era an enormous and impressive reshaping of our attitudes and our assumptions about what the constitution meant for individual liberties in the U.S.[30]

SELECTING JUDGES

Courts are part of the democratic electoral process in more than three-quarters of the states. In these states, voters are called upon to elect judges for various courts. Popular elections are used to choose judges, justices, and even the chief justice in some states. States still use partisan ballots for judicial elections, but many have begun to choose judges on nonpartisan ballots. Unlike federal judges who are appointed to serve for life, most state judges serve a limited term of office that is followed by a new election.

Increasingly, states have been moving to judicial retention elections based on some form of the **Missouri Plan.** In this type of system, the governor usually appoints the state's judges from a list of qualified persons recommended by the state bar or a committee of jurists and other officials. The judge serves until an election can be held, in which voters are asked whether the judge should be retained in office. If voters approve retention by a majority vote (Illinois requires 60 percent), then the judge continues in office for a specified term, after which another retention election is held. Few judges lose in this type of retention election.

Electing judges remains common and controversial. Allegations of bias in the judicial selection process have been made by minority groups and political parties. In 1990, for example, the U.S. Justice Department invalidated Georgia's system of electing judges because it was found to be discriminatory against African Americans. A 1994 federal court ruling held North Carolina's method of electing judges state-wide to be biased against the Republican Party because most of the state's trial court judges were Democrats.[31] And in 1997, the Illinois General Assembly changed the state's supreme court districts to make it harder for Democrats to dominate in these elections. This law was challenged by legal interest groups across the state, and a court declared it unconstitutional, with little opposition from the state.

LOCAL GOVERNMENTS

Grassroots democracy has a long history in this country, and Americans have shown a preference for local democracies. Many Americans believe that government closest to the people governs best. And in keeping with the principle of individualism, many local governments—especially in small, rural areas—are purposely kept small, inactive, and less obtrusive.

The U.S. Bureau of the Census counts not only people but also governments. Its latest count revealed an astonishing 84,955 American local governments (see Table 21.3). The sheer number of governments in the United States is, however, as much a burden as a boon to democracy. Program vendors say at baseball games that "you can't tell the players without a scorecard"; unfortunately, scorecards are not available for local governments, where the participants are numerous and sometimes seem to be playing different games.

In addition to being a citizen of the United States and of a state, an average citizen also resides within the jurisdiction of perhaps 10 to 20 local governments. The state of Illinois holds the current record for the largest number of individual governments: 6,722 at the latest count. The six-county Chicago-Illinois metropolitan area alone has more than 1,200 governments!

TABLE 21.3 LOCAL GOVERNMENTS IN THE UNITED STATES

TYPE OF GOVERNMENT	1962	1992	% CHANGE 1962-1992
All local governments	91,186	84,955	−6.8%
General-purpose governments:			
County	3,043	3,043	0.0
Municipal	18,000	19,279	+7.1
Township	17,142	16,656	−2.8
Single-purpose governments:			
School district	34,678	14,422	−58.4
Special district	18,323	31,555	+72.2

SOURCE: U.S. Bureau of the Census, *1992 Census of Governments,* Vol. 1, No. 1, Government Organization (Washington, DC: U.S. Government Printing Office, 1994)

Local governments are classified into five different varieties on the basis of their legal purposes and the scope of their responsibilities. In many states, citizens are governed by a complex maze of local governments—some with broad powers, others performing very specialized services. In many locales, for instance, residents are served by a county government, city government, township government, three school districts (elementary, secondary, and community college), and several special districts (transit, parks, airport, water, sewage, mosquito abatement, and so forth). Let us take a closer look at local governments.

COUNTIES AND TOWNSHIPS

The largest geographic unit of government at the local level is the **county** government. A county is called a "parish" in Louisiana and a "borough" in Alaska. County governments are the administrative arms of state government in most local areas. Texas has the largest number of counties with 254; Delaware and Hawaii have just 3 each. Los Angeles County serves the most people—over 8.8 million residents, whereas Loving County, Texas (a large geographic area) serves only 107 residents.

What is the job of the county government? Typically, counties are responsible for keeping records of births, deaths, and marriages, establishing a system of justice and law enforcement, maintaining roads and bridges, collecting taxes, conducting voter registration and elections, and providing for public welfare and education. Rural residents more often rely on county governments for services.

County governments usually consist of an elected **county commission,** which makes policy, and a collection of "row officers," including sheriffs, prosecutors, county clerks, and assessors, who run county services. Some urban counties, such as Milwaukee County, St. Louis County, and Wayne (Detroit) County, now elect a county executive (like a mayor). Or, as in the case of Dade (Miami) County and Sacramento County, they appoint a county administrator (like a city manager) to improve the administration of county policies.

Township governments are found in only 20 states, including Maine, Michigan, New Hampshire, New York, Vermont, and Wisconsin. Most township governments have limited powers to assist with county services in rural areas; however, some governments, such as those in New England, function much like city governments. Voters often elect a township board, a supervisor, and perhaps a very small number of other officials. Township officers oversee public highways and local law enforcement, keep records of vital statistics and tax collections, and administer elections. Most, however, lack power to pass local ordinances because they serve as administrative extensions of the state and county governments.

MUNICIPALITIES

Cities are more formally known as municipal governments or **municipalities,** and they supply most local programs and services for more than 19,275 communities in the United States. Municipalities typically provide police and fire protection, street maintenance, solid waste collection, water and sewer works, park and recreation services, and public planning. Some larger cities also operate school systems, run public hospitals and health programs, administer public welfare services, run public transit and utilities, and manage housing and urban development programs. Citizen satisfaction with the delivery of such services can vary greatly.

Originally, many local communities in the United States were operated under a form of direct democracy—the "**town meeting**" form of government. In this arrangement, all voting-age adults in a community gathered once a year to make public policy, such as passing new local laws, approving a town budget, and electing a small number of local residents to serve as government officials for the year. Historically, municipal corporations were chartered by state governments to operate government at the local level, under the direction of state legislatures that wrote and granted charters. After 1850, states began to allow cities to write their own charters and to change them without permission of the state legislature. Today, this practice,

The uniformed services are the most recognizable employees of local governments. Firefighters, police officers, and emergency medical personnel from Oklahoma City and surrounding municipalities led the rescue efforts in the aftermath of the bombing of the Murrah federal building.

known as **home rule,** is widely used to organize and modernize city governments. As cities became too large for the town meeting style of governance, three modern forms of municipal government came to be used in the United States.

- **Mayor-council government.** In a typical mayor-council government (Figure 21.2), local residents elect a mayor and a city council to represent them in city government. In strong-mayor cities, such as New York City, the city council makes public policy, and the mayor and city bureaucrats who report to the mayor are responsible for policy implementation. Strong mayors can also veto actions of the city council.
- The weak-mayor form of governance vests most power in the city council, which directs the activities of the city bureaucracy. The mayor serves as the presiding officer for city council meetings and as the ceremonial head of city government. Most mayor-council cities follow the weak-mayor form. Small cities of 10,000 or fewer residents are more likely to have a weak-mayor charter.
- **Council-manager government.** In this form of government, voters choose a city council and may choose a mayor (see Figure 21.3), who often acts as both presiding officer and voting member of the council. The council is responsible for political and policy decisions in the city. The implementation and administration of the council's actions are placed in the hands of an appointed city manager, who is expected to carry out policy with the city bureaucracy. More than one-third of cities use this form of government, including such major cities as Dallas, Kansas City, Phoenix, and San Diego.
- **Commission government.** In this type of government (Figure 21.4), voters elect a panel of city commissioners, each of whom serves as both legislator and executive. These legislators make public policy just as city council members do in the other two forms of government. But each member is also elected as a commissioner of a

FIGURE 21.2 MAYOR-COUNCIL GOVERNMENT

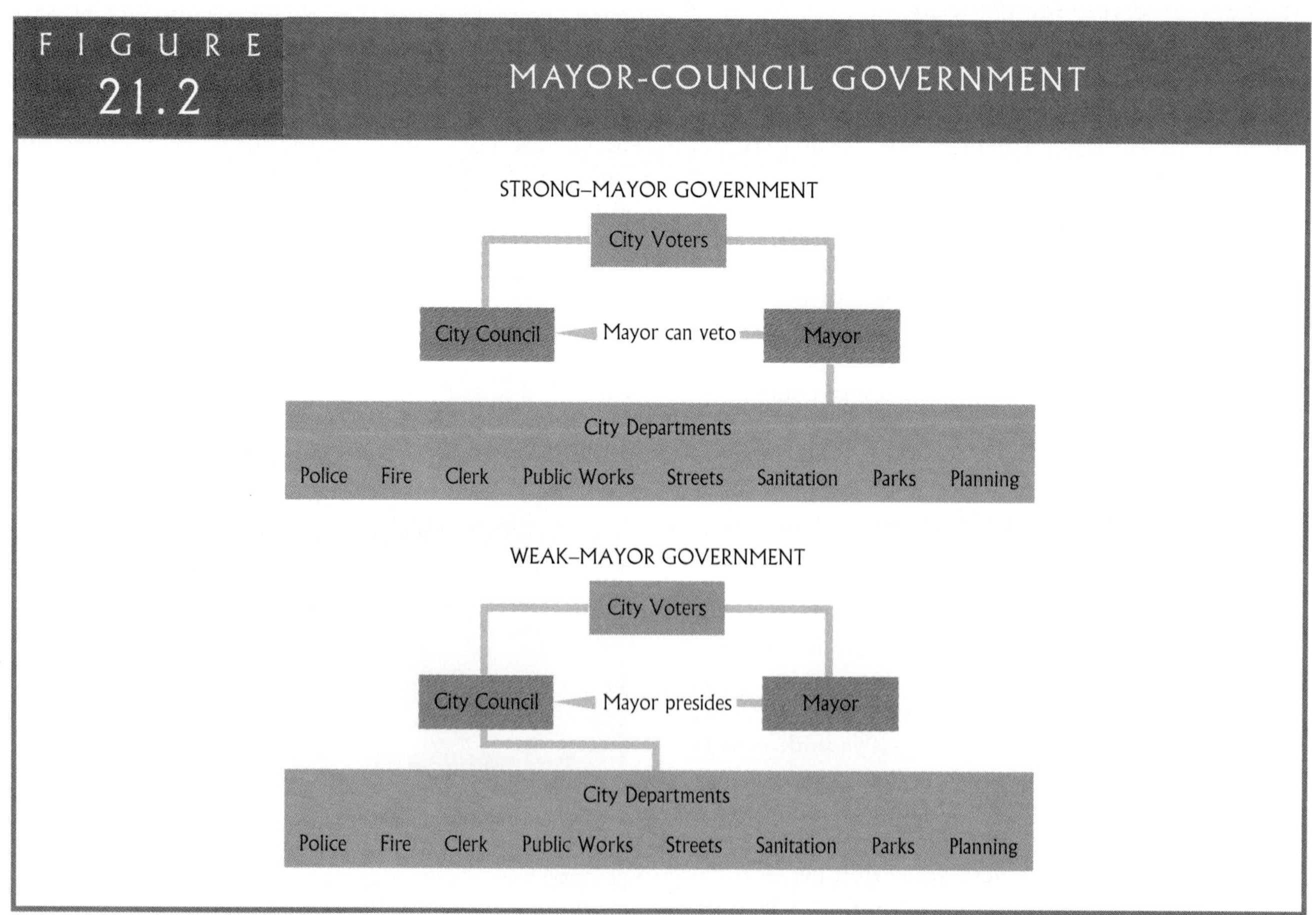

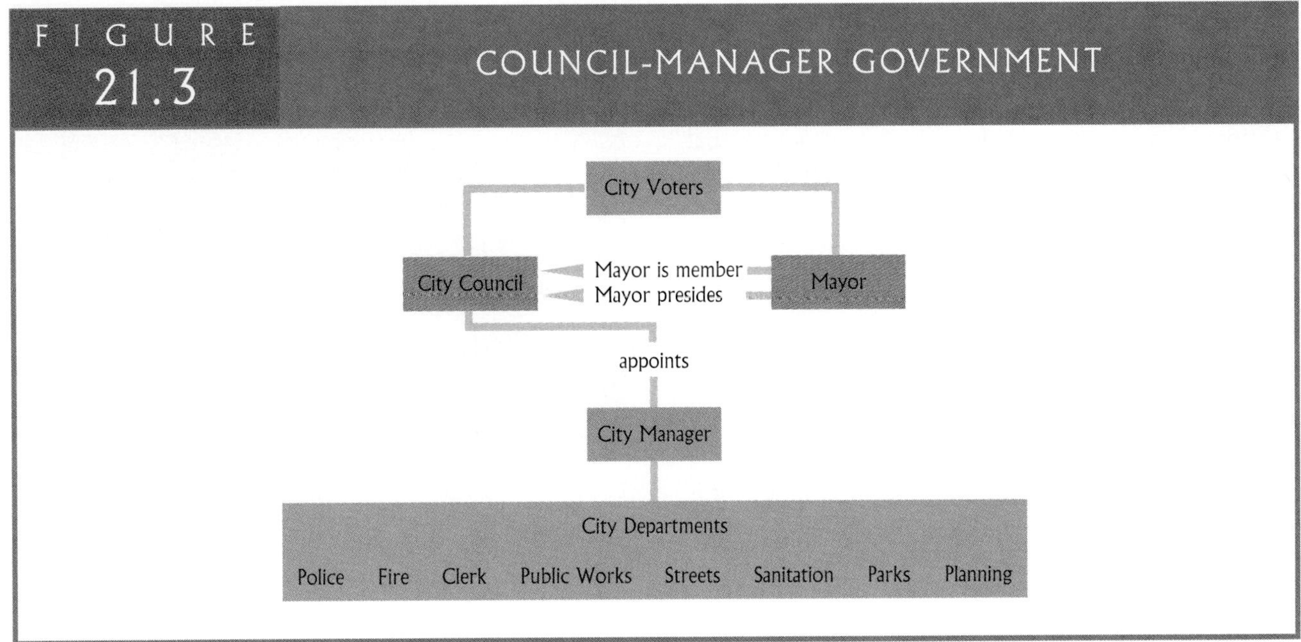

> functional area of city government (for example, public safety), and bureaucrats report to a single commissioner. Among the few cities that still use a commission government are Vicksburg, Mississippi, and St. Petersburg, Florida.[32]

Most city council members and many mayors are elected on a nonpartisan ballot. Traditionally, city council members represented a district or ward of the city—a practice that permitted the ward-based machine bosses to control elections and try to create public policies that were good for individual wards, rather than for the city as a whole. Reformers advocated at-large city elections, with all members of the city council chosen by voters across the city. These at-large representatives could not create public policies to benefit only their own neighborhoods because they would have to answer to all of the city's voters. A

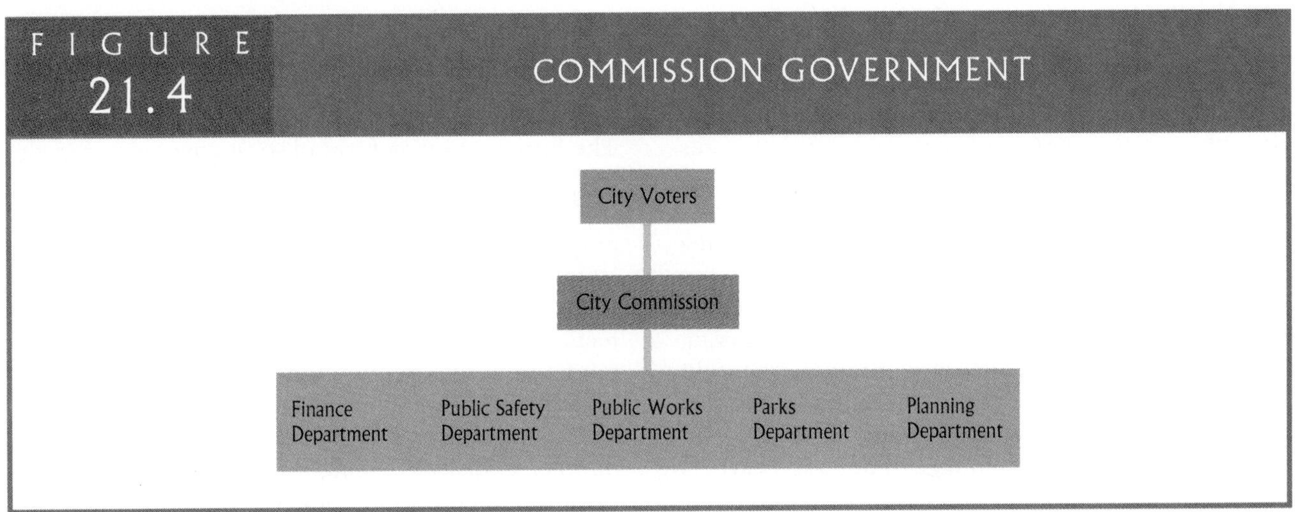

majority of cities use at-large elections today. An unintended consequence of at-large representation is that minority group members have had difficulty gaining election to the city council. Cities that employ district elections have a greater degree of representational equity for African Americans and Hispanics on city councils than cities that use at-large elections.[33]

Declining school revenues and growing enrollments in many of the nation's urban schools have led to makeshift classrooms, such as this scene in which students work in a hallway floor for a class period.

SCHOOL DISTRICTS

School districts are responsible for delivering education programs in over 14,000 areas of the country. Although a few cities, counties, and townships operate schools as part of their general budget, most school systems are run as independent local governments. The majority of districts provide both elementary and secondary education, but some operate only elementary schools or high schools. Consolidation of small, often rural districts with larger ones is the major reason for a nearly 60 percent drop in the number of school districts during the past 30 years.

In an independent school district, local voters within a geographically defined area are responsible for their own public education system, including electing a board of education, picking administrators and teachers, building and operating schools, designing and running education programs, and raising the revenues to meet a locally adopted school budget plan. Although states are ultimately responsible for public education, state governments adopt general standards for education policy and school buildings, mandate certain school programs, and provide a system of state aid for public schools. Within the guidelines of state policy and the parameters of state funding, locally elected school boards and appointed administrators deliver education services to the nation's children.

School districts have become the locus for many emotionally charged issues at the local level. Prayer in public schools, equity in school funding, and lingering racial discrimination are just a few of the more explosive issues surrounding schools in the 1990s. For example, although the Supreme Court declared that states have a responsibility to eliminate discrimination in education policy in such important decisions as *Brown v. Board of Education* (1954) and *Swann v. Charlotte-Mecklenberg County Schools* (1971) (see Chapter 5), our country continues to see inequities in the public school systems, with racial minorities still encountering poorly funded public education in many instances. In fact, political scientists have discovered an extensive pattern of "second-generation discrimination," in which we find a decided shortage of minority teachers in today's classrooms.[34]

This inequity is coupled with a financial crisis in many public school systems today. States have widely divergent school aid policies—some states being good providers to their neediest local schools, whereas others leave the financing responsibility largely to local districts.[35] Local revenue sources are disproportionately based on the local property tax—a policy choice that results in wealthier districts having an abundance of resources, while poorer districts have inadequate revenues for their schoolchildren. Schools around the country continue to struggle with providing quality education with limited resources. (See "You Are the Policymaker: Should Teachers' Salary Demands Be Met?")

SPECIAL DISTRICTS AND PUBLIC AUTHORITIES

The fastest-growing form of local government in the United States is the **special district.** The last official count showed 31,555 of these independent, limited-purpose governments, and they are found in every state. Generally, special districts provide only a single service, such as flood control, waste disposal, fire protection, public libraries, or public parks. No standard model of special district government organization is to be found in the United States—diversity of organizational arrangements is almost as plentiful as the number of districts. Some districts have elected policymaking boards; others are appointed by a governor

SHOULD TEACHERS' SALARY DEMANDS BE MET?

You Are the Policymaker

Public school districts in the United States must acquire the resources that are necessary to make schools successful. Perhaps the best resource in any school is the classroom teacher. For many years, public school teachers have been underpaid compared to other professionals. In recent years, this inequity has caught the attention of policymakers and the public and has led to unionization by teachers.

Suppose you are a member of an independent school district's board of education and you are negotiating a new contract with the local teachers' union for salary and benefits for the coming year. How far should you and your board go to continue paying teachers what they are worth?

The teachers' contracts have increased an average of 8 percent during the past 5 years as the local school board brought teacher salaries up to levels that equitably reflect their professional education and experience. These increases often were larger than the annual rate of inflation—the increase in the cost of living.

This year your school district's financial picture is bleak, and local taxpayers know it. The school system's local revenues are down, state aid has been cut, and the school has been borrowing money just to meet monthly expenses. The cost of living has increased by 3 percent during the past year.

Therefore, you and your fellow board members believe that offering the teachers a 3 percent pay increase is the prudent policy to pursue—one that will be acceptable to local residents. The teachers' union has asked for an 8 percent salary increase, maintaining that anything less than the recent average increase is an unacceptable sign that the board does not appreciate its teachers.

The teachers have threatened to strike if the board does not meet the union demand. The board knows that a strike will be costly. The board is willing to negotiate but believes that it owes the taxpayers a budget increase that is as close as possible to the increase in the cost of living.

Parents are caught in the middle. They want their taxes to remain low and expect the board to hold the line on spending. At the same time, they support the teachers who educate their children and they do not want the kids to miss out on school because of a teachers' strike.

Are the teachers being treated fairly? How far should the board go in meeting teacher demands to avoid a strike? What would you do?

or mayor. Illinois has the distinction of having the most special districts in the country.

Special districts are highly flexible units of local government, because their boundary lines can be drawn across the usual municipal, county, and township borders. By providing services on a larger scale, they help localities realize certain economies or savings. Public authorities (such as the Illinois Sports Facilities Authority mentioned at the beginning of this chapter) are similar to special districts but generally have even greater financing powers.

Important questions about democracy are inherent in the growth of special districts and public authorities. Special districts are, to a great extent, invisible governments; their operations are rarely covered by the local press, and there is little direct public participation in their decision making. Most citizens do not even know who serves on these district boards or when the boards meet. As a result, the public has a difficult time holding special districts accountable.

LIMITS OF LOCAL GOVERNMENT

Whatever the many virtues of local government, we find that local governments are also limited in their decision-making abilities. There are three distinct reasons for the limited nature of local government:

1. *Constitutional limitations.* Local governments have no constitutional right of existence. Strictly speaking, they are the administrative subunits of the state. Local governments have only the legislative, spending, and taxing authority that a state chooses to give them.

2. *Structural limitations.* Extensive metropolitan fragmentation results in limitations on local government power. The large number of governmental bodies fragments local government power in metropolitan areas. Each has jurisdiction over only a small geographic piece of the metropolis or responsibility for the provision of a narrow set of specialized services. No single unit of local government has the scope of action necessary to solve larger problems. Problems can be solved more effectively if the different units of local government work together. But such cooperation is difficult to achieve.
3. *Economic limitations.* Local governments find that they often must compete with one another in an effort to attract desirable businesses. This competition constrains local policymaking. Local officials are often reluctant to raise taxes, expand redistributional services, or otherwise undertake actions that would give the city a reputation for being a "bad" location for business.

The People Speak

How Well Do You Think Your State Government and Your Local Government Cooperate and Get Along With Each Other?

Very well	9%
Fairly well	50%
Not very well	19%
Not well at all	11%
Don't know/No answer	12%

SOURCE: The question as worded is taken directly from the U.S. Advisory Commission on Intergovernmental Relations, *Changing Public Attitudes on Governments and Taxes*, 1991 (Washington, DC: ACIR, 1991). Table 9.9.

FRAGMENTATION, COOPERATION, AND COMPETITION

Each governing body in a fragmented metropolis tends to look at problems from its own narrow, partial perspective. As a result, local bodies fail to cooperate with one another and plan effectively for the region's future needs. For example, the development of an effective mass transit system is often hindered when not all communities are willing to share in financing a new metropolitan bus network or light rail system. Also, narrow-based special districts or authorities devoted to maintaining the region's road network will be less willing to divert their money to help finance new rail construction. As you can see in "The People Speak" on this page, few citizens think that their state and local governments cooperate very well.

What prospects are there for promoting regional cooperation to correct the inequalities and coordination problems that result from metropolitan fragmentation? For the most part, the prospects have been dim. Generally speaking, the United States lacks the tradition of strong, regional planning evident in Europe (see "America in Perspective: Urban Planning in Western Europe and the United States"). But this fact also reflects the strong localism inherent in American democracy. In fact, very few metropolitan areas have attempted to create metropolitan or regional bodies capable of surmounting the problems that resulting from metropolitan fragmentation and local parochialism. The Miami Metro, the Seattle Metro, the Twin Cities (Minneapolis-St. Paul) Metropolitan Council, and Indianapolis' Unigov arrangements represent some of the more notable efforts at regional planning and decision-making. But these efforts are also noteworthy as exceptions. In the future, few, if any, state legislatures can be expected to antagonize powerful suburban constituencies by creating new metropolitan governments. Americans prefer living in small, autonomous communities. Suburbanites, in particular, profess a preference for their small-scale, easy-to-reach government over more distant and bureaucratized metropolitan arrangements.

Local governments do cooperate with one another extensively when they find it in their mutual interest to do so. Central cities and suburbs are often willing, for instance, to share the costs of a new sewage disposal facility. They will also cooperate in ventures to attract a major new employer to the area. Two or more governments may informally cooperate and share equipment and services. In many areas of the country, a **council of governments** (frequently referred to as a COG) exists wherein officials from various localities meet to discuss mutual problems and plan joint, cooperative action. But these councils are often extremely weak, because they tend to be underfunded, are poorly staffed, and lack any real legislative and taxing power.

Local governments in the 1990s are engaged in serious competition for economic development. That is, they seek to expand the local government tax base with new or existing commercial and residential development. Some analysts believe that cities are quite limited in their ability to control economic change in the community but should realize, nonetheless, that devel-

URBAN PLANNING IN WESTERN EUROPE AND THE UNITED STATES

America in Perspective

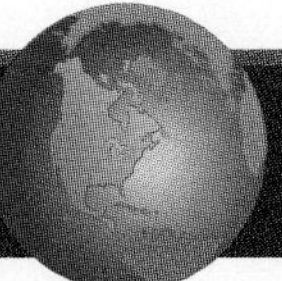

The nations of Western Europe play a much stronger role in guiding urban development than does the United States. Strong planning in Europe has helped to preserve cities, control the pace of development, protect agricultural land and the environment, and minimize urban sprawl to a degree that is hardly imaginable in the United States. Typically, these urban planning actions are initiated by regional agencies that get their authority from the central government.

In Great Britain, planners prevented the overgrowth of London by encircling the city with a "green belt"—a designated area of land in which the countryside would be preserved and no new development would be permitted. The growth of the region's population was absorbed in planned "new towns" that were built some distance from the central city. The result was a mixture of city and countryside in metropolitan areas and the avoidance of American-style urban sprawl.

In Paris, the nation's capital city was faced with the prospects of rapid growth and "Manhattanization." To avoid this, France's national agency for development steered new industries away from Paris into the suburbs and more distant cities. But still the lure of Paris proved attractive. If development continued at the then-existing pace, the old city of Paris was in danger of losing its character and would no longer be "Paris." Central government and regional planners came up with a solution. They built a new town of high-rise office buildings, convention centers, and hotels at La Defense, just outside the city's borders. Later, another center of new office parks was built north of the city, just next to Charles de Gaulle International Airport. These towns became the office centers, the virtual "Wall Streets," of the metropolitan Paris area. Other high-rise residential new towns were built in a ring around Paris to absorb the metropolitan area's rapidly growing population. All of these new commercial and residential centers were connected to the old city by a new commuter rail system. Paris was saved.

The Netherlands has similarly relied on strong government planning and controls over land use in order to prevent the city's limited supply of land from being eaten up by rapid urbanization. Dutch planners preserved valuable agricultural acreage and badly needed recreational space in a "green heart" in the midst of the metropolitan Amsterdam-The Hague-Rotterdam Randstad ("Ring City") area, one of the most densely populated areas in the world. A rider on any Dutch train today can look out the window and quickly see exactly where a city ends and the land designated for agricultural purposes begins. The planning boundaries are extremely strong.

But European planners now confront new problems. With the globalization of their economies, cities in Europe find that they are increasingly competing with one another for new business. As a result, spatial planning considerations are sometimes sacrificed in order to give a corporation a site it desires. Citizens' demands for individual homes of their own have also led to pressures for continued suburban development, sometimes compromising the integrity of regional land-use plans. Rush-hour traffic jams have become increasingly commonplace in major European metropolises.

Despite these new problems, European nations have been able to ward off the ills of uncontrolled growth. In the United States, by contrast, the private sector and the free market—not government—play a much greater role in deciding where growth will occur. The United States is unwilling to use strong, statist solutions to control and direct growth. Compared to Western Europe, regional planning in the United States is essentially toothless.

SOURCES: Peter Hall, *Urban and Regional Planning,* 2nd ed. (London: Allen and Unwin, 1982); H. V. Savitch, *Post-Industrial Cities: Politics and Planning in New York, Paris, and London* (Princeton, NJ: Princeton University Press, 1988); and Myron A. Levine and Jan Van Weesep, "The Changing Nature of Dutch Urban Planning," *Journal of the American Planning Association,* 54 (Summer 1988): 315-323.

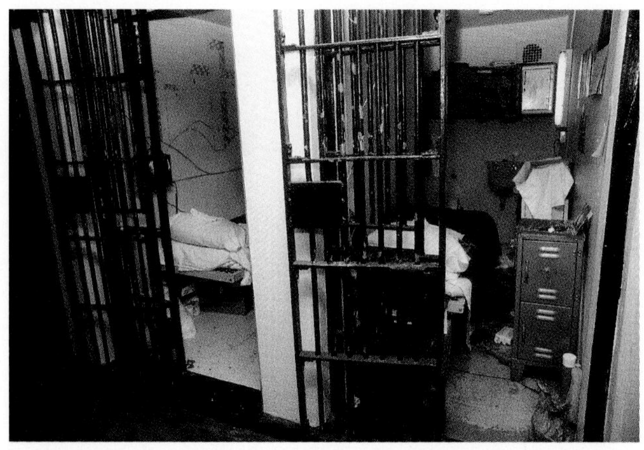

State prisons have become increasingly expensive programs for state governments to operate, leading to overcrowding, deferred maintenance, and calls for prison reform.

opment policies are the lifeblood of the community.[36] A business owner can simply threaten to leave a community or locate facilities in another town if the owner is unhappy with local policies. Thus, business owners and corporate officials great leverage in extracting concessions from a community, because no city wants to face the loss of its job or tax base. As a result, cities compete with one another for desirable business facilities by offering tax reductions, promises of subsidized infrastructure development, and other services demanded by business. But other analysts argue that cities have much more control over economic development and that development itself will not always be the top priority of city policymakers. Even amidst strong competition, local governing coalitions, or **urban regimes,** may pursue other policy goals than development, including progressive programs that favor neighborhood interests over commercial ones.[37]

STATE AND LOCAL FINANCE POLICY

When a state or local government approves its budget for the next fiscal year, the basic policy objectives of the government have also been approved. These objectives are contained in the taxing and spending plans for the coming year. Taxpayers increasingly demand more accountability and efficiency from their state and local governments, forcing legislators and executives to squeeze services and programs out of limited revenue dollars. Figure 21.5 shows where state governments obtain their money and the policy areas to which they allocate it.

The revenue picture reveals that state government revenues are derived from a variety of sources. States

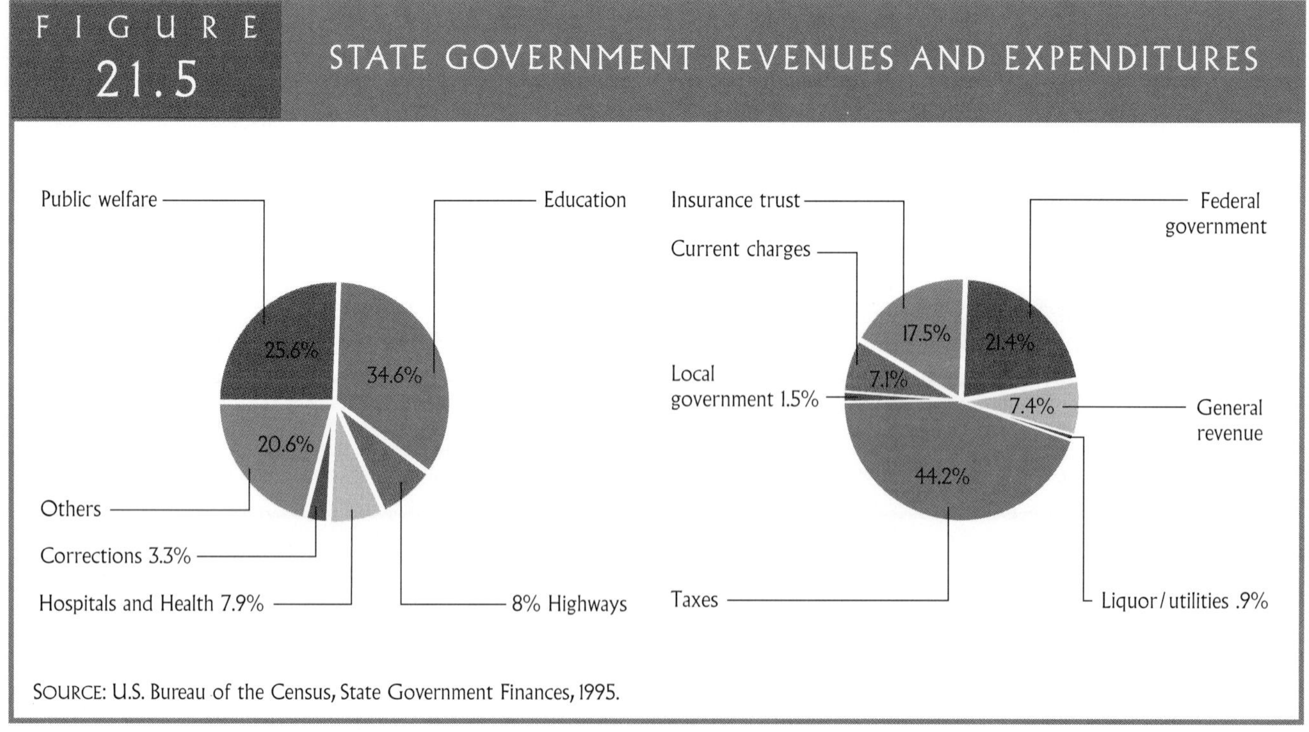

SOURCE: U.S. Bureau of the Census, State Government Finances, 1995.

receive the largest share of revenue, 44.2 percent, from taxes. States' major sources of tax revenue are sales taxes, income taxes, and motor vehicle and fuel taxes. The second largest source of state revenue is intergovernmental revenue—aid from the federal government (just over 21 percent) and a small amount from local governments. The third major revenue source is state insurance programs (17.5 percent). Other smaller revenue sources include charges and fees (for services such as state hospitals and college courses), state-operated liquor stores, utilities, payments from local governments, and a number of miscellaneous sources.

Changes in their constitutions have allowed the states to make more liberal use of income and sales taxes and other sources of revenue. By the beginning of the 1990s, 45 states levied a general sales tax; Alabama, Delaware, Montana, New Hampshire, and Oregon were the only holdouts. Only seven states—Alaska, Florida, Nevada, South Dakota, Texas, Washington, and Wyoming—lacked a personal income tax. The modernization of state revenue structures gave the states new money to finance public programs.

How do states spend their money? About 70 percent of total state money goes to operate state programs, construct state buildings, and provide direct assistance to individuals. The remaining 30 percent is allocated as aid to local governments. Figure 21.5 shows direct spending on programs and services by states in fiscal year 1995. State governments allocated the bulk of their money to education—about 30 percent for education programs at the primary, secondary, and college levels. Public welfare programs, including Medicaid, the medical care program for the poor, received 23 percent of state budgets. Hospitals and health programs claimed about 7 percent of the states' budgets, and state highways and other transportation projects received another 7 percent. Corrections and state police protection claimed just under 4 percent of the budget. In general, two-thirds of state monies are allocated to just five policy areas: education, social programs, health, transportation, and prisons. The remaining 20 percent of the budget is available to all other areas of state government: natural resources, employment security, administration, and interest payments on state bonds and other debts.

Local government finances can be a confusing matter because of the fragmentation of local governments and the varied ways in which states support and constrain their local authorities. This situation is primarily due to the different ways in which states and their local governments have sorted out the assignment of functional responsibilities among local governments. Figure 21.6 offers a snapshot of local government finances—representing county, city, township, or school and special district budgets—across the United States. Local governments receive their revenues from

FIGURE 21.6 LOCAL GOVERNMENT REVENUES AND EXPENDITURES

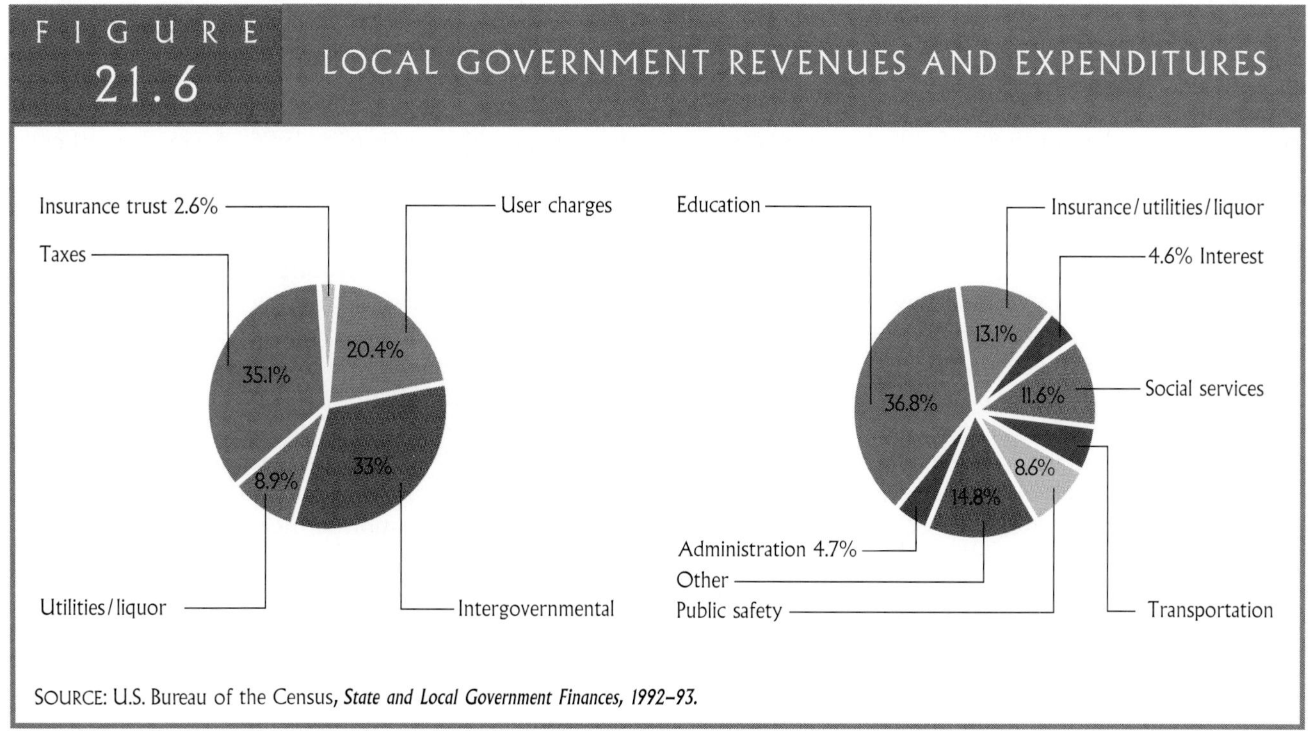

SOURCE: U.S. Bureau of the Census, *State and Local Government Finances, 1992–93.*

three main sources: taxes, user charges, and intergovernmental aid. The bulk of local revenues come from "own-source" taxes (35 percent)—mainly property taxes, sales taxes, and income taxes—and charges on the users of services (13 percent), such as libraries and recreation facilities. In addition, local governments continue to have a distinct dependence on intergovernmental funds (33 percent), primarily state aid, with some direct federal assistance. They also receive 8.5 percent of their revenues from the operation of municipally owned utilities. Compared to those in some other countries, U.S. local governments do not receive a large share of funds from the national government.

Local governments allocate their monies to a range of services, but the main areas are public education (about 37 percent), public safety (nearly 9 percent), transportation (about 6 percent), public works (5 percent), and welfare (over 4 percent). The remaining budget dollars must be devoted to administration, interest payments on debt, and a host of important local policies—from public health to land-use planning, from parks and recreation to mosquito abatement. Many of these are services that citizens need on a regular basis. Local governments also spend nearly 11 percent of their budgets on public utilities, especially water, and another 4.5 percent on interest payments on their general debt.

UNDERSTANDING STATE AND LOCAL GOVERNMENTS

A full understanding of the complexity of state and local governments cannot be gleaned from a single chapter in this book. But you should remember a few important points about these 85,000 governments.

DEMOCRACY AT THE STATE AND LOCAL LEVELS

The very existence of so many governments to handle complex as well as ordinary—but needed—services testifies to the health of our democracy. States have been willing to decentralize their governing arrangements to permit the creation of local governments to address citizens' policy demands. State governments first created county governments as local providers of state programs. Later, through constitutional change and legislation, the states created cities and townships to offer local residents a form of local democracy. Today, local voters choose their own representatives to serve on city councils, school boards, and some special district boards. As small legislatures elected from among the community's residents, these governing bodies are usually the policymaking institutions closest and most open to all citizens. In many ways, local governments encourage individual participation in government and promote the values of individualism at the local governing level.

States also operate in an open policymaking environment. Most states provide for popular democratic processes through the election of state officials. The direct primary permits eligible voters to select nominees for state offices. The constitutionally established power to recall officials from office before a term is over can be used by citizens in about one-third of the states. The state initiative process and the referendum provisions permit voters to make policy or amend their state constitutions directly.

Even so, state and local politics may not be as perfectly democratic as this initial assessment would seem to indicate. Politics at the state level is poorly covered by the media and, as a result, is relatively invisible to the public. Voters can hardly hold elected officials accountable if they know little about what is going on in the state capitol. Even at the local level, there is inadequate press coverage of anything other than the results of a city council meeting or a mayor's actions—and that doesn't happen with any regularity in smaller communities or in suburbs that lack their own daily newspaper.

When only 30 to 35 percent of state voters participate in statewide elections and fewer than 20 percent turn out for local elections, we have real concerns about the health of our grass-roots governments. Does citizen participation have to be so low? States have begun experimenting with vote-by-mail elections. Instead of having to show up on one day to cast a ballot, citizens in Oregon were able to mail in their ballots for a statewide vacancy in 1996. A small number of cities, including Birmingham, Dayton, Portland, and St. Paul, have undertaken vigorous programs of neighborhood democracy where citizen participation in public affairs goes far beyond voting. In these cities, neighborhood boards are given control over meaningful policy decisions and program resources; their actions are not merely advisory. Each city also rewards municipal officials who listen to the views of these neighborhood bodies. The experience in these and other cities shows that citizens will devote the considerable time necessary to participate in public affairs when they are convinced that participation is meaningful and that they are not just being manipulated by city officials.[38]

Interstate and interlocal competition for new businesses also raises significant questions about the democratic nature of subnational governments. As a result of this competition, state and local governments have been led to subsidize business growth and economic development, even at the cost of slighting redistributional services and human resource needs. Business interests have substantial leverage in state and city affairs as a result of their ability to threaten to leave or locate their facilities in another jurisdiction. The increasing importance of money in state and city elections has only added to the influence that special interests exert in state and local affairs.

Term limitations at the state and local levels also raise questions about democracy. On the one hand, term limits can be seen as contributing to democracy by limiting the power of a class of career politicians. Term limits will thereby allow citizen government and permit new ideas to enter government. Yet, as we have seen, there is more turnover in state legislatures and city councils than is commonly believed. Also, term limitations may be regarded as undemocratic, because they constrain voter choice. Term limitations deny voters the ability to reelect an official who they believe has served them well.

The workings of democracy are often difficult to see in the judicial branch of state government. Because most citizens do not attend trials and only lawyers and judges are directly involved in the appeals process, proceedings of the judiciary are seldom visible to the public until a significant case or decision is announced. This judicial process is not subject to quite the same scrutiny as the legislative and executive functions of state governments. Citizens will have to take more interest in the crucial role of courts in our democracy in order for courts to assume the same political importance in states as the other branches of government.

THE SCOPE OF STATE AND LOCAL GOVERNMENTS

Growth in state and local government employment has proceeded at a pace exceeding that of the federal government for most of this century, as we learned in Chapter 15. Most of this growth has been associated with heightened demands of state and local residents for more government programs. Although many voters expect their elected representatives to control the size of government and of public budgets, these same voters want government to provide them with more and better programs. Voters' requests often conflict with the notion of limited government.

Does reform of state and local governments make any difference for taxpayers? This is an appropriate question when so many governments have tried to reorganize their government structures to achieve more effective programs and more efficient use of taxpayers' dollars. In most cases, as we have seen, this process of reorganization has not resulted in smaller government. Even the "reform" of city governments has not always led to smaller budgets and payrolls. Consolidation of governments has also occurred, reducing the overall number of local governments by nearly 7 percent in the past 30 years. At the same time, declining numbers of school districts have been replaced with a growing demand for more special district governments, which have increased by over 72 percent in three decades.

Most state governments have experimented with sunset (or periodic review of) legislation to control the growth of government and eliminate unneeded agencies and programs. States have also empowered their legislatures to review executive branch regulations and rules to ensure that citizens or businesses are not overregulated by government. These practices limit the scope of state governments.

As demands of the later twentieth century have impelled growth in the areas of technology, communications, and public health and safety, state and local governments have had to grow, not diminish, in order to meet these challenges. More police, more health care providers, more computer technicians, and more social-welfare caseworkers have been needed to meet the expanding range of services and problems that confront state and local areas. Although some local governments are barely able to fulfill their basic responsibilities for public safety and maintenance of the local infrastructure, other cities and counties have become much more competent at managing local affairs. Indeed, recent research suggests that local governments often lead their states and the nation in devising innovative ways to deliver public services.[39]

SUMMARY

Our nation's states and its tens of thousands of local governments are responsible for most of the public policies with which we are most familiar: schools, fire protection, police patrolling, highway maintenance, public welfare, public health, and trash collection. Our 50 states are a diverse group, but each has a government that makes, enforces, and interprets laws for its citizens. The structure for state governments is specified in state constitutions—some very long, others quite short. Citizens may modify these state constitutions when necessary to keep pace with changing demands of government.

State legislatures include representatives and policymakers who make laws, appropriate money, oversee the executive branch, perform casework, and help manage conflict across the state. The elected legislators are diverse, but most tend to be from a somewhat higher socioeconomic position than the majority of the people they represent. Significant turnover takes place in state legislatures, and voters in some states have ensured that this will continue by enacting term limitations for their public officials.

The governors of our states are elected to be administrators of public policy and to attend to citizen needs. Once in office, a governor directs a complex state government and the programs that it administers; conducts state affairs with other governors and the president; initiates much of the legislation that state legislatures will adopt; and helps manage conflict. Governors must work with a number of other elected executive officials to produce public policy.

The state court systems are similar in organization to federal courts. Most states have a trial court level, intermediate courts of appeal, and one or more courts of last resort; all have jurisdiction over both civil and criminal cases. Judges are appointed in some states, whereas in others, they are elected on partisan or nonpartisan ballots. The actions of state judges, especially those on the court of last resort, often significantly affect policy.

The tremendous number of local governments in the United States—municipalities, counties, townships, school districts, and special districts—were established to perform policymaking at the local level with governments of either limited or broad responsibilities. Most cities are run by city councils with either a mayor or a city manager directing the day-to-day affairs of city bureaucracies. Counties and townships help states perform many local functions, such as record keeping and the administration of justice. School districts run public schools, and special districts provide limited services for multiple communities. Although nearly 85,000 local governments are found across the country, most of these units are effectively making public policy in a government that is closest to the people. Democracy truly thrives at the local level in the United States.

KEY TERMS

legislative proposal
popular initiative
governor
lieutenant governor
Missouri Plan
county
county commission
mayor-council government
council-manager government
commission government
school districts
township
municipalities
town meeting
home rule
special districts
council of governments
urban regimes

FOR FURTHER READING

Beyle, Thad L. *Governors and Hard Times.* Washington, DC: Congressional Quarterly Press, 1992. A timely monograph on the modern governor by one of the country's leading experts.

The Council of State Governments. *The Book of the States,* (biannual). Lexington, KY: CSG. An overview of annual developments in state government.

Dye, Thomas R. *Politics in States and Communities,* 9th ed. Englewood Cliffs, NJ: Prentice-Hall, 1996. A respected text that offers valuable explanations of the workings of state and local governments.

Gray, Virginia, and Herbert Jacob, *Politics in the American States: A Comparative Analysis,* 6th ed. Washington, DC: Congressional Quarterly Press, 1996. A superb collection of essays that reviews the empirical literature on state politics.

International City/County Management Association. *The Municipal Year Book.* Washington DC: ICMA, annual. Excellent current-affairs updates on local governments and informative directories on civic affairs and public officials.

Rosenthal, Alan. *Governors and Legislatures: Contending Powers.* Washington, DC: Congressional Quarterly Press, 1990. An insightful look at the dynamic relationship between the governors and state legislatures of this country.

Van Horn, Carl E. *The State of the States,* 3rd ed., Washington, DC: Congressional Quarterly Press, 1996. A timely update on government and politics in the states.

Welch, Susan, and Timothy Bledsoe. *Urban Reform and Its Consequences: A Study in Representation.* Chicago: University of Chicago Press, 1988. An important review and analysis of urban government today.

INTERNET RESOURCES

http://www.csg.org/
Council of State Governments Web Site with information on states and state public policies.

http://www.ncs.org/index.htm
National Conference of State Legislatures Web Site with information on state legislatures, elections, and members.

http://www.ncsc.dni.us/ncsc.htm
National Center for State Courts Web Site with information on state courts.

http://www.voxpop.org:80/jefferson/states
Information on the states.

http://www.btg.com/USCM/home.html
U.S. Conference of Mayors Web Site.

NOTES

1. Luther H. Gulick, "Reorganization of the State," *Civil Engineering* (August 1933): 420-421.
2. See Chapter 3 for a more extensive discussion of the changing shape of the intergovernmental system.
3. Ann O'M. Bowman and Richard C. Kearney, *The Resurgence of the States* (Englewood Cliffs, NJ: Prentice-Hall, 1986). For other important statements of the improved capacity of state governments to undertake innovative action, see David Osborne, *Laboratories of Democracy* (Boston: Harvard Business School Press, 1988); and David B. Walker, *The Rebirth of Federalism* (Chatham, NJ: Chatham House, 1995).
4. David C. Nice, "Interest Groups and State Constitutions: Another Look," *State and Local Government Review* 20 (Winter 1988): 21-27.
5. See Daniel J. Elazar, "The Principles and Traditions Underlying American State Constitutions," *Publius: The Journal of Federalism* 12 (Winter 1982): 11-25.
6. The Council of State Governments, *The Book of the States, 1996-97 Edition* (Lexington, KY: CSG, 1996), 12.
7. The states that permit citizen-initiated amendments to the constitution are Arizona, Arkansas, California, Colorado, Florida, Illinois, Massachusetts, Michigan, Mississippi, Missouri, Montana, Nebraska, Nevada, North Dakota, Ohio, Oklahoma, Oregon, and South Dakota. Over 20 states allow citizens to use the initiative process to pass new legislation.
8. Elaine Stuart, "Voters Make Laws," Council of State Governments, 1997.
9. Bowman and Kearney, *State and Local Government,* 125.
10. Samuel C. Patterson, "Legislative Politics in the States," Chapter 5 in Virginia Gray and Herbert Jacob, *Politics in the American States: A Comparative Analysis,* 6th ed. (Washington, DC: Congressional Quarterly Press, 1996).
11. Thomas R. Dye, *Politics in States and Communities,* 8th ed. (Englewood Cliffs, NJ: Prentice-Hall, 1994), 154.
12. Patterson, "Legislative Politics in the States," 177.
13. *Baker v. Carr* (1962); *Reynolds v. Sims* (1964).
14. V. O. Key, Jr., *Southern Politics in State and Nation* (New York: Knopf, 1949).
15. Dye, *Politics in States and Communities,* 162.
16. Rich Jones, "The State Legislatures," in Council of State Governments, *The Book of the States, 1992-93,* 127.
17. Alan Rosenthal, "The Legislature: Unraveling of Institutional Fabric," Chapter 6 in Carl E. Van Horn, *The State of the States,* 3rd ed. (Washington, DC: Congressional Quarterly Press, 1996), 128.
18. Patterson, "Legislative Politics in the States," 190.
19. Council of State Governments, *The Book of the States, 1996-97,* Table 3.2, 64-65.
20. Council of State Governments, *The Book of the States, 1996-97,* Table 3.6, 73-74.
21. Patterson, "Legislative Politics in the States," 193.
22. Thad Beyle, "Governors: The Middlemen and Women in our Political System," Chapter 6 in Gray and Jacobs, *Politics in the American States,* Table 6-17, 237.
23. *Ibid.,* 221-228.
24. The Council of State Governments, *The Book of the States, 1996-97,* Table 2.9, 33-34.
25. See Kenneth J. Meier, "Executive Reorganization of Government: Impact on Employment and Expenditures," *American Journal of Political Science* 24 (1980): 396-412.
26. Kenneth G. Pankey, Jr., "The State of the Judiciary," in *The Book of the States, 1992-93,* 210.
27. Delaware, Maine, Mississippi, Montana, Nevada, New Hampshire, North Dakota, Rhode Island, South Dakota, Vermont, West Virginia, and Wyoming.
28. G. Alan Tarr and Mary Cornelia Porter, "Gender Equality and Judicial Federalism: The Role of State Appellate Courts," in Marilyn Gittell, *State Politics and the New Federalism* (New York: Longman, 1986), 280-281.
29. Lawrence Baum, "Supreme Courts in the Policy Process," Chapter 7 in Van Horn, *The State of the States,* 3rd. ed., 146-150.
30. As quoted in Baum, *ibid.,* 148.
31. Thad Beyle, *State Government: CQ's Guide to Current Issues and Activities, 1996-97* (Washington, DC: Congressional Quarterly Press, 1996), 163.
32. *The Municipal Year Book, 1996,* Washington, DC: International City/County Management Association, 1996.
33. Susan Welch and Timothy Bledsoe, *Urban Reform and Its Consequences: A Study in Representation* (Chicago: University of Chicago Press, 1988), 12-15.
34. Kenneth J. Meier, Joseph Stewart, Jr., and Robert E. England, *Race, Class, and Education: The Politics of Second-Generation Discrimination* (Madison: University of Wisconsin Press, 1989).

35. John P. Pelissero and David R. Morgan, "Targeting Intergovernmental Aid to Local Schools: An Analysis of Federal and State Efforts," *Western Political Quarterly* 45 (1992): 985-999.

36. Paul E. Peterson, *City Limits* (Chicago, IL: University of Chicago Press, 1981).

37. See Clarence Stone and Heywood Sanders, eds., *The Politics of Urban Development* (Lawrence, KS: University Press of Kansas, 1987); and Mark Schneider, *The Competitive City* (Pittsburgh: University of Pittsburgh Press, 1989).

38. Jeffrey Berry, Kent Portney, and Ken Thomson, *The Rebirth of Urban Democracy* (Washington, DC: Brookings Institution, 1993).

39. David Osborne and Ted Gaebler, *Reinventing Government: How the Entrepreneurial Spirit IS Transforming the Public Sector* (Reading, MA: Addison-Wesley, 1992).

APPENDIXES

The Declaration of Independence

The Federalist No. 10

The Federalist No. 51

The Constitution of the United States of America

Presidents of the United States

Party Control of the Presidency, Senate, and House of Representatives in the Twentieth Century

Supreme Court Justices Serving in the Twentieth Century

*The Declaration of Independence**

In Congress, July 4, 1776

*This text retains the spelling, capitalization, and punctuation of the original.

THE UNANIMOUS DECLARATION OF THE THIRTEEN UNITED STATES OF AMERICA

When in the Course of human events it becomes necessary for one people to dissolve the political bands which have connected them with another, and to assume among the powers of the earth, the separate and equal station to which the Laws of Nature and of Nature's God entitle them, a decent respect to the opinions of mankind requires that they should declare the causes which impel them to the separation.

We hold these truths to be self-evident, that all men are created equal, that they are endowed by their Creator with certain unalienable Rights, that among these are Life, Liberty and the pursuit of Happiness. That to secure these rights, Governments are instituted among Men, deriving their just powers from the consent of the governed, That whenever any Form of Government becomes destructive of these ends, it is the Right of the People to alter or to abolish it, and to institute new Government, laying its foundation on such principles and organizing its powers in such form, as to them shall seem most likely to effect their Safety and Happiness. Prudence, indeed, will dictate that Governments long established should not be changed for light and transient causes; and accordingly all experience hath shewn that mankind are more disposed to suffer, while evils are sufferable, than to right themselves by abolishing the forms to which they are accustomed. But when a long train of abuses and usurpations, pursuing invariably the same Object evinces a design to reduce them under absolute Despotism, it is their right, it is their duty, to throw off such Government, and to provide new Guards for their future security. — Such has been the patient sufferance of these Colonies; and such is now the necessity which constrains them to alter their former Systems of Government. The history of the present King of Great Britain is a history of repeated injuries and usurpations, all having in direct object the establishment of an absolute Tyranny over these States. To prove this, let Facts be submitted to a candid world.

He has refused his Assent to Laws, the most wholesome and necessary for the public good.

He has forbidden his Governors to pass Laws of immediate and pressing importance, unless suspended in their operation till his Assent should be obtained; and when so suspended, he has utterly neglected to attend to them.

He has refused to pass other Laws for the accommodation of large districts of people, unless those people would relinquish the right of Representation in the Legislature, a right inestimable to them and formidable to tyrants only.

He has called together legislative bodies at places unusual, uncomfortable, and distant from the depository of their Public Records, for the sole purpose of fatiguing them into compliance with his measures.

He has dissolved Representative Houses repeatedly, for opposing with manly firmness his invasions on the rights of the people.

He has refused for a long time, after such dissolutions, to cause others to be elected; whereby the Legislative Powers, incapable of Annihilation, have returned to the People at large for their exercise; the State remaining in the mean time exposed to all the dangers of invasion from without, and convulsions within.

He has endeavored to prevent the population of these States; for that purpose obstructing the Laws for Naturalization of Foreigners; refusing to pass others to encourage their migration hither, and raising the conditions of new Appropriations of Lands.

He has obstructed the Administration of Justice, by refusing his Assent to Laws for establishing Judiciary powers.

He has made Judges dependent on his Will alone, for the tenure of their offices, and the amount and payment of their salaries.

He has erected a multitude of New Offices, and sent hither swarms of Officers to harass our people, and eat out their substance.

He has kept among us, in times of peace, Standing Armies without the Consent of our legislatures.

He has affected to render the Military independent of and superior to the Civil power.

He has combined with others to subject us to a jurisdiction foreign to our constitution, and unacknowledged by our laws; giving his Assent to their Acts of pretended Legislation:

For quartering large bodies of armed troops among us:

For protecting them, by a mock Trial, from punishment for any Murders which they should commit on the Inhabitants of these States:

For cutting off our Trade with all parts of the world:

For imposing Taxes on us without our Consent:

For depriving us in many cases, of the benefits of Trial by Jury:

For transporting us beyond Seas to be tried for pretended offences:

For abolishing the free System of English Laws in a neighboring Province, establishing therein an Arbitrary government, and enlarging its Boundaries so as to render it at once an example and fit instrument for introducing the same absolute rule into these Colonies:

For taking away our Charters, abolishing our most valuable Laws, and altering fundamentally the Forms of our Governments:

For suspending our own Legislatures, and declaring themselves invested with power to legislate for us in all cases whatsoever.

He has abdicated Government here, by declaring us out of his Protection and waging War against us.

He has plundered our seas, ravaged our Coasts, burnt our towns, and destroyed the lives of our people.

He is at this time transporting large Armies of foreign Mercenaries to compleat the works of death, desolation and tyranny, already begun with circumstances of Cruelty & perfidy scarcely paralleled in the most barbarous ages, and totally unworthy the Head of a civilized nation.

He has constrained our fellow Citizens taken Captive on the high Seas to bear Arms against their Country, to become the executioners of their friends and Brethren, or to fall themselves by their Hands.

He has excited domestic insurrections amongst us, and has endeavored to bring on the inhabitants of our frontiers, the merciless Indian Savages, whose known rule of warfare, is an undistinguished destruction of all ages, sexes and conditions.

In every stage of these Oppressions We have Petitioned for Redress in the most humble terms: Our repeated Petitions have been answered only by repeated injury. A Prince, whose character is thus marked by every act which may define a Tyrant, is unfit to be the ruler of a free people.

Nor have We been wanting in attention to our British brethren. We have warned them from time to time of attempts by their legislature to extend an unwarrantable jurisdiction over us. We have reminded them of the circumstances of our emigration and settlement here. We have appealed to their native justice and magnanimity, and we have conjured them by the ties of our common kindred to disavow these usurpations, which would inevitably interrupt our connections and correspondence. They too have been deaf to the voice of justice and consanguinity. We must, therefore, acquiesce in the necessity, which denounces our Separation, and hold them, as we hold the rest of mankind, Enemies in War, in Peace Friends.

We, therefore, the Representatives of the United States of America, in General Congress, Assembled, appealing to the Supreme Judge of the world for the rectitude of our intentions, do, in the Name, and by Authority of the good People of these Colonies, solemnly publish and declare, That these United Colonies are, and of Right ought to be Free and Independent States; that they are Absolved from all Allegiance to the British Crown, and that all political connection between them and the State of Great Britain, is and ought to be totally dissolved; and that as Free and Independent States, they have full Power to levy War, conclude Peace, contract Alliances, establish Commerce, and to do all other Acts and Things which Independent States may of right do. And for the support of this Declaration, with a firm reliance on the protection of divine Providence, we mutually pledge to each other our Lives, our Fortunes and our sacred Honor.

John Hancock

NEW HAMPSHIRE
Josiah Bartlett,
Wm. Whipple,
Matthew Thornton.

MASSACHUSETTS BAY
Saml. Adams,
John Adams,
Robt. Treat Paine,
Elbridge Gerry.

RHODE ISLAND
Step. Hopkins,
William Ellery.

CONNECTICUT
Roger Sherman,
Samuel Huntington,
Wm. Williams,
Oliver Wolcott.

NEW YORK
Wm. Floyd,
Phil. Livingston,
Frans. Lewis,
Lewis Morris.

NEW JERSEY
Richd. Stockton,
Jno. Witherspoon,
Fras. Hopkinson,
John Hart,
Abra. Clark.

PENNSYLVANIA
Robt. Morris,
Benjamin Rush,
Benjamin Franklin,
John Morton,
Geo. Clymer,
Jas. Smith,
Geo. Taylor,
James Wilson,
Geo. Ross.

DELAWARE
Caesar Rodney,
Geo. Read,
Tho. M'kean.

MARYLAND
Samuel Chase,
Wm. Paca,
Thos. Stone,
Charles Caroll of Carroll-ton.

VIRGINIA
George Wythe,
Richard Henry Lee,
Th. Jefferson,
Benjamin Harrison,
Thos. Nelson, jr.,
Francis Lightfoot Lee,
Carter Braxton.

NORTH CAROLINA
Wm. Hooper,
Joseph Hewes,
John Penn.

SOUTH CAROLINA
Edward Rutledge,
Thos. Heyward, Junr.,
Thomas Lynch, jnr.,
Arthur Middleton.

GEORGIA
Button Gwinnett,
Lyman Hall,
Geo. Walton.

The Federalist No. 10

JAMES MADISON

November 22, 1787

To the People of the State of New York.

Among the numerous advantages promised by a well constructed Union, none deserves to be more accurately developed than its tendency to break and control the violence of faction. The friend of popular governments, never finds himself so much alarmed for their character and fate, as when he contemplates their propensity to this dangerous vice. He will not fail therefore to set a due value on any plan which, without violating the principles to which he is attached, provides a proper cure for it. The instability, injustice and confusion introduced into the public councils, have in truth been the mortal diseases under which popular governments have every where perished; as they continue to be the favorite and fruitful topics from which the adversaries to liberty derive their most specious declamations. The valuable improvements made by the American Constitutions on the popular models, both ancient and modern, cannot certainly be too much admired; but it would be an unwarrantable partiality, to contend that they have as effectually obviated the danger on this side as was wished and expected. Complaints are every where heard from our most considerate and virtuous citizens, equally the friends of public and private faith, and of public and personal liberty; that our governments are too unstable; that the public good is disregarded in the conflicts of rival parties; and that measures are too often decided, not according to the rules of justice, and the rights of the minor party; but by the superior force of an interested and over-bearing majority. However anxiously we may wish that these complaints had no foundation, the evidence of known facts will not permit us to deny that they are in some degree true. It will be found indeed, on a candid review of our situation, that some of the distresses under which we labor, have been erroneously charged on the operation of our governments; but it will be found, at the same time, that other causes will not alone account for many of our heaviest misfortunes; and particularly, for that prevailing and increasing distrust of public engagements, and alarm for private rights, which are echoed from one end of the continent to the other. These must be chiefly, if not wholly, effects of the unsteadiness and injustice, with which a factious spirit has tainted our public administrations.

By a faction I understand a number of citizens, whether amounting to a majority or minority of the whole, who are united and actuated by some common impulse of passion, or of interest, adverse to the rights of other citizens, or to the permanent and aggregate interests of the community.

There are two methods of curing the mischiefs of faction: the one, by removing its causes; the other, by controlling its effects.

There are again two methods of removing the causes of faction: the one by destroying the liberty which is essential to its existence; the other, by giving to every citizen the same opinions, the same passions, and the same interests.

It could never be more truly said than of the first remedy, that it is worse than the disease. Liberty is to faction, what air is to fire, an aliment without which it instantly expires. But it could not be a less folly to abolish liberty, which is essential to political life, because it nourishes faction, than it would be to wish the annihilation of air, which is essential to animal life, because it imparts to fire its destructive agency.

The second expedient is as impracticable, as the first would be unwise. As long as the reason of man continues fallible, and he is at liberty to exercise it, different opinions will be formed. As long as the connection subsists between his reason and his self-love, his opinions and his passions will have a reciprocal influence on each other; and the former will be objects to which the latter will attach themselves. The diversity in the faculties of men from which the rights of property originate, is not less an insuperable obstacle to a uniformity of interests. The protection of these faculties is the first object of Government. From the protection of different and unequal faculties of acquiring property, the possession of different degrees and kinds of property immediately results: and from the influence of these on the sentiments and views of the respective proprietors, ensues a division of the society into different interests and parties.

The latent causes of faction are thus sown in the nature of man; and we see them every where brought into different degrees of activity, according to the different circumstances of civil society. A zeal for different opinions concerning religion, concerning Government and many other points, as well of speculation as of practice; an attachment to different leaders ambitiously contending for pre-eminence and power; or to persons of other descriptions whose fortunes have been interesting to the human passions, have in turn divided mankind into parties, inflamed them with mutual animosity, and rendered them much more disposed to vex and oppress each other, than to co-operate for their common good. So strong is this propensity of mankind to fall into mutual animosities, that where no substantial occasion presents itself, the most frivolous and fanciful distinctions have been sufficient to kindle their unfriendly passions, and excite their most violent conflicts. But the most common and durable source of factions, has been the various and unequal distribution of property. Those who hold, and those who are without property, have ever formed distinct interests in society. Those who are creditors, and those who are debtors, fall under a like discrimination. A landed interest, a manufacturing interest, a mercantile interest, a monied interest, with many lesser interests, grow up of necessity in civilized nations, and divide them into different classes, actuated by different sentiments and views. The regulation of these various and interfering interests forms the principal task of modern Legislation, and involves the spirit of party and faction in the necessary and ordinary operations of Government.

No man is allowed to be a judge in his own cause; because his interest would certainly bias his judgment, and, not improbably, corrupt his integrity. With equal, nay with greater reason, a body of men, are unfit to be both judges and parties, at the same time; yet, what are many of the most important acts of legislation, but so many judicial determinations, not indeed concerning the rights of single persons, but concerning the rights of large bodies of citizens, and what are the different classes of legislators, but advocates and parties to the causes which they determine? Is a law proposed concerning private debts? It is a question to which the creditors are parties on one side, and the debtors on the other. Justice ought to hold the balance between them. Yet the parties are and must be themselves the judges; and the most numerous party, or, in other words, the most powerful faction must be expected to prevail. Shall domestic manufactures be encouraged, and in what degree, by restrictions on foreign manufactures? are questions which would be differently decided by the landed and the manufacturing classes; and probably by neither, with a sole regard to justice and the public good. The apportionment of taxes on the various descriptions of property, is an act which seems to require the most exact impartiality; yet, there is perhaps no legislative act in which greater opportunity and temptation are given to a predominant party, to trample on the rules of justice. Every shilling with which they over-burden the inferior number, is a shilling saved to their own pockets.

It is in vain to say, that enlightened statesmen will be able to adjust these clashing interests, and render them all subservient to the public good. Enlightened statesmen will not always be at the helm: Nor, in many cases, can such an adjustment be made at all, without taking into view indirect and remote considerations, which will rarely prevail over the immediate interest which one party may find in disregarding the rights of another, or the good of the whole.

The inference to which we are brought, is, that the *causes* of faction cannot be removed; and that relief is only to be sought in the means of controlling its *effects*.

If a faction consists of less than a majority, relief is supplied by the republican principle, which enables the majority to defeat its sinister views by regular vote: It may clog the administration, it may convulse the society; but it will be unable to execute and mask its violence under the forms of the Constitution. When a majority is included in a faction, the form of popular government on the other hand enables it to sacrifice to its ruling passion or interest, both the public good and the rights of other citizens. To secure the public good, and private rights, against the danger of such a faction, and at the same time to preserve the spirit and the form of popular government, is then the great object to which our enquiries are directed: Let me add that it is the great desideratum, by which alone this form of government can be rescued from the opprobrium under which it has so long labored, and be recommended to the esteem and adoption of mankind.

By what means is this object attainable? Evidently by one of two only. Either the existence of the same passion or interest in a majority at the same time, must be prevented; or the majority, having such co-existent passion or interest, must be rendered, by their number and local situation, unable to concert and carry into effect schemes of oppression. If the impulse and the opportunity be suffered to coincide, we well know that neither moral nor religious motives can be relied on as an adequate control. They are not found to be such on the injustice and violence of individuals, and lose their efficacy in proportion to the number combined together; that is, in proportion as their efficacy becomes needful.

From this view of the subject, it may be concluded, that a pure Democracy, by which I mean, a Society, consisting of a small number of citizens, who assemble and administer the Government in person, can admit of no cure for the mischiefs of faction. A common passion or interest will, in almost every case, be felt by a majority of the whole; a communication and concert results from the form of Government itself; and there is nothing to check the inducements to sacrifice the weaker party, or an obnoxious individual. Hence it is, that such Democracies have ever been spectacles of turbulence and contention; have ever been found incompatible with personal security, or the rights of property; and have in general been as short in their lives, as they have been violent in their deaths. Theoretic politicians, who have patronized this species of Government, have erroneously supposed, that by reducing mankind to a perfect equality in their political rights, they would, at the same time, be perfectly equalized and assimilated in their possessions, their opinions, and their passions.

A republic, by which I mean a government in which the scheme of representation takes place, opens a different prospect, and promises the cure for which we are seeking. Let us examine the points in which it varies from pure democracy, and we shall comprehend both the nature of the cure and the efficacy which it must derive from the union.

The two great points of difference, between a democracy and a republic, are, first, the delegation of the government, in the latter, to a small number of citizens, elected by the rest; secondly, the greater number of citizens, and greater sphere of country, over which the latter may be extended.

The effect of the first difference is, on the one hand, to refine and enlarge the public views, by passing them through the medium of a chosen body of citizens, whose wisdom may best discern the true interest of their country, and whose patriotism and love of justice, will be least likely to sacrifice it to temporary or partial considerations. Under such a regulation, it may well happen, that the public voice, pronounced by the representatives of the people, will be more consonant to the public good, than if pronounced by the people themselves, convened for the purpose. On the other hand the effect may be inverted. Men of factious tempers, of local prejudices, or of sinister designs, may by intrigue, by corruption, or by other means, first obtain the suffrages, and then betray the interest of the people. The question resulting is, whether small or extensive republics are most favorable to the election of proper guardians of the public weal, and it is clearly decided in favor of the latter by two obvious considerations.

In the first place, it is to be remarked that, however small the republic may be, the representatives must be raised to a certain number, in order to guard against the cabals of a few; and that however large it may be, they must be limited to a certain number, in order to guard against the confusion of a multitude. Hence, the number of representatives in the two cases not being in proportion to that of the constituents, and being proportionally greatest in the small republic, it follows, that if the proportion of fit characters be not less in the large than in the small republic, the former will present a greater option, and consequently a greater probability of a fit choice.

In the next place, as each Representative will be chosen by a greater number of citizens in the large than in the small Republic, it will be more difficult for unworthy candidates to practise with success the vicious arts, by which elections are too often carried; and the suffrages of the people being more free, will be more likely to center on men who possess the most attractive merit, and the most diffusive and established characters.

It must be confessed, that in this, as in most other cases, there is a mean, on both sides of which inconveniences will be found to lie. By enlarging too much the number of electors, you render the representative too little acquainted with all their local circumstances and lesser interests; as by reducing it too much, you render him unduly attached to these, and too little fit to comprehend and pursue great and national objects. The Federal Constitution forms a happy combination in this respect; the great and aggregate interests being referred to the national, the local and particular, to the state legislatures.

The other point of difference is, the greater number of citizens and extent of territory which may be brought within the compass of Republican, than of Democratic Government; and it is this circumstance principally which renders factious combinations less to be dreaded in the former, than in the latter. The smaller the society, the fewer probably will be the distinct parties and interests composing it; the fewer the distinct parties and interests, the more frequently will a majority be found of the same party; and the smaller the number of individuals composing a majority, and the smaller the compass within which they are placed, the more easily will they concert and execute their plans of oppression. Extend the sphere, and you take in a greater variety of parties and interests; you make it less probable that a majority of the whole will have a common motive to invade the rights of other citizens; or if such a common motive exists, it will be more difficult for all who feel it to discover their own strength, and to act in unison with each other. Besides other impediments, it may be remarked, that where there is a consciousness of unjust or dishonorable purposes, communication is always checked by distrust, in proportion to the number whose concurrence is necessary.

Hence it clearly appears, that the same advantage, which a Republic has over a Democracy, in controlling the effects of faction, is enjoyed by a large over a small Republic—is enjoyed by the Union over the States composing it. Does this advantage consist in the substitution of Representatives, whose enlightened views and virtuous sentiments render them superior to local prejudices, and to schemes of injustice? It will not be denied, that the Representation of the Union will be most likely to possess these requisite endowments. Does it consist in the greater security afforded by a greater variety of parties, against the event of any one party being able to outnumber and oppress the rest? In an equal degree does the increased variety of parties, comprised within the Union, increase this security?

Does it, in fine, consist in the greater obstacles opposed to the concert and accomplishment of the secret wishes of an unjust and interested majority? Here, again, the extent of the Union gives it the most palpable advantage.

The influence of factious leaders may kindle a flame within their particular States, but will be unable to spread a general conflagration through the other States: a religious sect may degenerate into a political faction in a part of the Confederacy but the variety of sects dispersed over the entire face of it, must secure the national Councils against any danger from that source: a rage for paper money, for an abolition of debts, for an equal division of property, or for any other improper or wicked project, will be less apt to pervade the whole body of the Union, than a particular member of it; in the same proportion as such a malady is more likely to taint a particular county or district, than an entire State.

In the extent and proper structure of the Union, therefore, we behold a Republican remedy for the diseases most incident to Republican Government. And according to the degree of pleasure and pride, we feel in being Republicans, ought to be our zeal in cherishing the spirit, and supporting the character of Federalists.

PUBLIUS

The Federalist No. 51

JAMES MADISON

February 6, 1788

To the People of the State of New York.

To what expedient then shall we finally resort for maintaining in practice the necessary partition of power among the several departments, as laid down in the constitution? The only answer that can be given is, that as all these exterior provisions are found to be inadequate, the defect must be supplied, by so contriving the interior structure of the government, as that its several constituent parts may, by their mutual relations, be the means of keeping each other in their proper places. Without presuming to undertake a full development of this important idea, I will hazard a few general observations, which may perhaps place it in a clearer light, and enable us to form a more correct judgment of the principles and structure of the government planned by the convention.

In order to lay a due foundation for that separate and distinct exercise of the different powers of government, which to a certain extent, is admitted on all hands to be essential to the preservation of liberty, it is evident that each department should have a will of its own; and consequently should be so constituted, that the members of each should have as little agency as possible in the appointment of the members of the others. Were this principle rigorously adhered to, it would require that all the appointments for the supreme executive, legislative, and judiciary magistracies, should be drawn from the same fountain of authority, the people, through channels, having no communication whatever with one another. Perhaps such a plan of constructing the several departments would be less difficult in practice than it may in contemplation appear. Some difficulties however, and some additional expense, would attend the execution of it. Some deviations therefore from the principle must be admitted. In the constitution of the judiciary department in particular, it might be inexpedient to insist rigorously on the principle; first, because peculiar qualifications being essential in the members, the primary consideration ought to be to select that mode of choice, which best secures these qualifications; secondly, because the permanent tenure by which the appointments are held in that department, must soon destroy all sense of dependence on the authority conferring them.

It is equally evident that the members of each department should be as little dependent as possible on those of the others, for the emoluments annexed to their offices. Were the executive magistrate, or the judges, not independent of the legislature in this particular, their independence in every other would be merely nominal.

But the great security against a gradual concentration of the several powers in the same department, consists in giving to those who administer each department, the necessary constitutional means, and personal motives, to resist encroachments of the others. The provision for defense must in this, as in all other cases, be made commensurate to the danger of attack. Ambition must be made to counteract ambition. The interest of the man must be connected with the constitutional right of the place. It may be a reflection on human nature, that such devices should be necessary to control the abuses of government. But what is government itself but the greatest of all reflections on human nature? If men were angels, no government would be necessary. If angels were to govern men, neither external nor internal controls on government would be necessary. In framing a government which is to be administered by men over men, the great difficulty lies in this: You must first enable the government to control the governed; and in the next place, oblige it to control itself. A dependence on the people is no doubt the primary control on the government; but experience has taught mankind the necessity of auxiliary precautions.

This policy of supplying by opposite and rival interests, the defect of better motives, might be traced through the whole system of human affairs, private as well as public. We see it particularly displayed in all the subordinate distributions of power; where the constant aim is to divide and arrange the several offices in such a manner as that each may be a check on the other; that the private interest of every individual, may be a sentinel over the public rights. These inventions of prudence cannot be less requisite in the distribution of the supreme powers of the state.

But it is not possible to give to each department an equal power of self defense. In republican government the legislative authority, necessarily, predominates. The remedy for this inconveniency is, to divide the legislature into different branches; and to render them by different modes of election, and different principles of action, as little connected with each other, as the nature of their common functions, and their common dependence on the society, will admit. It may even be necessary to guard against dangerous encroachments by still further precautions. As the weight of the legislative authority requires that it should be thus

divided, the weakness of the executive may require, on the other hand, that it should be fortified. An absolute negative, on the legislature, appears at first view to be the natural defense with which the executive magistrate should be armed. But perhaps it would be neither altogether safe, nor alone sufficient. On ordinary occasions, it might not be exerted with the requisite firmness; and on extraordinary occasions, it might be prefidiously abused. May not this defect of an absolute negative be supplied, by some qualified connection between this weaker department, and the weaker branch of the stronger department, by which the latter may be led to support the constitutional rights of the former, without being too much detached from the rights of its own department?

If the principles on which these observations are founded be just, as I persuade myself they are, and they be applied as a criterion, to the several state constitutions, and to the federal constitution, it will be found, that if the latter does not perfectly correspond with them, the former are infinitely less able to bear such a test.

There are moreover two considerations particularly applicable to the federal system of America, which place that system in a very interesting point of view.

First. In a single republic, all the power surrendered by the people, is submitted to the administration of a single government; and usurpations are guarded against by a division of the government into distinct and separate departments. In the compound republic of America, the power surrendered by the people, is first divided between two distinct governments, and then the portion allotted to each, subdivided among distinct and separate departments. Hence a double security arises to the rights of the people. The different governments will control each other; at the same time that each will be controlled by itself.

Second. It is of great importance in a republic, not only to guard the society against the oppression of its rulers; but to guard one part of the society against the injustice of the other part. Different interests necessarily exist in different classes of citizens. If a majority be united by a common interest, the rights of the minority will be insecure. There are but two methods of providing against this evil: The one by creating a will in the community independent of the majority, that is, of the society itself, the other by comprehending in the society so many separate descriptions of citizens, as will render an unjust combination of a majority of the whole, very improbable, if not impracticable. The first method prevails in all governments possessing an hereditary or self appointed authority. This at best is but a precarious security; because a power independent of the society may as well espouse the unjust views of the major, as the rightful interests, of the minor party, and may possibly be turned against both parties. The second method will be exemplified in the federal republic of the United States. While all authority in it will be derived from and dependent on the society, the society itself will be broken into so many parts, interests and classes of citizens, that the rights of individuals or of the minority, will be in little danger from interested combinations of the majority. In a free government, the security for civil rights must be the same as for religious rights. It consists in the one case in the multiplicity of interests, and in the other, in the multiplicity of sects. The degree of security in both cases will depend on the number of interests and sects; and this may be presumed to depend on the extent of country and number of people comprehended under the same government. This view of the subject must particularly recommend a proper federal system to all the sincere and considerate friends of republican government: Since it shows that in exact proportion as the territory of the union may be formed into more circumscribed confederacies or states, oppressive combinations of a majority will be facilitated, the best security under the republican form, for the rights of every class of citizens, will be diminished; and consequently, the stability and independence of some member of the government, the only other security, must be proportionally increased. Justice is the end of government. It is the end of civil society. It ever has been, and ever will be pursued, until it be obtained, or until liberty be lost in the pursuit. In a society under the forms of which the stronger faction can readily unite and oppress the weaker, anarchy may as truly be said to reign, as in a state of nature where the weaker individual is not secured against the violence of the stronger: And as in the latter state even the stronger individuals are prompted by the uncertainty of their condition, to submit to a government which may protect the weak as well as themselves: So in the former state, will the more powerful factions or parties be gradually induced by a like motive, to wish for a government which will protect all parties, the weaker as well as the more powerful. It can be little doubted, that if the state of Rhode Island was separated from the confederacy, and left to itself, the insecurity of rights under the popular form of government within such narrow limits, would be displayed by such reiterated oppressions of factious majorities, that some power altogether independent of the people would soon be called for by the voice of the very factions whose misrule had proved the necessity of it. In the extended republic of the United States, and among the great variety of interests, parties and sects which it embraces, a coalition of a majority of the whole society could seldom take place

on any other principles than those of justice and the general good; and there being thus less danger to a minor from the will of the major party, there must be less pretext also, to provide for the security of the former, by introducing into the government a will not dependent on the latter; or in other words, a will independent of the society itself. It is no less certain than it is important, notwithstanding the contrary opinions which have been entertained, that the larger the society, provided it lie within a practicable sphere, the more duly capable it will be of self government. And happily for the *republican cause,* the practicable sphere may be carried to a very great extent, by a judicious modification and mixture of the *federal principle.*

PUBLIUS

The Constitution of the United States of America*

*This text retains the spelling, capitalization, and punctuation of the original. Brackets indicate passages that have been altered by amendments.

(PREAMBLE)

We the People of the United States, in Order to form a more perfect Union, establish Justice, insure domestic Tranquility, provide for the common defence, promote the general Welfare, and secure the Blessings of Liberty to ourselves and our Posterity, do ordain and establish this Constitution for the United States of America.

ARTICLE I.

(THE LEGISLATURE)

Section 1. All legislative Powers herein granted shall be vested in a Congress of the United States, which shall consist of a Senate and House of Representatives.

Section 2. The House of Representatives shall be composed of Members chosen every second Year by the People of the several States, and the Electors in each State shall have the Qualifications requisite for Electors of the most numerous Branch of the State Legislature.

No person shall be a Representative who shall not have attained to the Age of twenty five Years, and been seven Years a Citizen of the United States, and who shall not, when elected, be an Inhabitant of that State in which he shall be chosen.

Representatives and direct [Taxes][1] shall be apportioned among the several States which may be included within this Union, according to their respective Numbers [which shall be determined by adding to the whole Number of free Persons, including those bound to Service for a Term of Years, and excluding Indians not taxed, three fifths of all other Persons].[2] The actual Enumeration shall be made within three Years after the first Meeting of the Congress of the United States, and within every subsequent Term of ten Years, in such Manner as they shall by Law direct. The Number of Representatives shall not exceed one for every thirty Thousand, but each State shall have at Least one Representative; and until such enumeration shall be made, the State of New Hampshire shall be entitled to chuse three, Massachusetts eight, Rhode-Island and Providence Plantations one, Connecticut five, New-York six, New Jersey four, Pennsylvania eight, Delaware one, Maryland six, Virginia ten, North Carolina five, South Carolina five, and Georgia three.

When vacancies happen in the Representation from any State, the Executive Authority thereof shall issue Writs of Election to fill such Vacancies.

The House of Representatives shall chuse their speaker and other Officers; and shall have the sole Power of Impeachment.

Section 3. The Senate of the United States shall be composed of two Senators from each State [chosen by the Legislature thereof],[3] for six Years; and each Senator shall have one Vote.

Immediately after they shall be assembled in Consequence of the first Election, they shall be divided as equally as may be into three Classes. The Seats of the Senators of the first Class shall be vacated at the Expiration of the second year, of the second Class at the Expiration of the fourth Year, and of the third Class at the Expiration of the sixth Year, so that one third may be chosen every second Year [and if Vacancies happen by Resignation, or otherwise, during the Recess of the Legislature of any State, the Executive thereof may make temporary Appointments until the next Meeting of the Legislature, which shall then fill such Vacancies].[4]

No Person shall be a Senator who shall not have attained to the Age of thirty Years, and been nine Years a Citizen of the United States, and who shall not, when elected, be an Inhabitant of that State for which he shall be chosen.

The Vice President of the United States shall be President of the Senate, but shall have no Vote, unless they be equally divided.

[1] See Amendment XVI.

[2] See Amendment XIV.

[3] See Amendment XVII.

[4] See Amendment XVII.

The Senate shall chuse their other Officers, and also a President pro tempore, in the Absence of the Vice President, or when he shall exercise the Office of President of the United States.

The Senate shall have the sole Power to try all Impeachments. When sitting for that Purpose, they shall be on Oath or Affirmation. When the President of the United States is tried, the Chief Justice shall preside: And no Person shall be convicted without the Concurrence of two thirds of the Members present.

Judgment in Cases of Impeachment shall not extend further than to removal from Office, and disqualification to hold and enjoy any Office of honor, Trust or Profit under the United States; but the Party convicted shall nevertheless be liable and subject to Indictment, Trial, Judgment and Punishment, according to Law.

Section 4. The Times, Places and Manner of holding Elections for Senators and Representatives, shall be prescribed in each State by the Legislature thereof; but the Congress may at any time by Law make or alter such Regulations, except as to the Places of chusing Senators.

[The Congress shall assemble at least once in every Year, and such Meeting shall be on the first Monday in December, unless they shall by Law appoint a different Day.][5]

Section 5. Each House shall be the Judge of the Elections, Returns and Qualifications of its own Members, and a Majority of each shall constitute a Quorum to do Business; but a smaller Number may adjourn from day to day, and may be authorized to compel the Attendance of absent Members, in such Manner, and under such Penalties as each House may provide.

Each House may determine the Rules of its Proceedings, punish its Members for disorderly Behaviour, and, with the Concurrence of two thirds, expel a Member.

Each House shall keep a Journal of its Proceedings, and from time to time publish the same, excepting such Parts as may in their judgment require Secrecy; and the Yeas and Nays of the Members of either House on any question shall, at the Desire of one fifth of those present, be entered on the Journal.

Neither House, during the Session of Congress, shall, without the Consent of the other, adjourn for more than three days, nor to any other Place than that in which the two Houses shall be sitting.

[5] See Amendment XX.

Section 6. The Senators and Representatives shall receive a Compensation for their Services, to be ascertained by Law, and paid out of the Treasury of the United States. They shall in all Cases, except Treason, Felony and Breach of the Peace, be privileged from Arrest during their Attendance at the Session of their respective Houses, and in going to and returning from the same; and for any Speech or Debate in either House, they shall not be questioned in any other Place.

No Senator or Representative shall, during the Time for which he was elected, be appointed to any civil Office under the Authority of the United States, which shall have been created, or the Emoluments whereof shall have been encreased during such time; and no Person holding any Office under the United States, shall be a Member of either House during his Continuance in Office.

Section 7. All Bills for raising Revenue shall originate in the House of Representatives; but the Senate may propose or concur with Amendments as on other Bills.

Every Bill which shall have passed the House of Representatives and the Senate, shall, before it becomes a Law, be presented to the President of the United States; If he approves he shall sign it, but if not he shall return it, with his Objections to that House in which it shall have originated, who shall enter the Objections at large on their Journal, and proceed to reconsider it. If after such Reconsideration two thirds of that House shall agree to pass the Bill, it shall be sent, together with the Objections, to the other House, by which it shall likewise be reconsidered, and if approved by two thirds of that House, it shall become a Law. But in all such Cases the Votes of both Houses shall be determined by yeas and Nays, and the Names of the Persons voting for and against the Bill shall be entered on the Journal of each House respectively. If any Bill shall not be returned by the President within ten Days (Sundays excepted) after it shall have been presented to him, the Same shall be a Law, in like Manner as if he had signed it, unless the Congress by their Adjournment prevent its Return, in which Case it shall not be a Law.

Every Order, Resolution, or Vote to which the Concurrence of the Senate and House of Representatives may be necessary (except on a question of Adjournment) shall be presented to the President of the United States; and before the Same shall take Effect, shall be approved by him, or being disapproved by him, shall be repassed by two thirds of the Senate and House of Representatives, according to the Rules and Limitations prescribed in the Case of a Bill.

Section 8. The Congress shall have Power To lay and collect Taxes, Duties, Imposts and Excises, to pay the Debts and provide for the common Defence and general Welfare of the United States; but all Duties, Imposts and Excises shall be uniform throughout the United States;

To borrow Money on the credit of the United States;

To regulate Commerce with foreign Nations, and among the several States, and with the Indian Tribes;

To establish a uniform Rule of Naturalization, and uniform Laws on the subject of Bankruptcies throughout the United States;

To coin Money, regulate the Value thereof, and of foreign Coin, and fix the Standard of Weights and Measures;

To provide for the Punishment of counterfeiting the Securities and current Coin of the United States;

To establish Post Offices and post Roads;

To promote the Progress of Science and useful Arts, by securing for limited Times to Authors and Inventors the exclusive Right to their respective Writings and Discoveries;

To constitute Tribunals inferior to the supreme Court;

To define and punish Piracies and Felonies committed on the high Seas, and Offences against the Law of Nations;

To declare War, grant Letters of Marque and Reprisal, and make Rules concerning Captures on Land and Water;

To raise and support Armies, but no Appropriation of Money to that Use shall be for a longer Term than two Years;

To provide and maintain a Navy;

To make Rules for the Government and Regulation of the land and naval Forces;

To provide for calling forth the Militia to execute the Laws of the Union, suppress Insurrections and repel Invasions;

To provide for organizing, arming, and disciplining, the Militia, and for governing such Part of them as may be employed in the Service of the United States, reserving to the States respectively, the Appointment of the Officers, and the Authority of training the Militia according to the discipline prescribed by Congress;

To exercise exclusive Legislation in all Cases whatsoever, over such District (not exceeding ten Miles square) as may, by Cession of particular States, and the Acceptance of Congress, become the Seat of the Government of the United States, and to exercise like Authority over all Places purchased by the Consent of the Legislature of the State in which the Same shall be, for the Erection of Forts, Magazines, Arsenals, dock-Yards, and other needful Buildings;—And

To make all Laws which shall be necessary and proper for carrying into Execution the foregoing Powers, and all other Powers vested by this Constitution in the Government of the United States, or in any Department or Officer thereof.

Section 9. The Migration or Importation of such Persons as any of the States now existing shall think proper to admit, shall not be prohibited by the Congress prior to the Year one thousand eight hundred and eight, but a Tax or duty may be imposed on such Importation, not exceeding ten dollars for each Person.

The Privilege of the Writ of Habeas Corpus shall not be suspended, unless when in Cases of Rebellion or Invasion the public Safety may require it.

No Bill of Attainder or ex post facto Law shall be passed.

[No Capitation, or other direct, Tax shall be laid, unless in Proportion to the Census or Enumeration herein before directed to be taken.][6]

No Tax or Duty shall be laid on Articles exported from any State.

No Preference shall be given by any Regulation of Commerce or Revenue to the Ports of one State over those of another; nor shall Vessels bound to, or from, one State, be obliged to enter, clear, or pay Duties in another.

No Money shall be drawn from the Treasury, but in Consequence of Appropriations made by Law; and a regular Statement and Account of the Receipts and Expenditures of all public Money shall be published from time to time.

No Title of Nobility shall be granted by the United States: And no Person holding any Office of Profit or Trust under them, shall, without the Consent of the

[6] See Amendment XVI.

Congress, accept of any present, Emolument, Office, or Title, of any kind whatever, from any King, Prince, or foreign State.

Section 10. No State shall enter into any Treaty, Alliance, or Confederation; grant Letters of Marque and Reprisal; coin Money; emit Bills of Credit; make any Thing but gold and silver Coin a Tender in Payment of Debts; pass any Bill of Attainder, ex post facto Law, or Law impairing the Obligation of Contracts, or grant any Title of Nobility.

No State shall, without the Consent of the Congress, lay any Imposts or Duties on Imports or Exports, except what may be absolutely necessary for executing its inspection Laws: and the net Produce of all Duties and Imposts, laid by any State on Imports or Exports, shall be for the Use of the Treasury of the United States; and all such Laws shall be subject to the Revision and Controul of the Congress.

No State shall, without the Consent of Congress, lay any Duty of Tonnage, keep Troops, or Ships of War in time of Peace, enter into any Agreement or Compact with another State, or with a foreign Power, or engage in War, unless actually invaded, or in such imminent Danger as will not admit of delay.

ARTICLE II.

(THE EXECUTIVE)

Section 1. The executive Power shall be vested in a President of the United States of America. He shall hold his Office during the Term of four Years, and, together with the Vice President, chosen for the same Term, be elected, as follows.

Each State shall appoint, in such Manner as the Legislature thereof may direct, a Number of Electors, equal to the whole Number of Senators and Representatives to which the State may be entitled in the Congress; but no Senator or Representative, or Person holding an Office of Trust or Profit under the United States, shall be appointed an Elector.

[The Electors shall meet in their respective States, and vote by Ballot for two Persons, of whom one at least shall not be an Inhabitant of the same State with themselves. And they shall make a List of all the Persons voted for, and of the Number of Votes for each; which List they shall sign and certify, and transmit sealed to the Seat of the Government of the United States, directed to the President of the Senate. The President of the Senate shall, in the Presence of the Senate and House of Representatives, open all the Certificates, and the Votes shall then be counted. The Person having the greatest Number of Votes shall be the President, if such Number be a Majority of the whole Number of Electors appointed; and if there be more than one who have such Majority, and have an equal Number of Votes, then the House of Representatives shall immediately chuse by Ballot one of them for President; and if no Person have a Majority, then from the five highest on the List the said House shall in like Manner chuse the President. But in chusing the President, the Votes shall be taken by States, the Representation from each State having one Vote; A quorum for this Purpose shall consist of a Member or Members from two thirds of the States, and a Majority of all the States shall be necessary to a Choice. In every Case, after the Choice of the President, the Person having the greatest Number of Votes of the Electors shall be the Vice President. But if there should remain two or more who have equal Votes, the Senate shall chuse from them by Ballot the Vice President.][7]

The Congress may determine the Time of chusing the Electors, and the Day on which they shall give their Votes; which Day shall be the same throughout the United States.

No Person except a natural born Citizen, or a Citizen of the United States, at the time of the Adoption of this Constitution, shall be eligible to the Office of President; neither shall any Person be eligible to that Office who shall not have attained to the Age of thirty five Years, and been fourteen Years a Resident within the United States.

[In Case of the Removal of the President from Office, or of his Death, Resignation, or Inability to discharge the Powers and Duties of the said Office, the Same shall devolve on the Vice President, and the Congress may by Law provide for the Case of Removal, Death, Resignation or Inability, both of the President and Vice President, declaring what Officer shall then act as President, and such Officer shall act accordingly, until the Disability be removed, or a President shall be elected.][8]

The President shall, at stated Times, receive for his Services, a Compensation, which shall neither be encreased nor diminished during the Period for

[7] See Amendment XII.

[8] See Amendment XXV.

which he shall have been elected, and he shall not receive within that Period any other Emolument from the United States, or any of them.

Before he enter on the Execution of his Office, he shall take the following Oath or Affirmation:—"I do solemnly swear (or affirm) that I will faithfully execute the Office of President of the United States, and will to the best of my Ability, preserve, protect and defend the Constitution of the United States."

Section 2. The President shall be Commander in Chief of the Army and Navy of the United States, and of the Militia of the several States, when called into the actual Service of the United States; he may require the Opinion, in writing, of the principal Officer in each of the executive Departments, upon any Subject relating to the Duties of their respective Offices, and he shall have Power to grant Reprieves and Pardons for Offences against the United States, except in Cases of Impeachment.

He shall have Power, by and with the Advice and Consent of the Senate, to make Treaties, provided two thirds of the Senators present concur; and he shall nominate, and by and with the Advice and Consent of the Senate, shall appoint Ambassadors, other public Ministers and Consuls, Judges of the supreme Court, and all other Officers of the United States, whose Appointments are not herein otherwise provided for, and which shall be established by Law: but the Congress may by Law vest the Appointment of such inferior Officers, as they think proper, in the President alone, in the Courts of Law, or in the Heads of Departments.

The President shall have Power to fill up all Vacancies that may happen during the Recess of the Senate, by granting Commissions which shall expire at the end of their next Session.

Section 3. He shall from time to time give to the Congress Information of the State of the Union, and recommend to their Consideration such Measures as he shall judge necessary and expedient; he may, on extraordinary Occasions, convene both Houses, or either of them, and in Case of Disagreement between them, with Respect to the Time of Adjournment, he may adjourn them to such Time as he shall think proper; he shall receive Ambassadors and other public Ministers; he shall take Care that the Laws be faithfully executed, and shall Commission all the Officers of the United States.

Section 4. The President, Vice President and all civil Officers of the United States, shall be removed from Office on Impeachment for, and Conviction of, Treason, Bribery, or other high Crimes and Misdemeanors.

ARTICLE III.

(THE JUDICIARY)

Section 1. The judicial Power of the United States, shall be vested in one supreme Court, and in such inferior Courts as the Congress may from time to time ordain and establish. The Judges, both of the supreme and inferior Courts, shall hold their Offices during good Behaviour, and shall, at stated Times, receive for their Services, a Compensation, which shall not be diminished during their Continuance in Office.

Section 2. The judicial Power shall extend to all Cases, in Law and Equity, arising under this Constitution, the Laws of the United States, and Treaties made, or which shall be made, under their Authority;—to all Cases affecting Ambassadors, other public Ministers and Consuls;—to all Cases of admiralty and maritime Jurisdiction;—to Controversies to which the United States shall be a Party;—to Controversies between two or more States; [—between a State and Citizens of another State;—][9] between Citizens of different States,—between Citizens of the same State claiming Lands under Grants of different States, [and between a State, or the Citizens thereof, and foreign States, Citizens or Subjects.][10]

In all Cases affecting Ambassadors, other public Ministers and Consuls, and those in which a State shall be Party, the supreme Court shall have original Jurisdiction. In all the other Cases before mentioned, the supreme Court shall have appellate Jurisdiction, both as to Law and Fact, with such Exceptions, and under such Regulations as the Congress shall make.

The Trial of all Crimes, except in Cases of Impeachment, shall be by Jury; and such Trial shall be held in the State where the said Crimes shall have been committed; but when not committed within any State, the Trial shall be at such Place or Places as the Congress may by Law have directed.

Section 3. Treason against the United States, shall consist only in levying War against them, or in adhering to their Enemies, giving them Aid and Comfort. No Person shall be convicted of Treason unless on the Testimony of two Witnesses to the same overt Act, or on Confession in open Court.

The Congress shall have Power to declare the Punishment of Treason, but no Attainder of Treason shall

[9] See Amendment XI.

[10] See Amendment XI.

work Corruption of Blood, or Forfeiture except during the Life of the Person attainted.

ARTICLE IV.

(INTERSTATE RELATIONS)

Section 1. Full Faith and Credit shall be given in each State to the public Acts, Records, and judicial Proceedings of every other State. And the Congress may by general Laws prescribe the Manner in which such Acts, Records and Proceedings shall be proved, and the Effect thereof.

Section 2. The Citizens of each State shall be entitled to all Privileges and Immunities of Citizens in the several States.

A Person charged in any State with Treason, Felony, or other Crime, who shall flee from Justice, and be found in another State, shall on Demand of the executive Authority of the State from which he fled, be delivered up, to be removed to the State having Jurisdiction of the Crime.

[No Person held to Service or Labour in one State under the Laws thereof, escaping into another, shall, in Consequence of any Law or Regulation therein, be discharged from such Service or Labour, but shall be delivered up on Claim of the Party to whom such Service or Labour may be due.][11]

Section 3. New States may be admitted by the Congress into this Union; but no new State shall be formed or erected within the Jurisdiction of any other State; nor any State be formed by the Junction of two or more States, or Parts of States, without the Consent of the Legislatures of the States concerned as well as of the Congress.

The Congress shall have Power to dispose of and make all needful Rules and Regulations respecting the Territory or other Property belonging to the United States; and nothing in this Constitution shall be so construed as to Prejudice any Claims of the United States, or of any particular State.

Section 4. The United States shall guarantee to every State in this Union a Republican Form of Government, and shall protect each of them against Invasion, and on Application of the Legislature, or of the Executive (when the Legislature cannot be convened) against domestic Violence.

[11] See Amendment XIII.

ARTICLE V.

(AMENDING THE CONSTITUTION)

The Congress, whenever two thirds of both Houses shall deem it necessary, shall propose Amendments to this Constitution, or, on the Application of the Legislatures of two thirds of the several States, shall call a Convention for proposing Amendments, which, in either Case, shall be valid to all Intents and Purposes, as Part of this Constitution, when ratified by the Legislatures of three fourths of the several States, or by Conventions in three fourths thereof, as the one or the other Mode of Ratification may be proposed by the Congress; Provided that no Amendment which may be made prior to the Year One thousand eight hundred and eight shall in any Manner affect the first and fourth Clauses in the Ninth Section of the first Article; and that no State, without its Consent, shall be deprived of its equal Suffrage in the Senate.

ARTICLE VI.

(DEBTS, SUPREMACY, OATHS)

All Debts contracted and Engagements entered into, before the Adoption of this Constitution, shall be as valid against the United States under this Constitution, as under the Confederation.

This Constitution, and the laws of the United States which shall be made in Pursuance thereof; and all Treaties made, or which shall be made, under the Authority of the United States, shall be the supreme Law of the Land; and the Judges in every State shall be bound thereby, any Thing in the Constitution or Laws of any State to the Contrary notwithstanding.

The Senators and Representatives before mentioned, and the Members of the several State Legislatures, and all executive and judicial Officers, both of the United States and of the several States, shall be bound by Oath or Affirmation, to support this Constitution; but no religious Test shall ever be required as a Qualification to any Office or public Trust under the United States.

ARTICLE VII.

(RATIFYING THE CONSTITUTION)

The Ratification of the Conventions of nine States, shall be sufficient for the Establishment of this Constitution between the States so ratifying the Same.

Done in Convention by the Unanimous Consent of the States present the Seventeenth Day of September in the Year of our Lord one thousand seven hundred and Eighty seven and of the Independence of the United States of America the Twelfth. IN WITNESS whereof we have hereunto subscribed our Names.

Go. WASHINGTON
Presid't. and deputy from Virginia

Attest
William Jackson
Secretary

DELAWARE
Geo. Read
Gunning Bedford jun
John Dickinson
Richard Basset
Jaco. Broom

MASSACHUSETTS
Nathaniel Gorbam
Rufus King

CONNECTICUT
Wm. Saml. Johnson
Roger Sherman

NEW YORK
Alexander Hamilton

NEW JERSEY
Wh. Livingston
David Brearley
Wm. Paterson
Jona. Dayton

PENNSYLVANIA
B. Franklin
Thomas Mifflin
Robt. Morris
Geo. Clymer
Thos. FitzSimons
Jared Ingersoll
James Wilson
Gouv. Morris

NEW HAMPSHIRE
John Langdon
Nicholas Gilman

MARYLAND
James McHenry
Dan of St. Thos. Jenifer
Danl. Carroll

VIRGINIA
John Blair
James Madison Jr.

NORTH CAROLINA
Wm. Blount
Richd. Dobbs Spaight
Hu. Williamson

SOUTH CAROLINA
J. Rutledge
Charles Cotesworth Pinckney
Charles Pinckney
Pierce Butler

GEORGIA
William Few
Abr. Baldwin

Articles in addition to, and amendment of the Constitution of the United States of America, proposed by Congress and ratified by the Legislatures of the several states, pursuant to the Fifth Article of the original Constitution.

(The first ten amendments were passed by Congress on September 25, 1789, and were ratified on December 15, 1791.)

AMENDMENT I—*RELIGION, SPEECH, ASSEMBLY, PETITION*

Congress shall make no law respecting an establishment of religion, or prohibiting the free exercise thereof; or abridging the freedom of speech, or of the press; or the right of the people peaceably to assemble, and to petition the Government for a redress of grievances.

AMENDMENT II—*RIGHT TO BEAR ARMS*

A well regulated Militia, being necessary to the security of a free State, the right of the people to keep and bear Arms, shall not be infringed.

AMENDMENT III—*QUARTERING OF SOLDIERS*

No Soldier shall, in time of peace be quartered in any house, without the consent of the Owner, nor in time of war, but in a manner to be prescribed by law.

AMENDMENT IV—*SEARCHES AND SEIZURES*

The right of the people to be secure in their persons, houses, papers, and effects, against unreasonable searches and seizures, shall not be violated, and no warrants shall issue, but upon probable cause, supported by Oath or affirmation, and particularly describing the place to be searched, and the persons or things to be seized.

AMENDMENT V—*GRAND JURIES, DOUBLE JEOPARDY, SELF-INCRIMINATION, DUE PROCESS, EMINENT DOMAIN*

No person shall be held to answer for a capital, or otherwise infamous crime, unless on a presentment or indictment of a Grand Jury, except in cases arising in the land or naval forces, or in the Militia, when in actual service in time of War or public danger; nor shall any person be subject for the same offence to be twice put in jeopardy of life or limb; nor shall be compelled in any criminal case to be a witness against himself, nor be deprived of life, liberty, or property, without due process of law; nor shall private property be taken for public use, without just compensation.

AMENDMENT VI—*CRIMINAL COURT PROCEDURES*

In all criminal prosecutions, the accused shall enjoy the right to a speedy and public trial, by an impartial jury of the State and district wherein the crime shall have been committed, which district shall have been previously ascertained by law, and to be informed of the nature and cause of the accusation; to be confronted with the witnesses against him; to have compulsory process for obtaining witnesses in his favor, and to have the assistance of counsel for his defence.

AMENDMENT VII—*TRIAL BY JURY IN COMMON-LAW CASES*

In Suits at common law, where the value in controversy shall exceed twenty dollars, the right of trial by jury shall be preserved, and no fact tried by a jury, shall be otherwise re-examined in any Court of the United States, than according to the rules of the common law.

AMENDMENT VIII—*BAILS, FINES, AND PUNISHMENT*

Excessive bail shall not be required, nor excessive fines imposed, nor cruel and unusual punishments inflicted.

AMENDMENT IX—*RIGHTS RETAINED BY THE PEOPLE*

The enumeration in the Constitution, of certain rights, shall not be construed to deny or disparage others retained by the people.

AMENDMENT X—*RIGHTS RESERVED TO THE STATES*

The powers not delegated to the United States by the Constitution, nor prohibited by it to the States, are reserved to the States respectively, or to the people.

AMENDMENT XI—*SUITS AGAINST THE STATES (RATIFIED FEBRUARY 7, 1795)*

The Judicial power of the United States shall not be construed to extend to any suit in law or equity, commenced or prosecuted against one of the United States by Citizens of another State, or by Citizens or Subjects of any Foreign State.

AMENDMENT XII—*ELECTION OF THE PRESIDENT AND VICE-PRESIDENT (RATIFIED JUNE 15, 1804)*

The Electors shall meet in their respective states, and vote by ballot for President and Vice-President, one of whom, at least, shall not be an inhabitant of the same state with themselves; they shall name in their ballots the person voted for as President, and in distinct ballots the person voted for as Vice-President, and they shall make distinct lists of all persons voted for as President, and of all persons voted for as Vice-President, and of the number of votes for each, which lists they shall sign and certify, and transmit sealed to the seat of the government of the United States, directed to the President of the Senate;—The President of the Senate shall, in the presence of the Senate and House of Representatives, open all the certificates and the votes shall then be counted; — The person having the greatest number of votes for President, shall be the President, if such number be a majority of the whole number of Electors appointed; and if no person have such majority, then from the persons having the highest numbers not exceeding three on the list of those voted for as President, the House of Representatives shall choose immediately, by ballot, the President. But in choosing the President, the votes shall be taken by states, the representation from each state having one vote; a quorum for this purpose shall consist of a member or members from two-thirds of the states, and a majority of all the states shall be necessary to a Choice. [And if the House of Representatives shall not choose a President whenever the right of choice shall devolve upon them, before the fourth day of March next following, then the Vice-President shall act as President, as in the case of the death or other constitutional disability of the President.][12]—The person having the greatest number of votes as Vice-President, shall be the Vice-President, if such number be a majority of the whole number of Electors appointed, and if no person have a majority, then from the two highest numbers on the list, the Senate shall choose the Vice-President; a quorum for the purpose shall consist of two-thirds of the whole number of Senators, and a majority of the whole number shall be necessary to a choice. But no person constitutionally ineligible to the office of President shall be eligible to that of Vice-President of the United States.

AMENDMENT XIII—*SLAVERY (RATIFIED ON DECEMBER 6, 1865)*

Section 1. Neither slavery nor involuntary servitude, except as a punishment for crime whereof the party shall have been duly convicted, shall exist within the United States, or any place subject to their jurisdiction.

Section 2. Congress shall have power to enforce this article by appropriate legislation.

[12] Amendment XX.

AMENDMENT XIV—*CITIZENSHIP, DUE PROCESS, AND EQUAL PROTECTION OF THE LAWS (RATIFIED ON JULY 9, 1868)*

Section 1. All persons born or naturalized in the United States, and subject to the jurisdiction thereof, are citizens of the United States and of the State wherein they reside. No State shall make or enforce any law which shall abridge the privileges or immunities of citizens of the United States; nor shall any State deprive any person of life, liberty, or property, without due process of law; nor deny to any person within its jurisdiction the equal protection of the laws.

Section 2. Representatives shall be apportioned among the several States according to their respective numbers, counting the whole number of persons in each State, excluding Indians not taxed. But when the right to vote at any election for the choice of electors for President and Vice President of the United States, Representatives in Congress, the Executive and Judicial officers of a State, or the members of the Legislature thereof, is denied to any of the male inhabitants of such State, being twenty-one years of age, and citizens of the United States, or in any way abridged, except for participation in rebellion, or other crime, the basis of representation therein shall be reduced in the proportion which the number of such male citizens shall bear to the whole number of male citizens twenty-one years of age in such State.

Section 3. No person shall be a Senator or Representative in Congress, or elector of President and Vice President, or hold any office, civil or military, under the United States, or under any State, who, having previously taken an oath, as a member of Congress, or as an officer of the United States, or as a member of any State legislature, or as an executive or judicial officer of any State, to support the Constitution of the United States, shall have engaged in insurrection or rebellion against the same, or given aid or comfort to the enemies thereof. But Congress may by a vote of two-thirds of each House, remove such disability.

Section 4. The validity of the public debt of the United States, authorized by law, including debts incurred for payment of pensions and bounties for services in suppressing insurrection or rebellion, shall not be questioned. But neither the United States nor any State shall assume or pay any debt or obligation incurred in aid of insurrection or rebellion against the United States, or any claim for the loss or emancipation of any slave, but all such debts, obligations and claims shall be held illegal and void.

Section 5. The Congress shall have power to enforce, by appropriate legislation, the provisions of this article.

AMENDMENT XV—*THE RIGHT TO VOTE (RATIFIED ON FEBRUARY 3, 1870)*

Section 1. The right of citizens of the United States to vote shall not be denied or abridged by the United States or by any State on account of race, color, or previous condition of servitude.

Section 2. The Congress shall have power to enforce this article by appropriate legislation.

AMENDMENT XVI—*INCOME TAXES (RATIFIED ON FEBRUARY 3, 1913)*

The Congress shall have power to lay and collect taxes on incomes, from whatever source derived, without apportionment among the several States, and without regard to any census or enumeration.

AMENDMENT XVII—*ELECTION OF SENATORS (RATIFIED ON APRIL 8, 1913)*

The Senate of the United States shall be composed of two Senators from each State, elected by the people thereof, for six years; and each Senator shall have one vote. The electors in each State shall have the qualifications requisite for electors of the most numerous branch of the State legislatures.

When vacancies happen in the representation of any State in the Senate, the executive authority of such State shall issue writs of election to fill such vacancies: *Provided,* That the legislature of any State may empower the executive thereof to make temporary appointments until the people fill the vacancies by election as the legislature may direct.

This amendment shall not be so construed as to affect the election or term of any Senator chosen before it becomes valid as part of the Constitution.

AMENDMENT XVIII—*PROHIBITION (RATIFIED ON JANUARY 16, 1919)*

Section 1. After one year from the ratification of this article the manufacture, sale, or transportation of intoxicating liquors within, the importation thereof into, or the exportation thereof from the United States and all territory subject to the jurisdiction thereof for beverage purposes is hereby prohibited.

Section 2. The Congress and the several States shall have concurrent power to enforce this article by appropriate legislation.

---

[13] See Amendment XXI.

Section 3. This article shall be inoperative unless it shall have been ratified as an amendment to the Constitution by the legislatures of the several States, as provided in the Constitution, within seven years from the date of the submission hereof to the States by the Congress.[13]

AMENDMENT XIX—*WOMEN'S RIGHT TO VOTE (RATIFIED ON AUGUST 18, 1920)*

The right of citizens of the United States to vote shall not be denied or abridged by the United States or by any State on account of sex.

Congress shall have power to enforce this article by appropriate legislation.

AMENDMENT XX—*TERMS OF OFFICE, CONVENING OF CONGRESS, AND SUCCESSION (RATIFIED FEBRUARY 6, 1933)*

Section 1. The terms of the President and Vice President shall end at noon on the 20th day of January, and the terms of Senators and Representatives at noon on the 3d day of January, of the years in which such terms would have ended if this article had not been ratified; and the terms of their successors shall then begin.

Section 2. The Congress shall assemble at least once in every year, and such meeting shall begin at noon on the 3d day of January, unless they shall by law appoint a different day.

Section 3. If, at the time fixed for the beginning of the term of the President, the President elect shall have died, the Vice President elect shall become President. If a President shall not have been chosen before the time fixed for the beginning of his term, or if the President elect shall have failed to qualify, then the Vice President elect shall act as President until a President shall have qualified; and the Congress may by law provide for the case wherein neither a President elect nor a Vice President elect shall have qualified, declaring who shall then act as President, or the manner in which one who is to act shall be selected, and such person shall act accordingly until a President or Vice President shall have qualified.

Section 4. The Congress may by law provide for the case of the death of any of the persons from whom the House of Representatives may choose a President whenever the rights of choice shall have devolved upon them, and for the case of the death of any of the persons from whom the Senate may choose a Vice President whenever the right of choice shall have devolved upon them.

Section 5. Sections 1 and 2 shall take effect on the 15th day of October following the ratification of this article.

Section 6. This article shall be inoperative unless it shall have been ratified as an amendment to the Constitution by the legislatures of three-fourths of the several States within seven years from the date of its submission.

AMENDMENT XXI—*REPEAL OF PROHIBITION (RATIFIED ON DECEMBER 5, 1933)*

Section 1. The eighteenth article of amendment to the Constitution of the United States is hereby repealed.

Section 2. The transportation or importation into any State, Territory, or possession of the United States for delivery or use therein of intoxicating liquors, in violation of the laws thereof, is hereby prohibited.

Section 3. This article shall be inoperative unless it shall have been ratified as an amendment to the Constitution by conventions in the several States, as provided in the Constitution, within seven years from the date of the submission hereof to the States by the Congress.

AMENDMENT XXII—*NUMBER OF PRESIDENTIAL TERMS (RATIFIED ON FEBRUARY 27, 1951)*

No person shall be elected to the office of the President more than twice, and no person who has held the office of President, or acted as President, for more than two years of a term to which some other person was elected President shall be elected to the office of the President more than once. But this Article shall not apply to any person holding the office of President when this Article was proposed by the Congress, and shall not prevent any person who may be holding the office of President, or acting as President, during the term within which this Article becomes operative from holding the office of President or acting as President during the remainder of such term.

AMENDMENT XXIII—*PRESIDENTIAL ELECTORS FOR THE DISTRICT OF COLUMBIA (RATIFIED ON MARCH 29, 1961)*

Section 1. The District constituting the seat of Government of the United States shall appoint in such manner as the Congress may direct:

A number of electors of President and Vice President equal to the whole number of Senators and Representatives in Congress to which the District would be entitled if it were a State, but in no event more than the least populous State; they shall be in addition to those appointed by the States, but they shall be considered, for the purposes of the election of President and Vice President, to be electors appointed by a State; and they shall meet in the District and perform such duties as provided by the twelfth article of amendment.

Section 2. The Congress shall have power to enforce this article by appropriate legislation.

AMENDMENT XXIV—*POLL TAX (RATIFIED ON JANUARY 23, 1964)*

Section 1. The right of citizens of the United States to vote in any primary or other election for President or Vice President, for electors for President or Vice President, or for Senator or Representative in Congress, shall not be denied or abridged by the United States or any State by reason of failure to pay any poll tax or other tax.

Section 2. The Congress shall have power to enforce this article by appropriate legislation.

AMENDMENT XXV—*PRESIDENTIAL DISABILITY AND VICE PRESIDENTIAL VACANCIES (RATIFIED ON FEBRUARY 10, 1967)*

Section 1. In case of the removal of the President from office or of his death or resignation, the Vice President shall become President.

Section 2. Whenever there is a vacancy in the office of the Vice President, the President shall nominate a Vice President who shall take office upon confirmation by a majority vote of both Houses of Congress.

Section 3. Whenever the President transmits to the President pro tempore of the Senate and the Speaker of the House of Representatives his written declaration that he is unable to discharge the powers and duties of his office, and until he transmits to them a written declaration to the contrary, such powers and duties shall be discharged by the Vice President as Acting President.

Section 4. Whenever the Vice President and a majority of either the principal officers of the executive departments or of such other body as Congress may by law provide, transmit to the President pro tempore of the Senate and the Speaker of the House of Representatives their written declaration that the President is unable to discharge the powers and duties of his office, the Vice President shall immediately assume the powers and duties of the office as Acting President.

Thereafter, when the President transmits to the President pro tempore of the Senate and the Speaker of the House of Representatives his written declaration that no inability exists, he shall resume the powers and duties of his office unless the Vice President and a majority of either the principal officers of the executive department or of such other body as Congress may by law provide, transmit within four days to the President pro tempore of the Senate and the Speaker of the House of Representatives their written declaration that the President is unable to discharge the powers and duties of his office. Thereupon Congress shall decide the issue, assembling within forty-eight hours for that purpose if not in session. If the Congress, within twenty-one days after receipt of the latter written declaration, or, if Congress is not in session, within twenty-one days after Congress is required to assemble, determines by two-thirds vote of both Houses that the President is unable to discharge the powers and duties of his office, the Vice President shall continue to discharge the same as Acting President; otherwise, the President shall resume the powers and duties of his office.

AMENDMENT XXVI—*EIGHTEEN-YEAR-OLD VOTE (RATIFIED ON JULY 1, 1971)*

Section 1. The right of citizens of the United States, who are eighteen years of age or older, to vote shall not be denied or abridged by the United States or by any State on account of age.

Section 2. The Congress shall have power to enforce this article by appropriate legislation.

AMENDMENT XXVII—*CONGRESSIONAL SALARIES (RATIFIED ON MAY 18, 1992)*

Section 1. No law varying the compensation for the services of the Senators and Representatives, shall take effect, until an election of Representatives shall have intervened.

Supreme Court Justices Serving in the Twentieth Century

NAME	NOMINATED BY	SERVICE
John M. Harlan	Hayes	1877–1911
Horace Gray	Arthur	1882–1902
Melville W. Fuller*	Cleveland	1888–1910
David J. Brewer	Harrison	1890–1910
Henry B. Brown	Harrison	1890–1906
George Shiras, Jr.	Harrison	1892–1903
Edward D. White	Cleveland	1894–1910
Rufus W. Peckham	Cleveland	1895–1909
Joseph McKenna	McKinley	1898–1925
Oliver W. Holmes	T. Roosevelt	1902–1932
William R. Day	T. Roosevelt	1903–1922
William H. Moody	T. Roosevelt	1906–1910
Horace H. Lurton	Taft	1910–1914
Edward D. White	Taft	1910–1921
Charles E. Hughes	Taft	1910–1916
Willis Van Devanter	Taft	1911–1937
Joseph R. Lamar	Taft	1911–1916
Mahlon Pitney	Taft	1912–1922
James C. McReynolds	Wilson	1914–1941
Louis D. Brandeis	Wilson	1916–1939
John H. Clarke	Wilson	1916–1922
William H. Taft	Harding	1921–1930
George Sutherland	Harding	1922–1938
Pierce Butler	Harding	1922–1939
Edward T. Sanford	Harding	1923–1930
Harlan F. Stone	Coolidge	1925–1941
Charles E. Hughes	Hoover	1930–1941
Owen J. Roberts	Hoover	1930–1945
Benjamin N. Cardozo	Hoover	1932–1938
Hugo L. Black	F. Roosevelt	1937–1971
Stanley F. Reed	F. Roosevelt	1938–1957
Felix Frankfurter	F. Roosevelt	1939–1962
William O. Douglas	F. Roosevelt	1939–1975
Frank Murphy	F. Roosevelt	1940–1949
Harlan F. Stone	F. Roosevelt	1941–1946
James F. Byrnes	F. Roosevelt	1941–1942
Robert H. Jackson	F. Roosevelt	1941–1954
Wiley B. Rutledge	F. Roosevelt	1943–1949
Harold H. Burton	Truman	1945–1958
Fred M. Vinson	Truman	1946–1953
Tom C. Clark	Truman	1949–1967
Sherman Minton	Truman	1949–1956
Earl Warren	Eisenhower	1953–1969
John M. Harlan	Eisenhower	1955–1971
William J. Brennan, Jr.	Eisenhower	1956–1990
Charles E. Whittaker	Eisenhower	1957–1962

*Boldface type indicates service as chief justice.

NAME	NOMINATED BY	SERVICE
Potter Stewart	Eisenhower	1958–1981
Byron R. White	Kennedy	1962–1993
Arthur J. Goldberg	Kennedy	1962–1965
Abe Fortas	Johnson	1965–1969
Thurgood Marshall	Johnson	1967–1991
Warren E. Burger	Nixon	1969–1986
Harry A. Blackmun	Nixon	1970–1994
Lewis F. Powell, Jr.	Nixon	1971–1987
William H. Rehnquist	Nixon	1971–1986
John Paul Stevens	Ford	1975–
Sandra Day O'Connor	Reagan	1981–
William H. Rehnquist	Reagan	1986–
Antonin Scalia	Reagan	1986–
Anthony M. Kennedy	Reagan	1988–
David H. Souter	Bush	1990–
Clarence Thomas	Bush	1991–
Ruth Bader Ginsburg	Clinton	1993–
Stephen G. Breyer	Clinton	1994–

Glossary

A

activation. One of three key consequences of electoral campaigns for voters, in which the voter is activated to contribute money or ring doorbells instead of just voting. See also **reinforcement** and **conversion.**

actual group. That part of the **potential group** consisting of members who actually join. See also **interest group.**

Adarand Constructors v. Pena. 1995 Supreme Court decision holding that federal programs that classify people by race, even for an ostensibly benign purpose such as expanding opportunities for members of minorities, should be presumed to be unconstitutional. Such programs must be subject to the most searching judicial inquiry and can survive only if they are "narrowly tailored" to accomplish a "compelling governmental interest."

administrative discretion. The authority of administrative actors to select among various responses to a given problem. Discretion is greatest when routines, or **standard operating procedures,** do not fit a case.

advertising. According to David Mayhew, one of three primary activities undertaken by members of Congress to increase the probability of their reelection. Advertising involves contacts between members and their constituents between elections. See also **credit claiming** and **position taking.**

affirmative action. A policy designed to give special attention to or compensatory treatment of members of some previously disadvantaged group.

agenda. See **policy agenda.**

agents of socialization. Families, schools, television, peer groups, and other influences that contribute to **political socialization** by shaping formal and especially informal learning about politics.

Americans with Disabilities Act of 1990. A law passed in 1990 that requires employers and public facilities to make "reasonable accommodations" for people with disabilities and prohibits discrimination against these individuals in employment.

amicus curiae briefs. Legal briefs submitted by a "friend of the court" for the purpose of raising additional points of view and presenting information not contained in the briefs of the formal parties. These briefs attempt to influence a court's decision.

Anti-Federalists. Opponents of the American Constitution at the time when the states were contemplating its adoption. They argued that the Constitution was a class-based document, that it would erode fundamental liberties, and that it would weaken the power of the states. See also **Federalists** and **U.S. Constitution.**

antitrust policy. A policy designed to ensure competition and prevent monopoly, which is the control of a market by one company.

appellate jurisdiction. The jurisdiction of courts that hear cases brought to them on appeal from lower courts. These courts do not review the factual record, only the legal issues involved. Compare **original jurisdiction.**

appropriations bill. An act of Congress that actually funds programs within limits established by **authorization bills.** Appropriations usually cover 1 year.

arms race. A tense relationship beginning in the 1950s between the Soviet Union and the United States whereby one side's weaponry became the other side's goad to procure more weaponry, and so on.

Articles of Confederation. The first constitution of the United States, adopted by Congress in 1777 and enacted in 1781. The Articles established a national legislature, the Continental Congress, but most authority rested with the state legislatures.

authorization bill. An act of Congress that establishes, continues, or changes a discretionary government program or an entitlement. It specifies program goals and maximum expenditures for discretionary programs. Compare **appropriations bill.**

B

balance of trade. The ratio of what is paid for imports to what is earned from exports. When more is imported than exported, there is a balance-of-trade deficit.

balanced budget amendment. A proposed amendment to the Constitution that would instruct Congress to hold a national convention to propose to the states a requirement that peacetime federal budgets be balanced. The amendment has been passed in varied forms by the legislatures of nearly two-thirds of the states.

Barron v. Baltimore. The 1833 Supreme Court decision holding that the **Bill of Rights** restrained only the national government, not the states and cities. Almost a century later, the Court first ruled in ***Gitlow v. New York*** that state governments must respect some **First Amendment rights.**

beats. Specific locations from which news frequently eminates, such as Congress or the White House. Most top reporters work a particular beat, thereby becoming specialists in what goes on at that location.

bicameral legislature. A legislature divided into two houses. The U.S. Congress and every American state legislature except Nebraska's are bicameral.

bill. A proposed law, drafted in precise, legal language. Anyone can draft a bill, but only a member of the House of Representatives or the Senate can formally submit a bill for consideration.

Bill of Rights. The first ten amendments to the **U.S. Constitution,** drafted in response to some of the **Anti-Federalist** concerns. These amendments define such basic liberties as freedom of religion, speech, and press and offer protections against arbitrary searches by the police and being held without talking to a lawyer.

block grants. Federal grants given more or less automatically to states or communities to support broad programs in areas such as community development and social services. Compare **categorical grants.**

broadcast media. Television and radio, as compared with **print media.**

Brown v. Board of Education. The 1954 Supreme Court decision holding that school segregation in Topeka, Kansas, was inherently unconstitutional because it violated the **Fourteenth Amendment's** guarantee of **equal protection.** This case marked the end of legal segregation in the United States. See also ***Plessy v. Ferguson.***

budget. A policy document allocating burdens (taxes) and benefits (expenditures). See also **balanced budget amendment.**

budget resolution. A resolution binding Congress to a total expenditure level, supposedly the bottom line of all federal spending for all programs.

bureaucracy. According to Max Weber, a hierarchical authority structure that uses task specialization, operates on the merit principle, and behaves with impersonality. Bureaucracies govern modern states.

C

cabinet. A group of presidential advisors not mentioned in the Constitution, although every president has had one. Today the cabinet is composed of 13 secretaries and the attorney general.

campaign strategy. The master game plan candidates lay out to guide their electoral campaign.

capitalism. An economic system in which individuals and corporations, not the government, own the principal means of production and seek profits. Pure capitalism means the strict noninterference of the government in business affairs. Compare **mixed economy.**

casework. Activities of members of Congress in the course of helping constituents as individuals; cutting through bureaucratic red tape to get people what they think they have a right to get. See also **pork barrel.**

categorical grants. Federal grants that can be used only for specific purposes, or "categories," of state and local spending. They come with strings attached, such as nondiscrimination provisions. Compare **block grants.**

caucus (congressional). A group of members of Congress sharing some interest or characteristic. Most are composed of members from both parties and from both houses.

caucus (state party). A meeting of all state party leaders for selecting delegates to the **national party convention.** Caucuses are usually organized as a pyramid.

censorship. Governmental regulation of media content.

census. A valuable tool for understanding demographic changes. The Constitution requires that the government conduct an "actual enumeration" of the population every 10 years. See also **demography.**

Central Intelligence Agency (CIA). An agency created after World War II to coordinate American intelligence activities abroad. It became involved in intrigue, conspiracy, and meddling as well.

chains. See **newspaper chains.**

change. The degree to which **public opinion** is shifting or stable over time. See also **consensus** and **conflict.**

checks and balances. An important part of the Madisonian model designed to limit government's power by requiring that power be balanced among the different governmental institutions. These institutions continually check one another's activities. This system reflects Madison's goal of setting power against power. See also **separation of powers.**

civic duty. The belief that in order to support democratic government, a citizen should always vote.

civil disobedience. A form of **political participation** that reflects a conscious decision to break a law believed to be immoral and to suffer the consequences. See also **protest.**

civil law. The body of law involving cases without a charge of criminality. It concerns disputes between two parties and consists of both statutes and **common law.** Compare **criminal law.**

civil liberties. The legal constitutional protections against government. Although our civil liberties are formally set down in the **Bill of Rights,** the courts, police, and legislatures define their meaning.

civil rights. The policies extending basic rights to minority groups or other groups historically subject to discrimination. Many groups, especially African Americans and more recently women, have raised constitutional questions about slavery, segregation, equal pay, and other issues. See also **Civil Rights Act of 1964.**

Civil Rights Act of 1964. The law that made racial discrimination against any group in hotels, motels, and restaurants illegal and forbade many forms of job discrimination. See also **civil rights movement** and **civil rights policies.**

civil rights movement. A movement that began in the 1950s and organized both African Americans and whites to end the policies of segregation. It sought to establish equal opportunities in the political and economic sectors and to end policies that erected barriers between people because of race.

civil rights policies. Policies that extend government protection to particular disadvantaged groups. Compare **social welfare policies.**

civil service. A system of hiring and promotion based on the **merit principle** and the desire to create a nonpartisan government service. Compare **patronage.**

class action suits. Lawsuits permitting a small number of people to sue on behalf of all other people similarly situated.

Clean Air Act of 1970. The law that charged the Department of Transportation (DOT) with the responsibility of reducing automobile emissions.

clearance rate. The proportion of crimes resulting in an arrest. This statistic has remained stable for years.

coalition. A group of individuals with a common interest upon which every political party depends. See also **New Deal Coalition.**

coalition government. When two or more parties join together to form a majority in a national legislature. This form of government is quite common in the multiparty systems of Europe.

coattails. See **presidential coattails.**

cold war. War by other than military means usually emphasizing ideological conflict, such as that between the United States and the Soviet Union from the end of World War II until the 1990s.

collective bargaining. Negotiations between representatives of labor unions and management to determine acceptable working conditions.

collective good. Something of value (money, a tax write-off, prestige, clean air, and so on) that cannot be withheld from a group member.

command-and-control policy. According to Charles Schultze, the existing system of **regulation** whereby government tells business how to reach certain goals, checks that these commands are followed, and punishes offenders. Compare **incentive system.**

commercial speech. Communication in the form of advertising. It can be restricted more than many other types of speech but has been receiving increased protection from the Supreme Court.

commission government. A form of municipal government in which voters elect individuals to serve as city commissioners who will have legislative responsibilities to approve city policies and executive responsibilities to direct a functional area of city government, such as public safety or public works. See also **mayor–council government** and **council–manager government.**

committee chairs. The most important influencers of the congressional agenda. They play dominant roles in scheduling hearings, hiring staff, appointing subcommittees, and managing committee bills when these are brought before the full house.

committees (congressional). See **conference committees, joint committees, select committees,** and **standing committees.**

common law. The accumulation of judicial decisions applied in **civil law** disputes.

comparable worth. The issue raised when women who hold traditionally female jobs are paid less than men for working at jobs requiring comparable skill.

conference committees. Congressional committees formed when the Senate and the House pass a particular **bill** in different forms. Party leadership appoints members from each house who iron out the differences and bring back a single bill. See also **standing committees, joint committees,** and **select committees.**

conflict. A clash occurring when an issue is characterized by **public opinion** that is sharply divided. Compare **consensus** and **change.**

Congressional Budget and Impoundment Control Act of 1974. An act designed to reform the congressional budgetary process. Its supporters hoped that it would also make Congress less dependent on the president's budget and better able to set and meet its own budgetary goals.

Congressional Budget Office (CBO). A counterweight to the president's **Office of Management and Budget (OMB).** The CBO advises Congress on the probable consequences of budget decisions and forecasts revenues.

Connecticut Compromise. The compromise reached at the Constitutional Convention that established two houses of Congress: the House of Representatives, in which **representation** is based on a state's share of the U.S. population, and the Senate, in which each state has two representatives. Compare **New Jersey Plan** and **Virginia Plan.**

consensus. Agreement. Consensus is reflected by an opinion distribution in which a large majority see eye to eye. Compare **conflict** and **change.**

consent of the governed. According to John Locke, the required basis for government. **The Declaration of Independence** reflects Locke's view that governments derive their authority from the consent of the governed.

conservatism. A **political ideology** whose advocates fear the growth of government, deplore government's drag on private-sector initiatives, dislike permissiveness in society, and place a priority on military needs over social needs. Compare **liberalism.**

conservatives. Those who advocate **conservatism.** Compare **liberals.**

constitution. A nation's basic law. It creates political institutions, assigns or divides powers in government, and often provides certain guarantees to citizens. Constitutions can be either written or unwritten. See also **U.S. Constitution.**

constitutional convention. A method of amending a state constitution in which voters may approve the calling of a convention of state citizens to propose amendments to the state constitution; the proposals are submitted to state voters for approval. See also **legislative proposal** and **popular initiative.**

constitutional courts. Lower federal courts of original jurisdiction created by Congress by the Judiciary Act of 1789. Compare **legislative courts.**

consumer price index (CPI). The key measure of inflation that relates prices in one year to prices for a base year that are figured as 100.

containment doctrine. A **foreign policy** strategy advocated by George Kennan that called for the United States to isolate the Soviet Union, "contain" its advances, and resist its encroachments by peaceful means if possible, but by force if necessary.

continuing resolutions. When Congress cannot reach agreement and pass appropriations bills, these resolutions allow agencies to spend at the level of the previous year.

convention. See **national party convention.**

conversion. One of three key consequences of electoral campaigns for voters, in which the voter's mind is actually changed. See also **reinforcement** and **activation.**

cooperative federalism. A system of government in which powers and policy assignments are shared between states and the national government. They may also share costs, administration, and even blame for programs that work poorly. Compare **dual federalism.**

council–manager government. A common form of government used by municipalities in which voters elect a city council (and possibly an independent mayor) to make public policy for the city. The city council, in turn, appoints a professional city manager to serve as chief executive of the city and to administer public policy. See also **mayor-council government** and **commission government.**

Council of Economic Advisors (CEA). A three-member body appointed by the president to advise the president on economic policy.

council of governments (COG). Councils in many areas of the country where officials from various localities meet to discuss mutual problems and plan joint, cooperative action.

county. A political subdivision of state government that has a set of government officers to administer some local services—often on behalf of the state. Called a *parish* in Louisiana and a *borough* in Alaska. See also **county government.**

county government. A unit of local government that serves as the administrative arm of state government at the local level. It has many social service and record-keeping responsibilities. See also **county.**

court of last resort. The final appeals court in a state, often known as the state "supreme court."

courts. See **constitutional courts, legislative courts, district courts,** and **courts of appeal.**

courts of appeal. Appellate courts empowered to review all final decisions of district courts, except in rare cases. In addition, they also hear appeals to orders of many federal regulatory agencies. Compare **district courts.**

Craig v. Boren. In this 1976 Supreme Court decision, the Court determined that gender classification cases would have a "heightened" or "middle level" of scrutiny. In other words, the courts were to show less deference to gender classifications than to more routine classifications, but more deference than to racial classifications.

credit claiming. According to David Mayhew, one of three primary activities undertaken by members of Congress to increase the probability of their reelection. It involves personal and district service. See also **advertising** and **position taking.**

criminal law. The body of law involving a case in which an individual is charged with violating a specific law. The offense may be harmful to an individual or society and in either case warrants punishment, such as imprisonment or a fine. Compare **civil law.**

crisis. A sudden, unpredictable, and potentially dangerous event requiring the president to play the role of crisis manager.

critical election. An electoral "earthquake" whereby new issues emerge, new coalitions replace old ones, and the majority party is often displaced by the minority party. Critical election periods are sometimes marked by a national crisis and may require more than one election to bring about a new **party era.** See also **party realignment.**

cruel and unusual punishment. Court sentences prohibited by the **Eighth Amendment.** Although the Supreme Court has ruled that mandatory death sentences for certain offenses are unconstitutional, it has not held that the death penalty itself constitutes cruel and unusual punishment. See also ***Furman v. Georgia, Gregg v. Georgia,*** and ***McClesky v. Kemp.***

culture of poverty. Negative attitudes and values toward work, family, and success that condemn the poor to low levels of accomplishment. The view that there is a culture of poverty is most commonly held by **conservatives.**

D

Dartmouth College v. Woodward. The 1819 case in which the Supreme Court held that Dartmouth's charter, as well as the charter of any corporation, is a legal contract that cannot be tampered with by a government.

dealignment. See **party dealignment.**

debate. See **presidential debate.**

debt. See **federal debt.**

Declaration of Independence. The document approved by representatives of the American colonies in 1776 that stated their grievances against the British monarch and declared their independence.

deficit. An excess of federal **expenditures** over federal **revenues.** See also **budget.**

delegate. See **instructed delegate.**

democracy. A system of selecting policymakers and of organizing government so that policy represents and responds to the public's preferences.

democratic theory. See **traditional democratic theory.**

demography. The science of population changes. See also **census.**

Dennis v. United States. A 1951 Supreme Court decision that permitted the government to jail several American Communist Party leaders under the Smith Act, a law forbidding advocacy of the violent overthrow of the U.S. government.

dependency. See **interdependency.**

deregulation. The lifting of restrictions on business, industry, and other professional activities for which government rules had been established and that bureaucracies had been created to administer.

détente. A slow transformation from conflict thinking to cooperative thinking in **foreign policy** strategy and policymaking. It sought a relaxation of tensions between the superpowers, coupled with firm guarantees of mutual security.

Dillon's Rule. The prevailing constitutional doctrine under which cities and other local governments possess only those powers and responsibilities that a state chooses to confer on them. Furthermore, any power that a state gives a city it may amend, abridge, or take away. Only concerns of practicality, politics, and fairness limit how a state may treat its cities.

direct mail. A high-tech method of raising money for a political cause or candidate. It involves sending information and requests for money to people whose names appear on lists of those who have supported similar views or candidates in the past.

direct primaries. **Primaries** used to select party nominees for congressional and state offices.

district courts. The 91 federal courts of original jurisdiction. They are the only federal courts in which no trials are held and in which juries may be empaneled. Compare **courts of appeal.**

Dred Scott v. Sandford. The 1857 Supreme Court decision ruling that a slave who had escaped to a free state enjoyed no rights as a citizen and that Congress had no authority to ban slavery in the territories.

dual federalism. A system of government in which both the states and the national government remain supreme within their own spheres, each responsible for some policies. Compare **cooperative federalism.**

due process clause. Part of the **Fourteenth Amendment** guaranteeing that persons cannot be deprived of life, liberty, or property by the United States or state governments without due process of law. See also ***Gitlow v. New York.***

E

efficacy. See **political efficacy.**

Eighth Amendment. The constitutional amendment that forbids **cruel and unusual punishment,** although it does not define this phrase. Through the **Fourteenth Amendment,** this **Bill of Rights** provision applies to the states.

elastic clause. The final paragraph of Article I, Section 8, of the Constitution, which authorizes Congress to pass all laws "necessary and proper" to carry out the enumerated powers. See also **implied powers.**

electioneering. Direct group involvement in the electoral process. Groups can help fund campaigns, provide testimony, and get members to work for candidates, and some form **political action committees (PACs).**

electoral college. A unique American institution, created by the Constitution, providing for the selection of the president by electors chosen by the state parties. Although the electoral college vote usually reflects a popular majority, the winner-take-all rule gives clout to big states.

electoral mandate. A concept based on the idea that "the people have spoken." It is a powerful symbol in American electoral politics, according legitimacy and credibility to a newly elected president's proposals. See also **mandate theory of politics.**

elite. The upper class in a society that utilizes wealth for political power. According to the **elite and class theory** of government and politics, elites control policies because they control key institutions.

elite theory. A theory of government and politics contending that societies are divided along class lines and that an upper-class elite will rule, regardless of the formal niceties of governmental organization. Compare **hyperpluralism, pluralist theory,** and **traditional democratic theory.**

Endangered Species Act of 1973. This law requires the federal government to protect actively each of the hundreds of species listed as endangered—regardless of the economic effect on the surrounding towns or region.

Engel v. Vitale. The 1962 Supreme Court decision holding that state officials violated the **First Amendment** when they wrote a prayer to be recited by New York's schoolchildren. Compare ***School District of Abington Township, Pennsylvania v. Schempp.***

entitlements. Policies for which expenditures are uncontrollable because Congress has in effect obligated itself to pay *X* level of benefits to *Y* number of recipients. Each year, Congress' bill is a straightforward function of the *X* level of benefits times the *Y* number of beneficiaries. Social Security benefits are an example.

entrepreneur. See **political entrepreneur.**

enumerated powers. Powers of the federal government that are specifically addressed in the Constitution; for Congress, these powers are listed in Article I, Section 8, and include the power to coin money, regulate its value, and impose taxes. Compare **implied powers.**

environmental impact statement (EIS). A report filed with the **Environmental Protection Agency (EPA)** that specifies what environmental effects a proposed policy would have. The **National Environmental Policy Act** requires that whenever any agency proposes to undertake a policy that is potentially disruptive of the environment, the agency must file a statement with the EPA.

Environmental Protection Agency (EPA). An agency of the federal government created in 1970 and charged with administering all the government's environmental legislation. It also administers policies dealing with toxic wastes. The EPA is the largest federal **independent regulatory agency.**

equal opportunity. A policy statement about equality holding that the rules of the game should be the same for everyone. Most of our **civil rights** policies over the past three decades have presumed that equality of opportunity is a public policy goal. Compare **equal results.**

equal protection of the laws. Part of the **Fourteenth Amendment** emphasizing that the laws must provide equivalent "protection" to all people. As one member of Congress said during debate on the amendment, it should provide "equal protection of life, liberty, and property" to all a state's citizens.

equal results. A policy statement about equality holding that government has a duty to help break down barriers to **equal opportunity. Affirmative action** is an example of a policy justified as promoting equal results rather then merely equal opportunities.

Equal Rights Amendment. A constitutional amendment passed by Congress in 1978 and sent to the state legislatures for ratification, stating that "equality of rights under the law shall not be denied or abridged by the United States or by any state on account of sex." Despite substantial public support and an extended deadline, the amendment failed to acquire the necessary support from three-fourths of the state legislatures.

equity. See **intergenerational equity.**

establishment clause. Part of the **First Amendment** stating that "Congress shall make no law respecting an establishment of religion."

European Economic Community (EEC). An economic alliance of the major Western European nations, often called the Common Market. The EEC coordinates monetary, trade, immigration, and labor policies.

exclusionary rule. The rule that evidence, no matter how incriminating, cannot be introduced into a trial if it was not constitutionally obtained. The rule prohibits use of evidence obtained through **unreasonable search and seizure.**

executive agency. See **independent executive agency.**

executive orders. Regulations originating from the executive branch. Executive orders are one method presidents can use to control the bureaucracy; more often, though, presidents pass along their wishes through their aides.

exit polls. Public opinion surveys used by major media pollsters to predict electoral winners with speed and precision.

expenditures. Federal spending of **revenues.** Major areas of such spending are social services and the military.

extradition. A legal process whereby an alleged criminal offender is surrendered by the officials of one state to officials of the state in which the crime is alleged to have been committed.

F

facilitator. According to George Edwards, the effective leader who works at the margin of coalition building to recognize and exploit opportunities presented by a favorable configuration of political forces.

factions. Interest groups arising from the unequal distribution of property or wealth that James Madison attacked in **Federalist Paper** No. 10. Today's parties or interest groups are what Madison had in mind when he warned of the instability in government caused by factions.

federal debt. All the money borrowed by the federal government over the years and still outstanding. Today the federal debt is about $4.5 trillion.

Federal Election Campaign Act. A law passed in 1974 for reforming campaign finances. The act created the **Federal Election Commission (FEC),** provided public financing for presidential primaries and general elections, limited presidential campaign spending, required disclosure, and attempted to limit contributions.

Federal Election Commission (FEC). A six-member bipartisan agency created by the **Federal Election Campaign Act** of 1974. The FEC administers the campaign finance laws and enforces compliance with their requirements.

Federal Regulation of Lobbying Act. Passed in 1946, an act requiring congressional lobbyists to register and state their policy goals. According to the Supreme Court, the law applies only to groups whose "principal" purpose is **lobbying.**

Federal Reserve System. The main instrument for making **monetary policy** in the United States. It was created by Congress in 1913 to regulate the lending practices of banks and thus the money supply. The seven members of its Board of Governors are appointed to 14-year terms by the president with the consent of the Senate.

Federal Trade Commission (FTC). The **independent regulatory agency** traditionally responsible for regulating false and misleading trade practices. The FTC has recently become active in defending consumer interests through its truth-in-advertising rule and the Consumer Credit Protection Act.

federalism. A way of organizing a nation so that two levels of government have formal authority over the same land and people. It is a system of shared power between units of government. Compare **unitary government.**

Federalist Papers. A collection of 85 articles written by Alexander Hamilton, John Jay, and James Madison under the name "Publius" to defend the Constitution in detail. Collectively, these papers are second only to the **U.S. Constitution** in characterizing the framers' intents.

Federalists. Supporters of the **U.S. Constitution** at the time the states were contemplating its adoption. See also **Anti-Federalists** and **Federalist Papers.**

Fifteenth Amendment. The constitutional amendment adopted in 1870 to extend **suffrage** to African Americans.

Fifth Amendment. The constitutional amendment designed to protect the rights of persons accused of crimes, including protection against double jeopardy, **self-incrimination,** and punishment without due process of law.

filibuster. A strategy unique to the Senate whereby opponents of a piece of legislation try to talk it to death, based on the tradition of unlimited debate. Today, 60 members present and voting can halt a filibuster.

First Amendment. The constitutional amendment that establishes the four great liberties: freedom of the press, of speech, of religion, and of assembly.

fiscal federalism. The patterns of spending, taxing, and grants between governmental units in a federal system.

fiscal policy. The policy that describes the impact of the federal budget—taxes, spending, and borrowing—on the economy. Unlike **monetary policy,** which is mostly controlled by the **Federal Reserve System,** fiscal policy is almost entirely determined by Congress and the president, who are the budget makers. See also **Keynesian economic theory.**

Food and Drug Administration (FDA). The federal agency formed in 1913 and assigned the task of approving all food products and drugs sold in the United States. All drugs, with the exception of tobacco, must have FDA authorization.

foreign policy. A policy that involves choice taking, like domestic policy, but additionally involves choices about relations with the rest of the world. The president is the chief initiator of foreign policy in the United States.

formula grants. Federal **categorical grants** distributed according to a formula specified in legislation or in administrative regulations.

Fourteenth Amendment. The constitutional amendment adopted after the Civil War that states, "No State shall make or enforce any law which shall abridge the privileges or immunities of citizens of the United States; nor shall any state deprive any person of life, liberty, or property, without due process of law; nor deny to any person within its jurisdiction the **equal protection of the laws."** See also **due process clause.**

fragmentation. A situation in which responsibility for a policy area is dispersed among several units within the bureaucracy, making the coordination of policies both time-consuming and difficult.

free exercise clause. A **First Amendment** provision that prohibits government from interfering with the practice of religion.

free-rider problem. The problem faced by unions and other groups when people do not join because they can benefit from the group's activities without officially joining. The bigger the group, the more serious the free-rider problem. See also **interest group.**

full faith and credit clause. A clause in Article IV, Section 1, of the Constitution requiring each state to recognize the official documents and civil judgments rendered by the courts of other states.

G

General Schedule rating. See **GS (General Schedule) rating.**

Gibbons v. Ogden. A landmark case decided in 1824 in which the Supreme Court interpreted very broadly the clause in Article I, Section 8, of the Constitution giving Congress the power to regulate interstate commerce, encompassing virtually every form of commercial activity. The commerce clause has been the constitutional basis for much of Congress' regulation of the economy.

Gideon v. Wainwright. The 1963 Supreme Court decision holding that anyone accused of a felony where imprisonment may be imposed, however poor he or she might be, has a right to a lawyer. See also **Sixth Amendment.**

Gitlow v. New York. The 1925 Supreme Court decision holding that freedoms of press and speech are "fundamental personal rights and liberties protected by the **due process clause** of the **Fourteenth Amendment** from impairment by the states" as well as the federal government. Compare ***Barron v. Baltimore.***

government. The institutions and processes through which **public policies** are made for a society.

government corporation. A government organization that, like business corporations, provides a service that could be provided by the private sector and typically charges for its services. The U.S. Postal Service is an example. Compare **independent regulatory agency** and **independent executive agency.**

governor. The elected chief executive of state government who directs the administration of state government and the implementation of public policy in the state.

Gramm-Rudman-Hollings. Named for its sponsors and also known as the Balanced Budget and Emergency Deficit Act, legislation mandating maximum allowable deficit levels each year until 1991, when the budget was to be balanced. In 1987, the balanced budget year was shifted to 1993, but the Act was abandoned in 1991.

grandfather clause. One of the methods used by Southern states to deny African Americans the right to vote. In order to exempt illiterate whites from taking a literacy test before voting, the clause exempted people whose grandfathers were eligible to vote in 1860, thereby disenfranchising the grandchildren of slaves. The grandfather clause was declared unconstitutional by the Supreme Court in 1913. See also **poll taxes** and **white primary.**

grants. See **categorical grants** and **block grants.**

Gregg v. Georgia. The 1976 Supreme Court decision that upheld the constitutionality of the death penalty, stating that "It is an extreme sanction, suitable to the most extreme of crimes." The court did not, therefore, believe that the death sentence constitutes **cruel and unusual punishment.**

gross domestic product. The sum total of the value of all the goods and services produced in a nation.

GS (General Schedule) rating. A schedule for federal employees, ranging from GS 1 to GS 18, by which salaries can be keyed to rating and experience. See **civil service.**

H

Hatch Act. A federal law prohibiting government employees from active participation in partisan politics.

high-tech politics. A politics in which the behavior of citizens and policymakers and the political agenda itself are increasingly shaped by technology.

House Rules Committee. An institution unique to the House of Representatives that reviews all bills (except revenue, budget, and appropriations bills) coming from a House committee before they go to the full House.

House Ways and Means Committee. The House of Representatives committee that, along with the **Senate Finance Committee,** writes the tax codes, subject to the approval of Congress as a whole.

hyperpluralism. A theory of government and politics contending that groups are so strong that government is weakened. Hyperpluralism is an extreme, exaggerated, or perverted form of **pluralism.** Compare **elite and class theory, pluralist theory,** and **traditional democratic theory.**

I

ideology. See **political ideology.**

impacts. See **policy impacts.**

impeachment. The political equivalent of an indictment in criminal law, prescribed by the Constitution. The House of Representatives may impeach the president by a majority vote for "Treason, Bribery, or other high Crimes and Misdemeanors."

implementation. The stage of policymaking between the establishment of a policy and the consequences of the policy for the people whom it affects. Implementation involves translating the goals and objectives of a policy into an operating, ongoing program. See also **judicial implementation.**

implied powers. Powers of the federal government that go beyond those enumerated in the Constitution. The Constitution states that Congress has the power to "make all laws necessary and proper for carrying into execution" the powers enumerated in Article I. Many federal policies are justified on the basis of implied powers. See also ***McCulloch v. Maryland,*** **elastic clause,** and **enumerated powers.**

incentive system. According to Charles Shultze, a more effective and efficient policy than **command-and-control;** in the incentive system, marketlike strategies are used to manage public policy.

income. The amount of funds collected between any two points in time. Compare **wealth.**

income distribution. The "shares" of the national income earned by various groups.

income taxes. Shares of individual wages and corporate revenues collected by the government. The first income tax was declared unconstitutional by the Supreme Court in 1895, but the **Sixteenth Amendment** explicitly authorized Congress to levy a tax on income. See also **Internal Revenue Service.**

incorporation doctrine. The legal concept under which the **Supreme Court** has nationalized the **Bill of Rights** by making most of its provisions applicable to the states through the **Fourteenth Amendment.**

incrementalism. The belief that the best predictor of this year's **budget** is last year's budget, plus a little bit more (an increment). According to Aaron Wildavsky, "Most of the budget is a product of previous decisions."

incumbents. Those already holding office. In congressional elections, incumbents usually win.

independent executive agency. The government not accounted for by **cabinet** departments, **independent regulatory agencies,** and **government corporations.** Its administrators are typically appointed by the president and serve at the president's pleasure. The Veterans Administration is an example.

independent regulatory agency. A government agency responsible for some sector of the economy, making and enforcing rules supposedly to protect the public interest. It also judges disputes over these rules. The Interstate Commerce Commission is an example. Compare **government corporation** and **independent executive agency.**

individualism. The belief that individuals should be left on their own by the government. One of the primary reasons for the comparatively small scope of American government is the prominence of this belief in American political thought and practice.

industrial policy. An economic policy that advocates the federal government's supporting key strategic industries, such as the making of computer chips, and protecting these industries from foreign competition by tariffs and other measures.

INF Treaty. The elimination of intermediate range nuclear forces (INF) through an agreement signed by President Reagan and Mikhail Gorbachev during the May 1988 Moscow summit. It was the first treaty to reduce current levels of nuclear weapons.

initiative petition. A state-level method of direct legislation used by voters in 23 states to put proposed legislation on the ballot. See also **referendum.**

instructed delegate. A legislator who mirrors the preferences of his or her constituents. Compare **trustee.**

interdependency. Mutual dependency, in which the actions of nations reverberate and affect one another's economic lifelines.

interest group. An organization of people with shared policy goals entering the policy process at several points to try to achieve those goals. Interest groups pursue their goals in many arenas.

intergenerational equity. The issue of the distribution of government benefits and burdens among the generations and over time. Affected groups include children, the working and middle classes, and the aged, all of whom are beneficiaries of public policies.

intergovernmental relations. The workings of the federal system—the entire set of interactions among national, state, and local governments.

Internal Revenue Service. The office established to collect federal **income taxes,** investigate violations of the tax laws, and prosecute tax criminals.

investigative journalism. The use of detectivelike reporting to unearth scandals, scams, and schemes, putting reporters in adversarial relationships with political leaders.

isolationism. A **foreign policy** course followed throughout most of our nation's history, whereby the United States has tried to stay out of other nations' conflicts, particularly European wars. Isolationism was reaffirmed by the Monroe Doctrine.

issue. See **political issue.**

J

Joint Chiefs of Staff. The commanding officers of the armed services who advise the president on military policy.

joint committees. Congressional committees on a few subject-matter areas with membership drawn from both houses. See also **standing committees, conference committees,** and **select committees.**

judicial activism. A judicial philosophy in which judges make bold policy decisions, even charting new constitutional ground. Advocates of this approach emphasize that the courts can correct pressing needs, especially those unmet by the majoritarian political process.

judicial implementation. How and whether court decisions are translated into actual policy, affecting the behavior of others. The courts rely on other units of government to enforce their decisions.

judicial interpretation. A major informal way in which the Constitution is changed by the courts as they balance citizens' rights against those of the government. See also **judicial review.**

judicial restraint. A judicial philosophy in which judges play minimal policymaking roles, leaving that strictly to the legislatures. Compare **judicial activism.**

judicial review. The power of the courts to determine whether acts of Congress, and by implication the executive, are in accord with the **U.S. Constitution.** Judicial review was established by John Marshall and his associates in ***Marbury v. Madison.*** See also **judicial interpretation.**

jurisdiction. See **original jurisdiction** and **appellate jurisdiction.**

justiciable disputes. A constraint on the courts, requiring that a case must be capable of being settled by legal methods.

K

Keynesian economic theory. The theory emphasizing that government spending and deficits can help the economy weather its normal ups and downs. Proponents of this theory advocate using the power of government to stimulate the economy when it is lagging. See also **fiscal policy.**

Korematsu v. United States. A 1944 Supreme Court decision that upheld as constitutional the internment of more than 100,000 Americans of Japanese descent in encampments during World War II.

L

laissez-faire. The principle that government should not meddle in the economy. See also **capitalism.**

leak. See **news leak.**

legislative courts. Courts established by Congress for specialized purposes, such as the Court of Military Appeals. Judges who serve on these courts have fixed terms and lack the protections of **constitutional court** judges.

legislative proposal. A method of state constitutional revision in which the state legislature offers a proposed change to state voters for approval (or may be used to describe a bill proposed by a legislator). See also **constitutional convention** and **popular initiative.**

legislative turnover. The rate at which incumbent state legislators leave office by choice or by defeat during a bid for reelection.

legislative veto. The ability of Congress to override a presidential decision. Although the **War Powers Resolution** asserts this authority, there is reason to believe that, if challenged, the Supreme Court would find the legislative veto in violation of the doctrine of separation of powers.

legislators. The elected representatives of state citizens who serve in the state legislature and make public policy.

legitimacy. A characterization of elections by political scientists meaning that they are almost universally accepted as a fair and free method of selecting political leaders. When legitimacy is high, as in the United States, even the losers accept the results peacefully.

libel. The publication of false or malicious statements that damage someone's reputation.

liberalism. A **political ideology** whose advocates prefer a government active in dealing with human needs, support individual rights and liberties, and give higher priority to social needs than to military needs.

liberals. Those who advocate **liberalism.** Compare **conservatives.**

lieutenant governor. Often the second-highest executive official in state government, who is elected with the governor as a ticket in some states and is elected separately in others. May have legislative and executive branch responsibilities.

limited government. The idea that certain things are out of bounds for government because of the **natural rights** of citizens. Limited government was central to John Locke's philosophy in the seventeenth century, and it contrasted sharply with the prevailing view of the divine rights of monarchs.

line-item veto. A power that permits some state governors to veto parts of legislative bills sent to the governor for approval; most often used to change legislatively approved state budget bills.

linkage institutions. The channels or access points through which issues and people's policy preferences get on the government's **policy agenda.** In the United States, elections, **political parties,** and **interest groups** are the three main linkage institutions.

litigants. The **plaintiff** and the **defendant** in a **case.**

lobbying. According to Lester Milbrath, a "communication, by someone other than a citizen acting on his own behalf, directed to a governmental decision-maker with the hope of influencing his decision."

M

McCarthyism. The fear, prevalent in the 1950s, that international communism was conspiratorial, insidious, bent on world domination, and infiltrating American government and cultural institutions. It was named after Senator Joseph McCarthy and flourished after the Korean War.

McCulloch v. Maryland. An 1819 Supreme Court decision that established the supremacy of the national government over state governments. In deciding this case, Chief Justice John Marshall and his colleagues held that Congress had certain **implied powers** in addition to the **enumerated powers** found in the Constitution.

McGovern-Fraser Commission. A commission formed at the 1968 Democratic convention in response to demands for reform by minority groups and others who sought better representation.

machine. According to Edward C. Banfield and James Q. Wilson, a "party organization that depends crucially on inducements that are both specific and material." Machines and their local leaders exchange favors for votes and personalize politics.

majority leader. The principal partisan ally of the Speaker of the House or the party's wheel horse in the Senate. The majority leader is responsible for scheduling bills, influencing committee assignments, and rounding up votes in behalf of the party's legislative positions.

majority rule. A fundamental principle of **traditional democratic theory.** In a democracy, choosing among alternatives requires that the majority's desire be respected. See also **minority rights.**

mandate. See **electoral mandate** and **mandate theory of elections.**

mandate theory of elections. The idea that the winning candidate has a mandate from the people to carry out his or her platforms and politics. Politicians like the theory better than political scientists do.

Mapp v. Ohio. The 1961 Supreme Court decision ruling that the Fourth Amendment's protection against **unreasonable searches and seizures** must be extended to the states as well as the federal government. See also **exclusionary rule.**

Marbury v. Madison. The 1803 case in which Chief Justice John Marshall and his associates first asserted the right of the **Supreme Court** to determine the meaning of the **U.S. Constitution.** The decision established the Court's power of **judicial review** over acts of Congress, in this case the Judiciary Act of 1789.

mass media. Television, radio, newspapers, magazines, and other means of popular communication. They are a key part of **high-tech politics.** See also **broadcast media** and **print media.**

mayor–council government. One of three common forms of municipal government in which voters elect both a mayor and a city council. In the weak-mayor form, the city council is more powerful; in the strong-mayor form, the mayor is the chief executive of city government. See also **council–manager government** and **commission government.**

media events. Events purposely staged for the media that nonetheless look spontaneous. In keeping with politics as theater, media events can be staged by individuals, groups, and government officials, especially presidents.

Medicaid. A public assistance program designed to provide health care for poor Americans. Medicaid is funded by both the states and the national government. Compare **Medicare.**

Medicare. A program added to the Social Security system in 1965 that provides hospitalization insurance for the elderly and permits older Americans to purchase inexpensive coverage for doctor fees and other expenses. Compare **Medicaid.**

melting pot. The mixing of cultures, ideas, and peoples that has changed the American nation. The United States, with its history of immigration, has often been called a melting pot.

merit principle. The idea that hiring should be based on entrance exams and promotion ratings to produce administration by people with talent and skill. See also **civil service** and compare **patronage.**

Miami Herald Publishing Company v. Tornillo. A 1974 case in which the Supreme Court held that a state could not force a newspaper to print replies from candidates it had criticized, illustrating the limited power of government to restrict the **print media.** See ***Red Lion Broadcasting Company v. FCC.***

Miller v. California. A 1973 Supreme Court decision that avoided defining obscenity by holding that community standards be used to determine whether material is obscene in terms of appealing to a "prurient interest."

minority leader. The principal leader of the minority party in the House of Representatives or in the Senate.

minority majority. The emergence of a non-Caucasian majority, as compared with a white, generally Anglo-Saxon majority. It is predicted that, by about 2060, Hispanic Americans, African Americans, and Asian Americans together will outnumber white Americans.

minority rights. A principle of **traditional democratic theory** that guarantees rights to those who do not belong to majorities and allows that they might join majorities through persuasion and reasoned argument. See also **majority rule.**

Miranda v. Arizona. The 1966 Supreme Court decision that sets guidelines for police questioning of accused persons to protect them against **self-incrimination** and to protect their right to counsel.

Missouri Plan. A method of selecting judges in the states that begins with appointment to the bench by the governor from a list of names prepared by an advisory group of lawyers and laypersons. After serving on the bench for a year, the judge runs in a retention election in which voters decide whether the judge should be retained on the court for a specified number of years.

mixed economy. An economic system in which the government is deeply involved in economic decisions through its role as regulator, consumer, subsidizer, taxer, employer, and borrower. The United States can be considered a mixed economy. Compare **capitalism.**

monetarism. An economic theory holding that the supply of money is the key to a nation's economic health. Monetarists believe that too much cash and credit in circulation produces inflation. See also **monetary policy.**

monetary policy. Based on **monetarism,** monetary policy is the manipulation of the supply of money in private hands by which the government can control the economy. See also the **Federal Reserve System,** and compare **fiscal policy.**

Motor Voter Act. Passed in 1993, this Act went into effect for the 1996 election. It requires states to permit people to register to vote at the same time they apply for drivers' licenses. This should lessen the bureaucratic hassles of voter registration, though critics charge that it may also increase registration fraud.

multinational corporations. Large businesses with vast holdings in many countries. Many of these companies are larger than most governments.

municipalities. Another name for *cities,* also known by the legal term *municipal corporations;* denotes a government created by charter granted from the state government or by home rule charter approved by local voters.

N

NAACP v. Alabama. The Supreme Court protected the right to assemble peaceably in this 1958 case when it decided the NAACP did not have to reveal its membership list and thus subject its members to harassment.

national chairperson. One of the institutions that keeps the party operating between conventions. The national chairperson is responsible for the day-to-day activities of the party and is usually hand-picked by the presidential nominee. See also **national committee.**

national committee. One of the institutions that keeps the party operating between conventions. The national committee is composed of representatives from the states and territories. See also **national chairperson.**

national convention. The meeting of party delegates every 4 years to choose a presidential ticket and write the party's platform.

National Environmental Policy Act (NEPA). The law passed in 1969 that is the centerpiece of federal environmental policy in the United States. The NEPA established the requirements for **environmental impact statements.**

national health insurance. A compulsory insurance program for all Americans that would have the government finance citizens' medical care. First proposed by President Harry S Truman, the plan has been soundly opposed by the American Medical Association.

National Institutes of Health (NIH). Agencies of the national government that conduct research on health and medical issues—an example of how the government is involved in health policy.

National Labor Relations Act. A 1935 law, also known as the Wagner Act, that guarantees workers the right of **collective bargaining,** sets down rules to protect unions and organizers, and created the National Labor Relations Board to regulate labor–management relations.

national party convention. The supreme power within each of the parties. The convention meets every 4 years to nominate the party's presidential and vice-presidential candidates and to write the party's platform.

national primary. A proposal by critics of the **caucuses** and **presidential primaries** systems who would replace these electoral methods with a nationwide **primary** held early in the election year.

National Security Council. An office created in 1947 to coordinate the president's foreign and military policy advisors. Its formal members are the president, vice president, **secretary of state,** and **secretary of defense,** and it is managed by the president's national security advisor.

NATO. See **North Atlantic Treaty Organization.**

natural rights. Rights held to be inherent in human beings, not dependent on governments. John Locke asserted that natural law, which is superior to human law, specifies certain rights of "life, liberty, and property," a sentiment reflected in the **Declaration of Independence.**

Near v. Minnesota. The 1931 Supreme Court decision holding that the **First Amendment** protects newspapers from **prior restraint.**

necessary and proper clause. See **elastic clause.**

New Deal Coalition. A **coalition** forged by Franklin Roosevelt and the Democrats, who dominated American politics from the 1930s to the 1960s. Its basic elements were the urban working class, ethnic groups, Catholics and Jews, the poor, Southerners, African Americans, and Democratic intellectuals.

New Jersey Plan. The proposal at the Constitutional Convention that called for equal **representation** of each state in Congress regardless of the state's population. Compare **Virginia Plan** and **Connecticut Compromise.**

New York Times *v. Sullivan.* Decided in 1964, this case established the guidelines for determining whether public officials and public figures could win damage suits for libel. To do so, said the Court, such individuals must prove that the defamatory statements made about them were made with "actual malice" and reckless disregard for the truth.

news leak. A carefully placed bit of inside information given to a friendly reporter. Leaks can benefit both the leaker and the leakee.

newspaper chains. Newspapers published by massive media conglomerates that account for almost three-quarters of the nation's daily circulation. Often these chains control **broadcast media** as well.

Nineteenth Amendment. The constitutional amendment adopted in 1920 that guarantees women the right to vote. See also **suffrage.**

nomination. The official endorsement of a candidate for office by a **political party.** Generally, success in the nomination game requires momentum, money, and media attention.

nonrenewable resources. Minerals and other resources that nature does not replace when they are consumed. Many commonly used energy resources, such as oil and coal, are nonrenewable.

North Atlantic Treaty Organization (NATO). Created in 1949, an organization whose members include the United States, Canada, most Western European nations, and Turkey, all of whom agreed to combine military forces and to treat a war against one as a war against all. Compare **Warsaw Pact.**

O

Office of Management and Budget (OMB). An office that grew out of the Bureau of the Budget, created in 1921, consisting of a handful of political appointees and hundreds of skilled professionals. The OMB performs both managerial and budgetary functions, and although the president is its boss, the director and staff have considerable independence in the budgetary process. See also **Congressional Budget Office.**

Office of Personnel Management (OPM). The office in charge of hiring for most agencies of the federal government, using elaborate rules in the process.

Olson's law of large groups. Advanced by Mancur Olson, a principle stating that "the larger the group, the further it will fall short of providing an optimal amount of a collective good." See also **interest group.**

OPEC. See **Organization of Petroleum Exporting Countries.**

opinion. A statement of legal reasoning behind a judicial decision. The content of an opinion may be as important as the decision itself.

Organization of Petroleum Exporting Countries (OPEC). An economic organization, consisting primarily of Arab nations, that controls the price of oil and the amount of oil its members produce and sell to other nations. The Arab members of OPEC caused the oil boycott in the winter of 1973–1974.

original intent. A view that the Constitution should be interpreted according to the original intent of the framers. Many **conservatives** support this view.

original jurisdiction. The jurisdiction of courts that hear a case first, usually in a trial. These are the courts that determine the facts about a case. Compare **appellate jurisdiction.**

oversight. The process of monitoring the bureaucracy and its administration of policy, mainly through congressional hearings.

P

PACs. See **political action committees (PACs).**

parliamentary governments. Governments, like the one in Great Britain, that typically select the political leader from membership in the parliament (the legislature).

participation. See **political participation.**

party. See **political party.**

party competition. The battle of the parties for control of public offices. Ups and downs of the two major parties are one of the most important elements in American politics.

party dealignment. The gradual disengagement of people and politicians from the parties, as seen in part by shrinking **party identification.**

party eras. Historical periods in which a majority of voters cling to the party in power, which tends to win a majority of the elections. See also **critical election** and **party realignment.**

party identification. A citizen's self-proclaimed preference for one party or the other.

party image. The voter's perception of what the Republicans or Democrats stand for, such as **conservatism** or **liberalism.**

party machines. A type of political party organization that relies heavily on material inducements, such as patronage, to win votes and to govern.

party neutrality. A term used to describe the fact that many Americans are indifferent toward the two major political parties. See also **party dealignment.**

party realignment. The displacement of the majority party by the minority party, usually during a **critical election period.** See also **party era.**

patronage. One of the key inducements used by **machines.** A patronage job, promotion, or contract is one that is given for political reasons rather than for merit or competence alone. Compare **civil service** and the **merit principle.**

Pendleton Civil Service Act. Passed in 1883, an Act that created a federal **civil service** so that hiring and promotion would be based on merit rather than **patronage.**

per curiam decision. A court decision without explanation—in other words, without an **opinion.**

Planned Parenthood v. Casey. A 1992 case in which the Supreme Court loosened its standard for evaluating restrictions on abortion from one of "strict scrutiny" of any restraints on a "fundamental right" to one of "undue burden" that permits considerably more regulation.

plea bargaining. An actual bargain struck between the defendant's lawyer and the prosecutor to the effect that the defendant will plead guilty to a lesser crime in exchange for the state's promise not to prosecute the defendant for the more serious one.

Plessy v. Ferguson. An 1896 Supreme Court decision that provided a constitutional justification for segregation by ruling that a Louisiana law requiring "equal but separate accommodations for the white and colored races" was not unconstitutional.

pluralist theory. A theory of government and politics emphasizing that politics is mainly a competition among groups, each one pressing for its own preferred policies. Compare **elite and class theory, hyperpluralism,** and **traditional democratic theory.**

pocket veto. A veto taking place when Congress adjourns within 10 days of having submitted a **bill** to the president, who simply lets it die by neither signing nor vetoing it. See also **veto.**

policy. See **public policy.**

policy agenda. According to John Kingdon, "the list of subjects or problems to which government officials, and people outside of government closely associated with those officials, are paying some serious attention at any given time."

policy differences. The perception of a clear choice between the parties. Those who see such choices are more likely to vote.

policy entrepreneurs. People who invest their political "capital" in an issue. According to John Kingdon, a policy entrepreneur "could be in or out of government, in elected or appointed positions, in interest groups or research organizations."

policy gridlocks. A condition that occurs when no coalition is strong enough to form a majority and establish policy. The result is that nothing may get done.

policy impacts. The effects a policy has on people and problems. Impacts are analyzed to see how well a policy has met its goal and at what cost.

policy implementation. See **implementation.**

policy voting. Voting that occurs when electoral choices are made on the basis of the voters' policy preferences and on the basis of where the candidates stand on policy issues. For the voter, policy voting is hard work.

political action committees (PACs). Funding vehicles created by the 1974 campaign finance reforms. A corporation, union, or some other interest group can create a PAC and register it with the **Federal Election Commission (FEC),** which will meticulously monitor the PAC's expenditures.

political economy. The relationship between government and the economy.

political efficacy. The belief that one's **political participation** really matters—that one's vote can actually make a difference.

political ethics. Matters of right or wrong with respect to government, involving either the actions of individual politicians or policy choices.

political ideology. A coherent set of beliefs about politics, public policy, and public purpose. It helps give meaning to political events, personalities, and policies. See also **liberalism** and **conservatism.**

political issue. An issue that arises when people disagree about a problem and a public policy choice.

political participation. All the activities used by citizens to influence the selection of political leaders or the policies they pursue. The most common, but not the only, means of political participation in a **democracy** is voting. Other means include **protest** and **civil disobedience.**

political party. According to Anthony Downs, a "team of men [and women] seeking to control the governing apparatus by gaining office in a duly constituted election."

political questions. A doctrine developed by the federal courts and used as a means to avoid deciding some cases, principally those involving conflicts between the president and Congress.

political socialization. According to Richard Dawson, "the process through which an individual acquires his [or her] particular political orientations—his [or her] knowledge, feelings, and evaluations regarding his [or her] political world." See also **agents of socialization.**

political system. A set of institutions and activities that link together people, politics, and policy.

politics. According to Harold Lasswell, "who gets what, when, and how." Politics produces authoritative decisions about public issues.

poll taxes. Small taxes, levied on the right to vote, that often fell due at a time of year when poor African-American sharecroppers had the least cash on hand. This method was used by most Southern states to exclude African Americans from voting registers. Poll taxes were declared void by the **Twenty-fourth Amendment** in 1964. See also **grandfather clause** and **white primary.**

polls. See **exit polls.**

popular initiative. A process permitted in some states whereby voters may place proposed changes in the state constitution on a state referendum if sufficient signatures are obtained on petitions calling for such a referendum. See also **legislative proposal** and **constitutional convention.**

pork barrel. The mighty list of federal projects, grants, and contracts available to cities, businesses, colleges, and institutions in the district of a member of Congress.

position taking. According to David Mayhew, one of three primary activities undertaken by members of Congress to increase the probability of their reelection. It involves taking a stand on issues and responding to constituents about these positions. See also **advertising** and **credit taking.**

potential group. All the people who might be **interest group** members because they share some common interest. A potential group is almost always larger than an actual group.

poverty line. A method used to count the number of poor people, it considers what a family would need to spend for an "austere" standard of living.

power. The capacity to get people to do something that they would not otherwise do. The quest for power is a strong motivation to political activity.

precedents. How similar cases have been decided in the past.

presidential approval. An evaluation of the president based on many factors, but especially on the predisposition of many people to support the president. One measure is provided by the Gallup Poll.

presidential coattails. The situation occurring when voters cast their ballots for congressional candidates of the president's party because they support the president. Recent studies show that few races are won this way.

presidential debate. A debate between presidential candidates. The first televised debate was between Richard Nixon and John Kennedy during the 1960 campaign.

presidential primaries. Elections in which voters in a state vote for a candidate (or delegates pledged to him or her). Most delegates to the **national party conventions** are chosen this way.

press conferences. Meetings of public officials with reporters.

press secretary. The person on the White House staff who most often deals directly with the press, serving as a conduit of information. Press secretaries conduct daily press briefings.

price supports. The mechanism by which the federal government guarantees the prices of certain agricultural commodities by regularly buying surplus crops in order to keep prices high. In return, farmers agree to limit planting in a given year.

primaries. Elections that select candidates. In addition to **presidential primaries,** there are **direct primaries** for selecting party nominees for congressional and state offices and proposals for **regional primaries.**

print media. Newspapers and magazines, as compared with **broadcast media.**

prior restraint. A government's preventing material from being published. This is a common method of limiting the press in some nations, but it is unconstitutional in the United States, according to the **First Amendment** and as confirmed in the 1931 Supreme Court case of ***Near v. Minnesota.***

privacy. See **right to privacy.**

Privacy Act. A law passed in 1974 stipulating that information collected by one agency of the government cannot be used by another. For example, a driving record cannot be used to deny Social Security benefits.

privileges and immunities clause. A clause in Article IV, Section 2, of the Constitution according citizens of each state most of the privileges of citizens of other states.

probable cause. The situation occurring when the police have reason to believe that a person should be arrested. In making the arrest, the police are allowed legally to search for and seize incriminating evidence. Compare **unreasonable searches and seizures.**

progressive tax. A tax by which the government takes a greater share of the **income** of the rich than of the poor—for example, when a rich family pays 50 percent of its income in taxes and a poor family pays 5 percent. Compare **regressive tax** and **proportional tax.**

project grants. Federal grants given for specific purposes and awarded on the basis of the merits of applications. A type of the **categorical grants** available to states and localities.

proportional representation. An electoral system used throughout most of Europe that awards legislative seats to political parties in proportion to the number of votes won in an election. Compare with **winner-take-all system.**

proportional tax. A tax by which the government takes the same share of income from everyone, rich and poor alike—for example, when a rich family pays 20 percent and a poor family pays 20 percent. Compare **progressive tax** and **regressive tax.**

protest. A form of **political participation** designed to achieve policy change through dramatic and unconventional tactics. See also **civil disobedience.**

public goods. Goods, such as clean air and clean water, that everyone must share.

public interest. The idea that there are some interests superior to the private interest of groups and individuals, interests we all have in common. See also **public interest lobbies.**

public interest lobbies. According to Jeffrey Berry, organizations that seek "a collective good, the achievement of which will not selectively and materially benefit the membership or activities of the organization." See also **lobbying** and **public interest.**

public opinion. The distribution of the population's beliefs about politics and policy issues.

public policy. A choice that **government** makes in response to a political issue. A policy is a course of action taken with regard to some problem.

R

random digit dialing. A technique used by pollsters to place telephone calls randomly to both listed and unlisted numbers when conducting a survey. See also **random sampling.**

random sampling. The key technique employed by sophisticated survey researchers, which operates on the principle that everyone should have an equal probability of being selected for the sample. See also **sample.**

rational-choice theory. A popular theory in political science to explain the actions of voters as well as politicians. It assumes that individuals act in their own best interest, carefully weighing the costs and benefits of possible alternatives.

realignment. See **party realignment.**

reapportionment. The process of reallocating seats in the House of Representatives every 10 years on the basis of the results of the census.

reconciliation. A congressional process through which program authorizations are revised to achieve required savings. It usually also includes tax or other revenue adjustments.

Red Lion Broadcasting Company v. FCC. A 1969 case in which the Supreme Court upheld restrictions on radio and television broadcasting, such as giving adequate coverage to public issues and covering opposing views. These restrictions on the **broadcast media** are much tighter than those on the **print media,** because there are only a limited number of broadcasting frequencies available. See ***Miami Herald Publishing Company v. Tornillo.***

Reed v. Reed. The landmark case in 1971 in which the Supreme Court for the first time upheld a claim of gender discrimination.

referendum. A state-level method of direct legislation that gives voters a chance to approve or disapprove proposed legislation or a proposed constitutional amendment. See also **initiative petition.**

Regents of the University of California v. Bakke. A 1978 Supreme Court decision holding that a state university could not admit less qualified individuals solely because of their race. The Court did not, however, rule that such **affirmative action** policies and the use of race as a criterion for admission were unconstitutional, only that they had to be formulated differently.

regional primaries. A proposal by critics of the **caucuses** and **presidential primaries** to replace these electoral methods with regional primaries held early in the election year.

registration. See **voter registration.**

regressive tax. A tax in which the burden falls relatively more heavily upon low-income groups than upon wealthy taxpayers. The opposite of a **progressive tax,** in which tax rates increase as income increases.

regulation. The use of governmental authority to control or change some practice in the private sector. Regulations pervade the daily lives of people and institutions.

regulatory agency. See **independent regulatory agency.**

reinforcement. One of three key consequences of electoral campaigns for voters, in which the voter's candidate preference is reinforced. See also **activation** and **conversion.**

relative deprivation. A perception by a group that it is doing less well than is appropriate in relation to a reference group. The desire of a group to correct what it views as the unfair distribution of resources, such as income or government benefits, is a frequent motivator for political activism.

representation. A basic principle of **traditional democratic theory** that describes the relationship between the few leaders and the many followers.

republic. A form of government that derives its power, directly or indirectly, from the people. Those chosen to govern are accountable to those whom they govern. In contrast to a direct democracy, in which people themselves make laws, in a republic the people select representatives who make the laws.

responsible party model. A view favored by some political scientists about how parties should work. According to the model, parties should offer clear choices to the voters, who can then use those choices as cues to their own preferences of candidates. Once in office, parties would carry out their campaign promises.

retrospective voting. A theory of voting in which voters essentially ask this simple question: "What have you done for me lately?"

revenues. The financial resources of the federal government. The individual income tax and Social Security tax are two major sources of revenue. Compare **expenditures.**

right to privacy. According to Paul Bender, "the right to keep the details of [one's] life confidential; the free and untrammeled use and enjoyment of one's intellect, body, and private property . . . the right, in sum, to a private personal life free from the intrusion of government or the dictates of society." The right to privacy is implicitly protected by the **Bill of Rights.** See also **Privacy Act.**

right-to-work law. A state law forbidding requirements that workers must join a union to hold their jobs. State right-to-work laws were specifically permitted by the Taft-Hartley Act of 1947.

Roe v. Wade. The 1973 Supreme Court decision holding that a state ban on all abortions was unconstitutional. The decision forbade state control over abortions during the first trimester of pregnancy, permitted states to limit abortions to protect the mother's health in the second trimester, and permitted states to protect the fetus during the third trimester.

Roth v. United States. A 1957 Supreme Court decision ruling that "obscenity is not within the area of constitutionally protected speech or press."

S

sample. A relatively small proportion of people who are chosen in a survey so as to be representative of the whole.

sampling error. The level of confidence in the findings of a public opinion poll. The more people interviewed, the more confident one can be of the results.

Schenck v. United States. A 1919 decision upholding the conviction of a socialist who had urged young men to resist the draft during World War I. Justice Holmes declared that government can limit speech if the speech provokes a "clear and present danger" of substantive evils.

School District of Abington Township, Pennsylvania v. Schempp. A 1963 Supreme Court decision holding that a Pennsylvania law requiring Bible reading in schools violated the **establishment clause** of the **First Amendment.** Compare ***Engel v. Vitale.***

school districts. Units of local government that are normally independent of any other local government and are primarily responsible for operating public schools.

search warrant. A written authorization from a court specifying the area to be searched and what the police are searching for. The Fourth Amendment requires a search warrant to prevent **unreasonable searches and seizures.**

secretary of defense. The head of the Department of Defense and the president's key advisor on military policy; a key **foreign policy** actor.

secretary of state. The head of the Department of State and traditionally a key advisor to the president on **foreign policy.**

select committees. Congressional committees appointed for a specific purpose, such as the Watergate investigation. See also **joint committees, standing committees,** and **conference committees.**

selective benefits. Goods (such as information publications, travel discounts, and group insurance rates) that a group can restrict to those who pay their yearly dues. The American Association of Retired Persons (AARP) has built up a membership list of 32 million senior citizens through offering a variety of such goods.

selective perception. The phenomenon that people often pay the most attention to things they already agree with and interpret them according to their own predispositions.

self-incrimination. The situation occurring when an individual accused of a crime is compelled to be a witness against himself or herself in court. The **Fifth Amendment** forbids self-incrimination. See also ***Miranda v. Arizona.***

Senate Finance Committee. The Senate committee that, along with the **House Ways and Means Committee,** writes the tax codes, subject to the approval of Congress as a whole.

senatorial courtesy. An unwritten tradition whereby nominations for state-level federal judicial posts are not confirmed if they are opposed by the senator from the state in which the nominee will serve. The tradition also applies to courts of appeal when there is opposition from the nominee's state senator, if the senator belongs to the president's party.

Senior Executive Service (SES). An elite cadre of about 11,000 federal government managers, established by the Civil Service Reform Act of 1978, who are mostly career officials but include some political appointees who do not require Senate confirmation.

seniority system. A simple rule for picking **committee chairs,** in effect until the 1970s. The member who had served on the committee the longest and whose party controlled Congress became chair, regardless of party loyalty, mental state, or competence.

separation of powers. An important part of the **Madisonian model** that requires each of the three branches of government—executive, legislative, and judicial—to be relatively independent of the others so that one cannot control the others. Power is shared among these three institutions. See also **checks and balances.**

Shays' Rebellion. A series of attacks on courthouses by a small band of farmers led by revolutionary war Captain Daniel Shays to block foreclosure proceedings.

Simpson-Mazzolli Act. An immigration law, named after its legislative sponsors, that as of June 1, 1987, requires employees to document the citizenship of their employees. Civil and criminal penalties can be assessed against employers who knowingly employ illegal immigrants.

single-issue groups. Groups that have a narrow interest, tend to dislike compromise, and often draw membership from people new to politics. These features distinguish them from traditional **interest groups.**

Sixteenth Amendment. The constitutional amendment adopted in 1915 that explicitly permitted Congress to levy an **income tax.**

Sixth Amendment. The constitutional amendment designed to protect individuals accused of crimes. It includes the right to counsel, the right to confront witnesses, and the right to a speedy and public trial.

social policies. Policies that manipulate opportunities through public choice. They include policies related to income and policies related to opportunity.

Social Security Act. A 1935 law passed during the Great Depression that was intended to provide a minimal level of sustenance to older Americans and thus save them from poverty.

social welfare policies. Policies that provide benefits to individuals, particularly to those in need. Compare **civil rights policies.**

socialized medicine. A system in which the full cost of medical care is borne by the national government. Great Britain and the former Soviet Union are examples of countries that have socialized medicine. Compare **Medicaid** and **Medicare.**

soft money. Political contributions earmarked for party-building expenses at the grass-roots level (buttons, pamphlets, yard signs, etc.). Unlike money that goes to the campaign of a particular candidate, such party donations are not subject to contribution limits.

solicitor general. A presidential appointee and the third-ranking office in the Department of Justice. The solicitor general is in charge of the appellate court litigation of the federal government.

sound bites. Short video clips of approximately 15 seconds, which are typically all that is shown from a politician's speech or activities on the nightly television news.

Speaker of the House. An office mandated by the Constitution. The Speaker is chosen in practice by the majority party, has both formal and informal powers, and is second in line to succeed to the presidency should that office become vacant.

special districts. Limited-purpose local governments called *districts* or *public authorities* that are created to run a specific type of service, such as water distribution, airports, public transportation, libraries, and natural resource areas.

standard operating procedures. Better known as SOPs, these procedures are used by bureaucrats to bring uniformity to complex organizations. Uniformity improves fairness and makes personnel interchangeable. See also **administrative discretion.**

standing committees. Separate subject-matter committees in each house of Congress that handle **bills** in different policy areas. See also **joint committees, conference committees,** and **select committees.**

standing to sue. The requirement that **plaintiffs** have a serious interest in a **case,** which depends on whether they have sustained or are likely to sustain a direct and substantial injury from a party or an action of government.

stare decisis. A Latin phrase meaning "let the decision stand." The vast majority of cases reaching appellate courts are settled on this principle.

statutory construction. The judicial interpretation of an act of Congress. In some cases where statutory construction is an issue, Congress passes new legislation to clarify existing laws.

Strategic Defense Initiative (SDI). Renamed "Star Wars" by critics, a plan for defense against the Soviet Union unveiled by President Reagan in 1983. SDI would create a global umbrella in space, using computers to scan the skies and high-tech devices to destroy invading missiles.

street-level bureaucrats. A phrase coined by Michael Lipsky, referring to those bureaucrats who are in constant contact with the public and have considerable **administrative discretion.**

subgovernments. Also known as "iron triangles," subgovernments are composed of key interest group leaders interested in a policy, the government agency responsible for the policy's administration, and the members of the congressional committees and subcommittees handling the policy.

suffrage. The legal right to vote, extended to African Americans by the **Fifteenth Amendment,** to women by the **Nineteenth Amendment,** and to people over the age of 18 by the **Twenty-sixth Amendment.**

Super Tuesday. Created by a dozen or so Southern states when they held their **presidential primaries** in early March 1988. These states hoped to promote a regional advantage as well as a more conservative candidate.

superdelegates. National party leaders who automatically get a delegate slot at the Democratic **national party convention.**

Superfund. A $1.6 billion fund created by Congress in the late 1970s and renewed in the 1980s to clean up hazardous waste sites. Money for the fund comes from taxing chemical products.

supply-side economics. An economic theory, advocated by President Reagan, holding that too much income goes to taxes and too little money is available for purchasing and that the solution is to cut taxes and return purchasing power to consumers. Supply-side economics has widened the gap between government **revenues** and **expenditures.**

supremacy clause. Article VI of the Constitution, which makes the Constitution, national laws, and treaties supreme over state laws when the national government is acting within its constitutional limits.

Supreme Court. The pinnacle of the American judicial system. The Court ensures uniformity in interpreting national laws, resolves conflicts among states, and maintains national supremacy in law. It has both **original jurisdiction** and **appellate jurisdiction,** but unlike other federal courts, it controls its own agenda.

symbolic speech. Nonverbal communication, such as burning a flag or wearing an armband. The Supreme Court has accorded some symbolic speech protection under the **First Amendment.** See ***Texas v. Johnson.***

T

Taft-Hartley Act. A 1947 law giving the president power to halt major strikes by seeking a court injunction and permitting states to forbid requirements in labor contracts forcing workers to join a union. See also **right-to-work law.**

talking head. A shot of a person's face talking directly to the camera. Because this is visually unappealing, the major commercial networks rarely show a politician talking one-on-one for very long. See also **sound bites.**

tariff. A special tax added to imported goods to raise the price, thereby protecting American businesses and workers from foreign competition.

tax. See **proportional tax, progressive tax,** and **regressive tax.**

tax expenditures. Defined by the 1974 Budget Act as "revenue losses attributable to provisions of the federal tax laws which allow a special exemption, exclusion, or deduction." Tax expenditures represent the difference between what the government actually collects in taxes and what it would have collected without special exemptions.

Tenth Amendment. The constitutional amendment stating that "The powers not delegated to the United States by the Constitution, nor prohibited by it to the states, are reserved to the states respectively, or to the people."

Texas v. Johnson. A 1989 case in which the Supreme Court struck down a law banning the burning of the American flag on the grounds that such action was **symbolic speech** protected by the **First Amendment.**

third parties. Electoral contenders other than the two major parties. American third parties are not unusual, but they rarely win elections.

Thirteenth Amendment. The constitutional amendment passed after the Civil War that forbade slavery and involuntary servitude.

ticket splitting. Voting with one party for one office and with another party for other offices. It has become the norm in American voting behavior.

township. A political subdivision of local government that is found in 20 states and often serves to provide local government services in rural areas. It is a particularly strong form of local government—comparable to a municipality—in the Northeast.

trade-off. The sacrifice of one goal to achieve another.

traditional democratic theory. A theory about how a democratic government makes its decisions. According to Robert Dahl, its cornerstones are equality in voting, effective participation, enlightened understanding, final control over the agenda, and inclusion.

transfer payments. Benefits given by the government directly to individuals. Transfer payments may be either cash transfers, such as Social Security payments and retirement payments to former government employees, or in-kind transfers, such as Food Stamps and low-interest loans for college education.

trial balloons. An intentional **news leak** for the purpose of assessing the political reaction.

trial courts. The lowest tier in the trial court system, in which the facts of a case are considered. These courts hear both civil and criminal matters.

trustee. A legislator who uses his or her best judgment to make policy in the interests of the people.

This concept was favored by Edmund Burke. Compare **instructed delegate.**

Twenty-fifth Amendment. Passed in 1951, the amendment that permits the vice president to become acting president if both the vice president and the president's cabinet determine that the president is disabled. The amendment also outlines how a recuperated president can reclaim the job.

Twenty-fourth Amendment. The constitutional amendment passed in 1964 that declared **poll taxes** void.

Twenty-second Amendment. Passed in 1951, the amendment that limits presidents to two terms of office.

U

uncontrollable expenditures. Expenditures that are determined by how many eligible beneficiaries there are for some particular program. According to Lance LeLoup, an expenditure is classified as uncontrollable "if it is mandated under current law or by a previous obligation." Three-fourths of the federal **budget** is uncontrollable. Congress can change uncontrollable expenditures only by changing a law or existing benefit levels.

unemployment rate. As measured by the Bureau of Labor Statistics (BLS), the proportion of the labor force actively seeking work but unable to find jobs.

unfunded mandates. When the federal government requires state and local action but does not provide the funds to pay for the action.

union shop. A provision found in some collective bargaining agreements requiring all employees of a business to join the union within a short period, usually 30 days, and to remain members as a condition of employment.

unitary government. A way of organizing a nation so that all power resides in the central government. Most governments today, including those of Great Britain and Japan, are unitary governments. Compare **federalism.**

United Nations (UN). Created in 1945, an organization whose members agree to renounce war and to respect certain human and economic freedoms. The seat of real power in the UN is the Security Council.

United States v. Nixon. The 1974 case in which the Supreme Court unanimously held that the doctrine of executive privilege was implicit in the Constitution but could not be extended to protect documents relevant to criminal prosecutions.

unreasonable searches and seizures. Obtaining evidence in a haphazard or random manner, a practice prohibited by the Fourth Amendment. Both **probable cause** and a **search warrant** are required for a legal and proper search for and seizure of incriminating evidence.

unwritten constitution. The body of tradition, practice, and procedure that is as important as the written constitution. Changes in the unwritten **constitution** can change the spirit of the Constitution. **Political parties** and **national party conventions** are a part of the unwritten constitution in the United States.

urban underclass. The poorest of the poor in America. These are the Americans whose economic opportunities are severely limited in almost every way. They constitute a large percentage of the Americans afflicted by homelessness, crime, drugs, alcoholism, unwanted pregnancies, and other endemic social problems.

U.S. Constitution. The document written in 1787 and ratified in 1788 that sets forth the institutional structure of U.S. government and the tasks these institutions perform. It replaced the Articles of Confederation. See also **constitution** and **unwritten constitution.**

V

veto. The constitutional power of the president to send a **bill** back to Congress with reasons for rejecting it. A two-thirds vote in each house can override a veto. See also **pocket veto** and **legislative veto.**

Virginia Plan. The proposal at the Constitutional Convention that called for *representation* of each state in Congress in proportion to that state's share of the U.S. population. Compare **New Jersey Plan** and **Connecticut Compromise.**

voter registration. A system adopted by the states that requires voters to register well in advance of election day. Although a few states permit election day registration for presidential elections, advance registration dampens voter turnout.

Voting Rights Act of 1965. A law designed to help end formal and informal barriers to African-American **suffrage.** Under the law, federal registrars were sent to Southern states and counties that had long histories of discrimination; as a result, hundreds of thousands of African Americans were registered and the number of African-American elected officials increased dramatically.

W

War Powers Resolution. A law, passed in 1973 in reaction to American fighting in Vietnam and Cambodia, requiring presidents to consult with Congress whenever possible prior to using military force and to withdraw forces after 60 days unless Congress declares war or grants an extension. Presidents view the resolution as unconstitutional. See also **legislative veto.**

Water Pollution Control Act of 1972. A law intended to clean up the nation's rivers and lakes. It requires municipal, industrial, and other polluters to secure permits from the **Environmental Protection Agency** for discharging waste products into waters. According to the law, polluters are supposed to use "the best practicable [pollution] control technology."

Watergate. The events and scandal surrounding a break-in at the Democratic National Committee headquarters in 1972 and the subsequent cover-up of White House involvement, leading to the eventual resignation of President Nixon under the threat of **impeachment.**

wealth. The amount of funds already owned. Wealth includes stocks, bonds, bank deposits, cars, houses, and so forth. Throughout most of the last generation, wealth has been much less evenly divided than **income.**

whips. Party leaders who work with the **majority leader** to count votes beforehand and lean on waverers whose votes are crucial to a **bill** favored by the party.

white primary. One of the means used to discourage African-American voting that permitted political parties in the heavily Democratic South to exclude African Americans from primary elections, thus depriving them of a voice in the real contests. The Supreme Court declared white primaries unconstitutional in 1941. See also **grandfather clause** and **poll taxes.**

winner-take-all system. An electoral system in which legislative seats are awarded only to the candidates who come in first in their constituencies. In American presidential elections, the system in which the winner of the popular vote in a state receives all the electoral votes of that state. Compare with **proportional representation.**

writ of certiorari. A formal document issued from the **Supreme Court** to a lower federal or state court that calls up a case.

writ of habeas corpus. A court order requiring jailers to explain to a judge why they are holding a prisoner in custody.

writ of mandamus. A court order forcing action. In the dispute leading to ***Marbury v. Madison,*** Marbury and his associates asked the **Supreme Court** to issue a writ ordering Madison to give them their commissions.

Z

Zurcher v. Stanford Daily. A 1978 Supreme Court decision holding that a proper **search warrant** could be applied to a newspaper as well as to anyone else without necessarily violating the **First Amendment** rights to freedom of the press.

Acknowledgments

TEXT ACKNOWLEDGMENTS

Page 30: "Power Shift: Economic Status of State Legislators Before and After the Revolution War" from Jackson Turner Main, "Government by the People: The American Revolution and the Democratization of the Legislatures," *The William and Mary Quarterly,* 3rd ser. 23 (July 1966): Table 1. Reprinted by permission. *Page 57:* "Why Federalism?" from Central Intelligence Agency, *The World Factbook, 1994–95,* Brassey's, 1995. Reprinted by permission. *Page 73:* "National Government Responsibilities" from NBC News/ *Wall Street Journal* Polls, December 1994 and January 1995. Reprinted by permission. *Page 84:* "Prayer in the Public Schools" from CBS News/*New York Times* Poll, December 1994. Reprinted by permission. *Page 104:* "The Abortion Debate" from *The Wirthlin Report,* January 1997, page 3. Reprinted by permission. *Page 119:* "Percentage of Black Students Attending School with Any Whites in Southern States" from Lawrence Baum, *The Supreme Court,* 5th ed., 1995 Congressional Quarterly Press, p. 233. Reprinted with permission. *Page 128:* "Are Maternity Leaves a Form of Gender Discrimination?" from Judith A. Baer, *Women in American Law,* 2nd ed. Holmes & Meier Publishers, 1996. Copyright © 1996 Holmes & Meier Publishers, Inc. Reproduced by permission of the publisher. *Page 130:* "Mrs. In-the-Back-of-the-House Goes to Parliament" from Sherly WuDunn, "23 Women Break into a Male Citadel, " *New York Times,* October 26, 1996, p. 4. Copyright © 1996 by The New York Times Company. *Page 132:* "Discrimination Against Homosexuals" from Gallup Poll, November 1996. Reprinted by permission. *Page 135:* "Affirmative Action" from Gallup Poll, March 1995. Reprinted by permission. *Page 147:* "Shifting Population" from Richard Furno, *The Washington Post;* John Gunther, *Inside U.S.A.,* 1946. Reprinted by permission. *Page 148:* "Parent-Child Agreement on Party Identification" adapted from M. Kent Jennings and Richard G. Niemi, *The Political Character of Adolescence,* Princeton University Press, 1973, p. 39. Reprinted by permission. *Page 154:* "Citizens of the World Show Little Knowledge of Geography" from Warren E. Leary, "Two Superpowers' Citizens Do Badly in Geography," the *New York Times,* November 9, 1989. Copyright © 1989 by The New York Times Company. Reprinted by permission. *Page 157:* "Levels of Ideological Conceptualization" from Herbert B. Asher, *Presidential Elections and American Politics,* 3rd ed., Dorsey 1988. Copyright © 1988 by Dorsey Press. Reprinted by permission. *Page 160:* "Percentage Engaging in Various Kinds of Political Participation: 1967 and 1987" from Sidney Verba, Kay Lehman Schlozman, and Henry E. Brady, *Voice and Equality,* Harvard University Press, 1995, p. 72. Copyright © 1995 by Harvard University Press. Reprinted by permission. *Page 162:* "Public Opinion on the Scope of Government" from the 1964–1992 National Election Studies, conducted by the Center for Political Studies at the University of Michigan, 1994. Reprinted by permission. *Page 167:* Quote from *C-SPAN Update,* January 12, 1992, p. 6. *Page 169:* "Should Negative Political Ads Be Curbed?" from "Senators Divide on Proposals to Tame Negative TV Ads," *Congressional Quarterly Weekly Report,* July 22, 1989, 1890. Reprinted by permission. *Page 172:* "The Rise of the Negative Press" from Thomas E. Patterson, *Out of Order.* Copyright © 1993 by Thomas E. Patterson. Reprinted by permission of Alfred E. Knopf, Inc. *Page 177:* "Sources for Newspaper Stories" from Leon V. Sigal, *Reporters and Officials: The Organization and Politics of News Reporting.* Copyright © 1973 by Lexington Books. Reprinted by permission of Lexington Books. *Page 178:* "The Incredible Shrinking Soundbite" from Daniel Hallin, "Sound Bite News: Television Coverage of Elections," *Journal of Communications,* Spring 1992. Reprinted by permission of Oxford University Press. 1992 and 1996 data from studies by the Center for Media Public Affairs. Reprinted with permission. *Page 180:* "Stories People Have Tuned In and Stories They Have Tuned Out" from PEW Research Center for the People and the Press. Reprinted by permission. *Page 183:* "Time Devoted to the Three Branches of Government" from Doris A. Graber, *Mass Media and American Politics,* 4th ed., CQ Press, 1993, p. 291. Reprinted by permission. *Page 191:* "The Downs Model: How Rational Parties Match Voters' Policy Preferences," from the National Election Studies conducted by Center for Political Studies at the University of Michigan, 1996. Reprinted by permission. "Are There Differences Between the Parties?" from the National Election Studies, conducted by Center for Political Studies at the University of Michigan, 1996. Reprinted by permission. *Page 192:* "Party Identification in the United States, 1952–1996" from the 1952–1996 National Election Studies, conducted by Center for Political Studies at the University of Michigan, 1996. Reprinted by permission. *Page 201:* "Party Coalitions in 1996" from the National Election Studies, conducted by Center for Political Studies at the University of Michigan, 1996. Reprinted by permission. *Page 204:* "Party Identification and Ideology: 1996" from the National Election Studies, conducted by Center for Political Studies at the University of Michigan, 1996. Reprinted by permission. *Page 211:* "Are Political Parties Obsolete?" from CBS/*New York Times* Poll, June 1992. Copyright © 1992 by The New York Times Company. Reprinted by permission. *Page 219:* "Choosing Party Leaders in Great Britain" from Anthony King, "How Not to Select Presidential Candidates: A View from Europe," in Robert E. DiCierico, ed., *Analyzing the Presidency,* 2nd ed., Dushkin, 1990, p. 9–10. Reprinted by permission. *Page 223:* "The Inflated Importance of Iowa and New Hampshire in the Presidential Nomination Process" from William C. Adams, "As New Hampshire Goes . . ." in Gary R. Orren and Nelson W. Polsby (eds.), *Media and Momentum,* Chatham House, 1987, p. 43. Reprinted by permission. *Page 226:* "The Declining Coverage of Conventions on Network TV" from Byron E. Shafer, *Bifurcated Politics: Evolution and Reform in the National Party Convention,*

Harvard University Press, 1988, p. 274. Reprinted by permission. *Page 231:* "The Big PAC Spenders" from Center for Responsive Politics study archived at http://www.crp.org. Reprinted by permission. *Page 253:* "Do Elections Make Government Listen?" from the National Election Studies, conducted by Center for Political Studies at the University of Michigan, 1994. Reprinted by permission. *Page 262:* "Perceptions of the Dominance of Big Interests" from the National Election Studies, conducted by Center for Political Studies at the University of Michigan, 1996. Reprinted by permission. *Page 265.* "Why the AARP's 33 Million Members Say They Joined" from American Association of Retired Persons. Reprinted by permission. *Page 267:* "Percentage of Groups Using Various Lobbying Techniques" from Kay L. Schlozman and John T. Tierney, *Organized Interests and American Democracy*. Copyright ©1986 by Kay L. Schlozman and John T. Tierney. Reprinted by permission of HarperCollins Publishers, Inc. *Page 271:* "Washington Lawyers" from data provided by the Washington, D.C., Bar Association. Reprinted by permission. *Page 276:* "Restricting Lobbying for Foreign Interests" from Pat Choate, *Agents of Influence: How Japan Manipulates America's Political and Economic Systems.* Copyright © 1990 by Pat Choate. Reprinted by permission of Simon & Schuster. *Page 289:* "The Incumbency Factor in Congressional Elections" from Norman J. Ornstein, Thomas E. Mann, and Michael J. Malbin, *Vital Statistics on Congress, 1995–1996,* Congressional Quarterly Press, 1996. Copyright © 1996 by Congressional Quarterly Press. Reprinted by permission. *Page 291:* "Contact with Members of the House of Representatives" from the National Election Studies, conducted by Center for Political Studies at the University of Michigan, 1994. Reprinted by permission. *Page 306:* "Presidential Success on Votes in Congress" from George C. Edward III, *At the Margins: Presidential Leadership of Congress,* Yale University Press, 1989, Table 2.1. Copyright © 1989 by Yale University Press. Reprinted by permission. *Page 308:* "The People Speak" data from CBS/*New York Times* Poll, May 1987. Copyright 1987 by The New York Times Company. Reprinted by permission. *Page 310:* "The Russian Duma: A Reformer's Paradise" from Alessandra Stanley, "Russia's Gross National Legislature," *New York Times,* January 19, 1997, sec. 4, p. 3. Copyright © 1997 by The New York Times Company. Reprinted by permission. *Page 322:* "Barber's Classification of Presidents' Character" from James David Barber, *The Presidential Character* 4th ed., Prentice-Hall, 1992. Reprinted by permission of David James Barber. *Page 326:* "What a Difference a Border Makes" from Wayne A. Cornelius and Ann L. Craig, "Politics in Mexico," in Gabriel A. Almond and G. Bingham Powell, Jr., eds., *Comparative Politics Today: A World View,* 5th ed., pp. 475–478. Copyright © 1992. Reprinted by permission of Harper Collins Publishers. *Page 331:* "Principal Offices in the White House" adapted from George C. Edwards III and Stephen J. Wayne, *Presidential Leadership*, 4th ed. Copyright © 1997. Reprinted with permission of St. Martin's Press, Incorporated. *Page 343:* "Average Yearly Presidential Approval" from George C. Edwards III, *Presidential Approval*, Johns Hopkins University Press, Copyright 1990. Reprinted by permission. *Page 344:* "Average Presidential Approval for Entire Terms in Office" from George C. Edwards III, *Presidential Approval*, Johns Hopkins University Press, Copyright ©1990. Reprinted by permission. *Page 361:* "Taxes and Equity" from CBS News/*New York Times* Poll, February 1995. *Page 371:* "The Congressional Budget Process: Targets and Timetables" from Howard E. Shuman, *Politics and the Budget,* 3rd ed., Copyright © 1992, p. 67. Reprinted by permission of Prentice-Hall, Inc., Englewood Cliffs, NJ. *Page 393:* Quoted from M. S. Eccles, *Beckoning Frontiers,* Alfred Knopf, 1951, p. 336. Reprinted by permission of The Estate of M. S. Eccles. *Page 394:* Quoted from Albert Gore, *From Red Tape to Results: Creating A Government That Works Better and Costs Less,* p. 11. Copyright 1993, Random House, Inc. Reprinted by permission. *Page 396:* "A Full Day of Regulations" adapted from James Worsham, "A Typical Day is Full of Rules," *Chicago Tribune,* July 12, 1981, 1ff. Copyrighted Chicago Tribune Company. All rights reserved. Used with permission. *Page 403:* "The Death of an Iron Triangle" from Frank R. Baumgartner and Bryan D. Jones, *Agendas and Instability in American Politics,* University of Chicago Press, 1993. Reprinted by permission. *Page 416:* "Full Opinions in the Supreme Court's 1995–1996 Term" from "The Supreme Court, 1995 Term: The Statistics," *Harvard Law Review,* 108, November 1996, pp. 373–376. Copyright © 1996 by the Harvard Law Review Association. Reprinted by permission. *Page 421:* "Backgrounds of Recent Federal District and Appeals Court Judges" from Sheldon Goldman, "Clinton's First Term Judiciary: Many Bridges to Cross," *Judicature* 80, No. 6, 1997, pp. 261, 269. Reprinted by permission of *Judicature*, the Journal of the American Judicature Society. *Page 434:* "Supreme Court Rulings Which Federal Statutes Have Been Found Unconstitutional" adapted from *The Judicial Process: An Introductory Analysis of the Courts of the United States, England, and France,* 6th ed., by Henry J. Abraham. Copyright © 1993 by Henry J. Abraham. Reprinted by permission of Oxford University Press, Inc. *Page 448:* "Theories on the Economic Slowdown" from Paul Krugman, *Peddling Prosperity: Economic Sense and Nonsense in the Age of Diminished Expectations,* Norton, 1994, chap.2. Reprinted by permission. *Page 449:* "Percentage of Industrial Assets Controlled by the Top One Hundred Corporations" adapted from Thomas R. Dye, *Who's Running America: The Clinton Years*, 6th ed. Reprinted by permission of Prentice-Hall, Inc. *Page 450:* "America's Falling Share of the Worldwide Market for High-Tech Goods" from Derek Bok, *The State of the Nation,* Harvard University Press, 1996. Copyright © 1996 by Harvard University Press. Reprinted by permission. *Page 451:* "The People Speak" data from CBS News/*New York Times* Poll, November 1991. Copyright © The New York Times Company. Reprinted by permission. *Page 455:* "The Soviet Economic Morass" from Hedrick Smith, *The New Russians*, Random House, 1990, chaps. 10–12. Reprinted by permission. *Page 462:* "The Public's Perception of Welfare" from CBS News/*New York Times* Poll, December 6–9, 1994. Copyright © 1994 by The New York Times Company. Reprinted by permission. *Page 467:* "Maternity Leaves in Seven Countries" from *The Sydney Morning Herald,* June 3, 1994, p. 13. Copyright by *The Sydney Morning Herald.* Reprinted by permission. *Page 472:* "Should

Welfare Mothers Be Allowed to Save for Their Children's Education?" from Constance L. Hays, "Girl's Plan to Save for College Runs Afoul of Welfare Rules," *New York Times*, May 15, 1992, p. A1. Reprinted by permission. *Page 486:* "Comparing Sources of Electricity" from Frank R. Baumgartner, *Conflict and Rhetoric in French Policymaking*, University of Pittsburgh Press, 1989, p. 202. Reprinted by permission. *Page 488:* "The People Speak" data from *The Wirthlin Report,* Research Supplement, October 1996, p. 2. Copyright © 1996 by *The Wirthlin Report.* Reprinted by permission. *Page 489:* "Determining Standards for Clean Air" from George Hager, "Clean-Air Package, Part One: Toxic Air Pollutants," *Congressional Quarterly*, April 22, 1989, pp. 888–889. Reprinted by permission. *Page 513:* "The People Speak" data from Chicago Council on Foreign Relations Poll, October 1994. Reprinted by permission. *Page 518:* "The Global Connection and a Personal Computer" from *Business Week*, March 11, 1985. Copyright © 1985 by McGraw-Hill, Inc. Reprinted by special permission. *Page 537:* "Institutional Powers of the Governors" adapted from Thad L. Beyle, "Governors," Table 6.2, in Gray and Jacobs, *Politics in the American States*. Reprinted by permission. *Page 547:* "Urban Planning in Western Europe and the United States" from Peter Hall, *Urban and Regional Planning*, 2nd ed., Allen and Unwin, 1982; H.V. Savitch, *Post-Industrial Cities: Politics and Planning in New York, Paris, and London*, Princeton University Press, 1988; and Myron A. Levine and Jan Van Weesep, "The Changing Nature of Dutch Urban Planning," *Journal of the American Planning Association*, 54 (Summer 1988): 315–323. Reprinted by permission.

PHOTO ACKNOWLEDGMENTS

Unless otherwise acknowledged, all photographs are the property of Scott, Foresman and Company. Page abbreviations are as follows: (T)top, (C)center, (B)bottom, (L)left, (R)right.

1: © Paul Conklin/ PhotoEdit; 3: © Luke Frazza/ A.F.P./ Corbis-Bettmann; 4 left: Jim Argo/ Mercury; 4 right: AP/ Wide World; 5: Wiley/ Washington Post WritersGroup. Reprinted with permission.; 6: Rob Crandall/ Washington Post Writers Group. Reprinted with permission.; 7: Jane Rosett/ Sygma; 8 left: AP/ Wide World; 8 right: AP/ Wide World; 11: Reprinted with special permission of King Features Syndicate; 13 top: Reuters/ Corbis-Bettmann; 13 bottom: CESC Cartoonists and Writers Syndicate; 14: Larry Mayer/ NYT Pictures; 17: Owen Franken/ Sygma; 22: © Paul Conklin/ Monkmeyer; 23: ; 26 top: National Geographic Photographer George Mobley/ Courtesy U.S. Capitol Historical Society; 26 bottom: Brown Brothers; 31: Scribner's Popular History of the U.S. 1897.; 32 left: Copyright Yale University Art Gallery; 32 right: James Monroe Memorial Library; 33: New York Public Library , Astor , Lenox and Tilden Foundations.; 35 top left: Library of Congress; 35 bottom: DOONESBURY Copyright 1987, G.B. Trudeau/ UNIVERSAL PRESS SYNDICATE. Reprinted with permission.; 35 right: Brown Brothers; 42 top: National Geographic Photographer George Mobley/ Courtesy U.S. Capitol Historical Society; 42 bottom: Scott, Foresman and Company; 49: Drawing by Luckovich/ Creators Syndicate; 54: © Photri/ The Picture Cube; 56: AP/ Wide World; 58: U. S. Dept. of Transportation; 63: Stephen Frisch/. Stock Boston; 64: Scott, Foresman and Company; 65: AP/ Wide World; 68: Renato Rotolo/ Gamma -Liaison; 69: ©1992 Newspaper Enterprise Association, Inc.; 74: Sygma; 77: © Robert Ginn/ Unicorn ; 79 top: Christopher Lingg/ JB Pictures; 79 bottom: Scott, Foresman and Company; 85: AP/ Wide World; 88 top: AP/ Wide World; 88 bottom: Drawing by Mankoff; ©1992 The New Yorker Magazine, Inc.; 89: Pool/ Gamma-Liaison; 90 : Drawing by Richter; © 1991 The New Yorker Magazine, Inc.; 91: Bob Nelson/ Black Star; 93: AP/ Wide World; 96: AP/ Wide World; 99 top: Creators Syndicate & Johnny Hart; 99 bottom: AP/ Wide World; 100: ©1964 Flip Schulke/ Life Magazine Inc./ Time Warner Inc.; 105: Mobile Press Register/ Sygma; 106: Reuters/ Corbis-Bettmann; 111: William Johnson/ Stock Boston; 113: Drawing by Handelsman; 1992 The New Yorker Magazine Inc.; 114: Courtesy, Lyndon Baines Johnson Library, Austin TX.; 116: Bettmann Archive; 118: UPI/ Corbis-Bettmann; 121: Scott, Foresman and Company; 124: AP/ Wide World; 127: Reuters/ Corbis-Bettmann; 128: Allen Tannenbaum/ Sygma; 129: PALM BEACH POST/ Don Wright; 131: Paul Conklin; 140: AP/ Wide World; 141: Paul Hosefros/ NYT Pictures; 142 left: Ohman/ Reprinted by permission" Tribune Media Services; 142 right: Corbis-Bettmann; 144: Bart Bartholomew/ Black Star; 149: Bob Daemmrich/ Stock Boston; 150: © 1993 Gail Machlis/ Chronicle Features, San Francisco; 152: Bob Daemmrich; 158: Sygma; 159: Jeff Reinking/ Mercury; 161 left: Jeffrey Markowitz/ Sygma; 161 right: John Filo; 163: Bruce Brothers/ Photo Researchers; 166: Diana Walker/ Gamma-Liaison; 168: Reuters/ Corbis-Bettmann; 170 left: UPI/ Corbis-Bettmann; 170 right: AP/ Wide World; 171: AP/ Wide World; 177 left: Scott, Foresman and CVompany; 177 right: UPI/ Corbis-Bettmann; 178: Reprinted by permission: Tribune Media Services; 179: UPI/ Corbis-Bettmann; 181: THE MIAMI NEWS/ Don Wright; 182 top: Drawing by Luckovich/ Creators Syndicate; 182 bottom: AP/ Wide World; 184: Drawing by Modell ©1988 The New Yorker Magazine Inc.; 187: AP/ Wide World; 189: AP/ Wide World; 199: Bettmann Archive; 200: Reuters/ Corbis-Bettmann; 203: Joe Traver/ Gamma-Liaison; 204: AP/ Wide World; 206: THE PARTY GOES ON by Xandra Kayden/ reprinted by permission of Basic Books, Inc., New York (1985); 207: AP/ Wide World; 209 left: Archive Photos; 209 right: Corbis-Bettmann; 209 bottom: Reprinted with special prmission of King Features Syndicate; 210: Greg Mathieson/ Sygma; 216: AP/ Wide World; 218 right: AP/ Wide World; 218 left: AP/ Wide World; 220: Lee Corkran/ Sygma; 222: THE MIAMI NEWS: Don Wright; 225: AP/ Wide World; 226: Drawing by Bok/ Creators Syndicate; 227: Hopwell/ Gamma-Liaison; 228: Wally McNamee/ Sygma; 230: AP/ Wide World; 233 right: Reuters/ Archive Photos; 233 left: Jean-Marc Giboux/ Gamma-Liaison; 235: The White House; 238: © Bob Daemmrich/ Stock Boston; 240: © John Novrok/ PhotoEdit; 242 left: Reprinted by permission of United Feature Syndicate Inc.; 242 right: Library of Congress; 243: AP/ Wide World; 244: © B. Daemmrich/ The Image Works; 248:

SACRAMENTO BEE, Renault, with acknowledgment to the Simpsons; 253: Drawing by Martin; ©1988 The New Yorker Magazine, Inc.; 254 left: UYPI/ Corbis-Bettmann; 254 right: Reuters/ Corbis-Bettmann; 257: Gustavo Bilabert/ JB Pictures Ltd.; 259: © Cynthia Johnson/ Gamma-Liaison; 260: Stayskal/ Reprinted by permission: Tribune Media Services; 264 left: Corbis-Bettmann; 264 right: Corbis-Bettmann; 265: Reprinted with pecial permission of King Features Syndicate; 268: Reprinted courtesy of the National Rifle Association; 269: Reprinted with special permission of King Features Syndicate; 272: AP/ Wide World; 273: Alan D. Harkrader; 275 bottom: Gabe Kircheirmer/ Black Star; 275 top: Scott, Foresman and Company; 277 : Allen Tannenbaum/ Sygma; 278: UPI/ Corbis-Bewttmann; 284: AP/ Wide World; 287: AP/ Wide World; 290: Brad Markel/ Gamma- Liaison; 291: AP/ Wide World; 299 left: © Porter Gifford/ Gamma-Liaison; 299 center: © Brad Markel/ Gamma-Liaison; 299 right: Reuters/ MIke Theiler/ Archive Photos; 301: Paul Conklin/ Uniphoto; 303: Catherine Karnow/ Woodfin Camp & Associates; 309 left: Catherine Karnow/ Woodfin Camp & Associates; 309 right: Drawing by Handelsman © 1996 The New Yorker Magazine, Inc.; 311: Courtesy of C-SPAN; 312: Drawing by Fradon; 1987 The New Yorker Magazine, Inc.; 317: AP/ Wide World; 319: Copyright 1976/ Washington Post Writers Group. Reprinted with permission.; 322: Alex Webb/ Magnum Photos; 328: AP/ Wide World; 332: Reuters/ Win McNamee/ Archive Photos; 334: AP/ Wide World; 337 left: Terry Ashe/ Gamma-Liaison; 337 right: Copyright 1993, Toles/ UNIVERSAL PRESS SYNDICATE. Reprinted with permission. All Rights Reserved.; 338: Reuters/ Stephen Jaffe/ Archive Photos; 339 right: UPI/ Corbis -Bettmann; 339 left: AP/ Wide World; 342: AP/ Wide World; 345 right: Wayne Miller/ Magnum Photos; 345 left: Drawing by Zeigler; © 1984 The New Yorker Magazine, Inc.; 346: Diana Walker/ Gamma-Liaison; 353: © John Eastcott/ YVA/ Momatiuk/ Stock Boston; 357: Reuters/ Mark Cardwell/ Archive Photos; 359: UPI/ Corbis-Bettmann; 362: Sygma; 364: UPI/ Corbis-Bettmann; 371: AP/ Wide World; 375: Tony Korodny/ Sygma; 378: Reuters/ Dave Gatley/ Archive Photos; 384: DOONESBURY Copyright 1989. G. B. Trudeau/ UNIVERSAL PRESS SYNDICATE. Reprinted with permission. All Rights Reserved.; 389 top: Jeffrey D. Smith/ Woodfin Camp & Associates; 389 bottom: David H. Wells/ J.B. Pictures Ltd.; 391: AP/ Wide World; 393: Bob Daemmrich/ Stock Boston; 395: UPI/ Corbis-Bettmann; 396: Stacye Pick/ Stock Boston; 397: Alon Reininger/ Contact Press Images; 401: UPI/ Corbis-Bettmann; 408: © John Neubauer/ Monkmeyer; 410: Todd Bigelow/ Black Star; 411: LIFE Magazine © Time Warner Inc.; 420 top: Reuters/ Corbis-Bettmann; 420 bottom left: John Ficara/ Woodfin Camp & Associates; 420 bottom right: Diana Walker/ Gamma-Liaison; 424: Abe Frajndlich/ Sygma; 425: Drawing by Mirachi; ©1974 The New Yorker Magazine, Inc.; 427: UPI/ Corbis-Bettmann; 429: Supreme Court Historical Society; 430: UPI/ Corbis-Bettmann; 434 : Drawing by Handelsman. © 1992 The New Yorker Magazine, ; 435 top: Bob Daemmrich/ Stock Boston; 435 bottom: Ken Heinen; 440: © Mark Richards PhotoEdit; 445: Brooks Kraft/ Sygma; 446 left: Reuters/ Archive Photos; 446 right: Bettmann Archive; 447: Peters/ Reprinted by permission of United Feature Syndicate, Inc.; 449: Craig Aurness/ Woodfin Camp & Associates; 450: ; 452: Chuck Nache; 455: P. LeSegretain/ Sygma; 454: Bettmann Archive; 458: AP/ Wide World; 460: Bob Daemmrich; 461: UPI/ Corbis-Bettmann; 463: Shonna Zaleska; 464 left: Bob Daemmrich; 464 right: Bob Krist/ Black Star; 465: Alon Reininger/ Contact Press Images; 468: UPI/ Corbis-Bettmann; 470 left: Courtesy Lyndon Baines Johnson Library, Austin, TX.; 470 right: Drawing by Dana Fradon; © 1992 The New Yorker Magazine, Inc.; 472: Joyce Dopkeen/ NYT Pictures; 473: TANK McNAMARA, copyright 1992/ Miller/Hinds/ UNIVERSAL PRESS SYNDICATE. Reprinted with permission. All Rights Reserved.; 476: David Ulmer/ Stock Boston; 479: Dennis Brack/ Black Star; 483: D. Goldberg/ Sygma; 485: Mike Peters, Dayton Daily News; 487: M. L. Miller; 490: Stephen Ferry/ JB Pictures, Ltd.; 492: B. Nation/ Sygma; 493: Drawing by Handelsman © 1995 The New Yorker Magazine, Inc.; 494: Tannenbaum/ Sygma; 498: Reuters/ Carole DeVille/ Archive Photos; 502 left: AP/ Wide World; 502 right: AP/ Wide World; 506 left: UPI/ Corbis-Bettmann; 506 right: Tom Stoddart/ Woodfin Camp & Associates; 507: Wally McNamee/ Woodfin Camp & Associates; 508: Reuters/ Corbis-Bettmann; 512 top: Nemerofsky/ Mercury; 512 bottom: UPI/ Corbis-Bettmann; 523: Tannenbaum/ Sygma; 526: Courtesy of the Chicago White Sox; 528: AP/ Wide World; 530: Lester Sloan/ Gamma-Liaison; 535: AP/ Wide World; 541: Corbis-Bettmann; 544: Stephen Ferry/ Gamma-Liaison; 548: Roger Sandler/ Uniphoto.

Index

* Page numbers with *n* indicate endnotes